Acclaim for

CALIFORNIA GOLF
The Complete Guide

"The perfect guide with the lowdown on California Golf courses, *California Golf* cuts through the rough and shows golfers what California courses have to offer."

—Copley News Service

"*California Golf* is the bible of California golf courses."

—*The Desert Sun*

"*California Golf* is essential—a sage green scripture worn out by the best of the pros, the country club polish, and the Budweiser weekend muni hacks."

—Doug Miller, *The Oakland Tribune*

"Whether a beginning golfer or a seasoned pro, whatever the preferred terrain or price range, *California Golf* is the take-along guide to all California has to offer the golf enthusiast. Highly recommended!"   —*Reviewer's Bookwatch*

"Foghorn Press has done as good of a job as we've seen."

—*Golf Week*

"*California Golf* won't necessarily get you birdies, but it is unparalleled in finding places to try for them. *California Golf* doesn't miss a thing. Or a stroke."

—Art Spander, *Westways,* LA

> Avalon Travel Publishing
> Rights Department
> 5855 Beaudry St.
> Emeryville, CA 94608
> travel@moon.com

Foghorn Outdoors guidebooks are available wherever books are sold. To find a retailer near you or to order, call (800) FOGHORN (364-4676) or (510) 595-3664 or visit the Foghorn Outdoors website at www.foghorn. com. Foghorn Outdoors titles are available to the book trade through Publishers Group West (800) 788-3123 as well as through wholesalers.

Library of Congress ISSN Data:
September 1999

California Golf: The Complete Guide to Every Course in the Golden State
Ninth Edition

ISBN: 1-57354-091-9
ISSN: 1078-9618

Front cover photo courtesy of Cinnabar Hills Golf Club. For more about the course, see page 5.

Every effort has been made to ensure that the information in *California Golf* is as up-to-date as possible. However, details such as fees, telephone numbers, and discounts are subject to change. Please call each golf course for updated information.

CALIFORNIA GOLF

The Complete Guide to Every Course in the Golden State

by Shaw Kobre
with contributions from
Robert Fagan and Shannon Millhouse

Foghorn
Press
BOOKS BUILDING COMMUNITY™

ISBN 1-57354-091-9

About the Cover
Cinnabar Hills

Cinnabar Hills Golf Club, located in the hills just south of the Silicon Valley, is the first public course to open in San Jose in 30 years.

Designed by John Harbottle III, Cinnabar Hills offers golfers three distinct nine-hole courses: Lake, Canyon, and Mountain. The designer went to great lengths to incorporate the natural surroundings into theses layouts. Many of the holes are framed separately, so you're liable to encounter more wildlife than you are other golfers. None of the courses is particularly long, but that doesn't mean they are easy. When asked where first-time players make their biggest mistakes on the course, Scott Hoyt, PGA professional and general manager, said, "They make their biggest mistake before they even tee off. Golfers glance at the scorecard, see none of the courses is over 3,500 yards long, and tee it up from the back. By the end of the round, they realize that yardage is not the only factor in creating a challenging layout."

The Lake, Canyon, and Mountain Courses are maintained to tournament conditions, with firm fairways and smooth, fast greens. The courses are based on the principle of risk and reward. Players can gamble and cut corners, or go after pins. A good shot will be rewarded with a birdie or even an eagle. Take a risk and hit a poor shot, and you may find your ball in one of the well-placed traps, a creek, or a hazard. For the less-skilled or less-confident players, the course is very manageable. Many of the forced carries off the tee are either shortened or eliminated. From the fairways golfers are almost always given an option to bump-and-run the ball to the green.

At the hub of the Lake, Canyon, and Mountain Courses is an excellent snack bar, well-maintained grass-and-mat driving range, chipping area, and putting green.

Another unique feature of Cinnabar Hills is the clubhouse. The spectacular 25,000-square-foot facility is equal to any in Northern California. The clubhouse sits on a bluff, affording views of the courses as well as the surrounding areas. Inside the clubhouse you will find a well-stocked pro shop, restaurant, a large banquet area, and the Brandenburg Historic Golf Museum. The museum, located in the lounge area, is a must for golf enthusiasts. Make sure you give yourself a few extra minutes before or after your round to admire this extensive collection of golf photos and memorabilia. For more information on Cinnabar Hills Golf Club, see page 342.

Introduction

With each new edition comes a new challenge. The first year we wrote CALIFORNIA GOLF we changed software, which meant retyping nearly the entire book. It took a while, but our typing skills improved considerably. Last year we decided to make CALIFORNIA GOLF an annual publication, which gave us half the time to produce the book. With a little extra organization and a few more staff members, we produced an edition we were extremely proud of. This year's challenge is the most difficult yet: shrink CALIFORNIA GOLF.

The original CALIFORNIA GOLF was exactly 400 pages; this year's edition is just short of 1,200 pages. We consulted several experts on how to make the book smaller. They came back with several suggestions, but none as good as Greg Redmond's: "Just be happy you have so many new things to write about."

So enjoy our latest edition, and although we have had to change our motto slightly, we still think CALIFORNIA GOLF is a book every golf enthusiast should own.

Motto: Remember, CALIFORNIA GOLF should not be left behind. This book should be stuffed in the trunk of your car, resting on your dashboard, or tucked away in your briefcase. The pages should be scribbled with notes, dog-eared, and coffee stained. CALIFORNIA GOLF is meant to be used, not simply read.

California Golf

The Complete Guide to Every Course
in the Golden State

Table of Contents

CALIFORNIA AREA-BY-AREA

ARTICLES

CALIFORNIA GOLF COURSES

CENTRAL CALIFORNIA

SOUTHERN CALIFORNIA

INDEX

California Area-by-Area Map

Crescent City Area (2 crs) page 32

Eureka Area (5 crs) page 46

Yreka Area (4 crs) page 36

Weaverville Area (2 crs) page 54

Redding/ Shasta Area (11 crs) page 58

Tulelake Area (1 crs); page 42

Fall River Mills Area (1 crs) page 72

Alturas Area (2 crs) page 76

Benbow/ Ukiah Area (4 crs) page 80

Red Bluff/ Chico Area (9 crs) page 86

Lake Almanor/ Graeagle Area (10 crs) page 98

Susanville Area (1 crs) page 110

Mendocino/ Sonoma Coast Area (3 crs) page 114

Sonoma/ Napa Area (36 crs) page 120

Grass Valley/ Auburn Area (20 crs) page 210

Tahoe Area (12 crs) page 232

Stockton/ Modesto Area (38 crs) page 344

Central Valley Area (15 crs) page 384

Wawona Area (1 crs) page 402

Mammoth Lakes Area (2 crs) page 406

Sacramento Area (46 crs) page 160

San Francisco Bay Area (91 crs) page 248

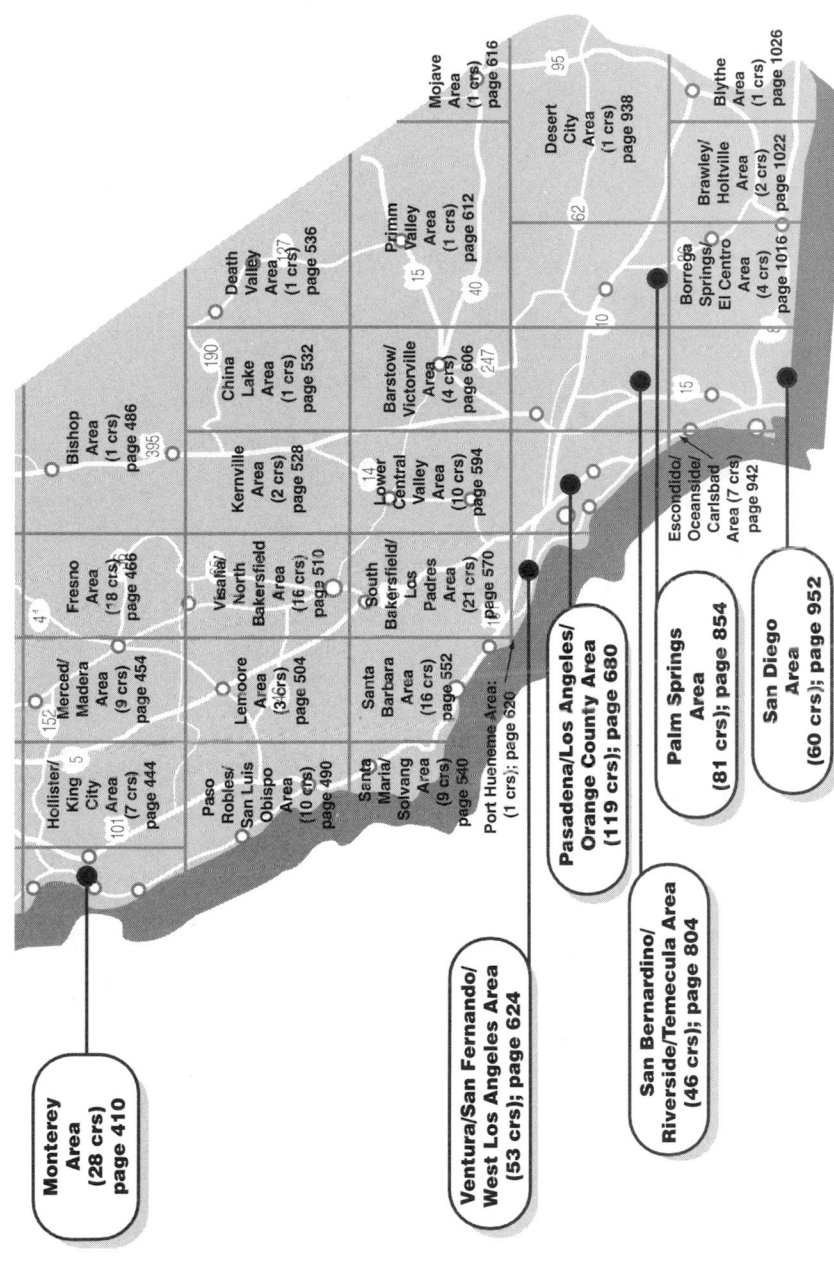

Mojave Area
(1 crs)
page 616

Desert City Area
(1 crs)
page 938

Blythe Area
(1 crs)
page 1026

Death Valley Area
(1 crs)
page 536

Primm Valley Area
(1 crs)
page 612

Brawley/ Holtville Area
(2 crs)
page 1022

Borrega Springs/ El Centro Area
(4 crs)
page 1016

China Lake Area
(1 crs)
page 532

Barstow/ Victorville Area
(4 crs)
page 606

Bishop Area
(1 crs)
page 486

Kernville Area
(2 crs)
page 528

Lower Central Valley Area
(10 crs)
page 594

Escondido/ Oceanside/ Carlsbad Area (7 crs)
page 942

Fresno Area
(18 crs)
page 466

Visalia/ North Bakersfield Area
(16 crs)
page 510

South Bakersfield/ Los Padres Area
(21 crs)
page 570

Merced/ Madera Area
(9 crs)
page 454

Lemoore Area
(3 crs)
page 504

Santa Barbara Area
(16 crs)
page 552

Hollister/ King City Area
(7 crs)
page 444

Paso Robles/ San Luis Obispo Area
(10 crs)
page 490

Santa Maria/ Solvang Area
(9 crs)
page 540

Port Hueneme Area:
(1 crs); page 620

Monterey Area
(28 crs)
page 410

Ventura/San Fernando/ West Los Angeles Area
(53 crs); page 624

Pasadena/Los Angeles/ Orange County Area
(119 crs); page 680

San Bernardino/ Riverside/Temecula Area
(46 crs); page 804

Palm Springs Area
(81 crs); page 854

San Diego Area
(60 crs); page 952

Editor in Chief	*Kyle Morgan*
Editor	*Carolyn Perkins*
Format Design	*Sandy Loam*
Head Researcher	*Shannon Millhouse*
Southern California Researchers	*Brad Sevier* *Scott Petersen* *Andy Lipscholtz* *Ray Wargnier*
Northern California Researchers	*Vince Mastracco* *Greg Fong* *Leigh Casey* *Bob Fagan*
Contributions	*George Tucker* *Jack Wolf* *Emmy Moore-Minister*
Cover Photo	*Photo of Cinnabar Hills* *(see page 5 for information)*
Cover Design	*Randi Morehead* *Studio M Graphic Design*

What's New in California

What's New in California: New Courses

This year California harvested a healthy crop of new courses. The majority of these courses are upscale public courses, but several new exclusive invitation only private clubs have emerged as well. Listed below are courses that opened in 1999, and even a few we sneaked in that will open sometime in the year 2000 or beyond.

For the golfer who wants to play all the new public facilities this year, here are a few tips. 1) Bring a steady hand — fast greens are in; 2) be prepared to be on the road; new courses are popping up in every region of the state, even golf-starved Los Angeles; and 3) those who plan to play on weekends before twilight, might want to open a line of credit to pay for green fees.

Course	Type	Region	Page
Aliso Viejo Golf Club	public	Los Angeles Area	790
Bridges Golf Club, The	public	San Francisco Bay Area	298
Cascade Golf Club	public	Los Angeles Area	636
CordeValle Golf Club	private	Monterey Area	414
Cypress Ridge	public	Santa Maria/Solvang	542
Darkhorse Golf Club	public	Auburn Area	216
Diamond Valley Golf Club	public	Riverside Area	842
Dragon at Gold Mountain, The	semi-private	Graeagle Area	108
Eagle Glen Golf Club	public	Los Angeles Area	752
Eagle Ridge Golf Club	public	Hollister/King City Area	446
Goose Creek Golf Club	public	Los Angeles Area	748
Landmark Golf Club	public	Palm Springs Area	936
Likely LInks Golf Club	public	Alturas Area	78
Lincoln Hills Golf Club	semi-private	Sacramento Area	172
Maderas Country Club	public	San Diego Area	17
Mission Hills of Hayward	public	San Francisco Bay Area	304
Ocean Trails Golf Club	public	West Los Angeles Area	678
Old River Golf Course	public	Stockton/Modesto Area	368
PGA WEST: Norman Course	semi-private	Palm Springs Area	926
Riverbend Golf Club	public	Merced/Madera Area	460
Sierra Star Golf Club	resort	Mammoth Lakes Area	408
Sterling Hills Golf Club	public	Los Angeles Area	626
Tehama Golf Club	private	Monterey Area	426

Links at River Lakes Ranch, The	public	North Bakersfield Area	524
Meadows Del Mar, The	public	San Diego Area	16
Palms Golf Club, The	private	Palm Springs Area	928
Plantation Golf Club, The	private	Palm Springs Area	934
Reserve at Spanos Park, The	public	Stockton/Modesto Area	356
Reserve, The	private	Palm Springs Area	934
Tierra Rejada Golf Club	public	Visalia Area	592
Turkey Creek Golf Club	public	Sacramento Area	170
Westridge Golf Club	public	Los Angeles Area	730
Wildhorse Golf Course	public	Sacramento Area	188
Winchester Country Club	private	Auburn Area	216
Yountville Golf Course	public	Sonoma/Napa Area	140
Yucaipa Golf Club	public	Riverside Area	822

***If you have information on new courses, please call us at (707) 523-6906.

What's New in California: Future Courses

Whether golf courses are in the proposal stage, construction phase, or hung up in financial or environmental red tape, more are being built in California than in any other state. Listed below are facilities under or nearing construction.

Warning: Changes of course names, designers, and production schedules are frequent. Don't be suprised if some of these clubs show up with a different name or designer or a year later than scheduled.

Gary Roger Baird
ASGCA MEMBER
Contra Costa County
Brentwood Lake is set to be an 18-hole championship golf course surrounded by 900 homes. The course will be managed by the Troon Golf Group and is expected to open in late 2000.

Bradford Benz
ASGCA MEMBER
Santa Clara
Boulder Ridge is a public course set to begin construction and will feature beautiful 360° views of the surrounding area. It is situated on the quarry that helped build Stanford University, so boulders will come into play. An opening date has not been set.

Redlands
Hampton Heights is starting the approval process. Hampton Heights will be part of a real estate development. The course will measure 7,010 yards from the back tees, and plans are to expand to 27 holes.

Cary Bickler

ASGCA MEMBER

Chula Vista

Auld Goff Course–that's not a mis-spelling, "goff" is the original name for golf. This public course is scheduled for construction in late summer of 1999 and will feature views of the Coronado Islands. A John Cook signature course, Auld will offer five sets of tees and will range from 4,800 to 6,900 yards.

Rancho Santa Fe

This unnamed course is being developed on the McCrink Ranch. McCrink will be a championship upscale public course. Ground breaking is due to begin in late 2000.

Fred Bliss

ASGCA MEMBER

Novato

Black Point Golf Course has been in the works for years, or maybe even a decade. Black Point will be a public 18-hole course and should be complete in the spring of 2000. Also working on this project are Johnny Miller and the design firm of Tatum and Summers.

Pete Dye

ASGCA MEMBER

Simi Valley

Lost Canyons is being built near or on the set of the 1970s television show, *Little House on the Prairie*. This 36-hole course is due to open in the year 2000.

Perry Dye

ASGCA MEMBER

Alpine

Viejas Turf Club and Casino will be an 18-hole championship golf course that will eventually be part of a 36-hole complex with a casino and turf club on site. Because of an ongoing battle between the state and the Indian tribes concerning gaming, this course is currently on hold.

Fremont

Central Park Golf Course will add a public nine-hole executive course and teaching center to the existing range and will be open in mid-2000. The course and teaching center will be run by Family Golf Centers.

Tom Fazio

ASGCA MEMBER

Carmel Valley

The Preserve Golf Club will be an 18-hole private club that will feature a non-returning front nine. The course will be part of an exclusive development and has a projected opening date of April 30, 2000.

San Diego

The Meadows Del Mar will open in fall 1999. The course will be an upscale daily-fee course and will eventually be part of a resort community. Green fees will range from $65 to $145. The par-71, 18-hole course will be over 6,800 yards in length from the back tees. Full details were not available at time of press. For more information call 619-792-6200.

Golf Plan

Folsom

Folsom Lake Golf Club will be a public 18-hole golf course that will play approximately 6,700 yards and meander through natural wetlands.

Graves & Pascuzzo

ASGCA MEMBER

Santa Clara

King Road Golf Club is on the site of the old Thunderbird Golf Course. Robert Muir Graves is redesigning this course from square one. It will be a 1,600-yard par 28, with eight par 3s and one par 4. The course will offer a driving range. The course is currently in the growing in stage and is expected to open in early 2000.

Poway

Maderas Country Club will be a high-end, daily-fee 18-hole course measuring over 7,100 yards from the back tees. The course is due to open in late 1999. For more information call 619-692-3220.

Morgan Hill

The Institute is set to be an exclusive private club with corporate membership set in Morgan Hill on the site of the former Flying Lady Golf Club.

Arthur Hills

ASGCA MEMBER

Yorba Linda

Black Gold Golf Club will be a private course that is routed within Shell Oil's operating oil fields. The course is due open in spring of 2001.

Peter Jacobson— Buzz Campion

Moor Park

Wild Canyon will be a 36-hole championship golf course due open in late 2000. The course, part of an upscale development, will offer spectacular views and challenge golfers' second shots. Eighteen holes will be designed by Robert Trent Jones, Jr. and 18 holes by Peter Jacobson and Buzz Campion.

Madera County

The Outlaw Course at River Bend will be a daily-fee course and reflect its name. Unpredictable and exciting, the course will wind through a canyon.

Sacramento

Rio La Paz is under construction and due to open in late 2000. This will be a family-oriented private course. The course will feature gentle slopes with an emphasis on fun.

Robert Trent Jones, Jr.

ASGCA MEMBER

Rancho Santa Fe

The Bridges at Rancho Santa Fe will be an 18-hole private club with 205 home sites and is due to open in 2000.

Riverside

Rancho La Sierra will be an upscale 36-hole facility. This course is currently pending construction. The other 18 holes are being designed by Jack Nicklaus and Jack Nicklaus II.

Jack Nicklaus
ASGCA MEMBER

Monterey

Pasadera Golf And Country Club will be a private club and is part of a real estate development. Construction is under way and should be completed in 2000.

Orinda

Montanera Country Club will be a private championship golf course offering a limited number of memberships. The course is due to begin construction in early 2000.

Riverside

Rancho La Sierra will be an upscale 36-hole facility. The first 18 holes is a collaboration between Jack Nicklaus and Jack Nicklaus II. The second 18 holes is being designed by Robert Trent Jones Jr.

Windsor

Mayacama Golf Club was rumored for years, but has finally become a reality. This will be an exclusive private course with more than half of its membership coming from outside the local area. Construction is due to begin in summer 1999.

Arnold Palmer
Palm Springs

The Preserve at Mountain Falls will be a semiprivate 18-hole championship course with a par of 72. An opening date has not been set.

Kyle Phillips
ASGCA MEMBER

Placer County

Morgan Creek Golf Club is currently in development with construction due to begin in spring 2000. This will be an 18-hole championship golf course that will play 7,100 yards from back tees. The course will be part of a housing development.

J. Michael Poellet
ASGCA MEMBER

Antioch

Roddy Ranch will be a private 18-hole course. The course will begin the seeding stage in the fall of 1999, with the driving range expected to be open late in 1999. Although no exact completion date has been set, the course is projected to be open in early 2000.

Pleasanton

Happy Valley Golf Club will be a public 18-hole championship course due to open in the year 2001. The site has diverse topography that includes oak trees, creeks, canyons, and barrancas. Ground breaking originally scheduled for fall 1998 is now projected for fall of 1999. The course will play approximately 7,000 yards from the back tees. Green fees are estimated at $40.

San Jose

San Jose municipal was originally slated to be named Coyote Creek, but since the name was recently taken by another facility, the San Jose municipal has yet to be named. The course is going to be a public 18-hole executive course with a par of 68. Construction will probably begin in 2000. Unlike most executive courses, this course will measure 6,000 yards and feature five par 5s.

Ted Robinson

ASGCA MEMBER

Fontana

Sierra Lakes is currently under construction and will be an 18-hole championship daily-fee golf course. A self-contained draining golf course, it will incorporate large waste areas into the design.

Palmdale

Rancho Vista Golf Club will be a public 18-hole championship golf course and is currently under construction. The course will measure 6,700 yards from the back tees.

Santa Clarita

Ted Robinson is a partner in **Robinson Ranch**, an upscale public course that will incorporate the natural landscape and old oak trees. This will be a 36-hole facility comprised of the Mountain Course and the Valley Course. Completion date for nine holes will be in the fall of 1999, with the rest to be completed the following year.

Schmidt-Curley

ASGCA MEMBER

Beaumont

The SCPGA Home Course will be a daily-fee course and feature two distinct 18 holes. One 18 will be a traditional golf course, while the other will be a rugged 18. The fee structure on this course is scheduled to put it within in most players' reach. The course is well under construction with an opening date projected to be in the late spring of 2000.

Elsinor

Liberty Golf Club will be an 18-hole daily-fee course with construction beginning in the fall of 1999.

Palm Desert

Marriot Palm Desert is the latest phase in the Marriot Springs development. In conjunction with Nick Faldo, this will be a high-end resort facility. Construction should begin in early fall of 1999.

Rancho Santa Fe

Santa Fe Valley Golf Club will be an 18-hole private course and is scheduled to open in the fall of 2000. This course will use the natural terrain and beauty to create a challenge for golfers.

Riverside

Oak Quarry will be an 18-hole daily-fee course and is currently under construction, due to open in late 2000.

San Clemente

Telega Golf Club will be an 18-hole daily-fee course and feature dramatic elevation changes. The course is being designed by Schmidt-Curley in conjunction with Fred Couples. The course is under construction with a scheduled completion date of mid-2000.

ASGCA stands for Association of Golf Course Architects

What's New in California: Great Ideas, Renovations, Additions, and Name Changes

Great Ideas

Benbow Valley RV Resort and Golf Course near Garberville has added a new junior golf course within the existing course. The course will be called the "Benbow Bear Junior Course" and come complete with its own scorecard.

Chalk Mountain Golf Course of Atascadero is offering free beginning golf lessons.

Colma Park Golf Course is constructing a million-dollar clubhouse. The facility will include a golf library, community room, classrooms, computer learning center, barbeque area, and toddler golf area. This facilty will be used for the ProKids program.

Del Rio Country Club, with the help of John Harbottle, has renovated the greens on the first 18, using William P. Bell's original design.

Ojai Valley Inn and Spa has announced an ambitious project to renovate its golf course by bringing back two signature holes that have been lost for a half century. During World War II, the U.S. Army took over the picturesque resort as a training camp, stationing 1,000 troops there from 1942 through 1944. When the government returned the course, the army did not rebuild it according to George Thomas's original design. With some good detective work and old photos, the reconstruction on the two lost holes has already begun. One them, a par 3, Thomas's favorite, resembles the famous number 3 at Pine Valley Golf Club. The opening date is planned for late fall of 1999.

Renovations and Additions

Alta Sierra Golf Club in Grass Valley has opened a new 21,000-square-foot clubhouse.

Bennett Valley Golf Course in Santa Rosa is in the process of rebuilding all the greens; six have been completed. A new cart path has been completed.

Bigfoot Golf and Country Club in Willow Creek has added outside dining.

Brighton Crest Golf and Country Club in Friant is under new management. The course has been renovated with the fairways being converted to a hybrid Bermuda grass.

CBC Port Hueneme Golf Club is now a public golf course. It has built a new clubhouse and added a lake with one million gallons of water that comes into play on the 10th and 17th holes.

Fallbrook Golf Club's clubhouse remodel is scheduled to be completed by the fall of 1999.

Hiddenbrooke Country Club of Vallejo has reconfigured the layout and added a brand-new clubhouse.

Lomas Santa Fe Executive Course has just added cart paths.

Mare Island Golf Course has upgraded the clubhouse and restaurant, and nine new holes and a driving range are being built and scheduled to open in 2000.

Merced Golf and Country Club rebuilt and repositioned the seventh green, bringing two eucalyptus trees into play. Holes 7 and 8 have been lengthened, and new tee boxes have been constructed for holes 4 and 17. The course has added another 90 yards.

Montebello Golf Course underwent major renovations in 1999, adding three new lakes, many new bunkers, and all-new greens.

Newport Beach Golf Course has a new, larger golf shop.

Old Ranch Country Club in Seal Beach is being completely redesigned by Ted Robinson. The course will have a double-ended driving range, and although the course will remain private, one end of the range will be open to the public.

Palo Alto Golf Course has just completed renovation of the golf course and facility.

Paso Robles Golf Club is constructing new tee boxes.

Pheasant Run Golf Club in Chowchilla started construction on the new nine in February 1999.

Pine Mountain Lake Country Club in Groveland has remodeled the clubhouse and built a new grill.

Presidio Golf Club in San Francisco has added a brand-new clubhouse and restaurant. It is the first new structure built in the Presidio since it was handed over from the military.

Rancho Bernardo Golf Club has a new 20,000-square-foot clubhouse.

Rancho Bernardo Inn and Country Club in San Diego has a remodeled golf shop, added a fourth set of tee boxes, remodeled the bunkers, and has new natural vegetation areas.

Rancho Park Golf Course in Los Angeles is in the process of rebuilding all the greens. A completion date is set for the end of 2000. Players should expect temporary greens.

Rio Vista Golf Club's new clubhouse is scheduled to open in the fall of 1999.

Saddle Creek Golf Club in Copperopolis has a new clubhouse scheduled to open in late 1999.

Salinas Fairways Golf Course has received a complete renovation.

San Leandro Golf Course has two 18-hole golf courses. The Marina Course has been closed for renovation and should be open in the fall of 1999. As soon as the Marina Course is complete, the Tony Lema Course will be closed for renovation. The renovation design was done by John Harbottle.

San Luis Obispo Golf and Country Club is due to open a new clubhouse in the summer of 2000.

San Mateo Golf Course is closed for renovation until May of 2000.

Seascape Golf Club in Aptos is undergoing major renovations, including new irrigation, drainage, bunker renovation, a new pro shop, bar and grill, snack bar, and locker rooms.

Sequoyah Country Club in Oakland is adding a new pro shop, lounge, and remodeled grill.

Shelter Cove Golf Course has added a new pro shop and lounge.

Summit Pointe Golf Course of Milpitas is undergoing renovation.

Temeku Hills Golf Course in Temecula has reversed the nines, one being ten, and ten being one.

Three Rivers Golf Course has re-opened with all new fairways and all new greens.

Thunderbird Country Club in Rancho Mirage has added a new driving range.

Name Changes

WAS:	IS:
Aspen Meadows (Beale Air Force Base)	Reece Point Golf Course
Gold Creek Golf Resort (Placerville)	Apple Mountain Golf Resort
Laguna Hills Golf Club	Laguna Woods Golf Club
Lake Don Pedro C.C. (La Grange)	Hidden Hills Resort and Golf Club
Rancho Bernardo Country Club	The Country Club at Rancho Bernardo
Rancho San Diego	Cottonwood at Rancho San Diego

Experts' Lists

Bob Fagan's California Golf "50"

GOLF 50

One of the joys of golfing in California is the wonderful diversity of courses available for everyone. One can enjoy golf in oceanside, desert, forest, mountain, parkland, or links-style environments. The following fifty are a cross section of the challenging, historic, and unique courses that you can play, representing all major areas of the state. Were you to play them all, you would certainly rate a Ph.D. in California Golf. (All courses listed below are at least 18-hole facilities.)

Aviara: Unsurpassed in greater San Diego, Aviara has an interesting layout that features remarkable waterscaping.

Bayonet Golf Course: Formerly known as Fort Ord, this is quietly one of the best tests of golf in California and has often hosted Regional PGA Tour qualifying. Another interesting 18 holes adjoin.

Bodega Harbour Golf Links: A rugged ocean view course, this Sonoma Coast course is one of the most challenging, yard for yard, you will ever encounter. Golfers will play two different styles of nines built at different times.

Carmel Valley Ranch Resort: Great resort and scenery belie a somewhat controversial Pete Dye–designed course that has been substantially softened. (Alternate course: Golf Club at Quail Lodge.)

Cinnabar Hills Golf Club: Course architect John Harbottle's 27-hole design features scenic undulating terrain, lightning-fast greens, and attractive bunkering, which combine for Silicon Valley's best golf experience.

Coronado Golf Course: This course offers a great walk in the park and a wonderful view of the San Diego skyline and harbor, where there is scarcely a bad day; it's a pretty fair course as well.

Del Monte Golf Course: Claiming to be the oldest course west of the Mississippi, it is not an overbearing test, but the small greens make par a challenge on this traditional layout in Monterey. (Alternate course: Laguna Seca Golf Club.)

Desert Dunes Golf Club: One of the desert's best evokes a links style; plan on wind in Desert Hot Springs.

Desert Willow Golf Resort, Firecliff Course: This upscale Palm Desert municipal facility is littered with bunkers that define the challenge and make a most dramatic impression. (Alternate course: Desert Willows Resort - Mountain View Course, and Mission Hills North - Player Course.)

Diablo Grande, Legends West Course: This Nicklaus-Sarazen collaboration near Patterson features a wonderfully scenic, versatile course that rates among the best new courses in California. The Ranch Course is also worthwhile and probably the more difficult of the two courses.

Edgewood Tahoe Golf Course: Long

considered the jewel of Lake Tahoe, the course affords wonderful vistas of the lake and the mountains, as well as a stout challenge. (Alternate Course: Lake Tahoe Golf Course.)

Fall River Valley Golf and Country Club: One of the hidden gems of the far northeast corner of the state, it affords great views and fun golf. (Alternate Course: Lake Shastina Resort - Championship Course.)

Furnace Creek Golf Course: This desert oasis course is remarkable because it is situated farther below sea level than any other course in the world. It was recently renovated by Perry Dye.

Griffith Park, Wilson Course: The historic parkland course in Los Angeles is the hub of one of the country's busiest golf complexes. (Alternate course: Empire Lakes Golf Course.)

Half Moon Bay, Ocean Course: This spectacular, playable new test boasts ocean views from nearly every hole. It nudges out the original wooded Links Course that plays tougher and has one of America's most dramatic finishing holes. (Alternate course: Crystal Springs Golf Club.)

Harding Park Golf Course: This historic, busy San Francisco muni boasts a challenging tree-lined layout. Not only a former tour site, it hosts the largest city amateur championship in the world.

Hidden Valley Golf Club: Head-twisting views and dramatic elevation changes highlight this unique layout that is naturally set amid high desert terrain near Norco. Designer Casey O'Callaghan produced a very playable design, provided you choose the proper tees.

Hunter Ranch Golf Course: This hilly course near Paso Robles is both challenging and scenic, featuring superb back-to-back par 5s.

Industry Hills, Eisenhower Course: One of the state's toughest tests, this course at the City of Industry is a beautiful reclamation of a former land dump, characterized by its flowering rough and elevation changes. The shorter Zaharias Course is also a testy layout.

La Costa Resort and Spa, Composite Course: Located in Carlsbad, the original 18, built by Dick Wilson, annually hosts the PGA Tour's Tournament of Champions and is well bunkered.

La Purisima: Nearby ocean winds and rolling terrain make this inland course one of the state's most formidable tests of golf. (Alternate course: The River Course at Alisal.)

La Quinta Hotel, Mountain Course: Considered one of the Southwest's premier courses, it combines spectacular mountainside vistas with a desert environment. (Alternate course: La Quinta Hotel - Dunes Course.)

Links at Spanish Bay: Formerly a quarried eyesore, this Pebble Beach course represents one of golf's outstanding examples of restoring and enhancing the environment and is the closest thing to a links-style course you can play in California.

Los Serranos, South Course: This long, hilly course in Chino is usually in excellent condition, and it's very popular as well.

Moreno Valley Ranch Golf Club: Twenty-seven holes of attractive vistas complement the challenging Pete Dye-designed layout that hosts many regional competitions.

Oak Valley Golf Club: This rolling layout near Beaumont boasts lots of sand and water together with very challenging green sites.

Oakhurst Country Club: Strong golf holes and views of Mt. Diablo make it the best all-around in the East Bay. (Alternate course: Canyon Lakes.)

Ojai Valley Inn and Country Club: The beautiful, playable old classic is set in idyllic surroundings with excellent resort hospitality.

Pacific Grove Golf Links: Often called the "poor man's Pebble Beach," the incoming nine features links-style play and great ocean views. It's a great golf experience.

Pasatiempo Golf Club: Regularly regarded among the 100 best courses in the nation, this Alister Mackenzie gem at Santa Cruz boasts some of the most attractive, interesting greens in golf. (Alternate course: DeLavega Golf Course.)

Pebble Beach Golf Links: Pebble Beach is simply the best and most famous golf course available for public play in the world. Terrific ocean and forest scenery combine with history and challenge to make the experience of a lifetime.

Pelican Hill, Ocean South Course: The original oceanside course along the Newport coast features spectacular ocean and canyon views and challenges, although many feel the newer North Course is the more difficult test of golf. (Alternate Course: Oak Creek Golf Club.)

PGA West, TPC Stadium Course: Famous or infamous for its difficulty, this La Quinta Pete Dye design is actually a very fair design and is perhaps the best of all the California courses to showcase his genius.

Poppy Hills Golf Course: Home of the Northern California Golf Association and a PGA Tour stop, it is a demanding thinker's course that takes full advantage of the Del Monte Forest at Pebble Beach.

Poppy Ridge Golf Course: These 27 Northern California Association holes at Livermore exude an inland treeless links feel and feature terrific bold bunkering.

Presido Golf Club: Formerly private, this venerable old San Francisco course is an exceptional, undulating, wooded layout that has undergone recent renovations.

Primm Valley Golf Resort, Lakes Course: Architect Tom Fazio has crafted the flat desert floor into his trademark mounding and framing. (Alternate Course: The sister course at Primm Valley is just as entertaining as the Lake Course.)

Redhawk: A scenic, challenging test at Temecula, Redhawk ranks high among the best in California and features dramatic elevation changes and excellent par threes. (Alternate course: Tijeras Creek Golf Club.)

Saddle Creek Golf Club: The classic, playable design is the gold standard of the Gold Country. (Alternate course: Greenhorn Creek, and Pine Moutain Lake Course.)

San Juan Oaks Golf Club: Attractively bunkered, and playable yet testy, this course is a "must play" when you are near Monterey.

Sandpiper Golf Club: The oceanside holes by Goleta are truly spectacular and worth the price of admission. Overall, Sandpiper is a very challenging course, especially with the ocean breeze, and is one of America's underrated courses.

SCGA Members' Club at Rancho California: Home course of the Southern California Golf Association, this is a well-maintained Robert Trent Jones beauty.

Sea Ranch Golf Links: Formerly one of the United States' best nine-hole courses, it now has 18 holes by the ocean.

Sonoma Mission Inn Golf Club: This beautiful, challenging course is built upon classic lines and is the "Quiet Gem of the Wine Country." (Alternate courses: Chardonnay Club, Hiddenbrooke Country Club, Fountaingrove Resort, and Silverado Resort.)

Spyglass Hill Golf: With premier scenery and challenge, Spyglass Hill is one of the top courses in the nation.

Stevinson Ranch: Level yet interesting, the Central Valley's best new course will delight the shot-maker in a golfer.

The Course at Wente Vineyards: This new upscale Greg Norman–designed course features spectacular terrain, making the holes the most exciting in the Livermore Valley.

The Golf Club at Whitehawk Ranch: A beautiful wooded location near Clio makes one of the Sierras' best courses. (Alternate course: Graeagle Meadow Golf Club.)

Torrey Pines, South Course: This busy La Jolla course annually hosts the PGA Tour and is noted for oceanside cliffs and deep canyons. Its companion, the North Course, is slightly shorter but shares similar terrain and photographic views. (Alternate courses: Singing Hills Resort - Willow Course, Steele Canyon, Mt. Woodson Country Club, Rancho Bernardo Inn.)

Twelve Bridges Golf Club: This LPGA site boasts a wonderful rolling wooded layout in Lincoln. (Alternate courses: Ancil Hoffman, Teal Bend, Dry Creek Ranch, Whitney Oaks, Plumas Lake, and Castle Oaks.)

PREVIEW: Ocean Trails Golf Club's opening was delayed due to earth slides that wiped out the 18th green and fairway. Provided construction can be completed in a timely manner, count this a future CALIFORNIA GOLF "50." This Pete Dye design enjoys a spectacular oceanside setting near Los Angeles.

Bob Fagan's California's 25 Best Private Courses

(Alphabetical Order)

Beauty is in the eye of the beholder. So too, for that matter, is the subjective rating of great golf courses. However, we've attempted to list California's best private clubs. Beauty, memorability, challenge, playability, conditioning, shot values, variety, and history all combine to determine a great course. If you are fortunate enough to play any of the following, you will be in store for a terrific golfing experience.

Bel-Air Country Club: This much-revised but sporty and enjoyable Los Angeles course has one of golf's most unusual routings.

California Golf Club: A quiet, scenic San Francisco gem, it requires accurate driving and thoughtful shotmaking.

CordeValle Golf Club: This new facility south of San Jose near Gilroy features an inspired routing, dramatic bunkering, and no houses bordering the property.

Cypress Point Club: Simply stated, it is one of the best most beautiful courses in the world, featuring oceanside, forest, and meadow holes.

Lahonton Golf Club: Tom Weiskopf's Sierra/Tahoe gem combines wonderful ambience and solid golf.

Lake Merced Golf and Country Club: This course in Daly City continues to be one of the Bay Area's most underrated layouts though it has undergone an extensive Rees Jones facelift.

Lakeside Golf Club: Located in Southern California's Toluca Lake, here is an excellent traditional-style course featuring rolling fairways and small greens.

Los Angeles Country Club, North Course: This rolling, tight, George Thomas masterpiece is always considered among America's best courses.

Mission Hills Country Club, Dinah Shore Course: The LPGA Tour stop by Desmond Muirhead has evolved into a desert classic in Rancho Mirage.

Monterey Peninsula Country Club, Dunes Course: As underrated as any course in America, this layout combines forest and coastal beauty.

Olympic Club, Lake Course: This U.S. Open course in San Francisco is one of America's most punishing courses with its avenues of trees and small treacherous greens guarding par.

Pauma Valley Golf Club: A "Top 100" course in America, it is both a tough and scenic Robert Trent Jones layout in the rugged mountainous area east of San Diego.

PGA West: Nicklaus Private Course - This desert layout in La Quinta is one of the toughest, most exacting Nicklaus courses you will ever encounter, but it's pleasing to the eye.

Plantation Club: Superb bunkering on this brand-new desert oasis course in the Palm Desert area makes it an instant classic, playable for the novice, yet a challenge for the expert.

Quarry at La Quinta: A Tom Fazio production, this desert course features some spectacular holes and a strong finish.

Rancho Sante Fe Golf Club: This residential parkland layout is rolling and features one of the best incoming nines anywhere.

Riviera Country Club: This historic, straightforward George Thomas design in Pacific Palisades emphasizes strategy and shotmaking. It ranks of America's best championship layouts.

San Francisco Golf Club: This exclusive golf club is considered among architect Tillinghast's very best, with raised, flashed bunkering imitated but never surpassed.

Saticoy Country Club: William F. Bell's design requires accurate driving and is a quiet Southern California gem in Camarillo.

Sherwood Country Club: This rolling, oak-studded Nicklaus design in Thousand Oaks features some wonderful holes and is the epitome of upscale country club courses.

The Club at Morningside: A natural-looking level Palm Springs Nicklaus design, the course is beautiful, testing, and very playable.

The Tradition Golf Club: This Arnold Palmer–designed layout built in La Quinta in 1998 features superb vistas, interesting golf strategies, and immaculate conditioning set in the desert adjoining the Santa Rosa Mountains.

Valencia Country Club: This stout tree-lined Robert Trent Jones course with bold bunkering among the trees gets great reviews from the pros who played there in the Los Angeles Open.

Valley Club of Montecito: This exclusive, publicity-shy club Santa Barbara course is widely considered among the country's very best, with wonderful Mackenzie-designed greens.

Vintage Club: Mountain Course: One of Tom Fazio's earlier works (1981), this spectacular desert garden-style course enjoys beautiful scenery at its Indian Wells mountainside location.

Honorable Mention Private Club (alphabetical order)

Southern California

Bakersfield Country Club

Bear Creek Golf Club, Murrieta

Coto de Caza Golf Club - North Course

Dove Canyon Country Club

Hacienda Country Club, La Habra Heights

La Cumbre Country Club, Santa Barbara

La Jolla Country Club

La Quinta Country Club

La Quinta Hotel and Spa - Citrus Course

Mission Hills Country Club - Pete Dye Challenge Course, Rancho Mirage

Oakmont Country Club, Glendale

Rancho La Quinta Country Club

San Diego Country Club

San Gabriel Country Club

Vintage Club - Desert Course, Indian Wells

Wilshire Country Club, Los Angeles

Northern California

Del Rio Country Club, Modesto

Diablo Country Club

Ft. Washington Golf and Country Club, Fresno

Granite Bay Golf Club

Green Hills Country Club, Millbrae

Meadow Club, Fairfax

Monterey Peninsula Country Club - Short Course

North Ridge Country Club, Fair Oaks

Olympic Club - Ocean Course, San Francisco

Peach Tree Country Club, Marysville

Rancho Murieta Country Club - North Course

Serrano Country Club, El Dorado Hills

Stanford Golf Course

Sunnyside Country Club, Fresno

California
Golf Listings

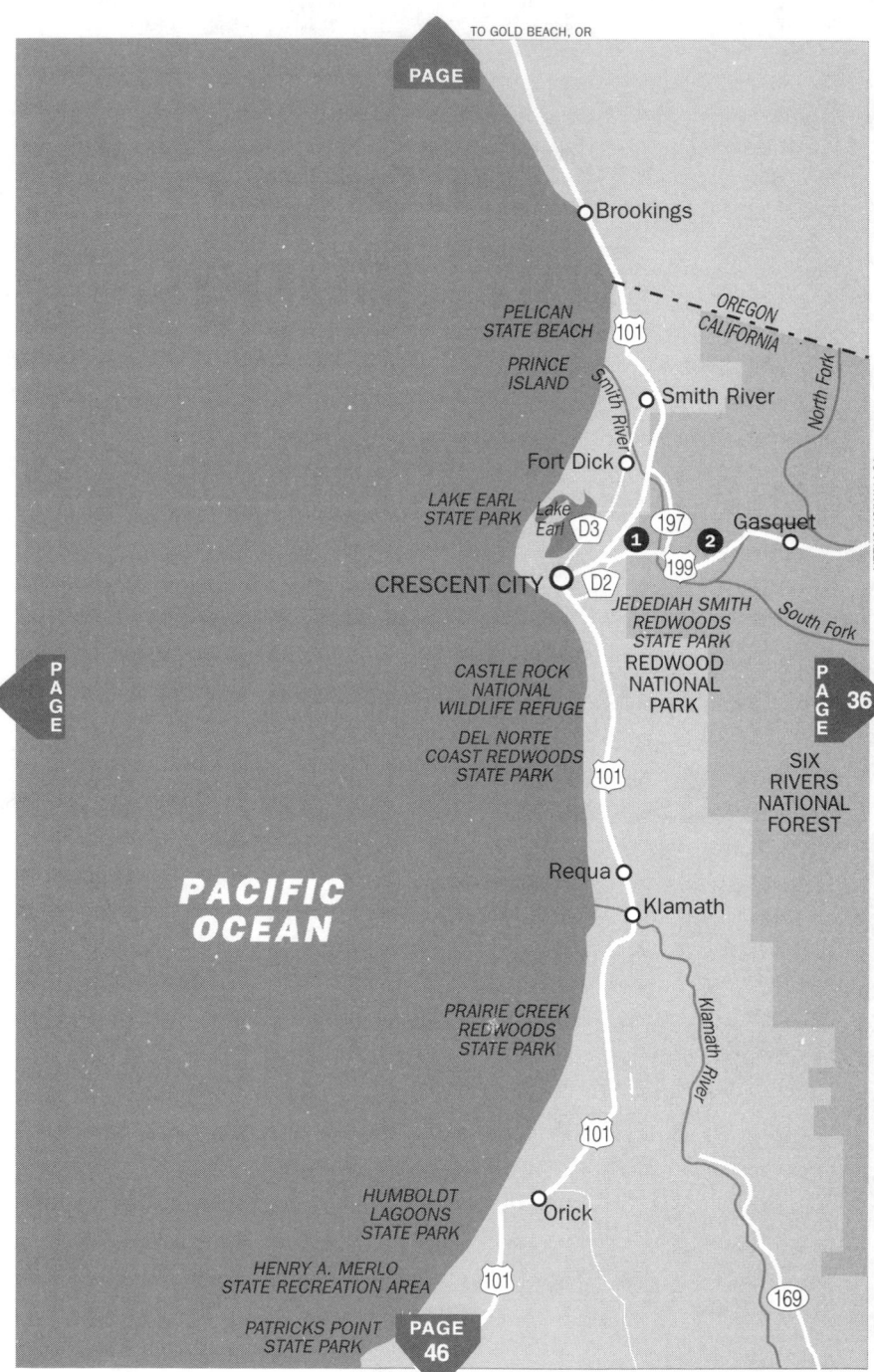

TO GOLD BEACH, OR

PAGE

O Brookings

PELICAN
STATE BEACH 101

OREGON
CALIFORNIA

PRINCE
ISLAND

Smith River

O Smith River

North Fork

TO PATRICK CREEK

Fort Dick O

LAKE EARL
STATE PARK

Lake
Earl D3

197

O Gasquet

1

2

CRESCENT CITY O D2

199

South Fork

JEDEDIAH SMITH
REDWOODS
STATE PARK

CASTLE ROCK
NATIONAL
WILDLIFE REFUGE

REDWOOD
NATIONAL
PARK

PAGE

PAGE 36

DEL NORTE
COAST REDWOODS
STATE PARK

101

SIX
RIVERS
NATIONAL
FOREST

PACIFIC
OCEAN

Requa O

Klamath O

PRAIRIE CREEK
REDWOODS
STATE PARK

Klamath River

101

HUMBOLDT
LAGOONS
STATE PARK

O Orick

HENRY A. MERLO
STATE RECREATION AREA

101

169

PATRICKS POINT
STATE PARK

PAGE 46

TO EUREKA

TO WILLOW CREEK

Crescent City Area

① KINGS VALLEY GOLF COURSE

3030 Lesina Road
Crescent City, CA 95531

PRO SHOP: 707-464-2886

Carl Haywood, Manager

Driving Range ●
Practice Greens ●
Clubhouse ●
Food / Beverage ●
Accommodations
Pull Carts ●
Power Carts ●
Club Rental ●
Special Offers

	1	2	3	4	5	6	7	8	9	OUT
BACK	-	-	-	-	-	-	-	-	-	-
REGULAR	125	102	128	232	170	140	107	132	123	1259
par	3	3	3	4	3	3	3	3	3	28
handicap	5	15	11	3	1	13	17	7	9	-
FORWARD	110	102	128	200	155	140	107	132	123	1197
par	3	3	3	4	3	3	3	3	3	28
handicap	5	15	13	1	3	11	17	7	9	-

	10	11	12	13	14	15	16	17	18	IN
BACK	-	-	-	-	-	-	-	-	-	-
REGULAR	125	102	128	232	170	140	107	132	123	1259
par	3	3	3	4	3	3	3	3	3	28
handicap	6	16	12	4	2	14	18	8	10	-
FORWARD	110	102	128	200	155	140	107	132	123	1197
par	3	3	3	4	3	3	3	3	3	28
handicap	6	16	14	2	4	12	18	8	10	-

BACK	
yardage	-
par	-
rating	-
slope	-

REGULAR	
yardage	2518
par	56
rating	55.0
slope	79

FORWARD	
yardage	2394
par	56
rating	54.1
slope	77

② DEL NORTE GOLF COURSE

130 Club Drive
Crescent City, CA 95531

PRO SHOP: 707-458-3214

Owen Westbrook, Manager
Wayne Bowlman, Tournament Director

Driving Range ●
Practice Greens ●
Clubhouse ●
Food / Beverage ●
Accommodations
Pull Carts ●
Power Carts ●
Club Rental ●
Special Offers

	1	2	3	4	5	6	7	8	9	OUT
BACK	-	-	-	-	-	-	-	-	-	-
REGULAR	430	375	125	386	185	320	340	490	345	2996
par	4	4	3	4	3	4	4	5	4	35
handicap	3	5	17	1	13	15	9	7	11	-
FORWARD	430	375	125	386	185	320	340	490	345	2996
par	5	4	3	4	3	4	4	5	4	36
handicap	3	5	17	1	13	15	9	7	11	-

	10	11	12	13	14	15	16	17	18	IN
BACK	-	-	-	-	-	-	-	-	-	-
REGULAR	475	380	130	386	220	350	340	495	345	3121
par	5	4	3	4	3	4	4	5	3	35
handicap	8	6	18	2	4	16	12	10	14	-
FORWARD	475	380	130	386	220	350	340	495	345	3121
par	5	4	3	4	4	4	4	5	4	37
handicap	4	6	18	2	16	14	10	8	12	-

BACK	
yardage	-
par	-
rating	-
slope	-

REGULAR	
yardage	6117
par	70
rating	66.5
slope	106

FORWARD	
yardage	6117
par	73
rating	74.0
slope	124

PLAY POLICY & FEES: Green fees are $7 for nine holes and $11 for 18 holes.

TEE TIMES: Reservations are not accepted. All play is on a first-come, first-served basis.

COURSE DESCRIPTION: Located in a remote country setting, this is a flat par-3 course with one par 4. It's a fun course for players of all abilities.

NOTES: Redwoods abound, and the course is walkable.

LOCATION: From U.S.101 in Crescent City, drive north to the Grants Pass/ Exit 199. Turn left on Elk Valley Road; then turn right on Lesina Road. The course is just down the road on the left.

. . . ● **TOURNAMENTS:** This course is available for outside tournaments. The banquet facility can accommodate up to 50 people.

1. KINGS VALLEY GOLF COURSE

PLAY POLICY & FEES: Green fees are $10 for nine holes and $18 for 18 holes everyday. Carts are $10 for nine holes, $18 for 18.

TEE TIMES: Reservations can be booked 30 days in advance.

DRESS CODE: Shirts and shoes are necessary.

COURSE DESCRIPTION: Del Norte is in a beautiful setting with redwoods lining each fairway and two creeks winding back and forth across the course. The par-4 fourth, the number-one handicap hole, is known as the Bell Hole since golfers up ahead must ring a bell to inform those on the tee that they are out of the way.

NOTES: Del Norte is the most northwestern course in the state. The men's course record is 64, held by Gary Parkhurst. The women's course record is 68, held by Vivienne Moran.

LOCATION: From U.S. 101 in Crescent City, drive north to Highway 197; turn right and then left on Club Drive. Drive north to the course.

. . . ● **TOURNAMENTS:** This course is available for outside tournaments.

2. DEL NORTE GOLF COURSE

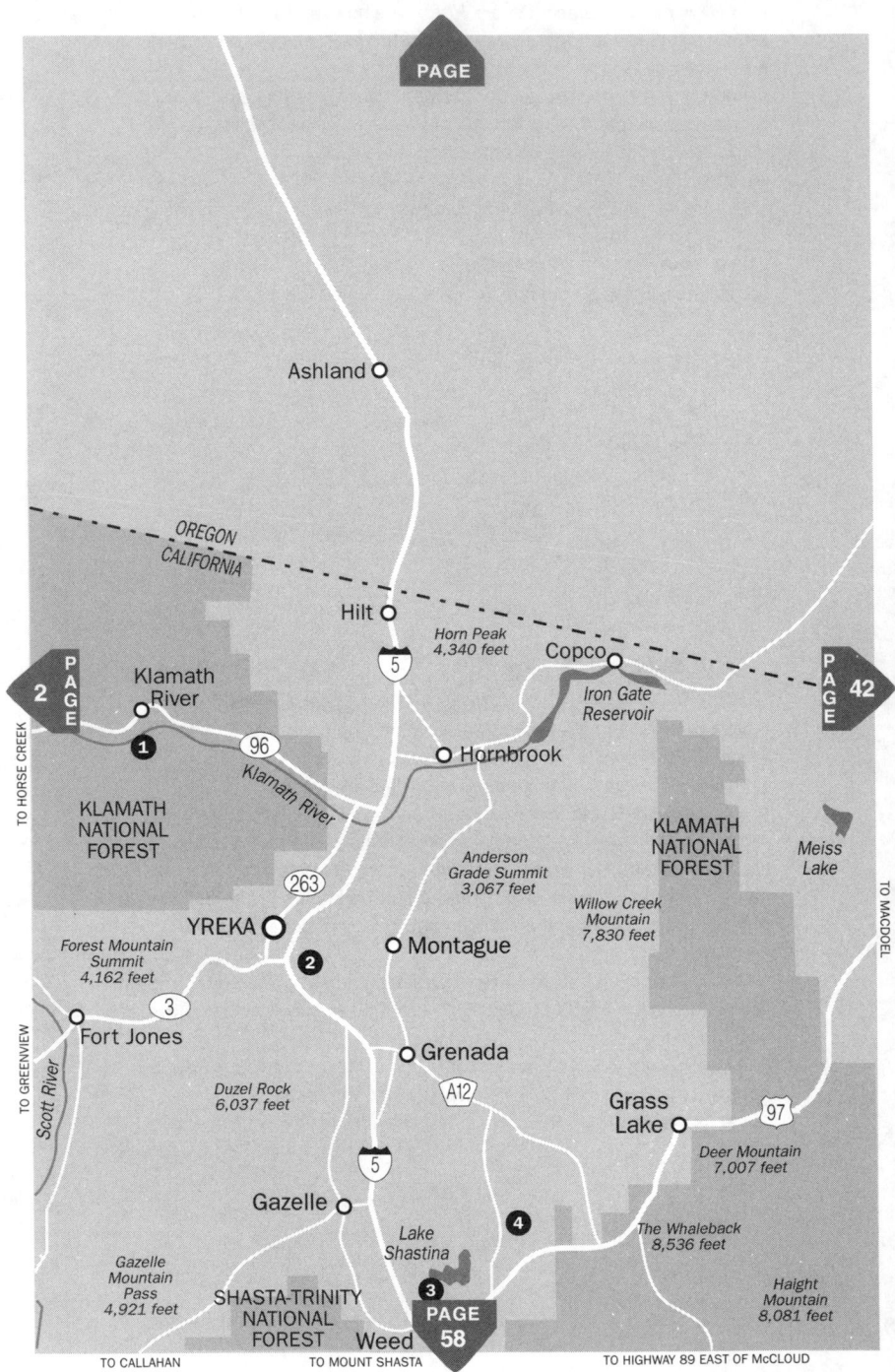

Ashland ○

OREGON
CALIFORNIA

Hilt ○

Horn Peak
4,340 feet

Copco ○

PAGE 2

TO HORSE CREEK

Klamath
River

1

96

Klamath River

Hornbrook ○

Iron Gate
Reservoir

PAGE 42

TO MACDOEL

KLAMATH
NATIONAL
FOREST

KLAMATH
NATIONAL
FOREST

Meiss
Lake

263

Anderson
Grade Summit
3,067 feet

Willow Creek
Mountain
7,830 feet

YREKA ○

Forest Mountain
Summit
4,162 feet

2

○ Montague

TO GREENVIEW

Scott River

3

○ Fort Jones

○ Grenada

Duzel Rock
6,037 feet

A12

Grass
Lake ○

97

Deer Mountain
7,007 feet

5

Gazelle ○

Lake
Shastina

4

The Whaleback
8,536 feet

Gazelle
Mountain
Pass
4,921 feet

SHASTA-TRINITY
NATIONAL
FOREST

3

PAGE 58

Haight
Mountain
8,081 feet

Weed

TO CALLAHAN

TO MOUNT SHASTA

TO HIGHWAY 89 EAST OF McCLOUD

Yreka Area

EAGLE'S NEST GOLF COURSE
ARCHITECT: ORVILLE REIRSGARD, 1971

22112 Klamath River Road
Klamath River, CA 96050

PRO SHOP: 530-465-2424

John Hinkle, General Manager

Driving Range
Practice Greens
Clubhouse ●
Food / Beverage ●
Accommodations
Pull Carts ●
Power Carts
Club Rental ●
$pecial Offers

	1	2	3	4	5	6	7	8	9	OUT
BACK	-	-	-	-	-	-	-	-	-	-
REGULAR	420	150	246	170	110	237	93	285	106	1817
par	5	3	4	3	3	4	3	4	3	32
handicap	1	13	9	5	11	7	17	3	15	-
FORWARD	420	150	246	170	110	237	93	285	106	1817
par	5	3	4	3	3	4	3	4	3	32
handicap	1	13	9	5	11	7	17	3	15	-

	10	11	12	13	14	15	16	17	18	IN
BACK	-	-	-	-	-	-	-	-	-	-
REGULAR	-	-	-	-	-	-	-	-	-	
par	-	-	-	-	-	-	-	-	-	
handicap	-	-	-	-	-	-	-	-	-	-
FORWARD	-	-	-	-	-	-	-	-	-	
par	-	-	-	-	-	-	-	-	-	
handicap	-	-	-	-	-	-	-	-	-	-

BACK	
yardage	-
par	-
rating	-
slope	-

REGULAR	
yardage	1817
par	32
rating	-
slope	-

FORWARD	
yardage	1817
par	32
rating	-
slope	-

SHASTA VALLEY GOLF COURSE
ARCHITECT: CLARK GLASSON

500 Golf Course Road
Montague, CA 96064

PRO SHOP: 530-842-2302

Cynthia Kirchen, Owner
Paul Kirchen, Professional

Driving Range ●
Practice Greens ●
Clubhouse ●
Food / Beverage ●
Accommodations
Pull Carts ●
Power Carts ●
Club Rental ●
$pecial Offers

	1	2	3	4	5	6	7	8	9	OUT
BACK	-	-	-	-	-	-	-	-	-	-
REGULAR	--	-	-	-	-	-	-	-	-	
par	-		-	-	-	-	-	-	-	
handicap	-	-	-	-	-	-	-	-	-	-
FORWARD	-	-	-	-	-	-	-	-	-	
par	-	-	-	-	-	-	-	-	-	
handicap	-	-	-	-	-	-	-	-	-	-

	10	11	12	13	14	15	16	17	18	IN
BACK	-	-	-	-	-	-	-	-	-	-
REGULAR	-	-	-	-	-	-	-	-	-	
par	-	-	-	-	-	-	-	-	-	
handicap	-	-	-	-	-	-	-	-	-	-
FORWARD	-	-	-	-	-	-	-	-	-	
par	-	-	-	-	-	-	-	-	-	
handicap	-	-	-	-	-	-	-	-	-	-

BACK	
yardage	-
par	-
rating	-
slope	-

REGULAR	
yardage	3140
par	36
rating	67.3
slope	110.

FORWARD	
yardage	2717
par	36
rating	71.4.
slope	105

38

PLAY POLICY & FEES: Green fees are $7 weekdays for nine holes and $10 for 18 holes. Weekend green fees are $9 for nine holes and $12 for 18 holes. The all-day rate is $15.

TEE TIMES: Reservations are not necessary, but call first to make sure a tournament is not scheduled.

COURSE DESCRIPTION: Located just south of the Oregon border, this course is tricky, with numerous trees and overhanging limbs that make fairways even narrower. The sixth hole is the most scenic, following alongside the Klamath River. This rarely played golf course could be one of the best values in California.

NOTES: This course is located on the Klamath River. Fishing, rafting, and hiking are other activities to enjoy. For those who pride themselves on finding golf balls on the course, try gold prospecting on the river instead. It could be more profitable, and you won't slow up play.

LOCATION: From Yreka drive eight miles north on Interstate 5. Take Highway 96 west to the city of Klamath River. Drive about three miles to Walker Bridge and turn left onto the bridge and Klamath River Road.

. . . ● **TOURNAMENTS:** This course is available for outside tournaments. A 24-player minimum is needed. Tournaments can be booked one month in advance. ● **TRAVEL:** The Sportsman's Lodge is located 10 minutes from the golf course and offers cabins. For more information call 530-465-2366.

1. EAGLE'S NEST GOLF COURSE

PLAY POLICY & FEES: Green fees are $10 for nine holes and $14 for 18 holes weekdays, and $11 for nine holes and $16 for 18 holes weekends. Carts are $9 for nine holes and $16 for 18 holes.

TEE TIMES: Reservations are not accepted. All play is on a first-come, first-served basis.

COURSE DESCRIPTION: There's a lot of water to contend with on this short course, so the premium is on accuracy.

NOTES: The men's course record is 68, set in 1979 by host pro Paul Kirchen and tied in 1991 by Darien Tucker, and the women's record is 72.

LOCATION: From Interstate 5 in Yreka drive east on Highway 3 to Monague. Exit south onto Golf Course Road.

. . . ● **TOURNAMENTS:** A 72-player minimum is needed for a shotgun tournament. ● **TRAVEL:** The Miners Inn B.W. (530-842-4355) and Amerihost Inn (530-841-1300) are recommended for lodging.

2. SHASTA VALLEY GOLF COURSE

27730 Old Edgewood Road
Weed, CA 96094

PRO SHOP: 530-938-9971

Dixie Nehring, Manager
Don Nehring, Superintendent

Driving Range ●
Practice Greens ●
Clubhouse ●
Food / Beverage ●
Accommodations
Pull Carts ●
Power Carts ●
Club Rental ●
$pecial Offers

	1	2	3	4	5	6	7	8	9	OUT
BACK	-	-	-	-	-	-	-	-	-	-
REGULAR	327	151	489	155	327	365	491	304	187	2796
par	4	3	5	3	4	4	5	4	3	35
handicap	5	17	3	13	11	7	1	15	9	-
FORWARD	327	140	418	133	325	300	404	238	163	2448
par	4	3	5	3	4	4	5	4	3	35
handicap	5	17	1	15	7	9	3	11	13	-

BACK	
yardage	-
par	-
rating	-
slope	-

	10	11	12	13	14	15	16	17	18	IN
BACK	-	-	-	-	-	-	-	-	-	-
REGULAR	327	132	468	134	327	329	491	304	161	2673
par	4	3	5	3	4	4	5	4	3	35
handicap	6	18	4	14	8	12	2	16	10	-
FORWARD	329	141	418	72	322	286	404	238	161	2371
par	4	3	5	3	4	4	5	4	3	35
handicap	6	16	2	18	8	10	4	12	14	-

REGULAR	
yardage	5469
par	70
rating	66.7
slope	115

FORWARD	
yardage	4819
par	70
rating	67.3
slope	116

5925 Country Club Drive
Weed, CA 96094

PRO SHOP: 530-938-3205

Ed McCarthy, General Manager, PGA
Bob Ledoux, Head Professional
Terry Zimmerman, Superintendent

Driving Range ●
Practice Greens ●
Clubhouse ●
Food / Beverage ●
Accommodations ●
Pull Carts ●
Power Carts ●
Club Rental ●
$pecial Offers

	1	2	3	4	5	6	7	8	9	OUT
BACK	562	345	181	402	342	442	399	190	572	3435
REGULAR	538	322	159	378	294	401	377	130	525	3124
par	5	4	3	4	4	4	4	3	5	36
handicap	5	11	17	1	13	3	7	15	9	-
FORWARD	496	297	123	313	283	374	339	97	457	2779
par	5	4	3	4	4	4	4	3	5	36
handicap	1	11	17	7	13	5	9	15	3	-

BACK	
yardage	6969
par	72
rating	72.6
slope	126

	10	11	12	13	14	15	16	17	18	IN
BACK	596	222	444	190	592	337	209	412	532	3534
REGULAR	566	157	413	141	520	300	183	360	504	3144
par	5	3	4	3	5	4	3	4	5	36
handicap	2	18	4	16	6	14	10	8	12	-
FORWARD	540	106	344	111	491	260	142	303	454	2751
par	5	3	4	3	5	4	3	4	5	36
handicap	2	18	8	16	4	12	14	10	6	-

REGULAR	
yardage	6268
par	72
rating	69.5
slope	119

FORWARD	
yardage	5530
par	72
rating	70.2
slope	114

PLAY POLICY & FEES: Summer green fees are $14 for nine holes and $19 for 18 holes weekdays, and $16 for nine holes and $21 for 18 holes weekends. After 3 p.m., green fees are $10 for unlimited play. Winter green fees are $10 for nine holes and $12 for 18 holes weekdays, $12 and $14 weekends. Carts are $10 for nine holes and $15 for 18 holes weekdays, and $12 for nine holes and $18 for 18 holes weekends.

TEE TIMES: Reservations are not needed but call ahead to make sure there are no tournaments in progress.

DRESS CODE: Shirts and shoes are necessary.

COURSE DESCRIPTION: This rolling course, bordered by trees and a creek, has magnificent views of Mount Shasta and Eddy Mountain. The greens are fast, and water comes into play on four holes. Watch out for the first hole, a tricky 327-yard par 4 with a dogleg left.

NOTES: Have you ever wanted to own part of a golf course? Here is your chance. Weed Golf Club is a membership-owned-and-operated corporation. The corporation is authorized to sell 200 shares of stock. Golf club members are are eligible to purchase one share. All dividends go to improve the golf course.

LOCATION: From Weed, drive one-half mile north on Interstate 5. Take the north Weed exit to the golf course.

. . . ● **TOURNAMENTS:** Outside tournaments are accepted with board of directors' approval.

3. WEED GOLF COURSE

PLAY POLICY & FEES: Green fees are $39 weekdays and $45 weekends for the 18-hole layout. Fees for the Scottish links course are $10 for nine holes and $14 for all day. Carts are $15 per person. Summer rules are played here year-round.

TEE TIMES: Reservations are accepted 30 days in advance.

DRESS CODE: Golf attire is encouraged. Collared shirts and nonmetal spikes are required.

COURSE DESCRIPTION: The large course is long and sprawling with five lakes. The 16th hole is one of the toughest par 3s in northern California. The short course is a nine-hole Scottish links layout. Par is 35. Both courses offer spectacular views of Mount Shasta.

NOTES: PGA Tour pro Peter Jacobsen earned his first pro win here at the 1976 Northern California Open. Craig Howard of Redding holds the course record at 63.

LOCATION: The Shastina Golf Resort is located seven miles north of Weed on U.S. 97. Turn right at Big Springs Road.

. . . ● **TOURNAMENTS:** A 48-player minimum is needed to book a tournament, and events should be booked 12 months in advance. The banquet facility can accommodate up to 135 people. ● **TRAVEL:** There is on-course lodging available. You can rent a condominium or a house. Play-and-stay packages are available at the resort. Call 800-358-4653 for information.

4. LAKE SHASTINA GOLF RESORT

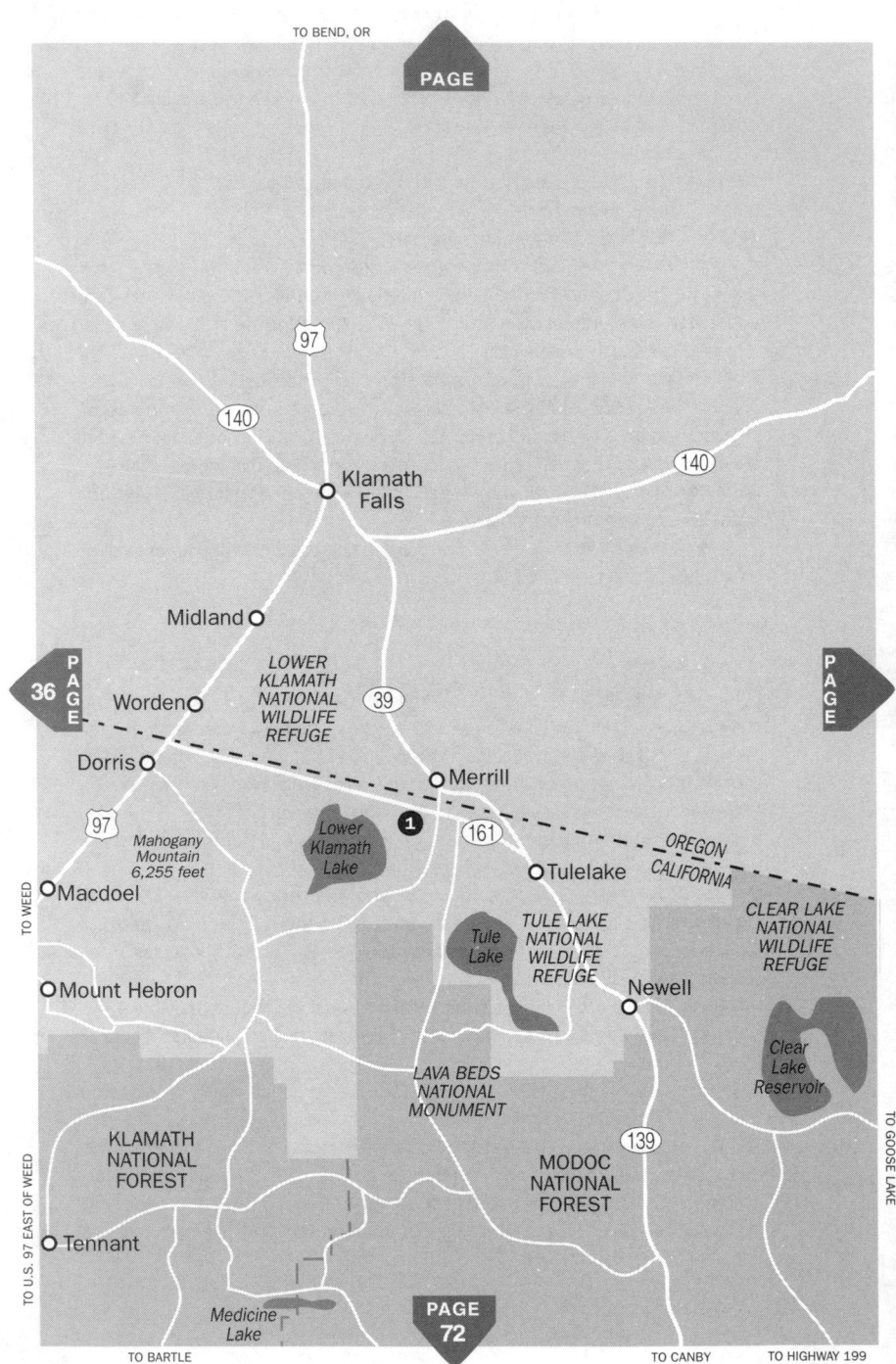

TO BEND, OR

PAGE

(97)

(140)

(140)

○ Klamath
Falls

Midland ○

LOWER
KLAMATH
NATIONAL
WILDLIFE
REFUGE

P
A
G
E
36

P
A
G
E

Worden ○

(39)

Dorris ○

○ Merrill

(97)

Mahogany
Mountain
6,255 feet

Lower
Klamath
Lake

❶

(161)

OREGON
CALIFORNIA

○ Macdoel

TO WEED

○ Tulelake

Tule
Lake

TULE LAKE
NATIONAL
WILDLIFE
REFUGE

CLEAR LAKE
NATIONAL
WILDLIFE
REFUGE

○ Mount Hebron

Newell
○

Clear
Lake
Reservoir

LAVA BEDS
NATIONAL
MONUMENT

TO U.S. 97 EAST OF WEED

KLAMATH
NATIONAL
FOREST

MODOC
NATIONAL
FOREST

(139)

TO GOOSE LAKE

○ Tennant

Medicine
Lake

PAGE
72

TO BARTLE

TO CANBY

TO HIGHWAY 199

Tulelake Area

17334 Stateline Road
Tulelake, CA 96134

PRO SHOP: 530-667-2922

Dan Crawford, Owner
Walter Zelensky, Manager

Driving Range
Practice Greens ●
Clubhouse
Food / Beverage
Accommodations
Pull Carts ●
Power Carts
Club Rental ●
$Special Offers

	1	2	3	4	5	6	7	8	9	OUT
BACK	-	-	-	-	-	-	-	-	-	-
REGULAR	179	255	153	186	146	100	180	157	156	1512
par	3	4	3	3	3	3	3	3	3	28
handicap	-	-	-	-	-	-	-	-	-	-
FORWARD	169	225	153	160	146	100	155	157	156	1421
par	3	4	3	3	3	3	3	3	3	28
handicap	-	-	-	-	-	-	-	-	-	-

	10	11	12	13	14	15	16	17	18	IN
BACK	-	-	-	-	-	-	-	-	-	-
REGULAR	179	255	153	186	146	100	180	157	156	1512
par	3	4	3	3	3	3	3	3	3	28
handicap	3	4	3	3	3	3	3	3	28	-
FORWARD	169	225	153	160	146	100	155	157	156	1421
par	3	4	3	3	3	3	3	3	3	28
handicap	-	-	-	-	-	-	-	-	-	-

BACK	
yardage	-
par	-
rating	-
slope	-

REGULAR	
yardage	3024
par	56
rating	-
slope	-

FORWARD	
yardage	2842
par	56
rating	-
slope	-

PLAY POLICY & FEES: Green fees are $7 for nine holes and $13 for 18 holes.

TEE TIMES: Reservations are not accepted. All play is on a first-come, first-served basis.

COURSE DESCRIPTION: The course is mostly flat, with scenic views and eight par-3 holes. The only par 4 is the 255-yard second hole.

NOTES: Indian Camp is the northernmost golf course in California. In fact, it's less than 300 yards from the Oregon border. According to archaeologists, the course is on the site of a historic Native American hunting and fishing camp. It is said that Captain Jack of the Modoc Indian tribe fished and hunted here in the 1870s when he wasn't skirmishing with the U.S. Army.

LOCATION: The course is located 25 miles southeast of Klamath Falls, Oregon. From Highway 39, turn right on Malon Road. Drive south two miles to Stateline Road and follow signs to the course.

. . . ● **TOURNAMENTS:** This course is available for outside tournaments.

1. INDIAN CAMP GOLF COURSE

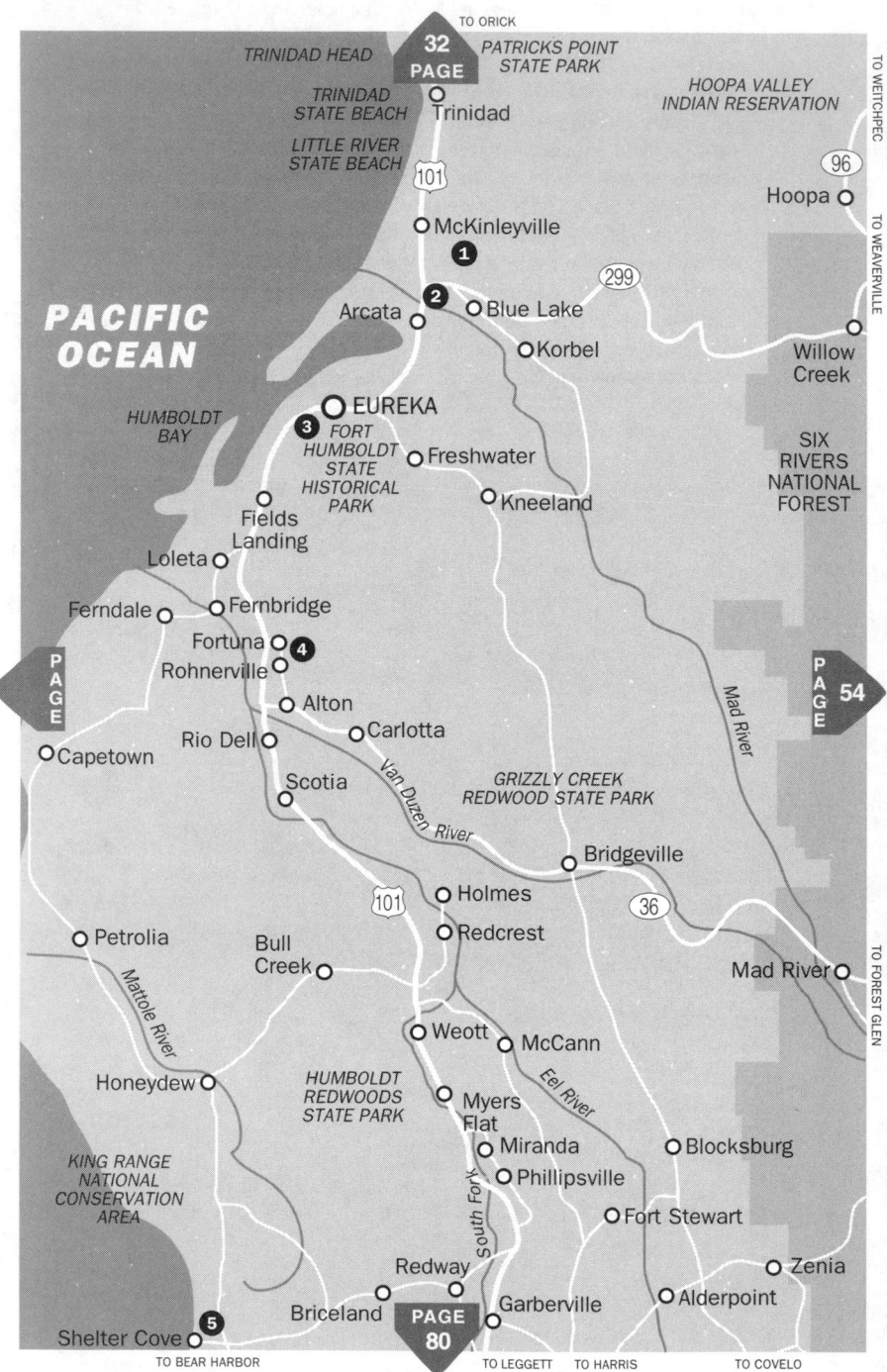

TO ORICK

TRINIDAD HEAD

PAGE 32

PATRICKS POINT
STATE PARK

HOOPA VALLEY
INDIAN RESERVATION

TO WEITCHPEC

TRINIDAD
STATE BEACH

Trinidad

LITTLE RIVER
STATE BEACH

96

101

Hoopa

McKinleyville

1

TO WEAVERVILLE

PACIFIC
OCEAN

2

299

Arcata

Blue Lake

Korbel

Willow
Creek

EUREKA

HUMBOLDT
BAY

3

FORT
HUMBOLDT
STATE
HISTORICAL
PARK

Freshwater

Kneeland

SIX
RIVERS
NATIONAL
FOREST

Fields
Landing

Loleta

Ferndale

Fernbridge

Fortuna

4

Rohnerville

PAGE

PAGE 54

Alton

Mad River

Rio Dell

Carlotta

Capetown

Scotia

GRIZZLY CREEK
REDWOOD STATE PARK

Van Duzen River

Bridgeville

36

Petrolia

101

Holmes

Redcrest

Mad River

TO FOREST GLEN

Bull
Creek

Mattole River

Weott

McCann

Eel River

Honeydew

HUMBOLDT
REDWOODS
STATE PARK

Myers
Flat

Miranda

Blocksburg

KING RANGE
NATIONAL
CONSERVATION
AREA

Phillipsville

Fort Stewart

South Fork

Zenia

Redway

PAGE 80

Garberville

Alderpoint

Briceland

Shelter Cove

5

TO BEAR HARBOR

TO LEGGETT   TO HARRIS

TO COVELO

Eureka Area

❶ BEAU PRE GOLF COURSE
ARCHITECT: DON HARLING, 1975

1777 Norton Road
McKinleyville, CA 95519

PRO SHOP: 707-839-2342

Don Harling, Director of Golf, PGA
Rex Denham, Professional
Paul Egbert, Superintendent

Driving Range ●
Practice Greens ●
Clubhouse ●
Food / Beverage ●
Accommodations
Pull Carts ●
Power Carts ●
Club Rental ●
Special Offers

	1	2	3	4	5	6	7	8	9	OUT
BACK	400	346	396	150	421	151	467	329	346	3006
REGULAR	369	302	355	134	403	121	419	309	325	2737
par	4	4	4	3	5	3	5	4	4	36
handicap	1	3	5	17	7	15	9	13	11	-
FORWARD	361	288	356	112	352	99	388	309	302	2567
par	4	4	4	3	5	3	5	4	4	36
handicap	1	3	5	17	7	15	9	13	11	-

	10	11	12	13	14	15	16	17	18	IN
BACK	463	424	197	293	143	452	375	141	330	2818
REGULAR	444	401	176	276	124	425	356	111	278	2591
par	5	4	3	4	3	5	4	3	4	35
handicap	4	2	8	12	16	10	6	18	14	-
FORWARD	332	393	164	253	98	400	308	92	262	2302
par	5	5	3	4	3	5	4	3	4	36
handicap	4	2	12	10	16	8	6	18	14	-

BACK	
yardage	5824
par	71
rating	69.0
slope	118

REGULAR	
yardage	5328
par	71
rating	66.8
slope	111

FORWARD	
yardage	4869
par	72
rating	68.4
slope	122

❷ BAYWOOD GOLF & COUNTRY CLUB
ARCHITECT: BOB BALDOCK, 1956

3600 Buttermilk Lane
Arcata, CA 95521

PRO SHOP: 707-822-3688
CLUBHOUSE: 707-822-3686

Don Witt, Manager
Jim Hosley, PGA Professional
Pete Williams, Superintendent

Driving Range ●
Practice Greens ●
Clubhouse ●
Food / Beverage ●
Accommodations
Pull Carts ●
Power Carts ●
Club Rental ●
Special Offers

	1	2	3	4	5	6	7	8	9	OUT
BACK	514	531	323	329	166	384	399	201	400	3247
REGULAR	493	509	306	318	136	369	385	185	383	3084
par	5	5	4	4	3	4	4	3	4	36
handicap	11	5	9	15	17	1	3	13	7	-
FORWARD	482	477	290	307	90	353	370	171	364	2904
par	5	5	4	4	3	4	4	3	4	36
handicap	3	5	9	11	15	7	1	17	13	-

	10	11	12	13	14	15	16	17	18	IN
BACK	345	451	165	338	509	207	458	282	409	3164
REGULAR	323	443	155	334	465	198	443	262	399	3022
par	4	4	3	4	5	3	5	4	4	36
handicap	14	2	16	6	10	12	8	18	4	-
FORWARD	319	429	144	328	401	153	430	241	390	2835
par	4	5	3	4	5	3	5	4	5	38
handicap	12	4	16	14	8	18	2	10	6	-

BACK	
yardage	6411
par	72
rating	71.6
slope	125

REGULAR	
yardage	6106
par	72
rating	70.4
slope	123

FORWARD	
yardage	5739
par	74
rating	73.9
slope	135

PLAY POLICY & FEES: Outside play is welcome. Green fees are $18 weekdays and $25 weekends. Twilight rates are $12 after 3 p.m. weekdays and after noon on weekends. Carts are $18

TEE TIMES: Reservations can be booked seven days in advance.

DRESS CODE: Shirts and shoes are necessary.

COURSE DESCRIPTION: This scenic course has lush fairways and ocean views. Pine and spruce trees line both sides of the fairways, sometimes interrupting a pleasant round of golf. Water comes into play on nine holes, and the bunkers are strategically placed. The par-5 seventh hole offers an excellent view of the Pacific Ocean.

NOTES: The men's course record is held by Jeff Arneson at 63, and the women's record is 71, held by Donna Stephens.

LOCATION: From U.S. 101 in McKinleyville, take the Murray Road exit to Central Avenue. Turn north on Central Avenue to Norton Road and drive to the course.

. . . ● **TOURNAMENTS:** This course is available for outside tournaments. A 24-player minimum is needed to book a tournament. Events can be booked two months in advance. The banquet facility can accommodate up to 50 people inside and 100 people outside. ● **TRAVEL:** The Double Tree Hotel in Eureka is located 15 minutes from the golf course. For reservations call 707-445-0844.

1. BEAU PRE GOLF COURSE

PLAY POLICY & FEES: Reciprocal play is accepted with members of other private clubs. Guest fees are $35 when accompanied by a member, $45 when sponsored by a member, and $60 for reciprocal players. Carts are $20. Reservations are recommended.

TEE TIMES: Tee times can be made seven days in advance for reciprocal play.

DRESS CODE: Golf attire is a must. No blue jeans, T-shirts, or short shorts may be worn. Nonmetal spikes are required during dry conditions, typically April to November.

COURSE DESCRIPTION: Situated in the midst of towering redwoods, this scenic course offers a challenging, tree-guarded layout. It's often foggy or misty. The downhill 11th hole is a 443-yard par 4, featuring a green surrounded by bunkers. The back nine is much tighter than the front.

LOCATION: From U.S. 101 in Arcata take the Sunny Brae exit east, past the California Highway Patrol station. Turn left on Buttermilk Lane and drive to the course.

. . . ● **TOURNAMENTS:** Outside tournaments are allowed on a limited basis. Events must have a member sponsor and a 50-player minimum. Events should be booked at least four months in advance. The banquet facility can accommodate 200 people.

2. BAYWOOD GOLF & COUNTRY CLUB

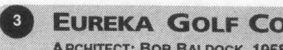

③ EUREKA GOLF COURSE
ARCHITECT: BOB BALDOCK, 1958

4750 Fairway Drive
Eureka, CA 95503

PRO SHOP: 707-443-4808

Daryl Parenteau, PGA Professional
Don Roller Jr., Superintendent

Driving Range ●
Practice Greens ●
Clubhouse ●
Food / Beverage ●
Accommodations
Pull Carts ●
Power Carts ●
Club Rental ●
$pecial Offers

	1	2	3	4	5	6	7	8	9	OUT
BACK	323	181	469	380	186	321	408	177	484	2929
REGULAR	315	174	456	362	164	305	395	157	469	2797
par	4	3	5	4	3	4	4	3	5	35
handicap	15	9	3	7	13	11	1	17	5	-
FORWARD	287	167	447	350	152	286	377	121	453	2640
par	4	3	5	4	3	4	4	3	5	35
handicap	11	13	3	7	15	9	1	17	5	-

	10	11	12	13	14	15	16	17	18	IN
BACK	407	314	139	471	417	160	304	553	174	2939
REGULAR	400	304	110	462	398	143	280	536	159	2792
par	4	4	3	5	4	3	4	5	3	35
handicap	2	10	18	8	6	16	14	4	12	-
FORWARD	443	322	127	309	350	104	280	413	287	2635
par	5	4	3	5	4	3	4	5	3	36
handicap	4	10	18	12	8	2	16	14	6	-

BACK	
yardage	5868
par	70
rating	68.0
slope	117

REGULAR	
yardage	5589
par	70
rating	67.0
slope	115

FORWARD	
yardage	5275
par	71
rating	69.8
slope	117

④ REDWOOD EMPIRE GOLF & COUNTRY CLUB

352 Country Club Drive
Fortuna, CA 95540

PRO SHOP: 707-725-5194

Greg Senestraro, PGA Professional
Barry Mueller, Superintendent

Driving Range ●
Practice Greens ●
Clubhouse ●
Food / Beverage ●
Accommodations
Pull Carts ●
Power Carts ●
Club Rental ●
$pecial Offers

	1	2	3	4	5	6	7	8	9	OUT
BACK	-	-	-	-	-	-	-	-	-	-
REGULAR	375	529	120	367	199	357	475	491	141	3054
par	4	5	3	4	3	4	5	5	3	36
handicap	1	5	13	3	7	11	9	15	17	-
FORWARD	322	430	120	367	204	330	436	358	141	2708
par	4	5	3	4	4	4	5	4	3	36
handicap	11	3	17	5	13	9	1	7	15	-

	10	11	12	13	14	15	16	17	18	IN
BACK	-	-	-	-	-	-	-	-	-	-
REGULAR	410	461	99	442	139	372	476	414	133	2946
par	4	5	3	5	3	4	5	4	3	36
handicap	2	10	18	12	16	6	8	4	14	-
FORWARD	371	422	99	423	139	302	341	414	133	2644
par	4	5	3	5	3	4	4	5	3	36
handicap	10	2	18	4	14	12	6	8	16	-

BACK	
yardage	-
par	-
rating	-
slope	-

REGULAR	
yardage	6000
par	72
rating	68.2
slope	109

FORWARD	
yardage	5352
par	72
rating	70.7
slope	115

18
HOLES

PLAY POLICY & FEES: Green fees are $11.75 weekdays and $14.75 weekends. Twilight, senior, and junior rates are available. Carts are $12 for nine holes and $17 for 18 holes. Reservations are recommended during the summer.

TEE TIMES: Reservations can be made at any time.

DRESS CODE: Shirts and shoes are necessary.

COURSE DESCRIPTION: An interesting layout with a creek that meanders throughout, Eureka Golf Course plays longer than its yardage indicates due to climatic conditions. If you want to score well, give your ego a break and club up. With pretty wide fairways, this is a great place to give your driver another chance. The par 4 10th hole doglegs 90 degrees and measures 400 yards from the regular tees.

NOTES: The course is surrounded by beautiful California redwoods.

LOCATION: From U.S.101 in Eureka take the Herrick exit east. Drive one-quarter mile to the golf course.

. . . ● **TOURNAMENTS:** This course is available for outside tournaments. ●

TRAVEL: The Ramada Limited is located 10 minutes from the golf course. For reservations call 707-443-2206.

3. EUREKA GOLF COURSE

9
HOLES

PLAY POLICY & FEES: Reciprocal play is accepted with members of other private clubs. Green fees are $25 for reciprocal players. Guest fees are $20 when accompanied by a member.

TEE TIMES: Reservations can be made at any time.

DRESS CODE: Appropriate golf attire is required.

COURSE DESCRIPTION: Situated on a ridge, this course is tight and hilly with lots of trees, sidehill lies, prevailing winds, and little roll. It's a great test of your short game. The greens are fast, but they hold well.

NOTES: The course record of 64 is held by Tim Crowley Jr.

LOCATION: From U.S. 101 in Fortuna take the Kenmar Road exit to Fortuna Boulevard. Drive east past Rhonerville Road to Mill Street, and turn right. Turn right on Country Club Drive.

. . . ● **TOURNAMENTS:** This course is available for outside tournaments with board approval.

4. REDWOOD EMPIRE GOLF & COUNTRY

1555 Upper Pacific Drive
Shelter Cove, CA 95589

PRO SHOP: 707-986-7000

Cheryl Taylor, Manager

Driving Range
Practice Greens
Clubhouse ●
Food / Beverage ●
Accommodations
Pull Carts ●
Power Carts ●
Club Rental ●
$pecial Offers

	1	2	3	4	5	6	7	8	9	OUT
BACK	-	-	-	-	-	-	-	-	-	-
REGULAR	185	470	309	352	135	275	323	200	216	2465
par	3	5	4	4	3	4	4	3	3	33
handicap	-	-	-	-	-	-	-	-	-	-
FORWARD	-	-	-	-	-	-	-	-	-	
par	-	-	-	-	-	-	-	-	-	
handicap	-	-	-	-	-	-	-	-	-	-

	10	11	12	13	14	15	16	17	18	IN
BACK	-	-	-	-	-	-	-	-	-	-
REGULAR	185	470	309	352	135	275	323	200	216	2465
par	3	5	4	4	3	4	4	3	3	33
handicap	-	-	-	-	-	-	-	-	-	-
FORWARD	-	-	-	-	-	-	-	-	-	
par	-	-	-	-	-	-	-	-	-	
handicap	-	-	-	-	-	-	-	-	-	-

BACK	
yardage	-
par	-
rating	
slope	

REGULAR	
yardage	4930
par	66
rating	-
slope	110

FORWARD	
yardage	
par	
rating	
slope	

PLAY POLICY & FEES: Green fees are $10 for unlimited play. Carts are $10 for nine holes and $18 for 18 holes.

TEE TIMES: Reservations can be made seven days in advance.

COURSE DESCRIPTION: This links course with one par 5 and four par 3s has spectacular ocean views from every hole. This course borders a daytime airstrip. One of the local rules is that if your ball lands near the airstrip it must be moved at least 10 yards away; no penalty.

NOTES: Camping, lodging, and dining are all within walking distance. A new pro shop and lounge opened in 1999.

LOCATION: From Garberville on U.S.101 go west 22 miles to Shelter Cove. Turn right onto Upper Pacific Drive, then left onto Lower Pacific Drive.

. . . ● **TOURNAMENTS:** A 12-player minimum is needed to book an event.

5. SHELTER COVE GOLF COURSE

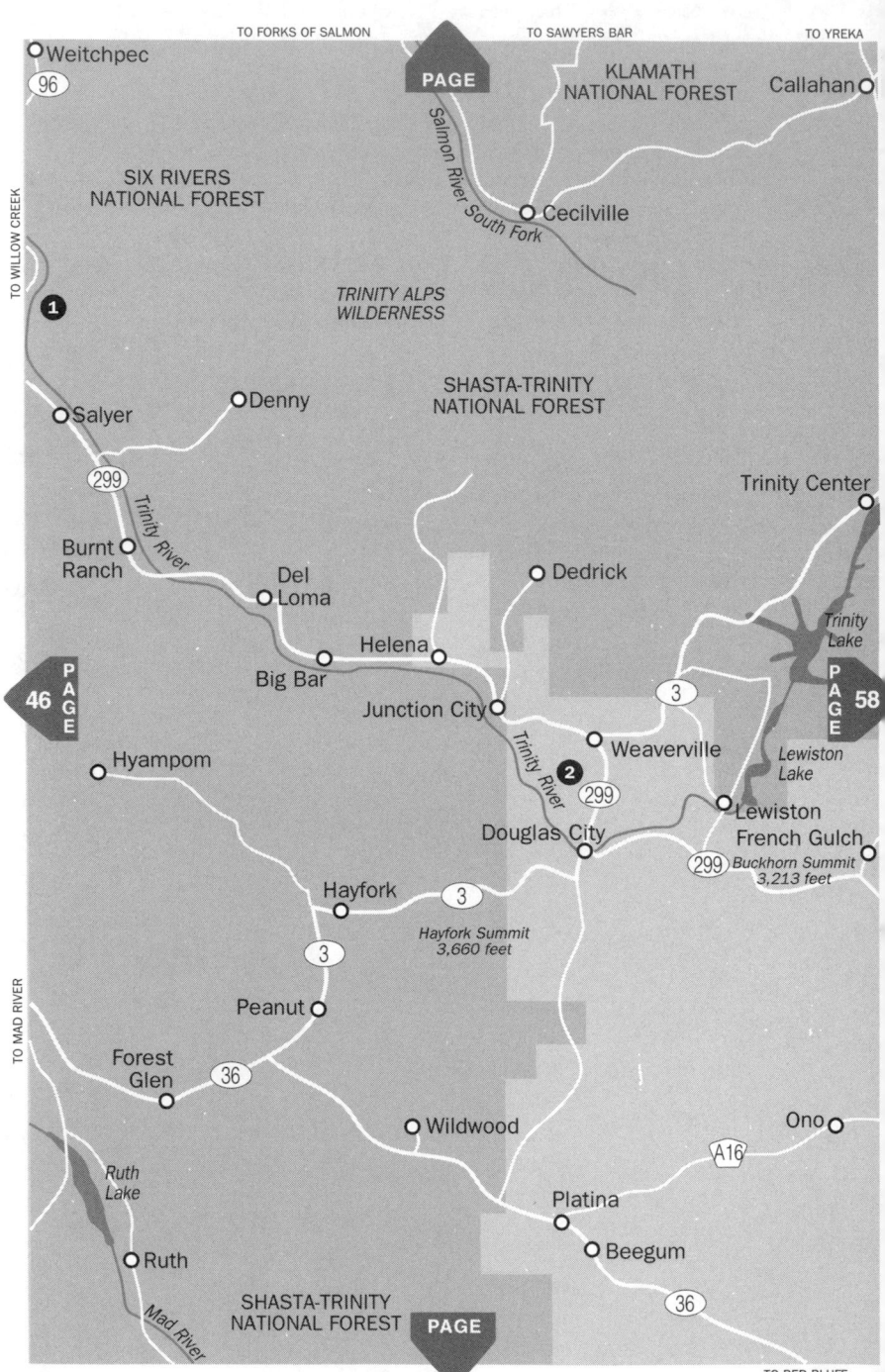

TO FORKS OF SALMON
TO SAWYERS BAR
TO YREKA

PAGE

KLAMATH
NATIONAL FOREST

Weitchpec
96
Callahan

TO WILLOW CREEK

SIX RIVERS
NATIONAL FOREST

Salmon River South Fork

Cecilville

TRINITY ALPS
WILDERNESS

SHASTA-TRINITY
NATIONAL FOREST

Denny

Salyer
299

Trinity River

Trinity Center

Burnt
Ranch

Del
Loma

Dedrick

Trinity
Lake

Helena

Big Bar

3

Junction City

46 PAGE

PAGE 58

Trinity River

Hyampom

Weaverville

Lewiston
Lake

2
299

Douglas City

Lewiston
French Gulch

299
Buckhorn Summit
3,213 feet

Hayfork
3

Hayfork Summit
3,660 feet

3

TO MAD RIVER

Peanut

Forest
Glen
36

Wildwood

A16

Ono

Ruth
Lake

Platina

Beegum

Ruth

36

Mad River

SHASTA-TRINITY
NATIONAL FOREST

PAGE

TO RED BLUFF

Weaverville Area

❶ BIGFOOT GOLF & COUNTRY CLUB

P.O. Box 836
Willow Creek, CA 95573

Patterson Road
Willow Creek, CA 95573

PRO SHOP: 800-788-9548
CLUBHOUSE: 530-629-2193

Carol Tonkin, Manager
Bob Newell, Tournament Director, PGA

Driving Range ●
Practice Greens ●
Clubhouse ●
Food / Beverage ●
Accommodations
Pull Carts ●
Power Carts ●
Club Rental ●
$pecial Offers

	1	2	3	4	5	6	7	8	9	OUT
BACK	-	-	-	-	-	-	-	-	-	-
REGULAR	304	141	271	487	155	299	267	489	145	2558
par	4	3	4	5	3	4	4	5	3	35
handicap	5	17	9	1	13	7	11	3	15	-
FORWARD	303	143	273	477	154	293	263	487	137	2530
par	4	3	4	5	3	4	4	5	3	35
handicap	5	17	9	1	13	7	11	3	15	-

	10	11	12	13	14	15	16	17	18	IN
BACK	-	-	-	-	-	-	-	-	-	-
REGULAR	298	126	252	468	135	292	244	490	139	2444
par	4	3	4	5	3	4	4	5	3	35
handicap	6	18	10	2	14	8	12	4	16	-
FORWARD	294	123	273	472	144	294	263	477	137	2477
par	4	3	4	5	3	4	4	5	3	35
handicap	6	18	10	2	14	8	12	4	16	-

BACK	
yardage	-
par	-
rating	-
slope	-

REGULAR	
yardage	5002
par	70
rating	64.4
slope	103

FORWARD	
yardage	5007
par	70
rating	68.5
slope	118

❷ TRINITY ALPS GOLF & COUNTRY CLUB
ARCHITECT: FRED EASTWOOD, 1973

P.O. Box 582
Weaverville, CA 96093

111 Fairway Drive
Weaverville, CA

PRO SHOP: 530-623-5411

Felix Claveran, PGA Professional

Driving Range ●
Practice Greens ●
Clubhouse ●
Food / Beverage ●
Accommodations
Pull Carts ●
Power Carts ●
Club Rental ●
$pecial Offers

	1	2	3	4	5	6	7	8	9	OUT
BACK	-	-	-	-	-	-	-	-	-	-
REGULAR	150	115	290	380	110	275	135	210	316	1981
par	3	3	4	4	3	4	3	3	4	31
handicap	13	17	9	1	15	11	15	7	3	-
FORWARD	150	115	290	360	110	265	135	210	316	1951
par	3	3	4	4	3	4	3	3	4	31
handicap	13	15	5	1	17	7	11	9	3	-

	10	11	12	13	14	15	16	17	18	IN
BACK	-	-	-	-	-	-	-	-	-	-
REGULAR	150	115	290	380	110	275	135	210	316	1981
par	3	3	4	4	3	4	3	3	4	31
handicap	14	18	10	2	16	12	6	8	4	-
FORWARD	150	115	290	360	110	265	135	210	316	1951
par	3	3	4	4	3	4	3	3	4	31
handicap	14	16	6	2	18	8	12	10	4	-

BACK	
yardage	-
par	-
rating	-
slope	-

REGULAR	
yardage	3962
par	62
rating	60.0
slope	-

FORWARD	
yardage	3902
par	62
rating	60.0
slope	-

PLAY POLICY & FEES: Outside play is accepted. No spectators are allowed. Green fees are $10 for nine holes and $15 for 18 holes weekdays, and $15 for nine holes and $20 for 18 holes on weekends. Carts are $10 for nine holes and $20 for 18 holes.

TEE TIMES: Reservations can be made at any time.

DRESS CODE: Shirts must be worn at all times.

COURSE DESCRIPTION: Although short from a yardage standpoint, Bigfoot requires accuracy with its small greens. It has water on five of nine holes. The par-4 seventh hole, for instance, is reachable for big hitters at 263 yards, but out-of-bounds lurks behind and to the left of the green. The par-5 fourth hole, at 477 yards, features a green that is just 15 yards deep from front to back, and water encircles two-thirds of the putting surface.

NOTES: The course record is 59, set by local pro Bob Newell. This facility offers outside dining.

LOCATION: From U.S. 101 in Arcata take Highway 299 east to Willow Creek. Turn left on Country Club Road and cross the Trinity River. Turn left on Patterson, then right on Bigfoot Avenue.

. . . ● **TOURNAMENTS:** This course is available for outside tournaments. A 60-player minimum is needed to book a tournament. Events should be booked four months in advance. The banquet facility can accommodate 100 people.

1. BIGFOOT GOLF & COUNTRY CLUB

PLAY POLICY & FEES: Green fees are $9 for nine holes and $14 for 18 holes every day. Carts are $9 for nine holes and $14 for 18 holes.

TEE TIMES: Reservations are accepted but not required.

DRESS CODE: Shirts must be worn at all times.

COURSE DESCRIPTION: There are two water hazards on this rolling, short, and walkable course. It's picturesque, with lots of trees and views of the Trinity Alps. The par-3 seventh hole has two water hazards. Four of the nine holes have water, and the greens are small.

NOTES: The course record of 55 is shared by Felix Claveran and Jay Berkowitz. The course was designed by Fred Eastwood, father of Senior PGA Tour pro Bob Eastwood.

LOCATION: From Redding drive 49 miles west on Highway 299 to Weaverville. Exit south on Glen Road and continue to Fairway Drive and the course.

. . . ● **TOURNAMENTS:** This course is available for outside tournaments and has a banquet facility that holds 140 people.

2. TRINITY ALPS GOLF & COUNTRY CLUB

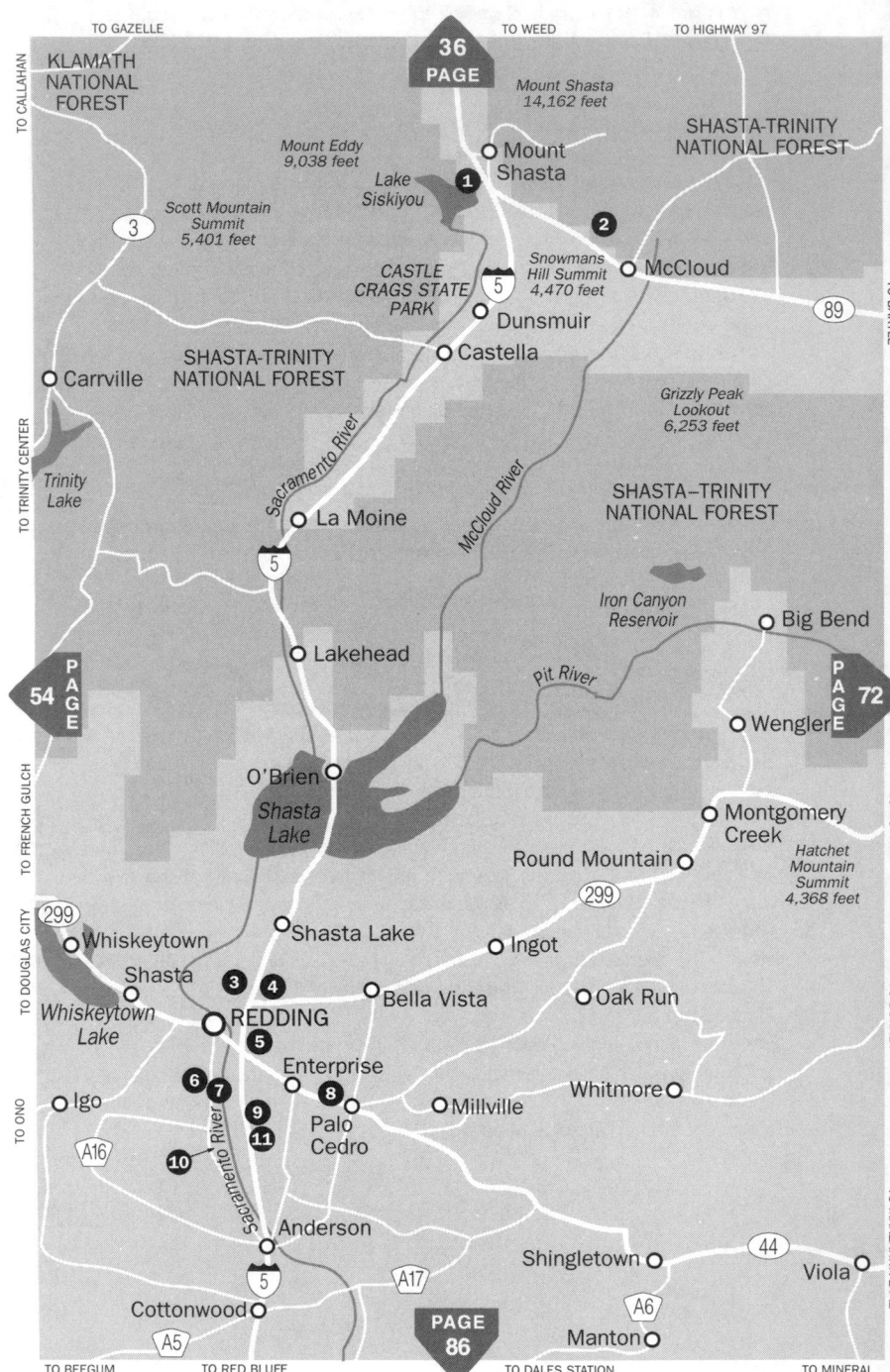

TO GAZELLE   TO WEED   TO HIGHWAY 97

36 PAGE

KLAMATH
NATIONAL
FOREST

TO CALLAHAN

Mount Shasta
14,162 feet

SHASTA-TRINITY
NATIONAL FOREST

Mount Eddy
9,038 feet

① Mount
Shasta

Lake
Siskiyou

Scott Mountain
Summit
5,401 feet

③

②

CASTLE
CRAGS STATE
PARK

Snowmans
Hill Summit
4,470 feet

McCloud

89

Dunsmuir

SHASTA-TRINITY
NATIONAL FOREST

Castella

TO TRINITY CENTER

Carrville

Grizzly Peak
Lookout
6,253 feet

Trinity
Lake

Sacramento River

McCloud River

SHASTA–TRINITY
NATIONAL FOREST

La Moine

5

Iron Canyon
Reservoir

54 PAGE

Lakehead

Big Bend

PAGE 72

Pit River

TO FRENCH GULCH

O'Brien

Wengler

Shasta
Lake

Round Mountain

Montgomery
Creek

Hatchet
Mountain
Summit
4,368 feet

299

TO DOUGLAS CITY

299

Whiskeytown

Shasta Lake

Ingot

Oak Run

Shasta

③ **④**

Whiskeytown
Lake

REDDING

Bella Vista

⑤

Enterprise

⑧

Whitmore

TO ONO

Igo

⑥ **⑦**

⑨

Millville

Palo
Cedro

⑪

⑩

Sacramento River

Anderson

5

A16

A17

Shingletown

44

Viola

PAGE 86

A6

Cottonwood

A5

Manton

TO BEEGUM   TO RED BLUFF   TO DALES STATION   TO MINERAL

Redding/Shasta Area

❶ MOUNT SHASTA RESORT GOLF COURSE
ARCHITECT: JIM SUMMERS, SANDY TATUM, 1994

1000 Siskiyou Lake
Mount Shasta, CA 96067

PRO SHOP: 530-926-3052

Jeremy Dunkason, PGA Professional
Thomas Jefferson, Superintendent

Driving Range ●
Practice Greens ●
Clubhouse ●
Food / Beverage ●
Accommodations ●
Pull Carts ●
Power Carts ●
Club Rental ●
$pecial Offers ●

	1	2	3	4	5	6	7	8	9	OUT
BACK	511	153	288	567	149	391	123	301	426	2909
REGULAR	498	142	270	537	139	379	117	292	402	2776
par	5	3	4	5	3	4	3	4	4	35
handicap	5	15	9	1	11	7	13	17	3	-
FORWARD	479	125	209	512	127	312	94	269	353	2480
par	5	3	4	5	3	4	3	4	4	35
handicap	5	15	11	1	9	7	13	17	3	-

	10	11	12	13	14	15	16	17	18	IN
BACK	482	399	419	141	341	409	350	136	479	3156
REGULAR	469	370	388	125	326	389	335	120	461	2983
par	4	4	4	3	4	4	4	3	5	35
handicap	2	10	4	18	14	8	6	12	16	-
FORWARD	428	342	351	109	270	346	313	78	349	2586
par	5	4	4	3	4	4	4	3	5	36
handicap	12	4	2	18	10	6	8	14	16	-

BACK	
yardage	6065
par	70
rating	68.8
slope	121

REGULAR	
yardage	5759
par	70
rating	66.9
slope	118

FORWARD	
yardage	5066
par	71
rating	66.7
slope	114

❷ MCCLOUD GOLF COURSE

P.O. Box 728
McCloud, CA 96057

1001 Squaw Valley Road
McCloud, CA 96057

PRO SHOP: 530-964-2535

Dottie Nelson, Manager
Rex Thrasher, Superintendent

Driving Range ●
Practice Greens ●
Clubhouse ●
Food / Beverage ●
Accommodations
Pull Carts ●
Power Carts ●
Club Rental ●
$pecial Offers

	1	2	3	4	5	6	7	8	9	OUT
BACK	-	-	-	-	-	-	-	-	-	-
REGULAR	346	354	482	154	274	477	167	222	507	2983
par	4	4	5	3	4	5	3	3	5	36
handicap	12	6	10	16	18	8	14	2	4	-
FORWARD	351	341	409	107	266	375	142	221	411	2623
par	4	4	5	3	4	4	3	4	5	36
handicap	5	3	9	13	17	1	7	15	11	-

	10	11	12	13	14	15	16	17	18	IN
BACK	-	-	-	-	-	-	-	-	-	-
REGULAR	346	354	502	197	274	497	167	323	417	3077
par	4	4	5	3	4	5	3	4	4	36
handicap	13	3	9	5	17	7	15	11	1	-
FORWARD	345	342	413	155	266	379	100	221	418	2639
par	4	4	5	3	4	5	3	4	5	37
handicap	4	6	8	10	12	2	18	16	14	-

BACK	
yardage	-
par	-
rating	-
slope	-

REGULAR	
yardage	6060
par	72
rating	68.2
slope	112

FORWARD	
yardage	5262
par	73
rating	69.4
slope	116

www.mountshastaresort.com

PLAY POLICY & FEES: Green fees are $25 for nine holes and $42 for 18 holes. Twilight fees are $30 starting at 2 p.m. Carts are $14 per person for 18 holes. Golf packages are available.

TEE TIMES: Reservations can be made seven days in advance.

DRESS CODE: No sleeveless shirts are allowed.

COURSE DESCRIPTION: This course features contoured fairways, though trees and water comes into play on five holes. The signature hole is the par-3 seventh, which features an elevated tee and great views over water. The course sits below snowcapped Mount Shasta and provides spectacular scenery and shot-making.

LOCATION: From Interstate 5 in Mount Shasta take the Central Mount Shasta exit. Follow the signs for the Mount Shasta Resort.

. . . ● **TOURNAMENTS:** There is a 20-player minimum to book a tournament. No shotgun starts are allowed on weekends. Carts must be used for tournament play. Events should be booked six months in advance. The banquet facility can accommodate up to 165 people. ● **TRAVEL:** For reservations at the resort call 530-926-3030. ● **$PECIAL OFFERS:** Overnight weekday golf packages are available. Contact the resort for details.

1. MOUNT SHASTA RESORT GOLF COURSE

PLAY POLICY & FEES: Green fees are $12 for nine holes and $17 for 18 holes. Carts are $9 for nine holes and $18 for 18 holes. The course is open April through November. Senior citizens can get a $2 discount on Monday.

TEE TIMES: Reservations are not accepted. All play is on a first-come, first-served basis.

COURSE DESCRIPTION: On a clear day, McCloud Golf Course offers one of the most beautiful sights in California golf: a majestic, bird's-eye view of Mount Shasta. The course features native pine and quaking aspen, with Squaw Creek meandering through it. Water comes into play on six of the nine holes. The par-3 seventh hole has a fountain offering 40-degree cold, pure water that is piped onto the course from Mount Shasta .

NOTES: The men's course record of 63 was set by former PGA Tour pro Rod Curl.

LOCATION: From Interstate 5 north of Redding and Dunsmuir, take the Highway 89 exit. Drive east to McCloud. In McCloud, turn right on Squaw Valley Road and follow it south to the course.

. . . ● **TOURNAMENTS:** This course is available for outside tournaments. A 72-player minimum is needed. Events should be booked nine months in advance. ● **TRAVEL:** When in town try Raymond's Restaurant on main street. The McCloud Hotel is recommended and located three miles from the golf course. For reservations or information call 800-964-2823. The Hogin House (530-964-2882) and The Timber Inn (530-964-2823) are also recommended.

2. MCCLOUD GOLF COURSE

③ LAKE REDDING GOLF COURSE

1795 Benton Drive
Redding, CA 96003

PRO SHOP: 530-243-5531

Dale Briggs, Professional

Driving Range ●
Practice Greens ●
Clubhouse ●
Food / Beverage ●
Accommodations
Pull Carts ●
Power Carts ●
Club Rental ●
$pecial Offers

	1	2	3	4	5	6	7	8	9	OUT
BACK	-	-	-	-	-	-	-	-	-	-
REGULAR	205	324	137	136	162	173	182	222	249	1790
par	4	4	3	3	3	3	4	4	4	31
handicap	4	3	16	18	14	8	6	12	10	-
FORWARD	205	324	137	136	162	173	182	222	249	1790
par	4	4	3	3	3	3	3	4	4	31
handicap	4	3	16	18	14	8	6	12	10	-

	10	11	12	13	14	15	16	17	18	IN
BACK	-	-	-	-	-	-	-	-	-	-
REGULAR	215	332	150	143	171	192	192	243	257	1895
par	4	4	3	3	3	3	3	4	4	31
handicap	2	1	15	17	13	7	5	11	9	-
FORWARD	215	332	150	143	171	192	192	243	257	1895
par	4	4	3	3	3	3	3	4	4	31
handicap	2	1	15	17	13	7	5	11	9	-

BACK	
yardage	-
par	-
rating	-
slope	-

REGULAR	
yardage	3685
par	62
rating	57.8
slope	87

FORWARD	
yardage	3685
par	62
rating	60.1
slope	88

④ GOLD HILLS COUNTRY CLUB
ARCHITECT: PHIL HOLCOMB, 1978

1950 Gold Hills Drive
Redding, CA 96003

PRO SHOP: 530-246-7867

Luis Miramontes, GM/Head Professional
Matt Valen, Tournament Director

Driving Range ●
Practice Greens ●
Clubhouse ●
Food / Beverage ●
Accommodations
Pull Carts ●
Power Carts ●
Club Rental ●
$pecial Offers

	1	2	3	4	5	6	7	8	9	OUT
BACK	405	542	131	354	356	424	381	199	497	3289
REGULAR	381	464	101	337	345	394	364	181	483	3050
par	4	5	3	4	4	4	4	3	5	36
handicap	3	9	17	5	13	1	15	7	11	-
FORWARD	308	340	84	242	274	331	303	108	406	2396
par	4	5	3	4	4	4	4	3	5	36
handicap	1	13	17	5	9	3	15	11	7	-

	10	11	12	13	14	15	16	17	18	IN
BACK	335	365	383	348	203	562	428	131	518	3273
REGULAR	325	342	366	341	171	544	394	125	506	3114
par	4	4	4	4	3	5	4	3	5	36
handicap	16	6	10	12	14	8	2	18	4	-
FORWARD	269	249	298	276	120	402	270	117	429	2430
par	4	4	4	4	3	5	4	3	5	36
handicap	14	12	8	2	18	10	4	16	6	-

BACK	
yardage	6562
par	72
rating	72.3
slope	135

REGULAR	
yardage	6164
par	72
rating	70.3
slope	132

FORWARD	
yardage	4826
par	72
rating	68.8
slope	120

PLAY POLICY & FEES: Green fees are $8 for nine holes and $13 for 18 holes. Senior rates are available Monday through Friday. Carts are $8 for nine holes and $15 for 18 holes. Pull carts are $2.

TEE TIMES: Tee times are generally not needed but can be reserved a couple of days in advance.

DRESS CODE: Shirts are required; no tank tops.

COURSE DESCRIPTION: This short executive course is known for requiring accuracy because of its narrow fairways lined with trees. There are four lakes that come into play. Lake Redding is popular with seniors and beginners.

NOTES: This course is open every day including Christmas.

LOCATION: Heading north on Interstate 5 in Redding, take the Highway 299 East exit. Turn left, drive to the second stop light, and turn left again. At the bottom of the hill, take the first right, which is Benton Drive. Take Benton Drive to the course.

. . . ● **TOURNAMENTS:** This course is available for outside tournaments.

3. LAKE REDDING GOLF COURSE

PLAY POLICY & FEES: Outside play is welcome. Green fees are $25 weekdays and $30 weekends. Carts are $20.

TEE TIMES: Reservations can be booked seven days in advance.

DRESS CODE: Collared shirts are required.

COURSE DESCRIPTION: This course is a challenging test in a beautiful setting. Golfers have views of Mount Lassen and Mount Shasta on clear days. The opening hole is formidable—405 yards with out-of-bounds left, Churn Creek right. Carts are recommended due to the hilly terrain.

NOTES: The course record is 62, set by Doren Granberry.

LOCATION: From Interstate 5 just north of Redding, take the Oasis Road exit east and drive one-half mile. Turn right on Gold Hills Drive and follow it to the course.

. . . ● **TOURNAMENTS:** A 20-player minimum is needed to book a tournament. Large tournaments should be booked six months in advance. The banquet facility will hold up to 200 people. ● **TRAVEL:** For golfers staying in the Redding area, the recently remodeled Holiday Inn is recommended. Reservations can be made by calling 530-221-7500 or 800-626-1900.

4. GOLD HILLS COUNTRY CLUB

THE GOLF CLUB OF TIERRA OAKS

ARCHITECTS: SANDY TATUM, JIM SUMMER, 1993; JIM SUMMER

19700 La Crescenta Drive
Redding, CA 96003

PRO SHOP: 530-275-0887
CLUBHOUSE: 530-275-0795

Jeffrey Kreafle, Manager
Brett Bieske, PGA Professional
Jim Aosit, Superintendent

Driving Range ●
Practice Greens ●
Clubhouse ●
Food / Beverage ●
Accommodations
Pull Carts ●
Power Carts ●
Club Rental ●
$pecial Offers

	1	2	3	4	5	6	7	8	9	OUT
BACK	411	512	161	419	436	509	185	400	386	3419
REGULAR	379	489	147	403	383	492	162	388	366	3209
par	4	5	3	4	4	5	3	4	4	36
handicap	5	1	17	7	9	11	15	3	13	-
FORWARD	278	434	102	292	346	400	103	323	299	2577
par	4	5	3	4	4	5	3	4	4	36
handicap	11	1	17	9	3	7	15	5	13	-

	10	11	12	13	14	15	16	17	18	IN
BACK	424	215	469	385	495	317	400	141	565	3411
REGULAR	395	175	429	368	481	303	367	113	535	3166
par	4	3	4	4	5	4	4	3	5	36
handicap	8	10	2	14	12	16	6	18	4	-
FORWARD	309	104	350	266	392	251	291	69	460	2492
par	4	3	5	4	5	4	4	3	5	37
handicap	8	14	6	12	10	16	4	18	2	-

BACK	
yardage	6830
par	72
rating	72.1
slope	130

REGULAR	
yardage	6375
par	72
rating	70.4
slope	126

FORWARD	
yardage	5069
par	73
rating	70.3
slope	117

---

6 RIVERVIEW GOLF & COUNTRY CLUB

4200 Bechelli Lane
Redding, CA 96002

PRO SHOP: 530-224-2250
CLUBHOUSE: 530-224-2255

Mr. Kim Thurman, PGA Professional
Lon Rickey, Manager
Bob Magladry, Tournament Director

Driving Range ●
Practice Greens ●
Clubhouse ●
Food / Beverage ●
Accommodations ●
Pull Carts ●
Power Carts ●
Club Rental ●
$pecial Offers

	1	2	3	4	5	6	7	8	9	OUT
BACK	-	-	-	-	-	-	-	-	-	-
REGULAR	580	369	208	341	346	338	347	183	536	3248
par	5	4	3	4	4	4	4	3	5	36
handicap	1	7	5	11	9	13	15	17	3	-
FORWARD	573	359	170	298	301	329	327	169	481	3007
par	5	4	3	4	4	4	4	3	5	36
handicap	1	5	15	13	11	9	7	17	3	-

	10	11	12	13	14	15	16	17	18	IN
BACK	-	-	-	-	-	-	-	-	-	-
REGULAR	193	346	351	417	475	525	406	138	382	3233
par	3	4	4	4	5	5	4	3	4	36
handicap	10	14	12	2	16	4	6	18	8	-
FORWARD	173	280	325	367	403	445	327	117	335	2772
par	3	4	4	4	5	5	4	3	4	36
handicap	14	61	8	4	6	2	10	18	12	-

BACK	
yardage	-
par	-
rating	-
slope	-

REGULAR	
yardage	6481
par	72
rating	70.1
slope	118

FORWARD	
yardage	5779
par	72
rating	73.0
slope	122

PLAY POLICY & FEES: Reciprocal play is accepted from other private clubs. Guest fees are $30 when accompanied by a member, $65 for reciprocal guests. Carts are $12 per person.

TEE TIMES: Reservations can be made two days in advance for reciprocal play. Call the head professional to make reservations.

DRESS CODE: Appropriate golf attire is required.

COURSE DESCRIPTION: Built in the rolling hills of north Redding, this course features oak- and pine-lined fairways, which give it a mature feel. The signature hole is the par-4 12th, a sharp dogleg right, with a creek guarding the left side of the fairway. Those who decide to play it safe will face a demanding second shot to an elevated green.

LOCATION: From Interstate 5 in Redding drive north to the Oasis Road exit. Drive east for 3.2 miles to the club entrance on the left.

. . . ● **TOURNAMENTS:** Fifteen outside events are allowed each year. Carts are required. A 16-player minimum is required. Events can be booked two to three months in advance. ● **TRAVEL:** For golfers staying in the Redding area, the recently remodeled Holiday Inn is recommended. Reservations can be made by calling 530-221-7500 or 800-626-1900.

5. THE GOLF CLUB OF TIERRA OAKS

PLAY POLICY & FEES: Reciprocal play is accepted with members of other private clubs. Reciprocal fees are $50. Carts are $20 for guests. The course is closed on Monday.

TEE TIMES: Reciprocal play is accepted with members of other private clubs. Tee times can be made one week in advance.

DRESS CODE: Collared shirts are required. Nonmetal spikes are required.

COURSE DESCRIPTION: Head pro Kim Thurman calls the first hole, a par 5 of 580 yards, "the most scenic in California." The Sacramento River borders the left side with a spectacular view of the mountains in the background. The traditional-style course is narrow with countless trees, and the greens are mostly small. The par 3s measure 208, 183, 193, and 138 yards.

NOTES: Some golfers sacrifice a ball into the Sacramento River as an act of resignation.

LOCATION: From Interstate 5 in Redding take the Bonneyview Road/Churn Creek exit. Cross the overpass and turn right on Bechelli Lane. Follow it to the course on the left.

. . . ● **TOURNAMENTS:** Board approval is a must for outside events. ● **TRAVEL:** The Holiday Inn can be reached by calling 530-221-7500

6. RIVERVIEW GOLF & COUNTRY CLUB

7 ALLEN'S GOLF COURSE

2780 Sacramento Dr.
Redding, CA 96001

PRO SHOP: 530-241-5055

Driving Range
Practice Greens •
Clubhouse
Food / Beverage •
Accommodations
Pull Carts •
Power Carts •
Club Rental •
$pecial Offers

	1	2	3	4	5	6	7	8	9	OUT
BACK	-	-	-	-	-	-	-	-	-	-
REGULAR	284	285	107	126	240	167	151	236	110	1706
par	4	4	3	3	4	3	3	4	3	31
handicap	3	5	17	15	1	7	9	11	13	-
FORWARD	284	285	107	126	196	167	151	236	110	1662
par	4	4	3	3	4	3	3	4	3	31
handicap	3	5	17	15	1	7	9	11	13	-

	10	11	12	13	14	15	16	17	18	IN
BACK	-	-	-	-	-	-	-	-	-	-
REGULAR	-	-	-	-	-	-	-	-	-	-
par	-	-	-	-	-	-	-	-	-	-
handicap	-	-	-	-	-	-	-	-	-	-
FORWARD	-	-	-	-	-	-	-	-	-	-
par	-	-	-	-	-	-	-	-	-	-
handicap	-	-	-	-	-	-	-	-	-	-

BACK	
yardage	-
par	-
rating	
slope	

REGULAR	
yardage	1706
par	31
rating	57.0
slope	92

FORWARD	
yardage	1662
par	31
rating	58.2
slope	89

8 PALO CEDRO GOLF CLUB
ARCHITECT: BERT STAMPS, 1992

22499 Golftime Drive
Palo Cedro, CA 96073

PRO SHOP: 530-547-3012

Ed Ochinero, Owner
Chad White, Head Professional, PGA
Debby Koopman, Manager

Driving Range •
Practice Greens •
Clubhouse •
Food / Beverage •
Accommodations
Pull Carts •
Power Carts •
Club Rental •
$pecial Offers

	1	2	3	4	5	6	7	8	9	OUT
BACK	375	260	169	416	522	183	361	279	534	3099
REGULAR	365	247	155	387	508	165	341	257	481	2906
par	4	4	3	4	5	3	4	4	5	36
handicap	7	15	9	3	1	11	13	17	5	-
FORWARD	342	235	109	384	481	139	318	246	462	2716
par	4	4	3	4	5	3	4	4	5	36
handicap	9	11	13	5	1	15	7	17	3	-

	10	11	12	13	14	15	16	17	18	IN
BACK	375	260	169	416	522	183	361	279	534	3099
REGULAR	365	247	155	387	508	165	341	257	481	2906
par	4	4	3	4	5	3	4	4	5	36
handicap	8	16	10	4	2	12	14	18	6	-
FORWARD	342	235	109	384	481	139	318	246	462	2716
par	4	4	3	4	5	3	4	4	5	36
handicap	10	12	14	6	2	16	8	18	4	-

BACK	
yardage	6198
par	72
rating	68.7
slope	116

REGULAR	
yardage	5812
par	72
rating	67.0
slope	113

FORWARD	
yardage	5432
par	72
rating	67.9
slope	114

PLAY POLICY & FEES: Weekday green fees are $6 for nine holes and $11.50 for 18 holes. Weekend green fees are $7 for nine holes and $13 for 18 holes. Senior and junior rates are $5.50 for nine holes and $9.50 for 18 holes on weekdays only.

TEE TIMES: Reservations are on a first-come, first-served basis.

DRESS CODE: Shirts and shoes are required.

COURSE DESCRIPTION: This course is located in a park-like setting with a lots of trees and a creek coming into play on five holes. The ninth hole has everything--a pond, trees and a blind shot to an elevated green. Most of the fairways are narrow and every hole has out-of-bounds areas.

LOCATION: From Redding on Interstate 5 take the Bechelli Lane exit and head west. After you cross the Sacramento River, you will take your second left on East Side Road. Follow East Side Road until you reach Start Road; turn left. The course is on the left.

. . . ● **TOURNAMENTS:** This course is available for outside events, and offers a nice barbecue area for banquets.

7. ALLEN'S GOLF COURSE

PLAY POLICY & FEES: Reciprocal play is accepted from other private clubs. Green fees are $10 for nine holes and $18 for 18 holes without a member. Carts are $10 for nine holes and $18 for 18 holes.

TEE TIMES: Reservations can be booked seven days in advance.

DRESS CODE: All shirts must have sleeves, and nonmetal spikes are required.

COURSE DESCRIPTION: There are lots of water hazards and many maturing trees on this slightly hilly layout. The par-5 ninth hole is 481 yards and doglegs left over a stream. The green is guarded on both sides by bunkers that will catch any errant shots. The signature hole is the 165-yard, par-3 sixth. It is flanked on the left by pine and oak trees and a creek, and on the right by two huge oak trees. Playing from the elevated tee, you have to channel your ball through the narrow fairway to reach the green.

LOCATION: From Redding take Interstate 5 north to Highway 44. Drive east on Highway 44 for eight miles to Silver Bridge Road and turn left. The course is on the left.

. . . ● **TOURNAMENTS:** Outside events are accepted. There is a 36-player minimum to reserve a nine-hole shotgun and a 56-player minimum for an 18-hole shotgun.

8. PALO CEDRO GOLF CLUB

7335 Churn Creek Road
Redding, CA 96002

PRO SHOP: 530-222-6353

Stephen Divine, Manager
June Szody, Professional

Driving Range ●
Practice Greens ●
Clubhouse ●
Food / Beverage ●
Accommodations
Pull Carts ●
Power Carts ●
Club Rental ●
$pecial Offers

	1	2	3	4	5	6	7	8	9	OUT
BACK	-	-	-	-	-	-	-	-	-	-
REGULAR	-	-	-	-	-	-	-	-	-	-
par	-	-	-	-	-	-	-	-	-	
handicap	-	-	-	-	-	-	-	-	-	-
FORWARD	-	-	-	-	-	-	-	-	-	
par	-	-	-	-	-	-	-	-	-	
handicap	-	-	-	-	-	-	-	-	-	-

BACK	
yardage	-
par	-
rating	-
slope	-

	10	11	12	13	14	15	16	17	18	IN
BACK	-	-	-	-	-	-	-	-	-	-
REGULAR	-	-	-	-	-	-	-	-	-	-
par	-	-	-	-	-	-	-	-	-	
handicap	-	-	-	-	-	-	-	-	-	-
FORWARD	-	-	-	-	-	-	-	-	-	-
par	-	-	-	-	-	-	-	-	-	
handicap	-	-	-	-	-	-	-	-	-	-

REGULAR	
yardage	3103
par	36
rating	69.8
slope	112

FORWARD	
yardage	2758
par	36
rating	71.4
slope	117

5369 Indianwood Drive
Redding, CA 96001

PRO SHOP: 530-246-9077
CLUBHOUSE: 530-246-9991

Dan and Sandy Kowall, Owners
Dan Kowall, PGA Professional
Rick White, Superintendent

Driving Range
Practice Greens ●
Clubhouse ●
Food / Beverage ●
Accommodations
Pull Carts ●
Power Carts ●
Club Rental ●
$pecial Offers

	1	2	3	4	5	6	7	8	9	OUT
BACK	-	-	-	-	-	-	-	-	-	-
REGULAR	295	332	105	155	288	282	153	326	139	2075
par	4	4	3	3	4	4	3	4	3	32
handicap	5	7	17	11	15	3	13	1	9	-
FORWARD	233	291	95	117	212	251	133	304	97	1733
par	4	4	3	3	4	4	3	4	3	32
handicap	3	7	17	13	15	5	11	1	9	-

BACK	
yardage	-
par	-
rating	-
slope	-

	10	11	12	13	14	15	16	17	18	IN
BACK	-	-	-	-	-	-	-	-	-	-
REGULAR	259	314	100	133	267	274	144	317	116	1924
par	4	4	3	3	4	4	3	4	3	32
handicap	6	8	18	12	16	4	14	2	10	-
FORWARD	233	291	95	117	212	251	133	304	97	1733
par	4	4	3	3	4	4	3	4	3	32
handicap	4	8	18	14	16	6	12	2	10	-

REGULAR	
yardage	3999
par	64
rating	59.0
slope	93

FORWARD	
yardage	3466
par	64
rating	60.0
slope	95

PLAY POLICY & FEES: Green fees are $9 for nine holes and $18 for 18 holes. Carts are $9 for nine holes and $18 for 18 holes.

TEE TIMES: Reservations can be made seven days in advance.

DRESS CODE: Dress can be casual, but shirts are required.

COURSE DESCRIPTION: The course is primarily flat, but numerous trees separate adjoining fairways, and there are out-of-bounds on all but two holes. The course is a good test of moderate length, with trees and small greens giving it a distinctive flavor.

LOCATION: From Interstate 5 in Redding take the Knighton Road exit east. Knighton Road turns into Churn Creek Road, which leads to the course.

. . . ● **TOURNAMENTS:** This course is available for outside events. A 72-player minimum is needed to book a shotgun tournament. Events should be booked 12 months in advance. The banquet facility holds 90 people.

9. CHURN CREEK GOLF COURSE

PLAY POLICY & FEES: Members and guests only. Only players with NCGA, SCGA, or out-of-state golf association handicaps, or guests of members are allowed to play the course. Guest fees are $10 to $12 for nine holes and $15 to $20 for 18 holes. Carts are $8 for nine holes, and $16 for 18 holes.

TEE TIMES: Reservations are accepted 48 hours in advance for reciprocal play.

DRESS CODE: A sleeved shirt is required to play this course.

COURSE DESCRIPTION: This course was designed and built by Bill Ralston with the assistance of retired pro Eric Batten. With its tight layout, two ponds, and the Sacramento River Slough coming into play on five holes, consider this a target course of the most demanding dimensions. The course is in outstanding condition. The eighth hole, a par 4 of 326 yards, is deceptively difficult with out-of-bounds right, water left, and a green that slopes heavily left.

LOCATION: From Interstate 5 in Redding take the Churn Creek/Bechelli exit and turn west. Cross over the Sacramento River and turn right onto Indianwood Drive, which leads to the River Bend Estate. Drive through the subdivision. The course is at the rear of the residential area.

. . . ● **TOURNAMENTS:** Shotgun tournaments are available weekdays only. Tournaments should be booked six months in advance. The banquet facility holds 175 people. ● **TRAVEL:** The recently remodeled Holiday Inn is recommended. Reservations can be made by calling 530-221-7500 or 800-626-1900.

10. RIVER BEND GOLF & COUNTRY CLUB

ANDERSON TUCKER OAKS GOLF COURSE
ARCHITECT: WILLIAM H. TUCKER JR.

P.O. Box 678
Anderson, CA 96007

6241 Churn Creek Road
Redding, CA 96002

PRO SHOP: 530-365-3350

Al Banuelos, Manager
Chuck Sherman, Professional
Mike Ervin, Superintendent

Driving Range ●
Practice Greens ●
Clubhouse ●
Food / Beverage ●
Accommodations
Pull Carts ●
Power Carts ●
Club Rental ●
$pecial Offers

	1	2	3	4	5	6	7	8	9	OUT
BACK	-	-	-	-	-	-	-	-	-	-
REGULAR	435	357	434	494	134	375	333	161	468	3191
par	4	4	4	5	3	4	4	3	5	36
handicap	3	11	1	9	15	5	13	17	7	-
FORWARD	435	357	434	494	134	375	333	161	468	3191
par	5	4	5	5	3	4	4	3	4	37
handicap	7	11	5	1	15	9	13	17	3	-

	10	11	12	13	14	15	16	17	18	IN
BACK	-	-	-	-	-	-	-	-	-	-
REGULAR	445	341	518	512	150	351	319	149	395	3180
par	4	4	4	5	3	4	4	3	5	36
handicap	3	11	1	9	15	5	13	17	7	-
FORWARD	435	357	434	494	134	375	333	161	468	3191
par	5	4	5	5	3	4	4	3	4	37
handicap	7	11	5	1	15	9	13	17	3	-

BACK	
yardage	-
par	-
rating	-
slope	-

REGULAR	
yardage	6371
par	72
rating	69.0
slope	106

FORWARD	
yardage	6382
par	74
rating	70.9
slope	109

PLAY POLICY & FEES: Green fees are $8 for nine holes and $16 for 18 holes. Carts are $8 for nine holes and $16 for 18 holes.

TEE TIMES: Reservations are not accepted. All play is on a first-come, first-served basis.

COURSE DESCRIPTION: Like most Redding-area courses, Tucker Oaks is distinguished by numerous trees. There are bunkers on every hole, and two lakes come into play. The best hole is No. 3, a 434-yard par 4 that doglegs left. Out-of-bounds come into play on the first three holes.

NOTES: The men's course record is 61 by host pro Chuck Sherman, and Betty Bennett has the women's record of 68.

LOCATION: From Interstate 5 in Anderson take the Riverside exit to Airport Road north. Drive across the Sacramento River and turn left on Churn Creek Road. Continue to the course.

. . . ● **TOURNAMENTS:** This course is available for outside tournaments. An 80-player minimum is required for shotgun tournaments, which should be booked six months in advance.

11. ANDERSON TUCKER OAKS GOLF COURSE

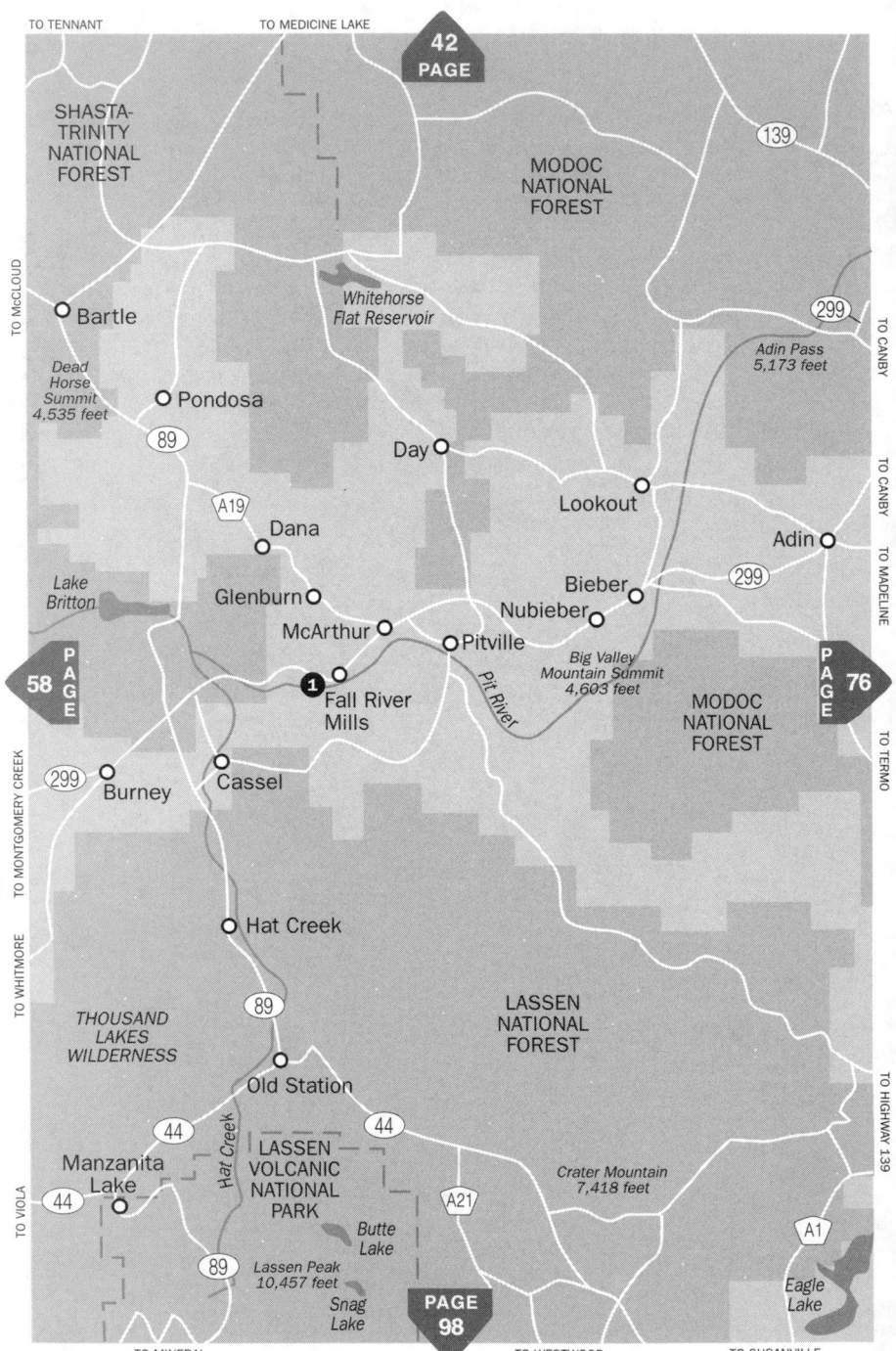

PAGE 42

TO TENNANT   TO MEDICINE LAKE

SHASTA-TRINITY NATIONAL FOREST

MODOC NATIONAL FOREST

139

TO McCLOUD

Bartle

Whitehorse Flat Reservoir

Dead Horse Summit 4,535 feet

Pondosa

89

Adin Pass 5,173 feet

299

TO CANBY

Day

A19

Lookout

Dana

Adin

TO CANBY

Lake Britton

Glenburn

Bieber

299

TO MADELINE

McArthur

Nubieber

Pitville

PAGE 58

1 Fall River Mills

Big Valley Mountain Summit 4,603 feet

Pit River

MODOC NATIONAL FOREST

PAGE 76

TO TERMO

299

Burney

Cassel

TO MONTGOMERY CREEK

TO WHITMORE

Hat Creek

89

THOUSAND LAKES WILDERNESS

LASSEN NATIONAL FOREST

TO HIGHWAY 139

Old Station

44

44

LASSEN VOLCANIC NATIONAL PARK

A21

Crater Mountain 7,418 feet

TO VIOLA

44

Manzanita Lake

Hat Creek

Butte Lake

A1

89

Lassen Peak 10,457 feet

Snag Lake

Eagle Lake

PAGE 98

TO MINERAL   TO WESTWOOD   TO SUSANVILLE

Fall River Mills Area

FALL RIVER VALLEY GOLF & COUNTRY CLUB
ARCHITECT: CLARK GLASSON, 1978

P.O. Box 827   42889 Highway 299 East
Fall River Mills, CA 96028   Fall River Mills, CA 96028

PRO SHOP: 530-336-5555

Karen Estes, Director of Golf
Susan Lauer, Professional
Mike Glasson, Owner/Superintendent

Driving Range ●
Practice Greens ●
Clubhouse
Food / Beverage ●
Accommodations
Pull Carts ●
Power Carts ●
Club Rental ●
$pecial Offers ●

GOLF 50

	1	2	3	4	5	6	7	8	9	OUT
BACK	392	442	666	227	400	449	435	198	579	3788
REGULAR	370	425	642	200	375	424	395	164	518	3513
par	4	4	5	3	4	4	4	3	5	36
handicap	15	5	1	13	17	3	7	11	9	-
FORWARD	353	379	549	179	338	385	361	136	450	3130
par	4	4	5	3	4	4	4	3	5	36
handicap	11	5	1	17	13	3	7	15	9	-

BACK	
yardage	7365
par	72
rating	74.9
slope	131

	10	11	12	13	14	15	16	17	18	IN
BACK	401	178	432	429	615	175	450	380	517	3577
REGULAR	377	166	407	390	561	151	421	354	492	3319
par	4	3	4	4	5	3	4	4	5	36
handicap	10	12	6	8	2	16	4	18	14	-
FORWARD	356	167	387	353	452	121	387	328	448	2999
par	4	3	4	4	5	3	4	4	5	36
handicap	12	16	4	10	2	18	6	14	8	-

REGULAR	
yardage	6832
par	72
rating	72.1
slope	126

FORWARD	
yardage	6129
par	72
rating	73.9
slope	129

PLAY POLICY & FEES: Green fees are $22 weekdays and $27 weekends. Senior rates are available. Carts are $22.

TEE TIMES: Reservations can be booked 14 days in advance.

DRESS CODE: Golf attire is encouraged.

COURSE DESCRIPTION: One of California's longest and toughest courses, at least when played from the blue tees, Fall River is located in a mountain valley best known for its first-rate fishing. But the golf course is a jewel, winding its way through the trees with a wide variety of holes.

NOTES: The eighth hole, a par 3 over a lake, is named "Bing's Bluff" in honor of the old crooner. Clark Glasson was building the course when he noticed Bing Crosby watching from a distance. Crosby owned the nearby Rising River Ranch, now owned by Clint Eastwood.

LOCATION: From Interstate 5 in Redding drive east on Highway 299 to Fall River Mills. The course is on the right.

. . . ● **TOURNAMENTS:** The banquet facility can accommodate up to 120 people. Carts are required. ● **TRAVEL:** The Fall River Hotel is located one-quarter mile from the golf course. For reservations call 530-336-5550. ● **$PECIAL OFFERS:** Play-and-stay packages are available that include lodging, green fees, cart, breakfast, and dinner.

1. FALL RIVER VALLEY GOLF & COUNTRY

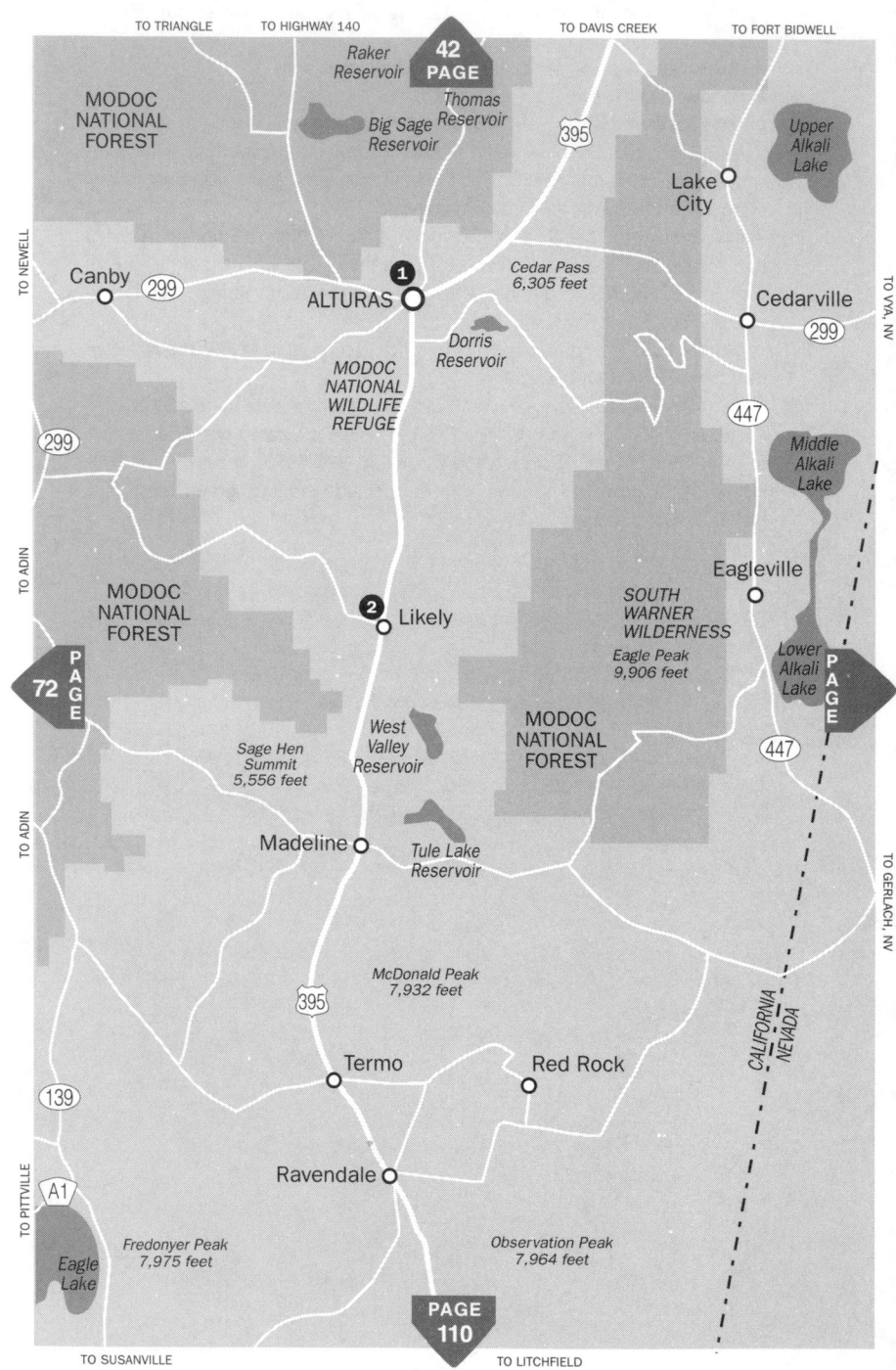

TO TRIANGLE   TO HIGHWAY 140   TO DAVIS CREEK   TO FORT BIDWELL

Raker Reservoir

42 PAGE

Thomas Reservoir

MODOC NATIONAL FOREST

Big Sage Reservoir

Upper Alkali Lake

395

Lake City

TO NEWELL

Canby 299

1 ALTURAS

Cedar Pass 6,305 feet

Cedarville 299

TO VYA, NV

Dorris Reservoir

MODOC NATIONAL WILDLIFE REFUGE

447

299

Middle Alkali Lake

TO ADIN

MODOC NATIONAL FOREST

2 Likely

Eagleville

SOUTH WARNER WILDERNESS
Eagle Peak 9,906 feet

Lower Alkali Lake

PAGE 72

PAGE

Sage Hen Summit 5,556 feet

West Valley Reservoir

MODOC NATIONAL FOREST

447

Madeline

Tule Lake Reservoir

TO ADIN

McDonald Peak 7,932 feet

395

TO GERLACH, NV

Termo

Red Rock

CALIFORNIA NEVADA

139

Ravendale

A1

TO PITTVILLE

Eagle Lake

Fredonyer Peak 7,975 feet

Observation Peak 7,964 feet

PAGE 110

TO SUSANVILLE   TO LITCHFIELD

Alturas Area

① ARROWHEAD GOLF COURSE
ARCHITECT: JOHN BRIGGS, 1969

1901 North Warner Street
Alturas, CA 96101

PRO SHOP: 530-233-3404
STARTER: 530-233-8494

Brad Server, General Manager, PGA
Red Gately, Superintendent

Driving Range ●
Practice Greens ●
Clubhouse ●
Food / Beverage ●
Accommodations
Pull Carts ●
Power Carts ●
Club Rental ●
Special Offers

	1	2	3	4	5	6	7	8	9	OUT
BACK	-	-	-	-	-	-	-	-	-	-
REGULAR	336	340	346	186	304	369	422	505	315	3123
par	4	4	4	3	4	4	4	5	4	36
handicap	13	1	15	3	17	5	7	11	9	-
FORWARD	320	331	346	93	149	363	422	445	325	2794
par	4	4	4	3	4	4	5	5	4	36
handicap	5	1	7	15	13	3	17	9	11	-

	10	11	12	13	14	15	16	17	18	IN
BACK	-	-	-	-	-	-	-	-	-	-
REGULAR	346	330	358	170	314	359	420	500	325	3122
par	4	4	4	3	4	4	4	5	4	36
handicap	14	2	16	8	18	4	6	12	10	-
FORWARD	336	331	272	93	149	318	422	445	325	2691
par	4	4	4	3	3	4	5	5	4	36
handicap	6	2	16	14	12	4	18	8	10	-

BACK	
yardage	-
par	-
rating	-
slope	-

REGULAR	
yardage	6245
par	72
rating	68.2
slope	112

FORWARD	
yardage	5485
par	72
rating	71.0
slope	112

② LIKELY LINKS GOLF CLUB
ARCHITECT: RICH HAMEL, 1999

Jess Valley Road
Likely, CA 96116

PRO SHOP: 530-233-6676

Gary McClellan, Professional

Driving Range ●
Practice Greens ●
Clubhouse ●
Food / Beverage ●
Accommodations ●
Pull Carts ●
Power Carts ●
Club Rental
Special Offers

	1	2	3	4	5	6	7	8	9	OUT
BACK	377	178	356	506	168	630	377	416	343	3351
REGULAR	361	150	347	491	156	606	362	377	326	3176
par	4	3	4	5	3	5	4	4	4	36
handicap										-
FORWARD	308	108	275	412	117	506	298	296	245	2565
par	4	3	4	5	3	5	4	4	4	36
handicap										-

	10	11	12	13	14	15	16	17	18	IN
BACK										
REGULAR										
par										
handicap										-
FORWARD										
par										
handicap										-

BACK	
yardage	3300
par	36
rating	70.2
slope	122

REGULAR	
yardage	3176
par	36
rating	68.8
slope	119

FORWARD	
yardage	2565
par	36
rating	
slope	

PLAY POLICY & FEES: Green fees are $10 for nine holes and $17 for 18 holes on weekdays. On weekends the green fees are $11 for nine holes and $20 for 18 holes. The clubhouse is closed November through February, but there is a drop box for collecting fees.

TEE TIMES: Reservations can be made one day in advance.

DRESS CODE: Golf attire is encouraged.

COURSE DESCRIPTION: This course has wide fairways and elevated greens. Irrigation ditches come into play on every hole, but there are no bunkers. The toughest hole is the par-5 eighth, which measures 450 yards for men.

NOTES: Because this course is located in a remote area of the most northeastern part of the state, Arrowhead is one of those rare spots where you can almost always drive up and tee off within minutes. Millard Porter and Jim Widby share the course record of 66.

LOCATION: From Interstate 5 in Redding drive east on Highway 299 to Alturas. Take the Warner Street exit and drive north to the course.

. . . ● **TOURNAMENTS:** A 40-player minimum is required to book a tournament. The banquet facility can accommodate 100 people. ● **TRAVEL:** The Best Western Trailside Inn is located five minutes from the golf course. For reservations call 530-233-4111.

1. ARROWHEAD GOLF COURSE

PLAY POLICY & FEES: Green fees are $10 for nine holes and $15 for 18 holes on weekdays, and $12 for nine holes and $17 for 18 holes on weekends. Carts are $10 for nine holes and $15 for 18 holes.

TEE TIMES: At this time reservations are not required.

DRESS CODE: Casual is OK, but shirts and shoes are required.

COURSE DESCRIPTION: Grip it and rip it; the average fairway on this course is 50 yards wide. Likely Links offers subtle elevation changes and large greens. Outside the fairways the rough is extemely rough, and if you can find your ball, it will be among the sagebrush and rocks. The signature hole is the slightly downhill 630-yard par-5 sixth hole from the championship tees. An afternoon breeze can be a factor.

NOTES: At 4,500 feet near both the Oregon and Nevada border, you will find an abundance of wildlife and fresh air. Yes, that's right—fresh air and California in the same sentence.

LOCATION: From Alturas take U.S. 395 south for 20 miles to Jess Valley Road. Take a right to the course.

. . . ● **TOURNAMENTS:** A few outside events will be allowed. Call the pro shop for more information.

2. LIKELY LINKS GOLF CLUB

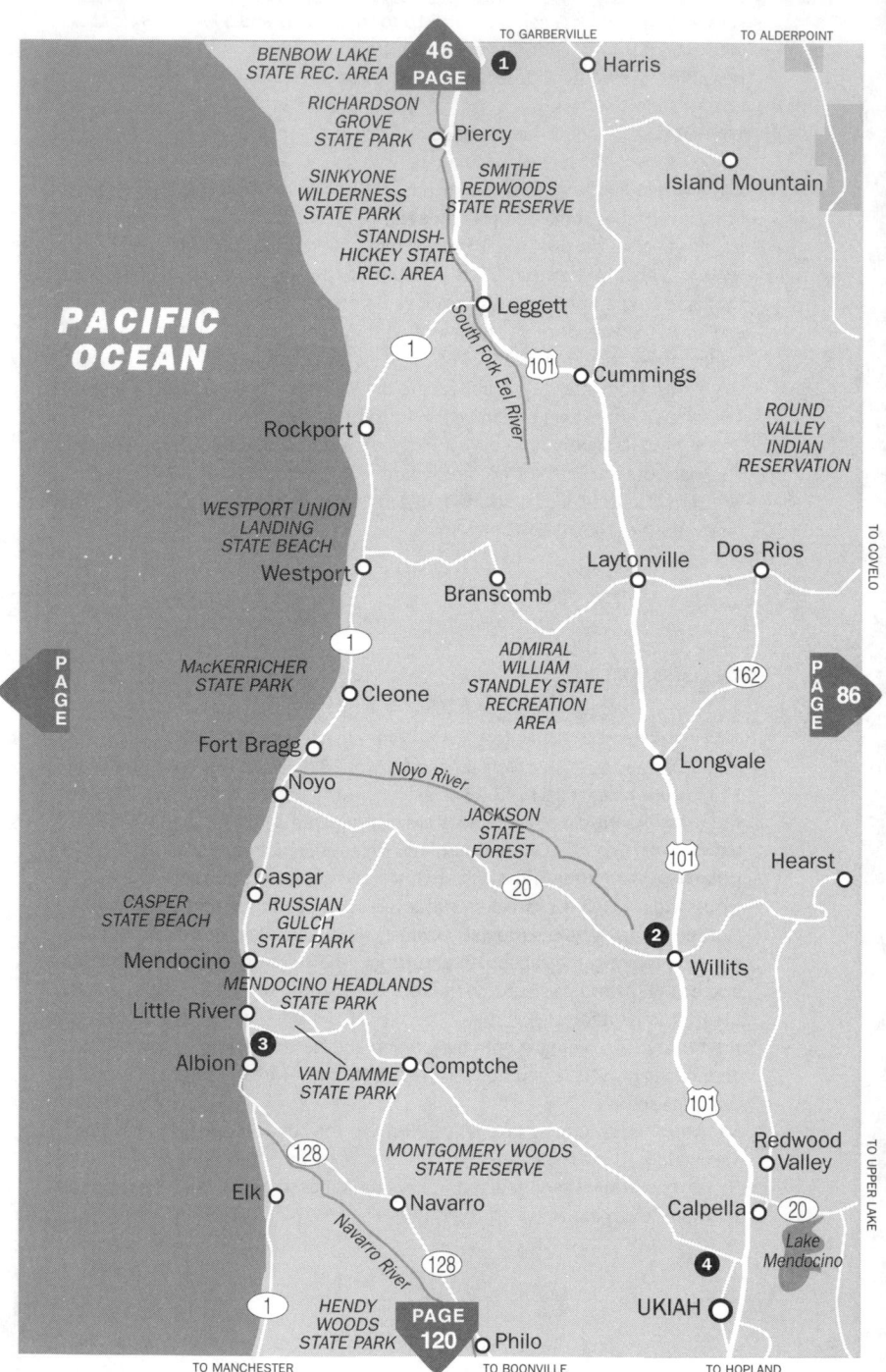

TO GARBERVILLE • TO ALDERPOINT

PAGE 46 • 1

BENBOW LAKE STATE REC. AREA

Harris

RICHARDSON GROVE STATE PARK • Piercy

SMITHE REDWOODS STATE RESERVE

Island Mountain

SINKYONE WILDERNESS STATE PARK

STANDISH-HICKEY STATE REC. AREA

PACIFIC OCEAN

1

Leggett

South Fork Eel River

101

Cummings

ROUND VALLEY INDIAN RESERVATION

Rockport

WESTPORT UNION LANDING STATE BEACH

Westport

Branscomb

Laytonville

Dos Rios

TO COVELO

PAGE

1

MacKERRICHER STATE PARK

Cleone

ADMIRAL WILLIAM STANDLEY STATE RECREATION AREA

162

PAGE 86

Fort Bragg

Noyo

Noyo River

JACKSON STATE FOREST

Longvale

20

101

Hearst

Caspar

CASPER STATE BEACH

RUSSIAN GULCH STATE PARK

2

Willits

Mendocino

MENDOCINO HEADLANDS STATE PARK

Little River

3

Albion

VAN DAMME STATE PARK

Comptche

101

128

MONTGOMERY WOODS STATE RESERVE

Redwood Valley

Elk

Navarro

Calpella

20

TO UPPER LAKE

Navarro River

128

4

Lake Mendocino

1

HENDY WOODS STATE PARK

PAGE 120

Philo

UKIAH

TO MANCHESTER • TO BOONVILLE • TO HOPLAND

Benbow/Ukiah Area

❶ BENBOW VALLEY RV RESORT & GOLF COURSE

7000 Benbow Drive
Garberville, CA 95542

PRO SHOP: 707-923-2777
CLUBHOUSE: 707-923-2777

Theodore Mattila, PGA Professional
Gerald Wendel, General Manager

Driving Range ●
Practice Greens ●
Clubhouse ●
Food / Beverage ●
Accommodations ●
Pull Carts ●
Power Carts ●
Club Rental ●
$pecial Offers ●

	1	2	3	4	5	6	7	8	9	OUT
BACK	-	-	-	-	-	-	-	-	-	-
REGULAR	242	166	299	126	334	484	441	144	319	2557
par	4	3	4	3	4	5	5	3	4	35
handicap	17	11	5	15	3	1	7	13	9	-
FORWARD	242	166	299	128	334	484	441	144	319	2557
par	4	3	4	3	4	5	5	3	4	35
handicap	11	15	7	13	5	1	3	17	9	-

	10	11	12	13	14	15	16	17	18	IN
BACK	-	-	-	-	-	-	-	-	-	-
REGULAR	255	167	324	144	324	464	462	98	303	2541
par	4	3	4	3	4	5	5	3	4	35
handicap	18	12	2	10	4	8	6	16	14	-
FORWARD	255	167	324	144	324	464	462	98	303	2541
par	4	3	4	3	4	5	5	3	4	35
handicap	12	14	6	16	8	4	2	18	10	-

BACK	
yardage	-
par	-
rating	-
slope	-

REGULAR	
yardage	5098
par	70
rating	64.7
slope	101

FORWARD	
yardage	5098
par	70
rating	68.5
slope	114

❷ BROOKTRAILS GOLF COURSE
ARCHITECT: ROBERT MUIR GRAVES, 1961

24860 Birch Street
Willits, CA 95490

PRO SHOP: 707-459-6761

Ron Runberg, PGA Professional
Doug Poulson, Superintendent

Driving Range
Practice Greens ●
Clubhouse ●
Food / Beverage ●
Accommodations
Pull Carts ●
Power Carts
Club Rental ●
$pecial Offers

	1	2	3	4	5	6	7	8	9	OUT
BACK	-	-	-	-	-	-	-	-	-	-
REGULAR	87	125	94	135	273	128	156	139	179	1316
par	3	3	3	3	4	3	3	3	3	28
handicap	18	13	15	6	1	11	5	12	4	-
FORWARD	87	125	94	135	273	128	156	139	179	1316
par	3	3	3	3	4	3	3	3	3	28
handicap	18	10	15	8	1	12	6	11	4	-

	10	11	12	13	14	15	16	17	18	IN
BACK	-	-	-	-	-	-	-	-	-	-
REGULAR	98	195	103	135	200	140	116	199	151	1337
par	3	3	3	3	4	3	3	3	3	28
handicap	17	3	14	10	7	9	16	2	8	-
FORWARD	98	195	103	135	200	140	116	199	151	1337
par	3	4	3	3	4	3	3	4	3	30
handicap	17	3	14	9	5	7	16	2	13	-

BACK	
yardage	-
par	-
rating	-
slope	-

REGULAR	
yardage	2653
par	56
rating	53.6
slope	80

FORWARD	
yardage	2653
par	58
rating	-
slope	-

PLAY POLICY & FEES: Green fees are $14 for unlimited play weekdays and $16 for unlimited play on weekends for those staying in the adjacent RV park. For outside guests, green fees are $14 for nine holes on weekdays and $16 for nine holes on weekends.

TEE TIMES: Reservations are not accepted. All play is on a first-come, first-served basis.

DRESS CODE: Shirts must be worn at all times, and no short shorts are allowed.

COURSE DESCRIPTION: This course is called the "Bowling Alley" for its tree-lined fairways. It features several severely sloping fairways, making it extremely difficult to keep the ball in play. Though it has its share of hills, the course is walkable.

NOTES: Located in a redwood forest, this course provides views of both the Eel River and Benbow Lake. Within the regular course is a junior golf course designed for beginning golfers ages 6 to 12 .

LOCATION: From U.S.101 two miles south of Garberville, take the Benbow exit directly to the course.

. . . ● **TOURNAMENTS:** This course is available for outside tournaments. A 40-player minimum is needed. Tournaments should be booked at least three months in advance. The banquet facility can accommodate 140 people. ● **TRAVEL:** The Benbow Inn is within walking distance of the course. For reservations call 707-923-2124. ● **$PECIAL OFFERS:** The Benbow Inn offers play-and-stay golf packages.

1. BENBOW VALLEY RV RESORT & GOLF

PLAY POLICY & FEES: Green fees are $8.50 for nine holes and $10.50 for 18 holes weekdays, and $9.50 for nine holes and $13 for 18 holes weekends. Senior rates are $8 for nine holes and $10 for 18 holes on weekdays.

TEE TIMES: Reservations can be made 14 days in advance.

COURSE DESCRIPTION: A wonderfully scenic course set in the redwoods, Brooktrails is short but tricky, with a creek winding across seven fairways. The greens are small but quick. The only par 4 is the fifth hole, a dogleg measuring 273 yards. The par 3s range in distance from 87 yards (the first hole) to 199 yards (the 17th).

NOTES: Eric McKillican holds the course record with a 51. Brooktrails Golf Course boasts 1,100 trees, all of which have been hit by errant shots.

LOCATION: Drive north on U.S.101 through Willits; then take the Sherwood exit northwest 2.5 miles to Brooktrails. Take a left on Brooktrails. Brooktrails meets Birch Street.

. . . ● **TOURNAMENTS:** A 20-player minimum is required to book a tournament. ● **TRAVEL:** The Baechtel Creek Inn is recommended. Reservations can be made by calling 707-459-9063.

2. BROOKTRAILS GOLF COURSE

7751 North Highway 1
Little River, CA 95456

PRO SHOP: 707-937-5667

Bob Fish, Head Professional
Terry Stratton, Superintendent

Driving Range •
Practice Greens •
Clubhouse •
Food / Beverage •
Accommodations •
Pull Carts •
Power Carts •
Club Rental •
$pecial Offers •

	1	2	3	4	5	6	7	8	9	OUT
BACK	-	-	-	-	-	-	-	-	-	-
REGULAR	385	150	460	510	295	245	210	335	185	2775
par	4	3	5	5	4	4	3	4	3	35
handicap	1	13	9	3	15	17	5	11	7	-
FORWARD	362	141	405	444	295	240	190	319	175	2571
par	4	3	5	5	4	4	3	4	3	35
handicap	3	13	5	1	15	17	7	11	9	-

	10	11	12	13	14	15	16	17	18	IN
BACK	-	-	-	-	-	-	-	-	-	-
REGULAR	375	140	450	500	275	235	140	325	270	2710
par	4	3	5	5	4	4	3	4	4	36
handicap	2	12	6	4	14	18	10	8	16	-
FORWARD	362	141	405	352	275	240	128	319	227	2449
par	4	3	5	4	4	4	3	4	4	35
handicap	4	12	8	2	14	18	6	10	16	-

BACK	
yardage	-
par	-
rating	-
slope	-

REGULAR	
yardage	5485
par	71
rating	67.3
slope	120

FORWARD	
yardage	5020
par	70
rating	68.3
slope	111

599 Park Boulevard
Ukiah, CA 95482

PRO SHOP: 707-467-2832

Jeff McMillen, Head Professional, PGA
Tad McCormick, Assistant Professional
Brian Steppe, Assistant Professional

Driving Range
Practice Greens •
Clubhouse •
Food / Beverage •
Accommodations
Pull Carts •
Power Carts •
Club Rental •
$pecial Offers

	1	2	3	4	5	6	7	8	9	OUT
BACK	275	377	198	441	114	394	307	357	155	2618
REGULAR	271	341	192	431	108	394	300	353	148	2538
par	4	4	3	5	3	4	4	4	3	34
handicap	5	1	11	15	3	7	17	13	9	-
FORWARD	267	310	167	414	108	390	290	353	142	2441
par	4	4	3	5	3	4	4	4	3	34
handicap	6	12	16	2	18	4	10	8	14	-

	10	11	12	13	14	15	16	17	18	IN
BACK	361	394	350	358	426	191	313	520	319	3232
REGULAR	351	383	337	350	396	185	307	495	315	3119
par	4	4	4	4	4	3	4	5	4	36
handicap	5	1	11	15	3	7	17	13	9	-
FORWARD	337	286	327	344	386	145	296	443	307	2871
par	4	4	4	4	4	3	4	5	4	36
handicap	3	15	11	7	1	17	13	9	5	-

BACK	
yardage	5850
par	70
rating	68.3
slope	120

REGULAR	
yardage	5657
par	70
rating	67.4
slope	118

FORWARD	
yardage	5312
par	70
rating	69.5
slope	120

PLAY POLICY & FEES: Outside play is accepted. Green fees are $15 for nine holes and $25 for 18 holes weekdays, and $20 for nine holes and $30 for 18 holes weekends and holidays. Carts are $16 for nine holes and $24 for 18 holes.

TEE TIMES: Reservations can be made one year in advance.

DRESS CODE: Sleeveless shirts are not allowed. Golf or tennis shoes are required.

COURSE DESCRIPTION: This favorite of Mendocino County tourists is tight and hilly with lots of sidehill, uphill, and downhill lies. The best hole is the 510-yard, par-5 fourth, a sharp dogleg left.

NOTES: Ocean views, deer, and other wildlife abound.

LOCATION: The course is located on Highway 1 south of Mendocino in the town of Little River.

. . . ● **TOURNAMENTS:** Shotgun tournaments are allowed, and the banquet facility holds up to 85 people. Carts are not mandatory ● **$PECIAL OFFERS:** All guests of the Little River Inn receive a 10% discount on green fees.

3. LITTLE RIVER INN GOLF & TENNIS RESORT

PLAY POLICY & FEES: Green fees are $11 for nine holes and $16 for 18 holes weekdays, and $13 for nine holes and $18 for 18 holes weekends. Twilight rates are available. Carts are $19.

TEE TIMES: Reservations can be made seven days in advance.

DRESS CODE: Shoes and shirts are required.

COURSE DESCRIPTION: Ukiah means "deep valley," and this municipal course does nothing to refute that definition. Don't be fooled by the scorecard. This short course with elevated greens has plenty of hills, oak trees, and other obstacles to keep you entertained, challenged, or frustrated. The first hole is the most picturesque, a par 4 of 275 yards heading straight uphill to an elevated green.

NOTES: The Mendocino County Men's Amateur is held here each year. John McMullen holds the course record with a 62.

LOCATION: From U.S. 101 in Ukiah take the Perkins Street exit west to North State Street. Turn left on Scott Street and follow it two blocks to Walnut Street. Walnut Street turns into Park Boulevard.

. . . ● **TOURNAMENTS:** A 100-player minimum is required for a shotgun tournament, and carts are required. The banquet facility holds 200 people. ● **TRAVEL:** The Broiler Steakhouse is recommended for dinner. The Discovery Inn is located two miles from the golf course, and reservations can be made by calling 707-462-8873.

4. UKIAH MUNICIPAL GOLF COURSE

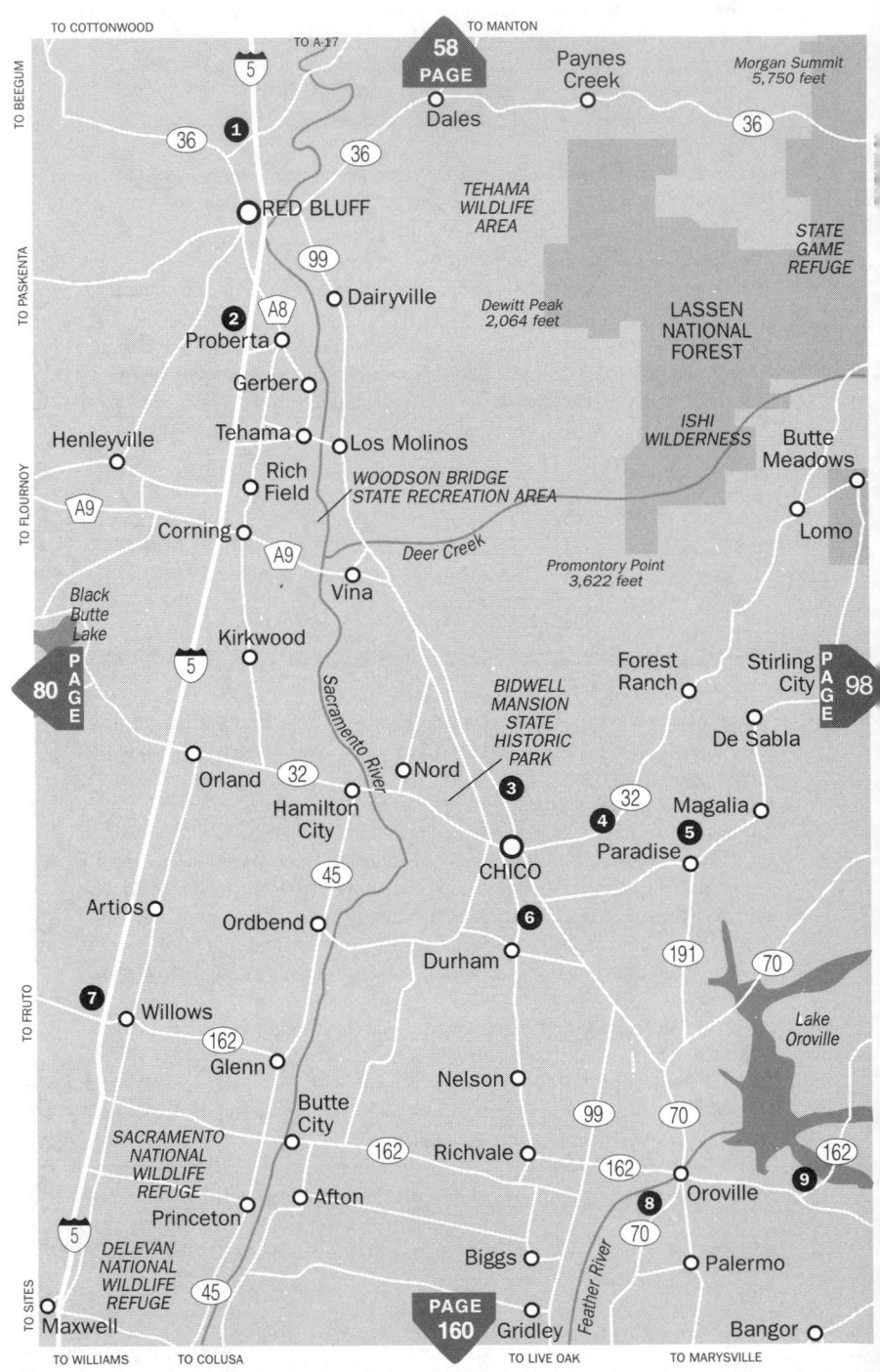

TO COTTONWOOD

TO A-17

TO MANTON

58 PAGE

Paynes Creek

Morgan Summit 5,750 feet

5

36

1

Dales

36

TO BEEGUM

36

RED BLUFF

TEHAMA WILDLIFE AREA

Dewitt Peak 2,064 feet

LASSEN NATIONAL FOREST

STATE GAME REFUGE

99

Dairyville

TO PASKENTA

2 A8

Proberta

Gerber

ISHI WILDERNESS

Butte Meadows

Henleyville

Tehama

Los Molinos

WOODSON BRIDGE STATE RECREATION AREA

Lomo

TO FLOURNOY

A9

Rich Field

Corning

A9

Deer Creek

Promontory Point 3,622 feet

Vina

Black Butte Lake

Kirkwood

Forest Ranch

Stirling City

P A G E 98

80 P A G E

5

Sacramento River

BIDWELL MANSION STATE HISTORIC PARK

De Sabla

Orland

32

Nord

3

32

Magalia

4

5

Hamilton City

CHICO

Paradise

Artios

45

Ordbend

6

Durham

191

70

Lake Oroville

TO FRUTO

7

Willows

162

Glenn

Nelson

99

70

Butte City

162

Richvale

162

162

9

SACRAMENTO NATIONAL WILDLIFE REFUGE

Afton

8

Oroville

Princeton

5

Biggs

70

Palermo

Feather River

DELEVAN NATIONAL WILDLIFE REFUGE

45

PAGE 160

Gridley

Bangor

TO SITES

Maxwell

TO WILLIAMS

TO COLUSA

TO LIVE OAK

TO MARYSVILLE

Red Bluff/Chico Area

① WILCOX OAKS GOLF CLUB
ARCHITECT: BEN HARMON, 1976

P.O. Box 127
Red Bluff, CA 96080

2 Wilcox Golf Road
Red Bluff, CA 96080

PRO SHOP: 530-527-7087
OFFICE: 530-527-6680

William DeWildt, Head Professional, PGA
Lin Westmoreland, Superintendent

Driving Range ●
Practice Greens ●
Clubhouse ●
Food / Beverage ●
Accommodations
Pull Carts ●
Power Carts ●
Club Rental ●
Special Offers

	1	2	3	4	5	6	7	8	9	OUT
BACK	-	-	-	-	-	-	-	-	-	-
REGULAR	309	489	323	189	504	378	311	144	395	3042
par	4	5	4	3	5	4	4	3	4	36
handicap	12	4	14	16	2	6	10	18	8	-
FORWARD	302	462	314	180	464	366	303	135	375	2901
par	4	5	4	3	5	4	4	3	4	36
handicap	13	1	9	15	3	5	11	17	7	-

	10	11	12	13	14	15	16	17	18	IN
BACK	-	-	-	-	-	-	-	-	-	-
REGULAR	311	335	513	378	383	188	379	479	130	3096
par	4	4	5	4	4	3	4	5	3	36
handicap	7	13	3	9	1	15	5	11	17	-
FORWARD	270	288	501	370	368	182	367	469	94	2909
par	4	4	5	4	4	3	4	5	3	36
handicap	8	14	2	10	6	16	12	14	18	-

BACK	
yardage	-
par	-
rating	-
slope	-

REGULAR	
yardage	6138
par	72
rating	69.2
slope	115

FORWARD	
yardage	5810
par	72
rating	73.4
slope	123

② OAK CREEK GOLF COURSE

2620 Montgomery Road
Red Bluff, CA 96080

PRO SHOP: 530-529-0674

Chris Goddard, Manager
Si Glover, Superintendent
Debbie Goddard, Tournament Director

Driving Range ●
Practice Greens ●
Clubhouse ●
Food / Beverage ●
Accommodations
Pull Carts ●
Power Carts ●
Club Rental ●
Special Offers

	1	2	3	4	5	6	7	8	9	OUT
BACK	249	284	160	297	336	366	333	167	484	2676
REGULAR	239	278	148	281	327	350	319	155	473	2570
par	4	4	3	4	4	4	4	3	5	35
handicap	9	11	13	7	1	3	5	17	15	-
FORWARD	236	276	142	277	323	345	318	149	465	2531
par	4	4	3	4	4	4	4	3	5	35
handicap	10	12	14	18	2	4	8	16	6	-

	10	11	12	13	14	15	16	17	18	IN
BACK	249	284	160	297	336	366	333	167	484	2676
REGULAR	239	278	148	281	327	350	319	155	473	2570
par	4	4	3	4	4	4	4	3	5	35
handicap	10	12	14	8	2	4	6	18	16	-
FORWARD	239	278	148	281	327	350	319	155	473	2570
par	4	4	3	4	4	4	4	3	5	35
handicap	9	11	13	17	1	3	7	15	5	-

BACK	
yardage	5352
par	70
rating	64.4
slope	105

REGULAR	
yardage	5140
par	70
rating	63.2
slope	103

FORWARD	
yardage	5101
par	70
rating	67.9
slope	115

PLAY POLICY & FEES: Reciprocal play is accepted with members of other private clubs for $45. Guest fees are $25 when accompanied by a member. Carts are $25.

TEE TIMES: Reservations can be made seven days in advance for reciprocal play.

DRESS CODE: Nonmetal spikes are required. Shirts for men and boys must have sleeves and collars. T-shirts and tank tops are not acceptable. Tops for women and girls should be appropriate for golf—no halter tops, tank tops, spaghetti straps, or bare midriffs. Shorts should be no less than five inches above the back of the knee or at least a six-inch inseam. Sweats and spandex pants are not acceptable. Men and boys must remove their hats in the dining room. If you ever wondered about the definition of appropriate golf attire, wonder no more.

COURSE DESCRIPTION: "The toughest 6,100-yard course in Northern California," head pro Bill DeWildt calls Wilcox Oaks. The back nine is appreciably more difficult than the front side, starting with the 311-yard 10th hole that doglegs up a steep hill.

NOTES: Wild turkeys frequent this course. The course record is 64, held by three men.

LOCATION: From Interstate 5 just north of Red Bluff, take the Wilcox Golf Road exit. The course is on the west side of Interstate 5.

. . . ● **TOURNAMENTS:** A 100-player minimum is needed to book a tournament. A banquet facility is available that can accommodate up to 120 people. Call Tournament Director Charlie Smith for more details.

1. WILCOX OAKS GOLF CLUB

PLAY POLICY & FEES: Green fees are $8 for nine holes and $15 for 18 holes. Senior rates are $7 for nine holes and $13 for 18 holes. Junior (under 16) rates are $5 for nine holes and $10 for 18 holes. Twilight green fees are $7 for 18 holes.

TEE TIMES: Reservations can be booked seven days in advance.

DRESS CODE: Golf attire is encouraged.

COURSE DESCRIPTION: Mount Shasta and Mount Lassen are visible from this flat course. The course is usually in fine shape. The seventh hole is only 319 yards but requires a carry of 200 yards.

NOTES: The Red Bluff Junior Golf Championship is held here the second Saturday in August.

LOCATION: From Interstate 5 in Red Bluff traveling north, take the Main Street exit. Turn north onto Main Street. Turn left on Montgomery Road and follow it to the course.

. . . ● **TOURNAMENTS:** This course is available for outside tournaments. A 20-player minimum in needed to book an event. Tournaments should be scheduled 12 months in advance.

2. OAK CREEK GOLF COURSE

③ BIDWELL PARK GOLF COURSE

3199 Golf Course Rd.
Chico, CA 95973

PRO SHOP: 530-891-8417

Roger Clark, PGA Professional
Matt Costa, Tournament Director
Santiago Carillo, Superintendent

Driving Range ●
Practice Greens ●
Clubhouse ●
Food / Beverage ●
Accommodations
Pull Carts ●
Power Carts ●
Club Rental ●
$pecial Offers

	1	2	3	4	5	6	7	8	9	OUT
BACK	-	-	-	-	-	-	-	-	-	-
REGULAR	362	123	368	147	385	399	140	452	465	2841
par	4	3	4	3	4	4	3	5	5	35
handicap	3	15	9	13	5	1	17	11	7	-
FORWARD	326	106	313	100	375	385	126	419	370	2520
par	4	3	4	3	4	4	3	5	5	35
handicap	5	15	7	17	3	1	13	11	9	-

	10	11	12	13	14	15	16	17	18	IN
BACK	-	-	-	-	-	-	-	-	-	-
REGULAR	390	171	365	403	390	366	398	354	376	3213
par	4	3	4	4	4	4	4	4	4	35
handicap	12	14	16	6	4	10	18	2	8	-
FORWARD	377	145	353	415	376	357	393	339	362	3117
par	4	3	4	5	4	4	4	4	4	36
handicap	8	14	18	4	12	10	16	2	6	-

BACK	
yardage	-
par	-
rating	-
slope	-

REGULAR	
yardage	6054
par	70
rating	68.5
slope	117

FORWARD	
yardage	5637
par	71
rating	70.8
slope	120

④ CANYON OAKS COUNTRY CLUB
ARCHITECT: JIM SUMMERS, 1985

999 Yosemite Drive
Chico, CA 95928

PRO SHOP: 530-343-1116
CLUBHOUSE: 530-343-2582

Mike Cress, Manager
David Lee, PGA Professional
Dave Ing, Superintendent

Driving Range ●
Practice Greens ●
Clubhouse ●
Food / Beverage ●
Accommodations ●
Pull Carts ●
Power Carts ●
Club Rental ●
$pecial Offers

	1	2	3	4	5	6	7	8	9	OUT
BACK	401	410	145	380	538	170	374	519	402	3339
REGULAR	360	326	104	336	497	135	345	480	367	2950
par	4	4	3	4	5	3	4	5	4	36
handicap	7	1	17	3	11/9	15/1	9/11	13/1	5	-
FORWARD	309	298	83	280	422	85	215	411	317	2420
par	4	4	3	4	5	3	4	5	4	36
handicap	7	1	15	11	9	17	13	3	5	-

	10	11	12	13	14	15	16	17	18	IN
BACK	509	157	369	337	187	400	579	441	486	3465
REGULAR	459	136	342	314	148	364	538	382	405	3088
par	5	3	4	4	3	4	5	4	4	36
handicap	14/1	18/1	12/1	10/1	16/1	8	6	4	2	-
FORWARD	429	116	247	275	125	325	466	319	308	2610
par	5	3	4	4	3	4	5	4	4	36
handicap	12	18	14	2	16	4	6	8	10	-

BACK	
yardage	6804
par	72
rating	72.7
slope	132

REGULAR	
yardage	6038
par	72
rating	69.4
slope	122

FORWARD	
yardage	5030
par	72
rating	70.8
slope	125

PLAY POLICY & FEES: Green fees are $17 weekdays and $22 weekends. This is an all-day rate; you can play as much or as little as you want. Carts are $10 for nine holes and $20 for 18 holes.

TEE TIMES: Reservations can be made one week in advance for weekends and holidays and two days in advance for weekdays.

COURSE DESCRIPTION: Situated in a beautiful part of upper Bidwell Park, this course is flanked by trees and water. The front nine is set in the foothills, and the back nine is longer and flat. Accuracy is important. The twelfth and thirteenth holes offer an excellent tandem of par 4s. The twelfth is 365 yards and a slight dogleg left over water, while the thirteenth is 403 yards with a blind, downhill fairway shot into the green.

NOTES: The course record is 65, held by David Osborne.

LOCATION: From Highway 99 in Chico take the East Avenue exit and drive east. Turn left and head two miles to Wildwood Avenue. Turn right on Golf Course Road and continue a short distance to the course.

. . . ● **TOURNAMENTS:** Shotgun starts are not allowed on Saturdays. Carts are required. ● **TRAVEL:** The Holiday Inn is a couple of miles from the golf course. For more information or reservations call 530-345-2491.

3. BIDWELL PARK GOLF COURSE

PLAY POLICY & FEES: Members and guests only. When accompanied by a member, guest fees are $20 Monday through Thursday and $45 Friday through Sunday and holidays. Carts are $22.

DRESS CODE: Collared shirts are required.

COURSE DESCRIPTION: At the mouth of Dead Horse Slough Canyon, this hilly course has narrow fairways and greens of varying size and contour. The course is tree lined, and a creek bed runs throughout. Water is everywhere but only comes into play on three holes. The sixth hole is a par 3 of 170 yards over water, and the 18th, a par 4, measures 486 yards from the back tees. Many consider the large greens some of the finest in Northern California.

LOCATION: From Highway 99 in Chico take Highway 32 east. Turn left on Bruce Road and then right on California Park Drive. Then turn right again on Yosemite Drive.

. . . ● **TOURNAMENTS:** This course is available for outside tournaments. A 72-player minimum is needed. The banquet facility can accommodate 200 people. Events should be booked 12 months in advance.

4. CANYON OAKS COUNTRY CLUB

PARADISE PINES GOLF COURSE
ARCHITECT: BOB BALDOCK

13917 South Park Drive
Magalia, CA 95954

PRO SHOP: 530-873-1111

Bob Fortina, Owner
Chuck Overmyer, Head Professional, PGA
Dave Roberts, Superintendent

Driving Range ●
Practice Greens ●
Clubhouse ●
Food / Beverage ●
Accommodations
Pull Carts ●
Power Carts ●
Club Rental ●
$pecial Offers

	1	2	3	4	5	6	7	8	9	OUT
BACK	-	-	-	-	-	-	-	-	-	-
REGULAR	295	234	201	323	188	364	486	265	139	2495
par	4	4	3	4	3	4	5	4	3	34
handicap	12	16	8	10	6	4	2	14	18	-
FORWARD	290	241	193	314	178	336	477	268	130	2427
par	4	4	3	4	3	4	5	4	3	34
handicap	12	16	8	10	6	4	2	14	18	-

	10	11	12	13	14	15	16	17	18	IN
BACK	-	-	-	-	-	-	-	-	-	-
REGULAR	313	255	196	347	198	385	500	284	149	2627
par	4	4	3	4	3	4	5	4	3	34
handicap	11	15	7	9	5	3	1	13	17	-
FORWARD	295	234	201	323	188	364	486	265	139	2495
par	4	4	3	4	3	4	5	4	3	34
handicap	11	15	7	9	5	3	1	13	17	-

BACK	
yardage	-
par	-
rating	-
slope	-

REGULAR	
yardage	5122
par	68
rating	64.6
slope	-

FORWARD	
yardage	4922
par	68
rating	68.4
slope	-

 ## BUTTE CREEK COUNTRY CLUB
ARCHITECT: BOB BALDOCK, 1965

175 Estates Drive
Chico, CA 95928

PRO SHOP: 530-343-8292
OFFICE: 530-343-7979

Al Farboud, Manager
Mike Mattingly, PGA Professional

Driving Range ●
Practice Greens ●
Clubhouse ●
Food / Beverage ●
Accommodations
Pull Carts
Power Carts ●
Club Rental
$pecial Offers

	1	2	3	4	5	6	7	8	9	OUT
BACK	388	528	149	375	403	162	357	372	525	3259
REGULAR	364	503	135	361	389	146	342	352	509	3101
par	4	5	3	4	4	3	4	4	5	36
handicap	5	7	17	1	3	15	9	11	13	-
FORWARD	298	441	135	298	323	131	317	282	410	2635
par	4	5	3	4	4	3	4	4	5	36
handicap	9	1	15	3	7	17	5	13	11	-

	10	11	12	13	14	15	16	17	18	IN
BACK	493	391	201	543	407	396	382	188	399	3400
REGULAR	478	374	180	483	390	380	343	138	381	3147
par	5	4	3	5	4	4	4	3	4	36
handicap	4	14	18	2	12	6	8	16	10	-
FORWARD	421	289	110	430	273	322	323	118	323	2609
par	5	4	3	5	4	4	4	3	4	36
handicap	4	14	18	2	12	6	8	16	10	-

BACK	
yardage	6659
par	72
rating	71.7
slope	122

REGULAR	
yardage	6248
par	72
rating	69.3
slope	117

FORWARD	
yardage	5244
par	72
rating	70.1
slope	117

PLAY POLICY & FEES: Green fees are $12 for nine holes and $15 for 18 holes on weekdays, and $13 for nine holes and $16 for 18 holes weekends and holidays. Carts are $11 for nine holes and $16 for 18 holes.

TEE TIMES: Reservations can be booked seven days in advance.

DRESS CODE: Shirts are required.

COURSE DESCRIPTION: This short course has tight, tree-lined fairways and offers diversity from hole to hole. Holes five through seven are the course's best. The fifth is a par 3 of 188 yards; the sixth is a narrow, dogleg par 4 measuring 364 yards; and the seventh is a dogleg par 5 of 486 yards. This is an interesting course with plenty of undulating lies and small greens.

LOCATION: From Highway 99 in Chico take the Skyway exit and drive to Magalia. In Magalia, turn left on South Park Drive.

. . . ● **TOURNAMENTS:** This course is available for outside tournaments, and the banquet facility can accommodate up to 98 people.

5. PARADISE PINES GOLF COURSE

PLAY POLICY & FEES: Reciprocal play is accepted with private clubs that allow reciprocal play; otherwise members and guests only. Reciprocal fees are $50. Guest fees are $25 when accompanied by a member and $50 unaccompanied. Carts are $20. The course is closed on Monday.

TEE TIMES: Reservations can be booked 30 days in advance.

DRESS CODE: Appropriate golf attire is required. No denim pants or denim shorts are allowed. Tucked-in collared shirts and nonmetal spikes are required.

COURSE DESCRIPTION: Butte Creek is arguably one of the top courses in the Sacramento Valley. The creek for which the course is named comes into play on five holes. Relatively open, this course has enough old oak trees to cause trouble, and the greens are large and undulating. The par-3 17th is a beauty, set over water, with flowers and railroad ties surrounding the green.

NOTES: Butte Creek played host to the US Open local qualifying round in 1992. The locker rooms and pro shop have recently been remodeled.

LOCATION: From Highway 99 in Chico, take the Estates Drive exit. Drive one mile west to the course.

. . . ● **TOURNAMENTS:** This course is available for outside tournaments on a limited basis, and the banquet facility will accommodate up to 300 people.

6. BUTTE CREEK COUNTRY CLUB

GLENN GOLF AND COUNTRY CLUB
ARCHITECT: BEN HARMON, 1960

6226 Country Road 39
Willows, CA 95988

PRO SHOP: 530-934-9918

Tony DeNapoli, Head Professional, PGA
Ron Golden, Superintendent

Driving Range ●
Practice Greens ●
Clubhouse
Food / Beverage ●
Accommodations
Pull Carts ●
Power Carts ●
Club Rental ●
$pecial Offers

	1	2	3	4	5	6	7	8	9	OUT
BACK	-	-	-	-	-	-	-	-	-	-
REGULAR	349	388	525	215	366	408	183	475	392	3301
par	4	4	5	3	4	4	3	5	4	36
handicap	15	8	9	1	13	3	11	17	5	-
FORWARD	330	368	498	177	341	386	162	427	370	3059
par	4	4	5	3	4	4	3	5	4	36
handicap	13	11	1	14	9	3	16	6	4	-

	10	11	12	13	14	15	16	17	18	IN
BACK	-	-	-	-	-	-	-	-	-	-
REGULAR	349	392	525	186	366	403	120	475	392	3208
par	4	4	5	3	4	4	3	5	4	36
handicap	14	6+	10	7	12	2	18	16	4	-
FORWARD	338	326	460	141	347	327	103	450	366	2858
par	4	4	5	3	4	4	3	5	4	36
handicap	10	12	2	17	8	15	18	5	7	-

BACK	
yardage	-
par	-
rating	-
slope	-

REGULAR	
yardage	6509
par	72
rating	69.9
slope	106

FORWARD	
yardage	5917
par	72
rating	72.7
slope	117

 # TABLE MOUNTAIN GOLF CLUB
ARCHITECT: BOB BALDOCK, 1956

P.O. Box 2769
Oroville, CA 95965

2700 West Oro Dam
Oroville, CA 95965

PRO SHOP: 530-533-3922
OFFICE: 530-533-3924

Courtney Foster, Director of Golf, PGA
Darryl McElmurray, Superintendent
Lonnie Hurst, Banquet Manager

Driving Range ●
Practice Greens ●
Clubhouse ●
Food / Beverage ●
Accommodations
Pull Carts ●
Power Carts ●
Club Rental ●
$pecial Offers

	1	2	3	4	5	6	7	8	9	OUT
BACK	371	499	155	380	506	363	179	407	416	3276
REGULAR	346	474	140	355	490	344	153	395	360	3057
par	4	5	3	4	5	4	3	4	4	36
handicap	14	10	18	8	12	6	16	2	4	-
FORWARD	321	451	124	316	419	319	129	354	335	2768
par	4	5	3	4	5	4	3	4	4	36
handicap	10	2	18	14	8	12	16	4	6	-

	10	11	12	13	14	15	16	17	18	IN
BACK	360	519	178	427	396	449	188	414	483	3414
REGULAR	347	491	137	401	371	424	163	389	474	3197
par	4	5	3	4	4	4	3	4	5	36
handicap	9	13	17	3	7	1	15	5	11	-
FORWARD	321	462	111	375	346	390	137	361	442	2945
par	4	5	3	4	4	4	3	4	5	36
handicap	11	1	17	9	13	3	15	5	7	-

BACK	
yardage	6690
par	72
rating	72.1
slope	118

REGULAR	
yardage	6254
par	72
rating	69.0
slope	114

FORWARD	
yardage	5713
par	72
rating	71.0
slope	114

PLAY POLICY & FEES: Outside play is accepted. Green fees are $12 Tuesday through Thursday and $20 Friday through Sunday. Senior rates are $9 during the week. Carts are $15 for 18 holes. The course is closed on Monday.

TEE TIMES: The public can call for weekend tee times on Wednesday.

DRESS CODE: No tank tops or short shorts are allowed. Nonmetal spikes are required.

COURSE DESCRIPTION: This long course is lined with weeping willows and eucalyptus. It has outstanding greens and a great view of the Sierras. There are four par-5 holes. The number-one handicap hole is the fourth, a par 3 of 215 yards. There are out-of-bounds to the left and in the back of the green, which is guarded by bunkers in the front. The average score on this par 3 is 4.3.

NOTES: The men's course record is 63, set by Ken Dunn in 1988.

LOCATION: From Interstate 5 in Willows drive five miles north and take the Bayliss Blue Gum Road exit west to the course.

. . . ● **TOURNAMENTS:** Shotgun tournaments are available weekdays only. Events should be scheduled two months in advance. The banquet facility can accommodate up to 200 people.

7. GLENN GOLF AND COUNTRY CLUB

PLAY POLICY & FEES: Green fees are $10 for nine holes and $16 for 18 holes Monday through Thursday. Friday through Sunday and holidays the fees are $12 for nine holes and $20 for 18 holes. Carts are $11 for nine holes and $18 for 18 holes.

TEE TIMES: Reservations can be booked seven days in advance.

DRESS CODE: Shirts must be worn that have either sleeves or a collar.

COURSE DESCRIPTION: Table Mountain is a wide-open course with firm fairways, considerable hard pan, and quick greens. Forty bunkers and nine ponds make things difficult. The signature hole is the 18th, a par 5 covering 474 yards. This course is a challenging test in a scenic setting.

LOCATION: From Sacramento take Highway 99 North to Highway 162 and head east. This course is located in Oroville on Highway 162 (Oro Dam Boulevard) between Highway 99 and Highway 70.

. . . ● **TOURNAMENTS:** A 100-player minimum is needed to book a shotgun tournament, and events should be booked six months in advance. The banquet facility can accommodate 144 people.

8. TABLE MOUNTAIN GOLF CLUB

5131 Royal Oaks Drive
Oroville, CA 95966

PRO SHOP: 530-589-0777
OFFICE: 530-589-5772

Donna McCutcheon, Manager
Bill Martz, Superintendent

Driving Range
Practice Greens ●
Clubhouse ●
Food / Beverage ●
Accommodations
Pull Carts ●
Power Carts ●
Club Rental ●
$pecial Offers

	1	2	3	4	5	6	7	8	9	OUT
BACK	-	-	-	-	-	-	-	-	-	-
REGULAR	293	297	133	245	95	333	108	228	264	1996
par	4	4	3	4	3	4	3	4	4	33
handicap	4	6	12	10	18	2	16	14	8	-
FORWARD	271	265	116	236	93	305	98	223	256	1863
par	4	4	3	4	3	4	3	4	4	33
handicap	4	6	12	10	18	2	16	14	8	-

	10	11	12	13	14	15	16	17	18	IN
BACK	-	-	-	-	-	-	-	-	-	-
REGULAR	314	316	142	260	97	351	127	244	314	2165
par	4	4	3	4	3	4	3	4	4	33
handicap	3	5	11	9	17	1	15	13	7	-
FORWARD	293	297	133	245	95	333	108	228	264	1996
par	4	4	3	4	3	4	3	4	4	33
handicap	3	5	11	9	17	1	15	13	7	-

BACK	
yardage	-
par	-
rating	-
slope	-

REGULAR	
yardage	4161
par	66
rating	62.5
slope	106

FORWARD	
yardage	3859
par	66
rating	64.4
slope	119

PLAY POLICY & FEES: Outside play and reciprocal play with members of other private clubs is accepted. Green fees are $9 for nine holes and $13 for 18 holes weekdays, $11 and $15 weekends and holidays. Carts are $13 for nine holes and $17 for 18 holes. Call for special rates.

TEE TIMES: Reservations are recommended at least 24 hours in advance.

DRESS CODE: Shirts are required.

COURSE DESCRIPTION: Situated in the Sierra Alton foothills near the Oroville Dam, this short course is hilly and tight, with narrow fairways and well-bunkered greens. Balls tend to kick right. Many players are intimidated by the 135-yard, par-3 third hole, which requires a carry over a deep ravine. There are six par-4s and three par-3 holes.

LOCATION: From Highway 70 in Oroville take the Oroville Dam Boulevard exit east for 1.5 miles to Olive Highway (Highway 162) and turn right. Drive 5.5 miles to Kelly Ridge Road and turn left. Turn left at Royal Oaks Drive and drive to the course.

. . . ● **TOURNAMENTS:** This course is available for outside tournaments. The banquet facility can accommodate 130 people.

9. KELLY RIDGE GOLF COURSE

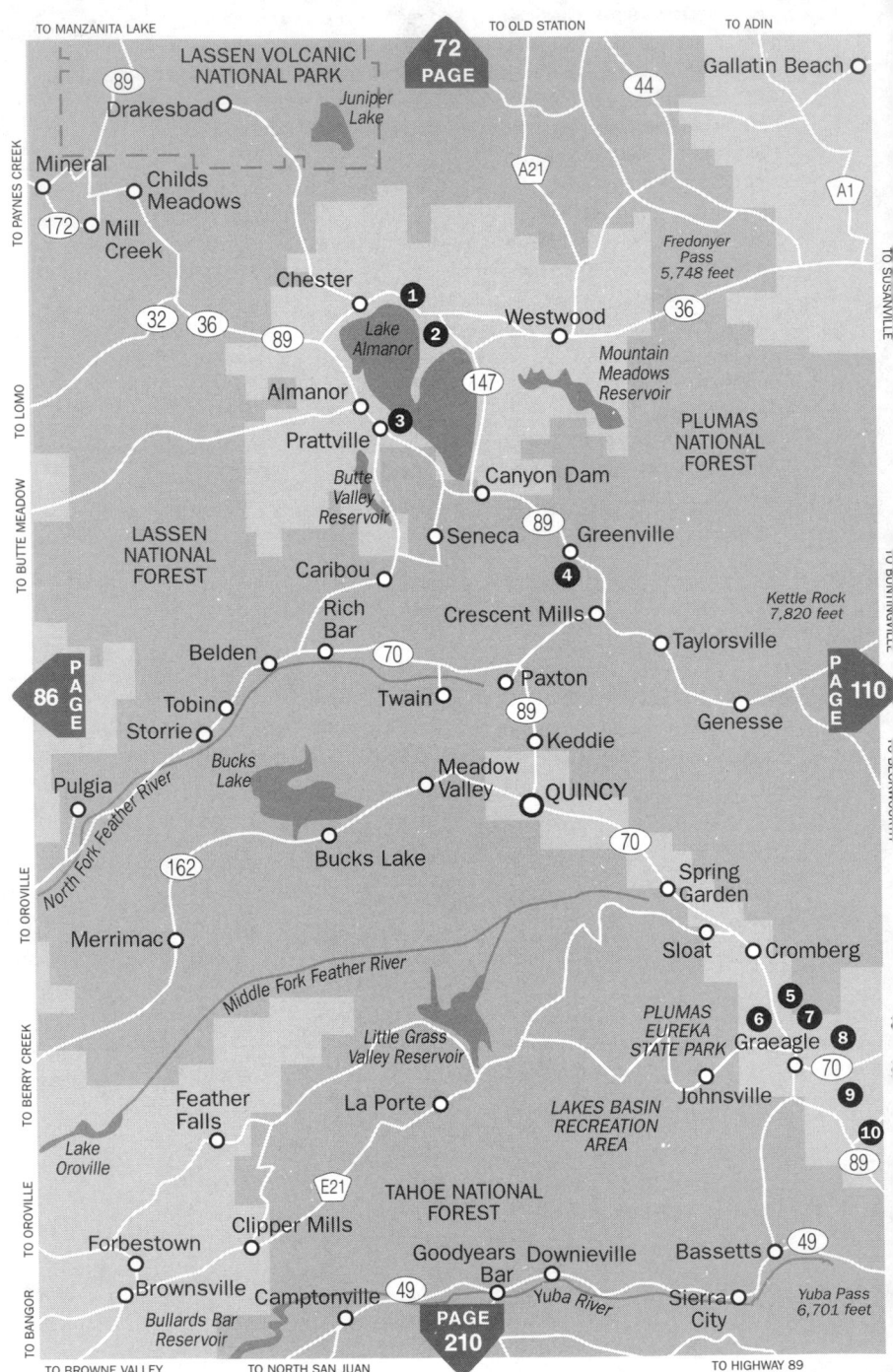

TO MANZANITA LAKE | TO OLD STATION | TO ADIN

LASSEN VOLCANIC
NATIONAL PARK

72 PAGE

Gallatin Beach

89
Drakesbad
Juniper Lake

44

A21

A1

Mineral
TO PAYNES CREEK

Childs
Meadows

172 Mill
Creek
TO LOMO

Chester

Fredonyer Pass 5,748 feet

1

Westwood

36

32 36 89

Lake Almanor

2

147

Mountain Meadows Reservoir

Almanor

Prattville

3

PLUMAS
NATIONAL
FOREST

TO BUTTE MEADOW

Butte Valley Reservoir

Canyon Dam

LASSEN
NATIONAL
FOREST

Seneca

89

Greenville

TO BUNTINGVILLE

Caribou

4

Kettle Rock 7,820 feet

Rich
Bar

Crescent Mills

Taylorsville

PAGE 86

Belden

70

Paxton

PAGE 110

Tobin

Twain

89

Genesse

Storrie

Keddie

TO BROWNSVILLE

Pulgia

Bucks Lake

Meadow
Valley

QUINCY

North Fork Feather River

Bucks Lake

70

162

Spring
Garden

Merrimac

Sloat

Cromberg

Middle Fork Feather River

5

PLUMAS
EUREKA
STATE PARK

6 **7** **8**

Graeagle

70

Feather
Falls

La Porte

Little Grass Valley Reservoir

LAKES BASIN
RECREATION
AREA

Johnsville

9

TO OROVILLE

Lake Oroville

10

89

E21

TAHOE NATIONAL
FOREST

TO BERRY CREEK

Clipper Mills

Bassetts

49

Forbestown

Goodyears
Bar

Downieville

TO BANGOR

Brownsville

Camptonville

49

Yuba River

Sierra
City

Yuba Pass 6,701 feet

Bullards Bar Reservoir

PAGE 210

TO BROWNE VALLEY | TO NORTH SAN JUAN | TO HIGHWAY 89

Lake Almanor/Graegle Area

Durkin Drive/Gateway
Lake Almanor, CA

PRO SHOP: 530-259-4653

Kevin Hughes, Director of Golf
Tom Maumoynier, Superintendent

Driving Range ●
Practice Greens ●
Clubhouse ●
Food / Beverage ●
Accommodations
Pull Carts ●
Power Carts ●
Club Rental ●
$pecial Offers

	1	2	3	4	5	6	7	8	9	OUT
BACK	-	-	-	-	-	-	-	-	-	-
REGULAR	-	-	-	-	-	-	-	-	-	
par	-	-	-	-	-	-	-	-	-	
handicap	-	-	-	-	-	-	-	-	-	-
FORWARD	-	-	-	-	-	-	-	-	-	
par	-	-	-	-	-	-	-	-	-	
handicap	-	-	-	-	-	-	-	-	-	-

BACK	
yardage	6900
par	72
rating	-
slope	-

	10	11	12	13	14	15	16	17	18	IN
BACK	-	-	-	-	-	-	-	-	-	-
REGULAR	-	-	-	-	-	-	-	-	-	
par	-	-	-	-	-	-	-	-	-	
handicap	-	-	-	-	-	-	-	-	-	-
FORWARD	-	-	-	-	-	-	-	-	-	
par	-	-	-	-	-	-	-	-	-	
handicap	-	-	-	-	-	-	-	-	-	-

REGULAR	
yardage	
par	
rating	-
slope	-

FORWARD	
yardage	
par	
rating	-
slope	-

951 Clifford Drive
Lake Almanor, CA 96137

PRO SHOP: 530-259-2868
CLUBHOUSE: 530-596-3282

David Cink, PGA Professional

Driving Range ●
Practice Greens ●
Clubhouse ●
Food / Beverage ●
Accommodations
Pull Carts ●
Power Carts ●
Club Rental ●
$pecial Offers

	1	2	3	4	5	6	7	8	9	OUT
BACK	-	-	-	-	-	-	-	-	-	-
REGULAR	506	331	321	194	387	220	474	131	355	2919
par	5	4	4	3	4	3	5	3	4	35
handicap	5	11	13	15	1	9	7	17	3	-
FORWARD	427	321	313	173	374	275	464	120	348	2815
par	5	4	4	3	4	4	5	3	4	36
handicap	1	13	11	15	5	7	9	17	3	-

BACK	
yardage	-
par	-
rating	
slope	

	10	11	12	13	14	15	16	17	18	IN
BACK	-	-	-	-	-	-	-	-	-	-
REGULAR	506	331	321	194	387	220	509	131	355	2954
par	5	4	4	3	4	3	5	3	4	35
handicap	6	12	14	16	2	10	8	18	4	-
FORWARD	427	321	313	173	374	275	464	120	348	2815
par	5	4	4	3	4	4	5	3	4	36
handicap	2	14	12	16	6	8	10	118	4	-

REGULAR	
yardage	5873
par	70
rating	68.3
slope	114

FORWARD	
yardage	5630
par	72
rating	70.8
slope	121

PLAY POLICY & FEES: This will be a public, daily-fee golf course.

TEE TIMES: Reservations can be made up to six months in advance with a deposit.

DRESS CODE: Appropriate golf attire and nonmetal spikes will be required.

COURSE DESCRIPTION: A course description was not available at press time.

NOTES: Bailey Creek has both on-course and off-course lots for sale. On-course lots start at $69,500 and off-course lots start at $49,500.

LOCATION: From Chico take Highway 32 east 55 miles to Highway 36. Take a right at the four-way stop and follow Highway 36 through Chester. Make a right turn on County Road A13 and then another right on Clifford Drive. The course will be on the right.

. . . ● **TOURNAMENTS:** Bailey Creek will be available for outside events. ●

TRAVEL: The Bidwell House is recommended by Bailey Creek. For reservations call 530-258-3338

1. BAILEY CREEK AT LAKE ALMANOR

PLAY POLICY & FEES: Public play is accepted after 3 p.m. in July and August. Green fees are $18 for nine holes and $36 for 18 holes for nonmembers. Outside players will not be permitted through the gate without a prearranged tee time.

TEE TIMES: Reservations are taken day of play.

DRESS CODE: Golfers must wear a collared shirt.

COURSE DESCRIPTION: This rolling, scenic mountain course is tight and has big trees and undulating greens. The par-4 second hole provides a breathtaking view of Mount Lassen, and the seventh hole offers a view of Lake Almanor.

NOTES: Mark Soltau's 63 is the course record. Osprey and deer are frequent visitors.

LOCATION: From Interstate 5 in Red Bluff take Highway 36 through Chester. Turn right on County Road A13 and drive about one mile. Turn right on Walker Road and drive to the gate.

. . . ● **TOURNAMENTS:** Outside events are limited.

2. LAKE ALMANOR COUNTRY CLUB

❸ ALMANOR WEST GOLF COURSE
ARCHITECT: HOMER FLINT, 1976

P.O. Box 1040
Chester, CA 96020

111 Slim Drive
Chester, CA 96020

PRO SHOP: 530-259-4555

Robert Delgado, PGA Professional
Dave Delay, Superintendent

Driving Range ●
Practice Greens ●
Clubhouse ●
Food / Beverage ●
Accommodations
Pull Carts ●
Power Carts ●
Club Rental ●
$pecial Offers

	1	2	3	4	5	6	7	8	9	OUT
BACK	-	-	-	-	-	-	-	-	-	-
REGULAR	489	341	176	389	354	162	470	440	323	3144
par	5	4	3	4	4	3	5	4	4	36
handicap	11	17	5	3	9	15	7	1	13	-
FORWARD	454	308	131	364	306	120	411	324	266	2684
par	5	4	3	4	4	3	5	4	4	36
handicap	1	9	5	3	13	17	11	7	15	-

	10	11	12	13	14	15	16	17	18	IN
BACK	-	-	-	-	-	-	-	-	-	-
REGULAR	474	375	137	402	329	155	411	522	369	3174
par	5	4	3	4	4	3	4	5	4	36
handicap	8	14	18	2	16	12	4	6	10	-
FORWARD	408	318	97	345	304	109	363	440	279	2663
par	5	4	3	4	4	3	4	5	4	36
handicap	2	12	16	6	14	18	8	4	10	-

BACK	
yardage	-
par	-
rating	
slope	

REGULAR	
yardage	6318
par	72
rating	69.9
slope	119

FORWARD	
yardage	5347
par	72
rating	69.6
slope	115

❹ MOUNT HUFF GOLF COURSE

P.O. Box 569
Greenville, CA 95947

Hwy 89 at Taylorsville "T"
Crescent Mills, CA 95934

PRO SHOP: 530-284-6204

Loren and Virginia Lindner, Owners

Driving Range ●
Practice Greens ●
Clubhouse ●
Food / Beverage ●
Accommodations
Pull Carts ●
Power Carts ●
Club Rental ●
$pecial Offers

	1	2	3	4	5	6	7	8	9	OUT
BACK	201	304	279	135	163	304	314	100	501	2301
REGULAR	189	286	257	121	143	290	285	100	467	2138
par	3	4	4	3	3	4	4	3	5	33
handicap	1	15	12	2	6	10	3	17	8	-
FORWARD	179	259	249	121	132	263	247	95	371	1916
par	3	4	4	3	3	4	4	3	5	33
handicap	1	15	12	2	6	10	3	17	8	-

	10	11	12	13	14	15	16	17	18	IN
BACK	201	304	279	135	163	304	314	100	501	2301
REGULAR	189	286	257	121	143	290	285	100	467	2138
par	3	4	4	3	3	4	4	3	5	33
handicap	4	14	13	3	10	16	7	18	8	-
FORWARD	179	259	249	121	132	263	227	86	371	1887
par	3	4	4	3	3	4	4	3	5	33
handicap	4	12	6	2	10	16	8	18	14	-

BACK	
yardage	4602
par	66
rating	60.2
slope	92

REGULAR	
yardage	4276
par	66
rating	60.2
slope	92

FORWARD	
yardage	3803
par	66
rating	61.1
slope	93

PLAY POLICY & FEES: Green fees are $18 for nine holes and $26 for 18 holes. Carts are $10 for nine holes and $20 for 18 holes.

TEE TIMES: Reservations can be booked seven days in advance.

DRESS CODE: Shirts must be worn at all times. Cutoffs are not allowed.

COURSE DESCRIPTION: This picturesque mountain layout offers dramatic views of Mount Lassen. It has towering pines and large, undulating greens. Most fairways are spacious. The third hole—a par 3 of 176 yards for men and 131 yards for women—requires a firm shot over water. Deer abound on this fun, interesting layout.

LOCATION: From Interstate 5 in Red Bluff take Highway 36 to Highway 89. Drive south on Highway 89 to Lake Almanor West. Turn left on Slim Drive to the course. The course is 65 miles from Chico. Take Highway 99 north.

. . . ● **TOURNAMENTS:** A 16-player minimum is required to book a tournament. Tournaments should be booked at least one month in advance. A banquet facility is available that can accommodate 75 people. ● **TRAVEL:** The Chester Manor (530-258-2441) and the Bidwell House (530-258-3338) are recommended for lodging.

3. ALMANOR WEST GOLF COURSE

PLAY POLICY & FEES: Green fees are $10 for nine holes and $15 for 18 holes weekdays, and $11 and $16 weekends and holidays. Carts are $9 for nine holes and $16 for 18 holes.

TEE TIMES: Reservations can be booked seven days in advance.

DRESS CODE: Nonmetal spikes are preferred.

COURSE DESCRIPTION: The course originated as a six-hole layout about 25 years ago and was expanded into nine holes in 1981. Many seniors enjoy this course because it isn't too hilly. However, flat doesn't mean easy. The par 3s are long, although the best might be No. 4, which measures just 135 yards but plays much tougher because of water.

NOTES: The course record is 57, set by Greg Hockenson.

LOCATION: From Interstate 5 in Red Bluff take Highway 36 to Highway 89. Follow Highway 89 to Crescent Mills (between Greenville and Quincy). The course is located on Highway 89 at the Taylorsville junction. From Oroville take Highway 70 east to Highway 89. Turn left on Highway 89 and drive six miles to the course.

. . . ● **TOURNAMENTS:** A 44-player minimum is needed to book a tournament. Tournaments should be booked three months in advance.

4. MOUNT HUFF GOLF COURSE

ARCHITECT: HOMER FLINT, 1980

P.O. Box 1210
Graeagle, CA 96103

402 Poplar Valley Road
Blairsden, CA 96103

PRO SHOP: 530-836-1420

Tom Godman, Director of Golf, PGA
Brandon Bowling, Assistant Professional
Mark Callihan, Superintendent

Driving Range ●
Practice Greens ●
Clubhouse ●
Food / Beverage ●
Accommodations ●
Pull Carts
Power Carts ●
Club Rental ●
$pecial Offers ●

	1	2	3	4	5	6	7	8	9	OUT
BACK	591	419	201	484	378	310	157	414	395	3349
REGULAR	548	359	155	458	364	293	126	362	363	3028
par	5	4	3	5	4	4	3	4	4	36
handicap	9	3	5	11	13	15	17	7	1	-
FORWARD	469	309	135	318	344	254	109	410	312	2660
par	5	4	3	5	4	4	3	5	4	37
handicap	1	9	17	11	7	13	15	3	5	-

	10	11	12	13	14	15	16	17	18	IN
BACK	295	177	379	460	398	155	354	398	539	3155
REGULAR	257	135	349	450	352	139	298	373	513	2866
par	4	3	4	5	4	3	4	4	5	36
handicap	16	14	4	12	10	18	8	6	2	-
FORWARD	233	98	329	360	265	128	267	340	426	2446
par	4	3	4	4	4	3	4	4	5	35
handicap	14	18	6	8	16	10	12	4	2	-

BACK	
yardage	6504
par	72
rating	71.6
slope	127

REGULAR	
yardage	5894
par	72
rating	69.0
slope	120

FORWARD	
yardage	5106
par	72
rating	68.5
slope	122

ARCHITECT: ELLIS VAN GORDER, 1968

P.O. Box 310
Graeagle, CA 96103

Highway 89
Graeagle, CA 96103

PRO SHOP: 530-836-2323

Daniel E. West, Manager
Bob Klein Jr., PGA Professional
Ross Ripple, Superintendent

Driving Range ●
Practice Greens ●
Clubhouse ●
Food / Beverage ●
Accommodations
Pull Carts ●
Power Carts ●
Club Rental ●
$pecial Offers

	1	2	3	4	5	6	7	8	9	OUT
BACK	-	-	-	-	-	-	-	-	-	-
REGULAR	435	394	110	413	512	386	543	139	357	3289
par	4	4	3	4	5	4	5	3	4	36
handicap	3	11	17	1	7	9	5	13	15	-
FORWARD	370	284	110	366	440	354	481	139	290	2834
par	4	4	3	4	5	4	5	3	4	36
handicap	7	13	17	5	3	9	1	15	11	-

	10	11	12	13	14	15	16	17	18	IN
BACK	-	-	-	-	-	-	-	-	-	-
REGULAR	437	504	135	431	401	422	161	395	505	3391
par	4	5	3	4	4	4	3	4	5	36
handicap	4	16	18	2	12	6	8	10	14	-
FORWARD	369	416	135	351	307	358	139	304	427	2806
par	4	5	3	4	4	4	3	4	5	36
handicap	4	2	48	10	12	6	14	16	8	-

BACK	
yardage	-
par	-
rating	-
slope	-

REGULAR	
yardage	6680
par	72
rating	70.7
slope	119

FORWARD	
yardage	5640
par	72
rating	71.3
slope	127

5. PLUMAS PINES GOLF RESORT

PLAY POLICY & FEES: Green fees are $50 Monday through Thursday and $55 Friday through Sunday. Twilight rates are offered Sunday through Thursday. The course is open from April to November.

TEE TIMES: Reservations can be made at any time. Reservations can be made for a fee through Tee Time Central. Call 888-236-8725.

DRESS CODE: No tank tops or short shorts are allowed on the course.

COURSE DESCRIPTION: This scenic, hilly course is situated in the midst of Plumas National Forest and is bordered by the Middle Fork of the Feather River. The fairways are tight with lots of trees. One notable hole is the second, a 419-yard par 4, with the river to the left and trees to the right. Another tough hole is the 201-yard, par-3 third over water. Accuracy is more important than length here, so smart players use irons off many tees.

LOCATION: From Truckee take Highway 89 north toward Graeagle. Just before Graeagle, turn left on County Road A14 and follow the signs (about two miles) to the course.

. . . ● **TOURNAMENTS:** A 12-player minimum is needed to book an event. Tournaments should be booked 12 months in advance. The banquet facility can accommodate up to 250 people. ● **$PECIAL OFFERS:** Plumas Pines offers both play-and-stay and play-and-dine golf packages.

6. GRAEAGLE MEADOWS GOLF COURSE

PLAY POLICY & FEES: Green fees are $35 weekdays and $40 weekends. The twilight rate (after 3 p.m.) is $20. Carts are $30. The course is open from April until about mid-November.

TEE TIMES: Reservations can be made one year in advance.

DRESS CODE: Shoes and shirts must remain on at all times.

COURSE DESCRIPTION: This popular mountain course is set in a picturesque valley with the Feather River running through it. Though pine trees abound, most holes are fairly wide open off the tee. Graeagle's signature hole is No. 6, a 386-yard par 4 with a bunker across the fairway and a stunning view of Eureka Peak.

NOTES: The course record of 63 is held by Dick Lotz. Head pro Bob Klein Jr. is an accomplished player. His sister, Emilee, won the 1994 NCAA Championship competing for Arizona State and now competes on the LPGA Tour representing Graeagle Meadows.

LOCATION: From Truckee drive 50 miles north on Highway 89. The course is on Highway 89 in Graeagle, three miles south of Highway 70.

. . . ● **TOURNAMENTS:** A 144-player minimum is needed to book a shotgun tournament. ● **TRAVEL:** The River Pines lodge is located one mile from the course. For reservations call 530-836-2552. Condominiums at Graeagle are available by calling 530-836-1100.

7 FEATHER RIVER INN GOLF COURSE
ARCHITECT: HAROLD SAMPSON, 1915

P.O. Box 67
Graeagle, CA 96103

65899 Highway 70

PRO SHOP: 530-836-2722

Jody Lindroth, PGA Professional
Richard Horton, Superintendent

Driving Range
Practice Greens •
Clubhouse
Food / Beverage •
Accommodations •
Pull Carts •
Power Carts •
Club Rental •
$Special Offers

	1	2	3	4	5	6	7	8	9	OUT
BACK	393	405	318	346	424	365	118	146	272	2787
REGULAR	393	405	318	346	424	365	118	146	272	2787
par	4	4	4	4	5	4	3	3	4	35
handicap	5	1	13	7	9	3	17	15	11	-
FORWARD	393	405	318	346	424	365	118	146	272	2787
par	4	5	4	4	5	4	3	3	4	36
handicap	5	1	13	7	9	3	17	15	11	-

	10	11	12	13	14	15	16	17	18	IN
BACK	398	409	306	351	511	393	124	130	278	2900
REGULAR	398	409	306	351	511	393	124	130	278	2900
par	4	4	4	4	5	4	3	3	4	35
handicap	6	2	14	8	10	4	18	16	12	-
FORWARD	398	409	306	351	459	393	124	130	278	2848
par	4	5	4	4	5	4	3	3	4	36
handicap	6	2	14	8	10	4	18	16	12	-

BACK	
yardage	5687
par	70
rating	66.0
slope	105

REGULAR	
yardage	5687
par	70
rating	65.8
slope	104

FORWARD	
yardage	5635
par	72
rating	69.2
slope	112

8 THE GOLF CLUB AT WHITEHAWK RANCH
ARCHITECT: DICK BAILEY, 1995

GOLF 50

P.O. Box 170
Clio, CA 96106

1137 Highway 89
Clio, CA 96106

PRO SHOP: 530-836-0394

Van Batchelder, Head Professional, PGA
Craig Pearson, Superintendent

Driving Range •
Practice Greens •
Clubhouse •
Food / Beverage •
Accommodations •
Pull Carts •
Power Carts •
Club Rental •
$Special Offers •

	1	2	3	4	5	6	7	8	9	OUT
BACK	396	412	231	481	348	392	178	543	310	3291
REGULAR	366	368	203	449	328	363	152	519	276	3024
par	4	4	3	4	4	4	3	5	4	35
handicap	9	3	11	1	17	5	15	7	13	-
FORWARD	274	283	117	329	248	272	111	412	238	2284
par	4	4	3	4	4	4	3	5	4	35
handicap	9	3	11	1	17	5	15	7	13	-

	10	11	12	13	14	15	16	17	18	IN
BACK	464	202	419	434	417	536	175	431	558	3636
REGULAR	445	191	370	408	372	510	163	411	528	3398
par	4	3	4	4	4	5	3	4	5	36
handicap	2	16	14	8	12	10	18	4	6	-
FORWARD	300	129	285	302	242	396	117	319	442	2532
par	4	3	4	4	4	5	3	4	5	36
handicap	2	16	14	8	12	10	18	4	6	-

BACK	
yardage	6927
par	71
rating	69.8
slope	124

REGULAR	
yardage	6422
par	71
rating	66.6
slope	110

FORWARD	
yardage	4816
par	71
rating	64.2
slope	115

PLAY POLICY & FEES: Green fees are $12 for nine holes and $18 for 18 holes every day. Senior and junior rates are $15 for 18 holes. Twilight rates are $12 beginning at 2:30 p.m. Carts are $16 for nine holes and $24 for 18 holes. The course is open from April to mid-October.

TEE TIMES: There are no restrictions for making a tee time.

DRESS CODE: Casual dress is OK, but shirts must remain on at all times.

COURSE DESCRIPTION: This scenic course is tight, with lots of trees and small, elevated greens. It opened in 1915, making it the oldest course in the Mohawk Valley. The ninth hole has strong character. It measures 275 yards but plays longer to an elevated green.

NOTES: It is said that Dwight D. Eisenhower played here during his many travels. Harry Weis, the former head pro, holds the course record with a 58.

LOCATION: The course is located 49 miles north of Truckee and 60 miles northwest of Reno. From Highway 70 the course is just one-eighth mile west of the intersection of Highway 70 and Highway 89 in Graeagle.

. . . ● **TOURNAMENTS:** A 16-player minimum is needed to book a tournament. A 60-player minimum is needed to book a shotgun start. Events should be booked six to 12 months in advance. The banquet facility can accommodate up to 200 people. ● **TRAVEL:** For reservations at the Feather River Inn call 530-836-2623.

7. FEATHER RIVER INN GOLF COURSE

PLAY POLICY & FEES: From May 1 through May 22, green fees are $75. From May 23 through September 28 green fees are $95, and from October 1 until October 26 green fees are $75. Price includes cart and use of the practice facility.

TEE TIMES: Reservations can be booked six months in advance. Group (12 players or more) reservations are booked beginning January 1 each year. Regular tee times may be made March 1.

DRESS CODE: Traditional golf attire is required. This is a nonmetal-spike facility.

COURSE DESCRIPTION: This scenic mountain course is bordered by five lakes and numerous streams. Five holes are situated in a meadow while the rest of the course meanders through trees. There is lots of mounding but only 30 bunkers. Greens are medium-sized and several have tiers. The course also features a complete practice facility.

NOTES: This course was named the 18th best course in California by "Golf Digest" in May 1999.

LOCATION: From Truckee drive 38 miles north on Highway 89 to the course.

. . . ● **TOURNAMENTS:** A minimum of 12 players is needed to book an event, and tournaments should be scheduled six months in advance. ● **TRAVEL:** The River Pine Resort is recommended. Call 530-836-0313. ● **$PECIAL OFFERS:** Several golf packages with local hotels are available. Call the pro shop for details.

8. THE GOLF CLUB AT WHITEHAWK RANCH

⑨ FEATHER RIVER PARK RESORT
ARCHITECT: BURT STAMP, 1922

P.O. Box 37
Blairsden, CA 96103

Highway 89
Blairsden, CA 96103

PRO SHOP: 530-836-2328

Mike Boyd, Manager

Driving Range
Practice Greens
Clubhouse
Food / Beverage ●
Accommodations
Pull Carts ●
Power Carts ●
Club Rental ●
$pecial Offers

	1	2	3	4	5	6	7	8	9	OUT
BACK	-	-	-	-	-	-	-	-	-	-
REGULAR	162	433	179	307	240	351	352	170	439	2633
par	3	5	3	4	4	4	4	3	5	35
handicap	9	11	15	7	13	5	1	17	3	-
FORWARD	-	-	-	-	-	-	-	-	-	
par	-	-	-	-	-	-	-	-	-	
handicap	-	-	-	-	-	-	-	-	-	-

	BACK	
yardage	-	
par	-	
rating	-	
slope	-	

	10	11	12	13	14	15	16	17	18	IN
BACK	-	-	-	-	-	-	-	-	-	-
REGULAR	162	433	179	307	240	351	352	170	439	2633
par	3	5	3	4	4	4	4	3	5	35
handicap	10	12	16	8	14	6	2	18	4	-
FORWARD	-	-	-	-	-	-	-	-	-	
par	-	-	-	-	-	-	-	-	-	
handicap	-	-	-	-	-	-	-	-	-	-

	REGULAR	
yardage	5266	
par	70	
rating	-	
slope	-	

	FORWARD	
yardage		
par		
rating	-	
slope	-	

⑩ THE DRAGON AT GOLD MOUNTAIN
ARCHITECT: ROBIN NELSON, 1997

P.O. BOX 880
Graeagle, CA 96103

3887 CR A-15
Clio, CA 96106

PRO SHOP: 877-DRAGON1

Norm Blandel, Director of Golf, PGA

Driving Range
Practice Greens
Clubhouse
Food / Beverage
Accommodations
Pull Carts
Power Carts
Club Rental
$pecial Offers ●

	1	2	3	4	5	6	7	8	9	OUT
BACK										
REGULAR										
par										
handicap										
FORWARD										
par										
handicap										

	BACK	
yardage		
par		
rating		
slope		

	10	11	12	13	14	15	16	17	18	IN
BACK										
REGULAR										
par										
handicap										
FORWARD										
par										
handicap										

	REGULAR	
yardage		
par		
rating		
slope		

	FORWARD	
yardage		
par		
rating		
slope		

PLAY POLICY & FEES: Green fees are $16 for 18 holes on weekdays and $18 on weekends. Carts are $10 for nine holes and $15 for 18 holes. The course is open from April to mid-October.

TEE TIMES: Reservations are not accepted. All play is on a first-come, first-served basis.

DRESS CODE: Casual dress is OK.

COURSE DESCRIPTION: This scenic course is level, open, and walkable. There are two par 5s, both reachable in two, and three par 3s, the 179-yard third being the longest one. This course is particularly popular with women, seniors, and juniors, who can learn to play in a low-pressure environment.

LOCATION: From Truckee drive about 50 miles north on Highway 89. The course is on Highway 89 just past the town of Graeagle.

. . . ● **TOURNAMENTS:** This course is available for outside events.

9. FEATHER RIVER PARK RESORT

PLAY POLICY & FEES: Nine holes are currently open to members only. No pricing or fee structure has been established at press time. The back nine opens in 2000.

DRESS CODE: Appropriate golf attire and nonmetal spikes are required.

COURSE DESCRIPTION: The Dragon at Gold Mountain is an unusual name for a course, which is fitting, because nothing about Gold Mountain is ordinary. First, before opening the back nine, Gold Mountain is waiting another season to allow the course to mature, unheard of in this day and age. Second, the course is one of the few courses admitted into the Audubon International Signature Program for the preservation of animal wildlife and conservation. Finally, the course uses the natural surroundings to create a challenging layout instead of forcing itself upon the land. With several tee boxes available and playing at 7,000 yards from the back tees, the course should be playable for all skill levels. If that wasn't enough, there are some outstanding views of the Sierras and the Feather River.

NOTES: The clubhouse is a Frank Loyd Wright design that will inspire as much conversation as the golf course itself.

LOCATION: From Sacramento take Interstate 80 north to Highway 89. North of Truckee 35 miles you will come to County Road A-15. Make a right and follow County Road A-15 for five miles to the course.

. . . ● **TOURNAMENTS:** Tournament play is accepted. Call the pro shop for more information. ● **TRAVEL:** A lodge is under construction and should be completed in 2000. ● **$PECIAL OFFERS:** When the lodge opens, play-and-stay packages will be available.

10. THE DRAGON AT GOLD MOUNTAIN

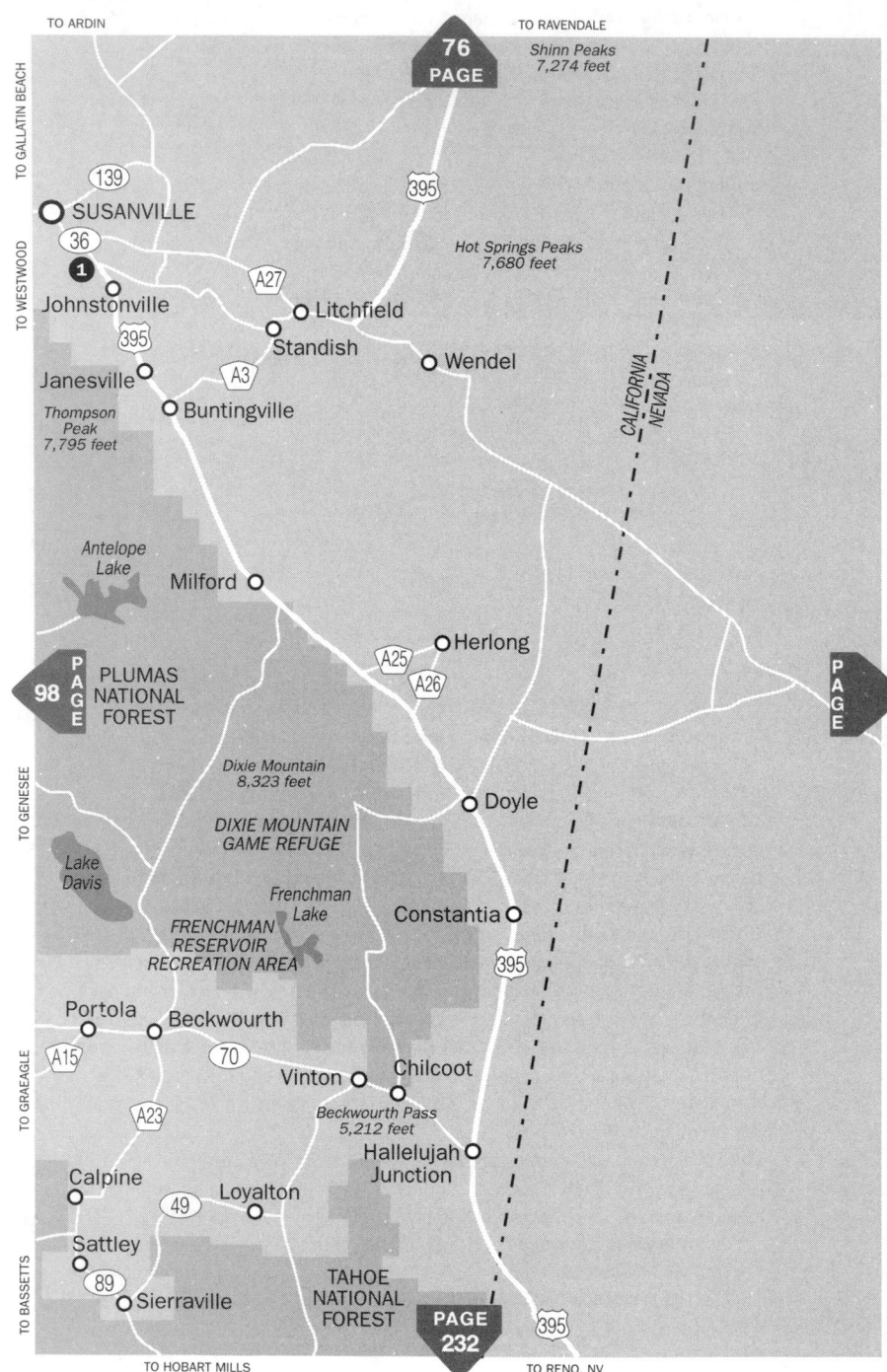

TO ARDIN
TO RAVENDALE

76
PAGE

Shinn Peaks
7,274 feet

TO GALLATIN BEACH

139

395

○ SUSANVILLE

36

Hot Springs Peaks
7,680 feet

1

TO WESTWOOD

Johnstonville ○

A27

○ Litchfield

395

○ Standish

Janesville ○

A3

○ Wendel

Thompson
Peak
7,795 feet

○ Buntingville

Antelope
Lake

Milford ○

CALIFORNIA
NEVADA

P
A 98 PLUMAS
G   NATIONAL
E   FOREST

A25

○ Herlong

A26

P
A
G
E

TO GENESEE

Dixie Mountain
8,323 feet

DIXIE MOUNTAIN
GAME REFUGE

○ Doyle

Lake
Davis

Frenchman
Lake

Constantia ○

FRENCHMAN
RESERVOIR
RECREATION AREA

395

Portola ○

Beckwourth

○

TO GRAEAGLE

A15

70

Vinton ○

Chilcoot
○

A23

Beckwourth Pass
5,212 feet

Hallelujah ○
Junction

Calpine
○

Loyalton

49   ○

TO BASSETTS

Sattley
○

89

TAHOE
NATIONAL
FOREST

PAGE
232

395

○ Sierraville

TO HOBART MILLS

TO RENO, NV

Susanville Area

470-835 Wingfield Road
Susanville, CA 96130

PRO SHOP: 530-257-6303

Todd Sickles, PGA Professional
Walt DeWitt, Superintendent

Driving Range ●
Practice Greens ●
Clubhouse ●
Food / Beverage ●
Accommodations
Pull Carts ●
Power Carts ●
Club Rental ●
$pecial Offers

	1	2	3	4	5	6	7	8	9	OUT
BACK	-	-	-	-	-	-	-	-	-	-
REGULAR	513	218	391	284	156	370	378	513	362	3185
par	5	3	4	4	3	4	4	5	4	36
handicap	7	9	3	17	13	15	1	5	11	-
FORWARD	497	208	283	273	118	296	298	443	261	2677
par	5	3	4	4	3	4	4	5	4	36
handicap	1	5	11	13	17	9	7	3	15	-

	10	11	12	13	14	15	16	17	18	IN
BACK	-	-	-	-	-	-	-	-	-	-
REGULAR	488	157	379	296	218	402	339	513	371	3163
par	5	3	4	4	3	4	4	5	4	36
handicap	8	16	2	18	6	4	14	10	12	-
FORWARD	416	147	365	283	152	327	284	408	339	2721
par	5	3	4	4	3	4	4	5	4	36
handicap	8	16	2	18	12	10	14	6	4	-

BACK	
yardage	-
par	-
rating	-
slope	-

REGULAR	
yardage	6348
par	72
rating	68.8
slope	107

FORWARD	
yardage	5398
par	72
rating	68.9
slope	112

PLAY POLICY & FEES: Green fees are $10 for nine holes and $14 for 18 holes. Carts are $8 for nine holes and $15 for 18 holes.

TEE TIMES: Reservations can be booked 14 days in advance.

DRESS CODE: Shirts must be worn.

COURSE DESCRIPTION: This rolling course is well maintained and walkable. It has two creeks, one lake, which is frequently dry, and some hills. Evergreens flank the entire course. The greens are excellent, and there is a beautiful view of Diamond Mountain.

NOTES: The men's record is 64, set by Tom Swickard. The Susanville Open is held here each July, drawing a full field of 150.

LOCATION: From Interstate 5 in Red Bluff take Highway 36 to Susanville. Turn right on Weatherlow, which turns into Richmond Road. Make a right turn on Wingfield Road. From Reno take U.S. 395 to Susanville. Turn left on Richmond Road and drive about three miles. Turn left on Wingfield Road and drive one-quarter mile to the clubhouse.

. . . ● **TOURNAMENTS:** A 40-player minimum is needed to book an event. Tournaments should be scheduled at least four months in advance.

1. EMERSON LAKE GOLF COURSE

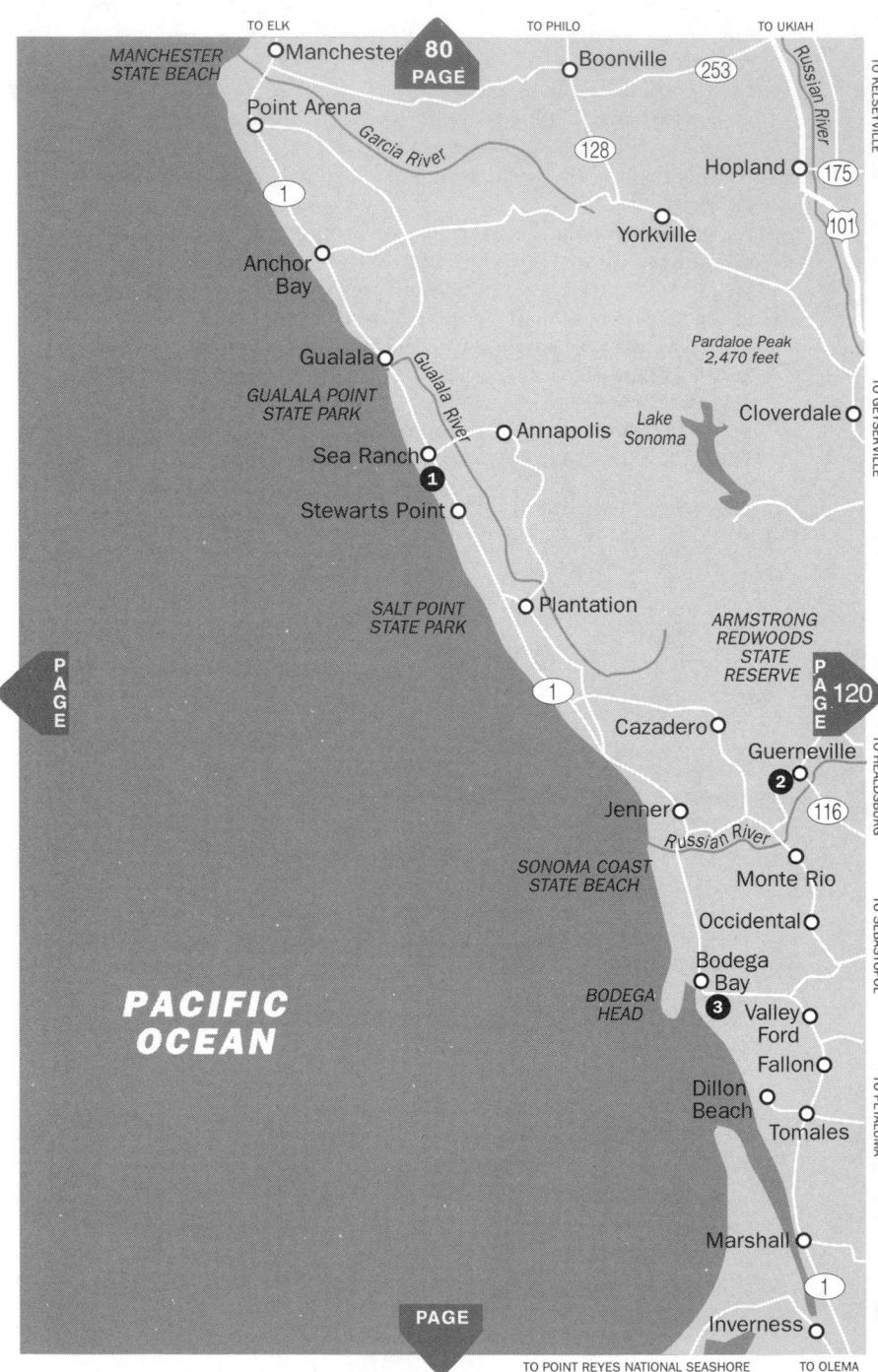

TO ELK
TO PHILO
TO UKIAH
TO KELSEYVILLE

MANCHESTER
STATE BEACH
Manchester

80
PAGE

Boonville

253

Russian River

Point Arena

Garcia River

128

Hopland
175

101

1

Yorkville

Anchor
Bay

Gualala

Gualala River

GUALALA POINT
STATE PARK

Pardaloe Peak
2,470 feet

Annapolis

Lake
Sonoma

Cloverdale

TO GEYSERVILLE

Sea Ranch
1

Stewarts Point

SALT POINT
STATE PARK

Plantation

ARMSTRONG
REDWOODS
STATE
RESERVE

P
A
G
E

120

P
A
G
E

1

Cazadero

Guerneville

2

TO HEALDSBURG

Jenner

Russian River

116

SONOMA COAST
STATE BEACH

Monte Rio

Occidental

TO SEBASTOPOL

PACIFIC
OCEAN

BODEGA
HEAD

Bodega
Bay

3

Valley
Ford

Fallon

TO PETALUMA

Dillon
Beach

Tomales

Marshall

1

PAGE

Inverness

TO POINT REYES NATIONAL SEASHORE
TO OLEMA

Mendocino/Sonoma Coast Area

THE SEA RANCH GOLF LINKS
ARCHITECT: ROBERT MUIR GRAVES, 1973

GOLF
50

P.O. Box 10
Sea Ranch, CA 95497

42000 Highway 1
The Sea Ranch, CA 95497

PRO SHOP: 707-785-2468

Wally Eskew, Tournament Director
Greg Sherwood, Superintendent

Driving Range •
Practice Greens •
Clubhouse •
Food / Beverage •
Accommodations
Pull Carts •
Power Carts •
Club Rental •
$pecial Offers •

	1	2	3	4	5	6	7	8	9	OUT
BACK	277	370	217	501	547	374	385	158	422	3251
REGULAR	277	358	202	486	525	344	373	146	410	3121
par	4	4	3	5	5	4	4	3	4	36
handicap	13	5	15	3	7	11	1	17	9	-
FORWARD	215	277	90	395	392	301	269	80	310	2329
par	4	4	3	5	5	4	4	3	4	36
handicap	5	1	17	13	11	9	7	15	3	-

	10	11	12	13	14	15	16	17	18	IN
BACK	525	341	222	355	406	545	379	182	390	3345
REGULAR	501	321	195	333	382	518	334	152	369	3105
par	5	4	3	4	4	5	4	3	4	36
handicap	4	12	16	10	8	6	14	18	2	-
FORWARD	411	253	138	267	308	457	270	107	297	2508
par	5	4	3	4	4	5	4	3	4	36
handicap	8	10	18	14	4	2	12	16	6	-

BACK	
yardage	6596
par	72
rating	73.2
slope	136

REGULAR	
yardage	6226
par	72
rating	71.9
slope	130

FORWARD	
yardage	4837
par	72
rating	70.2
slope	120

 # NORTHWOOD GOLF COURSE
ARCHITECT: ALISTER MACKENZIE, 1928

P.O. Box 930
Monte Rio, CA 95462

19400 Highway 116
Monte Rio, CA 95462

PRO SHOP: 707-865-1116

Vern Ayres, Professional
Gaylord R. Schaap, Manager
Edwin Bale, Superintendent

Driving Range
Practice Greens •
Clubhouse •
Food / Beverage •
Accommodations •
Pull Carts •
Power Carts •
Club Rental •
$pecial Offers •

	1	2	3	4	5	6	7	8	9	OUT
BACK	-	-	-	-	-	-	-	-	-	-
REGULAR	296	385	145	282	465	286	368	104	527	2858
par	4	4	3	4	5	4	4	3	5	36
handicap	11	7	17	9	5	13	3	15	1	-
FORWARD	296	385	144	280	460	285	366	103	461	2780
par	4	4	3	4	5	4	4	3	5	36
handicap	11	7	17	9	5	13	3	15	1	-

	10	11	12	13	14	15	16	17	18	IN
BACK	-	-	-	-	-	-	-	-	-	-
REGULAR	296	385	145	282	465	286	368	104	527	2858
par	4	4	3	4	5	4	4	3	5	36
handicap	12	8	18	10	6	14	4	16	2	-
FORWARD	296	385	144	280	460	285	366	103	461	2780
par	4	4	3	4	5	4	4	3	5	36
handicap	12	8	18	10	6	14	4	16	2	-

BACK	
yardage	-
par	-
rating	
slope	

REGULAR	
yardage	5716
par	72
rating	67.7
slope	113

FORWARD	
yardage	5560
par	72
rating	72.2
slope	127

PLAY POLICY & FEES: Green fees Monday through Friday are $45. Green fees for Saturday, Sunday, and holidays are $65. Carts are $12.50 per person everyday. Twilight and nine-hole rates are available.

TEE TIMES: Reservations can be booked up to six months in advance.

DRESS CODE: Appropriate golf attire is required.

COURSE DESCRIPTION: Sea Ranch Golf Links is a seaside Scottish-style course. Although the course is not long in distance, the prevailing northwest winds add a significant challenge to golfers of all levels. There is a view of the ocean from every hole. To score well here, you not only have to be hitting the ball well, but you also need to be creative.

LOCATION: From the south drive 40 miles northwest from Jenner on Highway 1 to the course, located in the Sea Ranch development. From the north the course is one mile south of Gualala.

. . . ● **TOURNAMENTS:** A 16-player minimum is needed to book a tournament. Tournaments should be booked three months in advance. ● **TRAVEL:** The Sea Ranch Lodge is located 15 minutes from the golf course. For reservations call 707-785-2371. ● **$PECIAL OFFERS:** Play-and-stay packages are available with the Sea Ranch Lodge and several other hotels. Call the pro shop for information.

1. THE SEA RANCH GOLF LINKS

PLAY POLICY & FEES: Green fees are $15 for nine holes and $25 for 18 holes weekdays, and $20 for nine holes and $35 for 18 holes weekends. Carts are $12 for nine holes and $20 for 18 holes.

TEE TIMES: Reservations are accepted two weeks in advance.

DRESS CODE: Nonmetal spikes are preferred.

COURSE DESCRIPTION: Situated in the Russian River resort area near the Bohemian Grove, this course was designed in 1928 by Alister Mackenzie. The huge redwoods and firs give this course a quiet, peaceful feeling before before you tee off. After you tee off, the huge redwoods and firs can become quite disturbing for the golfer who can't hit it straight. If that weren't enough, the greens are small and guarded by mounds, blind shots, and a few bunkers. The course condition has improved dramatically over the last few years and is a round is a must for golfers with a sense of history.

LOCATION: From Guerneville drive three miles west on Highway 116. The course is on the left.

. . . ● **TOURNAMENTS:** This course is available for outside tournaments. ● **$PECIAL OFFERS:** Play-and-stay packages are available on weekdays at the Rio Villa Resort. For more information call 707-865-1143.

2. NORTHWOOD GOLF COURSE

BODEGA HARBOUR GOLF LINKS
ARCHITECT: ROBERT TRENT JONES JR., 1977

P.O. Box 368
Bodega Bay, CA 94923

21301 Heron Drive
Bodega Bay, CA 94923

PRO SHOP: 707-875-3538

Dennis Kalkowski, Director of Golf, PGA
Chester Manni, Superintendent

Driving Range
Practice Greens •
Clubhouse •
Food / Beverage •
Accommodations
Pull Carts
Power Carts •
Club Rental •
$pecial Offers •

GOLF 50

	1	2	3	4	5	6	7	8	9	OUT
BACK	407	334	203	407	496	155	216	487	327	3032
REGULAR	389	308	175	371	488	136	172	451	301	2791
par	4	4	3	4	5	3	3	5	4	35
handicap	3	7	5	1	15	17	11	13	9	-
FORWARD	283	251	135	305	415	88	128	400	270	2275
par	4	4	3	4	5	3	3	5	4	35
handicap	3	7	5	1	11	17	15	13	9	-

	10	11	12	13	14	15	16	17	18	IN
BACK	332	399	186	413	510	291	192	467	3233
REGULAR	292	363	158	377	400	476	271	152	405	2894
par	4	4	3	4	4	5	4	3	4	35
handicap	18	6	12	8	4	14	16	10	2	-
FORWARD	267	346	117	353	355	458	164	88	326	2474
par	4	4	3	4	4	5	4	3	5	36
handicap	10	6	14	8	2	12	18	16	4	-

BACK	
yardage	6265
par	70
rating	72.4
slope	134

REGULAR	
yardage	5685
par	70
rating	69.3
slope	125

FORWARD	
yardage	4749
par	71
rating	67.7
slope	120

3. BODEGA HARBOUR GOLF LINKS

PLAY POLICY & FEES: Outside play is accepted. Property owners on the golf course are eligible for membership. Green fees are $55 Monday through Thursday and $65 Friday. Weekend and holiday green fees are $85. Fees include carts. Twilight rates are available.

TEE TIMES: Reservations are required and are accepted as far as 90 days in advance with a credit card.

DRESS CODE: Appropriate golf attire is required.

COURSE DESCRIPTION: This is two courses in one. On the front side you will play a hilly, links-style course with few level lies, and narrow fairways. On the back side (the original nine) you will play a meadow course that is slightly more open off the tee. Although completely different designs, both have several things in common. Both nines are well maintained, with fast tricky greens and beautiful ocean views. A steady ocean breeze is common, making this challenging course, downright difficult. We can't guarantee even the best golfers a good score, but we can promise that the controversial layout and three finishing holes will give you something to talk about on your ride home.

NOTES: Intensive drainage work has greatly improved playability in the winter months. The course record for men is 68, held by Charlie Gibson and Bob Borowicz. The women's record is 71, held by Lois Hodge.

LOCATION: From Bodega Bay drive south on Highway 1. Take the South Harbour Way exit to the right and drive 150 yards to Heron Drive. Turn right on Heron Drive and drive a half mile to the course.

. . . ● **TOURNAMENTS:** A 16-player tournament can be booked with a credit card. Any tournament over 20 players must have a contract. Events should be scheduled 12 months in advance. The banquet facility can accommodate up to 150 people. ● **TRAVEL:** The Bodega Bay Lodge is located three minutes from the golf course. For reservations call 707-875-3525. The Inn at the Tides (800-541-7788) is also recommended. ● **$PECIAL OFFERS:** Play-and-stay packages are available with Bodega Bay Lodge and other nearby hotels. Call the pro shop for more information.

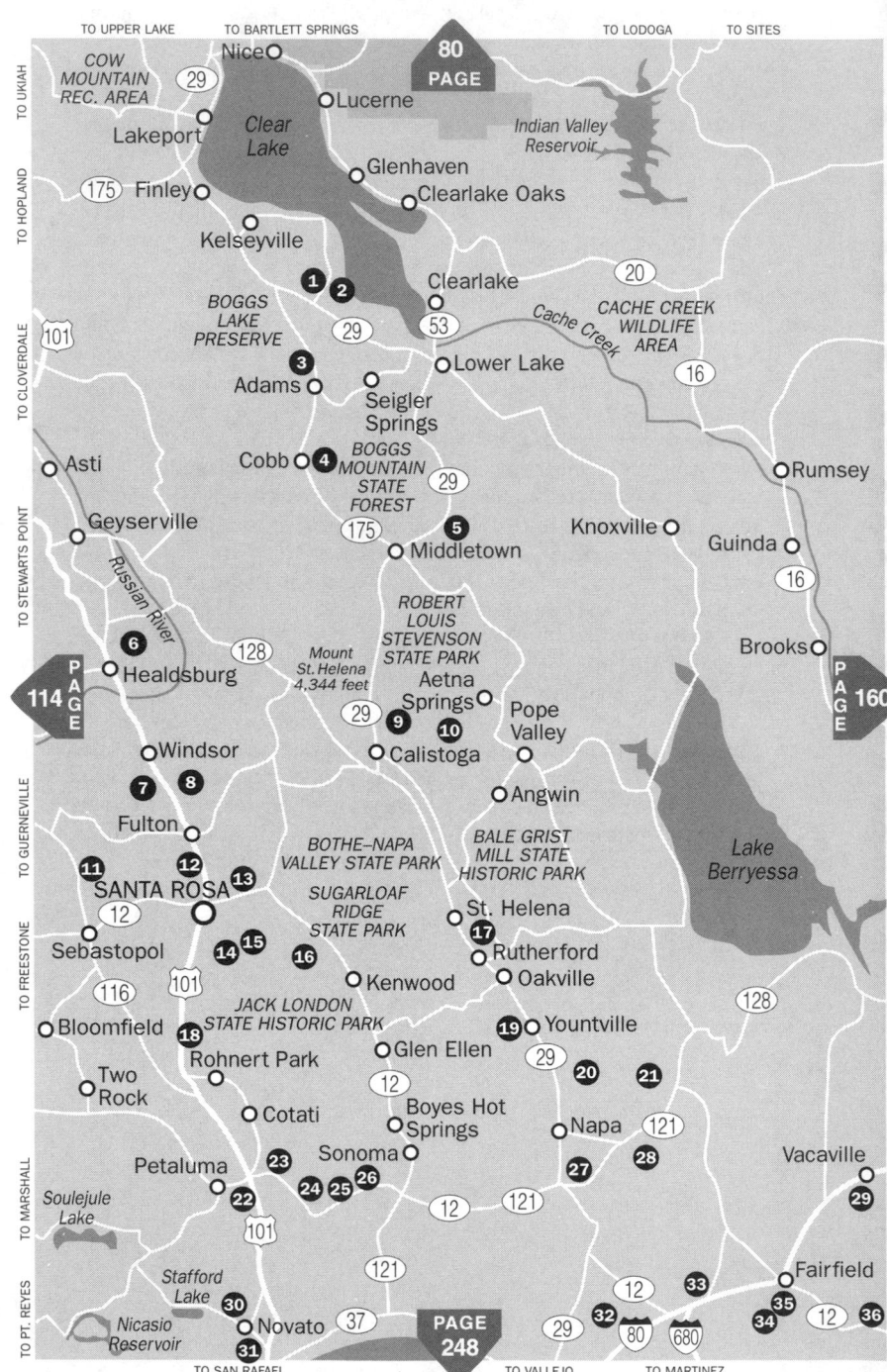

TO UKIAH

COW MOUNTAIN REC. AREA

Nice

Lucerne

(29)

Lakeport

Clear Lake

Indian Valley Reservoir

TO HOPLAND

(175) Finley

Glenhaven

Clearlake Oaks

Kelseyville

❶ ❷   Clearlake

(20)

CACHE CREEK WILDLIFE AREA

TO CLOVERDALE

(101)

BOGGS LAKE PRESERVE

(29)

(53)

Cache Creek

(16)

❸

Adams

Seigler Springs

Lower Lake

Asti

Cobb ❹

BOGGS MOUNTAIN STATE FOREST

(29)

Rumsey

TO STEWARTS POINT

Geyserville

(175)

❺

Middletown

Knoxville

Guinda

(16)

Russian River

ROBERT LOUIS STEVENSON STATE PARK

Brooks

P A G E 160

❻

PAGE 114

Healdsburg

(128)

Mount St. Helena 4,344 feet

(29)

Aetna Springs

❾ ❿

Pope Valley

Lake Berryessa

TO GUERNEVILLE

Windsor

❽

Calistoga

Angwin

❼

Fulton

❶❶

❶❷

SANTA ROSA

❶❸

BOTHE–NAPA VALLEY STATE PARK

BALE GRIST MILL STATE HISTORIC PARK

(12)

SUGARLOAF RIDGE STATE PARK

St. Helena

❶❼

TO FREESTONE

Sebastopol

❶❹ ❶❺

❶❻

Rutherford

Oakville

(128)

(116)

(101)

Kenwood

JACK LONDON STATE HISTORIC PARK

Bloomfield

❶❽

❶❾ Yountville

Two Rock

Rohnert Park

Glen Ellen

(29)

❷⓿

❷❶

TO MARSHALL

Cotati

Boyes Hot Springs

Napa

(121)

Vacaville

Petaluma

❷❸

Sonoma

❷❼

❷❽

❷❹ ❷❺ ❷❻

❷❷

(101)

(12)

(121)

❷❾

Soulejule Lake

Stafford Lake

(121)

PAGE 248

❸❸

Fairfield

TO PT. REYES

❸⓿

Novato

(37)

(29)

❸❷

(12)

❸❺

Nicasio Reservoir

❸❶

(80)

(680)

❸❹

(12)

❸❻

Sonoma/Napa Area

❶ BUCKINGHAM GOLF & COUNTRY CLUB
ARCHITECT: JAMES YOUNG, 1960

2855 Eastlake Drive
Kelseyville, CA   95451

PRO SHOP: 707-279-4863
CLUBHOUSE: 707-229-1140

Mark Wotherspoon, Director of Golf, PGA

Driving Range ●
Practice Greens ●
Clubhouse ●
Food / Beverage ●
Accommodations ●
Pull Carts ●
Power Carts ●
Club Rental ●
$pecial Offers

	1	2	3	4	5	6	7	8	9	OUT
BACK	-	-	-	-	-	-	-	-	-	-
REGULAR	366	172	160	508	241	197	422	382	532	2980
par	4	3	3	5	4	3	5	4	5	36
handicap	3	17	15	9	13	7	11	1	5	-
FORWARD	366	149	162	480	199	179	423	401	473	2832
par	4	3	3	5	4	3	5	5	5	37
handicap	5	17	13	1	15	11	7	9	3	-

	10	11	12	13	14	15	16	17	18	IN
BACK	-	-	-	-	-	-	-	-	-	-
REGULAR	345	160	258	493	210	211	423	382	496	2978
par	4	3	4	5	3	3	5	4	5	36
handicap	8	18	16	12	2	6	14	4	10	-
FORWARD	351	146	156	471	196	172	418	401	473	2784
par	4	3	3	5	4	3	5	5	5	37
handicap	6	18	14	2	16	12	8	10	4	-

BACK	
yardage	-
par	-
rating	-
slope	-

REGULAR	
yardage	5958
par	72
rating	68.2
slope	114

FORWARD	
yardage	5616
par	74
rating	71.9
slope	127

❷ CLEAR LAKE RIVIERA YACHT & GOLF CLUB
ARCHITECT: ED DEFELICE, 1965

10200 Fairway Drive
Kelseyville, CA 95451

PRO SHOP: 707-277-7129

Alice Doyle, Manager

Driving Range
Practice Greens ●
Clubhouse ●
Food / Beverage ●
Accommodations
Pull Carts ●
Power Carts ●
Club Rental ●
$pecial Offers ●

	1	2	3	4	5	6	7	8	9	OUT
BACK	-	-	-	-	-	-	-	-	-	-
REGULAR	276	387	303	273	151	439	283	254	362	2728
par	4	4	4	4	3	5	4	4	4	36
handicap	9	3	7	13	11	5	17	15	1	-
FORWARD	227	370	304	210	152	431	276	232	361	2563
par	4	4	4	3	3	5	4	4	5	36
handicap	15	5	7	11	13	1	17	9	3	-

	10	11	12	13	14	15	16	17	18	IN
BACK	-	-	-	-	-	-	-	-	-	-
REGULAR	309	519	321	213	161	459	353	262	313	2910
par	4	5	4	3	3	5	4	4	4	36
handicap	12	2	8	14	16	10	4	18	6	-
FORWARD	273	368	304	238	151	431	279	238	260	2542
par	4	4	4	4	3	5	4	4	4	36
handicap	10	8	4	12	16	2	18	14	6	-

BACK	
yardage	-
par	-
rating	-
slope	-

REGULAR	
yardage	5638
par	72
rating	68.0
slope	119

FORWARD	
yardage	5105
par	72
rating	69.9
slope	125

PLAY POLICY & FEES: Outside play and reciprocal play is accepted with members of other private clubs. Green fees are $15 for nine holes and $22 for 18 holes weekdays, and $18 for nine holes and $26 for 18 holes weekends and holidays. Carts are $9 for nine holes and $14 for 18 holes.

TEE TIMES: Reservations can be booked 30 days in advance.

DRESS CODE: No tank tops or short shorts are allowed. Nonmetal spikes are required.

COURSE DESCRIPTION: This flat course circles a 25-acre lake called Little Borax. Pine and oak trees come into play, and large boulders dot the fairways. The par-5 fourth features a sand trap around an oak tree 50 yards short of the green.

NOTES: Buckingham has added new tee boxes, bunkers, and water hazards.

LOCATION: From U.S. 101 north of Ukiah, exit on Highway 20 and drive to Highway 29. Bear south on Highway 29 through Lakeport to Highway 281. Turn left (it becomes Soda Bay Road) and proceed six miles to Crystal Drive. Turn right. Crystal Drive runs into Eastlake Drive.

. . . ● **TOURNAMENTS:** This course is available for outside tournaments. A 28-player minimum is needed to book an event. Tournaments should be booked two months in advance. The banquet facility can accommodate up to 200 people. ● **TRAVEL:** The Konocti Harbor Resort is five minutes from the golf course. For reservations call 707-279-4281.

1. BUCKINGHAM GOLF & COUNTRY CLUB

PLAY POLICY & FEES: Outside play is accepted. Memberships are available. Green fees are $13 for nine holes and $16 for 18 holes on weekdays, and $16 for nine holes and $22 for 18 holes on weekends. Carts are $6 for nine holes and $9 for 18 holes weekdays, $8 and $11 weekends.

TEE TIMES: Reservations can be made any time.

DRESS CODE: No tank tops or jeans are allowed on the golf course.

COURSE DESCRIPTION: This hilly, picturesque course offers views of Clear Lake. It has sidehill lies, big greens, and elevated tees. This course features dramatic elevation changes that offer breathtaking panoramic views. There are no adjacent fairways.

NOTES: There is also a six-hole, pitch-and-putt course. Volunteers run the course.

LOCATION: From Napa on Highway 29 drive to Lower Lake, turn left, and drive to Soda Bay Road. Turn right and drive to Fairway Drive. From Ukiah take Highway 20 to Lakeport and Kelseyville. Turn left on Soda Bay Road and travel to Fairway Drive.

. . . ● **TOURNAMENTS:** This course is available for outside tournaments. A 20-player minimum is required to book a tournament. The banquet facility can accommodate up to 80 people. ● **TRAVEL:** The Konocti Harbor Resort and Spa is near the course. For information and reservations call 707-279-4281.

2. CLEAR LAKE RIVIERA YACHT & GOLF

❸ ADAMS SPRINGS GOLF COURSE
ARCHITECT: JACK FLEMING, 1962

14347 Snead Court at Hwy
Loch Lomond, CA 95426

PRO SHOP: 707-928-9992

Eddie Mullins, Owner
Carolynn Mann, Manager
Sean Mullins, Superintendent

Driving Range
Practice Greens ●
Clubhouse ●
Food / Beverage ●
Accommodations
Pull Carts ●
Power Carts ●
Club Rental ●
$pecial Offers

	1	2	3	4	5	6	7	8	9	OUT
BACK	-	-	-	-	-	-	-	-	-	
REGULAR	-	-	-	-	-	-	-	-	-	
par	-	-	-	-	-	-	-	-	-	
handicap	-	-	-	-	-	-	-	-	-	-
FORWARD	-	-	-	-	-	-	-	-	-	
par	-	-	-	-	-	-	-	-	-	
handicap	-	-	-	-	-	-	-	-	-	-

	10	11	12	13	14	15	16	17	18	IN
BACK	-	-	-	-	-	-	-	-	-	
REGULAR	-	-	-	-	-	-	-	-	-	
par	-	-	-	-	-	-	-	-	-	
handicap	-	-	-	-	-	-	-	-	-	-
FORWARD	-	-	-	-	-	-	-	-	-	
par	-	-	-	-	-	-	-	-	-	
handicap	-	-	-	-	-	-	-	-	-	-

BACK	
yardage	-
par	-
rating	-
slope	-

REGULAR	
yardage	2640
par	34
rating	64.6
slope	111

FORWARD	
yardage	2499
par	34
rating	68.1-
slope	119

❹ HOBERG'S FOREST LAKE GOLF & COUNTRY CLUB
ARCHITECT: NORMAN S. WREN, 1954

P.O. Box 350
Cobb, CA 95426

10200 Golf Road
Cobb, CA 95426

PRO SHOP: 707-928-5276

George Hoberg, Owner
Kit Huston, Director of Golf, PGA

Driving Range
Practice Greens ●
Clubhouse ●
Food / Beverage ●
Accommodations
Pull Carts ●
Power Carts ●
Club Rental ●
$pecial Offers

	1	2	3	4	5	6	7	8	9	OUT
BACK	-	-	-	-	-	-	-	-	-	
REGULAR	264	152	310	241	110	358	130	398	299	2262
par	4	3	4	4	3	4	3	4	4	33
handicap	9	13	7	11	15	3	17	1	5	-
FORWARD	264	152	310	241	110	358	130	398	299	2262
par	4	3	4	4	3	4	3	5	4	34
handicap	11	9	7	13	15	1	17	3	5	-

	10	11	12	13	14	15	16	17	18	IN
BACK	-	-	-	-	-	-	-	-	-	
REGULAR	264	152	310	241	110	358	130	398	356	2319
par	4	3	4	4	3	4	3	4	4	33
handicap	10	14	8	12	16	6	18	2	4	-
FORWARD	264	152	310	241	110	358	130	398	356	2319
par	4	3	4	4	3	4	3	5	5	35
handicap	12	10	8	14	16	2	18	6	4	-

BACK	
yardage	-
par	-
rating	-
slope	-

REGULAR	
yardage	4581
par	66
rating	61.2
slope	109

FORWARD	
yardage	4581
par	69
rating	62.2
slope	107

PLAY POLICY & FEES: Green fees are $10 for nine holes and $16 for 18 holes weekdays, and $14 for nine holes and $20 for 18 holes weekends. Thursday is "Senior Day"; green fees are $7. Carts are $12 for nine holes and $20 for 18 holes.

TEE TIMES: Reservations can be booked 30 days in advance.

DRESS CODE: No tank tops allowed on the course.

COURSE DESCRIPTION: This walkable mountain course has rolling terrain with generous fairways. Three lakes come into play on five holes. The par-3 fourth hole, 181 yards long, has a great view. You'll see lots of wildlife.

LOCATION: From Highway 29 in Middletown take Highway 175 west. Drive 11 miles to the course (one mile past Hoberg and one mile south of Loch Lomond). There are signs on the road to direct you.

. . . ● **TOURNAMENTS:** This course is available for outside tournaments.

3. ADAMS SPRINGS GOLF COURSE

PLAY POLICY & FEES: Green fees are $12 for nine holes and $17 for 18 holes weekdays, and $14 for nine holes and $20 for 18 holes weekends. Carts are $12 for nine holes and $20 for 18 holes.

TEE TIMES: Reservations can be booked seven days in advance.

DRESS CODE: Nonmetal spikes are required.

COURSE DESCRIPTION: A creek meanders through this pretty mountain course located 3,600 feet above sea level. There are bunkers on every hole, and many pine trees come into play. This course is open for play year-round, weather permitting. There are six par 4s and three par 3s. The pride of the course is the 398-yard, par-4 eighth.

LOCATION: Drive north on Highway 29 to Highway 175. Take Highway 175 north to the town of Cobb. The course is set at Highway 175 and Golf Road.

. . . ● **TOURNAMENTS:** This course is available for outside tournaments. Tournaments should be booked six months in advance.

4. HOBERG'S FOREST LAKE GOLF &

HIDDEN VALLEY LAKE GOLF & COUNTRY CLUB
ARCHITECT: WILLIAM F. BELL, 1970

19210 Hartman Road
Middletown, CA 95461

PRO SHOP: 707-987-3035

Bill Stewart, Manager
Bob Archer, PGA Professional

Driving Range ●
Practice Greens ●
Clubhouse ●
Food / Beverage ●
Accommodations
Pull Carts
Power Carts ●
Club Rental ●
$pecial Offers

	1	2	3	4	5	6	7	8	9	OUT
BACK	434	483	442	189	354	567	461	210	393	3533
REGULAR	420	458	436	143	347	505	433	201	341	3284
par	4	5	4	3	4	5	4	3	4	36
handicap	5	17	1	15	13	7	3	9		-
FORWARD	326	431	431	125	342	453	335	134	333	2910
par	4	5	5	3	4	5	4	3	4	37
handicap	11	5	7	17	1	3	15	13		-

BACK	
yardage	6667
par	72
rating	72.5
slope	124

	10	11	12	13	14	15	16	17	18	IN
BACK	429	146	466	399	114	401	483	344	352	3134
REGULAR	407	131	458	388	99	389	463	336	342	3013
par	4	3	5	4	3	4	5	4	4	36
handicap	4	18	8	2	16	12	6	10	14	-
FORWARD	416	103	405	321	98	251	430	328	284	2636
par	5	3	5	4	3	4	5	4	4	37
handicap	10	16	2	4	18	14	8	6	12	-

REGULAR	
yardage	6297
par	72
rating	70.6
slope	122

FORWARD	
yardage	5546
par	74
rating	71.5
slope	124

HEALDSBURG TAYMAN PARK GOLF COURSE
ARCHITECT: W.H. TAYMAN, 1922

927 South Fitch Mountain
Healdsburg, CA 95448

PRO SHOP: 707-433-4275

Frank L. Johnson, Director of Golf
Dale Wights, Superintendent

Driving Range
Practice Greens ●
Clubhouse ●
Food / Beverage ●
Accommodations
Pull Carts ●
Power Carts ●
Club Rental ●
$pecial Offers

	1	2	3	4	5	6	7	8	9	OUT
BACK	315	403	141	349	182	290	298	252	385	2615
REGULAR	310	395	137	339	160	285	298	242	378	2544
par	4	5	3	4	3	4	4	4	4	35
handicap	10	16	18	6	12	4	8	14	2	-
FORWARD	307	385	134	329	124	281	245	222	320	2347
par	4	5	3	4	4	4	4	4	4	35
handicap	9	1	17	5	15	3	13	11	7	-

BACK	
yardage	5230
par	70
rating	65.6
slope	112

	10	11	12	13	14	15	16	17	18	IN
BACK	315	403	141	349	182	290	298	252	385	2615
REGULAR	310	395	137	339	160	285	298	242	378	2544
par	4	5	3	4	3	4	4	4	4	35
handicap	9	15	17	5	11	3	7	13	1	-
FORWARD	307	385	134	329	124	281	245	222	320	2347
par	4	5	3	4	3	4	4	4	4	35
handicap	10	2	18	6	16	4	14	12	8	-

REGULAR	
yardage	5088
par	70
rating	65.6
slope	112

FORWARD	
yardage	4694
par	70
rating	68.4
slope	113

PLAY POLICY & FEES: Green fees are $13 for nine holes and $20 for 18 holes Monday through Friday, and $18 for nine holes and $30 for 18 holes weekends and holidays. Senior, twilight, and resident rates are available. Carts are $7 for nine holes and $12 for 18 holes per person. Carts are mandatory until noon on weekends and on holidays. Fees are subject to change.

TEE TIMES: Reservations can be booked seven days in advance.

DRESS CODE: Shirts with collars must be worn. Nonmetal spikes are required.

COURSE DESCRIPTION: This sprawling course is scenic and hilly. The front nine is long and flat. The back nine is shorter with elevated tees. Water comes into play on 10 holes, mostly during the winter months. The most dramatic hole is the 389-yard, par-4 15th. The tee is 200 feet above the fairway. It's a spectacular shot, with Sutter Home vineyards on the left and Mount St. Helena in the background. It looks like you have to hit it a country mile, but you don't. Try aiming for the swimming pool and you're safe.

NOTES: Charlie Gibson holds the course record with a 64.

LOCATION: From Middletown drive five miles north on Highway 29. The course is on the right.

. . . ● **TOURNAMENTS:** An 80-player minimum is needed to book a shotgun tournament, and a 20-player minimum is required for a regular tournament. Carts are required. Events should be booked 12 months in advance. The banquet facility holds 100 people.

5. HIDDEN VALLEY LAKE GOLF & COUNTRY

PLAY POLICY & FEES: Green fees are $10 for nine holes and $16 for 18 holes weekdays, and $12 for nine holes and $18 for 18 holes weekends and holidays. Carts are $10 for nine holes and $20 for 18 holes.

TEE TIMES: Reservations can be booked seven days in advance.

COURSE DESCRIPTION: This is a hilly, tree-lined course with small greens. It's walkable. The 378-yard ninth, usually into the wind, is across a creek and down into a sloping fairway. The approach goes back uphill to the green next to the clubhouse. The course offers picturesque views of Healdsburg and the surrounding area. The greens are fast, and many have two tiers.

LOCATION: Driving north on U.S. 101 into Healdsburg, take the Central Healdsburg exit onto Healdsburg Avenue. Drive on Healdsburg Avenue through two lights before turning right on Matheson Street (Matheson turns into Fitch Mountain Road). The course is on the left.

. . . ● **TOURNAMENTS:** A 16-player minimum is needed to book a tournament. Carts are required. Events should be scheduled three months in advance. The banquet facility can accommodate 75 people.

6. HEALDSBURG TAYMAN PARK GOLF

7 WINDSOR GOLF CLUB
ARCHITECTS: GOLF PLAN, 1989; FRED BLISS

1340 19th Hole Drive
Windsor, CA 95492

PRO SHOP: 707-838-7888
CLUBHOUSE: 707-838-8802

Charlie Gibson, Director of Golf, PGA
Mike Folden, Manager
Bill Mish, PGA Professional

Driving Range ●
Practice Greens ●
Clubhouse ●
Food / Beverage ●
Accommodations
Pull Carts ●
Power Carts ●
Club Rental ●
$Special Offers

	1	2	3	4	5	6	7	8	9	OUT
BACK	386	432	327	502	162	428	217	368	546	3368
REGULAR	361	404	297	477	152	397	195	336	516	3135
par	4	4	4	5	3	4	3	4	5	36
handicap	13	1	17	7	15	9	11	5	3	-
FORWARD	300	325	234	401	127	341	141	300	437	2606
par	4	4	4	5	3	4	3	4	5	36
handicap	9	7	15	3	5	13	17	11	1	-

	10	11	12	13	14	15	16	17	18	IN
BACK	569	186	371	194	338	362	354	494	414	3282
REGULAR	537	160	347	163	316	340	325	464	382	3034
par	5	3	4	3	4	4	4	5	4	36
handicap	6	18	4	12	16	14	10	8	2	-
FORWARD	468	111	285	117	277	278	276	381	317	2510
par	5	3	4	3	4	4	4	5	4	36
handicap	4	18	16	14	12	8	6	2	10	-

BACK	
yardage	6650
par	72
rating	72.3
slope	126

REGULAR	
yardage	6169
par	72
rating	70.1
slope	121

FORWARD	
yardage	5116
par	72
rating	69.3
slope	125

8 WIKIUP GOLF COURSE
ARCHITECT: CLARK GLASSON, 1963

5001 Carriage Lane
Santa Rosa, CA 95403

PRO SHOP: 707-546-8787

Ernest Langbein, Owner
Tom Langbein, Manager

Driving Range
Practice Greens ●
Clubhouse
Food / Beverage ●
Accommodations
Pull Carts ●
Power Carts
Club Rental ●
$Special Offers

	1	2	3	4	5	6	7	8	9	OUT
BACK	-	-	-	-	-	-	-	-	-	-
REGULAR	115	264	130	181	117	113	138	375	117	1550
par	3	4	3	3	3	3	3	4	3	29
handicap	14	6	10	4	16	12	8	2	18	-
FORWARD	115	264	130	181	117	113	138	375	117	1550
par	3	4	3	3	3	3	3	4	3	29
handicap	14	6	10	4	16	12	8	2	18	-

	10	11	12	13	14	15	16	17	18	IN
BACK	-	-	-	-	-	-	-	-	-	-
REGULAR	133	283	143	190	128	135	149	386	126	1673
par	3	4	3	3	3	3	3	5	3	30
handicap	13	5	11	3	15	9	7	1	17	-
FORWARD	133	283	143	190	128	135	149	386	126	1673
par	3	4	3	3	3	3	3	5	3	30
handicap	13	5	11	3	15	9	7	1	17	-

BACK	
yardage	-
par	-
rating	-
slope	-

REGULAR	
yardage	3223
par	59
rating	54.8
slope	80

FORWARD	
yardage	3223
par	59
rating	54.8
slope	80

PLAY POLICY & FEES: Green fees are $24 Monday through Thursday, $29 Friday, and $42 on weekends. Twilight, senior, and junior rates are available. Carts are $22 for 18 holes and $16 for a single rider.

TEE TIMES: Reservations can be booked seven days in advance.

DRESS CODE: Nonmetal spikes are required.

COURSE DESCRIPTION: This course boasts a winding creek, four lakes, and many mature oaks. The pride of the course is the par-3 13th, a 194-yarder to a rock-banked green. The par-4 second at 432 yards and the 217-yard par-3 seventh were among the toughest holes on the Nike Tour from 1990 to 1995. The course is driver friendly, but don't miss the small greens if you want to score well.

NOTES: David Duval's 63 is the course record.

LOCATION: From U.S. 101 in Santa Rosa take the Shiloh Road exit. Drive one-half mile west of the freeway. Turn right on Golf Course Drive and left on 19th Hole Drive.

. . . ● **TOURNAMENTS:** A 12-player minimum is needed for tournament play. Carts are required. Events should be booked 24 months in advance. The banquet facility can accommodate 300 people. ● **TRAVEL:** The Sonoma County Hilton is about seven minutes from the golf course. For reservations call 707-523-7555 or 800-445-8667.

7. WINDSOR GOLF CLUB

PLAY POLICY & FEES: The green fees are $10 for nine holes and $13 for 18 holes on weekdays, $12 for nine holes and $6 for each replay on weekends. Student and senior rates are $10 for nine or 18 holes weekdays.

TEE TIMES: Reservations are not accepted. All play is on a first-come, first-served basis.

DRESS CODE: Shirts are required.

COURSE DESCRIPTION: This is a challenging, short course with no adjacent holes. It is scenic and well bunkered, with two par 4s. The short 264-yard, par-4 second hole is a temptation. It makes players choose between laying up or carrying a water hazard. The gentle slopes make the course easily walkable.

NOTES: Power carts are available for seniors only.

LOCATION: From Santa Rosa drive four miles north on U.S. 101 to River Road. Turn east on River Road. Turn north on Old Redwood Highway and drive one-half mile. Turn east on Wikiup Drive and turn right on Carriage Lane.

. . . ● **TOURNAMENTS:** This course is available for outside tournaments.

8. WIKIUP GOLF COURSE

P.O. Box 344
Calistoga, CA 94515

PRO SHOP: 707-942-9966

Larry Casey, Professional
Craig Tresidder, Superintendent

2025 Grant Street, Napa
Calistoga, CA 94515

Driving Range
Practice Greens ●
Clubhouse
Food / Beverage ●
Accommodations
Pull Carts ●
Power Carts ●
Club Rental ●
$pecial Offers

	1	2	3	4	5	6	7	8	9	OUT
BACK	-	-	-	-	-	-	-	-	-	-
REGULAR	278	326	161	306	144	435	391	397	312	2750
par	4	4	3	4	3	4	4	4	4	34
handicap	13	11	15	9	17	1	5	3	7	-
FORWARD	273	320	132	291	139	426	380	384	302	2647
par	4	4	3	4	3	5	4	4	4	35
handicap	13	11	15	9	17	3	5	1	7	-

BACK	
yardage	-
par	-
rating	-
slope	-

	10	11	12	13	14	15	16	17	18	IN
BACK	-	-	-	-	-	-	-	-	-	-
REGULAR	278	326	161	306	144	433	391	397	312	2748
par	4	4	3	4	3	4	4	4	4	34
handicap	14	12	16	10	18	2	6	4	8	-
FORWARD	273	320	132	291	139	426	380	384	302	2647
par	4	4	3	4	3	5	4	4	4	35
handicap	14	12	16	10	18	4	6	2	8	-

REGULAR	
yardage	5498
par	68
rating	65.9
slope	105

FORWARD	
yardage	5294
par	70
rating	69.1
slope	113

10 AETNA SPRINGS GOLF
ARCHITECT: E.F. MUTTON, 1891

1600 Aetna Springs Road
Pope Valley, CA 94567

PRO SHOP: 707-965-2115

Joel Larson, General Manager
Dan Reed, Head Professional
Jaime Espinoza, Superintendent

Driving Range ●
Practice Greens ●
Clubhouse ●
Food / Beverage ●
Accommodations
Pull Carts ●
Power Carts ●
Club Rental ●
$pecial Offers

	1	2	3	4	5	6	7	8	9	OUT
BACK	-	-	-	-	-	-	-	-	-	-
REGULAR	331	282	141	452	138	312	381	336	317	2690
par	4	4	3	5	3	4	4	4	4	35
handicap	12	16	14	4	18	6	1	10	8	-
FORWARD	293	245	131	427	131	267	331	320	275	2420
par	4	4	3	5	3	4	4	4	4	35
handicap	11	15	16	4	18	9	2	6	13	-

BACK	
yardage	-
par	-
rating	-
slope	-

	10	11	12	13	14	15	16	17	18	IN
BACK	-	-	-	-	-	-	-	-	-	-
REGULAR	331	282	184	452	138	312	339	336	317	2691
par	4	4	3	5	3	4	4	4	4	35
handicap	11	15	2	3	17	5	13	9	7	-
FORWARD	293	245	147	427	131	267	331	320	275	2436
par	4	4	3	5	3	4	4	4	4	35
handicap	10	14	7	3	17	8	1	5	12	-

REGULAR	
yardage	5381
par	70
rating	65.9
slope	106

FORWARD	
yardage	4856
par	70
rating	66.7
slope	111

PLAY POLICY & FEES: Green fees are $12 on weekdays and $18 on weekends. Senior rates are $9 on weekdays and $12 weekends. Carts are $8 for nine holes and $15 for 18 holes. The course is closed during the Napa County Fair over the Fourth of July weekend.

TEE TIMES: Reservations are not accepted. All play is on a first-come, first-served basis.

DRESS CODE: Shirts must be worn at all times. No short shorts are allowed on the course.

COURSE DESCRIPTION: This course is located in the middle of the Napa County Fairgrounds. It's short and flat, with narrow fairways. Accuracy is important. There are no par 5s from the men's regular tees. The sixth hole, formerly a par 5, is now a 435-yard par 4. Water comes into play on two holes.

LOCATION: Driving north into Calistoga off Highway 29, turn left on Stephenson Street and take it to Grant Street. Turn left and follow the road to the course at the fairgrounds on the left.

. . . ● **TOURNAMENTS:** A 20-player minimum is needed to book a tournament. Events should be scheduled two months in advance.

9. MOUNT SAINT HELENA GOLF COURSE

PLAY POLICY & FEES: Green fees are $15 weekdays and $20 weekends for 18 holes. Senior, twilight, and nine-hole rates are available. Carts are $9 for nine holes and $16 for 18 holes.

TEE TIMES: Reservations can be booked 30 days in advance.

DRESS CODE: Nonmetal spikes are required.

COURSE DESCRIPTION: Built in 1891 as part of the Aetna Springs Resort, this is one of the oldest courses in California. It's nestled in the mountains, with gentle hills and two creeks running through it. It has six par 4s, two par 3s, and one par 5. The course is marked by towering oak trees, meandering creeks, and excellent greens.

NOTES: Bring the family—picnic tables border the course. There is also a barbecue area. Walk the resort grounds and relive Napa history.

LOCATION: From Napa on Highway 29 heading north toward Calistoga, drive one mile past Saint Helena. Turn right on Deer Park Road. Stay on this road and drive through Angwin. The road turns into Howell Mountain Road. Once in Pope Valley veer to the left where the road branches at the service station. Drive four miles to Aetna Springs Road (just past the Hub Cap Ranch). Turn onto Aetna Springs Road and drive one mile to the course.

. . . ● **TOURNAMENTS:** A 32-player minimum is need to book an event, and tournaments should be scheduled four to six months in advance. A banquet facility is available that holds up to 100 people.

10. AETNA SPRINGS GOLF COURSE

2881 Scotts Right-of-Way
Sebastopol, CA 95472

PRO SHOP: 707-823-9852

Lee Farris, Owner
Gene Phillips, Professional
Jean Rossini, Tournament Director

Driving Range
Practice Greens ●
Clubhouse ●
Food / Beverage ●
Accommodations
Pull Carts ●
Power Carts ●
Club Rental ●
$pecial Offers

	1	2	3	4	5	6	7	8	9	OUT
BACK	-	-	-	-	-	-	-	-	-	-
REGULAR	147	195	190	200	206	140	150	195	240	1663
par	3	3	3	4	4	3	3	4	4	31
handicap	15	11	9	5	7	17	13	3	1	-
FORWARD	147	195	190	200	206	140	150	195	240	1663
par	3	4	4	4	4	3	3	4	4	33
handicap	15	11	9	5	7	17	13	3	1	-

	10	11	12	13	14	15	16	17	18	IN
BACK	-	-	-	-	-	-	-	-	-	-
REGULAR	147	195	190	200	206	140	150	195	240	1663
par	3	3	3	4	4	3	3	4	4	31
handicap	16	12	10	6	8	18	14	4	2	-
FORWARD	147	195	190	200	206	140	150	195	240	1663
par	3	4	4	4	4	3	3	4	4	33
handicap	16	12	10	6	8	18	14	4	2	-

BACK	
yardage	-
par	-
rating	-
slope	-

REGULAR	
yardage	3326
par	62
rating	55.0
slope	86

FORWARD	
yardage	3326
par	66
rating	55.0
slope	86

5110 Oak Meadow Drive
Santa Rosa, CA 95401

PRO SHOP: 707-546-6617
CLUBHOUSE: 707-546-3485

Jeff Ogden, Head Professional, PGA
John Hamilton, Tournament Director
Richard McAllister, Superintendent

Driving Range ●
Practice Greens ●
Clubhouse ●
Food / Beverage ●
Accommodations
Pull Carts ●
Power Carts ●
Club Rental ●
$pecial Offers

	1	2	3	4	5	6	7	8	9	OUT
BACK	378	490	439	194	537	174	400	426	367	3405
REGULAR	361	474	422	184	508	158	391	390	352	3240
par	4	5	4	3	5	3	4	4	4	36
handicap	7	13	1	15	11	17	5	3	9	-
FORWARD	350	413	416	142	480	124	381	340	342	2988
par	4	5	5	3	5	3	4	4	4	37
handicap	11	3	5	17	1	15	7	13	9	-

	10	11	12	13	14	15	16	17	18	IN
BACK	367	584	401	344	368	213	355	197	515	3344
REGULAR	347	540	373	312	362	188	319	150	490	3081
par	4	5	4	4	4	3	4	3	5	36
handicap	14	2	6	16	4	10	12	18	8	-
FORWARD	337	495	341	305	352	144	304	121	411	2810
par	4	5	4	4	4	3	4	3	5	36
handicap	12	2	8	10	6	16	14	18	4	-

BACK	
yardage	6749
par	72
rating	72.5
slope	128

REGULAR	
yardage	6321
par	72
rating	70.5
slope	124

FORWARD	
yardage	5798
par	73
rating	72.7
slope	123

PLAY POLICY & FEES: Green fees are $10 for nine holes and $5 for each replay weekdays, and $12 for nine holes and $5 for each replay on weekends. Senior rates are $7 on weekdays. Carts are $10 for nine holes and $12 for 18 holes.

TEE TIMES: Reservations are not accepted. All play is on a first-come, first-served basis.

COURSE DESCRIPTION: This short course is all par 3s and par 4s, with the longest hole measuring 240 yards. The most notable is the 195-yard, par-3 second hole, which requires an uphill shot to a two-tiered green. Water comes into play on the 195-yard, par-4 eighth hole.

LOCATION: From Sebastopol drive three miles north on Highway 116 to Scotts Right-of-Way. Turn right and drive to the course.

. . . ● **TOURNAMENTS:** A 54-player minimum is needed to book a private event.

11. SEBASTOPOL GOLF COURSE

PLAY POLICY & FEES: Reciprocal play is accepted with members of other private clubs; otherwise, members and guests only. Reciprocal fees are $50 on weekdays and $70 on weekends. Guest fees are $40 when accompanied by a club member. Carts are mandatory.

DRESS CODE: Shirts must have a collar, and shorts must have a six-inch inseam. No blue jeans, halter tops, or tank tops may be worn. Nonmetal spikes are required.

COURSE DESCRIPTION: This sprawling course is lined with beautiful oak trees and is tougher than it looks. Out-of-bounds areas come into play on six holes, so accurate tee shots are essential for good play. On the par-4 eighth, the tee shot must carry over a lake, and an oak tree comes into play on the approach. The course has small greens and many false fronts, so good touch is essential.

NOTES: The 17th hole has been remodeled and now includes a lake guarding the left front portion of the green. The course record for men is 63, set by Tom Costello.

LOCATION: From U.S. 101 take Highway 12 west toward Sebastopol. Turn right on Fulton Road and left on Hall Road. Turn left on Country Club Road and drive to the parking lot.

. . . ● **TOURNAMENTS:** Only six outside events are allowed here each year.

12. SANTA ROSA GOLF & COUNTRY CLUB

FOUNTAINGROVE RESORT & COUNTRY CLUB
ARCHITECTS: TED ROBINSON, 1985; TED ROBINSON, 1998

1525 Fountaingrove
Santa Rosa, CA 95403

PRO SHOP: 707-579-GOLF

John Theilade, Director of Golf, PGA
Byron Cone, Head Professional, PGA
Gary Skolnik, Superintendent

Driving Range ●
Practice Greens ●
Clubhouse ●
Food / Beverage ●
Accommodations ●
Pull Carts
Power Carts ●
Club Rental ●
$pecial Offers ●

	1	2	3	4	5	6	7	8	9	OUT
BACK	378	407	398	510	153	405	376	612	173	3412
REGULAR	353	379	372	490	130	381	340	583	148	3176
par	4	4	4	5	3	4	4	5	3	36
handicap	15	1	11	5	17	7	9	3	13	-
FORWARD	302	326	329	434	97	316	296	492	117	2709
par	4	4	4	5	3	4	4	5	3	36
handicap	15	5	7	3	17	9	11	1	13	-

	10	11	12	13	14	15	16	17	18	IN
BACK	392	566	179	405	552	394	440	215	385	3528
REGULAR	370	535	158	373	532	359	375	200	361	3263
par	4	5	3	4	5	4	4	3	4	36
handicap	14	2	18	10	6	8	4	12	16	-
FORWARD	290	430	123	325	477	314	316	129	311	2715
par	4	5	3	4	5	4	4	3	4	36
handicap	12	4	18	8	2	10	6	14	16	-

BACK	
yardage	6940
par	72
rating	73.7
slope	136

REGULAR	
yardage	6439
par	72
rating	71.7
slope	132

FORWARD	
yardage	5424
par	72
rating	71.0
slope	125

 BENNETT VALLEY GOLF COURSE
ARCHITECT: BEN HARMON, 1969

3330 Yulupa Avenue
Santa Rosa, CA 95405

PRO SHOP: 707-528-3673
CLUBHOUSE: 707-528-1192

Bob Borowicz, Director of Golf, PGA
John Flachman, Superintendent
Bruce Smith, Banquet Manager

Driving Range ●
Practice Greens ●
Clubhouse ●
Food / Beverage ●
Accommodations
Pull Carts ●
Power Carts ●
Club Rental ●
$pecial Offers

	1	2	3	4	5	6	7	8	9	OUT
BACK	491	441	368	309	519	176	365	212	377	3258
REGULAR	444	432	347	297	501	156	340	201	365	3083
par	5	4	4	4	5	3	4	3	4	36
handicap	3	1	9	17	5	15	7	13	11	-
FORWARD	420	422	340	293	449	143	331	191	337	2926
par	5	5	4	4	5	3	4	3	4	37
handicap	3	5	9	15	1	17	7	13	11	-

	10	11	12	13	14	15	16	17	18	IN
BACK	499	171	424	393	392	168	367	433	478	3325
REGULAR	482	160	413	359	369	138	356	425	436	3138
par	5	3	4	4	4	3	4	4	5	36
handicap	12	18	4	10	6	16	8	2	14	-
FORWARD	458	148	403	350	359	133	343	420	418	3032
par	5	3	5	4	4	3	4	5	5	38
handicap	2	18	14	12	10	16	4	6	8	-

BACK	
yardage	6583
par	72
rating	70.6
slope	112

REGULAR	
yardage	6221
par	72
rating	69.0
slope	109

FORWARD	
yardage	5958
par	75
rating	72.5
slope	116

PLAY POLICY & FEES: Outside play is accepted. Green fees are $55 on weekdays and $75 on weekends. Carts are mandatory and included in the green fees. Carts are allowed on paths only.

TEE TIMES: Reservations can be booked seven days in advance.

DRESS CODE: Collared shirts are required, and metal spikes are prohibited.

COURSE DESCRIPTION: Demanding off the tee is an understatement. This is a tight, hilly layout with lots of trees and excellent greens. The picturesque 17th hole is a par 3 that requires a 215-yard shot downhill over water. The course is situated in a very pretty setting in north Santa Rosa.

NOTES: Ted Robinson's work in renovating this challenging course is a success. The new design makes the course more difficult, but it is both functionally and aesthetically pleasing.

LOCATION: In Santa Rosa on U.S.101, take the Mendocino Avenue/Old Redwood Highway exit. Drive east and turn left on Fountaingrove Parkway. Continue up the hill to the course, which is on the left.

. . . ● **TOURNAMENTS:** This course is available for outside tournaments. A 16-player minimum is needed to book an event. The banquet facility can accommodate up to 250 people. ● **TRAVEL:** The Sonoma County Hilton (707-523-7555) and the Fountaingrove Inn (707-578-6101) are within five minutes of the golf course. ● **$PECIAL OFFERS:** The Fountaingrove Inn offers play-and-stay packages. Call the hotel for more information.

13. FOUNTAINGROVE RESORT & COUNTRY

PLAY POLICY & FEES: Green fees are $18 weekdays and $25 weekends. Senior rates are $11 for nine holes and $14 for 18 holes, weekdays only. Carts are $20 for 18 holes.

TEE TIMES: Reservations are issued a week in advance and eight days for Sunday.

COURSE DESCRIPTION: This is a level, well-conditioned course with lots of trees. The greens are fast, and the course is walkable. A creek wanders through the course, providing some water hazard encounters. In the summer the course averages 350 to 400 players a day. The 433-yard 17th hole is the toughest on the course, and overall this course is a good test for all golfers.

NOTES: Every green on the course is being rebuilt over the next few years under the supervision of Golf Plan. As of summer 1999, six greens have been completed. Expect one or two temporary greens throughout the year. New cart paths for all 18 holes have been completed. The course record is 61 held by Don Tarvid.

LOCATION: In Santa Rosa take Highway 12 east towards Sonoma/Napa At the first stop light (Farmers Lane) take a right. Farmers Lane dead ends at Bennett Valley Road. Turn left at the stoplight. Bennett Valley Road leads to the course.

. . . ● **TOURNAMENTS:** Shotgun tournaments are available weekdays only. A 20-player minimum is needed to book an event. Tournaments can be booked two months in advance. The banquet facility can accommodate 65 people. ● **TRAVEL:** The Days Inn is located ten minutes from the golf course. For reservations call 707-573-9000.

14. BENNETT VALLEY GOLF COURSE

1350 Bennett Valley Road
Santa Rosa, CA 95405

PRO SHOP: 707-577-0755

Robert Braun, Manager
John Russell, PGA Professional
Jerry McCart, Superintendent

Driving Range ●
Practice Greens ●
Clubhouse
Food / Beverage ●
Accommodations
Pull Carts ●
Power Carts
Club Rental ●
$pecial Offers

	1	2	3	4	5	6	7	8	9	OUT
BACK	-	-	-	-	-	-	-	-	-	-
REGULAR	185	90	305	120	145	170	310	320	155	1800
par	3	3	4	3	3	3	4	4	3	30
handicap	3	17	1	13	15	7	5	9	11	-
FORWARD	185	90	305	120	145	170	310	320	155	1800
par	3	3	4	3	3	3	4	4	3	30
handicap	3	17	1	13	15	7	5	9	11	-

BACK	
yardage	-
par	-
rating	-
slope	-

	10	11	12	13	14	15	16	17	18	IN
BACK	-	-	-	-	-	-	-	-	-	-
REGULAR	175	80	300	110	135	160	300	300	175	1735
par	3	3	4	3	3	3	4	4	3	30
handicap	4	18	2	14	16	8	6	10	12	-
FORWARD	175	80	300	110	135	160	300	300	175	1735
par	3	3	4	3	3	3	4	4	3	30
handicap	4	18	2	14	16	8	6	10	12	-

REGULAR	
yardage	3535
par	60
rating	57.3
slope	78

FORWARD	
yardage	3535
par	60
rating	57.3
slope	78

16 **OAKMONT GOLF COURSE**
ARCHITECT: TED ROBINSON, 1963

7025 Oakmont Drive
Santa Rosa, CA 95409

PRO SHOP: 707-539-0415

Dean James, Director of Golf, PGA
Jeff Pace, PGA Professional
Mike Clark, Superintendent

Driving Range ●
Practice Greens ●
Clubhouse ●
Food / Beverage ●
Accommodations
Pull Carts ●
Power Carts ●
Club Rental ●
$pecial Offers ●

	1	2	3	4	5	6	7	8	9	OUT
BACK	481	352	384	173	384	537	145	399	403	3258
REGULAR	469	335	375	147	371	521	127	381	374	3100
par	5	4	4	3	4	5	3	4	4	36
handicap	11	9	5	15	7	13	17	1	3	-
FORWARD	436	319	361	113	340	487	107	356	352	2871
par	5	4	4	3	4	5	3	4	4	36
handicap	3	13	9	15	11	1	17	5	7	-

BACK	
yardage	6379
par	72
rating	70.5
slope	120

	10	11	12	13	14	15	16	17	18	IN
BACK	352	403	477	360	213	343	463	145	365	3121
REGULAR	330	387	456	342	198	330	453	136	327	2959
par	4	4	5	4	3	4	5	3	4	36
handicap	8	2	14	6	4	10	16	18	12	-
FORWARD	298	321	424	326	170	302	443	122	296	2702
par	4	4	5	4	3	4	5	3	4	36
handicap	10	8	4	6	14	12	2	18	16	-

REGULAR	
yardage	6059
par	72
rating	69.0
slope	117

FORWARD	
yardage	5573
par	72
rating	71.9
slope	128

PLAY POLICY & FEES: Green fees are $9 for 18 holes and $3 for replays weekdays. Weekend green fees are $12 for nine holes and $4 replays. Senior and junior rates are available. Pull carts are $2. The course is closed for two weeks during the fair in July, Thanksgiving, and Christmas.

TEE TIMES: Reservations are not accepted. All play is on a first-come, first-served basis.

DRESS CODE: No metal spikes are allowed on the course.

COURSE DESCRIPTION: This course, situated in the center of the Santa Rosa Fairgrounds racetrack, is a good practice course. There are two water hazards and some sand traps. The course is flat and the greens are fairly small. The course is well-maintained, and the greens are in better shape than more than a few country clubs.

NOTES: A night driving range is available (hours vary).

LOCATION: In Santa Rosa on U.S. 101 north, take the Highway 12 exit east; then take the first offramp (the Downtown exit), which leads straight to the fairgrounds and the course on the right.

. . . ● **TOURNAMENTS:** This course is available for outside events. A 36-player minimum is needed to book a tournament. Tournaments can be booked two months in advance.

15. FAIRGROUNDS GOLF CENTER

PLAY POLICY & FEES: Outside play is accepted. West Course green fees are $29 on weekdays and $39 on weekends. East Course green fees are $24 on weekdays and $32 on weekends. Twilight rates are available. Carts are $24.

TEE TIMES: Reservations are recommended, one day in advance for weekdays and one week for weekends.

DRESS CODE: Shirts must have collars. No tank tops may be worn.

COURSE DESCRIPTION: The West Course is short with lots of trees. There is water on 14 holes. The pride of the West Course is the 381-yard, par-4 eighth hole, which boasts two lakes and out-of-bounds on both sides. The East Course is a challenging executive course with some tough par 3s. The 171-yard, par 3 14th hole, for example, requires a longish carry over a creek to a green surrounded by trees. Both courses are busy and in excellent shape.

NOTES: Par is 63 for the East Course. The East Course is 4,293 yards and rated 59.8 from the regular tees. The slope rating is 94. The West Course: See scorecard for yardage and rating information.

LOCATION: From Santa Rosa take Highway 12 east toward Sonoma. Turn right on Oakmont Drive into the community of Oakmont. The course is on the right, eight miles east of U.S. 101.

. . . ● **TOURNAMENTS:** A 24-player minimum is required to book a tournament.

16. OAKMONT GOLF COURSE

MEADOWOOD RESORT HOTEL GOLF COURSE
ARCHITECT: JACK FLEMING, 1964

900 Meadowood Lane
Saint Helena, CA 94574

PRO SHOP: 707-963-3646

Doug Pike, PGA Professional

Driving Range
Practice Greens ●
Clubhouse ●
Food / Beverage ●
Accommodations ●
Pull Carts ●
Power Carts
Club Rental ●
Special Offers ●

	1	2	3	4	5	6	7	8	9	OUT
BACK	-	-	-	-	-	-	-	-	-	-
REGULAR	174	185	334	142	187	325	270	123	281	2021
par	3	3	4	3	3	4	4	3	4	31
handicap	9	1	5	13	3	11	7	17	15	-
FORWARD	174	107	334	142	187	325	270	123	281	1943
par	3	3	4	3	3	4	4	3	4	31
handicap	11	15	3	13	5	9	7	17	1	-

	10	11	12	13	14	15	16	17	18	IN
BACK	-	-	-	-	-	-	-	-	-	-
REGULAR	161	171	324	122	174	258	259	106	273	1848
par	3	3	4	3	3	4	4	3	4	31
handicap	10	2	6	14	4	12	8	18	16	-
FORWARD	161	100	324	122	174	258	259	106	273	1777
par	3	3	4	3	3	4	4	3	4	31
handicap	12	16	4	14	6	10	8	18	2	-

BACK	
yardage	-
par	-
rating	-
slope	-

REGULAR	
yardage	3869
par	62
rating	60.1
slope	101

FORWARD	
yardage	3720
par	62
rating	60.8
slope	97

 ## MOUNTAIN SHADOWS GOLF COURSES
ARCHITECTS: BOB BALDOCK, 1963; GARY ROGER BAIRD, 1978

100 Golf Course Drive
Rohnert Park, CA 94928

PRO SHOP: 707-584-7766

Tom Terra, Manager
Dave Johnson, PGA Professional
Tim Woods, Tournament Director

Driving Range ●
Practice Greens ●
Clubhouse ●
Food / Beverage ●
Accommodations
Pull Carts ●
Power Carts ●
Club Rental ●
Special Offers ●

	1	2	3	4	5	6	7	8	9	OUT
BACK	545	465	180	530	455	150	440	400	375	3540
REGULAR	539	397	162	505	394	143	353	387	320	3200
par	5	4	3	5	4	3	4	4	4	36
handicap	11	7	5	15	3	17	1	9	13	-
FORWARD	476	336	144	438	318	105	278	338	298	2731
par	5	4	3	5	4	3	4	4	4	36
handicap	3	13	17	1	7	15	5	11	9	-

	10	11	12	13	14	15	16	17	18	IN
BACK	370	445	580	155	380	220	520	395	425	3490
REGULAR	339	383	552	152	385	139	483	384	383	3200
par	4	4	5	3	4	3	5	4	4	36
handicap	8	12	10	16	6	18	14	4	2	-
FORWARD	299	330	477	131	356	110	437	341	321	2802
par	4	4	5	3	4	3	5	4	4	36
handicap	10	12	2	16	6	18	8	14	4	-

BACK	
yardage	7030
par	72
rating	69.2
slope	112

REGULAR	
yardage	6400
par	72
rating	67.5
slope	108

FORWARD	
yardage	5533
par	72
rating	70.5
slope	117

PLAY POLICY & FEES: Reciprocal play is accepted with members of other private clubs. Hotel guests are welcome. Green fees are $35 for all day.

TEE TIMES: Guests can make tee times up to six months in advance.

DRESS CODE: Shirts with collars must be worn. No jeans are allowed on the course.

COURSE DESCRIPTION: This is a short, tight, and tricky course with lots of trees. There are some hills and undulating greens. It's an excellent course for beginners and intermediates. The 334-yard third hole is a par 4 that doglegs to the right. Although Meadowood is short, the setting in the oaks with the beautiful resort nearby is pretty and peaceful.

NOTES: A world-class croquet pitch is located next to the golf course.

LOCATION: From Napa drive north on Highway 29. Turn right on Pope Street and take Pope Street to Silverado Trail. Take a left on Silverado Trail, then a quick right onto Howell Mountain Road. Follow Howell Mountain Road to Meadowood Lane and the course.

. . . ● **TOURNAMENTS:** This course is available for outside tournaments. ● **$PECIAL OFFERS:** Play-and-stay golf packages with the resort are available.

PLAY POLICY & FEES: The green fees are $20 Monday through Friday and $35 on weekends and holidays for both the Redwoods (North) Course and the Willows (South) Course. Carts are mandatory after 10 a.m. on the Redwoods Course. Twilight and other special rates are available.

TEE TIMES: Reservations can be booked seven days in advance.

DRESS CODE: No cutoffs of any kind are allowed on the course, and shirts must have sleeves. Translation: No tank tops.

COURSE DESCRIPTION: Both courses are tight, with a rolling terrain and large, undulating greens. Notable is the seventh hole on the Redwoods Course. It's long, and every shot is tough to negotiate. Off the tee you face out-of-bounds to the left and a lake running down the entire right side. If you hit it down the middle, you're faced with a green that sits on a well-bunkered peninsula.

NOTES: The Willows (South) Course is 6,496 yards and rated 70.1 from the championship tees, with a slope of 115. The Redwoods Course: see scorecard.

LOCATION: From Santa Rosa drive seven miles south on U.S. 101. Take the Wilfred exit east to Golf Course Drive.

. . . ● **TOURNAMENTS:** A 20-player minimum is required to book a tournament. The banquet facility can accommodate 250 people. ● **TRAVEL:** The DoubleTree Sonoma County is within walking distance. For reservations call 707-584-5466. ● **$PECIAL OFFERS:** Play-and-stay golf packages are available with the DoubleTree.

⑲ YOUNTVILLE GOLF COURSE
ARCHITECT: CASEY O'CALLAGHAN, 1999

7901 Solano Ave.
Yountville, CA 94599

PRO SHOP: 707-944-1992

Terry Sullivan, PGA Professional
Sean Battistini, Superintendent

Driving Range ●
Practice Greens ●
Clubhouse
Food / Beverage ●
Accommodations
Pull Carts ●
Power Carts ●
Club Rental ●
$pecial Offers

	1	2	3	4	5	6	7	8	9	OUT
BACK	357	165	311	159	293	484	362	157	348	2636
REGULAR										
par	4	3	4	3	4	5	4	3	4	34
handicap	1	9	17	7	15	3	13	11	5	-
FORWARD	321	147	264	121	264	433	332	97	274	2253
par	4	3	4	3	4	5	4	3	4	34
handicap	1	9	17	7	15	3	13	11	4	-

	10	11	12	13	14	15	16	17	18	IN
BACK	327	156	311	128	274	484	341	135	348	2504
REGULAR										
par	4	3	4	3	4	5	4	3	4	34
handicap	2	10	18	8	16	4	14	12	6	-
FORWARD	274	137	236	114	239	433	288	85	243	2049
par	4	3	4	3	4	5	4	3	4	34
handicap	2	10	18	8	16	4	14	12	6	-

BACK	
yardage	5140
par	68
rating	62.8
slope	108

REGULAR	
yardage	
par	68
rating	
slope	

FORWARD	
yardage	4302
par	68
rating	62.8
slope	108

⑳ CHIMNEY ROCK GOLF COURSE
ARCHITECT: BOB BALDOCK, 1965

5320 Silverado Trail
Napa, CA 94558

PRO SHOP: 707-255-3363

Scott Pajak, Superintendent

Driving Range
Practice Greens ●
Clubhouse
Food / Beverage ●
Accommodations
Pull Carts ●
Power Carts ●
Club Rental ●
$pecial Offers

	1	2	3	4	5	6	7	8	9	OUT
BACK	384	426	221	534	418	302	200	505	422	3412
REGULAR	373	415	208	527	408	290	188	497	406	3312
par	4	4	3	5	4	4	3	5	4	36
handicap	9	1	15	7	5	11	17	13	3	-
FORWARD	362	300	147	485	396	257	139	473	374	2933
par	4	4	3	5	4	4	3	5	4	36
handicap	9	13	15	1	5	11	17	3	7	-

	10	11	12	13	14	15	16	17	18	IN
BACK	384	426	221	534	418	302	200	505	422	3412
REGULAR	373	415	208	527	408	290	188	497	406	3312
par	4	4	3	5	4	4	3	5	4	36
handicap	10	2	16	8	6	12	18	14	4	-
FORWARD	362	300	147	485	396	257	140	473	374	2934
par	4	4	3	5	4	4	3	5	4	36
handicap	10	14	16	2	6	12	18	4	8	-

BACK	
yardage	6824
par	72
rating	71.5
slope	115

REGULAR	
yardage	6624
par	72
rating	70.6
slope	113

FORWARD	
yardage	5867
par	72
rating	73.0
slope	122

PLAY POLICY & FEES: Green fees for nine holes are $18 Monday through Thursday and $24 Friday through Sunday and holidays. Green fees for 18 holes are $24 Monday through Thursday, $30 Friday through Sunday and holidays. Junior rates are $14 for nine holes, $18 for 18 holes Monday through Thursday. Resident and senior rates are available for Napa County residents. Carts are $16 for nine holes,$24 for 18 holes.

TEE TIMES: Reservations can be made 30 days in advance. If possible let the pro-shop know whether you plan to play nine or 18.

DRESS CODE: Appropriate golf attire is required. Metal spikes are not allowed.

COURSE DESCRIPTION: Yountville is an upscale nine-hole course and practice center. The course, set next the Domaine Chandon Winery, is a perfect place to play for golfers who need a fix while touring the wine country. For the serious golfer the course is challenging enough to have fun, while for the recreational golfer the course is fun but not overly demanding. The course offers spacious greens and holes ranging from 85 to 501 yards.

NOTES: The driving range is covered and lighted. Mats and grass areas available.

LOCATION: From Highway 29 in Napa head north toward St. Helena. Take the Yountville exit, head west, and make a left on Solano Avenue to the clubhouse.

. . . ● **TOURNAMENTS:** A 72-player minimum is required to book a shotgun event. Tournament packages include green fees, golf cart rental, and a $5 per player credit in the golf shop for gift certificates or merchandise. Banquet, scoring, and contests for special events are available.

19. YOUNTVILLE GOLF COURSE

PLAY POLICY & FEES: Green fees are $15 for nine holes and $20 for 18 holes weekdays, and $18 and $24 weekends. Carts are $16 for nine holes and $22 for 18 holes. Twilight rates start at 3 p.m. Twilight fees are $14 on weekdays and $17 on weekends.

TEE TIMES: Reservations can be booked 14 days in advance.

COURSE DESCRIPTION: Located on the picturesque Silverado Trail, this scenic course is situated at the base of the Napa foothills in the midst of vineyards and wineries. Offering one of the most beautiful sites in the Napa Valley, this championship course (3,412 yards) is lined with weeping willows and California oak trees. Three lakes come into play on this flat, challenging layout.

NOTES: Chimney Rock is owned by the winery of the same name. This is the longest permanent nine-hole course in California.

LOCATION: From Napa heading north on Highway 29, go right on Oak Knoll Avenue. At the end, turn left and make an immediate right onto Oak Knoll. Turn left onto Silverado Trail and travel 1.5 miles to the course.

. . . ● **TOURNAMENTS:** A 16-player minimum is needed to book a tournament. Tournaments should be booked six months in advance.

20. CHIMNEY ROCK GOLF COURSE

1600 Atlas Peak Road
Napa, CA 94558

PRO SHOP: 707-257-5460
STARTER: 800-362-4727

Kirk Candland, General Manager
Jeff Goodwin, Head Professional, PGA
Brian Morris, Superintendent

Driving Range ●
Practice Greens ●
Clubhouse ●
Food / Beverage ●
Accommodations ●
Pull Carts
Power Carts ●
Club Rental ●
$pecial Offers ●

	1	2	3	4	5	6	7	8	9	OUT
BACK	436	195	405	382	536	435	212	375	528	3504
REGULAR	404	150	348	371	512	405	182	323	493	3188
par	4	3	4	4	5	4	3	4	5	36
handicap	1	17	7	5	9	3	15	13	11	-
FORWARD	382	132	337	303	483	396	153	289	478	2953
par	4	3	4	4	5	4	3	4	5	36
handicap	5	17	9	13	1	7	15	11	3	-

	10	11	12	13	14	15	16	17	18	IN
BACK	418	183	362	420	400	195	525	357	536	3396
REGULAR	381	122	348	400	375	176	500	336	521	3159
par	4	3	4	4	4	3	5	4	5	36
handicap	4	18	16	2	12	10	6	14	8	-
FORWARD	358	116	316	336	351	138	485	298	506	2904
par	4	3	4	4	4	3	5	4	5	36
handicap	6	18	14	10	12	16	2	8	4	-

BACK	
yardage	6900
par	72
rating	73.4
slope	131

REGULAR	
yardage	6347
par	72
rating	70.9
slope	126

FORWARD	
yardage	5857
par	72
rating	73.1
slope	128

PLAY POLICY & FEES: Reciprocal play with other private clubs is accepted, but reservations may be made no more than two days in advance. Hotel guests are welcome. Green fees are $120 for hotel guests and $140 for reciprocal players. Carts are mandatory and included in the green fees.

TEE TIMES: Tee times can be made up to one year in advance for resort guests.

DRESS CODE: Collared shirts are required. No denim is allowed.

COURSE DESCRIPTION: Although the North Course is longer, the South Course requires more finesse shots. Both are sprawling layouts with large, undulating greens. Water and oak trees guard the courses. The back nine on the North Course offers demanding par 4s. The South Course is not as long, but it's equally challenging. There are three par 5s on the back nine—Nos. 11, 13, and 18—and two are guarded by water. This is one of northern California's premier resorts.

NOTES: See scorecard for yardage and rating information for the North Course. The Sourth Course is 6,685 yards long with a rating of 72.4 and a slope of 129. Redesigned by Robert Trent Jones Jr., the North Course was formerly used for the PGA Tour's Kaiser International and Anheuser-Busch Classic. The South Course is the site of the Senior PGA Tour's Transamerica Open.

LOCATION: From Highway 29 in Napa take a right on Trancas Street. Take a left on Atlas Peak and drive less than a mile to the course.

. . . ● **TOURNAMENTS:** Shotgun tournaments are available Monday, Wednesday, and Friday, and carts are required. Events should be booked nine to 12 months in advance. The banquet facility holds up to 250 people. ● **TRAVEL:** The Silverado Resort is one of the finest golf resorts in Northern California. The resort now offers a full service spa, salon, and fitness facility. Call 707-257-0200 for information and reservations. ● **$PECIAL OFFERS:** Play-and-stay packages are available.

22 PETALUMA GOLF & COUNTRY CLUB

ARCHITECT: ROGER BAIRD, 1922

P.O. Box 26
Petaluma, CA 94953

1500 Country Club Drive
Petaluma, CA 94953

PRO SHOP: 707-762-7041

John D. Moore, Head Professional, PGA
Bill Maeder, Superintendent

Driving Range ●
Practice Greens ●
Clubhouse ●
Food / Beverage ●
Accommodations
Pull Carts ●
Power Carts ●
Club Rental ●
$pecial Offers

	1	2	3	4	5	6	7	8	9	OUT
BACK	-	-	-	-	-	-	-	-	-	-
REGULAR	381	281	306	170	565	136	311	159	480	2789
par	4	4	4	3	5	3	4	3	5	35
handicap	3	15	9	7	1	17	13	11	5	-
FORWARD	377	270	303	160	554	131	303	154	476	2728
par	4	4	4	3	5	3	4	3	5	35
handicap	3	13	9	7	1	17	11	15	5	-

	10	11	12	13	14	15	16	17	18	IN
BACK	-	-	-	-	-	-	-	-	-	-
REGULAR	362	288	348	195	513	146	311	159	486	2808
par	4	4	4	3	5	3	4	3	5	35
handicap	6	18	8	4	2	10	16	14	12	-
FORWARD	358	270	329	163	505	144	303	154	478	2704
par	4	4	4	3	5	3	4	3	5	35
handicap	4	14	10	8	2	18	12	16	6	-

BACK	
yardage	-
par	-
rating	-
slope	-

REGULAR	
yardage	5597
par	70
rating	67.2
slope	111

FORWARD	
yardage	5432
par	70
rating	72.3
slope	125

23 ADOBE CREEK GOLF CLUB

ARCHITECT: ROBERT TRENT JONES JR., 1990

1901 Frates Road
Petaluma, CA 94954

PRO SHOP: 707-765-3000 EXT. 100

Norm Smith, Head Professional, PGA
Cliff Peterson, Superintendent

Driving Range ●
Practice Greens ●
Clubhouse ●
Food / Beverage ●
Accommodations
Pull Carts ●
Power Carts ●
Club Rental ●
$pecial Offers

	1	2	3	4	5	6	7	8	9	OUT
BACK	547	390	390	483	132	320	388	160	352	3162
REGULAR	501	363	367	444	118	276	363	124	322	2878
par	5	4	4	5	3	4	4	3	4	36
handicap	3	7	9	13	17	15	1	11	5	-
FORWARD	454	330	339	405	94	255	298	98	267	2540
par	5	4	4	5	3	4	4	3	4	36
handicap	1	5	9	7	17	13	3	15	11	-

	10	11	12	13	14	15	16	17	18	IN
BACK	357	533	128	382	476	379	140	326	407	3128
REGULAR	318	503	97	349	442	344	135	303	374	2865
par	4	5	3	4	5	4	3	4	4	36
handicap	4	2	16	8	12	14	18	10	6	-
FORWARD	277	463	85	299	416	297	96	280	332	2545
par	4	5	3	4	5	4	3	4	4	36
handicap	10	4	16	8	2	14	18	12	6	-

BACK	
yardage	6290
par	72
rating	71.3
slope	125

REGULAR	
yardage	5743
par	72
rating	68.7
slope	123

FORWARD	
yardage	5085
par	72
rating	69.4
slope	120

PLAY POLICY & FEES: Reciprocal play is accepted with members of other private clubs.

DRESS CODE: Collared shirts are required.

COURSE DESCRIPTION: This short course is called "Goat Hill." It has plenty of well-positioned bunkers, good putting surfaces, and many rolling hills. The sixth hole is a 136-yard par 3, guarded on the right by a huge oak tree.

LOCATION: Heading north on U.S. 101 toward Petaluma, take the Petaluma Boulevard South exit into town. Take McNear Avenue south to Country Club Drive and the course.

. . . ● **TOURNAMENTS:** This course is available for outside tournaments.

22. PETALUMA GOLF & COUNTRY CLUB

PLAY POLICY & FEES: Green fees are $27 weekdays and $47 weekends and holidays. Carts are included on weekend rates. Carts are $13 per rider. Senior and twilight rates are available.

TEE TIMES: Reservations can be booked seven days in advance.

DRESS CODE: Nonmetal spikes are required.

COURSE DESCRIPTION: This sprawling, links-style course is situated in the Sonoma County countryside. Five lakes, a stream, and 70 bunkers make accuracy a must. Beware of the seventh hole. It's a par-4, 388-yard challenge with a creek on the right and another creek fronting the large green. The 9th, 16th, 17th, and 18th holes will test golfers of every ability.

NOTES: Adobe Creek is a great place to play in the rainy, winter months. Built on adobe, this course has been blessed with exceptional natural drainage.

LOCATION: From U.S.101 in Petaluma take the Highway 116 exit east and drive 1.25 miles. Turn left on Frates Road and drive three-quarters of a mile to the course on the left.

. . . ● **TOURNAMENTS:** A 16-player minimum is needed to book a tournament. Events should be booked at least six months in advance. The banquet facility can accommodate 200 people. ● **TRAVEL:** The Quality Inn is four miles from the golf course. For information and reservations call 707-664-1155.

23. ADOBE CREEK GOLF CLUB

ROOSTER RUN GOLF CLUB
ARCHITECT: FRED BLISS, 1998

2301 East Washington
Petaluma, CA 94954

PRO SHOP: 707-778-1211
CLUBHOUSE: 707-778-1232

Rob Watson, Head Professional, PGA
Val Verhunce, Director of Golf Instruction
David Saly, Superintendent

Driving Range •
Practice Greens •
Clubhouse
Food / Beverage •
Accommodations
Pull Carts •
Power Carts •
Club Rental •
$pecial Offers

	1	2	3	4	5	6	7	8	9	OUT
BACK	550	174	354	360	420	173	415	408	529	3383
REGULAR	481	148	305	312	376	107	348	310	472	2859
par	5	3	4	4	4	3	4	4	5	36
handicap	9	11	17	3	1	15	5	7	13	-
FORWARD	371	120	266	271	336	90	299	282	415	2450
par	5	3	4	4	4	3	4	4	5	36
handicap	9	11	17	3	1	15	5	7	13	-

	10	11	12	13	14	15	16	17	18	IN
BACK	398	560	408	404	380	172	460	230	606	3618
REGULAR	354	495	349	334	333	118	366	166	515	3030
par	4	5	4	4	4	3	4	3	5	36
handicap	10	8	14	18	12	16	2	6	4	-
FORWARD	307	435	314	299	292	103	353	141	445	2689
par	4	5	4	4	4	3	4	3	5	36
handicap	10	8	14	18	12	16	2	6	4	-

BACK	
yardage	7001
par	72
rating	73.9
slope	128

REGULAR	
yardage	5889
par	72
rating	71.2
slope	124

FORWARD	
yardage	5139
par	72
rating	69.1
slope	113

 SONOMA MISSION INN GOLF AND COUNTRY CLUB
ARCHITECTS: SAM WHITING, 1926; ROBERT MUIR GRAVES, 1991

GOLF 50

17700 Arnold Drive
Sonoma, CA 95476

PRO SHOP: 707-996-0300
CLUBHOUSE: 707-996-4852

Jeff Hall, Manager
August Thompson, Head Professional, PGA
Mark H. Bunte, Dir. of Golf Maintenance

Driving Range •
Practice Greens •
Clubhouse •
Food / Beverage •
Accommodations
Pull Carts
Power Carts •
Club Rental •
$pecial Offers •

	1	2	3	4	5	6	7	8	9	OUT
BACK	386	552	409	204	431	417	219	596	345	3559
REGULAR	340	481	352	163	375	359	171	551	303	3095
par	4	5	4	3	4	4	3	5	4	36
handicap	15	3	9	13	1	11	7	5	17	-
FORWARD	302	442	321	140	347	338	131	498	264	2783
par	4	5	4	3	4	4	3	5	4	36
handicap	15	5	9	13	1	7	11	3	17	-

	10	11	12	13	14	15	16	17	18	IN
BACK	425	359	427	587	215	436	541	142	396	3528
REGULAR	387	302	364	474	170	376	486	118	351	3028
par	4	4	4	5	3	4	5	3	4	36
handicap	10	14	4	12	6	2	16	18	8	-
FORWARD	303	272	328	455	150	347	446	105	322	2728
par	4	4	4	5	3	4	5	3	4	36
handicap	14	16	8	6	10	2	4	18	12	-

BACK	
yardage	7087
par	72
rating	74.1
slope	132

REGULAR	
yardage	6123
par	72
rating	69.4
slope	125

FORWARD	
yardage	5511
par	72
rating	66.6
slope	118

PLAY POLICY & FEES: Green fees are $26 Monday through Thursday, $32 Friday, and $42 weekends and holidays. Senior green fees are $15 Monday through Wednesday. Discounts are available for juniors and residents of Petaluma. Seasonal twilight rates range from $18 to $26. Golf carts are $24.

TEE TIMES: Reservations can be booked seven days in advance.

DRESS CODE: Appropriate golf attire and nonmetal spikes are required.

COURSE DESCRIPTION: This course epitomizes the saying, "Drive for show, and putt for dough." The majority of the fairways on this level course are driver friendly, but the greens are sloping, undulating, and quick. Aiming straight at the cup on even the shortest putts can make for a three-putt day. Water comes into play on 15 holes, and wind can be a factor. With four sets of tee boxes, Rooster Run is accommodating and challenging for all skill levels. From the back tees, the 18th hole is a 606-yard par 5 into the wind--hitting your driver off the tee is mandatory, not for show but for survival.

NOTES: For those who like to pilot small planes, the golf course is located next to the Petaluma Airport.

LOCATION: On U.S. 101 in Petaluma take the East Washington exit. Head east on East Washington one mile to the course.

. . . ● **TOURNAMENTS:** This course is available for outside tournaments. Tournaments should be booked six to 12 months in advance.

24. ROOSTER RUN GOLF CLUB

PLAY POLICY & FEES: Green fees include cart and are $70 Monday through Thursday, $85 Friday, and $100 Saturday, Sunday, and holidays. Twilight and late-afternoon walking rates are available starting at $50.

TEE TIMES: Reservations can be booked 30 days in advance.

DRESS CODE: T-shirts and jeans are not allowed, and nonmetal spikes are required.

COURSE DESCRIPTION: This is considered one of the top-rated places to play in the state. The course features plenty of mounding and subtle elevation changes. The greens are also very subtle and maintain a traditional flavor. Lots of oaks and redwoods guard several tight doglegs. If you love a traditional straight-forward golfing experience, this is the course for you.

NOTES: Sonoma plays host to U.S. Open sectional and U.S. amateur qualifying.

LOCATION: From San Francisco drive north on U.S. 101. Take Highway 37 east to Highway 121 north. Follow Highway 121 to Highway 116. Continue north on Highway 116 for two miles. Take the Arnold Drive exit and drive about four miles to the club.

. . . ● **TOURNAMENTS:** Shotgun tournaments are available Monday through Thursday. A 24-player minimum is needed to book a tournament. Events should be booked 12 months in advance. The banquet facility can hold 300 people. ●

TRAVEL: The world-famous Sonoma Mission Inn now owns the golf course. The inn is five minutes from the course. For reservations call 707-938-9000. ●

$PECIAL OFFERS: Play-and-stay packages are available.

25. SONOMA MISSION INN GOLF AND

26 LOS ARROYOS GOLF CLUB

5000 Stage Gulch Road
Sonoma, CA 95476

PRO SHOP: 707-938-8835

Charles Reynolds, Director of Golf

Driving Range
Practice Greens
Clubhouse
Food / Beverage ●
Accommodations
Pull Carts ●
Power Carts
Club Rental ●
$pecial Offers

	1	2	3	4	5	6	7	8	9	OUT
BACK	-	-	-	-	-	-	-	-	-	
REGULAR	143	150	285	95	305	100	144	160	157	1539
par	3	3	4	3	4	3	3	3	3	29
handicap	11	5	3	15	9	17	7	1	13	
FORWARD	143	150	285	95	305	100	144	160	157	1539
par	3	3	4	3	4	3	3	3	3	29
handicap	11	5	3	15	9	17	7	1	13	

BACK		
yardage	-
par	-
rating	
slope	-

	10	11	12	13	14	15	16	17	18	IN
BACK	-	-	-	-	-	-	-	-	-	
REGULAR	143	150	285	95	305	100	144	160	157	1539
par	3	3	4	3	4	3	3	3	3	29
handicap	12	6	4	16	10	18	8	2	14	
FORWARD	143	150	285	95	305	100	144	160	157	1539
par	3	3	4	3	4	3	3	3	3	29
handicap	12	6	4	16	10	18	8	2	14	

REGULAR		
yardage	3078
par	58
rating	
slope	

FORWARD		
yardage	3078
par	58
rating	
slope	

27 NAPA GOLF COURSE
ARCHITECT: JACK FLEMING, 1967

2295 Streblow Drive
Napa, CA 94558

PRO SHOP: 707-255-4333

Jeff Dennis, Professional/Manager
Jack Noonkester, Superintendent

Driving Range ●
Practice Greens ●
Clubhouse ●
Food / Beverage ●
Accommodations
Pull Carts ●
Power Carts ●
Club Rental ●
$pecial Offers

	1	2	3	4	5	6	7	8	9	OUT
BACK	391	422	409	199	510	433	164	350	527	3405
REGULAR	371	408	401	188	494	417	148	336	513	3276
par	4	4	4	3	5	4	3	4	5	36
handicap	7	1	5	9	11	3	17	15	13	-
FORWARD	359	398	388	143	438	335	133	323	461	2978
par	4	5	4	3	5	4	3	4	5	37
handicap	3	13	5	15	9	7	17	11	1	-

BACK		
yardage	6730
par	72
rating	71.7
slope	127

	10	11	12	13	14	15	16	17	18	IN
BACK	415	329	429	202	549	372	161	490	378	3325
REGULAR	405	318	418	187	538	362	157	478	367	3230
par	4	4	4	3	5	4	3	5	4	36
handicap	4	18	2	8	12	10	16	14	6	-
FORWARD	395	307	338	139	474	351	154	464	356	2978
par	4	4	4	3	5	4	3	5	4	36
handicap	2	4	10	18	12	8	16	4	6	-

REGULAR		
yardage	6506
par	72
rating	70.7
slope	123

FORWARD		
yardage	5956
par	73
rating	73.6
slope	120

PLAY POLICY & FEES: Green fees for 18 holes are $15 weekdays and $17 weekends. The rate for the pitch-and-putt course is $5. Pull carts are $2.

TEE TIMES: Reservations are not accepted. All play is on a first-come, first-served basis.

COURSE DESCRIPTION: This tree-lined executive course is level and ideal for sharpening iron play. There are only two par 4s. The best hole on the course is the par-3 eighth, at 160 yards.

NOTES: Los Arroyos also features a nine-hole course for chipping and putting. Some of the best Sonoma Valley wineries are within minutes of Los Arroyos.

LOCATION: From San Francisco heading north on U.S. 101, take the Highway 116 exit east to Sonoma. The course is at the intersection of Highway 116 and Highway 121.

. . . ● **TOURNAMENTS:** No shotgun tournaments are allowed. A 12-player minimum is needed to book a tournament. ● **TRAVEL:** Sonoma Mission Inn (707-938-9000), Sonoma Best Western (707-938-9200) and MacArthur Place (707-938-2929) are recommended for lodging.

26. LOS ARROYOS GOLF CLUB

PLAY POLICY & FEES: Green fees for nonresidents are $23.50 weekdays and $27.75 weekends and holidays. Resident green fees are $16.25 weekdays and $20.50 weekends and holidays. Twilight rates are available. Carts are $23 for 18 holes. No spectators are allowed.

TEE TIMES: Reservations are recommended seven days in advance.

DRESS CODE: Let common sense be your guide.

COURSE DESCRIPTION: This underrated course is long, tough, and tight. It has many trees, and water comes into play on 14 holes. Nicknamed Kennedy Park because it is situated in Napa's John F. Kennedy Park, this course was used for U.S. Open qualifying in 1972 and for several PGA Tour events at the Silverado Country Club.

NOTES: Napa was the site of qualifying for two PGA Tour stops as well as the 1972 U.S. Open.

LOCATION: From Highway 12 in Napa, take Highway 29 north. Take the Lake Berryessa exit at the fork. Drive two miles to Streblow Drive and turn left to get to the course.

. . . ● **TOURNAMENTS:** A 16-player minimum is needed to book a tournament. Tournaments should be booked 12 months in advance. There is a banquet facility that can accommodate 130 people.

27. NAPA GOLF COURSE

3385 Hagen Road
Napa, CA 94558

PRO SHOP: 707-252-1114
CLUBHOUSE: 707-252-1111

Bruce Bennetts, General Manager
Mitch Johnson, PGA Professional
Ray Layland, Superintendent

Driving Range •
Practice Greens •
Clubhouse •
Food / Beverage •
Accommodations
Pull Carts •
Power Carts •
Club Rental •
$pecial Offers

	1	2	3	4	5	6	7	8	9	OUT
BACK	120	444	393	413	143	380	474	361	296	3024
REGULAR	120	430	371	377	134	345	455	346	287	2865
par	3	5	4	4	3	4	5	4	4	36
handicap	17	1	3	11	15	7	9	5	13	-
FORWARD	109	423	367	364	114	310	444	326	277	2734
par	3	5	4	4	3	4	5	4	4	36
handicap	17	3	1	13	15	5	11	7	9	-

	10	11	12	13	14	15	16	17	18	IN
BACK	306	140	485	429	357	181	530	352	394	3174
REGULAR	279	120	444	401	311	142	494	323	335	2849
par	4	3	5	4	4	3	5	4	4	36
handicap	16	18	6	4	12	14	2	8	10	-
FORWARD	259	100	426	360	295	119	450	303	240	2552
par	4	3	5	4	4	3	5	4	4	36
handicap	12	18	8	4	10	14	2	6	16	-

BACK	
yardage	6198
par	72
rating	70.0
slope	125

REGULAR	
yardage	5714
par	72
rating	69.0
slope	122

FORWARD	
yardage	5286
par	72
rating	70.2
slope	124

29 GREEN TREE GOLF CLUB
ARCHITECT: WILLIAM F. BELL, 1963

P.O. Box 1056
Vacaville, CA 95696

999 Leisure Town Road
Vacaville, CA 95687

PRO SHOP: 707-448-1420

Bob Peterson, General Manager, PGA
Bob Miller, Tournament Director

Driving Range •
Practice Greens •
Clubhouse •
Food / Beverage •
Accommodations
Pull Carts •
Power Carts •
Club Rental •
$pecial Offers

	1	2	3	4	5	6	7	8	9	OUT
BACK	539	514	347	385	115	502	197	440	160	3199
REGULAR	510	483	340	379	108	495	186	404	146	3051
par	5	5	4	4	3	5	3	4	3	36
handicap	3	13	9	5	17	11	7	1	15	-
FORWARD	424	401	320	348	91	415	154	352	82	2587
par	5	5	4	4	3	5	3	4	3	36
handicap	5	13	9	7	17	11	7	1	15	-

	10	11	12	13	14	15	16	17	18	IN
BACK	335	416	395	168	335	152	303	417	581	3102
REGULAR	320	409	382	144	325	141	286	397	553	2957
par	4	4	4	3	4	3	4	5	5	35
handicap	18	4	8	10	12	14	16	6	2	-
FORWARD	292	392	364	127	293	122	268	379	438	2675
par	4	4	4	3	4	3	4	5	5	35
handicap	18	2	6	10	12	14	16	8	4	-

BACK	
yardage	6301
par	71
rating	70.2
slope	119

REGULAR	
yardage	6008
par	71
rating	68.5
slope	114

FORWARD	
yardage	5262
par	71
rating	69.5
slope	117

PLAY POLICY & FEES: Reciprocal play is accepted with members of other private clubs. Green fees for reciprocators are $90, including cart. Guest fees are $45 when accompanied by a member weekdays, and $60 weekends. Call to make arrangements. Carts are $10 per rider. Rates are subject to change.

DRESS CODE: Collared shirts are required. No denim, tank tops, or short shorts are allowed.

COURSE DESCRIPTION: This scenic course has tight fairways and small, undulating greens. There are many oak trees. The course was expanded in the spring of 1990 to 18 holes by Ron Fream. Many holes offer views of the Bay Area and Napa Valley. From the 11th tee the Golden Gate Bridge is visible. When you're not looking at the view, check out this par 3; it's 120 yards to an island green. If you miss the green, you're not in water, but in a mean barranca. The course has small greens on the front and bigger greens on the back. It's a member's course, where local knowledge prevails over talent.

NOTES: The 16th green, a par five, has a new green and tee box. The new yardage is 530 yards.

LOCATION: From Highway 121 in Napa drive 1.5 miles on Hagen Road to the course.

. . . ● **TOURNAMENTS:** Outside events must receive board approval and are usually limited to Monday. A 72-player minimum is needed to book a tournament. Events can be booked two to four months in advance. The banquet facility can accommodate 130 people.

28. NAPA VALLEY COUNTRY CLUB

PLAY POLICY & FEES. Monday through Thursday green fees are $18. Friday through Sunday and holidays green fees are $25. Junior and senior green fees are available Monday through Thursday, excluding holidays. Carts are $22.

TEE TIMES: Reservations can be booked seven days in advance.

DRESS CODE: Appropriate golf attire and nonmetal spikes are required.

COURSE DESCRIPTION: The course is well maintained. The length is not too demanding, but the greens have subtle breaks that make local knowledge a big advantage. The course has undergone extensive changes and renovation during the past two years. Hundreds of trees have been planted, and new tees have been built, along with the new two-tiered 18th green capping a par-5, double-dogleg finish over water. You will find Green Tree easy to walk.

NOTES: The executive course is 3,120 yards, and par is 29. "Golf Digest" calls the greens some of the best in the area.

LOCATION: The course is located one-quarter mile south of Interstate 80 on Leisure Town Road at the east end of Vacaville.

. . . ● **TOURNAMENTS:** A 12-player minimum is needed for tournament play. Events should be booked 12 months in advance. The banquet facility can accommodate up to 150 people. ● **TRAVEL:** The Black Oak Restaurant is recommended.

29. GREEN TREE GOLF CLUB

30 INDIAN VALLEY GOLF CLUB
ARCHITECT: ROBERT NYBERG, 1957

P.O. Box 351
Novato, CA 94948

3035 Novato Boulevard
Novato, CA 94947

PRO SHOP: 415-897-1118
CLUBHOUSE: 415-892-5885

Jeff McAndrew, Director of Golf, PGA
Ron Hoyt, PGA Professional
Terry Leach, Superintendent

Driving Range ●
Practice Greens ●
Clubhouse ●
Food / Beverage ●
Accommodations
Pull Carts ●
Power Carts ●
Club Rental ●
$pecial Offers

	1	2	3	4	5	6	7	8	9	OUT
BACK	528	408	485	120	289	367	420	158	365	3140
REGULAR	523	389	464	110	261	332	387	148	323	2937
par	5	4	5	3	4	4	4	3	4	36
handicap	1	5	9	18	13	3	7	15	11	-
FORWARD	504	374	474	96	239	298	327	138	264	2714
par	5	4	5	3	4	4	4	3	4	36
handicap	1	7	3	17	15	9	5	13	11	-

	10	11	12	13	14	15	16	17	18	IN
BACK	360	324	425	146	395	365	475	148	475	3113
REGULAR	300	313	415	134	379	323	450	139	452	2905
par	4	4	4	3	4	4	5	3	5	36
handicap	14	12	2	16	4	6	8	17	10	-
FORWARD	232	301	374	119	359	250	429	123	357	2544
par	4	4	4	3	5	4	5	3	4	36
handicap	16	6	4	14	10	8	12	18	2	-

BACK	
yardage	6253
par	72
rating	69.2
slope	119

REGULAR	
yardage	5842
par	72
rating	67.8
slope	116

FORWARD	
yardage	5258
par	72
rating	70.9
slope	128

31 MARIN COUNTRY CLUB
ARCHITECTS: LAWRENCE HUGHES, 1959; ROBERT MUIR GRAVES, 1986

500 Country Club Drive
Novato, CA 94949

PRO SHOP: 415-382-6707
CLUBHOUSE: 415-382-6700

Bob Stangron, Manager
Ed Hester, PGA Professional
Stanley Burgess, Superintendent

Driving Range ●
Practice Greens ●
Clubhouse ●
Food / Beverage ●
Accommodations
Pull Carts ●
Power Carts ●
Club Rental ●
$pecial Offers

	1	2	3	4	5	6	7	8	9	OUT
BACK	481	167	388	357	411	352	178	394	506	3234
REGULAR	475	145	373	343	395	342	160	368	490	3091
par	5	3	4	4	4	4	3	4	5	36
handicap	70.5	17	15	5	7	1	13	11	3	-
FORWARD	460	134	371	330	301	331	146	320	479	2872
par	5	3	4	4	4	4	3	4	5	36
handicap	6	18	4	8	14	10	16	12	2	-

	10	11	12	13	14	15	16	17	18	IN
BACK	370	385	385	319	360	150	479	364	382	3194
REGULAR	362	377	375	307	352	135	472	349	368	3097
par	4	4	4	4	4	3	5	4	4	36
handicap	2	12	4	16	6	18	10	8	14	-
FORWARD	357	370	368	297	303	114	437	327	359	2932
par	4	4	4	4	4	3	5	4	4	36
handicap	1	13	5	15	11	17	3	9	7	-

BACK	
yardage	6428
par	72
rating	71.6
slope	130

REGULAR	
yardage	6188
par	72
rating	70.5
slope	127

FORWARD	
yardage	5804
par	72
rating	74.8
slope	133

PLAY POLICY & FEES: Green fees are $28 Monday through Thursday, $35 Friday, and $45 weekends. Senior fees are $21 Monday through Thursday. Carts are $22. The course is closed Christmas Day.

TEE TIMES: Reservations can be booked seven days in advance.

DRESS CODE: No tank tops or cut-off shorts are allowed.

COURSE DESCRIPTION: This scenic course is challenging and diverse. There are rolling hills and many trees. Water comes into play on 10 holes. A premium is placed on chipping and putting. One of the best holes is the 16th, a par 5 that drops 250 feet from the tee.

NOTES: There is an elevator from the 13th to the 14th hole.

LOCATION: From U.S. 101 in Novato take the San Marin Drive exit west to Novato Boulevard. Turn right on Novato Boulevard to the course.

. . . ● **TOURNAMENTS:** Shotgun tournaments are available weekdays only. There is a 24-player minimum for tournament play, and carts are required. Events should be booked 12 months in advance. The banquet facility can accommodate up to 120 people. ● **TRAVEL:** The Embassy Suites in San Rafael is located about 20 minutes from the golf course. For reservations call 415-499-9222.

30. INDIAN VALLEY GOLF CLUB

PLAY POLICY & FEES: Reciprocal play is accepted with members of other private clubs. Reciprocal play is $55. Fees for guests accompanied by a member are $40 weekdays and $50 weekends. Carts are $22.

TEE TIMES: Reservations can be booked seven days in advance.

DRESS CODE: Appropriate golf attire and nonmetal spikes are required.

COURSE DESCRIPTION: This sprawling course winds through a posh suburban neighborhood, offering tight fairways, fast and undulating greens, and sidehill lies. Wind can become a factor, but club selection is the key here on any day. The 411-yard fifth hole is a dogleg right, with water on the right and out-of-bounds on the left. All the par 3s are demanding, and the greens are typically fast, placing a premium on the short game.

LOCATION: From U.S. 101 in Novato take the Ignacio Boulevard exit west. Drive 1.5 miles. Turn left on Country Club Drive to the course.

. . . ● **TOURNAMENTS:** This course is available for outside tournaments.

31. MARIN COUNTRY CLUB

P.O. Box 3779
Napa, CA 94558

2555 Jameson Canyon
Napa, CA 94558

PRO SHOP: 707-257-1900

Ray Graziani, Head Professional, PGA
Kevin Buckles, Tournament Director
Gary Cozart, Superintendent

Driving Range ●
Practice Greens ●
Clubhouse ●
Food / Beverage ●
Accommodations
Pull Carts
Power Carts ●
Club Rental ●
$pecial Offers ●

	1	2	3	4	5	6	7	8	9	OUT
BACK	441	162	516	176	348	441	492	154	513	3243
REGULAR	427	155	482	153	341	392	478	138	465	3031
par	4	3	5	3	4	4	5	3	5	36
handicap	-	-	-	-	-	-	-	-	-	-
FORWARD	388	129	452	124	333	321	416	115	424	2702
par	4	3	5	3	4	4	5	3	5	36
handicap	-	-	-	-	-	-	-	-	-	-

	10	11	12	13	14	15	16	17	18	IN
BACK	493	383	182	389	151	539	164	421	445	3167
REGULAR	466	343	151	374	132	505	151	401	429	2952
par	5	4	3	4	3	5	3	4	5	36
handicap	-	-	-	-	-	-	-	-	-	-
FORWARD	443	299	109	337	104	410	126	325	345	2498
par	5	4	3	4	3	5	3	4	5	36
handicap	-	-	-	-	-	-	-	-	-	-

BACK	
yardage	6410
par	72
rating	71.7
slope	127

REGULAR	
yardage	5983
par	72
rating	69.8
slope	122

FORWARD	
yardage	5200
par	72
rating	70.1
slope	126

PLAY POLICY & FEES: For the Vineyards Course, green fees are $65 Monday through Friday and $85 weekends. Carts are included. For the Club Shakespeare Course, reciprocal play is accepted. Fees for reciprocal play are $125 every day.

TEE TIMES: Reservations may be made up to 14 days in advance with a credit card.

DRESS CODE: Appropriate golf attire is required.

COURSE DESCRIPTION: The Club Shakespeare Course features open par 4s, back-to-back par 3s and par 5s, and plenty of character. The 200-yard sixth, with the pin-tucked left, is a great par 3. The 392-yard 14th offers a severe descent to a dogleg-left fairway. The course is a good test that can be made brutal by an incessant wind. The Vineyards has a rougher feel to it and seems more exposed to the wind. It has long carries over crevasses and creeks, with punishing par 4s on eight and nine.

NOTES: This is rumored to be one of Michael Jordan's favorite golf courses when he's in California. The courses are surrounded by 150 acres of working vines. The front and back nines have been reversed on the Vineyards Course. The Club Shakespeare Course is a private 18-hole course, with a par of 72 from all tees. The course ranges from 5,448 yards to 7,001 yards long.

LOCATION: From Highway 29 south of Napa, take Highway 12 east. The entrance to the course is 1.3 miles from the intersection.

. . . ● **TOURNAMENTS:** Both courses are available for tournament play. There are several rooms available for banquets, with the largest holding up to 200 people. ● **TRAVEL:** Embassy Suites of Napa is located about 15 minutes from the golf course. For reservations call 707-253-9540 ● **SPECIAL OFFERS:** Golf discounts at Chardonnay are provided for hotel guests at Embassy Suites. Call for more information.

32. CHARDONNAY GOLF CLUB

GREEN VALLEY COUNTRY CLUB

ARCHITECTS: ELMER G. BORDERS, 1950; ROBERT MUIR GRAVES, 1965

35 Country Club Drive
Suisun City, CA 94585

PRO SHOP: 707-864-0473
CLUBHOUSE: 707-864-1101

Mark Sherman, PGA Professional
Ray Story, Superintendent
Claude Capozzo, Manager

Driving Range ●
Practice Greens ●
Clubhouse ●
Food / Beverage ●
Accommodations
Pull Carts ●
Power Carts ●
Club Rental ●
$pecial Offers

	1	2	3	4	5	6	7	8	9	OUT
BACK	450	344	524	366	196	349	148	385	389	3151
REGULAR	443	337	513	355	175	340	132	371	382	3048
par	5	4	5	4	3	4	3	4	4	36
handicap	16	8	12	2	10	14	18	6	4	-
FORWARD	428	340	516	364	132	341	128	351	382	2982
par	5	4	5	4	3	4	3	4	4	36
handicap	7	9	1	3	15	13	17	11	5	-

	10	11	12	13	14	15	16	17	18	IN
BACK	464	400	349	168	378	519	445	209	388	3320
REGULAR	457	382	335	149	378	486	420	172	378	3157
par	5	4	4	3	4	5	4	3	4	36
handicap	13	9	5	15	11	17	1	3	7	-
FORWARD	440	365	304	143	318	442	381	144	362	2899
par	5	4	4	3	4	5	4	3	4	36
handicap	2	12	10	14	16	6	4	18	8	-

BACK	
yardage	6471
par	72
rating	71.0
slope	130

REGULAR	
yardage	6205
par	72
rating	69.7
slope	128

FORWARD	
yardage	5881
par	72
rating	73.7
slope	131

 RANCHO SOLANO GOLF COURSE

ARCHITECT: GARY ROGER BAIRD, 1990

3250 Rancho Solano
Fairfield, CA 94533

PRO SHOP: 707-429-4653

Mike Ash, Director of Golf, PGA
Eric Eguaras, Superintendent

Driving Range ●
Practice Greens ●
Clubhouse ●
Food / Beverage ●
Accommodations
Pull Carts ●
Power Carts ●
Club Rental ●
$pecial Offers

	1	2	3	4	5	6	7	8	9	OUT
BACK	502	348	384	382	194	370	482	217	387	3266
REGULAR	479	330	364	366	170	339	466	176	345	3035
par	5	4	4	4	3	4	5	3	4	36
handicap	3	9	1	13	7	17	5	11	15	-
FORWARD	417	297	272	323	138	289	388	114	307	2545
par	5	4	4	4	3	4	5	3	4	36
handicap	3	7	11	9	15	13	1	17	5	-

	10	11	12	13	14	15	16	17	18	IN
BACK	572	429	233	372	442	158	355	522	356	3439
REGULAR	528	376	197	336	421	147	331	494	345	3175
par	5	4	3	4	4	3	4	5	4	36
handicap	8	2	4	16	6	18	14	12	10	-
FORWARD	443	322	127	309	376	104	280	413	287	2661
par	5	4	3	4	4	3	4	5	4	36
handicap	8	6	16	12	2	18	14	10	4	-

BACK	
yardage	6705
par	72
rating	72.6
slope	127

REGULAR	
yardage	6210
par	72
rating	70.4
slope	121

FORWARD	
yardage	5206
par	72
rating	69.6
slope	117

PLAY POLICY & FEES: Reciprocal play is accepted with members of other private clubs. Guest fees are $40 with a member weekdays and $60 without a member weekdays. On weekends, guest fees are $50 with a member and $70 without a member. Carts are $22 with a member and $26 without. The course is closed on Monday.

DRESS CODE: No jeans are allowed on the course. Appropriate golf attire is required.

COURSE DESCRIPTION: This is a rolling, tree-lined layout with good, fast greens. The front nine is flat, while the back winds through the hills. The 12th requires a long-iron off the tee, then a mid- to short-iron to a green that is severely contoured. It's a good example of Green Valley's charm, which includes a creek running through four holes. The wind can become a factor.

LOCATION: From Vallejo take Interstate 80 to Green Valley Road. Head north to Country Club Drive and turn left to the course.

. . . ● **TOURNAMENTS:** Outside events are held on Monday only. A 100-player minimum is needed to book a tournament, and carts are required. Events should be scheduled 12 months in advance. A banquet facility is available and can accommodate 200 people.

33. GREEN VALLEY COUNTRY CLUB

PLAY POLICY & FEES: Green fees are $27 to walk and $41 to ride Monday through Thursday, $31 to walk and $45 to ride Friday, and $40 to walk and $54 to ride on Saturday, Sunday, and holidays. Resident, senior, junior, and twilight rates are offered.

TEE TIMES: Reservations can be booked seven days in advance.

DRESS CODE: No tank tops are allowed.

COURSE DESCRIPTION: Rancho Solano has some of the largest greens in California. The green on the ninth hole measures 150 feet front to back. The course is situated in rolling hills that are dotted with oak trees. There are five lakes and 87 bunkers. Practicing long putts on the putting green is a must at Rancho Solano. The enormous greens demand a good putting touch; it's one of the few places where pros have been known to four putt.

NOTES: The course record is 64 held by Jeff Wilson from the blue tees and Charles Millard from the white tees.

LOCATION: From Interstate 80 in Fairfield take Waterman Boulevard west and follow it two miles. Go right on Rancho Solano Parkway and continue to the course.

. . . ● **TOURNAMENTS:** A 16-player minimum is required for tournament play. Carts are mandatory. Events should be booked 12 months in advance. A banquet facility can accommodate 300 people.

34. RANCHO SOLANO GOLF COURSE

35 PARADISE VALLEY GOLF COURSE
ARCHITECT: ROBERT MUIR GRAVES, 1993

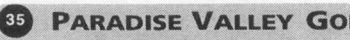

3950 Paradise Valley Drive
Fairfield, CA 94533

PRO SHOP: 707-426-1600

Steve Walker, Head Professional, PGA
Shane Howe, Superintendent

Driving Range ●
Practice Greens ●
Clubhouse ●
Food / Beverage ●
Accommodations
Pull Carts ●
Power Carts ●
Club Rental ●
$pecial Offers

	1	2	3	4	5	6	7	8	9	OUT
BACK	549	358	189	528	438	370	375	206	364	3377
REGULAR	518	338	164	495	384	337	322	185	320	3063
par	5	4	3	5	4	4	4	3	4	36
handicap	5	7	17	9	1	3	11	15	13	-
FORWARD	481	296	147	437	344	295	295	130	266	2691
par	5	4	3	5	4	4	4	3	4	36
handicap	1	7	15	9	3	5	11	17	13	-

	10	11	12	13	14	15	16	17	18	IN
BACK	498	407	151	433	318	185	526	376	433	3327
REGULAR	457	372	129	397	296	154	509	361	390	3065
par	5	4	3	4	4	3	5	4	4	36
handicap	4	10	18	6	14	16	8	12	2	-
FORWARD	419	339	89	340	259	121	468	326	361	2722
par	5	4	3	4	4	3	5	4	4	36
handicap	4	10	18	8	14	16	6	12	2	-

BACK	
yardage	6704
par	72
rating	73.0
slope	133

REGULAR	
yardage	6128
par	72
rating	70.6
slope	127

FORWARD	
yardage	5413
par	72
rating	71.1
slope	119

36 CYPRESS LAKES GOLF COURSE
ARCHITECT: JOESPH FINGER, 1960

5601 Meridian
Vacaville, CA 95687

PRO SHOP: 707-448-7186
CLUBHOUSE: 707-424-5797

Joesph Goldbronn, Superintendent
Debra Joyce, Head Professional, PGA

Driving Range ●
Practice Greens ●
Clubhouse ●
Food / Beverage ●
Accommodations
Pull Carts ●
Power Carts ●
Club Rental ●
$pecial Offers

	1	2	3	4	5	6	7	8	9	OUT
BACK	503	383	176	403	523	376	362	194	405	3325
REGULAR	461	363	151	383	512	351	342	163	383	3109
par	5	4	3	4	5	4	4	3	4	36
handicap	11	5	17	1	9	7	13	15	3	-
FORWARD	448	343	138	345	443	327	327	154	368	2893
par	5	4	3	4	5	4	4	3	4	36
handicap	1	11	17	7	3	9	13	15	5	-

	10	11	12	13	14	15	16	17	18	IN
BACK	522	179	429	427	141	367	408	553	445	3471
REGULAR	508	148	413	410	123	342	391	523	417	3275
par	5	3	4	4	3	4	4	5	4	36
handicap	12	16	6	10	18	14	2	8	4	-
FORWARD	404	118	338	341	115	323	311	422	404	2776
par	5	3	4	4	3	4	4	5	5	37
handicap	4	16	14	12	18	10	8	2	6	-

BACK	
yardage	6796
par	72
rating	72.6
slope	122

REGULAR	
yardage	6384
par	72
rating	71.0
slope	119

FORWARD	
yardage	5669
par	73
rating	72.9
slope	120

PLAY POLICY & FEES: Green fees are $30 weekdays and $40 weekends. Senior and twilight rates are available.

TEE TIMES: Reservations can be booked seven days in advance.

DRESS CODE: There are no tank tops, bare midriffs, or short shorts allowed on the golf course.

COURSE DESCRIPTION: This is a mostly flat, challenging course where wind plays a major role. When it's calm, the course lets down its guard. Most days, however, wind influences almost every shot. Water comes into play on nine holes, and accurate driving is a must. One of the signature holes is the 433-yard, par-4 18th, a dogleg right guarded by a lake on the right. Don't get too greedy on your tee shot. This is one of the best draining courses in Northern California.

NOTES: All golf carts are equipped with ProShot Electronic Caddy. What's that? From anywhere on the course, your cart can tell you the exact yardage to the middle of the green.

LOCATION: From San Francisco take Interstate 80 east to the North Texas Street exit. Turn right on North Texas Street to Dixon Hill and turn left. Follow Dixon Hill to Dover Street and turn left. Follow Dover Street one-half mile to the club.

. . . ● **TOURNAMENTS:** A 20-player minimum is needed for tournament play, and carts are required. Tournaments should be booked 12 months in advance. A banquet facility is available and can accommodate 200 people.

35. PARADISE VALLEY GOLF COURSE

PLAY POLICY & FEES: Military and guests only. Guest green fees are $20 weekdays, $25 weekends. Carts are $18 for 18 holes.

DRESS CODE: Collared shirts are required, and nonmetal spikes required.

COURSE DESCRIPTION: This course boasts big greens, seven lakes, and lots of trees. It's flat and easily walkable. Plan to play into the wind. The greens are usually in great condition, and the course can become a challenge from the blue tees. The last three holes are the best: the par-4 16th, which doglegs right over a lake; the par-5 17th, which doglegs left over a lake; and the par-4 18th, which requires an approach shot over a lake.

LOCATION: From Vallejo drive east on Interstate 80. Take the Elmira exit east. Turn right on Meridian and continue to the course.

. . . ● **TOURNAMENTS:** Shotgun tournaments are available weekdays only.

36. CYPRESS LAKES GOLF COURSE

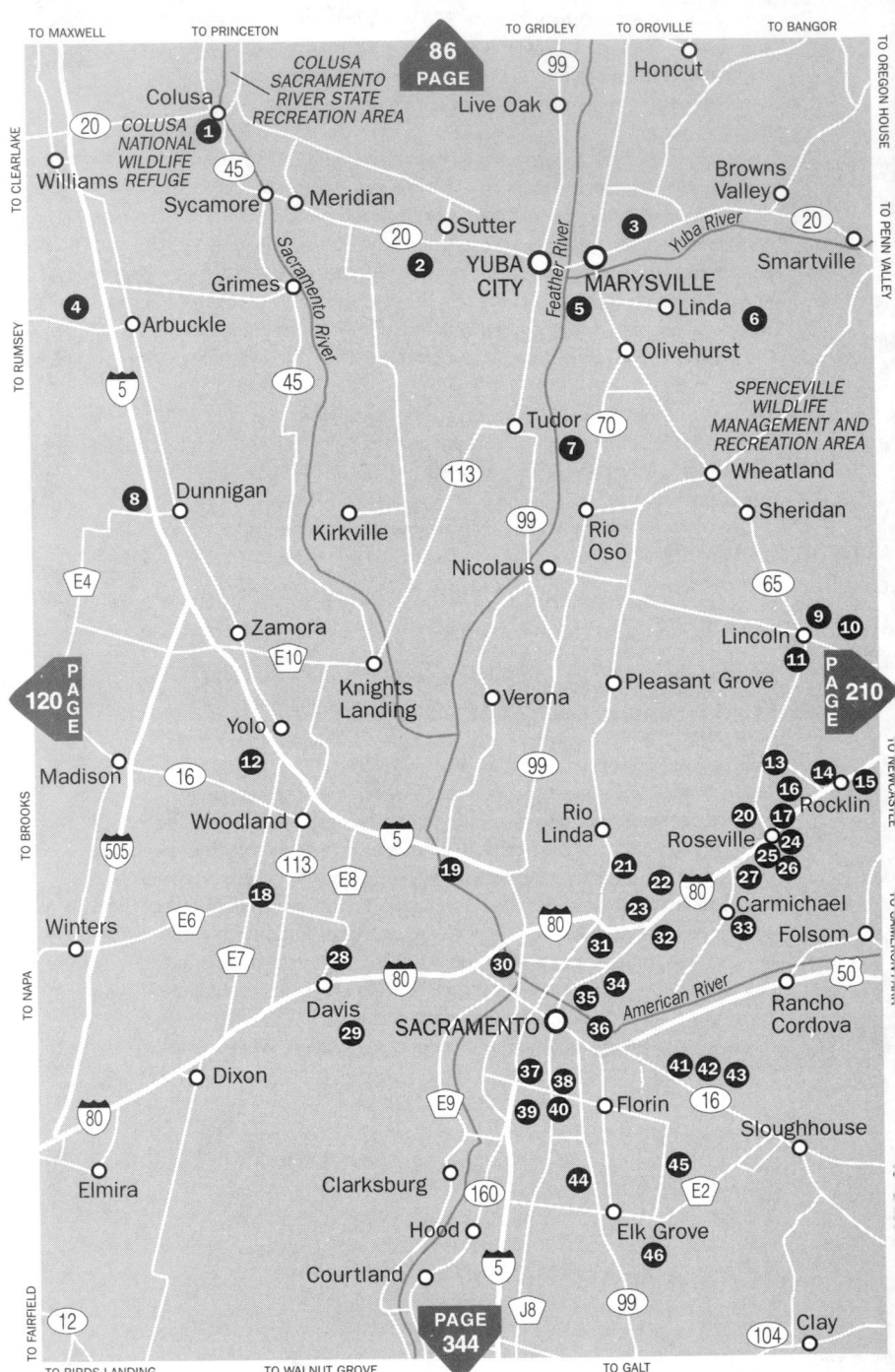

TO MAXWELL   TO PRINCETON   TO GRIDLEY   TO OROVILLE   TO BANGOR

86 PAGE

99 Honcut

COLUSA SACRAMENTO RIVER STATE RECREATION AREA

Colusa   Live Oak

20   ❶   COLUSA NATIONAL WILDLIFE REFUGE

Williams   Browns Valley

Sycamore   45   Meridian

20   Sutter   ❸   Yuba River   20   Smartville

❷   YUBA CITY   MARYSVILLE

Grimes   ❺   Linda   ❻

❹   Arbuckle   Olivehurst

45   SPENCEVILLE WILDLIFE MANAGEMENT AND RECREATION AREA

5   Tudor   70   ❼

❽   Dunnigan   113   Wheatland

99   Sheridan

Kirkville   Rio Oso

E4   Nicolaus   65

Zamora   Lincoln   ❾ ❿

E10   ❶❶

PAGE 120   Knights Landing   Verona   Pleasant Grove   **PAGE 210**

Yolo   99   ❶❸   ❶❹ ❶❺

Madison   16   ❶❷   ❶❻ ❶❼   Rocklin

Woodland   Rio Linda   ❷⓿ ❶❼   Roseville   ❷❹

505   113   E8   ❷❺ ❷❻

❶❽   ❶❾   ❷❶   ❷❷   80   ❷❼

Winters   80   ❷❸   Carmichael   ❸❸   Folsom

E6   ❷❽   ❸❷   ❸❸

E7   ❸⓿   ❸❶   50

Davis   ❷❾   ❸❺   ❸❹   American River   Rancho Cordova

SACRAMENTO   ❸❻

Dixon   ❸❼ ❸❽   ❹❶ ❹❷ ❹❸

80   E9   ❸❾ ❹⓿   Florin   16   Sloughhouse

Elmira   ❹❺   E2

Clarksburg   ❹❹

160   Hood   Elk Grove   ❹❻

Courtland   5

PAGE 344   99   104   Clay

12   J8

TO FAIRFIELD   TO BIRDS LANDING   TO WALNUT GROVE   TO GALT

160

Sacramento Area

❶ COLUSA COUNTRY CLUB

P.O. Box 827
Colusa, CA 95932

2224 Highway 20
Colusa, CA 95932

PRO SHOP: 530-458-5577

Rick Burgess, PGA Professional
Cotton Triplett, Superintendent

Driving Range ●
Practice Greens ●
Clubhouse
Food / Beverage ●
Accommodations
Pull Carts ●
Power Carts ●
Club Rental ●
$pecial Offers

	1	2	3	4	5	6	7	8	9	OUT
BACK	-	-	-	-	-	-	-	-	-	-
REGULAR	414	198	362	393	161	503	400	490	390	3311
par	4	3	4	4	3	5	4	5	4	36
handicap	1	11	15	3	17	5	7	13	9	-
FORWARD	405	176	299	296	143	428	378	444	355	2924
par	5	3	4	4	3	5	4	5	4	37
handicap	5	15	11	13	17	1	7	3	9	-

	10	11	12	13	14	15	16	17	18	IN
BACK	-	-	-	-	-	-	-	-	-	-
REGULAR	408	201	347	406	158	517	392	497	380	3306
par	4	3	4	4	3	5	4	5	4	36
handicap	2	12	16	4	18	6	8	14	10	-
FORWARD	395	186	294	301	86	433	373	454	350	2872
par	5	3	4	4	3	5	4	5	4	37
handicap	6	16	12	14	18	2	8	4	10	-

BACK	
yardage	-
par	-
rating	-
slope	-

REGULAR	
yardage	6617
par	72
rating	71.1
slope	118

FORWARD	
yardage	5796
par	74
rating	72.2
slope	120

❷ SOUTHRIDGE GOLF COURSE
ARCHITECT: CAL OLSON, 1991

9413 South Butte Road
Sutter, CA 95982

PRO SHOP: 530-755-4653
CLUBHOUSE: 530-755-0457

Lucy Kumar, Owner
Terry Taylor, Head Professional, PGA

Driving Range ●
Practice Greens ●
Clubhouse ●
Food / Beverage ●
Accommodations
Pull Carts ●
Power Carts ●
Club Rental ●
$pecial Offers

	1	2	3	4	5	6	7	8	9	OUT
BACK	406	383	372	177	495	358	150	416	478	3235
REGULAR	375	356	306	146	471	330	131	382	472	2969
par	4	4	4	3	5	4	3	4	5	36
handicap	4	6	10	16	14	8	18	2	12	-
FORWARD	345	336	261	98	439	283	95	364	420	2641
par	4	4	4	3	5	4	3	4	5	36
handicap	4	6	10	16	14	8	18	2	12	-

	10	11	12	13	14	15	16	17	18	IN
BACK	423	515	347	357	184	118	619	417	396	3376
REGULAR	414	477	309	341	168	109	556	400	362	3136
par	4	5	4	4	3	3	5	4	4	36
handicap	9	15	3	11	13	17	1	5	7	-
FORWARD	382	443	273	325	150	92	530	373	332	2900
par	4	5	4	4	3	3	5	4	4	36
handicap	9	15	3	11	13	17	1	5	7	-

BACK	
yardage	6611
par	72
rating	71.2
slope	123

REGULAR	
yardage	6105
par	72
rating	68.9
slope	118

FORWARD	
yardage	5541
par	72
rating	69.8
slope	123

PLAY POLICY & FEES: Outside play is accepted. Green fees are $10 for nine holes and $14 for 18 holes weekdays, and $20 for nine or 18 holes weekends and holidays. Carts are $9 for nine holes and $18 for 18 holes. Twilight, senior, and junior rates are available. The course is closed on Monday.

TEE TIMES: Reservations can be made Tuesday prior to the weekend.

DRESS CODE: Shirts with sleeves or collars and nonmetal spikes are required. No gym shorts or ice chests are allowed.

COURSE DESCRIPTION: This flat, tree-lined course is tight and walkable. It's more challenging than meets the eye. A new sprinkler system has improved fairway conditions. The par-5 sixth hole (503 yards) is a challenge, requiring a difficult second shot to avoid trees in the fairway.

LOCATION: From Interstate 5 in Williams drive east on Highway 20 to Colusa. The course is on Highway 20.

. . . ● **TOURNAMENTS:** This course is available for outside tournaments.

1. COLUSA COUNTRY CLUB

PLAY POLICY & FEES: Outside play is accepted. Green fees are $29, including cart, weekdays. Weekend rates are $39, including cart. Carts are a necessity due to the severe terrain on the back nine.

TEE TIMES: Reservations can be booked 14 days in advance.

COURSE DESCRIPTION: A most interesting layout, Southridge features a back nine that would fatigue a mountain goat, and a links-style front nine. The Sutter Buttes (back) nine are picturesque and feature one of the most challenging (and exasperating) holes in Northern California, a 619-yard par 5 that requires a radar-straight drive and a well-placed second shot, among other skills. Love it or loathe it, you'll remember it. The links side is easier, though not by much, with water coming into play on seven holes. If you want diversity, this is the course.

LOCATION: From Yuba City drive west on Highway 20. The course is seven miles west of Yuba City and can be seen from the highway on the north.

. . . ● **TOURNAMENTS:** A 20-player minimum is needed to book a tournament. Events should be scheduled at least four months in advance. A banquet facility is available that can accommodate up to 250 people.

2. SOUTHRIDGE GOLF COURSE

③ PEACH TREE GOLF & COUNTRY CLUB
ARCHITECT: BOB BALDOCK, 1958

P.O. Box 231
Marysville, CA 95901

2043 Simpson-Dantoni
Marysville, CA 95901

PRO SHOP: 530-743-2039
CLUBHOUSE: 530-743-1897

Mel Brim, Manager, PGA
Pat Gould, Head Professional, PGA
Mike Shelly, Tournament Director

Driving Range ●
Practice Greens ●
Clubhouse ●
Food / Beverage ●
Accommodations
Pull Carts ●
Power Carts ●
Club Rental ●
$pecial Offers

	1	2	3	4	5	6	7	8	9	OUT
BACK	402	527	165	432	450	503	218	384	360	3441
REGULAR	387	511	150	414	432	485	203	364	342	3288
par	4	5	3	4	4	5	3	4	4	36
handicap	7	9	17	3	1	15	5	13	11	-
FORWARD	374	494	139	397	418	466	147	346	329	3110
par	4	5	3	4	5	5	3	4	4	37
handicap	9	1	17	5	7	3	15	11	13	-

	10	11	12	13	14	15	16	17	18	IN
BACK	363	513	429	380	181	378	401	184	541	3370
REGULAR	351	488	411	358	167	366	389	169	519	3218
par	4	5	4	4	3	4	4	3	5	36
handicap	16	10	2	8	18	14	4	12	12	-
FORWARD	341	461	395	342	158	353	381	157	505	3093
par	4	5	4	4	3	4	4	3	5	36
handicap	73	12	2	4	14	18	10	8	16	-

BACK	
yardage	6811
par	72
rating	72.8
slope	125

REGULAR	
yardage	6506
par	72
rating	71.4
slope	122

FORWARD	
yardage	6203
par	73
rating	76.0
slope	136

④ ARBUCKLE GOLF CLUB

P.O. Box 1009
Arbuckle, CA 95912

5918 Hillgate Road
Arbuckle, CA 95912

PRO SHOP: 530-476-2470

Ross Farley, PGA Professional
Jim Stone, Superintendent

Driving Range ●
Practice Greens ●
Clubhouse ●
Food / Beverage ●
Accommodations
Pull Carts ●
Power Carts ●
Club Rental ●
$pecial Offers

	1	2	3	4	5	6	7	8	9	OUT
BACK	-	-	-	-	-	-	-	-	-	-
REGULAR	502	167	416	383	548	338	182	390	336	3262
par	5	3	4	4	5	4	3	4	4	36
handicap	3	15	7	9	1	11	17	5	13	-
FORWARD	408	132	393	360	509	314	182	368	317	2983
par	5	3	4	4	5	4	3	4	4	36
handicap	7	17	5	3	1	13	15	9	11	-

	10	11	12	13	14	15	16	17	18	IN
BACK	-	-	-	-	-	-	-	-	-	-
REGULAR	486	132	403	371	521	326	197	379	383	3198
par	5	3	4	4	5	4	3	4	4	36
handicap	4	18	8	10	2	14	16	12	6	-
FORWARD	408	122	403	371	426	326	169	379	325	2929
par	5	3	4	4	5	4	3	4	4	36
handicap	6	18	4	2	14	12	16	8	10	-

BACK	
yardage	-
par	-
rating	-
slope	-

REGULAR	
yardage	6460
par	72
rating	69.9
slope	111

FORWARD	
yardage	5912
par	72
rating	72.7
slope	120

PLAY POLICY & FEES: Reciprocal play is accepted with members of other private clubs. Guest fees are $25 weekdays and $30 weekends when accompanied by a member. The fee for reciprocal players is $50 weekdays and $60 weekends. Carts are $20. The course is closed on Monday.

TEE TIMES: Reservations can be booked seven days in advance.

DRESS CODE: Appropriate golf attire and nonmetal spikes are required.

COURSE DESCRIPTION: This course is characterized by its mature trees—walnut and cypress, but only one peach tree. The fairways are Bermuda, and the greens are bent grass. Peach Tree is a very tight course with fairway bunkers strategically placed. The greens are fast and bowl-shaped. The seventh, a par 3 of 218 yards from the blues, is the signature hole. It requires a carry over water that fronts about half the green, and there's a bunker on the left side.

NOTES: The course record of 62 was set before the trees matured; since then, the best is a 66.

LOCATION: From Sacramento take Highway 70 through Marysville to Highway 20. Turn right on Ramirez Road and drive to Simpson-Dantoni Road. Turn left and drive to the course.

. . . ● **TOURNAMENTS:** A 100-player minimum is needed to book a tournament, and carts are mandatory.

3. PEACH TREE GOLF & COUNTRY CLUB

PLAY POLICY & FEES: Outside play is accepted. Green fees are $14 Tuesday through Friday and $25 weekends and holidays. Carts are $20 for one or two riders.

TEE TIMES: Reservations can be booked seven days in advance.

DRESS CODE: Appropriate golf attire is required. Nonmetal spikes are recommended.

COURSE DESCRIPTION: This challenging course has rolling hills, tight fairways, and some of the fastest greens in the Sacramento Valley. The par-4, 416-yard third hole presents a postcard setting with a view of the Sacramento Valley and Sutter Buttes. Arbuckle is one of the finest nine-hole courses in the state—challenging and exceptionally conditioned.

NOTES: This course was built in 1924 by the residents of the town. Arbuckle was voted the best nine-hole course in Northern California by the "Lake County Record-Bee."

LOCATION: From Sacramento travel 35 minutes north on Interstate 5. Take the Arbuckle/College City exit. Head west on Hillgate Road for 4.6 miles, and the course will be on the left.

. . . ● **TOURNAMENTS:** Carts are required for tournament play, and a 24-player minimum is needed to book a tournament. A banquet facility is available that can accommodate 120 people. ● **TRAVEL:** Granzella's Inn is located 15 minutes from the golf course. For reservations call 530-473-3301.

4. ARBUCKLE GOLF CLUB

4238 South Highway 99
Yuba City, CA 95991

PRO SHOP: 530-674-0475

Terry Sutton, Head Professional, PGA
Jerry McCardel, Superintendent

Driving Range ●
Practice Greens ●
Clubhouse ●
Food / Beverage
Accommodations
Pull Carts ●
Power Carts ●
Club Rental ●
$pecial Offers

	1	2	3	4	5	6	7	8	9	OUT
BACK	-	-	-	-	-	-	-	-	-	-
REGULAR	361	148	385	357	327	329	301	160	344	2712
par	4	3	4	4	4	4	4	3	4	34
handicap	5	17	3	1	7	11	13	15	9	-
FORWARD	342	133	313	336	276	314	286	150	320	2470
par	4	3	4	4	4	4	4	3	4	34
handicap	1	17	5	11	9	13	7	15	3	-

	10	11	12	13	14	15	16	17	18	IN
BACK	-	-	-	-	-	-	-	-	-	-
REGULAR	361	148	385	357	327	329	301	160	344	2712
par	4	3	4	4	4	4	4	3	4	34
handicap	6	18	4	2	8	12	14	16	10	-
FORWARD	342	133	313	336	276	314	286	150	320	2470
par	4	3	4	4	4	4	4	3	4	34
handicap	2	18	6	12	10	14	8	16	4	-

BACK	
yardage	-
par	-
rating	-
slope	-

REGULAR	
yardage	5424
par	68
rating	65.0
slope	110

FORWARD	
yardage	4940
par	68
rating	67.6
slope	112

17440 Warren Shingle
Beale AFB, CA 95903

PRO SHOP: 530-788-0192

Bob Anderson, Director of Golf
Jim Callahan, Tournament Director
Allan Miners, Superintendent

Driving Range ●
Practice Greens ●
Clubhouse ●
Food / Beverage ●
Accommodations
Pull Carts ●
Power Carts ●
Club Rental ●
$pecial Offers

	1	2	3	4	5	6	7	8	9	OUT
BACK	186	351	444	328	219	505	408	435	553	3429
REGULAR	167	323	429	295	187	481	373	414	522	3191
par	3	4	4	4	3	5	4	4	5	36
handicap	7	5	3	17	11	15	9	1	13	-
FORWARD	124	225	289	236	107	388	281	328	442	2420
par	3	4	4	4	3	5	4	4	5	36
handicap	7	5	3	17	11	15	9	1	13	-

	10	11	12	13	14	15	16	17	18	IN
BACK	351	385	497	457	179	425	188	402	501	3385
REGULAR	338	369	481	380	150	392	164	393	489	3156
par	4	4	5	4	3	4	3	4	5	36
handicap	14	6	10	4	18	2	16	12	8	-
FORWARD	255	243	357	263	106	254	135	253	338	2204
par	4	4	5	4	3	4	3	4	5	36
handicap	14	6	10	4	18	2	16	12	8	-

BACK	
yardage	6814
par	72
rating	72.4
slope	132

REGULAR	
yardage	6347
par	72
rating	70.3
slope	124

FORWARD	
yardage	4624
par	72
rating	-
slope	-

PLAY POLICY & FEES: Green fees are $8 for nine holes and $12 for 18 holes weekdays, and $10 for nine holes and $14 for 18 holes on weekends. Twilight rates are available. Carts are $11 for nine holes and $16 for 18 holes.

TEE TIMES: Reservations can be booked seven days in advance.

DRESS CODE: Tank tops and coolers are not allowed.

COURSE DESCRIPTION: This mostly flat course has water on all nine holes. It's short and tough with small, well-maintained greens. The toughest hole is the fourth (357 yards), with out-of-bounds on both sides of the fairway and a pond situated right where the average hitter usually drives.

LOCATION: From Yuba City drive south approximately four miles on Highway 99. The course is a quarter mile south of Oswald Road on Highway 99.

. . . ● **TOURNAMENTS:** This course is available for outside tournaments. ●

TRAVEL: The Fireside Inn is recommended for lodging.

5. MALLARD LAKE GOLF COURSE

PLAY POLICY & FEES: Public play is accepted with prior arrangement. Guest fees are $20. Carts are $15.

TEE TIMES: Reservations can be made seven days in advance on weekends for military personnel. Civilians can make tee times one day in advance on weekends.

DRESS CODE: Appropriate golf attire and nonmetal spikes are required.

COURSE DESCRIPTION: Reece Point is a flat course with some elevated greens. There are enough trees to make things challenging, and the fifth hole is distinguished by a large lake, one of three on the course.

NOTES: Golf Plan has just finished a complete remodel that includes additional yardage, new lakes, creeks, 10 new greens, and four sets of tee boxes.

LOCATION: From Highway 70 in Marysville, take the North Beale Road exit east. Drive to the main gate of Beale Air Force Base.

. . . ● **TOURNAMENTS:** A 80-player minimum is needed to book a shotgun tournament. Carts are mandatory. A 20-player minimum is needed to book a regular tournament. The banquet facility holds up to 250 people. Events should be booked 12 months in advance. ● **TRAVEL:** Base lodging is available for military personnel. Call 530-634-2953. The Amerihost Inn (530-742-2700) and The Best Western Bonanza Inn (530-674-8824) are recommended for lodging.

6. REECE POINT GOLF COURSE

⑦ PLUMAS LAKE GOLF & COUNTRY CLUB
ARCHITECTS: JACK BEASLEY, 1926; BOB BALDOCK, 1960

1551 Country Club Road
Marysville, CA 95901

PRO SHOP: 530-742-3201
OFFICE: 530-742-3202

Ron Anderson, General Manager, PGA
Doug Levy, PGA Professional
Odis Evans, Superintendent

Driving Range ●
Practice Greens ●
Clubhouse ●
Food / Beverage ●
Accommodations
Pull Carts ●
Power Carts ●
Club Rental ●
$Special Offers

	1	2	3	4	5	6	7	8	9	OUT
BACK	421	407	188	348	520	341	166	408	340	3139
REGULAR	406	386	158	339	509	329	161	399	327	3014
par	4	4	3	4	5	4	3	4	4	35
handicap	3	5	15	13	9	7	17	1	11	-
FORWARD	392	377	146	329	414	310	161	337	316	2782
par	4	4	3	4	5	4	3	4	4	35
handicap	4	8	18	6	2	10	16	12	14	-

	10	11	12	13	14	15	16	17	18	IN
BACK	486	394	433	219	424	501	162	347	332	3298
REGULAR	473	361	423	208	414	490	142	319	309	3139
par	5	4	4	3	4	5	3	4	4	36
handicap	8	6	2	12	4	10	18	16	14	-
FORWARD	457	350	413	195	351	479	128	305	299	2977
par	5	4	5	3	4	5	3	4	4	37
handicap	3	5	7	13	9	1	17	15	11	-

BACK	
yardage	6437
par	71
rating	70.5
slope	122

REGULAR	
yardage	6153
par	71
rating	69.3
slope	120

FORWARD	
yardage	5759
par	72
rating	73.2
slope	126

⑧ CAMPERS INN GOLF COURSE & RV RESORT

P.O. Box 71
Dunnigan, CA 95937

2501 Road 88
Dunnigan, CA 95937

PRO SHOP: 530-724-3350

Tom Lynch, Owner

Driving Range
Practice Greens ●
Clubhouse
Food / Beverage ●
Accommodations
Pull Carts ●
Power Carts
Club Rental ●
$Special Offers

	1	2	3	4	5	6	7	8	9	OUT
BACK	-	-	-	-	-	-	-	-	-	-
REGULAR	-	-	-	-	-	-	-	-	-	-
par	-	-	-	-	-	-	-	-	-	
handicap	-	-	-	-	-	-	-	-	-	-
FORWARD	-	-	-	-	-	-	-	-	-	
par	-	-	-	-	-	-	-	-	-	
handicap	-	-	-	-	-	-	-	-	-	-

	10	11	12	13	14	15	16	17	18	IN
BACK	-	-	-	-	-	-	-	-	-	-
REGULAR	-	-	-	-	-	-	-	-	-	
par	-	-	-	-	-	-	-	-	-	
handicap	-	-	-	-	-	-	-	-	-	-
FORWARD	-	-	-	-	-	-	-	-	-	-
par	-	-	-	-	-	-	-	-	-	
handicap	-	-	-	-	-	-	-	-	-	-

BACK	
yardage	-
par	-
rating	-
slope	-

REGULAR	
yardage	1600
par	27
rating	-
slope	-

FORWARD	
yardage	1580
par	27
rating	-
slope	-

PLAY POLICY & FEES: Outside play is accepted. Green fees are $19 Monday through Thursday and $24 Friday through Sunday. Carts are $18.

TEE TIMES: Reservations can be booked seven days in advance.

DRESS CODE: No tank tops or short shorts allowed on the course. Nonmetal spikes are encouraged.

COURSE DESCRIPTION: Plumas Lake is a well-known jewel among golf insiders throughout Northern California. It is mostly flat and not exceedingly tight, but there are a number of monster holes, starting with the eighth, a 399-yarder with a giant oak blocking the entrance to the green. Holes 12 (423 yards), 13 (208 yards), and 14 (414 yards) are Plumas Lake's answer to Amen Corner. This course is also known for its excellent greens.

NOTES: The course record is a superb 60, held by Ray Arinno. LPGA star Alice Miller grew up playing Plumas Lake—from the men's tees.

LOCATION: From Marysville drive south on Highway 70. Take the Feather River Boulevard exit and drive about 6.5 miles. Turn left on Country Club Road.

. . . ● **TOURNAMENTS:** A 40-player minimum is required to book a tournament. Carts are mandatory. Tournaments should be scheduled 12 months in advance. A banquet facility is available and can hold up to 144 players.

7. PLUMAS LAKE GOLF & COUNTRY CLUB

PLAY POLICY & FEES: Green fees are $5.50 for nine holes and $10.50 for 18 holes, and $15.50 all day on weekdays. Green fees are $6.50 for nine holes and $12 for 18 holes, and $18 for all day on weekends. Pull carts are $2. Night golf fees are $25 for a minimum of 20 players.

TEE TIMES: Reservations can be booked seven days in advance.

DRESS CODE: Nonmetal spikes are required.

COURSE DESCRIPTION: This short par-3 course is excellent for beginners and seniors. The course features ponds, sand traps, mature trees, and is often windy. This is a good test for the short game.

NOTES: RV and tent sites are available. Facilities include showers and a pool.

LOCATION: From Sacramento take Interstate 5 north to the Dunnigan exit. Turn left over the freeway and drive one mile. Turn right on Road 88 and drive 1.6 miles to course.

. . . ● **TOURNAMENTS:** This course is available for outside tournaments. The banquet facility can accommodate 100 people. ● **TRAVEL:** Best Western Country is located five minutes from the course. For reservations call 530-724-3471.

8. CAMPERS INN GOLF COURSE & RV

9 TWELVE BRIDGES GOLF CLUB
ARCHITECT: DICK PHELPS, 1996

3070 Twelve Bridges Drive
Lincoln, CA 95648

PRO SHOP: 916-645-7200
STARTER: 916-645-6729

Noni Schneider, LPGA Master Professional
Michael Lucena, Tournament Coordinator
Neil Hladik, Superintendent

Driving Range ●
Practice Greens ●
Clubhouse ●
Food / Beverage ●
Accommodations
Pull Carts
Power Carts ●
Club Rental ●
Special Offers

	1	2	3	4	5	6	7	8	9	OUT
BACK	435	395	548	180	418	216	356	604	415	3567
REGULAR	374	340	495	140	330	170	313	537	356	3055
par	4	4	5	3	4	3	4	5	4	36
handicap	11	9	5	17	7	13	15	1	3	-
FORWARD	313	297	451	92	279	133	273	487	265	2590
par	4	4	5	3	4	3	4	5	4	36
handicap	11	9	5	17	7	13	15	1	3	-

	10	11	12	13	14	15	16	17	18	IN
BACK	386	499	367	186	475	595	412	218	445	3583
REGULAR	330	458	314	137	414	562	355	159	390	3119
par	4	5	4	3	4	5	4	3	4	36
handicap	10	12	16	18	4	6	8	14	2	-
FORWARD	284	410	274	111	365	478	318	133	347	2720
par	4	5	4	3	4	5	4	3	4	36
handicap	10	12	16	18	4	6	8	14	2	-

BACK	
yardage	7150
par	72
rating	74.6
slope	139

REGULAR	
yardage	6174
par	72
rating	71.8
slope	123

FORWARD	
yardage	5310
par	72
rating	71.0
slope	123

10 TURKEY CREEK GOLF CLUB
ARCHITECT: BRAD BELL, 1999

1525 Highway 193
Lincoln, CA 95648

PRO SHOP: 916-434-9100

Kevin Williams, Head Professional, PGA
Jeff Wilson, General Manager, PGA

Driving Range ●
Practice Greens ●
Clubhouse ●
Food / Beverage ●
Accommodations
Pull Carts
Power Carts ●
Club Rental ●
Special Offers

	1	2	3	4	5	6	7	8	9	OUT
BACK	331	364	191	567	449	462	549	186	432	3531
REGULAR	326	351	171	538	432	423	529	168	403	3341
par	4	4	3	5	4	4	5	3	4	36
handicap										-
FORWARD	271	259	139	417	304	318	434	124	291	2557
par	4	4	3	5	4	4	5	3	4	36
handicap										-

	10	11	12	13	14	15	16	17	18	IN
BACK	446	189	581	377	173	344	533	409	429	3481
REGULAR	416	176	546	359	152	324	522	382	399	3276
par	4	3	5	4	3	4	5	4	4	36
handicap										-
FORWARD	314	109	444	238	99	221	336	238	331	2330
par	4	3	5	4	3	4	5	4	4	36
handicap										-

BACK	
yardage	7012
par	72
rating	73.4
slope	136

REGULAR	
yardage	6617
par	72
rating	71.3
slope	131

FORWARD	
yardage	4887
par	72
rating	73.4
slope	121

PLAY POLICY & FEES: Green fees are $45 Monday through Thursday, and $60 Friday through Sunday and holidays. Carts are $15 per person.

TEE TIMES: Reservations can be booked 14 days in advance at the course. Reservations can be made up to 60 days in advance by calling Tee Time Central at 888-236-8725.

DRESS CODE: Collared shirts and nonmetal spikes are required. No denim is allowed on the course.

COURSE DESCRIPTION: The course is situated in a bowl surrounded by oak trees. This challenging and beautiful layout has no parallel fairways, and 10-minute tee times are designed to give golfers a feeling of solitude. The pride of the course is the 218-yard, par-3 17th hole, flanked by water and traps on the right side.

NOTES: Twelve Bridges hosts the LPGA Longs Drugs Challenge and is noted for its friendly staff and excellent teaching facility.

LOCATION: From Roseville take Interstate 80 east to the Sierra College Boulevard exit. Follow Sierra College Boulevard 5.3 miles north to Twelve Bridges Drive and the course entrance.

. . . ● **TOURNAMENTS:** Tournament packages are an additional $15 per person and include prize fund, range balls, yardage guide, and tournament scoring. A 24-player minimum is required to book an event. The banquet facility can accommodate 250 people. With tents, Twelve Bridges has hosted events of over 600 people.

PLAY POLICY & FEES: Green fees for 18 holes are $45 Monday through Thursday, and $65 Friday through Sunday. Nine-hole rates are $25 Monday through Thursday, and $40 Friday through Sunday. Twilight rates are available. Carts and range balls are included. Golfers can repeat their round for a fee of $15.

TEE TIMES: Reservations can be made by calling Tee Time Central at 888-236-8725. Tee times at the course can be made seven days in advance. Fivesomes are allowed on the course.

DRESS CODE: Proper golf attire and nonmetal spikes are required.

COURSE DESCRIPTION: Turkey Creek is set on rolling foothills featuring tree-lined fairways and a natural quarry. The course offers generous landing areas, but for those golfers who like to use more room than the fairways have to offer, trouble awaits in the form of trees–many trees. With yardages ranging from 4,800 to 7,000 yards, this is truly a course for all skill levels.

LOCATION: From the Sacramento area take Interstate 80 east to Highway 65, head north to Highway 193, and turn right (east). This course is a couple of miles on the left.

. . . ● **TOURNAMENTS:** A 20-player minimum is required to book an event. One hundred players are needed to book a shotgun event. An outdoor facility can accommodate up to 152 people.

LINCOLN HILLS GOLF CLUB
ARCHITECT: GREG NASH, 1999

1005 Sun City Lane
Lincoln, CA 95648

PRO SHOP: 916-434-3366

Craig Sloan, Director of Golf, PGA
Scott Perterson, General Manager
John Martin, Superintendent

Driving Range •
Practice Greens •
Clubhouse •
Food / Beverage •
Accommodations
Pull Carts
Power Carts •
Club Rental
Special Offers

	1	2	3	4	5	6	7	8	9	OUT
BACK										
REGULAR										
par										
handicap										
FORWARD										
par										
handicap										

BACK	
yardage	
par	
rating	
slope	

REGULAR	
yardage	
par	
rating	
slope	

	10	11	12	13	14	15	16	17	18	IN
BACK										
REGULAR										
par										
handicap										
FORWARD										
par										
handicap										

FORWARD	
yardage	
par	
rating	
slope	

YOLO FLIERS COUNTRY CLUB
ARCHITECTS: BOB BALDOCK, 1950; MICHAEL J. MCDONAGH, 1955

17980 Country Road
Woodland, CA 95695

PRO SHOP: 530-662-8050

Steve Bryant, Manager
Jeff Burger, Head Professional, PGA
Mike Azevedo, Superintendent

Driving Range •
Practice Greens •
Clubhouse •
Food / Beverage •
Accommodations
Pull Carts •
Power Carts •
Club Rental •
Special Offers

	1	2	3	4	5	6	7	8	9	OUT
BACK	528	398	380	210	418	512	165	388	398	3397
REGULAR	525	384	370	190	399	505	145	360	358	3236
par	5	4	4	3	4	5	3	4	4	36
handicap	3	11	13	17	5	1	15	7	9	-
FORWARD	491	329	357	178	388	481	130	331	331	3016
par	5	4	4	3	4	5	3	4	4	36
handicap	3	13	11	17	9	1	15	8	7	-

BACK	
yardage	6782
par	72
rating	71.7
slope	121

REGULAR	
yardage	6459
par	72
rating	70.1
slope	118

	10	11	12	13	14	15	16	17	18	IN
BACK	450	510	157	369	465	138	348	517	431	3385
REGULAR	441	480	150	339	445	130	330	504	404	3223
par	4	5	3	4	4	3	4	5	4	36
handicap	6	8	16	12	4	18	14	2	10	-
FORWARD	432	423	143	333	420	119	320	493	382	3065
par	5	5	3	4	5	3	4	5	4	38
handicap	10	4	16	14	5	18	12	2	6	-

FORWARD	
yardage	6081
par	74
rating	74.0
slope	125

PLAY POLICY & FEES: Lincoln Hills will be a daily-fee golf course open to the public and residents of Del Webb's Sun City Lincoln Hills. Green fees including cart will range from $45 to $65.

DRESS CODE: Proper golf attire and nonmetal spikes are required.

COURSE DESCRIPTION: The course description was not available at time of press.

LOCATION: From Sacramento take Interstate 80 toward Reno. Exit at Highway 65 heading north torward Lincoln. The entrance to the course is one-half mile before the town of Lincoln.

. . . ● **TOURNAMENTS:** A 20-player minimum will be required to book an event. A banquet facility will be available that can accommodate up to 250 people. ●

TRAVEL: For reservations at the Hilton, call 916-773-7171. For reservations at the Rocklin Park Hotel, call 916-630-9400, and for reservations at the Courtyard by Marriot, call 916-772-5555.

11. LINCOLN HILLS GOLF CLUB

PLAY POLICY & FEES: Reciprocal play is accepted with members of other private clubs on Tuesday afternoon, Thursday, and Friday. Guest fees are $27.50 with a member and $55 without a member. Reciprocal fees are $55 per person. Carts are $22.

DRESS CODE: Appropriate golf attire and nonmetal spikes are required.

COURSE DESCRIPTION: This one has the feel of an old course, with mature trees and well-maintained greens. The number-one handicap hole is the 14th, a par 4 measuring 445 yards. There is a fair amount of out-of-bounds.

NOTES: The name of the course came from the adjacent airport. It's not uncommon for people to fly in for a round of golf, hence Yolo Fliers.

LOCATION: From Interstate 505 in Woodland take Highway 16 east. Drive four miles and turn north on Road 94-B. The course is located next to the Watts Municipal Airport.

. . . ● **TOURNAMENTS:** Shotgun tournaments are available weekdays only.

12. YOLO FLIERS COUNTRY CLUB

⑬ DIAMOND OAKS GOLF COURSE
ARCHITECT: TED ROBINSON, 1963

349 Diamond Oaks Blvd.
Roseville, CA 95678

PRO SHOP: 916-783-4947

Ed Vasconcellos, PGA Professional

Driving Range ●
Practice Greens ●
Clubhouse ●
Food / Beverage ●
Accommodations
Pull Carts ●
Power Carts ●
Club Rental ●
$pecial Offers

	1	2	3	4	5	6	7	8	9	OUT
BACK	366	486	143	358	162	475	374	375	405	3144
REGULAR	356	476	134	348	144	465	363	360	390	3036
par	4	5	3	4	3	5	4	4	4	36
handicap	7	13	17	5	15	9	3	11	1	-
FORWARD	331	449	123	268	133	414	344	342	381	2785
par	4	5	3	4	3	5	4	4	4	36
handicap	9	3	15	13	17	1	7	11	5	-

	10	11	12	13	14	15	16	17	18	IN
BACK	497	357	136	370	319	177	473	370	440	3139
REGULAR	470	345	120	360	314	170	465	355	430	3029
par	5	4	3	4	4	3	5	4	4	36
handicap	10	6	18	4	16	8	14	12	2	-
FORWARD	407	340	119	336	312	137	412	340	420	2823
par	5	4	3	4	4	3	5	4	5	37
handicap	4	12	18	8	14	16	2	10	6	-

BACK	
yardage	6283
par	72
rating	69.5
slope	115

REGULAR	
yardage	6065
par	72
rating	68.4
slope	113

FORWARD	
yardage	5608
par	73
rating	70.5
slope	112

⑭ SUNSET WHITNEY COUNTRY CLUB

P.O. Box 788
Rocklin, CA 95677

4201 Midas Avenue
Rocklin, CA 95677

PRO SHOP: 916-624-2610
CLUBHOUSE: 916-624-2402

Kathleen Tucker, General Manager
Andy Gonzalez, Head Professional, PGA
Mike Kaveney, Superintendent

Driving Range ●
Practice Greens ●
Clubhouse ●
Food / Beverage ●
Accommodations
Pull Carts ●
Power Carts ●
Club Rental ●
$pecial Offers

	1	2	3	4	5	6	7	8	9	OUT
BACK	463	423	183	346	410	529	167	346	128	2995
REGULAR	452	404	169	316	375	504	146	331	113	2810
par	5	4	3	4	4	5	3	4	3	35
handicap	7	1	13	11	3	5	15	9	17	-
FORWARD	444	385	141	304	326	411	87	317	88	2503
par	5	4	3	4	4	5	3	4	3	35
handicap	3	1	16	13	10	14	18	6	17	-

	10	11	12	13	14	15	16	17	18	IN
BACK	458	380	439	541	371	373	194	447	409	3612
REGULAR	446	359	411	516	351	345	171	428	381	3408
par	5	4	4	5	4	4	3	4	4	37
handicap	18	14	2	6	10	12	16	4	8	-
FORWARD	433	339	311	447	342	303	152	319	358	3004
par	5	4	4	5	4	4	3	4	4	37
handicap	9	7	4	5	2	11	15	12	8	-

BACK	
yardage	6607
par	72
rating	72.3
slope	129

REGULAR	
yardage	6218
par	72
rating	70.2
slope	125

FORWARD	
yardage	5507
par	72
rating	72.9
slope	132

PLAY POLICY & FEES: Green fees are $12 for nine holes and $19 for 18 holes on weekdays. Green fees are $14 for nine holes and $22 for 18 holes on weekends. Carts are $10 for nine holes and $19 for 18 holes. The front nine is closed until 9 a.m. on Monday. Twilight, junior, and senior rates are available.

TEE TIMES: Reservations can be booked seven days in advance.

DRESS CODE: Shirts and shoes are necessary. No tank tops are allowed on the course.

COURSE DESCRIPTION: Mature oaks line the fairways of this rolling course. Diamond Oaks is fairly forgiving for the most part, and the greens are in excellent shape for a municipal course which hosts 90,000 rounds per year. The ninth hole (par 4 and 405 yards) has oak trees right and left. The 18th is a superb finishing hole, measuring 440 yards uphill with a large oak tree dominating the right side of the fairway.

NOTES: Lou Alvarez holds the lowest score here, a 62.

LOCATION: From Interstate 80 in Roseville take the Atlantic Street exit to Yosemite Street. Turn right and drive to Diamond Oaks Road. Turn left and drive 400 yards to the course.

. . . ● **TOURNAMENTS:** A 24-player minimum is required to book a tournament. No shotgun tournaments are allowed.

13. DIAMOND OAKS GOLF COURSE

PLAY POLICY & FEES: Reciprocal play is accepted with members of other private clubs. Green fees for reciprocal players are $50 weekdays and $60 weekends, carts included. Guest fees are $30 weekdays and $40 weekends with a member. Carts for guests are $22. The course is closed on Monday.

TEE TIMES: Reservations can be booked seven days in advance.

DRESS CODE: Shirts with collars must be worn, and no blue jeans are allowed.

COURSE DESCRIPTION: Situated in the Sierra Nevada foothills, this tight, twisting course has water, bunkers, and undulating greens. It plays longer than the scorecard since fairways allow minimal roll. Sunset has one of Northern California's best short par 3s in the ninth, a 113-yarder. From the elevated tee, it seems as though the golfer can almost reach across the small pond and touch the green. But the two-tiered green is wide and shallow. The tee shot had better bite or it's sand city. Then there is the par-4 12th, a 411-yarder requiring a tee shot to carry over a large pond.

LOCATION: From Interstate 80 in Rocklin take the Taylor Road exit, north. Turn left on Midas Avenue and drive to the course.

. . . ● **TOURNAMENTS:** Shotgun tournaments are available Monday, Thursday, and Friday. Carts are required, and a 50-player minimum is needed. Events should be scheduled six months in advance. The banquet facility can accommodate 300 people.

14. SUNSET WHITNEY COUNTRY CLUB

P.O. Box 303
Loomis, CA 95650

4487 Barton Road
Loomis, CA 95650

PRO SHOP: 916-652-5546

Patty Snyder, Head Professional, LPGA

Driving Range ●
Practice Greens ●
Clubhouse ●
Food / Beverage ●
Accommodations
Pull Carts ●
Power Carts ●
Club Rental ●
$pecial Offers

	1	2	3	4	5	6	7	8	9	OUT
BACK	268	348	174	296	410	108	325	116	170	2215
REGULAR	255	336	168	290	402	108	325	116	170	2170
par	4	4	3	4	4	3	4	3	3	32
handicap	13	1	7	5	11	17	9	15	3	-
FORWARD	243	318	154	278	361	108	248	116	170	1996
par	4	4	3	4	4	3	4	3	3	32
handicap	13	1	7	5	11	17	9	15	3	-

	10	11	12	13	14	15	16	17	18	IN
BACK	268	348	174	296	410	108	325	116	170	2215
REGULAR	255	336	168	290	402	108	325	116	170	2170
par	4	4	3	4	4	3	4	3	3	32
handicap	14	2	8	6	12	18	10	16	4	-
FORWARD	243	318	154	278	361	108	248	116	170	1996
par	4	4	3	4	4	3	4	3	3	32
handicap	14	2	8	6	12	18	10	16	4	-

BACK	
yardage	4430
par	64
rating	-
slope	-

REGULAR	
yardage	4340
par	64
rating	60.7
slope	98

FORWARD	
yardage	3992
par	64
rating	-
slope	-

16 **WHITNEY OAKS GOLF CLUB**
ARCHITECT: JOHNNY MILLER & FRED BLISS, 1997

2305 Clubhouse Dr.
Rocklin, CA 95765

PRO SHOP: 916-632-8333

Dave Rowe, G.M./Director of Golf, PGA
Bruce Mullen, Head Professional, PGA
Jim Ferrin, Superintendent

Driving Range ●
Practice Greens ●
Clubhouse ●
Food / Beverage ●
Accommodations
Pull Carts
Power Carts ●
Club Rental ●
$pecial Offers ●

	1	2	3	4	5	6	7	8	9	OUT
BACK	377	386	510	211	417	430	462	199	458	3450
REGULAR	347	370	489	190	395	407	429	182	428	3237
par	4	4	5	3	4	4	4	3	4	35
handicap	17	3	15	11	1	7	9	5	13	-
FORWARD	270	305	406	133	324	312	327	119	320	2516
par	4	4	5	3	4	4	4	3	4	35
handicap	17	3	15	11	1	9	5	7	13	-

	10	11	12	13	14	15	16	17	18	IN
BACK	297	568	179	436	383	329	150	462	540	3344
REGULAR	282	546	164	411	355	315	137	423	513	3146
par	4	5	3	4	4	4	3	4	5	36
handicap	14	2	40	6	8	18	12	4	16	-
FORWARD	243	441	118	318	258	264	89	284	429	2444
par	4	5	3	4	4	4	3	4	5	36
handicap	10	2	14	6	8	18	16	4	12	-

BACK	
yardage	6794
par	71
rating	73.7
slope	132

REGULAR	
yardage	6383
par	71
rating	71.7
slope	125

FORWARD	
yardage	4960
par	71
rating	70.9
slope	127

PLAY POLICY & FEES: Green fees are $9 for nine holes and $15 for 18 holes weekdays, and $10 for nine holes and $17 for 18 holes weekends. Senior (65 and over) rates are available. Carts are $14 for nine holes and $21 for 18 holes. Pull carts are $3 for nine holes and $4 for 18 holes.

TEE TIMES: Reservations can be made at any time.

COURSE DESCRIPTION: A short course, Indian Creek is a natural layout set in the rolling hills of Placer County. Low-handicappers are often surprised at the difficulty of these holes. The second hole is a downhill dogleg over water, with the second shot played to an elevated green.

NOTES: Indian Creek made some fairway improvements and constructed a new parking lot.

LOCATION: From Interstate 80 east in Rocklin take the Rocklin Road exit (not the exit for the town of Rocklin). Turn right on Rocklin Road and drive about two miles to the end. Turn left on Barton Road and drive one mile to the course.

. . . ● **TOURNAMENTS:** This course is available for outside tournaments. A private room and patio is available.

15. INDIAN CREEK COUNTRY CLUB

PLAY POLICY & FEES: Green fees are seasonal and range from $40 to $70. Call for current rates. Twilight fees are available year round. All green fees include cart and range balls.

TEE TIMES: Reservations can be made seven days in advance.

DRESS CODE: Collared shirts and nonmetal spikes are required.

COURSE DESCRIPTION: Whitney Oaks has it all--wetlands, meadows, ancient oak trees, granite outcroppings, picturesque hills, and views of the Sacramento skyline. The par-4 fifth hole forces you to lay up off the tee to avoid a ravine. This leaves a long second shot into a narrow and sloping green. The green is guarded by bunkers on the left and a hazard on the right.

NOTES: Whitney Oaks is located on a portion of the J. Parker Whitney Ranch, site of what is believed to be the first golf course in Northern California. A new 12,000 square foot clubhouse is due to open at the end of 1999.

LOCATION: From Interstate 80 east of Roseville take Highway 65 north to Stanford Ranch Road exit. Follow Stanford Ranch Road three miles to Park Drive. Turn right on Park Drive and go to Whitney Oaks Drive. Turn left and continue to Clubhouse Drive.

. . . ● **TOURNAMENTS:** A 16-player minimum is required to book an event. The banquet facility can accommodate 175 people. ● **TRAVEL:** The Rocklin Park Hotel is 10 minutes from the course. Call 888-630-9400. For reservations at the Marriot Courtyard call 916-772-5555. ● **$PECIAL OFFERS:** Golf packages with Rocklin Park Hotel and Marriot Courtyard are available.

16. WHITNEY OAKS GOLF CLUB

⑰ SIERRA VIEW COUNTRY CLUB
ARCHITECT: JACK FLEMING, 1956

105 Alta Vista
Roseville, CA 95678

PRO SHOP: 916-783-4600
CLUBHOUSE: 916-782-3741

Bill Wampler, Manager
James Salazar, PGA Professional
Ben Hartley, Superintendent

Driving Range ●
Practice Greens ●
Clubhouse ●
Food / Beverage ●
Accommodations
Pull Carts ●
Power Carts ●
Club Rental ●
Special Offers

	1	2	3	4	5	6	7	8	9	OUT
BACK	526	375	459	484	146	349	392	183	392	3306
REGULAR	511	366	429	478	123	342	350	156	339	3094
par	5	4	4	5	3	4	4	3	4	36
handicap	11	7	1	13	17	15	3	9	9	-
FORWARD	511	366	429	478	123	342	350	156	339	3094
par	5	4	5	5	3	4	4	3	4	37
handicap	1	3	13	5	17	11	7	15	9	-

BACK	
yardage	6481
par	72
rating	70.5
slope	121

	10	11	12	13	14	15	16	17	18	IN
BACK	515	399	178	375	311	340	333	170	554	3175
REGULAR	491	384	147	366	271	266	321	131	465	2842
par	5	4	3	4	4	4	4	3	5	36
handicap	12	2	10	4	18	14	16	8	6	-
FORWARD	491	384	147	366	271	266	321	131	465	2842
par	5	4	3	4	4	4	4	3	5	36
handicap	2	6	18	4	12	14	10	16	8	-

REGULAR	
yardage	5936
par	72
rating	68.0
slope	115

FORWARD	
yardage	5936
par	73
rating	74.2
slope	130

⑱ DAVIS GOLF COURSE
ARCHITECT: BOB BALDOCK, 1964

P.O. Box 928
Davis, CA 95617

24439 Fairway Drive
Davis, CA 95616

PRO SHOP: 530-756-4010

Jerry Lilliedoll, Manager, PGA
Mark Hansen, PGA Professional
Gary Lipelt, Tournament Director, PGA

Driving Range ●
Practice Greens ●
Clubhouse
Food / Beverage ●
Accommodations
Pull Carts ●
Power Carts ●
Club Rental ●
Special Offers

	1	2	3	4	5	6	7	8	9	OUT
BACK	343	331	158	299	142	352	121	318	237	2301
REGULAR	322	306	132	267	128	328	103	274	216	2076
par	4	4	3	4	3	4	3	4	4	33
handicap	4	6	10	8	12	2	16	14	18	-
FORWARD	322	306	132	267	128	328	103	274	216	2076
par	4	4	3	4	3	4	3	4	4	33
handicap	4	6	12	16	14	2	8	10	18	-

BACK	
yardage	4953
par	67
rating	62.3
slope	97

	10	11	12	13	14	15	16	17	18	IN
BACK	324	176	295	476	200	301	141	350	389	2652
REGULAR	306	154	272	438	167	259	120	313	367	2396
par	4	3	4	5	3	4	3	4	4	34
handicap	13	7	15	1		17	11	9	3	-
FORWARD	306	154	272	394	167	259	120	313	367	2352
par	4	3	4	5	3	4	3	4	4	34
handicap	5	15	13	1	9	11	17	7	3	-

REGULAR	
yardage	4472
par	67
rating	60.1
slope	92

FORWARD	
yardage	4428
par	67
rating	63.9
slope	95

PLAY POLICY & FEES: Reciprocal play is accepted with members of other private clubs; otherwise, members and guests only. Guest fees are $35 weekdays and $40 weekends when accompanied by a member. Carts are $20. Green fees for reciprocal play are the same as the visitor's home course fees (at least $40).

TEE TIMES: Reservations can be booked one day in advance.

DRESS CODE: No denim is allowed on the course, and nonmetal spikes are required.

COURSE DESCRIPTION: Sierra View, a rolling course with mature trees and exceptional greens, is located at the base of the Sierra foothills. Designed by Jack Fleming, the right-hand man of famed architect Alister Mackenzie, it offers a wide variety of short and long par 4s. The toughest is the third hole, a 459-yarder, which plays like a par 5 for all but the biggest hitters. The par-5 18th hole (554 yards) is an outstanding test, tightening as it goes along.

NOTES: Robert Meyer holds the course record with a 62. Sierra View has served as a qualifying site for the U.S. Senior Open and the U.S. Women's Amateur.

LOCATION: From Interstate 80 in Roseville, exit at Atlantic Street and take the second right onto Yosemite Street. Drive a few blocks until the road bends. Look for Alta Vista and go left to the course.

. . . ● **TOURNAMENTS:** Shotgun tournaments are available Monday only.

17. SIERRA VIEW COUNTRY CLUB

PLAY POLICY & FEES: Green fees are $11 weekdays, $15 weekends. Seniors and juniors during the week pay $8 and $5 respectively. Carts are $17 for 18 holes.

TEE TIMES: Reservations can be booked seven days in advance.

COURSE DESCRIPTION: This short, level course has strategically placed trees and six lakes that come into play on 12 holes. The seventh hole may be short, but that doesn't make it easy. The green is surrounded by water.

NOTES: The course is extremely popular with seniors and women. Chris Hallee and Bob Neri share the course record with a 56.

LOCATION: From Interstate 80 in Davis take the Highway 113 exit. Drive five miles north to County Road 29. The course is on the left.

. . . ● **TOURNAMENTS:** A 24-player minimum is needed to book a tournament. The banquet facility can accommodate up to 60 people. Events should be scheduled at least two months in advanced. ● **TRAVEL:** The Hallmark Inn is located 10 minutes from the golf course. For reservations call 530-753-3600.

18. DAVIS GOLF COURSE

19 TEAL BEND GOLF CLUB
ARCHITECT: BRAD BELL, 1997

7200 Garden Highway
Sacramento, CA 95837

PRO SHOP: 916-922-5209

Nate Pomeroy, Director of Golf, PGA
Mike Sharp, Tournament Director, PGA
Troy Thompson, Superintendent

Driving Range ●
Practice Greens ●
Clubhouse ●
Food / Beverage ●
Accommodations
Pull Carts
Power Carts ●
Club Rental ●
$pecial Offers

	1	2	3	4	5	6	7	8	9	OUT
BACK	446	535	353	196	363	407	426	587	175	3488
REGULAR	381	464	294	133	319	351	368	507	141	2958
par	4	5	4	3	4	4	4	5	3	36
handicap	5	7	13	17	11	9	3	1	15	-
FORWARD	318	411	259	95	269	314	295	418	123	2502
par	4	5	4	3	4	4	4	5	3	36
handicap	5	7	13	17	11	9	3	1	15	-

	10	11	12	13	14	15	16	17	18	IN
BACK	515	448	194	386	461	438	201	512	418	3573
REGULAR	484	391	165	306	402	366	146	451	353	3064
par	5	4	3	4	4	4	3	5	4	36
handicap	8	6	18	16	2	4	14	12	10	-
FORWARD	391	328	143	286	320	304	116	394	293	2575
par	5	4	3	4	4	4	3	5	4	36
handicap	8	6	18	16	2	4	14	12	10	-

BACK	
yardage	7061
par	72
rating	73.5
slope	126

REGULAR	
yardage	6022
par	72
rating	68.5
slope	117

FORWARD	
yardage	5077
par	72
rating	68.8
slope	112

20 SUN CITY GOLF CLUB
ARCHITECTS: BILLY CASPER, 1996; GREG NASH

7050 Del Webb Boulevard
Roseville, CA 95747

PRO SHOP: 916-774-3851

Jim Carra, Head Professional, PGA
Leonard Theis, Superintendent

Driving Range ●
Practice Greens ●
Clubhouse ●
Food / Beverage ●
Accommodations
Pull Carts ●
Power Carts ●
Club Rental ●
$pecial Offers

	1	2	3	4	5	6	7	8	9	OUT
BACK	360	474	372	155	522	124	466	385	384	3242
REGULAR	334	436	329	128	488	105	409	345	358	2932
par	4	5	4	3	5	3	4	4	4	36
handicap	11	9	15	17	5	13	1	7	3	-
FORWARD	277	404	284	95	437	83	360	302	286	2528
par	4	5	4	3	5	3	4	4	4	36
handicap	13	3	11	17	5	15	1	7	9	-

	10	11	12	13	14	15	16	17	18	IN
BACK	403	429	478	336	156	379	133	413	516	3243
REGULAR	384	409	467	318	138	361	121	393	484	3075
par	4	4	5	4	3	4	3	4	5	36
handicap	12	2	10	14	16	8	18	4	6	-
FORWARD	328	328	428	286	100	313	107	315	449	2654
par	4	4	5	4	3	4	3	4	5	36
handicap	12	2	4	14	18	10	16	8	6	-

BACK	
yardage	6485
par	72
rating	70.9
slope	124

REGULAR	
yardage	6007
par	72
rating	68.9
slope	117

FORWARD	
yardage	5182
par	72
rating	70.2
slope	116

PLAY POLICY & FEES: Green fees are $39 Monday through Thursday and $52 Friday through Sunday and holidays. Twilight rates are $28 Monday through Thursday and $38 Friday through Sunday and holidays. All fees include cart and use of the range.

TEE TIMES: Reservations can be booked seven days in advance. For tee times beyond seven days, call 1-888- CENTRAL.

DRESS CODE: Nonmetal spikes are required.

COURSE DESCRIPTION: Built on 250 acres, this course features gently rolling hills and natural wetlands. The greens are undulating and true. Open in the front, they lend themselves to a variety of shots, including bump and run. With four sets of tees, this is a great course for players of all abilities.

LOCATION: From Sacramento take Interstate 5 north to Highway 99 North. Exit at Elverta Road and take a left. Follow Elverta Road and make a left on Garden Highway to the course.

. . . ● **TOURNAMENTS:** Shotgun tournaments are available weekdays only. A 16-player minimum is needed to book a tournament, and carts are mandatory.

● **TRAVEL:** The Hyatt Regency Sacramento at Capitol Park is located 20 minutes from the course. For reservations call 916-443-1234. The Marriott Courtyard (916-443-1234) and The Doubletree Inn (916-929-8855) are also recommended.

19. TEAL BEND GOLF CLUB

PLAY POLICY & FEES. Public play is accepted. Green fees are $45 weekdays and $50 weekends. Carts are included.

TEE TIMES: Reservations can be booked three days in advance.

DRESS CODE: Collared shirts and nonmetal spikes are required, and no jeans are allowed.

COURSE DESCRIPTION: This course features native California oak trees and large undulating greens. Water comes into play on six of the nine holes on the front side.

NOTES: The Sierra Pines Course is 3,175 from the championship tees with a rating of 35.2 and a slope of 113. Par is 36. The other two nines are named the Lakes Course and the Oaks Course. See scorecard for more information.

LOCATION: From Interstate 80 heading toward Reno take Highway 65 towards Yuba City. Exit on Blue Oaks. Follow Blue Oaks all the way to the golf course.

. . . ● **TOURNAMENTS:** A 16-player minimum is needed to book a tournament. The banquet facility can hold 350 people.

20. SUN CITY GOLF CLUB

㉑ ANTELOPE GREENS GOLF COURSE
ARCHITECT: DON REINERS, 1994

2721 Elverta Road
Antelope, CA 95843

PRO SHOP: 916-334-5764

John Anderson, Manager
John Christiano, Superintendent

Driving Range ●
Practice Greens ●
Clubhouse
Food / Beverage ●
Accommodations
Pull Carts ●
Power Carts ●
Club Rental ●
$pecial Offers

	1	2	3	4	5	6	7	8	9	OUT
BACK	114	298	139	77	101	126	129	355	330	1669
REGULAR	137	288	131	71	93	121	99	344	319	1603
par	3	4	3	3	3	3	3	4	4	30
handicap	6	18	2	16	14	10	8	4	12	-
FORWARD	90	248	83	63	83	116	66	311	260	1320
par	3	4	3	3	3	3	3	4	4	30
handicap	6	18	2	16	14	10	8	4	12	-

	10	11	12	13	14	15	16	17	18	IN
BACK	152	277	155	109	205	115	128	200	175	1516
REGULAR	145	261	147	98	183	108	119	187	156	1404
par	3	4	3	3	3	3	3	3	3	28
handicap	9	15	7	17	1	13	11	3	5	-
FORWARD	138	212	139	89	147	101	108	159	133	1226
par	3	4	3	3	3	3	3	3	3	28
handicap	9	15	7	17	1	13	11	3	5	-

BACK	
yardage	3185
par	58
rating	57.6
slope	81

REGULAR	
yardage	3007
par	58
rating	57.0
slope	80

FORWARD	
yardage	2546
par	58
rating	55.4
slope	79

㉒ CHERRY ISLAND GOLF COURSE
ARCHITECT: ROBERT MUIR GRAVES, 1990

2360 Elverta Road
Elverta, CA 95626

PRO SHOP: 916-575-GOLF
STARTER: 916-575-4653

Curt David, PGA Professional
Rick Chavez, Superintendent

Driving Range ●
Practice Greens ●
Clubhouse ●
Food / Beverage ●
Accommodations
Pull Carts ●
Power Carts ●
Club Rental ●
$pecial Offers

	1	2	3	4	5	6	7	8	9	OUT
BACK	331	384	543	133	516	352	183	393	341	3176
REGULAR	295	371	531	110	499	334	171	380	317	3008
par	4	4	5	3	5	4	3	4	4	36
handicap	11	1	5	17	7	15	13	9	3	-
FORWARD	230	274	489	66	453	277	138	321	285	2533
par	4	4	5	3	5	4	3	4	4	36
handicap	14	8	2	18	6	12	16	10	4	-

	10	11	12	13	14	15	16	17	18	IN
BACK	425	402	421	158	376	544	391	168	501	3386
REGULAR	401	381	393	138	359	519	374	154	474	3193
par	4	4	4	3	4	5	4	3	5	36
handicap	2	8	10	18	14	12	4	16	6	-
FORWARD	357	333	340	113	283	429	275	100	400	2630
par	4	4	4	3	4	5	4	3	5	36
handicap	1	9	7	17	13	11	5	15	3	-

BACK	
yardage	6562
par	72
rating	71.6
slope	122

REGULAR	
yardage	6201
par	72
rating	70.1
slope	118

FORWARD	
yardage	5163
par	72
rating	70.0
slope	117

PLAY POLICY & FEES: Green fees are $13.50 weekdays and $17 weekends. Twilight rates are $8 weekdays and $10 weekends for 18 holes. Carts are $16.

TEE TIMES: Reservations can be booked seven days in advance.

COURSE DESCRIPTION: This course features four par 4s, and water comes into play on five holes. The signature hole is the par-3 seventh, which features a three-tiered island green.

LOCATION: From Interstate 80 north of Sacramento, turn north onto Watt Avenue. Drive six miles to Elverta Road. Turn left onto Elverta and drive one-half mile. The course will be on your right.

. . . ● **TOURNAMENTS:** This course is available for outside tournaments. Events should be booked two months in advance.

21. ANTELOPE GREENS GOLF COURSE

PLAY POLICY & FEES: Green fees are $18 weekdays, $22 weekends. The twilight rate is $11. Carts are $22 for 18 holes.

TEE TIMES: Reservations can be booked seven days in advance.

COURSE DESCRIPTION: Cherry Island is an unusual course in that it forces a golfer with average or above-average length to leave the driver in the bag on several holes. Water comes into play on 10 holes, requiring numerous layup shots off the tee. The front nine has two in-course out-of-bounds areas. The third hole (par 5,543 yards) wraps around a large lake and forces a difficult decision on the second shot. The par 3s are excellent, including the 158-yard 13th hole over a creek onto a green framed by trees. The 15th hole, a par 5 of 544 yards, is a tough nut. There are out-of-bounds areas left, water on the right, and an elevated green surrounded by bunkers.

LOCATION: From Interstate 80 in Sacramento take the Watt Avenue exit north. Drive five miles to Elverta Road and turn left. Drive one mile to the course on the left.

. . . ● **TOURNAMENTS:** Shotgun tournaments are available weekdays only. A 20-player minimum is needed to book a tournament.

22. CHERRY ISLAND GOLF COURSE

LAWRENCE LINKS GOLF COURSE
ARCHITECT: BERT STAMPS

McClellan AFB/3825
Antelope, CA 95843

PRO SHOP: 916-643-3313

Charles Gilbert, Manager
Larry Rehberg, PGA Professional
David Anderson, Superintendent

Driving Range
Practice Greens ●
Clubhouse ●
Food / Beverage ●
Accommodations
Pull Carts ●
Power Carts ●
Club Rental ●
$pecial Offers ●

	1	2	3	4	5	6	7	8	9	OUT
BACK	-	-	-	-	-	-	-	-	-	-
REGULAR	503	422	298	134	485	165	475	360	132	2974
par	5	4	4	3	5	3	5	4	3	36
handicap	3	1	11	17	5	13	9	7	15	-
FORWARD	481	394	205	103	444	160	329	361	125	2602
par	5	5	4	3	5	3	4	4	3	36
handicap	1	9	13	17	3	11	7	5	15	-

	10	11	12	13	14	15	16	17	18	IN
BACK	-	-	-	-	-	-	-	-	-	-
REGULAR	503	422	298	134	485	165	475	360	132	2974
par	5	4	4	3	5	3	5	4	3	36
handicap	3	1	11	17	5	13	9	7	15	-
FORWARD	481	394	205	103	444	160	329	361	125	2602
par	5	5	4	3	5	3	4	4	3	36
handicap	1	9	13	17	3	11	7	5	15	-

BACK	
yardage	-
par	-
rating	-
slope	-

REGULAR	
yardage	5948
par	72
rating	69.7
slope	123

FORWARD	
yardage	5204
par	72
rating	70.2
slope	120

GRANITE BAY GOLF CLUB
ARCHITECT: ROBERT TRENT JONES JR., 1994

9600 Golf Club Drive
Granite Bay, CA 95746

PRO SHOP: 916-791-5379
CLUBHOUSE: 916-791-7578

Jack Deal, Manager
Bob Sykora, Director of Golf
Ken Mentzer, Superintendent

Driving Range ●
Practice Greens ●
Clubhouse ●
Food / Beverage ●
Accommodations
Pull Carts ●
Power Carts ●
Club Rental
$pecial Offers

	1	2	3	4	5	6	7	8	9	OUT
BACK	354	422	172	538	451	327	169	448	434	3315
REGULAR	341	397	162	513	434	302	157	432	409	3147
par	4	4	3	5	4	4	3	4	4	35
handicap	11	5	13	9	1	15	17	7	3	-
FORWARD	220	316	75	463	334	261	122	375	379	2545
par	4	4	3	5	4	4	3	4	4	35
handicap	11	5	13	9	3	15	17	7	1	-

	10	11	12	13	14	15	16	17	18	IN
BACK	396	202	578	374	212	550	416	397	469	3594
REGULAR	367	183	543	356	200	501	400	368	455	3373
par	4	3	5	4	3	5	4	4	4	36
handicap	14	18	2	16	10	12	4	8	6	-
FORWARD	244	114	452	291	95	436	360	300	390	2682
par	4	3	5	4	3	5	4	4	4	36
handicap	14	18	2	12	16	6	4	10	8	-

BACK	
yardage	6909
par	71
rating	73.5
slope	136

REGULAR	
yardage	6520
par	71
rating	71.7
slope	132

FORWARD	
yardage	5227
par	71
rating	70.0
slope	122

23. LAWRENCE LINKS GOLF COURSE

PLAY POLICY & FEES: Reciprocal play is accepted with members of other military clubs. Green fees for military personnel E5 and above are $7 for nine holes and $12 for 18 holes weekdays, and $8 for nine holes and $14 for 18 holes weekends. Guest fees for civilians are $10 for nine holes and $20 for 18 holes every day. Carts are $18 for 18 holes. The course is closed on Monday.

DRESS CODE: No fatigues, tank tops, white T-shirts, or gym shorts are allowed on the course. Nonmetal spikes are required.

COURSE DESCRIPTION: This tough, demanding course has four lakes that provide water hazards on every hole. Golfers play from the red tees the first nine and the blue tees the next time around. The 10th is the longest hole, a par 5 stretching out to 603 yards, and the best par 3 is the sixth, a 160-yarder over a hazard.

NOTES: The clubhouse has recently been remodeled. McClellan AFB is due to close in 2001. Most likely this will become a civilian golf course in the near future.

LOCATION: From Interstate 80 in Sacramento take the Watt Avenue exit north and drive past the entrance to McClellan Air Force Base. Turn right on Blackfoot Way and drive to the end.

. . . ● **TOURNAMENTS:** Shotgun tournaments are available weekdays only. A minimum of 60 players is needed to book a tournament. Tournaments should be booked six months in advance.

---

24. GRANITE BAY GOLF CLUB

PLAY POLICY & FEES: Outside play is accepted on Monday. Otherwise, members and guests only. Guests must be accompanied by a member. Green fees are $90. Carts are $15 per person for 18 holes.

DRESS CODE: Proper golf attire and nonmetal spikes are required.

COURSE DESCRIPTION: Architect Robert Trent Jones Jr. combined the influence of the old-style designers with a modern-day touch to create one of the best new courses in the state. This sprawling, oak-lined layout was set into the existing topography and has a natural look and feel. Granite outcroppings abound, Linda Creek meanders through the course, and most holes provide scenic vistas. The par-4 16th and 18th holes are already among the most talked-about holes in the Sacramento area. This one is a real gem.

LOCATION: From Sacramento take Interstate 80 east. Exit at Douglas Boulevard in Roseville. Proceed two miles to Roseville Parkway. Turn right on Roseville Parkway and drive three miles to the course entry gate on the right.

. . . ● **TOURNAMENTS:** This course is open to outside tournaments on Monday only. A 120-player minimum is needed to book a tournament. Tournaments should be booked 12 months in advance. The banquet facility can accommodate 250 people.

5572 Eureka Road
Roseville, CA 95746

PRO SHOP: 916-797-9986

Robert Peterson, Owner
Richard Dudleston, Teaching Professional
Lynn Barker, Superintendent

Driving Range
Practice Greens ●
Clubhouse
Food / Beverage ●
Accommodations
Pull Carts ●
Power Carts
Club Rental ●
$pecial Offers

	1	2	3	4	5	6	7	8	9	OUT
BACK	-	-	-	-	-	-	-	-	-	-
REGULAR	187	127	141	117	234	223	181	155	135	1500
par	3	3	3	3	3	3	3	3	3	27
handicap	5	17	11	15	3	1	7	9	13	-
FORWARD	190	130	144	120	235	225	185	160	140	1529
par	3	3	3	3	4	4	3	3	3	29
handicap	3	17	7	15	11	13	1	5	9	-

	10	11	12	13	14	15	16	17	18	IN
BACK	-	-	-	-	-	-	-	-	-	-
REGULAR	187	127	141	117	234	223	181	155	135	1500
par	3	3	3	3	3	3	3	3	3	27
handicap	6	18	12	16	4	2	8	10	14	-
FORWARD	190	130	144	120	235	225	185	160	140	1529
par	3	3	3	3	4	4	3	3	3	29
handicap	4	18	8	16	12	14	2	6	10	-

BACK	
yardage	-
par	-
rating	-
slope	-

REGULAR	
yardage	3000
par	54
rating	53.9
slope	79

FORWARD	
yardage	3058
par	58
rating	56.5
slope	92

26 WOODCREEK GOLF CLUB
ARCHITECT: ROBERT MUIR GRAVES, 1995

5880 Woodcreek Oaks
Roseville, CA 95747

PRO SHOP: 916-771-4653

Rob Frederick, Head Professional, PGA
Scott Prenez, Tournament Director, PGA

Driving Range ●
Practice Greens ●
Clubhouse ●
Food / Beverage ●
Accommodations
Pull Carts ●
Power Carts ●
Club Rental ●
$pecial Offers

	1	2	3	4	5	6	7	8	9	OUT
BACK	398	348	375	174	533	427	319	219	525	3318
REGULAR	376	311	345	148	499	399	300	128	504	3010
par	4	4	4	3	5	4	4	3	5	36
handicap	7	11	9	17	1	3	15	13	5	-
FORWARD	294	257	258	100	417	293	255	89	336	2299
par	4	4	4	3	5	4	4	3	4	35
handicap	3	11	9	15	1	7	13	17	5	-

	10	11	12	13	14	15	16	17	18	IN
BACK	552	306	321	367	197	426	486	133	412	3200
REGULAR	523	292	293	341	183	408	474	119	398	3031
par	5	4	4	4	3	4	5	3	4	36
handicap	2	14	16	10	12	4	8	18	6	-
FORWARD	406	246	238	262	164	329	389	82	324	2440
par	5	4	4	4	3	4	4	3	4	35
handicap	2	14	16	10	12	4	8	18	6	-

BACK	
yardage	6518
par	72
rating	72.4
slope	128

REGULAR	
yardage	6041
par	72
rating	70.5
slope	121

FORWARD	
yardage	4739
par	70
rating	66.2
slope	112

PLAY POLICY & FEES: Green fees are $9 for nine holes and $13 for 18 holes weekdays, and $10 for nine holes and $15 for 18 holes weekends. The course is open after 10 a.m. on Monday.

TEE TIMES: Reservations are not accepted. All play is on a first-come, first-served basis.

DRESS CODE: Shirts must be worn.

COURSE DESCRIPTION: This short, par-3 course has rolling terrain and can be tough, especially the 223-yard, par-3 sixth, which has only been aced once.

NOTES: The course record is 50 for 18 holes.

LOCATION: From Interstate 80 in Roseville take the Douglas Street exit east. Turn right on Sierra College Boulevard and left on Eureka Road.

. . . ● **TOURNAMENTS:** This course is available for outside tournaments.

25. ROSEVILLE ROLLING GREENS GOLF

PLAY POLICY & FEES: Green fees for nine holes are $15.50 weekdays and $19 weekends. Green fees for 18 holes are $25.50 weekdays and $31 weekends. Junior, senior and twilight rates are available. Carts are $24.

TEE TIMES: Reservations can be booked seven days in advance.

DRESS CODE: No tank tops are allowed on the course.

COURSE DESCRIPTION: Woodcreek is spread out over 210 acres of gently rolling terrain. More than 1,000 mature oaks are scattered throughout and give the course an older feel. Natural wetlands, lakes, streams, and 80 bunkers give golfers plenty to think about, along with the large greens. This course has great finishing holes.

LOCATION: From Sacramento take Interstate 80 north to the Riverside exit in Roseville. Turn left on Cirby Way. Take Cirby Way to Foothills and turn right. Take Foothills to Pleasant Grove Road and turn left. Take Pleasant Grove Road to Woodcreek Oaks Boulevard and turn right. Continue one-quarter mile to the course.

. . . ● **TOURNAMENTS:** A 24-player minimum is needed for tournament play, and carts are mandatory.

26. WOODCREEK GOLF CLUB

27

SUNRISE GOLF COURSE

6412 Sunrise Boulevard
Citrus Heights, CA 95610

PRO SHOP: 916-723-8854
STARTER: 916-723-0481

Larry Lowe, Jim Mackey, Owner/Operators
and Gary Mills,
Mike Griggs, Professional

Driving Range ●
Practice Greens ●
Clubhouse ●
Food / Beverage ●
Accommodations
Pull Carts ●
Power Carts ●
Club Rental
$pecial Offers

	1	2	3	4	5	6	7	8	9	OUT
BACK	-	-	-	-	-	-	-	-	-	-
REGULAR	149	142	165	283	342	130	274	155	428	2068
par	3	3	3	4	4	3	4	3	5	32
handicap	15	9	11	7	3	13	5	17	1	-
FORWARD	149	142	165	283	342	130	274	155	428	2068
par	3	3	3	4	4	3	4	3	5	32
handicap	15	9	11	7	3	13	5	17	1	-

BACK		
yardage	-
par	-
rating	-
slope	-

	10	11	12	13	14	15	16	17	18	IN
BACK	-	-	-	-	-	-	-	-	-	-
REGULAR	149	142	165	283	342	130	274	155	428	2068
par	3	3	3	4	4	3	4	3	5	32
handicap	16	10	12	8	4	14	6	18	2	-
FORWARD	149	142	165	283	342	130	274	155	428	2068
par	3	3	3	4	4	3	4	3	5	32
handicap	16	10	12	8	4	14	6	18	2	-

REGULAR		
yardage	4136
par	64
rating	60.4
slope	98

FORWARD		
yardage	4136
par	64
rating	62.3
slope	105

28

WILDHORSE GOLF COURSE
ARCHITECT: JEFF BRAUER, 1999

2323 Rockwell Drive
Davis, CA 95616

PRO SHOP: 530-753-4900

John Hoag, Head Professional, PGA
Craig McDonald, Superintendent

Driving Range ●
Practice Greens ●
Clubhouse
Food / Beverage ●
Accommodations
Pull Carts ●
Power Carts
Club Rental ●
$pecial Offers

	1	2	3	4	5	6	7	8	9	OUT
BACK	460	193	581	159	506	473	359	305	392	3428
REGULAR	385	145	514	128	448	417	297	241	336	2911
par	4	3	5	3	5	4	4	4	4	36
handicap	3	13	7	17	11	1	5	15	9	-
FORWARD	338	127	459	98	398	375	214	227	252	2488
par	4	3	5	3	4	4	4	4	4	35
handicap	3	13	7	17	11	1	5	15	9	-

BACK		
yardage	6736
par	72
rating	
slope	135

	10	11	12	13	14	15	16	17	18	IN
BACK	341	344	203	594	137	508	465	388	328	3308
REGULAR	300	307	172	554	120	487	433	348	309	3030
par	4	4	3	5	3	5	4	4	4	36
handicap	8	16	14	10	18	4	2	6	12	-
FORWARD	230	267	108	499	93	420	346	237	237	2437
par	4	4	3	5	3	5	4	4	4	36
handicap	8	16	14	10	18	4	2	6	12	-

REGULAR		
yardage	5941
par	72
rating	
slope	

FORWARD		
yardage	4925
par	71
rating	
slope	

PLAY POLICY & FEES: Reciprocal play is accepted with members of other private clubs. Guest and reciprocal fees are $7 and $11 (respectively) weekdays, and $8 and $15 weekends when accompanied by a member.

TEE TIMES: Reservations can be booked seven days in advance.

DRESS CODE: Appropriate golf attire and nonmetal spikes are required.

COURSE DESCRIPTION: This executive-style course has rolling hills, tree-lined fairways, and small greens. The par-5 ninth hole has a creek running through the fairway and is very tight—a demanding finish.

NOTES: While the course is private, the driving range is open to the public until 10 p.m. nightly.

LOCATION: From Interstate 80 in Citrus Heights (northeast of Sacramento) take the Greenback Lane exit east. Drive four miles to Sunrise Boulevard and turn left. The course is located on the right.

. . . ● **TOURNAMENTS:** This course is available for outside tournaments. A 20-player minimum is needed. Events should be booked three months in advance.

27. SUNRISE GOLF COURSE

PLAY POLICY & FEES: Green fees are $25 Monday through Friday and $45 on weekends and holidays. Carts are $11 per player.

TEE TIMES: Reservations can be made seven days in advance.

DRESS CODE: Collared shirts and soft spikes are required.

COURSE DESCRIPTION: This is a links-style course with five lakes, 64 traps, and an enviromentally sensitive area running throughout. The greens are good size, true, firm, fast, and well protected by bunkers. Although the course only plays 6,700 yards from the back tees, the slope rating is 135. The back tees present a great challenge for even experienced golfers; however, the forward tees make the course playable for the less-experienced player.

LOCATION: From Interstate 80 take the Mace exit and head north to Covel, take a right on Wright Boulevard, and turn left on Moore Street until you get to Rockwell. Take a right on Rockwell to the course.

. . . ● **TOURNAMENTS:** A 16-player minimum is required to book an event. Tournaments should be scheduled 12 to 24 months in advance.

28. WILDHORSE GOLF COURSE

44571 Clubhouse Drive
El Macero, CA 95618

PRO SHOP: 530-753-5621

Nick Nicoloudis, Manager
Eric Pollard, PGA Professional
Jeff Gorham, Superintendent

Driving Range ●
Practice Greens ●
Clubhouse ●
Food / Beverage ●
Accommodations
Pull Carts ●
Power Carts ●
Club Rental
$pecial Offers

	1	2	3	4	5	6	7	8	9	OUT
BACK	515	226	467	560	437	157	381	381	389	3513
REGULAR	346	503	210	443	543	407	133	363	367	3315
par	4	5	3	4	5	4	3	4	4	36
handicap	15	13	5	1	7	3	17	11	9	-
FORWARD	325	481	141	353	524	331	113	345	355	2968
par	4	5	3	4	5	4	3	4	4	36
handicap	11	3	18	13	1	14	16	8	7	-

	10	11	12	13	14	15	16	17	18	IN
BACK	408	416	177	382	354	516	176	398	520	3347
REGULAR	386	402	152	361	338	488	162	384	501	3174
par	4	4	3	4	4	5	3	4	5	36
handicap	4	2	18	8	12	14	16	6	10	-
FORWARD	350	365	135	347	307	473	145	372	490	2984
par	4	4	3	4	4	5	3	4	5	36
handicap	12	5	15	10	9	4	17	6	2	-

BACK	
yardage	6860
par	72
rating	72.3
slope	125

REGULAR	
yardage	6489
par	72
rating	70.4
slope	119

FORWARD	
yardage	5952
par	72
rating	74.5
slope	129

500 Douglas Street
West Sacramento, CA
95605
PRO SHOP: 916-372-4949

Robert Halpenny, PGA Professional

Driving Range ●
Practice Greens ●
Clubhouse ●
Food / Beverage ●
Accommodations
Pull Carts ●
Power Carts ●
Club Rental ●
$pecial Offers

	1	2	3	4	5	6	7	8	9	OUT
BACK	416	465	256	197	374	491	133	129	280	2741
REGULAR	416	454	256	188	348	485	123	116	275	2661
par	5	5	4	3	4	5	3	3	4	36
handicap	7	9	15	3	5	1	11	13	17	-
FORWARD	403	401	219	174	325	463	101	93	221	2400
par	5	5	4	3	4	5	3	3	4	36
handicap	1	9	15	3	11	7	5	13	17	-

	10	11	12	13	14	15	16	17	18	IN
BACK	464	188	155	185	169	491	269	268	379	2568
REGULAR	464	162	144	175	158	484	262	251	347	2447
par	5	3	3	3	3	5	4	4	4	34
handicap	14	4	16	10	8	2	12	18	6	-
FORWARD	412	101	107	115	125	469	237	234	321	2121
par	5	3	3	3	3	5	4	4	4	34
handicap	8	4	16	14	12	2	10	18	6	-

BACK	
yardage	5309
par	70
rating	67.3
slope	115

REGULAR	
yardage	5108
par	70
rating	66.4
slope	113

FORWARD	
yardage	4521
par	70
rating	65.6
slope	116

PLAY POLICY & FEES: Reciprocal play is accepted with members of other private clubs. Guest fees are $35. Reciprocal fees are $60. Carts are $20.

DRESS CODE: Appropriate golf attire and nonmetal spikes are required.

COURSE DESCRIPTION: This long, narrow course has lots of out-of-bounds areas, challenging fairway bunkers, and excellent greens. There are three lakes. The talk of this course is the 516-yard, par-5 15th hole. There are two fairway bunkers in the right landing zone, and the undulating green is surrounded by more bunkers. Trees are everywhere. Out-of-bounds areas mark both sides of the wide fairway. If shots stray, the player is hitting out of the trees.

NOTES: Joe Acosta of Visalia set the course record of 63 in U.S. Amateur qualifying.

LOCATION: From Davis drive two miles east on Interstate 80. Take the Mace Boulevard exit south in El Macero to Clubhouse Road.

. . . ● **TOURNAMENTS:** A 100-player minimum is needed to book a shotgun tournament.

29. EL MACERO COUNTRY CLUB

PLAY POLICY & FEES: Green fees are $18 weekdays and $25 weekends. Carts are $20 for 18 holes.

TEE TIMES: Reservations can be booked seven days in advance.

COURSE DESCRIPTION: Extensive work was done on this course in 1993. The old course, formerly the River Bend Golf and Country Club, was plowed up and redesigned. There is now water on 13 holes, guarded by many mature trees. Surfacing as a spectacularly tough hole is the par-5, 491-yard 15th. There is water left and right. The elevated green is narrow in the front and deep in the back. The pin position often makes this a particularly difficult hole. Lighthouse Golf Course is known for its excellent condition, beautiful greens, and challenging layout. The course drains very well in wet weather.

LOCATION: From the Interstate 80 Business Loop in West Sacramento, take the Jefferson exit north. Turn right on Sacramento Avenue. Drive 1.5 blocks to Douglas Street and turn left. The course is at the end of Douglas.

. . . ● **TOURNAMENTS:** This course is available for outside tournaments. Carts are required. There is an outside eating area that can accommodate 180 people.

● **TRAVEL:** The Hyatt Regency (916-443-1234) and Best Western Harbor Inn (800-371-2101) are recommended for lodging.

30. LIGHTHOUSE GOLF COURSE

3645 Fulton Avenue
Sacramento, CA 95821

PRO SHOP: 916-575-2525

Mike Wood, PGA Professional
Lynn Sisler, Tournament Director
Joe Andrade, Superintendent

Driving Range ●
Practice Greens ●
Clubhouse ●
Food / Beverage ●
Accommodations
Pull Carts ●
Power Carts ●
Club Rental ●
$pecial Offers

	1	2	3	4	5	6	7	8	9	OUT
BACK	521	402	410	343	129	383	381	155	330	3054
REGULAR	512	390	395	333	114	373	370	139	320	2946
par	5	4	4	4	3	4	4	3	4	35
handicap	11	3	1	9	17	5	7	15	13	-
FORWARD	482	375	373	325	111	308	335	140	311	2760
par	5	4	4	4	3	4	4	3	4	35
handicap	6	4	8	2	18	12	10	16	14	-

BACK	
yardage	6592
par	72
rating	70.6
slope	113

	10	11	12	13	14	15	16	17	18	IN
BACK	389	387	548	350	176	422	191	560	515	3538
REGULAR	375	371	534	336	147	395	165	528	499	3350
par	4	4	5	4	3	4	3	5	5	37
handicap	10	14	12	4	16	2	8	6	18	-
FORWARD	285	345	520	304	125	364	132	495	426	2996
par	4	4	5	4	3	4	3	5	5	37
handicap	13	9	5	1	15	7	17	3	11	-

REGULAR	
yardage	6296
par	72
rating	69.3
slope	110

FORWARD	
yardage	5756
par	72
rating	71.4
slope	113

PLAY POLICY & FEES: Green fees for the Alister Mackenzie course are $20 Monday through Thursday, $22 Friday, and $24 weekends and holidays. Green fees for the Arcade Creek Course are $9 Monday through Thursday, $11 Friday, and $12 weekends and holidays. Carts are $22. Haggin Oaks offers a number of off-peak rates as well as senior and junior rates.

TEE TIMES: Reservations can be booked seven days in advance for weekdays. Weekend and holiday reservations are taken on the Tuesday prior starting at 6 a.m., by calling the Sacramento City Tee Time Hotline at 916-665-1202. The phone number for the Arcade Creek Course is 916-481-4508.

DRESS CODE: Nonmetal spikes are required.

COURSE DESCRIPTION: The Alister Mackenzie Course is tree-lined with large greens and extensive bunkering. The best hole on the course is either No. 16, a par 3 of 165 yards, or the par-5 18th hole. The Arcade Creek Course is much longer but more wide open.

NOTES: The South Course (now called the Alister Mackenzie) played host to the Sacramento Open in the late 1930s. Among those who competed were Sam Snead, Walter Hagen, Gene Sarazen, and Ben Hogan.The North Course is now called Arcade Creek. Haggin Oaks features a 24-hour driving range and a super pro shop. The Arcade Creek Course is 6,660 yards and rated 69.9 with a slope rating of 112 from the regular tees. Forward tees are 5,853 yards and rated 70.6 with a slope of 107. The Alister MacKenzie Course: See scorecard for more information.

LOCATION: Take the Fulton Road exit north off Business 80 in Sacramento and follow it to the course.

. . . ● **TOURNAMENTS:** A 24-player minimum is needed to book a tournament. A 128-player minimum is needed for a shotgun start, and carts are required.

31. HAGGIN OAKS GOLF COURSE

32

ANCIL HOFFMAN GOLF COURSE
ARCHITECT: WILLIAM F. BELL, 1965

6700 Tarshes Drive
Carmichael, CA 95608

PRO SHOP: 916-575-GOLF
OFFICE: 916-482-3284

Art Leuang, PGA Professional
Rich Sizelove, Superintendent

Driving Range ●
Practice Greens ●
Clubhouse ●
Food / Beverage ●
Accommodations
Pull Carts ●
Power Carts ●
Club Rental ●
$pecial Offers

	1	2	3	4	5	6	7	8	9	OUT
BACK	348	552	406	339	189	438	583	405	197	3457
REGULAR	340	531	374	335	168	421	542	367	182	3260
par	4	5	4	4	3	4	5	4	3	36
handicap	9	5	11	13	15	3	1	7	17	-
FORWARD	320	470	359	319	140	368	499	359	148	2982
par	4	5	4	4	3	4	5	4	3	36
handicap	11	3	9	13	17	5	1	7	15	-

	10	11	12	13	14	15	16	17	18	IN
BACK	512	373	440	376	127	347	449	179	534	3337
REGULAR	502	361	422	367	112	318	422	155	515	3174
par	5	4	4	4	3	4	4	3	5	36
handicap	8	6	4	10	18	14	2	16	12	-
FORWARD	493	350	376	330	107	305	411	127	473	2972
par	5	4	4	4	3	4	5	3	5	37
handicap	2	8	4	14	18	10	12	16	6	-

BACK	
yardage	6794
par	72
rating	72.8
slope	128

REGULAR	
yardage	6434
par	72
rating	70.9
slope	125

FORWARD	
yardage	5954
par	73
rating	73.4
slope	123

33

NORTH RIDGE COUNTRY CLUB
ARCHITECT: WILLIAM F. BELL, 1952

7600 Madison Ave.
Fair Oaks, CA 95628

7600 Madison Avenue
Fair Oaks, CA 95628

PRO SHOP: 916-967-5716

Ron Witt, Manager
Michael Silva, PGA Professional
Fritz Howell, Superintendent

Driving Range ●
Practice Greens ●
Clubhouse ●
Food / Beverage ●
Accommodations
Pull Carts ●
Power Carts ●
Club Rental ●
$pecial Offers

	1	2	3	4	5	6	7	8	9	OUT
BACK	510	402	202	426	456	154	329	191	521	3191
REGULAR	501	391	180	405	445	131	309	183	497	3042
par	5	4	3	4	5	3	4	3	5	36
handicap	8	4	10	2	14	18	16	12	6	-
FORWARD	495	352	169	386	419	116	296	172	465	2870
par	5	4	3	4	5	3	4	3	5	36
handicap	6	8	16	2	10	18	12	14	4	-

	10	11	12	13	14	15	16	17	18	IN
BACK	369	182	430	388	344	523	358	208	559	3361
REGULAR	354	176	411	381	327	512	341	176	538	3216
par	4	3	4	4	4	5	4	3	5	36
handicap	9	15	1	5	17	3	13	7	11	-
FORWARD	341	169	383	371	317	494	316	172	445	3008
par	4	3	4	4	4	5	4	3	5	36
handicap	11	15	7	5	13	1	9	17	3	-

BACK	
yardage	6552
par	72
rating	71.6
slope	129

REGULAR	
yardage	6258
par	72
rating	70.3
slope	125

FORWARD	
yardage	5878
par	72
rating	75.2
slope	131

PLAY POLICY & FEES: Green fees are $19 Monday through Thursday and $24 Friday through Sunday. Twilight, senior, junior and nine-hole rates are available. Carts are $20 for 18 holes.

TEE TIMES: Reservations can be booked seven days in advance for weekdays. For weekend reservations call on the Monday prior, starting at 6:30 a.m.

DRESS CODE: Shirts must be worn.

COURSE DESCRIPTION: Situated in Ancil Hoffman Park on the American River, oak and pine trees come into play on nearly every hole. The fairways are tight, and the greens are contoured. Although it shows the wear of nearly 100,000 rounds each year, Hoffman is one of the premier public courses in Northern California. The seventh hole, a par 5 of 542 yards, is outstanding, requiring a pinpoint drive down a tree-lined fairway. The second shot is almost as difficult to place, and the green is large.

NOTES: "Golf Digest" ranks this course among the top 75 public courses in the country.

LOCATION: From Business 80 in Sacramento take the Marconi Avenue exit east. Drive five miles to Fair Oaks Boulevard and turn right. Turn left on Kenneth Avenue. Turn right on California Avenue and left on Ancil Hoffman Park Road (Tarshes Drive) and follow it to the course.

. . . ● **TOURNAMENTS:** Shotgun tournaments are limited and must have a full field of 144. Carts are required.

32. ANCIL HOFFMAN GOLF COURSE

PLAY POLICY & FEES: Reciprocal play is accepted with members of other private clubs for $70, including cart. Guest fees are $40 weekdays, $50 weekends with a member, and $70 without. Carts are $20. The course is closed on Monday.

DRESS CODE: Appropriate golf attire is required, shirts must be collared and tucked in. No jeans are allowed on the course, and hats must be removed in the clubhouse.

COURSE DESCRIPTION: This tree-lined course has Bermuda grass fairways and long par 4s. It tends to play longer than the yardage because of the number of uphill holes. North Ridge features a classic par 5, the 15th hole. It narrows each step of the way and demands a precise second shot to the left of the tree line. The small green caps things off.

NOTES: Robert Meyer holds the course record with a 62.

LOCATION: From Sacramento drive east on Interstate 80. Take the Madison Avenue exit east. Follow Madison Avenue for five miles and make a right into the club at Mariposa Avenue.

. . . ● **TOURNAMENTS:** A minimum of 130 players is needed to book a shotgun tournament. Shotgun tournaments are available Monday only.

33. NORTH RIDGE COUNTRY CLUB

DEL PASO COUNTRY CLUB
ARCHITECT: HERBERT FOWLER, 1916

3333 Marconi Avenue
Sacramento, CA 95821

PRO SHOP: 916-483-0401
CLUBHOUSE: 916-489-2681

Mike Green, PGA Professional

Driving Range ●
Practice Greens ●
Clubhouse ●
Food / Beverage ●
Accommodations
Pull Carts ●
Power Carts ●
Club Rental
$pecial Offers

	1	2	3	4	5	6	7	8	9	OUT
BACK	-	-	-	-	-	-	-	-	-	-
REGULAR	338	488	156	402	376	125	517	527	260	3189
par	4	5	3	4	4	3	5	5	4	37
handicap	9	5	15	1	7	17	11	3	13	-
FORWARD	337	432	138	405	361	125	501	492	218	3009
par	4	5	3	5	4	3	5	5	4	38
handicap	8	6	16	11	7	18	2	4	15	-

	10	11	12	13	14	15	16	17	18	IN
BACK	-	-	-	-	-	-	-	-	-	-
REGULAR	322	393	162	491	354	390	200	403	396	3111
par	4	4	3	5	4	4	3	4	4	35
handicap	12	2	18	14	10	8	16	4	6	-
FORWARD	317	316	128	476	318	391	181	408	387	2922
par	4	4	3	5	4	4	3	5	4	36
handicap	9	14	17	5	10	1	13	12	3	-

BACK	
yardage	-
par	-
rating	-
slope	-

REGULAR	
yardage	6300
par	72
rating	70.0
slope	117

FORWARD	
yardage	5931
par	74
rating	74.2
slope	130

 CAMPUS COMMONS GOLF COURSE
ARCHITECT: BILL MCDOWELL, 1973

2 Cadillac Drive
Sacramento, CA 95825

PRO SHOP: 916-922-5861

Ray Arinno, Manager
Mike Fancolli, Head Professional, PGA
Dale Arinno, Superintendent

Driving Range
Practice Greens ●
Clubhouse ●
Food / Beverage ●
Accommodations
Pull Carts ●
Power Carts ●
Club Rental ●
$pecial Offers

	1	2	3	4	5	6	7	8	9	OUT
BACK	-	-	-	-	-	-	-	-	-	-
REGULAR	150	138	276	135	187	168	160	287	172	1673
par	3	3	4	3	3	3	3	4	3	29
handicap	16	18	6	12	1	8	4	14	10	-
FORWARD	127	116	264	118	187	152	142	260	142	1508
par	3	3	4	3	4	3	3	4	3	30
handicap	13	15	1	17	5	11	7	3	9	-

	10	11	12	13	14	15	16	17	18	IN
BACK	-	-	-	-	-	-	-	-	-	-
REGULAR	150	138	276	135	187	168	160	287	172	1673
par	3	3	4	3	3	3	3	4	3	29
handicap	16	18	6	12	1	8	4	14	10	-
FORWARD	127	116	264	118	187	152	142	260	142	1508
par	3	3	4	3	4	3	3	4	3	30
handicap	13	15	1	17	5	11	7	3	9	-

BACK	
yardage	-
par	-
rating	-
slope	-

REGULAR	
yardage	3346
par	58
rating	54.0
slope	-

FORWARD	
yardage	3016
par	60
rating	56.0
slope	-

PLAY POLICY & FEES: Reciprocal play is accepted only with clubs at least 50 miles away. Call for specifics. Guest fees are $40 with a member and $85 without.

TEE TIMES: Reservations can be booked seven days in advance.

DRESS CODE: Appropriate golf attire is required. A seven-inch inseam is required for all shorts.

COURSE DESCRIPTION: This rolling, tree-lined layout is narrow with small, undulating greens. The fairways and greens are well bunkered. The most distinct holes are the second, a par 5 of 488 yards that horseshoes around a creek and trees; the 16th, a 200-yard par 3; the 17th, a par 4 of 403 yards into a well-bunkered green; and the 18th, a 396-yarder with the stately clubhouse serving as a backdrop.

NOTES: The men's course record is 63, set by Lee Elder and Bob E. Smith during the old "Swing at Cancer" benefits. Del Paso has hosted several USGA events: the 1957 and 1976 U.S. Women's Amateur and the 1964 Senior Women's Amateur. The 1982 U.S. Women's Open was held here.

LOCATION: From Business 80 in Sacramento take the Marconi Avenue exit east. Drive one-half mile to the course on the left. From Interstate 80 take the Watt Avenue exit. Travel on Watt Avenue to Marconi Avenue and turn right on Marconi. Follow it to the course.

. . . ● **TOURNAMENTS:** This course is available for outside tournaments. Call the pro shop for more information.

34. DEL PASO COUNTRY CLUB

PLAY POLICY & FEES: Outside play is accepted. Green fees are $8 for nine holes and $13 for 18 holes weekdays, and $9 for nine holes and $14 for 18 holes weekends. Carts are $8.50 per nine holes.

TEE TIMES: Reservations can be booked seven days in advance.

COURSE DESCRIPTION: This rolling executive course is bordered by the American River. The greens are elevated, and there is a lot of roll to the fairways. The river comes into play on the fifth, seventh, and eighth holes. The fifth plays 187 yards, with the river an intimidating presence on the right.

NOTES: The course record is 51, set by Tony Alvarado.

LOCATION: From U.S. 50 in Sacramento take the Howe Avenue North exit. Take a left on Fair Oaks Boulevard and a right on Cadillac Drive. Follow Cadillac Drive to the course.

. . . ● **TOURNAMENTS:** This course is available for outside events.

35. CAMPUS COMMONS GOLF COURSE

36 SWALLOW'S NEST GOLF COURSE

2245 Orchard Lane
Sacramento, CA 95833

PRO SHOP: 916-927-6481

Driving Range
Practice Greens
Clubhouse ●
Food / Beverage
Accommodations
Pull Carts
Power Carts
Club Rental
$pecial Offers

	1	2	3	4	5	6	7	8	9	OUT
BACK										
REGULAR										
par										
handicap										
FORWARD										
par										
handicap										

	10	11	12	13	14	15	16	17	18	IN
BACK										
REGULAR										
par										
handicap										
FORWARD										
par										
handicap										

BACK	
yardage	
par	
rating	
slope	

REGULAR	
yardage	2968
par	60
rating	53.2
slope	82

FORWARD	
yardage	2968
par	60
rating	55.8
slope	83

37 WILLIAM LAND PARK GOLF COURSE

1701 Sutterville Road
Sacramento, CA 95822

PRO SHOP: 916-455-5014

Ruben Samaniego, General Manager, PGA
Doug Hocking, Superintendent

Driving Range
Practice Greens ●
Clubhouse ●
Food / Beverage ●
Accommodations
Pull Carts ●
Power Carts ●
Club Rental ●
$pecial Offers

	1	2	3	4	5	6	7	8	9	OUT
BACK	-	-	-	-	-	-	-	-	-	-
REGULAR	144	328	153	358	383	296	147	456	334	2599
par	3	4	3	4	4	4	3	5	4	34
handicap	15	3	9	11	1	13	17	7	5	-
FORWARD	144	328	153	358	383	296	147	436	334	2579
par	3	4	3	4	4	4	3	5	4	34
handicap	15	3	9	11	1	13	17	5	7	-

	10	11	12	13	14	15	16	17	18	IN
BACK	-	-	-	-	-	-	-	-	-	-
REGULAR	144	328	153	358	383	296	147	456	334	2599
par	3	4	3	4	4	4	3	5	4	34
handicap	16	4	10	12	2	14	18	6	8	-
FORWARD	144	328	153	358	383	296	147	436	334	2579
par	3	4	3	4	4	4	3	5	4	34
handicap	16	4	10	12	2	14	18	6	8	-

BACK	
yardage	-
par	-
rating	-
slope	-

REGULAR	
yardage	5198
par	68
rating	63.3
slope	101

FORWARD	
yardage	5158
par	68
rating	63.0
slope	100

PLAY POLICY & FEES: Members and guests only.

COURSE DESCRIPTION: This short course has three par 4s.

LOCATION: In Sacramento take the El Camino exit. Turn right on El Camino, then right on Orchard. The course is two blocks down.

. . . ● **TOURNAMENTS:** This course is not available for outside tournaments.

36. SWALLOW'S NEST GOLF COURSE

PLAY POLICY & FEES: Weekday greens fees are $8.50. Weekend green fees are $9.50. Senior, junior, early-bird, afternoon and twilight rates are available.

TEE TIMES: Weekday reservations can be booked seven days in advance. Weekend and holiday reservations are taken on the Tuesday prior, starting at 6 a.m., by calling the Sacramento City Tee Tme Hotline at 916-665-1202.

DRESS CODE: Nonmetal spikes are required.

COURSE DESCRIPTION: Set in beautiful William Land Park, this course is a favorite of women, seniors, and locals interested in a peaceful round of golf. The par-3 third hole (153 yards) has long been considered one of the area's best, with its two huge cottonwoods guarding the green.

NOTES: Former U.S. Women's Amateur champion Barbara Romack learned how to play here, as did "Mr. 59," Al Geiberger. When the city threatened to close the golf course in the early 1950s, one of its staunchest defenders was Sis Kennedy, mother of Supreme Court Justice Anthony Kennedy.

LOCATION: From Interstate 5 heading north to Sacramento, take the Sutterville exit and head east to Land Park. The course will be on the left.

. . . ● **TOURNAMENTS:** This course is available for outside tournaments.

37. WILLIAM LAND PARK GOLF COURSE

8915 Gerber Road
Sacramento, CA 95828

PRO SHOP: 916-688-9120
OFFICE: 916-688-8791

Matt Holm, Co-Head Professional, PGA
Vic Pitton, Co-Head Professional, PGA
Bob Morris, Superintendent

Driving Range ●
Practice Greens ●
Clubhouse ●
Food / Beverage ●
Accommodations
Pull Carts ●
Power Carts ●
Club Rental ●
$pecial Offers

	1	2	3	4	5	6	7	8	9	OUT
BACK	134	409	302	122	166	150	142	410	111	1946
REGULAR	105	351	278	106	151	109	111	352	97	1660
par	3	4	4	3	3	3	3	4	3	30
handicap	17	1	5	15	9	7	11	3	13	-
FORWARD	97	300	209	98	143	95	81	154	97	1274
par	3	4	4	3	3	3	3	4	3	30
handicap	17	1	5	15	9	7	11	3	13	-

	10	11	12	13	14	15	16	17	18	IN
BACK	134	409	302	122	166	150	142	410	111	1946
REGULAR	105	351	278	106	151	109	111	352	97	1660
par	3	4	4	3	3	3	3	4	3	30
handicap	18	2	6	16	10	8	12	4	14	-
FORWARD	97	300	209	98	143	95	81	154	97	1274
par	3	4	4	3	3	3	3	4	3	30
handicap	18	2	6	16	10	8	12	4	14	-

BACK	
yardage	3892
par	60
rating	59.1
slope	94

REGULAR	
yardage	3320
par	60
rating	57.8
slope	92

FORWARD	
yardage	2548
par	60
rating	-
slope	-

6801 Freeport Boulevard
Sacramento, CA 95822

PRO SHOP: 916-428-9401

Tim Walsh, Director of Golf, PGA
Joe Findley, PGA Professional
Linda Drake, Tournament Director

Driving Range ●
Practice Greens ●
Clubhouse
Food / Beverage ●
Accommodations
Pull Carts ●
Power Carts ●
Club Rental ●
$pecial Offers

	1	2	3	4	5	6	7	8	9	OUT
BACK	-	-	-	-	-	-	-	-	-	-
REGULAR	392	385	123	355	169	493	400	352	516	3185
par	4	4	3	4	3	5	4	4	5	36
handicap	2	6	16	14	18	8	4	12	10	-
FORWARD	383	380	100	345	157	450	342	349	493	2999
par	4	4	3	4	3	5	4	4	5	36
handicap	5	3	15	13	17	7	9	11	1	-

	10	11	12	13	14	15	16	17	18	IN
BACK	-	-	-	-	-	-	-	-	-	-
REGULAR	372	490	414	130	462	379	149	344	356	3096
par	4	5	4	3	5	4	3	4	4	36
handicap	3	5	1	11	15	9	13	17	7	-
FORWARD	363	475	413	128	468	295	145	340	346	2973
par	4	5	4	3	5	4	3	4	4	36
handicap	4	6	12	18	2	14	16	10	8	-

BACK	
yardage	-
par	-
rating	-
slope	-

REGULAR	
yardage	6281
par	72
rating	70.1
slope	113

FORWARD	
yardage	5972
par	72
rating	72.6
slope	121

PLAY POLICY & FEES: Green fees are $10 weekdays for 9 holes and $14 for 18 holes. Weekend green fees are $14 for 9 holes and $18 for 18 holes. Senior and junior rates are available. Carts are $8 for 9 holes and $12 for 18 holes. Champions Club and Champions Gold Club card holders receive additional discounts.

TEE TIMES: Reservations can be booked seven days in advance.

DRESS CODE: Shirts and shoes are necessary.

COURSE DESCRIPTION: This links-style executive course features one par 4. Most greens have at least two tiers. Three lakes come into play, notably on the ninth, the signature hole.

LOCATION: From Sacramento take Highway 99 south to Florin Road exit. Go east on Florin Road to Elk Grove/Florin Road. Turn right on Elk Grove/Florin Road. Drive about one mile to Gerber Road and the course.

. . . ● **TOURNAMENTS:** This course is available for outside tournaments. A 28-player minimum is required. Events should be booked two months in advance. A banquet facility is available that will accommodate 100 people.

38. CHAMPIONS GOLF LINKS

PLAY POLICY & FEES: Green fees are $20 weekdays and $24 weekends. Twilight rates are available. Carts are $22.

TEE TIMES: Weekday reservations can be booked seven days in advance. Weekend and holiday reservations are taken on the Tuesday prior, starting at 6 a.m., by calling the Sacramento City Tee Time Hotline at 916-665-1202.

DRESS CODE: Nonmetal spikes are required.

COURSE DESCRIPTION: A flat course, Bing Maloney requires accurate tee shots because large trees border each fairway. Site of the Sacramento Regional Four-Ball Championship each year, this heavily used course (upwards of 95,000 rounds a year) has large greens surrounded by bunkers. The most difficult hole, without question, is the 12th, a par 4 measuring 414 yards. A huge cottonwood tree stands out like a sore thumb directly in front of the tee, forcing the golfer to A) bail out right; B) hook it around the tree and risk going out-of-bounds; or C) hit a sharp cut shot. Good luck. Bing Maloney is a shot-maker's course.

NOTES: Bing Maloney also has a short executive course that is 1,332 yards and rated 58.0.

LOCATION: From Sacramento drive six miles south on Interstate 5. Take the Florin Road exit east. Turn left on Freeport Road and drive toward the Sacramento Executive Airport. The course is on the right.

. . . ● **TOURNAMENTS:** Shotgun tournaments are available weekdays only. There is a 24-player minimum to book a tournament.

39. BING MALONEY GOLF COURSE

BARTLEY CAVANAUGH GOLF COURSE
ARCHITECT: PERRY DYE, 1995

8301 Freeport Boulevard
Sacramento, CA 95832

PRO SHOP: 916-665-2020

Eric Pohl, PGA Professional
Sam Samelson, Superintendent
Linda Drake, Tournament Director

Driving Range ●
Practice Greens ●
Clubhouse ●
Food / Beverage ●
Accommodations
Pull Carts ●
Power Carts ●
Club Rental ●
$pecial Offers

	1	2	3	4	5	6	7	8	9	OUT
BACK	364	331	512	543	191	330	322	182	400	3175
REGULAR	333	311	482	519	174	312	309	160	372	2972
par	4	4	5	5	3	4	4	3	4	36
handicap	15	7	17	3	13	5	9	11	1	-
FORWARD	277	267	425	434	108	219	252	112	308	2402
par	4	4	5	5	3	4	4	3	4	36
handicap	13	7	15	3	17	5	9	11	1	-

	10	11	12	13	14	15	16	17	18	IN
BACK	398	509	143	289	351	445	351	107	390	2983
REGULAR	364	485	137	275	335	430	334	85	371	2816
par	4	5	3	4	4	4	4	3	4	35
handicap	8	18	10	14	12	2	6	16	4	-
FORWARD	299	419	106	222	298	344	267	57	300	2312
par	4	5	3	4	4	4	4	3	4	35
handicap	8	18	12	10	14	2	6	16	4	-

BACK	
yardage	6158
par	71
rating	69.0
slope	114

REGULAR	
yardage	5788
par	71
rating	67.3
slope	109

FORWARD	
yardage	4714
par	71
rating	66.3
slope	107

 BRADSHAW RANCH GOLF COURSE
ARCHITECT: STEVE LEGARRA, 1989

7350 Bradshaw Road
Sacramento, CA 95829

PRO SHOP: 916-363-6549

Marshall Cain, PGA Professional
Stephen J. Legarra, Superintendent

Driving Range
Practice Greens ●
Clubhouse ●
Food / Beverage ●
Accommodations
Pull Carts ●
Power Carts
Club Rental ●
$pecial Offers

	1	2	3	4	5	6	7	8	9	OUT
BACK	-	-	-	-	-	-	-	-	-	-
REGULAR	92	178	87	111	115	97	199	107	110	1096
par	3	3	3	3	3	3	3	3	3	27
handicap	9	2	6	3	4	7	1	8	5	-
FORWARD	-	-	-	-	-	-	-	-	-	-
par	-	-	-	-	-	-	-	-	-	-
handicap	-	-	-	-	-	-	-	-	-	-

	10	11	12	13	14	15	16	17	18	IN
BACK	-	-	-	-	-	-	-	-	-	-
REGULAR	-	-	-	-	-	-	-	-	-	-
par	-	-	-	-	-	-	-	-	-	-
handicap	-	-	-	-	-	-	-	-	-	-
FORWARD	-	-	-	-	-	-	-	-	-	-
par	-	-	-	-	-	-	-	-	-	-
handicap	-	-	-	-	-	-	-	-	-	-

BACK	
yardage	-
par	-
rating	-
slope	-

REGULAR	
yardage	1096
par	27
rating	--
slope	--

FORWARD	
yardage	
par	
rating	--
slope	-

PLAY POLICY & FEES: Monday through Thursday green fees are $20 from opening until 11 a.m., $14 from 11a.m. to 4 p.m. Friday green fees are $22 from opening until 11 a.m., $14 from 11 a.m. to 4 p.m. Weekend and holiday rates are $24 from opening until 1 p.m., $15 1 p.m. to 4 p.m. Super twilight, junior, and senior rates are available.

TEE TIMES: Weekday reservations can be booked seven days in advance. Weekend and holiday reservations are taken on the prior Tuesday starting at 6 a.m., by calling the Sacramento City Tee Time Hotline at 916-665-1202.

DRESS CODE: Shirts and shoes are necessary. Nonmetal spikes are required.

COURSE DESCRIPTION: This Perry Dye design has a links feel because of extensive mounding and frequency of wind. The course is adjacent to the Sacramento River and is built on 91 acres, so accuracy is important. The signature hole is the par-3 17th, which is played to an island green.

LOCATION: From Sacramento take Interstate 5 south to the Pocket Road exit. Turn left over the freeway to Freeport Boulevard. Turn right on Freeport Boulevard. Drive 1.5 miles to the course on the left.

. . . ● **TOURNAMENTS:** A 24-player minimum is needed to book a tournament.

40. BARTLEY CAVANAUGH GOLF COURSE

PLAY POLICY & FEES: Green fees are $5.50 weekdays and $7 weekends and holidays. Pull carts are $1. Club rentals are $4.

TEE TIMES: Reservations can be booked seven days in advance.

DRESS CODE: Nonmetal spikes are preferred.

COURSE DESCRIPTION: A short course that is particularly popular with seniors and women, it is well maintained with good greens. The 111-yard fourth hole has a lake and features the only real sloping green on the course. This is a good place to sharpen your iron play.

NOTES: No observers are allowed on the golf course.

LOCATION: Take Bradshaw exit south off U.S. 50 or Florin Road east off Highway 99 and drive several miles to Bradshaw Road. Turn left on Bradshaw.

. . . ● **TOURNAMENTS:** This course is available for outside tournaments. A 20-player minimum is needed to book an event. Tournaments should be scheduled two months in advance.

41. BRADSHAW RANCH GOLF COURSE

MATHER GOLF COURSE

ARCHITECT: JACK FLEMING, 1958

4103 Eagles Nest Road
Mather, CA 95655

PRO SHOP: 916-575-GOLF

Paul Henderson, PGA Professional
Asa Jennings, Tournament Director

Driving Range ●
Practice Greens ●
Clubhouse ●
Food / Beverage ●
Accommodations
Pull Carts ●
Power Carts ●
Club Rental ●
$pecial Offers

	1	2	3	4	5	6	7	8	9	OUT
BACK	395	534	156	423	426	353	183	382	522	3374
REGULAR	385	521	144	388	416	342	162	371	503	3232
par	4	5	3	4	4	4	3	4	5	36
handicap	5	7	17	3	1	13	15	11	9	-
FORWARD	377	473	135	374	409	308	150	331	471	3028
par	4	5	3	4	5	4	3	4	5	37
handicap	5	1	13	7	15	11	17	9	3	-

	10	11	12	13	14	15	16	17	18	IN
BACK	448	168	473	296	182	356	541	463	420	3347
REGULAR	417	144	458	281	167	345	523	428	402	3165
par	4	3	5	4	3	4	5	4	4	36
handicap	4	18	10	16	12	14	6	2	8	-
FORWARD	376	134	452	273	157	328	427	415	386	2948
par	4	3	5	4	3	4	5	5	4	37
handicap	6	12	2	14	18	10	8	16	4	-

BACK	
yardage	6721
par	72
rating	71.7
slope	121

REGULAR	
yardage	6397
par	72
rating	70.3
slope	119

FORWARD	
yardage	5976
par	74
rating	72.4
slope	119

 CORDOVA GOLF COURSE

9425 Jackson Road
Sacramento, CA 95826

PRO SHOP: 916-362-1196

Jim Marta, Professional
Stanley E. Flood, Superintendent

Driving Range ●
Practice Greens ●
Clubhouse ●
Food / Beverage ●
Accommodations
Pull Carts ●
Power Carts ●
Club Rental ●
$pecial Offers

	1	2	3	4	5	6	7	8	9	OUT
BACK	-	-	-	-	-	-	-	-	-	-
REGULAR	390	265	201	170	211	471	381	154	389	2632
par	4	4	3	3	3	5	4	3	4	33
handicap	7	17	1	13	5	11	9	15	3	-
FORWARD	390	265	214	170	221	471	381	154	389	2655
par	4	4	4	3	4	5	4	3	4	35
handicap	3	13	17	9	15	7	5	11	1	-

	10	11	12	13	14	15	16	17	18	IN
BACK	-	-	-	-	-	-	-	-	-	-
REGULAR	383	178	190	180	407	306	143	177	191	2155
par	4	3	3	3	4	4	3	3	3	30
handicap	4	12	8	14	2	18	16	10	6	-
FORWARD	301	178	190	180	407	306	143	177	191	2073
par	4	3	3	3	5	4	3	3	3	31
handicap	6	10	4	8	14	18	16	12	2	-

BACK	
yardage	-
par	-
rating	-
slope	-

REGULAR	
yardage	4787
par	63
rating	61.2
slope	90

FORWARD	
yardage	4728
par	66
rating	64.9
slope	96

PLAY POLICY & FEES: Green fees are $19 weekdays and $24 weekends.

TEE TIMES: Reservations can be booked seven days in advance.

DRESS CODE: Nonmetal spikes are encouraged.

COURSE DESCRIPTION: This long course is lined with mature trees. It demands length off the tee. There are five par 4s that are 420 yards or longer. The final two holes are a tough finish. The 17th is 463 yards and par 4. It is straight away and long with trees left and right. The front of the large green is open, but there is a bunker to the left. The 18th hole is a 420-yard, par-4 dogleg left with trees down both sides.

NOTES: In 1998 new carts and new cart paths were added.

LOCATION: From U.S. 50 south take the Sunrise exit east 3.5 miles. Take a right on Douglas Avenue and a left onto Eagles Nest.

. . . ● **TOURNAMENTS:** Shotgun tournaments are available weekdays only. A 20-player minimum is needed to book a tournament.Tournaments should be booked 12 months in advance.

42. MATHER GOLF COURSE

PLAY POLICY & FEES: Green fees are $8 weekdays and $10 weekends. Carts are $8 for nine holes and $15 for 18 holes.

TEE TIMES: Weekend tee times are made after 10 a.m. on Mondays. Weekday tee times are made after 10 a.m. on Fridays.

COURSE DESCRIPTION: Cordova is a flat course with small greens and tough par 3s. The third hole, for instance, is 201 yards in length, and the 18th is 191 yards. The only par 5 is the sixth hole. This is the busiest course in the Sacramento area, numbering 120,000 rounds a year, because of its low rates and short yardage.

NOTES: Dave Keck's 56 is the lowest round ever shot here. New cart paths were added throughout the course in 1998.

LOCATION: From U.S. 50 in Sacramento take the Bradshaw exit south to Jackson Road. The course is between Bradshaw Road and south Watt Avenue.

. . . ● **TOURNAMENTS:** No shotgun starts are allowed. A 24-player minimum is needed to book a tournament. Arrangements must be made through the Cordova Park District. Events should be booked six months in advance.

43. CORDOVA GOLF COURSE

VALLEY HI COUNTRY CLUB
ARCHITECT: WILLIAM P. BELL, 1959

P.O. Box 850
Elk Grove, CA 95759

9595 Franklin Boulevard
Elk Grove, CA 95624

PRO SHOP: 916-423-2170
CLUBHOUSE: 916-423-2093

Nick West, General Manager
Dave Bingham, Head Professional, PGA
Mike Azevedo, Superintendent

Driving Range ●
Practice Greens ●
Clubhouse ●
Food / Beverage ●
Accommodations
Pull Carts
Power Carts ●
Club Rental ●
$pecial Offers

	1	2	3	4	5	6	7	8	9	OUT
BACK	366	445	389	488	175	371	194	538	376	3342
REGULAR	358	434	380	478	140	360	183	528	367	3228
par	4	4	4	5	3	4	3	5	4	36
handicap	9	1	3	13	17	7	15	11	5	-
FORWARD	340	381	337	465	112	334	172	480	328	2949
par	4	4	4	5	3	4	3	5	4	36
handicap	9	5	11	1	17	7	16	2	13	-

	10	11	12	13	14	15	16	17	18	IN
BACK	334	424	365	566	168	436	185	396	571	3445
REGULAR	326	409	352	549	158	412	170	381	558	3315
par	4	4	4	5	3	4	3	4	5	36
handicap	14	2	12	10	18	4	16	8	6	-
FORWARD	311	403	341	468	106	361	147	372	485	2994
par	4	5	4	5	3	4	3	4	5	37
handicap	12	14	10	3	18	8	15	6	4	-

BACK	
yardage	6787
par	72
rating	71.7
slope	123

REGULAR	
yardage	6543
par	72
rating	70.7
slope	121

FORWARD	
yardage	5943
par	73
rating	73.9
slope	126

 WILDHAWK GOLF CLUB
ARCHITECT: J. MICHAEL POELLOT, 1997

7713 Vineyard Road
Sacramento, CA 95829

PRO SHOP: 916-688-4653

Edward Lombard III, Director of Golf, PGA
Bruce Mullen, Head Professional, PGA
Gerry Levesque, Superintendent

Driving Range ●
Practice Greens ●
Clubhouse ●
Food / Beverage ●
Accommodations
Pull Carts ●
Power Carts ●
Club Rental ●
$pecial Offers

	1	2	3	4	5	6	7	8	9	OUT
BACK	349	407	540	159	325	398	227	418	502	3325
REGULAR	320	379	515	143	305	377	204	391	474	3108
par	4	4	5	3	4	4	3	4	5	36
handicap	17	7	5	9	15	11	3	1	13	-
FORWARD	239	290	422	93	236	298	115	308	396	2397
par	4	4	5	3	4	4	3	4	5	36
handicap	17	7	5	9	15	11	3	1	13	-

	10	11	12	13	14	15	16	17	18	IN
BACK	372	374	195	433	527	438	319	182	530	3370
REGULAR	341	349	181	411	501	410	290	162	507	3152
par	4	4	3	4	5	4	4	3	5	36
handicap	16	14	12	2	8	4	10	18	6	-
FORWARD	275	254	113	321	428	326	216	93	424	2450
par	4	4	3	4	5	4	4	3	5	36
handicap	16	14	12	2	8	4	10	18	6	-

BACK	
yardage	6695
par	72
rating	71.2
slope	124

REGULAR	
yardage	6260
par	72
rating	69.7
slope	118

FORWARD	
yardage	4847
par	72
rating	67.2
slope	109

PLAY POLICY & FEES: Reciprocal play is accepted with members of other private clubs. Guest fees are $30 with a member and reciprocal fees are $55. Carts are $20 and mandatory.

DRESS CODE: Appropriate golf attire and nonmetal spikes are required.

COURSE DESCRIPTION: Valley Hi's reputation grows with each year as the trees and the course mature. It has three large lakes that seem to crop up everywhere. The toughest holes are the second (434 yards), the 11th (409 yards), and the 15th (412 yards). Those three par 4s invariably play into the wind. The greens are bent grass, without much undulation, but are fairly fast and difficult to read.

NOTES: Valley Hi holds numerous amateur tournaments for men and women.

LOCATION: From Sacramento drive south on Highway 99. Take the Elk Grove Boulevard exit west. Drive 3.5 miles to Franklin Boulevard. Turn right. The course is on the right.

. . . ● **TOURNAMENTS:** This course is available for outside tournaments. Weekend shotgun tournaments are reserved for member play.

44. VALLEY HI COUNTRY CLUB

PLAY POLICY & FEES: Green fees are $36 weekdays and $49 weekends. Senior, junior, and twilight rates are available. All prices include cart, but walking is allowed.

TEE TIMES: Reservations can be made seven days in advance starting at seven in the morning. Advance reservations can be made for a $10 fee per player.

DRESS CODE: Appropriate golf attire and nonmetal spikes are required. No denim is allowed.

COURSE DESCRIPTION: J. Michael Poellot has created an intriguing course out of what was once a flat and featureless piece of land. By adding extensive mounding, well-placed bunkers, and contoured greens this is a challenging course where wind is a factor. There are two lakes, and a creek runs throughout.

LOCATION: From U.S. 50 take the Bradshaw Road exit. Take Bradshaw south to Gerbar Road. Take Gerbar east one mile. Make a right on Vineyard; the course will be on the left.

. . . ● **TOURNAMENTS:** A 12-player minimum is required to book an event. Events should be scheduled 12 months in advance. The banquet facility can accommodate up to 200 people. ● **TRAVEL:** The Sheraton Rancho Cordova is located 12 minutes from the golf course. For reservations call 916-638-1100. Holiday Inn (916-638-1111) is also recommended.

45. WILDHAWK GOLF CLUB

10651 E. Stockton
Elk Grove, CA 95624

PRO SHOP: 916-685-4653

Jim Roeder, General Manager
Nelson Hirst, PGA Professional
Jay Guttridge, Superintendent

Driving Range ●
Practice Greens ●
Clubhouse
Food / Beverage ●
Accommodations
Pull Carts ●
Power Carts ●
Club Rental ●
$pecial Offers

	1	2	3	4	5	6	7	8	9	OUT
BACK	-	-	-	-	-	-	-	-	-	-
REGULAR	300	206	129	505	123	353	173	285	342	2416
par	4	3	3	5	3	4	3	4	4	33
handicap	9	13	17	1	7	3	15	11	5	-
FORWARD	236	148	100	461	97	333	148	250	244	2017
par	4	3	3	5	3	4	3	4	4	33
handicap	9	15	17	3	7	1	13	11	5	-

BACK		
yardage	-
par	-
rating	-
slope	-

	10	11	12	13	14	15	16	17	18	IN
BACK	-	-	-	-	-	-	-	-	-	-
REGULAR	300	206	129	505	123	353	173	285	342	2416
par	4	3	3	5	3	4	3	4	4	33
handicap	10	14	18	2	8	4	16	12	6	-
FORWARD	236	148	100	461	97	333	148	250	244	2017
par	4	3	3	5	3	4	3	4	4	33
handicap	10	16	18	6	8	2	14	12	4	-

REGULAR	
yardage	4832
par	66
rating	62.7
slope	98

FORWARD	
yardage	4034
par	66
rating	61.8
slope	99

PLAY POLICY & FEES: Green fees are $9 for nine holes and $14 for 18 holes weekdays, and $11 for nine holes and $17 for 18 holes weekends. The senior rate is $8 for nine holes weekdays. The rate for juniors holding an etiquette card is $6 for nine holes and $10 for 18 holes weekdays. On weekends junior green fees are $8 for nine holes and $12 for 18 holes. Twilight green fees Monday through Friday after 3 p.m. are $6 for nine holes and $11 for 18 holes. Carts are $9 for nine holes.

TEE TIMES: Reservations can be booked seven days in advance. There is a $1 reservation fee on weekends.

COURSE DESCRIPTION: The layout consists of one par 5, four par 4s, and four par 3s. The fairways are relatively narrow. Three lakes come into play on six holes. The greens, which are the best part of this young course, are undulating and fast. Two of the greens are two-tiered. The signature hole is the par-3 fifth, a 123-yarder to an island green.

NOTES: The lighted driving range is open in summer months until 10 p.m. and 7 p.m. in the winter.

LOCATION: From Highway 99 in Elk Grove take the Grant Line Road exit east. Drive south on East Stockton Boulevard (frontage road). East Stockton Boulevard dead-ends in the parking lot of the course.

. . . ● **TOURNAMENTS:** This course is available for outside tournaments.

46. EMERALD LAKES GOLF CENTER

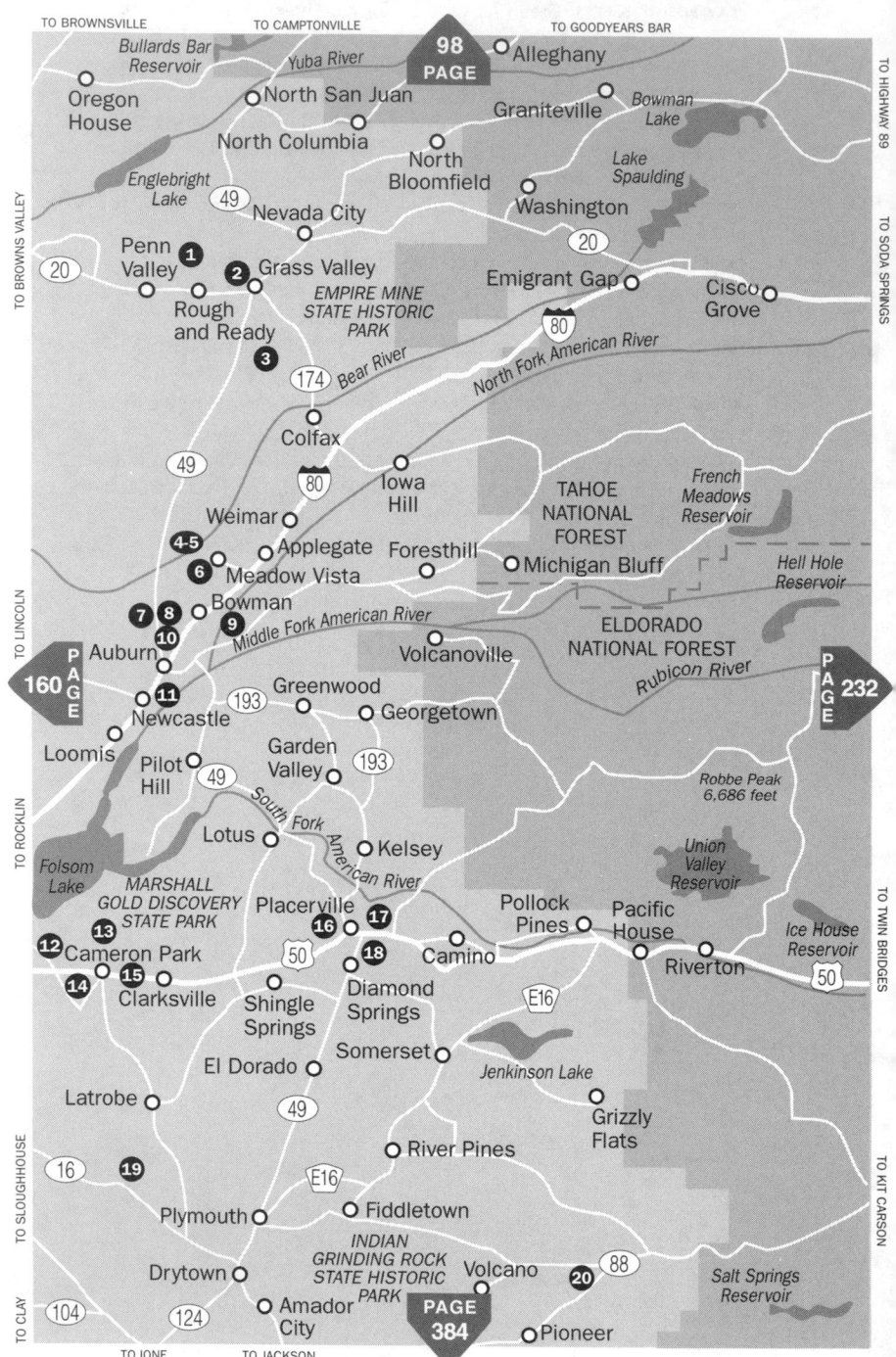

TO BROWNSVILLE TO CAMPTONVILLE TO GOODYEARS BAR

Bullards Bar
Reservoir

Yuba River

98 PAGE

Alleghany

Oregon
House

North San Juan

Graniteville

Bowman
Lake

North Columbia

North
Bloomfield

Lake
Spaulding

Englebright
Lake

49

Nevada City

Washington

TO HIGHWAY 89

20

Penn
Valley ❶

❷ Grass Valley

EMPIRE MINE
STATE HISTORIC
PARK

Emigrant Gap

Cisco
Grove

TO SODA SPRINGS

Rough
and Ready

❸

174 Bear River

80

North Fork American River

TO BROWNS VALLEY

20

Colfax

49

80

Iowa
Hill

TAHOE
NATIONAL
FOREST

French
Meadows
Reservoir

Weimar

4-5

Applegate

Foresthill

Michigan Bluff

Hell Hole
Reservoir

❻ Meadow Vista

TO LINCOLN

❼ ❽ Bowman

❾

Middle Fork American River

ELDORADO
NATIONAL
FOREST

❿

Auburn

Volcanoville

Rubicon River

PAGE 160

PAGE 232

⓫

193

Greenwood

Georgetown

Newcastle

Loomis

Pilot
Hill

Garden
Valley

193

Robbe Peak
6,686 feet

TO ROCKLIN

49

South Fork

American River

Lotus

Kelsey

Union
Valley
Reservoir

Folsom
Lake

MARSHALL
GOLD DISCOVERY
STATE PARK

Placerville

⓰ ⓱

Pollock
Pines

Pacific
House

Ice House
Reservoir

⓬ ⓭ Cameron Park

50

⓲

Camino

Riverton

50

TO TWIN BRIDGES

⓮ ⓯ Clarksville

Shingle
Springs

Diamond
Springs

E16

El Dorado

Somerset

Jenkinson Lake

Latrobe

49

Grizzly
Flats

TO SLOUGHHOUSE

16 ⓳

River Pines

E16

Plymouth

Fiddletown

INDIAN
GRINDING ROCK
STATE HISTORIC
PARK

Volcano

⓴

88

Salt Springs
Reservoir

TO KIT CARSON

TO CLAY

104

124

Drytown

Amador
City

PAGE 384

Pioneer

TO IONE TO JACKSON

Grass Valley/Auburn Area

① LAKE WILDWOOD COUNTRY CLUB

ARCHITECTS: WILLIAM F. BELL, 1971; ROBERT MUIR GRAVES, 1977

11255 Cottontail Way
Penn Valley, CA 95946

PRO SHOP: 530-432-1163
CLUBHOUSE: 530-432-1152

Jim Knight, PGA Professional
Mark Bunte, Superintendent

Driving Range ●
Practice Greens ●
Clubhouse ●
Food / Beverage ●
Accommodations
Pull Carts ●
Power Carts ●
Club Rental ●
$pecial Offers

	1	2	3	4	5	6	7	8	9	OUT
BACK	304	354	162	523	474	434	392	400	155	3198
REGULAR	286	345	153	472	466	406	379	389	136	3032
par	4	4	3	5	5	4	4	4	3	36
handicap	13	9	17	7	11	1	3	5	15	-
FORWARD	253	270	134	443	431	409	367	355	131	2793
par	4	4	3	5	5	5	4	4	3	37
handicap	14	12	18	6	8	10	4	2	16	-

	10	11	12	13	14	15	16	17	18	IN
BACK	400	160	382	373	428	546	171	471	371	3302
REGULAR	393	156	364	356	422	528	161	471	363	3214
par	4	3	4	4	4	5	3	5	4	36
handicap	6	18	4	8	2	10	16	14	12	-
FORWARD	363	125	330	351	421	495	131	420	314	2950
par	4	3	4	4	5	5	3	5	4	37
handicap	5	15	1	7	9	3	17	11	13	-

BACK	
yardage	6500
par	72
rating	71.0
slope	125

REGULAR	
yardage	6246
par	72
rating	69.7
slope	123

FORWARD	
yardage	5743
par	74
rating	73.0
slope	130

② NEVADA COUNTY COUNTRY CLUB

1040 East Main Street
Grass Valley, CA 95945

PRO SHOP: 530-273-6436

Jeff Fish, PGA Professional
Robert Brueggeman, Superintendent

Driving Range
Practice Greens ●
Clubhouse ●
Food / Beverage
Accommodations
Pull Carts ●
Power Carts ●
Club Rental ●
$pecial Offers

	1	2	3	4	5	6	7	8	9	OUT
BACK	-	-	-	-	-	-	-	-	-	-
REGULAR	315	152	324	318	150	309	353	416	357	2694
par	4	3	4	4	3	4	4	5	4	35
handicap	6	18	16	8	10	14	12	2	4	-
FORWARD	318	153	328	328	147	264	370	417	277	2602
par	4	3	4	4	3	4	4	5	4	35
handicap	5	17	9	7	15	13	3	1	11	-

	10	11	12	13	14	15	16	17	18	IN
BACK	-	-	-	-	-	-	-	-	-	-
REGULAR	320	152	330	328	170	309	353	423	384	2769
par	4	3	4	4	3	4	4	4	4	34
handicap	5	17	15	7	9	13	11	1	3	-
FORWARD	299	156	315	316	129	311	356	408	261	2551
par	4	3	4	4	3	4	4	5	4	35
handicap	8	16	12	6	16	10	4	2	14	-

BACK	
yardage	-
par	-
rating	-
slope	-

REGULAR	
yardage	5463
par	69
rating	65.6
slope	110

FORWARD	
yardage	5153
par	70
rating	68.1
slope	112

PLAY POLICY & FEES: Reciprocal play is accepted with members of other private clubs. Guest fees are $24 for nine holes and $30 for 18 holes when accompanied by a member. Reciprocal fees are $50 for 18 holes. Carts for reciprocators are $22 for guests.

DRESS CODE: Appropriate golf attire and nonmetal spikes are required.

COURSE DESCRIPTION: This rolling course is lined with mature oaks. Water comes into play on five holes, and the back nine is hilly. The most memorable hole is the par -4 12th. It requires a difficult carry over water on the second shot. Appropriately, there is an old "hanging" tree behind the green. Three of the course's par 5s are reachable in two by good players.

NOTES: Lake Wildwood member Kirk Lyford claims the course record of 62.

LOCATION: From Marysville drive 30 miles east on Highway 20 to Pleasant Valley Road. Turn left and drive one mile to the four-way stop. Turn right onto Cottontail Way.

. . . ● **TOURNAMENTS:** This course is not available for outside events.

1. LAKE WILDWOOD COUNTRY CLUB

PLAY POLICY & FEES: Outside play is accepted. Members only until noon on Monday, Tuesday, Thursday, and Friday, and 2 p.m. on Wednesday. Green fees are $12 for nine holes and $18 for 18 holes. Green fees for juniors under 17 are $6 for nine holes and $9 for 18 holes. Carts are $12 for nine holes and $18 for 18 holes seven days a week.

TEE TIMES: Reservations are not accepted. All play is on a first-come, first-served basis.

DRESS CODE: No tank tops are allowed on the course. Nonmetal spikes are encouraged.

COURSE DESCRIPTION: This course is relatively wide open except for the fifth and sixth holes. The greens are small and tricky, invariably breaking toward the nearby (but unseen) hospital. The par-5 eighth is the toughest, a 416-yard hole with a tiny green.

NOTES: Some of the older members caddied here in the 1920s, and many of them were miners in the nearby gold country.

LOCATION: From Highway 49 in Grass Valley take the Idaho Maryland exit. At the end of the ramp, turn left and drive to East Main Street. Turn right and drive to the course on the left.

. . . ● **TOURNAMENTS:** This course is available for outside tournaments.

2. NEVADA COUNTY COUNTRY CLUB

ALTA SIERRA GOLF & COUNTRY CLUB
ARCHITECT: BOB BALDOCK, 1965

11897 Tammy Way
Grass Valley, CA 95949

PRO SHOP: 530-273-2010
CLUBHOUSE: 530-273-2041

Jeff Chleboun, Director of Golf, PGA
Sean O'Brien, Superintendent

Driving Range ●
Practice Greens ●
Clubhouse ●
Food / Beverage ●
Accommodations
Pull Carts ●
Power Carts ●
Club Rental ●
$pecial Offers

	1	2	3	4	5	6	7	8	9	OUT
BACK	497	444	184	344	365	503	180	389	402	3308
REGULAR	487	426	176	330	355	498	172	379	394	3217
par	5	4	3	4	4	5	3	4	4	36
handicap	3	1	15	13	11	9	17	5	7	-
FORWARD	446	371	170	322	326	482	170	369	369	3025
par	5	4	3	4	4	5	3	4	4	36
handicap	3	1	15	11	13	5	17	9	7	-

	10	11	12	13	14	15	16	17	18	IN
BACK	384	365	142	351	515	204	367	393	508	3229
REGULAR	375	355	137	341	505	195	356	370	493	3127
par	4	4	3	4	5	3	4	4	5	36
handicap	2	16	18	12	8	14	6	10	4	-
FORWARD	363	325	135	324	483	164	336	352	477	2959
par	4	4	3	4	5	3	4	4	5	36
handicap	2	16	18	12	6	14	8	10	4	-

BACK	
yardage	6537
par	72
rating	71.2
slope	128

REGULAR	
yardage	6344
par	72
rating	70.3
slope	126

FORWARD	
yardage	5984
par	72
rating	75.6
slope	126

 LAKE OF THE PINES COUNTRY CLUB

11665 Lakeshore North
Auburn, CA 95602

PRO SHOP: 530-269-1544
CLUBHOUSE: 530-269-1133

Chris Beachley, Professional/Manager
Ed Vicano, Manager

Driving Range ●
Practice Greens ●
Clubhouse ●
Food / Beverage ●
Accommodations
Pull Carts
Power Carts ●
Club Rental
$pecial Offers

	1	2	3	4	5	6	7	8	9	OUT
BACK	-	-	-	-	-	-	-	-	-	-
REGULAR	-	-	-	-	-	-	-	-	-	-
par	-	-	-	-	-	-	-	-	-	-
handicap	-	-	-	-	-	-	-	-	-	-
FORWARD	-	-	-	-	-	-	-	-	-	-
par	-	-	-	-	-	-	-	--		
handicap	-	-	-	-	-	-	-	-	-	-

	10	11	12	13	14	15	16	17	18	IN
BACK	-	-	-	-	-	-	-	-	-	-
REGULAR	-	-	-	-	-	-	-	-	-	-
par	-	-	-	-	-	-	-	-	-	-
handicap	-	-	-	-	-	-	-	-	-	-
FORWARD	-	-	-	-	-	-	-	-	-	-
par	-	-	-	-	-	-	-	-		
handicap	-	-	-	-	-	-	-	-	-	-

BACK	
yardage	6150
par	71
rating	69.3
slope	119

REGULAR	
yardage	5843
par	71
rating	68.2
slope	117

FORWARD	
yardage	5598
par	71
rating	71.5
slope	129

PLAY POLICY & FEES: Outside play is accepted after 2 p.m. Green fees are $45 for 18 holes Monday through Thursday and $50 Friday through Sunday. Nine-hole rates are available. Carts are $20 for 18 holes and $12 for nine holes.

TEE TIMES: Reservations can be made seven days before the first of each month for the entire month

DRESS CODE: Collared shirts and nonmetal spikes are required. Shorts must be Bermuda length.

COURSE DESCRIPTION: This hilly, scenic course has a links-style layout with big greens. There are no parallel fairways. Deer and other wildlife are plentiful. The 18th hole is a challenging par 5 that doglegs right with water on the right and a hazard that interferes with the second shot. Alta Sierra is a well-conditioned course that is particularly challenging for women because there is little difference in yardage from the forward tees on several tough holes.

NOTES: A new 21,000 square foot clubhouse was completed in 1999. Bryan Pemberton's 61 is the course record.

LOCATION: From Highway 49 between Grass Valley and Auburn, take the Alta Sierra Drive East exit two miles to the course on Tammy Way.

. . . ● **TOURNAMENTS:** A 20-player minimum is required for tournaments. Carts are required. Events should be scheduled 12 months in advance. ● **TRAVEL:** For information on the Alta Sierra Village Inn call 530-273-9102.

3. ALTA SIERRA GOLF & COUNTRY CLUB

PLAY POLICY & FEES: Reciprocal play is accepted with members of other private clubs; otherwise, members and guests only. Reciprocal fees are $37. Guest fees are $27 weekends and $37 weekends.

DRESS CODE: Appropriate golf attire is required. Nonmetal spikes are encouraged.

COURSE DESCRIPTION: This hilly course is about 25 years old. It's narrow with lots of out-of-bounds. Water comes into play on seven holes. The eighth hole can be a headache. At 505 yards, it's a tough par 5 with hazards everywhere. Your drive must clear a creek; then the fairway doglegs to the left, and there are out-of-bounds stakes on both sides. The green is small but holds well.

LOCATION: In Auburn drive north on Highway 49 to Combie Road East. Turn right and drive to Lakeshore North. Turn right and drive to the course.

. . . ● **TOURNAMENTS:** A 40-player minimum is needed to book an event. Carts are mandatory.

4. LAKE OF THE PINES COUNTRY CLUB

⑤ DARKHORSE GOLF CLUB
ARCHITECT: KEITH FOSTER, 1999

13450 Combie Road
Auburn, CA 95602-8917

PRO SHOP: 530-269-7900

Russell Sylte, Director of Golf, PGA

Driving Range ●
Practice Greens ●
Clubhouse ●
Food / Beverage ●
Accommodations
Pull Carts
Power Carts ●
Club Rental ●
Special Offers

	1	2	3	4	5	6	7	8	9	OUT
BACK										
REGULAR										
par										
handicap										
FORWARD										
par										
handicap										

BACK	
yardage	
par	
rating	
slope	

	10	11	12	13	14	15	16	17	18	IN
BACK										
REGULAR										
par										
handicap										
FORWARD										
par										
handicap										

REGULAR	
yardage	
par	
rating	
slope	

FORWARD	
yardage	
par	
rating	
slope	

⑥ WINCHESTER COUNTRY CLUB
ARCHITECT: ROBERT TRENT JONES, SR. & JR., 1999

P.O. Box 125
Auburn, CA 95604

PRO SHOP: 530-878-6500

David Hall, Director of Golf, PGA
Bob Marshall, Superintendent

Driving Range ●
Practice Greens ●
Clubhouse ●
Food / Beverage ●
Accommodations
Pull Carts
Power Carts ●
Club Rental ●
Special Offers

	1	2	3	4	5	6	7	8	9	OUT
BACK										
REGULAR										
par										
handicap										
FORWARD										
par										
handicap										

BACK	
yardage	7040
par	72
rating	
slope	

	10	11	12	13	14	15	16	17	18	IN
BACK										
REGULAR										
par										
handicap										
FORWARD										
par										
handicap										

REGULAR	
yardage	5955
par	72
rating	
slope	

FORWARD	
yardage	5265
par	72
rating	
slope	

PLAY POLICY & FEES: The course is due to open in the summer of 2000. Green fees are expected to range from $35 to $50. Cart fees are projected at $15.

COURSE DESCRIPTION: The course was not available for review.

NOTES: The practice facility and teaching center will feature a three-hole course, 1,500-square-foot classroom, two short-game practice greens, a practice bunker, and a place to practice uneven lie shots. The course will also be home to the Darkhorse Golf Academy.

LOCATION: From Highway 49 in Auburn head north. Take a right on Combie Road heading east. The golf course will be on the left.

. . . ● **TOURNAMENTS:** Events will be allowed.

5. DARKHORSE GOLF CLUB

PLAY POLICY & FEES: Play is restricted to members and their guests; limited reciprocal play is accepted.

DRESS CODE: Appropriate golf attire is required.

COURSE DESCRIPTION: Winchester Country Club was not available for play at time of press. The course is set to open in fall of 1999. Set in the foothills, the course will offer views of both the Sierra Nevada and the Sacramento Valley.

NOTES: The course is one of only three collaborations between Robert Trent Jones, Sr. and Jr.

LOCATION: The course is located five miles east of Auburn. From Interstate 80 take the Meadow Vista exit; go north one mile. Turn west on Sugar Pine Road to the course.

. . . ● **TOURNAMENTS:** This course is not available for outside events.

6. WINCHESTER COUNTRY CLUB

7 AUBURN VALLEY COUNTRY CLUB
ARCHITECT: BOB BISSETT, 1959

8800 Auburn Valley Road
Auburn, CA 95602

PRO SHOP: 530-269-1837
CLUBHOUSE: 530--269-2775

Larry Johnson, General Manager
Craig Ballard, Head Professional, PGA
Rene John, Banquet Manager

Driving Range •
Practice Greens •
Clubhouse •
Food / Beverage •
Accommodations
Pull Carts •
Power Carts •
Club Rental •
$pecial Offers

	1	2	3	4	5	6	7	8	9	OUT
BACK	423	320	507	377	576	143	408	218	357	3329
REGULAR	415	292	483	367	569	134	397	184	326	3167
par	4	4	5	4	5	3	4	3	4	36
handicap	1	15	9	3	7	17	5	13	11	-
FORWARD	412	265	422	356	548	111	386	119	312	2931
par	5	4	5	4	5	3	4	3	4	37
handicap	9	13	5	3	1	17	7	15	11	-

	10	11	12	13	14	15	16	17	18	IN
BACK	425	433	190	507	397	435	221	376	508	3492
REGULAR	410	424	163	500	364	409	187	367	495	3319
par	4	4	3	5	4	4	3	4	5	36
handicap	8	4	10	18	14	2	12	6	16	-
FORWARD	383	317	142	414	297	393	128	295	475	2844
par	4	4	3	5	4	4	3	4	5	36
handicap	6	14	16	10	12	4	18	8	2	-

BACK	
yardage	6821
par	72
rating	72.6
slope	129

REGULAR	
yardage	6486
par	72
rating	71.0
slope	125

FORWARD	
yardage	5775
par	73
rating	73.3
slope	127

8 BLACK OAK GOLF COURSE
ARCHITECT: JOHN WALKER, 1984

2455 Black Oak Road
Auburn, CA 95602

PRO SHOP: 530-878-1900
CLUBHOUSE: 530-878-8261

Norman Morrice, Manager
Brent Perkins, PGA Professional
Matt Dillon, Superintendent

Driving Range •
Practice Greens •
Clubhouse •
Food / Beverage •
Accommodations
Pull Carts •
Power Carts •
Club Rental •
$pecial Offers

	1	2	3	4	5	6	7	8	9	OUT
BACK	348	376	530	134	336	530	202	297	360	3113
REGULAR	330	355	503	117	318	514	186	277	345	2945
par	4	4	5	3	4	5	3	4	4	36
handicap	15	1	7	17	11	9	15	13	3	-
FORWARD	314	309	450	109	285	468	141	259	285	2620
par	4	4	5	3	4	5	3	4	4	36
handicap	15	1	7	17	11	9	5	13	3	-

	10	11	12	13	14	15	16	17	18	IN
BACK	348	376	530	134	336	530	202	297	360	3113
REGULAR	330	355	503	117	318	514	186	277	345	2945
par	4	4	5	3	4	5	3	4	4	36
handicap	16	2	8	18	12	10	16	14	4	-
FORWARD	314	309	450	109	285	468	141	259	285	2620
par	4	4	5	3	4	5	3	4	4	36
handicap	16	2	8	18	12	10	6	14	4	-

BACK	
yardage	6226
par	72
rating	70.1
slope	130

REGULAR	
yardage	5890
par	72
rating	68.8
slope	121

FORWARD	
yardage	5240
par	72
rating	70.0
slope	119

PLAY POLICY & FEES: Reciprocal play is accepted with members of other private clubs. Guest and reciprocal fees are $60 weekdays and $70 weekends. Carts are included. The course is closed on Monday.

TEE TIMES: Guests can make reservations seven days in advance.

DRESS CODE: Collared shirts and nonmetal spikes are required. No denim is allowed on the course.

COURSE DESCRIPTION: This is a long, hilly, and challenging course with fast greens and 11 lakes that come into play. It is a beautiful course, set in the foothills, with numerous elevated tees that afford excellent views. The fairways are generally narrow and the greens fast. Auburn Valley has one of the most difficult starting holes around, measuring 415 yards onto an elevated green. This course is one of Northern California's hidden jewels.

NOTES: In 2000 Auburn Valley will host the women's Trans-International, an event that features the best female amateurs from around the world.

LOCATION: From Auburn drive eight miles north on Highway 49. Take the Lone Star Road exit west to Auburn Valley Road.

. . . ● **TOURNAMENTS:** The course is available six Fridays each year, with a minimum fee of $10,000. Tournaments should be booked three to nine months in advance. A banquet facility is available and can accommodate 200 people. ●

TRAVEL: The Auburn Inn is about 20 minutes from the golf course. For reservations call 530-885-1800.

7. AUBURN VALLEY COUNTRY CLUB

PLAY POLICY & FEES: Green fees are $11 for nine holes and $17 for 18 holes weekdays, and $12 for nine holes and $20 for 18 holes weekends. Senior and junior rates are $8 for nine holes and $15 for 18 holes weekdays. Carts are $10 per nine holes.

TEE TIMES: Reservations can be booked seven days in advance.

DRESS CODE: Nonmetal spikes are encouraged.

COURSE DESCRIPTION: This challenging, nine-hole course is one of the toughest of its kind in Northern California. It has an up-and-down, wide-open terrain with mature oaks, water, and sand. The greens are fast and undulating. Every hole is a killer, but a standout is the par-4, 376-yard second. It plays uphill and is longer than it looks. The green is guarded by a bunker on the right, and everything slopes to the left. You can three- or four-putt this hole easily if you're careless.

NOTES: New cart paths have been installed.

LOCATION: From Interstate 80 take the Dry Creek Road exit west and drive two miles. Turn right on Black Oak Road and follow it to the course.

. . . ● **TOURNAMENTS:** A 64-player minimum is required for shotgun tournaments. Tournaments should be booked six months in advance. ● **TRAVEL:** The Auburn Inn is located about 10 minutes from the golf course. For reservations call 530-885-1800.

8. BLACK OAK GOLF COURSE

9 COURSE AT RASPBERRY HILL
ARCHITECTS: FRED STRONG, 1982; RANDALL DAWSON, 1996

14500 Musso Road
Auburn, CA 95603

PRO SHOP: 530-878-7818

Brandy Jones, Manager
Jon Turbosky, Professional
Kelly McLaughlin, Superintendent

Driving Range ●
Practice Greens ●
Clubhouse ●
Food / Beverage ●
Accommodations
Pull Carts ●
Power Carts
Club Rental ●
$Special Offers

	1	2	3	4	5	6	7	8	9	OUT
BACK	-	-	-	-	-	-	-	-	-	-
REGULAR	279	201	187	178	128	83	125	269	83	1533
par	4	3	3	3	3	3	3	4	3	29
handicap	3	9	5	7	11	15	13	1	17	-
FORWARD	279	201	187	178	128	83	125	269	83	1533
par	4	3	3	3	3	3	3	4	3	29
handicap	3	9	5	7	11	15	13	1	17	-

BACK	
yardage	-
par	-
rating	-
slope	-

	10	11	12	13	14	15	16	17	18	IN
BACK	-	-	-	-	-	-	-	-	-	-
REGULAR	279	201	187	178	128	83	125	269	83	1533
par	4	3	3	3	3	3	3	4	3	29
handicap	4	10	6	8	12	16	14	2	18	-
FORWARD	279	201	187	178	128	83	125	269	83	1533
par	4	3	3	3	3	3	3	4	3	29
handicap	4	10	6	8	12	16	14	2	18	-

REGULAR	
yardage	3066
par	58
rating	56.6
slope	89

FORWARD	
yardage	3066
par	58
rating	56.3
slope	84

10 THE RIDGE GOLF COURSE
ARCHITECT: ROBERT TRENT JONES, JR., 1998

2020 Golf Course Road
Auburn, CA 95602

PRO SHOP: 530-888-7888

Greg French, Head Professional, PGA
Fred Bateta, General Manager
Steve Fackler, Superintendent

Driving Range ●
Practice Greens ●
Clubhouse
Food / Beverage ●
Accommodations
Pull Carts
Power Carts ●
Club Rental
$Special Offers

	1	2	3	4	5	6	7	8	9	OUT
BACK	433	578	183	408	208	344	360	356	562	3432
REGULAR	404	551	163	383	173	328	344	333	541	3220
par	4	5	3	4	3	4	4	4	5	36
handicap										-
FORWARD	343	455	116	290	101	264	243	237	479	2528
par	4	5	3	4	3	4	4	4	5	36
handicap										-

BACK	
yardage	6734
par	71
rating	
slope	

REGULAR	
yardage	6345
par	71
rating	
slope	

	10	11	12	13	14	15	16	17	18	IN
BACK	405	517	195	416	182	549	433	178	427	3302
REGULAR	382	511	177	409	175	540	392	152	387	3125
par	4	5	3	4	3	5	4	3	4	35
handicap										-
FORWARD	317	425	124	314	114	443	303	103	283	2426
par	4	5	3	4	3	5	4	3	4	35
handicap										-

FORWARD	
yardage	4954
par	71
rating	
slope	

PLAY POLICY & FEES: Green fees are $8 weekdays and $9.50 weekends for nine holes. Eighteen-hole rates are $14 weekdays and $17.50 weekends. Twilight rates are available.

TEE TIMES: Reservations can be booked seven days in advance.

DRESS CODE: Shirts and shoes are necessary.

COURSE DESCRIPTION: This short course has several water hazards and is tougher than it looks. The Course at Raspberry Hill has small greens that require accurate approaches. There is a moderate amount of water. The toughest hole is the second, a par 3 with a new tee box location, that demands a long iron or wood downhill to a small target.

NOTES: The men's course record is 25 (nine holes), set by Andy Arvay. The women's record is 27 (nine holes), set by Susan Parnell.

LOCATION: From Interstate 80 east in Auburn take the Belle Road exit. Take a right on Belle and a left onto Musso Road. The course can be seen from Musso Road.

. . . ● **TOURNAMENTS:** This course is available for outside tournaments. A 20-player minimum is needed to book an event. Tournaments should be scheduled two months in advance. A banquet facility is available that can accommodate 350 people. ● **TRAVEL:** The Holiday Inn is located five minutes from the golf course. For reservations call 530-887-8787.

9. COURSE AT RASPBERRY HILL

PLAY POLICY & FEES: Green fees are $40 weekdays and $54 weekends. Twilight, junior, and local senior rates are available.

TEE TIMES: Tee times can be made seven days in advance.

DRESS CODE: Proper golf attire and nonmetal spikes are mandatory.

COURSE DESCRIPTION: With natural rock outcroppings, rambling creeks, and plenty of mature oaks, Robert Trent Jones Jr. has created a new course with a mature feel. The 13th hole is a long par 4 that requires an uphill drive to an elevated and visually deceptive green.

NOTES: A clubhouse is under construction and due to be completed late fall of 1999.

LOCATION: From Sacramento take Interstate 80 east to the Bell Road exit in Auburn. Head north on Bell Road for 1.8 miles. Make a right on Airport Road and then turn right on Golf Course Road.

. . . ● **TOURNAMENTS:** A 16-player minimum will be required for tournament play. ● **TRAVEL:** The course is a 40-minute drive from the Sacramento airport.

10. THE RIDGE GOLF COURSE

⑪ AUBURN LAKE TRAILS GOLF COURSE

P.O. Box 728
Cool, CA 95614

1400 American River Trail
Cool, CA 95614

Driving Range
Practice Greens •
Clubhouse •

PRO SHOP: 530-885-2919

Ken Herr, Manager/Superintendent

Food / Beverage
Accommodations
Pull Carts •
Power Carts
Club Rental
$pecial Offers

	1	2	3	4	5	6	7	8	9	OUT
BACK	-	-	-	-	-	-	-	-	-	-
REGULAR	266	111	153	133	70	139	80	104	296	1352
par	4	3	3	3	3	3	3	3	4	29
handicap	5	13	1	7	15	11	17	9	3	-
FORWARD	266	111	153	133	70	139	80	104	296	1352
par	4	3	3	3	3	3	3	3	4	29
handicap	5	13	1	7	15	11	17	9	3	-

	10	11	12	13	14	15	16	17	18	IN
BACK	-	-	-	-	-	-	-	-	-	-
REGULAR	286	99	134	168	131	108	92	104	271	1393
par	4	3	3	3	3	3	3	3	4	29
handicap	4	18	10	2	8	14	16	12	6	-
FORWARD	286	99	134	168	131	108	92	104	271	1393
par	4	3	3	3	3	3	3	3	4	29
handicap	4	18	10	2	8	14	16	12	6	-

BACK	
yardage	-
par	-
rating	-
slope	-

REGULAR	
yardage	2745
par	58
rating	54.8
slope	77

FORWARD	
yardage	2745
par	58
rating	55.5
slope	80

⑫ EL DORADO HILLS GOLF CLUB

ARCHITECT: ROBERT TRENT JONES SR., 1963

3775 El Dorado Hills
El Dorado Hills, CA 95762

Driving Range •
Practice Greens •
Clubhouse •

PRO SHOP: 916-933-6552

Jay Pott, PGA Professional
Dallas Davis, Tournament Director
Griffin Cheek, Superintendent

Food / Beverage •
Accommodations
Pull Carts •
Power Carts •
Club Rental •
$pecial Offers

	1	2	3	4	5	6	7	8	9	OUT
BACK	303	461	195	189	117	198	155	192	290	2100
REGULAR	294	461	185	174	117	198	155	185	290	2059
par	4	5	3	3	3	3	3	3	4	31
handicap	17	11	1	3	13	5	9	7	15	-
FORWARD	289	395	180	156	117	185	155	135	290	1902
par	4	5	3	3	3	3	3	3	4	31
handicap	3	1	9	7	17	11	13	15	5	-

	10	11	12	13	14	15	16	17	18	IN
BACK	178	311	121	300	185	192	202	142	281	1912
REGULAR	168	311	98	278	175	183	188	132	268	1801
par	3	4	3	4	3	3	3	3	4	30
handicap	6	16	14	8	2	12	4	10	18	-
FORWARD	144	293	98	268	161	119	173	116	256	1628
par	3	4	3	4	3	3	3	3	4	30
handicap	12	4	18	2	10	14	6	16	8	-

BACK	
yardage	4012
par	61
rating	61.8
slope	103

REGULAR	
yardage	3860
par	61
rating	61.1
slope	102

FORWARD	
yardage	3530
par	61
rating	59.2
slope	91

PLAY POLICY & FEES: Members and guests only. Guest fees are $10 weekdays and $15 weekends when authorized by a property owner.

DRESS CODE: Appropriate golf attire is required.

COURSE DESCRIPTION: This is an executive-type course that is maintained for and by the local property owners. The course is short and hilly with lots of out-of-bounds. There are two par 4s, one of which, the ninth, is the most compelling hole. It measures 296 yards with a slight bend to the right around oak trees, with the green guarded on the left and right by a lake.

LOCATION: From Auburn drive six miles south on Highway 49. Turn left onto Highway 193 and drive three-fourths of a mile to the course.

. . . ● **TOURNAMENTS:** All outside events must be approved by the manager. No weekend shotgun tournaments are allowed.

11. AUBURN LAKE TRAILS GOLF COURSE

PLAY POLICY & FEES: Green fees are $17 weekdays and $22 weekends. Nine-hole rates are $11 weekdays and $14 weekends. Carts are $18 weekdays and $20 weekends.

TEE TIMES: Reservations can be booked 14 days in advance for weekdays and seven days in advance for weekends.

DRESS CODE: Golf attire is encouraged.

COURSE DESCRIPTION: Although primarily a test for irons, this course does have five par 4s and one par 5. The front nine is hilly. The course is well maintained and has lots of trees and water. The par-3 14th (185 yards) is one of the Sacramento area's finest, a challenging shot onto a green fronted by a bunker with water on the left.

LOCATION: From Sacramento drive 25 miles east on U.S.50. Take the El Dorado Hills Boulevard exit north and drive to the course, which is on the right.

. . . ● **TOURNAMENTS:** This course is available for outside tournaments.

12. EL DORADO HILLS GOLF CLUB

13 GREEN VALLEY OAKS
ARCHITECT: GENE THORNE, 1996

3000 Alexandrite Drive
Rescue, CA 95672

PRO SHOP: 530-677-4653

Bob Mack, Owner
Jacob Angel, Head Professional, PGA

- Driving Range •
- Practice Greens •
- Clubhouse •
- Food / Beverage •
- Accommodations
- Pull Carts •
- Power Carts •
- Club Rental •
- $pecial Offers

	1	2	3	4	5	6	7	8	9	OUT
BACK										
REGULAR										
par										
handicap										
FORWARD										
par										
handicap										

	10	11	12	13	14	15	16	17	18	IN
BACK										
REGULAR										
par										
handicap										
FORWARD										
par										
handicap										

BACK	
yardage	
par	
rating	
slope	

REGULAR	
yardage	5950
par	70
rating	69.2
slope	127

FORWARD	
yardage	5687
par	69
rating	68.0
slope	122

14 CAMERON PARK COUNTRY CLUB
ARCHITECT: BERT STAMPS, 1963

3201 Royal Drive
Cameron Park, CA 95682

PRO SHOP: 530-672-7900

Scotty Moran, Manager
Steve Frye, PGA Professional
Amby Mrozek, Superintendent

- Driving Range •
- Practice Greens •
- Clubhouse •
- Food / Beverage •
- Accommodations
- Pull Carts •
- Power Carts •
- Club Rental •
- $pecial Offers

	1	2	3	4	5	6	7	8	9	OUT
BACK	327	518	169	523	430	380	140	399	347	3233
REGULAR	318	504	152	516	417	366	139	385	338	3135
par	4	5	3	5	4	4	3	4	4	36
handicap	15	9	13	7	1	3	17	5	11	-
FORWARD	280	497	132	506	416	291	133	328	328	2911
par	4	5	3	5	5	4	3	4	4	37
handicap	9	1	15	3	13	11	17	7	5	-

	10	11	12	13	14	15	16	17	18	IN
BACK	443	327	123	377	402	533	376	215	488	3284
REGULAR	433	320	117	365	396	513	347	204	473	3168
par	4	4	3	4	4	5	4	3	4	35
handicap	2	16	18	8	4	12	14	6	10	-
FORWARD	391	296	106	350	390	497	341	151	462	2984
par	4	4	3	4	4	5	4	3	5	36
handicap	2	14	18	8	4	12	10	16	6	-

BACK	
yardage	6517
par	71
rating	71.0
slope	128

REGULAR	
yardage	6303
par	71
rating	70.2
slope	126

FORWARD	
yardage	5895
par	73
rating	74.0
slope	134

PLAY POLICY & FEES: Green fees Monday through Thursday are $10 for nine holes and $16 for 18 holes. On Friday, Saturday, Sunday, and holidays, green fees are $12 for nine holes and $19 for 18 holes. Carts are $10 for nine holes and $15 for 18 holes. Junior, senior, and twilight rates are available.

TEE TIMES: Reservations can be booked seven days in advance.

DRESS CODE: No tank tops are allowed on the course. Golf shoes are highly recommended.

COURSE DESCRIPTION: This well-maintained course has plenty of pine and oak trees and an eight-acre pond. One of the more unusual holes has you teeing off from an elevated deck over the water. Those less daring can hit from the tees in front of the pond.

NOTES: Nine additional holes are due to be completed in fall of 1999.

LOCATION: From U.S. 50 near Cameron Park take the Bass Lake Road exit. Head north on Bass Lake Road for three miles to the golf course.

. . . ● **TOURNAMENTS:** This course is available for outside tournaments. A 12-player minimum is needed to book a tournament.

13. GREEN VALLEY OAKS

PLAY POLICY & FEES: Reciprocal play is accepted with members of other private clubs. Green fees for reciprocal players are $60. Guest fees are $40 Tuesday through Thursday and $45 Friday through Sunday. Carts are $20.

TEE TIMES: Reservations can be booked seven days in advance. You must have your club professional call to book a time.

DRESS CODE: Appropriate golf attire is required. No denim is allowed.

COURSE DESCRIPTION: Cameron Park would be a tough course due to its tightness alone, but the real trick to scoring well is in mastering the greens. They are fast—so fast that some putts simply won't stop short of the hole. Holes of particular note are the 14th and 17th. The 17th is a par 3 of 204 yards over water, and the 14th is a par 4 measuring 389 yards with out-of-bounds to the right.

NOTES: Lance Nielsen holds the course record at 63.

LOCATION: From Sacramento drive 30 miles east on U.S. 50. Take the Cameron Park Drive exit. Turn left and drive under the overpass. Make the first left (don't get back on the freeway) onto Country Club Drive. Drive one-half mile to just past the driving range. Make the first right past the driving range (Royal Drive) and drive to the course entrance.

. . . ● **TOURNAMENTS:** Outside events must be approved by the tournament committee.

14. CAMERON PARK COUNTRY CLUB

15 SERRANO COUNTRY CLUB
ARCHITECT: ROBERT TRENT JONES JR., 1996

5005 Serrano Parkway
El Dorado Hills, CA 95762

PRO SHOP: 916-933-5716

Bruce Kaiser, Director of Golf, PGA
Tim Sedgley, Superintendent

Driving Range ●
Practice Greens ●
Clubhouse ●
Food / Beverage ●
Accommodations
Pull Carts
Power Carts ●
Club Rental
$pecial Offers

	1	2	3	4	5	6	7	8	9	OUT
BACK	406	416	441	158	427	577	153	510	409	3497
REGULAR	379	375	417	140	405	549	140	469	385	3259
par	4	4	4	3	4	5	3	5	4	36
handicap	15	5	1	13	7	9	11	17	3	-
FORWARD	324	292	344	109	334	453	85	403	320	2664
par	4	4	4	3	4	5	3	5	4	36
handicap	15	1	5	13	11	7	17	9	3	-

	10	11	12	13	14	15	16	17	18	IN
BACK	369	183	408	505	537	230	597	175	455	3459
REGULAR	352	171	383	496	515	202	563	149	435	3266
par	4	3	4	5	5	3	5	3	4	36
handicap	16	14	2	10	12	6	8	18	4	-
FORWARD	282	84	290	407	443	121	501	98	342	2568
par	4	3	4	5	5	3	5	3	4	36
handicap	16	14	8	12	6	10	2	18	4	-

BACK	
yardage	6956
par	72
rating	73.0
slope	132

REGULAR	
yardage	6525
par	72
rating	71.3
slope	128

FORWARD	
yardage	5232
par	72
rating	69.7
slope	121

16 COLD SPRINGS GOLF & COUNTRY CLUB
ARCHITECT: BERT STAMPS, 1960/1981

6500 Clubhouse Drive
Placerville, CA 95667

PRO SHOP: 530-622-4567
OFFICE: 530-622-7642

Randy Thomas, PGA Professional
Robert Leas, Superintendent

Driving Range ●
Practice Greens ●
Clubhouse ●
Food / Beverage ●
Accommodations
Pull Carts ●
Power Carts ●
Club Rental ●
$pecial Offers

	1	2	3	4	5	6	7	8	9	OUT
BACK	307	257	271	402	307	461	207	158	549	2919
REGULAR	288	237	271	358	307	458	180	138	489	2726
par	4	4	4	4	4	5	3	3	5	36
handicap	8	18	14	2	10	12	6	16	4	-
FORWARD	276	237	269	362	302	452	182	127	495	2702
par	4	4	4	4	4	5	3	3	5	36
handicap	9	15	11	5	7	3	13	17	1	-

	10	11	12	13	14	15	16	17	18	IN
BACK	375	369	158	413	553	333	436	186	413	3236
REGULAR	365	362	155	349	473	329	416	110	353	2912
par	4	4	3	4	5	4	5	3	4	36
handicap	5	11	15	1	7	9	17	13	3	-
FORWARD	351	359	147	349	459	323	428	124	355	2895
par	4	4	3	4	5	4	5	3	4	36
handicap	6	10	16	14	2	4	12	18	8	-

BACK	
yardage	6155
par	72
rating	70.0
slope	120

REGULAR	
yardage	5638
par	72
rating	67.9
slope	115

FORWARD	
yardage	5597
par	72
rating	73.0
slope	128

PLAY POLICY & FEES: Reciprocal play is accepted with members of other private clubs on a limited basis. The reciprocal fee is $125, including cart. The guest fees are $60 Tuesday through Thursday and $80 Friday through Sunday. Guests may play unaccompanied by a member. The course is closed on Monday.

TEE TIMES: Have your club pro call in advance to arrange tee times.

DRESS CODE: Appropriate golf attire and nonmetal spikes are required. No cellular phones are allowed on the course.

COURSE DESCRIPTION: This sprawling course is packed with mature oak trees that come into play on ten holes. The rolling terrain is mostly forgiving, and the majority of greens are open in front. Water comes into play on six holes, and wind is often a factor. Set in the Sierra foothills, this course offers spectacular views of Folsom Lake and the snowcapped Sierras to the east.

NOTES: Serrano plays host to the Raley's Gold Rush Classic, a Senior PGA Tour event. The course is patterned after Shinnecock Hills Golf Club in New York.

LOCATION: From downtown Sacramento drive 25 miles east on U.S. 50. Take El Dorado Hills Boulevard exit. Drive one-quarter mile north on El Dorado Hills Boulevard to Serrano Parkway and turn right. Drive east to the course.

. . . ● **TOURNAMENTS:** Outside events are allowed on an extremely limited basis. Shotgun tournaments are available Monday only. Carts are required. ●

TRAVEL: The Lake Notoma Inn in Folsom and the Sheraton in Rancho Cordova are recommended for lodging.

15. SERRANO COUNTRY CLUB

PLAY POLICY & FEES: Reciprocal play is accepted with members of other private clubs; otherwise, members and guests only. The green fees for reciprocal players are $40. Guest fees are $25 weekdays and $30 weekends. Carts are $10 for nine holes and $20 for 18 holes.

DRESS CODE: Collared shirts and nonmetal spikes are required. Shorts must have a four-inch inseam.

COURSE DESCRIPTION: Weber Creek winds through this course, which is very tight with a preponderance of short, dogleg par 4s. Cold Springs is moderately hilly and has plenty of oaks and pines. The fourth hole (par 4, 402 yards) is a handful. It doglegs right with out-of-bounds right and hard pan left for those driving through the fairway. There is a huge oak on the right side of the green, which slopes severely.

NOTES: The course record is 64 for men, set by Jim Sorum. Karen Beckman's 77 is the women's record.

LOCATION: From U.S. 50 in Placerville take the Placerville Drive/Forni Road exit. Drive over the overpass to the second stop sign. Turn left on Cold Springs Road. Drive three miles and turn left on Richard Avenue, which turns into Clubhouse Drive.

. . . ● **TOURNAMENTS:** This course is available for outside events on Monday and approved alternate days. The banquet facility can accommodate at least 200 people.

16. COLD SPRINGS GOLF & COUNTRY CLUB

APPLE MOUNTAIN GOLF RESORT

ARCHITECT: ALGIE PULLEY, 1997

3455 Carson Rd.
Camino, CA 95709

3455 Carson Rd.
Camino, CA 95709

PRO SHOP: 530-647-7400
CLUBHOUSE: 530-647-7400

Benny Campos, PGA Professional
P.J. Spellman, Superintendent
Dan Ward, Tournament Director

Driving Range ●
Practice Greens ●
Clubhouse ●
Food / Beverage ●
Accommodations
Pull Carts
Power Carts ●
Club Rental ●
$pecial Offers

	1	2	3	4	5	6	7	8	9	OUT
BACK	456	375	418	203	402	129	546	169	496	3194
REGULAR	443	332	361	154	330	104	473	131	433	2761
par	5	4	4	3	4	3	5	3	5	36
handicap	13	11	3	9	7	15	5	17	1	-
FORWARD	382	273	303	115	247	72	373	85	362	2212
par	5	4	4	3	4	3	5	3	5	36
handicap	13	11	3	9	7	15	5	17	1	-

	10	11	12	13	14	15	16	17	18	IN
BACK	400	154	381	170	571	449	200	356	552	3233
REGULAR	373	128	330	138	531	413	169	310	510	2902
par	4	3	4	3	5	4	3	4	5	35
handicap	8	18	10	14	2	4	6	16	12	-
FORWARD	331	78	278	109	428	359	135	299	423	2440
par	4	3	4	3	5	4	3	4	5	35
handicap	8	18	10	14	2	4	6	16	12	-

BACK	
yardage	6427
par	71
rating	70.6
slope	127

REGULAR	
yardage	5663
par	71
rating	67.8
slope	116

FORWARD	
yardage	4652
par	71
rating	67.4
slope	117

SIERRA GOLF COURSE

1822 Country Club Drive
Placerville, CA 95667

PRO SHOP: 530-622-0760

Dean Peterson, Professional

Driving Range
Practice Greens ●
Clubhouse ●
Food / Beverage ●
Accommodations
Pull Carts ●
Power Carts
Club Rental
$pecial Offers

	1	2	3	4	5	6	7	8	9	OUT
BACK	-	-	-	-	-	-	-	-	-	-
REGULAR	148	115	248	176	120	213	242	176	236	1674
par	3	3	4	3	3	4	4	3	4	31
handicap	5	13	11	3	7	15	17	1	9	-
FORWARD	130	105	232	157	114	207	204	166	213	1528
par	3	3	4	3	3	4	4	3	4	31
handicap	5	13	15	3	9	11	17	1	7	-

	10	11	12	13	14	15	16	17	18	IN
BACK	-	-	-	-	-	-	-	-	-	-
REGULAR	148	115	248	176	120	213	242	176	236	1674
par	3	3	4	3	3	4	4	3	4	31
handicap	6	14	12	4	8	16	18	2	10	-
FORWARD	130	105	232	157	114	207	204	166	213	1528
par	3	3	4	3	3	4	4	3	4	31
handicap	6	14	16	4	10	12	18	2	8	-

BACK	
yardage	-
par	-
rating	-
slope	-

REGULAR	
yardage	3348
par	62
rating	55.4
slope	82

FORWARD	
yardage	3056
par	62
rating	58.1
slope	92

PLAY POLICY & FEES: Green fees are $40 weekdays and $50 weekends. Green fees include cart and unlimited range balls.

TEE TIMES: Reservations can be booked 10 days in advance. Advance reservations can be made by calling Tee Time Central: 888-236-8725.

DRESS CODE: Collared shirts are required. No sweat pants or blue or denim jeans are allowed on the course. Shorts must be worn no more than three inches above the knee.

COURSE DESCRIPTION: This new course is characterized by uneven lies, numerous grass hollows, and plenty of trees. The par-4, uphill, dogleg-right fifth hole, and the 603-yard, double-dogleg 14th are two of the most challenging holes in the area. The 18th hole provides breathtaking views of the Sierra Nevada.

NOTES: An elevation of 2,500 feet above sea level allows escape from the extreme valley heat during the summer and yet sits below the Sierra snow line.

LOCATION: From Sacramento take U.S. 50 east toward South Lake Tahoe. Five miles east of Placerville take the Carson Road exit. At the intersection turn right and proceed one-quarter mile to the entrance.

. . . ● **TOURNAMENTS:** A 16-player minimum is needed to book a tournament. Tournaments can be booked up to two years in advance. A banquet facility that can accommodate 200 people will be available in fall 1999. Call for tournament information. ● **TRAVEL:** Powell Bros. Steamer in Placerville is recommended for dinner. The Best Western Placerville Inn is 15 minutes from Gold Creek. For reservations call 530-622-9100.

17. APPLE MOUNTAIN GOLF RESORT

PLAY POLICY & FEES: Green fees are $8 for nine holes and $10 for 18 holes weekdays, and $9 for nine holes and $12 for 18 holes weekends. Junior and twilight rates are available.

TEE TIMES: Reservations are not accepted. All play is on a first-come, first-served basis.

DRESS CODE: Shirts and shoes are required.

COURSE DESCRIPTION: This short course is flat, with sloping greens. Oak, pine, and cedar trees line the fairways, but there is no water. The eighth hole features a challenging green.

LOCATION: From U.S. 50 in Placerville take the Main Street exit. Take Cedar Ravine to Country Club Drive and the course. Watch for the airport sign and you'll find the course.

. . . ● **TOURNAMENTS:** This course is available for outside tournaments.

18. SIERRA GOLF COURSE

RANCHO MURIETA COUNTRY CLUB
ARCHITECTS: TED ROBINSON, 1980 (N); BERT STAMPS, 1971

7000 Alameda Drive
Rancho Murieta, CA 95683

PRO SHOP: 916-354-2400

Zoe Girelli, Manager
Paul Fakundiny, Head Professional, PGA
Mark Murphy, Tournament Director

Driving Range ●
Practice Greens ●
Clubhouse ●
Food / Beverage ●
Accommodations ●
Pull Carts
Power Carts ●
Club Rental ●
$Special Offers

	1	2	3	4	5	6	7	8	9	OUT
BACK	395	395	553	182	385	514	190	402	423	3439
REGULAR	375	350	523	157	360	494	156	362	387	3164
par	4	4	5	3	4	5	3	4	4	36
handicap	7	9	13	17	5	11	15	1	3	-
FORWARD	334	310	445	119	329	434	126	325	325	2747
par	4	4	5	3	4	5	3	4	4	36
handicap	5	7	3	17	13	1	15	9	11	-

	10	11	12	13	14	15	16	17	18	IN
BACK	201	400	543	404	538	175	386	392	416	3455
REGULAR	166	356	513	364	490	150	361	367	376	3143
par	3	4	5	4	5	3	4	4	4	36
handicap	10	2	12	8	16	18	14	4	6	-
FORWARD	140	314	438	312	454	122	325	355	320	2780
par	3	4	5	4	5	3	4	4	4	36
handicap	16	8	2	14	6	18	10	4	12	-

BACK	
yardage	6894
par	72
rating	72.6
slope	127

REGULAR	
yardage	6307
par	72
rating	70.0
slope	121

FORWARD	
yardage	5527
par	72
rating	71.6
slope	122

 # MACE MEADOW GOLF & COUNTRY CLUB
ARCHITECT: JACK FLEMING, 1972

26570 Fairway Drive
Pioneer, CA 95666

PRO SHOP: 209-295-7020

Driving Range ●
Practice Greens ●
Clubhouse ●
Food / Beverage ●
Accommodations
Pull Carts ●
Power Carts ●
Club Rental ●
$Special Offers

	1	2	3	4	5	6	7	8	9	OUT
BACK	508	155	342	184	316	483	334	390	368	3080
REGULAR	491	130	330	158	304	471	327	367	360	2938
par	5	3	4	3	4	5	4	4	4	36
handicap	3	15	9	17	11	1	5	7	13	-
FORWARD	425	90	280	142	267	421	316	353	352	2646
par	5	3	4	3	4	5	4	4	4	36
handicap	4	18	12	16	14	2	10	6	8	-

	10	11	12	13	14	15	16	17	18	IN
BACK	357	379	176	361	490	404	332	181	525	3205
REGULAR	336	370	165	350	473	382	323	172	501	3072
par	4	4	3	4	5	4	4	3	5	36
handicap	14	6	18	8	4	2	12	16	10	-
FORWARD	294	331	143	321	401	317	307	160	467	2741
par	4	4	3	4	5	4	4	3	5	36
handicap	13	7	17	5	3	11	9	15	1	-

BACK	
yardage	6285
par	72
rating	70.0
slope	125

REGULAR	
yardage	6010
par	72
rating	68.7
slope	122

FORWARD	
yardage	5387
par	72
rating	70.0
slope	114

19. RANCHO MURIETA COUNTRY CLUB

PLAY POLICY & FEES: Reciprocal play is accepted with members of other private clubs. Guest fees are $35 weekday and $45 weekends; guests must be accompanied by a member. Reciprocal fees are $50 to $70. The course is closed on Monday.

TEE TIMES: Reciprocal guests should have their golf pro call three days in advance.

DRESS CODE: Appropriate golf attire and nonmetal spikes are required.

COURSE DESCRIPTION: The North Course is generally considered to be the Sacramento area's top layout. It features out-of-bounds areas on virtually every hole and gigantic, undulating greens. The 4th, 10th, and 18th holes are outstanding par 4s. The 3rd and 15th holes are rugged par 5s. On the South Course, water comes into play on 10 of 18 holes, and scoring is almost as difficult as on the North Course.

NOTES: The North Course was home to the Senior PGA Tour's Raley's Senior Gold Rush. The North Course is 6,839 yards and rated 72.8 with a slope rating of 131 from the championship tees. See scorecard for South Course information.

LOCATION: From Sacramento drive east on U.S. 50. Take the Bradshaw Road exit south. Turn left on Highway 16/Jackson Road to Rancho Murieta. The club entrance is on the left.

. . . ● **TOURNAMENTS:** A 120-player minimum is needed to book a shotgun tournament.

20. MACE MEADOW GOLF & COUNTRY CLUB

PLAY POLICY & FEES: Green fees are $19 weekdays and $29 weekends. Carts are $22. Twilight and junior rates are available.

TEE TIMES: Reservations can be booked 14 days in advance.

DRESS CODE: Appropriate golf attire is required.

COURSE DESCRIPTION: The most picturesque hole on this scenic course is the first, a par 5 with a red barn and a noisy rooster behind the green.

NOTES: Originally a nine-hole course designed by Jack Fleming, Mace Meadow was expanded into 18 holes in 1988 by the club membership. The old and new nines were mixed together.

LOCATION: The course is located 18 miles east of Jackson on Highway 88, and five miles east of Pioneer in Buckhorn. In Buckhorn, look for Meadow Drive and the parking lot. Fairway Drive is right there.

. . . ● **TOURNAMENTS:** This course is available for outside tournaments.

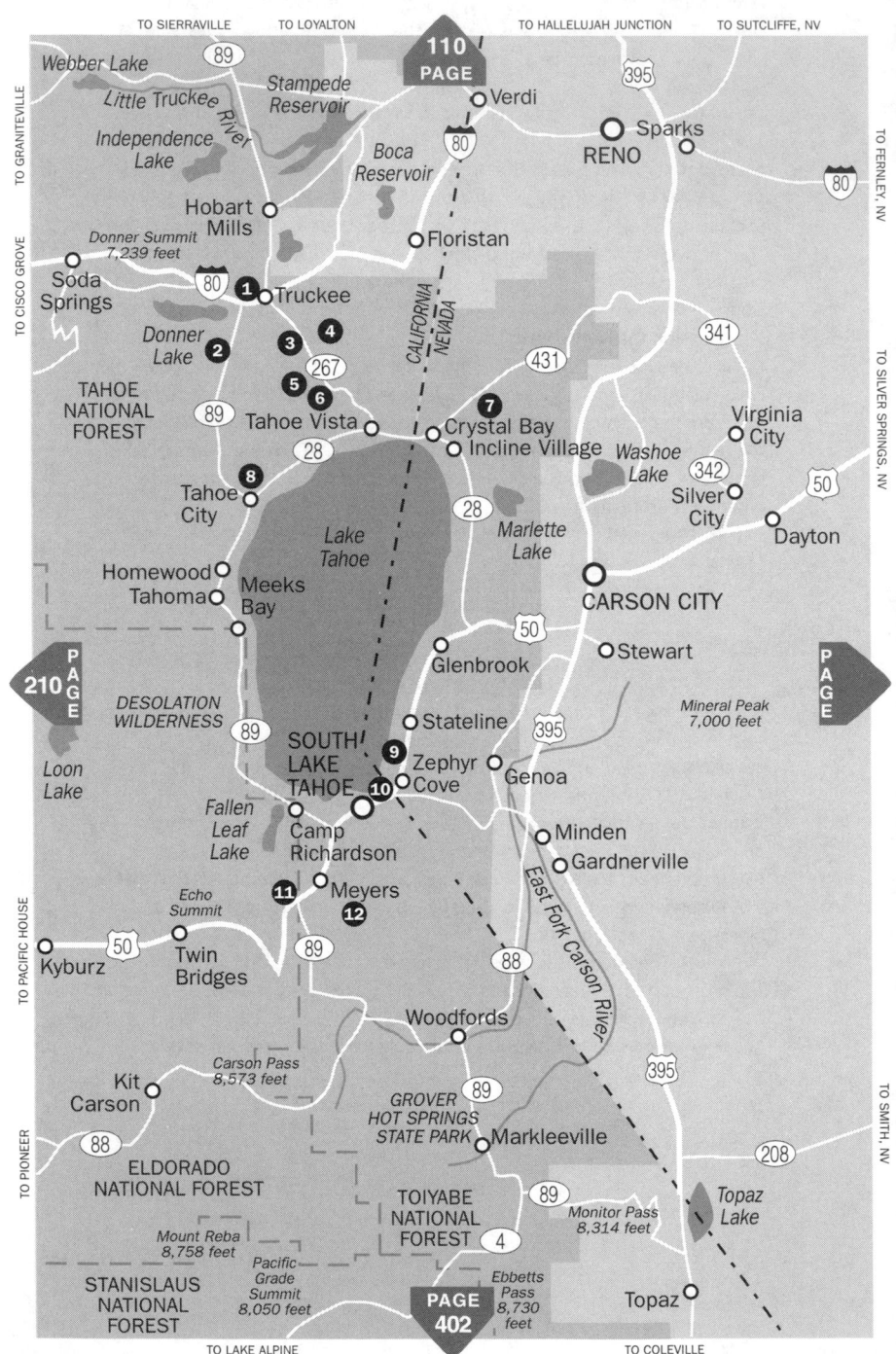

TO SIERRAVILLE   TO LOYALTON   TO HALLELUJAH JUNCTION   TO SUTCLIFFE, NV

89

110 PAGE

Webber Lake

Stampede Reservoir

395

Verdi

Sparks

TO GRANITEVILLE

Little Truckee River

Independence Lake

Boca Reservoir

80

RENO

80

TO FERNLEY, NV

Hobart Mills

Floristan

Donner Summit 7,239 feet

TO CISCO GROVE

Soda Springs

80 **1** Truckee

CALIFORNIA NEVADA

341

TO SILVER SPRINGS, NV

Donner Lake

4

2

3

267

431

Virginia City

TAHOE NATIONAL FOREST

5 **6**

7

342

Silver City

50

89

Tahoe Vista

Crystal Bay

Incline Village

Washoe Lake

28

Dayton

8

Tahoe City

28

Marlette Lake

Homewood

Lake Tahoe

CARSON CITY

Tahoma

Meeks Bay

50

PAGE 210

Glenbrook

Stewart

PAGE

DESOLATION WILDERNESS

89

SOUTH LAKE TAHOE

Stateline

Mineral Peak 7,000 feet

Loon Lake

9

Zephyr Cove

395

10

Genoa

Fallen Leaf Lake

Camp Richardson

Minden

Gardnerville

Echo Summit

11 Meyers

12

East Fork Carson River

TO PACIFIC HOUSE

50

Kyburz

Twin Bridges

89

88

Woodfords

395

Carson Pass 8,573 feet

Kit Carson

GROVER HOT SPRINGS STATE PARK

89

TO PIONEER

88

ELDORADO NATIONAL FOREST

Markleeville

208

TO SMITH, NV

TOIYABE NATIONAL FOREST

89

Monitor Pass 8,314 feet

Topaz Lake

Mount Reba 8,758 feet

Pacific Grade Summit 8,050 feet

4

STANISLAUS NATIONAL FOREST

Ebbetts Pass 8,730 feet

PAGE 402

Topaz

TO LAKE ALPINE   TO COLEVILLE

Tahoe Area

① TAHOE DONNER GOLF & COUNTRY CLUB
ARCHITECT: JOSEPH B. WILLIAMS, 1976

11509 Northwoods
Truckee, CA 96161

PRO SHOP: 530-587-9440

Bruce Towle, Head Professional, PGA
Bob Broyer, General Manager
Joel Blaker, Superintendent

Driving Range ●
Practice Greens ●
Clubhouse ●
Food / Beverage ●
Accommodations
Pull Carts ●
Power Carts ●
Club Rental ●
$pecial Offers

	1	2	3	4	5	6	7	8	9	OUT
BACK	450	513	439	201	377	357	163	464	550	3514
REGULAR	432	483	430	192	369	349	146	439	532	3372
par	4	5	4	3	4	4	3	4	5	36
handicap	1	9	5	11	17	13	15	3	7	-
FORWARD	422	471	359	147	308	340	132	429	453	3061
par	5	5	4	3	4	4	3	5	5	38
handicap	3	1	5	13	11	7	17	15	9	-

	10	11	12	13	14	15	16	17	18	IN
BACK	424	449	200	320	391	519	453	226	421	3403
REGULAR	394	441	152	310	369	503	442	203	401	3215
par	4	5	3	4	4	5	4	3	4	36
handicap	4	6	12	18	14	8	2	16	10	-
FORWARD	349	430	130	301	352	491	356	182	380	2971
par	4	5	3	4	4	5	4	3	4	36
handicap	4	10	16	12	8	6	14	18	2	-

BACK	
yardage	6917
par	72
rating	72.4
slope	133

REGULAR	
yardage	6587
par	72
rating	71.2
slope	128

FORWARD	
yardage	6032
par	74
rating	73.1
slope	138

② RESORT AT SQUAW CREEK
ARCHITECT: ROBERT TRENT JONES JR., 1991

P.O. Box 3333   400 Squaw Creek Road
Olympic Valley, CA 96146 Olympic Valley, CA 96146

PRO SHOP: 530-581-6637
OFFICE: 530-583-6300

Chris Lynch, Head Professional, PGA
Mike Carlson, Superintendent, CGCS

Driving Range ●
Practice Greens ●
Clubhouse ●
Food / Beverage ●
Accommodations ●
Pull Carts
Power Carts ●
Club Rental ●
$pecial Offers ●

	1	2	3	4	5	6	7	8	9	OUT
BACK	406	430	242	554	386	210	365	338	514	3445
REGULAR	368	404	205	525	371	176	343	318	488	3198
par	4	4	3	5	4	3	4	4	5	36
handicap	11	15	17	9	13	5	7	1	3	-
FORWARD	305	344	150	467	281	124	286	243	436	2636
par	4	4	3	5	4	3	4	4	5	36
handicap	11	15	17	9	13	5	7	1	3	-

	10	11	12	13	14	15	16	17	18	IN
BACK	385	402	445	513	221	403	204	429	484	3486
REGULAR	365	387	412	496	202	378	184	407	424	3255
par	4	4	4	5	3	4	3	4	4	35
handicap	10	14	6	12	18	8	16	2	4	-
FORWARD	300	213	346	441	126	273	124	312	326	2461
par	4	4	4	5	3	4	3	4	4	35
handicap	10	14	6	12	18	8	16	2	4	-

BACK	
yardage	6931
par	71
rating	72.9
slope	140

REGULAR	
yardage	6453
par	71
rating	70.9
slope	132

FORWARD	
yardage	5097
par	71
rating	68.9
slope	127

PLAY POLICY & FEES: Outside play is accepted. Green fees are $100 every day, including cart. A $43 twilight rate is available.

TEE TIMES: Reservations can be made 10 days in advance on weekdays. For weekend play, reservations can be made the Friday before the weekend you want to play. For twilight play, reservations can be made up to 30 days in advance. Restrictions apply.

DRESS CODE: Collared shirts and golf shoes are required. Shorts must be mid-thigh length.

COURSE DESCRIPTION: A golfer must search high and low to find a tighter golf course than Tahoe Donner. Pines line both sides of all 18 fairways, none of which runs parallel to another. There are no out-of-bounds, and the course is walkable despite its 6,600-foot altitude. The 18th hole (401 yards from the regular tees, 380 for women) features a vertical drop of 180 feet.

NOTES: Members joke about having to walk single file down the fairways of this spectacular, but extremely tight, course.

LOCATION: From Interstate 80 east take the first Truckee exit (Donner Pass Road). Turn left on Donner Pass Road and drive to the blinking red light. Turn left on Northwoods Boulevard. The course is located three miles from Interstate 80.

. . . ● **TOURNAMENTS:** This course is available for outside tournaments; restrictions apply in July and August. Call for details. A 13-player minimum is needed to book a tournament. Events should be booked 12 months in advance. The banquet facility can hold 120 people.

1. TAHOE DONNER GOLF & COUNTRY CLUB

PLAY POLICY & FEES. Green fees are $115 weekdays and weekends. Carts are included; however, walking is permitted. Squaw Creek is generally open from May 15 through October 28, depending on the weather.

TEE TIMES: Reservations can be made for the season beginning May 1.

DRESS CODE: Collared shirts are required. No blue jeans are allowed on the course.

COURSE DESCRIPTION: This is a challenging target golf course with four sets of tee boxes to accommodate most skill levels. The mountain layout meanders through pine trees and parallels the granite peaks of the famed Sqaw Valley Ski area before making a transition into a scenic meadowland. The par-4 17th requires a long drive over wetlands, followed by an equally difficult second shot to a green bordered by Squaw Creek.

NOTES: In the winter, Squaw Creek doubles as a first-class ski resort.

LOCATION: Take Highway 89 from Truckee south toward Squaw Valley. Turn right on Squaw Valley Road, then left on Squaw Creek Road.

. . . ● **TOURNAMENTS:** This course is available for outside tournaments. Carts are required. The banquet facility can accommodate up to 600 people. Events can be booked 12 months in advance. ● **TRAVEL:** This first-class resort has rooms ranging in price from $250 to $1800 a night. For reservations call 800-327-3353. ● **SPECIAL OFFERS:** Several play-and-stay packages are available.

2. RESORT AT SQUAW CREEK

LAHONTAN GOLF CLUB
ARCHITECT: TOM WEISKOPF, 1998

12000 Lodgetrail Road
Truckee, CA 96161

PRO SHOP: 530-550-2424

Sean Farren, PGA Professional
Mark Johnson, General Manager
Mike Kosak, Superintendent

Driving Range ●
Practice Greens ●
Clubhouse ●
Food / Beverage ●
Accommodations
Pull Carts
Power Carts ●
Club Rental ●
Special Offers

	1	2	3	4	5	6	7	8	9	OUT
BACK	423	627	182	386	210	482	563	427	328	3628
REGULAR	398	590	154	358	190	435	543	393	302	3363
par	4	5	3	4	3	4	5	4	4	36
handicap	9	3	17	11	15	1	5	7	13	-
FORWARD	303	498	101	248	122	333	447	314	259	2625
par	4	5	3	4	3	4	5	4	4	36
handicap	9	3	17	11	15	1	5	7	13	-

	10	11	12	13	14	15	16	17	18	IN
BACK	428	198	594	388	449	239	158	621	511	3586
REGULAR	386	184	591	379	403	213	147	603	484	3390
par	4	3	5	4	3	3	5	5	5	36
handicap	8	16	4	10	6	14	18	2	12	-
FORWARD	4	3	5	4	4	3	3	5	5	36
par	227	146	468	241	300	164	118	473	396	2533
handicap	4	3	5	4	4	3	3	5	5	-

BACK	
yardage	7214
par	72
rating	-
slope	-

REGULAR	
yardage	6753
par	72
rating	-
slope	-

FORWARD	
yardage	2661
par	2569
rating	-
slope	-

PONDEROSA GOLF COURSE
ARCHITECT: BOB BALDOCK, 1961

P.O. Box 729
Truckee, CA 96160

PRO SHOP: 530-587-3501

Al Bailey, Manager
Brad Gorsuch, Superintendent

Highway 267 and Reynold
Truckee, CA 96160

Driving Range
Practice Greens ●
Clubhouse ●
Food / Beverage ●
Accommodations
Pull Carts ●
Power Carts ●
Club Rental ●
Special Offers

	1	2	3	4	5	6	7	8	9	OUT
BACK	389	300	145	360	354	174	436	353	511	3022
REGULAR	375	289	135	350	337	163	424	331	496	2900
par	4	4	3	4	4	3	4	4	5	35
handicap	5	13	17	3	11	9	7	15	1	-
FORWARD	309	266	118	327	313	134	347	281	461	2556
par	4	4	3	4	4	3	4	4	5	35
handicap	5	13	17	3	11	9	7	15	1	-

	10	11	12	13	14	15	16	17	18	IN
BACK	389	300	145	360	354	174	436	353	511	3022
REGULAR	375	289	135	350	337	163	424	331	496	2900
par	4	4	3	4	4	3	4	4	5	35
handicap	6	14	18	4	12	10	8	16	2	-
FORWARD	309	266	118	327	313	134	347	281	461	2556
par	4	4	3	4	4	3	4	4	5	35
handicap	5	13	17	3	11	9	7	15	1	-

BACK	
yardage	6044
par	70
rating	67.8
slope	113

REGULAR	
yardage	5800
par	70
rating	66.6
slope	111

FORWARD	
yardage	5112
par	70
rating	68.2
slope	108

PLAY POLICY & FEES: This course is for members and accompanied guests only. Caddies are available.

DRESS CODE: Appropriate golf attire and nonmetal spikes are required.

COURSE DESCRIPTION: This course takes full advantage of the natural surroundings, which include mature trees, constant elevation changes, water features, and mountain vistas.

NOTES: Tom Weiskopf considers Lahontan the best site in the U.S. he's ever worked with.

LOCATION: From Highway 267 in Truckee heading towards Northstar, take the Schaffer Mill exit. Turn right onto Schaffer Mill Road. The golf course will be on the left.

. . . ● **TOURNAMENTS:** Outside events are not available.

3. LAHONTAN GOLF CLUB

PLAY POLICY & FEES: Green fees are $40 for 18 holes weekdays and weekends. Nine-hole rates are $26. Carts are $16 for nine holes and $24 for 18 holes. The course is open from May to October.

TEE TIMES: Reservations can be booked 10 days in advance.

DRESS CODE: Shirts must be worn at all times on the course.

COURSE DESCRIPTION: The first three holes are heavily wooded, after which things open up a bit. The ninth hole, a par 5 covering 496 yards from the white tee box, doglegs right. Ponderosa is popular with golfers of all ages and abilities.

LOCATION: From Interstate 80 in Truckee take the Northshore Boulevard (Highway 267) exit south and drive to the course. The course is a 12-minute drive from Lake Tahoe.

. . . ● **TOURNAMENTS:** Shotgun tournaments are not allowed.

4. PONDEROSA GOLF COURSE

5 OLD BROCKWAY GOLF COURSE

ARCHITECT: JOHN DUNCAN DUNN, 1924

P.O. Box 1368
Kings Beach, CA 96143

7900 North Lake
Kings Beach, CA 96143

PRO SHOP: 530-546-9909

Lane Lewis, Owner
Garrett Good, PGA Professional
Dave Laurie, Superintendent

Driving Range ●
Practice Greens ●
Clubhouse ●
Food / Beverage ●
Accommodations
Pull Carts ●
Power Carts ●
Club Rental ●
$pecial Offers

	1	2	3	4	5	6	7	8	9	OUT
BACK	414	376	203	503	368	178	553	346	373	3314
REGULAR	388	360	180	439	302	145	528	325	360	3027
par	4	4	3	4	4	3	5	4	4	35
handicap	3	5	9	7	15	11	1	17	13	-
FORWARD	349	324	109	429	240	111	396	207	297	2462
par	4	4	3	5	4	3	5	4	4	36
handicap	3	5	17	13	7	15	1	9	11	-

	10	11	12	13	14	15	16	17	18	IN
BACK	414	376	203	503	368	178	553	346	373	3314
REGULAR	388	360	180	439	302	145	528	325	360	3027
par	4	4	3	4	4	3	5	4	4	35
handicap	4	6	10	8	16	12	2	18	14	-
FORWARD	349	324	109	429	240	111	396	207	297	2462
par	4	4	3	5	4	3	5	4	4	36
handicap	4	6	18	14	8	16	2	10	12	-

BACK	
yardage	6628
par	70
rating	-
slope	118

REGULAR	
yardage	6054
par	70
rating	-
slope	113

FORWARD	
yardage	4924
par	72
rating	-
slope	113

6 NORTHSTAR-AT-TAHOE GOLF COURSE

ARCHITECT: ROBERT MUIR GRAVES, 1975

P.O. Box 129
Truckee, CA 96160

168 Basque Drive
Truckee, CA 96161

PRO SHOP: 530-562-2490
OFFICE: 530-562-1010

Jim Anderson, PGA Professional
Tom Neadeau, Superintendent
Pete Chow, Assistant Superintendent

Driving Range ●
Practice Greens ●
Clubhouse ●
Food / Beverage ●
Accommodations ●
Pull Carts ●
Power Carts ●
Club Rental ●
$pecial Offers ●

	1	2	3	4	5	6	7	8	9	OUT
BACK	398	520	130	369	356	181	562	375	362	3253
REGULAR	383	486	128	350	345	161	520	359	346	3078
par	4	5	3	4	4	3	5	4	4	36
handicap	5	3	17	13	11	15	1	9	7	-
FORWARD	348	475	125	325	333	130	485	332	322	2875
par	4	5	3	4	4	3	5	4	4	36
handicap	5	3	17	13	11	15	1	9	7	-

	10	11	12	13	14	15	16	17	18	IN
BACK	380	330	314	162	489	180	376	359	552	3142
REGULAR	343	330	314	150	465	122	344	359	510	2937
par	4	4	4	3	5	3	4	4	5	36
handicap	8	14	16	10	2	18	12	6	4	-
FORWARD	312	305	286	135	445	78	321	307	406	2595
par	4	4	4	3	5	3	4	4	5	36
handicap	8	14	16	10	2	18	12	6	4	-

BACK	
yardage	6395
par	72
rating	70.5
slope	129

REGULAR	
yardage	6015
par	72
rating	69.0
slope	125

FORWARD	
yardage	5470
par	72
rating	71.2
slope	134

PLAY POLICY & FEES: Green fees are $35 for nine holes and $55 for 18 holes. Fees are $30 for nine holes and $50 for 18 holes after Labor Day. Carts are $16 for nine and $25 for 18 holes. Weather permitting, the course is open from about April 15 to November 15.

TEE TIMES: Reservations can be booked 30 days in advance.

COURSE DESCRIPTION: This scenic mountain course, flanked by trees, is tight with narrow fairways and small greens. The most notable hole is the seventh, a par 5 of 553 yards.

NOTES: Old Brockway has a new log-cabin style clubhouse.

LOCATION: This course is located on the north shore of Lake Tahoe where Highway 28 (North Lake Boulevard) and Highway 267 intersect.

. . . ● **TOURNAMENTS:** This course is available for outside tournaments.

5. OLD BROCKWAY GOLF COURSE

PLAY POLICY & FEES: Green fees are $75. For guests of the lodge, fees are $64. Afternoon, twilight, and nine-hole rates are available. All fees include carts. This course is open from May 1 to October 30.

TEE TIMES: Reservations can be booked 21 days in advance.

DRESS CODE: Golf attire is encouraged.

COURSE DESCRIPTION: The two nines contrast sharply. There are either wide-open tee shots or tight, tree-lined fairways. The front side is set in a meadow, while the back nine is set in a forest. Water comes into play on 14 holes. The 15th hole (par 3, 180 yards from the back tees) features a 120-foot drop to a postage-stamp green.

NOTES: Among the celebrities who have played this interesting course are Bill Murray and Bobby Riggs. Former U.S. Women's Open champ Susie Berning once lost eight balls on the back nine.

LOCATION: In Truckee drive six miles south on Highway 267. Exit at Northstar Drive. Turn right on Basque Drive and follow it to the clubhouse.

. . . ● **TOURNAMENTS:** This course is available for outside tournaments. ●

TRAVEL: For information about the Northstar Resort call 800-GO-NORTH. ●

$PECIAL OFFERS: Play-and-stay packages and weekend golf schools are available.

6. NORTHSTAR-AT-TAHOE GOLF COURSE

P.O. Box 7590
Incline Village, NV 89452

PRO SHOP: 775-832-1146
OFFICE: 775-832-1143

955 Fairway Blvd.
Incline Village, NV, CA
89451

John Hughes, Director of Golf, PGA
Brian Eilders, Head Professional, PGA
Kim Reuter, Tournament Director

Driving Range ●
Practice Greens ●
Clubhouse ●
Food / Beverage ●
Accommodations
Pull Carts
Power Carts ●
Club Rental ●
$pecial Offers

	1	2	3	4	5	6	7	8	9	OUT
BACK	400	487	419	622	223	423	401	169	406	3550
REGULAR	364	461	394	600	176	397	386	146	402	3326
par	4	5	4	5	3	4	4	3	4	36
handicap	9	15	5	1	13	7	11	17	3	-
FORWARD	312	355	291	505	124	325	356	105	269	2642
par	4	5	4	5	3	4	4	3	4	36
handicap	7	13	11	1	15	3	5	17	9	-

BACK		
yardage	6931
par	72
rating	72.2
slope	133

	10	11	12	13	14	15	16	17	18	IN
BACK	371	468	427	393	486	198	419	197	422	3381
REGULAR	352	456	395	380	449	179	365	182	363	3121
par	4	5	4	4	5	3	4	3	4	36
handicap	8	18	2	6	16	10	12	14	4	-
FORWARD	288	370	373	307	400	99	339	112	315	2603
par	4	4	5	4	5	3	4	3	4	36
handicap	10	8	2	12	4	14	6	18	16	-

REGULAR		
yardage	6447
par	72
rating	70.2
slope	129

FORWARD		
yardage	5245
par	72
rating	70.1
slope	131

PLAY POLICY & FEES: Green fees are $115. Twilight rates are available. Carts are included. The course is open from mid-May through mid-October depending on the weather.

TEE TIMES: Reservations can be booked up to 90 days in advance for a fee through Tee Time Central. Call 888-236-8725.

DRESS CODE: No tennis shorts, cutoffs, tank tops, or T-shirts are allowed. Collared shirts are required. Nonmetal spikes are preferred.

COURSE DESCRIPTION: The Championship Course is cut out of the Sierras and runs through pine tree–laden terrain to an elevation of 6,500 feet. A creek cuts through a number of holes. The 16th par 4 offers spectacular views of Lake Tahoe. Tightly cut fairways bordered by towering pines demand accuracy and distance. On approach shots golfers are faced with bunkered greens and water hazards on almost every hole. The executive-style Mountain Course has 18 holes that require target golf.

NOTES: "Golf Digest" gives the courses at Incline Village a four-star rating. The Championship Course: See scorecard for information. The executive-length Mountain Course: From the white tees the course is 3,513 yards long with a rating of 56.6 and a slope of 94. From the red tees the course is 3,002 yards long with a rating of 57.3 and a slope of 85. The course features fourteen par 3s that all average over 150 yards.

LOCATION: Located in Nevada just five miles across the California border, the course can be reached by following Highway 267 from Truckee to Lake Tahoe. Turn left onto Highway 28 and go six miles into Incline Village.

. . . ● **TOURNAMENTS:** A 20-player minimum is needed to book a tournament. Call 702-832-1172.

7. THE GOLF COURSES AT INCLINE VILLAGE

P.O. Box 5400
Stateline, NV 89449

180 Lake Parkway and
Stateline, NV, CA 89449

PRO SHOP: 775-588-3566
OFFICE: 775-588-3042

Paul Martin, PGA Professional
Steve Seibel, Superintendent
Donovan Calderon, Tournament Director

GOLF 50

Driving Range ●
Practice Greens ●
Clubhouse ●
Food / Beverage ●
Accommodations
Pull Carts
Power Carts ●
Club Rental ●
Special Offers ●

	1	2	3	4	5	6	7	8	9	OUT
BACK	436	417	599	612	231	442	169	458	461	3825
REGULAR	370	362	558	528	157	368	149	377	414	3283
par	4	4	5	5	3	4	3	4	4	36
handicap	15	9	1	7	11	5	17	13	3	-
FORWARD	343	322	469	413	101	352	112	315	399	2826
par	4	4	5	5	3	4	3	4	4	36
handicap	9	13	5	11	17	1	15	7	3	-

BACK	
yardage	7470
par	72
rating	75.7
slope	139

	10	11	12	13	14	15	16	17	18	IN
BACK	441	407	205	434	421	394	564	207	572	3645
REGULAR	383	328	167	387	388	341	533	140	489	3156
par	4	4	3	4	4	4	5	3	5	36
handicap	6	12	10	2	4	16	8	18	14	-
FORWARD	353	259	127	344	334	309	451	107	437	2721
par	4	4	3	4	4	4	5	3	5	36
handicap	4	14	12	2	8	16	6	18	10	-

REGULAR	
yardage	6439
par	72
rating	70.2
slope	127

FORWARD	
yardage	5547
par	72
rating	71.3
slope	136

PLAY POLICY & FEES: Green fees for reservations made up to 14 days in advance are $150. Green fees for reservations made 15-90 days in advance are $175. Carts are included. For reservations call 888-881-8659.

TEE TIMES: Tee times can be made two weeks in advance or 90 days in advance with an additional $25 per person nonrefundable booking fee.

DRESS CODE: Golf attire and nonmetal spikes are encouraged.

COURSE DESCRIPTION: Situated at 6,200 feet with breathtaking views of Lake Tahoe, this course requires accurate approach shots and an ability to putt fast, undulating greens. Some holes are wide open; others, such as the beautiful par-5 16th, require length and precision. The 17th and 18th holes border the lake. All of the par 3s—particularly the 12th, which measures 167 yards (white tees) over a pond to a narrow green—are outstanding.

NOTES: Tom Fazio has completed dramatic changes on holes one through three. The course is actually in Nevada, though the state line is a few yards from the eighth green. Edgewood, site of the 1985 U.S. Senior Open, has been rated among the nation's top 100 courses by "Golf Digest." The Isuzu Celebrity Golf Championship is played here.

LOCATION: From U.S. 50 in South Lake Tahoe, take the Lake Parkway Drive exit north and drive to the course located between the casinos and Lake Tahoe.

. . . ● **TOURNAMENTS:** No shotgun tournaments are allowed. A 20-player minimum is required to book a tournament. Events should be booked 12 months in advance. The banquet facility can accommodate 200 people. ● **TRAVEL:** Harvey's at Lake Tahoe is across the street from Edgewood. For reservations call 800-553-1022. Caesars (775-588-3515) and Harrahs (775-588-6611) are also recommended. ● **$PECIAL OFFERS:** Golf packages are available with America West Golf Vacations. For more information call 1-800-356-6611.

8. EDGEWOOD TAHOE GOLF COURSE

9 TAHOE CITY GOLF COURSE

ARCHITECT: MAY DUNN, 1917

P.O. Box 226
Tahoe City, CA 95730

251 North Lake Boulevard
Tahoe City, CA 95730

PRO SHOP: 530-583-1516

Bob Bonino, Manager
Mark Landry, Head Professional, PGA
Greg Virrey, Superintendent

- Driving Range •
- Practice Greens •
- Clubhouse •
- Food / Beverage •
- Accommodations
- Pull Carts •
- Power Carts •
- Club Rental •
- $pecial Offers

	1	2	3	4	5	6	7	8	9	OUT
BACK	-	-	-	-	-	-	-	-	-	-
REGULAR	485	201	419	151	294	170	360	318	172	2570
par	5	3	4	3	4	3	4	4	3	33
handicap	10	8	2	12	4	18	6	14	16	-
FORWARD	473	185	403	136	229	163	350	301	163	2403
par	5	3	5	3	4	3	4	4	3	34
handicap	2	14	4	18	6	16	8	10	12	-

	10	11	12	13	14	15	16	17	18	IN
BACK	-	-	-	-	-	-	-	-	-	-
REGULAR	491	212	425	160	316	177	375	344	191	2691
par	5	3	4	3	4	3	4	4	3	33
handicap	9	7	1	11	3	17	5	13	15	-
FORWARD	473	185	403	136	229	163	350	301	163	2403
par	5	3	5	3	4	3	4	4	3	34
handicap	1	13	3	17	5	15	7	9	11	-

BACK	
yardage	-
par	-
rating	-
slope	-

REGULAR	
yardage	5261
par	66
rating	64.3
slope	108

FORWARD	
yardage	4806
par	68
rating	65.7
slope	105

10 BIJOU MUNICIPAL GOLF COURSE

1180 Rufus Allen
South Lake Tahoe, CA
96150
PRO SHOP: 530-542-6097

Stan Bobman, Manager
Steve Weiss, Superintendent

- Driving Range
- Practice Greens •
- Clubhouse •
- Food / Beverage •
- Accommodations
- Pull Carts •
- Power Carts
- Club Rental •
- $pecial Offers

	1	2	3	4	5	6	7	8	9	OUT
BACK	-	-	-	-	-	-	-	-	-	-
REGULAR	310	143	264	143	237	347	211	202	207	2064
par	4	3	4	3	4	4	4	3	3	32
handicap	3	13	9	17	15	1	11	7	5	-
FORWARD	292	125	249	115	214	234	191	178	166	1764
par	4	3	4	3	4	4	4	3	3	32
handicap	3	15	5	17	11	1	13	9	7	-

	10	11	12	13	14	15	16	17	18	IN
BACK	-	-	-	-	-	-	-	-	-	-
REGULAR	310	143	264	143	237	347	211	202	207	2064
par	4	3	4	3	4	4	4	3	3	32
handicap	3	13	9	17	15	1	11	7	5	-
FORWARD	292	125	249	115	214	234	191	178	166	1764
par	4	3	4	3	4	4	4	3	3	32
handicap	3	15	5	17	11	1	13	9	7	-

BACK	
yardage	-
par	-
rating	-
slope	-

REGULAR	
yardage	4128
par	64
rating	-
slope	-

FORWARD	
yardage	3528
par	64
rating	-
slope	-

PLAY POLICY & FEES: Green fees are $30 for nine holes and $50 for 18 holes. Carts are $16 for nine holes and $24 for 18 holes. The course is open from April to November, depending on the weather.

TEE TIMES: Reservations can be booked 14 days in advance.

COURSE DESCRIPTION: This is the oldest course on Lake Tahoe. Offering great views of Lake Tahoe, Tahoe City Golf Course is lined with pine, fir, and cedar trees. The greens are well maintained, and the fairways are tight.

NOTES: This layout has the rare distinction of being designed by a woman. Among the luminaries who have played here are Bob Hope, Bing Crosby, and Frank Sinatra.

LOCATION: This course is located near the intersection of Highway 89 and Highway 28 in Tahoe City. At the junction, turn onto Highway 28 (North Lake Boulevard) and follow it to the course.

. . . ● **TOURNAMENTS:** An eight-player minimum is needed to book an event. The banquet facility can accommodate up to 100 people. ● **TRAVEL:** The Tahoe City Travel Lodge is located within walking distance of the golf course. For reservations call 530-583-3766.

9. TAHOE CITY GOLF COURSE

PLAY POLICY & FEES: The green fee is $12 for nine holes, and $20 for 18 holes. Resident, senior, and twilight rates are available.

TEE TIMES: Reservations are not accepted. All play is on a first-come, first-served basis.

DRESS CODE: Shirts and shoes are necessary.

COURSE DESCRIPTION: This scenic mountain course is set in a meadow and offers spectacular views. The course is mostly flat and walkable and is bordered by trees. No water comes into play. There are five par 4s and four par 3s. Be wary of the eighth and ninth holes.

LOCATION: From Sacramento take U.S. 50 through South Lake Tahoe. Turn right at the Johnson Boulevard Safeway. Turn left on Fairway and proceed to the course driveway.

. . . ● **TOURNAMENTS:** Shotgun tournaments are not allowed, and a 36-player minimum is need to book an event. Tournaments should be booked at least one month in adance.

10. BIJOU MUNICIPAL GOLF COURSE

ARCHITECT: WILLIAM F. BELL, 1960

2500 Emerald Bay Road
South Lake Tahoe, CA
96150
PRO SHOP: 530-577-0788

Ronda Gangelhoff, Director of Golf
Mike Durst, PGA Professional
John Stanowski, Superintendent

Driving Range ●
Practice Greens ●
Clubhouse ●
Food / Beverage ●
Accommodations
Pull Carts ●
Power Carts ●
Club Rental ●
$pecial Offers ●

	1	2	3	4	5	6	7	8	9	OUT
BACK	505	202	410	417	409	186	364	414	589	3496
REGULAR	495	158	362	377	362	154	338	384	515	3145
par	5	3	4	4	4	3	4	4	5	36
handicap	10	12	14	4	2	16	18	8	6	-
FORWARD	485	154	356	362	350	120	300	376	433	2936
par	5	3	4	4	4	3	4	4	5	36
handicap	1	17	9	5	11	15	13	7	3	-

BACK	
yardage	6707
par	71
rating	70.9
slope	120

	10	11	12	13	14	15	16	17	18	IN
BACK	427	208	393	447	379	280	357	160	560	3211
REGULAR	406	182	375	427	363	270	351	123	527	3024
par	4	3	4	4	4	4	4	3	5	35
handicap	3	13	5	1	7	17	11	15	9	-
FORWARD	285	143	355	415	353	269	341	101	489	2751
par	4	3	4	5	4	4	4	3	5	36
handicap	12	18	6	14	8	10	4	16	2	-

REGULAR	
yardage	6169
par	71
rating	68.8
slope	116

FORWARD	
yardage	5687
par	72
rating	70.1
slope	115

ARCHITECT: BRUCE BEEMAN, 1959

3021 Highway 50
Meyers, CA 96150

PRO SHOP: 530-577-2121
CLUBHOUSE: 530-577-2125

Dawn Beeman, Director of Golf
Dave Beeman, Professional/Manager
Colby Gunsch, Superintendent

Driving Range ●
Practice Greens ●
Clubhouse ●
Food / Beverage ●
Accommodations
Pull Carts ●
Power Carts ●
Club Rental ●
$pecial Offers

	1	2	3	4	5	6	7	8	9	OUT
BACK	-	-	-	-	-	-	-	-	-	-
REGULAR	237	209	95	195	110	234	241	268	338	1927
par	4	4	3	3	3	4	4	4	4	33
handicap	14	10	18	8	12	6	16	4	2	-
FORWARD	215	199	85	180	105	229	228	268	328	1837
par	4	4	3	4	3	4	4	4	5	35
handicap	12	5	18	16	9	8	15	4	1	-

BACK	
yardage	-
par	-
rating	-
slope	-

	10	11	12	13	14	15	16	17	18	IN
BACK	-	-	-	-	-	-	-	-	-	-
REGULAR	268	257	257	128	295	131	241	147	377	2101
par	4	4	4	3	4	4	4	3	4	33
handicap	13	9	3	7	5	15	17	11	1	-
FORWARD	258	231	247	128	260	100	203	147	357	1931
par	4	4	4	3	4	3	4	3	5	34
handicap	6	11	2	10	13	14	17	7	3	-

REGULAR	
yardage	4028
par	66
rating	59.9
slope	94

FORWARD	
yardage	3768
par	69
rating	61.7
slope	96

PLAY POLICY & FEES: Green fees are $44. Carts are $20 per player. Twilight rates are also available. Carts are required Friday through Sunday. The course is open from mid-April through October.

TEE TIMES: Reservations can be booked eight to 60 days in advance with a major credit card, plus a $7 per player nonrefundable fee. Reservations made within seven days require a credit card, but there is no reservation fee.

DRESS CODE: No tank tops or short shorts are allowed.

COURSE DESCRIPTION: The Truckee River runs through this scenic course, which also features five ponds. Water comes into play on 14 holes. The greens are smooth and true, particularly in late summer and early fall. The front nine is relatively wide open, though water comes into play on six holes. The back nine is the strength of the course, beginning with a tee shot against the mountain backdrop on the 10th. The 14th, 15th, 16th, and 17th holes are a wonderful series of tight, scenic holes alongside the river.

LOCATION: This course is located on U.S. 50 between South Lake Tahoe and Meyers.

. . . ● **TOURNAMENTS:** A 16-player minimum is required to book a tournament. Events can be scheduled up to one year in advance. The banquet facility can accommodate up to 200 people. ● **TRAVEL:** The Embassy Suites South Lake Tahoe is located 15 minutes from the course. ● **$PECIAL OFFERS:** Play-and-stay packages are available at the Embassy-Suites that include green fees, range balls, carts, accommodations, and breakfast.

11. LAKE TAHOE GOLF COURSE

PLAY POLICY & FEES: Green fees are $32 for 18 holes any day of the week. Twilight rates after 3 p.m. are $19. Carts are $28 for 18 holes and $18 for twilight play.

TEE TIMES: Reservations can be booked seven days in advance. Groups of twelve or more players can book tee times one month in advance with a deposit.

DRESS CODE: Nonmetal spikes are recommended.

COURSE DESCRIPTION: This valley course has hilly, rolling terrain with narrow, tree-lined fairways. The greens are small, and there are very few bunkers. The longest and the number-one handicap hole is the ninth—a par 4 for men, but a par 5 for women.

NOTES: This is a seasonal golf course.

LOCATION: This course is located in Meyers on U.S.50, three miles south of the Lake Tahoe Airport.

. . . ● **TOURNAMENTS:** Shotgun tournaments are available weekdays only. No shotgun tournaments are held in July or August.

12. TAHOE PARADISE GOLF COURSE

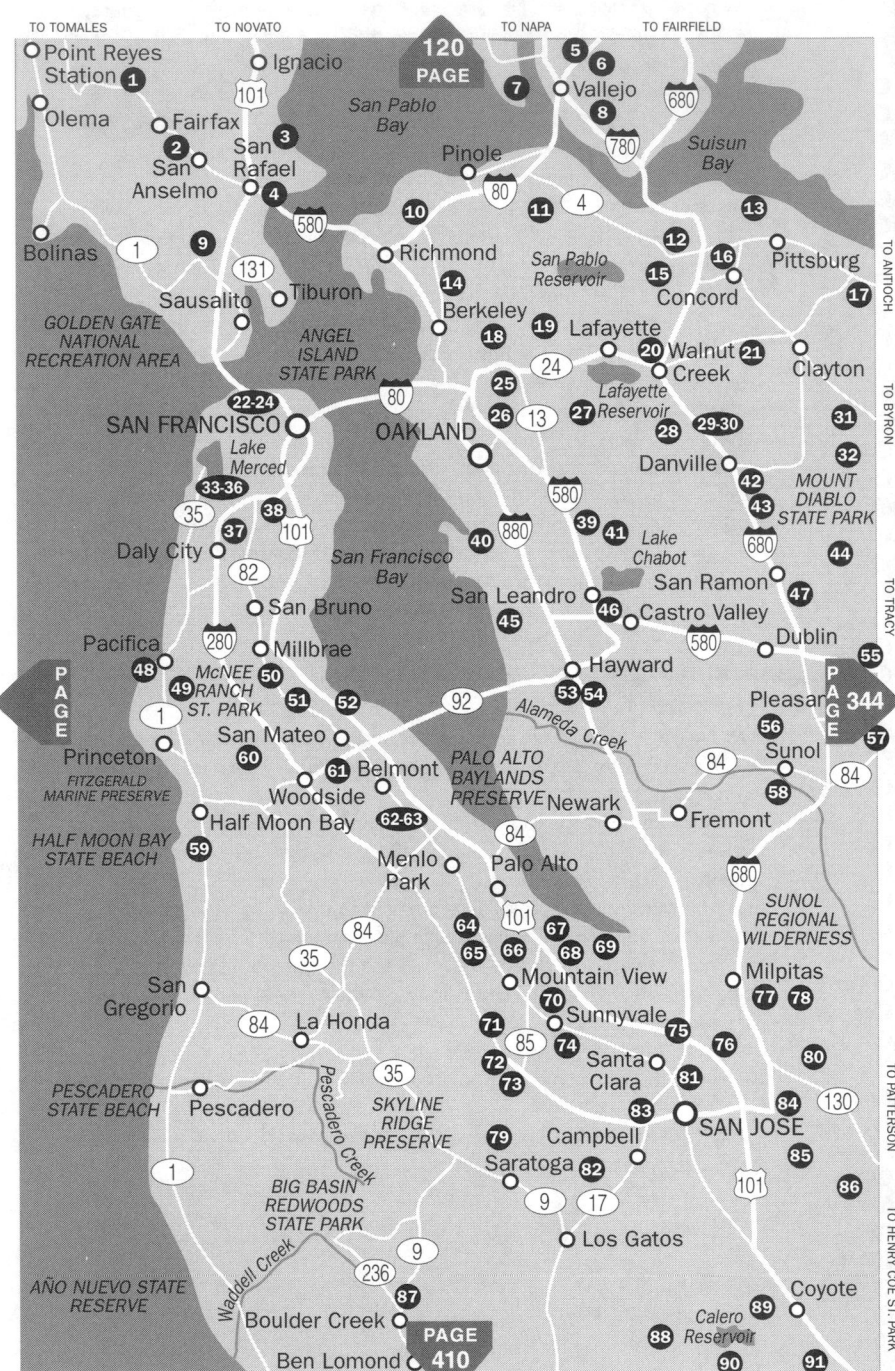

120
PAGE

TO TOMALES   TO NOVATO   TO NAPA   TO FAIRFIELD

Point Reyes Station **1**

Ignacio

San Pablo Bay

5 **6**

7

Vallejo

8

680

Olema

Fairfax

101

Pinole

Suisun Bay

2 San Anselmo

San Rafael **3**

780

4

580

10

80

11

4

13

Bolinas

1

9

131

Richmond

San Pablo Reservoir

12

15 **16**

Pittsburg

17

Sausalito

Tiburon

14

Berkeley

Concord

GOLDEN GATE NATIONAL RECREATION AREA

ANGEL ISLAND STATE PARK

18 **19** Lafayette

20 Walnut **21**
Creek

Clayton

SAN FRANCISCO

Lake Merced

80

OAKLAND

24

25

Lafayette Reservoir

22-24

26 **13** **27**

28 **29-30**

31

32

Danville

42

MOUNT DIABLO STATE PARK

33-36

43

680

44

35

37 **38**

101

580

39 **41**

Lake Chabot

San Ramon

47

40 880

Daly City

82

San Francisco Bay

San Leandro

46 Castro Valley

Dublin

580

55

San Bruno

45

Pacifica

280

Millbrae

Hayward

Pleasar

48

McNEE RANCH ST. PARK

50

53 **54**

344

PAGE

49

51 **52**

92

56

Sunol

57

1

Alameda Creek

84

Princeton

San Mateo

60

84

58

FITZGERALD MARINE PRESERVE

61 Belmont

PALO ALTO BAYLANDS PRESERVE

Newark

Woodside

62-63

Fremont

HALF MOON BAY STATE BEACH

Half Moon Bay

59

Menlo Park

84

Palo Alto

680

San Gregorio

84

64

101

67

SUNOL REGIONAL WILDERNESS

35

65 **66**

68 **69**

Milpitas

La Honda

Mountain View

77 **78**

84

70 Sunnyvale

PESCADERO STATE BEACH

35

71

85 **74**

75

76

80

Pescadero

72

Santa Clara

SKYLINE RIDGE PRESERVE

73

81

84

130

1

79 Campbell

83 SAN JOSE

BIG BASIN REDWOODS STATE PARK

Saratoga **82**

85

9 17

86

AÑO NUEVO STATE RESERVE

9

Los Gatos

Coyote

236

87

89

Boulder Creek

Calero Reservoir

88

Ben Lomond

PAGE
410

90 **91**

TO SANTA CRUZ

TO ANTIOCH

TO BYRON

TO TRACY

TO PATTERSON

TO HENRY COE ST. PARK

San Francisco Bay Area

SAN GERONIMO GOLF COURSE
ARCHITECT: ROBERT MUIR GRAVES, 1970

P.O. Box 130
San Geronimo, CA 94963

5800 Sir Francis Drake
San Geronimo, CA 94963

PRO SHOP: 415-488-4030

Tim Grove, Manager, PGA
Robert Francischine, Superintendent, GCSA

Driving Range
Practice Greens •
Clubhouse •
Food / Beverage •
Accommodations
Pull Carts •
Power Carts •
Club Rental •
$pecial Offers

	1	2	3	4	5	6	7	8	9	OUT
BACK	387	482	205	550	450	394	190	377	380	3415
REGULAR	357	464	172	500	388	325	155	306	314	2981
par	4	5	3	5	4	4	3	4	4	36
handicap	5	17	11	13	1	3	9	7	15	-
FORWARD	306	442	128	426	345	254	125	284	250	2560
par	4	5	3	5	5	4	3	4	4	37
handicap	9	3	15	1	5	11	17	7	13	-

BACK		
yardage	6801
par	72
rating	73.8
slope	135

REGULAR		
yardage	6003
par	72
rating	69.8
slope	126

	10	11	12	13	14	15	16	17	18	IN
BACK	516	421	415	150	397	227	358	496	406	3386
REGULAR	484	384	386	121	320	177	327	472	351	3022
par	5	4	4	3	4	3	4	5	4	36
handicap	14	2	8	18	4	10	12	16	6	-
FORWARD	406	351	344	106	228	158	290	424	273	2580
par	5	4	4	3	4	3	4	5	4	36
handicap	10	4	8	18	12	16	14	2	6	-

FORWARD		
yardage	5140
par	73
rating	69.9
slope	125

 MEADOW CLUB
ARCHITECT: ALISTER MACKENZIE, 1926

1001 Bolinas Road
Fairfax, CA 94930

PRO SHOP: 415-456-9393

Steve Snyder, Head Professional, PGA
John McMullen, PGA Professional
Dave Sexton, Superintendent

Driving Range •
Practice Greens •
Clubhouse •
Food / Beverage •
Accommodations
Pull Carts •
Power Carts •
Club Rental •
$pecial Offers

	1	2	3	4	5	6	7	8	9	OUT
BACK	494	444	382	379	202	410	420	170	450	3351
REGULAR	482	424	369	365	172	397	404	151	434	3198
par	5	4	4	4	3	4	4	3	4	35
handicap	15	5	9	11	13	1	7	17	3	-
FORWARD	481	420	361	356	150	349	345	141	373	2976
par	5	5	4	4	3	4	4	3	4	36
handicap	5	13	1	11	15	7	9	17	3	-

BACK		
yardage	6611
par	71
rating	70.7
slope	125

REGULAR		
yardage	6276
par	71
rating	69.6
slope	122

	10	11	12	13	14	15	16	17	18	IN
BACK	378	153	389	524	203	502	333	415	363	3260
REGULAR	347	144	360	505	171	494	311	399	347	3078
par	4	3	4	5	3	5	4	4	4	36
handicap	4	18	14	10	8	6	16	2	12	-
FORWARD	345	139	349	485	132	488	293	393	342	2966
par	4	3	4	5	3	5	4	5	4	37
handicap	8	18	12	4	16	2	10	14	6	-

FORWARD		
yardage	5942
par	73
rating	73.5
slope	132

PLAY POLICY & FEES: Green fees are $40 weekdays and $55 weekends for nonresidents. Resident green fees are $30 Monday through Thursday, $40 Friday, and $50 weekends after noon. Twilight rates are available starting at $25 weekdays and $35 weekends. Carts are $10 per player.

TEE TIMES: Reservations can be booked ten days in advance.

DRESS CODE: No tank tops are allowed on the course. Nonmetal spikes are required.

COURSE DESCRIPTION: The greens are tough, and there are a few blind holes at San Geronimo. Playing into a prevailing wind, the 394-yard sixth requires a 210-yard carry off the tee. Trees and a creek guard the right side. The 11th hole is one of the toughest holes in the area. It's 421 yards, and the tee shot has to be left-center to open up an approach shot to the green, which is guarded on the right and front by a creek and trees. The 358-yard 16th can be a challenge with the pin tucked left behind a hazard.

LOCATION: Driving on U.S. 101 south of San Rafael, take the San Anselmo exit to Sir Francis Drake Boulevard and drive 12 miles west to the course.

. . . ● **TOURNAMENTS:** This course is available for morning shotguns. Carts are required. A 20-player minimum is required to book a tournament. Tournaments can be booked one month in advance. The banquet facility holds 150 people. ●

TRAVEL: The Best Western Inn (415-924-1502), the Courtyard by Marriott (415-925-1800) and the Two Bird (415-488-9952) are recommended for lodging.

1. SAN GERONIMO GOLF COURSE

PLAY POLICY & FEES: Limited reciprocal play is accepted with members of other private clubs. Reciprocal fees are $120, cart included. Guest fees are $50 Tuesday through Thursday, and $75 Friday through Sunday when accompanied by a member. Carts are $22. The course is closed on Monday.

DRESS CODE: Appropriate golf attire and nonmetal spikes are required.

COURSE DESCRIPTION: This is a tight course nestled in the foothills of Mount Tamalpais; it's built on light rolling terrain that used to be Marin County Water District property. All the bunkers have been redone, and the greens are tricky. Five par 4s over 400 yards make the course a real challenge. The par-4, 333-yard 16th requires tight shot placement with a creek down the right side, willow trees, and a two-tiered green, which is heavily bunkered.

NOTES: Former tour pro Ray Leach owns the course record, a 60.

LOCATION: From U.S. 101 take the Sir Francis Drake Boulevard exit west (toward Fairfax). Turn left on Bolinas Road and follow it to the course.

. . . ● **TOURNAMENTS:** This course is available for outside tournaments on Monday only.

2. MEADOW CLUB

③ PEACOCK GAP GOLF & COUNTRY CLUB
ARCHITECT: WILLIAM F. BELL, 1957

333 Biscayne Drive
San Rafael, CA 94901

PRO SHOP: 415-453-4940
CLUBHOUSE: 415-453-3111

Bob Yokoi, General Manager, PGA
Brain Tawa, Head Professional, PGA
Richard Lavine, Superintendent

Driving Range ●
Practice Greens ●
Clubhouse ●
Food / Beverage ●
Accommodations
Pull Carts ●
Power Carts ●
Club Rental ●
$pecial Offers

	1	2	3	4	5	6	7	8	9	OUT
BACK	398	395	173	506	426	305	185	391	502	3281
REGULAR	366	382	159	500	413	292	158	367	489	3126
par	4	4	3	5	4	4	3	4	5	36
handicap	11	5	15	3	1	13	17	9	7	-
FORWARD	358	371	136	453	403	232	128	354	471	2906
par	4	4	3	5	5	4	3	4	5	37
handicap	5	9	11	3	13	15	17	7	1	-

	10	11	12	13	14	15	16	17	18	IN
BACK	137	391	543	180	516	362	155	348	441	3073
REGULAR	121	376	522	173	465	313	145	334	421	2870
par	3	4	5	3	5	4	3	4	4	35
handicap	18	6	8	16	2	12	14	10	4	-
FORWARD	119	359	469	138	464	302	138	326	408	2723
par	3	4	5	3	5	4	3	4	5	36
handicap	18	6	4	16	2	14	12	8	10	-

BACK	
yardage	6354
par	71
rating	69.7
slope	121

REGULAR	
yardage	5996
par	71
rating	67.9
slope	118

FORWARD	
yardage	5629
par	73
rating	71.9
slope	126

④ McINNIS PARK GOLF CENTER
ARCHITECT: FRED BLISS, 1994

350 Smith Ranch Road
San Rafael, CA 94903

PRO SHOP: 415-492-1800

Marsha O'Neill, Manager
Mark Scott, Superintendent

Driving Range ●
Practice Greens ●
Clubhouse ●
Food / Beverage ●
Accommodations
Pull Carts ●
Power Carts ●
Club Rental ●
$pecial Offers

	1	2	3	4	5	6	7	8	9	OUT
BACK	343	105	204	279	92	276	180	100	263	1842
REGULAR	337	100	164	274	84	248	154	90	244	1695
par	4	3	3	4	3	4	3	3	4	31
handicap	3	8	5	1	9	2	6	7	4	-
FORWARD	315	82	129	253	57	204	134	71	213	1458
par	4	3	3	4	3	4	3	3	4	31
handicap	3	8	5	1	9	2	6	7	4	-

	10	11	12	13	14	15	16	17	18	IN
BACK	-	-	-	-	-	-	-	-	-	-
REGULAR	-	-	-	-	-	-	-	-	-	-
par	-	-	-	-	-	-	-	-	-	-
handicap	-	-	-	-	-	-	-	-	-	-
FORWARD	-	-	-	-	-	-	-	-	-	-
par	-	-	-	-	-	-	-	-	-	-
handicap	-	-	-	-	-	-	-	-	-	-

BACK	
yardage	1842
par	31
rating	59.3
slope	94

REGULAR	
yardage	1695
par	31
rating	58.4
slope	92

FORWARD	
yardage	1458
par	31
rating	60.6
slope	92

3. PEACOCK GAP GOLF & COUNTRY CLUB

PLAY POLICY & FEES: Green fees are $30 Monday through Thursday, $34 on Friday, and $52 on weekends. Twilight rates are available. Carts, which are mandatory on weekends and holidays before noon, are $22.

TEE TIMES: Reservations are recommended seven days in advance for weekdays and call Thursday at noon for the following weekend. Nonmembers may call after noon on Thursday for reservations.

DRESS CODE: Men must wear shirts. No tank tops or cutoffs may be worn. Nonmetal spikes are preferred.

COURSE DESCRIPTION: This sprawling, tree-lined course is mostly flat and features water on 12 holes. A creek meanders through the course. On the 16th hole there's a 155-yard shot over an inlet of San Pablo Bay. The sixth, a dogleg left of 305 yards, demands a mid-iron off the tee and an approach over a lagoon—a fun hole.

NOTES: PGA Tour legend Raymond Floyd holds the course record of 63.

LOCATION: From U.S.101 in San Rafael, take the Central San Rafael exit. Turn east onto Second Street and drive five miles. Turn left on Biscayne Drive.

. . . ● **TOURNAMENTS:** Tournaments must start after 10:30 a.m. on weekends. Carts are required. A 20-player minimum is required to book an event. Tournaments should be scheduled 10 months in advance. The banquet facility can accommodate 500 people. ● **TRAVEL:** The Embassy Suites is located 15 minutes from the golf course. For reservations call 415-499-9222. Wydham Gardens (415-479-8800) and Novato Oaks (415-883-4128) are also recommended.

4. McINNIS PARK GOLF CENTER

PLAY POLICY & FEES: Green fees are $13 for nine holes and $21 for 18 holes Monday through Thursday. Friday through Sunday green fees are $16 for nine holes and $25 for 18 holes. Senior rates are $10 for nine holes and $18 for 18 holes on weekdays. Carts are $9 for nine holes and $15 for 18 holes.

TEE TIMES: Reservations can be booked seven days in advance.

DRESS CODE: Appropriate golf attire required.

COURSE DESCRIPTION: This well-maintained executive course has four par 4s and five par 3s, with water coming into play on four holes. The hardest hole on the course is the fourth hole, a dogleg right to a green guarded by water.

NOTES: McInnis Park features a double-decker driving range, a putting and chipping practice area, miniature golf, batting cages, and a four-star restaurant (reservations are a must). The driving range is open until 9:45 p.m., and in the spring and summer, range players can hit off grass tees from 7 a.m. to 10 a.m. Monday through Thursday.

LOCATION: From U.S.101 in San Rafael, take the Smith Ranch Road exit. Go east on Smith Ranch Road to the golf course.

. . . ● **TOURNAMENTS:** This course is available for outside tournaments. A 16-player minimum is required to book a tournament. Events should be booked at least one month in advance. The banquet facility can accommodate 200 people. ● **TRAVEL:** The Embassy Suites is a few minutes from the course. For reservations call 415-419-9222.

1095 Hiddenbrooke
Vallejo, CA 94591

PRO SHOP: 707-557-8181

Tom Sims, PGA Professional
Gary Sayre, Superintendent

Driving Range ●
Practice Greens ●
Clubhouse ●
Food / Beverage ●
Accommodations
Pull Carts
Power Carts ●
Club Rental ●
$pecial Offers

	1	2	3	4	5	6	7	8	9	OUT
BACK	528	369	481	151	330	586	207	333	489	3474
REGULAR	520	359	462	135	300	539	172	327	440	3254
par	5	4	5	3	4	5	3	4	5	38
handicap	7	9	3	13	17	1	15	11	5	-
FORWARD	446	279	387	91	260	468	133	265	374	2703
par	5	4	5	3	4	5	3	4	5	38
handicap	7	9	3	13	17	1	15	11	5	-

	10	11	12	13	14	15	16	17	18	IN
BACK	389	415	415	426	169	433	184	529	204	3164
REGULAR	373	385	385	393	149	400	163	512	177	2937
par	4	4	4	4	3	4	3	5	3	34
handicap	16	8	10	2	12	4	18	6	14	-
FORWARD	321	346	341	289	100	334	138	467	124	2460
par	4	4	4	4	3	4	3	5	3	34
handicap	16	6	10	2	12	4	18	6	14	-

BACK	
yardage	6638
par	72
rating	72.8
slope	137

REGULAR	
yardage	6191
par	72
rating	70.8
slope	129

FORWARD	
yardage	5163
par	72
rating	70.0
slope	123

900 Fairgrounds Drive
Vallejo, CA 94590

PRO SHOP: 707-642-5146

Tim Berg, Manager, PGA
Joe Mortara Jr., PGA Professional

Driving Range
Practice Greens ●
Clubhouse ●
Food / Beverage ●
Accommodations
Pull Carts ●
Power Carts
Club Rental ●
$pecial Offers

	1	2	3	4	5	6	7	8	9	OUT
BACK	-	-	-	-	-	-	-	-	-	-
REGULAR	200	150	160	172	212	140	320	126	112	1592
par	3	3	3	3	3	3	4	3	3	28
handicap	3	11	9	7	1	13	5	15	17	-
FORWARD	200	150	160	172	212	140	320	126	112	1592
par	3	3	3	3	3	3	4	3	3	28
handicap	3	11	9	7	1	13	5	15	17	-

	10	11	12	13	14	15	16	17	18	IN
BACK	-	-	-	-	-	-	-	-	-	-
REGULAR	200	150	160	172	212	140	320	125	112	1591
par	3	3	3	3	3	3	4	3	3	28
handicap	4	12	10	8	2	14	6	16	18	-
FORWARD	200	150	160	172	212	140	320	125	112	1591
par	3	3	3	3	3	3	4	3	3	28
handicap	4	12	10	8	2	14	6	16	18	-

BACK	
yardage	-
par	-
rating	-
slope	-

REGULAR	
yardage	3183
par	56
rating	54.4
slope	-

FORWARD	
yardage	3183
par	56
rating	54.4
slope	-

PLAY POLICY & FEES: Outside play is accepted. Green fees are $75 Monday through Wednesday, $85 Thursday and Friday, and $100 Saturday, Sunday, and holidays. Price includes carts and use of the driving range.

TEE TIMES: Reservations can be booked four days in advance Friday through Sunday, and seven days in advance Monday through Thursday.

DRESS CODE: Golfers must wear collared shirts. No short shorts or jeans are allowed on the course. Nonmetal spikes are required.

COURSE DESCRIPTION: Gorgeous views are afforded from many elevated tees at this Arnold Palmer–designed course. It is well-bunkered with rolling hills and large greens. Water comes into play on eight holes. One of the most spectacular holes is the 200-yard, par-3 18th, which is guarded by a waterfall and four ponds.

NOTES: A new clubhouse opened in 1999.

LOCATION: From Vallejo take Interstate 80 north to the American Canyon exit. Turn right and proceed to the golf course.

. . . ● **TOURNAMENTS:** Shotgun tournaments are available weekdays only.

5. HIDDENBROOKE COUNTRY CLUB

PLAY POLICY & FEES: Green fees are $7 for nine holes weekdays with $4 for each additional nine holes, and $8 for nine holes weekends with $5 for each additional nine holes. Junior and senior green fees are $5 for nine holes and $1 for each additional nine. Pull carts are $2 for the day. The course is closed two weeks in July for the fair.

TEE TIMES: Reservations are not accepted. All play is on a first-come, first-served basis.

COURSE DESCRIPTION: This short course is flat and a good test for beginners or for brushing up on the irons. There is only one par 4, the 320-yard seventh. The course is situated in the middle of the track of the Solano County Fairgrounds. A total of 75,000 rounds are played here each year.

LOCATION: From Interstate 80 at the north end of Vallejo, take the Redwood exit. Turn right on Fairgrounds Drive. The course is located at the Solano County Fairgrounds.

. . . ● **TOURNAMENTS:** This course is not available for outside events.

6. JOE MORTARA GOLF COURSE

1800 Club Drive/Mare
Vallejo, CA 94590

PRO SHOP: 707-562-4653

Dennis Walker, Head Professional
Rhonda Carter, General Manager

Driving Range ●
Practice Greens ●
Clubhouse ●
Food / Beverage ●
Accommodations
Pull Carts ●
Power Carts ●
Club Rental ●
$Special Offers

	1	2	3	4	5	6	7	8	9	OUT
BACK	-	-	-	-	-	-	-	-	-	-
REGULAR	374	188	521	257	386	193	510	335	348	3112
par	4	3	5	4	4	3	5	4	4	36
handicap	7	17	3	9	1	11	5	15	13	-
FORWARD	364	136	498	185	375	79	403	320	342	2702
par	4	3	5	4	4	3	5	4	4	36
handicap	7	15	1	13	3	17	5	11	9	-

BACK	
yardage	-
par	-
rating	-
slope	-

	10	11	12	13	14	15	16	17	18	IN
BACK	-	-	-	-	-	-	-	-	-	-
REGULAR	434	173	501	184	386	193	510	284	372	3037
par	4	3	5	3	4	3	5	4	4	35
handicap	4	18	8	14	2	10	6	16	12	-
FORWARD	345	136	430	137	367	79	403	279	342	2518
par	4	3	5	3	4	3	5	4	4	35
handicap	8	16	2	14	4	18	6	12	10	-

REGULAR	
yardage	6149
par	71
rating	68.8
slope	-

FORWARD	
yardage	5220
par	71
rating	69.6
slope	116

8 **BLUE ROCK SPRINGS GOLF COURSE**
ARCHITECT: ROBERT MUIR GRAVES, 1993

P.O. Box 5207
Vallejo, CA 94591

655 Columbus Parkway
Vallejo, CA 94591

PRO SHOP: 707-643-8476
OFFICE: 707-642-0247

Tim Berg, Manager, PGA
Tom Wade, PGA Professional
Pete Badaracco, Tournament Director

Driving Range ●
Practice Greens ●
Clubhouse ●
Food / Beverage ●
Accommodations
Pull Carts ●
Power Carts ●
Club Rental ●
$Special Offers

	1	2	3	4	5	6	7	8	9	OUT
BACK	360	136	356	366	488	161	523	141	372	2903
REGULAR	343	119	344	358	473	148	502	104	349	2740
par	4	3	4	4	5	3	5	3	4	35
handicap	9	17	7	3	1	11	13	15	5	-
FORWARD	306	80	314	316	420	103	428	65	313	2345
par	4	3	4	4	5	3	5	3	4	35
handicap	9	17	11	5	3	15	1	13	7	-

BACK	
yardage	6064
par	70
rating	69.0
slope	122

	10	11	12	13	14	15	16	17	18	IN
BACK	346	167	355	380	551	413	159	412	378	3161
REGULAR	319	130	342	366	542	406	141	391	363	3000
par	4	3	4	4	5	4	3	4	4	35
handicap	12	16	4	10	18	2	14	6	8	-
FORWARD	243	109	292	316	474	346	99	331	296	2506
par	4	3	4	4	5	4	3	4	4	35
handicap	14	6	8	16	2	4	18	10	12	-

REGULAR	
yardage	5740
par	70
rating	67.5
slope	118

FORWARD	
yardage	4851
par	70
rating	68.2
slope	117

PLAY POLICY & FEES: Formerly a military course, this course is now open to the public. Green fees are $10 for nine holes, and $16 for 18 holes Monday through Thursday. Friday through Sunday green fees are $12 for nine holes, and $18 for 18 holes. Carts are $9 for nine holes and $16 for 18 holes. Twilight rates are available.

TEE TIMES: Reservations can be booked 14 days in advance.

DRESS CODE: No tank tops or short shorts are allowed.

COURSE DESCRIPTION: Water comes into play on four holes, and the course is very hilly. Look out for the 10th hole. This 434-yard par 4 doglegs slightly right. The course forces players to be accurate with the irons. Locals like to think of it as a small version of the Olympic Club.

NOTES: The clubhouse and restaurant was upgraded in 1999. A new nine holes and driving range will be completed by July, 2000.

LOCATION: From Vallejo take Interstate 80 to Highway 37. Take Highway 37 to the Mare Island exit. Follow Walnut Street to the north gate. Enter the gate and drive two miles to the course.

. . . ● **TOURNAMENTS:** This course is available for outside tournaments. A 60-player minimum is needed to book a tournament. Tournaments can be booked one month in advance.

7. MARE ISLAND GOLF CLUB

PLAY POLICY & FEES: Green fees for the East Course are $24 on weekdays and $28 on weekends. Green fees for Vallejo residents are $20 weekdays and $24 weekends. Carts are $22 for 18 holes. Green fees for the West Course are $21 weekdays and $25 weekends. Vallejo residents' green fees are $17 weekdays and $21 weekends. Carts are $24 for 18 holes.

TEE TIMES: Reservations can be made the Tuesday before the weekend.

DRESS CODE: Appropriate golf attire is required, and nonmetal spikes are encouraged.

COURSE DESCRIPTION: The new East Course is a sprawling, hilly layout with sidehill lies and large undulating greens. Wind is usually a factor. The signature holes are the uphill, par-4 15th hole, measuring 413 yards, and the 159-yard, par-3 16th, featuring a plateau green surrounded by rocks.

LOCATION: From Interstate 80 in Vallejo, take the Columbus Parkway exit and drive three miles east to the course on the right.

. . . ● **TOURNAMENTS:** Shotgun tournaments are available weekdays only. A 24-player minimum is needed to book an event. Tournaments should be scheduled 12 months in advance. A banquet facility is available that can accommodate up to 100 people. ● **TRAVEL:** The Ramada Inn in Vallejo is two minutes from the golf course. For reservations call 707-643-2700.

8. BLUE ROCK SPRINGS GOLF COURSE

280 Buenta Vista Avenue
Mill Valley, CA 94941

PRO SHOP: 415-388-9982

Stephen Yuhas, Professional
Charles Schultz, Superintendent

Driving Range
Practice Greens •
Clubhouse
Food / Beverage •
Accommodations
Pull Carts •
Power Carts •
Club Rental •
$pecial Offers

	1	2	3	4	5	6	7	8	9	OUT
BACK	-	-	-	-	-	-	-	-	-	-
REGULAR	241	186	241	365	130	250	121	343	263	2140
par	4	3	4	4	3	4	3	4	4	33
handicap	13	3	11	1	17	9	15	5	7	-
FORWARD	237	176	241	356	130	250	121	343	228	2082
par	4	4	4	5	3	4	3	4	4	35
handicap	9	11	13	1	17	5	15	3	7	-

BACK	
yardage	-
par	-
rating	-
slope	-

	10	11	12	13	14	15	16	17	18	IN
BACK	-	-	-	-	-	-	-	-	-	-
REGULAR	241	224	217	365	130	250	108	312	228	2075
par	4	3	3	4	3	4	3	4	4	32
handicap	14	4	8	2	18	10	16	6	12	-
FORWARD	237	224	217	356	130	250	103	296	228	2041
par	4	3	4	5	3	4	3	4	4	34
handicap	10	12	14	2	18	6	16	4	8	-

REGULAR	
yardage	4215
par	65
rating	63.1
slope	107

FORWARD	
yardage	4123
par	69
rating	62.8
slope	104

10 **RICHMOND COUNTRY CLUB**
ARCHITECTS: EDS AWYER, 1924; PAT MARKOVICH, 1939

1 Markovich Lane
Richmond, CA 94806

PRO SHOP: 510-232-7815
CLUBHOUSE: 510-232-1080

Ron G. Svien, Manager
Tom Zahradka, Head Professional, PGA
Jorge Bartholomeu, Superintendent

Driving Range •
Practice Greens •
Clubhouse •
Food / Beverage •
Accommodations
Pull Carts •
Power Carts •
Club Rental •
$pecial Offers

	1	2	3	4	5	6	7	8	9	OUT
BACK	340	356	163	404	305	377	235	372	510	3062
REGULAR	331	340	158	398	301	366	215	324	494	2927
par	4	4	3	4	4	4	3	4	5	35
handicap	13	3	7	1	17	5	9	11	15	-
FORWARD	248	258	146	304	251	293	178	268	395	2341
par	4	4	3	4	4	4	3	4	5	35
handicap	8	7	15	5	14	6	16	13	4	-

BACK	
yardage	6571
par	72
rating	72.0
slope	127

	10	11	12	13	14	15	16	17	18	IN
BACK	420	165	421	525	341	554	196	367	520	3509
REGULAR	407	137	408	503	332	544	188	360	507	3386
par	4	3	4	5	4	5	3	4	5	37
handicap	4	18	2	8	14	12	16	10	6	-
FORWARD	346	118	321	420	286	471	158	315	438	2873
par	4	3	4	5	4	5	3	4	5	37
handicap	9	18	11	3	12	2	17	10	1	-

REGULAR	
yardage	6313
par	72
rating	70.9
slope	125

FORWARD	
yardage	5214
par	72
rating	69.1
slope	116

PLAY POLICY & FEES: Green fees are $12 for nine holes and $18 for 18 holes on weekdays, and $15 for nine holes and $21 for 18 holes on weekends. Senior rates are available. Power carts are $12 for nine holes and $20 for 18 holes.

TEE TIMES: Reservations can be booked seven days in advance.

DRESS CODE: Golf spikes are mandatory October through April.

COURSE DESCRIPTION: A creek comes into play on half the holes. This short, hilly course is walkable. The par-4 fourth is tight, so most players hit long irons off the tee. It's a dogleg uphill. The redwood groves make this a very scenic course.

NOTES: The men's course record is 56, held by Malcolm Brown, and the women's is 64, held by Karen Zielenski.

LOCATION: From U.S. 101 in Mill Valley take the East Blithedale Avenue exit west. Turn right on Carmelita Avenue and then right again on Buena Vista Avenue to the course.

. . . ● **TOURNAMENTS:** A 60-player minimum is needed to book a tournament. Events should be scheduled at least three months in advance.

9. MILL VALLEY GOLF COURSE

PLAY POLICY & FEES: Reciprocal play is accepted with members of other private clubs. Have your club pro call ahead. Green fees for reciprocal guests are $65 on weekdays and $85 on weekends and holidays. Carts are $22. The course is closed on Monday.

TEE TIMES: Make reservations one week in advance.

DRESS CODE: Wear suitable golf attire. No tank tops, blue jeans, or shorts of inappropriate length may be worn.

COURSE DESCRIPTION: This mature course is short and very secluded. The fairways are tight and tree-lined. The terrain is gentle and rolling with very tall and broad pine and eucalyptus trees. This is the norm among old East Bay courses: short holes with slanted greens—very tricky. The 16th, 17th, and 18th holes offer views of the bay through the trees. On the third tee you can catch a glimpse of the Golden Gate Bridge, fog permitting.

NOTES: In the late 1940s and '50s, men's and women's professional tournaments were held here featuring such players as Patty Berg, Babe Zaharias, Ben Hogan, and Sam Snead. The men's course record is 63, set by George Archer; the women's course record is 64, set by Patty Berg.

LOCATION: From Interstate 80 take the Richmond Parkway to the Giant Highway and follow it to Markovich Lane, which leads to the golf course.

. . . ● **TOURNAMENTS:** Outside events are held Monday only with board approval. ● **TRAVEL:** The Hotel Mac in Richmond is recommended as the place to eat after your round.

10. RICHMOND COUNTRY CLUB

FRANKLIN CANYON GOLF COURSE
ARCHITECT: ROBERT MUIR GRAVES, 1969

Highway 4
Rodeo, CA 94572

PRO SHOP: 510-799-6191

Greg Williams, Manager
Kevin Estrella, Assistant General Manager
Jacob Angel, Head Professional, PGA

Driving Range ●
Practice Greens ●
Clubhouse ●
Food / Beverage ●
Accommodations
Pull Carts ●
Power Carts ●
Club Rental ●
$pecial Offers

	1	2	3	4	5	6	7	8	9	OUT
BACK	396	242	370	525	373	457	373	157	535	3428
REGULAR	356	189	338	504	335	401	353	138	461	3075
par	4	3	4	5	4	4	4	3	5	36
handicap	4	8	12	2	14	6	10	16	18	-
FORWARD	340	133	320	425	312	363	278	135	445	2751
par	4	3	4	5	4	4	4	3	5	36
handicap	8	16	10	2	12	6	14	18	4	-

	10	11	12	13	14	15	16	17	18	IN
BACK	532	193	368	183	383	207	528	420	519	3333
REGULAR	472	183	345	169	360	189	511	392	505	3126
par	5	3	4	3	4	3	5	4	5	36
handicap	11	5	17	13	15	9	7	1	3	-
FORWARD	441	157	315	145	325	165	490	317	410	2765
par	5	3	4	3	4	3	5	4	5	36
handicap	3	13	11	17	7	15	1	9	5	-

BACK	
yardage	6761
par	72
rating	70.9
slope	118

REGULAR	
yardage	6201
par	72
rating	68.9
slope	114

FORWARD	
yardage	5516
par	72
rating	71.2
slope	123

 # CONTRA COSTA COUNTRY CLUB
ARCHITECT: ROBERT MUIR GRAVES, 1992

801 Golf Club Road
Pleasant Hill, CA 94523

PRO SHOP: 925-685-8288

Scott Steele, PGA Professional
Anthony Steers, Superintendent

Driving Range ●
Practice Greens ●
Clubhouse ●
Food / Beverage ●
Accommodations
Pull Carts ●
Power Carts ●
Club Rental
$pecial Offers

	1	2	3	4	5	6	7	8	9	OUT
BACK	427	185	481	400	137	544	366	225	470	3235
REGULAR	405	160	477	380	125	526	349	188	465	3075
par	4	3	5	4	3	5	4	3	5	36
handicap	5	13	11	1	17	3	7	9	15	-
FORWARD	391	146	462	363	115	492	321	166	404	2860
par	4	3	5	4	3	5	4	3	5	36
handicap	5	13	11	1	17	3	7	9	15	-

	10	11	12	13	14	15	16	17	18	IN
BACK	350	382	343	352	145	550	368	405	420	3315
REGULAR	342	370	336	337	134	535	348	377	376	3155
par	4	4	4	4	3	5	4	4	4	36
handicap	14	2	16	6	18	12	10	4	8	-
FORWARD	325	356	313	322	126	521	321	360	316	2960
par	4	4	4	4	3	5	4	4	4	36
handicap	14	2	16	6	18	12	10	4	8	-

BACK	
yardage	6550
par	72
rating	71.5
slope	128

REGULAR	
yardage	6230
par	72
rating	70.1
slope	124

FORWARD	
yardage	5820
par	72
rating	73.3
slope	130

PLAY POLICY & FEES: Green fees are $25 to walk and $37 to ride Monday through Thursday, $30 to walk and $42 to ride Friday, and $40 to walk and $52 to ride on weekends and holidays. Call for early-bird and twilight rates.

TEE TIMES: Reservations can be booked seven days in advance.

DRESS CODE: Golf attire is encouraged, and nonmetal spikes are recommended but not mandatory.

COURSE DESCRIPTION: This hilly, sprawling course has two ponds that come into play on four holes. Several tight doglegs require accurate positioning. The wind often affects play, and the large undulating greens are difficult to read. Locals seem to prefer the front nine, including the par-3 second and the par-4 third, a dogleg right over a barranca. The fifth hole, downhill with pine trees on the right side, seems easy, but bunkers and a tricky green can wreck a scorecard. The lateral hazards make this course.

NOTES: The golf course has been reversed. The 10th hole is now the first hole. Junior golf programs are held for children ages 6 to 17 from June through September.

LOCATION: Follow Highway 4 in Rodeo. The course is three miles east of the junction with Interstate 80.

. . . ● **TOURNAMENTS:** This course is available for outside tournaments and has a complete banquet facility.

11. FRANKLIN CANYON GOLF COURSE

PLAY POLICY & FEES: Reciprocal play is accepted with members of other private clubs. Fees are $65 weekdays and $75 weekends.

TEE TIMES: Have your club pro call for arrangements.

DRESS CODE: Appropriate golf attire and nonmetal spikes are required.

COURSE DESCRIPTION: Redesigned greens and new tees and bunkers, coupled with a beautiful setting, should make this one of the better courses in Northern California. Designer Robert Muir Graves was in charge of the project. Originally this course dates back to the 1920s and was designed and built by members. It offers scenic views of Mount Diablo. The greens are large, with lots of undulation. Almost every green is bunkered, and there are barrancas on the 13th and 17th holes.

LOCATION: From Interstate 680 in Pleasant Hill take either the Willow Pass or Concord Avenue exit, turning onto Contra Costa Boulevard and then onto Golf Club Road.

. . . ● **TOURNAMENTS:** This course is available for outside events.

12. CONTRA COSTA COUNTRY CLUB

DIABLO CREEK GOLF COURSE
ARCHITECTS: BOB BALDOCK, 1963; ROBERT MUIR GRAVES, 1966

4050 Port Chicago
Concord, CA 94520

PRO SHOP: 925-686-6262

Joe Fernandez, Head Professional, PGA
Sandy Sanderson, Tournament Director
Rod Kilcoyne, Superintendent

Driving Range ●
Practice Greens ●
Clubhouse ●
Food / Beverage ●
Accommodations
Pull Carts ●
Power Carts ●
Club Rental ●
$pecial Offers

	1	2	3	4	5	6	7	8	9	OUT
BACK	391	356	660	237	439	564	134	416	430	3627
REGULAR	373	340	600	208	401	509	114	405	419	3369
par	4	4	5	3	4	5	3	4	4	36
handicap	11	15	1	7	9	13	17	5	3	-
FORWARD	357	319	477	178	352	495	96	381	388	3043
par	4	4	5	3	4	5	3	4	4	36
handicap	7	13	1	17	11	3	15	5	9	-

BACK	
yardage	6863
par	71
rating	72.2
slope	122

	10	11	12	13	14	15	16	17	18	IN
BACK	394	393	407	200	492	429	450	111	360	3236
REGULAR	365	371	387	182	478	417	420	99	341	3060
par	4	4	4	3	5	4	4	3	4	35
handicap	4	10	8	12	14	6	2	18	16	-
FORWARD	273	355	372	146	453	392	432	78	328	2829
par	4	4	4	3	5	4	5	3	4	36
handicap	10	6	12	18	2	8	4	16	14	-

REGULAR	
yardage	6429
par	71
rating	70.0
slope	118

FORWARD	
yardage	5872
par	72
rating	72.5
slope	119

 MIRA VISTA COUNTRY CLUB
ARCHITECT: WILLIE WATSON, 1924

7901 Cutting Boulevard
El Cerrito, CA 94530

PRO SHOP: 510-237-7045

Carol Pence, LPGA, PGA Professional
Frank Barberio, Superintendent

Driving Range ●
Practice Greens ●
Clubhouse ●
Food / Beverage ●
Accommodations
Pull Carts ●
Power Carts ●
Club Rental ●
$pecial Offers

	1	2	3	4	5	6	7	8	9	OUT
BACK	376	412	335	426	442	219	503	365	145	3223
REGULAR	361	393	317	417	424	195	497	343	126	3073
par	4	4	4	4	4	3	5	4	3	35
handicap	11	3	13	1	9	5	17	7	15	-
FORWARD	340	376	302	410	412	154	472	333	114	2913
par	4	4	4	5	4	3	5	4	3	36
handicap	7	1	9	13	5	15	11	3	17	-

BACK	
yardage	6501
par	71
rating	72.0
slope	128

	10	11	12	13	14	15	16	17	18	IN
BACK	516	338	204	443	423	352	480	178	344	3278
REGULAR	516	320	188	410	402	312	468	156	322	3094
par	5	4	3	4	4	4	5	3	4	36
handicap	18	8	10	2	4	12	16	14	6	-
FORWARD	510	311	178	389	394	295	446	148	312	2983
par	5	4	3	5	4	4	5	3	4	37
handicap	4	8	16	12	2	14	10	18	6	-

REGULAR	
yardage	6167
par	71
rating	70.4
slope	126

FORWARD	
yardage	5896
par	73
rating	69.2
slope	123

PLAY POLICY & FEES: Green fees are $17.50 weekdays and $20.50 weekends for Concord residents. Nonresident fees are $20 weekdays and $23 weekends. Carts are $22.

TEE TIMES: Call the pro shop for more information on the tee time policy.

DRESS CODE: No tank tops or cutoffs allowed on the course.

COURSE DESCRIPTION: This is one of the best-kept municipal courses in Northern California. The course has its own water, so it's always in good shape despite 100,000 rounds a year. There are five lakes on the front nine, and the back nine is tight and narrow. The third hole is tough; at 660 yards from the back tees, this par 5 requires a shot into the wind around two ponds. The course is flat, but wind can be a factor.

NOTES: Diablo is currently in the process of remodeling. The remodeling includes new greens on the first three holes, new cart paths, new drainage and irrigation systems, and a new parking lot. Call the pro shop for more details.

LOCATION: From Highway 4 in Concord, exit on Port Chicago Highway and go north to the course.

. . . ● **TOURNAMENTS:** Shotgun tournaments are available weekdays only. Carts are required.

13. DIABLO CREEK GOLF COURSE

PLAY POLICY & FEES: Reciprocal play is accepted with members of other private clubs. For guests accompanied by a member, green fees are $35 weekdays and $50 weekends. For unaccompanied guests, the fees are $65 on weekdays and $85 on weekends.

TEE TIMES: Have the golf pro from your club call in advance to arrange tee times.

DRESS CODE: Appropriate golf attire is required.

COURSE DESCRIPTION: This sprawling course has small, severe greens with great views of San Francisco. It often gets windy. The course is undulating with lots of trees. Water comes into play on one hole. All greens are elevated and require precise shot making. Stay below the hole whenever possible.

LOCATION: From Interstate 80 in Oakland take the Potrero exit straight across San Pablo Avenue, go up Hill Street, and turn left on Elm. Elm flows into Cutting Boulevard. Follow Cutting to the end and the course.

. . . ● **TOURNAMENTS:** Outside events are limited, and board approval is necessary.

14. MIRA VISTA COUNTRY CLUB

⑮ PINE MEADOWS GOLF COURSE
ARCHITECT: JIM COWARD, 1966

451 Vine Hill Way
Martinez, CA 94553

PRO SHOP: 925-228-2881

John Dodson, Manager/Superintendent

Driving Range
Practice Greens ●
Clubhouse ●
Food / Beverage ●
Accommodations
Pull Carts ●
Power Carts ●
Club Rental ●
$pecial Offers

	1	2	3	4	5	6	7	8	9	OUT
BACK	-	-	-	-	-	-	-	-	-	-
REGULAR	-	-	-	-	-	-	-	-	-	
par	-	-	-	-	-	-	-	-	-	
handicap	-	-	-	-	-	-	-	-	-	-
FORWARD	-	-	-	-	-	-	-	-	-	
par	-	-	-	-	-	-	-	-	-	
handicap	-	-	-	-	-	-	-	-	-	-

BACK	
yardage	-
par	-
rating	-
slope	-

REGULAR	
yardage	1501
par	28
rating	57.6
slope	86

	10	11	12	13	14	15	16	17	18	IN
BACK	-	-	-	-	-	-	-	-	-	-
REGULAR	-	-	-	-	-	-	-	-	-	
par	-	-	-	-	-	-	-	-	-	
handicap	-	-	-	-	-	-	-	-	-	-
FORWARD	-	-	-	-	-	-	-	-	--	
par	-	-	-	-	-	-	-	-	-	
handicap	-	-	-	-	-	-	-	-	-	

FORWARD	
yardage	
par	
rating	-
slope	-

⑯ BUCHANAN FIELDS GOLF COURSE
ARCHITECT: ROBERT MUIR GRAVES, 1960

1091 Concord Avenue
Concord, CA 94520

PRO SHOP: 925-682-1846

Tim Sullivan, Director of Golf
Dave Fowler, PGA Professional

Driving Range ●
Practice Greens ●
Clubhouse ●
Food / Beverage ●
Accommodations
Pull Carts ●
Power Carts ●
Club Rental ●
$pecial Offers

	1	2	3	4	5	6	7	8	9	OUT
BACK	290	156	160	298	142	144	162	294	336	1982
REGULAR	270	142	135	282	117	122	143	279	321	1811
par	4	3	3	4	3	3	3	4	4	31
handicap	-	-	-	-	-	-	-	-	-	
FORWARD	220	111	100	261	85	104	128	258	278	1545
par	4	3	3	4	3	3	3	4	4	31
handicap	-	-	-	-	-	-	-	-	-	-

BACK	
yardage	3964
par	62
rating	-
slope	-

REGULAR	
yardage	3622
par	62
rating	-
slope	-

	10	11	12	13	14	15	16	17	18	IN
BACK	290	156	160	298	142	144	162	294	336	1982
REGULAR	270	142	135	282	117	122	143	279	321	1811
par	4	3	3	4	3	3	3	4	4	31
handicap	-	-	-	-	-	-	-	-	-	
FORWARD	220	111	100	261	85	104	128	258	278	1545
par	4	3	3	4	3	3	3	4	4	31
handicap	-	-	-	-	-	-	-	-	-	

FORWARD	
yardage	3090
par	62
rating	-
slope	-

PLAY POLICY & FEES: Green fees are $9 for nine holes and $15 for 18 holes weekdays. Senior rates are $8 for nine holes and $11 for 18 holes Monday through Thursday. Weekend green fees are $11 for nine holes and $18 for 18 holes.

TEE TIMES: Reservations can be booked seven days in advance.

DRESS CODE: Shirts must be worn.

COURSE DESCRIPTION: This course has rolling hills and lots of trees. The longest hole is the 215-yard seventh. Although short in length, this course is no cakewalk.

LOCATION: From Interstate 80 take Highway 4 to the Morrelo exit in Martinez. Drive past two stop signs and turn left on Center. Turn left again at Vine Hill Way. The course is on the left.

. . . ● **TOURNAMENTS:** This course is available for outside tournaments.

15. PINE MEADOWS GOLF COURSE

PLAY POLICY & FEES: Green fees are $10 for nine holes and $15.50 for 18 holes on weekdays, $11.50 for nine holes and $18 for 18 holes on weekends. Senior and junior rates are $8 for nine holes and $13.50 for 18 holes on weekdays only. Juniors must be over 12 years in age. Carts are $18 for 18 holes.

TEE TIMES: Reservations can be booked seven days in advance.

DRESS CODE: Shirts and shoes must be worn on the golf course at all times.

COURSE DESCRIPTION: This course is relatively short and flat, with a creek and a large lake. The greens are undulating. This is a great practice course for any golfer and an excellent test for juniors and seniors.

NOTES: Buchanan Fields provides lessons for all ages and has a strong youth program.

LOCATION: From Interstate 80 in Concord take the Concord Avenue exit. Take a left on Diamond Avenue. Take a right on Concord Avenue to the course.

. . . ● **TOURNAMENTS:** This course is available for outside tournaments.

16. BUCHANAN FIELDS GOLF COURSE

PITTSBURG'S DELTA VIEW GOLF COURSE
ARCHITECTS: ALISTER MACKENZIE, 1947; ROBERT MUIR GRAVES, 1991

2242 Golf Club Road
Pittsburg, CA 94565

PRO SHOP: 925-439-4040

Ken Yuson, Head Professional, PGA
Doug Holcomb, Superintendent

Driving Range ●
Practice Greens ●
Clubhouse ●
Food / Beverage ●
Accommodations
Pull Carts ●
Power Carts ●
Club Rental ●
Special Offers

	1	2	3	4	5	6	7	8	9	OUT
BACK	318	543	189	377	491	178	427	344	220	3087
REGULAR	287	519	168	346	470	145	395	303	181	2814
par	4	5	3	4	5	3	4	4	3	35
handicap	13	1	11	15	9	7	5	17	3	-
FORWARD	287	483	130	326	405	117	309	270	150	2477
par	4	5	3	4	5	3	4	4	3	35
handicap	11	1	17	9	3	13	7	15	5	-

	10	11	12	13	14	15	16	17	18	IN
BACK	350	547	375	138	434	203	398	395	403	3243
REGULAR	342	510	333	120	411	186	378	364	372	3016
par	4	5	4	3	5	3	4	4	4	36
handicap	16	2	14	18	12	8	6	10	4	-
FORWARD	332	495	290	99	387	159	373	332	350	2817
par	4	5	4	3	5	3	4	4	4	36
handicap	6	2	10	18	8	16	14	12	4	-

BACK	
yardage	6330
par	71
rating	70.9
slope	128

REGULAR	
yardage	5830
par	71
rating	68.7
slope	124

FORWARD	
yardage	5294
par	71
rating	71.4
slope	125

 ## TILDEN PARK GOLF COURSE
ARCHITECT: WILLIAM P. BELL, 1935

Grizzly Peak and Shasta Road
Berkeley, CA 94708

PRO SHOP: 510-848-7373

Cam Stephens, Manager
Trisha Hinze, PGA Professional

Driving Range ●
Practice Greens ●
Clubhouse ●
Food / Beverage ●
Accommodations
Pull Carts ●
Power Carts ●
Club Rental ●
Special Offers

	1	2	3	4	5	6	7	8	9	OUT
BACK	411	399	464	143	366	316	221	475	334	3129
REGULAR	404	385	377	137	327	297	201	467	320	2915
par	4	4	4	3	4	4	3	5	4	35
handicap	3	11	9	15	1	13	17	5	7	-
FORWARD	401	376	356	123	316	270	170	460	286	2758
par	5	4	4	3	4	4	3	5	4	36
handicap	3	13	17	11	5	9	15	1	7	-

	10	11	12	13	14	15	16	17	18	IN
BACK	395	234	350	504	352	329	206	395	400	3165
REGULAR	387	199	300	438	311	322	186	395	370	2908
par	4	3	4	5	4	4	3	4	4	35
handicap	6	14	2	8	4	16	12	18	10	-
FORWARD	381	120	264	431	284	309	138	379	335	2641
par	4	3	4	5	4	4	3	4	4	35
handicap	6	18	4	2	12	14	16	8	10	-

BACK	
yardage	6294
par	70
rating	69.9
slope	120

REGULAR	
yardage	5823
par	70
rating	67.8
slope	116

FORWARD	
yardage	5399
par	71
rating	69.8
slope	116

PLAY POLICY & FEES: Green fees are $18 for 18 holes Monday through Thursday, $20 for 18 holes on Friday, and $24 for 18 holes weekends and holidays. Senior and junior rates are available. Pittsburg residents receive a discount.

TEE TIMES: Reservations can be booked seven days in advance.

DRESS CODE: Shirts and shoes must be worn at all times.

COURSE DESCRIPTION: Formerly the Pittsburg Golf and Country Club, this layout expanded to a full 18 holes in June 1991. This sporty course gets windy, but it rewards the accurate driver. Hills abound as do an assortment of trees. The course plays harder than the yardage would indicate. It's murder for the slicer, particularly on the new nine.

NOTES: Pittsburg's Delta View has an extensive junior program in which over 103 children participated last year.

LOCATION: From Concord drive east on Highway 4. Take the Bailey Road exit south. Turn left on West Leland Road to Golf Club Road.

. . . ● **TOURNAMENTS:** This course is available for outside tournaments. Carts are required.

17. PITTSBURG'S DELTA VIEW GOLF COURSE

PLAY POLICY & FEES: Green fees are $25 Monday through Thursday, $35 Friday, and $40 on weekends. Carts are $12 for nine holes and $24 for 18 holes. Junior, twilight, early-bird, and nine-hole rates are available. Tilden also offers seniors' and women's discount passes.

TEE TIMES: Reservations can be booked seven days in advance.

COURSE DESCRIPTION: Situated in the Berkeley hills, this course has squirrels, raccoons, and deer. Overall, it's a course that allows little margin for error with lots of trees and tricky greens. This course has a lot of fun holes, with the 10th through the 12th particularly interesting. The 411-yard, par-4 first hole is straight uphill and plays like a par 5. The first is the toughest, but the 400-yard 18th is no bargain.

NOTES: Extensive work has been done on the entire course that includes remodeled greens, practice greens, and new cart paths. The course now offers a three-tiered driving range, and carts can be rented with the Pro-Shot electrontric caddy/distance finder. The men's record is 64 and is held jointly by Al Norris and Greg Anderson.

LOCATION: From Highway 24 in Berkeley take the Fish Ranch Road exit (on the east side of the Caldecott Tunnel) and drive one mile north. Turn right on Grizzly Peak Boulevard and follow it to the course.

. . . ● **TOURNAMENTS:** Shotgun tournaments are available weekdays only. Carts are required. A 16-player minimum is required to book a tournament.

18. TILDEN PARK GOLF COURSE

ORINDA COUNTRY CLUB
ARCHITECT: WILLIE WATSON

315 Camino Sobrante
Orinda, CA 94563

PRO SHOP: 925-254-0811

Shim LaGoy, Head Professional, PGA
Bob Lapic, Superintendent
John Bethe, General Manager

Driving Range
Practice Greens ●
Clubhouse ●
Food / Beverage ●
Accommodations
Pull Carts ●
Power Carts ●
Club Rental ●
$pecial Offers

	1	2	3	4	5	6	7	8	9	OUT
BACK	354	321	244	458	354	569	337	120	432	3189
REGULAR	334	309	237	450	343	556	316	116	428	3089
par	4	4	3	5	4	5	4	3	4	36
handicap	15	11	7	9	5	1	13	17	3	-
FORWARD	310	307	230	448	334	496	299	101	423	2948
par	4	4	3	5	4	5	4	3	5	37
handicap	15	9	13	3	7	1	11	17	5	-

	10	11	12	13	14	15	16	17	18	IN
BACK	308	442	463	192	290	186	414	347	521	3163
REGULAR	298	434	441	178	282	162	394	339	510	3038
par	4	4	5	3	4	3	4	4	5	36
handicap	16	2	12	14	18	8	4	10	6	-
FORWARD	252	426	403	155	272	127	354	328	453	2770
par	4	5	5	3	4	3	4	4	5	37
handicap	14	2	6	18	12	16	8	10	4	-

BACK	
yardage	6352
par	72
rating	71.0
slope	125

REGULAR	
yardage	6127
par	72
rating	70.0
slope	123

FORWARD	
yardage	5718
par	74
rating	73.0
slope	129

 ## DIABLO HILLS GOLF COURSE
ARCHITECT: ROBERT MUIR GRAVES, 1975

1551 Marchbanks Drive
Walnut Creek, CA 94598

PRO SHOP: 925-939-7372

Tony Singh, Manager
Nick Andrakin, PGA Professional

Driving Range
Practice Greens ●
Clubhouse ●
Food / Beverage ●
Accommodations
Pull Carts ●
Power Carts ●
Club Rental ●
$pecial Offers

	1	2	3	4	5	6	7	8	9	OUT
BACK	-	-	-	-	-	-	-	-	-	-
REGULAR	264	328	106	88	323	254	140	489	310	2302
par	4	4	3	3	4	4	3	5	4	34
handicap	16	4	12	18	2	14	6	10	8	-
FORWARD	251	305	94	63	323	254	126	466	291	2173
par	4	4	3	3	4	4	3	5	4	34
handicap	7	5	15	18	3	11	13	1	9	-

	10	11	12	13	14	15	16	17	18	IN
BACK	-	-	-	-	-	-	-	-	-	-
REGULAR	264	328	106	88	323	254	140	489	310	2302
par	4	4	3	3	4	4	3	5	4	34
handicap	15	3	11	17	1	13	5	9	7	-
FORWARD	251	305	94	63	323	254	126	466	291	2173
par	4	4	3	3	4	4	3	5	4	34
handicap	8	6	16	18	4	12	14	2	10	-

BACK	
yardage	-
par	-
rating	-
slope	-

REGULAR	
yardage	4604
par	68
rating	62.5
slope	100

FORWARD	
yardage	4346
par	68
rating	65.7
slope	104

PLAY POLICY & FEES: Reciprocal play is accepted with members of other private clubs. Guest fees are $125. No reciprocal play is allowed on weekends.

DRESS CODE: Appropriate golf attire is required.

COURSE DESCRIPTION: This tight, rolling course has traditional small greens. A creek winds through it. Two long par 4s, the 9th and 11th holes, create the most trouble. The ninth is a rolling 432-yard demon. You can see the green from the tee box, but you're driving over two mounds to a blind fairway. Long hitters can fly both hills on the fairway, but most will land in the second bank, requiring a long iron or wood for the second shot. It's considered the best hole on the course. The 11th hole is 442 yards from the back and doglegs 220 yards out to the left. There is a creek 75 yards short of the green that you must carry if you're going for it. Beware: The green has very interesting natural mounds all around it and out-of-bounds to the left.

LOCATION: From Highway 24 take the Orinda-Moraga exit. Turn left on San Pablo Dam Road. Turn right at the second stop light at Camino Sobrante. Follow Camino Sobrante and take a left at the stop sign in front of the lake. The course is on the left.

. . . ● **TOURNAMENTS:** Outside events are limited and must be member sponsored.

19. ORINDA COUNTRY CLUB

PLAY POLICY & FEES: Green fees are $13 for nine holes and $26 for 18 holes on weekdays, and $16 for nine holes and $32 for 18 holes on weekends and holidays. Senior rates are $11 Monday through Thursday. Carts are $14 for nine holes and $24 for 18 holes.

TEE TIMES: Reservations can be booked seven days in advance.

DRESS CODE: Shirts with collars must be worn.

COURSE DESCRIPTION: This course winds through condominiums, but it is wide open. There are slightly rolling yet walkable hills with many sand traps. This is an ideal course for beginning and junior golfers.

NOTES: Host pro Nick Andrakin holds the course record of 60. Ed Rolloson holds the course record for nine holes at 28.

LOCATION: From Interstate 680 in Walnut Creek take the Ygnacio Valley Road exit to Marchbanks Drive. Drive approximately one-half mile to the course.

. . . ● **TOURNAMENTS:** This course is available for outside tournaments. A 16-player minimum is needed to book a tournament. The banquet facility can hold 150 people. ● **TRAVEL:** The Embassy Suites is located about 10 minutes from the golf course. For reservations call 510-934-2500.

20. DIABLO HILLS GOLF COURSE

21 BOUNDARY OAK GOLF COURSE
ARCHITECT: ROBERT MUIR GRAVES, 1969

3800 Valley Vista Road
Walnut Creek, CA 94598

PRO SHOP: 925-934-6211

Bob Boldt, Director of Golf, PGA
George Claus, General Manager

Driving Range
Practice Greens ●
Clubhouse ●
Food / Beverage ●
Accommodations
Pull Carts ●
Power Carts ●
Club Rental ●
$pecial Offers

	1	2	3	4	5	6	7	8	9	OUT
BACK	405	160	519	402	503	188	357	335	391	3260
REGULAR	396	140	483	392	470	167	343	294	373	3058
par	4	3	5	4	5	3	4	4	4	36
handicap	6	18	8	2	12	16	10	14	4	-
FORWARD	382	119	473	331	424	148	315	272	332	2796
par	4	3	5	4	5	3	4	4	4	36
handicap	3	17	1	5	11	15	7	13	9	-

	10	11	12	13	14	15	16	17	18	IN
BACK	365	400	186	415	563	428	408	200	514	3479
REGULAR	343	376	170	393	548	408	394	185	497	3314
par	4	4	3	4	5	4	4	3	5	36
handicap	13	11	17	9	1	3	7	15	5	-
FORWARD	305	323	128	355	489	361	351	146	445	2903
par	4	4	3	4	5	4	4	3	5	36
handicap	14	6	18	12	2	10	8	16	4	-

BACK	
yardage	6739
par	72
rating	72.1
slope	127

REGULAR	
yardage	6372
par	72
rating	70.5
slope	124

FORWARD	
yardage	5699
par	72
rating	72.1
slope	123

22 GOLDEN GATE PARK GOLF COURSE
ARCHITECT: JACK FLEMING, 1950

47th Avenue and Fulton
San Francisco, CA 94117

PRO SHOP: 415-751-8987

Jim Thigpin, Manager

Driving Range
Practice Greens ●
Clubhouse
Food / Beverage ●
Accommodations
Pull Carts ●
Power Carts ●
Club Rental ●
$pecial Offers

	1	2	3	4	5	6	7	8	9	OUT
BACK	-	-	-	-	-	-	-	-	-	-
REGULAR	-	-	-	-	-	-	-	-	-	-
par	-	-	-	-	-	-	-	-	-	-
handicap	-	-	-	-	-	-	-	-	-	-
FORWARD	-	-	-	-	-	-	-	-	-	-
par	-	-	-	-	-	-	-	-	-	-
handicap	-	-	-	-	-	-	-	-	-	-

	10	11	12	13	14	15	16	17	18	IN
BACK	-	-	-	-	-	-	-	-	-	-
REGULAR	-	-	-	-	-	-	-	-	-	-
par	-	-	-	-	-	-	-	-	-	-
handicap	-	-	-	-	-	-	-	-	-	-
FORWARD	-	-	-	-	-	-	-	-	-	-
par	-	-	-	-	-	-	-	-	-	-
handicap	-	-	-	-	-	-	-	-	-	-

BACK	
yardage	-
par	-
rating	-
slope	-

REGULAR	
yardage	1357
par	27
rating	--
slope	--

FORWARD	
yardage	
par	
rating	-
slope	-

PLAY POLICY & FEES: Green fees for residents of Walnut Creek are $11 for nine holes and $16 for 18 holes weekdays and $19 for 18 holes weekends. Nonresident fees are $14 for nine holes and $20 for 18 holes weekdays and $25 for 18 holes weekends. Carts are $25.

TEE TIMES: Reservations can be booked seven days in advance.

DRESS CODE: Collared shirts are required. Nonmetal spikes are encouraged.

COURSE DESCRIPTION: This is a sprawling, demanding layout with both trees and water coming into play. It's a good driving course. Coincidentally, head pro Bob Boldt led the Senior PGA Tour in driving distance in 1988. The 11th, at 400 yards, requires a big drive to reach the green in two. The second shot is over a lake. When the greens are in good condition, this is a fun, challenging course.

LOCATION: From Interstate 680 take the Ygnacio Valley Road exit east. Drive three miles into Walnut Creek. Turn right on Oak Grove Road, then left on Valley Vista Road.

. . . ● **TOURNAMENTS:** This course is available for outside tournaments.

21. BOUNDARY OAK GOLF COURSE

PLAY POLICY & FEES: Green fees are $10 weekdays and $13 weekends; San Francisco residents pay $6 weekdays, $8 weekends. Senior rates are $4 weekdays, $7 weekends. Carts are $8 for nine holes. Pull carts are $3.50. Club rental is $6 per bag.

TEE TIMES: Reservations are not accepted. All play is on a first-come, first-served basis.

COURSE DESCRIPTION: Situated at the end of Golden Gate Park near the ocean, this short course is tight and curvy with lots of trees. The longest hole is the 193-yard fifth, and the shortest is the 109-yard eighth. The course offers good practice for your iron game.

NOTES: The course hosts the annual San Francisco Family Championship.

LOCATION: This course is set at the far west end of Golden Gate Park on Fulton Street off 47th Avenue. Take the 19th Avenue exit off U.S. 101 into San Francisco. Follow 19th Avenue (Park Presidio) until you reach Fulton Street. Turn right and follow it along the park to 47th Avenue. Turn into the park and the course.

. . . ● **TOURNAMENTS:** This course is available for outside tournaments.

22. GOLDEN GATE PARK GOLF COURSE

PRESIDIO GOLF CLUB
ARCHITECT: ROBERT JOHNSTONE, 1895

GOLF 50

300 Finley Road/P.O. Box
San Francisco, CA   94129

PRO SHOP: 415-561-4653

Jeff Levine, Manager
Jack Baker, PGA Professional
Colleen Daily, Tournament Director

Driving Range ●
Practice Greens ●
Clubhouse ●
Food / Beverage ●
Accommodations
Pull Carts
Power Carts ●
Club Rental ●
$pecial Offers

	1	2	3	4	5	6	7	8	9	OUT
BACK	398	528	395	145	312	363	245	379	526	3291
REGULAR	385	473	379	127	302	350	221	365	491	3093
par	4	5	4	3	4	4	3	4	5	36
handicap	8	16	2	18	14	4	6	10	12	-
FORWARD	368	412	371	111	292	344	171	354	449	2872
par	4	5	4	3	4	4	3	4	5	36
handicap	14	4	2	18	12	8	16	10	6	-

BACK	
yardage	6599
par	72
rating	71.8
slope	129

	10	11	12	13	14	15	16	17	18	IN
BACK	508	398	453	173	349	182	368	353	524	3308
REGULAR	488	381	436	159	326	153	346	344	483	3116
par	5	4	4	3	4	3	4	4	5	36
handicap	7	5	1	13	11	17	9	3	15	-
FORWARD	468	302	424	153	325	133	332	335	464	2936
par	5	4	5	3	4	3	4	4	5	37
handicap	1	13	5	15	9	17	11	7	3	-

REGULAR	
yardage	6209
par	72
rating	70.2
slope	126

FORWARD	
yardage	5808
par	73
rating	73.5
slope	128

PLAY POLICY & FEES: Green fees are $42 to walk and $57 to ride Monday through Thursday and $52 to walk and $67 to ride Friday through Sunday. Twilight rates are available. Pull carts are not allowed.

TEE TIMES: Reservations can be made up to 30 days in advance and are subject to a fee of $8 per person Monday through Thursday and $12 per person Friday through Sunday and holidays. There is no fee for tee times booked less than a week in advance.

DRESS CODE: Collared shirts must be worn. Proper golf attire is required.

COURSE DESCRIPTION: This is a must play for golf enthusiasts. The course originated as a member-built, nine-hole layout in 1895 and expanded to 18 holes in 1910. Operated by the military since the 1950s, the course opened for public play on September 1, 1995. Arnold Palmer Golf Company has done an excellent job of restoring and improving the Presidio Golf Club. This hilly course meanders through the San Francisco Presidio and offers spectacular views of the city. The course is challenging, steep, and heavily wooded with cypress and eucalyptus. Beware of the 528-yard, par-5 second hole. It has a blind elevated green that is guarded by bunkers.

NOTES: The grand opening for the new pro shop and dining facility opened to rave reviews on June 30,1999. The course record of 64, probably dating back to the late 1920s, is held by the late Lawson Little.

LOCATION: Driving into San Francisco over the Golden Gate Bridge on U.S. 101, take the 19th Avenue exit south. At the first light after passing through the tunnel (Lake Street), turn right. Make a U-turn and head east on Lake to Arguello Boulevard and turn left. The course is at the top of the hill.

. . . ● **TOURNAMENTS:** The course is available for outside tournaments. Carts are required.

23. PRESIDIO GOLF CLUB

LINCOLN PARK GOLF COURSE
ARCHITECT: TOM BENDELOW, 1910

34th Avenue and Clement
San Francisco, CA 94121

PRO SHOP: 415-750-GOLF

Mike Gerber, Manager
Lance Wong, PGA Professional

Driving Range
Practice Greens ●
Clubhouse ●
Food / Beverage ●
Accommodations
Pull Carts ●
Power Carts ●
Club Rental ●
$pecial Offers

	1	2	3	4	5	6	7	8	9	OUT
BACK	-	-	-	-	-	-	-	-	-	-
REGULAR	318	260	160	323	354	286	338	170	305	2514
par	4	4	3	4	4	4	4	3	4	34
handicap	3	13	17	5	7	11	9	15	1	-
FORWARD	310	247	156	314	338	272	321	153	292	2403
par	4	4	3	4	4	4	4	3	4	34
handicap	3	13	15	11	1	7	9	17	5	-

BACK	
yardage	-
par	-
rating	-
slope	-

	10	11	12	13	14	15	16	17	18	IN
BACK	-	-	-	-	-	-	-	-	-	-
REGULAR	269	266	201	498	259	282	237	242	381	2635
par	4	4	3	5	4	4	3	3	4	34
handicap	14	4	12	2	6	18	10	16	8	-
FORWARD	258	270	197	487	250	277	231	238	373	2581
par	4	4	3	5	4	4	4	4	4	36
handicap	12	10	14	2	8	6	16	18	4	-

REGULAR	
yardage	5149
par	68
rating	65.3
slope	-

FORWARD	
yardage	4984
par	70
rating	68.2
slope	-

CLAREMONT COUNTRY CLUB

5295 Broadway Terrace
Oakland, CA 94618

PRO SHOP: 510-655-2431

Jay S. McDaniel, PGA Professional
Randy Gai, Superintendent

Driving Range
Practice Greens ●
Clubhouse ●
Food / Beverage ●
Accommodations ●
Pull Carts ●
Power Carts ●
Club Rental ●
$pecial Offers

	1	2	3	4	5	6	7	8	9	OUT
BACK	-	-	-	-	-	-	-	-	-	-
REGULAR	430	215	126	341	332	260	385	170	391	2650
par	5	3	3	4	4	4	4	3	4	34
handicap	10	8	18	4	14	12	2	16	6	-
FORWARD	430	215	126	341	332	260	385	170	376	2635
par	5	4	3	4	4	4	5	3	4	36
handicap	8	16	18	6	10	12	2	14	4	-

BACK	
yardage	-
par	-
rating	-
slope	-

	10	11	12	13	14	15	16	17	18	IN
BACK	-	-	-	-	-	-	-	-	-	-
REGULAR	160	391	400	225	291	345	372	130	505	2819
par	3	4	4	3	4	4	4	3	5	34
handicap	15	3	1	11	13	7	5	17	9	-
FORWARD	120	391	400	198	291	345	372	130	505	2752
par	3	4	5	3	4	4	4	3	5	35
handicap	17	3	1	13	11	9	7	15	5	-

REGULAR	
yardage	5469
par	68
rating	67.0
slope	119

FORWARD	
yardage	5387
par	71
rating	71.4
slope	127

PLAY POLICY & FEES: Green fees are $23 weekdays and $27 weekends. Carts are $22. Residents of San Francisco may purchase discount cards for $20; green fees with the discount card are $8 weekdays and $9 weekends.

TEE TIMES: Reservations can be booked six days in advance for the general public starting at 7 p.m. by calling the automated reservations number listed above. A $1 charge will be added to your green fee at the time of play for using this system. San Francisco residents with a reservation card can make tee times seven days in advance.

COURSE DESCRIPTION: Situated around the Palace of the Legion of Honor with views of San Francisco below, this extremely scenic course is tight and twisty. Part of the course runs along steep cliffs above the ocean. The 242-yard 17th hole is a brutal but spectacular par 3, with a stunning view of the Golden Gate Bridge. There are lots of trees, and good placement shots are vital. Lincoln Park is hilly but walkable.

NOTES: Pro golfers Johnny Miller and George Archer grew up playing here. This is a very busy course with 100,000 rounds played annually. Architects Herbert Fowler and Jack Fleming remodeled the original design.

LOCATION: Crossing over the Golden Gate Bridge on U.S. 101 into San Francisco, take the 19th Avenue exit south, follow it through the tunnel, and then turn right onto Clement Street. Follow Clement a few miles to the entrance of the course on the right.

. . . ● **TOURNAMENTS:** Shotgun tournaments are available weekdays only. Carts are required. A 24-player minimum is needed to book a tournament.

24. LINCOLN PARK GOLF COURSE

PLAY POLICY & FEES: Members and guests only. Guests must be accompanied by a member. Green fees are $40 weekdays and $50 weekends and holidays for guests. Carts are $40.

DRESS CODE: Appropriate golf attire is required.

COURSE DESCRIPTION: Alister Mackenzie remodeled this tight, rolling course in the Oakland hills. Built in 1904, Claremont is one of the oldest courses in Northern California. The 225-yard, par-3 13th requires a tee shot through a narrow opening. Sam Snead is credited with saying it's the only fairway that requires players to walk single file. The course looks easy on the card, but the par 3s and contoured greens make this a tough test. It's also one of the few courses that still has caddies.

NOTES: Sam Snead won the Oakland Open here in 1937.

LOCATION: From Highway 24 in Oakland exit onto Broadway southwest. Turn left on Broadway Terrace. The course is one-half mile on the right. Or take Highway 13 and exit on Broadway Terrace west.

. . . ● **TOURNAMENTS:** This course is not available for outside events.

25. CLAREMONT COUNTRY CLUB

26 MONTCLAIR GOLF COURSE

2477 Monterey Boulevard
Oakland, CA 94611

PRO S HOP: 510-482-0422

Pillim Lee, Owner
Chris Lee, Manager
Jim Collins, PGA Professional

Driving Range ●
Practice Greens
Clubhouse ●
Food / Beverage ●
Accommodations
Pull Carts
Power Carts
Club Rental ●
$pecial Offers

	1	2	3	4	5	6	7	8	9	OUT
BACK										
REGULAR										
par										
handicap										
FORWARD										
par										
handicap										

BACK	
yardage	
par	
rating	-
slope	-

REGULAR	
yardage	567
par	27
rating	-
slope	-

	10	11	12	13	14	15	16	17	18	IN
BACK										
REGULAR										
par										
handicap										
FORWARD										
par										
handicap										

FORWARD	
yardage	
par	
rating	-
slope	-

27 MORAGA COUNTRY CLUB
ARCHITECT: ROBERT M UIR G RAVES, 1974

1600 Saint Andrews Drive
Moraga, CA 94556

PRO S HOP: 925-376-2253
CLUBHOUSE: 510-376-2200

Greg Gonsalves, General Manager
Randy Kahn, PGA Professional

Driving Range ●
Practice Greens ●
Clubhouse ●
Food / Beverage ●
Accommodations
Pull Carts ●
Power Carts ●
Club Rental ●
$pecial Offers

	1	2	3	4	5	6	7	8	9	OUT
BACK	402	376	412	323	129	395	182	268	505	2992
REGULAR	391	366	399	305	124	384	174	259	486	2888
par	4	4	4	4	3	4	3	4	5	35
handicap	3	1	5	15	17	7	9	11	13	-
FORWARD	378	326	327	269	124	350	128	255	435	2592
par	4	4	4	4	3	4	3	4	5	35
handicap	1	3	7	13	17	5	15	9	4	-

BACK	
yardage	6151
par	71
rating	70.5
slope	127

REGULAR	
yardage	5757
par	71
rating	68.5
slope	124

	10	11	12	13	14	15	16	17	18	IN
BACK	167	302	353	503	489	224	391	170	560	3159
REGULAR	155	291	340	460	448	185	333	147	510	2869
par	3	4	4	5	5	3	4	3	5	36
handicap	6	14	2	18	8	10	16	12	4	-
FORWARD	131	247	281	419	412	156	302	120	449	2517
par	3	4	4	5	5	3	4	3	5	36
handicap	6	12	10	8	4	16	6	18	2	-

FORWARD	
yardage	5109
par	71
rating	69.7
slope	128

PLAY POLICY & FEES: Green fees are $3 weekdays and $4 weekends. There is a $2 replay fee.

TEE TIMES: Reservations are not accepted. All play is on a first-come, first-served basis.

COURSE DESCRIPTION: This short, par-3 course is situated in the Oakland Hills and is mostly flat. It's a good beginner's course. The 85-yard first hole is the longest.

NOTES: Montclair has redesigned and lengthened the second hole. Over the next the year, Montclair will also be remodeling the practice greens, driving range, and parking lot.

LOCATION: From Highway 13 in Oakland take the Park Boulevard exit west. Follow it to Monterey Boulevard and drive one-quarter mile to the course.

. . . ● **TOURNAMENTS:** This course is available for outside tournaments.

26. MONTCLAIR GOLF COURSE

PLAY POLICY & FEES: Reciprocal play is accepted with members of other private clubs in the area. Guest fees are $35 weekdays and $50 for weekends with a member. Carts are $22. Reciprocal play is $75 including cart. Carts are mandatory.

TEE TIMES: Reservations can be booked one day in advance.

DRESS CODE: Appropriate golf attire is required. Nonmetal spikes are encouraged. No jeans are allowed.

COURSE DESCRIPTION: This course demands a good short game. It's tight and hilly with bunkers and slick greens. The course expanded to 18 holes in the fall of 1992 under the design expertise of Algie Pulley. The new ninth, a 505-yard par 5, has water on the right, big mounds on the left, and plays into a breeze. The green is long and narrow. The par-3 10th, a 167-yarder over a creek, is a beauty. From there the course goes uphill. Some deceptive par 4s with mounds in the greens make this course memorable and exasperating. The 489-yard, par-5 14th, for example, has a five-tiered green.

NOTES: Three new bunkers were added to the course, and a new driving range opened in 1998.

LOCATION: From Highway 24 in Moraga take the Moraga Way exit south four miles to Saint Andrews Drive.

. . . ● **TOURNAMENTS:** Shotgun tournaments are available weekdays only. Carts are required. An 80-player minimum is needed to book a tournament. The banquet facility can accommodate 100 people.

27. MORAGA COUNTRY CLUB

ROSSMOOR GOLF COURSE
ARCHITECT: ROBERT MUIR GRAVES, 1965

1010 Stanley Dollar Drive
Walnut Creek, CA 94595

PRO SHOP: 925-933-2607

Mark Heptig, Director of Golf, PGA
Joe Rodriquez, Superintendent

Driving Range ●
Practice Greens ●
Clubhouse ●
Food / Beverage
Accommodations
Pull Carts ●
Power Carts ●
Club Rental ●
$pecial Offers

	1	2	3	4	5	6	7	8	9	OUT
BACK	322	366	168	522	373	494	363	369	157	3134
REGULAR	310	353	149	490	361	459	344	355	147	2968
par	4	4	3	5	4	5	4	4	3	36
handicap	13	5	17	1	11	3	9	7	15	-
FORWARD	305	349	145	479	356	445	338	303	125	2845
par	4	4	3	5	4	5	4	4	3	36
handicap	13	3	15	1	7	5	9	11	17	-

	10	11	12	13	14	15	16	17	18	IN
BACK	554	390	295	158	499	147	303	494	151	2991
REGULAR	521	366	291	148	486	132	297	483	130	2854
par	5	4	4	3	5	3	4	5	3	36
handicap	2	6	12	14	4	18	8	10	16	-
FORWARD	451	362	285	143	428	124	296	454	127	2670
par	5	4	4	3	5	3	4	5	3	36
handicap										-

BACK	
yardage	6125
par	72
rating	69.2
slope	124

REGULAR	
yardage	5822
par	72
rating	68.1
slope	120

FORWARD	
yardage	5515
par	72
rating	70.0
slope	120

 ROUND HILL COUNTRY CLUB
ARCHITECT: LAWRENCE HUGHES, 1960

3169 Round Hill Road
Alamo, CA 94507

PRO SHOP: 925-837-7424
OFFICE: 925-934-8212

Al Krueger, PGA Professional
Jack Mahoney, General Manager
Troy Flanagan, Superintendent

Driving Range ●
Practice Greens ●
Clubhouse ●
Food / Beverage ●
Accommodations
Pull Carts
Power Carts ●
Club Rental ●
$pecial Offers

	1	2	3	4	5	6	7	8	9	OUT
BACK	398	350	402	502	207	455	140	341	388	3183
REGULAR	380	350	378	487	191	455	140	341	354	3076
par	4	4	4	5	3	5	3	4	4	36
handicap	5	11	1	3	9	7	17	15	13	-
FORWARD	374	333	367	482	182	415	122	327	332	2934
par	4	4	4	5	3	5	3	4	4	36
hand.cap	7	9	1	3	17	5	15	13	11	-

	10	11	12	13	14	15	16	17	18	IN
BACK	384	319	419	188	492	385	199	420	486	3292
REGULAR	374	301	408	173	492	368	192	399	479	3186
par	4	4	4	3	5	4	3	4	5	36
handicap	10	18	2	12	8	6	14	4	16	-
FORWARD	366	289	402	165	479	315	174	398	434	3022
par	4	4	5	3	5	4	3	5	5	38
handicap	10	14	4	16	2	8	18	6	12	-

BACK	
yardage	6475
par	72
rating	71.8
slope	131

REGULAR	
yardage	6262
par	72
rating	70.7
slope	128

FORWARD	
yardage	5956
par	74
rating	74.9
slope	134

PLAY POLICY & FEES: Members and guests only. Guest fees are $14 for nine holes and $25 for 18 holes weekdays, and $20 for nine holes and $36 for 18 holes weekends and holidays. Carts are $20. The course is closed on Monday.

DRESS CODE: Golf attire is encouraged.

COURSE DESCRIPTION: These are retirement community courses that are mostly flat and walkable, although the South Course has some hills. The South's 372-yard second hole requires an uphill approach. The par-5 10th hole doglegs left, with two big oak trees at the turn. Both layouts feature tricky greens and are a good test of irons and short-game strategy.

NOTES: This course is the home of the Rossmoor Pro-Am, which benefits Children's Hospital of Oakland. The Creekside Course is 2,930 yards from the regular tees with a slope of 123 and is rated 67.7 with a par of 36. For more information on the Dollar Ranch Course, see scorecard.

LOCATION: From Highway 24 east of Lafayette take the Pleasant Hill Road exit south to Olympic Boulevard east. Then turn right on Tice Valley Boulevard and right again on Rossmoor Parkway. From there turn right on Stanley Dollar Drive. . . . ● **TOURNAMENTS:** A limited number of outside events is allowed with approval of the board of directors. A 50-player minimum is needed. Events should be booked six months in advance. The banquet facility can hold 200 people. ● **TRAVEL:** The Lafayette Park Hotel is located 15 minutes from the golf course. For reservations call 925-283-3700.

28. ROSSMOOR GOLF COURSE

PLAY POLICY & FEES: Reciprocal play is accepted with members of other private clubs. Guest fees are $50 when accompanied by a member and $100 unaccompanied. Carts are $36 for guests.

TEE TIMES: Have your head professional call for a tee time.

DRESS CODE: Appropriate golf attire is required. Nonmetal spikes are mandatory from the beginning of April to the end of Novemeber.

COURSE DESCRIPTION: This tight, rolling course is located in the San Ramon Valley. It has undulating greens, many trees, lots of sidehill lies, and narrow approach shots. The 402-yard third is a great par 4. There's a lake in front of the tee and a huge oak in the middle of the fairway. Holes 12 through 16, a 419-yard severe dogleg right, a 188-yard par 3, a 492-yard par 5, a 385-yard par 4, and a 199-yard par 3, are the pride of the course.

NOTES: LPGA events have been held at this course.

LOCATION: From Interstate 680 in Alamo take the Stone Valley Road east to Round Hill Road north. The course is one mile from Interstate 680. . . . ● **TOURNAMENTS:** This course is available for outside tournaments on Monday only. The banquet facility can accommodate up to 300 people.

29. ROUND HILL COUNTRY CLUB

30 DIABLO COUNTRY CLUB
ARCHITECT: JACK NEVILLE, 1914

1700 Clubhouse Road
Diablo, CA 94528

PRO SHOP: 925-837-9233

Jerry Zan Houten, Manager
Paul Wilcox Jr., PGA Professional
Sohan Singh, Superintendent

Driving Range
Practice Greens ●
Clubhouse ●
Food / Beverage ●
Accommodations
Pull Carts
Power Carts ●
Club Rental ●
$pecial Offers

	1	2	3	4	5	6	7	8	9	OUT
BACK	391	388	166	419	540	192	490	157	436	3179
REGULAR	358	378	157	401	529	179	485	141	401	3029
par	4	4	3	4	5	3	5	3	4	35
handicap	7	5	13	1	9	11	17	15	3	-
FORWARD	360	373	141	347	453	158	472	113	369	2786
par	4	4	3	4	5	3	5	3	4	35
handicap	9	7	15	11	1	13	3	17	5	-

	10	11	12	13	14	15	16	17	18	IN
BACK	536	441	430	238	338	421	181	397	479	3461
REGULAR	513	379	390	213	326	404	164	385	474	3248
par	5	4	4	3	4	4	3	4	5	36
handicap	12	4	6	8	14	2	16	10	18	-
FORWARD	429	373	376	160	310	408	145	334	431	2966
par	5	4	4	3	4	5	3	4	5	37
handicap	2	8	12	16	14	4	18	10	6	-

BACK	
yardage	6640
par	71
rating	71.5
slope	123

REGULAR	
yardage	6277
par	71
rating	71.0
slope	120

FORWARD	
yardage	5752
par	72
rating	72
slope	129

31 OAKHURST COUNTRY CLUB
ARCHITECT: RON FREAM, 1990

1001 Peacock Creek Drive
Clayton, CA 94517

PRO SHOP: 925-672-9737

Tom Norton, General Manager
Art Gaoiran, Head Professional, PGA

Driving Range ●
Practice Greens ●
Clubhouse ●
Food / Beverage ●
Accommodations
Pull Carts
Power Carts ●
Club Rental ●
$pecial Offers

	1	2	3	4	5	6	7	8	9	OUT
BACK	517	380	163	362	374	402	495	144	361	3198
REGULAR	488	340	123	342	351	372	466	123	340	2945
par	5	4	3	4	4	4	5	3	4	36
handicap	5	1	17	13	7	3	11	15	9	-
FORWARD	457	313	92	324	323	344	432	105	316	2706
par	5	4	3	4	4	4	5	3	4	36
handicap	1	11	17	13	5	9	3	15	7	-

	10	11	12	13	14	15	16	17	18	IN
BACK	405	181	535	122	340	274	480	325	415	3077
REGULAR	381	160	513	118	315	258	471	302	380	2898
par	4	3	5	3	4	4	5	4	4	36
handicap	4	10	8	18	6	14	12	16	2	-
FORWARD	349	126	469	95	295	239	404	272	330	2579
par	4	3	5	3	4	4	5	4	4	36
handicap	8	16	2	18	6	14	12	10	4	-

BACK	
yardage	6275
par	72
rating	70.9
slope	127

REGULAR	
yardage	5843
par	72
rating	69.1
slope	122

FORWARD	
yardage	5285
par	72
rating	70.3
slope	123

PLAY POLICY & FEES: Reciprocal play is accepted with members of other private clubs. Guest fees are $55 Tuesday through Thursday and $65 Friday through Sunday with a member. Carts are $12 per person. Reciprocal fees are $120, including cart. The course is closed on Monday.

TEE TIMES: Have your club pro call for arrangements.

DRESS CODE: Appropriate golf attire is required. Nonmetal spikes are encouraged.

COURSE DESCRIPTION: This traditional, tree-lined layout has small, demanding greens and tough par 3s. The 436-yard 9th, 536-yard 10th, 441-yard 11th, 430-yard 12th, and 238-yard, par-3 13th could be the best string of holes in Northern California. Huge oak trees come into play often. The 397-yard 17th and 479-yard 18th play through oaks that are 300 years old.

LOCATION: From Interstate 680 in Danville take the Diablo Road exit into the Village of Diablo development. Go a quarter of a mile, veering left at the fork in the road; then turn left on Clubhouse Road.

. . . ● **TOURNAMENTS:** Call the head professional for tournament information.

30. DIABLO COUNTRY CLUB

PLAY POLICY & FEES: Outside play is accepted. Green fees are $60 weekdays and $80 weekends. Twilight fees are available. Carts are included and required.

TEE TIMES: Reservations can be booked seven days in advance by calling 877-625-4877.

DRESS CODE: Collared shirts and nonmetal spikes are encouraged. No blue jeans are allowed on the course.

COURSE DESCRIPTION: This course has quickly become a solid test of any player's game. It's a highly rated semiprivate layout, with lots of lateral hazards and out-of-bounds. The fairways are undulating with few even lies. The large greens are quick and true. The 535-yard 12th hole plays along a barranca on the right, and the next two par 4s require precision tee shots. The 18th hole, which plays over a huge barranca, can be misleading if not downright deceptive. You have to play the tee shot just left of the right fairway bunkers.

LOCATION: From Interstate 680 take the Ygnacio Valley exit east to Clayton Road. Turn right on Clayton Road and drive two miles. Turn left on Peacock Creek Drive.

. . . ● **TOURNAMENTS:** This course is available for outside tournaments.

31. OAKHURST COUNTRY CLUB

BLACKHAWK COUNTRY CLUB

ARCHITECTS: ROBERT VON HAGGE, 1981; BRUCE DEVLIN (L); TED ROBINSON (F)

599 Blackhawk Club Drive
Danville, CA 94506

PRO SHOP: 925-736-6565
OFFICE: 925-736-6520

Mark Caufield, Head Professional, PGA
Mike Nunemacher, Superintendent
Paul Lonestar, Tournament Director

Driving Range ●
Practice Greens ●
Clubhouse ●
Food / Beverage ●
Accommodations
Pull Carts
Power Carts ●
Club Rental ●
$pecial Offers

	1	2	3	4	5	6	7	8	9	OUT
BACK	428	340	591	209	460	401	209	404	538	3580
REGULAR	389	317	576	172	439	393	182	356	520	3344
par	4	4	5	3	5	4	3	4	5	37
handicap	7	11	1	13	17	9	5	3	15	-
FORWARD	316	291	551	144	427	317	108	310	416	2880
par	4	4	5	3	5	4	3	4	5	37
handicap	7	11	3	17	1	13	15	9	5	-

	10	11	12	13	14	15	16	17	18	IN
BACK	201	583	155	343	385	627	227	330	404	3255
REGULAR	167	562	133	321	359	609	210	316	370	3047
par	3	5	3	4	4	5	3	4	4	35
handicap	16	4	10	12	6	2	16	18	8	-
FORWARD	139	452	103	309	270	495	132	302	350	2552
par	3	5	3	4	4	5	3	4	4	35
handicap	16	6	14	8	12	2	18	10	4	-

BACK	
yardage	6835
par	72
rating	74.1
slope	136

REGULAR	
yardage	6391
par	72
rating	71.8
slope	135

FORWARD	
yardage	5432
par	72
rating	71.5
slope	131

 # HARDING PARK GOLF COURSE

ARCHITECT: WILLIE WATSON, 1925

Harding Park/Skyline
San Francisco, CA 94132

PRO SHOP: 415-750-GOLF

Jack Baker, Head Professional, PGA
John Larner, General Manager

Driving Range ●
Practice Greens ●
Clubhouse ●
Food / Beverage ●
Accommodations
Pull Carts ●
Power Carts ●
Club Rental ●
$pecial Offers

	1	2	3	4	5	6	7	8	9	OUT
BACK	382	346	166	571	370	401	404	201	503	3344
REGULAR	377	339	161	572	337	396	386	204	495	3267
par	4	4	3	5	4	4	4	3	5	36
handicap	7	17	11	3	13	1	5	9	15	-
FORWARD	346	348	146	550	325	372	319	185	481	3072
par	4	4	3	5	4	4	4	3	5	36
handicap	9	7	17	1	11	3	13	15	5	-

	10	11	12	13	14	15	16	17	18	IN
BACK	558	185	492	406	425	405	337	170	417	3395
REGULAR	552	182	492	401	401	404	334	169	384	3319
par	5	3	5	4	4	4	4	3	4	36
handicap	4	10	16	2	8	6	18	14	12	-
FORWARD	528	139	468	400	366	375	320	155	364	3115
par	5	3	5	4	4	4	3	4	37	
handicap	2	18	4	6	10	8	14	16	12	-

BACK	
yardage	6739
par	72
rating	72.1
slope	124

REGULAR	
yardage	6586
par	72
rating	71.3
slope	119

FORWARD	
yardage	6187
par	73
rating	74.5
slope	-

PLAY POLICY & FEES: Reciprocal play is allowed. Green fees for reciprocal play are $125. Guests must be accompanied by a member at time of play. Guest fees are $50 weekdays and $65 weekends. Carts are $24 and mandatory on both courses.

DRESS CODE: No denim clothing is allowed on the golf course or in the clubhouse. Nonmetal spikes are required.

COURSE DESCRIPTION: The Lakeside Course is rolling and imaginative. It has large, undulating greens, lots of water, and tight fairways. There are many up-and-down holes threading through oak trees. The course requires precise shot-making. The 404-yard eighth has a creek all the way down the right side. The Falls Course is a shorter version with emphasis on placement. It is rolling and hilly between holes. The first hole is a straight drop, but after that it flattens out. The Falls' 14th, a 384-yard dogleg, has a barranca on the right side. A moon crater in the green puts precision on the approach. Each course has a clubhouse and pro shop.

NOTES: The Falls Course is 6,738 yards and rated 72.5 from the championship tees with a slope of 134. The Lakeside Course: See scorecard for yardage and rating information.

LOCATION: From Interstate 680 take the Crow Canyon exit, head east, and take a right on Blackhawk Club Drive.

. . . ● **TOURNAMENTS:** Shotgun tournaments are available weekdays only. Carts are required.

32. BLACKHAWK COUNTRY CLUB

PLAY POLICY & FEES: Green fees are $26 weekdays and $31 weekends at the Harding Course. Golfers with a resident card pay $17 weekdays, $20 weekends. The Fleming Course fees are $13. Golfers with a resident card pay $7 weekdays and $9 weekends. Senior rates are also available. Carts are $11 for nine holes and $22 for 18 holes with a $5 deposit.

TEE TIMES: Reservations can be booked six days in advance for the general public by calling the automated reservations at 415-750-GOLF. A $1 charge will be added to your green fee at the time of play for using this system. Players with a resident card can make tee times seven days in advance.

COURSE DESCRIPTION: This sprawling course surrounded by Lake Merced is mostly flat, but well guarded by trees. The back nine, designed by Jack Fleming, is one of the best in Northern California.

NOTES: This course is the site for the San Francisco City Golf Championship, the biggest and oldest city tournament in the country. The Fleming Course, a nine-hole, par-3 beginner layout, is 2,700 yards, and par is 32.

LOCATION: Heading north into San Francisco on Interstate 280, take 19th Avenue and make a left on Skyline Boulevard. Follow Skyline to Morton Drive and turn left to the course.

. . . ● **TOURNAMENTS:** A 12-player minimum is required to book a tournament.

33. HARDING PARK GOLF COURSE

34 SAN FRANCISCO GOLF CLUB
ARCHITECT: A.W. TILLINGHAST, 1915

Junipero Serra
San Francisco, CA 94132

PRO SHOP: 415-469-4122

Rick Rhoads, PGA Professional
Robert Klinesteker, Superintendent

Driving Range ●
Practice Greens ●
Clubhouse ●
Food / Beverage ●
Accommodations
Pull Carts
Power Carts ●
Club Rental ●
$Special Offers

	1	2	3	4	5	6	7	8	9	OUT
BACK	523	424	388	220	381	422	190	378	582	3508
REGULAR	505	409	358	211	375	408	170	337	550	3323
par	5	4	4	3	4	4	3	4	5	36
handicap	15	1	5	11	7	3	17	9	13	-
FORWARD	480	387	347	168	340	381	154	310	526	3093
par	5	5	4	3	4	4	3	4	5	37
handicap	3	11	9	15	7	5	17	13	1	-

	10	11	12	13	14	15	16	17	18	IN
BACK	410	161	408	381	344	169	375	430	530	3208
REGULAR	380	152	373	376	337	157	368	422	512	3077
par	4	3	4	4	4	3	4	4	5	35
handicap	6	18	4	8	14	16	10	2	12	-
FORWARD	368	138	336	343	319	138	362	410	508	2922
par	4	3	4	4	4	3	4	5	5	36
handicap	2	18	4	14	12	16	10	8	6	-

BACK	
yardage	6716
par	71
rating	73.0
slope	134

REGULAR	
yardage	6400
par	71
rating	71.7
slope	131

FORWARD	
yardage	6015
par	73
rating	75.2
slope	135

35 LAKE MERCED GOLF & COUNTRY CLUB
ARCHITECTS: WILLIAM LOCK, 1922; ALISTER MACKENZIE, 1927; REES JONES, 1997

2300 Junipero Serra
Daly City, CA 94015

PRO SHOP: 650-755-2239
CLUBHOUSE: 650-755-2233

Woody Wright, Director of Golf, PGA
Lou Tonelli, Superintendent

Driving Range ●
Practice Greens ●
Clubhouse ●
Food / Beverage ●
Accommodations
Pull Carts
Power Carts ●
Club Rental
$Special Offers

	1	2	3	4	5	6	7	8	9	OUT
BACK	432	390	186	441	399	503	458	206	516	3531
REGULAR	419	370	162	405	381	479	434	184	502	3336
par	4	4	3	4	4	5	4	3	5	36
handicap	3	9	15	1	7	17	5	11	13	-
FORWARD	408	350	146	392	370	466	413	159	492	3196
par	4	4	3	4	4	5	4	3	5	36
handicap	3	9	15	1	7	17	5	11	13	-

	10	11	12	13	14	15	16	17	18	IN
BACK	391	380	196	376	496	220	335	382	556	3332
REGULAR	373	359	175	364	475	197	320	366	538	3167
par	4	4	3	4	5	3	4	4	5	36
handicap	2	6	16	12	18	8	14	4	10	-
FORWARD	363	340	152	347	460	178	309	359	532	3040
par	4	4	3	4	5	3	4	4	5	36
handicap	2	6	16	12	18	8	14	4	10	-

BACK	
yardage	6863
par	72
rating	74.4
slope	138

REGULAR	
yardage	6503
par	72
rating	72.7
slope	134

FORWARD	
yardage	6236
par	72
rating	71.5
slope	131

PLAY POLICY & FEES: Reciprocal play is not accepted. Members and guests only. Guest fees are $50 when accompanied by a member and $150 unaccompanied. Carts are reserved for players with medical excuses; the fee is $25 when accompanied by a member and $30 unaccompanied.

DRESS CODE: Appropriate golf attire is mandatory and enforced. No shorts are allowed on the golf course. Nonmetal spikes are required.

COURSE DESCRIPTION: This serene, immaculate course is rated among the top in the country. It's a medium-length, sprawling course with fast, undulating greens and 100 bunkers. Every hole is a treat. Designed in 1915 by A.W. Tillinghast, the course has strategically placed bunkers and pine trees that make accuracy essential. The 408-yard dogleg-right 12th and the 430-yard dogleg-right 17th are examples of Tillinghast's subtle touch.

NOTES: The course played host to the 1974 Curtis Cup Match and has been used for U.S. Open sectional qualifying. Adjacent to the seventh tee are monuments commemorating the last dueling spot in California.

LOCATION: Heading into San Francisco on U.S.101, take the 19th Avenue exit through town until it turns into Junipero Serra Boulevard (past San Francisco State University). Turn right on Brotherhood Way and take the first left onto Saint Thomas More Way to the course on the left.

. . . ● **TOURNAMENTS:** This course is not available for outside events.

34. SAN FRANCISCO GOLF CLUB

PLAY POLICY & FEES: Reciprocal play is at the discretion of the pro. Guest fees when accompanied by a member are $45 weekdays and $50 weekends. Green fees for reciprocal guests range from $100 to $200. Carts are $12 with a member and $15 without. Reciprocal guests are required to use a cart or a caddy.

DRESS CODE: Appropriate golf attire and nonmetal spikes are required.

COURSE DESCRIPTION: This is a long, challenging course with big, undulating greens, huge pines, and San Francisco weather. There are some difficult par 3s, especially the 15th hole. This course is well maintained and walkable. The uphill, dogleg-right fourth hole and dogleg-left seventh are among the toughest holes in the area.

LOCATION: On 19th Avenue in San Francisco or Highway 1, merge onto Junipero Serra Boulevard toward Daly City and follow it to the course.

. . . ● **TOURNAMENTS:** This course is not available for outside events.

35. LAKE MERCED GOLF & COUNTRY CLUB

524 Post Street
San Francisco, CA 94102

PRO SHOP: 415-587-8338
CLUBHOUSE: 415-587-4800

Paul Kennedy, General Manager
Jim Lucius, Head Professional, PGA
John Fleming, Superintendent

Driving Range ●
Practice Greens ●
Clubhouse ●
Food / Beverage ●
Accommodations
Pull Carts
Power Carts ●
Club Rental ●
$pecial Offers

	1	2	3	4	5	6	7	8	9	OUT
BACK	533	394	223	438	457	437	288	137	433	3340
REGULAR	515	380	205	417	434	427	280	125	426	3209
par	5	4	3	4	4	4	4	3	4	35
handicap	13	5	11	1	3	7	15	17	9	-
FORWARD	504	370	187	370	411	418	259	113	418	3050
par	5	4	3	4	5	5	4	3	5	38
handicap	5	1	13	3	11	9	15	17	7	-

	10	11	12	13	14	15	16	17	18	IN
BACK	422	430	396	186	417	157	609	522	347	3486
REGULAR	383	422	375	172	408	133	579	483	332	3287
par	4	4	4	3	4	3	5	5	4	36
handicap	8	4	10	16	6	18	2	14	12	-
FORWARD	377	416	358	165	392	125	507	458	309	3107
par	4	5	4	3	5	3	5	5	4	38
handicap	10	6	12	14	16	18	2	4	8	-

BACK	
yardage	6826
par	71
rating	74.0
slope	135

REGULAR	
yardage	6496
par	71
rating	72.1
slope	133

FORWARD	
yardage	6157
par	76
rating	76.2
slope	138

2001 Hillside Boulevard
Colma, CA 94014

PRO SHOP: 650-992-5155

Donald Giovannini, General Manager, PGA
Brian Hall, Superintendent
Ron Barels, Owner

Driving Range ●
Practice Greens ●
Clubhouse ●
Food / Beverage ●
Accommodations
Pull Carts ●
Power Carts ●
Club Rental ●
$pecial Offers

	1	2	3	4	5	6	7	8	9	OUT
BACK	-	-	-	-	-	-	-	-	-	-
REGULAR	365	460	163	478	530	372	394	355	326	3443
par	4	4	3	5	5	4	4	4	4	37
handicap	4	1	7	9	2	3	8	5	6	-
FORWARD	365	460	163	478	530	372	394	355	326	3443
par	4	4	3	5	5	4	4	4	4	37
handicap	4	1	7	9	2	3	8	5	6	-

	10	11	12	13	14	15	16	17	18	IN
BACK	-	-	-	-	-	-	-	-	-	-
REGULAR	-	-	-	-	-	-	-	-	-	-
par	-	-	-	-	-	-	-	-	-	-
handicap	-	-	-	-	-	-	-	-	-	-
FORWARD	-	-	-	-	-	-	-	-	-	-
par	-	-	-	-	-	-	-	-	-	-
handicap	-	-	-	-	-	-	-	-	-	-

BACK	
yardage	-
par	-
rating	-
slope	-

REGULAR	
yardage	3443
par	37
rating	-
slope	-

FORWARD	
yardage	3443
par	37
rating	-
slope	-

PLAY POLICY & FEES: All guests must be accompanied by a member.

DRESS CODE: Appropriate golf attire is required.

COURSE DESCRIPTION: The Lake Course, perennially among the top 10 in the country, has been the site of four U.S. Opens (1955, 1966,1987, 1998). It is long and tight, with lots of trees and small, undulating greens. Long par 4s dominate the Lake Course, making it seem like the longest 6,800-yard course in golf. The Ocean Course is shorter and tighter but equally challenging. Wind and fog often come into play. The Cliffs Course, a scenic new nine-hole, par-3 course overlooking the ocean and designed by Jay Morrish and Tom Weiskopf, opened in October 1994.

NOTES: The nine-hole Cliffs Course is 1,506 yards from the long tees and 780 yards from the short tees. Par is 27. The course is not rated. The Lakes Course is 6,496 yards and rated 72.1 from the regular tees with a slope of 133. Par is 71. Women's tees are 6,157 yards and rated 76.2 with a slope of 138. See scorecard for ratings and slope on the Ocean Course.

LOCATION: Driving south on 19th Avenue through San Francisco, turn right on Sloat Boulevard. Follow it until it splits into a "Y" (before the San Francisco Zoo). Turn left onto Skyline Boulevard. The course is at the top of the hill on the left.

. . . ● **TOURNAMENTS:** This course is not available for outside events.

36. OLYMPIC CLUB

PLAY POLICY & FEES: Green fees are $12 weekdays and $15 weekends and holidays for nine holes. Senior rates are $10 before 10 a.m. Monday through Friday. Carts are $12 for nine holes.

TEE TIMES: Reservations can be made starting on Monday for Monday through Sunday.

DRESS CODE: Appropriate golf attire is required.

COURSE DESCRIPTION: This course is tight and well guarded by trees. The course is currently open but is under renovation to be completed by January 2000. Playing conditions will be greatly improved.

NOTES: Cypress Golf Course is under new management.

LOCATION: Take Interstate 280 north to Hickey Boulevard and turn right. Take Hickey Boulevard to El Camino Real and turn left. Take El Camino Real one mile to Serramonte Boulevard, turn right, and take Serramonte Boulevard to Hillside Boulevard. Turn right onto Hillside Boulevard to the course. From the north take Interstate 280 south to Serramonte. Follow Serramonte to Hillside. The course is 800 yards south on the left.

. . . ● **TOURNAMENTS:** Shotgun tournaments are available weekdays only. A 16-player minimum is required to book a tournament.

37. CYPRESS GOLF COURSE

GLENEAGLES INTERNATIONAL GOLF COURSE

ARCHITECT: JACK FLEMING, 1963

2100 Sunnydale Avenue
San Francisco, CA 94134

PRO SHOP: 415-587-2425

Bill Smith, Manager
Erik DeLambert, Superintendent

Driving Range
Practice Greens ●
Clubhouse ●
Food / Beverage ●
Accommodations
Pull Carts
Power Carts ●
Club Rental
$pecial Offers

	1	2	3	4	5	6	7	8	9	OUT
BACK										
REGULAR										
par										
handicap										
FORWARD										
par										
handicap										

BACK	
yardage	3321
par	36
rating	73.6
slope	136

	10	11	12	13	14	15	16	17	18	IN
BACK										
REGULAR										
par										
handicap										
FORWARD										
par										
handicap										

REGULAR	
yardage	3210
par	36
rating	69.9
slope	129

FORWARD	
yardage	
par	
rating	-
slope	-

 SEQUOYAH COUNTRY CLUB

4550 Heafey Road
Oakland, CA 94605

PRO SHOP: 510-632-4069
CLUBHOUSE: 510-632-2900

John R. Bearden, Head Professional, PGA

Driving Range ●
Practice Greens ●
Clubhouse ●
Food / Beverage ●
Accommodations
Pull Carts ●
Power Carts ●
Club Rental ●
$pecial Offers

	1	2	3	4	5	6	7	8	9	OUT
BACK	311	191	400	374	137	528	329	389	348	3007
REGULAR	311	191	387	369	137	509	314	366	333	2917
par	4	3	4	4	3	5	4	4	4	35
handicap	17	3	5	1	15	3	11	7	9	-
FORWARD	304	188	380	359	119	496	304	327	299	2776
par	4	3	4	4	3	5	4	4	4	35
handicap	13	15	3	5	17	1	7	9	11	-

BACK	
yardage	6061
par	70
rating	70.4
slope	129

	10	11	12	13	14	15	16	17	18	IN
BACK	380	445	172	337	238	330	482	220	450	3054
REGULAR	380	421	154	324	217	323	469	192	441	2921
par	4	4	3	4	3	4	5	3	5	35
handicap	4	2	16	12	10	14	6	8	18	-
FORWARD	373	448	126	307	231	316	452	177	432	2862
par	4	5	3	4	4	4	5	3	5	37
handicap	4	6	16	10	18	12	2	14	8	-

REGULAR	
yardage	5838
par	70
rating	69.7
slope	128

FORWARD	
yardage	5638
par	72
rating	73.3
slope	131

PLAY POLICY & FEES: Green fees are $11 for nine holes and $17 for 18 holes weekdays. On weekends, the fees are $14 for nine holes and $24 for 18 holes. Carts are $12 for nine holes and $22 for 18 holes.

TEE TIMES: Reservations can be booked seven days in advance for weekends and holidays. Reservations for weekdays are on a first-come, first served basis.

DRESS CODE: No tanks tops are allowed. Golf spikes are mandatory.

COURSE DESCRIPTION: This sleeper course is patterned after a Scottish links-type course with a rolling terrain. You'll find tight, tree-lined fairways and tricky greens. Good target shots are required. The course is well maintained and often foggy and windy. The greens and tee boxes are usually in great shape.

NOTES: Lee Trevino played the course. According to legend, he shot 71 on his first try and 72 on his second try. There is another local legend, however: no one has ever broken par the first time out. The course record is 65, set by local amateur John Camozzi.

LOCATION: Driving north on U.S. 101 into San Francisco, take the Cow Palace/Brisbane exit to Old Bayshore and go left at Geneva Street. In 1.5 miles, turn right on Moscow and then right again on Persia. It's three blocks to Sunnydale Avenue.

. . . ● **TOURNAMENTS:** This course is not available for outside events.

38. GLENEAGLES INTERNATIONAL GOLF

PLAY POLICY & FEES: Reciprocal play is accepted with members of other private clubs weekdays only. Guest green fees are $60 weekdays and $75 weekends. Carts are mandatory .

TEE TIMES: Have your club pro call to make arrangements.

DRESS CODE: Appropriate golf attire is required. Nonmetal spikes are required April through September.

COURSE DESCRIPTION: This mature course is short, hilly, and tight. The elevated tees and fast greens make for exciting par 3s. Member Dr. Wayne Wright has scored a hole in one on all of the five par 3s. This exclusive course is very tough, and local knowledge of the greens is the only way to survive. The 445-yard 11th, with a panoramic view of the bay, is a great challenge.

NOTES: This course was the site of the PGA Tour's Oakland Open in the 1930s, featuring players such as Ben Hogan and Sam Snead. The course record, set by Don Witt, is 60.

LOCATION: From Interstate 580 in Oakland take the 98th Avenue exit off the left side of the freeway. Turn left onto Mountain Boulevard. Turn right on Sequoyah Road and go three-fourths of a mile. Turn right at the stop sign onto Heafey Road and drive to the course.

. . . ● **TOURNAMENTS:** Shotgun tournaments are available Monday only. Carts are required. A 100-player minimum is required to book a tournament. Events should be scheduled 12 months in advance. A banquet facility is available that can accommodate 250 people.

39. SEQUOYAH COUNTRY CLUB

CHUCK CORICA GOLF COMPLEX
ARCHITECTS: WILLIAM P. BELL, 1927; WILLIAM F. BELL, 1955

1 Clubhouse Memorial
Alameda, CA 94501

PRO SHOP: 510-522-4321

Dana Banke, General Manager, PGA
Matt Plumlee, Head Professional, PGA
Doug Poole, Superintendent

Driving Range ●
Practice Greens ●
Clubhouse ●
Food / Beverage ●
Accommodations
Pull Carts ●
Power Carts ●
Club Rental ●
$pecial Offers

	1	2	3	4	5	6	7	8	9	OUT
BACK	371	493	345	177	330	459	176	386	400	3137
REGULAR	358	479	335	169	317	446	160	363	367	2994
par	4	5	4	3	4	5	3	4	4	36
handicap	7	3	13	17	15	5	11	1	9	-
FORWARD	326	450	314	154	284	439	150	412	340	2869
par	4	5	4	3	4	5	3	5	4	37
handicap	7	1	15	17	11	3	13	5	9	-

BACK	
yardage	6141
par	71
rating	69.2
slope	119

	10	11	12	13	14	15	16	17	18	IN
BACK	389	166	364	403	450	192	393	281	366	3004
REGULAR	367	139	356	385	434	154	385	268	344	2832
par	4	3	4	4	5	3	4	4	4	35
handicap	12	18	10	8	4	2	6	16	14	-
FORWARD	366	134	329	376	423	99	381	250	333	2691
par	4	3	4	4	5	3	4	4	4	35
handicap	4	14	12	8	2	16	6	18	10	-

REGULAR	
yardage	5826
par	71
rating	67.6
slope	116

FORWARD	
yardage	5560
par	72
rating	71.0
slope	114

PLAY POLICY & FEES: Green fees for the 18-hole Earl Fry and Jack Clark Courses are $16 Monday through Thursday and $19 Friday through Saturday for residents. For nonresidents Monday through Thursday fees are $24, and Friday through Sunday fees are $27. Carts are $24. Green fees for the Mel Albright nine-hole course are $7 Monday through Thursday and $9 Friday through Sunday. Senior, junior, and twilight rates are available for all courses.

TEE TIMES: Reservations can be booked seven days in advance.

DRESS CODE: No tank tops or cutoffs are allowed.

COURSE DESCRIPTION: These are flat, challenging courses. The Jack Clark Course, designed by William Francis Bell and remodeled by Robert Muir Graves, is longer and more difficult. It is the more popular course, with the par-3 15th—bunkers left and right and a water hazard behind the green—serving as the signature hole. The Earl Fry Course was designed by William Park Bell and remodeled by Desmond Muirhead. Both are well maintained and walkable courses with lots of trees and some water.

NOTES: The course now features a lighted, state-of-the-art driving range and teaching academy. The Chuck Corica Complex also includes a nine-hole executive course. Par is 27 for the nine-hole executive course. The Jack Clark Course is 6,107 yards and is rated 68.5 from the regular tees, with a slope of 100. Forward tees are 5,473 yards and rated 70.0. For more information on the Earl Fry course, see scorecard.

LOCATION: From Interstate 880 south of the Oakland Coliseum, take the Hegenberger Road exit west one mile. Turn right on Doolittle Road to Island Drive and turn left. Turn left again on Memorial Drive to the course.

. . . ● **TOURNAMENTS:** A 16-player minimum is required to book a tournament. Carts are required Friday through Sunday and holidays. Tournaments should be scheduled 12 months in advance. A banquet facility is available and can accommodate 100 people. ● **TRAVEL:** The Oakland Hyatt is recommended for convenient lodging.

40. CHUCK CORICA GOLF COMPLEX

ARCHITECTS: WILLIAM LOCK, 1917; ROBERT MUIR GRAVES, 1989

11450 Golf Links Road
Oakland, CA 94605

PRO SHOP: 510-351-5812

Raymond Chester, Director of Golf
Gloria Armstrong, Professional
Linda Rawls, Director of Operations

Driving Range ●
Practice Greens ●
Clubhouse ●
Food / Beverage ●
Accommodations
Pull Carts
Power Carts ●
Club Rental ●
$pecial Offers

	1	2	3	4	5	6	7	8	9	OUT
BACK	375	151	461	488	385	315	191	491	178	3035
REGULAR	366	145	453	470	375	306	183	485	144	2927
par	4	3	5	5	4	4	3	5	3	36
handicap	1	13	9	7	15	11	5	3	17	-
FORWARD	362	136	446	426	328	294	169	337	143	2641
par	4	3	5	5	4	4	3	4	3	35
handicap	3	13	5	1	17	7	11	9	15	-

	10	11	12	13	14	15	16	17	18	IN
BACK	301	389	170	296	375	269	326	180	677	2983
REGULAR	287	338	127	275	366	254	300	173	665	2785
par	4	4	3	4	4	4	4	3	6	36
handicap	16	2	18	10	4	14	6	8	12	-
FORWARD	277	337	118	253	284	232	286	168	638	2593
par	4	4	3	4	4	4	4	3	6	36
handicap	12	8	18	4	10	16	6	14	2	-

BACK	
yardage	6018
par	72
rating	68.6
slope	115

REGULAR	
yardage	5712
par	72
rating	67.3
slope	113

FORWARD	
yardage	5234
par	71
rating	68.5
slope	116

 CROW CANYON COUNTRY CLUB

ARCHITECT: TED ROBINSON, 1977

711 Silverlake Drive
Danville, CA 94526

PRO SHOP: 925-735-8300
CLUBHOUSE: 510-735-5700

Brent Mulanax, PGA Professional
Ernie Martin, Superintendent

Driving Range ●
Practice Greens ●
Clubhouse ●
Food / Beverage ●
Accommodations
Pull Carts
Power Carts ●
Club Rental ●
$pecial Offers

	1	2	3	4	5	6	7	8	9	OUT
BACK	370	544	401	165	326	196	373	167	388	2930
REGULAR	344	523	372	148	304	161	349	148	375	2724
par	4	5	4	3	4	3	4	3	4	34
handicap	9	7	3	13	15	1	11	17	5	-
FORWARD	344	523	372	148	304	161	349	148	375	2724
par	4	5	4	3	4	3	4	3	4	34
handicap	7	1	5	15	13	11	9	17	3	-

	10	11	12	13	14	15	16	17	18	IN
BACK	340	369	146	519	344	336	170	395	400	3019
REGULAR	307	345	134	497	327	330	137	377	388	2842
par	4	4	3	5	4	4	3	4	4	35
handicap	14	4	18	8	16	10	12	6	2	-
FORWARD	307	345	134	497	327	330	137	377	388	2842
par	4	4	3	5	4	4	3	4	5	36
handicap	14	10	16	2	12	4	18	6	8	-

BACK	
yardage	5949
par	69
rating	68.7
slope	121

REGULAR	
yardage	5566
par	69
rating	67.0
slope	117

FORWARD	
yardage	5566
par	70
rating	72.3
slope	126

18
HOLES

PLAY POLICY & FEES: Green fees are $15 for Oakland residents and $18 for nonresidents weekdays. On weekends the fees are $20 for Oakland residents and $23 for nonresidents. Seniors are $9. Twilight rates are available. Carts are $9 per person weekdays and $11 per person weekends.

DRESS CODE: Golf attire is encouraged.

COURSE DESCRIPTION: This course is hilly but walkable. The 18th hole is a unique 677-yard par 6, which starts off level and slopes down and then up. Out-of-bounds is to the left, and trees are on the right.

NOTES: Take your complaints to course manager Raymond Chester, former All-Pro tight end with the Oakland Raiders. The course is one of the oldest in Northern California. Tony Lema, 1964 British Open champion, grew up near Lake Chabot. The course record of 60 is shared by John Fry and Gary Vanier.

LOCATION: From Interstate 580 in Oakland, take the Golf Links Road exit and follow the road to the end.

. . . ● **TOURNAMENTS:** This course is available for outside tournaments.

41. LAKE CHABOT GOLF COURSE

18
HOLES

PLAY POLICY & FEES: Reciprocal play is accepted with members of other private clubs. Guest fees are $45 Tuesday through Thursday and $55 Friday and weekends. The course is closed on Monday.

TEE TIMES: Have your club pro call for arrangements.

DRESS CODE: Shirts with collars are required. No jeans, tank tops, T-shirts, short shorts, gym shorts, or tennis shorts may be worn. Nonmetal spikes are mandatory.

COURSE DESCRIPTION: This is a hilly, tight, rolling course. The sixth hole is a notable par 3. It's 196 yards against the wind to an elevated green. The par-4 third can get you into trouble. The fairway is only 15 yards from out-of-bounds on the right. Watch out for the 400-yard, par-4 18th hole with an elevated tee and water along the left side. This course is known for being very well manicured, with great drainage during the rainy season. The course is well bunkered with water coming into play on nine holes.

NOTES: The Diablo Advocates Pro-Am initially started at Crow Canyon with such golfers as Johnny Miller, George Archer, Larry Nelson, Bill Russell, Joe Morgan, and Jim Rice. The men's and women's course records are held by Duane Robertson (62) and Jane Crafter (64).

LOCATION: From Interstate 680 in San Ramon, take the Crow Canyon exit east. Turn left on El Capitan and right on Silver Lake Drive.

. . . ● **TOURNAMENTS:** Tournaments are allowed on Monday only. Carts are required. A 72-player minimum is required to book a tournament.

42. CROW CANYON COUNTRY CLUB

CANYON LAKES COUNTRY CLUB
ARCHITECT: TED ROBINSON, 1987

640 Bollinger Canyon Way
San Ramon, CA 94583

PRO SHOP: 925-735-6511
CLUBHOUSE: 925-735-6224

Russ Dicks, PGA Professional
Bobby Cox, Superintendent

Driving Range
Practice Greens •
Clubhouse •
Food / Beverage •
Accommodations
Pull Carts
Power Carts •
Club Rental •
$pecial Offers

	1	2	3	4	5	6	7	8	9	OUT
BACK	340	550	213	292	152	347	501	403	390	3188
REGULAR	319	524	201	274	135	328	478	380	355	2994
par	4	5	3	4	3	4	5	4	4	36
handicap	17	9	5	11	15	13	7	1	3	-
FORWARD	287	433	171	207	120	303	446	346	294	2607
par	4	5	3	4	3	4	5	4	4	36
handicap	15	3	11	13	17	7	1	5	9	-

	10	11	12	13	14	15	16	17	18	IN
BACK	205	368	385	195	523	163	365	548	433	3185
REGULAR	181	347	362	171	500	154	348	508	405	2976
par	3	4	4	3	5	3	4	5	4	35
handicap	8	14	12	16	4	10	18	2	6	-
FORWARD	138	340	314	119	442	108	324	452	347	2584
par	3	4	4	3	5	3	4	5	4	35
handicap	16	6	14	18	2	12	10	4	8	-

BACK	
yardage	6373
par	71
rating	71.4
slope	129

REGULAR	
yardage	5970
par	71
rating	69.7
slope	126

FORWARD	
yardage	5191
par	71
rating	69.9
slope	121

44

SAN RAMON ROYAL VISTA GOLF COURSE
ARCHITECT: CLARK GLASSON, 1962

9430 Fircrest Lane
San Ramon, CA 94583

PRO SHOP: 925-828-6100

Russell Davies, Director of Golf, PGA
Michael J. Reed, PGA Professional
Ed Ferriera, Superintendent

Driving Range •
Practice Greens •
Clubhouse •
Food / Beverage •
Accommodations
Pull Carts •
Power Carts •
Club Rental •
$pecial Offers

	1	2	3	4	5	6	7	8	9	OUT
BACK	331	206	437	429	336	488	213	504	356	3300
REGULAR	325	192	426	416	320	478	170	460	346	3133
par	4	3	4	4	4	5	3	5	4	36
handicap	13	9	3	1	15	17	5	11	7	-
FORWARD	311	174	301	407	309	455	146	434	312	2849
par	4	3	4	5	4	5	3	5	4	37
handicap	1	17	13	7	15	3	11	9	5	-

	10	11	12	13	14	15	16	17	18	IN
BACK	345	400	361	519	203	503	413	171	384	3299
REGULAR	332	385	347	497	193	485	402	159	372	3172
par	4	4	4	5	3	5	4	3	4	36
handicap	16	2	12	8	4	14	6	18	10	-
FORWARD	322	358	334	475	180	450	356	131	315	2921
par	4	4	4	5	3	5	4	3	4	36
handicap	8	10	12	4	16	2	6	18	14	-

BACK	
yardage	6599
par	72
rating	71.0
slope	120

REGULAR	
yardage	6305
par	72
rating	69.7
slope	117

FORWARD	
yardage	5770
par	73
rating	72.7
slope	119

PLAY POLICY & FEES: Green fees are $65 Tuesday through Thursday and $75 Friday through Sunday, mandatory carts included. The course is closed on Monday.

TEE TIMES: Reservations can be booked seven days in advance.

DRESS CODE: Shirts must have collars and sleeves. No blue jeans are allowed.

COURSE DESCRIPTION: Situated in the foothills of San Ramon, this course has lots of water, trees, bunkers, contoured fairways, and undulating greens. The 405-yard eighth and 392-yard ninth are strong holes, but the 287-yard fourth, with its green surrounded by water, is a lot of fun. The 526-yard 14th, a par-5 that plays over a creek, requires a precise 250-yard shot to a narrow fairway. It's possible to reach the green in two shots, but the green is severely sloped and fast—home of the four-putt. The par-5 17th is an uphill shot into the prevailing wind—a maddening hole. The 435-yard 18th has a blind second shot.

LOCATION: From Interstate 680 in San Ramon take the Bollinger Canyon exit east over the freeway. Turn left on Canyon Lakes Drive and left again on Bollinger Canyon Way to the course.

. . . ● **TOURNAMENTS:** Shotgun tournaments are available weekdays only. You must have 16 players to book a tournament. Events can be booked 12 months in advance. The banquet facility holds 140 people.

43. CANYON LAKES COUNTRY CLUB

PLAY POLICY & FEES: Green fees are $27 weekdays and $37 weekends. There is a $19 rate for nine holes before 7:30 a.m. Twilight rate is $16 weekdays and $19 weekends. Senior rates are available. Carts are $14 for nine holes and $29 for 18 holes.

TEE TIMES: Reservations can be booked seven days in advance.

DRESS CODE: Shirts with collars are required. No T-shirts or tank tops are allowed on the course or at the driving range. Nonmetal spikes are required.

COURSE DESCRIPTION: This is a relatively flat course with large greens. Homes line almost every fairway. More than 300 new trees have been planted. The course is usually in great condition, thanks to on-site well water and a new irrigation system. The 9th hole features an island green. The 11th hole requires a layup off the tee due to a hazard halfway down the hole. The 16th doglegs right and has out-of-bounds on the right.

NOTES: The driving range is lighted.

LOCATION: Driving south on Interstate 680 in San Ramon, take the Alcosta Boulevard exit. Cross back over the freeway and drive one mile east. Turn left on Fircrest Lane to the course.

. . . ● **TOURNAMENTS:** A 20-player minimum is required to book a tournament. Carts are required. A banquet facility is available that can accommodate up to 250 people.

44. SAN RAMON ROYAL VISTA GOLF COURSE

45

SAN LEANDRO GOLF CLUB
ARCHITECTS: WILLIAM F. BELL, 1982; JOHN HARBOTTLE, 1999

13800 Neptune Drive
San Leandro, CA 94577

PRO SHOP: 510-895-2162

Bill Cahoon, General Manager
Dave Gannon, Head Professional, PGA
Ken Schwark, Superintendent

Driving Range ●
Practice Greens ●
Clubhouse ●
Food / Beverage ●
Accommodations
Pull Carts ●
Power Carts ●
Club Rental ●
$pecial Offers

	1	2	3	4	5	6	7	8	9	OUT
BACK	413	397	358	146	505	420	537	191	381	3348
REGULAR	401	377	346	132	471	392	505	178	252	3054
par	4	4	4	3	5	4	5	3	4	36
handicap	5	7	15	17	13	1	3	9	11	-
FORWARD	395	365	348	119	452	359	451	148	242	2879
par	4	4	4	3	5	4	5	3	4	36
handicap	1	5	9	17	7	3	11	13	15	-

	10	11	12	13	14	15	16	17	18	IN
BACK	160	399	549	486	296	411	210	371	406	3288
REGULAR	146	385	507	465	278	406	192	351	391	3121
par	3	4	5	5	4	4	3	4	4	36
handicap	18	8	4	14	16	2	10	12	6	-
FORWARD	123	369	373	465	267	400	169	338	335	2839
par	3	4	5	5	4	4	3	4	4	36
handicap	18	4	2	8	12	14	16	10	6	-

BACK	
yardage	6636
par	72
rating	70.7
slope	115

REGULAR	
yardage	6175
par	72
rating	68.6
slope	107

FORWARD	
yardage	5718
par	72
rating	71.3
slope	108

46

WILLOW PARK GOLF COURSE
ARCHITECT: BOB BALDOCK, 1967

P.O. Box 2407
Castro Valley, CA 94546

17007 Redwood Road
Castro Valley, CA 94546

PRO SHOP: 510-537-8989
STARTER: 510-537-8989

Robert Bruce, Professional
Jeff Roberts, Superintendent

Driving Range ●
Practice Greens ●
Clubhouse
Food / Beverage ●
Accommodations
Pull Carts ●
Power Carts ●
Club Rental
$pecial Offers

	1	2	3	4	5	6	7	8	9	OUT
BACK	417	384	157	494	182	352	191	333	582	3092
REGULAR	377	362	120	440	140	310	150	291	487	2677
par	4	4	3	5	3	4	3	4	5	35
handicap	1	7	13	3	11	15	9	17	5	-
FORWARD	365	340	112	430	127	296	136	283	472	2561
par	4	4	3	5	3	4	3	4	5	35
handicap	5	7	17	3	15	9	13	11	1	-

	10	11	12	13	14	15	16	17	18	IN
BACK	416	288	499	144	332	390	190	367	509	3135
REGULAR	353	258	485	130	275	365	160	329	475	2830
par	4	4	5	3	4	4	3	4	5	36
handicap	2	18	8	16	12	4	6	10	14	-
FORWARD	328	237	450	120	258	358	148	318	415	2632
par	4	4	5	3	4	4	3	4	5	36
handicap	10	14	2	18	12	6	16	8	4	-

BACK	
yardage	6227
par	71
rating	69.2
slope	115

REGULAR	
yardage	5507
par	71
rating	67.4
slope	110

FORWARD	
yardage	5193
par	71
rating	69.2
slope	117

PLAY POLICY & FEES: Green fees are $20 weekdays and $25 weekends for the Tony Lema Course, with a $5 discount for residents. Fees are $9 for nine holes weekdays and $12 for nine holes weekends for the Marina Course, with a $2 discount for residents. Call for discount rates. Carts are $24. Pull carts are $4.

TEE TIMES: Reservations can be booked seven days in advance.

DRESS CODE: No tank tops or gym shorts are allowed.

COURSE DESCRIPTION: The course has large greens and is easy to walk. Play early to miss the prevailing southeast wind off the bay. One of the more difficult holes is the sixth, a par-4, 420-yarder dead into the wind with a lake on the left. The hole plays like a par 5 because of the wind. The course can be played by all skill levels.

NOTES: Call before coming out. The Marina Course has been closed for renovation. It is due to open October 1999. At that time the Tony Lema Course will close for a complete renovation. Estimated completion time is one to two years. Par is 58 on the Marina Course for 18 holes. It is 3,316 yards and rated 53.8 from the regular tees. The slope is 73.

LOCATION: From Interstate 880 in San Leandro take the Marina Boulevard exit west, which curves left into Neptune Drive to the course.

. . . ● **TOURNAMENTS:** Shotgun tournaments are available weekdays only. Carts are required. A 16-player minimum is needed to book a tournament.

45. SAN LEANDRO GOLF CLUB

PLAY POLICY & FEES: Green fees are $15 for nine holes and $20 for 18 holes weekdays, and $17 for nine holes and $27 for 18 holes weekends. Carts are $14 for nine holes and $20 for 18 holes.

TEE TIMES: Call the pro shop for further information.

DRESS CODE: Shirts must be worn.

COURSE DESCRIPTION: This course is mostly flat with narrow fairways. A creek borders the front nine holes. There are often deer in the outlying areas.

NOTES: The driving range has an unusual feature: You hit into a lake about 175 yards out. Floating balls are provided. A total of 100,000 rounds are played here each year. Sam Ross holds the course record with a 62.

LOCATION: The course is in Castro Valley, two miles north of Interstate 580 on Redwood Road.

. . . ● **TOURNAMENTS:** Shotgun tournaments are not allowed. Events should be booked 12 months in advance.

46. WILLOW PARK GOLF COURSE

THE BRIDGES GOLF CLUB
ARCHITECTS: GRAVES/PASCUZZO, 1999; JOHNNY MILLER

9000 S. Gale Ridge Rd.
San Ramon, CA 94583

PRO SHOP: 877-278-8837

Joey Pickavance, Director of Golf, PGA
Ryan Mitchell, Professional
Stacey Gates, Tournament Director

Driving Range ●
Practice Greens ●
Clubhouse ●
Food / Beverage ●
Accommodations
Pull Carts ●
Power Carts ●
Club Rental ●
Special Offers

	1	2	3	4	5	6	7	8	9	OUT
BACK										
REGULAR										
par										
handicap										
FORWARD										
par										
handicap										

	10	11	12	13	14	15	16	17	18	IN
BACK										
REGULAR										
par										
handicap										
FORWARD										
par										
handicap										

BACK	
yardage	7200
par	72
rating	
slope	

REGULAR	
yardage	
par	
rating	
slope	

FORWARD	
yardage	
par	
rating	
slope	

SHARP PARK GOLF COURSE
ARCHITECT: ALISTER MACKENZIE, 1929

P.O. Box 1275
Pacifica, CA 94044

Sharp Park Road and Highway
Pacifica, CA 94044

PRO SHOP: 650-355-8546
STARTER: 650-359-3380

Joan W. Lantz, Manager
Gregory Ritschy, Head Professional, PGA
John Farley, Superintendent

Driving Range
Practice Greens ●
Clubhouse ●
Food / Beverage ●
Accommodations
Pull Carts ●
Power Carts ●
Club Rental ●
Special Offers

	1	2	3	4	5	6	7	8	9	OUT
BACK	-	-	-	-	-	-	-	-	-	-
REGULAR	362	320	357	457	193	408	375	100	458	3030
par	4	4	4	5	3	4	4	3	5	36
handicap	9	11	3	15	5	1	7	17	13	-
FORWARD	347	315	352	457	171	395	355	95	458	2945
par	4	4	4	5	3	4	4	3	5	36
handicap	11	15	7	1	13	3	9	17	5	-

	10	11	12	13	14	15	16	17	18	IN
BACK	-	-	-	-	-	-	-	-	-	-
REGULAR	414	402	170	525	397	135	366	340	494	3243
par	4	4	3	5	4	3	4	4	5	36
handicap	2	4	10	14	8	18	6	12	16	-
FORWARD	417	406	154	511	360	124	374	317	487	3150
par	5	5	3	5	4	3	4	4	5	38
handicap	10	12	16	2	8	18	4	14	6	-

BACK	
yardage	-
par	-
rating	-
slope	-

REGULAR	
yardage	6273
par	72
rating	70
slope	115

FORWARD	
yardage	6095
par	74
rating	73
slope	120

PLAY POLICY & FEES: Green fees are $75 Monday through Thursday and $95 Friday through Sunday, and holidays. Senior rates are $55 Monday through Thursday, and Junior fees are $50 Monday through Thursday, and $60 Friday through Sunday. A six-hole lighted loop is available for $30 every day. Twilight rates are available beginning 4.5 hours before sunset. Carts are included.

TEE TIMES: Reservations can be made 30 days in advance.

DRESS CODE: Blue jeans, T-shirts, and gym-type shorts are not allowed.

COURSE DESCRIPTION: The Bridges at Gale Ranch will be a par 73 and measure 7,200 yards from the championship tees. This links-style course, inspired from the great courses in Scotland, will play deep in a valley with a natural creek running throughout. Players will be given the chance to loft the ball in or bump and run.

NOTES: Caddies are available for $40 per player.

LOCATION: From Pleasanton drive north on Interstate 680. Take the Bollinger Canyon exit and go east about three miles to S. Gale Ridge. Turn right to the course entrance.

. . . ● **TOURNAMENTS:** Events may be booked one year in advance. A 16-player minimum is need to book an event. Tournament rates are $90 Monday through Thursday and $110 Friday through Sunday and holidays. All tournaments include range balls, carts, and tournament amenities. The banquet facility can accommodate up to 150 people indoors and 250 indoors and out.

47. THE BRIDGES GOLF CLUB

PLAY POLICY & FEES: Green fees are $23 weekdays and $27 weekends and holidays. Reduced rates are available. Carts are $22.

TEE TIMES: Reservations can be booked six days in advance for the general public starting at 7 p.m. by calling 415-750-GOLF. A $1 charge will be added to your green fee at the time of play for using this system. San Francisco residents with a reservation card can make tee times seven days in advance.

DRESS CODE: Casual dress and metal spikes are OK.

COURSE DESCRIPTION: This is a flat, tree-lined course located at sea level. The front nine is set inland, and the back nine runs along the ocean. The fairways are tight with medium-sized greens. You'll find sand, water, views, and challenging golf. The 13th hole is a par-5, 525-yard dogleg left over water, and it's a doozie. The par-3 15th, at 135 yards over water, is also a tester.

LOCATION: From Highway 280 take Skyline Boulevard. Follow Skyline Boulevard to Sharp Park Road. Take a left on Sharp Park Road to the golf course.

. . . ● **TOURNAMENTS:** A 32-player minimum is needed to book a tournament. Carts are mandatory. Events should be scheduled at least eight months in advance. The banquet facility can accommodate up to 150 people. ● **TRAVEL:** The Lighthouse Hotel is five minutes from the golf course. For reservations call 650-355-6300.

48. SHARP PARK GOLF COURSE

CALIFORNIA GOLF CLUB
ARCHITECT: A. VERNON MACAAN, 1918

844 West Orange Avenue
South San Francisco, CA
94080
PRO SHOP: 650-589-0144
OFFICE: 650-761-0210

Dennis Mahoney, Manager
Mark Doss, PGA Professional
Roger Robarge, Superintendent

Driving Range ●
Practice Greens ●
Clubhouse ●
Food / Beverage ●
Accommodations
Pull Carts
Power Carts ●
Club Rental ●
$Special Offers

	1	2	3	4	5	6	7	8	9	OUT
BACK	510	363	154	525	370	338	183	387	422	3252
REGULAR	500	355	148	513	354	330	179	376	389	3144
par	5	4	3	5	4	4	3	4	4	36
handicap	5	7	17	1	11	9	13	15	3	-
FORWARD	485	321	122	475	300	311	166	357	336	2873
par	5	4	3	5	4	4	3	4	4	36
handicap	3	7	17	1	11	9	15	13	5	-

	10	11	12	13	14	15	16	17	18	IN
BACK	394	399	225	368	442	489	160	552	396	3425
REGULAR	386	392	194	363	437	471	154	547	386	3330
par	4	4	3	4	4	5	3	5	4	36
handicap	4	12	14	8	2	16	18	6	10	-
FORWARD	380	358	177	354	388	416	117	535	330	3055
par	4	4	3	4	4	5	3	5	4	36
handicap	6	10	16	2	12	8	18	4	14	-

BACK	
yardage	6677
par	72
rating	73.1
slope	137

REGULAR	
yardage	6474
par	72
rating	72.1
slope	135

FORWARD	
yardage	5928
par	72
rating	75.3
slope	136

 ## GREEN HILLS COUNTRY CLUB
ARCHITECT: ALISTER MACKENZIE, 1930

End of Ludeman Lane
Millbrae, CA 94030

PRO SHOP: 650-583-0882
CLUBHOUSE: 650-588-4616

Steve Martino, PGA Professional
Carolyn Parmele, Clubhouse Manager
Walt Barret, Superintendent

Driving Range ●
Practice Greens ●
Clubhouse ●
Food / Beverage ●
Accommodations
Pull Carts
Power Carts ●
Club Rental ●
$Special Offers

	1	2	3	4	5	6	7	8	9	OUT
BACK	348	508	511	178	384	400	150	381	364	3224
REGULAR	341	487	501	165	352	388	138	364	356	3092
par	4	5	5	3	4	4	3	4	4	36
handicap	9	17	1	11	5	7	15	13	3	-
FORWARD	336	469	480	155	323	379	129	355	345	2971
par	4	5	5	3	4	4	3	4	4	36
handicap	7	5	1	15	11	9	17	13	3	-

	10	11	12	13	14	15	16	17	18	IN
BACK	361	353	364	166	349	180	520	358	442	3093
REGULAR	348	343	358	150	336	146	507	338	435	2961
par	4	4	4	3	4	3	5	4	4	35
handicap	8	12	10	18	2	16	14	4	6	-
FORWARD	335	326	346	140	327	132	443	317	415	2781
par	4	4	4	3	4	3	5	4	5	36
handicap	10	12	8	18	6	16	2	4	14	-

BACK	
yardage	6317
par	71
rating	71.4
slope	130

REGULAR	
yardage	6053
par	71
rating	70.3
slope	128

FORWARD	
yardage	5752
par	72
rating	73.7
slope	138

PLAY POLICY & FEES: Members and guests only. Guest fees are $75 with a member and $150 without. Carts are $10.

DRESS CODE: Appropriate golf attire is required.

COURSE DESCRIPTION: This rolling, challenging course is situated above San Francisco International Airport. It's hilly, windy, and loaded with 185 bunkers. The par 5s and par 3s are especially challenging. Lakes have been added, one on the right side of the 11th and another on the left of the 18th green. This is a real sleeper course, giving the best golfers everything they want. The par-5 fourth is a 525-yard double dogleg, with heavy trees on the right—a true three-shot hole, with six bunkers guarding the approach. The 14th, a dogleg left through a chute, is 442 yards.

NOTES: San Mateo professional Dennis Trixler holds the course record with a 64. Trees were removed to let in air and light. The open space does not make the course any easier.

LOCATION: From San Francisco take Interstate 280 south to the Westborough Avenue exit east. At the bottom of the hill, turn right on West Orange Avenue and follow it to the course.

. . . ● **TOURNAMENTS:** This course is not available for outside events.

49. CALIFORNIA GOLF CLUB

PLAY POLICY & FEES: Reciprocal play is accepted with members of some other private clubs within 50 miles. Guest fees are $70 weekdays and $90 weekends when accompanied by a member, and $100 unaccompanied (cart included). Fees for reciprocators are $100. Carts are $11 per rider. Four-bagger prices are available if you'd like a cart to tow your bag while you walk.

DRESS CODE: Appropriate golf attire is required. Nonmetal spikes are encouraged.

COURSE DESCRIPTION: This short but tricky Alister Mackenzie course is situated in the foothills among eucalyptus, pine, and cypress trees. It has small, undulating greens and is well bunkered. The pride of the course is the uphill 180-yard, par-3 15th hole, which crosses a ravine. You must hit to a two-level green with severe undulation between the levels. Count on the back level to be the toughest. When you play here bring your nerves; it's the longest 6,300 yards you may ever play.

NOTES: John Joseph holds the course record of 63.

LOCATION: This course is located between Interstate 280 and U.S.101 in Millbrae. Exit on Millbrae Avenue off Highway 101 and drive north on El Camino Real. Turn left on Ludeman Lane and drive up the hill to the course.

. . . ● **TOURNAMENTS:** Shotgun tournaments are allowed Monday only. A 100-player minimum is needed to book an event. Carts are required.

50. GREEN HILLS COUNTRY CLUB

ARCHITECTS: HERBERT FOWLER, 1893; HAROLD S AMPSON

80 New Place Road
Hillsborough, CA 94010

PRO S HOP: 650-342-0750

Hartmut Hofacker, Manager
Maurice VerBrugge, PGA Professional
Terry Grasso, Superintendent

Driving Range •
Practice Greens •
Clubhouse •
Food / Beverage •
Accommodations
Pull Carts •
Power Carts •
Club Rental •
$pecial Offers

	1	2	3	4	5	6	7	8	9	OUT
BACK										
REGULAR										
par										
handicap										
FORWARD										
par										
handicap										

	10	11	12	13	14	15	16	17	18	IN
BACK										
REGULAR										
par										
handicap										
FORWARD										
par										
handicap										

BACK	
yardage	
par	
rating	
slope	

REGULAR	
yardage	6394
par	70
rating	70.3
slope	126

FORWARD	
yardage	5731
par	70
rating	73.0
slope	125

P.O. Box 634
San Mateo, CA 94401

1700 Coyote Point Drive
San Mateo, CA 94401

PRO S HOP: 650-522-4653

Gary Monisteri, PGA Professional
Tim Heck, Manager
Dulbag Dubria, Superintendent

Driving Range
Practice Greens •
Clubhouse •
Food / Beverage •
Accommodations
Pull Carts •
Power Carts •
Club Rental •
$pecial Offers

	1	2	3	4	5	6	7	8	9	OUT
BACK	286	431	468	187	401	373	332	425	169	3072
REGULAR	275	421	458	150	397	364	316	415	142	2938
par	4	4	5	3	4	4	4	4	3	35
handicap	13	1	11	9	7	5	17	3	15	-
FORWARD	266	418	450	159	393	360	296	400	139	2881
par	4	5	5	3	4	4	4	5	3	37
handicap	13	5	1	15	3	9	11	7	17	-

	10	11	12	13	14	15	16	17	18	IN
BACK	308	292	338	319	169	381	529	164	347	2847
REGULAR	298	282	320	277	156	335	507	132	333	2640
par	4	4	4	4	3	4	5	3	4	35
handicap	10	18	14	8	12	2	6	16	4	-
FORWARD	291	274	296	263	148	311	499	118	328	2528
par	4	4	4	4	3	4	5	3	4	35
handicap	10	12	14	2	16	8	4	18	6	-

BACK	
yardage	5919
par	70
rating	68.3
slope	112

REGULAR	
yardage	5578
par	70
rating	66.7
slope	108

FORWARD	
yardage	5409
par	72
rating	69.8
slope	115

PLAY POLICY & FEES: Members and guests only. Guest fees are $40 when accompanied by a member and $80 unaccompanied. Carts are $30.

DRESS CODE: Collared shirts are required.

COURSE DESCRIPTION: Significant changes to the course have been made by various architects, most notably Robert Trent Jones Sr. in 1954. Today it has a sprawling, tree-lined layout and narrow fairways that require precise shots off the tee. It's fairly flat and walkable. This course has been used for U.S. Open sectional qualifying.

NOTES: This course is the oldest west of the Mississippi, dating back to 1893. It premiered as a three-hole course, then expanded to nine in 1899. Bing Crosby was one of the many prominent members of this highly exclusive club. Head pro Maurice Ver Brugge set the course record of 60.

LOCATION: Driving on U.S. 101 in Burlingame, take the Broadway exit southwest to El Camino Real. Go left on El Camino Real and turn right on Floribunda Avenue. When it dead-ends, turn left on Eucalyptus Avenue. Turn right on New Place Road. The course is on the right.

. . . ● **TOURNAMENTS:** This course is not available for outside events.

51. BURLINGAME COUNTRY CLUB

PLAY POLICY & FEES: The course is closed for renovation until May 1, 2000.

TEE TIMES: Reservations can be hooked seven days in advance.

DRESS CODE: Golf attire is encouraged.

COURSE DESCRIPTION: This course is short and flat with tight eucalyptus-lined fairways. The greens are in the traditional style: very small, elevated, well bunkered, and well contoured. Because of this, there is a premium on approach shots and putting. This walkable course is usually windy and has several water hazards.

NOTES: A total of 102,000 rounds are played here each year. Sil DeLuca set the course record of 59.

LOCATION: This course is on the east side of U.S. 101 in San Mateo and visible from the freeway. From the north take the Poplar Avenue exit. From the south take the Dore exit. Follow the signs marked Coyote Point Drive from both exits to the course.

. . . ● **TOURNAMENTS:** No shotgun tournaments are allowed. A 12-player minimum is needed to book a tournament.

52. SAN MATEO GOLF COURSE

SKYWEST GOLF COURSE
ARCHITECT: BOB BALDOCK, 1964

1401 Golf Course Road
Hayward, CA 94541

PRO SHOP: 510-278-6188

Gordon Campbell, Professional/Manager
David Suh, Tournament Director

Driving Range ●
Practice Greens ●
Clubhouse ●
Food / Beverage ●
Accommodations
Pull Carts ●
Power Carts ●
Club Rental ●
$Special Offers

	1	2	3	4	5	6	7	8	9	OUT
BACK	391	441	157	409	475	390	188	520	381	3352
REGULAR	367	422	147	396	465	379	166	490	369	3201
par	4	4	3	4	5	4	3	5	4	36
handicap	9	1	17	3	15	13	7	11	5	-
FORWARD	355	410	135	386	440	350	144	472	349	3041
par	4	5	3	4	5	4	3	5	4	37
handicap	13	1	17	3	15	11	9	7	5	-

	10	11	12	13	14	15	16	17	18	IN
BACK	428	140	404	547	360	427	543	220	441	3510
REGULAR	412	121	387	525	338	406	520	199	421	3329
par	4	3	4	5	4	4	5	3	4	36
handicap	4	18	14	6	16	2	12	10	8	-
FORWARD	389	100	367	506	320	391	502	156	399	3130
par	4	3	4	5	4	4	5	3	4	36
handicap	4	18	10	8	16	2	6	14	12	-

BACK	
yardage	6862
par	72
rating	72.9
slope	121

REGULAR	
yardage	6530
par	72
rating	71.0
slope	117

FORWARD	
yardage	6171
par	73
rating	74.3
slope	123

 # MISSION HILLS OF HAYWARD GOLF COURSE
ARCHITECT: RAINVILLE-BYE, 1999

Hayward, CA

Driving Range
Practice Greens
Clubhouse
Food / Beverage
Accommodations
Pull Carts
Power Carts
Club Rental
$Special Offers

	1	2	3	4	5	6	7	8	9	OUT
BACK										
REGULAR										
par										
handicap										
FORWARD										
par										
handicap										

	10	11	12	13	14	15	16	17	18	IN
BACK										
REGULAR										
par										
handicap										
FORWARD										
par										
handicap										

BACK	
yardage	1720
par	30
rating	
slope	

REGULAR	
yardage	
par	
rating	
slope	

FORWARD	
yardage	
par	
rating	
slope	

PLAY POLICY & FEES: Green fees are $18 for nine holes and $23 for 18 holes weekdays, and $21 for nine holes and $31 for 18 holes weekends. Carts are $12 per person for 18 holes. Junior and resident rates are available.

TEE TIMES: Reservations can be booked eight days in advance. For reservations call 510-888-0106.

DRESS CODE: Collared shirts are required.

COURSE DESCRIPTION: This flat course has lush, well-maintained, wide fairways and lots of trees. It tests every club in the bag. The most talked-about hole on this course is the seventh. It's a 192-yard par 3, playing especially difficult against the wind. There is a lake on the right and out-of-bounds on the left. The green slopes back to front, but fortunately it holds well.

NOTES: This course holds many tournaments, including a Player's West tour event for aspiring women pros. Mike Powers set the men's record of 65, and Muffin Spencer-Devlin set the women's record of 68.

LOCATION: From Interstate 880 in Hayward take the A Street exit west to Hesperian and turn right on Hesperian. Take the first left at Golf Course Road. The course is located next to the Hayward Air Terminal.

. . . ● **TOURNAMENTS:** A 20-player minimum is required to book a tournament. Carts are required.

53. SKYWEST GOLF COURSE

PLAY POLICY & FEES: At the time of press, the golf course was completed, but no parking, permanent address, or phone number existed. For more information call 510-278-6188. The course is due to open in late fall of 1999.

COURSE DESCRIPTION: The par-30 course is 1,720 yards long with six par 3s and three par 4s. Both the fairways and greens are undulating. The greens are extremely large, averaging over 7,000 square feet. The course will be challenging enough for the good golfer, yet accessible to the entire family.

NOTES: An extensive practice area will be on site, featuring a lit, two-tier, 43-station driving range, plus 10 grass stations. There will also be two chipping greens and a large putting green.

LOCATION: From Oakland take Highway 880 south to Industrial Boulevard. Go east on Industrial. The course is at the corner of Industrial and Mission Boulevards.

54. MISSION HILLS OF HAYWARD GOLF

PLEASANTON FAIRWAYS GOLF COURSE
ARCHITECT: RON CURTOLA, 1974

P.O. Box 123
Pleasanton, CA 94566

PRO SHOP: 925-462-4653

Connie Curtola, Manager
Ronnie Juarez, Tournament Director
Paul Marty, Superintendent

Driving Range •
Practice Greens •
Clubhouse •
Food / Beverage •
Accommodations
Pull Carts •
Power Carts
Club Rental •
$pecial Offers

	1	2	3	4	5	6	7	8	9	OUT
BACK										
REGULAR										
par										
handicap										
FORWARD										
par										
handicap										

	10	11	12	13	14	15	16	17	18	IN
BACK										
REGULAR										
par										
handicap										
FORWARD										
par										
handicap										

BACK	
yardage	
par	
rating	-
slope	-

REGULAR	
yardage	1714
par	30
rating	55.9
slope	82

FORWARD	
yardage	1586
par	30
rating	-
slope	-

 # CASTLEWOOD COUNTRY CLUB
ARCHITECT: WILLIAM P. BELL, 1923

707 Country Club Circle
Pleasanton, CA 94566

PRO SHOP: 925-846-5151
CLUBHOUSE: 925-846-2871

John Hughes, Director of Golf, PGA
Jon Hughes, PGA Professional

Driving Range •
Practice Greens •
Clubhouse •
Food / Beverage •
Accommodations
Pull Carts •
Power Carts •
Club Rental •
$pecial Offers

	1	2	3	4	5	6	7	8	9	OUT
BACK	424	472	396	186	421	141	482	406	335	3263
REGULAR	424	457	388	172	412	130	457	389	325	3154
par	4	5	4	3	4	3	4	4	4	35
handicap	3	13	15	11	5	17	7	1	9	-
FORWARD	408	390	360	117	397	107	454	382	313	2928
par	5	5	4	3	5	3	5	4	4	38
handicap	9	5	13	15	3	17	11	1	7	-

	10	11	12	13	14	15	16	17	18	IN
BACK	276	479	139	326	360	404	397	211	413	3005
REGULAR	264	463	139	316	348	394	354	201	370	2849
par	4	5	3	4	4	4	4	3	4	35
handicap	12	14	16	10	4	2	6	8	18	-
FORWARD	239	426	114	301	297	381	338	183	316	2595
par	4	5	3	4	4	4	4	3	4	35
handicap	12	6	18	10	8	2	4	16	14	-

BACK	
yardage	6268
par	70
rating	70.7
slope	124

REGULAR	
yardage	6003
par	70
rating	69.8
slope	123

FORWARD	
yardage	5523
par	73
rating	72.0
slope	129

55. PLEASANTON FAIRWAYS GOLF COURSE

PLAY POLICY & FEES: Green fees are $11 for nine holes and $21 for 18 holes weekdays, and $14 for nine holes and $27 for 18 holes weekends. Senior, junior, and twilight fees are available. The course is closed during the Alameda County Fair in late June and early July.

TEE TIMES: Reservations can be booked seven days in advance.

COURSE DESCRIPTION: This short, flat course is located in the middle of the racetrack at the Alameda County Fairgrounds. This is not a course for beginners. The greens are all elevated, and a driver is needed on three holes. You must be accurate to hold the par-3 greens.

NOTES: The Curtola family owns a large driving range on the west end of the fairgrounds, about a half mile from the course. Irons only on the driving range.

LOCATION: From Interstate 680 in Pleasanton driving south, take the Bernal exit to the right, make a loop, and head east on Bernal. Turn left on Pleasanton Avenue and left again at the fairgrounds entrance.

. . . ● **TOURNAMENTS:** This course is not available for outside events.

---

56. CASTLEWOOD COUNTRY CLUB

PLAY POLICY & FEES: Reciprocal play is accepted with members of other private clubs. Guest fees are $50 Monday through Thursday and $75 Friday and weekends, plus $12 for a cart when accompanied by a member. Fees are $80 plus $12 for a cart when unaccompanied. The Hill Course is closed on Monday. The Valley Course is closed every other Thursday. Reciprocal play is not allowed Friday, Saturday, or Sunday.

TEE TIMES: Have your club pro call for arrangements.

DRESS CODE: Appropriate golf attire is required. Nonmetal spikes are mandatory.

COURSE DESCRIPTION: The Valley Course is now one of the best in the East Bay. Robert Muir Graves added contours and mounds to define the fairways, and also redesigned all of the greens. This course is a tough, demanding test.

NOTES: The men's course record is held by former PGA Tour winner Ron Cerrudo, who scored 62 on both courses in 1962. Don't expect to see anyone break that record; the course is tougher now because the trees are taller and the fairways aren't rock hard as they were in '62. The Valley Course is 6,401 yards and rated 70.8 with a slope of 124 from the regular tees. The Hill Course: See scorecard for yardage and rating information.

LOCATION: From Interstate 680 in Pleasanton take the Sunol–Castlewood Drive exit. Drive one block. The Valley Course is on the right, and the Hill Course is farther up the hill.

. . . ● **TOURNAMENTS:** Outside events are allowed on Monday.

ARCHITECT: JACK NICKLAUS, 1996

3404 West Ruby Hill Drive
Pleasanton, CA 94566

PRO SHOP: 925-417-5850

Chuck Notestone, PGA Master Professional
Hossein Bahri, General Manager
Mark Licon, Superintendent

Driving Range ●
Practice Greens ●
Clubhouse ●
Food / Beverage ●
Accommodations
Pull Carts
Power Carts ●
Club Rental ●
$pecial Offers

	1	2	3	4	5	6	7	8	9	OUT
BACK	430	450	212	520	469	177	435	499	467	3659
REGULAR	386	380	173	475	420	158	378	454	401	3225
par	4	4	3	5	4	3	4	5	4	36
handicap	10	6	16	14	4	18	8	12	2	-
FORWARD	305	293	153	406	327	127	336	399	314	2660
par	4	4	3	5	4	3	4	5	4	36
handicap	10	6	16	14	4	18	8	12	2	-

	10	11	12	13	14	15	16	17	18	IN
BACK	473	464	456	549	193	436	414	202	602	3789
REGULAR	402	406	409	472	145	396	366	161	559	3316
par	4	4	4	5	3	4	4	3	5	36
handicap	5	13	3	9	15	1	7	17	11	-
FORWARD	315	309	314	417	94	294	285	107	504	2639
par	4	4	4	5	3	4	4	3	5	36
handicap	5	13	3	9	15	1	7	17	11	-

BACK	
yardage	7448
par	72
rating	76.7
slope	134

REGULAR	
yardage	6541
par	72
rating	72.6
slope	127

FORWARD	
yardage	5299
par	72
rating	70.0
slope	121

ARCHITECT: CLARK GLASSON, 1969

6900 Mission Road
Sunol, CA 94586

PRO SHOP: 925-862-0414

Mike Rubio, Head Professional, PGA
Dave Martinez, Tournament Director
Bryan Richardson, Manager

Driving Range
Practice Greens ●
Clubhouse ●
Food / Beverage ●
Accommodations
Pull Carts
Power Carts ●
Club Rental ●
$pecial Offers

	1	2	3	4	5	6	7	8	9	OUT
BACK	375	343	525	420	195	305	333	231	584	3311
REGULAR	350	324	485	383	175	284	319	217	547	3084
par	4	4	5	4	3	4	4	3	5	36
handicap	3	7	9	1	13	17	11	15	5	-
FORWARD	313	292	473	410	150	269	300	195	527	2929
par	4	4	5	5	3	4	4	3	5	37
handicap	7	11	3	9	17	15	5	13	1	-

	10	11	12	13	14	15	16	17	18	IN
BACK	561	369	409	197	369	207	540	434	433	3519
REGULAR	537	329	385	177	356	193	519	401	425	3322
par	5	4	4	3	4	3	5	4	4	36
handicap	6	14	2	18	12	16	8	10	4	-
FORWARD	495	260	357	155	355	172	508	368	418	3088
par	5	4	4	3	4	3	5	4	5	37
handicap	4	12	6	16	8	14	2	10	18	-

BACK	
yardage	6830
par	72
rating	72.4
slope	126

REGULAR	
yardage	6406
par	72
rating	70.4
slope	120

FORWARD	
yardage	6017
par	74
rating	74.4
slope	124

PLAY POLICY & FEES: Members and guests only. The course is closed on Monday.

DRESS CODE: Appropriate golf attire and nonmetal spikes are required.

COURSE DESCRIPTION: This course is very long with 10 par 4s over 400 yards from the back tees. If that isn't challenging enough, there are two lakes and creeks running throughout. The highlight of Ruby Hills is the greens, which are some of the best in Northern California.

LOCATION: From Interstate 680 in Pleasanton, take the Bernal Road exit east. Make a right on Vineyard Road, and the course will be on the right.

. . . ● **TOURNAMENTS:** Outside events are available on a very limited basis (Monday only).

57. RUBY HILL GOLF CLUB

PLAY POLICY & FEES: Green fees are $25 to walk weekdays, or $37 with a cart. Weekend fees are $50; carts are mandatory and included. Sunrise and twilight rates are available.

TEE TIMES: Reservations can be booked seven days in advance.

COURSE DESCRIPTION: Nestled in the Mission Hills, the Palm Course, with palm trees lining the wide fairways, is aptly named. There's plenty to worry about on both courses: tight, rolling hills, lots of trees, water hazards, and bunkers. The greens are true but tricky.

NOTES: An estimated 500 tournaments were played on these two courses last year. Sunol Valley was the site of the Alameda County Open in the early 1970s.

LOCATION: From Interstate 680 in Sunol exit on Andrade Road North. The course is located adjacent to the freeway.

. . . ● **TOURNAMENTS:** A 16-player minimum is needed to book a tournament. Carts are required weekends and holidays only.

58. SUNOL VALLEY GOLF COURSE

2000 Fairway Drive
Half Moon Bay, CA 94019

PROSHOP: 650-726-4438

Jim Wagner, PGA Professional
Dan Miller, Superintendent
James Monroe, Tournament Director

Driving Range
Practice Greens ●
Clubhouse ●
Food / Beverage ●
Accommodations
Pull Carts
Power Carts ●
Club Rental ●
$pecial Offers ●

	1	2	3	4	5	6	7	8	9	OUT
BACK	546	409	232	378	496	418	207	435	365	3486
REGULAR	513	389	130	336	476	388	180	407	341	3160
par	5	4	3	4	5	4	3	4	4	36
handicap	11	5	7	13	7	3	9	1	15	-
FORWARD	468	322	117	332	416	338	166	396	327	2882
par	5	4	3	4	5	4	3	4	4	36
handicap	3	11	15	7	1	13	17	5	9	-

	10	11	12	13	14	15	16	17	18	IN
BACK	560	417	439	208	424	573	426	170	428	3645
REGULAR	495	390	416	168	350	536	378	145	396	3274
par	5	4	4	3	4	5	4	3	4	36
handicap	12	10	4	16	14	2	6	18	8	-
FORWARD	432	357	358	106	325	469	358	135	347	2887
par	5	4	4	3	4	5	4	3	4	36
handicap	6	14	10	16	12	4	2	18	8	-

BACK	
yardage	7131
par	72
rating	75.0
slope	135

REGULAR	
yardage	6434
par	72
rating	71.8
slope	130

FORWARD	
yardage	5769
par	72
rating	73.3
slope	125

PLAY POLICY & FEES: Green fees for the Links Course are $95 Monday through Friday, and $115 weekends and holidays. Green fees for the Ocean Course are $115 Monday through Friday, and $135 weekends and holidays. Twilight green fees are available. Carts are included in fees and mandatory on the links course.

TEE TIMES: Reservations can be booked three weeks in advance.

DRESS CODE: Appropriate golf attire and nonmetal spikes are required.

COURSE DESCRIPTION: This Links Course is long and demanding. The 18th hole spans 428 yards along an ocean cliff and has been rated one of the top 100 holes in the country. Be wary of the back pin placement on this hole. Fog and wind often come into play. Big, undulating greens and long par 3s add to the challenge. The Ocean Course offers ocean views from every hole, and the three finishing holes sit directly on the Pacific Ocean.

NOTES: The Ocean Course is a par 72 and 6,732 yards long from the championship tees. For more information on Links Course: see scorecard.

LOCATION: Heading toward Half Moon Bay via Highway 1 or Highway 92, the course is located three miles south of the junction of Highway 1 and 92, south of Half Moon Bay on the oceanside.

. . . ● **TOURNAMENTS:** Carts are required. Shotgun tournaments can be held Monday through Thursday. A 72-player minimum is needed for a semi-shotgun start and 120 players are needed for a full shotgun start. A 24-player minimum is needed for a regular tournament. Events should be booked 12 months in advance.The banquet facility can accommodate up to 144 people. ● **TRAVEL:** The Half Moon Bay Lodge is located a couple of minutes from the course. Many of the rooms overlook the fourth fairway of the Links Course. For reservations call 800-368-2468. ● **$PECIAL OFFERS:** Play-and-stay packages at the Half Moon Bay Lodge are available for both courses Monday through Thursday.

59. HALF MOON BAY: LINKS & OCEAN

CRYSTAL SPRINGS GOLF COURSE

ARCHITECT: HERBERT FOWLER, 1924

6650 Golf Course Drive
Burlingame, CA 94010

PRO SHOP: 650-342-0603
CLUBHOUSE: 650-342-4188

Roger Billings, PGA Professional
Ray Davies, Superintendent

Driving Range ●
Practice Greens ●
Clubhouse ●
Food / Beverage ●
Accommodations
Pull Carts
Power Carts ●
Club Rental ●
$pecial Offers

	1	2	3	4	5	6	7	8	9	OUT
BACK	397	413	234	499	390	431	483	226	402	3475
REGULAR	389	397	224	474	380	426	467	178	386	3321
par	4	4	3	5	4	4	5	3	4	36
handicap	7	5	9	17	1	13	15	11	3	-
FORWARD	372	384	204	467	379	419	451	168	366	3210
par	4	4	3	5	4	4	5	3	4	36
handicap	5	1	15	13	3	9	11	17	7	-

	10	11	12	13	14	15	16	17	18	IN
BACK	375	161	373	154	425	313	479	402	526	3208
REGULAR	344	151	348	149	408	295	451	349	505	3000
par	4	3	4	3	4	4	5	4	5	36
handicap	6	18	4	16	2	14	12	8	10	-
FORWARD	335	103	276	142	342	274	422	342	474	2710
par	4	3	4	3	4	4	5	4	5	36
handicap	12	18	6	16	10	14	4	8	2	-

BACK	
yardage	6683
par	72
rating	72.1
slope	125

REGULAR	
yardage	6321
par	72
rating	70.7
slope	122

FORWARD	
yardage	5920
par	72
rating	74.0
slope	130

THE PENINSULA GOLF & COUNTRY CLUB

ARCHITECT: DONALD ROSS, 1922

701 Madera Drive
San Mateo, CA 94403

PRO SHOP: 650-638-2239
CLUBHOUSE: 650-638-2200

John Hightower, Manager
Tom Toschi, Head Professional, PGA
Bill Davis, Superintendent

Driving Range ●
Practice Greens ●
Clubhouse ●
Food / Beverage ●
Accommodations
Pull Carts ●
Power Carts ●
Club Rental ●
$pecial Offers

	1	2	3	4	5	6	7	8	9	OUT
BACK	374	423	468	193	461	364	183	328	445	3239
REGULAR	365	395	463	173	445	358	174	319	432	3124
par	4	4	5	3	4	4	3	4	4	35
handicap	7	3	11	15	1	9	17	13	5	-
FORWARD	349	363	445	102	421	339	155	309	404	2887
par	4	4	5	3	5	4	3	4	4	36
handicap	9	11	1	17	5	3	15	13	7	-

	10	11	12	13	14	15	16	17	18	IN
BACK	447	521	164	457	354	151	425	294	527	3340
REGULAR	438	496	158	457	342	134	411	288	507	3231
par	4	5	3	4	4	3	4	4	5	36
handicap	2	10	16	4	8	18	6	14	12	-
FORWARD	431	415	126	439	325	125	334	275	433	2903
par	5	5	3	5	4	3	4	4	5	38
handicap	8	2	18	10	6	16	14	12	4	-

BACK	
yardage	6579
par	71
rating	72.8
slope	132

REGULAR	
yardage	6355
par	71
rating	71.7
slope	130

FORWARD	
yardage	5790
par	74
rating	73.5
slope	131

PLAY POLICY & FEES: Green fees are $40 Monday through Thursday and $60 Friday through Sunday. Carts are $13 per person. Twilight rates are available.

TEE TIMES: Reservations can be booked seven days in advance.

DRESS CODE: No tanks tops are allowed on the course.

COURSE DESCRIPTION: This hilly, meandering course has sidehill lies and requires good placement shots. Situated in the midst of a California State game preserve, wildlife abounds. The weather ranges from San Francisco fog to Peninsula sun. It has some steep holes, but it is walkable. The view from the sixth tee opens up on the game preserve. Deer regularly come onto the course. The first hole is a hard dogleg left, 397 yards, requiring a long, accurate tee shot, and the green is severely sloped.

NOTES: Charlie Leider set the course record of 62.

LOCATION: On Interstate 280 heading north or south in Burlingame, take the Hayne and Black Mountain Road exit. Head west and follow the road until it dead ends at Golf Course Drive. Turn right onto Golf Course Drive. The course is visible from the highway.

. . . ● **TOURNAMENTS:** A 16-player minimum is required to book a tournament. Carts are required. Events should be booked 12 months in advance. The banquet facility can accommodate 200 people. ● **TRAVEL:** The Sheraton Gateway (650-340-8500), the San Francisco Airport Marriott (415-692-9100), and the Downtown San Francisco Marriott (415-896-1600) are recommended for lodging.

60. CRYSTAL SPRINGS GOLF COURSE

PLAY POLICY & FEES: Reciprocal play is accepted with members of other private clubs. Guest fees are $50 when accompanied by a member on weekdays and $60 Friday through Sunday. The green fee for reciprocators is $100. Carts are $11.50 per person for 18 holes. The course is closed on Monday.

TEE TIMES: Have your club pro call to make arrangements.

DRESS CODE: Appropriate golf attire is required.

COURSE DESCRIPTION: This mature course offers undulating greens and tight fairways lined with redwood, Monterey pine, stone pine, and eucalyptus trees. The par-4 10th hole measures 445 yards and is especially challenging. You hit from an elevated tee to a fairly wide-open fairway with trees on both sides and out-of-bounds on the left. The green is sizable and is surrounded by bunkers. Play left-center off the tee and aim for the middle of the slightly undulating green. The 425-yard 16th has a blind tee shot, then a downhill approach to a green bordered on the left by a huge stand of eucalyptus. From a few other, tee boxes you can see a full view of Mount Diablo in the East Bay.

NOTES: This is the only Donald Ross–designed golf course on the West Coast.

LOCATION: The course is located between U.S. 101 and Interstate 280. Take Highway 92 to Alameda De Las Pulgas and bear south. Turn right on Madera Drive.

. . . ● **TOURNAMENTS:** This course is available for outside events on Monday.

61. THE PENINSULA GOLF & COUNTRY CLUB

62 MENLO COUNTRY CLUB
ARCHITECT: TOM NICOLL, 1900

P.O. Box 729
Redwood City, CA 94064

2300 Woodside Road
Woodside, CA 94062

PRO SHOP: 650-366-9910
OFFICE: 650-366-4469

Scott Farr, PGA Professional
Scott Lewis, Superintendent
Michael Dubes, Banquet Manager

Driving Range ●
Practice Greens ●
Clubhouse ●
Food / Beverage ●
Accommodations ●
Pull Carts ●
Power Carts ●
Club Rental ●
$pecial Offers

	1	2	3	4	5	6	7	8	9	OUT
BACK	361	388	524	201	429	319	160	400	393	3175
REGULAR	342	372	510	187	405	293	154	385	384	3032
par	4	4	5	3	4	4	3	4	4	35
handicap	9	11	3	13	1	15	17	5	7	-
FORWARD	327	324	481	171	411	259	130	340	368	2811
par	4	4	5	3	5	4	3	4	4	36
handicap	9	11	1	15	3	13	17	7	5	-

	10	11	12	13	14	15	16	17	18	IN
BACK	394	410	376	183	519	330	379	175	379	3145
REGULAR	355	392	364	173	498	320	370	165	373	3010
par	4	4	4	3	5	4	4	3	4	35
handicap	12	6	8	16	2	14	10	18	4	-
FORWARD	319	400	348	145	467	306	352	134	359	2830
par	4	5	4	3	5	4	4	3	4	36
handicap	12	4	8	16	2	14	10	18	6	-

BACK	
yardage	6320
par	70
rating	70.9
slope	128

REGULAR	
yardage	6042
par	70
rating	69.6
slope	126

FORWARD	
yardage	5641
par	72
rating	72.6
slope	128

63 EMERALD HILLS GOLF CLUB

938 Wilmington Way
Redwood City, CA 94062

PRO SHOP: 650-368-7820

Bruce Olson, Director of Golf
Julie Harris, Head Professional
Jim Irvine, Superintendent

Driving Range ●
Practice Greens ●
Clubhouse
Food / Beverage ●
Accommodations
Pull Carts ●
Power Carts
Club Rental ●
$pecial Offers

	1	2	3	4	5	6	7	8	9	OUT
BACK	-	-	-	-	-	-	-	-	-	-
REGULAR	209	164	172	104	112	117	105	122	100	1205
par	3	3	3	3	3	3	3	3	3	27
handicap	3	1	2	6	5	9	4	8	7	-
FORWARD	160	156	105	92	103	106	93	108	90	1013
par	3	3	3	3	3	3	3	3	3	27
handicap	4	6	1	3	2	9	7	5	8	-

	10	11	12	13	14	15	16	17	18	IN
BACK	-	-	-	-	-	-	-	-	-	-
REGULAR	209	164	172	104	112	117	105	122	100	1205
par	3	3	3	3	3	3	3	3	3	27
handicap	4	6	1	3	2	9	7	5	8	-
FORWARD	160	156	105	92	103	106	93	108	90	1013
par	3	3	3	3	3	3	3	3	3	27
handicap	4	6	1	3	2	9	7	5	8	-

BACK	
yardage	-
par	-
rating	-
slope	-

REGULAR	
yardage	2410
par	54
rating	-
slope	-

FORWARD	
yardage	2026
par	54
rating	-
slope	-

PLAY POLICY & FEES: Guests must be accompanied by a member. Reciprocal play is not accepted. Guest fees are $35 weekdays and $40 weekends when accompanied by a member. Carts are $24.

DRESS CODE: Appropriate golf attire is required.

COURSE DESCRIPTION: This is a short but sneaky course. Overhanging old oaks add character and line the fairways. Beware of the 16th hole where there's a massive oak in the middle of the fairway. The course mixes traditional small greens with recent innovations by Robert Trent Jones Jr. It's mostly flat and walkable. A very exclusive club, this course is known for its pristine condition and traditional presence.

LOCATION: Take interstate 280 to Redwood City. Exit on Woodside Road. The course is on the north side of the street, 0.7 mile from Interstate 280.

. . . ● **TOURNAMENTS:** This course is not available for outside events.

62. MENLO COUNTRY CLUB

PLAY POLICY & FEES: Green fees are $8 for nine holes weekdays and $12 for nine holes weekends and holidays. Senior and junior rates are $5 for nine holes weekdays only. Carts are $2.

TEE TIMES: Reservations are not accepted. All play is on a first-come, first-served basis.

DRESS CODE: Shoes and shirts are required.

COURSE DESCRIPTION: This is a short starter course composed of par 3s. It's hilly but walkable and is a perfect layout for juniors, seniors, and beginners. This is a good course for the advanced golfer to sharpen his short game. With a driving range and putting green, this a good place to learn the game.

NOTES: The course is owned by the Redwood City Elks Lodge.

LOCATION: From Interstate 280 in Redwood City, exit on Edgewood Road southwest and turn left on Cañada Road. Drive 1.5 miles to Jefferson Avenue and turn left again, following it to Wilmington Way. Turn right to the course.

. . . ● **TOURNAMENTS:** A 40-player minimum is required to book an event. A banquet facility is available that can accommodate up to 300 people. Events should be booked three months in advance.

63. EMERALD HILLS GOLF CLUB

ARCHITECT: JACK FLEMING, 1962

2900 Sand Hill Road
Menlo Park, CA 94025

PRO SHOP: 650-854-6429
CLUBHOUSE: 650-854-6422

David Nightingale, Manager
James Knipp, Director of Golf, PGA
Mike Rothenberg, Superintendent

Driving Range ●
Practice Greens ●
Clubhouse ●
Food / Beverage ●
Accommodations
Pull Carts ●
Power Carts ●
Club Rental ●
$pecial Offers

	1	2	3	4	5	6	7	8	9	OUT
BACK	426	173	504	372	585	151	368	430	373	3382
REGULAR	412	149	485	352	562	133	355	407	354	3209
par	4	3	5	4	5	3	4	4	4	36
handicap	10	16	14	12	4	18	6	2	8	-
FORWARD	382	116	435	311	522	100	322	339	312	2839
par	4	3	5	4	5	3	4	4	4	36
handicap	8	16	12	10	2	18	4	14	6	-

	10	11	12	13	14	15	16	17	18	IN
BACK	539	435	425	201	324	431	400	172	528	3455
REGULAR	515	409	399	179	312	410	383	157	503	3267
par	5	4	4	3	4	4	4	3	5	36
handicap	11	7	3	15	13	5	1	17	9	-
FORWARD	475	349	360	140	277	370	351	120	453	2895
par	5	4	4	3	4	4	4	3	5	36
handicap	9	13	5	15	11	7	1	17	3	-

BACK	
yardage	6837
par	72
rating	73.7
slope	137

REGULAR	
yardage	6476
par	72
rating	72.0
slope	134

FORWARD	
yardage	5734
par	72
rating	73.7
slope	132

ARCHITECT: WILLIAM P. BELL, 1930

198 Junipero Serra
Stanford, CA 94305

PRO SHOP: 650-323-0944

Don Chelemedos, Manager, PGA
Ken Williams, Superintendent

Driving Range ●
Practice Greens ●
Clubhouse ●
Food / Beverage ●
Accommodations
Pull Carts ●
Power Carts ●
Club Rental ●
$pecial Offers

	1	2	3	4	5	6	7	8	9	OUT
BACK	511	439	188	371	417	430	520	173	358	3407
REGULAR	488	425	166	344	388	402	484	142	342	3181
par	5	4	3	4	4	4	5	3	4	36
handicap	13	3	15	5	9	1	11	17	7	-
FORWARD	482	413	105	339	338	398	480	119	334	3008
par	5	5	3	4	4	5	5	3	4	38
handicap	5	9	17	3	13	7	1	15	11	-

	10	11	12	13	14	15	16	17	18	IN
BACK	435	345	474	424	182	363	503	192	445	3363
REGULAR	403	337	443	408	157	328	494	173	422	3165
par	4	4	4	4	3	4	5	3	4	35
handicap	4	14	2	8	16	12	6	18	10	-
FORWARD	343	331	404	400	118	308	491	153	415	2963
par	4	4	5	5	3	4	5	3	5	38
handicap	8	14	4	6	18	12	2	16	10	-

BACK	
yardage	6770
par	71
rating	72.9
slope	131

REGULAR	
yardage	6346
par	71
rating	70.9
slope	127

FORWARD	
yardage	5971
par	76
rating	74.2
slope	135

PLAY POLICY & FEES: Reciprocal play is accepted with members of other private clubs upon approval of the head pro. Guests must be sponsored by a member. Guest fees are $55 on weekdays and $80 on weekends when accompanied by a member, and $135 when unaccompanied. Carts are $24.

DRESS CODE: Appropriate golf attire is required.

COURSE DESCRIPTION: This course is long and challenging. Redwoods ranging in height from 40 to 80 feet often come into play. The course boasts some of the best greens between San Francisco and Monterey. They're large, smooth, and fast. The course is hilly but walkable.

LOCATION: From Interstate 280 in Menlo Park take the Sand Hill Road exit toward Stanford University. The course is located on the left, less than a quarter mile off Sand Hill Road.

. . . ● **TOURNAMENTS:** Outside events are allowed on an extremely limited basis.

64. SHARON HEIGHTS GOLF & COUNTRY

PLAY POLICY & FEES: Stanford students, alumni, faculty, staff, and guests only. Guests must be accompanied by a constituant. Guest fees are $75 weekdays and $90 weekends and holidays. Carts are $28. The course is closed on Monday except on university holidays.

TEE TIMES: Stanford students, alumni, faculty and staff can make reservations one day in advance.

DRESS CODE: Nonmetal spikes are required.

COURSE DESCRIPTION: This sprawling layout is dotted with eucalyptus and oak trees. It has large, contoured greens and many bunkers. There are no breathers, especially on the infamous, nerve-wracking par-4 12th hole. It's extremely long, with two oak trees in the middle of the fairway. The second and the tenth holes are cast-iron tests. This course can get very crowded, but it's worth the wait.

NOTES: Stanford has played host to several NCAA Men's Championships, NCAA Women's Championships, the USGA Junior Championship, and the Western Amateur.

LOCATION: From Interstate 280 take the Sand Hill Road exit in Menlo Park. Drive east toward Stanford University. Turn right on Junipero Serra Boulevard and proceed a half mile to West Campus Drive. Turn right and proceed to the course. From U.S. 101 take the University Avenue exit, which turns into Palm Drive. Turn right on West Campus Drive and continue to the course.

. . . ● **TOURNAMENTS:** Outside events are limited to Monday. Carts are required. A 120-player minimum is required. Tournaments should be booked 12 months in advance. The banquet facilities can accommodate up to 150 people.

65. STANFORD UNIVERSITY GOLF COURSE

PALO ALTO HILLS GOLF & COUNTRY CLUB

ARCHITECTS: CLARK GLASSON, 1960; NEAL MEAGER, 1998

3000 Alexis Drive
Palo Alto, CA 94304

PRO SHOP: 650-948-2320
CLUBHOUSE: 650-948-1800

Lyn Nelson, Manager
Jim O'Neal, Head Professional, PGA
Mike Garvale, Superintendent

Driving Range ●
Practice Greens ●
Clubhouse ●
Food / Beverage ●
Accommodations
Pull Carts ●
Power Carts ●
Club Rental ●
$pecial Offers

	1	2	3	4	5	6	7	8	9	OUT
BACK	331	121	413	389	194	390	497	372	392	3099
REGULAR	307	101	358	359	154	371	317	357	384	2708
par	4	3	4	4	3	4	5	4	4	35
handicap	16	18	6	2	12	8	14	4	10	-
FORWARD	307	83	294	351	148	364	253	242	355	2387
par	4	3	4	5	3	4	4	4	5	36
handicap	12	18	6	12	14	2	4	8	16	-

	10	11	12	13	14	15	16	17	18	IN
BACK	385	214	497	461	285	145	353	353	477	3170
REGULAR	358	149	470	441	257	122	330	320	450	2897
par	4	3	5	4	4	3	4	4	5	36
handicap	3	9	15	1	17	13	5	7	11	-
FORWARD	284	144	438	414	235	115	297	288	430	2645
par	4	3	5	4	4	3	4	4	5	36
handicap	3	15	9	13	11	17	5	7	1	-

BACK	
yardage	6269
par	71
rating	-
slope	-

REGULAR	
yardage	5605
par	71
rating	-
slope	-

FORWARD	
yardage	5032
par	72
rating	-
slope	-

PALO ALTO GOLF COURSE

ARCHITECT: WILLIAM F. BELL, 1956

1875 Embarcadero Road
Palo Alto, CA 94303

PRO SHOP: 650-856-0881
CLUBHOUSE: 650-856-0133

Brad Lozares
Richard Bin, Head Professional, PGA
Dave Davies, Superintendent

Driving Range ●
Practice Greens ●
Clubhouse ●
Food / Beverage ●
Accommodations
Pull Carts ●
Power Carts ●
Club Rental ●
$pecial Offers

	1	2	3	4	5	6	7	8	9	OUT
BACK	539	418	201	431	392	439	351	192	536	3499
REGULAR	517	411	189	422	382	428	342	176	521	3388
par	5	4	3	4	4	4	4	3	5	36
handicap	5	7	13	1	9	3	11	17	15	-
FORWARD	491	359	96	377	353	370	278	133	500	2957
par	5	4	3	4	4	4	4	3	5	36
handicap	1	9	17	7	11	5	13	15	3	-

	10	11	12	13	14	15	16	17	18	IN
BACK	319	155	489	363	226	499	425	443	402	3321
REGULAR	313	155	480	343	208	469	415	428	381	3192
par	4	3	5	4	3	5	4	4	4	36
handicap	18	12	14	8	4	16	6	2	10	-
FORWARD	257	103	461	302	127	410	348	386	328	2722
par	4	3	5	4	3	5	4	4	4	36
handicap	14	18	2	10	16	4	8	6	12	-

BACK	
yardage	6820
par	72
rating	
slope	

REGULAR	
yardage	6580
par	72
rating	
slope	

FORWARD	
yardage	5679
par	72
rating	
slope	

PLAY POLICY & FEES: Reciprocal play is accepted with members of other private clubs. The green fee for reciprocators is $125, including carts. Guest fees are $55 weekdays and $70 weekends when accompanied by a member. Carts are $22. The course is closed on Monday.

DRESS CODE: Appropriate golf attire is required.

COURSE DESCRIPTION: Although this tight, hilly course is short, it plays considerably longer than the yardage indicates. It's a defensive course, with undulating fairways and elevated fast greens. Water comes into play on five holes. Watch out for the par-4 third hole, a nasty, downhill tester. The par-5 18th hole is the signature hole with a lake and waterfall fronting the green, resulting in a risky approach shot. Situated in the hills, the course offers picturesque views of the San Francisco Bay, so don't forget to look up.

NOTES: The first head professional was Ken Venturi in 1960. The course records are held by Steve Burrell with a 65.

LOCATION: From Interstate 280 west, take the Page Mill exit. Drive one mile to Alexis Drive and continue a half mile to the course. From U.S. 101, take Oregon Expressway. Cross El Camino Real and the road turns into Page Mill. Continue to the course.

. . . ● **TOURNAMENTS:** Outside tournaments are available on Monday only. A 100-player minimum is required to book an event. Tournaments should be scheduled 12 months in advance. The banquet facility can accommodate 400 people.

66. PALO ALTO HILLS GOLF & COUNTRY

PLAY POLICY & FEES: Green fees are $25 weekdays and $30 weekends. Twilight rates are available. Carts are $20.

TEE TIMES: Reservations can be booked seven days in advance.

COURSE DESCRIPTION: A recent remodel has made this well-run and well-maintained facility even more popular. The addition of several bunkers and new greens has improved playing conditions dramatically. Palo Alto has a links feel with wide open, driver-friendly fairways and large greens. Although wind is a factor, the greens allow players several approach options, including bump and run.

NOTES: Annual tournaments played at the Palo Alto Golf Course include the Palo Alto City Women's Amateur (April), the Santa Clara Valley Best-Ball (May), and the Palo Alto City Seniors Amateur (October). The course record of 64 is held by Brad Henninger.

LOCATION: From U.S. 101 in Palo Alto take the Embarcadero Road exit east. The course is located on the left about a half mile from the highway. It's just before the airport.

. . . ● **TOURNAMENTS:** This course is available for outside tournaments.

67. PALO ALTO GOLF COURSE

750 MSS/SVBG–Box 42
Onizuka Air Station, CA
94089
PRO SHOP: 650-603-8026

Doug Carlton, PGA Professional
Mike Hill, Superintendent

1080 Lockhead Way
Sunnyvale, CA 94089

Driving Range ●
Practice Greens ●
Clubhouse ●
Food / Beverage ●
Accommodations
Pull Carts ●
Power Carts ●
Club Rental ●
$pecial Offers

	1	2	3	4	5	6	7	8	9	OUT
BACK										
REGULAR										
par										
handicap										
FORWARD										
par										
handicap										

	10	11	12	13	14	15	16	17	18	IN
BACK										
REGULAR										
par										
handicap										
FORWARD										
par										
handicap										

BACK	
yardage	6491
par	72
rating	70.0
slope	119

REGULAR	
yardage	6329
par	72
rating	70.8
slope	116

FORWARD	
yardage	5936
par	72
rating	73.0
slope	116

 SHORELINE GOLF LINKS
ARCHITECT: ROBERT TRENT JONES JR., 1983

2940 North Shoreline
Mountain View, CA 94043

PRO SHOP: 650-969-2041
OFFICE: 650-903-6178

Dave Collins, Director of Golf
Joe DeBode, Head Professional, PGA
Greg Stemel, Tournament Director

Driving Range ●
Practice Greens ●
Clubhouse ●
Food / Beverage ●
Accommodations
Pull Carts ●
Power Carts ●
Club Rental ●
$pecial Offers

	1	2	3	4	5	6	7	8	9	OUT
BACK	497	386	388	162	378	409	394	174	498	3286
REGULAR	470	370	358	137	347	375	370	143	475	3045
par	5	4	4	3	4	4	4	3	5	36
handicap	8	4	14	6	10	12	2	16	18	-
FORWARD	434	329	336	108	269	340	323	115	415	2669
par	5	4	4	3	4	4	4	3	5	36
handicap	8	2	12	10	16	6	4	18	14	-

	10	11	12	13	14	15	16	17	18	IN
BACK	513	155	375	372	382	396	519	161	417	3290
REGULAR	475	119	338	346	361	366	496	136	379	3016
par	5	3	4	4	4	4	5	3	4	36
handicap	7	15	5	9	17	13	11	3	1	-
FORWARD	443	101	298	311	329	333	453	117	346	2731
par	5	3	4	4	4	4	5	3	4	36
handicap	9	17	11	13	7	3	5	15	1	-

BACK	
yardage	6576
par	72
rating	71.9
slope	124

REGULAR	
yardage	6061
par	72
rating	69.3
slope	117

FORWARD	
yardage	5400
par	72
rating	71.2
slope	120

18 HOLES

PLAY POLICY & FEES: Active and retired military personnel, reservists, Department of Defense personnel, federal employees, NASA employees, and sponsored guests only. Rates vary according to military status. Call for information. Carts are $11 for nine holes and $20 for 18 holes.

TEE TIMES: Reservations on weekends are according to rank.

DRESS CODE: Appropriate golf attire and nonmetal spikes are required.

COURSE DESCRIPTION: This course is mostly flat, with more than 7,000 pine, poplar, and cedar trees. Three lakes come into play. The course is easily walkable. Kikuyu grass makes the course distinctive, and it tends to create flier lies, requiring the golfer to pick the ball clean for best results. This isn't a demanding course, but out-of-bounds areas come into play on several holes.

LOCATION: From U.S. 101 in Mountain View take the Moffett Field exit. Drive north to the main gate of Moffett Field for instructions.

. . . ● **TOURNAMENTS:** This course is not available for outside events.

68. MOFFETT FIELD GOLF COURSE

PUBLIC: $18-$42
FAX: 650-969-8383

18 HOLES

PLAY POLICY & FEES: Green fees are $30 Monday through Thursday, $35 on Friday, and $42 weekends. Twilight rates are $18 Monday through Thursday, $20 on Friday, and $22 weekends. Carts are $22.

TEE TIMES: Reservations can be booked seven days in advance.

DRESS CODE: Shirts and shoes are necessary. Nonmetal spikes are required.

COURSE DESCRIPTION: This sprawling, flat, links-style course demands accuracy with the long irons. The greens are large and undulating, the fairways are narrow, and there are more than 80 bunkers. Water guards the 4th, 11th, and 17th holes, all par 3s. The wind can blow here, but it's a fun course.

NOTES: The driving range has both grass and mats. The facility has a short game practice area.

LOCATION: From U.S. 101 in Mountain View take the Shoreline Boulevard exit north and drive toward the bay. Follow Shoreline Boulevard to Shoreline Park. The golf course is one-fourth mile inside the park.

. . . ● **TOURNAMENTS:** A 12-player minimum is required to book a tournament. There is a premium charge for shotgun tournaments. Carts are required. A banquet facility is available that can accommodate up to 200 people.

69. SHORELINE GOLF LINKS

SUNNYVALE GOLF COURSE
ARCHITECT: CLARK G LASSON, 1968

605 Macara Lane
Sunnyvale, CA 94086

PRO SHOP: 408-738-3666

Mark Petersen, Manager, PGA
Jerry Thormann, Head Professional, PGA
Curtis Black, Superintendent

Driving Range
Practice Greens •
Clubhouse •
Food / Beverage •
Accommodations
Pull Carts •
Power Carts •
Club Rental •
$pecial Offers

	1	2	3	4	5	6	7	8	9	OUT
BACK	381	404	509	175	296	389	161	341	432	3088
REGULAR	363	368	492	149	286	341	136	322	402	2859
par	4	4	5	3	4	4	3	4	4	35
handicap	7	3	11	17	15	13	9	1	5	-
FORWARD	306	286	472	126	274	320	117	298	380	2579
par	4	4	5	3	4	4	3	4	5	36
handicap	7	3	11	17	15	13	9	1	5	-

	10	11	12	13	14	15	16	17	18	IN
BACK	529	417	387	198	368	201	323	386	358	3167
REGULAR	499	392	346	161	340	178	303	353	333	2905
par	5	4	4	3	4	3	4	4	4	35
handicap	18	8	16	6	12	14	4	10	2	-
FORWARD	481	369	330	123	323	161	290	322	301	2700
par	5	4	4	3	4	3	4	4	4	35
handicap	18	8	16	6	12	14	4	10	2	-

BACK	
yardage	6255
par	70
rating	70.1
slope	121

REGULAR	
yardage	5764
par	70
rating	67.6
slope	114

FORWARD	
yardage	5279
par	71
rating	75.5
slope	107

 # LOS ALTOS GOLF & COUNTRY CLUB
ARCHITECT: TOM NICOLL, 1923

1560 County Club Drive
Los Altos, CA 94024

PRO SHOP: 650-948-2146
CLUBHOUSE: 650-948-1024

Kenneth Kelley, Manager
Brian Inkster, PGA Professional
Mike Simpson, Superintendent

Driving Range
Practice Greens •
Clubhouse •
Food / Beverage •
Accommodations
Pull Carts •
Power Carts •
Club Rental •
$pecial Offers

	1	2	3	4	5	6	7	8	9	OUT
BACK	519	390	231	347	349	143	388	424	412	3203
REGULAR	507	366	221	332	329	133	378	412	412	3090
par	5	4	3	4	4	3	4	4	4	35
handicap	3	13	17	11	7	15	5	1	9	-
FORWARD	492	347	189	315	314	113	364	398	403	2935
par	5	4	3	4	4	3	4	5	5	37
handicap	1	7	13	5	9	17	3	15	11	-

	10	11	12	13	14	15	16	17	18	IN
BACK	412	340	385	333	429	155	344	545	388	3331
REGULAR	387	315	366	322	413	145	334	490	388	3160
par	4	4	4	4	4	3	4	5	4	36
handicap	10	16	12	2	4	18	8	14	6	-
FORWARD	338	309	352	299	406	115	328	459	370	2976
par	4	4	4	4	5	3	4	5	4	37
handicap	12	6	10	14	16	18	8	4	2	-

BACK	
yardage	6534
par	71
rating	71.5
slope	128

REGULAR	
yardage	6250
par	71
rating	70.5
slope	125

FORWARD	
yardage	5911
par	74
rating	75.0
slope	134

PLAY POLICY & FEES: Green fees are $26 weekdays and $36 weekends. Twilight rates are available. Carts are $23.

TEE TIMES: Reservations can be booked seven days in advance for weekdays and on Monday for weekends.

COURSE DESCRIPTION: The short, flat course boasts several long par 3s. Conspiring trees, wind, lakes, and doglegs all demand good positioning. Beware of the 358-yard 18th hole, a par 4 over water with a three-tiered green guarded by bunkers.

NOTES: This public course has one of the largest pro shops in the country, offering full-service sales and repairs. A total of 100,000 rounds are played here each year.

LOCATION: From U.S.101 in northern Sunnyvale, exit onto Mathilda Avenue south. Turn right on Maude Avenue and right again on Macara Lane.

. . . ● **TOURNAMENTS:** No shotgun tournaments are allowed. A 24-player minimum is needed to book a tournament. Events should be booked 24 months in advance. A banquet facility is available that can accommodate up to 200 people.

70. SUNNYVALE GOLF COURSE

PLAY POLICY & FEES: Reciprocal play is accepted with members of other selected private clubs. Members and guests only. Green fees for reciprocators are $125, plus $22 for a cart. Guest fees are $70 when accompanied by a member. Carts are $22. The course is closed on Monday.

TEE TIMES: Have your club pro call for arrangements.

DRESS CODE: Appropriate golf attire and nonmetalspikes are required.

COURSE DESCRIPTION: The course is tight, tree-lined, and has undulating greens. The par-3 third hole requires a 231-yard carry over a barranca from an elevated tee.

NOTES: Three-time U.S. Amateur champion and LPGA standout, Juli Inkster, holds the women's record of 68; head pro Brian Inkster, her husband, grew up on the course. The men's course record is 64, set by Jeff Brehaut in 1989.

LOCATION: From Interstate 280 in Los Altos, take the Magdelena Avenue exit northeast. Turn right on the Foothill Expressway and continue to Loyola Drive. Turn right on Loyola. Turn right onto Country Club Drive and then turn left 100 yards up the road into the course driveway.

. . . ● **TOURNAMENTS:** Shotgun tournaments are Monday only, May through October. Carts are required. A 100-player minimum is needed to book a tournament.

71. LOS ALTOS GOLF & COUNTRY CLUB

BLACKBERRY FARM GOLF COURSE
ARCHITECT: ROBERT MUIR GRAVES, 1962

22100 Stevens Creek
Cupertino, CA 95041

PRO SHOP: 408-253-9200

Mike O'Dowd, Manager
Jeff Piserchio, PGA Professional
Nick Alverez, Superintendent

Driving Range ●
Practice Greens ●
Clubhouse ●
Food / Beverage ●
Accommodations
Pull Carts ●
Power Carts
Club Rental ●
$Special Offers

	1	2	3	4	5	6	7	8	9	OUT
BACK										
REGULAR										
par										
handicap										
FORWARD										
par										
handicap										

	10	11	12	13	14	15	16	17	18	IN
BACK										
REGULAR										
par										
handicap										
FORWARD										
par										
handicap										

BACK	
yardage	
par	
rating	
slope	

REGULAR	
yardage	3182
par	58
rating	55.9
slope	78

FORWARD	
yardage	3182
par	58
rating	58.5
slope	83

 DEEP CLIFF GOLF COURSE
ARCHITECT: CLARK GLASSON, 1960

10700 Clubhouse Lane
Cupertino, CA 95014

PRO SHOP: 408-253-5357

Chris Kulpa, Manager
Mark Francetic, Superintendent

Driving Range ●
Practice Greens ●
Clubhouse ●
Food / Beverage ●
Accommodations
Pull Carts ●
Power Carts ●
Club Rental ●
$Special Offers

	1	2	3	4	5	6	7	8	9	OUT
BACK	-	-	-	-	-	-	-	-	-	-
REGULAR	271	136	128	164	165	224	118	105	254	1565
par	4	3	3	3	3	4	3	3	4	30
handicap	3	15	13	11	9	1	7	17	5	-
FORWARD	242	121	117	146	150	160	95	88	232	1351
par	4	3	3	3	3	4	3	3	4	30
handicap	3	15	13	11	9	1	7	17	5	-

	10	11	12	13	14	15	16	17	18	IN
BACK	-	-	-	-	-	-	-	-	-	-
REGULAR	142	289	276	199	168	289	132	117	180	1792
par	3	4	4	3	3	4	3	3	3	30
handicap	14	2	10	4	12	6	16	18	8	-
FORWARD	115	266	254	185	153	247	113	97	148	1578
par	3	4	4	3	3	4	3	3	3	30
handicap	14	2	10	4	12	6	16	18	8	-

BACK	
yardage	-
par	-
rating	-
slope	-

REGULAR	
yardage	3357
par	60
rating	59.0
slope	96

FORWARD	
yardage	2929
par	60
rating	56.8
slope	91

PLAY POLICY & FEES: Green fees for residents of Cupertino are $9 weekdays and $11 weekends. Nonresident green fees are $10 weekdays and $12 weekends.

TEE TIMES: Reservations are accepted one week in advance starting at 7 a.m.

DRESS CODE: Shirts must be worn.

COURSE DESCRIPTION: This flat, narrow course has lots of water and trees. It's relatively short with dome-shaped greens. The 120-yard, par-3 eighth hole is over water.

NOTES: A total of 80,000 rounds are played here each year.

LOCATION: From Interstate 280 in Cupertino take Highway 85 south to the Stevens Creek Boulevard exit. Go west and drive one-third mile to the course, which is on the left.

. . . ● **TOURNAMENTS:** Shotgun tournaments are not allowed. A 16-player minimum is required to book a tournament.

72. BLACKBERRY FARM GOLF COURSE

PLAY POLICY & FEES: Green fees are $25 weekdays and $33 weekends.

TEE TIMES: Reservations can be booked seven days in advance.

DRESS CODE: Shirts and shoes are necessary. Nonmetal spikes are encouraged.

COURSE DESCRIPTION: This mid-length course has three par 4s on the front nine and three par 4s on the back nine. It requires good placement shots because of the narrow corridor-type fairways. Stevens Creek bisects the course and comes into play on several holes.

NOTES: A total of 90,000 rounds are played here each year.

LOCATION: From Interstate 280 in Sunnyvale, take the Foothill Expressway exit south to McClellan Road. Turn left and then turn right onto Clubhouse Lane.

. . . ● **TOURNAMENTS:** This course is available for outside events. Tournaments should be booked six months in advance. ● **TRAVEL:** The Cupertino Inn is located about 10 minutes from the golf course.

73. DEEP CLIFF GOLF COURSE

SUNKEN GARDENS GOLF COURSE
ARCHITECT: ROBERT DEAN PUTMAN, 1959

1010 South Wolfe Road
Sunnyvale, CA 94086

PRO SHOP: 408-739-6588
CLUBHOUSE: 408-732-2046

Jerry Thormann, Head Professional, PGA
Curtis Black, Superintendent

Driving Range ●
Practice Greens ●
Clubhouse ●
Food / Beverage ●
Accommodations
Pull Carts ●
Power Carts ●
Club Rental ●
$pecial Offers

	1	2	3	4	5	6	7	8	9	OUT
BACK	-	-	-	-	-	-	-	-	-	-
REGULAR	140	259	150	108	130	261	102	150	138	1438
par	3	4	3	3	3	4	3	3	3	29
handicap	6	4	3	8	1	7	9	2	5	-
FORWARD	140	259	150	108	130	261	102	150	138	1438
par	3	4	3	3	3	4	3	3	3	29
handicap	6	4	3	8	1	7	9	2	5	-

	10	11	12	13	14	15	16	17	18	IN
BACK	-	-	-	-	-	-	-	-	-	-
REGULAR	140	259	150	108	130	261	102	150	138	1438
par	3	4	3	3	3	4	3	3	3	29
handicap	15	13	12	17	10	16	18	11	14	-
FORWARD	140	259	150	108	130	261	102	150	138	1438
par	3	4	3	3	3	4	3	3	3	29
handicap	15	13	12	17	10	16	18	11	14	-

BACK	
yardage	-
par	-
rating	-
slope	-

REGULAR	
yardage	2876
par	58
rating	56.8
slope	86

FORWARD	
yardage	2876
par	58
rating	-
slope	-

 # SANTA CLARA GOLF & TENNIS CLUB
ARCHITECT: ROBERT MUIR GRAVES, 1986

5155 Stars and Stripes
Santa Clara, CA 95054

PRO SHOP: 408-980-9515

David Tuttle, Manager
Mike Paul, Professional, PGA
Mike Basile, Superintendent

Driving Range ●
Practice Greens ●
Clubhouse
Food / Beverage ●
Accommodations
Pull Carts ●
Power Carts ●
Club Rental ●
$pecial Offers

	1	2	3	4	5	6	7	8	9	OUT
BACK	539	387	370	397	421	232	557	146	372	3421
REGULAR	511	366	338	378	400	205	541	131	351	3221
par	5	4	4	4	4	3	5	3	4	36
handicap	9	11	13	7	1	5	3	17	15	-
FORWARD	475	330	290	347	363	174	486	100	318	2883
par	5	4	4	4	4	3	5	3	4	36
handicap	3	9	13	7	5	15	1	17	11	-

	10	11	12	13	14	15	16	17	18	IN
BACK	382	362	398	186	524	440	425	189	495	3401
REGULAR	358	335	382	168	503	430	404	172	484	3236
par	4	4	4	3	5	4	4	3	5	36
handicap	14	10	8	16	12	2	4	6	18	-
FORWARD	316	292	302	116	441	361	366	123	439	2756
par	4	4	4	3	5	4	4	3	5	36
handicap	10	14	12	18	2	6	8	16	4	-

BACK	
yardage	6822
par	72
rating	73.2
slope	126

REGULAR	
yardage	6457
par	72
rating	71.5
slope	123

FORWARD	
yardage	5639
par	72
rating	71.5
slope	115

PLAY POLICY & FEES: Green fees are $11.50 weekdays and $15 weekends. Power carts may be used by the physically challenged only.

TEE TIMES: Weekend reservations must be made Monday prior to the weekend.

DRESS CODE: Shirts must be worn, and no tank tops are allowed.

COURSE DESCRIPTION: This mostly flat course borders a former quarry and is somewhat tight. There are two par 4s, and the rest are par 3s. The course is an excellent layout for beginners, juniors, and seniors.

LOCATION: This course is located between U.S. 101 and Interstate 280 in Sunnyvale. Exit on Wolfe Road toward El Camino Real. The course is on the east side of the street.

. . . ● **TOURNAMENTS:** A 16-player minimum is needed to book a tournament.

74. SUNKEN GARDENS GOLF COURSE

PLAY POLICY & FEES: Green fees for residents of the city of Santa Clara are $14 weekdays and $19 weekends. Nonresident green fees are $26 weekdays and $34 weekends. Twilight rates are available. Carts are $11 for nine holes and $22 for 18 holes. A single-rider cart is $13.

TEE TIMES: Residents can reserve tee times eight days in advance, and nonresidents can reserve tee times seven days in advance. Residents must have an ID card issued by the pro shop.

COURSE DESCRIPTION: This course has rolling hills and is long and open, with a links-style rough on the fairway. It's walkable. There are doglegs and blind shots, and the wind can blow. The par-4 15th, at 440-yards, is brutal in the afternoon wind. Water comes into play on two par 4s on the front nine.

NOTES: The course is located across the street from the San Francisco 49ers' headquarters. A total of 110,000 rounds are played here each year.

LOCATION: From Sunnyvale take U.S.101 south to the Great America Parkway exit. Go east on Tasman Drive and the course is on the left.

. . . ● **TOURNAMENTS:** Shotgun tournaments are available weekdays only. Carts are required. A 16-player minimum player is needed to book a tournament. Events should be scheduled 12 months in advance. The banquet facility can accommodate 400 people. ● **TRAVEL:** The Westin Santa Clara is located within walking distance of the course. For reservations call 408-986-0700.

75. SANTA CLARA GOLF & TENNIS CLUB

1560 Oakland Road
San Jose, CA 95131

PRO SHOP: 408-441-4653

Mike Rawitser, Director of Golf
Bob McGrath, Head Professional, PGA
Dave Parks, Tournament Director

Driving Range ●
Practice Greens ●
Clubhouse ●
Food / Beverage ●
Accommodations
Pull Carts ●
Power Carts ●
Club Rental ●
$pecial Offers

	1	2	3	4	5	6	7	8	9	OUT
BACK	492	403	402	144	364	383	184	418	502	3292
REGULAR	478	390	381	131	349	373	159	403	478	3142
par	5	4	4	3	4	4	3	4	5	36
handicap	11	3	9	5	17	7	15	1	13	-
FORWARD	429	318	311	109	305	340	122	371	436	2741
par	5	4	4	3	4	4	3	4	5	36
handicap	17	11	9	5	7	3	13	1	15	-

	10	11	12	13	14	15	16	17	18	IN
BACK	377	543	147	394	361	415	381	194	498	3310
REGULAR	361	530	139	379	350	404	361	165	478	3167
par	4	5	3	4	4	4	4	3	5	36
handicap	12	4	18	6	16	2	8	10	14	-
FORWARD	328	461	121	321	317	346	338	153	468	2853
par	4	5	3	4	4	4	4	3	5	36
handicap	12	16	14	6	10	2	4	8	18	-

BACK	
yardage	6602
par	72
rating	70.1
slope	108

REGULAR	
yardage	6309
par	72
rating	68.7
slope	105

FORWARD	
yardage	5594
par	72
rating	69.7
slope	112

 SUMMITPOINTE GOLF COURSE

1500 Country Club Drive
Milpitas, CA 95035

PRO SHOP: 408-262-8813
CLUBHOUSE: 408-262-2500

Ruth Kirk, Head Pro/Operations Manager
Bob Poitrowski, Director of Instruction, PGA
Bill Conrad, Superintendent

Driving Range ●
Practice Greens ●
Clubhouse ●
Food / Beverage ●
Accommodations
Pull Carts ●
Power Carts ●
Club Rental ●
$pecial Offers

	1	2	3	4	5	6	7	8	9	OUT
BACK	322	528	122	362	183	384	338	401	515	3155
REGULAR	300	483	117	351	175	375	329	393	505	3028
par	4	5	3	4	3	4	4	4	5	36
handicap	15	3	17	5	7	11	9	1	13	-
FORWARD	273	448	107	342	169	274	326	383	462	2784
par	4	5	3	4	3	4	4	4	5	36
handicap	15	3	17	5	9	13	11	1	7	-

	10	11	12	13	14	15	16	17	18	IN
BACK	358	329	364	154	488	498	199	388	398	3176
REGULAR	346	322	352	143	473	492	178	381	348	3035
par	4	4	4	3	5	5	3	4	4	36
handicap	8	16	2	18	14	12	6	10	4	-
FORWARD	330	310	329	112	458	438	122	291	322	2712
par	4	4	4	3	5	5	3	4	4	36
handicap	14	16	6	18	2	4	12	10	8	-

BACK	
yardage	6331
par	72
rating	70.9
slope	125

REGULAR	
yardage	6063
par	72
rating	69.7
slope	122

FORWARD	
yardage	5496
par	72
rating	70.6
slope	121

PLAY POLICY & FEES: Green fees are $28 weekdays and $38 weekends. Call for special afternoon and twilight rates. Carts are $13 for nine holes and $24 for 18 holes.

TEE TIMES: Reservations can be booked seven days in advance for weekdays and on Tuesday for the upcoming weekend.

COURSE DESCRIPTION: This course is relatively flat and undemanding, making it a good intermediate test of golf. There are a few long par 4s. Most fairways are wide, but watch out for doglegs and large, undulating greens. The course is usually in excellent condition, and it is one of the busiest in Northern California, with 108,000 rounds played here annually.

NOTES: This course averages 400 to 450 players a day, depending on the season. San Jose has a complete club-fitting center.

LOCATION: From U.S. 101 heading south in San Jose, take the 13th Street exit and cross back over the freeway on Oakland Road. Follow it for one mile to the course on your right.

. . . ● **TOURNAMENTS:** This course is available for outside tournaments. A 20-player minimum is needed. Tournaments should be booked at least one month in advance.

76. SAN JOSE MUNICIPAL GOLF COURSE

PLAY POLICY & FEES: Green fees are $25 weekdays and $68 weekends and holidays. Carts are $15 per person and included in the weekend fees. Call for twilight rates.

TEE TIMES: Reservations can be booked seven days in advance.

DRESS CODE: Collared shirts are required. Blue jeans are not allowed. Nonmetal spikes are encouraged.

COURSE DESCRIPTION: The front nine is open but very hilly, while the back nine is flat and tight with water on nearly every hole. The greens are tough and fast. The 16th hole, a 199-yard par 3, is described as one of the best holes in Northern California. The short, par-4 11th hole is a member of the Bay Area's "Dream 18."

NOTES: Summit Pointe is renovating the irrigation system, leveling fairways, reconstructing bunkers, planting more trees, and improving the fourth and eighth greens. Renovations should be completed by the end of 1999. The course record is 64, held by Esteban Toledo.

LOCATION: From Interstate 680 in Milpitas take the Jacklin Road exit east to Park Victoria. Turn left and then right onto Country Club Drive.

. . . ● **TOURNAMENTS:** A 16-player minimum is required to book a tournament. Tournaments should be booked three to six months in advance. The banquet facility can accommodate 150 people. ● **TRAVEL:** The Embassy Suites in Milpitas is recommended.

77. SUMMITPOINTE GOLF COURSE

3441 East Calaveras
Milpitas, CA 95035

PRO SHOP: 408-262-1722

Dana Jetter, Director of Golf, PGA
Denise Fitzgerald, Tournament Director

Driving Range ●
Practice Greens ●
Clubhouse ●
Food / Beverage ●
Accommodations
Pull Carts ●
Power Carts ●
Club Rental ●
$pecial Offers

	1	2	3	4	5	6	7	8	9	OUT
BACK	373	168	296	171	315	508	171	415	416	2833
REGULAR	359	162	290	159	295	502	160	407	403	2737
par	4	3	4	3	4	5	3	4	4	34
handicap	7	9	11	13	15	1	17	5	3	-
FORWARD	345	155	284	146	273	496	149	401	401	2650
par	4	3	4	3	4	5	3	5	5	36
handicap	5	13	7	17	9	1	15	11	3	-

	10	11	12	13	14	15	16	17	18	IN
BACK	499	182	309	342	374	379	188	498	469	3240
REGULAR	477	170	292	328	363	368	178	478	456	3110
par	5	3	4	4	4	4	3	5	4	36
handicap	4	12	18	16	2	8	14	10	6	-
FORWARD	454	129	275	314	353	355	168	459	442	2949
par	5	3	4	4	4	4	3	5	5	37
handicap	4	18	16	14	2	12	10	8	6	-

BACK	
yardage	6073
par	70
rating	68.8
slope	112

REGULAR	
yardage	5847
par	70
rating	67.7
slope	110

FORWARD	
yardage	5599
par	73
rating	71.2
slope	120

P.O. Box 2759   21990 Prospect Road
Saratoga, CA 95070   Saratoga, CA 95070

PRO SHOP: 408-253-5494

Grant Barnes, PGA Professional
Tracy Shanahan, Superintendent

Driving Range ●
Practice Greens ●
Clubhouse ●
Food / Beverage ●
Accommodations
Pull Carts ●
Power Carts ●
Club Rental ●
$pecial Offers

	1	2	3	4	5	6	7	8	9	OUT
BACK	-	-	-	-	-	-	-	-	-	-
REGULAR	326	291	272	271	127	312	309	340	199	2447
par	4	4	4	4	3	4	4	4	3	34
handicap	17	11	5	9	15	13	7	1	3	-
FORWARD	326	291	272	271	127	312	309	340	199	2447
par	4	4	4	4	3	4	4	4	3	34
handicap	11	9	15	13	17	5	3	1	7	-

	10	11	12	13	14	15	16	17	18	IN
BACK	-	-	-	-	-	-	-	-	-	-
REGULAR	295	284	253	258	159	320	283	335	191	2378
par	4	4	4	4	3	4	4	4	3	34
handicap	18	10	16	12	4	14	8	6	2	-
FORWARD	295	284	253	258	159	320	283	335	191	2378
par	4	4	4	4	3	4	4	4	3	34
handicap	18	10	14	16	8	12	4	2	6	-

BACK	
yardage	-
par	-
rating	-
slope	-

REGULAR	
yardage	4825
par	68
rating	65.0
slope	119

FORWARD	
yardage	4825
par	68
rating	69.5
slope	121

PLAY POLICY & FEES: Green fees are $29 weekdays and $42 weekends. Twilight rates are $19 weekdays and $21weekends. Carts are $24.

TEE TIMES: Reservations can be booked seven days in advance at 7 a.m. the Monday prior to the weekend.

COURSE DESCRIPTION: This rolling course is set in the foothills outside Milpitas. It's a gambler's paradise. Doglegs and water plus cypress, pine, and elm trees all come into play. There aren't many bunkers, but as a consolation they made the bunkers extra tricky. Stay below the pin. There are three holes over water, including the 182-yard 11th.

NOTES: The course record of 61 is held by John Kennaday. The Mark Dorcak's Complete Golf School is located at Spring Valley. A total of 85,000 rounds are played here each year.

LOCATION: From Interstate 880 or Interstate 680 in Milpitas, exit on Highway 237/Calaveras Boulevard and drive east to the course.

. . . ● **TOURNAMENTS:** Shotgun tournaments are available weekdays only. A 16-player minimum is required to book an event. The banquet facility can accommodate 150 people. ● **TRAVEL:** The Embassy Suites Milpitas is located less than 10 minutes from the course. For reservations call 408-942-0400.

78. SPRING VALLEY GOLF COURSE

PLAY POLICY & FEES: Reciprocal play is accepted with members of other private clubs. Guest fees are $20 for nine holes and $30 for 18 holes Tuesday through Thurday, and $35 for nine holes and $45 for 18 holes Friday through Sunday and holidays. Carts are $11 for nine holes and $22 for 18 holes.

TEE TIMES: Guests can make reservations up to 14 days in advance.

DRESS CODE: Collared shirts and nonmetal spikes are encouraged.

COURSE DESCRIPTION: Two holes have been added to lengthen the course, and a driving range opened in 1992. This hilly course has extremely narrow, tree-lined fairways. The par-4 seventh and 199-yard, par-3 ninth are unarguably the best holes on the course.

LOCATION: From Interstate 280 in Cupertino take the Highway 85/Sunnyvale Road exit south to the Saratoga city line. Turn right on Prospect Road to the course.

. . . ● **TOURNAMENTS:** Outside events are available on Monday only.

79. SARATOGA COUNTRY CLUB

80 SAN JOSE COUNTRY CLUB
ARCHITECT: TOM NICOLL, 1915

15571 Alum Rock Avenue
San Jose, CA 95127

PRO SHOP: 408-258-3636
CLUBHOUSE: 408-258-4901

Chris Simpson, Manager
Jay Walkinshaw, Head Professional, PGA
Joel Ahearn, Superintendent

Driving Range •
Practice Greens •
Clubhouse •
Food / Beverage •
Accommodations
Pull Carts •
Power Carts •
Club Rental •
$pecial Offers

	1	2	3	4	5	6	7	8	9	OUT
BACK	303	316	174	432	145	392	156	436	353	2707
REGULAR	293	301	159	420	145	381	125	421	353	2598
par	4	4	3	4	3	4	3	4	4	33
handicap	14	10	12	2	18	6	16	4	8	-
FORWARD	274	250	149	347	132	362	106	421	343	2384
par	4	4	3	5	3	4	3	5	4	35
handicap	10	8	12	6	16	2	18	14	4	-

	10	11	12	13	14	15	16	17	18	IN
BACK	209	477	439	404	158	366	536	516	367	3472
REGULAR	190	454	429	392	142	357	516	496	349	3325
par	3	5	4	4	3	4	5	5	4	37
handicap	13	15	1	9	17	11	5	3	7	-
FORWARD	178	443	418	373	123	282	467	470	336	3090
par	3	5	4	4	3	4	5	5	4	38
handicap	15	11	13	7	17	9	5	1	3	-

BACK	
yardage	6179
par	70
rating	69.8
slope	124

REGULAR	
yardage	5923
par	70
rating	68.7
slope	122

FORWARD	
yardage	5474
par	73
rating	71.9
slope	126

81 PIN HIGH FAMILY GOLF CENTER

P.O. Box 280
Alviso, CA 95002-0280

4701 North Street
San Jose, CA 95002

PRO SHOP: 408-934-1111

Don Rumpf, Director of Golf, PGA

Driving Range •
Practice Greens •
Clubhouse •
Food / Beverage •
Accommodations
Pull Carts   v
Power Carts
Club Rental   v
$pecial Offers

	1	2	3	4	5	6	7	8	9	OUT
BACK	246	139	273	246	139	273	246	139	273	1974
REGULAR	235	131	265	235	131	265	235	131	265	1893
par	3	3	4	3	3	4	3	3	4	30
handicap	1	7	4	2	8	5	3	9	6	-
FORWARD	224	122	260	224	122	260	224	122	260	1818
par	3	3	4	3	3	4	3	3	4	30
handicap	1	7	4	2	8	5	3	9	6	-

	10	11	12	13	14	15	16	17	18	IN
BACK	-	-	-	-	-	-	-	-	-	-
REGULAR	-	-	-	-	-	-	-	-	-	-
par	-	-	-	-	-	-	-	-	-	-
handicap	-	-	-	-	-	-	-	-	-	-
FORWARD	-	-	-	-	-	-	-	-	-	-
par	-	-	-	-	-	-	-	-	-	-
handicap	-	-	-	-	-	-	-	-	-	-

BACK	
yardage	1974
par	30
rating	57.9
slope	83

REGULAR	
yardage	1893
par	30
rating	57.9
slope	83

FORWARD	
yardage	1818
par	30
rating	57.9
slope	83

18
HOLES

PLAY POLICY & FEES: Reciprocal play is accepted with members of other private clubs. Guest fees are $55 every day when accompanied by a member and $75 without a member. Carts are $11.

TEE TIMES: Have your professional call in advance for arrangements.

DRESS CODE: Appropriate golf attire and nonmetal spikes are required. The dress code is strictly enforced.

COURSE DESCRIPTION: Situated in the foothills overlooking the Santa Clara Valley, this course is one of the oldest in Northern California with a history dating back to 1915. The course is short, hilly, and tight. The small greens require accurate iron play and a deft short game. From the tee on the fourth hole, you have a view of much of the course. On a clear day you can see San Francisco. The course has two of the finest finishing holes in the region: the 17th, a par 5 across a ravine, at 516 yards; and the 18th, a 367-yard par 4 requiring a layup shot off the tee. Both greens are well bunkered. Precise approach shots are needed.

NOTES: The men's record is 59 and the women's is 69. The Santa Clara County Championship is held here annually.

LOCATION: From Interstate 680 in San Jose take the Alum Rock Avenue exit east. Drive 2.5 miles to the course entrance.

. . . ● **TOURNAMENTS:** Shotgun tournaments are available on weekdays. An 80-player minimum is needed to close the course. Carts are required.

80. SAN JOSE COUNTRY CLUB

3
HOLES

PLAY POLICY & FEES: Green fees are $5 for the first round, $4 for the next time around, and $3 for every round thereafter.

TEE TIMES: Reservations are accepted, or play is on a first-come, first-served basis.

DRESS CODE: Tank tops are not allowed on the golf course.

COURSE DESCRIPTION: This is the perfect course for beginners and those who want to sneak out and play a few holes. Heck, if you have a long layover at San Jose International, take a cab, play three holes and be back in time to find out the flight has been delayed. There are no tricks on this three-hole course. The holes are all straight away. The first hole is a 246-yard par 3. If you don't like your score on the first go around, play eighteen holes and you'll have five more chances to make par.

NOTES: This facility was designed to introduce people to golf and has PGA-trained teaching professionals on staff. Pin High has a lighted driving range that is open until 10 p.m. on weekdays and 9 p.m. on weekends.

LOCATION: From San Jose take Highway 880 north to Highway 237. Travel west on Highway 237 for two miles; then exit at North First Street. Take a right on North First Street. The course is a quarter mile on the left side.

. . . ● **TOURNAMENTS:** This course is available for outside events. The banquet facility can hold 50 to 75 people.

81. PIN HIGH FAMILY GOLF CENTER

14597 Clearview Drive
Los Gatos, CA 95030

PRO SHOP: 408-395-4220
CLUBHOUSE: 408-395-4181

Dick Maynes, Manager
Charlie Eddie, PGA Professional
Jesse Pifferini, Superintendent

Driving Range ●
Practice Greens ●
Clubhouse ●
Food / Beverage ●
Accommodations
Pull Carts ●
Power Carts ●
Club Rental ●
$pecial Offers

	1	2	3	4	5	6	7	8	9	OUT
BACK	404	312	281	432	200	374	141	354	418	2916
REGULAR	393	312	281	421	176	374	135	336	409	2837
par	4	4	4	4	3	4	3	4	4	34
handicap	5	13	15	3	11	7	17	9	1	-
FORWARD	384	287	273	413	130	365	121	318	403	2694
par	4	4	4	5	3	4	3	4	5	36
handicap	3	13	11	7	15	5	17	9	1	-

	10	11	12	13	14	15	16	17	18	IN
BACK	366	150	544	194	306	321	436	404	494	3215
REGULAR	360	140	523	184	306	321	414	385	484	3117
par	4	3	5	3	4	4	4	4	5	36
handicap	10	18	6	16	14	12	4	2	8	-
FORWARD	350	116	453	135	301	289	347	341	476	2808
par	4	3	5	3	4	4	4	4	5	36
handicap	2	18	6	16	8	10	12	14	4	-

BACK	
yardage	6131
par	70
rating	70.5
slope	126

REGULAR	
yardage	5954
par	70
rating	69.6
slope	124

FORWARD	
yardage	5502
par	72
rating	67.7
slope	120

83 **PRUNERIDGE GOLF CLUB**
ARCHITECT: ROBERT TRENT JONES JR., 1977

400 North Saratoga
Santa Clara, CA 95050

PRO SHOP: 408-248-4424

Karen Wallick, Manager
Jeff Johnson, Head Professional, PGA

Driving Range ●
Practice Greens ●
Clubhouse ●
Food / Beverage ●
Accommodations
Pull Carts ●
Power Carts
Club Rental ●
$pecial Offers

	1	2	3	4	5	6	7	8	9	OUT
BACK	262	104	353	285	148	131	130	113	288	1814
REGULAR	240	91	322	273	130	115	109	98	250	1628
par	4	3	4	4	3	3	3	3	4	31
handicap	4	9	1	3	5	6	7	8	2	-
FORWARD	158	77	180	177	104	83	61	66	225	1131
par	4	3	4	4	4	3	3	3	5	33
handicap	4	9	2	3	5	6	7	8	1	-

	10	11	12	13	14	15	16	17	18	IN
BACK	-	-	-	-	-	-	-	-	-	-
REGULAR	-	-	-	-	-	-	-	-	-	-
par	-	-	-	-	-	-	-	-	-	-
handicap	-	-	-	-	-	-	-	-	-	-
FORWARD	-	-	-	-	-	-	-	-	-	-
par	-	-	-	-	-	-	-	-	-	-
handicap	-	-	-	-	-	-	-	-	-	-

BACK	
yardage	1814
par	31
rating	-
slope	-

REGULAR	
yardage	1628
par	31
rating	-
slope	-

FORWARD	
yardage	1131
par	33
rating	-
slope	-

PLAY POLICY & FEES: Reciprocal play is accepted with members of other private clubs Tuesday, Thursday, and Friday. Advance arrangements are required. Green fees for reciprocators are $55 when unaccompanied by a member, plus cart. Guest fees are $50 when playing with a member and $95 without. Carts are $6 for nine holes and $11 for 18 holes. The course is closed on Monday.

DRESS CODE: Appropriate golf attire and nonmetal spikes are required.

COURSE DESCRIPTION: This mature layout is short and narrow with tree-lined fairways and undulating greens. A lake comes into play on the 14th and 15th holes. Located in the foothills of Los Gatos, this course offers a scenic view of the southern Santa Clara Valley. The best hole is the uphill, 418-yard, par-4 ninth.

LOCATION: From Highway 17 in San Jose take the Lark Avenue exit. Turn left on Winchester Boulevard. Turn right on La Rinconada Drive and follow it to Clearview Drive. Turn left to the course.

. . . ● **TOURNAMENTS:** All outside events must have board approval.

82. LA RINCONADA COUNTRY CLUB

PLAY POLICY & FEES: Green fees are $14 weekdays and $15 weekends.

TEE TIMES: Reservations can be booked seven days in advance.

COURSE DESCRIPTION: This short, flat, and walkable course was redesigned in 1977 by Robert Trent Jones Jr. Watch out for ducks on the lake at the ninth hole. They can get aggressive if they aren't fed on the spot. This is a tight, high-quality executive course featuring four par 4s.

NOTES: A total of 100,000 rounds are played here each year.

LOCATION: The course is located between U.S. 101 and Interstate 280 in Santa Clara on Saratoga Avenue, which is off the San Tomas Expressway. From Interstate 280, take the Saratoga Avenue exit north.

. . . ● **TOURNAMENTS:** This course is available for outside tournaments. Tournaments can be booked one month in advance. The banquet facility can hold 60 people.

83. PRUNERIDGE GOLF CLUB

SILVER CREEK VALLEY COUNTRY CLUB
ARCHITECT: TED ROBINSON, 1992

5460 Country Club
San Jose, CA 95138

PRO SHOP: 408-239-5775
CLUBHOUSE: 408-239-5888

Robert Lee, Manager
Jay W. Jackson, Head Professional, PGA
Tonya McElwee, Tournament Director, PGA

Driving Range ●
Practice Greens ●
Clubhouse ●
Food / Beverage ●
Accommodations
Pull Carts
Power Carts ●
Club Rental ●
$pecial Offers

	1	2	3	4	5	6	7	8	9	OUT
BACK	440	390	416	195	394	515	161	508	428	3447
REGULAR	403	333	373	154	347	469	124	470	370	3043
par	4	4	4	3	4	5	3	5	4	36
handicap	9	15	7	11	13	5	17	1	3	-
FORWARD	359	267	333	117	295	429	106	405	312	2623
par	4	4	4	3	4	5	3	5	4	36
handicap	9	15	5	17	11	3	13	1	7	-

	10	11	12	13	14	15	16	17	18	IN
BACK	437	501	237	393	367	185	524	377	400	3421
REGULAR	393	458	176	349	314	156	467	331	370	3014
par	4	5	3	4	4	3	5	4	4	36
handicap	12	10	8	4	14	16	2	18	6	-
FORWARD	370	405	148	306	271	103	432	287	344	2666
par	4	5	3	4	4	3	5	4	4	36
handicap	10	4	16	8	12	18	2	14	6	-

BACK	
yardage	6868
par	72
rating	74.0
slope	140

REGULAR	
yardage	6057
par	72
rating	70.5
slope	129

FORWARD	
yardage	5289
par	72
rating	71.1
slope	127

 PLEASANT HILLS GOLF COURSE
ARCHITECTS: HENRY DUINO SR., 1959; JOESEPH SOTO

2050 South White Road
San Jose, CA 95152

PRO SHOP: 408-238-3485

Henry Duino, Head Professional

Driving Range
Practice Greens ●
Clubhouse ●
Food / Beverage ●
Accommodations
Pull Carts ●
Power Carts ●
Club Rental ●
$pecial Offers

	1	2	3	4	5	6	7	8	9	OUT
BACK	490	176	398	234	559	183	470	552	463	3525
REGULAR	470	148	379	210	538	169	456	517	435	3322
par	5	3	4	3	5	3	4	5	4	36
handicap	17	15	5	7	9	13	1	11	3	-
FORWARD	429	129	359	175	517	145	432	482	416	3084
par	5	3	4	3	5	3	5	5	5	38
handicap	11	17	5	13	1	15	7	3	9	-

	10	11	12	13	14	15	16	17	18	IN
BACK	368	532	437	211	391	503	170	361	390	3363
REGULAR	342	519	421	185	380	485	156	332	377	3197
par	4	5	4	3	4	5	3	4	4	36
handicap	16	10	2	6	4	14	12	18	8	-
FORWARD	326	485	382	160	358	474	138	313	354	2990
par	4	5	5	3	4	5	3	4	4	37
handicap	12	2	6	16	8	4	18	14	10	-

BACK	
yardage	6888
par	72
rating	-
slope	-

REGULAR	
yardage	6519
par	72
rating	-
slope	-

FORWARD	
yardage	6074
par	75
rating	-
slope	-

PLAY POLICY & FEES: Reciprocal play is accepted.Guest fees range from $70 to $115 (including cart). The course is closed on Monday.

TEE TIMES: Have your pro call for details.

DRESS CODE: Appropriate golf attire and nonmetal spikes are required.

COURSE DESCRIPTION: The golf course takes you from a panoramic ridge to a valley floor and ends on a high plateau where a waterfall plummets into a serene but treacherous lake guarding the signature 18th hole. Natural rock outcroppings, groves of eucalyptus trees, and majestic oaks protect many of the landing areas, while sculpted rock walls hold back armies of flowers surrounding the greens. The par-4 14th hole requires a well-played tee shot around a grove of oaks to a contoured fairway guarded left, right, and long by lateral hazards. The green is nestled at the base of a rocky canyon wall and is tiered, requiring a short, accurate approach. The capper on the front nine is the ninth hole, which offers breathtaking views of the Santa Clara Valley and the entire golf course.

LOCATION: From San Jose take U.S. 101 south to the Silver Creek Valley Road/Blossom Hill exit. Turn east onto Silver Creek Valley Road and follow the signs to the club.

. . . ● **TOURNAMENTS:** All tournaments must be approved by the head professional. A 125-player minimum is needed to book an event. Tournaments should be scheduled 12 months in advance. The banquet facility can accommodate 275 people.

84. SILVER CREEK VALLEY COUNTRY CLUB

PLAY POLICY & FEES: Green fees are $22 weekdays and $30 weekends. Twilight rates are available. Carts are $13 for nine holes and $22 for 18 holes.

TEE TIMES: Reservations can be booked seven days in advance. The executive course is played on a first-come, first-served basis.

DRESS CODE: No tank tops or T-shirts are allowed on the course.

COURSE DESCRIPTION: Owned by the Duino family and situated at the base of the foothills, this course has a half million trees (or so it seems), including fig, apple, and eucalyptus, which all come into play. A flat course dominated by trees, it's always in good shape.

NOTES: This public course has an 18-hole course and a nine-hole executive course. Par is 72 for the championship course. See scorecard for yardage and rating information. The par-3 executive course is 2,600 yards and unrated.

LOCATION: From U.S. 101 in San Jose take the Tully Road East exit. Drive northeast past Capitol Expressway and turn left on South White Road to the course.

. . . ● **TOURNAMENTS:** This course is available for outside tournaments.

85. PLEASANT HILLS GOLF COURSE

86 THE VILLAGES GOLF & COUNTRY CLUB
ARCHITECT: ROBERT MUIR GRAVES, 1970

5000 Cribari Lane
San Jose, CA 95135

PRO SHOP: 408-274-3220

Kevin Cullen, Director of Golf, PGA
Brian Bagley, Superintendent

Driving Range •
Practice Greens •
Clubhouse •
Food / Beverage •
Accommodations
Pull Carts •
Power Carts •
Club Rental •
$pecial Offers

	1	2	3	4	5	6	7	8	9	OUT
BACK	354	486	445	155	369	209	363	430	516	3327
REGULAR	335	468	422	144	361	187	348	383	508	3156
par	4	5	4	3	4	3	4	4	5	36
handicap	13	11	1	17	3	15	7	9	5	-
FORWARD	324	455	411	131	324	168	342	337	453	2945
par	4	5	5	3	4	3	4	4	5	37
handicap	11	3	5	17	7	15	9	13	1	-

	10	11	12	13	14	15	16	17	18	IN
BACK	364	151	384	388	365	407	482	414	425	3380
REGULAR	342	141	373	367	344	365	478	389	383	3182
par	4	3	4	4	4	4	5	4	4	36
handicap	8	18	2	12	14	16	6	4	10	-
FORWARD	332	133	321	350	327	315	441	354	333	2906
par	4	3	4	4	4	4	5	4	4	36
handicap	4	18	12	10	14	16	2	6	8	-

BACK	
yardage	6707
par	72
rating	71.7
slope	122

REGULAR	
yardage	6338
par	72
rating	70.0
slope	119

FORWARD	
yardage	5851
par	73
rating	72.2
slope	120

87 BOULDER CREEK GOLF & COUNTRY
ARCHITECT: JACK FLEMING, 1961

16901 Big Basin Highway
Boulder Creek, CA 95006

PRO SHOP: 831-338-2121
OFFICE: 831-338-2111

Bill Aragona, General Manager
Hal Wells, Professional
Andy Barrick, Tournament Director

Driving Range
Practice Greens •
Clubhouse •
Food / Beverage •
Accommodations •
Pull Carts
Power Carts •
Club Rental •
$pecial Offers •

	1	2	3	4	5	6	7	8	9	OUT
BACK	-	-	-	-	-	-	-	-	-	-
REGULAR	225	177	310	387	139	189	159	157	265	2008
par	4	5	4	4	3	3	3	3	4	31
handicap	17	7	5	1	13	3	9	15	11	-
FORWARD	225	177	310	387	139	189	159	157	207	1950
par	4	3	4	5	3	3	3	3	4	32
handicap	15	5	1	17	9	3	13	7	11	-

	10	11	12	13	14	15	16	17	18	IN
BACK	-	-	-	-	-	-	-	--	-	-
REGULAR	182	168	440	325	138	410	169	436	120	2388
par	3	3	5	4	3	5	3	5	3	34
handicap	2	4	8	14	18	10	6	12	16	-
FORWARD	182	125	355	325	96	410	169	325	90	2077
par	4	3	5	4	3	5	3	5	3	35
handicap	8	4	14	12	16	2	6	18	10	-

BACK	
yardage	-
par	-
rating	-
slope	-

REGULAR	
yardage	4396
par	65
rating	61.5
slope	98

FORWARD	
yardage	4027
par	67
rating	63.3
slope	98

PLAY POLICY & FEES: Reciprocal play is accepted with members of other private clubs. Green fees for reciprocators are $45 weekdays and $55 weekends. With a member, guest fees are $32 weekdays and $37 weekends. Carts are $20 for nine holes and $30 for 18 holes.

TEE TIMES: Reservations can be booked four days in advance.

DRESS CODE: No jeans are allowed on the course, and shorts may be no shorter than four inches above the knee. Shirts must have collars.

COURSE DESCRIPTION: This resident-community course has water hazards on 10 holes, and bunkers come into play for the longer hitters. The 17th and 18th are long par 4s, with out-of-bounds left. The 17th has water on the right, and the 18th has water in front of the green. All three nines are enjoyable and usually in excellent shape.

NOTES: The nine-hole course is a par 27. The course record for the championship course is 63 by Roger Maltbie. The Villages hosts the Alzheimers Benefit Pro-Am golf tournament annually.

LOCATION: From U.S. 101 in eastern San Jose take Yerba Buena Ave. northeast about four miles. Turn right on San Felipe Road and drive 2.5 miles to the Villages Parkway. Turn left and drive to Cribari Lane and the course.

. . . ● **TOURNAMENTS:** Shotgun tournaments are available Monday only, requiring a 120-player minimum. Carts are required. Tournaments should be booked 12 months in advance. The banquet facility can accommodate up to 350 people.

86. THE VILLAGES GOLF & COUNTRY CLUB

PLAY POLICY & FEES: Green fees are $22 Monday through Thursday, $20 Friday, and $40 weekends. Special discount rates are available. Carts are $18.

TEE TIMES: Reservations can be booked seven days in advance.

DRESS CODE: No tank tops are allowed, and shirts must be worn.

COURSE DESCRIPTION: This scenic course is situated in the midst of redwoods. It is well maintained, short, slightly rolling, and tight. The immaculate and demanding greens are the great neutralizer for the lack of length. The front nine has five par 3s, and the back plays as a regular nine-hole course. All holes are tight and demanding.

NOTES: A hole in one was made on the first shot on the first hole on opening day in June 1961.

LOCATION: From Santa Cruz drive 12 miles north on Highway 9 to Boulder Creek. In Boulder Creek take Highway 236 three miles northwest to the course on the left.

. . . ● **TOURNAMENTS:** Shotgun tournaments are available weekdays only. A 16-player minimum is required for tournament play. Events should be booked 12 months in advance. ● **TRAVEL:** For condominium reservations and golf package information, call 408-338-2111. ● **$PECIAL OFFERS:** Golf packages are available that include two-night, three-day stays, green fees, food coupons, and lodging.

87. BOULDER CREEK GOLF & COUNTRY

ALMADEN GOLF & COUNTRY CLUB
ARCHITECT: JACK FLEMING, 1955

6663 Hampton Drive
San Jose, CA 95120

PRO SHOP: 408-268-3959
CLUBHOUSE: 408-268-4653

Avery Cook, Head Professional, PGA

Driving Range ●
Practice Greens ●
Clubhouse ●
Food / Beverage ●
Accommodations
Pull Carts ●
Power Carts ●
Club Rental ●
$pecial Offers

	1	2	3	4	5	6	7	8	9	OUT
BACK	489	369	354	423	444	153	514	177	423	3346
REGULAR	477	351	343	412	398	146	492	162	412	3193
par	5	4	4	4	4	3	5	3	4	36
handicap	9	13	11	1	3	17	7	15	5	-
FORWARD	412	340	338	424	378	117	480	152	364	3005
par	5	4	4	5	4	3	5	3	4	37
handicap	13	7	9	11	5	17	1	15	3	-

	10	11	12	13	14	15	16	17	18	IN
BACK	541	421	412	187	352	191	449	416	509	3478
REGULAR	520	402	400	164	336	166	416	395	502	3301
par	5	4	4	3	4	3	4	4	5	36
handicap	12	4	6	10	16	18	2	8	14	-
FORWARD	486	374	383	129	314	137	410	357	465	3055
par	5	4	4	3	4	3	5	4	5	37
handicap	4	6	2	18	12	16	14	8	10	-

BACK	
yardage	6824
par	72
rating	72.5
slope	128

REGULAR	
yardage	6494
par	72
rating	71.0
slope	125

FORWARD	
yardage	6060
par	74
rating	74.3
slope	130

 SANTA TERESA GOLF CLUB
ARCHITECT: G. SANTANA, 1963; SHORT COURSE, 1996

260 Bernal Road
San Jose, CA 95199

PRO SHOP: 408-225-2650

Jim McGrath, Manager, PGA
Ellen Lorance, Dir. of instruction, LPGA

Driving Range ●
Practice Greens ●
Clubhouse ●
Food / Beverage ●
Accommodations
Pull Carts ●
Power Carts ●
Club Rental ●
$pecial Offers

	1	2	3	4	5	6	7	8	9	OUT
BACK	416	512	351	384	166	409	190	408	436	3272
REGULAR	404	492	343	368	151	396	162	400	426	3142
par	4	5	4	4	3	4	3	4	4	35
handicap	1	13	15	11	17	5	9	3	7	-
FORWARD	380	482	324	359	142	385	145	350	420	2987
par	4	5	4	4	3	4	3	4	5	36
handicap	5	1	11	7	17	3	15	13	9	-

	10	11	12	13	14	15	16	17	18	IN
BACK	383	498	417	405	184	371	220	571	421	3470
REGULAR	373	479	397	393	171	349	190	529	407	3288
par	4	5	4	4	3	4	3	5	4	36
handicap	10	16	8	4	18	14	12	6	2	-
FORWARD	352	434	361	384	161	334	148	471	400	3045
par	4	5	4	4	3	4	3	5	5	37
handicap	12	2	6	8	16	14	18	4	10	-

BACK	
yardage	6742
par	71
rating	72.1
slope	124

REGULAR	
yardage	6430
par	71
rating	70.6
slope	122

FORWARD	
yardage	6032
par	73
rating	73.5
slope	125

PLAY POLICY & FEES: Reciprocal play is accepted with members of other private clubs Tuesday, Thursday, and Friday. Green fees for reciprocators are $50 when accompanied by a member and $90 unaccompanied. Carts are $12 for nine holes and $22 for 18 holes. The course is closed on Monday.

DRESS CODE: Appropriate golf attire and nonmetal spikes are required.

COURSE DESCRIPTION: This scenic, demanding course set in the Silicon Valley has a tree-lined, rolling terrain. The greens are undulating. The difficult par-4 16th requires a strong tee shot, and trees on the right guard a heavy slope down to "Death Valley." The dogleg-left 17th forces most players to bail out again into "Chicken Alley" on the right.

NOTES: Almaden was the site of several LPGA events and currently plays host to the Nike Tour. The women's course record is 62, set by Palo Alto native Vicki Fergon during the 1984 San Jose Classic. The men's course record is 64.

LOCATION: From U.S.101 in San Jose take Highway 85 to Almaden Expressway. Take Almaden Expressway to Crown Boulevard. Turn right to Hampton Drive.

. . . ● **TOURNAMENTS:** Outside events are accepted with board approval.

88. ALMADEN GOLF & COUNTRY CLUB

PLAY POLICY & FEES: Green fees are $30 weekdays and $44 weekends. Afternoon rates are $18 weekdays and $25 weekends and holidays. Carts are $24 for 18 holes. The short course fees are $11 on weekdays and $14 weekends. Twilight, senior, student, and nine-hole rates are available.

TEE TIMES: Reservations can be booked seven days in advance for weekdays and the Monday prior for weekends. Tee times for the Short Course are first-come, first-served.

DRESS CODE: Shirts and shoes are necessary.

COURSE DESCRIPTION: This challenging course, the pride of the South Bay public courses, is long, with tree-lined fairways. The front nine is flat and the back nine is hilly. This course has been voted the best municipal course in Santa Clara Valley. The testy 16th hole is one reason why: It's a tough par 3 of 220 yards, into a strong prevailing wind. The winds make various holes more difficult. The dogleg-left first hole stretches 416 yards into the wind.

LOCATION: From U.S. 101 in San Jose take the Bernal Road exit west. Drive two miles to the course.

. . . ● **TOURNAMENTS:** A 20-player minimum is needed to book a tournament. Tournaments may start after 10 a.m. on weekdays and 11 a.m. on weekends and holidays. Shotgun tournaments are not allowed on weekends.

89. SANTA TERESA GOLF CLUB

CINNABAR HILLS GOLF CLUB
ARCHITECT: JOHN F. HARBOTTLE, 97-98

23600 McKean Road
San Jose, CA 95141

PRO S HOP: 408-323-5200

D. Scott Hoyt, General Manager, PGA
Robert Kambourian, PGA Professional
Adam Schiro, Tournament Director

GOLF 50

Driving Range •
Practice Greens •
Clubhouse •
Food / Beverage •
Accommodations
Pull Carts
Power Carts •
Club Rental •
$pecial Offers

	1	2	3	4	5	6	7	8	9	OUT
BACK	496	157	437	433	361	196	503	424	396	3403
REGULAR	461	136	409	409	349	164	486	387	373	3174
par	5	3	4	4	4	3	5	4	4	36
handicap	6	9	2	1	7	5	8	3	4	-
FORWARD	408	97	356	308	284	111	428	335	281	2608
par	5	3	4	4	4	3	5	4	4	36
handicap	3	9	5	4	7	8	1	2	6	-

	10	11	12	13	14	15	16	17	18	IN
BACK	523	175	445	382	360	387	567	172	439	3450
REGULAR	498	168	427	351	341	363	535	147	393	3223
par	5	3	4	4	4	4	5	3	4	36
handicap	5	9	4	1	8	6	3	7	2	-
FORWARD	424	124	371	260	297	315	477	79	313	2660
par	5	3	4	4	4	4	5	3	4	36
handicap	2	9	4	5	6	7	1	8	3	-

BACK	
yardage	6853
par	72
rating	73.1
slope	135

REGULAR	
yardage	6397
par	72
rating	70.8
slope	130

FORWARD	
yardage	5268
par	72
rating	68.1
slope	120

 RIVERSIDE/COYOTE CREEK GOLF COURSE
ARCHITECTS: JACK FLEMING, 1957; JACK NICKLAUS, 1999

9770 Monterey Road
Coyote, CA 95013

PRO S HOP: 408-463-0622

John McMahon, Head Professional, PGA
John Jorgensen, Superintendent

Driving Range •
Practice Greens •
Clubhouse •
Food / Beverage •
Accommodations
Pull Carts •
Power Carts •
Club Rental •
$pecial Offers

	1	2	3	4	5	6	7	8	9	OUT
BACK	519	210	514	373	336	212	424	379	443	3410
REGULAR	501	195	484	357	324	189	411	365	434	3260
par	5	3	5	4	4	3	4	4	4	36
handicap	12	18	8	6	16	14	4	10	2	-
FORWARD	479	145	443	316	293	164	374	330	402	2946
par	5	3	5	4	4	3	4	4	5	37
handicap	3	17	7	11	13	15	1	9	5	-

	10	11	12	13	14	15	16	17	18	IN
BACK	459	386	205	378	540	212	377	415	499	3471
REGULAR	420	350	182	364	528	172	367	405	483	3271
par	4	4	3	4	5	3	4	4	5	36
handicap	1	7	9	5	11	17	15	3	13	-
FORWARD	377	335	154	340	483	157	346	357	447	2996
par	4	4	3	4	5	3	4	4	5	36
handicap	6	14	16	10	2	18	12	8	4	-

BACK	
yardage	6881
par	72
rating	72.2
slope	127

REGULAR	
yardage	6531
par	72
rating	71.0
slope	124

FORWARD	
yardage	5942
par	73
rating	72.7
slope	119

PLAY POLICY & FEES: Green fees Monday through Thursday are $75, and $100 Friday through Sunday and holidays. Twilight rates beginning five hours before dark are $45 Monday through Thursday, and $55 Friday through Sunday and holidays. A supertwilight rate is available starting at $30 approximately three hours before darkness. All green fees include a cart.

TEE TIMES: Reservations can be made 14 days in advance without a fee. Golfers can make tee times 15 to 90 days in advance for an additional charge. For automated reservations call 408-323-7880.

DRESS CODE: Nonmetal spikes are required.

COURSE DESCRIPTION: Cinnabar Hills Golf Club is a collection of three well-maintained and distinctive golf courses: Lake, Canyon, and Mountain. The Canyon Course is a tight, undulating course, surrounded by trees, with creeks running throughout. The Mountain Course features several elevated tee boxes, spacious landing areas, and well-protected greens. The Lake Course has a four-acre lake and two creeks, bringing water into play on eight of nine holes.

NOTES: Inside the clubhouse make sure you visit the Brandenburg Historic Golf Museum. The Mountain/Lake Course: see scorecard for more information. For other scorecard combinations check www.cinnabarhills.com.

LOCATION: From San Francisco take Interstate 280 to Highway 85 south. Exit at the Almaden Expressway and head south for five miles to Harry Road. Turn right on Harry Road and left on McKean Road. Follow McKean Road for five miles around the Calero Reservoir to the the golf course on the left.

90. CINNABAR HILLS GOLF CLUB

PLAY POLICY & FEES: Green fees for the Riverside Course are $26 weekdays and $36 weekends. Carts are $24. Fees for Coyote Creek are $70 Monday through Thursday and $90 Friday through Sunday. Fees include carts.

TEE TIMES: Reservations can be booked seven days in advance.

DRESS CODE: Appropriate golf attire and nonmetal spikes are required.

COURSE DESCRIPTION: Coyote Creek is a demanding course. Off the tee you will find plenty of room, and there are few mature trees to get in your way, but many of the greens are multi-tiered and guarded by deep pot bunkers. The front nine is characterized by rolling terrain, while the back nine is relatively flat. Water comes in to play on several of the closing holes.

NOTES: The new course, Coyote Creek, should be fully open in October 1999. In March of 2000, the Riverside Course will close for reconstruction. When complete it will open as the Valley Course. A new clubhouse has opened and a driving range is under construction.

LOCATION: From U.S. 101 in Morgan Hill take the Cochrane Road exit. From U.S. 101 in San Jose, exit at Bernal Road. Turn onto Monterey Road heading south toward Morgan Hill. Turn at Palm Avenue and look for the signs.

. . . ● **TOURNAMENTS:** Shotgun tournaments are available weekdays only. A 20-player minimum is needed to book a tournament. Carts are required.

91. RIVERSIDE/COYOTE CREEK GOLF COURSE

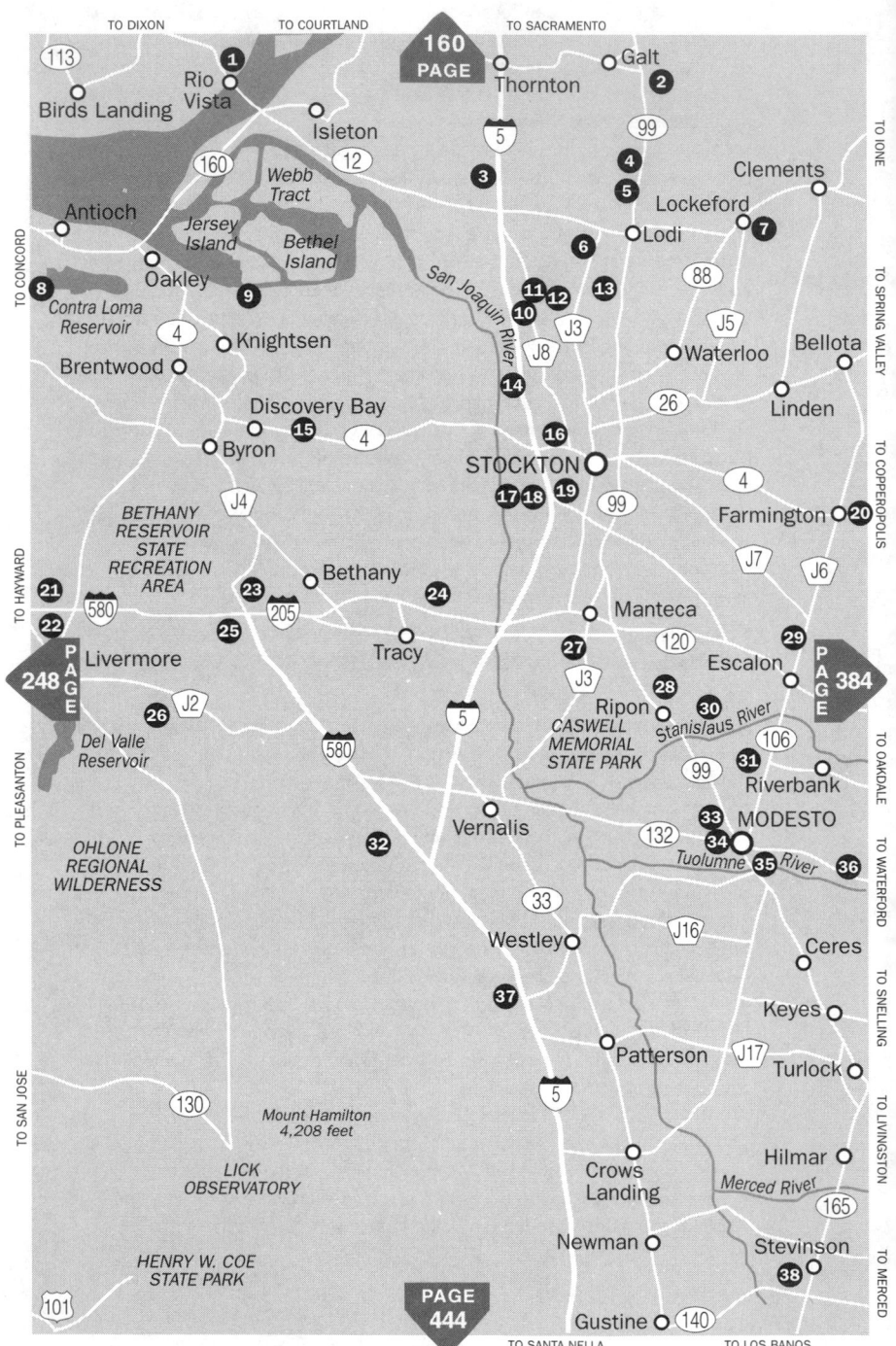

TO DIXON   TO COURTLAND   TO SACRAMENTO

113

160
PAGE

Rio Vista
Birds Landing

1

Thornton

Galt

2

Isleton

12

5

99

160

Webb
Tract

3

4

Clements

Antioch

Jersey
Island

Bethel
Island

5

Lockeford

Lodi

7

Oakley

8

9

6

88

Contra Loma
Reservoir

4

Knightsen

San Joaquin River

11 12 13

J5

Waterloo   Bellota

Brentwood

10

J3

26

Linden

Discovery Bay

J8

14

Byron

15

4

16

STOCKTON

4

Farmington

20

BETHANY
RESERVOIR
STATE
RECREATION
AREA

J4

17 18 19

99

J7

J6

Bethany

23

24

Manteca

29

P
A
G
E
384

21

580

205

Tracy

25

27

120

Escalon

22

P
A
G
E
248

Livermore

J3

28

30

Stanislaus River

106

26

J2

Ripon
CASWELL
MEMORIAL
STATE PARK

99

31

Riverbank

Del Valle
Reservoir

5

33

MODESTO

OHLONE
REGIONAL
WILDERNESS

32

Vernalis

132

34

Tuolumne River

35

36

33

J16

Ceres

Westley

37

Keyes

130

Mount Hamilton
4,208 feet

J17

Turlock

5

LICK
OBSERVATORY

Patterson

Hilmar

HENRY W. COE
STATE PARK

Crows
Landing

Merced River

165

101

Newman

Stevinson

38

PAGE
444

Gustine

140

TO SANTA NELLA   TO LOS BANOS

TO IONE

TO SPRING VALLEY

TO COPPEROPOLIS

TO OAKDALE

TO WATERFORD

TO SNELLING

TO LIVINGSTON

TO MERCED

TO CONCORD

TO HAYWARD

TO PLEASANTON

TO SAN JOSE

344

Stockton/Modesto Area

① RIO VISTA GOLF CLUB
ARCHITECT: TED ROBINSON, 1996

1000 Summerset Drive
Rio Vista, CA 94571

PRO SHOP: 707-374-2900

Michael A. Kieser, Director of Golf, PGA
Charlie Johnson, Superintendent

Driving Range •
Practice Greens •
Clubhouse
Food / Beverage •
Accommodations
Pull Carts
Power Carts •
Club Rental •
$pecial Offers

	1	2	3	4	5	6	7	8	9	OUT
BACK	363	502	426	546	195	365	416	216	443	3472
REGULAR	346	487	391	516	175	343	396	198	391	3243
par	4	5	4	5	3	4	4	3	4	36
handicap	17/1	11	7/5	1	9/15	13/7	3	15/1	5/9	-
FORWARD	304	430	315	448	120	294	325	154	313	2703
par	4	5	4	5	3	4	4	3	4	36
handicap	7	5	13	1	17	9	3	15	11	-

	10	11	12	13	14	15	16	17	18	IN
BACK	321	388	422	198	488	222	428	491	372	3330
REGULAR	309	366	398	170	469	199	405	478	356	3150
par	4	4	4	3	5	3	4	5	4	36
handicap	18/1	10/1	6/4	14/1	16/1	8/14	4/2	12/8	2/6	-
FORWARD	281	302	299	131	403	158	326	453	274	2627
par	4	4	4	3	5	3	4	5	4	36
handicap	6	4	16	18	14	8	12	10	2	-

BACK	
yardage	6802
par	72
rating	73.9
slope	131

REGULAR	
yardage	6393
par	72
rating	71.9
slope	126

FORWARD	
yardage	5330
par	72
rating	72.4
slope	124

② DRY CREEK RANCH GOLF COURSE
ARCHITECT: JACK FLEMING, 1962

809 Crystal Way
Galt, CA 95632

PRO SHOP: 209-745-2330
CLUBHOUSE: 209-745-2978

Rod Sims, PGA Professional
Tom Park, Manager
Jim Sweagle, Superintendent

Driving Range •
Practice Greens •
Clubhouse •
Food / Beverage •
Accommodations
Pull Carts •
Power Carts •
Club Rental •
$pecial Offers

	1	2	3	4	5	6	7	8	9	OUT
BACK	421	365	552	358	161	442	202	495	331	3327
REGULAR	409	352	533	350	151	424	192	480	319	3210
par	4	4	5	4	3	4	3	5	4	36
handicap	3	11	7	13	17	1	9	5	15	-
FORWARD	291	333	524	337	138	408	170	383	306	2890
par	4	4	5	4	3	5	3	4	4	36
handicap	11	7	1	9	17	5	15	3	13	-

	10	11	12	13	14	15	16	17	18	IN
BACK	551	159	531	431	322	467	358	190	437	3446
REGULAR	539	142	521	397	302	434	350	180	427	3292
par	5	3	5	4	4	4	4	3	4	36
handicap	8	18	6	10	14	2	12	16	4	-
FORWARD	532	128	435	373	278	423	335	161	397	3062
par	5	3	5	4	4	5	4	3	5	38
handicap	2	18	4	10	14	6	12	16	8	-

BACK	
yardage	6773
par	72
rating	72.7
slope	129

REGULAR	
yardage	6502
par	72
rating	71.3
slope	126

FORWARD	
yardage	5952
par	74
rating	73.9
slope	128

PLAY POLICY & FEES: Green fees are $24 for nine holes and $32 for 18 holes on weekdays. On weekends and holidays green fees are $28 for nine holes and $47 for 18 holes. Carts are $9 for nine holes and $13 for 18 holes.

TEE TIMES: Reservations can be booked 30 days in advance by calling Tee Time Central at 1-888-CENTRAL, or seven days in advance by calling the pro shop.

DRESS CODE: Collared shirts are preferred, and nonmetal spikes are required.

COURSE DESCRIPTION: This course is based on the philosophy of risk and reward, giving the golfer plenty of options. The signature hole is the 18th hole, a par-4 dogleg left that plays into a prevailing wind. A bunker is strategically placed at the corner of the dogleg. Once around the corner, you are faced with a lake guarding the majority of the green, with waterfalls on both sides.

NOTES: A new clubhouse is scheduled to open in the fall of 1999.

LOCATION: Travel two miles west of Rio Vista on Highway 12 and exit on Summerset Road.

. . . ● **TOURNAMENTS:** A 16-player minimum is needed to book a tournament. Carts are required. Tournaments should be scheduled 12 months in advance.

1. RIO VISTA GOLF CLUB

PLAY POLICY & FEES: Green fees are $18 weekdays and $30 weekends and holidays. Carts are $20.

TEE TIMES: Reservations can be booked 14 days in advance.

DRESS CODE: Golf attire is encouraged.

COURSE DESCRIPTION: This testy tree-lined course has a difficult combination of first and last holes. The first hole tees off into a narrow chute with a grove of oaks as out-of-bounds. The 18th hole doglegs to the left with oak trees and a creekbed that provide headaches. Rounds are made or ruined on either hole. There are numerous other outstanding holes: the par-4 sixth, a monster of 442 yards from the back tees; and the 13th, par 4 of moderate length that, due to placement of the trees, leaves little room for error on either the drive or the approach.

NOTES: Dry Creek has been listed as one of the top 25 public golf courses in California by "Golf Today."

LOCATION: From Sacramento drive 24 miles south on Highway 99 to Galt. Take the Central Galt exit onto C Street and drive east. Turn right on Crystal Way and drive to the course. From Stockton take Highway 99 north and exit at Crystal Way.

. . . ● **TOURNAMENTS:** A 20-player minimum is needed to book a tournament. Events can be booked 12 months in advance. Carts are required. A banquet facility can accommodate up to 120 people. ● **TRAVEL:** The Holiday Inn Express in Galt is located five minutes from the golf course. For reservations call 209-745-9500.

2. DRY CREEK RANCH GOLF COURSE

3 WOODBRIDGE GOLF & COUNTRY CLUB
ARCHITECT: HAROLD SAMPSON, 1923

P.O. Box 806
Woodbridge, CA 95258

800 E. Woodbridge Road
Woodbridge, CA 95258

PRO SHOP: 209-369-2371

Rick Morgan, Manager
Robert E. Vocker, Head Professional, PGA

Driving Range ●
Practice Greens ●
Clubhouse ●
Food / Beverage ●
Accommodations
Pull Carts ●
Power Carts ●
Club Rental ●
$pecial Offers

	1	2	3	4	5	6	7	8	9	OUT
BACK	-	-	-	-	-	-	-	-	-	-
REGULAR	504	363	177	365	404	380	355	165	494	3207
par	5	4	3	4	4	4	4	3	5	36
handicap	7	3	6	4	1	2	5	8	9	-
FORWARD	500	345	166	348	392	373	346	129	490	3089
par	5	4	3	4	4	4	4	3	5	36
handicap	1	7	8	5	2	4	6	9	3	-

	10	11	12	13	14	15	16	17	18	IN
BACK	-	-	-	-	-	-	-	-	-	-
REGULAR	482	170	418	202	345	518	215	364	398	3112
par	5	3	4	3	4	5	3	4	4	35
handicap	9	8	1	5	6	2	4	7	3	-
FORWARD	474	144	415	184	335	478	184	340	383	2937
par	5	3	5	3	4	5	3	4	4	36
handicap	3	9	5	7	4	1	8	6	2	-

BACK	
yardage	-
par	-
rating	-
slope	-

REGULAR	
yardage	6319
par	71
rating	70.1
slope	121

FORWARD	
yardage	6026
par	72
rating	75.4
slope	131

4 FOREST LAKE GOLF COURSE

2450 East Woodson Road
Acampo, CA 95220

PRO SHOP: 209-369-5451

David Ring, PGA Professional
Bill Frasier, Superintendent

Driving Range ●
Practice Greens ●
Clubhouse ●
Food / Beverage ●
Accommodations
Pull Carts ●
Power Carts ●
Club Rental ●
$pecial Offers

	1	2	3	4	5	6	7	8	9	OUT
BACK										
REGULAR										
par										
handicap										
FORWARD										
par										
handicap										

	10	11	12	13	14	15	16	17	18	IN
BACK										
REGULAR										
par										
handicap										
FORWARD										
par										
handicap										

BACK	
yardage	
par	
rating	
slope	

REGULAR	
yardage	4915
par	66
rating	61.3
slope	90

FORWARD	
yardage	4915
par	72
rating	64.0
slope	95

27
HOLES

PLAY POLICY & FEES: Reciprocal play is accepted on a limited basis with members of other private clubs; otherwise, members and guests only. The green fee for reciprocators is the reciprocal fee charged at their course. Guest rates are $40 weekday and $50 on weekends. Carts are $18. The course is closed on Monday.

DRESS CODE: Appropriate golf attire and nonmetal spikes are required.

COURSE DESCRIPTION: Built in 1923, the greens are small and traditional. Of the three nines at Woodbridge, the River Course is the oldest. The Middle Course has rolling terrain, and the Lake Course is the youngest and boasts lots of water. All three reward accuracy over distance. Of the 18-hole setups, the Middle River is the oldest and best regarded, hosting the University of Pacific Invitational every other year.

NOTES: The three nine-hole course combinations are Lake-Middle, River-Lake, and Middle-River. The Lake-Middle Course is 6,489 yards and rated 70.9 for 18 holes from the regular tees. The slope rating is 125. The River-Lake Course is 6,394 yards and rated 70.8 from the regular tees. The slope rating is 122. The Middle-River Course: See scorecard yardage and rating information.

LOCATION: The course is located between Interstate 5 and Highway 99 in Woodbridge on Woodbridge Road.

. . . ● **TOURNAMENTS:** All tournaments must have board approval.

3. WOODBRIDGE GOLF & COUNTRY CLUB

18
HOLES

PLAY POLICY & FEES: Green fees are $8 for nine holes and $11 for 18 holes weekdays, and $10 for nine holes and $14 for 18 holes weekends and holidays. Carts are $9 for nine holes and $17 for 18 holes.

TEE TIMES: Reservations can be booked seven days in advance.

DRESS CODE: Nonmetal spikes are preferred.

COURSE DESCRIPTION: This short course offers tight fairways with a variety of mature trees and some water. The new front nine with some elevated greens and tees is slightly tougher than the back nine. The alternate white (also called the blue) course is the newer of the two combinations.

NOTES: Par is 60 on Monday and Tuesday and 66 the rest of the week. There are actually 24 holes consisting of two different 18-hole layouts (white and alternate white) for men and women. The white course is par 60 (4,005 yards, 56.0 rating, 83 slope). The alternate white: see scorecard. For women the white course plays to a par of 64 (3,685 yards, 58.4 rating, 83 slope). The alternate white for women: See scorecard for more information.

LOCATION: From Highway 99 in Acampo (just north of Lodi), take the Jahant Road exit west, which turns into Woodson Road. Take Woodson Road one mile to the course on the left.

. . . ● **TOURNAMENTS:** Shotgun tournaments are available weekdays only, and a 150- player minimum is required.

4. FOREST LAKE GOLF COURSE

⑤ MICKE GROVE GOLF LINKS
ARCHITECT: BOB DORHAM, 1990

11401 North Micke Grove
Lodi, CA 95240

PRO SHOP: 209-369-4410

Stan Seifert, Head Professional
Mike Granzella, Superintendent
Sara Snider, Tournament Director

Driving Range ●
Practice Greens ●
Clubhouse ●
Food / Beverage ●
Accommodations
Pull Carts ●
Power Carts ●
Club Rental ●
$pecial Offers

	1	2	3	4	5	6	7	8	9	OUT
BACK	399	378	335	149	500	179	489	356	434	3219
REGULAR	372	349	307	125	471	154	471	332	402	2983
par	4	4	4	3	5	3	5	4	4	36
handicap	3	7	9	17	1	13	15	11	5	-
FORWARD	334	319	283	100	425	132	405	300	363	2661
par	4	4	4	3	5	3	5	4	4	36
handicap	7	9	13	17	1	15	3	11	5	-

	10	11	12	13	14	15	16	17	18	IN
BACK	364	532	367	330	179	584	223	378	389	3346
REGULAR	332	496	338	303	143	541	179	350	361	3043
par	4	5	4	4	3	5	3	4	4	36
handicap	14	4	12	18	8	2	16	10	6	-
FORWARD	303	441	309	246	109	444	133	314	326	2625
par	4	5	4	4	3	5	3	4	4	36
handicap	12	2	8	14	18	4	16	10	6	-

BACK	
yardage	6565
par	72
rating	71.1
slope	118

REGULAR	
yardage	6026
par	72
rating	68.5
slope	112

FORWARD	
yardage	5286
par	72
rating	69.7
slope	111

⑥ VENETIAN GARDENS COMMUNITY GOLF COURSE

1555 Mosaic Way
Stockton, CA 95207

PRO SHOP: 209-477-3871

George Winges, Manager

Driving Range
Practice Greens ●
Clubhouse
Food / Beverage
Accommodations
Pull Carts
Power Carts
Club Rental
$pecial Offers

	1	2	3	4	5	6	7	8	9	OUT
BACK	-	-	-	-	-	-	-	-	-	-
REGULAR	89	52	57	83	87	109	140	87	73	777
par	3	3	3	3	3	3	3	3	3	27
handicap	-	-	-	-	-	-	-	-	-	-
FORWARD	-	-	-	-	-	-	-	-	-	-
par	-	-	-	-	-	-	-	-	-	-
handicap	-	-	-	-	-	-	-	-	-	-

	10	11	12	13	14	15	16	17	18	IN
BACK	-	-	-	-	-	-	-	-	-	-
REGULAR	-	-	-	-	-	-	-	-	-	-
par	-	-	-	-	-	-	-	-	-	-
handicap	-	-	-	-	-	-	-	-	-	-
FORWARD	-	-	-	-	-	-	-	-	-	-
par	-	-	-	-	-	-	-	-	-	-
handicap	-	-	-	-	-	-	-	-	-	-

BACK	
yardage	-
par	-
rating	-
slope	-

REGULAR	
yardage	777
par	27
rating	-
slope	-

FORWARD	
yardage	
par	
rating	-
slope	-

PLAY POLICY & FEES: Green fees are $18 to walk and $24 to ride weekdays and $27 to walk and $38 to ride weekends. Afternoon, twilight, senior and junior rates are available.

TEE TIMES: Reservations can be booked 30 days in advance for a $2 fee per person.

DRESS CODE: Hemmed shorts and sleeved shirts are a must.

COURSE DESCRIPTION: This highly acclaimed links-style course is set among the vineyards. The greens are large, and there is plenty of water. The signature hole is the 14th, a par 3 of 179 yards over water. Beware of the strong winds that often blow. This is a well-maintained course that stays lush and green in the hot summer months.

NOTES: Bryan Pemberton's 65 is the course record.

LOCATION: Take Highway 99 south from Sacramento and north from Modesto to Armstrong Road. Take Armstrong about a half mile west. Then turn left on Micke Grove Road. The course is on the right.

. . . ● **TOURNAMENTS:** A 16-player minimum is required to book a tournament. Carts are required. Events should be scheduled 12 months in advance. The banquet facility can accommodate up to 144 people. ● **TRAVEL:** The Comfort Inn is located 15 minutes from the golf course. For reservations call 209-367-4848.

5. MICKE GROVE GOLF LINKS

PLAY POLICY & FEES: Members and guests only. No outside or reciprocal play is accepted.

COURSE DESCRIPTION: This course is located in Venetian Gardens, a private residential community.

LOCATION: From Interstate 5 in Stockton, turn onto March Lane and drive one mile east to Venetian Drive North. Turn right on Mosaic Way to the Venetian Gardens Community Golf Course.

. . . ● **TOURNAMENTS:** This course is not available for outside events.

6. VENETIAN GARDENS COMMUNITY GOLF

LOCKEFORD SPRINGS GOLF COURSE
ARCHITECT: JIM SUMMERS/ SANDY TATUM, 1995

P.O. Box 1315
Lockeford, CA 95237

16360 North Highway 88
Lodi, CA 95240

PRO SHOP: 209-333-6275

Gary Reiff, Director of Golf
Mitch Lowe, Head Professional, PGA

Driving Range ●
Practice Greens ●
Clubhouse ●
Food / Beverage ●
Accommodations
Pull Carts ●
Power Carts ●
Club Rental ●
$pecial Offers

	1	2	3	4	5	6	7	8	9	OUT
BACK	388	422	161	470	420	542	406	182	516	3507
REGULAR	363	391	145	450	400	517	383	161	488	3298
par	4	4	3	4	4	5	4	3	5	36
handicap	15	5	17	3	7	1	11	13	9	-
FORWARD	331	331	129	392	360	486	359	122	472	2982
par	4	4	3	4	4	5	4	3	5	36
handicap	15	5	17	3	7	1	11	13	5	-

	10	11	12	13	14	15	16	17	18	IN
BACK	359	436	548	311	437	202	403	144	514	3354
REGULAR	349	414	532	296	414	178	386	130	486	3185
par	4	4	5	4	4	3	4	4	5	37
handicap	14	6	4	16	2	12	8	18	10	-
FORWARD	334	394	488	278	396	150	354	115	460	2969
par	4	4	5	4	4	3	4	4	5	37
handicap	14	6	4	16	2	12	8	18	10	-

BACK	
yardage	6861
par	73
rating	72.8
slope	121

REGULAR	
yardage	6483
par	73
rating	71.1
slope	116

FORWARD	
yardage	5951
par	73
rating	74.0
slope	123

 LONE TREE GOLF COURSE
ARCHITECT: BOB BALDOCK, 1957

4800 Golf Course Road
Antioch, CA 94509

PRO SHOP: 925-757-5200

Pat Cain, Director of Golf, PGA
Jack Oakley, Head Professional, PGA

Driving Range ●
Practice Greens ●
Clubhouse ●
Food / Beverage ●
Accommodations
Pull Carts ●
Power Carts ●
Club Rental ●
$pecial Offers

	1	2	3	4	5	6	7	8	9	OUT
BACK	469	180	294	515	389	382	422	184	379	3214
REGULAR	460	134	281	488	357	370	405	144	367	3006
par	5	3	4	5	4	4	4	3	4	36
handicap	9	17	15	7	3	13	1	11	5	-
FORWARD	450	120	271	434	329	338	373	121	340	2776
par	5	3	4	5	4	4	4	3	4	36
handicap	7	17	13	1	5	11	9	15	3	-

	10	11	12	13	14	15	16	17	18	IN
BACK	426	171	518	382	117	362	496	492	303	3267
REGULAR	417	153	509	373	105	341	476	473	292	3139
par	4	3	5	4	3	4	5	5	4	37
handicap	2	8	4	10	16	6	14	12	18	-
FORWARD	399	142	500	368	100	307	459	451	281	3007
par	5	3	5	4	3	4	5	5	4	38
handicap	8	16	2	10	18	12	4	6	14	-

BACK	
yardage	6481
par	73
rating	70.5
slope	122

REGULAR	
yardage	6145
par	73
rating	68.9
slope	119

FORWARD	
yardage	5783
par	74
rating	72.4
slope	121

PLAY POLICY & FEES: Green fees for 18 holes are $20 weekdays and $30 weekends. Carts are $12 per rider for 18 holes. Call for special rates.

TEE TIMES: Reservations can be booked seven days in advance.

DRESS CODE: No tank tops or swimwear are allowed on the course.

COURSE DESCRIPTION: This traditional, flat valley course opened in July 1995. It features lots of mounding and contours, large, undulating greens, and mature trees. Fourteen holes wander through an old walnut grove. The 512-yard, par-5 18th hole is one of the best on the course. It's a dogleg left around a lake and includes an eye-catching waterfall.

NOTES: PGA Tour player Ron Ewing owns the course record with a 65.

LOCATION: From Sacramento take Highway 99 south to the Highway 12 exit. Drive east approximately six miles to Highway 88 and turn right. The course is approximately one mile up on the left.

. . . ● **TOURNAMENTS:** A 16-player minimum is needed to book a tournament. Carts are required. Tournaments can be booked six to 12 months in advance.

7. LOCKEFORD SPRINGS GOLF COURSE

PLAY POLICY & FEES: Green fees for residents of the city of Antioch are $15 for 18 holes weekdays, and $18 for 18 holes weekends. Nonresident green fees are $19 for 18 holes Monday through Thursday, and $22 for 18 holes Friday through Sunday. Carts are $12 for nine holes and $22 for 18 holes. Many special rates are available. Call for information.

TEE TIMES: Reservations can be booked seven days in advance. Players should check in 30 minutes prior to teeing off.

DRESS CODE: Shirts must be worn, and nonmetal spikes are required.

COURSE DESCRIPTION: This hilly yet open course has a unique par of 73. It's a walkable course, and in spite of its name, there are lots of trees. The best hole is probably the fifth, 389 yards from the back tees. Golfers must carry a creek 185 yards off the tee. The green is the biggest on the course.

LOCATION: From Highway 4 in Antioch take the Lone Tree Way exit south. Veer to the right and continue six lights. Turn right onto Golf Course Road.

. . . ● **TOURNAMENTS:** This course is available for outside tournaments.

8. LONE TREE GOLF COURSE

9 BETHEL ISLAND GOLF COURSE
ARCHITECT: BOB BALDOCK, 1966

3303 Gateway Road
Bethel Island, CA 94511

PRO SHOP: 925-684-2654
CLUBHOUSE: 925-684-2775

Jim Adams, Superintendent

Driving Range ●
Practice Greens ●
Clubhouse ●
Food / Beverage ●
Accommodations
Pull Carts ●
Power Carts ●
Club Rental ●
$pecial Offers

	1	2	3	4	5	6	7	8	9	OUT
BACK	332	533	175	390	416	468	418	190	300	3222
REGULAR	321	520	167	380	400	456	403	176	290	3113
par	4	5	3	4	4	5	4	3	4	36
handicap	13	5	15	7	1	11	3	9	17	-
FORWARD	295	491	147	362	370	433	381	149	280	2908
par	4	5	3	4	4	5	4	3	4	36
handicap	11	1	17	9	7	3	5	15	13	-

	10	11	12	13	14	15	16	17	18	IN
BACK	308	347	437	272	164	498	158	510	417	3111
REGULAR	298	332	417	267	161	493	142	502	395	3007
par	4	4	4	4	3	5	3	5	4	36
handicap	14	8	2	16	10	6	18	12	4	-
FORWARD	266	312	402	242	128	462	112	470	411	2805
par	4	4	5	4	3	5	3	5	5	38
handicap	14	10	6	12	16	2	18	4	8	-

BACK	
yardage	6333
par	72
rating	-
slope	-

REGULAR	
yardage	6120
par	72
rating	69.2
slope	114

FORWARD	
yardage	5713
par	74
rating	71.9
slope	113

10 SWENSON PARK GOLF COURSE
ARCHITECT: JACK FLEMING, 1952

6803 Alexandria Place
Stockton, CA 95207

PRO SHOP: 209-937-7360

Ernie George, Manager, PGA
Greg Rice, Tournament Director
Tom Noack, Superintendent

Driving Range ●
Practice Greens ●
Clubhouse ●
Food / Beverage ●
Accommodations
Pull Carts ●
Power Carts ●
Club Rental ●
$pecial Offers

	1	2	3	4	5	6	7	8	9	OUT
BACK										
REGULAR										
par										
handicap										
FORWARD										
par										
handicap										

	10	11	12	13	14	15	16	17	18	IN
BACK										
REGULAR										
par										
handicap										
FORWARD										
par										
handicap										

BACK	
yardage	
par	
rating	-
slope	-

REGULAR	
yardage	6407
par	72
rating	70.1
slope	110

FORWARD	
yardage	6266
par	72
rating	73.8
slope	114

PLAY POLICY & FEES: Green fees are $17 for 18 holes weekdays until noon. From noon until 3 p.m. green fees are $12; after 3 p.m. green fees drop to $10. On weekends green fees are $23 for 18 holes until 3 p.m. Green fees are $14 after 3 p.m. Carts are $11 per person until noon on weekdays and $8 afternoon. On weekends, carts are $11per person until 3 p.m. and $8 per person thereafter.

TEE TIMES: Reservations can be booked seven days in advance.

DRESS CODE: Collared shirts with sleeves are required.

COURSE DESCRIPTION: This links-style layout has been around for nearly 30 years. It is flat and windy, with lots of trees, water, and bunkers. It's a challenging but fair test.

NOTES: The parking lot and cart paths have been repaved, and the clubhouse and restrooms have been remodeled.

LOCATION: Take Highway 4 through Oakley to Brentwood and exit at Cypress Road east. Turn left at Bethel Island Road and then right at Gateway Road to the course.

. . . ● **TOURNAMENTS:** This course is available for outside tournaments.

9. BETHEL ISLAND GOLF COURSE

PLAY POLICY & FEES: Green fees are $15.75 weekdays and $17.25 weekends for 18 holes. The executive course is $9.25 weekdays and $10 weekends. Carts are $20 for 18 holes. There is a $2 key deposit.

TEE TIMES: Reservations can be booked seven days in advance.

COURSE DESCRIPTION: Swenson Park offers some of the lowest green fees in Northern California for a regulation track. It is a wide-open layout with fewer than a dozen traps and just two water holes. The 15th and 16th holes, however, feature extremely demanding tee shots through narrow chutes. The executive course is dotted with water hazards, though only two holes are longer than 150 yards.

NOTES: The par-27 executive course measures 2,760 yards and is not rated. Rick Burgess holds the course record at 63.

LOCATION: Heading north on Interstate 5 on the north side of Stockton, take the Benjamin Holt Drive exit east. Turn left on Alexandria Place and drive to the course on the left.

. . . ● **TOURNAMENTS:** This course is available for outside tournaments.

10. SWENSON PARK GOLF COURSE

11 THE RESERVE AT SPANOS PARK
ARCHITECT: ANDY RAUGUST

6301 West Eight Mile Rd.
Stockton, CA 95219

PRO SHOP: 209-477-4653

Mark Stevens, General Manager, PGA
Tony Troncale, Head Professional, PGA
John Jorgenson, Superintendent

Driving Range •
Practice Greens •
Clubhouse •
Food / Beverage •
Accommodations
Pull Carts
Power Carts •
Club Rental •
Special Offers

	1	2	3	4	5	6	7	8	9	OUT
BACK	353	554	435	182	413	540	446	198	410	3531
REGULAR	300	501	372	138	355	492	372	162	366	3058
par	4	5	4	3	4	5	4	3	4	36
handicap	15	1	5	17	7	9	3	13	11	-
FORWARD										
par	4	5	4	3	4	5	4	3	4	36
handicap	13	1	5	17	11	3	9	15	7	-

	10	11	12	13	14	15	16	17	18	IN
BACK	393	519	390	166	421	179	535	467	399	3469
REGULAR	347	471	334	149	372	150	480	366	363	3032
par	4	5	4	3	4	3	5	4	4	36
handicap	12	4	8	16	6	18	10	2	14	-
FORWARD										
par	4	5	4	3	4	3	5	4	4	36
handicap	8	4	14	18	12	16	2	6	10	-

BACK	
yardage	7000
par	72
rating	73.1
slope	

REGULAR	
yardage	6090
par	72
rating	70.0
slope	

FORWARD	
yardage	5204
par	72
rating	
slope	

12 ELKHORN COUNTRY CLUB
ARCHITECT: BERT STAMPS, 1963

1050 Elkhorn Drive
Stockton, CA 95209

PRO SHOP: 209-477-0252
OFFICE: 209-477-8896

Bob Young, General Manager, PGA
Dennis Blinn, Superintendent

Driving Range •
Practice Greens •
Clubhouse •
Food / Beverage •
Accommodations
Pull Carts •
Power Carts •
Club Rental
Special Offers

	1	2	3	4	5	6	7	8	9	OUT
BACK	404	155	449	419	301	476	416	532	163	3315
REGULAR	391	152	430	395	271	471	358	474	140	3082
par	4	3	4	4	4	5	4	5	3	36
handicap	7	17	5	9	11	13	3	1	15	-
FORWARD	273	90	368	252	251	409	242	402	122	2409
par	4	3	5	4	4	5	4	5	3	37
handicap	13	15	7	3	11	1	9	5	17	-

	10	11	12	13	14	15	16	17	18	IN
BACK	430	506	361	171	414	336	213	395	418	3244
REGULAR	426	494	356	140	393	303	188	362	381	3043
par	4	5	4	3	4	4	3	4	4	35
handicap	2	4	6	16	14	8	18	10	12	-
FORWARD	418	407	241	76	268	217	130	253	237	2247
par	5	5	4	3	4	4	3	4	4	36
handicap	10	2	4	18	8	14	16	12	6	-

BACK	
yardage	6559
par	71
rating	70.9
slope	124

REGULAR	
yardage	6125
par	71
rating	69.2
slope	120

FORWARD	
yardage	4656
par	73
rating	67.5
slope	116

PLAY POLICY & FEES: Green fees are $30 weekdays and $45 on weekends. Carts are $12 per person.

TEE TIMES: Reservations can be made seven days in advance.

DRESS CODE: Collared shirts and nonmetal spikes required. No denim is allowed on the course.

COURSE DESCRIPTION: Spanos Park is part of a working farm, and you will find corn fields throughout. This is a links-style course with eight lakes that come into play on 12 holes. The fairways give you plenty of room for error, and there are plenty of places to bail out, but if you miss the fairways and greens badly, trouble awaits. Many of the greens are protected by well-placed pot bunkers but allow players to approach in a variety of ways. The greens are small, with subtle undulations.

LOCATION: From Stockton take Interstate 5 north to the Eight Mile road exit. Go west on Eight Mile Drive for a quarter mile to the course on the north side of the road.

. . . ● **TOURNAMENTS:** A minimum of 16-players is required for an event. A banquet facility can accommodate up to 160 people.

11. THE RESERVE AT SPANOS PARK

PLAY POLICY & FEES: Reciprocal play is accepted with members of other private clubs. Members and guests only. Guest fees are $30 on weekdays and $50 on weekends and holidays. Guest fees after 2 p.m. are $20. Fees for reciprocal players are $30 on weekdays and $50 on weekends. Carts are $24.

TEE TIMES: Reservations can be booked seven days in advance.

DRESS CODE: Appropriate golf attire is required, including collared shirts for men.

COURSE DESCRIPTION: This tough course rewards accuracy over distance. More than 63 bunkers guard the fairways and the elevated greens. Trees abound.

NOTES: Sean Corte-Real holds the men's course record of 61. The women's mark of 69 is held by Dana Arnold. The late Ty Caplin, a fixture among NorCal PGA pros, purchased the course in 1978 with his wife Nancy. She remains the current owner.

LOCATION: From Interstate 5 take the Eight Mile Road exit and drive three miles east. Turn right on Davis Road and drive a quarter mile. Turn left on Elkhorn Drive.

. . . ● **TOURNAMENTS:** This course is available Monday only. A 72-player minimum is required for an afternoon shotgun start. A 48-player minimum is required for a morning start. Tournaments should be booked 12 months in advance. The banquet facility can accommodate 375 people. ● **TRAVEL:** The Courtyard by Marriot is located 15 minutes from the golf course. Call 209-472-9700 for reservations. The Radisson of Stockton (209-975-9090) and the Stockton Holiday Inn (209-474-3301) are also recommended.

12. ELKHORN COUNTRY CLUB

⑬ OAKMOORE GOLF COURSE
ARCHITECT: DONALD A. CRUMP, 1959

3737 North Wilson Way
Stockton, CA 95205

PRO SHOP: 209-462-6712
OFFICE: 209-943-1983

Jean Lawton, Manager
Antonio Garcia, Tournament Director

Driving Range ●
Practice Greens ●
Clubhouse ●
Food / Beverage ●
Accommodations
Pull Carts
Power Carts ●
Club Rental
$pecial Offers

	1	2	3	4	5	6	7	8	9	OUT
BACK	-	-	-	-	-	-	-	-	-	-
REGULAR	368	415	200	474	346	197	335	370	531	3236
par	4	4	3	5	4	3	4	4	5	36
handicap	11	1	7	13	17	9	15	3	5	-
FORWARD	368	415	200	474	346	197	335	370	531	3236
par	4	5	3	5	4	3	4	4	5	37
handicap	7	15	3	9	11	13	17	5	1	-

	10	11	12	13	14	15	16	17	18	IN
BACK	-	-	-	-	-	-	-	-	-	-
REGULAR	388	395	245	464	366	167	350	350	556	3281
par	4	4	3	5	4	3	4	4	5	36
handicap	10	2	8	16	18	12	14	4	6	-
FORWARD	388	395	245	464	366	167	350	350	556	3281
par	4	4	3	5	4	3	4	5	5	37
handicap	6	4	8	12	10	18	14	16	2	-

BACK	
yardage	-
par	-
rating	-
slope	-

REGULAR	
yardage	6517
par	72
rating	72.0
slope	-

FORWARD	
yardage	6517
par	74
rating	74.5
slope	-

⑭ STOCKTON GOLF & COUNTRY CLUB
ARCHITECT: ALISTER MACKENZIE, 1914

3800 West Country Club
Stockton, CA 95204

PRO SHOP: 209-466-6221
CLUBHOUSE: 209-466-4313

David Morris, Manager
Jeff Foreman, Head Professional, PGA
Mike Phillips, Superintendent

Driving Range ●
Practice Greens ●
Clubhouse ●
Food / Beverage ●
Accommodations
Pull Carts ●
Power Carts ●
Club Rental ●
$pecial Offers

	1	2	3	4	5	6	7	8	9	OUT
BACK	332	511	188	408	395	375	323	141	365	3038
REGULAR	325	505	179	390	382	368	323	126	356	2954
par	4	5	3	4	4	4	4	3	4	35
handicap	15	9	11	1	3	7	13	17	5	-
FORWARD	311	493	168	364	373	356	318	111	346	2840
par	4	5	3	4	4	4	4	3	4	35
handicap	13	1	15	5	3	11	9	17	7	-

	10	11	12	13	14	15	16	17	18	IN
BACK	368	212	352	412	531	202	515	422	374	3388
REGULAR	351	206	352	406	526	194	499	414	368	3316
par	4	3	4	4	5	3	5	4	4	36
handicap	8	14	16	2	4	18	12	6	10	-
FORWARD	328	180	348	400	518	185	464	409	351	3183
par	4	3	4	4	5	3	5	5	4	37
handicap	4	18	10	6	2	16	8	14	12	-

BACK	
yardage	6426
par	71
rating	70.8
slope	124

REGULAR	
yardage	6270
par	71
rating	70.1
slope	122

FORWARD	
yardage	6023
par	72
rating	75.0
slope	126

PLAY POLICY & FEES: Don't you hate it when you walk up to the pro shop only to find out there is a tournament in progress? Well, at Oakmoore there's always a tournament in progress. This is a most unusual course in that it is solely used for tournaments. The approximate cost to each member of a visiting group is $24 Monday through Thursday, $29 on Friday and $34 on weekends, which includes golf, cart, and use of the clubhouse.

TEE TIMES: This is a very popular tournament course where previous events receive the first rights for the same date. Call in January for open dates.

COURSE DESCRIPTION: The course is wooded, with three lakes and mostly elevated greens.

NOTES: Oakmoore just purchased a new fleet of golf carts and has further improved maintenance of the course.

LOCATION: From Highway 99 in Stockton, exit at Business 99/Wilson Way south and drive to the course.

. . . ● **TOURNAMENTS:** For tournaments there is a 40-player minimum Monday through Thursday, a 44-player minimum on Friday, and a 50-player minimum on weekends.

13. OAKMOORE GOLF COURSE

PLAY POLICY & FEES: Reciprocal play is accepted with members of other private clubs. Guest fees are $20 when accompanied by a member. Reciprocal fees are $70. Carts are $10 for nine holes and $20 for 18 holes. The course is closed on Monday.

TEE TIMES: Reservations can be booked seven days in advance.

DRESS CODE: Collared shirts and nonmetal spikes are required. No denim is allowed on the course.

COURSE DESCRIPTION: The flavor of Alister Mackenzie's original design remains 80 years later on this course bordered by Stockton's deep-water channel. The fairways are primarily Bermuda grass, and the greens are bent. It is a tight course with countless eucalyptus trees. The par 3s are outstanding, three of them measuring from 188 to 212 yards. The first hole is bordered by the channel.

LOCATION: From Interstate 5 in Stockton take the Country Club Boulevard exit west and drive 1.5 miles to the course.

. . . ● **TOURNAMENTS:** Outside events are allowed Monday only with board and manager approval. A 72-player minimum is required to book a tournament, and carts are required.

14. STOCKTON GOLF & COUNTRY CLUB

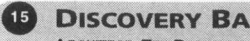

1475 Clubhouse Drive
Byron, CA 94514

PRO SHOP: 925-634-0705

Mark Tissot, General Manager
Scott A. Smith, Director of Golf, PGA
Rich Eichner, Superintendent

Driving Range ●
Practice Greens ●
Clubhouse ●
Food / Beverage ●
Accommodations
Pull Carts ●
Power Carts ●
Club Rental ●
$pecial Offers

	1	2	3	4	5	6	7	8	9	OUT
BACK	500	162	427	415	406	406	166	316	372	3170
REGULAR	492	143	405	402	389	393	151	298	359	3032
par	5	3	4	4	4	4	3	4	4	35
handicap	11	15	3	1	9	5	17	13	7	-
FORWARD	411	108	336	345	329	313	124	245	315	2526
par	5	3	4	4	4	4	3	4	4	35
handicap	3	13	5	1	7	11	17	15	9	-

BACK	
yardage	6552
par	71
rating	72.1
slope	126

	10	11	12	13	14	15	16	17	18	IN
BACK	524	346	426	376	162	500	425	178	445	3382
REGULAR	507	337	398	361	150	485	395	156	377	3166
par	5	4	4	4	3	5	4	3	4	36
handicap	8	14	2	10	18	12	4	16	6	-
FORWARD	446	294	335	325	123	425	324	100	341	2713
par	5	4	4	4	3	5	4	3	4	36
handicap	8	12	2	14	18	10	4	16	6	-

REGULAR	
yardage	6198
par	71
rating	69.8
slope	123

FORWARD	
yardage	5239
par	71
rating	70.2
slope	123

16 **BROOKSIDE COUNTRY CLUB**
ARCHITECT: ROBERT TRENT JONES JR., 1990

3603 St. Andrews Drive
Stockton, CA 95219

PRO SHOP: 209-956-7888

Bob Johnson, Manager
Tom Braun, Director of Golf, PGA
Pete Fredeen, Superintendent

Driving Range ●
Practice Greens ●
Clubhouse ●
Food / Beverage ●
Accommodations
Pull Carts ●
Power Carts ●
Club Rental ●
$pecial Offers

	1	2	3	4	5	6	7	8	9	OUT
BACK	390	418	160	531	396	335	587	163	450	3430
REGULAR	367	396	122	512	372	301	556	126	427	3179
par	4	4	3	5	4	4	5	3	4	36
handicap	12	8	16	10	4	14	2	18	6	-
FORWARD	272	316	86	452	298	248	464	91	318	2545
par	4	4	3	5	4	4	5	3	4	36
handicap	11	7	15	5	9	13	1	17	3	-

BACK	
yardage	6720
par	72
rating	72.6
slope	125

	10	11	12	13	14	15	16	17	18	IN
BACK	548	380	131	387	152	420	559	181	532	3290
REGULAR	503	347	113	353	141	401	530	165	512	3065
par	5	4	3	4	3	4	5	3	5	36
handicap	11	9	17	3	15	7	1	13	5	-
FORWARD	434	264	74	295	89	342	444	115	420	2477
par	5	4	3	4	3	4	5	3	5	36
handicap	6	12	18	10	16	8	2	14	4	-

REGULAR	
yardage	6244
par	72
rating	69.8
slope	118

FORWARD	
yardage	5022
par	72
rating	68.2
slope	112

PLAY POLICY & FEES: Reciprocal play is accepted with members of other private clubs on weekdays only. Guests must be accompanied by a member. Carts are $22. Green fees for reciprocators are $65. Guest fees are $36 weekdays and $52 weekends. The course is closed on Monday.

TEE TIMES: Have your club pro call to make arrangements.

DRESS CODE: Appropriate golf attire and nonmetal spikes are required.

COURSE DESCRIPTION: Water can be—and often is—found on 16 of 18 holes. Set in rolling terrain, Discovery Bay is wide open with undulating greens. The par-3 17th hole features an island green, though there is room to bail out left on the 178-yard (blue tees) hole.

LOCATION: From Highway 4 take the Discovery Bay Boulevard exit. Take the first right onto Clubhouse Drive.

. . . ● **TOURNAMENTS:** Tournament play is on Monday only. A 100-player minimum is needed to book a shotgun tournament.

15. DISCOVERY BAY

PLAY POLICY & FEES: This course accepts reciprocal play with members of other clubs. The reciprocal fee is $64. The rate for guests accompanied by a member is $35 weekdays, $50 weekends. Carts are $22.

DRESS CODE: Appropriate golf attire and nonmetal spikes are required.

COURSE DESCRIPTION: Brookside is a links-style layout that offers a spellbinding view of ocean freighters floating down the inland channel to the Port of Stockton. Water comes into play on 10 of 18 holes, the most notorious being the 16th, a double dogleg of 559 yards. The holes here offer a nice change of pace, from the 450-yard uphill 9th to the chip-shot 12th of 131 yards.

NOTES: The course records are held by Mike Baty, 64 on the white tees, and Mike Omlansky, 66 on the blues.

LOCATION: Take Interstate 5 to the March Lane exit on the north end of Stockton. Follow March Lane west into the Brookside real estate development. The gated entrance is on the left.

. . . ● **TOURNAMENTS:** Outside events are booked for Monday only. A 100-player minimum is needed to reserve a tournament.

16. BROOKSIDE COUNTRY CLUB

17 LYONS GOLF COURSE

Rough and Ready Island
Stockton, CA 95203

PRO SHOP: 209-937-7905

Eric Molgaard, Professional

Driving Range
Practice Greens x
Clubhouse x
Food / Beverage x
Accommodations
Pull Carts x
Power Carts x
Club Rental
$pecial Offers

	1	2	3	4	5	6	7	8	9	OUT
BACK	332	129	256	376	169	297	164	112	272	2107
REGULAR	320	10	251	349	161	285	156	103	261	1896
par	4	3	4	4	3	4	3	3	4	32
handicap	4	18	10	2	12	6	14	16	8	-
FORWARD	307	90	235	342	148	278	151	91	255	1897
par	4	3	4	4	3	4	3	3	4	32
handicap	4	18	10	2	12	6	14	16	8	-

	10	11	12	13	14	15	16	17	18	IN
BACK										
REGULAR										
par										
handicap										-
FORWARD										
par										
handicap										-

BACK	
yardage	2107
par	32
rating	
slope	

REGULAR	
yardage	1896
par	32
rating	
slope	

FORWARD	
yardage	1897
par	32
rating	
slope	

18 VAN BUSKIRK GOLF COURSE
ARCHITECT: LARRY NORDSTROM, 1961

1740 Houston Avenue
Stockton, CA 95206

PRO SHOP: 209-937-7357

Jose Santiago, Head Professional, PGA
Tom Nowak, Superintendent

Driving Range ●
Practice Greens ●
Clubhouse ●
Food / Beverage ●
Accommodations
Pull Carts ●
Power Carts ●
Club Rental ●
$pecial Offers

	1	2	3	4	5	6	7	8	9	OUT
BACK	402	545	366	414	198	357	601	152	373	3408
REGULAR	379	519	345	384	180	334	510	145	350	3146
par	4	5	4	4	3	4	5	3	4	36
handicap	5	7	15	3	9	11	1	17	13	-
FORWARD	363	491	326	360	169	334	566	128	280	3017
par	4	5	4	4	3	4	6	3	4	37
handicap	7	3	9	5	15	11	1	17	13	-

	10	11	12	13	14	15	16	17	18	IN
BACK	466	221	578	467	260	393	400	224	511	3520
REGULAR	456	183	551	510	243	370	379	224	440	3356
par	4	3	5	5	4	4	4	3	4	36
handicap	2	14	8	16	18	12	10	6	4	-
FORWARD	367	156	456	464	218	357	327	165	400	2910
par	4	3	5	5	4	4	4	3	5	37
handicap	10	18	2	4	14	8	12	16	6	-

BACK	
yardage	6928
par	72
rating	72.2
slope	118

REGULAR	
yardage	6502
par	72
rating	70.3
slope	113

FORWARD	
yardage	5927
par	74
rating	72.2
slope	113

PLAY POLICY & FEES: Weekday green fees are $9.25 for nine holes and $11.25 for 18 holes. Green fees on weekends are $10 for nine holes and $12 for 18 holes. Seniors and student green fees are $8.50 weekdays and $10.50 weekends. A sunset rate is available.

TEE TIMES: Reservations are recommended for weekend mornings. Tee times can be made seven days in advance.

DRESS CODE: No tank tops or cutoff shorts are allowed on the course.

COURSE DESCRIPTION: This is a level course with ponds that come into play on two holes.

LOCATION: From Lodi travel south on Interstate 5 . Take the Fresno Avenue exit. Go right on Fresno Avenue, take the first left on Washington, and continue until you cross over the bridge. You will see the course on the right. Take the first right into the course.

17. LYONS GOLF COURSE

PLAY POLICY & FEES: Green fees are $15.75 weekdays and $17.25 weekends. Carts are $20 for 18 holes.

TEE TIMES: Reservations can be booked seven days in advance.

DRESS CODE: Golf attire is encouraged.

COURSE DESCRIPTION: This flat, open course has three ponds, with water coming into play on nearly every hole on the front nine. Notable is the seventh hole, a long par 5 with out-of-bounds on the left and water on the right. On the back nine the greens are somewhat elevated.

NOTES: The Stockton City Championship is held here each August.

LOCATION: From Interstate 5 in Stockton, exit at Eighth Street west to Fresno Street. Turn left and drive to the course.

. . . ● **TOURNAMENTS:** Shotgun tournaments are not allowed. A 24-player minimum is required to book a tournament. Events can be scheduled up to 12 months in advance. ● **TRAVEL:** The Stockton Hilton is recommended. For reservations call 209-957-9090.

18. VAN BUSKIRK GOLF COURSE

⑲ FRENCH CAMP GOLF COURSE & RV PARK
ARCHITECT: LLOYD ZASTRE, 1995

P.O. Box 1500
French Camp, CA 95231

PRO SHOP: 209-234-3030

Steve Videtta, PGA Professional
Mike Aguilera, Superintendent
Diana Soto, Banquet Manager

3919 E. French Camp Road

Driving Range ●
Practice Greens ●
Clubhouse ●
Food / Beverage ●
Accommodations ●
Pull Carts ●
Power Carts ●
Club Rental ●
Special Offers ●

	1	2	3	4	5	6	7	8	9	OUT
BACK	417	511	368	189	415	506	381	191	429	3407
REGULAR	399	451	346	164	381	487	366	143	366	3103
par	4	5	4	3	4	5	4	3	4	36
handicap	1	11	13	9	7	17	15	5	3	-
FORWARD	326	386	319	130	330	433	312	108	269	2613
par	4	5	4	3	4	5	4	3	4	36
handicap	1	11	13	9	7	17	15	5	3	-

	10	11	12	13	14	15	16	17	18	IN
BACK	417	511	368	189	415	506	381	191	429	3407
REGULAR	399	451	346	164	381	487	366	143	366	3103
par	4	5	4	3	4	5	4	3	4	36
handicap	2	12	14	10	8	18	16	6	4	-
FORWARD	326	386	319	130	330	433	312	108	269	2613
par	4	5	4	3	4	5	4	3	4	36
handicap	2	12	14	10	8	18	16	6	4	-

BACK	
yardage	6814
par	72
rating	-
slope	-

REGULAR	
yardage	6206
par	72
rating	-
slope	-

FORWARD	
yardage	5226
par	72
rating	-
slope	-

⑳ J.B. GOLF COURSE

24305 E. Highway 4
Farmington, CA 95230

PRO SHOP: 209-886-5670

Jim Boone, Owner

Driving Range
Practice Greens ●
Clubhouse ●
Food / Beverage ●
Accommodations
Pull Carts ●
Power Carts
Club Rental ●
Special Offers ●

	1	2	3	4	5	6	7	8	9	OUT
BACK	127	80	107	135	39	100	87	86	127	888
REGULAR										
par	3	3	3	3	3	3	3	3	3	27
handicap	7	8	6	1	9	2	3	4	5	-
FORWARD										
par										
handicap										-

	10	11	12	13	14	15	16	17	18	IN
BACK										
REGULAR										
par										
handicap										-
FORWARD										
par										
handicap										-

BACK	
yardage	888
par	27
rating	
slope	

REGULAR	
yardage	
par	27
rating	
slope	

FORWARD	
yardage	
par	
rating	
slope	

PLAY POLICY & FEES: Green fees are $10 for nine holes and $18 for 18 holes on weekdays. On weekends and holidays, green fees are $12 for nine holes and $20 for 18 holes. Fees for juniors, seniors, and campers are available. Twilight rates are also available. Carts are $5 per person for nine holes and $10 per person for 18 holes.

TEE TIMES: Reservations can be booked seven days in advance for the general public and one year in advance for RVers.

DRESS CODE: Shirts must be worn, and nonmetal spikes are required.

COURSE DESCRIPTION: French Camp is one of the longest nine-hole courses in California. From the back tees three of the five par 4s are over 400 yards long. Water comes into play on every hole on this well-maintained golf course.

NOTES: If you love golf and recreational vehicles are your thing, this is the place for you. French Camp has 197 landscaped spaces with full hookups, a swimming pool, clubhouse with kitchen, showers, laundry room, 18-hole putting course, lighted driving range, and practice course.

LOCATION: From Stockton take Highway 99 south five miles. From Manteca take Highway 99 three miles north. The course is located at the junction of Highway 99 and French Camp Road.

. . . ● **TOURNAMENTS:** An eight-player minimum is needed to book a tournament. The banquet facility can accommodate 200 people. ● **TRAVEL:** The Radisson in Stockton is located 15 minutes from the golf course. For reservations call 209-957-9090.

19. FRENCH CAMP GOLF COURSE & RV

PLAY POLICY & FEES: Green fees are $5 for nine holes and $8 for 18 holes.

TEE TIMES: Reservations are not accepted; golfers are sent out on a first-come, first-served basis.

DRESS CODE: Casual attire is OK.

COURSE DESCRIPTION: This is a family-oriented golf course that is a good tune up for your iron game. A creek comes into play on two holes.

NOTES: For those who like to fly, there is an airstrip on site.

LOCATION: Driving north on Highway 99 from Modesto, take the Farmington Road exit, Highway 4, and head east. The course is on the left-hand side.

20. J.B. GOLF COURSE

939 Larkspur Drive
Livermore, CA 94550

PRO SHOP: 925-455-5695

Les Edwards, Manager
Mulkh Raj, Superintendent

Driving Range ●
Practice Greens ●
Clubhouse ●
Food / Beverage ●
Accommodations
Pull Carts ●
Power Carts ●
Club Rental ●
$pecial Offers

	1	2	3	4	5	6	7	8	9	OUT
BACK	-	-	-	-	-	-	-	-	-	-
REGULAR	472	190	355	202	353	90	285	355	467	2769
par	5	3	4	3	4	3	4	4	5	35
handicap	6	8	2	4	12	13	16	10	14	-
FORWARD	411	149	318	190	343	76	276	343	457	2563
par	5	3	4	3	4	3	4	4	5	35
handicap	10	16	8	12	4	18	14	6	2	-

	10	11	12	13	14	15	16	17	18	IN
BACK	-	-	-	-	-	-	-	-	-	-
REGULAR	473	209	428	202	386	122	298	364	480	2962
par	5	3	4	3	4	3	4	4	5	35
handicap	5	7	1	3	11	17	15	9	13	-
FORWARD	472	190	355	202	353	90	285	355	467	2769
par	5	3	4	3	4	3	4	4	5	35
handicap	1	15	7	11	3	17	13	5	9	-

BACK	
yardage	-
par	-
rating	-
slope	-

REGULAR	
yardage	5731
par	70
rating	67.1
slope	114

FORWARD	
yardage	5332
par	70
rating	70.1
slope	112

917 Clubhouse Drive
Livermore, CA 94550

PRO SHOP: 925-443-3122
OFFICE: 925-455-7820

Dan Lippstreu, Director of Golf, PGA
Mulkh Raj, Superintendent

Driving Range ●
Practice Greens ●
Clubhouse ●
Food / Beverage ●
Accommodations
Pull Carts ●
Power Carts ●
Club Rental ●
$pecial Offers

	1	2	3	4	5	6	7	8	9	OUT
BACK	375	520	154	394	350	562	191	391	432	3369
REGULAR	367	494	145	377	334	549	163	363	418	3210
par	4	5	3	4	4	5	3	4	4	36
handicap	5	13	17	9	3	11	15	7	1	-
FORWARD	304	461	105	282	281	492	111	287	329	2652
par	4	5	3	4	4	5	3	4	4	36
handicap	9	7	17	13	11	3	15	5	1	-

	10	11	12	13	14	15	16	17	18	IN
BACK	349	165	347	588	434	190	412	347	524	3356
REGULAR	340	156	338	558	396	172	370	336	501	3167
par	4	3	4	5	4	3	4	4	5	36
handicap	8	16	12	6	4	14	2	18	10	-
FORWARD	265	130	285	449	351	106	317	255	460	2618
par	4	5	3	4	4	5	3	4	4	36
handicap	6	14	12	10	4	18	8	16	2	-

BACK	
yardage	6725
par	72
rating	72.1
slope	127

REGULAR	
yardage	6377
par	72
rating	70.8
slope	123

FORWARD	
yardage	5270
par	72
rating	70.1
slope	120

PLAY POLICY & FEES: Green fees are $14 for nine holes and $22 for 18 holes on weekdays and $16 for nine holes and $25 for 18 holes on weekends. Carts are $22 for 18 holes. The course is closed Christmas Day.

TEE TIMES: Reservations can be booked seven days in advance.

DRESS CODE: Shirts must be worn.

COURSE DESCRIPTION: This short course is well maintained, with water on two holes, undulating greens, and two long par 3s of 190 and 202 yards. This is a test for golfers of all abilities. The third hole is perhaps the most memorable, with a large palm tree and bunker next to the par-4 green.

LOCATION: From Interstate 580 in Livermore, take the Springtown Boulevard exit north. Turn right on Bluebell, which turns into Larkspur Drive.

. . . ● **TOURNAMENTS:** There is a 100-player minimum for shotgun tournaments and 24-player minimum for regular tournaments.

21. SPRINGTOWN GOLF COURSE

PLAY POLICY & FEES: Green fees for residents of Livermore are $15 for nine holes and $24 for 18 holes weekdays, and $18 for nine holes and $31 for 18 holes weekends. Nonresident green fees are $16 for nine holes and $26 for 18 holes weekdays, and $24 for nine holes and $36 for 18 holes weekends. Carts are $24. The course is closed Christmas.

TEE TIMES: Reservations can be booked seven days in advance beginning at 5 a.m.

COURSE DESCRIPTION: This level, tree-lined course has four lakes and a creek that come into play on seven holes. The greens are large and the fairways are wide and lush. The par-4 fifth hole doglegs around a lake and tempts long hitters to go for the green on the tee shot. But with a carry of at least 235 yards—good luck. Las Positas also has an executive course with four par 4s.

NOTES: The executive course is 2,034 yards from the back tees and 1,537 yards from the forward tees. The course is neither rated nor sloped.

LOCATION: Driving east on Interstate 580 at Livermore, exit on Airway Boulevard. This course is located near the Livermore Airport on the south side of the street.

. . . ● **TOURNAMENTS:** Shotgun tournaments are available weekdays only. A 16-player minimum is required to book an event. Tournaments should be scheduled 12 months in advance. A banquet facility is available that can accommodate 150 people.

22. LAS POSITAS GOLF COURSE

㉓ BRENTWOOD COUNTRY CLUB
ARCHITECT: TED ROBINSON, 1994

1740 Balfour Road
Brentwood, CA 94513

PRO SHOP: 925-516-3400

Steve Caulkins, PGA Professional
Nancy Caulkins, Tournament Director
Mark Condos, Superintendent

Driving Range ●
Practice Greens ●
Clubhouse
Food / Beverage ●
Accommodations
Pull Carts
Power Carts ●
Club Rental ●
Special Offers

	1	2	3	4	5	6	7	8	9	OUT
BACK	369	297	344	356	166	533	176	529	354	3124
REGULAR	369	297	344	356	166	533	176	529	354	3124
par	4	4	4	4	3	5	3	5	4	36
handicap	3	17	15	13	7	1	11	5	9	-
FORWARD	302	256	303	305	121	451	136	454	287	2615
par	4	4	4	4	3	5	3	5	4	36
handicap	5	13	9	11	15	1	17	3	7	-

	10	11	12	13	14	15	16	17	18	IN
BACK	516	221	393	518	379	552	292	190	424	3485
REGULAR	498	194	371	490	351	529	278	176	386	3273
par	5	3	4	5	4	5	4	3	4	37
handicap	16	8	6	4	12	10	18	14	2	-
FORWARD	440	135	293	426	279	465	250	144	322	2754
par	5	3	4	5	4	5	4	3	4	37
handicap	8	14	10	6	12	2	18	16	4	-

BACK	
yardage	6609
par	73
rating	
slope	132

REGULAR	
yardage	6397
par	73
rating	
slope	120

FORWARD	
yardage	5369
par	73
rating	
slope	128

㉔ OLD RIVER GOLF COURSE
ARCHITECT: HIRAM SIBLEY, 1999

18007 MacArthur
Tracy, CA 95376

PRO SHOP: 209-830-8585

Curtis Matsuno, Head Professional

Driving Range ●
Practice Greens ●
Clubhouse
Food / Beverage ●
Accommodations
Pull Carts ●
Power Carts ●
Club Rental
Special Offers

	1	2	3	4	5	6	7	8	9	OUT
BACK	339	347	357	386	153	373	142	504	503	3104
REGULAR	329	333	323	376	138	346	132	474	471	2922
par	4	4	4	4	3	4	3	5	5	36
handicap	5	6	4	2	3	8	1	7	9	-
FORWARD	307	316	295	354	121	326	118	474	471	2782
par	4	4	4	4	3	4	3	5	5	36
handicap	8	4	5	2	3	6	1	7	9	-

	10	11	12	13	14	15	16	17	18	IN
BACK										
REGULAR										
par										
handicap										-
FORWARD										
par										
handicap										-

BACK	
yardage	3104
par	36
rating	
slope	

REGULAR	
yardage	2922
par	36
rating	
slope	

FORWARD	
yardage	2782
par	36
rating	
slope	

PLAY POLICY & FEES: Green fees for 18 holes are $45 from Monday through Thursday and $60 from Friday through Sunday and holidays, including cart. Carts are mandatory. Green fees for the executive course are $12 Monday through Thursday, $14 Friday through Sunday and holidays.

TEE TIMES: Tee times can be booked three days in advance.

DRESS CODE: Appropriate golf attire and nonmetal spikes are required.

COURSE DESCRIPTION: The 18-hole course is long, level, and has water on several holes. The greens are large and challenging. The trees are mostly small and immature.

NOTES: Brentwood also features a nine-hole executive course.

LOCATION: From Livermore take Interstate 580 to the Vasco Road exit. Take Vasco Road to Balfour Road. Turn left on Balfour and drive to the course clubhouse on the left.

. . . ● **TOURNAMENTS:** This course is available for outside tournaments.

23. BRENTWOOD COUNTRY CLUB

PLAY POLICY & FEES: Green fees for nine holes are $12 weekdays and $14 on weekends. Green fees for 18 holes are $20 weekdays and $22 on weekends. Carts are $10 per nine holes.

TEE TIMES: Reservations can be made seven days in advance for nonresidents and nine days in advance for residents of Tracy.

DRESS CODE: Casual attire is OK, but nonmetal spikes are required.

COURSE DESCRIPTION: Old River Course has water coming into play on eight of nine holes. The course lets golfers use their creativity when approaching the green, giving them several different options. The greens are undulating, and water comes into play on eight of nine holes.

NOTES: The course will eventually expand to 18 holes.

LOCATION: From Stockton take Interstate 5 south to Highway 205 west. Exit at MacArthur Road and head north for 2.3 miles. The course is on the left.

. . . ● **TOURNAMENTS:** A 16-player minimum is required to book an event. Shotgun tournaments are allowed.

24. OLD RIVER GOLF COURSE

POPPY RIDGE GOLF COURSE
ARCHITECT: REES JONES, 1996

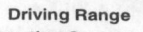

4280 Greenville Road
Livermore, CA 94550

PRO SHOP: 925-447-6779

Rick Hickman, Director of Golf, PGA
Kevin Earl, Head Professional, PGA

Driving Range ●
Practice Greens ●
Clubhouse ●
Food / Beverage ●
Accommodations
Pull Carts
Power Carts ●
Club Rental ●
$pecial Offers

	1	2	3	4	5	6	7	8	9	OUT
BACK	415	170	368	421	518	426	422	151	505	3396
REGULAR	397	131	349	394	487	404	404	131	490	3187
par	4	3	4	4	5	4	4	3	5	36
handicap	4	8	7	2	6	1	3	9	5	-
FORWARD	279	96	268	315	436	336	345	111	419	2605
par	4	3	4	4	5	4	4	3	5	36
handicap	6	9	7	5	2	4	3	8	1	-

	10	11	12	13	14	15	16	17	18	IN
BACK	381	277	193	363	565	425	162	421	503	3290
REGULAR	345	261	171	345	534	404	141	394	477	3072
par	4	4	3	4	5	4	3	4	5	36
handicap	4	8	7	6	3	2	9	1	5	-
FORWARD	264	229	137	282	461	323	124	368	419	2607
par	4	4	3	4	5	4	3	4	5	36
handicap	3	6	8	7	2	5	9	4	1	-

BACK	
yardage	6686
par	72
rating	72.4
slope	131

REGULAR	
yardage	6259
par	72
rating	70.4
slope	124

FORWARD	
yardage	5212
par	72
rating	70.3
slope	120

 # THE COURSE AT WENTE VINEYARDS
ARCHITECT: GREG NORMAN, 1998

5050 Arroyo Road
Livermore, CA 94550

PRO SHOP: 925-456-2475

George Price, Director of Golf, PGA

Driving Range ●
Practice Greens ●
Clubhouse ●
Food / Beverage ●
Accommodations
Pull Carts
Power Carts ●
Club Rental ●
$pecial Offers

	1	2	3	4	5	6	7	8	9	OUT
BACK	426	307	138	388	526	351	228	600	467	3431
REGULAR	402	279	121	341	479	293	182	542	405	3044
par	4	4	3	4	5	4	3	5	4	36
handicap	7	15	17	11	13	9	5	3	1	-
FORWARD	300	254	101	289	419	240	122	429	315	2469
par	4	4	3	4	5	4	3	5	4	36
handicap	9	15	17	7	11	5	13	3	1	-

	10	11	12	13	14	15	16	17	18	IN
BACK	302	170	564	420	174	554	407	453	474	3518
REGULAR	278	157	542	375	147	499	372	405	416	3191
par	4	3	5	4	3	5	4	4	4	36
handicap	18	16	6	10	12	14	8	4	2	-
FORWARD	216	120	413	302	112	423	286	319	315	2506
par	4	3	5	4	3	5	4	4	4	36
handicap	16	14	6	8	18	12	10	4	2	-

BACK	
yardage	6949
par	72
rating	74.5
slope	142

REGULAR	
yardage	6235
par	72
rating	71.3
slope	130

FORWARD	
yardage	4975
par	72
rating	69.4
slope	122

PLAY POLICY & FEES: Outside play is welcome. If you are a member of the NCGA, green fees are $35 Monday through Thursday and $40 Friday through Sunday and holidays. Guests of members are $45 Monday through Thursday and $55 Friday through Sunday and holidays. Nonmember green fees are $55 Monday through Thursday and $70 Friday through Sunday and holidays. Seasonal twilight rates are available. Carts are $24.

TEE TIMES: Reservations can be booked 30 days in advance. To make automated tee times call 925-455-2035.

DRESS CODE: Collared shirts are required, and nonmetal spikes are mandatory.

COURSE DESCRIPTION: This facility, the second built by the Northern California Golf Association (the first was Poppy Hills), is a links-style golf course. Greens are open in front, allowing players to run the ball onto the putting surfaces. There is only one tree on the site, but several lakes and sidehill lies will test the skills of every golfer.

LOCATION: From Livermore take Interstate 580 to the Greenville Road exit. Take Greenville Road five miles south to the course.

. . . ● **TOURNAMENTS:** Outside events need board approval. Carts are required.

25. POPPY RIDGE GOLF COURSE

---

wentegolf.com

PLAY POLICY & FEES: Green fees are $80 Monday through Thursday and $100 Friday through Sunday. Green fees include range balls and carts.

TEE TIMES: Reservations can be made 30 days in advance and are recommended.

DRESS CODE: Nonmetal spikes are required.

COURSE DESCRIPTION: This challenging course allows golfers a chance to play every shot in their bags—and maybe a few in someone else's. The excellent use of land, varied terrain, and well-thought-out design make this one of the more interesting and demanding new courses in Northern California.

LOCATION: From San Jose take Interstate 680 north. Take the Livermore/Highway 84 exit east. Drive 7.7 miles to the first stoplight. Take a right on Concannon Road and another right on Arroyo Road. The course will be on the left.

. . . ● **TOURNAMENTS:** Outside events are allowed. A 20-player minimum is needed to book a tournament. Events should be scheduled 12 months in advance. The banquet facility holds up to 144 people. ● **TRAVEL:** The Purple Orchid Bed & Breakfast (925-606-8855), Residence Inn (800-331-3131), and Holiday Inn (925-443-4950) are recommended for lodging.

26. THE COURSE AT WENTE VINEYARDS

---

305 North Union Road
Manteca, CA 95337

PRO SHOP: 209-825-2500

Alan Thomas, PGA Professional

Driving Range •
Practice Greens •
Clubhouse •
Food / Beverage •
Accommodations
Pull Carts •
Power Carts •
Club Rental •
$pecial Offers

	1	2	3	4	5	6	7	8	9	OUT
BACK	528	283	442	504	177	346	339	145	522	3286
REGULAR	519	276	414	485	174	336	324	129	513	3170
par	5	4	4	5	3	4	4	3	5	37
handicap	5	15	1	17	3	9	11	13	7	-
FORWARD	512	262	393	457	165	312	299	101	480	2981
par	5	4	4	5	3	4	4	3	5	37
handicap	1	13	7	5	15	9	11	17	3	-

	10	11	12	13	14	15	16	17	18	IN
BACK	394	433	297	484	176	407	394	174	421	3180
REGULAR	384	430	294	477	170	402	389	168	413	3127
par	4	4	4	5	3	4	4	3	4	35
handicap	12	2	10	18	16	8	6	14	4	-
FORWARD	309	377	287	451	136	366	327	132	373	2758
par	4	4	4	5	3	4	4	3	4	35
handicap	12	4	14	2	16	8	10	18	6	-

BACK	
yardage	6466
par	72
rating	70.7
slope	119

REGULAR	
yardage	6297
par	72
rating	69.9
slope	117

FORWARD	
yardage	5739
par	72
rating	72.1
slope	115

1500 Ruess Rd.
Ripon, CA 95366

PRO SHOP: 209-599-2973

George Buzzini, Manager
Tim Buzzini, Professional
Jacob Perez, Superintendent

Driving Range •
Practice Greens •
Clubhouse
Food / Beverage
Accommodations
Pull Carts •
Power Carts •
Club Rental •
$pecial Offers

	1	2	3	4	5	6	7	8	9	OUT
BACK	321	132	451	111	157	117	148	86	332	1855
REGULAR	302	127	437	100	151	105	140	80	302	1744
par	4	3	5	3	3	3	3	3	4	31
handicap	3	7	1	11	9	15	13	17	5	-
FORWARD	290	115	403	94	142	98	132	72	290	1636
par	4	3	5	3	3	3	3	3	4	31
handicap	3	7	1	11	9	15	13	17	5	-

	10	11	12	13	14	15	16	17	18	IN
BACK	328	142	123	90	254	102	285	127	387	1838
REGULAR	317	130	114	85	242	92	274	123	368	1745
par	4	3	3	3	4	3	4	3	4	31
handicap	2	18	12	16	8	14	6	10	4	-
FORWARD	305	119	105	77	232	85	265	108	338	1634
par	4	3	3	3	4	3	4	3	4	31
handicap	2	18	12	16	8	14	6	10	4	-

BACK	
yardage	3693
par	62
rating	
slope	

REGULAR	
yardage	3489
par	62
rating	
slope	

FORWARD	
yardage	3270
par	62
rating	
slope	

PLAY POLICY & FEES: Green fees are $15 weekdays and $18 weekends for residents of Manteca. Fees for nonresidents are $18 weekdays and $24 weekends. Nine-hole rates are $12 weekdays and $14 weekends. Carts are $22 weekdays and $24 weekends.

TEE TIMES: Reservations can be booked seven days in advance with a credit card.

COURSE DESCRIPTION: A magnificent clubhouse makes this municipal course seem like a country club. The golf course is both fun and demanding. The 11th hole is probably the most difficult hole, a 430-yard par 4 that used to be a par 5. The 18th hole is an excellent finisher, a long dogleg of 413 yards, and the par 3s offer variety. The 17th is a tough, 168 yarder to a sloping, bunkered green.

NOTES: Pat Biocini and Kevin Wentworth share the course record of 65.

LOCATION: The course is located in Manteca off Highway 120 between Interstate 5 and Highway 99. From Highway 120, take the Union Road exit heading north. The course is on the left, past Center Street.

. . . ● **TOURNAMENTS:** This course is available for outside tournaments. A banquet facility is available that holds 160 people.

27. MANTECA GOLF COURSE

PLAY POLICY & FEES: Green fees are $15 weekdays, and $17 weekends for 18 holes. Twilight, senior and junior rates are available.

TEE TIMES: Reservations are taken Monday for the upcoming week.

DRESS CODE: No tank tops are allowed on the course. Nonmetal spikes are required.

COURSE DESCRIPTION: Jack Tone is an executive golf course featuring 11 par 3's, sand traps around the greens, and one water hazard. The third hole is a tricky 450-yard par 5 with out-of-bounds areas on the left and traps surrounding the green.

LOCATION: From Manteca drive south on Highway 99. Take the Jack Tone Road exit and turn right. Follow Jack Tone Road until it dead-ends. Turn right and make the first left to the course.

. . . ● **TOURNAMENTS:** This course is available for outside events.

28. JACK TONE GOLF COURSE

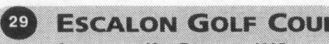

29 ESCALON GOLF COURSE
ARCHITECT: KEN ROBERTS, 1985

17051 South
Escalon, CA 95320

PRO SHOP: 209-838-1277

John DeFilippi, Professional
Lorie Hagan, Tournament Director
Tom Hagen, Owner/Superintendent

Driving Range ●
Practice Greens ●
Clubhouse ●
Food / Beverage ●
Accommodations
Pull Carts ●
Power Carts
Club Rental ●
$Special Offers

	1	2	3	4	5	6	7	8	9	OUT
BACK	-	-	-	-	-	-	-	-	-	-
REGULAR	185	80	70	190	195	175	250	220	165	1530
par	4	3	3	4	3	3	4	4	3	31
handicap	-	-	-	-	-	-	-	-	-	-
FORWARD	185	80	70	190	195	175	250	220	165	1530
par	4	3	3	4	3	3	4	4	3	31
handicap	-	-	-	-	-	-	-	-	-	-

	10	11	12	13	14	15	16	17	18	IN
BACK	-	-	-	-	-	-	-	-	-	-
REGULAR	185	80	70	190	195	175	250	220	165	1530
par	4	3	3	4	3	3	4	4	3	31
handicap	-	-	-	-	-	-	-	-	-	-
FORWARD	185	80	70	190	195	175	250	220	165	1530
par	4	3	3	4	3	3	4	4	3	31
handicap	-	-	-	-	-	-	-	-	-	-

BACK	
yardage	-
par	-
rating	-
slope	-

REGULAR	
yardage	3060
par	62
rating	59.6
slope	67

FORWARD	
yardage	3060
par	62
rating	59.6
slope	67

30 SPRING CREEK GOLF & COUNTRY CLUB
ARCHITECT: JACK FLEMING, 1976

P.O. Box 535
Ripon, CA 95366

16436 E. Spring Creek
Ripon, CA 95366

PRO SHOP: 209-599-3630
CLUBHOUSE: 209-599-3258

Greg Sabens, Manager
Jim Toal, Head Professional, PGA
David Piper, Superintendent

Driving Range ●
Practice Greens ●
Clubhouse ●
Food / Beverage ●
Accommodations
Pull Carts ●
Power Carts ●
Club Rental ●
$Special Offers

	1	2	3	4	5	6	7	8	9	OUT
BACK	474	394	391	383	183	289	154	482	453	3203
REGULAR	461	384	381	373	169	280	142	456	432	3078
par	5	4	4	4	3	4	3	5	4	36
handicap	11	3	7	5	13	17	15	9	1	-
FORWARD	436	339	376	363	144	220	126	429	420	2853
par	5	4	4	4	3	4	3	5	5	37
handicap	11	9	7	1	13	17	15	5	3	-

	10	11	12	13	14	15	16	17	18	IN
BACK	382	365	147	524	318	161	393	493	394	3177
REGULAR	369	355	137	506	312	152	377	473	385	3066
par	4	4	3	5	4	3	4	5	4	36
handicap	6	8	18	10	14	16	2	12	4	-
FORWARD	340	299	120	465	299	130	342	440	338	2773
par	4	4	3	5	4	3	4	5	4	36
handicap	10	12	18	4	14	16	2	8	6	-

BACK	
yardage	6380
par	72
rating	70.6
slope	121

REGULAR	
yardage	6144
par	72
rating	69.5
slope	119

FORWARD	
yardage	5626
par	73
rating	75.0
slope	128

PLAY POLICY & FEES: Green fees are $5 for nine holes and $9 for 18 holes weekdays, and $5.50 for nine holes and $10 for 18 holes weekends.

TEE TIMES: Reservations can be made at any time.

COURSE DESCRIPTION: This short course is flat and has one pond. There are four par-4 and five par-3 holes. It is easy to walk and is particularly popular among seniors.

NOTES: The course record is 25 for nine holes.

LOCATION: From Highway 99 take the Mariposa exit east. Drive about 15 miles through Collegeville (Mariposa Road turns into Escalon-Bellota Road). The course is on the right.

. . . ● **TOURNAMENTS:** This course is available for outside tournaments.

29. ESCALON GOLF COURSE

PLAY POLICY & FEES: Reciprocal play is accepted with members of other private clubs. Reciprocal fees match those of the visitor's home club. Guest fees are $30 when accompanied by a member and $45 when unaccompanied. Carts are $20. This course is closed on Monday.

TEE TIMES: Have your club pro call for arrangements after 2 p.m.

DRESS CODE: Appropriate golf attire and nonmetal spikes are required.

COURSE DESCRIPTION: This flat course is tight with lots of oak trees, two of which are stationed in the middle of narrow fairways. The ninth hole is a notable par 4 that crosses water. At 432 yards, it places a premium on accuracy.

NOTES: The men's course record is 64, held jointly by Ron Brown and Robert Warren. The women's course record is 68, held by Keri Arnold-Cusenza.

LOCATION: From Highway 99 in Ripon (north of Modesto) take the Ripon exit to the east side of the freeway. Drive two miles to Spring Creek Drive and the course.

. . . ● **TOURNAMENTS:** This course is available for outside tournaments on Monday only. An 80-player minimum is needed to book an event. Tournaments should be scheduled five months in advance. The banquet facility can accommodate up to 175 people. ● **TRAVEL:** The Best Western Mallards Inn is located 15 minutes from the golf course. For reservations call 209-577-3825.

30. SPRING CREEK GOLF & COUNTRY CLUB

DEL RIO COUNTRY CLUB
ARCHITECTS: WILLIAM P. BELL, 1947; P ASCUZZO & GRAVES, 1996; JOHN HARBOTTLE, 1999

801 Stewart Road
Modesto, CA 95356

PRO SHOP: 209-545-0013
CLUBHOUSE: 206-545-0723

Duncan Reno, Manager
Glenn Mahler, Professional
Brian Ash, Superintendent

Driving Range ●
Practice Greens ●
Clubhouse ●
Food / Beverage ●
Accommodations
Pull Carts ●
Power Carts ●
Club Rental ●
$pecial Offers

	1	2	3	4	5	6	7	8	9	OUT
BACK	387	190	465	546	361	367	478	195	472	3461
REGULAR	374	182	455	536	350	337	462	182	464	3342
par	4	3	4	5	4	4	5	3	4	36
handicap	7	5	1	4	3	6	9	8	2	-
FORWARD	359	151	387	455	340	327	452	173	351	2995
par	4	3	4	5	4	4	5	3	4	36
handicap	5	9	1	4	6	7	3	8	2	-

	10	11	12	13	14	15	16	17	18	IN
BACK	509	141	374	392	416	572	411	180	406	3401
REGULAR	496	135	344	384	406	566	401	161	394	3287
par	5	3	4	4	4	5	4	3	4	36
handicap	7	9	6	5	2	3	1	8	4	-
FORWARD	471	125	314	364	377	506	368	151	366	3042
par	5	3	4	4	4	5	4	3	4	36
handicap	6	9	5	7	1	2	4	8	3	-

BACK	
yardage	6862
par	72
rating	72.9
slope	126

REGULAR	
yardage	6629
par	72
rating	71.8
slope	124

FORWARD	
yardage	6037
par	72
rating	76.5
slope	131

  TRACY GOLF & COUNTRY CLUB
ARCHITECT: ROBERT TRENT JONES SR., 1956

35200 South Chrisman
Tracy, CA 95376

PRO SHOP: 209-835-9463

Frank Elston, PGA Professional
Ron Carney, Superintendent

Driving Range ●
Practice Greens ●
Clubhouse ●
Food / Beverage ●
Accommodations
Pull Carts ●
Power Carts ●
Club Rental ●
$pecial Offers

	1	2	3	4	5	6	7	8	9	OUT
BACK	429	330	305	200	497	174	406	526	454	3321
REGULAR	413	319	297	185	485	160	374	482	409	3124
par	4	4	4	3	5	3	4	5	4	36
handicap	1	9	17	5	15	13	7	11	3	-
FORWARD	406	259	275	148	485	113	369	435	394	2884
par	5	4	4	3	5	3	4	5	4	37
handicap	9	13	11	15	1	17	3	5	7	-

	10	11	12	13	14	15	16	17	18	IN
BACK	353	140	386	156	551	465	321	394	532	3298
REGULAR	339	134	378	146	523	441	304	323	515	3103
par	4	3	4	3	5	4	4	4	5	36
handicap	14	16	4	12	8	2	18	6	10	-
FORWARD	322	128	360	130	472	404	298	282	492	2888
par	4	3	4	3	5	4	4	4	5	37
handicap	8	16	4	18	6	14	12	10	2	-

BACK	
yardage	6619
par	72
rating	70.7
slope	118

REGULAR	
yardage	6227
par	72
rating	69.5
slope	115

FORWARD	
yardage	5772
par	74
rating	72.7
slope	125

PLAY POLICY & FEES: Reciprocal play with members of other private clubs is accepted on Tuesday, Thursday, and Friday. The fee is $75 for reciprocal play. Guest fees are $30 with a member and $40 weekends. No play is allowed without a member. Carts are $20. The course is closed on Monday.

TEE TIMES: Have your club professional call for tee times.

DRESS CODE: Appropriate golf attire and nonmetal spikes are required.

COURSE DESCRIPTION: This course was designed in 1926 by William Park Bell. It's a challenging, rolling country course that demands good shot placement. The greens are fast, undulating, and have subtle breaks. This is a classic layout from the old school of golf course architecture.

NOTES: The new nine-hole River Course has been completed. The course is 3,467 yards long from the back tees. In 1999 John Harbottle renovated the greens on the original 18 holes, using William P. Bell's original design.

LOCATION: From Highway 99 in Modesto take the Salida exit onto Kerinin Avenue north. Turn left at Dale Road and follow it to the "T." Turn right on Ladd, drive one mile to Saint John, and go left up to the club.

. . . ● **TOURNAMENTS:** This course is available for limited outside tournaments. A 100-player minimum is needed to book a tournament. Tournaments can be booked up to a year in advance. The banquet facility can accommodate 250 people.

31. DEL RIO COUNTRY CLUB

PLAY POLICY & FEES: Reciprocal play is accepted with members of other private clubs. Reciprocal rates are $30 weekdays, $40 weekends (including cart). Guest fees are $25 when accompanied by a member. Carts are $16.

TEE TIMES: Have your club pro call ahead for arrangements.

DRESS CODE: Collared shirts are required.

COURSE DESCRIPTION: This flat course has rolling terrain, fast, elevated greens, four ponds, and numerous bunkers. The original nine holes were designed by Robert Trent Jones Sr. The front nine is tight, while the newer back side is more wide open. The first hole is a monster, 429 yards into the wind. The par-5 fifth hole (497 yards) is an excellent hole as well. All out-of-bounds areas are on the left, so big hooks are deadly.

NOTES: Steve Moreland holds the course record at 63.

LOCATION: From Interstate 580 take the Chrisman Road exit. The course is located next to the highway.

. . . ● **TOURNAMENTS:** Shotgun starts are available weekdays only. Carts are mandatory for tournament play.

32. TRACY GOLF & COUNTRY CLUB

400 Tuolumne Boulevard
Modesto, CA 95351

PRO SHOP: 209-577-5360

Sue Fiscoe, Director of Golf, PGA
Mike Roberson, PGA Professional
Chris Mendez, PGA Professional

Driving Range
Practice Greens ●
Clubhouse ●
Food / Beverage ●
Accommodations
Pull Carts ●
Power Carts ●
Club Rental ●
$pecial Offers

	1	2	3	4	5	6	7	8	9	OUT
BACK										
REGULAR										
par										
handicap										
FORWARD										
par										
handicap										

	10	11	12	13	14	15	16	17	18	IN
BACK										
REGULAR										
par										
handicap										
FORWARD										
par										
handicap										

BACK	
yardage	
par	
rating	-
slope	-

REGULAR	
yardage	6074
par	70
rating	68.2
slope	113

FORWARD	
yardage	5868
par	70
rating	72.0
slope	112

920 Sunset Boulevard
Modesto, CA 95351

PRO SHOP: 209-577-5359

Sue Fiscoe, Director of Golf, PGA
Mike Roberson, PGA Professional
Chris Mendez, PGA Professional

Driving Range ●
Practice Greens ●
Clubhouse ●
Food / Beverage ●
Accommodations
Pull Carts ●
Power Carts ●
Club Rental ●
$pecial Offers

	1	2	3	4	5	6	7	8	9	OUT
BACK										
REGULAR										
par										
handicap										
FORWARD										
par										
handicap										

	10	11	12	13	14	15	16	17	18	IN
BACK										
REGULAR										
par										
handicap										
FORWARD										
par										
handicap										

BACK	
yardage	6514
par	72
rating	69.8
slope	119

REGULAR	
yardage	6214
par	72
rating	68.3
slope	116

FORWARD	
yardage	5910
par	72
rating	72.5
slope	115

PLAY POLICY & FEES: Green fees are $10 for nine holes weekdays and $12 for nine holes on weekends. Carts are $10 for nine holes and $20 for 18 holes. Afternoon, twilight, senior and junior rates are available.

TEE TIMES: Reservations can be booked seven days in advance. For tee times call 209-491-4653.

DRESS CODE: A six-inch inseam on shorts is required, and shoes are mandatory.

COURSE DESCRIPTION: This course is walkable and fairly flat. The fairways are narrow, and the trees are mature. The ninth is considered one of the top holes in the area. At 424 yards it's a par-4 dogleg right with out-of-bounds on the right and trees on both sides. You can't see the green from the tee, but there is a bunker to the left front and a cart path to the right. The green will hold well-struck shots. This is one of the better nine-hole layouts around.

LOCATION: On Highway 99 off Tuolumne Boulevard, take the B Street off-ramp and make a right at the stop sign. Drive one-half block on Neece Drive and stay left along the river to the course.

. . . ● **TOURNAMENTS:** A 28-player minimum is needed to book a tournament.

33. MODESTO MUNICIPAL GOLF COURSE

PLAY POLICY & FEES: Green fees are $16 weekdays and $22 weekends. The twilight rate is $12. Carts are $10 for nine holes and $20 for 18 holes.

TEE TIMES: Reservations can be booked seven days in advance by calling the tee-time reservations number at 209-491-4653.

DRESS CODE: A six-inch inseam on shorts is required. Collared shirts and shoes are mandatory.

COURSE DESCRIPTION: The Tuolumne River runs adjacent to this course. The front nine is flat, and the back nine is somewhat hilly. Numerous pine trees make Dryden a nice test despite its relatively modest length.

NOTES: Dryden Park has a lighted golf range. The course record is 64.

LOCATION: This course is located right off Highway 99 in Modesto. Take the Tuolumne Boulevard/B Street exit and make a right on Tuolumne.

. . . ● **TOURNAMENTS:** A 28-player minimum is needed to book a tournament. Events should be scheduled at least six tmonths in advance. The banquet facility can accommodate 80 people. ● **TRAVEL:** The Doubletree Hotel is located five minutes from the golf course. For reservations call 209-526-6000.

34. DRYDEN PARK GOLF COURSE

RIVER OAKS GOLF COURSE
ARCHITECT: JIM D. PHIPPS, 1979

P.O. Box 97
Ceres, CA 95307

3441 East Hatch Road
Ceres, CA 95307

PRO SHOP: 209-537-4653

Robert Phipps, Director of Golf, PGA
Linda Collins-Maurer, LPGA Professional
Greg Silva, PGA Professional

Driving Range ●
Practice Greens ●
Clubhouse
Food / Beverage ●
Accommodations
Pull Carts ●
Power Carts
Club Rental ●
$pecial Offers

	1	2	3	4	5	6	7	8	9	OUT
BACK	-	-	-	-	-	-	-	-	-	-
REGULAR	128	171	110	136	94	133	103	133	111	1119
par	3	3	3	3	3	3	3	3	3	27
handicap	10	2	12	4	18	6	16	8	14	-
FORWARD	108	160	105	127	85	122	95	125	100	1027
par	3	3	3	3	3	3	3	3	3	27
handicap	10	2	12	4	18	6	16	8	14	-

	10	11	12	13	14	15	16	17	18	IN
BACK	-	-	-	-	-	-	-	-	-	-
REGULAR	266	135	356	103	173	252	86	113	252	1736
par	4	3	4	3	3	4	3	3	4	31
handicap	5	7	1	17	3	11	15	13	9	-
FORWARD	250	125	348	105	165	230	80	85	225	1613
par	4	3	4	3	3	4	3	3	4	31
handicap	5	7	1	17	3	11	15	13	9	-

BACK	
yardage	-
par	-
rating	-
slope	-

REGULAR	
yardage	2855
par	58
rating	52.7
slope	74

FORWARD	
yardage	2640
par	58
rating	54.3
slope	-

 MODESTO CREEKSIDE GOLF COURSE
ARCHITECT: STEVE HALSEY, 1991

701 Lincoln Avenue
Modesto, CA 95354

PRO SHOP: 209-571-5123

Sue Fiscoe, Director of Golf, PGA
Larry Alvarado, Head Professional, PGA

Driving Range ●
Practice Greens ●
Clubhouse
Food / Beverage ●
Accommodations
Pull Carts ●
Power Carts ●
Club Rental ●
$pecial Offers

	1	2	3	4	5	6	7	8	9	OUT
BACK										
REGULAR										
par										
handicap										
FORWARD										
par										
handicap										

	10	11	12	13	14	15	16	17	18	IN
BACK										
REGULAR										
par										
handicap										
FORWARD										
par										
handicap										

BACK	
yardage	6610
par	72
rating	71.2
slope	117

REGULAR	
yardage	6021
par	72
rating	68.5
slope	

FORWARD	
yardage	5496
par	72
rating	69.5
slope	108

PLAY POLICY & FEES: Green fees are $11 weekdays and $14 weekends and holidays.

TEE TIMES: Reservations can be booked seven days in advance.

DRESS CODE: Appropriate golf attire is required. Nonmetal spikes would be appreciated.

COURSE DESCRIPTION: This tree-lined course runs along the Tuolumne River. It has some ponds and no bunkers. The front nine is all par 3s, while the back nine has four short par 4s, the longest (the 12th) measuring 349 yards.

NOTES: River Oaks has a junior golf program that enrolls over 500 kids each summer.

LOCATION: From Modesto drive south on Highway 99. Take the Hatch Road exit east. The course is located on the left past Mitchell Road.

. . . ● **TOURNAMENTS:** An 80-player minimum is needed to book a shotgun tournament.

35. RIVER OAKS GOLF COURSE

PLAY POLICY & FEES: Green fees are $18 weekdays and $25 weekends. Twilight and super-twilight rates are available. Carts are $20.

TEE TIMES: Reservations can be booked seven days in advance. For tee times call 209-491-4653.

DRESS CODE: A six-inch inseam on shorts is required, and shoes are mandatory.

COURSE DESCRIPTION: This course, opened in 1991, is relatively flat, with two holes playing into the creekside. Three ponds come into play on six holes. There are also several two-tiered greens. Once the trees mature, this course will be demonstrably tougher. The par-4 18th hole is 392 yards from the white tees, with water on both sides of the fairway.

LOCATION: From Highway 99 in Modesto take Highway 132 to Lincoln Avenue. Turn left on Lincoln and follow it to the course.

. . . ● **TOURNAMENTS:** A 28-player minimum is needed to book a tournament.

36. MODESTO CREEKSIDE GOLF COURSE

DIABLO GRANDE GOLF CLUB
ARCHITECT: DENNIS GRIFFITHS, 1996

P.O. Box 655
Patterson, CA 95363

10001 Oak Flat Road
Patterson, CA 95363

PRO SHOP: 209-892-4653

Shane Balfour, PGA Professional
John Silveira, Tournament Director

Driving Range ●
Practice Greens ●
Clubhouse ●
Food / Beverage ●
Accommodations
Pull Carts
Power Carts ●
Club Rental ●
$pecial Offers

	1	2	3	4	5	6	7	8	9	OUT
BACK	369	384	369	156	545	383	209	449	509	3373
REGULAR	339	344	352	149	519	354	192	376	491	3116
par	4	4	4	3	5	4	3	4	5	36
handicap	17	5	3	13	9	15	7	1	11	-
FORWARD	223	290	313	130	446	304	148	305	416	2575
par	4	4	4	3	5	4	3	4	5	36
handicap	17	5	3	13	9	15	7	1	11	-

	10	11	12	13	14	15	16	17	18	IN
BACK	402	180	621	375	461	444	517	130	412	3542
REGULAR	379	161	583	352	414	397	472	118	386	3262
par	4	3	5	4	4	4	5	3	4	36
handicap	10	12	4	16	2	6	14	18	8	-
FORWARD	296	136	254	304	327	336	404	65	329	2451
par	4	3	4	4	4	4	5	3	4	35
handicap	10	12	4	16	2	6	14	18	8	-

BACK	
yardage	6915
par	72
rating	73.5
slope	134

REGULAR	
yardage	6378
par	72
rating	71.4
slope	127

FORWARD	
yardage	5026
par	71
rating	69.5
slope	120

 # STEVINSON RANCH GOLF CLUB
ARCHITECT: JOHN HARBOTTLE, GEORGE H. KELLEY, 1995

P.O. Box 96
Stevinson, CA 95374

2700 North Van Clief Road

PRO SHOP: 209-668-8200

George Kelley, Bob Lurie, Owners
Ken Campbell, General Manager
Jeff Yost, Head Professional

Driving Range ●
Practice Greens ●
Clubhouse ●
Food / Beverage ●
Accommodations
Pull Carts ●
Power Carts ●
Club Rental ●
$pecial Offers ●

	1	2	3	4	5	6	7	8	9	OUT
BACK	575	454	388	179	446	511	204	338	464	3559
REGULAR	541	431	369	148	422	486	192	315	437	3341
par	5	4	4	3	4	5	3	4	4	36
handicap	5	7	15	13	3	17	9	11	1	-
FORWARD	474	356	304	110	367	433	116	256	387	2803
par	5	4	4	3	4	5	3	4	4	36
handicap	5	7	17	9	1	11	15	13	3	-

	10	11	12	13	14	15	16	17	18	IN
BACK	449	513	155	417	334	437	236	420	540	3501
REGULAR	429	503	142	387	306	423	205	398	512	3305
par	4	5	3	4	4	4	3	4	5	36
handicap	6	16	18	10	14	4	12	2	8	-
FORWARD	340	413	90	326	233	348	137	342	429	2658
par	4	5	3	4	4	4	3	4	5	36
handicap	6	14	18	10	16	2	12	4	8	-

BACK	
yardage	7060
par	72
rating	73.9
slope	137

REGULAR	
yardage	6646
par	72
rating	72.0
slope	130

FORWARD	
yardage	5461
par	72
rating	71.9
slope	124

PLAY POLICY & FEES: Green fees for the Ranch Course are $65 Monday through Thursday and $80 Friday through Sunday and holidays. Twilight rates are available. The Legends West Course is $85 Monday through Thursday and $100 Friday through Sunday and holidays. A 36-hole rate to play both courses is $100 Monday through Thursday and $150 Friday through Sunday. Twilight rates are not available. All prices include carts.

TEE TIMES: Reservations can be booked seven days in advance.

DRESS CODE: Collared shirts and nonmetal spikes are encouraged. Slacks or Bermuda-type shorts are preferred.

COURSE DESCRIPTION: Amid the rolling terrain of western Stanislaus County, the Ranch Course rolls through 400-year-old oak trees with the beautiful Salado Creek meandering throughout. On the Ranch Course each hole is named after a breed of horse. Sounds peaceful, but beware of the par-5 12th Mustang Hole. If the length doesn't stop you from going for it in two, the thought of hitting in the ravine that lies in wait should. Take your par and move on. The Legends West Course is just as scenic and well designed, but easier.

NOTES: Legends West is the first-ever design collaboration between Gene Sarazen and Jack Nicklaus. From the blue tees the course is 6,680 yards long, and from the women's tees the course is 4,905 yards long.

LOCATION: Traveling north on Interstate 5, take the Crows Landing Road exit east and turn left onto Ward Avenue. Head north on Ward about two miles until you reach Oak Flat Road. Turn left and go six miles to the course.

. . . ● **TOURNAMENTS:** A 24-player minimum is needed to book a tournament.

37. DIABLO GRANDE GOLF CLUB

PLAY POLICY & FEES: Green fees are $35 Monday through Thursday, $45 Friday, and $60 Saturday and Sunday.

TEE TIMES: Reservations can be booked 60 days in advance with a credit card.

DRESS CODE: Collared shirts and nonmetal spikes are mandatory. No tank tops or cutoffs are allowed.

COURSE DESCRIPTION: Former San Francisco Giants owner Bob Lurie is a partner in this John Harbottle design. The course has a links feel and is characterized by large tees and greens, and distinctive bunkering. Greens have extended collars, giving golfers the option of chipping or putting. One of the more spectacular holes is the 179-yard, par-3 fourth over a lake.

NOTES: If you like awards, this is the club for you. "Golf Digest" gave the course a four-star rating in 1998 and was included in that magazine's 1997 top-25 listing of the best courses in California. The facility has added a new western-style restaurant.

LOCATION: From Turlock drive south on Highway 99 to the Lander Avenue/Highway 165 exit. Drive south 10 miles to Stevinson. At the center of Stevinson take a left on Third Avenue. Proceed one mile east to the entrance of the course.

. . . ● **TOURNAMENTS:** This course is available for outside tournaments. A 16-player minimum is needed. ● **TRAVEL:** Twenty on-site cottages have just been completed. The cottages can be used for meetings or overnight accommodations . A conference facility is available. ● $**PECIAL OFFERS:** Stay-and-play packages are available. For more information call 888-606-7529

38. STEVINSON RANCH GOLF CLUB

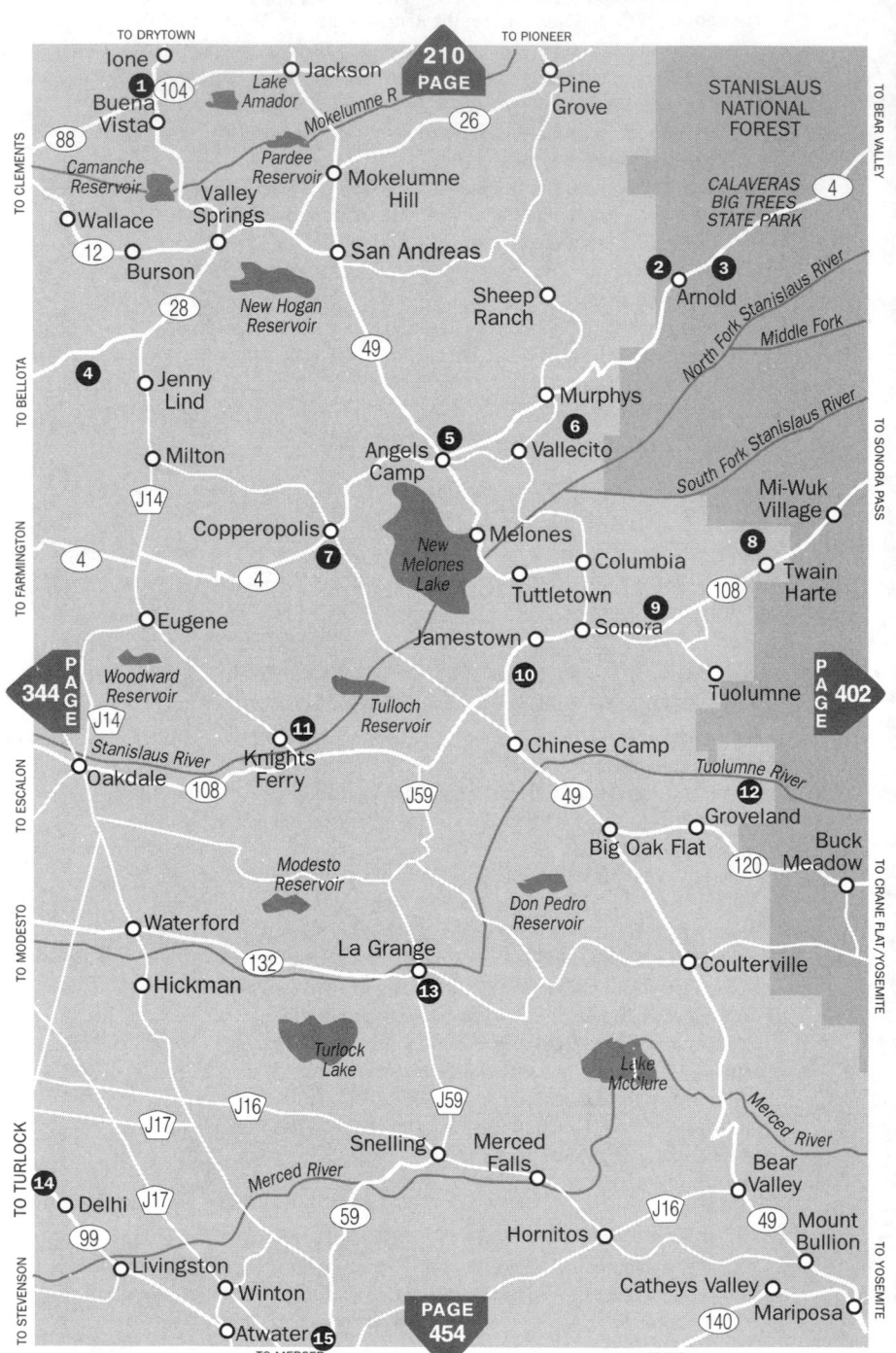

TO DRYTOWN   TO PIONEER

210 PAGE

STANISLAUS NATIONAL FOREST

TO BEAR VALLEY

Ione
104
Jackson
Lake Amador
Pine Grove

Buena Vista
88
Mokelumne R

CALAVERAS BIG TREES STATE PARK
4

TO CLEMENTS

Camanche Reservoir
Pardee Reservoir
Valley Springs
Mokelumne Hill

Wallace
12
Burson
San Andreas

② Arnold ❸

28
New Hogan Reservoir
Sheep Ranch

North Fork Stanislaus River

Middle Fork

TO BELLOTA

❹
Jenny Lind
49
Murphys

Milton
Angels Camp ❺
Vallecito ❻

South Fork Stanislaus River

TO SONORA PASS

J14
Mi-Wuk Village

TO FARMINGTON

4
Copperopolis
❼
New Melones Lake
Melones
Columbia
❽
Twain Harte

4
Tuttletown
108

Eugene
Jamestown
Sonora ❾

PAGE 344
Woodward Reservoir
Tulloch Reservoir

J14
Stanislaus River
Knights Ferry ⑪

⑩
Tuolumne

PAGE 402

TO ESCALON

Oakdale
108

Chinese Camp
Tuolumne River

J59
49
Groveland ⑫

TO CRANE FLAT/YOSEMITE

Modesto Reservoir
Big Oak Flat
120
Buck Meadow

TO MODESTO

Waterford
Don Pedro Reservoir

Hickman
132
La Grange
Coulterville

⑬

Turlock Lake
Lake McClure

Merced River

TO TURLOCK

J17
J16
J59

Snelling
Merced Falls
Bear Valley

⑭
Merced River
J16
49
Mount Bullion

Delhi
J17

99
Hornitos

Livingston

Winton
Catheys Valley

Atwater ⑮
140
Mariposa

PAGE 454

TO STEVENSON
TO MERCED   TO MERCED

TO YOSEMITE

Central Valley Area

① CASTLE OAKS GOLF CLUB
ARCHITECT: BRADFORD BENZ, 1994

P.O. Box 1368
Ione, CA 95640

1000 Castle Oaks Drive
Ione, CA 95640

PRO SHOP: 209-274-0167

Hal Ingram, Director of Golf
Dominic Atlan, PGA Professional
Mike Lahmann, Superintendent

Driving Range ●
Practice Greens ●
Clubhouse
Food / Beverage ●
Accommodations
Pull Carts ●
Power Carts ●
Club Rental ●
$pecial Offers ●

	1	2	3	4	5	6	7	8	9	OUT
BACK	577	215	420	370	529	369	424	195	394	3493
REGULAR	554	178	400	352	500	355	402	181	373	3295
par	5	3	4	4	5	4	4	3	4	36
handicap	3	11	5	15	7	17	1	13	9	-
FORWARD	452	121	319	286	410	279	324	125	293	2609
par	5	3	4	4	5	4	4	3	4	36
handicap	3	11	5	15	7	17	1	13	9	-

	10	11	12	13	14	15	16	17	18	IN
BACK	416	173	355	535	342	410	155	422	438	3246
REGULAR	387	157	332	521	321	382	145	400	416	3061
par	4	3	4	5	4	4	3	4	4	35
handicap	8	18	12	10	14	6	16	2	4	-
FORWARD	300	76	253	424	243	292	94	338	324	2344
par	4	3	4	5	4	4	3	4	4	35
handicap	8	18	12	10	14	6	16	2	4	-

BACK	
yardage	6739
par	71
rating	72.7
slope	131

REGULAR	
yardage	6356
par	71
rating	70.8
slope	127

FORWARD	
yardage	4953
par	71
rating	67.3
slope	114

② MEADOWMONT GOLF COURSE
ARCHITECT: DICK FRY, 1962

Highway 4 and Country
Arnold, CA 95223

P.O. Box 586
Arnold, CA 95223

PRO SHOP: 209-795-1313

Jim Dillashaw, Director of Golf, PGA

Driving Range
Practice Greens ●
Clubhouse
Food / Beverage ●
Accommodations ●
Pull Carts ●
Power Carts ●
Club Rental ●
$pecial Offers

	1	2	3	4	5	6	7	8	9	OUT
BACK	-	-	-	-	-	-	-	-	-	-
REGULAR	307	258	437	453	354	416	317	140	249	2931
par	4	4	4	5	4	4	4	3	4	36
handicap	17	15	1	11	3	5	7	13	9	-
FORWARD	286	242	428	371	341	419	302	126	157	2672
par	4	4	5	4	4	5	4	3	3	36
handicap	9	11	1	3	5	7	13	17	15	-

	10	11	12	13	14	15	16	17	18	IN
BACK	-	-	-	-	-	-	-	-	-	-
REGULAR	304	250	437	458	352	416	312	134	230	2893
par	4	4	4	5	4	4	4	3	4	36
handicap	18	16	2	12	4	6	8	14	10	-
FORWARD	304	250	437	458	352	416	312	134	230	2893
par	4	4	4	5	4	4	4	3	4	36
handicap	10	14	4	2	8	6	12	18	16	-

BACK	
yardage	-
par	-
rating	-
slope	-

REGULAR	
yardage	5824
par	72
rating	67.6
slope	113

FORWARD	
yardage	5565
par	72
rating	71.0
slope	114

PLAY POLICY & FEES: Green fees are $35 for 18 holes Monday through Thursday, $39 on Friday, and $45 on Saturday and Sunday, carts included. Twilight rates are available. Senior rates are also available.

TEE TIMES: Reservations can be booked seven days in advance.

DRESS CODE: Collared shirts are required. No tank tops, short shorts, or halter tops allowed on the course.

COURSE DESCRIPTION: Rolling hills, water, and strategically-placed oak trees characterize this new course. There are few flat lies and several elevated greens. The premium is on accuracy, not length. The par-4 finishing hole, measuring 438 yards from the back tees, is one of the best in Northern California. The dogleg left features a split fairway—the safe right side or the shorter left side, an island fairway surrounded by water. The left side shortens the hole, but it requires a 200-yard carry.

LOCATION: From Sacramento take Highway 16 to Ione Road. Turn right on Ione Road and go to Highway 104. Turn left at Highway 104 and continue 2.2 miles to the course entrance.

. . . ● **TOURNAMENTS:** Shotgun tournaments are available weekdays only. A 16-player minimum is needed for a regular tournament. Tournaments can be booked up to 12 months in advance. ● **TRAVEL:** The Ione Hotel is located two minutes from the golf course. For reservations call 209-274-6082. ● **$PECIAL OFFERS:** The renovated historic hotel offers play-and-stay packages that include upgraded rooms, green fees, carts, and dinner.

1. CASTLE OAKS GOLF CLUB

PLAY POLICY & FEES: Green fees are $12.50 for nine holes and $18.75 for 18 holes weekdays, and $15.50 for nine holes and $23 for 18 holes weekends. Carts are $12 for nine holes and $20 for 18 holes. Senior and twilight rates are available. Meadowmont is generally open from March through November.

TEE TIMES: Reservations can be booked 14 days in advance.

COURSE DESCRIPTION: This flat course is narrow, thanks to the forest of pine trees lining each fairway. The greens are small, and Rae's Creek—no relation to the more famous Rae's Creek of Augusta National fame—runs through the entire course. The fifth hole (354 yards) is an absolute beauty, with out-of-bounds left and a lake right. The green is tucked into the pines.

NOTES: Gary Plato holds the course record of 64.

LOCATION: From Highway 99 drive 70 miles east on Highway 4 past Murphys to Arnold. The course is on the left.

. . . ● **TOURNAMENTS:** A 24-player minimum is required to book a tournament. ● **TRAVEL:** The Yellow Dog Inn is recommended. For reservations or more information call 209-795-1980.

2. MEADOWMONT GOLF COURSE

SEQUOIA WOODS COUNTRY CLUB
ARCHITECT: BOB BALDOCK, 1976

P.O. Box 930
Arnold, CA 95223

1000 Cypress Point Drive
Arnold, CA 95223

PRO SHOP: 209-795-2141
OFFICE: 209-795-2141

Larry Babica, General Manager, PGA
Rob Cobb, Superintendent
Lynne Babica, Banquet Manager

Driving Range ●
Practice Greens ●
Clubhouse ●
Food / Beverage ●
Accommodations
Pull Carts ●
Power Carts ●
Club Rental ●
$pecial Offers

	1	2	3	4	5	6	7	8	9	OUT
BACK	397	405	254	480	384	527	167	304	537	3455
REGULAR	387	396	243	466	369	433	155	291	529	3269
par	4	4	4	5	4	5	3	4	5	38
handicap	3	7	17	9	11	1	13	15	5	-
FORWARD	376	388	226	402	354	419	139	274	520	3098
par	4	4	4	5	4	5	3	4	5	38
handicap	7	5	17	9	11	3	13	15	1	-

	10	11	12	13	14	15	16	17	18	IN
BACK	165	195	304	297	252	165	250	82	399	2109
REGULAR	119	175	290	281	243	160	216	78	375	1937
par	3	3	4	4	4	3	4	3	4	32
handicap	8	4	14	12	6	10	16	18	2	-
FORWARD	107	173	278	267	235	152	205	73	352	1842
par	3	3	4	4	4	3	4	3	4	32
handicap	16	6	12	14	8	4	10	18	2	-

BACK	
yardage	5564
par	70
rating	67.3
slope	114

REGULAR	
yardage	5206
par	70
rating	65.8
slope	111

FORWARD	
yardage	4940
par	70
rating	67.8
slope	111

 LA CONTENTA GOLF CLUB
ARCHITECT: RICHARD BIGLER, 1973

P.O. Box 249
Valley Springs, CA 95252

1653 Highway 26
Valley Springs, CA 95252

PRO SHOP: 209-772-1081

Marty Davis, Manager, PGA
Cliff Rourke, Superintendent

Driving Range
Practice Greens ●
Clubhouse ●
Food / Beverage ●
Accommodations ●
Pull Carts ●
Power Carts ●
Club Rental ●
$pecial Offers

	1	2	3	4	5	6	7	8	9	OUT
BACK	440	175	485	215	315	350	475	210	410	3075
REGULAR	370	160	465	185	285	305	455	165	380	2770
par	4	3	5	3	4	4	5	3	4	35
handicap	7	17	3	9	15	11	5	13	1	-
FORWARD	335	120	440	150	235	255	380	110	335	2360
par	4	3	5	3	4	4	4	3	4	34
handicap	5	15	1	13	11	9	3	17	7	-

	10	11	12	13	14	15	16	17	18	IN
BACK	420	405	340	185	460	350	415	315	460	3350
REGULAR	380	375	315	165	440	325	390	300	435	3125
par	4	4	4	3	5	4	4	4	4	36
handicap	8	14	10	12	6	16	4	18	2	-
FORWARD	365	315	265	105	410	260	385	250	405	2760
par	4	4	4	3	5	4	4	4	5	37
handicap	8	10	12	18	2	14	6	16	4	-

BACK	
yardage	6425
par	71
rating	70.2
slope	125

REGULAR	
yardage	5895
par	71
rating	68.4
slope	123

FORWARD	
yardage	5120
par	71
rating	70.8
slope	120

PLAY POLICY & FEES: Reciprocal play is accepted with members of other private clubs. Guest fees are $30 weekdays and $50 weekends with a member. Reciprocal fees are $35 weekdays and $50 weekends. Nine-hole and twilight rates are available.

DRESS CODE: Appropriate golf attire is required. Nonmetal spikes are encouraged.

COURSE DESCRIPTION: This sprawling, mountain course is tougher than the rating indicates. The front nine is situated in a spacious meadow and is long and open. Trade the woods for irons on the back nine because it gets narrow and steep. Out-of-bounds run along both sides of the fairways. Par is 38 on the front side, with the par-5 sixth hole measuring 527 yards uphill. The sixth hole doglegs right around a creek and offers no room for error off the tee.

NOTES: Club member John Trench shot a record 62 in 1984.

LOCATION: From Highway 99 drive east on Highway 4 to Arnold. Exit right on Blue Lake Springs and follow the signs to the club. The course is a 90-minute drive from Stockton.

. . . ● **TOURNAMENTS:** This course is available for outside tournaments. A 24-player minimum is needed. Events can be booked one month in advance. A banquet facility is available that can accommodate 120 people. An outdoor deck area accommodates 200 people. ● **TRAVEL:** The Yellow Dog Inn is only 10 minutes from Sequoia Woods. For reservations or more information call 209-795-1980.

3. SEQUOIA WOODS COUNTRY CLUB

PLAY POLICY & FEES: Green fees are $21 Monday through Thursday, $25 Friday, and $33 weekends and holidays. Carts are $22. Twilight rates are also available. The course is closed Christmas Day.

TEE TIMES: Reservations can be booked 14 days in advance.

DRESS CODE: No tank tops, halter tops, or short shorts are allowed.

COURSE DESCRIPTION: Set in the rolling foothills 35 miles east of Stockton, this tight, hilly course challenges a player with out-of-bounds areas on 14 holes and water on nine. The trademark hole is the 13th, a par 3 that drops 100 feet from the tee to an L-shaped green almost completely surrounded by water. Be ready to hit plenty of blind shots as well as approaches from sidehill lies, but La Contenta is in excellent shape and affords outstanding vistas on virtually every hole.

LOCATION: From Highway 99 in Stockton, take the Fremont (Highway 26) exit east. Drive 28 miles on Highway 26 to the course on the right.

. . . ● **TOURNAMENTS:** A 16-player minimum is required to book a tournament. Events should be scheduled 12 months in advance. The banquet facility can accommodate up to 200 people. ● **TRAVEL:** The 10th Green Inn is located behind the 10th green. For reservations call 209-772-1084.

4. LA CONTENTA GOLF CLUB

ARCHITECT: DON BOOS, 1996

P.O. Box 1419   676 McCauley Ranch
Angels Camp, CA 95222   Angels Camp, CA 95222

PRO SHOP: 209-736-8110

Tim J. Hovancsek, PGA Professional
Scott Bowers, Superintendent

Driving Range ●
Practice Greens ●
Clubhouse ●
Food / Beverage ●
Accommodations ●
Pull Carts
Power Carts ●
Club Rental ●
$pecial Offers ●

	1	2	3	4	5	6	7	8	9	OUT
BACK	369	339	129	481	362	175	507	180	473	3015
REGULAR	343	295	95	455	343	135	468	156	445	2735
par	4	4	3	5	4	3	5	3	5	36
handicap	12	14	18	10	2	6	8	16	4	-
FORWARD	323	261	86	441	310	97	432	138	409	2497
par	4	4	3	5	4	3	5	3	5	36
handicap	10	12	14	2	8	18	6	16	4	-

	10	11	12	13	14	15	16	17	18	IN
BACK	563	425	327	136	421	157	313	405	451	3198
REGULAR	526	396	293	121	397	130	286	388	427	2964
par	5	4	4	3	4	3	4	4	5	36
handicap	1	9	11	17	3	15	13	5	7	-
FORWARD	496	367	265	113	364	105	258	346	403	2717
par	5	4	4	3	4	3	4	4	5	36
handicap	1	5	11	15	7	17	13	9	3	-

BACK	
yardage	6213
par	72
rating	70.0
slope	124

REGULAR	
yardage	5699
par	72
rating	67.3
slope	119

FORWARD	
yardage	5214
par	72
rating	70.1
slope	119

ARCHITECT: ROBERT TRENT JONES JR., 1971

633 Forest Meadows Drive
Murphys, CA 95247

PRO SHOP: 209-728-3439
CLUBHOUSE: 209-728-3440

Norby Wilson, PGA Professional
Curtis Johnson, Superintendent

Driving Range
Practice Greens
Clubhouse ●
Food / Beverage ●
Accommodations
Pull Carts ●
Power Carts ●
Club Rental ●
$pecial Offers

	1	2	3	4	5	6	7	8	9	OUT
BACK	-	-	-	-	-	-	-	-	-	-
REGULAR	509	139	184	333	191	157	132	172	207	2024
par	5	3	3	4	3	3	3	3	3	30
handicap	1	15	11	3	5	13	17	9	7	-
FORWARD	485	107	151	305	144	125	92	118	151	1678
par	5	3	3	4	3	3	3	3	3	30
handicap	1	15	5	3	7	11	17	13	9	-

	10	11	12	13	14	15	16	17	18	IN
BACK	-	-	-	-	-	-	-	-	-	-
REGULAR	351	119	120	130	102	195	366	149	330	1862
par	4	3	3	3	3	3	4	3	4	30
handicap	4	12	18	14	16	8	2	10	6	-
FORWARD	318	90	84	108	77	141	318	112	295	1543
par	4	3	3	3	3	3	4	3	4	30
handicap	4	14	16	12	18	8	2	10	6	-

BACK	
yardage	-
par	-
rating	-
slope	-

REGULAR	
yardage	3886
par	60
rating	58.3
slope	95

FORWARD	
yardage	3221
par	60
rating	58.0
slope	90

PLAY POLICY & FEES: Green fees are $38 Monday through Thursday and $53 Friday through Sunday and holidays. Junior, twilight, and nine-hole rates are available. Carts are $12 per person for 18 holes.

TEE TIMES: Reservations can be booked seven days in advance.

DRESS CODE: Collared shirts and nonmetal spikes are mandatory. No denim is allowed on the course.

COURSE DESCRIPTION: Greenhorn Creek is a hidden gem in a serene setting with gently rolling fairways surrounded by oaks, pines, ponds, creeks, and excellent greens. Do not let the surroundings fool you—this course is no walk in the park. Although several tees boxes accommodate players for all skill levels, better golfers will find this a course that is taxing on the brain and scorecard for those who can't manage their game. A driver on many holes is not a good option as the oak trees, ponds, creeks, and out-of bounds come into play.

NOTES: Historical landmarks from the Gold Rush are incorporated into the course.

LOCATION: From Highway 99 between Modesto and Stockton take Highway 4 east. The course is on the corner of Highway 4 and Highway 49.

. . . ● **TOURNAMENTS:** A 20-player minimum is needed to book a tournament. Carts are required. Tournaments can be booked 12 months in advance. ● **TRAVEL:** On-site cottages are available. ● **$PECIAL OFFERS:** Play-and-stay packages are available Monday through Thursday. Call 800-736-6203.

5. GREENHORN CREEK

PLAY POLICY & FEES: Green fees are $15 for nine holes and $25 for 18 holes on weekdays. Weekend green fees are $20 for nine holes and $30 for 18 holes. Carts are $15 for nine holes and $22 for 18 holes. Winter play is subject to weather conditions.

TEE TIMES: Reservations can be booked 14 days in advance.

DRESS CODE: Shirts and shoes are required. No short shorts may be worn. Nonmetal spikes are preferred.

COURSE DESCRIPTION: This is a beautiful Sierra Nevada course traversed by the Stanislaus River canyon. Situated at 3,500 feet, its panoramic layout mixes aesthetics and serious play, offering a challenge to low and high handicappers alike. Known for its excellent, fast greens, the course places a premium on putting.

NOTES: Mike Lane, a former Northern California Golf Association points champion, holds the course record with a 51.

LOCATION: From Highway 99 drive east on Highway 4 to Murphys. The course is about 3.5 miles east of Murphys on Highway 4.

. . . ● **TOURNAMENTS:** A 72-player minimum is required for shotgun tournaments and a 20-player minimum for regular tournaments. Carts are required.

6. FOREST MEADOWS GOLF COURSE

SADDLE CREEK GOLF CLUB
ARCHITECT: CARTER MORRISH, 1996

1001 Saddle Creek Drive
Copperopolis, CA 95228

PRO SHOP: 209-785-3700

Billy Graham, PGA Professional
Rich Reynolds, Tournament Director, PGA
Chris Weaver, Superintendent

Driving Range	●
Practice Greens	●
Clubhouse	
Food / Beverage	●
Accommodations	●
Pull Carts	
Power Carts	●
Club Rental	●
$pecial Offers	●

	1	2	3	4	5	6	7	8	9	OUT
BACK	397	433	477	206	377	417	153	519	390	3369
REGULAR	329	396	437	169	322	379	132	485	355	3004
par	4	4	5	3	4	4	3	5	4	36
handicap	13	3	11	7	15	1	17	5	9	-
FORWARD	239	278	359	102	249	278	97	374	239	2215
par	4	4	5	3	4	4	3	5	4	36
handicap	13	3	11	7	15	1	17	5	9	-

	10	11	12	13	14	15	16	17	18	IN
BACK	422	150	338	556	245	370	444	399	535	3459
REGULAR	368	127	307	488	187	343	399	353	473	3045
par	4	3	4	5	3	4	4	4	5	36
handicap	6	18	14	2	8	16	4	12	10	-
FORWARD	271	88	223	424	123	241	283	265	355	2273
par	4	3	4	5	3	4	4	4	5	36
handicap	6	18	14	2	8	16	4	12	10	-

BACK	
yardage	6828
par	72
rating	73.0
slope	134

REGULAR	
yardage	6049
par	72
rating	69.4
slope	125

FORWARD	
yardage	4488
par	72
rating	65.4
slope	111

7. SADDLE CREEK GOLF CLUB

PLAY POLICY & FEES: Members receive priority for tee times, but public play is accepted. Green fees are $47 Monday through Thursday and $62 Friday through Sunday and holidays. Carts are $13 per person and optional but must remain on the cart path at all times. This is strictly enforced and there are no exceptions.

TEE TIMES: Reservations can be booked 14 days in advance without a fee, up to 60 days in advance for a fee. Call 888-852-5787 for reservations.

DRESS CODE: Appropriate golf attire and nonmetal spikes are required.

COURSE DESCRIPTION: This scenic, traditional-style course is characterized by rolling terrain, mature oak trees, ponds, lakes, and natural wetlands. The goal was to blend the course and land together naturally, and the owners succeeded. Water comes into play on eight holes.The layout is well balanced, enabling golfers to use every club in their bag, and five sets of tees provide a challenging course for players of all skill levels.

NOTES: This is the home course of the Northern California PGA. Saddle Creek was ranked the seventh best upscale public access course in the country by "Golf Digest." A clubhouse is scheduled to open November 1999.

LOCATION: From Stockton take Highway 4 east to Copperopolis and Obyrnes Ferry Road. Turn right and follow the signs to the course. From Oakdale take Highway 108/120 east to Obyrnes Ferry Road. Turn left and follow the signs to the course.

. . . ● **TOURNAMENTS:** A 20-player minimum is required to book an event. Tournaments should be booked 12 months in advance. The banquet facility holds 300 people. Call for special winter rates. ● **TRAVEL:** The Lake Tulloch Resort is located minutes away from the course. For reservations call 888-785-8200 or visit their website at www.tullochresort.com ● **$PECIAL OFFERS:** Stay-and-play golf packages are available with Lake Tulloch Resort and other Gold Country Properties. Package rates vary by season. Call the pro shop for information.

⑧ TWAIN HARTE GOLF & COUNTRY CLUB

ARCHITECTS: BOB BALDOCK, 1961; ROBERT PUTMAN

22909 Meadow Lane
Twain Harte, CA   95383

PRO SHOP: 209-586-3131

Derek Claveran, Professional/Manager
Rich Garrison, Superintendent

Driving Range
Practice Greens ●
Clubhouse ●
Food / Beverage ●
Accommodations
Pull Carts ●
Power Carts ●
Club Rental ●
$pecial Offers

	1	2	3	4	5	6	7	8	9	OUT
BACK										
REGULAR										
par										
handicap										
FORWARD										
par										
handicap										

	10	11	12	13	14	15	16	17	18	IN
BACK										
REGULAR										
par										
handicap										
FORWARD										
par										
handicap										

BACK	
yardage	1718
par	29
rating	57.1
slope	88

REGULAR	
yardage	1663
par	29
rating	56.4
slope	87

FORWARD	
yardage	1716
par	29
rating	59.7
slope	92

⑨ PHOENIX LAKE GOLF COURSE

ARCHITECT: BERT STAMPS, 1968

21448 Paseo de Los
Sonora, CA   95370

PRO SHOP: 209-532-0111

Jeff Christensen, Director of Golf, PGA
Dan Bacci, Professional

Driving Range ●
Practice Greens
Clubhouse ●
Food / Beverage ●
Accommodations
Pull Carts ●
Power Carts ●
Club Rental ●
$pecial Offers

	1	2	3	4	5	6	7	8	9	OUT
BACK	-	-	-	-	-	-	-	-	-	-
REGULAR	520	361	177	438	329	231	254	141	290	2741
par	5	4	3	5	4	3	4	3	4	35
handicap	3	1	9	11	7	5	17	13	15	-
FORWARD	510	274	119	335	329	224	254	103	272	2420
par	5	4	3	4	4	4	4	3	4	35
handicap	1	7	15	3	5	13	11	17	9	-

	10	11	12	13	14	15	16	17	18	IN
BACK	-	-	-	-	-	-	-	-	-	-
REGULAR	515	340	167	428	384	187	250	133	276	2680
par	5	4	3	5	4	3	4	3	4	35
handicap	4	6	8	10	2	12	18	14	16	-
FORWARD	506	282	113	400	373	182	250	96	263	2465
par	5	4	3	5	4	3	4	3	4	35
handicap	2	8	16	4	6	14	12	18	10	-

BACK	
yardage	-
par	-
rating	-
slope	-

REGULAR	
yardage	5421
par	70
rating	66.4
slope	115

FORWARD	
yardage	4885
par	70
rating	67.8
slope	114

PLAY POLICY & FEES: Green fees are $10 for nine holes and $15 for 18 holes. Senior and junior rates are available.

TEE TIMES: Reservations can be booked seven days in advance.

DRESS CODE: Casual dress is acceptable.

COURSE DESCRIPTION: Plenty of trees make this executive course a challenge. There are two ponds. The best hole is the seventh, a par 3 where the player is hitting to an elevated green with a large bunker in front. This is an excellent course for beginners in a setting all players can enjoy.

LOCATION: From Highway 108 in Twain Harte (10 miles east of Sonora), turn left on Meadow Lane and follow it to the course.

. . . ● **TOURNAMENTS:** This course is available for outside tournaments.

PLAY POLICY & FEES: Green fees are $8 for nine holes and $12 for 18 holes weekdays, and $10 for nine holes and $14 for 18 holes weekends. Carts are $12 for nine holes and $20 for 18 holes.

TEE TIMES: Reservations can be booked 30 days in advance.

DRESS CODE: Shirts and shoes are required.

COURSE DESCRIPTION: The relatively short yardage of this course is deceptive because Phoenix Lake Golf Course is extremely narrow with pines and oaks lining the fairways. Only two holes run parallel to one another. Sullivan's Creek comes into play on five holes. The second hole (par 4,361 yards) requires a tee shot that carries 180 yards over the creek down a narrow fairway. The par-3 sixth hole is a bear, measuring 231 yards downhill.

LOCATION: From Highway 108 in Sonora, take the Phoenix Lake Road exit left. The course is on the left on Paseo de Los Portales, about three miles from Highway 108.

. . . ● **TOURNAMENTS:** This course is available for outside tournaments. ●
TRAVEL: The Best Western Sonora Oaks is 10 minutes from the golf course. For reservations call 209-533-4400.

⑩ MOUNTAIN SPRINGS GOLF COURSE
ARCHITECT: ROBERT MUIR GRAVES, 1990

17566 Lime Kiln Road
Sonora, CA 95370

PRO SHOP: 209-532-1000
CLUBHOUSE: 209-532-8278

Mike Cook, Director of Golf, PGA
Ty Abraham, Superintendent

Driving Range ●
Practice Greens ●
Clubhouse ●
Food / Beverage ●
Accommodations
Pull Carts
Power Carts ●
Club Rental ●
$pecial Offers

	1	2	3	4	5	6	7	8	9	OUT
BACK	360	370	330	380	180	515	185	425	545	3290
REGULAR	350	355	320	360	160	445	165	460	525	3140
par	4	4	4	4	3	5	3	4	5	36
handicap	13	9	17	7	15	3	11	1	5	-
FORWARD	270	310	300	305	100	335	110	330	445	2505
par	4	4	4	4	3	4	3	4	5	35
handicap	9	7	13	11	17	3	15	5	1	-

	10	11	12	13	14	15	16	17	18	IN
BACK	380	340	160	420	575	370	390	200	540	3375
REGULAR	365	320	135	400	550	360	370	170	520	3190
par	4	4	3	4	5	4	4	3	5	36
handicap	14	18	16	2	4	6	12	8	10	-
FORWARD	300	280	105	320	475	310	300	105	475	2670
par	4	4	3	4	5	4	4	3	5	36
handicap	6	10	18	8	4	12	14	16	2	-

BACK	
yardage	6665
par	72
rating	71.9
slope	128

REGULAR	
yardage	6330
par	72
rating	70.2
slope	125

FORWARD	
yardage	5175
par	71
rating	68.8
slope	114

⑪ OAKDALE GOLF & COUNTRY CLUB
ARCHITECT: BOB BALDOCK, 1961

243 North Stearns Road
Oakdale, CA 95361

PRO SHOP: 209-847-2924

Jay D. Ward, PGA Professional
Mike Olson, Superintendent

Driving Range ●
Practice Greens ●
Clubhouse ●
Food / Beverage ●
Accommodations
Pull Carts ●
Power Carts ●
Club Rental ●
$pecial Offers

	1	2	3	4	5	6	7	8	9	OUT
BACK										
REGULAR										
par										
handicap										
FORWARD										
par										
handicap										

	10	11	12	13	14	15	16	17	18	IN
BACK										
REGULAR										
par										
handicap										
FORWARD										
par										
handicap										

BACK	
yardage	6720
par	72
rating	72.5
slope	126

REGULAR	
yardage	6445
par	72
rating	71.2
slope	123

FORWARD	
yardage	5826
par	72
rating	67.5
slope	114

PLAY POLICY & FEES: Outside play is accepted. Green fees are $21 Monday through Thursday, $24 Friday, $32 on weekends. Senior, nine-hole green fees, and cart rates are available. Call for special golf package rates. Carts are $11 per rider.

TEE TIMES: Reservations can be booked 14 days in advance.

DRESS CODE: Collared shirts are required.

COURSE DESCRIPTION: This rolling layout is located in the heart of the gold country and offers sweeping vistas. Six lakes and 70 bunkers come into play. Scenic views are offered on the 1st, 5th, 10th, 15th, and 17th holes. The pride of the course is the 200-yard, par-3 17th hole across water.

LOCATION: Driving east on Highway 108 in Sonora, turn right on Lime Kiln Road. Drive 2.5 miles to the course entrance on the right.

. . . ● **TOURNAMENTS:** A 12-player minimum is needed to book a tournament. Tournaments should be booked 12 months in advance. The banquet facility can hold 140 people. ● **TRAVEL:** The Sonora Oaks Best Western is recommended for lodging. Call 800-533-1944 for reservations.

10. MOUNTAIN SPRINGS GOLF COURSE

PLAY POLICY & FEES: Reciprocal play is accepted with members of other private clubs. Guest fees are $30 weekdays and $35 weekends. Guests must be accompanied by a member. The green fees for reciprocators are $45. Carts are $13 for nine holes and $20 for 18 holes.

TEE TIMES: Have your club pro call in advance to make arrangements.

DRESS CODE: Appropriate golf attire and nonmetal spikes are required.

COURSE DESCRIPTION: Long and rolling, Oakdale Country Club is medium tight with average-sized greens. A number of the tees and greens are elevated. The par-3 ninth is 200 yards downhill to a well-bunkered green with water on the right. The fifth hole is a 600-yard par 5 that doglegs left with a large elevated green.

LOCATION: Driving east on Highway 108, turn left on Stearns Road. The course is located north of Oakdale.

. . . ● **TOURNAMENTS:** Outside events can be held Monday only with board approval.

11. OAKDALE GOLF & COUNTRY CLUB

PINE MOUNTAIN LAKE COUNTRY CLUB
ARCHITECT: WILLIAM F. BELL, 1969

19228 Pine Mountain Drive
Groveland, CA 95321

PRO SHOP: 209-962-8620
OFFICE: 209-962-8600

John Gray, Executive Manager
Chris Borrego, Head Professional, PGA
Reza Bahri, Club Manager

Driving Range ●
Practice Greens ●
Clubhouse ●
Food / Beverage ●
Accommodations
Pull Carts ●
Power Carts ●
Club Rental ●
$pecial Offers

	1	2	3	4	5	6	7	8	9	OUT
BACK	406	325	189	471	430	406	189	360	310	3086
REGULAR	378	317	184	466	408	403	169	342	302	2969
par	4	4	3	5	4	4	3	4	4	35
handicap	11	13	15	5	3	1	9	7	17	-
FORWARD	364	315	173	450	391	398	144	346	295	2876
par	4	4	3	5	4	5	3	4	4	36
handicap	9	5	17	1	3	7	15	11	13	-

	10	11	12	13	14	15	16	17	18	IN
BACK	429	489	396	372	168	320	525	185	381	3265
REGULAR	419	475	370	367	136	317	525	172	366	3147
par	4	4	4	4	3	4	5	3	4	35
handicap	8	2	12	10	18	14	1	16	6	-
FORWARD	417	410	364	331	127	305	439	158	343	2894
par	5	4	4	4	3	4	5	3	4	36
handicap	8	10	4	12	18	14	2	16	6	-

BACK	
yardage	6351
par	70
rating	70.6
slope	125

REGULAR	
yardage	6116
par	70
rating	69.5
slope	122

FORWARD	
yardage	5770
par	72
rating	73.4
slope	130

HIDDEN HILLS RESORT AND GOLF CLUB
ARCHITECT: WILLIAM F. BELL, 1970

7643 Fachada Way
La Grange, CA 95329

PRO SHOP: 209-852-2242

Kit Vaille, PGA Professional
Kit Vaille, Superintendent

Driving Range ●
Practice Greens ●
Clubhouse ●
Food / Beverage ●
Accommodations
Pull Carts ●
Power Carts ●
Club Rental ●
$pecial Offers

	1	2	3	4	5	6	7	8	9	OUT
BACK	367	470	365	351	185	343	246	533	315	3175
REGULAR	361	457	358	340	176	335	207	501	305	3040
par	4	5	4	4	3	4	3	5	4	36
handicap	7	17	5	11	13	9	3	1	15	-
FORWARD	311	450	325	326	145	321	154	480	300	2812
par	4	5	4	4	3	4	3	5	4	36
handicap	11	3	7	9	17	5	15	1	13	-

	10	11	12	13	14	15	16	17	18	IN
BACK	206	472	365	391	402	190	478	533	175	3212
REGULAR	194	462	350	384	392	176	469	522	156	3105
par	3	5	4	4	4	3	5	5	3	36
handicap	4	16	8	6	2	14	12	10	18	-
FORWARD	168	412	315	346	375	126	411	482	121	2756
par	3	5	4	4	4	3	5	5	3	36
handicap	14	8	12	10	6	16	4	2	18	-

BACK	
yardage	6387
par	72
rating	69.8
slope	120

REGULAR	
yardage	6145
par	72
rating	68.4
slope	118

FORWARD	
yardage	5568
par	72
rating	71.2
slope	112

PLAY POLICY & FEES: Outside play is welcome. Green fees for the public are $53, including cart.

TEE TIMES: Reservations are taken 14 days in advance for members and 10 days in advance for public play.

DRESS CODE: Appropriate golf attire and nonmetal spikes are required.

COURSE DESCRIPTION: Pine Mountain Lake is a hilly course set at 3,500 feet. The fairways are outlined by trees, and the greens are large, with pronounced undulation. Hitting the driver straight is the key to scoring well here. The par-4 11th hole measures an outrageous 475 yards. It plays shorter, however, due to a 75-foot drop in elevation.

NOTES: Steve Caulkins holds the course record at 62. In 1999 the clubhouse was remodeled and a new grill was built.

LOCATION: From Interstate 5 in Manteca take Highway 120 east to Groveland. The course is located north of Groveland on Mueller Drive.

. . . ● **TOURNAMENTS:** All tournaments must be approved by the golf professional. A 16-player minimum is needed to book a tournament. A banquet facility is available that can accommodate up to 200 people.

12. PINE MOUNTAIN LAKE COUNTRY CLUB

PLAY POLICY & FEES: Green fees are $15 Monday through Thursday and $25 Friday through Sunday and holidays. Carts are $24. The course is closed Thanksgiving and Christmas.

TEE TIMES: Reservations can be booked seven days in advance.

DRESS CODE: Collared shirts and nonmetal spikes are required. No torn or frayed jeans are allowed on the course.

COURSE DESCRIPTION: Ninety-nine percent of the players ride carts because the course is quite hilly. There are a lot of semiblind shots and even more sidehill, uphill, and downhill lies. The eighth hole is a par 5 that measures 533 yards from the blues and 480 from the reds, with two lakes to negotiate.

NOTES: Nearby accommodations are under construction.

LOCATION: From Highway 99 in Modesto drive 30 miles east on Highway 132 to La Grange. After six miles, exit on Hayward Road south and follow it a mile. Turn left on Ranchito (where the pavement ends) and follow it to the course.

. . . ● **TOURNAMENTS:** A 40-player minimum is required to book an event. Tournaments should be scheduled at least three months in advance. The banquet facility can accommodate up to 200 people.

13. HIDDEN HILLS RESORT AND GOLF CLUB

14 TURLOCK GOLF & COUNTRY CLUB

ARCHITECTS: ROBERT DEAN PUTMAN, 1959; ANDY RAUGUST, 1995

10532 Golf Links Road
Turlock, CA 95380

PRO SHOP: 209-634-4976

Michael Blevins, Manager
Nick Dimond, Head Professional, PGA
Kevin Friesen, Superintendent

Driving Range ●
Practice Greens ●
Clubhouse ●
Food / Beverage ●
Accommodations
Pull Carts ●
Power Carts ●
Club Rental
Special Offers

	1	2	3	4	5	6	7	8	9	OUT
BACK	424	492	431	202	509	436	179	379	286	3338
REGULAR	407	482	420	184	495	422	152	368	260	3190
par	4	5	4	3	5	4	3	4	4	36
handicap	3	9	1	13	11	5	15	7	17	-
FORWARD	384	449	410	171	483	358	124	311	228	2918
par	4	5	5	3	5	4	3	4	4	37
handicap	3	5	9	13	1	7	17	11	15	-

	10	11	12	13	14	15	16	17	18	IN
BACK	368	191	382	480	365	219	479	432	400	3316
REGULAR	356	158	354	471	347	204	475	424	389	3178
par	4	3	4	5	4	3	5	4	4	36
handicap	10	18	4	16	6	12	14	2	8	-
FORWARD	341	142	334	453	297	185	421	411	320	2904
par	4	3	4	5	4	3	5	5	4	37
handicap	10	18	8	4	6	16	2	12	14	-

BACK	
yardage	6654
par	72
rating	71.9
slope	123

REGULAR	
yardage	6368
par	72
rating	70.6
slope	121

FORWARD	
yardage	5822
par	74
rating	73.4
slope	129

15 RANCHO DEL REY GOLF COURSE

ARCHITECT: BOB BALDOCK, 1963

5250 Green Sands Avenue
Atwater, CA 95301

PRO SHOP: 209-358-7131

Phil Greenhill, General Manager
Ron Ewing, Professional
Jack Greenhill, Manager

Driving Range ●
Practice Greens ●
Clubhouse ●
Food / Beverage ●
Accommodations
Pull Carts ●
Power Carts ●
Club Rental ●
Special Offers

	1	2	3	4	5	6	7	8	9	OUT
BACK	500	367	480	216	321	441	404	199	450	3378
REGULAR	481	352	461	191	318	413	388	158	431	3193
par	5	4	5	3	4	4	4	3	4	36
handicap	5	7	1	15	13	9	11	17	3	-
FORWARD	465	334	445	216	306	361	370	147	412	3056
par	5	4	5	4	4	4	4	3	5	38
handicap	3	7	1	15	13	11	9	17	5	-

	10	11	12	13	14	15	16	17	18	IN
BACK	349	364	419	505	177	448	513	188	362	3325
REGULAR	340	348	353	487	161	420	497	166	349	3121
par	4	4	4	5	3	4	5	3	4	36
handicap	4	14	12	2	18	8	6	16	10	-
FORWARD	333	331	304	471	144	423	439	152	334	2931
par	4	4	4	5	3	5	5	3	4	37
handicap	6	14	12	4	18	2	8	16	10	-

BACK	
yardage	6703
par	72
rating	72.5
slope	124

REGULAR	
yardage	6314
par	72
rating	70.6
slope	121

FORWARD	
yardage	5987
par	75
rating	73.6
slope	125

PLAY POLICY & FEES: Reciprocal play is accepted with members of other private clubs. Reciprocal fees are $40. Guest fees are $30. Carts are $20.

TEE TIMES: Reservations can be booked seven days in advance.

DRESS CODE: Collared shirts and nonmetal spikes are required.

COURSE DESCRIPTION: This flat course is deceiving. It's tight and the rough is difficult. The 14th hole is a rugged test. At 365 yards, this par 4 requires a carry over water and then doglegs 90 degrees. It's primarily a placement course with tricky greens.

NOTES: The 1991 California State Amateur qualifying and the 1993 NCAA Division II Men's Championship were held here.

LOCATION: From Highway 99 south in Turlock, exit on Lander Avenue south and turn left on Bradbury. Turn right onto Golf Links Road.

. . . ● **TOURNAMENTS:** Tournaments are limited to Monday and Friday with board approval.

14. TURLOCK GOLF & COUNTRY CLUB

PLAY POLICY & FEES: Green fees for 18 holes are $18 before 12 p.m. and $13 thereafter. Weekend green fees for 18 holes are $22 before noon and $15 after noon. Carts are $11 for nine holes and $18 for 18 holes.

TEE TIMES: Reservations can be made seven days in advance.

DRESS CODE: Shirts must be worn at all times. Nonmetal spikes are required.

COURSE DESCRIPTION: This course is mostly level, with lots of trees and water. The signature hole is the 17th, a par 3 of 158 yards from the white tees, with two willows and large bunkers framing the green.

NOTES: A complete overhaul of the greens and fairways has recently been completed. The course record of 63 is held by Pete Culver.

LOCATION: From Highway 99 in Atwater, exit north onto Buhach Road. Turn left on Green Sands Avenue and follow it to the course.

. . . ● **TOURNAMENTS:** A 20-player minimum is needed to book an event. The banquet facility can accommodate up to 60 people.

15. RANCHO DEL REY GOLF COURSE

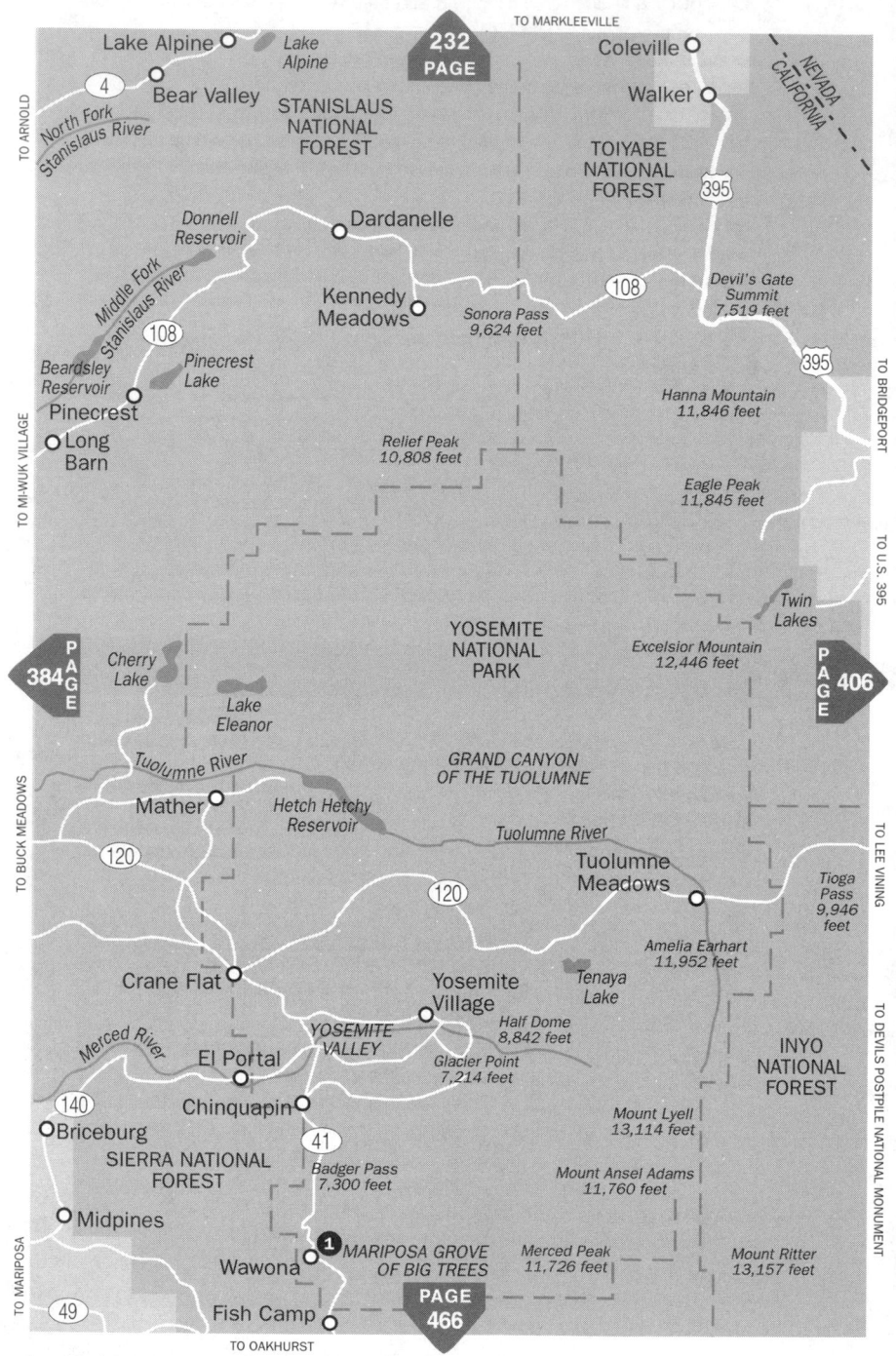

TO MARKLEEVILLE

232 PAGE

Lake Alpine ○ Lake Alpine

4 Bear Valley

North Fork Stanislaus River

STANISLAUS NATIONAL FOREST

Coleville ○

Walker ○

TOIYABE NATIONAL FOREST

395

Donnell Reservoir

Dardanelle

Middle Fork Stanislaus River

108

Kennedy Meadows

Sonora Pass 9,624 feet

108

Devil's Gate Summit 7,519 feet

395

Beardsley Reservoir

Pinecrest Lake

Pinecrest

Long Barn

Relief Peak 10,808 feet

Hanna Mountain 11,846 feet

Eagle Peak 11,845 feet

Twin Lakes

384 PAGE

Cherry Lake

Lake Eleanor

YOSEMITE NATIONAL PARK

Excelsior Mountain 12,446 feet

PAGE 406

Tuolumne River

Mather

Hetch Hetchy Reservoir

GRAND CANYON OF THE TUOLUMNE

Tuolumne River

120

120

Tuolumne Meadows

Tioga Pass 9,946 feet

Crane Flat

Yosemite Village

Tenaya Lake

Amelia Earhart 11,952 feet

Merced River

El Portal

YOSEMITE VALLEY

Half Dome 8,842 feet

Glacier Point 7,214 feet

Mount Lyell 13,114 feet

INYO NATIONAL FOREST

140

○ Briceburg

Chinquapin

41

Badger Pass 7,300 feet

Mount Ansel Adams 11,760 feet

Mount Ritter 13,157 feet

SIERRA NATIONAL FOREST

○ Midpines

49

Wawona

1 MARIPOSA GROVE OF BIG TREES

Fish Camp

Merced Peak 11,726 feet

PAGE 466

TO OAKHURST

NEVADA
CALIFORNIA

TO ARNOLD

TO MI-WUK VILLAGE

TO BUCK MEADOWS

TO MARIPOSA

TO BRIDGEPORT

TO U.S. 395

TO LEE VINING

TO DEVILS POSTPILE NATIONAL MONUMENT

Wawona Area

WAWONA HOTEL GOLF COURSE
ARCHITECT: ALISTER MACKENZIE, 1918

P.O. Box 2005
Wawona, CA 95389

PRO SHOP: 209-375-6572

Barry Ferris, Professional
Kim Porter, Superintendent

Driving Range
Practice Greens ●
Clubhouse ●
Food / Beverage ●
Accommodations ●
Pull Carts ●
Power Carts ●
Club Rental ●
Special Offers

	1	2	3	4	5	6	7	8	9	OUT
BACK	-	-	-	-	-	-	-	-	-	-
REGULAR	464	229	470	393	349	185	402	167	358	3017
par	5	3	5	4	4	3	4	3	4	35
handicap	11	5	15	7	3	13	1	17	9	-
FORWARD	394	183	457	366	339	157	385	113	329	2723
par	5	3	5	4	4	3	4	3	4	35
handicap	1	13	3	9	7	15	5	17	11	-

	10	11	12	13	14	15	16	17	18	IN
BACK	-	-	-	-	-	-	-	-	-	-
REGULAR	474	217	479	380	353	154	417	153	371	2998
par	5	3	5	4	4	3	4	3	4	35
handicap	12	8	14	6	4	16	2	18	10	-
FORWARD	429	223	444	375	350	154	355	135	318	2783
par		5	4	5	4	4	3	4	4	33
handicap		4	14	2	10	8	16	6	12	-

BACK	
yardage	-
par	-
rating	-
slope	-

REGULAR	
yardage	6015
par	70
rating	69.1
slope	117

FORWARD	
yardage	5506
par	68
rating	70.9
slope	119

PLAY POLICY & FEES: Green fees are $13.75 for nine holes and $22 for 18 holes. Carts are $12.50 for nine holes and $20 for 18 holes. The course is open April 1 to November 1.

TEE TIMES: Guests of the Wawona Hotel should make golf reservations at the same time they make room reservations.

COURSE DESCRIPTION: This is a short, scenic course in Yosemite National Park. There are lots of trees, and the course is well maintained. Deer and other wildlife abound. The adjacent Wawona Hotel is a wonderful place to stay and dine. Wawona Golf Course is one of numerous Northern California courses designed by Scottish architectural giant Alister Mackenzie.

LOCATION: This course is located between Oakhurst and Yosemite on Highway 41 at the south end of the park.

. . . ● **TOURNAMENTS:** This course is available for outside tournaments.

1. WAWONA HOTEL GOLF COURSE

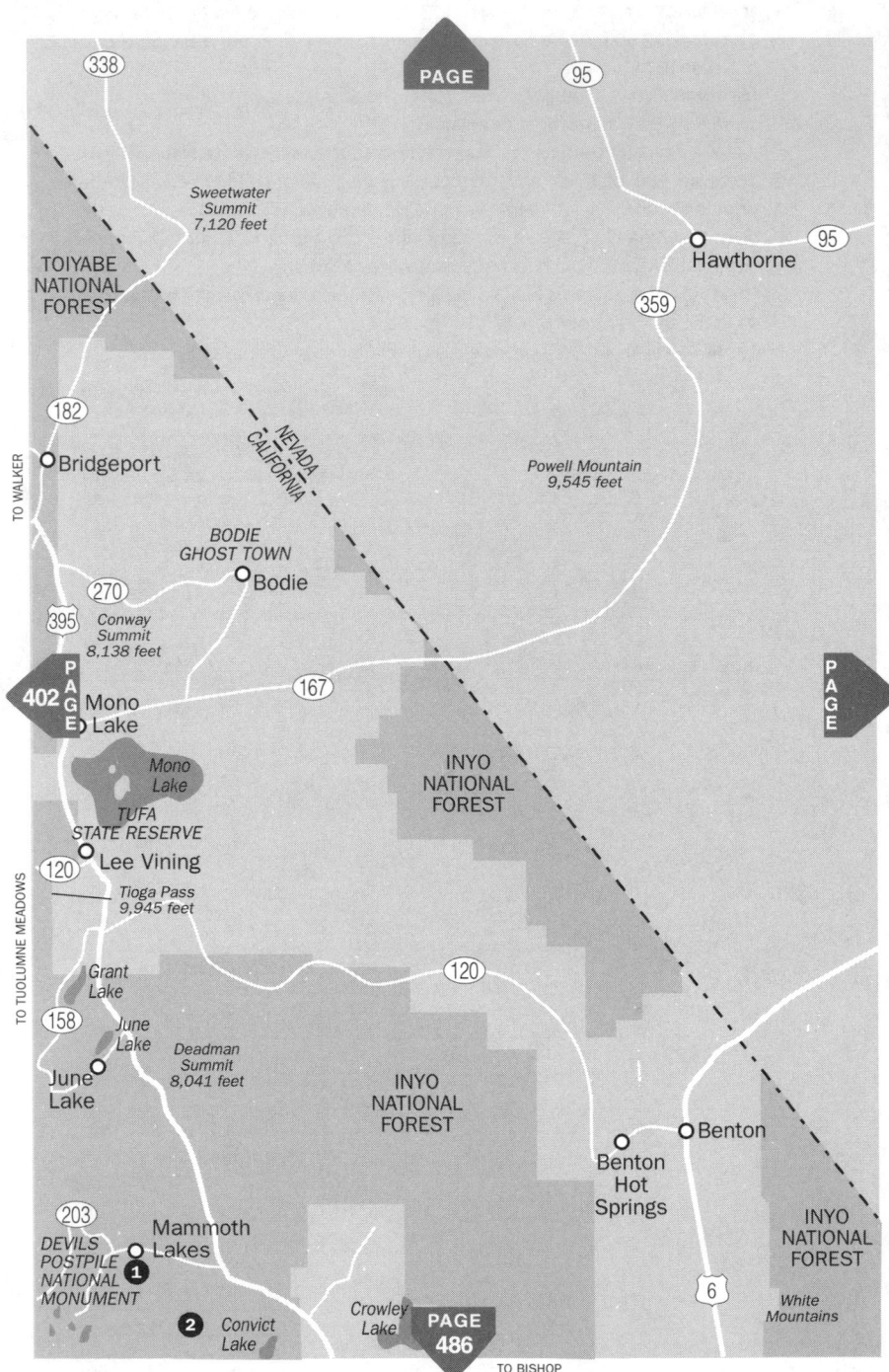

PAGE

338

95

Sweetwater
Summit
7,120 feet

95

○ Hawthorne

TOIYABE
NATIONAL
FOREST

359

NEVADA
|
CALIFORNIA

182

○ Bridgeport

TO WALKER

Powell Mountain
9,545 feet

BODIE
GHOST TOWN
○ Bodie

270

395 Conway
Summit
8,138 feet

167

402 PAGE Mono
Lake

PAGE

Mono
Lake

INYO
NATIONAL
FOREST

TUFA
STATE RESERVE

○ Lee Vining

120

Tioga Pass
9,945 feet

TO TUOLUMNE MEADOWS

Grant
Lake

120

158

June
Lake

Deadman
Summit
8,041 feet

INYO
NATIONAL
FOREST

June
Lake

○ Benton

Benton
Hot
Springs

203

DEVILS
POSTPILE
NATIONAL
MONUMENT

Mammoth
Lakes

1

INYO
NATIONAL
FOREST

White
Mountains

6

2 Convict
Lake

Crowley
Lake

PAGE
486

TO BISHOP

Mammoth Lakes Area

SIERRA STAR GOLF CLUB
ARCHITECT: CAL OLSON, 1999

P.O. Box 1942
Mammoth Lakes, CA 93546

2001 Sierra Star Parkway
Mammoth Lakes, CA 93546

PRO SHOP: 760-924-GOLF

David Schacht, Head Professional

Driving Range
Practice Greens •
Clubhouse •
Food / Beverage •
Accommodations •
Pull Carts •
Power Carts •
Club Rental
Special Offers •

	1	2	3	4	5	6	7	8	9	OUT
BACK	374	118	413	440	424	469	203	525	423	3389
REGULAR	364	113	408	434	420	466	198	519	417	3339
par	4	3	4	4	4	4	3	5	4	35
handicap	15	17	3	7	11	1	13	9	5	-
FORWARD	263	73	328	329	345	371	145	407	277	2538
par	4	3	4	4	4	4	3	5	4	35
handicap	11	17	5	9	7	1	15	3	13	-

	10	11	12	13	14	15	16	17	18	IN
BACK	555	437	321	413	190	380	443	365	215	3319
REGULAR	550	432	317	409	186	375	438	362	209	3278
par	5	4	4	4	3	4	4	4	3	35
handicap	10	4	18	6	14	16	2	8	12	-
FORWARD	422	316	235	276	122	258	337	291	117	2374
par	5	4	4	4	3	4	4	4	3	35
handicap	2	6	14	12	16	10	4	8	18	-

BACK	
yardage	6708
par	70
rating	71.0
slope	133

REGULAR	
yardage	6617
par	70
rating	70.6
slope	133

FORWARD	
yardage	4912
par	70
rating	-
slope	-

 SNOWCREEK GOLF COURSE
ARCHITECT: TED ROBINSON, 1991

P.O. Box 569
Mammoth Lakes, CA 93546

Old Mammoth Road
Mammoth Lakes, CA 93546

PRO SHOP: 760-934-6633

Tim Standifer, Manager
Dennis Hurlburt, Head Professional, PGA
Tim Schobert, Superintendent

Driving Range •
Practice Greens •
Clubhouse •
Food / Beverage •
Accommodations •
Pull Carts •
Power Carts •
Club Rental •
Special Offers

	1	2	3	4	5	6	7	8	9	OUT
BACK	545	397	173	350	330	430	155	383	340	3103
REGULAR	521	370	149	335	320	401	145	368	322	2931
par	5	4	3	4	4	4	3	4	4	35
handicap	4	1	3	6	9	5	8	2	7	-
FORWARD	487	293	128	323	293	344	131	324	294	2617
par	5	4	3	4	4	4	3	4	4	35
handicap	4	1	3	6	9	5	8	2	7	-

	10	11	12	13	14	15	16	17	18	IN
BACK	545	397	173	350	330	430	155	383	340	3103
REGULAR	521	370	149	335	320	401	145	368	322	2931
par	5	4	3	4	4	4	3	4	4	35
handicap	4	1	3	6	9	5	8	2	7	-
FORWARD	487	293	128	323	293	344	131	324	294	2617
par	5	4	3	4	4	4	3	4	4	35
handicap	4	1	3	6	9	5	8	2	7	-

BACK	
yardage	6206
par	70
rating	67.8
slope	121

REGULAR	
yardage	5862
par	70
rating	66.0
slope	118

FORWARD	
yardage	5234
par	70
rating	69.2
slope	114

PLAY POLICY & FEES: Green fees are $115 every day. Nine-hole green fees are $85 before 9:30 a.m. only. The twilight rate is $85 starting at 3 p.m. All green fees include a cart. Pull carts are available for those who prefer to walk.

TEE TIMES: Reservations can be made six months in advance.

DRESS CODE: Alternative spikes are preferred, and golf attire is required.

COURSE DESCRIPTION: This tree-lined mountain course offers spectacular views on nearly every hole. With narrow fairways and high elevation, the smart player will keep the driver in the bag or better yet, take it out and leave it in the trunk of the car. The greens are firm, holding shots well; and with five sets of tee boxes, Sierra Star can accommodate players of all skill levels.

NOTES: Because of the high elevation, the course is open approximately five and a half months a year starting mid-May.

LOCATION: From Los Angeles take U.S.395 to Highway 203. Head west on 203 to Mammoth Lake; turn left on Minaret and right on Meridian. The course will be on the right-hand side.

. . . ● **TOURNAMENTS:** A 36-player minimum is needed to book an event. Shotgun tournaments must have a minimum field of 120-players. ● **$PECIAL OFFERS:** Golf packages that include lodging, breakfast, and golf are available with the Mammoth Mountain Inn. For more information call 800-228-4947.

1. SIERRA STAR GOLF CLUB

PLAY POLICY & FEES: Green fees are $25 for nine holes and $45 for 18 holes. Carts are $7 per person for nine holes and $12 per person for 18 holes. Twilight rates are available. The course is open from Memorial Day weekend through mid-October, weather permitting.

TEE TIMES: Reservations can be booked seven days in advance.

DRESS CODE: No tank tops are allowed. Nonmetal spikes are mandatory.

COURSE DESCRIPTION: Golfers tend to be overcome by the scenery, but the course itself is also an eyeful. The fairways are narrow, and water comes into play on nearly every hole. The greens are relatively large for a course of this distance, which is a plus.

NOTES: There are rumors of another nine holes being built in the next few years.

LOCATION: From U.S. 395 take Highway 203 west to Old Mammoth Road. Turn left on Old Mammoth Road and drive about one mile to the course. The course is on the left side.

. . . ● **TOURNAMENTS:** This course is available for outside tournaments.

2. SNOWCREEK GOLF COURSE

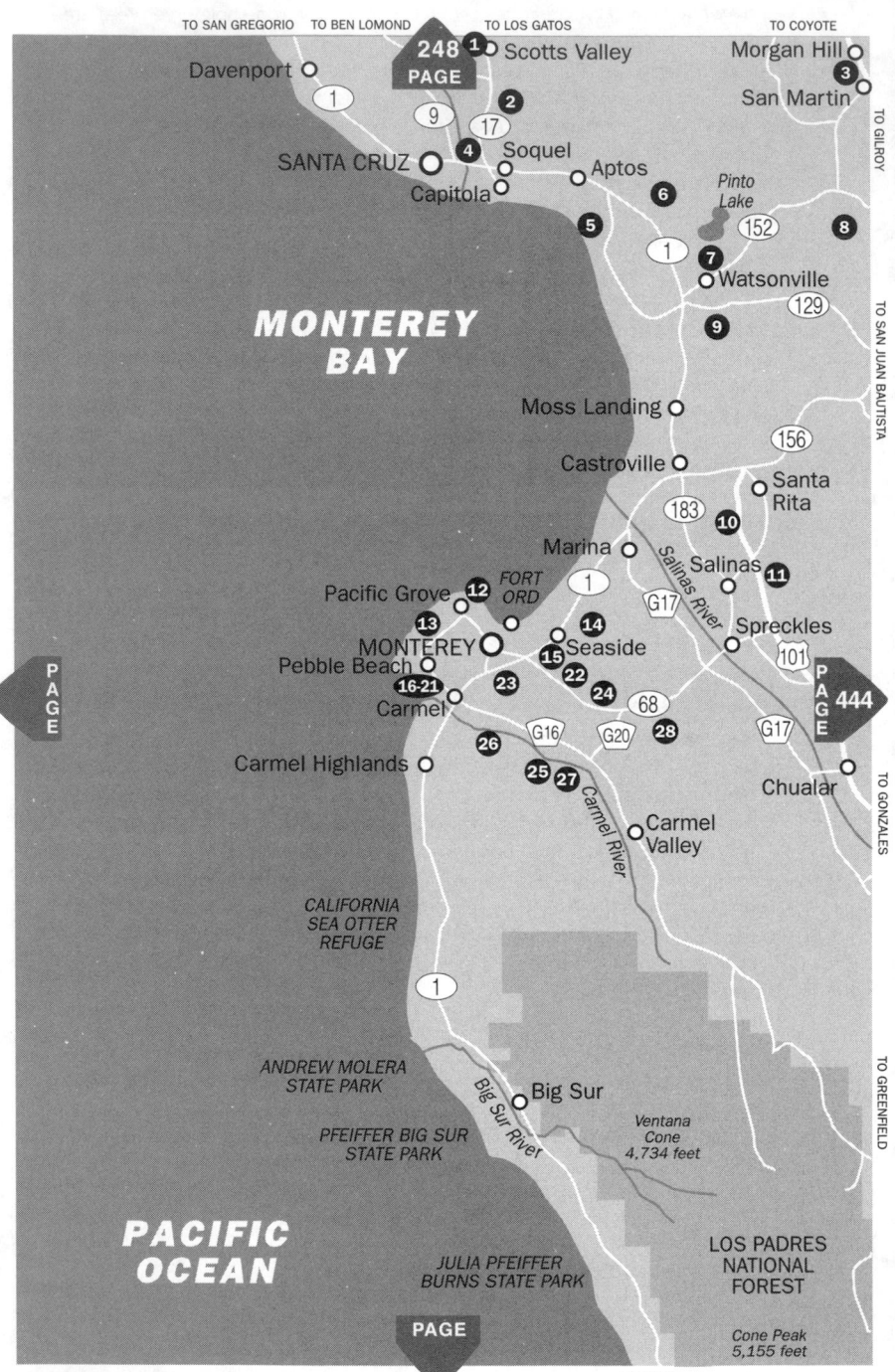

Monterey Area

① VALLEY GARDENS GOLF COURSE
ARCHITECT: BOB BALDOCK, 1971

263 Mount Hermon Road
Scotts Valley, CA 95066

PRO SHOP: 831-438-3058

Jim Knowlton, Head Professional, PGA
Robert Hayes, Superintendent

Driving Range
Practice Greens •
Clubhouse •
Food / Beverage •
Accommodations
Pull Carts •
Power Carts
Club Rental •
$pecial Offers

	1	2	3	4	5	6	7	8	9	OUT
BACK	-	-	-	-	-	-	-	-	-	-
REGULAR	247	248	108	217	178	367	218	161	121	1865
par	4	4	3	3	3	4	4	3	3	31
handicap	11	9	15	1	5	3	13	7	17	-
FORWARD	236	231	96	211	153	214	206	96	114	1557
par	4	4	3	4	3	4	4	3	3	32
handicap	1	7	15	11	13	3	5	9	17	-

	10	11	12	13	14	15	16	17	18	IN
BACK	-	-	-	-	-	-	-	-	-	-
REGULAR	247	248	108	217	178	367	218	161	121	1865
par	4	4	3	3	3	4	4	3	3	31
handicap	12	10	16	2	6	4	14	8	18	-
FORWARD	236	231	96	211	153	214	206	96	114	1557
par	4	4	3	4	3	4	4	3	3	32
handicap	2	8	16	12	14	4	6	10	18	-

BACK	
yardage	-
par	-
rating	-
slope	-

REGULAR	
yardage	3730
par	62
rating	56.5
slope	82

FORWARD	
yardage	3114
par	64
rating	55.0
slope	-

② DE LAVEAGA GOLF COURSE
ARCHITECT: BERT STAMPS, 1970

401 Upper Park Road, Box
Santa Cruz, CA 95065

PRO SHOP: 831-423-7212

Gary Loustalot, Director of Golf, PGA
David Loustalot, Head Professional, PGA
Don Paul, Superintendent

Driving Range •
Practice Greens •
Clubhouse •
Food / Beverage •
Accommodations
Pull Carts •
Power Carts •
Club Rental •
$pecial Offers

	1	2	3	4	5	6	7	8	9	OUT
BACK	-	-	-	-	-	-	-	-	-	-
REGULAR	496	334	150	325	157	459	350	135	379	2785
par	5	4	3	4	3	5	4	3	4	35
handicap	3	9	13	11	17	1	7	15	5	-
FORWARD	478	315	104	297	127	441	326	94	353	2535
par	5	4	3	4	3	5	4	3	4	35
handicap	2	10	14	12	16	4	6	18	8	-

	10	11	12	13	14	15	16	17	18	IN
BACK	-	-	-	-	-	-	-	-	-	-
REGULAR	537	162	345	322	337	162	381	504	475	3225
par	5	3	4	4	4	3	4	5	5	37
handicap	2	18	12	14	10	16	8	4	6	-
FORWARD	445	125	329	283	237	145	369	437	426	2796
par	5	3	4	4	4	3	4	5	5	37
handicap	1	17	11	9	15	13	7	5	3	-

BACK	
yardage	-
par	-
rating	-
slope	-

REGULAR	
yardage	6010
par	72
rating	70.4
slope	133

FORWARD	
yardage	5331
par	72
rating	70.6
slope	125

PLAY POLICY & FEES: Green fees are $11 weekdays and $12.50 weekends for nine holes.

TEE TIMES: Reservations are recommended one week in advance.

DRESS CODE: This is Santa Cruz County—casual dress is appropriate.

COURSE DESCRIPTION: This course is short, tight, and flat. There are 27 different varieties of trees that come into play. Beginners, juniors, and seniors will find it an excellent layout.

NOTES: Hal Wells, the PGA Professional from Boulder Creek Golf Course, holds the course record with a 23.

LOCATION: From Highway 17 in Scotts Valley, drive one mile west on Mount Hermon Road.

. . . ● **TOURNAMENTS:** A 12-player minimum is needed to book a tournament.

1. VALLEY GARDENS GOLF COURSE

PLAY POLICY & FEES: Green fees are $35 weekdays and $45 weekends. Twilight rates are $21 weekdays and $27 weekends after 3 p.m. Carts are $15 per rider.

TEE TIMES: Reservations can be booked seven days in advance. Reservations are possible 30 days in advance for a $10 per player service fee.

DRESS CODE: Traditional or ceramic-tipped spikes are not allowed.

COURSE DESCRIPTION: This tight, rolling course in the Santa Cruz mountains has lateral hazards on nearly every hole. Staying on the fairways off the tee is vital. The course may give the appearance of birdie opportunities, but they don't come easily.

NOTES: The men's course record of 63 is held by Tim Loustalot, son of host pro, Gary.

LOCATION: From San Francisco take Interstate 280 to Highway 17 toward Santa Cruz. Take Highway 1 south to the Morrisey exit. Turn right on Fairmount and right again on Branciforte Ave. Turn left on Upper Park Road and proceed to the course.

. . . ● **TOURNAMENTS:** A 16-player minimum is needed to book a tournament. Carts are required. Events should be scheduled 12 months in advance. A banquet facility is available that can accommodate up to 150 people.

2. DE LAVEAGA GOLF COURSE

CORDEVALLE GOLF CLUB
ARCHITECT: ROBERT TRENT JONES., JR., 1999

150 Almaden Blvd., Ste. 1380
San Jose, CA 95113

1005 Highland Rd.
Morgan Hill, CA

PRO SHOP: 408-278-7280
CLUBHOUSE: 408-924-0427

Joe Root, Director of Golf, PGA
Jimmy Stewart, Director of Sales
Jim McPhilomy, Superintendent

Driving Range •
Practice Greens •
Clubhouse •
Food / Beverage •
Accommodations •
Pull Carts
Power Carts •
Club Rental •
Special Offers

	1	2	3	4	5	6	7	8	9	OUT
BACK	425	185	573	407	461	540	210	358	425	3584
REGULAR	405	160	555	394	428	520	188	325	397	3372
par	4	3	5	4	4	5	3	4	4	36
handicap										-
FORWARD	335	92	464	325	356	454	118	262	340	2746
par	4	3	5	4	4	5	3	4	4	36
handicap										-

	10	11	12	13	14	15	16	17	18	IN
BACK	422	390	230	418	454	480	166	478	547	3585
REGULAR	404	360	195	382	429	460	148	449	504	3331
par	4	4	3	4	4	5	3	4	5	36
handicap										-
FORWARD	331	291	106	317	328	374	105	358	429	2639
par	4	4	3	4	4	5	3	4	5	36
handicap										-

BACK	
yardage	7169
par	72
rating	
slope	

REGULAR	
yardage	6703
par	72
rating	
slope	

FORWARD	
yardage	5385
par	72
rating	
slope	

PLAY POLICY & FEES: Play is for members and guests only.

DRESS CODE: Appropriate golf attire and nonmetal spikes are required.

COURSE DESCRIPTION: Every once in a while a course comes along that has it all. Set in rolling hills dotted with native oaks, this Robert Trent Jones Jr.–designed course is truly inspiring. There is nothing fancy about this golf course—what you see is what you get—but everything works. The fairways are wide enough to hit driver and even provide players with ample bail-out areas. But if you cut a corner or miss the fairway in the wrong spot, you'll find yourself in a fairway bunker, a creek, or the thick native grasses. The greens are subtle and roll true, but leave the ball in the wrong spot and you'll have to work for a two putt. Around the greens are even more bail-out areas that will allow players a variety of shots to come back, including putting. Although the rough isn't long around the greens, it's dense and tricky. Hitting it over the side of the green will spell disaster. With five sets of tees, this is truly a course every skill level can enjoy. CordeValle Golf Club is what all new country clubs should aspire to be.

NOTES: Located in the Silicon Valley, CordeValle has both individual and corporate memberships available. Besides an excellent practice facility, members will also enjoy their own private resort for themselves and their guests.

LOCATION: From San Jose take U.S.101 south to Morgan Hill. Take the San Martin exit and head west. Take a left on Monterey Avenue and a right on Highland Drive to the course.

. . . ● **TOURNAMENTS:** Outside events are not allowed.

3. CORDEVALLE GOLF CLUB

PASATIEMPO GOLF COURSE
ARCHITECT: ALISTER MACKENZIE, 1929

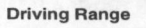

20 Clubhouse Road
Santa Cruz, CA 95060

PRO SHOP: 831-459-9155

Rick Forney, Manager
Shawn McEntee, Head Professional, PGA
Dean Gump, Superintendent

Driving Range •
Practice Greens •
Clubhouse •
Food / Beverage •
Accommodations
Pull Carts •
Power Carts •
Club Rental •
$pecial Offers

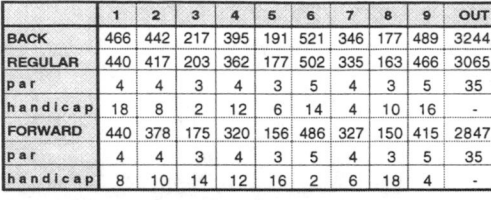

	1	2	3	4	5	6	7	8	9	OUT
BACK	466	442	217	395	191	521	346	177	489	3244
REGULAR	440	417	203	362	177	502	335	163	466	3065
par	4	4	3	4	3	5	4	3	5	35
handicap	18	8	2	12	6	14	4	10	16	-
FORWARD	440	378	175	320	156	486	327	150	415	2847
par	4	4	3	4	3	5	4	3	5	35
handicap	8	10	14	12	16	2	6	18	4	-

	10	11	12	13	14	15	16	17	18	IN
BACK	444	384	376	492	426	145	395	366	173	3201
REGULAR	440	375	372	478	390	125	372	354	157	3063
par	4	4	4	5	4	3	4	4	3	35
handicap	5	3	13	17	9	15	1	7	11	-
FORWARD	440	311	371	447	331	96	353	345	88	2782
par	5	4	4	5	4	3	4	4	3	36
handicap	5	1	11	7	13	17	3	9	15	-

BACK	
yardage	6445
par	70
rating	72.9
slope	138

REGULAR	
yardage	6128
par	70
rating	71.4
slope	134

FORWARD	
yardage	5629
par	71
rating	73.6
slope	135

SEASCAPE GOLF CLUB

610 Clubhouse Drive
Aptos, CA 95003

PRO SHOP: 831-688-3213
CLUBHOUSE: 831-688-3254

Bruce Pluim, Manager, PGA
Mike Higuera, Superintendent

Driving Range •
Practice Greens •
Clubhouse •
Food / Beverage •
Accommodations
Pull Carts •
Power Carts •
Club Rental •
$pecial Offers

	1	2	3	4	5	6	7	8	9	OUT
BACK	369	441	433	370	349	207	343	126	364	3002
REGULAR	351	431	423	362	325	201	333	118	353	2897
par	4	5	4	4	4	3	4	3	4	35
handicap	5	15	1	3	13	9	7	17	11	-
FORWARD	334	425	397	355	307	183	316	109	333	2759
par	4	5	5	4	4	3	4	3	4	36
handicap	1	9	13	3	15	11	5	17	7	-

	10	11	12	13	14	15	16	17	18	IN
BACK	524	361	128	452	192	349	192	398	436	3032
REGULAR	510	354	118	446	173	336	175	376	428	2916
par	5	4	3	4	3	4	3	4	5	36
handicap	16	8	18	12	6	10	4	2	14	-
FORWARD	484	346	110	436	135	323	151	355	415	2755
par	5	4	3	5	3	4	3	4	5	36
handicap	6	10	18	2	16	12	14	8	4	-

BACK	
yardage	6034
par	71
rating	69.4
slope	125

REGULAR	
yardage	5813
par	71
rating	68.4
slope	123

FORWARD	
yardage	5514
par	72
rating	67.0
slope	120

PLAY POLICY & FEES: Outside play is accepted. Green fees are $115 Monday through Thursday and $125 Friday through Sunday. Optional carts are $34.

TEE TIMES: To reserve a weekday tee time, call one week before, and for the upcoming weekend, call on Monday at 10 a.m. Reservations can be made 90 days in advance for a $20 per player surcharge.

DRESS CODE: Appropriate golf attire and nonmetal spikes are required.

COURSE DESCRIPTION: This Alister Mackenzie–designed course opened in 1929 and still ranks as one of the best in the nation. The par-4, 395-yard 16th was Mackenzie's favorite hole in golf. It's a blind driving hole that requires a difficult uphill approach across a creek to a three-tiered green. There are hazards and out-of-bounds on both sides of the fairway, which doglegs to the left. The course overlooks the Pacific Ocean and Monterey Bay.

NOTES: The men's course record of 63 is held by Ken Venturi, Brian Pini, and Forrest Fezler. The women's record is 70, held by Sandy Woodruff. Pasatiempo played host to the 1986 U.S. Women's Amateur.

LOCATION: From San Francisco drive south on Interstate 280. Take Highway 17 toward Santa Cruz. Exit onto Pasatiempo Drive and follow the signs.

. . . ● **TOURNAMENTS:** A 16-player minimum is required to book a tournament. Tournaments can be booked at least six months in advance. Shotgun tournaments are available Monday and Thursday only. The banquet facility can accommodate up to 200 people. ● **TRAVEL:** The Inn at Pasatiempo (831-423-5000), the Chaminade (831-475-5600) and the Seascape Resort (831-688-6800) are recommended for lodging.

4. PASATIEMPO GOLF COURSE

PLAY POLICY & FEES: Green fees are $45 Monday through Thursday, $55 Friday, and $65 weekends and holidays. Twilight rates are available. Carts are $14 for nine holes and $18 for 18 holes.

TEE TIMES: Reservations can be booked seven days in advance. For a $5 charge, reservations can be made 30 days out.

COURSE DESCRIPTION: This scenic course has rolling, oceanside character, although you can't actually see the ocean. Cypress trees and bunkers border every hole. The course is tight, and accuracy is vital. Par 3s are the key to success here.

NOTES: The 180-yard driving range is for iron practice only. The course record of 62 is held by Jeff McMillen. In 1999 the course underwent major renovations including upgrades to the irrigation and drainage systems, bunker renovations, a new proshop, bar and grill, snack bar, and locker rooms.

LOCATION: From Santa Cruz drive seven miles south on Highway 1. Exit on Rio Del Mar and go right. Turn left on Clubhouse Drive.

. . . ● **TOURNAMENTS:** A 20-player minimum is required to book a tournament. Events should be scheduled 12 months in advance. The banquet facility can accommodate up to 350 people. ● **TRAVEL:** The Seascape Resort is located one mile from the golf course. For reservations call 408-688-6800. The Seacliff Inn (831-688-7300) is also recommended.

5. SEASCAPE GOLF CLUB

CASSERLY PAR-3 GOLF COURSE
ARCHITECT: ROBERT SANFORD, 1966

626 Casserly Road
Watsonville, CA 95076

PRO SHOP: 831-724-1654

Robert Sanford, Owner & Superintendent

Driving Range
Practice Greens ●
Clubhouse
Food / Beverage
Accommodations
Pull Carts ●
Power Carts
Club Rental ●
$pecial Offers

	1	2	3	4	5	6	7	8	9	OUT
BACK	-	-	-	-	-	-	-	-	-	-
REGULAR	105	158	128	132	147	176	112	88	112	1158
par	3	3	3	3	3	3	3	3	3	27
handicap	-	-	-	-	-	-	-	-	-	-
FORWARD	105	158	128	132	147	176	112	88	112	1158
par	3	3	3	3	3	3	3	3	3	27
handicap	-	-	-	-	-	-	-	-	-	-

	10	11	12	13	14	15	16	17	18	IN
BACK	-	-	-	-	-	-	-	-	-	-
REGULAR	105	158	159	132	180	218	112	88	112	1264
par	3	3	3	3	3	3	3	3	3	27
handicap	-	-	-	-	-	-	-	-	-	-
FORWARD	105	158	159	132	180	218	112	88	112	1264
par	3	3	3	3	3	3	3	3	3	27
handicap	-	-	-	-	-	-	-	-	-	-

BACK	
yardage	-
par	-
rating	-
slope	-

REGULAR	
yardage	2422
par	54
rating	-
slope	-

FORWARD	
yardage	2422
par	54
rating	-
slope	-

SPRING HILLS GOLF CLUB
ARCHITECT: HANK SCHIMPELER, 1965

501 Spring Hills Drive
Watsonville, CA 95076

PRO SHOP: 831-724-1404

Amy Candau, Manager
Stan Hutchison, Professional
Hank Schimpeler, Superintendent

Driving Range ●
Practice Greens ●
Clubhouse ●
Food / Beverage ●
Accommodations
Pull Carts ●
Power Carts ●
Club Rental ●
$pecial Offers

	1	2	3	4	5	6	7	8	9	OUT
BACK	393	428	353	340	350	462	190	398	177	3091
REGULAR	385	417	350	335	341	458	181	385	165	3017
par	4	4	4	4	4	5	3	4	3	35
handicap	7	1	9	5	13	17	11	3	15	-
FORWARD	368	341	325	325	278	413	157	350	144	2701
par	4	4	4	4	4	5	3	4	3	35
handicap	3	9	13	7	11	5	15	1	17	-

	10	11	12	13	14	15	16	17	18	IN
BACK	165	473	340	107	369	168	525	510	267	2924
REGULAR	158	465	333	102	361	165	519	506	257	2866
par	3	5	4	3	4	3	5	5	4	36
handicap	8	14	2	18	4	10	6	12	16	-
FORWARD	133	435	316	99	350	155	495	477	236	2696
par	3	5	4	3	4	3	5	5	4	36
handicap	14	4	10	18	8	16	2	6	12	-

BACK	
yardage	6015
par	71
rating	69.4
slope	117

REGULAR	
yardage	5883
par	71
rating	68.8
slope	115

FORWARD	
yardage	5397
par	71
rating	70.8
slope	114

418   Monterey Area (map page 410)

PLAY POLICY & FEES: Green fees are $5 for nine holes. Pull carts are 50 cents.

TEE TIMES: Reservations are not accepted. All play is on a first-come, first-served basis.

COURSE DESCRIPTION: This par-3 course has two water hazards as well as hills that come into play. It's a good beginner's course. You can play nine holes in an hour during your lunch break.

NOTES: The course record of 22 is held by Ed Rhoades.

LOCATION: This course is located between U.S. 101 and Highway 1. From Highway 1 heading east toward Watsonville, take the Airport Boulevard exit and follow it to Green Valley Road. Turn left and follow Green Valley Road 1.5 miles to Casserly Road.

. . . ● **TOURNAMENTS:** No shotgun tournaments are allowed.

6. CASSERLY PAR-3 GOLF COURSE

PLAY POLICY & FEES: Green fees are $25 weekdays and $35 weekends. Twilight rates are available. Carts are $24. A pull cart is $3.

TEE TIMES: Reservations can be booked one month in advance.

DRESS CODE: Shirts and nonmetal spikes are required.

COURSE DESCRIPTION: Situated in the foothills, this challenging course is tight with lots of trees. The many doglegs make placement important. The back nine is rolling and scenic.

NOTES: During your round you may see deer, bobcats, rabbits, quail, coyotes, foxes, and hawks in this country setting. The clubhouse is an old farmhouse built in 1911.

LOCATION: From south of Watsonville on Highway 1, take the Green Valley Road exit, drive four or five miles to Casserly Road, and turn right. Drive one mile to Smith Road and turn left. From north of Watsonville on Highway 1, take the Airport Boulevard exit. Go two miles and turn left onto Green Valley Road. Go two miles and turn right on Casserly Road. Turn left on Smith Road.

. . . ● **TOURNAMENTS:** Shotgun tournaments are available weekdays only. A 16-player minimum is required to book a tournament. ● **TRAVEL:** Best Western Inn Watsonville is located about seven minutes from the golf course. For reservations cal 408-724-3367.

7. SPRING HILLS GOLF CLUB

8 GAVILAN GOLF COURSE

5055 Santa Teresa
Gilroy, CA 95020

PRO SHOP: 408-846-4920

Mike Fish, PGA Professional

Driving Range ●
Practice Greens ●
Clubhouse ●
Food / Beverage ●
Accommodations
Pull Carts ●
Power Carts ●
Club Rental ●
$Special Offers

	1	2	3	4	5	6	7	8	9	OUT
BACK	-	-	-	-	-	-	-	-	-	-
REGULAR	117	276	356	227	145	166	266	87	159	1799
par	3	4	4	4	3	3	4	3	3	31
handicap	18	2	6	12	16	4	14	10	8	-
FORWARD	117	276	356	227	145	166	266	87	159	1799
par	3	4	4	4	3	3	4	3	3	31
handicap	18	2	6	12	16	4	14	10	8	-

	10	11	12	13	14	15	16	17	18	IN
BACK	-	-	-	-	-	-	-	-	-	-
REGULAR	127	286	366	215	190	170	256	92	137	1839
par	3	4	4	3	3	4	3	3	3	31
handicap	17	3	7	13	1	5	15	11	9	-
FORWARD	127	286	366	215	190	170	256	92	137	1839
par	3	4	4	4	4	3	4	3	3	32
handicap	17	3	7	13	1	5	15	11	9	-

BACK	
yardage	-
par	-
rating	-
slope	-

REGULAR	
yardage	3638
par	62
rating	55.6
slope	73

FORWARD	
yardage	3638
par	63
rating	55.6
slope	73

9 PAJARO VALLEY GOLF CLUB
ARCHITECT: FLOYD MCFARLAND, 1926

967 Salinas Road
Watsonville, CA 95076

PRO SHOP: 831-724-3851
OFFICE: 831-724-9390

Robert Bowker, Director of Golf, PGA
Patrick Larkin, Head Professional, PGA
Gary Feliciano, Superintendent

Driving Range ●
Practice Greens ●
Clubhouse ●
Food / Beverage ●
Accommodations
Pull Carts ●
Power Carts ●
Club Rental ●
$Special Offers

	1	2	3	4	5	6	7	8	9	OUT
BACK	455	389	189	504	286	360	103	393	355	3034
REGULAR	440	378	179	481	282	348	98	392	348	2946
par	5	4	3	5	4	4	3	4	4	36
handicap	8	4	14	10	16	6	18	2	12	-
FORWARD	443	354	130	401	272	339	96	379	337	2751
par	5	4	3	4	4	4	3	4	4	35
handicap	6	8	16	4	14	10	18	2	12	-

	10	11	12	13	14	15	16	17	18	IN
BACK	345	171	417	376	160	468	393	515	355	3200
REGULAR	341	171	412	370	146	459	375	505	340	3119
par	4	3	4	4	3	5	4	5	4	36
handicap	15	7	1	13	17	9	3	5	11	-
FORWARD	345	151	404	312	149	428	352	487	322	2950
par	4	3	5	4	3	5	4	5	4	37
handicap	9	15	7	13	17	3	5	1	11	-

BACK	
yardage	6234
par	72
rating	70.0
slope	122

REGULAR	
yardage	6065
par	72
rating	69.1
slope	119

FORWARD	
yardage	5701
par	72
rating	72.3
slope	123

PLAY POLICY & FEES: Green fees are $11 for nine holes and $15 for 18 holes weekdays and $14 for nine holes and $20 for 18 holes weekends. Senior and junior rates are available. Carts are $12 for nine holes and $20 for 18 holes.

TEE TIMES: Reservations can be booked seven days in advance.

DRESS CODE: Shirts must be worn.

COURSE DESCRIPTION: This course, owned by Gavilan Community College, dates back to the 1960s. It is a short, mostly flat course and excellent for beginners. The greens are small, tricky, and challenging.

NOTES: Don DeLorenzo holds the course record with 54.

LOCATION: From U.S. 101 in Gilroy take the Castro Valley exit and follow it until it dead ends. Turn right on Santa Teresa Boulevard. Enter at the south gate at the Gavilan Community College campus.

. . . ● **TOURNAMENTS:** This course is available for outside tournaments.

8. GAVILAN GOLF COURSE

PLAY POLICY & FEES: Green fees are $40 Monday through Thursday and $55 Friday through Sunday and holidays. Twilight rates are available. Carts are $14 per rider and optional.

TEE TIMES: Reservations for weekends and holidays are taken seven days in advance starting at 6 a.m.

DRESS CODE: No tank tops are allowed on the course. Nonmetal spikes are mandatory.

COURSE DESCRIPTION: The serene and verdant Pajaro Valley provides an exquisite setting for the beautiful Pajaro Valley Golf Course. Dating back to the late 1920s, this course is short and wide with rolling fairways. This 18-hole course with groves of Monterey cypress trees presents a challenge for every golfer. The 12th hole, a long par 4, features a three-tiered green surrounded by bunkers.

LOCATION: Take Highway 1 south past Watsonville. After the Riverside Drive exit, head to the top of the hill where the lanes merge. Turn left at the flashing yellow lights on Salinas Road and go three-fourths of a mile to the course on the right.

. . . ● **TOURNAMENTS:** This course is available for outside tournaments. A 24-player minimum is needed to book an event. Events should be scheduled six to 12 months in advance. A banquet facility is available that can accommodate 100+ people. ● **TRAVEL:** The Red Roof Inn (831-740-4520) and Pajaro Dunes (831-722-4671) are recommended for lodging.

9. PAJARO VALLEY GOLF CLUB

⑩ SALINAS GOLF & COUNTRY CLUB
ARCHITECT: STEPHEN HALSEY, 1939

P.O. Box 4277
Salinas, CA 93912

475 San Juan Grade Road
Salinas, CA 93906

PRO SHOP: 831-449-1527
CLUBHOUSE: 831-449-1526

Robert Hedberg, Manager
Holly Jurgens, Professional
David Hayes, Superintendent

Driving Range •
Practice Greens •
Clubhouse •
Food / Beverage •
Accommodations
Pull Carts •
Power Carts •
Club Rental •
Special Offers

	1	2	3	4	5	6	7	8	9	OUT
BACK	463	138	353	326	187	310	336	346	513	2972
REGULAR	463	114	335	326	187	302	336	338	513	2914
par	5	3	4	4	3	4	4	4	5	36
handicap	5	17	9	3	13	15	1	7	11	-
FORWARD	439	105	304	312	164	277	319	331	493	2744
par	5	3	4	4	3	4	4	4	5	36
handicap	3	18	14	8	16	12	2	6	1	-

	10	11	12	13	14	15	16	17	18	IN
BACK	478	359	376	204	340	376	125	380	492	3130
REGULAR	478	359	376	204	332	357	125	380	492	3103
par	5	4	4	3	4	4	3	4	5	36
handicap	16	8	6	12	10	4	18	2	14	-
FORWARD	467	349	337	185	308	355	106	316	454	2877
par	5	4	4	3	4	4	3	4	5	36
handicap	9	10	13	15	11	5	17	4	7	-

BACK	
yardage	6102
par	72
rating	70.1
slope	123

REGULAR	
yardage	6017
par	72
rating	69.6
slope	122

FORWARD	
yardage	5621
par	72
rating	74.0
slope	129

⑪ SALINAS FAIRWAYS GOLF COURSE
ARCHITECT: JACK FLEMING, 1961

45 Skyway Boulevard
Salinas, CA 93905

PRO SHOP: 831-758-7300
OFFICE: 831-78-7163

Glen Stubblefield, PGA Professional
Rick Key, Superintendent

Driving Range •
Practice Greens •
Clubhouse •
Food / Beverage •
Accommodations
Pull Carts •
Power Carts •
Club Rental •
Special Offers

	1	2	3	4	5	6	7	8	9	OUT
BACK	380	342	166	465	418	550	404	189	353	3267
REGULAR	369	342	142	458	404	536	394	160	343	3148
par	4	4	3	5	4	5	4	3	4	36
handicap	6	10	14	16	2	4	12	18	8	-
FORWARD	323	328	128	443	326	451	329	156	328	2812
par	4	4	3	5	4	5	4	3	4	36
handicap	10	16	16	2	8	4	6	14	12	-

	10	11	12	13	14	15	16	17	18	IN
BACK	433	550	341	192	388	415	411	137	533	3400
REGULAR	415	529	331	163	378	400	398	130	519	3263
par	4	5	4	3	4	4	4	3	5	36
handicap	3	1	11	17	7	9	13	15	5	-
FORWARD	406	464	319	165	304	332	321	125	426	2862
par	5	5	4	3	4	4	4	3	5	37
handicap	5	1	11	13	7	15	9	17	3	-

BACK	
yardage	6667
par	72
rating	70.4
slope	114

REGULAR	
yardage	6411
par	72
rating	69.3
slope	111

FORWARD	
yardage	5674
par	73
rating	71.0
slope	115

PLAY POLICY & FEES: Reciprocal play is accepted with members of other private clubs. On weekdays, guest fees are $30 when accompanied by a member and $50 unaccompanied. On weekends, guest fees are $40 when accompanied by a member and $60 unaccompanied. Carts are $30. The course is closed on Monday.

DRESS CODE: No blue jeans are allowed, and shirts must have collars.

COURSE DESCRIPTION: This short course is tight and hilly with small, tricky greens. It has lots of trees. Many up-and-down holes require finesse shots from sidehill lies. It's a good test for the irons and the short game.

NOTES: This course was the site of a battle fought by General Fremont during the Mexican-American War. The men's course record of 60 is held by Kurt Dillard, and the women's by Pat Cornett at 67.

LOCATION: From U.S. 101 in Salinas, take the Boronda Road exit. Turn right on Main Street (the first stoplight) and follow it to San Juan Grade Road. Turn left on San Juan Grade Road and drive 2.5 miles to the course.

. . . ● **TOURNAMENTS:** Shotgun tournaments are available weekdays only. Carts are required. A 50-player minimum is required to book a tournament.

10. SALINAS GOLF & COUNTRY CLUB

PLAY POLICY & FEES: Green fees are $20 weekdays and $24 weekends. Twilight rates are $12 after 2:30 p.m. Resident rates are available. Carts are $18.

TEE TIMES: Reservations can be booked seven days in advance.

COURSE DESCRIPTION: This flat, tight course, has lots of trees and is often windy. Most greens are large and user-friendly. The course is located next to the Salinas Airport.

NOTES: The men's course record is 64, held by host pro Glen Stubblefield. The course underwent a complete renovation in 1999.

LOCATION: From U.S. 101 in Salinas, exit on Airport Boulevard east and follow it until it dead ends at the airport. Turn left on Skyway Boulevard to the course.

. . . ● **TOURNAMENTS:** This course has limited availability for tournaments. A 24-player minimum is needed to book an event. Tournaments should be scheduled six to 12 months in advance. ● **TRAVEL:** The Days Inn and the Good Nite Inn are recommended.

11. SALINAS FAIRWAYS GOLF COURSE

PACIFIC GROVE GOLF COURSE
ARCHITECT: JACK NEVILLE, 1932

GOLF 50

77 Asilomar Boulevard
Pacific Grove, CA 93950

PRO SHOP: 831-648-3177
CLUBHOUSE: 831-648-3175

Peter Vitarisi, Head Professional, PGA
Jeff Bushnell, Tournament Director
Mike Leach, Superintendent

Driving Range •
Practice Greens •
Clubhouse •
Food / Beverage •
Accommodations
Pull Carts •
Power Carts •
Club Rental •
$pecial Offers

	1	2	3	4	5	6	7	8	9	OUT
BACK	151	199	312	265	520	533	310	424	218	2932
REGULAR	146	193	305	259	510	527	304	419	213	2876
par	3	3	4	4	5	5	4	4	3	35
handicap	15	9	13	17	7	1	11	3	5	-
FORWARD	141	187	298	253	504	521	300	409	207	2820
par	3	3	4	4	5	5	4	5	4	37
handicap	17	15	9	11	3	1	7	5	13	-

	10	11	12	13	14	15	16	17	18	IN
BACK	109	303	513	316	356	397	355	153	298	2800
REGULAR	104	273	497	307	348	383	351	138	294	2695
par	3	4	5	4	4	4	4	3	4	35
handicap	18	12	4	10	6	2	8	16	14	-
FORWARD	97	265	480	283	328	305	336	100	291	2485
par	3	4	5	4	4	4	4	3	4	35
handicap	18	12	2	14	4	8	10	16	6	-

BACK	
yardage	5732
par	70
rating	67.7
slope	119

REGULAR	
yardage	5571
par	70
rating	66.9
slope	117

FORWARD	
yardage	5305
par	72
rating	70.1
slope	112

THE LINKS AT SPANISH BAY
ARCHITECTS: TOM WATSON, 1987; ROBERT TRENT JONES, JR.; FRANK TATUM

GOLF 50

P.O. Box 1418
Pebble Beach, CA 93953

2700 17-mile Drive
Pebble Beach, CA 93953

PRO SHOP: 831-647-7495

R.J. Harper, Director of Golf, PGA
Rich Cosand, PGA Professional
Forrest Arthur, Superintendent

Driving Range •
Practice Greens •
Clubhouse •
Food / Beverage •
Accommodations •
Pull Carts
Power Carts •
Club Rental •
$pecial Offers

	1	2	3	4	5	6	7	8	9	OUT
BACK	500	307	405	190	459	395	418	163	394	3231
REGULAR	461	265	334	176	405	345	382	148	357	2873
par	5	4	4	3	4	4	4	3	4	35
handicap	9	13	5	15	1	11	3	17	7	-
FORWARD	434	224	285	127	349	301	342	120	326	2508
par	5	4	4	3	4	4	4	3	4	35
handicap	9	13	5	15	1	11	3	17	7	-

	10	11	12	13	14	15	16	17	18	IN
BACK	520	365	432	126	571	390	200	414	571	3589
REGULAR	464	318	406	99	535	342	157	369	515	3205
par	5	4	4	3	5	4	3	4	5	37
handicap	8	12	6	18	2	12	16	4	10	-
FORWARD	401	285	341	76	475	296	130	321	476	2801
par	5	4	4	3	5	4	3	4	5	37
handicap	8	14	6	18	2	12	16	4	10	-

BACK	
yardage	6820
par	72
rating	74.8
slope	146

REGULAR	
yardage	6078
par	72
rating	71.7
slope	134

FORWARD	
yardage	5309
par	72
rating	70.6
slope	129

PUBLIC: $31-$36

18 HOLES

PLAY POLICY & FEES: Green fees are $31 Monday through Thursday and $36 Friday through Sunday and holidays. Twilight, senior, junior, and nine-hole rates are available. Carts are $26; pull carts are $2 for nine holes and $4 for 18.

TEE TIMES: Reservations are recommended seven days in advance.

DRESS CODE: Casual attire is OK.

COURSE DESCRIPTION: This tight, scenic oceanside course has a Scottish links-style flavor and is fun to play. The front nine weaves through the forest and is flanked by trees, while the back nine is bordered by sand dunes and ice plant. An old lighthouse stands guard over the course.

NOTES: The course used to be one of Monterey Peninsula's best-kept secrets, but with an estimated 98,000 rounds played each year, you may want to make reservations.

LOCATION: From Highway 1 in Monterey, take Highway 68/W.R. Holman (Pacific Grove Highway) west. Remain in the left lane after the second stop light and continue on Highway 68 to Asilomar. Turn right at Asilomar Avenue and follow it to the cemetery and lighthouse. The clubhouse is across from the lighthouse.

. . . ● **TOURNAMENTS:** Shotgun tournaments are not allowed. A 20-player minimum is required to book a tournament. Carts are required. Events should be scheduled 12 months in advance.

12. PACIFIC GROVE GOLF COURSE

RESORT: $165-$185

FAX: 831-644-7956

18 HOLES

PLAY POLICY & FEES: Green fees are $165 for Pebble Beach Resort guests and $185 for the public. Carts are $25. Players may carry their own bag, but caddies are available.

TEE TIMES: Resort guests may make tee times with their room reservations 18 months in advance. Outside players (two or more) may make reservations 60 days in advance. For tee times call 800-654-9300.

DRESS CODE: No cutoffs are allowed, and collared shirts are required.

COURSE DESCRIPTION: This fast-rolling course is tailored in the pure Scottish fashion, complete with fescue-grass fairways, pot bunkers, and mounds. Here the architects want golfers to hit run-up shots, keeping the ball low. All but four holes flank the ocean, so this strategy is especially advantageous when the wind kicks up. This is said to be the most authentic Scottish-links course in America.

LOCATION: From Highway 1 in Monterey, exit at Highway 68/W.R. Holman (Pacific Grove/Carmel Highway) west. The highway becomes Forest Avenue. Turn left at Sunset Drive, and drive to 17-Mile Drive. Turn left and drive one-eighth mile to the gate. The course is 500 yards past the gate on the right.

. . . ● **TOURNAMENTS:** A 16-player minimum is for a tournament. Events should be scheduled 24 months in advance. The banquet facility can accommodate 900 people. ● **TRAVEL:** For those who are flying in, the San Jose Airport is 60 minutes away. For reservations at the Lodge at Pebble Beach or the Inn at Spanish Bay call 800-654-9300.

13. THE LINKS AT SPANISH BAY

BAYONET/BLACK HORSE GOLF COURSE
ARCHITECT: GEN. ROBERT MCCLURE, 1954

1 McClure Way
Seaside, CA 93955

PRO SHOP: 831-899-7271

Joe Priddy, Director of Golf, PGA
Al Luna, PGA Professional
Leonard Theis, Superintendent

Driving Range ●
Practice Greens ●
Clubhouse ●
Food / Beverage ●
Accommodations
Pull Carts ●
Power Carts ●
Club Rental ●
$pecial Offers ●

	1	2	3	4	5	6	7	8	9	OUT
BACK	537	438	360	626	459	182	342	206	343	3493
REGULAR	508	423	354	620	450	176	334	192	334	3391
par	5	4	4	5	4	3	4	3	4	36
handicap	7	5	9	3	1	17	11	15	13	-
FORWARD	470	318	298	507	368	156	308	163	311	2899
par	5	4	4	5	5	3	4	3	4	37
handicap	11	13	5	1	3	17	7	15	9	-

BACK	
yardage	6982
par	72
rating	74.6
slope	138

	10	11	12	13	14	15	16	17	18	IN
BACK	504	423	390	453	215	403	348	201	552	3489
REGULAR	499	403	376	448	209	386	338	191	535	3385
par	5	4	4	4	3	4	4	3	5	36
handicap	12	10	2	4	16	6	14	18	8	-
FORWARD	461	371	315	357	135	336	292	164	434	2865
par	5	5	4	4	3	4	4	3	5	37
handicap	6	12	2	10	18	14	4	16	8	-

REGULAR	
yardage	6776
par	72
rating	73.6
slope	135

FORWARD	
yardage	5764
par	74
rating	73.7
slope	134

 TEHAMA GOLF CLUB
ARCHITECT: JAY MORRISH, 1999

7145 Carmel Valley Road
Carmel, CA

PRO SHOP: 831-624-5549

Bob Hickam, Director of Golf, PGA

Driving Range ●
Practice Greens ●
Clubhouse
Food / Beverage ●
Accommodations
Pull Carts
Power Carts ●
Club Rental
$pecial Offers

	1	2	3	4	5	6	7	8	9	OUT
BACK										
REGULAR										
par										
handicap										
FORWARD										
par										
handicap										

BACK	
yardage	
par	
rating	
slope	

	10	11	12	13	14	15	16	17	18	IN
BACK										
REGULAR										
par										
handicap										
FORWARD										
par										
handicap										

REGULAR	
yardage	
par	
rating	
slope	

FORWARD	
yardage	
par	
rating	
slope	

PLAY POLICY & FEES: Bayonet green fees are $50 Monday through Thursday, $70 Friday through Sunday and holidays, Carts are required before 1 p.m. on Saturday, Sunday, and holidays. Black Horse fees are $40 Monday through Thursday, and $60 Friday through Sunday and holidays. Carts are required before 1 p.m. on Saturday, Sunday, and holidays. Twilight fees are available for both courses. Cart fees are $20 per person. All fees Friday through Sunday and holidays include a registration fee.

TEE TIMES: Reservations can be booked 30 days in advance.

DRESS CODE: Collared shirts and hemmed pants are required. Metal spikes are discouraged.

COURSE DESCRIPTION: The Bayonet Course is long and difficult. The front nine is longer and more open, while the back nine has several tight doglegs and tricky greens. The Black Horse Course is shorter and more forgiving. It has a meandering layout bordered by tall trees and bunkers. Both courses offer ocean views, but can be foggy and windy.

NOTES: Both courses have undergone improvements. The clubhouse includes a full restaurant and banquet facility that will accommodate 144 people.

LOCATION: The main gate of Fort Ord is off Highway 1 at Light Fighter Drive. Drive through the gate and turn right on North South Road. Follow North South Road and turn right on McClure Way.

. . . ● **TOURNAMENTS:** Events can be booked 12 months in advance. ● **TRAVEL:** The Embassy Suites Monterey Bay Seaside (408-393-1115) is located 10 minutes from the course. ● **$PECIAL OFFERS:** Golf packages are available.

14. BAYONET/BLACK HORSE GOLF COURSE

PRIVATE   **18**

HOLES

PLAY POLICY & FEES: Members and guest only. No reciprocal play is allowed.

DRESS CODE: Appropriate golf attire is required.

COURSE DESCRIPTION: This course was not available for review at time of press. Tehama is expected to be one of the more challenging private courses to come out in years. Off the tee on many holes players must confront narrow, undulating fairways with few level lies and severe penalties for those who miss the short grass. From the fairways players will be aiming at tricky greens that present their own challenges.

LOCATION: From Highway 1 near Carmel take Highway 68 east toward Salinas. Make a right on Olmstead Road and a left on Via Malpaso to the front gate.

. . . ● **TOURNAMENTS:** Outside events are not allowed.

15. TEHAMA GOLF CLUB

16 PETER HAY GOLF COURSE
ARCHITECT: PETER HAY, 1957

P.O. Box 658　　　　17-Mile Drive
Pebble Beach, CA 93953

PRO SHOP: 831-625-8518
OFFICE: 831-625-8518

R.J. Harper, Director of Golf, PGA
Chris Pryor, Head Professional, PGA
Mark Michaud, Superintendent

Driving Range ●
Practice Greens ●
Clubhouse ●
Food / Beverage ●
Accommodations ●
Pull Carts ●
Power Carts
Club Rental ●
Special Offers

	1	2	3	4	5	6	7	8	9	OUT
BACK	-	-	-	-	-	-	-	-	-	-
REGULAR	72	70	106	92	115	96	71	118	79	819
par	3	3	3	3	3	3	3	3	3	27
handicap	-	-	-	-	-	-	-	-	-	-
FORWARD	72	70	106	92	115	96	71	118	79	819
par	3	3	3	3	3	3	3	3	3	27
handicap	-	-	-	-	-	-	-	-	-	-

	10	11	12	13	14	15	16	17	18	IN
BACK	-	-	-	-	-	-	-	-	-	-
REGULAR	72	70	106	92	115	96	71	118	79	819
par	3	3	3	3	3	3	3	3	3	27
handicap	-	-	-	-	-	-	-	-	-	-
FORWARD	72	70	106	92	115	96	71	118	79	819
par	3	3	3	3	3	3	3	3	3	27
handicap	-	-	-	-	-	-	-	-	-	-

BACK	
yardage	-
par	-
rating	-
slope	-

REGULAR	
yardage	1638
par	54
rating	-
slope	-

FORWARD	
yardage	1638
par	54
rating	-
slope	-

17 PEBBLE BEACH GOLF LINKS
ARCHITECT: JACK NEVILLE, 1919

GOLF 50

P.O. Box 658　　　　17-Mile Drive
Pebble Beach, CA 93953

PRO SHOP: 831-624-3811
OFFICE: 831-625-8518

R.J. Harper, Director of Golf, PGA
Chris Pryor, Head Professional, PGA
Mark Michaud, Superintendent

Driving Range ●
Practice Greens ●
Clubhouse ●
Food / Beverage ●
Accommodations ●
Pull Carts
Power Carts ●
Club Rental ●
Special Offers

	1	2	3	4	5	6	7	8	9	OUT
BACK	373	502	388	327	166	516	107	431	464	3274
REGULAR	338	439	341	303	156	487	103	405	439	3011
par	4	5	4	4	3	5	3	4	4	36
handicap	8	10	12	16	14	2	18	6	4	-
FORWARD	322	363	275	256	140	385	88	350	330	2509
par	4	5	4	4	3	5	3	4	4	36
handicap	8	10	12	16	14	2	18	6	4	-

	10	11	12	13	14	15	16	17	18	IN
BACK	426	384	202	392	565	397	402	209	548	3525
REGULAR	395	374	184	373	553	366	388	175	538	3346
par	4	4	3	4	5	4	4	3	5	36
handicap	7	5	17	9	1	13	11	15	3	-
FORWARD	296	316	166	285	420	308	307	164	426	2688
par	4	4	3	4	5	4	4	3	5	36
handicap	7	5	17	9	1	13	11	15	3	-

BACK	
yardage	6799
par	72
rating	74.4
slope	142

REGULAR	
yardage	6357
par	72
rating	72.1
slope	138

FORWARD	
yardage	5197
par	72
rating	71.9
slope	130

PLAY POLICY & FEES: Green fees are $15 for all-day play. Juniors under 12 are free when accompanied by an adult.

TEE TIMES: Reservations are not accepted. All play is on a first-come, first-served basis.

COURSE DESCRIPTION: This par-3 course provides an excellent opportunity to sharpen your short game. The course has been replanted with rye grass. Additional tees allow playing the holes from a different location on a second round. This course is short and tight, with some hills and lots of trees; the longest hole is 118 yards.

NOTES: The course is named for the late Peter Hay, the designer and longtime pro at Pebble Beach.

LOCATION: From Highway 1 take the Pebble Beach exit. The guard will give you instructions and a map. The course is across from Pebble Beach Golf Links.

. . . ● **TOURNAMENTS:** A 16-player minimum is needed to book an event. Tournaments should be scheduled three months in advance. The banquet facility can accommodate 400 people. ● **TRAVEL:** For reservations at the Lodge at Pebble Beach or the Inn at Spanish Bay call 800-654-9300.

16. PETER HAY GOLF COURSE

PLAY POLICY & FEES: Green fees for Pebble Beach Resort guests are $275 including cart. For other players, the fee is $305. Carts are $25 per person and $25 for spectators. Caddies are available.

TEE TIMES: Reservations can be booked one day in advance for nonlodge guests, and 18 months for lodge guests. For tee times call 800-654-9300.

DRESS CODE: Collared shirts are required. Nonmetal spikes are requested, and no jeans are allowed.

COURSE DESCRIPTION: Designed by Jack Neville in 1919, this is one of the most scenic and demanding courses in the world. Eight holes flank the ocean, placing the entire course under the influence of fog, mist, and wind. The par-5 18th hole is considered by many to be the finest finishing hole in golf.

NOTES: This course is used regularly for the AT&T Pebble Beach National Pro-Am, the U.S. Open, the PGA Championship, and the U.S. Amateur. The course will host the 2000 U.S. Open.

LOCATION: From Highway 1 take the Pebble Beach exit and drive to the Pebble Beach Resort gate for instructions and a map.

. . . ● **TOURNAMENTS:** A 16-player minimum is needed to book a tournament. Events should be booked three months in advance. The banquet facility can accommodate 400 people. ● **TRAVEL:** For those who are flying in, the San Jose Airport is 60 minutes away. For reservations at the Lodge at Pebble Beach or the Inn at Spanish Bay call 800-654-9300. Recommended restaurants include the Tap Room, Club XIX, and the Stillwater Bar & Grill.

17. PEBBLE BEACH GOLF LINKS

MONTEREY PENINSULA COUNTRY CLUB
ARCHITECT: SETH J. RAYNOR

3000 Club Road
Pebble Beach, CA 93953

PRO SHOP: 831-372-8141

David Vivolo, PGA Professional
Bob Zoller, Superintendent

Driving Range ●
Practice Greens ●
Clubhouse ●
Food / Beverage ●
Accommodations ●
Pull Carts ●
Power Carts ●
Club Rental ●
$pecial Offers

	1	2	3	4	5	6	7	8	9	OUT
BACK										
REGULAR										
par										
handicap										
FORWARD										
par										
handicap										

	10	11	12	13	14	15	16	17	18	IN
BACK										
REGULAR										
par										
handicap										
FORWARD										
par										
handicap										

BACK	
yardage	6361
par	72
rating	71.4
slope	129

REGULAR	
yardage	6173
par	72
rating	70.5
slope	127

FORWARD	
yardage	5935
par	72
rating	74.4
slope	130

CYPRESS POINT CLUB
ARCHITECT: ALISTER MACKENZIE, 1928

P.O. Box 466
Pebble Beach, CA 93953

3150 17-Mile Drive
Pebble Beach, CA 93953

PRO SHOP: 831-624-2223

Jim Langley, PGA Professional
Jeff Markow, Superintendent

Driving Range ●
Practice Greens ●
Clubhouse ●
Food / Beverage ●
Accommodations ●
Pull Carts
Power Carts ●
Club Rental ●
$pecial Offers

	1	2	3	4	5	6	7	8	9	OUT
BACK	421	548	162	384	493	518	168	363	292	3349
REGULAR	409	538	155	373	471	509	161	347	282	3245
par	4	5	3	4	5	5	3	4	4	37
handicap	5	1	17	7	11	3	15	9	13	-
FORWARD	409	510	142	366	416	475	155	319	247	3039
par	5	5	3	4	5	5	3	4	4	38
handicap	11	1	17	7	5	3	13	9	15	-

	10	11	12	13	14	15	16	17	18	IN
BACK	480	437	404	365	388	143	231	393	346	3187
REGULAR	480	428	397	343	382	127	219	382	329	3087
par	5	4	4	4	4	3	3	4	4	35
handicap	16	4	2	14	8	18	6	10	12	-
FORWARD	480	401	310	285	323	119	208	355	296	2777
par	5	5	4	4	4	3	4	4	4	37
handicap	2	10	8	14	6	18	16	4	12	-

BACK	
yardage	6536
par	72
rating	72.3
slope	134

REGULAR	
yardage	6332
par	72
rating	71.2
slope	130

FORWARD	
yardage	5816
par	75
rating	74.1
slope	139

PLAY POLICY & FEES: Guest fees are $60 when accompanied by a member and $185 to $215 unaccompanied. All guests must be member sponsored. Fees include carts.

DRESS CODE: No denim is allowed, and skirts must be knee length. Women may wear knee-length shorts. Nonmetal spikes are required.

COURSE DESCRIPTION: These meandering, scenic courses are flanked by pine trees, the ocean, and sand dunes. The greens are tricky and immaculate with a lot of undulation. Keep the ball below the hole. The picturesque Dunes Course is longer and situated farther inland. It was used for the Bing Crosby National Pro-Am for 18 years. The Shore Course is shorter and tighter. Designed by Bob Baldock, it flanks the ocean and is more exposed to the elements. The short par 5s are reachable in two for the long hitters.

NOTES: The Dunes Course was remodeled and reopened in 1999.

LOCATION: From Highway 1 in Monterey take Highway 68/W.R. Holman (Pacific Grove exit) to David Avenue. Turn left on David Avenue and drive less than a quarter of a mile. Turn right on Congress Avenue. Turn left at Forest Lodge Road and drive to the entrance gate of 17-Mile Drive. Head south on Sloat Road and turn right on Club Road.

. . . ● **TOURNAMENTS:** This course is not available for outside events.

18. MONTEREY PENINSULA COUNTRY CLUB

PLAY POLICY & FEES: Members and guests only.

DRESS CODE: Appropriate golf attire is required

COURSE DESCRIPTION: This spectacular course is the best-known work of the Scottish architect Alister Mackenzie, who designed it in 1928. Flanked by sand and sea, the course makes the most of its natural resources. The greens are fast and undulating. The famous par-3 16th hole requires a scenic and spectacular 200-yard carry over the ocean. The shorter par-3 15th hole flanks the ocean and is one of the prettiest in the world.

NOTES: The club is exclusive. The course was used for the AT&T Pebble Beach National Pro-Am (formerly the Bing Crosby National Pro-Am) from 1947 to 1990. Gay Brewer holds the course record with a 62.

LOCATION: From Highway 1 take the Pacific Grove exit. At the first stop sign, drive to the Carmel Hill gate leading into Pebble Beach. Ask for instructions and a map at the gate.

. . . ● **TOURNAMENTS:** This course is not available for outside events.

19. CYPRESS POINT CLUB

SPYGLASS HILL GOLF COURSE
ARCHITECT: ROBERT T. JONES SR., 1966

GOLF
50

P.O. Box 658
Pebble Beach, CA 93953

Spyglass Hill Road at
Pebble Beach, CA 93953

PRO SHOP: 831-625-8563

R.J. Harper, Director of Golf, PGA
Mark Brenneman, Head Professional, LPGA
Eric Johnson, Superintendent

Driving Range ●
Practice Greens ●
Clubhouse ●
Food / Beverage ●
Accommodations ●
Pull Carts
Power Carts ●
Club Rental ●
$pecial Offers

	1	2	3	4	5	6	7	8	9	OUT
BACK	600	351	152	370	186	412	529	396	430	3426
REGULAR	565	327	131	361	144	374	485	363	411	3161
par	5	4	3	4	3	4	5	4	4	36
handicap	3	13	17	9	15	7	11	1	5	-
FORWARD	487	246	92	299	110	325	467	300	391	2717
par	5	4	3	4	3	4	5	4	5	37
handicap	1	13	17	11	15	7	3	9	5	-

BACK	
yardage	6855
par	72
rating	75.3
slope	148

	10	11	12	13	14	15	16	17	18	IN
BACK	408	528	178	441	560	121	464	322	407	3429
REGULAR	379	491	145	419	519	99	431	311	392	3186
par	4	5	3	4	5	3	4	4	4	36
handicap	12	10	16	4	6	18	2	14	8	-
FORWARD	367	419	96	393	481	84	399	301	361	2901
par	4	5	3	4	5	3	5	4	4	37
handicap	10	4	18	8	2	16	6	14	12	-

REGULAR	
yardage	6347
par	72
rating	72.8
slope	141

FORWARD	
yardage	5618
par	74
rating	73.7
slope	133

PLAY POLICY & FEES: Outside play is accepted. Green fees are $220 for NCGA members, $225 for nonmembers, and $195 including cart for Pebble Beach Resort guests (the Inn at Spanish Bay or the Lodge at Pebble Beach). Carts are $25 per person.

TEE TIMES: Resort guests may book tee times 18 months ahead, and nonguests 30 days ahead. For tee times call 800-654-9300.

DRESS CODE: Golf attire is encouraged. No blue jeans are allowed.

COURSE DESCRIPTION: This long, demanding course, designed by Robert Trent Jones Sr. in 1966, is unforgiving. Used annually for the AT&T Pebble Beach National Pro-Am, it almost always produces the highest scoring average. The first five holes wind through sand dunes and offer magnificent ocean views. It's surrounded by Monterey pines. The large, undulating greens are well protected. The names given to each of the holes were derived from Robert Louis Stevenson's classic, "Treasure Island." You'll find Treasure Island--an island in the sand--on the first hole, Long John Silver on the 14th (a double dogleg par 5), and Black Dog on the 16th (an infamous par 4).

NOTES: Spyglass is part of the AT&T Pebble Beach Pro-Am and the annual site of the NCGA Amateur Championship. It will host qualifying rounds for the 1999 U.S. Amateur. It ranked in the country's top 100 courses in 1991,1994, and 1997.

LOCATION: From Highway 1 take the Pebble Beach exit and drive to the Highway 1 gate for instructions and a map.

. . . ● **TOURNAMENTS:** A four-player minimum is required to book a tournament. Tournaments can be booked one month in advance. The banquet facility at the Lodge at Pebble Beach can accommodate 400 people. ● **TRAVEL:** For those flying in, the San Jose Airport is 60 minutes away. For reservations at the Lodge at Pebble Beach, or the Inn at Spanish Bay, call 800-654-9300. Recommended dining in the area: The Tap Room, Club XIX, and the Stillwater Bar & Grill.

20. SPYGLASS HILL GOLF COURSE

21 POPPY HILLS GOLF COURSE
ARCHITECT: ROBERT TRENT JONES JR., 1986

GOLF 50

3200 Lopez Road
Pebble Beach, CA 93953

3200 Lopez on 17-Mile
Pebble Beach, CA 93953

PRO SHOP: 831-622-8239

Bob Higgins, Director of Golf, PGA
Tyler Jones, Head Professional, PGA

Driving Range •
Practice Greens •
Clubhouse •
Food / Beverage •
Accommodations
Pull Carts
Power Carts •
Club Rental •
$pecial Offers

	1	2	3	4	5	6	7	8	9	OUT
BACK	413	174	406	550	426	181	388	390	557	3485
REGULAR	390	142	369	513	381	149	351	370	508	3173
par	4	3	4	5	4	3	4	4	5	36
handicap	7	15	5	1	9	17	11	13	3	-
FORWARD	316	110	255	454	337	120	313	330	446	2681
par	4	3	4	5	4	3	4	4	5	36
handicap	7	15	5	1	9	17	11	13	3	-

BACK		
yardage	6835
par	72
rating	74.6
slope	144

	10	11	12	13	14	15	16	17	18	IN
BACK	511	203	531	393	400	210	439	163	500	3350
REGULAR	472	163	502	377	385	175	402	126	474	3076
par	5	3	5	4	4	3	4	3	5	36
handicap	4	16	2	10	12	14	6	18	8	-
FORWARD	402	144	456	343	341	148	367	115	411	2727
par	5	3	5	4	4	3	4	3	5	36
handicap	4	16	2	10	12	14	6	18	8	-

REGULAR		
yardage	6249
par	72
rating	71.5
slope	140

FORWARD		
yardage	5408
par	72
rating	74.8
slope	143

---

22 MONTEREY PINES GOLF COURSE
ARCHITECT: ROBERT MUIR GRAVES, 1962

MWR Department, 1
NPS Monterey, CA 93943

1250 Garden Road
Monterey, CA 93943

PRO SHOP: 831-656-2167
OFFICE: 831-656-4029

Mike Valleau, General Manager
Daniel R. Tracy, Superintendent

Driving Range •
Practice Greens •
Clubhouse •
Food / Beverage •
Accommodations
Pull Carts •
Power Carts •
Club Rental •
$pecial Offers

	1	2	3	4	5	6	7	8	9	OUT
BACK	-	-	-	-	-	-	-	-	-	-
REGULAR	359	156	358	194	365	340	500	323	404	2999
par	4	3	4	3	4	4	5	4	4	35
handicap	3	17	5	15	13	7	9	11	1	-
FORWARD	337	122	325	180	323	317	464	310	402	2780
par	4	3	4	3	4	4	5	4	5	36
handicap	11	17	9	15	13	7	1	5	3	-

BACK		
yardage	-
par	-
rating	-
slope	-

	10	11	12	13	14	15	16	17	18	IN
BACK	-	-	-	-	-	-	-	-	-	-
REGULAR	435	141	157	466	373	251	142	171	540	2676
par	4	3	3	5	4	4	3	3	5	34
handicap	2	14	10	12	6	18	16	8	4	-
FORWARD	410	102	140	442	347	239	127	164	444	2415
par	5	3	3	5	4	4	3	3	5	35
handicap	8	14	10	4	2	16	18	12	6	-

REGULAR		
yardage	5675
par	69
rating	67.6
slope	119

FORWARD		
yardage	5195
par	71
rating	69.3
slope	115

21. POPPY HILLS GOLF COURSE

PLAY POLICY & FEES: Green fees are $45 for NCGA members and $75 for NCGA guests (limited to three per day), and $115 for nonmembers on Monday through Thursday. Green fees are $50 for NCGA members and $80 for NCGA guests, and $130 for nonmembers Friday, Saturday, Sunday, and holidays. Carts are $30. Caddies are available with advance notice.

TEE TIMES: Reservations are available one month in advance, or call the golf shop for available tee times.

DRESS CODE: Appropriate golf attire and nonmetal spikes are required.

COURSE DESCRIPTION: This course is long and tight, with plenty of trees, water, and sand. The large, undulating greens are well guarded by bunkers. Many of the greens are flanked by areas that give the player an option to chip or putt. On most holes a golfer can play it safe or go for broke, especially on the par-5 9th and 18th holes. This is the home of the Northern California Golf Association.

NOTES: This course is one of three in rotation for the annual AT&T Pebble Beach National Pro-Am. Clark Dewars holds the course record of 63.

LOCATION: From Highway 1 take the Pebble Beach exit and proceed to the gate for instructions.

. . . ● **TOURNAMENTS:** Shotgun tournaments are limited. Group reservations are available one year in advance. For more information call 831-622-8244 Monday through Friday, 8 a.m. to 4 p.m. The banquet facility can accommodate 120 people. ● **TRAVEL:** The Hyatt (831-372-1234), the Double Tree (831-649-4511) and the Marriott (831-649-4234) are all recommended for lodging.

22. MONTEREY PINES GOLF COURSE

PLAY POLICY & FEES: Green fees for military personnel are $10 weekdays and $12 weekends. Green fees for civilians are $18 weekdays and $25 weekends. Carts are $10 for nine holes and $16 for 18 holes. No children under eight years of age are permitted.

TEE TIMES: Military personnel can make reservations seven days in advance. Military dependent civilians can make reservations five days in advance. Civilians can make reservations three days in advance.

DRESS CODE: Appropriate golf attire and nonmetal spikes are required.

COURSE DESCRIPTION: This short, level course has narrow fairways and lots of trees. Four lakes come into play. The course has greatly improved conditions and has some of the best greens on the Monterey Peninsula. Monterey Pines is a good value for those wanting to play on the Monterey Peninsula.

NOTES: The course, formerly known as the U.S. Navy Course, is still operated by the military, but anyone can play here now. The men's course record is 63, held by Peter Niles. The women's course record is 70.

LOCATION: From Highway 1 in Monterey take the Casa Verde Way exit south to Fairgrounds Road. Turn right on Fairgrounds and continue to Garden Road; then turn left. The course is immediately on the left.

. . . ● **TOURNAMENTS:** This course is available for outside tournaments. A 24-player minimum is needed to book a tournament. Tournaments can be booked six months in advance.

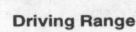

1300 Sylvan Road
Monterey, CA 93940

PRO SHOP: 831-373-2700

R.J. Harper, Director of Golf, PGA
Chuck Dunbar, PGA Professional
Cindy Minor, Tournament Director

Driving Range
Practice Greens ●
Clubhouse ●
Food / Beverage ●
Accommodations
Pull Carts ●
Power Carts ●
Club Rental ●
$pecial Offers

	1	2	3	4	5	6	7	8	9	OUT
BACK	511	328	379	181	323	196	380	385	527	3210
REGULAR	496	311	364	166	295	188	368	370	516	3074
par	5	4	4	3	4	3	4	4	5	36
handicap	9	17	5	15	13	3	1	11	7	-
FORWARD	424	307	354	143	284	180	299	311	426	2728
par	5	4	4	3	4	3	4	4	5	36
handicap	1	11	5	17	13	15	9	7	3	-

	10	11	12	13	14	15	16	17	18	IN
BACK	290	329	160	516	219	346	423	477	369	3129
REGULAR	282	321	145	502	211	320	423	463	328	2995
par	4	4	3	5	3	4	4	5	4	36
handicap	16	14	12	10	4	8	2	18	6	-
FORWARD	277	314	121	414	204	298	416	438	316	2798
par	4	4	3	5	4	4	5	5	4	38
handicap	14	12	18	4	16	10	6	2	8	-

BACK	
yardage	6339
par	72
rating	71.6
slope	125

REGULAR	
yardage	6069
par	72
rating	70.3
slope	123

FORWARD	
yardage	5526
par	74
rating	71.0
slope	120

PLAY POLICY & FEES: For hotel guests of the Inn at Spanish Bay, the Lodge at Pebble Beach, and the Hyatt, green fees are $75. Outside green fees are $80. The course has special arrangements with other hotels in the area, and guests of those hotels receive courtesy discount rates. Carts are $18 per rider. Caddies are available upon request.

TEE TIMES: Reservations can be booked 60 days in advance.

DRESS CODE: Golf attire is encouraged. No cut-off shorts or tank tops allowed. Nonmetal spikes are recommended.

COURSE DESCRIPTION: Originally built as a nine-hole course in 1897, it was expanded to 18 holes in 1901. It was reported in the early days to be the first course in the world to have green fairways throughout the seasons. This inland course offers a meandering, hilly layout with lots of trees and tight doglegs. The short, but infuriating, par-4 18th hole looks like an easy birdie, but don't count on it. It will drive you crazy.

NOTES: In 1997 Del Monte Golf Course celebrated its 100th birthday. This is the oldest course west of the Mississippi in continuous use. The 40-plus-year-old record of 62 was recently tied by Todd Gjesvold.

LOCATION: In Monterey heading south on Highway 1 take the central Monterey exit. Go left on Aguajito Road and go back under the highway. Turn left at Mark Thomas Drive and turn right at Sylvan Road to the course.

. . . ● **TOURNAMENTS:** A 16-player minimum is required to book a tournament. Carts are required. The banquet facility can accommodate 180 people. Events can be booked 24 months in advance. ● **TRAVEL:** For those who are flying in, the San Jose Airport is 60 minutes away. For reservations at the Lodge at Pebble Beach, or the Inn at Spanish Bay, call 800-654-9300.

23. DEL MONTE GOLF COURSE

LAGUNA SECA GOLF CLUB
ARCHITECT: ROBERT TRENT JONES SR. & JR., 1970

10520 York Road
Monterey, CA 93940

PRO SHOP: 831-373-3701
CLUBHOUSE: 888-524-8629

Gary Cursio, Director of Golf
Mark W. Darby, Head Professional, PGA
Jeff Hardy, Superintendent

Driving Range ●
Practice Greens ●
Clubhouse ●
Food / Beverage ●
Accommodations
Pull Carts ●
Power Carts ●
Club Rental ●
$pecial Offers

	1	2	3	4	5	6	7	8	9	OUT
BACK	344	151	505	377	499	326	363	157	404	3126
REGULAR	333	139	493	368	477	302	332	137	386	2967
par	4	3	5	4	5	4	4	3	4	36
handicap	13	15	7	3	9	11	5	17	1	-
FORWARD	303	132	479	354	472	288	316	105	374	2823
par	4	3	5	4	5	4	4	3	5	37
handicap	11	15	1	7	3	13	9	17	5	-

	10	11	12	13	14	15	16	17	18	IN
BACK	425	321	178	558	154	548	382	127	338	3031
REGULAR	379	279	165	507	132	511	365	111	310	2759
par	4	4	3	5	3	5	4	3	4	35
handicap	6	12	14	8	16	2	4	18	10	-
FORWARD	342	242	118	488	116	419	265	93	298	2381
par	4	4	3	5	3	5	4	3	4	35
handicap	6	12	14	4	16	2	10	18	8	-

BACK	
yardage	6157
par	71
rating	70.7
slope	127

REGULAR	
yardage	5726
par	71
rating	68.9
slope	122

FORWARD	
yardage	5204
par	72
rating	70.8
slope	121

 # QUAIL LODGE RESORT AND COUNTRY CLUB
ARCHITECT: ROBERT MUIR GRAVES, 1963

8000 Valley Greens Drive
Carmel, CA 93923

PRO SHOP: 831-620-8808
CLUBHOUSE: 831-624-2888

Edgar Haber, President
Dave Anderson, PGA Professional
Lisa Autrey, Tournament Director

Driving Range ●
Practice Greens ●
Clubhouse ●
Food / Beverage ●
Accommodations ●
Pull Carts ●
Power Carts ●
Club Rental ●
$pecial Offers ●

	1	2	3	4	5	6	7	8	9	OUT
BACK	549	209	401	407	197	352	371	219	537	3242
REGULAR	536	196	387	329	189	337	362	208	525	3069
par	5	3	4	4	3	4	4	3	5	35
handicap	5	13	3	1	15	11	17	9	7	-
FORWARD	455	156	338	320	171	311	357	178	450	2736
par	5	3	4	4	3	4	4	3	5	35
handicap	3	17	11	5	15	7	9	13	1	-

	10	11	12	13	14	15	16	17	18	IN
BACK	345	346	223	386	507	522	411	161	373	3274
REGULAR	321	333	135	375	494	509	399	149	356	3071
par	4	4	3	4	5	5	4	3	4	36
handicap	12	16	4	6	14	8	2	18	8	-
FORWARD	294	323	125	319	437	418	348	108	343	2715
par	4	4	3	4	5	5	4	3	4	36
handicap	14	12	18	10	2	4	8	16	6	-

BACK	
yardage	6516
par	71
rating	72.1
slope	129

REGULAR	
yardage	6140
par	71
rating	70.4
slope	125

FORWARD	
yardage	5451
par	71
rating	72.2
slope	126

PLAY POLICY & FEES: Green fees are $60 every day. Twilight rates are $30. The course provides powered golf carts for $35.

TEE TIMES: Reservations can be booked at any time.

DRESS CODE: Appropriate golf attire is required. Nonmetal spikes are mandatory.

COURSE DESCRIPTION: A Robert Trent Jones–design, this challenging course has a number of elevated tees and greens. It's a sprawling course that follows the oak-studded coastal hills, and it will require every club in your bag--a great challenge!

NOTES: Laguna Seca is known as the "Sunshine Golf Course" because it has some of the best weather on the Monterey Peninsula.

LOCATION: On the east side of Monterey off Highway 68 exit north on York Road and drive to the end.

. . . ● **TOURNAMENTS:** A 20-player minimum is required to book a tournament. Events should be scheduled 12 months in advance. A banquet facility is available that can accommodate up to 200 people. ● **TRAVEL:** The Embassy Suites Monterey Bay-Seaside is about 15 minutes from the golf course. Call 408-393-1115 for reservations.

24. LAGUNA SECA GOLF CLUB

PLAY POLICY & FEES: Green fees are $145 Monday through Thursday and $165 weekends and holidays during the peak season (April through October). Off-season green fees are $125. Twilight guest fees are $75 during peak season and $65 during the off season.Carts and range balls are included.

TEE TIMES: Reservations can be made 180 days in advance.

DRESS CODE: Shirts with collars and nonmetal spikes are required. Walking shorts are permitted, but no jeans, tank tops, or hard rubber golf shoes are allowed.

COURSE DESCRIPTION: The front nine is level with generous landing areas off the tee, but most greens are usually well protected requiring an accurate second shot. On the back nine you will find the fairways and greens getting smaller as your chances of hitting into atrap or water hazard become greater. Quail Lodge gives the average golfer a chance to score well, yet still remains a challenge for low handicappers.

NOTES: The California State Women's Amateur is held here each December.

LOCATION: From Highway 1 in Carmel, take the Carmel Valley Road exit. Drive 3.5 miles to Valley Greens Drive. Turn right on Valley Greens Drive and follow it to the course.

. . . ● **TOURNAMENTS:** A 12-player minimum is needed to book an event, and tournaments should be made 18 months in advance. The banquet facility can accommodate 200 people. ● **TRAVEL:** For reservations at Quail Lodge call 831-624-2888. ● **$PECIAL OFFERS:** Play-and-stay packages are available.

25. QUAIL LODGE RESORT AND COUNTRY

26 RANCHO CAÑADA GOLF CLUB
ARCHITECT: ROBERT DEAN PUTMAN, 1970

P.O. Box 22590
Carmel, CA 93922

Carmel Valley Rd. 1 Mile

PRO SHOP: 800-536-9459
CLUBHOUSE: 831-624-0111

Todd Pontti, Director of Golf, PGA
Mark Stoddard, Head Professional, PGA
Tim Greenwald, Superintendent, GCSA

Driving Range ●
Practice Greens ●
Clubhouse ●
Food / Beverage ●
Accommodations
Pull Carts ●
Power Carts ●
Club Rental ●
$Special Offers ●

	1	2	3	4	5	6	7	8	9	OUT
BACK	416	438	196	344	366	521	187	385	485	3338
REGULAR	406	424	167	326	347	508	177	371	468	3194
par	4	4	3	4	4	5	3	4	5	36
handicap	9	5	17	15	11	1	13	7	3	-
FORWARD	380	394	117	300	326	477	151	347	437	2929
par	4	5	3	4	4	5	3	4	5	37
handicap	14	10	18	12	6	4	16	8	2	-

	10	11	12	13	14	15	16	17	18	IN
BACK	405	159	415	300	338	372	156	503	363	3011
REGULAR	395	151	415	289	326	366	139	494	347	2922
par	4	3	4	4	4	4	3	5	4	35
handicap	10	16	6	14	2	12	18	4	8	-
FORWARD	368	129	375	260	292	350	108	438	319	2639
par	4	3	4	4	4	4	3	5	4	35
handicap	13	9	7	15	1	3	17	5	11	-

BACK	
yardage	6349
par	71
rating	70.4
slope	125

REGULAR	
yardage	6116
par	71
rating	69.3
slope	123

FORWARD	
yardage	5568
par	72
rating	71.9
slope	118

PLAY POLICY & FEES: Peak season green fees for the West Course are $75 in the morning, and $40 in the afternoon. Morning green fees for the East Course are $60. Afternoon rates are $35. Rates are subject to change, and super twilight fees are available. Carts are $32.

TEE TIMES: Reservations are recommended seven days in advance for weekends and holidays, and up to 180 days for credit card bookings.

DRESS CODE: Collared shirts and nonmetal spikes are required. No cut-off shorts are allowed on the course.

COURSE DESCRIPTION: Nestled in the scenic Carmel River Valley, these beautiful courses are tight with plenty of mature pine and oak trees. Both courses offer excellent greens that hold your approach shot and roll true. The West Course is tougher and tighter. The 15th hole is one of the tightest par 4s you'll ever play. The East Course is short, surrounded by trees, and crosses the Carmel River five times. Yard for yard these are two of the more challenging golf courses you will ever play.

NOTES: See scorecard for information on the West Course. The East Course is 6,109 yards from the back tees with a rating of 68.7 and a slope of 120. The white tees are 5,832 yards with a rating of 67.4 and a slope of 117. The forward tees are 5,267 yards with a rating of 69.4 and a slope of 114.

LOCATION: From Highway 1 in Carmel take the Carmel Valley Road exit. Drive 1.5 miles east to the course. The entrance is on the right.

. . . ● **TOURNAMENTS:** A 20-player minimum is required for group reservations and rates. Tournaments can be up to 24 months in advance. The banquet facility can accommodate 400 people. ● **TRAVEL:** Alternative lodging can be found at the Carmel Mission Inn. For reservations call 831-373-3252. ● **$PECIAL OFFERS:** Play-and-stay packages are available at the Mariposa Inn. For reservations call 831-649-1414.

26. RANCHO CAÑADA GOLF CLUB

CARMEL VALLEY RANCH RESORT
ARCHITECT: PETE DYE, 1981

GOLF 50

1 Old Ranch Road
Carmel, CA 93923

PRO SHOP: 831-626-2510

Martin Nicholson, General Manager
Michael L. Chapman, Director of Golf, PGA

Driving Range ●
Practice Greens ●
Clubhouse ●
Food / Beverage ●
Accommodations ●
Pull Carts
Power Carts ●
Club Rental ●
$Special Offers

	1	2	3	4	5	6	7	8	9	OUT
BACK	353	299	318	402	161	548	127	415	383	3006
REGULAR	339	285	297	311	130	484	111	394	352	2703
par	4	4	4	4	3	5	3	4	4	35
handicap	7	15	9	11	13	3	17	1	5	-
FORWARD	327	275	269	291	119	442	99	378	325	2525
par	4	4	4	4	3	5	3	4	4	35
handicap	5	13	15	9	11	7	17	3	1	-

	10	11	12	13	14	15	16	17	18	IN
BACK	458	438	397	150	358	416	229	360	422	3228
REGULAR	430	402	355	138	298	393	182	323	339	2860
par	5	4	4	3	4	4	3	4	4	35
handicap	10	2	8	18	16	6	14	12	4	-
FORWARD	389	360	346	114	265	324	140	295	288	2521
par	5	4	4	3	4	4	3	4	4	35
handicap	6	2	8	18	14	4	16	10	12	-

BACK	
yardage	6234
par	70
rating	70.5
slope	134

REGULAR	
yardage	5563
par	70
rating	67.6
slope	126

FORWARD	
yardage	5046
par	70
rating	68.6
slope	120

 CORRAL DE TIERRA COUNTRY CLUB
ARCHITECT: BOB BALDOCK, 1959

81 Corral de Tierra Road
Salinas, CA 93908

PRO SHOP: 831-484-1325
CLUBHOUSE: 831-484-1112

Scott Domnie, Director of Golf
Gerry Greenfield, PGA Professional
Scott Domnie, Superintendent

Driving Range ●
Practice Greens ●
Clubhouse ●
Food / Beverage ●
Accommodations
Pull Carts ●
Power Carts ●
Club Rental ●
$Special Offers

	1	2	3	4	5	6	7	8	9	OUT
BACK	431	377	501	171	470	388	366	181	502	3387
REGULAR	418	342	488	148	446	352	351	154	472	3171
par	4	4	5	3	4	4	4	3	5	36
handicap	3	7	9	17	1	5	13	15	11	-
FORWARD	418	333	442	112	385	346	344	109	445	2934
par	5	4	5	3	5	4	4	3	5	38
handicap	13	9	1	15	11	3	7	17	5	-

	10	11	12	13	14	15	16	17	18	IN
BACK	387	160	335	487	439	365	482	187	409	3251
REGULAR	374	131	321	477	423	344	471	171	370	3082
par	4	3	4	5	4	4	5	3	4	36
handicap	8	18	16	10	2	12	6	14	4	-
FORWARD	368	79	284	454	420	340	420	123	360	2848
par	4	3	4	5	5	4	5	3	4	37
handicap	10	18	14	4	12	6	2	16	8	-

BACK	
yardage	6638
par	72
rating	71.8
slope	125

REGULAR	
yardage	6253
par	72
rating	70.4
slope	122

FORWARD	
yardage	5782
par	75
rating	73.3
slope	129

PLAY POLICY & FEES: Reciprocal play is accepted with members of other private clubs. Guest fees are $65 when accompanied by a member, $145 for hotel guests, and $155 weekdays and $175 holidays for unaccompanied guests and reciprocators (includes carts and range balls). Carts are mandatory.

TEE TIMES: After receiving hotel confirmation, guests can book a tee time at their convenience. Reciprocal players must have their club pro call to make arrangements.

DRESS CODE: Golf attire is the only acceptable dress on the golf course. No blue jeans, tank tops, or short shorts may be worn. Nonmetal spikes are required.

COURSE DESCRIPTION: This imaginative Pete Dye design features large greens and deep bunkers. Most holes are tight and unforgiving. The back nine is especially hilly and creative. Elevation changes of up to 350 feet on several holes create interesting golf shots and spectacular views.

NOTES: The men's course record is 63 held by Matt Gogel.

LOCATION: From Highway 1 in Carmel take the Carmel Valley Road exit and drive seven miles. Turn right on Robinson Canyon Road and left on Old Ranch Road.

. . . ● **TOURNAMENTS:** An eight-player minimum is required to book a tournament. Carts are required. The banquet facility can accommodate up to 280 people. ● **TRAVEL:** The Carmel Valley Ranch is recommended for lodging. Call 800-422-7635 for reservations.

27. CARMEL VALLEY RANCH RESORT

PLAY POLICY & FEES: Reciprocal play is accepted with members of other private clubs on Thursday and Friday only. Guest fees are $50 when accompanied by a member and $90 unaccompanied. Carts are $20 accompanied by a member and $24 without a member. The course is closed on Monday.

DRESS CODE: No blue jeans may be worn, and shirts must remain tucked in. Nonmetal spikes are required.

COURSE DESCRIPTION: This challenging, rolling, tree-lined course has undulating greens. Water comes into play on several holes. The par-4 first hole starts from a scenic, elevated tee. The par 5s are tight but reachable in two for long hitters.

NOTES: The men's course record is 63. The women's record is 70.

LOCATION: From Highway 68 between Salinas and Monterey, take the Corral de Tierra Road exit south. Drive three-quarters of a mile to the course.

. . . ● **TOURNAMENTS:** Outside events need board approval. An 80-player minimum is needed to book an event. Players should book tournaments 12 months in advance. A banquet facility is available that can accommodate 300 people.

28. CORRAL DE TIERRA COUNTRY CLUB

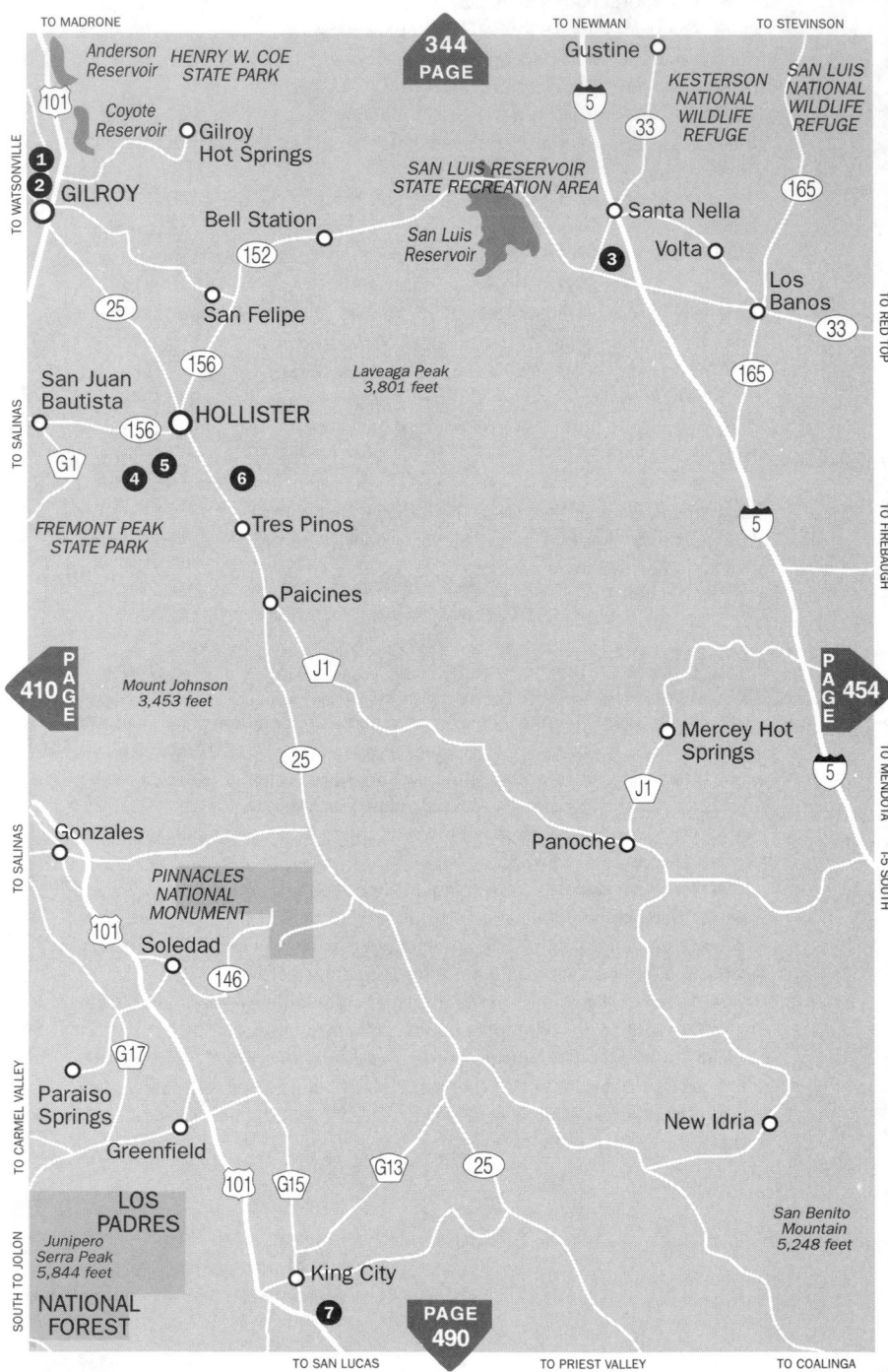

TO MADRONE

TO NEWMAN

TO STEVINSON

344 PAGE

Anderson Reservoir

HENRY W. COE STATE PARK

Gustine

KESTERSON NATIONAL WILDLIFE REFUGE

SAN LUIS NATIONAL WILDLIFE REFUGE

101

Coyote Reservoir

Gilroy Hot Springs

33

TO WATSONVILLE

1
2 GILROY

SAN LUIS RESERVOIR STATE RECREATION AREA

165

Bell Station

San Luis Reservoir

Santa Nella

152

3 Volta

Los Banos

25

San Felipe

Laveaga Peak 3,801 feet

33

156

165

TO SALINAS

San Juan Bautista

156 HOLLISTER

G1

4 5   6

5

FREMONT PEAK STATE PARK

Tres Pinos

Paicines

P A G E 410

Mount Johnson 3,453 feet

J1

P A G E 454

TO RED TOP

TO FIREBAUGH

25

Mercey Hot Springs

5

TO SALINAS

Gonzales

PINNACLES NATIONAL MONUMENT

J1

Panoche

5

TO MENDOTA

I-5 SOUTH

101

Soledad

146

TO CARMEL VALLEY

G17

Paraiso Springs

New Idria

Greenfield

LOS PADRES

Junipero Serra Peak 5,844 feet

G13   25

G15

SOUTH TO JOLON

NATIONAL FOREST

101

King City

San Benito Mountain 5,248 feet

7

PAGE 490

TO SAN LUCAS

TO PRIEST VALLEY

TO COALINGA

444

Hollister/King City Area

2951 Club Drive
Gilroy, CA 95020

PRO SHOP: 877-813-2453

Scot Hathaway, General Manager, PGA

Driving Range ●
Practice Greens ●
Clubhouse ●
Food / Beverage ●
Accommodations
Pull Carts ●
Power Carts ●
Club Rental ●
$pecial Offers

	1	2	3	4	5	6	7	8	9	OUT
BACK	330	163	358	565	438	150	503	407	442	3356
REGULAR	315	150	347	545	417	142	478	397	422	3213
par	4	3	4	5	4	3	5	4	4	36
handicap										-
FORWARD	257	90	273	433	307	85	418	300	317	2480
par	4	3	4	5	4	3	5	4	4	36
handicap										-

	10	11	12	13	14	15	16	17	18	IN
BACK	385	413	455	233	597	337	168	533	427	3548
REGULAR	360	392	450	210	568	324	150	516	412	3382
par	4	4	4	3	5	4	3	5	4	36
handicap										
FORWARD	238	302	345	141	429	247	85	407	317	2511
par	4	4	4	3	5	4	3	5	4	36
handicap										-

BACK	
yardage	6904
par	72
rating	
slope	

REGULAR	
yardage	6595
par	72
rating	
slope	

FORWARD	
yardage	4991
par	72
rating	
slope	

2695 Hecker Pass Highway
Gilroy, CA 95020

PRO SHOP: 408-848-0490

Don DeLorenzo, PGA Professional
Ted Hernandez, Superintendent

Driving Range ●
Practice Greens ●
Clubhouse ●
Food / Beverage ●
Accommodations
Pull Carts ●
Power Carts ●
Club Rental ●
$pecial Offers

	1	2	3	4	5	6	7	8	9	OUT
BACK	-	-	-	-	-	-	-	-	-	-
REGULAR	394	343	374	520	151	374	393	261	169	2979
par	4	4	4	5	3	4	4	3	3	34
handicap	3	11	5	13	15	9	1	7	17	-
FORWARD	380	330	369	474	123	370	373	225	142	2786
par	5	4	4	5	3	4	5	4	3	37
handicap	9	11	3	7	13	5	1	15	17	-

	10	11	12	13	14	15	16	17	18	IN
BACK	-	-	-	-	-	-	-	-	-	-
REGULAR	371	366	352	500	128	388	350	345	168	2968
par	4	4	4	5	3	4	4	4	3	35
handicap	2	10	8	16	12	6	4	18	14	-
FORWARD	365	360	341	450	95	365	342	240	157	2715
par	4	4	4	5	3	4	4	4	3	35
handicap	4	12	10	8	18	2	6	14	16	-

BACK	
yardage	-
par	-
rating	-
slope	-

REGULAR	
yardage	5947
par	69
rating	67.8
slope	109

FORWARD	
yardage	5501
par	72
rating	70.5
slope	112

PLAY POLICY & FEES: The course is due to open in fall of 1999. Green fees are projected to be in the range of $50 weekdays and $75 on weekends. Cart fees are $15.

TEE TIMES: Reservations can be made 30 days in advance.

DRESS CODE: Collared shirts and nonmetal spikes are required.

COURSE DESCRIPTION: This course set up against the hills and features rolling fairways, native oaks, and dramatic fairway and greenside bunkers. There are no long carries for the average player, but for the low handicapper the course will play close to 7,000 yards. On some holes the golfers can rip the driver without fear of needing pin-point accuracy; on other holes players would be foolish to even think about pulling a driver out of the bag. Around the greens players are given friendly areas for errant shots, but if you bail out and miss the green on the wrong side, trouble awaits. The greens are undulating, but not overly sloped.

NOTES: The course features a 25,000-square-foot clubhouse that can hold banquets, business meetings, and special events.

LOCATION: From San Jose take U.S. 101 to Gilroy, take the Masten exit, and head west. Take a left on Santa Teresa and follow it for three miles. Make a right on Club Drive to the course.

. . . ● **TOURNAMENTS:** Outside events are allowed, and the banquet facility can accommodate up to 250 people.

1. EAGLE RIDGE GOLF CLUB

PLAY POLICY & FEES: Green fees are $20 weekdays and $26 weekends and holidays. Twilight, senior, and junior rates are available.

TEE TIMES: Reservations can be booked seven days in advance.

COURSE DESCRIPTION: There are actually 11 holes on this course, changing the back nine into a different layout. This mature course is situated in oak-studded foothills. The terrain is rolling and hilly, with tricky, small greens. Panoramic views of the valley are offered on the eighth and 17th holes.

NOTES: The course record is 60, held by George Archer and Jon Bettencourt.

LOCATION: From U.S. 101 drive two miles west on Hecker Pass Highway (Highway 152) in Gilroy. The course is on the right.

. . . ● **TOURNAMENTS:** This course is available for outside tournaments.

2. GILROY GOLF COURSE

FOREBAY GOLF COURSE
ARCHITECT: JOE SONTOR, 1964

29500 Bayview Road
Santa Nella, CA 95322

PRO SHOP: 209-826-3637
CLUBHOUSE: 209-826-4858

Greg Arnaudo, Owner/Manager

Driving Range ●
Practice Greens ●
Clubhouse ●
Food / Beverage ●
Accommodations
Pull Carts ●
Power Carts ●
Club Rental ●
$pecial Offers

	1	2	3	4	5	6	7	8	9	OUT
BACK	-	-	-	-	-	-	-	-	-	-
REGULAR	337	382	173	505	338	172	467	381	409	3164
par	4	4	3	5	4	3	5	4	4	36
handicap	13	3	11	7	15	17	9	5	1	-
FORWARD	295	245	132	446	304	137	399	352	387	2697
par	4	4	3	5	4	3	5	4	5	37
handicap	11	13	15	1	9	17	3	7	5	-

	10	11	12	13	14	15	16	17	18	IN
BACK	-	-	-	-	-	-	-	-	-	-
REGULAR	365	400	190	520	349	186	399	401	492	3302
par	4	4	3	5	4	3	4	4	5	36
handicap	14	4	12	10	16	18	2	6	8	-
FORWARD	295	245	132	446	304	137	399	352	387	2697
par	4	4	3	5	4	3	5	4	5	37
handicap	12	14	16	2	10	18	4	8	6	-

BACK	
yardage	-
par	-
rating	-
slope	-

REGULAR	
yardage	6466
par	72
rating	70.2
slope	112

FORWARD	
yardage	5394
par	74
rating	-
slope	-

 SAN JUAN OAKS GOLF CLUB
ARCHITECT: FRED COUPLES, GENE BATES, 1996

GOLF 50

P.O. Box 1060
San Juan Bautista, CA
95045
PRO SHOP: 831-636-6113
OFFICE: 831-636-6118

3825 Union Road at Hwy
Hollister, CA 95023

Scott Fuller, Manager
Bruce Lewis, Head Professional, PGA
Marc Henry, Tournament Director, PGA

Driving Range ●
Practice Greens ●
Clubhouse ●
Food / Beverage ●
Accommodations
Pull Carts ●
Power Carts ●
Club Rental ●
$pecial Offers

	1	2	3	4	5	6	7	8	9	OUT
BACK	377	578	359	431	425	204	407	179	513	3473
REGULAR	358	538	353	403	357	186	380	169	489	3233
par	4	5	4	4	4	3	4	3	5	36
handicap	18	12	14	6	10	4	2	16	8	-
FORWARD	273	415	213	304	269	116	292	114	375	2371
par	4	5	4	4	4	3	4	3	5	36
handicap	6	2	10	12	8	18	16	14	4	-

	10	11	12	13	14	15	16	17	18	IN
BACK	423	543	182	462	397	539	166	487	461	3660
REGULAR	414	536	161	440	378	523	142	446	439	3479
par	4	5	3	4	4	5	3	4	4	36
handicap	15	13	9	1	3	11	17	5	7	-
FORWARD	274	392	110	346	295	263	77	326	316	2399
par	4	5	3	5	4	4	3	4	4	36
handicap	9	1	15	11	7	13	17	3	5	-

BACK	
yardage	7133
par	72
rating	74.8
slope	135

REGULAR	
yardage	6712
par	72
rating	72.8
slope	131

FORWARD	
yardage	4770
par	72
rating	71.0
slope	125

PLAY POLICY & FEES: Green fees are $11.50 for nine holes and $13.50 for 18 holes weekdays, and $15 for nine holes and $19 for 18 holes weekends and holidays. Senior and twilight rates are available. Carts are $14 for nine holes and $18 for 18 holes.

TEE TIMES: Reservations are recommended one week in advance.

COURSE DESCRIPTION: This is a flat course with new trees and a creek. The testy, 424-yard, par-4 ninth hole requires a second-shot carry over the creek.

LOCATION: In Santa Nella on Interstate 5, exit onto Highway 33 south. Turn right on Bayview Road and continue to the course.

. . . ● **TOURNAMENTS:** This course is available for outside tournaments.

3. FOREBAY GOLF COURSE

PLAY POLICY & FEES: Green fees are $45 Monday through Thursday, and $70 Friday through Sunday and holidays. Carts are $12 per person. Twilight rates are available. Call for more information.

TEE TIMES: Reservations can be booked one month in advance.

DRESS CODE: Collared shirts and nonmetal spikes are required. No tank tops or cutoffs are allowed.

COURSE DESCRIPTION: Every hole of this well-designed, old-style course is different. The course meanders through rolling hills, where players encounter native oaks, plenty of bunkers, and undulating, well-paced greens. Don't let the scenic beauty of San Juan Oaks fool you; it is a good, fair test of golf.

NOTES: Some of Fred Couples' mementos are featured in the clubhouse.

LOCATION: From San Jose take U.S. 101 to Highway 156 east. Follow Highway 156 four miles east of San Juan Bautista. Turn right on Union Road. The golf course entry road is one-quarter mile on the right.

. . . ● **TOURNAMENTS:** Shotgun tournaments are available weekdays only. A 24-player minimum is needed to book an event. Carts are mandatory. Events should be scheduled six months in advance. A spectacular mission-style clubhouse is available for banquets, weddings, and conferences and can accommodate 300 people. ● **TRAVEL:** Posada de San Juan is located five minutes from the golf course. For reservations call 831-623-4030. Arboleda (831-623-1066) is also recommended.

4. SAN JUAN OAKS GOLF CLUB

⑤ RIDGEMARK GOLF & COUNTRY CLUB
ARCHITECT: RICHARD BIGLER, 1972

3800 Airline Highway
Hollister, CA 95023

PRO SHOP: 831-637-1010
OFFICE: 800-637-8151

Kathy Wake, Dir. of Golf, PGA/LPGA
Dave Lewelen, Superintendent
Cathy Guajardo, Tournament Director

Driving Range ●
Practice Greens ●
Clubhouse ●
Food / Beverage ●
Accommodations ●
Pull Carts
Power Carts ●
Club Rental ●
$pecial Offers ●

	1	2	3	4	5	6	7	8	9	OUT
BACK	391	509	536	200	386	386	390	383	190	3371
REGULAR	362	491	513	186	349	372	380	362	178	3193
par	4	5	5	3	4	4	4	4	3	36
handicap	10	14	7	15	11	4	2	6	12	-
FORWARD	320	435	452	166	301	348	368	333	131	2854
par	4	5	5	3	4	4	4	4	3	36
handicap	9	12	1	16	10	5	2	7	17	-

	10	11	12	13	14	15	16	17	18	IN
BACK	350	402	212	470	433	209	337	397	540	3350
REGULAR	340	378	190	454	401	186	304	371	519	3143
par	4	4	3	5	4	3	4	4	5	36
handicap	16	1	8	17	3	13	18	5	9	-
FORWARD	314	295	97	415	330	160	275	337	435	2658
par	4	4	3	5	4	3	4	4	5	36
handicap	13	3	18	11	6	15	14	8	4	-

BACK	
yardage	6721
par	72
rating	72.7
slope	126

REGULAR	
yardage	6336
par	72
rating	71.0
slope	123

FORWARD	
yardage	5512
par	72
rating	71.6
slope	118

⑥ BOLADO PARK GOLF COURSE
ARCHITECT: W.I. HAWKINS, COL. GEORGE E. SIKES, 1928

P.O. Box 419
Tres Pinos, CA 95075

7777 Airline Highway 25
Tres Pinos, CA 95075

PRO SHOP: 831-628-9995

Gary Churhill, Manager
Sal Hernandez, Superintendent

Driving Range ●
Practice Greens ●
Clubhouse ●
Food / Beverage ●
Accommodations
Pull Carts ●
Power Carts ●
Club Rental
$pecial Offers

	1	2	3	4	5	6	7	8	9	OUT
BACK										
REGULAR										
par										
handicap										
FORWARD										
par										
handicap										

	10	11	12	13	14	15	16	17	18	IN
BACK										
REGULAR										
par										
handicap										
FORWARD										
par										
handicap										

BACK	
yardage	
par	
rating	
slope	

REGULAR	
yardage	2993
par	35
rating	67.6
slope	110

FORWARD	
yardage	2818
par	35
rating	71.6
slope	114

5. RIDGEMARK GOLF & COUNTRY CLUB

PLAY POLICY & FEES: Green fees are $52 Monday through Friday, and $62 weekends and holidays. Twilight rates are available after 3 p.m. Courses rotate daily between membership and public play. Call to find out which course is open for public play.

TEE TIMES: Reservations can be booked 30 days in advance.

DRESS CODE: Collared shirts are required, and slacks are preferred. No jeans are allowed on the course.

COURSE DESCRIPTION: These par-72 courses hug the rolling terrain of the foothills, and feature large, contoured greens. The Diablo Course is steeper and requires more placement. It's shorter than the Gabilan Course and also has more water hazards. The Gabilan Course is flatter and less deceptive.

NOTES: The Diablo Course record is held by Greg Beaulieu (63), and the Gabilan Course record is held by John Bedell (63). The Diablo Course is 6,603 yards and rated 71.9 from the championship tees with a slope of 123.

LOCATION: From U.S. 101 south take the Highway 25 exit and drive 13 miles to the golf course. The course is located five miles south of Hollister.

. . . ● **TOURNAMENTS:** A 16-player minimum is needed to book an event. Tournaments should be scheduled 10 months in advance. The banquet facility holds up to 250 people. ● **TRAVEL:** Ridgemark has 32 lodging units overlooking the golf course. For reservations call 800-637-8151. ● **$PECIAL OFFERS:** Play-and-stay packages are available.

6. BOLADO PARK GOLF COURSE

PLAY POLICY & FEES: Green fees are $15 weekdays and $20 weekends. Student and senior rates are available. Carts are $12 for nine holes and $20 for 18 holes.

TEE TIMES: Reservations are not accepted. All play is on a first-come, first-served basis.

DRESS CODE: Nonmetal spikes are encouraged.

COURSE DESCRIPTION: This flat course has well-maintained greens.

NOTES: Senior PGA Tour pro George Archer uses these greens for practice. The course was rebuilt in 1958 in its present location by George Santana. The course record is 63, held by General M.I. Moncado.

LOCATION: This course is located five miles south of Hollister on Highway 25/Airline Highway in Tres Pinos.

. . . ● **TOURNAMENTS:** This course is available for outside tournaments.

613 South Vanderhurst
King City, CA 93930

PRO SHOP: 831-385-4546

Jon Christensen, PGA Professional

Driving Range ●
Practice Greens ●
Clubhouse ●
Food / Beverage ●
Accommodations
Pull Carts ●
Power Carts ●
Club Rental ●
$pecial Offers

	1	2	3	4	5	6	7	8	9	OUT
BACK	-	-	-	-	-	-	-	-	-	-
REGULAR	199	259	404	161	501	532	361	169	231	2817
par	3	4	4	3	5	5	4	3	4	35
handicap	11	15	1	13	7	5	3	9	17	-
FORWARD	199	259	350	161	465	480	361	169	231	2675
par	3	4	4	3	5	5	4	3	4	35
handicap	11	15	5	17	7	3	1	13	9	-

	10	11	12	13	14	15	16	17	18	IN
BACK	-	-	-	-	-	-	-	-	-	-
REGULAR	199	259	404	161	501	532	361	169	231	2817
par	3	4	4	3	5	5	4	3	4	35
handicap	12	16	2	14	8	6	4	10	18	-
FORWARD	199	259	350	161	465	480	361	169	231	2675
par	3	4	4	3	5	5	4	3	4	35
handicap	12	16	6	18	8	4	2	14	10	-

BACK	
yardage	-
par	-
rating	-
slope	-

REGULAR	
yardage	5634
par	70
rating	66.4
slope	107

FORWARD	
yardage	5350
par	70
rating	68.3
slope	110

PLAY POLICY & FEES: Green fees are $9 for nine holes and $14 for 18 holes on weekdays; $11 for nine holes and $16 for 18 holes on weekends and holidays. Twilight, senior. and junior rates are available.

TEE TIMES: Reservations can be booked seven days in advance.

COURSE DESCRIPTION: The course opened in 1953. In 1976 Robert Dean Putman redesigned it. This flat, short course has tree-lined fairways and small, tricky greens. A creek meanders through the terrain and comes into play on four holes.

NOTES: The men's course record is 62, set in 1984 by Mark Pumphrey. The women's course record is 72.

LOCATION: From U.S. 101 in King City take the Canal Street exit. Turn right on Division Street. At the second stop sign, turn right on South Vanderhurst Street and drive to the course.

. . . ● **TOURNAMENTS:** This course is available for outside tournaments.

7. KING CITY GOLF COURSE

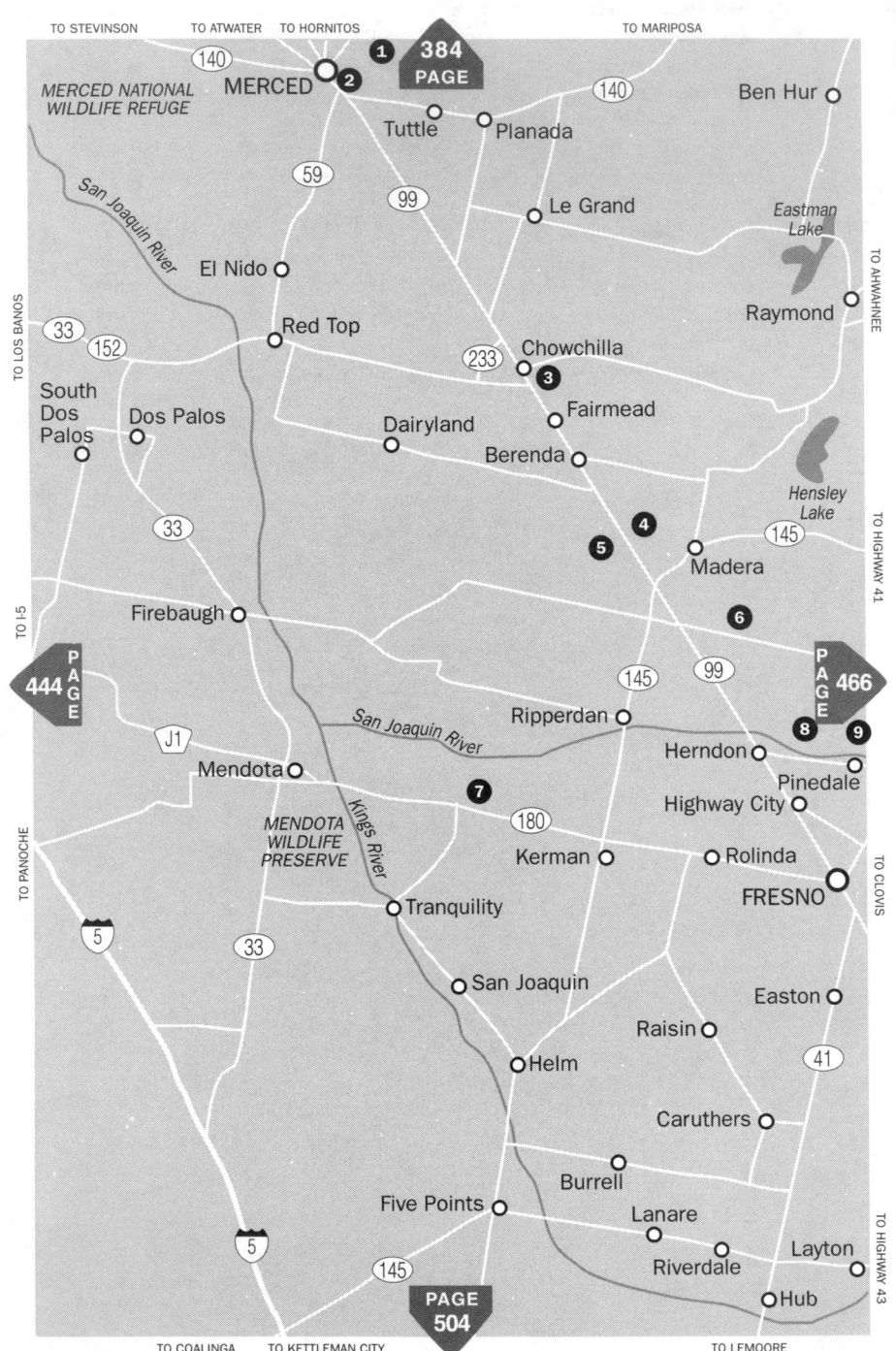

TO STEVINSON TO ATWATER TO HORNITOS TO MARIPOSA

MERCED NATIONAL WILDLIFE REFUGE

MERCED

140

1

384 PAGE

140

Ben Hur

Tuttle Planada

59

99

Le Grand

Eastman Lake

El Nido

Red Top

233 Chowchilla **3**

Raymond

TO AHWAHNEE

TO LOS BANOS

33 152

South Dos Palos

Dos Palos

Dairyland

Fairmead

Berenda

Hensley Lake

TO HIGHWAY 41

San Joaquin River

33

4
5

145

Madera

6

Firebaugh

TO I-5

PAGE 444

145 99

PAGE 466

J1

San Joaquin River

Ripperdan

Herndon

8 **9**

Pinedale

TO CLOVIS

Mendota

MENDOTA WILDLIFE PRESERVE

Kings River

7

180

Highway City

Kerman

Rolinda

TO PANOCHE

5

Tranquility

FRESNO

33

San Joaquin

Easton

Raisin

41

Helm

Caruthers

5

Burrell

Five Points

Lanare

145

PAGE 504

Layton

Riverdale

Hub

TO HIGHWAY 43

TO COALINGA TO KETTLEMAN CITY TO LEMOORE

Merced/Madera Area

① MERCED HILLS GOLF CLUB
ARCHITECT: CHARLES HOWARD, 1995

5320 North Lake Road
Merced, CA 95340

PRO SHOP: 209-383-4943

Ron Porter, Manager
Lance Johnson, Head Professional, PGA

Driving Range ●
Practice Greens ●
Clubhouse ●
Food / Beverage ●
Accommodations
Pull Carts ●
Power Carts ●
Club Rental ●
Special Offers

	1	2	3	4	5	6	7	8	9	OUT
BACK	506	376	438	153	454	533	181	392	424	3457
REGULAR	477	351	397	135	424	507	171	371	367	3200
par	5	4	4	3	4	5	3	4	4	36
handicap	17	5	1	15	3	7	11	13	9	-
FORWARD	458	275	339	109	369	430	140	331	312	2763
par	5	4	4	3	4	5	3	4	4	36
handicap	7	11	5	17	3	1	15	9	13	-

	10	11	12	13	14	15	16	17	18	IN
BACK	403	379	195	360	497	412	182	525	421	3374
REGULAR	387	336	180	33	477	386	170	499	389	3158
par	4	4	3	4	5	4	3	5	4	36
handicap	8	4	12	14	18	6	16	10	2	-
FORWARD	370	288	123	308	423	315	116	428	263	2634
par	4	4	3	4	5	4	3	5	4	36
handicap	4	6	16	14	8	10	18	2	12	-

BACK	
yardage	6831
par	72
rating	72.6
slope	125

REGULAR	
yardage	6358
par	72
rating	70.2
slope	119

FORWARD	
yardage	5397
par	72
rating	70.6
slope	115

② MERCED GOLF & COUNTRY CLUB
ARCHITECTS: BOB BALDOCK, 1961; MUIR GRAVES, 1998

6333 North Golf Road
Merced, CA 95340

PRO SHOP: 209-722-3357

Bernadette Lucas, Manager
Ed Leinenkugel, Director of Golf, PGA
Carl King, Superintendent

Driving Range ●
Practice Greens ●
Clubhouse ●
Food / Beverage ●
Accommodations
Pull Carts ●
Power Carts ●
Club Rental ●
Special Offers

	1	2	3	4	5	6	7	8	9	OUT
BACK	323	387	420	181	519	204	559	323	413	3329
REGULAR	308	373	399	148	507	184	532	310	403	3164
par	4	4	4	3	5	3	5	4	4	36
handicap	17	3	1	13	9	15	7	11	5	-
FORWARD	292	361	341	117	491	169	479	269	387	2906
par	4	4	4	3	5	3	5	4	4	36
handicap	13	7	9	17	1	15	5	11	3	-

	10	11	12	13	14	15	16	17	18	IN
BACK	508	197	413	478	189	364	367	144	530	3190
REGULAR	497	173	397	460	169	353	348	130	515	3042
par	5	3	4	5	3	4	4	3	5	36
handicap	16	8	2	4	12	10	6	18	14	-
FORWARD	455	157	372	441	158	308	324	113	462	2790
par	5	3	4	5	3	4	4	3	5	36
handicap	4	14	6	2	16	10	12	18	8	-

BACK	
yardage	6519
par	72
rating	70.7
slope	125

REGULAR	
yardage	6206
par	72
rating	69.5
slope	123

FORWARD	
yardage	5696
par	72
rating	72.9
slope	128

PLAY POLICY & FEES: Green fees are $13 weekdays and $20 on weekends and holidays. Cart fees are $10 per rider.

TEE TIMES: Reservations can be booked seven days in advance.

DRESS CODE: Appropriate golf attire and nonmetal spikes are required.

COURSE DESCRIPTION: This is a links-style course with rolling terrain and a creek meandering throughout. The creek and water come into play on nine holes.

LOCATION: From Highway 99 in Merced take Highway 59 north to Bellevue Road. Take a right onto Bellevue Road and follow it to North Lake Road. Make a left on North Lake Road. The course will be on the right.

. . . ● **TOURNAMENTS:** This course is available for outside tournaments. A 20-player tournament is needed to book a tournament. Tournaments should be booked six months in advance.

1. MERCED HILLS GOLF CLUB

PLAY POLICY & FEES: Reciprocal play is accepted with members of other private clubs. Green fees for reciprocators are $35. Guest fees are $25 when accompanied by a member and $35 unaccompanied. Carts are $9 for nine holes and $18 for 18 holes. The course is closed on Monday.

DRESS CODE: Appropriate golf attire and nonmetal spikes are required.

COURSE DESCRIPTION: Redesigned by Robert Muir Graves in 1977, this quiet valley course is short and challenging, with rolling hills and lots of trees.

NOTES: Merced Golf and Country Club is home to the Merced County Amateur and has hosted the US Amateur Qualifying, the NCGA San Joaquin Valley Amateur, the Oldsmobile Sectional Qualifier, and the Player's West Merced Women's Classic. In 1999 the course underwent renovations that included rebuilding, repositioning and lengthening the seventh hole. New tee boxes were built for holes 4 and 17, and a new lake was added to 16. The changes added 90 yards to the course.

LOCATION: From Highway 99 in Merced take G Street north. Follow it to Bellevue Road; turn right and then turn left onto North Golf Road.

. . . ● **TOURNAMENTS:** An 80-player minimum is needed to book a tournament. Carts are required. Events should be booked 12 months in advance.

2. MERCED GOLF & COUNTRY CLUB

PHEASANT RUN GOLF CLUB
ARCHITECT: RICHARD BIGLER, 1998

3125 Arcadian Street
Chowchilla, CA 93610

PRO SHOP: 559-665-3411

Ted Fernandes, Head Professional

Driving Range ●
Practice Greens ●
Clubhouse ●
Food / Beverage ●
Accommodations
Pull Carts ●
Power Carts ●
Club Rental ●
$pecial Offers

	1	2	3	4	5	6	7	8	9	OUT
BACK	-	-	-	-	-	-	-	-	-	-
REGULAR	453	487	484	406	197	467	375	428	156	3453
par	4	5	5	4	3	4	4	4	3	36
handicap	3	7	6	4	5	1	8	2	9	-
FORWARD	428	445	449	373	93	391	351	365	134	3029
par	4	5	5	4	3	4	4	4	3	36
handicap	2	8	5	4	7	1	6	3	9	-

	10	11	12	13	14	15	16	17	18	IN
BACK	-	-	-	-	-	-	-	-	-	-
REGULAR	494	523	468	430	185	416	404	395	179	3494
par	5	5	4	4	3	4	4	4	3	36
handicap	7	6	1	3	5	2	8	4	9	-
FORWARD	428	445	363	373	133	353	351	365	134	2945
par	5	5	4	4	3	4	4	4	3	36
handicap	8	7	4	2	5	1	6	3	9	-

BACK	
yardage	-
par	-
rating	-
slope	-

REGULAR	
yardage	6947
par	72
rating	-
slope	-

FORWARD	
yardage	5974
par	72
rating	70.0
slope	113

MADERA GOLF & COUNTRY CLUB
ARCHITECT: BOB BALDOCK, 1955

19297 Road 26
Madera, CA 93638

PRO SHOP: 559-674-2682
CLUBHOUSE: 559-674-1527

Eric Costa, PGA Professional
Bob Stucky, Superintendent

Driving Range ●
Practice Greens ●
Clubhouse ●
Food / Beverage ●
Accommodations
Pull Carts ●
Power Carts ●
Club Rental ●
$pecial Offers

	1	2	3	4	5	6	7	8	9	OUT
BACK	416	462	497	203	326	505	399	154	369	3331
REGULAR	405	440	490	200	320	485	395	145	355	3235
par	4	4	5	3	4	5	4	3	4	36
handicap	5	1	9	7	15	13	3	17	11	-
FORWARD	366	425	410	198	309	456	333	120	342	2959
par	4	5	5	3	4	5	4	3	4	37
handicap	1	13	15	9	11	5	3	17	7	-

	10	11	12	13	14	15	16	17	18	IN
BACK	530	386	319	378	226	381	177	423	533	3353
REGULAR	520	375	315	360	220	365	165	390	525	3235
par	5	4	4	4	3	4	3	4	5	36
handicap	10	4	18	12	6	14	16	2	8	-
FORWARD	517	334	301	336	188	349	134	316	446	2921
par	5	4	4	4	3	4	3	4	5	36
handicap	2	12	16	4	14	6	18	8	10	-

BACK	
yardage	6684
par	72
rating	71.0
slope	123

REGULAR	
yardage	6470
par	72
rating	70.2
slope	122

FORWARD	
yardage	5880
par	73
rating	74.3
slope	126

PLAY POLICY & FEES: Green fees Monday through Thursday are $8 for nine holes and $16 for 18 holes. Friday through Sunday green fees are $11 for nine holes and $18 for 18 holes. Twilight, senior, and junior rates are available.

TEE TIMES: Reservations can be made seven days in advance

DRESS CODE: Shirts and nonmetal spikes are required.

COURSE DESCRIPTION: This is a desert-style course with a stadium feel, palm trees, and plenty of water. The greens are fairly fast and undulating. Pheasant Run features Putter Bent, a new type of bent grass. The hardest hole is the 197-yard par-3 fifth hole. You tee off from a slightly elevated tee box to a green with water front and back, surrounded by palm trees and guarded by bunkers. A constant northern breeze from 5 to 15 miles per hour makes wind a factor.

NOTES: A new nine holes began construction in February 1999. This is currently the longest nine-hole course in California.

LOCATION: From Madera drive 12 miles north on Highway 99. Take the Chowchilla Robertson exit. Make a right on Robertson and follow to the course. From the north take the same exit and make a left onto Robertson.

. . . ● **TOURNAMENTS:** The course is available for outside events.

3. PHEASANT RUN GOLF CLUB

PLAY POLICY & FEES: Reciprocal play is accepted with members of other private clubs. Green fees for reciprocators are $35. Guest fees are $20 accompanied by a member and $35 unaccompanied. Carts are $10. The course is closed on Monday.

TEE TIMES: Reservations can be booked seven days in advance.

DRESS CODE: Collared shirts are a must, and shorts must be mid-thigh or longer. Nonmetal spikes are required.

COURSE DESCRIPTION: This sporty course has lots of rolling hills. Tall eucalyptus trees come into play on the front nine, maturing pine trees on the back nine. It's easily walkable.

NOTES: Howard Roseen holds the course record of 64, set in 1967.

LOCATION: From Highway 99 north of downtown Madera, take the Avenue 17 exit east. Turn left onto County Road 26. The course is at Avenue 19.

. . . ● **TOURNAMENTS:** This course is available for outside events on a very limited basis.

4. MADERA GOLF & COUNTRY CLUB

⑤ MADERA MUNICIPAL GOLF COURSE
ARCHITECT: ROBERT DEAN PUTMAN, 1991

23200 Avenue 17
Madera, CA 93637

PRO SHOP: 559-675-3504
CLUBHOUSE: 559-675-3533

Mike Catanesi, PGA Professional
Lowell Stone, Superintendent

Driving Range ●
Practice Greens ●
Clubhouse ●
Food / Beverage ●
Accommodations
Pull Carts ●
Power Carts ●
Club Rental ●
Special Offers

	1	2	3	4	5	6	7	8	9	OUT
BACK	425	398	191	506	381	188	343	387	541	3360
REGULAR	404	342	158	497	365	147	329	356	523	3121
par	4	4	3	5	4	3	4	4	5	36
handicap	1	5	3	11	7	9	15	17	13	-
FORWARD	353	307	130	400	321	112	296	331	456	2706
par	4	4	3	5	4	3	4	4	5	36
handicap	3	15	13	9	7	17	11	5	1	-

	10	11	12	13	14	15	16	17	18	IN
BACK	417	187	529	420	401	202	416	522	379	3473
REGULAR	390	167	512	410	389	150	378	493	359	3248
par	4	3	5	4	4	3	4	5	4	36
handicap	4	14	18	2	6	12	8	16	10	-
FORWARD	342	110	395	395	346	114	340	452	312	2806
par	4	3	5	4	4	3	4	5	4	36
handicap	2	18	16	12	8	14	4	6	10	-

BACK	
yardage	6833
par	72
rating	71.3
slope	119

REGULAR	
yardage	6369
par	72
rating	69.1
slope	115

FORWARD	
yardage	5512
par	72
rating	70.3
slope	112

⑥ RIVERBEND GOLF CLUB
ARCHITECT: GARY BAIRD, 1999

43369 Avenue 12
Fresno, CA 93638

PRO SHOP: 559-432-3020

Flint Nelson, Head Professional, PGA
Gary McClung, PGA Professional

Driving Range ●
Practice Greens ●
Clubhouse ●
Food / Beverage ●
Accommodations
Pull Carts ●
Power Carts ●
Club Rental
Special Offers

	1	2	3	4	5	6	7	8	9	OUT
BACK	393	422	182	517	396	397	175	555	465	3502
REGULAR	366	382	160	488	362	365	144	517	445	3229
par	4	4	3	5	4	4	3	5	4	36
handicap	11	5	13	17	9	3	15	7	1	-
FORWARD	301	265	109	427	282	329	115	449	336	2613
par	4	4	3	5	4	4	3	5	4	36
handicap	11	5	13	17	9	3	15	7	1	-

	10	11	12	13	14	15	16	17	18	IN
BACK	443	538	150	335	198	535	367	362	428	3356
REGULAR	409	528	131	299	161	502	343	337	395	3105
par	4	5	3	4	3	5	4	4	4	36
handicap	4	12	18	14	16	8	6	10	2	-
FORWARD	335	407	101	232	114	445	284	272	303	2493
par	4	5	3	4	3	5	4	4	4	36
handicap	4	12	18	14	16	8	6	10	2	-

BACK	
yardage	6858
par	72
rating	
slope	

REGULAR	
yardage	6334
par	72
rating	
slope	

FORWARD	
yardage	5106
par	72
rating	
slope	

5. MADERA MUNICIPAL GOLF COURSE

PLAY POLICY & FEES: Green fees for 18 holes are $12 before 1 p.m., $10 after 1 p.m., and $9 after 3 p.m. on weekdays. On weekends green fees are $17 before 1 p.m., $13 after 1 p.m., and $10 after 3 p.m. Senior discount cards are available. Carts are $11 for nine holes and $19 for 18 holes.

TEE TIMES: Reservations can be booked seven days in advance.

COURSE DESCRIPTION: Robert Dean Putman tested his course on opening day, June 8, 1991, and shot a 68. He has designed a course with wide appeal. The greens are large, undulating, and well bunkered. The fairways are bunkered, too, and four lakes come into play on eight holes.

NOTES: Mike Facciani holds the course record at 62.

LOCATION: From Highway 99 north of Madera, take the Avenue 17 exit and follow it west one mile to the course.

. . . ● **TOURNAMENTS:** This course is available for outside tournaments. A 20-player minimum is needed to book a tournament. Events should be booked 8 to 12 months in advance. The banquet facility can hold 275 people. ● **TRAVEL:** The Madera Valley Inn is recommended for lodging. Call 559-673-5164 for reservations.

6. RIVERBEND GOLF CLUB

PLAY POLICY & FEES: Green fees are $25 Monday, $35 Tuesday through Thursday, and $45 Friday through Sunday and holidays. Twilight green fees are $25 every day. Carts are included in green fees.

TEE TIMES: Reservations can be made seven days in advance.

DRESS CODE: No denim is allowed on the course. Collared shirts and nonmetal spikes are required.

COURSE DESCRIPTION: Riverbend is a links-style course featuring large greens, old native oaks and attractive bunkering that allows players several options in attacking the greens. The number nine hole, the hardest hole on the course, is a 465-yard par 4. The rolling fairway is fairly open, but don't overlook the fairway bunkers to the right. Long hitters who can get over the second hill are looking at a nice 150-yard shot in to a deep green. The rest of us are looking at a long iron or a wood into the deep green guarded by a lake to the right with three bunkers in between. Translation: take a bogey if you can, be happy, get something to eat at the snack bar, and enjoy the back nine.

NOTES: Riverbend will be adding an 18-hole championship course, and a 9-hole executive course designed by Peter Jacobson. Plans also call for a resort hotel.

LOCATION: From Highway 99 in Fresno take the Avenue 12 exit and head east for 10 miles to the golf course.

. . . ● **TOURNAMENTS:** A 20-player minimum is required to book an event, and shotgun tournaments are allowed.

FRESNO WEST GOLF COURSE
ARCHITECT: BOB BALDOCK, 1966

23986 West Whitesbridge
Kerman, CA 93630

PRO SHOP: 559-846-8655

Ron Goering, PGA Professional
Carlos Rodriguez, Superintendent

Driving Range ●
Practice Greens ●
Clubhouse ●
Food / Beverage ●
Accommodations
Pull Carts ●
Power Carts ●
Club Rental ●
$pecial Offers

	1	2	3	4	5	6	7	8	9	OUT
BACK	404	179	590	408	364	579	407	192	417	3540
REGULAR	383	164	561	388	348	560	383	174	410	3371
par	4	3	5	4	4	5	4	3	4	36
handicap	5	15	3	7	17	13	1	9	11	-
FORWARD	369	148	488	370	328	483	376	156	345	3063
par	4	3	5	4	4	5	4	3	4	36
handicap	7	17	1	9	13	3	5	15	11	-

	10	11	12	13	14	15	16	17	18	IN
BACK	388	389	543	467	213	506	147	327	439	3419
REGULAR	360	378	523	445	196	498	128	311	397	3236
par	4	4	5	4	3	5	3	4	4	36
handicap	4	12	8	2	6	14	18	16	10	-
FORWARD	342	319	503	436	183	403	118	297	336	2937
par	4	4	5	5	3	5	3	4	4	37
handicap	8	12	2	6	16	4	18	14	10	-

BACK	
yardage	6959
par	72
rating	72.6
slope	118

REGULAR	
yardage	6607
par	72
rating	70.6
slope	114

FORWARD	
yardage	6000
par	73
rating	74.1
slope	118

 # SAN JOAQUIN COUNTRY CLUB
ARCHITECT: BOB BALDOCK, 1961

3484 West Bluff Avenue
Fresno, CA 93711

PRO SHOP: 559-439-3359
CLUBHOUSE: 559-439-3483

Mike Paniccia, PGA Professional
David Stone, Superintendent

Driving Range ●
Practice Greens ●
Clubhouse ●
Food / Beverage ●
Accommodations
Pull Carts ●
Power Carts ●
Club Rental
$pecial Offers

	1	2	3	4	5	6	7	8	9	OUT
BACK	430	409	593	177	355	533	199	391	432	3519
REGULAR	401	385	541	145	343	510	160	375	380	3240
par	4	4	5	3	4	5	3	4	4	36
handicap	7	3	1	13	17	5	15	11	9	-
FORWARD	349	377	465	108	298	489	144	360	352	2942
par	4	4	5	3	4	5	3	4	4	36
handicap	11	3	7	15	13	1	17	5	9	-

	10	11	12	13	14	15	16	17	18	IN
BACK	401	177	502	419	364	423	226	384	555	3451
REGULAR	370	160	485	389	345	410	181	333	525	3198
par	4	3	5	4	4	4	3	4	5	36
handicap	6	18	8	2	14	4	16	12	10	-
FORWARD	337	123	452	375	311	309	145	292	474	2818
par	4	3	5	4	4	4	3	4	5	36
handicap	8	18	4	2	10	12	16	14	6	-

BACK	
yardage	6970
par	72
rating	73.4
slope	133

REGULAR	
yardage	6438
par	72
rating	71.6
slope	129

FORWARD	
yardage	5760
par	72
rating	73.4
slope	129

PLAY POLICY & FEES: Green fees are $13 weekdays and $16 weekends. Carts are $10 for nine holes and $22 for 18 holes. Junior, senior, and twilight rates are available.

TEE TIMES: Reservations can be booked seven days in advance.

DRESS CODE: Nonmetal spikes are recommended.

COURSE DESCRIPTION: This is a very quiet championship golf course. It's long, flat, and often windy. There's water on eight holes. Among the tougher holes is the 174-yard, par-3 eighth, which features water to the left and behind the green.

NOTES: Harold Chuhlantseff holds the course record with a 65.

LOCATION: From Highway 99 in Fresno take the Highway 180/Whitesbridge Road exit. Drive past Kerman to the course.

. . . ● **TOURNAMENTS:** This course is available for outside tournaments. Events should be booked six months in advance. A banquet facility is available that can accommodate 180 people.

7. FRESNO WEST GOLF COURSE

PLAY POLICY & FEES: Reciprocal play is accepted with members of other private clubs. Guest fees are $35 with a member and $75 for reciprocal players. Carts are $11 per person

DRESS CODE: Appropriate golf attire and nonmetal spikes are required.

COURSE DESCRIPTION: This is a long, rolling course with lots of trees. The San Joaquin River comes into play on the north side of three holes. The highlight here is the well-maintained greens, which are fast and tricky.

NOTES: The men's course record from the back tees is 63, held by Mike Barr, and Gary Bauer shot a 61 from the regular tees. The women's course record is 67, held by Kathleen Scrivner.

LOCATION: From Highway 99 in Herndon take the West Herndon Avenue exit. Drive east to North Marks Avenue and turn left. North Marks Avenue will take you to the course driveway.

. . . ● **TOURNAMENTS:** This course is not available for outside tournaments.

8. SAN JOAQUIN COUNTRY CLUB

7700 North Van Ness
Fresno, CA 93711

PRO SHOP: 559-439-2928
OFFICE: 559-439-1573

Gordon T. Knott, Owner
Gary Bauer, Director of Golf, PGA
David T. Knott, Superintendent

Driving Range	●
Practice Greens	●
Clubhouse	●
Food / Beverage	●
Accommodations	
Pull Carts	
Power Carts	●
Club Rental	●
Special Offers	

	1	2	3	4	5	6	7	8	9	OUT
BACK	340	385	170	560	453	595	210	370	314	3397
REGULAR	340	378	142	500	442	560	169	356	305	3192
par	4	4	3	5	4	5	3	4	4	36
handicap	15	9	13	5	1	7	3	11	17	-
FORWARD	329	335	90	483	393	491	107	337	267	2832
par	4	4	3	5	4	5	3	4	4	36
handicap	11	5	17	1	7	3	15	9	13	-

	10	11	12	13	14	15	16	17	18	IN
BACK	408	175	344	352	390	418	542	189	485	3303
REGULAR	400	165	316	341	362	390	489	178	472	3113
par	4	3	4	4	4	4	5	3	5	36
handicap	4	12	18	16	8	2	10	6	14	-
FORWARD	345	158	236	282	309	417	382	127	422	2678
par	4	3	4	4	4	5	4	3	5	36
handicap	6	18	12	10	14	4	8	16	2	-

BACK	
yardage	6700
par	72
rating	70.6
slope	117

REGULAR	
yardage	6305
par	72
rating	68.7
slope	113

FORWARD	
yardage	5510
par	72
rating	70.4
slope	117

PLAY POLICY & FEES: Outside play is accepted. Green fees are $50 in the morning, $23 after 12 p.m., and $17 after 2 p.m. Carts are $15 for nine holes and $26 for 18 holes.

TEE TIMES: Reservations can be booked seven days in advance.

DRESS CODE: Appropriate golf attire is required.

COURSE DESCRIPTION: Robert Dean Putman redesigned this course in 1973. It's a tight course and has two lakes and a river. The 406-yard, par-4 16th hole is a monster with the river flanking the left side.

NOTES: A new tee box has added length to the 16th hole. Gary Bauer holds the men's course record with a 61. Veteran LPGA golfer Shelly Hamlin holds the women's record with a 68.

LOCATION: Heading south toward Fresno on Highway 99, take the Herndon exit east. Turn left on North Van Ness Boulevard and drive one mile to the course.

. . . ● **TOURNAMENTS:** A 24-player minimum is needed to book an event. Carts are required. Events should be scheduled 12 months in advance. A banquet facility is available that can accommodate 150 people.

9. FIG GARDEN GOLF COURSE

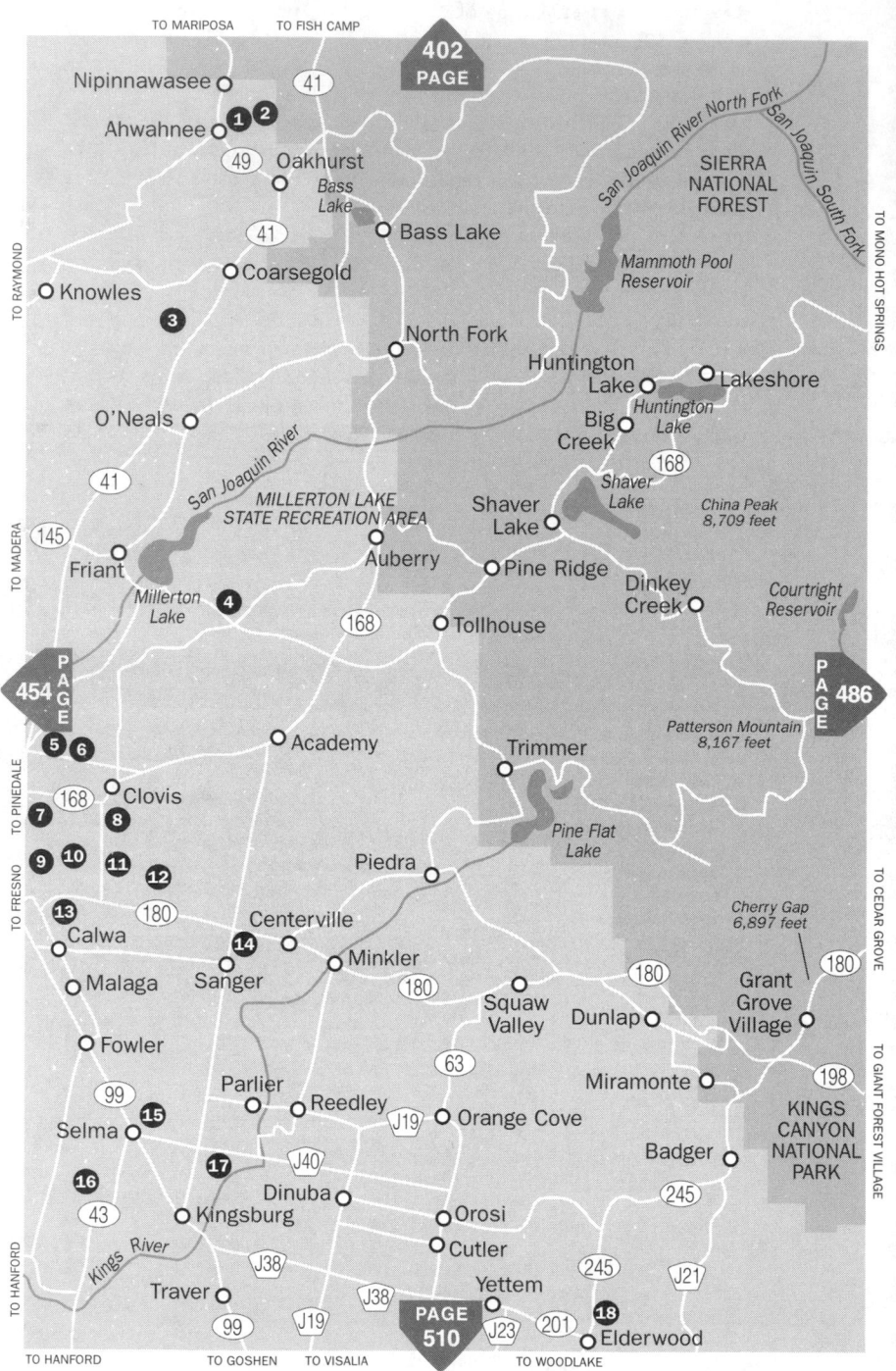

TO MARIPOSA   TO FISH CAMP

402
PAGE

Nipinnawasee ○

41

Ahwahnee ○ ①②

49   Oakhurst
Bass
Lake

41   Bass Lake

○ Coarsegold

TO RAYMOND

○ Knowles   ③

North Fork

O'Neals ○

41

TO MADERA

145

Friant ○

Millerton
Lake   ④

San Joaquin River

MILLERTON LAKE
STATE RECREATION AREA

Auberry ○

168   ○ Tollhouse

San Joaquin River North Fork

San Joaquin River South Fork

SIERRA
NATIONAL
FOREST

TO MONO HOT SPRINGS

Mammoth Pool
Reservoir

Huntington
Lake ○   ○ Lakeshore

Big   Huntington
Creek ○   Lake

168

Shaver
Lake   China Peak
8,709 feet

Shaver
Lake ○

○ Pine Ridge   Dinkey
Creek ○

Courtright
Reservoir

PAGE
454   ○⑤ ⑥   Academy ○

TO PINEDALE

168   ○ Clovis
⑦   ⑧

⑨ ⑩ ⑪   ⑫

TO FRESNO

⑬
Calwa ○

180

Centerville
○

⑭   ○ Minkler

○ Malaga   Sanger ○

180

○ Fowler

99   ⑮

Selma ○

⑯

43

Kingsburg ○

Kings River

TO HANFORD

Traver ○

99

TO HANFORD   TO GOSHEN   TO VISALIA

⑰

J40

Dinuba ○

J38

J38

Piedra ○

Pine Flat
Lake

Trimmer ○

Patterson Mountain
8,167 feet

PAGE
486

Squaw   Dunlap ○
Valley

63

Miramonte ○

○ Orange Cove

J19

○ Orosi

○ Cutler

Yettem ○

J23

201   ⑱
○ Elderwood

PAGE
510

TO WOODLAKE

Parlier ○   ○ Reedley

Cherry Gap
6,897 feet

180   180

Grant
Grove
Village

198

KINGS
CANYON
NATIONAL
PARK

Badger ○

245

245   J21

TO CEDAR GROVE

TO GIANT FOREST VILLAGE

466

Fresno Area

① RIVER CREEK GOLF COURSE
ARCHITECT: JOHN HILBORN, 1991

41709 Road 600
Ahwahnee, CA 93607

PRO SHOP: 559-683-3388

Larry Vaccaro, Manager
Roger Lyon, Professional

Driving Range ●
Practice Greens ●
Clubhouse ●
Food / Beverage ●
Accommodations
Pull Carts ●
Power Carts ●
Club Rental ●
$pecial Offers

	1	2	3	4	5	6	7	8	9	OUT
BACK	542	365	166	387	346	343	503	151	349	3152
REGULAR	523	348	156	373	325	322	490	144	333	3014
par	5	4	3	4	4	4	5	3	4	36
handicap	1	7	15	5	11	13	3	17	9	-
FORWARD	428	272	91	293	290	301	460	118	309	2562
par	5	4	3	4	4	4	5	3	4	36
handicap	3	13	17	11	9	7	1	15	5	-

	10	11	12	13	14	15	16	17	18	IN
BACK	542	365	166	387	346	343	503	151	349	3152
REGULAR	523	348	156	373	325	322	490	144	333	3014
par	5	4	3	4	4	4	5	3	4	36
handicap	2	8	16	6	12	14	4	18	10	-
FORWARD	428	272	91	293	290	301	460	118	309	2562
par	5	4	3	4	4	4	5	3	4	36
handicap	4	14	18	12	10	8	2	16	6	-

BACK	
yardage	6304
par	72
rating	69.4
slope	125

REGULAR	
yardage	6028
par	72
rating	68.3
slope	123

FORWARD	
yardage	5124
par	72
rating	69.8
slope	118

② AHWAHNEE GOLF CLUB
ARCHITECTS: ALAN THOMAS, 1988; JOHN SIRMAN, 1997

46516 Opah Drive
Ahwahnee, CA 93644

PRO SHOP: 559-642-1343
OFFICE: 559-642-1340

John Sirman, Manager
Mike Best, Professional
Mike Stieler, Superintendent

Driving Range ●
Practice Greens ●
Clubhouse ●
Food / Beverage ●
Accommodations
Pull Carts ●
Power Carts ●
Club Rental ●
$pecial Offers

	1	2	3	4	5	6	7	8	9	OUT
BACK	396	429	417	377	170	386	373	191	521	3260
REGULAR	344	428	382	342	154	321	347	146	497	2961
par	4	5	4	4	3	4	4	3	5	36
handicap	13	1	7	11	9	15	3	17	5	-
FORWARD	277	376	280	317	114	278	333	116	460	2551
par	4	5	4	4	3	4	4	3	5	36
handicap	15	1	13	5	11	9	3	17	7	-

	10	11	12	13	14	15	16	17	18	IN
BACK	323	401	526	311	185	243	381	179	551	3100
REGULAR	301	375	479	286	156	176	346	149	523	2791
par	4	4	5	4	3	4	4	3	5	36
handicap	14	4	12	16	10	6	2	18	8	-
FORWARD	244	327	402	260	86	155	308	111	497	2390
par	4	4	5	4	3	4	4	3	5	36
handicap	14	6	12	10	8	18	2	16	4	-

BACK	
yardage	6360
par	72
rating	71.1
slope	135

REGULAR	
yardage	5752
par	72
rating	68.4
slope	126

FORWARD	
yardage	4941
par	72
rating	68.6
slope	119

PLAY POLICY & FEES: Green fees are $10 for nine holes and $18 for 18 holes weekdays, and $13 for nine holes and $22 for 18 holes weekends. Carts are $12 for nine and $20 for 18 holes.

TEE TIMES: Reservations can be booked seven days in advance.

COURSE DESCRIPTION: Trees guard many holes on this scenic and challenging course. Water comes into play on three holes. The par-4 fourth hole is a 387-yard tester.

NOTES: The course record of 65 is held by Michael Best.

LOCATION: From Fresno take Highway 41 to Oakhurst. Take a left on Highway 49 for five miles to Road 600. Take a right on Road 600 for one-half mile to the course.

. . . ● **TOURNAMENTS:** Tournaments should be scheduled 12 months in advance.

● **TRAVEL:** The Oakhurst Lodge is located 20 minutes from the golf course. For reservations call 209-683-4417.

1. RIVER CREEK GOLF COURSE

PLAY POLICY & FEES: Green fees are $13 for nine and $25 for 18 holes. Carts are $12 for nine and $20 for 18 holes. Senior and twilight rates are available.

TEE TIMES: Reservations can be booked 30 days in advance.

DRESS CODE: Collared shirts and nonmetal spikes are required.

COURSE DESCRIPTION: This is a mountain course that demands shot-making accuracy. Good iron play is essential for a successful round. The course has small greens, but they are fast and challenging.

LOCATION: From Mariposa, take Highway 49 for 28 miles heading to Oakhurst. Turn left on Harmony Lane and continue 2.7 miles to the course.

. . . ● **TOURNAMENTS:** A 40-player minimum is required to book an event. The banquet facility can accommodate up to 200 people.

2. AHWAHNEE GOLF CLUB

③ YOSEMITE LAKES PARK GOLF COURSE
ARCHITECT: BUCK NOONKESTER, 1970

30250 Yosemite Springs
Coarsegold, CA 93614

PRO SHOP: 559-658-7468
CLUBHOUSE: 559-658-7466

Buck Noonkester, Superintendent

Driving Range
Practice Greens ●
Clubhouse ●
Food / Beverage ●
Accommodations
Pull Carts ●
Power Carts ●
Club Rental ●
$pecial Offers

	1	2	3	4	5	6	7	8	9	OUT
BACK										
REGULAR										
par										
handicap										
FORWARD										
par										
handicap										

	10	11	12	13	14	15	16	17	18	IN
BACK										
REGULAR										
par										
handicap										
FORWARD										
par										
handicap										

BACK	
yardage	
par	
rating	
slope	

REGULAR	
yardage	3534
par	62
rating	57.9
slope	98

FORWARD	
yardage	3069
par	62
rating	57.1
slope	85

④ BRIGHTON CREST GOLF & COUNTRY CLUB
ARCHITECT: JOHNNY MILLER, 1990

21722 Fairway Oaks Lane
Friant, CA 93626

PRO SHOP: 559-299-8586
OFFICE: 559-299-8570

Eric Peterson, PGA Professional
Bret Billeadeau, Superintendent
Darren M. Myers, Tournament Director

Driving Range ●
Practice Greens ●
Clubhouse ●
Food / Beverage ●
Accommodations
Pull Carts
Power Carts ●
Club Rental ●
$pecial Offers

	1	2	3	4	5	6	7	8	9	OUT
BACK	360	185	440	337	433	505	390	199	429	3278
REGULAR	342	158	405	319	412	482	364	174	395	3051
par	4	3	4	4	4	5	4	3	4	35
handicap	-	-	-	-	-	-	-	-	-	-
FORWARD	268	103	352	260	331	392	311	114	323	2454
par	4	3	4	4	4	5	4	3	4	35
handicap	-	-	-	-	-	-	-	-	-	-

	10	11	12	13	14	15	16	17	18	IN
BACK	525	136	340	466	517	464	187	404	514	3553
REGULAR	499	130	312	443	481	431	167	379	480	3322
par	5	3	4	4	5	4	3	4	5	37
handicap	-	-	-	-	-	-	-	-	-	-
FORWARD	426	102	255	363	420	326	112	331	406	2741
par	5	3	4	4	5	4	3	4	5	37
handicap	-	-	-	-	-	-	-	-	-	-

BACK	
yardage	6831
par	72
rating	-
slope	-

REGULAR	
yardage	6373
par	72
rating	-
slope	-

FORWARD	
yardage	5195
par	72
rating	-
slope	-

PLAY POLICY & FEES: Reciprocal play is accepted with members of other private clubs. Guest fees are $12 and $6 for juniors. Carts are $9 for nine holes and $15 for 18 holes.

TEE TIMES: On weekdays play is on a first-come, first-served basis. Reservations are required on Friday, weekends, and holidays.

DRESS CODE: Golf attire is encouraged.

COURSE DESCRIPTION: This is a fun, short course. Hills and water come into play on five holes, and the fairways are narrow. Don't expect this to be an easy stroll in the park.

NOTES: Diane Staurum holds the women's course record of 64, and Gene Templeton holds the men's record of 59.

LOCATION: Driving toward Yosemite National Park on Highway 41, before Coarsegold, turn left on Yosemite Springs Parkway. Drive three miles to the course.

. . . ● **TOURNAMENTS:** This course is available for outside tournaments.

3. YOSEMITE LAKES PARK GOLF COURSE

PLAY POLICY & FEES: Green fees are $40 weekdays and $50 weekends. Twilight rates are available.

TEE TIMES: Reservations can be booked seven days in advance.

DRESS CODE: Appropriate golf attire is required. Nonmetal spikes are optional.

COURSE DESCRIPTION: At the 800-foot elevation, the course is above the winter fog level and is somewhat cooler during the summer months. The terrain is rolling, and the course is dotted with native blue and valley oaks. The greens, which Miller sized to fit the difficulty of the hole, are subtle but undulating. One of Miller's favorite holes is the par-5, 505-yard third. There is a slight dogleg right, and the second shot must negotiate two oaks. There is a lateral hazard down the entire left side. Water runs in front of the small, two-tiered green.

NOTES: This is the first Johnny Miller–designed course in California. The course record is 65 by Mike Springer. In 1999 the course underwent a turf-conversion program to hybrid Bermuda fairways.

LOCATION: From Fresno take Highway 41 north to the Friant Road/Millerton Lake exit. The course is five miles past the town of Friant on Friant Road.

. . . ● **TOURNAMENTS:** A 24-player minimum is required to book an event. Carts are required. Events should be scheduled six months in advance. ● **TRAVEL:** The Courtyard by Marriott (209-221-6000) and Days Inn (209-222-5641) are recommended for lodging.

4. BRIGHTON CREST GOLF & COUNTRY CLUB

⑤ FORT WASHINGTON GOLF & COUNTRY CLUB
ARCHITECT: WILLIE WATSON, 1923

10272 North Millbrook
Fresno, CA 93720

PRO SHOP: 559-434-9120
OFFICE: 559-434-1702

Alan Ehnes, Director of Golf, PGA
Owen Stone

Driving Range ●
Practice Greens ●
Clubhouse ●
Food / Beverage ●
Accommodations
Pull Carts ●
Power Carts ●
Club Rental ●
$pecial Offers

	1	2	3	4	5	6	7	8	9	OUT
BACK	487	427	174	448	331	425	208	407	502	3409
REGULAR	478	395	164	414	319	411	201	393	473	3248
par	5	4	3	4	4	4	3	4	5	36
handicap	11	3	17	5	13	1	9	7	15	-
FORWARD	459	381	149	404	310	401	167	365	424	3060
par	5	4	3	4	4	4	3	4	5	36
handicap	1	7	17	3	13	5	15	11	9	-

	10	11	12	13	14	15	16	17	18	IN
BACK	427	161	537	413	422	327	520	146	403	3356
REGULAR	414	158	496	394	383	313	514	141	385	3198
par	4	3	5	4	4	4	5	3	4	36
handicap	2	18	16	6	4	14	10	12	8	-
FORWARD	409	147	481	385	369	301	463	102	374	3031
par	5	3	5	4	4	4	5	3	4	37
handicap	10	16	4	6	12	14	2	18	8	-

BACK	
yardage	6765
par	72
rating	72.2
slope	128

REGULAR	
yardage	6446
par	72
rating	70.6
slope	125

FORWARD	
yardage	6091
par	73
rating	74.7
slope	129

⑥ RIVERSIDE OF FRESNO GOLF COURSE
ARCHITECT: WILLIAM P. BELL, 1939

7672 North Josephine
Fresno, CA 93711

PRO SHOP: 559-275-5900
OFFICE: 559-275-6561

Bruce Ballou, Director of Golf, PGA
Robert Tillema, Jr., Superintendent
Lance Rohrman, Tournament Director

Driving Range ●
Practice Greens ●
Clubhouse
Food / Beverage ●
Accommodations
Pull Carts ●
Power Carts ●
Club Rental ●
$pecial Offers

	1	2	3	4	5	6	7	8	9	OUT
BACK	380	174	379	423	158	546	363	178	554	3155
REGULAR	372	153	371	411	147	535	355	168	547	3059
par	4	3	4	4	3	5	4	3	5	35
handicap	13	9	7	1	17	5	15	11	3	-
FORWARD	327	130	300	404	136	489	344	153	515	2798
par	4	3	4	5	3	5	4	3	5	36
handicap	7	17	9	11	15	3	5	13	1	-

	10	11	12	13	14	15	16	17	18	IN
BACK	424	143	364	437	542	206	522	383	469	3490
REGULAR	414	134	354	408	532	185	507	375	457	3366
par	4	3	4	4	5	3	5	4	5	37
handicap	4	16	12	2	14	6	10	8	18	-
FORWARD	404	122	312	401	433	157	492	364	441	3126
par	5	3	4	5	5	3	5	4	5	39
handicap	18	14	6	16	8	16	2	4	12	-

BACK	
yardage	6645
par	72
rating	71.1
slope	123

REGULAR	
yardage	6425
par	72
rating	70.1
slope	121

FORWARD	
yardage	5924
par	75
rating	73.8
slope	125

PLAY POLICY & FEES: Reciprocal play is accepted with members of other private clubs. Guest fees are $35 with a member and $75 without, and $100 if not a resident of the area. Carts are $8. The course is closed on Monday.

TEE TIMES: Have your club pro call to make arrangements.

DRESS CODE: Collared shirts and nonmetal spikes are required. Bermuda shorts must be knee length, and no denim is allowed.

COURSE DESCRIPTION: This is a classic valley course, and it ranks among the top courses in Central California. It is a walkable course with rolling hills, tree-lined fairways, and fast, undulating greens.

NOTES: The Pro-Scratch is played here annually in May. Fort Washington will host the USGA mid-amateur in 2000.

LOCATION: From Highway 99 in Fresno take the Herndon Avenue exit east. Turn left on Blackstone Avenue. Turn right on Friant Road and then turn right again on Fort Washington, which leads to the course.

. . . ● **TOURNAMENTS:** A 100-player minimum is required to book a tournament. Carts are required. Events should be booked 12 months in advance. The banquet facility can accommodate up to 300 people. ● **TRAVEL:** The Piccadilly Inn is recommended. For reservations call 209-251-6000.

5. FORT WASHINGTON GOLF & COUNTRY

PLAY POLICY & FEES: Green fees are $12.75 weekdays and $20 weekends and holidays. Carts are $10 for nine holes and $18 for 18 holes.

TEE TIMES: Reservations can be booked seven days in advance starting at 6 a.m.

DRESS CODE: Shirts must be worn. Golf shoes or flat-soled shoes are required.

COURSE DESCRIPTION: This rolling course is long and well guarded by trees. It's testy, with a number of sidehill lies to medium-sized greens. Bring every club. Notable is the par-4 10th hole which tees off from a bluff and requires a difficult second shot to a green guarded on the right by an overhanging tree.

NOTES: Both Bruce Sanders and Harold Chuhlantseff hold the course record of 63.

LOCATION: From Highway 99 in Fresno, exit onto Herndon Avenue east. Cross the railroad tracks and turn left on Van Buren. Turn right on Josephine Avenue and follow it to the course.

. . . ● **TOURNAMENTS:** This course is available for outside tournaments. A 24-player minimum is needed. Tournaments should be booked three to six months in advance.

6. RIVERSIDE OF FRESNO GOLF COURSE

COPPER RIVER COUNTRY CLUB
ARCHITECT: DAVID PFAFF, 1995

11500 North Friant Road
Fresno, CA 93720

PRO SHOP: 559-434-5200

Doug Scrivner, PGA Professional
Jean Thysse, General Manager
Bill Griffith, Superintendent

Driving Range ●
Practice Greens ●
Clubhouse ●
Food / Beverage ●
Accommodations
Pull Carts ●
Power Carts ●
Club Rental ●
$pecial Offers

	1	2	3	4	5	6	7	8	9	OUT
BACK	402	511	421	531	189	406	419	168	451	3498
REGULAR	387	488	397	515	160	378	405	138	410	3278
par	4	5	4	5	3	4	4	3	4	36
handicap	9	15	3	13	7	11	5	17	1	-
FORWARD	336	405	326	432	122	291	330	108	323	2673
par	4	5	4	5	3	4	4	3	4	36
handicap	7	3	11	1	15	13	5	17	9	-

	10	11	12	13	14	15	16	17	18	IN
BACK	396	208	522	415	442	541	424	171	426	3545
REGULAR	385	178	497	400	422	513	387	157	403	3342
par	4	3	5	4	4	5	4	3	4	36
handicap	10	12	16	6	4	18	8	14	2	-
FORWARD	320	119	412	324	368	462	302	76	318	2701
par	4	3	5	4	4	5	4	3	4	36
handicap	14	16	4	12	6	2	10	18	8	-

BACK	
yardage	7043
par	72
rating	74.3
slope	132

REGULAR	
yardage	6620
par	72
rating	72.0
slope	126

FORWARD	
yardage	5374
par	72
rating	70.5
slope	120

 ## VILLAGE GREEN GOLF COURSE
ARCHITECT: ROBERT DEAN PUTMAN, 1959

236 South Clovis Avenue
Fresno, CA 93727

PRO SHOP: 559-255-2786

Gordon Israelsky Jr., Director of Golf, PGA

Driving Range
Practice Greens ●
Clubhouse ●
Food / Beverage ●
Accommodations
Pull Carts ●
Power Carts ●
Club Rental ●
$pecial Offers

	1	2	3	4	5	6	7	8	9	OUT
BACK	-	-	-	-	-	-	-	-	-	-
REGULAR	318	85	148	127	120	128	121	249	335	1631
par	4	3	3	3	3	3	3	4	4	30
handicap	2	18	6	14	16	10	8	12	4	-
FORWARD	-	-	-	-	-	-	-	-	-	
par	-	-	-	-	-	-	-	-	-	
handicap	-	-	-	-	-	-	-	-	-	-

	10	11	12	13	14	15	16	17	18	IN
BACK	-	-	-	-	-	-	-	-	-	-
REGULAR	333	95	172	137	130	138	157	291	345	1798
par	4	3	3	3	3	3	3	4	4	30
handicap	1	17	7	13	15	9	3	11	5	-
FORWARD	-	-	-	-	-	-	-	-	-	
par	-	-	-	-	-	-	-	-	-	
handicap	-	-	-	-	-	-	-	-	-	-

BACK	
yardage	-
par	-
rating	
slope	

REGULAR	
yardage	3429
par	60
rating	56.8
slope	-

FORWARD	
yardage	
par	
rating	-
slope	

PLAY POLICY & FEES: Reciprocal play is accepted; otherwise, members and guests only. Guest fees are $35 Monday through Thursday and $45 Friday through Sunday. All guests must be accompanied by a member.

DRESS CODE: Appropriate golf attire and nonmetal spikes are required.

COURSE DESCRIPTION: This links-style course is driver friendly, but bring a light touch because the greens are fast. There is water on nine holes.

LOCATION: From Fresno take Highway 41 toward Yosemite to the North Friant Road exit. Follow North Friant to the golf course on the right.

. . . ● **TOURNAMENTS:** This course is available for outside tournaments. A banquet facility is available that can accommodate 280 people.

7. COPPER RIVER COUNTRY CLUB

PLAY POLICY & FEES: Green fees are $5 for nine holes and $8 for 18 holes weekdays, and $6 for nine holes and $9 for 18 holes weekends. Carts are $8 for nine holes and $14 for 18 holes. Junior and senior rates are also available.

TEE TIMES: Reservations are not accepted. All play is on a first-come, first-served basis.

COURSE DESCRIPTION: There are three par 4s and six par 3s on this course. All holes are well bunkered from tee to green and well maintained, with lots of trees. On the seventh hole, the ball must carry over trees and a duck pond to the green. You can barely see the green.

LOCATION: From Highway 99 in Fresno take the Belmont Avenue exit east to Clovis Avenue. Go south on Clovis just past Tulare Street. The course is located in the Village Green Country Club Apartments.

. . . ● **TOURNAMENTS:** This course is available for outside tournaments, and shotgun tournaments are welcome. A 12-player minimum is needed to book an event.

8. VILLAGE GREEN GOLF COURSE

⑨ HANK'S SWANK PAR 3
ARCHITECT: HENRY BOCCHINI JR., 1983

6101 East Olive Avenue
Fresno, CA 93727

PRO SHOP: 559-252-7077

Henry Bocchini III, PGA Professional
Hank Bocchini Jr., PGA Professional

Driving Range ●
Practice Greens ●
Clubhouse ●
Food / Beverage ●
Accommodations
Pull Carts ●
Power Carts ●
Club Rental ●
$pecial Offers

	1	2	3	4	5	6	7	8	9	OUT
BACK	-	-	-	-	-	-	-	-	-	-
REGULAR	120	130	210	140	175	185	110	85	150	1305
par	3	3	3	3	3	3	3	3	3	27
handicap	7	8	1	5	3	2	4	9	6	-
FORWARD	-	-	-	-	-	-	-	-	-	
par	-	-	-	-	-	-	-	-	-	
handicap	-	-	-	-	-	-	-	-	-	-

	10	11	12	13	14	15	16	17	18	IN
BACK	-	-	-	-	-	-	-	-	-	-
REGULAR	-	-	-	-	-	-	-	-	-	-
par	-	-	-	-	-	-	-	-	-	-
handicap	-	-	-	-	-	-	-	-	-	-
FORWARD	-	-	-	-	-	-	-	-	-	-
par	-	-	-	-	-	-	-	-	-	-
handicap	-	-	-	-	-	-	-	-	-	-

BACK	
yardage	-
par	-
rating	-
slope	

REGULAR	
yardage	1305
par	27
rating	-
slope	-

FORWARD	
yardage	
par	
rating	-
slope	-

⑩ PALM LAKES GOLF COURSE
ARCHITECT: RICHARD BIGLER, 1986

5025 East Dakota Avenue
Fresno, CA 93727

PRO SHOP: 559-291-4050

Bruce Ballou, Director of Golf, PGA
Ronald Hill, Superintendent

Driving Range
Practice Greens ●
Clubhouse ●
Food / Beverage ●
Accommodations
Pull Carts ●
Power Carts ●
Club Rental ●
$pecial Offers

	1	2	3	4	5	6	7	8	9	OUT
BACK	-	-	-	-	-	-	-	-	-	-
REGULAR	318	386	159	121	172	180	249	165	328	2078
par	4	4	3	3	3	3	3	3	4	30
handicap	13	1	7	18	12	9	2	14	15	-
FORWARD	318	386	159	121	172	180	249	165	328	2078
par	4	4	3	3	3	3	4	3	4	31
handicap	5	1	15	17	11	13	7	9	3	-

	10	11	12	13	14	15	16	17	18	IN
BACK	-	-	-	-	-	-	-	-	-	-
REGULAR	313	161	182	211	381	358	260	195	323	2384
par	4	3	3	3	4	4	4	3	4	32
handicap	8	17	5	6	10	11	4	3	16	-
FORWARD	313	161	182	211	381	358	260	195	323	2384
par	4	3	3	4	4	4	4	3	4	33
handicap	10	18	16	12	2	4	8	14	6	-

BACK	
yardage	-
par	-
rating	-
slope	-

REGULAR	
yardage	4462
par	62
rating	60.7
slope	100

FORWARD	
yardage	4462
par	64
rating	60.7
slope	100

PLAY POLICY & FEES: Green fees for nine holes are $7 weekdays and $8 on weekends. Fees for juniors and seniors are $6 weekdays and $7 on weekends. An additional nine holes is $3.50.

TEE TIMES: Reservations are not accepted. All play is on a first-come, first-served basis.

COURSE DESCRIPTION: This pretty course features rolling terrain, plenty of sand, and large well-kept greens.

NOTES: If your clubs are in need of repair, you're in luck. Hank Bocchini can repair your clubs on site. For the golf purist he also custom makes persimmon woods.

LOCATION: The course is one mile east of the Fresno Airport on East Olive Avenue.

. . . ● **TOURNAMENTS:** This course is available for outside tournaments.

9. HANK'S SWANK PAR 3

PLAY POLICY & FEES: Green fees are $10.50 weekdays and $12 weekends and holidays. Senior and student rates are available. Carts are $8 for nine holes and $16 for 18 holes.

TEE TIMES: Reservations can be booked seven days in advance.

COURSE DESCRIPTION: This short, walkable executive course has one large lake, which comes into play on four holes.

LOCATION: Driving south on Highway 99 from Madera, take the Shaw exit east past California State University Fresno. Turn right on Willow and then left at East Dakota Avenue. The course is located across from the airport.

. . . ● **TOURNAMENTS:** This course is available for outside tournaments.

10. PALM LAKES GOLF COURSE

AIRWAYS GOLF COURSE
ARCHITECT: BERT STAMPS, 1948

5440 East Shields Avenue
Fresno, CA 93727

PRO SHOP: 559-291-6254

Jim Cooke, PGA Professional
Bob Weitz, Superintendent

Driving Range •
Practice Greens •
Clubhouse •
Food / Beverage •
Accommodations
Pull Carts •
Power Carts •
Club Rental •
$pecial Offers

	1	2	3	4	5	6	7	8	9	OUT
BACK	-	-	-	-	-	-	-	-	-	-
REGULAR	329	332	407	302	130	319	116	516	217	2668
par	4	4	4	4	3	4	3	5	3	34
handicap	11	13	1	9	15	7	17	5	3	-
FORWARD	329	332	407	302	130	319	116	516	217	2668
par	4	4	5	4	3	4	3	5	4	36
handicap	5	7	3	11	15	9	17	1	13	-

	10	11	12	13	14	15	16	17	18	IN
BACK					-	-	-	-	-	-
REGULAR	352	176	277	301	363	166	445	255	283	2618
par	4	3	4	4	4	3	5	4	3	34
handicap	4	10	18	16	2	6	12	14	8	-
FORWARD	352	176	277	301	363	138	445	255	283	2590
par	4	3	4	4	4	3	5	4	3	34
handicap	6	14	18	8	4	12	2	10	16	-

BACK	
yardage	-
par	-
rating	-
slope	-

REGULAR	
yardage	5286
par	68
rating	64.0
slope	107

FORWARD	
yardage	5258
par	70
rating	67.9
slope	110

 BELMONT COUNTRY CLUB
ARCHITECT: BERT STAMPS, 1956

8253 East Belmont
Fresno, CA 93727

PRO SHOP: 559-251-5076
CLUBHOUSE: 559-251-5078

Kenny Collins, PGA Professional
Tom Casey, Superintendent
Jack Costa, Banquet Manager

Driving Range •
Practice Greens •
Clubhouse •
Food / Beverage •
Accommodations
Pull Carts •
Power Carts •
Club Rental
$pecial Offers

	1	2	3	4	5	6	7	8	9	OUT
BACK	368	129	450	407	506	378	326	211	481	3256
REGULAR	363	109	442	401	492	372	326	193	470	3168
par	4	3	4	4	5	4	4	3	5	36
handicap	9	17	1	3	11	5	15	7	13	-
FORWARD	257	81	308	322	413	311	276	131	403	2502
par	4	3	5	4	5	4	4	3	5	37
handicap	13	17	9	5	1	7	11	15	3	-

	10	11	12	13	14	15	16	17	18	IN
BACK	424	175	540	178	374	317	376	317	524	3225
REGULAR	414	168	516	144	367	305	351	307	516	3088
par	4	3	5	3	4	4	4	4	5	36
handicap	2	12	6	18	10	14	4	16	8	-
FORWARD	297	141	432	109	289	283	298	285	408	2542
par	4	3	5	3	4	4	4	4	5	36
handicap	8	16	4	18	10	14	6	12	2	-

BACK	
yardage	6481
par	72
rating	70.4
slope	124

REGULAR	
yardage	6256
par	72
rating	69.5
slope	121

FORWARD	
yardage	5044
par	73
rating	68.5
slope	113

PLAY POLICY & FEES: Green fees are $12.50 weekdays and $15 weekends. Carts are $20. Senior, junior, and twilight rates are available.

TEE TIMES: Reservations can be booked seven days in advance.

DRESS CODE: Shirts and shoes must be worn.

COURSE DESCRIPTION: This flat, tree-lined course is short and sporty. It's a mature course and excellent for beginners and intermediate players.

NOTES: Rounds are usually completed in less than four hours. The course record is 58.

LOCATION: From Highway 99 in Fresno, exit on Ashlon Avenue and drive east for eight miles. Turn right on Peach Avenue and proceed one-half mile to the course entrance on the right.

. . . ● **TOURNAMENTS:** This course is available for outside tournaments. Carts are required.

11. AIRWAYS GOLF COURSE

PLAY POLICY & FEES: Reciprocal play is accepted with members of other private clubs. Guest and reciprocal fees are $35. Carts are $9 for one person and $18 for two people. The course is closed on Monday.

TEE TIMES: Have your club pro call for arrangements.

DRESS CODE: Appropriate golf attire and nonmetal spikes are required.

COURSE DESCRIPTION: This course is well maintained, short, and tight, with big greens and lots of trees. It's a good test of irons and the short game.

NOTES: Renovations include green side mounding, improved bunkers, and new water hazards. Gary Bauer and Steve Gutilla both hold the course record with a 62.

LOCATION: In Fresno on Highway 99 take the Belmont Avenue exit east. Drive 13.5 miles to the course on the right.

. . . ● **TOURNAMENTS:** This course has limited availability for outside tournaments. An 80-player minimum is needed to book an event.

12. BELMONT COUNTRY CLUB

SUNNYSIDE COUNTRY CLUB
ARCHITECT: WILLIAM P. BELL, 1911

5704 East Butler
Fresno, CA 93727

PRO SHOP: 559-255-6871
CLUBHOUSE: 559-251-6011

Steve Menchinella, Head Professional, PGA
Diana McGrath, Banquet Manager
Rick Stone, Superintendent

Driving Range ●
Practice Greens ●
Clubhouse ●
Food / Beverage ●
Accommodations
Pull Carts ●
Power Carts ●
Club Rental ●
$pecial Offers

	1	2	3	4	5	6	7	8	9	OUT
BACK	415	387	441	207	527	135	404	421	548	3485
REGULAR	404	367	427	186	511	122	383	402	534	3336
par	4	4	4	3	5	3	4	4	5	36
handicap	3	7	1	11	15	17	9	5	13	-
FORWARD	354	302	405	160	452	93	335	347	457	2905
par	4	4	5	3	5	3	4	4	5	37
handicap	3	7	1	11	15	17	9	5	13	-

	10	11	12	13	14	15	16	17	18	IN
BACK	344	436	340	158	385	548	352	188	551	3302
REGULAR	323	419	325	149	373	527	322	159	511	3108
par	4	4	4	3	4	5	4	3	5	36
handicap	16	2	8	14	6	4	12	18	10	-
FORWARD	295	371	252	137	330	440	265	120	424	2634
par	4	4	4	3	4	5	4	3	5	36
handicap	16	2	10	14	8	4	12	18	6	-

BACK	
yardage	6787
par	72
rating	72.3
slope	126

REGULAR	
yardage	6444
par	72
rating	70.4
slope	121

FORWARD	
yardage	5539
par	73
rating	71.8
slope	124

 SHERWOOD FOREST GOLF COURSE
ARCHITECT: BOB BALDOCK, 1968

79 North Frankwood
Sanger, CA 93657

PRO SHOP: 559-787-2611

Don Siler, Shop Manager
Randy Hansen, PGA Professional
Robert Tillema, Superintendent

Driving Range ●
Practice Greens ●
Clubhouse ●
Food / Beverage ●
Accommodations
Pull Carts ●
Power Carts ●
Club Rental ●
$pecial Offers

	1	2	3	4	5	6	7	8	9	OUT
BACK	315	357	400	163	367	548	417	338	381	3286
REGULAR	314	351	381	159	359	546	410	338	369	3227
par	4	4	4	3	4	5	4	4	4	36
handicap	17	5	11	15	13	3	1	7	9	-
FORWARD	284	333	298	129	329	516	391	302	338	2920
par	4	4	4	3	4	5	4	4	4	36
handicap	15	5	11	17	13	1	3	7	9	-

	10	11	12	13	14	15	16	17	18	IN
BACK	323	533	470	188	517	140	405	178	305	3059
REGULAR	313	516	445	184	515	131	384	164	302	2954
par	4	5	4	3	5	3	4	3	4	35
handicap	12	6	2	14	4	18	10	8	16	-
FORWARD	298	455	430	124	491	111	361	125	282	2677
par	4	5	5	3	5	3	4	3	4	36
handicap	12	6	8	16	2	18	4	10	14	-

BACK	
yardage	6345
par	71
rating	69.2
slope	118

REGULAR	
yardage	6181
par	71
rating	68.5
slope	116

FORWARD	
yardage	5597
par	72
rating	71.4
slope	118

PLAY POLICY & FEES: Reciprocal play is accepted with members of other private clubs. Guest fees are $35 when accompanied by a member and $75 unaccompanied. Carts are $10 per person. The course is closed on Monday.

TEE TIMES: Have your club pro call for arrangements.

DRESS CODE: No denim of any kind may be worn. Shorts must have a six-inch inseam, and shirts must have collars. Nonmetal spikes are required.

COURSE DESCRIPTION: This long, demanding course has tight fairways and lots of sand and trees. Be careful of the greens—they look innocent, but they're small, fast, and tricky.

NOTES: This is the oldest course in the San Joaquin Valley and one of the original four clubs to start the California State Golf Association. Kevin Sutherland holds the course record at 61. The women's record of 67 is owned by LPGA golfer Shelly Hamlin. The USGA Junior Championship was played here in 1981.

LOCATION: From Highway 99 in Fresno take the Ventura Avenue/Kings Canyon Road exit east for seven miles to Clovis Avenue. Turn right on Clovis Avenue and turn left on East Butler Avenue to the course.

. . . ● **TOURNAMENTS:** All tournaments must be member sponsored. A 20-player minimum is needed. Tournaments can be booked six months in advance. The banquet facility can hold 300 people. ● **TRAVEL:** The Piccadilly Inn is about 10 minutes away from the golf course. For reservations call 559-251-6000.

13. SUNNYSIDE COUNTRY CLUB

PLAY POLICY & FEES: Green fees are $17 Monday through Thursday and $20 Friday, weekends, and holidays. Carts are $20.

TEE TIMES: Reservations can be booked seven days in advance.

DRESS CODE: No tank tops are allowed.

COURSE DESCRIPTION: This scenic course runs along the Kings River and offers views of the mountains throughout. True to its name, the course has trees on every hole. All but five holes demand accuracy off the tee.

LOCATION: From north of Fresno take Highway 99 south to Jensen Avenue. Take Jensen east to McCall Avenue. Take McCall Avenue north to Kings Canyon/Highway 180 east to Frankwood Avenue. Take Frankwood Avenue north one mile to the course.

. . . ● **TOURNAMENTS:** Shotgun tournaments are available weekdays only. Carts are required for shotgun starts. A 20-player minimum is required to book a regular tournament. Events should be booked six months in advance. ● **TRAVEL:** The Edgewater Inn is recommended for lodging. Call 800-479-5855 for reservations.

14. SHERWOOD FOREST GOLF COURSE

SELMA VALLEY GOLF COURSE
ARCHITECT: ROBERT DEAN PUTMAN, 1956

12389 East Rose Avenue
Selma, CA 93662

PRO SHOP: 559-896-2424

Walter Short, Owner
Duffy Allison, Director of Golf
Jerry Lopez, Superintendent

Driving Range ●
Practice Greens ●
Clubhouse ●
Food / Beverage ●
Accommodations
Pull Carts ●
Power Carts ●
Club Rental ●
$pecial Offers

	1	2	3	4	5	6	7	8	9	OUT
BACK	-	-	-	-	-	-	-	-	-	-
REGULAR	403	379	165	381	283	305	155	486	310	2867
par	4	4	3	4	4	4	3	5	4	35
handicap	1	3	9	5	15	17	13	7	11	-
FORWARD	399	367	142	370	277	304	136	416	300	2711
par	5	4	3	4	4	4	3	5	4	36
handicap	3	5	15	7	13	11	17	1	9	-

	10	11	12	13	14	15	16	17	18	IN
BACK	-	-	-	-	-	-	-	-	-	-
REGULAR	271	260	397	358	365	105	390	122	256	2524
par	4	4	4	4	4	3	4	3	4	34
handicap	12	10	4	8	6	14	2	16	18	-
FORWARD	270	259	385	353	362	80	379	119	252	2459
par	4	4	4	4	4	3	4	3	4	34
handicap	10	12	2	8	6	18	4	16	14	-

BACK	
yardage	-
par	-
rating	-
slope	-

REGULAR	
yardage	5391
par	69
rating	64.7
slope	107

FORWARD	
yardage	5170
par	70
rating	69.8
slope	118

 KINGS COUNTRY CLUB
ARCHITECT: WILLIAM LOCK, 1923

3529 12th Avenue
Hanford, CA 93230

PRO SHOP: 559-582-0740
CLUBHOUSE: 559-582-2264

John Echols, PGA Professional
Joe Elias, Superintendent

Driving Range ●
Practice Greens ●
Clubhouse ●
Food / Beverage ●
Accommodations
Pull Carts ●
Power Carts ●
Club Rental ●
$pecial Offers

	1	2	3	4	5	6	7	8	9	OUT
BACK	477	394	505	205	291	439	173	419	421	3324
REGULAR	473	377	471	192	286	421	155	399	403	3177
par	5	4	5	3	4	4	3	4	4	36
handicap	17	7	15	5	13	1	11	9	3	-
FORWARD	451	363	467	170	259	370	134	397	383	2994
par	5	4	5	3	4	4	3	4	4	36
handicap	5	11	3	15	13	9	17	1	7	-

	10	11	12	13	14	15	16	17	18	IN
BACK	192	407	331	474	368	623	436	140	426	3397
REGULAR	178	394	320	463	355	580	428	118	416	3252
par	3	4	4	5	4	5	4	3	4	36
handicap	10	8	14	12	16	2	4	18	6	-
FORWARD	167	363	302	443	315	514	380	98	412	2994
par	3	4	4	5	4	5	4	3	5	37
handicap	14	8	10	4	12	2	6	18	16	-

BACK	
yardage	6721
par	72
rating	71.5
slope	115

REGULAR	
yardage	6429
par	72
rating	70.1
slope	112

FORWARD	
yardage	5988
par	73
rating	74.2
slope	126

PLAY POLICY & FEES: Green fees are $12 weekdays and $16 weekends. Carts are $12 for nine holes and $22 for 18 holes. The course is closed Christmas, New Year's Day, Thanksgiving, and Easter.

TEE TIMES: Reservations can be booked seven days in advance.

DRESS CODE: Golf shoes or flat-bottom athletic shoes are required.

COURSE DESCRIPTION: This mostly flat course is short with many doglegs and tree-lined fairways. The course is easy to walk and is particularly good for beginning and intermediate players. It's a fast course to play. Most rounds can be completed in fewer than four hours on a weekend, a rarity.

LOCATION: From Highway 99 in Selma (20 miles south of Fresno) take the Floral Avenue exit for two miles to Bethel. Turn right on Bethel and drive a half mile to Rose Avenue. Turn left on Rose Avenue and drive a quarter of a mile to the course on the right.

. . . ● **TOURNAMENTS:** This course is available for outside tournaments, but shotgun tournaments are not allowed. Dates are booked the second week in January for the year. A 16-player minimum is needed to schedule an event.

15. SELMA VALLEY GOLF COURSE

PLAY POLICY & FEES: Reciprocal play is accepted with members of other private clubs. Green fees for reciprocators are $35 weekdays and $45 weekends. Guest fees are $20 when accompanied by a member weekdays and $30 weekends. Guest fees are $35 weekdays and $45 weekends when unaccompanied. Carts are $16.

TEE TIMES: Reciprocal members should have their pro call to set up a tee time.

DRESS CODE: Appropriate golf attire and nonmetal spikes are required.

COURSE DESCRIPTION: This tough course plays longer than the yardage suggests. Towering oak trees and two lakes conspire against the golfer. Don't take the 623-yard, par-5 15th for granted. It may appear to be a dull straight-away stretch, but it usually gives players all they can handle.

NOTES: Craig Stadler holds the course record of 63.

LOCATION: Driving south on Highway 99 from Fresno, take the Highway 43 exit south and turn right on Dover Avenue. Drive two miles to 12th Avenue, turn right, and follow it to the end.

. . . ● **TOURNAMENTS:** This course is not available for outside events.

16. KINGS COUNTRY CLUB

KINGS RIVER GOLF & COUNTRY CLUB
ARCHITECTS: B. BALDOCK, 1955; NICK LOMBARDO; ROBERT DEAN PUTMAN, 1957

3100 Avenue 400
Kingsburg, CA 93631

PRO SHOP: 559-897-2077

Chuck Blanks, PGA Professional

Driving Range ●
Practice Greens ●
Clubhouse ●
Food / Beverage ●
Accommodations
Pull Carts ●
Power Carts ●
Club Rental
Special Offers

	1	2	3	4	5	6	7	8	9	OUT
BACK	519	369	518	411	419	372	164	432	164	3368
REGULAR	513	342	504	392	407	351	155	416	151	3231
par	5	4	5	4	4	4	3	4	3	36
handicap	9	11	7	5	3	13	15	1	17	-
FORWARD	508	328	490	363	393	337	146	354	106	3025
par	5	4	5	4	4	4	3	4	3	36
handicap	3	11	1	5	7	13	15	9	17	-

	10	11	12	13	14	15	16	17	18	IN
BACK	405	382	141	404	526	208	532	370	359	3327
REGULAR	392	371	127	387	510	199	519	352	343	3200
par	4	4	3	4	5	3	5	4	4	36
handicap	2	12	18	4	8	6	10	14	16	-
FORWARD	369	354	82	374	490	181	510	337	290	2987
par	4	4	3	4	5	3	5	4	4	36
handicap	6	12	18	8	4	16	2	10	14	-

BACK	
yardage	6695
par	72
rating	71.5
slope	122

REGULAR	
yardage	6431
par	72
rating	70.2
slope	119

FORWARD	
yardage	6012
par	72
rating	74.3
slope	130

OAK PATCH GOLF COURSE

30400 Road 158
Visalia, CA 93291

PRO SHOP: 559-733-5000

Rich Freeman, Owner, PGA
Ryan Wiezycki, Owner, PGA

Driving Range
Practice Greens ●
Clubhouse ●
Food / Beverage ●
Accommodations
Pull Carts ●
Power Carts
Club Rental ●
Special Offers

	1	2	3	4	5	6	7	8	9	OUT
BACK	-	-	-	-	-	-	-	-	-	-
REGULAR	79	125	248	286	79	102	186	103	106	1314
par	3	3	4	4	3	3	3	3	3	29
handicap	15	7	1	5	17	11	3	9	13	-
FORWARD	79	120	211	260	75	97	175	103	107	1227
par	3	3	4	4	3	3	3	3	3	29
handicap	15	7	1	5	17	11	3	9	13	-

	10	11	12	13	14	15	16	17	18	IN
BACK										-
REGULAR										
par										
handicap										-
FORWARD										
par										
handicap										

BACK	
yardage	-
par	-
rating	
slope	

REGULAR	
yardage	1314
par	29
rating	-
slope	-

FORWARD	
yardage	1227
par	29
rating	-
slope	-

PLAY POLICY & FEES: Reciprocal play is accepted with members of other private clubs. Guest fees are $24 weekdays and $30 weekends with a member; fees for unaccompanied guests are equal to the visitor's rate at the guest's home club. Carts are $16. The course is closed on Monday and the day after holidays.

TEE TIMES: Reciprocal members should have their head pro call to make a tee time.

DRESS CODE: Appropriate golf attire and nonmetal spikes are required.

COURSE DESCRIPTION: This course is tight, mostly flat, and walkable. The Kings River borders the course. The signature hole is the 519-yard, par-5 16th, which crosses the Kings River. Bold players can cut as much yardage as they dare off the tee to reach the green in two shots. The greens are small, fast, and usually in good shape.

LOCATION: This course is located between Fresno and Visalia. From Highway 99 take the Canejo exit east for four miles to the course on the left.

. . . ● **TOURNAMENTS:** This course is not available for outside events.

17. KINGS RIVER GOLF & COUNTRY CLUB

PLAY POLICY & FEES: Green fees are $6 for nine holes and $11 for 18 holes on weekdays, and $7 for nine holes and $13 for 18 holes on weekends. Pull carts are $1.

TEE TIMES: Reservations are not accepted. All play is on a first-come, first-served basis.

COURSE DESCRIPTION: This course has one par 4, "the toughest hole in the valley," according to former pro Harry Harrison. This hole is 240 yards and runs along the Kaweah River.

LOCATION: From Visalia drive seven miles east on Highway 198 to Ivanhoe. Turn off on County Road 158. Follow signs under the bridge, turn right after the bridge, and continue to the course.

. . . ● **TOURNAMENTS:** This course is available for outside tournaments.

18. OAK PATCH GOLF COURSE

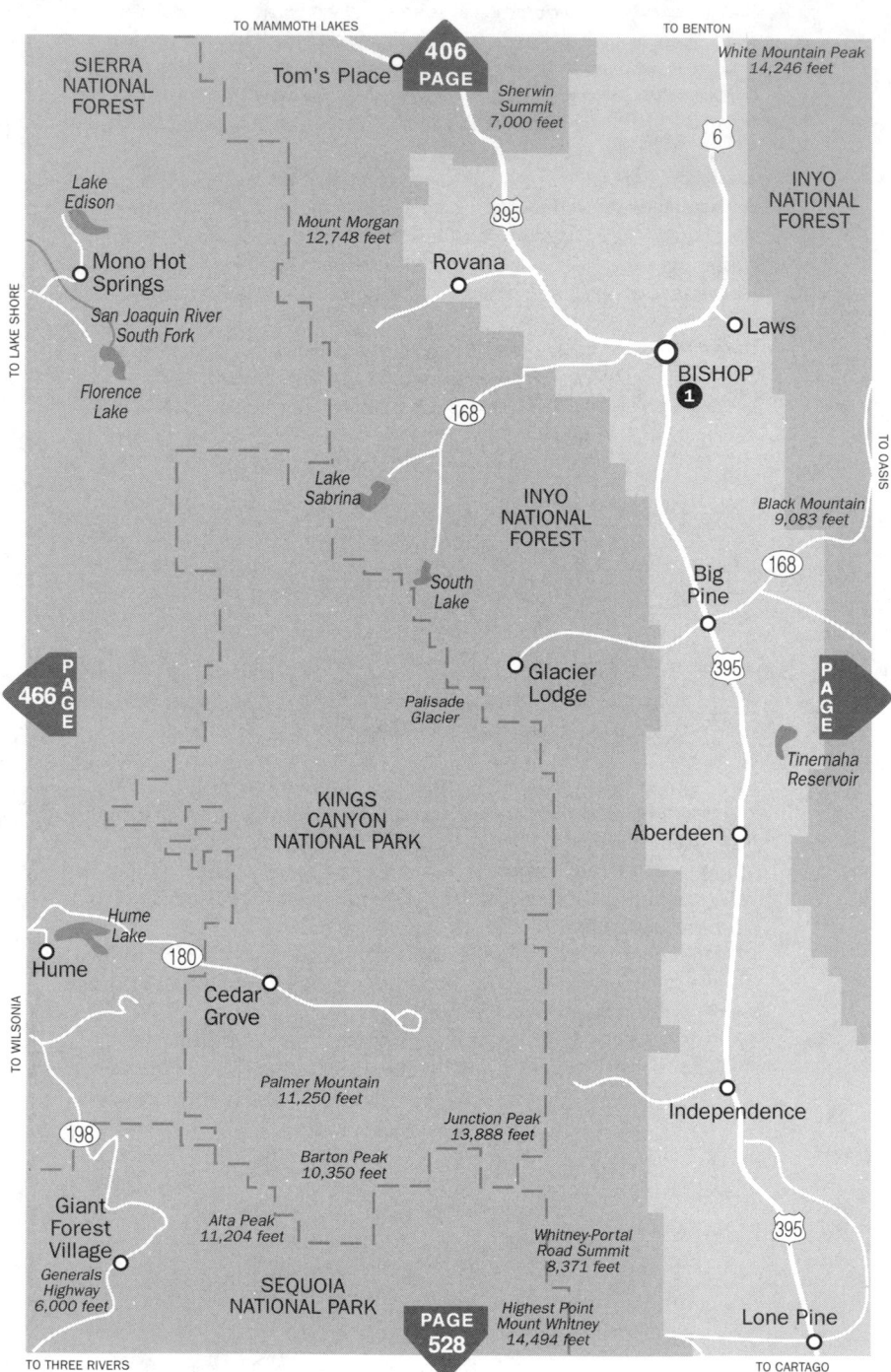

TO MAMMOTH LAKES

TO BENTON

SIERRA
NATIONAL
FOREST

Tom's Place

406 PAGE

White Mountain Peak
14,246 feet

Sherwin
Summit
7,000 feet

6

Lake
Edison

INYO
NATIONAL
FOREST

Mount Morgan
12,748 feet

395

Mono Hot
Springs

Rovana

San Joaquin River
South Fork

Laws

BISHOP
1

Florence
Lake

168

TO LAKE SHORE

Lake
Sabrina

INYO
NATIONAL
FOREST

Black Mountain
9,083 feet

South
Lake

TO OASIS

Big
Pine

168

466 PAGE

Glacier
Lodge

395

PAGE

Palisade
Glacier

Tinemaha
Reservoir

KINGS
CANYON
NATIONAL PARK

Aberdeen

Hume
Lake

180

Hume

Cedar
Grove

TO WILSONIA

Palmer Mountain
11,250 feet

Junction Peak
13,888 feet

Independence

Barton Peak
10,350 feet

198

Alta Peak
11,204 feet

Giant
Forest
Village

395

Generals
Highway
6,000 feet

SEQUOIA
NATIONAL PARK

Whitney-Portal
Road Summit
8,371 feet

PAGE 528

Highest Point
Mount Whitney
14,494 feet

Lone Pine

TO THREE RIVERS

TO CARTAGO

486

Bishop Area

P.O. Box 1586
Bishop, CA 93515

South Highway 395
Bishop, CA 93514

PRO SHOP: 760-873-5828

Mike Landry, Director of Golf, PGA
Mike Apted, Superintendent

Driving Range ●
Practice Greens ●
Clubhouse ●
Food / Beverage ●
Accommodations
Pull Carts ●
Power Carts ●
Club Rental ●
$pecial Offers

	1	2	3	4	5	6	7	8	9	OUT
BACK	381	531	385	196	488	424	422	207	417	3451
REGULAR	361	479	360	181	473	406	386	179	390	3215
par	4	5	4	3	5	4	4	3	4	36
handicap	5	13	9	15	17	3	1	11	7	-
FORWARD	352	424	309	150	420	330	329	166	329	2809
par	4	5	4	3	5	4	4	3	4	36
handicap	1	5	7	17	9	13	3	15	11	-

	10	11	12	13	14	15	16	17	18	IN
BACK	562	403	401	208	322	196	527	169	422	3210
REGULAR	527	367	360	189	268	179	506	130	397	2923
par	5	4	4	3	4	3	5	3	4	35
handicap	8	6	4	12	14	10	16	18	2	-
FORWARD	485	401	348	166	259	124	445	113	403	2744
par	5	5	4	3	4	3	5	3	5	37
handicap	6	2	10	16	14	18	8	12	4	-

BACK	
yardage	6661
par	71
rating	70.9
slope	122

REGULAR	
yardage	6138
par	71
rating	68.5
slope	118

FORWARD	
yardage	5553
par	73
rating	70.8
slope	119

PLAY POLICY & FEES: Outside play is accepted. Green fees are $27 weekdays and $32 weekends. Senior green fees are $18 Monday through Friday. Twilight green fees are $18 every day. Carts are $10 per person.

TEE TIMES: Reservations can be booked seven days in advance.

DRESS CODE: Golf attire is encouraged, and no tank tops are allowed.

COURSE DESCRIPTION: The first nine opened for play in 1952, and the second nine opened in 1984. This difficult course has lots of trees and bunkers. Water hazards spice up 15 holes. Keep the ball out of the rough. This is a course that demands accuracy.

NOTES: During the summer the driving range is lighted.

LOCATION: This course is located one mile south of Bishop on U.S. 395.

. . . ● **TOURNAMENTS:** This course is available for outside tournaments.

1. BISHOP COUNTRY CLUB

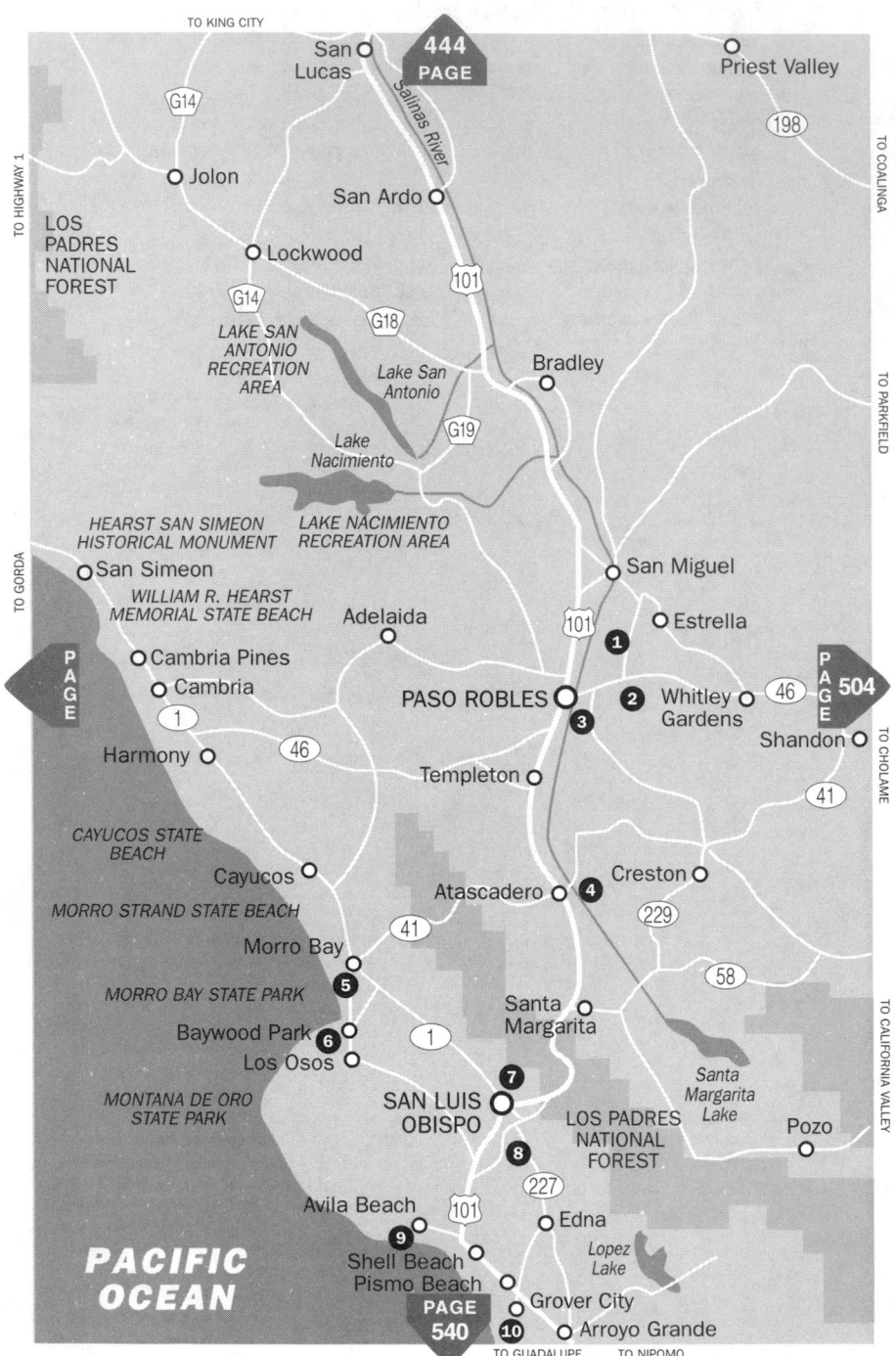

TO KING CITY

San Lucas ○

444 PAGE

○ Priest Valley

G14

198

TO HIGHWAY 1

○ Jolon

San Ardo ○

○ Lockwood

LOS PADRES NATIONAL FOREST

G14

G18

101

LAKE SAN ANTONIO RECREATION AREA

Lake San Antonio

○ Bradley

Lake Nacimiento

G19

TO GORDA

HEARST SAN SIMEON HISTORICAL MONUMENT

LAKE NACIMIENTO RECREATION AREA

○ San Simeon

WILLIAM R. HEARST MEMORIAL STATE BEACH

Adelaida ○

○ San Miguel

101

○ Estrella

PAGE

○ Cambria Pines

○ Cambria

PASO ROBLES ○

❶

❷ ○ Whitley Gardens

46

PAGE 504

1

❸

Shandon ○

Harmony ○

46

Templeton ○

41

TO CHOLAME

TO COALINGA

TO PARKFIELD

CAYUCOS STATE BEACH

Cayucos ○

MORRO STRAND STATE BEACH

Atascadero ○ ❹

○ Creston

229

58

Morro Bay ○

41

MORRO BAY STATE PARK

❺

Baywood Park ○ ❻

Los Osos ○

MONTANA DE ORO STATE PARK

Santa Margarita ○

1

❼

SAN LUIS OBISPO

Santa Margarita Lake

○ Pozo ○

LOS PADRES NATIONAL FOREST

❽

227

Avila Beach ○

101

❾

PACIFIC OCEAN

Shell Beach ○
Pismo Beach ○

PAGE 540

○ Edna

Lopez Lake

○ Grover City

❿ ○ Arroyo Grande

TO GUADALUPE   TO NIPOMO

TO CALIFORNIA VALLEY

Paso Robles/
San Luis Obispo Area

LINKS COURSE AT PASO ROBLES
ARCHITECT: RUDY DURAN, 1996

5151 Jardine Road
Paso Robles, CA 93446

PRO SHOP: 805-227-4567

Keith Doshier, PGA Professional

Driving Range ●
Practice Greens ●
Clubhouse ●
Food / Beverage ●
Accommodations
Pull Carts ●
Power Carts ●
Club Rental ●
$pecial Offers

	1	2	3	4	5	6	7	8	9	OUT
BACK	548	564	393	241	250	585	184	423	346	3534
REGULAR	530	545	355	210	231	569	168	406	334	3348
par	5	5	4	3	3	5	3	4	4	36
handicap	5	1	9	11	15	3	17	7	13	-
FORWARD	470	460	276	166	188	512	119	347	306	2844
par	5	5	4	3	3	5	3	4	4	36
handicap	5	1	9	11	15	3	17	7	13	-

	10	11	12	13	14	15	16	17	18	IN
BACK	373	553	177	427	250	497	382	424	439	3522
REGULAR	357	536	161	414	181	484	368	379	414	3294
par	4	5	3	4	3	5	4	4	4	36
handicap	14	4	18	2	16	12	10	6	8	-
FORWARD	293	482	117	373	118	387	319	333	344	2766
par	4	5	3	4	3	5	4	4	4	36
handicap	14	4	18	2	16	12	10	6	8	-

BACK	
yardage	7056
par	72
rating	73.3
slope	118

REGULAR	
yardage	6642
par	72
rating	69.5
slope	109

FORWARD	
yardage	5610
par	72
rating	66.6
slope	103

 # HUNTER RANCH GOLF COURSE
ARCHITECT: HUNTER RESOURCES, 1994

GOLF 50

4041 Highway 46 East
Paso Robles, CA 93446

PRO SHOP: 805-237-7444

Michael McGinnis, Director of Golf, PGA
Michael Bremer, PGA Professional
Doug Westbrook, Superintendent

Driving Range ●
Practice Greens ●
Clubhouse ●
Food / Beverage ●
Accommodations
Pull Carts ●
Power Carts ●
Club Rental ●
$pecial Offers ●

	1	2	3	4	5	6	7	8	9	OUT
BACK	405	424	197	400	339	509	586	187	334	3381
REGULAR	383	397	169	372	312	495	570	167	326	3191
par	4	4	3	4	4	5	5	3	4	36
handicap	9	3	17	5	11	7	1	15	13	-
FORWARD	356	355	138	341	276	426	498	135	287	2812
par	4	4	3	4	4	5	5	3	4	36
handicap	9	3	17	5	11	7	1	15	13	-

	10	11	12	13	14	15	16	17	18	IN
BACK	325	396	415	403	186	518	173	544	400	3360
REGULAR	308	346	396	371	156	505	138	526	355	3101
par	4	4	4	4	3	5	3	5	4	36
handicap	12	8	4	10	14	6	18	2	16	-
FORWARD	291	287	368	343	127	471	121	489	330	2827
par	4	4	4	4	3	5	3	5	4	36
handicap	12	8	4	10	14	6	18	2	16	-

BACK	
yardage	6741
par	72
rating	72.6
slope	136

REGULAR	
yardage	6292
par	72
rating	70.7
slope	131

FORWARD	
yardage	5639
par	72
rating	72.8
slope	132

PLAY POLICY & FEES: All green fees are for as much golf as you can play in one day! Green fees are $11 Monday through Thursday and $18 Friday through Sunday. Carts are $18 for 18 holes.

TEE TIMES: Reservations can be booked seven days in advance.

DRESS CODE: Shirts must be worn.

COURSE DESCRIPTION: This is a traditional links-style course. The fairways are generous, and wind is a factor. The course gives you plenty of options for several types of shots. Course management is a must if you are going to score well.

LOCATION: On U.S. 101 take the 46 East exit, and follow it to Jardine Road. Take a left on Jardine Road. The course is 1.5 miles down Jardine Road on the left.

. . . ● **TOURNAMENTS:** This course is available for outside tournaments. A 20-player minimum is needed to book a tournament.

1. LINKS COURSE AT PASO ROBLES

PLAY POLICY & FEES: The green fees are $45 Monday through Thursday prior to 2 p.m. and $25 thereafter. Friday through Sunday green fees are $55 prior to 2 p.m. and $35 thereafter. Carts are $24 until 2 p.m. and $15 after 2 p.m.

TEE TIMES: Reservations can be booked seven days in advance.

DRESS CODE: Collared shirts are preferred; no tank tops or cutoffs are allowed. Nonmetal spikes are required.

COURSE DESCRIPTION: This heavily-bunkered course has rolling hills and an abundance of mature oak trees. This is a championship layout where water comes into play on four holes, and several greens are tiered. The tricky stretch of holes 11 through 14 is Hunter Ranch's version of Amen Corner at Augusta National Golf Club.

NOTES: Hunter Ranch was designed by Kenneth Hunter, Mike McGinnis, and Paul Casas. The course record of 65 is held by Roger Tambellini. The course features an excellent practice facility.

LOCATION: From U.S. 101 drive east on Highway 46 for 3.5 miles to the course.

. . . ● **TOURNAMENTS:** A 16-player minimum is needed to book a tournament. Tournaments can be booked 12 months in advance. The banquet facility can accommodate up to 200 people. ● **TRAVEL:** The Paso Robles Inn is located seven minutes from the course. For reservations call 800-676-1713. The Arbor Inn (805-227-4673) and the Adelaide Motor Inn (805-238-2770) are also recommended. ● **$PECIAL OFFERS:** Play-and-stay packages with the Paso Robles Inn are available.

2. HUNTER RANCH GOLF COURSE

PASO ROBLES GOLF CLUB
ARCHITECT: BERT STAMPS, 1960

P.O. Box 517 1600 Country Club Drive
Paso Robles, CA 93447 Paso Robles, CA 93446

PRO SHOP: 805-238-4722

Ed Anshen, GM/Director of Golf, PGA
Steve Hahn, PGA Professional
Ben Swinney, Superintendent

Driving Range ●
Practice Greens ●
Clubhouse ●
Food / Beverage ●
Accommodations
Pull Carts ●
Power Carts ●
Club Rental ●
$pecial Offers ●

	1	2	3	4	5	6	7	8	9	OUT
BACK	494	400	500	167	315	225	391	157	344	2993
REGULAR	486	381	487	142	308	217	386	150	339	2896
par	5	4	5	3	4	3	4	3	4	35
handicap	11	1	13	15	5	3	7	17	9	-
FORWARD	452	351	477	110	302	213	384	142	330	2761
par	5	4	5	3	4	3	5	3	4	36
handicap	5	9	1	17	7	13	3	15	11	-

	10	11	12	13	14	15	16	17	18	IN
BACK	461	335	524	178	484	326	391	186	340	3225
REGULAR	451	326	506	153	480	316	367	181	335	3115
par	4	4	5	3	5	4	4	3	4	36
handicap	2	18	6	12	8	16	4	14	10	-
FORWARD	449	307	502	117	478	305	354	173	320	3005
par	5	4	5	3	5	4	4	3	4	37
handicap	10	14	2	18	4	12	6	16	8	-

BACK	
yardage	6218
par	71
rating	71.0
slope	123

REGULAR	
yardage	6011
par	71
rating	70.1
slope	121

FORWARD	
yardage	5766
par	73
rating	73.5
slope	126

 CHALK MOUNTAIN GOLF COURSE
ARCHITECT: ROBERT MUIR GRAVES, 1980

10000 El Bordo Road
Atascadero, CA 93422

PRO SHOP: 805-466-8848

Tammy Doshier
Bob Schneiderhan, Superintendent

Driving Range ●
Practice Greens ●
Clubhouse ●
Food / Beverage ●
Accommodations
Pull Carts ●
Power Carts ●
Club Rental ●
$pecial Offers

	1	2	3	4	5	6	7	8	9	OUT
BACK	520	318	333	406	134	463	221	567	354	3316
REGULAR	504	311	317	381	113	438	202	547	337	3150
par	5	4	4	4	3	5	3	5	4	37
handicap	5	13	7	1	17	15	11	3	9	-
FORWARD	483	262	281	326	100	409	186	514	291	2852
par	5	4	4	4	3	5	3	5	4	37
handicap	5	13	7	3	17	9	15	1	11	-

	10	11	12	13	14	15	16	17	18	IN
BACK	531	357	194	352	173	470	154	337	415	2983
REGULAR	512	336	176	300	152	451	115	329	405	2776
par	5	4	3	4	3	5	3	4	4	35
handicap	8	6	12	14	10	2	18	16	4	-
FORWARD	466	286	156	272	136	414	97	299	352	2478
par	5	4	3	4	3	5	3	4	4	35
handicap	6	8	16	12	10	2	18	14	4	-

BACK	
yardage	6299
par	72
rating	70.9
slope	126

REGULAR	
yardage	5926
par	72
rating	69.2
slope	122

FORWARD	
yardage	5330
par	72
rating	66.5
slope	118

PLAY POLICY & FEES: Green fees are $15 weekdays and $20 weekends. Carts are $20. The course offers many discounts and specials; call for details.

TEE TIMES: Reservations can be booked seven days in advance.

COURSE DESCRIPTION: Formerly a country club, this is a very walkable course. Paso Robles is a shot-maker's course, with water coming into play on 15 holes. Don't let the yardage fool you; this course will test your golf skills.

LOCATION: Travel 27 miles north of San Luis Obispo on U.S.101 to the Spring Street exit in Paso Robles. Turn right onto Niblick Bridge and drive to Country Club Drive.

. . . ● **TOURNAMENTS:** A 24-player minimum is required to book a tournament. Events should be booked at least two months in advance. The banquet facility can accommodate 200 people. ● **TRAVEL:** The Paso Robles Inn is located three minutes from the course. For reservations call 800-676-1713. The Adelaide Inn (805-238-2770) and Black Oak Motor Lodge (805-238-4770) are also recommended. ● **$PECIAL OFFERS:** Golf packages are available.

3. PASO ROBLES GOLF CLUB

PLAY POLICY & FEES: Green fees are $11 for nine holes and $22 for 18 holes weekdays, and $13.50 for nine holes and $28 for 18 holes weekends. Senior rates are $13 weekdays. Carts are $20.

TEE TIMES: Reservations can be booked seven days in advance starting at 6:15 a.m.

COURSE DESCRIPTION: This is a short, narrow course set in the mountains among groves of oak trees. It's the kind of course you have to play a few times before you can actually score well. A hole to watch out for is the fourth, par 4. Known as "Cardiac Hill," it plays straight uphill. You can see the green from the tee, but it isn't much help. The hole is deceptive in its distance, and the tendency is to come up short. Accuracy off the tee is a must.

NOTES: Dean Greene and Paul D'Ambra hold the men's course record with a 64. Paul shot a 64 during a junior amateur championship. Tammy Doshier holds the women's record of 67. This course offers free lessons for beginners. Call the pro shop for information.

LOCATION: Off U.S.101 at the south end of Atascadero, exit at Santa Rosa Avenue heading east. Follow the Heilman Regional Park signs out El Camino Real and El Bordo Road to the course.

. . . ● **TOURNAMENTS:** This course is available for outside tournaments. A 20-player minimum is needed to book an event. Tournaments should be scheduled 12 months in advance.

4. CHALK MOUNTAIN GOLF COURSE

MORRO BAY GOLF COURSE
ARCHITECTS: RUSSELL NEYES, 1929; AL LAPE, 1949

201 State Park Road
Morro Bay, CA 93442

PRO SHOP: 805-782-8060

Pat Comerford, General Manager
Aaron S. Williams, Professional
Tom Massey, Superintendent

Driving Range ●
Practice Greens ●
Clubhouse ●
Food / Beverage ●
Accommodations
Pull Carts ●
Power Carts ●
Club Rental ●
$pecial Offers

	1	2	3	4	5	6	7	8	9	OUT
BACK	496	440	317	130	311	375	334	232	442	3077
REGULAR	486	432	302	118	304	356	322	217	436	2973
par	5	4	4	3	4	4	4	3	4	35
handicap	7	1	15	17	11	13	5	9	3	-
FORWARD	419	360	261	101	237	291	263	157	369	2458
par	5	4	4	3	4	4	4	3	4	35
handicap	1	5	13	17	9	11	7	15	3	-

	10	11	12	13	14	15	16	17	18	IN
BACK	192	333	373	439	468	347	512	239	380	3283
REGULAR	171	322	363	423	454	308	490	233	370	3134
par	3	4	4	4	5	4	5	3	4	36
handicap	18	16	8	2	12	14	10	6	4	-
FORWARD	139	250	306	402	400	257	419	145	279	2597
par	3	4	4	5	5	4	5	3	4	37
handicap	18	10	4	16	8	12	2	14	6	-

BACK	
yardage	6360
par	71
rating	70.4
slope	118

REGULAR	
yardage	6107
par	71
rating	69.3
slope	116

FORWARD	
yardage	5055
par	72
rating	69.5
slope	117

 SEA PINES GOLF RESORT

1945 Solano Ave.
Los Osos, CA 93402

PRO SHOP: 805-528-1788

Gary Setting, Head Professional, PGA
Kurt Sugarman, Assistant Professional

Driving Range ●
Practice Greens ●
Clubhouse ●
Food / Beverage ●
Accommodations ●
Pull Carts ●
Power Carts ●
Club Rental ●
$pecial Offers

	1	2	3	4	5	6	7	8	9	OUT
BACK	-	-	-	-	-	-	-	-	-	-
REGULAR	95	145	350	255	265	260	195	145	185	1895
par	3	3	4	4	4	4	3	3	3	31
handicap	17	11	3	15	13	7	1	9	5	-
FORWARD	95	145	350	255	265	260	195	145	185	1895
par	3	3	4	4	4	4	3	3	3	31
handicap	17	11	3	15	13	7	1	9	5	-

	10	11	12	13	14	15	16	17	18	IN
BACK	-	-	-	-	-	-	-	-	-	-
REGULAR	95	145	350	255	265	260	195	145	185	1895
par	3	3	4	4	4	4	3	3	3	31
handicap	18	12	4	16	14	8	2	10	8	-
FORWARD	95	145	350	255	265	260	195	145	185	1895
par	3	3	4	4	4	4	3	3	3	31
handicap	18	12	4	16	14	8	2	10	8	-

BACK	
yardage	-
par	-
rating	-
slope	-

REGULAR	
yardage	3790
par	62
rating	-
slope	-

FORWARD	
yardage	3790
par	62
rating	-
slope	-

PLAY POLICY & FEES: Green fees are $28 weekdays and $35 weekends. Senior and junior rates are available. Call for other special rates. Carts are $20.

TEE TIMES: For weekend tee times, reservations must be made the preceding week of play starting at 6:15 a.m. For reservations call 805-782-8060.

DRESS CODE: Nonmetal spikes are recommended.

COURSE DESCRIPTION: This picturesque layout is located in Morro Bay State Park and has fantastic ocean views from almost every hole. It's slightly hilly with tree-lined fairways. It is one of the busiest courses in the state. The long, undulating greens remind some of Poppy Hills and Spyglass Hill. To speed up play, most of the bunkers were removed in the 1960s. There are only four traps on the course. Wildlife is part of this course, which has an Audubon certification.

NOTES: The course record is 64.

LOCATION: Heading north from San Luis Obispo, take U.S. 101 and exit on Highway 1 to Morro Bay. Follow the Morro Bay State Park signs to the course.

. . . ● **TOURNAMENTS:** This course is available for outside tournaments. A 20-player minimum is needed. Tournaments should be booked two weeks in advance. ● **TRAVEL:** The Inn at Morro Bay (805-772-5651), Ascott Suites (805-772-4437) and Days Inn (805-247-5076) are recommended for lodging.

5. MORRO BAY GOLF COURSE

PLAY POLICY & FEES: Green fees are $10 weekdays and $11 weekends. There is a $6 replay fee.

TEE TIMES: Reservations can be booked seven days in advance.

COURSE DESCRIPTION: This well-maintained course has more than 200 trees lining the narrow fairways. Most are pine trees that are over 25 years old. The first fairway has been removed and relocated to make way for a parking lot, so watch out for the new row of small connecting ponds along the left side.

LOCATION: Off U.S. 101 in Los Osos take the Los Osos Valley Road exit and drive west to the course, which is about 11 miles from the highway. Take the entrance to Montana de Oro State Park.

. . . ● **TOURNAMENTS:** This course is available for outside tournaments. A 20-player minimum is needed. Tournaments can be booked 12 months in advance. The banquet facility can accommodate up to 100 people. ● **TRAVEL:** The Sea Pines Golf Resort is located at the course. Call 805-528-5252 for reservations.

6. SEA PINES GOLF RESORT

7 DAIRY CREEK GOLF COURSE
ARCHITECT: JOHN HARBOTTLE, 1997

2990A Dairy Creek Road
San Luis Obispo, CA
93405
PRO SHOP: 805-782-8060

Patrick Comerford, General Manager
Jim Coles, Director of Instruction
Charles Proft, Head Professional

Driving Range ●
Practice Greens ●
Clubhouse ●
Food / Beverage ●
Accommodations
Pull Carts ●
Power Carts ●
Club Rental ●
$pecial Offers

	1	2	3	4	5	6	7	8	9	OUT
BACK	389	427	204	370	466	398	518	135	418	3325
REGULAR	355	367	130	311	372	322	474	97	370	2798
par	4	4	3	4	4	4	4	5	3	35
handicap	11	1	9	7	5	13	15	17	3	-
FORWARD	329	271	123	288	351	293	429	85	317	2486
par	4	4	3	4	4	4	4	5	3	35
handicap	5	7	11	13	1	17	9	15	3	-

	10	11	12	13	14	15	16	17	18	IN
BACK	500	438	372	164	549	206	310	500	184	3223
REGULAR	439	393	324	121	481	134	245	452	144	2733
par	5	4	4	3	5	3	4	5	3	36
handicap	8	2	10	16	4	6	18	12	14	-
FORWARD	404	370	297	91	447	111	215	430	114	2479
par	5	4	4	3	5	3	4	5	3	36
handicap	4	6	14	18	2	8	16	10	12	-

BACK	
yardage	6548
par	71
rating	71.9
slope	127

REGULAR	
yardage	5531
par	71
rating	67.1
slope	117

FORWARD	
yardage	4965
par	71
rating	67.7
slope	120

8 SAN LUIS OBISPO GOLF & COUNTRY CLUB
ARCHITECT: BERT STAMPS, 1957

255 Country Club Drive
San Luis Obispo, CA
93401
PRO SHOP: 805-543-4035
CLUBHOUSE: 805-543-3400

Scott Cartwright, PGA Professional
Joe Tompkins, Superintendent

Driving Range ●
Practice Greens ●
Clubhouse ●
Food / Beverage ●
Accommodations
Pull Carts ●
Power Carts ●
Club Rental ●
$pecial Offers

	1	2	3	4	5	6	7	8	9	OUT
BACK	567	423	204	356	492	365	426	153	369	3355
REGULAR	558	402	188	346	474	356	418	143	355	3240
par	5	4	3	4	5	4	4	3	4	36
handicap	5	1	13	11	15	7	3	17	9	-
FORWARD	492	323	167	336	456	309	410	136	338	2967
par	5	4	3	4	5	4	5	3	4	37
handicap	3	7	15	1	9	11	13	17	5	-

	10	11	12	13	14	15	16	17	18	IN
BACK	472	496	390	379	172	401	395	164	390	3259
REGULAR	467	477	378	370	162	391	379	157	369	3150
par	5	5	4	4	3	4	4	3	4	36
handicap	18	16	4	10	14	2	6	12	8	-
FORWARD	455	460	361	352	95	408	312	144	358	2945
par	5	5	4	4	3	5	4	3	4	37
handicap	8	6	2	10	18	14	12	16	4	-

BACK	
yardage	6614
par	72
rating	72.5
slope	129

REGULAR	
yardage	6390
par	72
rating	70.8
slope	124

FORWARD	
yardage	5912
par	74
rating	73.6
slope	124

PLAY POLICY & FEES: Green fees are $23 weekdays and $29 weekends and holidays. Seniors play for $14 weekdays. Green fees for juniors are $8 every day. Carts are $20.

TEE TIMES: Reservations can be booked seven days in advance starting at 6:15 a.m.

DRESS CODE: Nonmetal spikes are preferred.

COURSE DESCRIPTION: This links-style course is defined by rolling hills, large greens, and plenty of wind. The number-one handicap hole is the par-5, 549-yard double-dogleg fifth hole with a creek running through the fairway.

NOTES: The course record is 64, held by Roger Tamellini.

LOCATION: On Highway 1 just north of San Luis Obispo, exit at El Chorro Regional Park. Take a right and make your first left. The course will be on the left.

. . . ● **TOURNAMENTS:** A 20-player minimum is needed to book a tournament. No shotgun tournaments are allowed. Carts are required. A banquet facility is available that can accommodate up to 300 people. ● **TRAVEL:** The Inn on Morro Bay (805-772-5651), the Ascot Suites (805-772-4437), and Days Inn (800-247-5076) are recommended for lodging.

7. DAIRY CREEK GOLF COURSE

PLAY POLICY & FEES: Reciprocal play is accepted with members of other private clubs; otherwise, members and guests only. Fees for reciprocators are $65. Carts are $20.

DRESS CODE: Appropriate golf attire and nonmetal spikes are required.

COURSE DESCRIPTION: This rolling course along the central coast plays longer than it looks because of the lush fairways that provide little roll. Thick stands of pine trees line the fairways, waiting for errant tee shots. The greens are protected by strategically placed bunkers.

NOTES: The course record is 64, held by PGA Tour winner Loren Roberts. A new clubhouse is being built with completion expected summer of 2000.

LOCATION: Take the Marsh Street exit off U.S. 101 in San Luis Obispo and turn right. Travel to Broad Street (Highway 227) and turn right. Drive 4.5 miles to Los Ranchos Road, then right to Country Club Drive and right again to the club.

. . . ● **TOURNAMENTS:** This course is available for outside tournaments on Monday with board approval.

8. SAN LUIS OBISPO GOLF & COUNTRY CLUB

P.O. Box 2140   Avila Beach Road
Avila Beach, CA 93424   Avila Beach, CA 93424

PRO SHOP: 805-595-4000 EXT. 1

Mike Barbenec, Director of Golf
Billy Gibbs, Teaching Professional
Tom Stankowski, PGA Touring Professional

Driving Range ●
Practice Greens ●
Clubhouse ●
Food / Beverage ●
Accommodations
Pull Carts ●
Power Carts ●
Club Rental ●
$Special Offers ●

	1	2	3	4	5	6	7	8	9	OUT
BACK	415	234	470	363	373	188	376	171	540	3130
REGULAR	397	200	446	327	359	159	327	144	523	2882
par	4	3	5	4	4	3	4	3	5	35
handicap	3	5	13	7	15	9	1	17	11	-
FORWARD	370	133	433	282	336	133	263	102	410	2462
par	4	3	5	4	4	3	4	3	5	35
handicap	3	17	1	11	5	13	7	15	9	-

	10	11	12	13	14	15	16	17	18	IN
BACK	434	502	388	529	326	207	389	185	353	3313
REGULAR	419	495	375	504	318	178	383	169	325	3166
par	4	5	4	5	4	3	4	3	4	36
handicap	6	12	2	14	18	15	4	10	8	-
FORWARD	338	437	293	408	279	140	318	157	284	2654
par	4	5	4	5	4	3	4	3	4	36
handicap	4	6	2	16	12	18	8	14	10	-

BACK	
yardage	6443
par	71
rating	70.9
slope	122

REGULAR	
yardage	6048
par	71
rating	69.0
slope	116

FORWARD	
yardage	5116
par	71
rating	69.9
slope	126

PLAY POLICY & FEES: Green fees are $32 weekdays and $42 weekends. Carts are $24. Fees are subject to change.

TEE TIMES: Reservations can be made up to seven days in advance. Reservations can be made 8 to t30 days in advance through EZ-Links Internet Tee Times. See the facility's website.

DRESS CODE: Collared shirts are required.

COURSE DESCRIPTION: In the heart of California's central coast, this course is both beautiful and challenging. The front nine is nestled in an oak-lined canyon bisected by a gentle, flowing creek. Accuracy and club selection are important. The back nine calls for distance and placement, as it traverses back and forth across San Luis Creek and a tidal lagoon. Some holes have been reworked, resulting in slightly shorter yardage.

NOTES: The course record is 63, held by Tom Stankowski. Avila Beach has hosted several concerts, and past performers have included the Neville Brothers, Jackson Browne, Bonnie Raitt, and Don Henly.

LOCATION: Take the Avila Beach exit off U.S. 101 north of Pismo Beach and drive west for three miles to the entrance of the San Luis Bay Inn. Turn right and follow the signs to the club.

. . . ● **TOURNAMENTS:** A 12-player minimum is needed to book an event. Tournaments should be scheduled 10 to 12 months in advance. The banquet facility can accommodate 100 to 1,500 people. ● **TRAVEL:** Recommended restaurants include Fat Cats, Custom House, and Sea Cliff Restaurant. Several nearby hotels are recommended: The Embassy Suites (805-549-0800); Sycamore Mineral Springs (805-595-7302); the Cliffs Hotel (805-773-5000), and Shelter Cove (805-773-3511). ● **$PECIAL OFFERS:** Play-and-stay packages with the Embassy Suites are available. Several other hotels in the area also offer golf packages; call the pro shop or check out the website for more information.

9. AVILA BEACH RESORT

25 Grand Avenue
Grover Beach, CA 93433

PRO SHOP: 805-481-5215

Jay Fetters, Manager
Al Carlin, Professional

Driving Range
Practice Greens ●
Clubhouse ●
Food / Beverage ●
Accommodations
Pull Carts ●
Power Carts
Club Rental ●
$pecial Offers

	1	2	3	4	5	6	7	8	9	OUT
BACK	-	-	-	-	-	-	-	-	-	-
REGULAR	175	220	135	115	170	110	170	180	190	1465
par	3	3	3	3	3	3	3	3	3	27
handicap	9	1	13	15	11	17	7	5	3	-
FORWARD	175	220	135	115	170	110	170	180	190	1465
par	4	4	3	3	4	3	4	4	4	33
handicap	9	1	13	15	11	17	7	5	3	-

	10	11	12	13	14	15	16	17	18	IN
BACK	-	-	-	-	-	-	-	-	-	-
REGULAR	165	180	110	115	150	100	160	170	180	1330
par	3	3	3	3	3	3	3	3	3	27
handicap	10	4	16	14	12	18	8	6	2	-
FORWARD	165	180	100	110	150	100	160	170	180	1315
par	3	3	3	3	3	3	3	3	3	27
handicap	10	8	16	14	12	18	6	4	2	-

BACK	
yardage	-
par	-
rating	-
slope	-

REGULAR	
yardage	2795
par	54
rating	-
slope	-

FORWARD	
yardage	2780
par	60
rating	-
slope	-

PLAY POLICY & FEES: Green fees are $7 weekdays and $8 weekends for nine holes. Weekday twilight rates after 4 p.m. are $6.50, and weekend twilight rates are $7.50. Senior green fees are $5 weekdays and $6 weekends for nine holes.

TEE TIMES: Reservations are not accepted. All play is on a first-come, first-served basis.

COURSE DESCRIPTION: This flat course has water on seven holes, plus excellent ocean views. There are no sand traps. Monterey pines line the fairways and get a lot of action. This is a good course for beginners.

LOCATION: On Highway 1 in Grover City, turn right on Grand Avenue toward the beach and follow it to the course.

. . . ● **TOURNAMENTS:** This course is available for outside tournaments.

10. PISMO STATE BEACH GOLF COURSE

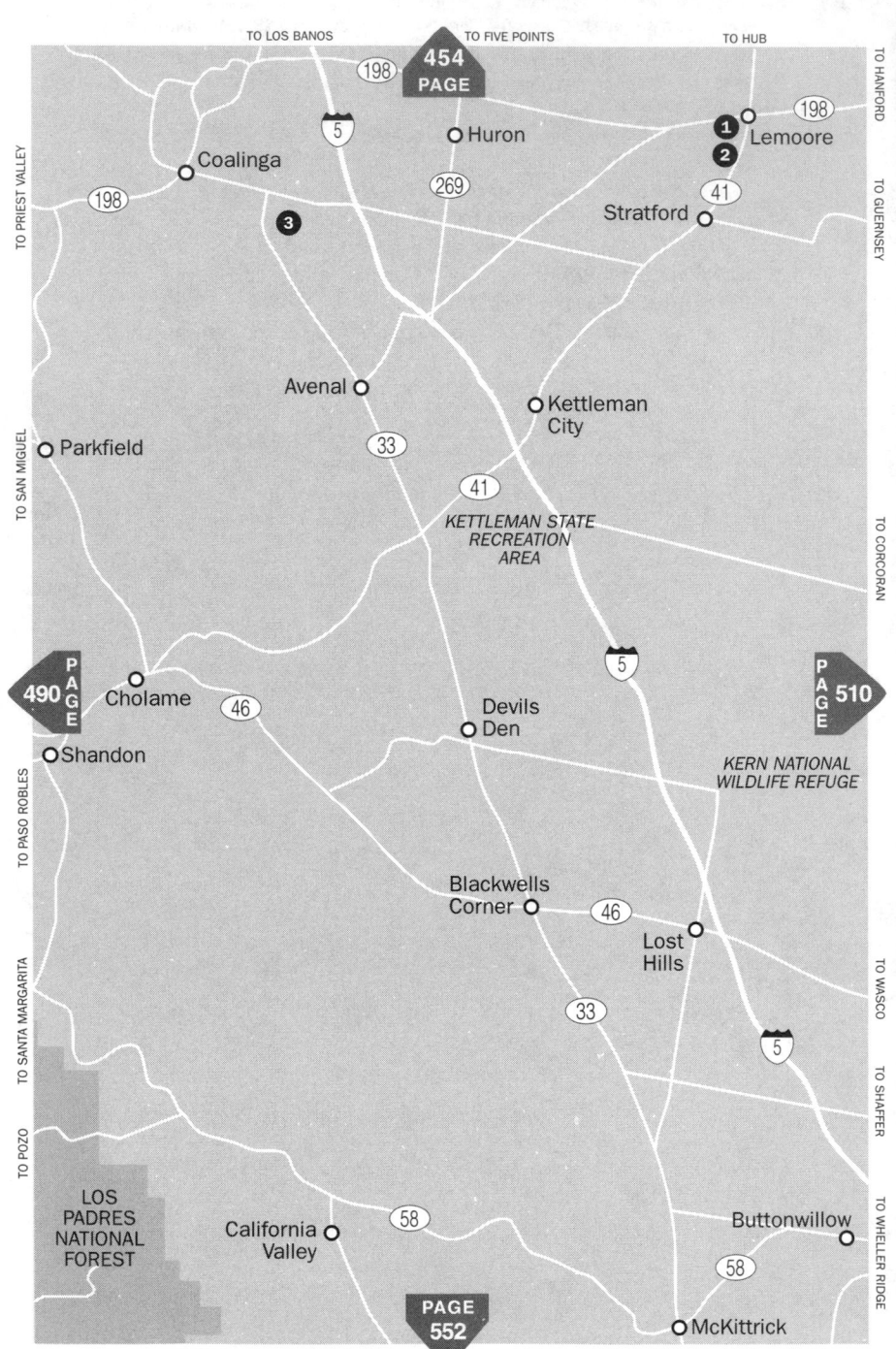

TO LOS BANOS
TO FIVE POINTS
TO HUB
TO HANFORD

454 PAGE

198

5

Huron

Coalinga

198

269

1
2
Lemoore
198

41
Stratford

TO GUERNSEY

3

TO PRIEST VALLEY

Avenal

Kettleman City

33

41

KETTLEMAN STATE RECREATION AREA

TO SAN MIGUEL

Parkfield

TO CORCORAN

5

PAGE 490

Cholame

46

Devils Den

PAGE 510

Shandon

KERN NATIONAL WILDLIFE REFUGE

TO PASO ROBLES

Blackwells Corner

46

Lost Hills

TO SANTA MARGARITA

33

5

TO WASCO
TO SHAFFER

TO POZO

LOS PADRES NATIONAL FOREST

California Valley

58

Buttonwillow

58

TO WHEELER RIDGE

PAGE 552

McKittrick

TO DERBY

Lemoore Area

LEMOORE GOLF COURSE
ARCHITECT: BOB BALDOCK, 1963

350 West Iona Avenue
Lemoore, CA 93245

PRO SHOP: 559-924-9658

Rich Rhoads, Head Professional, PGA
George Sula, Superintendent
Alan Fish, Superintendent

Driving Range ●
Practice Greens ●
Clubhouse ●
Food / Beverage ●
Accommodations
Pull Carts ●
Power Carts ●
Club Rental ●
$pecial Offers

	1	2	3	4	5	6	7	8	9	OUT
BACK	320	469	313	180	353	340	182	342	509	3008
REGULAR	302	452	277	163	335	309	160	308	487	2793
par	4	5	4	3	4	4	3	4	5	36
handicap	12	10	18	6	2	14	4	16	8	-
FORWARD	251	403	255	142	312	247	139	278	433	2460
par	4	5	4	4	3	4	3	4	5	36
handicap	13	3	17	9	11	7	5	15	1	-

	10	11	12	13	14	15	16	17	18	IN
BACK	356	179	405	429	553	399	190	540	372	3423
REGULAR	328	153	370	399	529	370	167	518	351	3185
par	4	3	4	4	5	4	3	5	4	36
handicap	13	17	9	1	3	15	7	5	11	-
FORWARD	277	110	332	347	467	266	144	448	275	2666
par	4	3	4	4	5	4	3	5	4	36
handicap	10	18	12	4	2	16	14	6	8	-

BACK	
yardage	6431
par	72
rating	69.8
slope	118

REGULAR	
yardage	5978
par	72
rating	67.8
slope	112

FORWARD	
yardage	5126
par	72
rating	67.9
slope	115

JACKSON LAKES GOLF COURSE
ARCHITECT: BOB BALDOCK, 1960

14868 18th Avenue
Lemoore, CA 93245

PRO SHOP: 559-925-8513

Jack Pasquale, Owners
Mike Schy, Head Professional, PGA

Driving Range ●
Practice Greens ●
Clubhouse ●
Food / Beverage ●
Accommodations
Pull Carts ●
Power Carts ●
Club Rental ●
$pecial Offers

	1	2	3	4	5	6	7	8	9	OUT
BACK										
REGULAR										
par										
handicap										
FORWARD										
par										
handicap										

	10	11	12	13	14	15	16	17	18	IN
BACK										
REGULAR										
par										
handicap										
FORWARD										
par										
handicap										

BACK	
yardage	6356
par	70
rating	-
slope	-

REGULAR	
yardage	6025
par	70
rating	-
slope	-

FORWARD	
yardage	5517
par	70
rating	-
slope	-

PUBLIC: $12-$19
FAX: 559-924-4131

18

HOLES

PLAY POLICY & FEES: Green fees are $12 for nine holes and $16 for 18 holes weekdays. The weekend fee is $19. Twilight rates are available. Carts are $12 for nine holes and $18 for 18.

TEE TIMES: Reservations can be booked seven days in advance.

COURSE DESCRIPTION: The old front nine is made up of narrow fairways surrounded by lots of trees and lakes. The newer front nine was designed to look like the course at the Links at Spanish Bay.

LOCATION: Take Highway 198 west fromVisalia to the18th Avenue exit in Lemoore. Take 18th Avenue south to Iona Avenue. Turn right on Iona and drive to the course.

. . . ● **TOURNAMENTS:** A 20-player minimum is required to book an event. Tournaments should be scheduled four to eight months in advance. ● **TRAVEL:** Best Western Vineyards Inn is located about five minutes from the golf course. For reservations call 209-924-1261.

1. LEMOORE GOLF COURSE

SEMIPRIVATE: $10-$14

18

HOLES

PLAY POLICY & FEES: Green fees are $10 weekdays and $14 weekends. Carts are $16.

TEE TIMES: Reservations can be booked seven days in advance.

COURSE DESCRIPTION: Water comes into play on 14 holes, so accuracy off the tee is a must. This flat course has a links-style feel because of the water and greens that are small and traditional in character. Standout holes include the par-3 16th, which features an island green, and the short but tempting par-4 17th, which is surrounded by water.

NOTES: Jackson Lakes was formerly named the Harvest Valley Golf Course.

LOCATION: From Highway 99 take Highway 198 west to Lemoore. From Lemoore, take 18th Avenue south three miles to the course, which is on the corner of 18th and Jackson.

. . . ● **TOURNAMENTS:** This course is available for outside tournaments.

2. JACKSON LAKES GOLF COURSE

③ POLVADERO GOLF COURSE
ARCHITECT: BOB BALDOCK, 1963

41605 Sutter Avenue
Coalinga, CA 93210

PRO SHOP: 559-935-3578

Jeff Christensen, General Manager
James Mize, Head Professional, PGA
Jorge Lopez, Superintendent

Driving Range ●
Practice Greens ●
Clubhouse
Food / Beverage ●
Accommodations
Pull Carts ●
Power Carts ●
Club Rental ●
Special Offers

	1	2	3	4	5	6	7	8	9	OUT
BACK	-	-	-	-	-	-	-	-	-	-
REGULAR	450	159	364	405	382	531	145	320	477	3233
par	4	3	4	4	4	5	3	4	5	36
handicap	3	10	11	2	5	14	17	15	9	-
FORWARD	435	155	293	396	347	540	131	305	435	3037
par	5	3	4	4	4	5	3	4	5	37
handicap	3	17	13	9	5	7	15	11	1	-

	10	11	12	13	14	15	16	17	18	IN
BACK	-	-	-	-	-	-	-	-	-	-
REGULAR	445	198	324	425	367	548	130	367	438	3242
par	4	3	4	4	4	5	3	4	5	36
handicap	8	7	16	1	6	13	18	4	12	-
FORWARD	447	123	255	364	356	486	96	293	368	2788
par	4	3	4	4	4	5	3	4	5	36
handicap	10	16	14	4	2	6	18	12	8	-

BACK	
yardage	-
par	-
rating	-
slope	-

REGULAR	
yardage	6475
par	72
rating	70.4
slope	119

FORWARD	
yardage	5825
par	73
rating	70.2
slope	115

PLAY POLICY & FEES: Green fees are $9 for nine holes and $13 for 18 holes weekdays, and $11 for nine holes and $14 for 18 holes weekends. Carts are $12 for nine holes and $20 for 18 holes.

TEE TIMES: Reservations can be booked seven days in advance.

COURSE DESCRIPTION: This hilly course is walkable. Mature trees and two lakes come into play on two holes. The course is a good exercise for players of all abilities. A few holes to watch out for are the 11th and 13th. The 11th hole, a par 3, is a long iron into a small green with water guarding three sides. The 13th hole is a par 4 that dares you to cut off as much of the dogleg as possible.

NOTES: Polvadero sits next to Interstate 5 between Los Angeles and the San Francisco Bay area. Many people like to take a break from the grueling drive and play a round.

LOCATION: From Interstate 5 near Coalinga take the Jayne Avenue exit west to Sutter Avenue. Turn left, and the course is on the right.

. . . ● **TOURNAMENTS:** A 16-player minimum is required to book a tournament.

3. POLVADERO GOLF COURSE

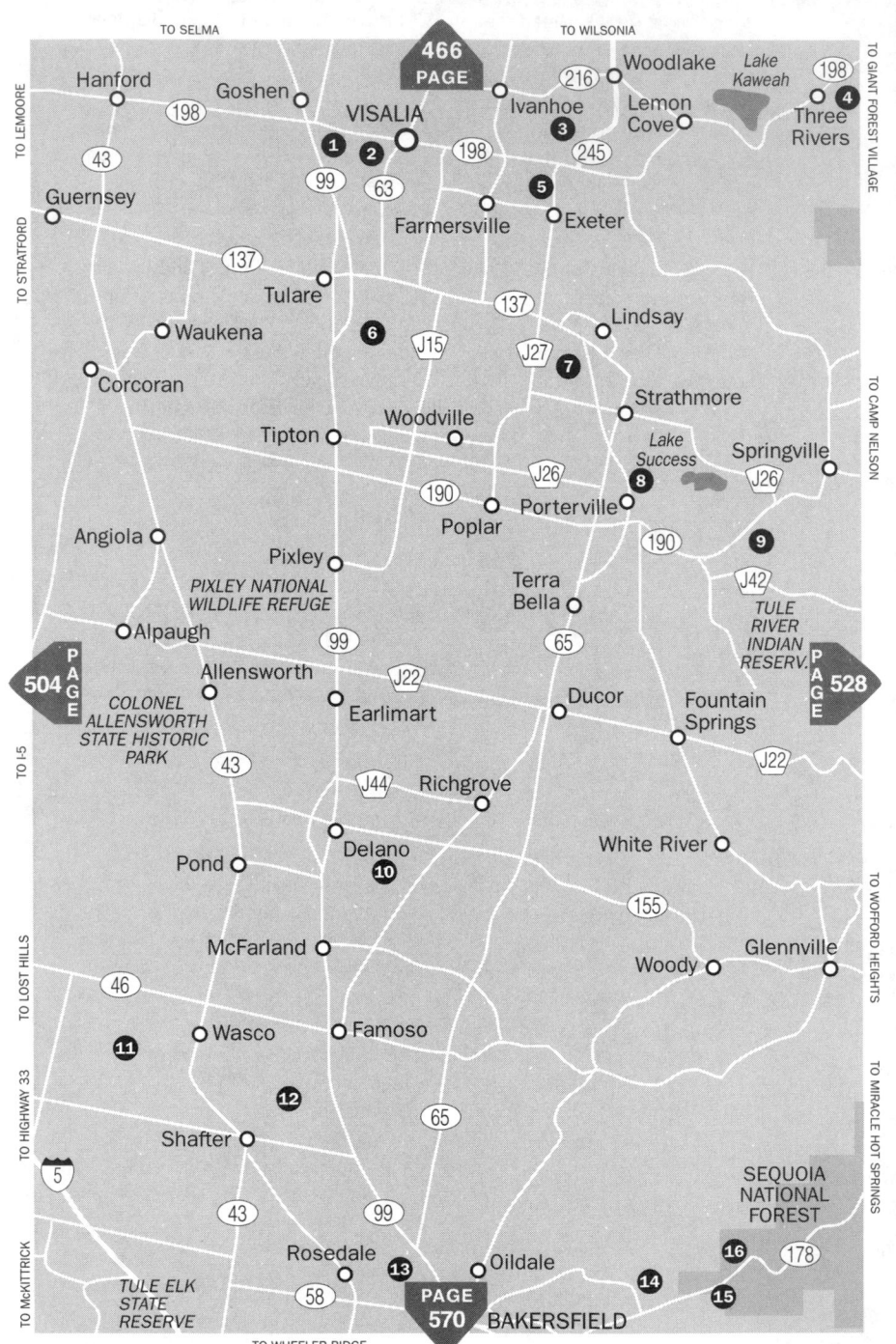

TO SELMA

TO WILSONIA

PAGE 466

Hanford

Goshen

VISALIA

Woodlake

Lake Kaweah

TO GIANT FOREST VILLAGE

198

216

Ivanhoe

Lemon Cove

Three Rivers

4

TO LEMOORE

198

1   2

99

63

198

245

3

5

Guernsey

43

Farmersville

Exeter

TO STRATFORD

137

Tulare

137

Lindsay

Waukena

6

J15

J27

7

Corcoran

Strathmore

TO CAMP NELSON

Tipton

Woodville

Lake Success

Springville

J26

J26

190

Angiola

Pixley

J26

Porterville

Poplar

9

190

J42

PIXLEY NATIONAL WILDLIFE REFUGE

Terra Bella

TULE RIVER INDIAN RESERV.

Alpaugh

65

Allensworth

J22

Ducor

Fountain Springs

PAGE 504

PAGE 528

COLONEL ALLENSWORTH STATE HISTORIC PARK

Earlimart

TO I-5

43

J22

J44

Richgrove

White River

Pond

Delano

155

10

TO WOFFORD HEIGHTS

McFarland

Woody

Glennville

TO LOST HILLS

46

Wasco

Famoso

11

12

TO HIGHWAY 33

Shafter

65

SEQUOIA NATIONAL FOREST

TO MIRACLE HOT SPRINGS

5

43

99

178

Rosedale

13

Oildale

16

TO McKITTRICK

TULE ELK STATE RESERVE

58

PAGE 570

14

15

BAKERSFIELD

TO WHEELER RIDGE

510

Visalia/North Bakersfield Area

❶ VALLEY OAKS GOLF COURSE
ARCHITECTS: ROBERT PUTNAM, 1972; CARY BICKLER, 1984; J.M. POELLOT, 1996

1800 South Plaza Drive
Visalia, CA 93277

PRO SHOP: 559-651-1441
CLUBHOUSE: 559-651-0840

Donna Bailey, Manager
Ryan Wiezycki, Director of Golf, PGA
Rich Freeman, Head Professional, PGA

Driving Range ●
Practice Greens ●
Clubhouse ●
Food / Beverage ●
Accommodations
Pull Carts ●
Power Carts ●
Club Rental ●
$pecial Offers

	1	2	3	4	5	6	7	8	9	OUT
BACK	476	374	361	396	168	354	209	402	490	3230
REGULAR	468	359	335	386	152	341	200	389	482	3112
par	5	4	4	4	3	4	3	4	5	36
handicap	15	7	9	1	13	11	3	5	17	-
FORWARD	422	343	307	373	139	323	174	369	465	2915
par	5	4	4	4	3	4	3	4	5	36
handicap	3	9	15	5	17	13	11	7	1	-

	10	11	12	13	14	15	16	17	18	IN
BACK	369	376	517	509	151	381	395	204	432	3334
REGULAR	351	331	492	501	140	369	385	189	408	3166
par	4	4	5	5	3	4	4	3	4	36
handicap	10	6	14	12	18	16	8	2	4	-
FORWARD	336	321	385	476	109	316	363	174	400	2880
par	4	4	5	5	3	4	4	3	5	37
handicap	8	12	4	2	18	16	10	14	6	-

BACK	
yardage	6564
par	72
rating	70.7
slope	119

REGULAR	
yardage	6278
par	72
rating	69.4
slope	116

FORWARD	
yardage	5795
par	73
rating	73.0
slope	122

❷ SIERRA VIEW GOLF COURSE OF VISALIA
ARCHITECT: ROBERT DEAN PUTMAN, 1956

12608 Avenue 264
Visalia, CA 93277

PRO SHOP: 559-732-2078

Brett Shuman

Driving Range ●
Practice Greens ●
Clubhouse ●
Food / Beverage ●
Accommodations
Pull Carts ●
Power Carts ●
Club Rental ●
$pecial Offers

	1	2	3	4	5	6	7	8	9	OUT
BACK	349	409	154	474	339	415	173	480	395	3188
REGULAR	339	394	138	457	329	404	164	466	380	3071
par	4	4	3	5	4	4	3	5	4	36
handicap	13	3	17	15	11	1	7	9	5	-
FORWARD	322	383	120	441	314	392	146	452	331	2901
par	4	4	3	5	4	4	3	5	4	36
handicap	11	7	17	5	13	3	15	1	9	-

	10	11	12	13	14	15	16	17	18	IN
BACK	205	378	490	397	123	389	426	480	312	3200
REGULAR	196	365	478	389	118	374	418	467	293	3098
par	3	4	5	4	3	4	4	5	4	36
handicap	4	6	14	10	16	8	2	12	18	-
FORWARD	177	350	469	373	108	363	407	454	284	2985
par	3	4	5	4	3	4	5	5	4	37
handicap	12	10	2	6	18	8	14	4	16	-

BACK	
yardage	6388
par	72
rating	68.9
slope	107

REGULAR	
yardage	6169
par	72
rating	67.8
slope	105

FORWARD	
yardage	5886
par	73
rating	71.6
slope	114

PLAY POLICY & FEES: Green fees are $12 for nine holes and $16 for 18 holes weekdays, and $16 for nine holes and $20 for 18 holes weekends. Carts are $12 for nine holes and $20 for 18 holes.

TEE TIMES: Reservations can be booked five days in advance.

DRESS CODE: Shirts and shoes are necessary.

COURSE DESCRIPTION: These are level courses with trees and water, featuring fast, large, well-maintained greens. Good putting is essential to scoring well.

LOCATION: In Visalia on Highway 99 take the Highway 198 turnoff east. Drive one mile and exit at South Plaza Drive. Continue to the course, which is located next to the airport.

. . . ● **TOURNAMENTS:** A 16-player minimum is needed to book an event. Tournaments can be booked 12 months in advance. The banquet facility can accommodate up to 180 people. ● **TRAVEL:** The Holiday Inn is located about one-quarter mile from the course. For reservations call 559-651-5000.

1. VALLEY OAKS GOLF COURSE

PLAY POLICY & FEES: Green fees are $11 for nine holes and $15 for 18 holes weekdays, and $15 for nine holes and $20 for 18 holes weekends. Carts are $12 for nine holes and $18 for 18 holes.

TEE TIMES: For weekend tee times, call the preceding Tuesday.

DRESS CODE: Nonmetal spikes are required.

COURSE DESCRIPTION: Situated in the San Joaquin Valley, this course has fast greens and lots of trees and bunkers. Mostly flat, the four par 5s measure under 500 yards and are easily reachable for long hitters.

NOTES: The course record is 61, held by Jerry Heard. Built in 1956, this is the oldest course in Visalia.

LOCATION: On Highway 99 in south Visalia, take the Avenue 264 exit (Tagus exit) east. Continue four miles to the course.

. . . ● **TOURNAMENTS:** An 80-player minimum is needed to book a shotgun start. A 16-player minimum is needed for regular tournaments. Tournaments should be booked at least one month in advance.

2. SIERRA VIEW GOLF COURSE OF VISALIA

③ VISALIA COUNTRY CLUB
ARCHITECTS: UNKNOWN, 1922; DESMOND MUIRHEAD, 1964

625 Ranch Road
Visalia, CA 93291

PRO SHOP: 559-734-1458
CLUBHOUSE: 559-734-3733

Jean Thysse, General Manager
Tom Ringer, Head Professional, PGA
Bob Dalton, Superintendent

Driving Range ●
Practice Greens ●
Clubhouse ●
Food / Beverage ●
Accommodations
Pull Carts ●
Power Carts ●
Club Rental ●
$pecial Offers

	1	2	3	4	5	6	7	8	9	OUT
BACK	357	493	363	205	441	388	388	203	548	3386
REGULAR	337	479	341	181	413	370	360	193	515	3189
par	4	5	4	3	4	4	4	3	5	36
handicap	15	17	11	7	1	5	3	13	9	-
FORWARD	319	462	313	156	388	339	336	172	464	2949
par	4	5	4	3	4	4	4	3	5	36
handicap	11	7	13	17	3	9	1	15	5	-

	10	11	12	13	14	15	16	17	18	IN
BACK	361	559	331	164	321	440	142	532	398	3248
REGULAR	348	534	329	156	316	421	110	508	387	3109
par	4	5	4	3	4	4	3	5	4	36
handicap	12	4	10	14	16	2	18	8	6	-
FORWARD	335	465	327	147	316	336	97	486	365	2874
par	4	5	4	3	4	4	3	5	4	36
handicap	8	6	10	16	12	14	18	2	4	-

BACK	
yardage	6634
par	72
rating	72.0
slope	122

REGULAR	
yardage	6298
par	72
rating	69.9
slope	117

FORWARD	
yardage	5823
par	72
rating	73.6
slope	128

④ THREE RIVERS GOLF COURSE
ARCHITECT: ROBERT DEAN PUTMAN, 1962

P.O. Box 839
Three Rivers, CA 93271

41117 Sierra Drive
Three Rivers, CA 93271

PRO SHOP: 559-561-3133
CLUBHOUSE: 559-561-4156

Driving Range
Practice Greens ●
Clubhouse ●
Food / Beverage ●
Accommodations
Pull Carts ●
Power Carts ●
Club Rental ●
$pecial Offers

	1	2	3	4	5	6	7	8	9	OUT
BACK										
REGULAR										
par										
handicap										
FORWARD										
par										
handicap										

	10	11	12	13	14	15	16	17	18	IN
BACK										
REGULAR										
par										
handicap										
FORWARD										
par										
handicap										

BACK	
yardage	5478
par	
rating	
slope	

REGULAR	
yardage	5208
par	
rating	
slope	

FORWARD	
yardage	4042
par	
rating	
slope	

PRIVATE: $30-$60

18 HOLES

PLAY POLICY & FEES: Reciprocal play is accepted with members of other private clubs. Guest green fees are $30 to $60. Carts are $10. The course is closed on Monday.

TEE TIMES: Have your golf professional call to make arrangements.

DRESS CODE: Nonmetal spikes are required; check with golf shop for apparel regulations.

COURSE DESCRIPTION: This level course has lots of trees and bunkers with water on eight holes. Visalia demands accuracy off the tee, and the well-kept greens are large and tricky, requiring a deft putting touch.

NOTES: This is one of the few valley courses that overseed in the winter months. The course record is 63, held by Sean McHenry.

LOCATION: From Highway 99 take the Visalia exit. Go three stoplights and turn left onto West Main. Turn left again on Ranch Road and follow it to the end.

. . . ● **TOURNAMENTS:** The course is available for outside events on a limited basis. A 100-player minimum is required to book an event. Events should be scheduled 12 months in advance. The banquet facility can accommodate 250 people. ● **TRAVEL:** The Radisson Hotel is located three minutes from the golf course. For reservations call 559-636-1111.

3. VISALIA COUNTRY CLUB

PUBLIC: $12-$28

9 HOLES

PLAY POLICY & FEES: Green fees are $12 for nine holes and $18 for 18 holes on weekdays and $15 for nine holes and $28 for 18 holes on weekends. Twilight, senior and junior rates are available. Call for information.

TEE TIMES: Tee times can be made one week in advance and are recommended for weekends and holidays.

DRESS CODE: Nonmetal spikes are required.

COURSE DESCRIPTION: Located about 800 feet above sea level in the Sequoias, this course is packed with trees and hilly, but walkable.

NOTES: This course reopened in 1999 after considerable renovation, including all new fairways and greens. Three Rivers has added a new clubhouse and restaurant.

LOCATION: From Highway 99 in Tulare, take Highway 198 east through Visalia to Three Rivers. The course is next to the highway.

. . . ● **TOURNAMENTS:** This course is available for outside events.

4. THREE RIVERS GOLF COURSE

EXETER PUBLIC GOLF COURSE
ARCHITECT: BOB BALDOCK, 1963

510 West Visalia
Exeter, CA 93211

PRO SHOP: 559-592-4783

Steve Maaske, Owner

Driving Range
Practice Greens ●
Clubhouse
Food / Beverage ●
Accommodations
Pull Carts ●
Power Carts
Club Rental ●
$pecial Offers

	1	2	3	4	5	6	7	8	9	OUT
BACK	-	-	-	-	-	-	-	-	-	-
REGULAR	300	165	108	100	400	85	110	105	270	1643
par	4	3	3	3	4	3	3	3	4	30
handicap	7	3	9	13	1	15	5	11	17	-
FORWARD	300	165	108	100	400	85	110	105	270	1643
par	4	3	3	3	5	3	3	3	4	31
handicap	7	3	9	13	1	15	5	11	17	-

	10	11	12	13	14	15	16	17	18	IN
BACK	-	-	-	-	-	-	-	-	-	-
REGULAR	300	165	108	100	400	85	110	105	270	1643
par	4	3	3	3	4	3	3	3	4	30
handicap	8	4	10	14	2	16	6	12	18	-
FORWARD	300	165	108	100	400	85	110	105	270	1643
par	4	3	3	3	5	3	3	3	4	31
handicap	8	4	10	14	2	16	6	12	18	-

BACK	
yardage	-
par	-
rating	-
slope	-

REGULAR	
yardage	3286
par	60
rating	-
slope	-

FORWARD	
yardage	3286
par	62
rating	-
slope	-

TULARE GOLF COURSE
ARCHITECT: BOB BALDOCK, 1956

5310 South Laspina
Tulare, CA 93274

PRO SHOP: 559-686-5300

Dave Vogt, Head Professional, PGA
Brett Miller, Superintendent

Driving Range ●
Practice Greens ●
Clubhouse ●
Food / Beverage ●
Accommodations
Pull Carts ●
Power Carts ●
Club Rental ●
$pecial Offers

	1	2	3	4	5	6	7	8	9	OUT
BACK	375	489	367	210	410	530	158	414	411	3364
REGULAR	367	471	358	197	394	515	148	396	397	3243
par	4	5	4	3	4	5	3	4	4	36
handicap	13	17	7	9	5	15	11	3	1	-
FORWARD	355	432	334	162	293	449	131	267	296	2719
par	4	5	4	3	4	5	3	4	4	36
handicap	3	7	5	15	11	1	17	13	9	-

	10	11	12	13	14	15	16	17	18	IN
BACK	382	517	386	142	354	405	202	467	515	3370
REGULAR	376	510	377	134	346	398	192	453	505	3291
par	4	5	4	3	4	4	3	4	5	36
handicap	6	14	10	18	12	4	8	2	16	-
FORWARD	364	436	373	125	337	289	174	380	429	2907
par	4	5	4	3	4	4	3	4	5	36
handicap	12	2	6	18	10	14	16	8	4	-

BACK	
yardage	6734
par	72
rating	71.3
slope	118

REGULAR	
yardage	6534
par	72
rating	70.4
slope	116

FORWARD	
yardage	5626
par	72
rating	71.6
slope	117

PLAY POLICY & FEES: Green fees are $6 for nine holes and $10 for 18 holes weekdays, and $7 for nine holes and $12 for 18 holes weekends. Pull carts are $1.

TEE TIMES: Reservations are not accepted. All play is on a first-come, first-served basis.

COURSE DESCRIPTION: A lot of water comes into play on this tree-lined, mature course. Three of the holes are par 4s; the longest is the 400-yard fifth.

LOCATION: From Highway 99 in Visalia drive east on Highway 198 (toward Three Rivers). Turn right on Anderson Road (Highway 180). Follow it to Visalia Road and turn left to the course.

. . . ● **TOURNAMENTS:** This course is available for outside tournaments.

5. EXETER PUBLIC GOLF COURSE

PLAY POLICY & FEES: Green fees are $11 for nine holes and $17 for 18 holes weekdays, and $14 for nine holes and $22 for 18 holes weekends. Carts are $12 for nine holes and $20 for 18 holes.

TEE TIMES: Reservations can be made on Tuesday prior to the weekend.

DRESS CODE: Shirts must be worn.

COURSE DESCRIPTION: This course is mostly flat and open with several lakes. This is a course that plows its money back into the greens, fairways, and irrigation system, and it shows in the yearly improvements.

NOTES: The course record is 61, held by Jimmy Hill.

LOCATION: From Highway 99 in Tulare head east on Avenue 200. Turn left on South Laspina. The course is on the right.

. . . ● **TOURNAMENTS:** This course is available for outside tournaments.

6. TULARE GOLF COURSE

7 LINDSAY MUNICIPAL GOLF COURSE
ARCHITECT: BOB BALDOCK, 1961

801 North Elmwood
Lindsay, CA 93247

PRO SHOP: 559-562-1144

Steve Maaske, Manager, Pro

Driving Range ●
Practice Greens ●
Clubhouse
Food / Beverage ●
Accommodations
Pull Carts ●
Power Carts
Club Rental ●
$pecial Offers

	1	2	3	4	5	6	7	8	9	OUT
BACK	-	-	-	-	-	-	-	-	-	-
REGULAR	85	144	119	131	125	117	95	140	134	1090
par	3	3	3	3	3	3	3	3	3	27
handicap	6	2	8	12	14	16	18	4	10	-
FORWARD	85	144	119	131	125	117	95	140	134	1090
par	3	3	3	3	3	3	3	3	3	27
handicap	6	2	8	12	14	16	18	4		-

	10	11	12	13	14	15	16	17	18	IN
BACK	-	-	-	-	-	-	-	-	-	-
REGULAR	85	144	119	131	125	117	95	140	134	1090
par	3	3	3	3	3	3	3	3	3	27
handicap	5	1	7	10	13	15	17	3	9	-
FORWARD	85	144	119	131	125	117	95	140	134	1090
par	3	3	3	3	3	3	3	3	3	27
handicap	5	1	7	10	13	15	17	3	9	-

BACK	
yardage	-
par	-
rating	-
slope	-

REGULAR	
yardage	2180
par	54
rating	50.0
slope	-

FORWARD	
yardage	2180
par	54
rating	50.0
slope	-

8 PORTERVILLE GOLF COURSE

702 East Isham Avenue
Porterville, CA 93257

PRO SHOP: 559-784-9468

Dale Bartlett, Head Professional, PGA
David Zorn, Superintendent

Driving Range ●
Practice Greens ●
Clubhouse ●
Food / Beverage ●
Accommodations
Pull Carts ●
Power Carts ●
Club Rental ●
$pecial Offers

	1	2	3	4	5	6	7	8	9	OUT
BACK	-	-	-	-	-	-	-	-	-	-
REGULAR	350	184	385	260	400	140	345	450	380	2894
par	4	3	4	4	4	3	4	5	4	35
handicap	9	3	13	17	1	15	5	11	7	-
FORWARD	350	184	385	232	400	140	280	450	380	2801
par	4	3	4	4	5	3	4	5	4	36
handicap	7	15	9	13	3	17	11	1	5	-

	10	11	12	13	14	15	16	17	18	IN
BACK	-	-	-	-	-	-	-	-	-	-
REGULAR	350	184	385	260	400	140	345	450	380	2894
par	4	3	4	4	4	3	4	5	4	35
handicap	10	4	14	18	2	16	6	12	8	-
FORWARD	350	184	385	232	400	140	280	450	380	2801
par	4	3	4	4	5	3	4	5	4	36
handicap	8	16	10	14	4	18	12	2	6	-

BACK	
yardage	-
par	-
rating	-
slope	-

REGULAR	
yardage	5788
par	70
rating	66.2
slope	109

FORWARD	
yardage	5602
par	72
rating	70.2
slope	117

PLAY POLICY & FEES: Green fees are $3.50 for nine holes and $6 for 18 holes weekdays, and $4 for nine holes and $7 for 18 holes weekends. Pull carts are $1.
TEE TIMES: Reservations are not accepted. All play is on a first-come, first-served basis.
COURSE DESCRIPTION: This is a short course that you can play twice. Set in Lindsay City Park, it's flat, with lots of trees and small greens. It's a good course for beginners, seniors, and players wanting to work on their irons.
NOTES: The driving range is for irons only.
LOCATION: This course is located in the city park eight blocks east of Highway 65 between Exeter and Porterville.
. . . ● **TOURNAMENTS:** This course is available for outside tournaments.

7. LINDSAY MUNICIPAL GOLF COURSE

PLAY POLICY & FEES: Green fees are $8.50 for nine holes and $12.50 for 18 holes weekdays, and $9.50 for nine holes and $13.50 for 18 holes weekends. Carts are $8 for nine holes and $16 for 18 holes. The course is closed on Monday.
TEE TIMES: Reservations on weekdays are not accepted. All play is on a first-come, first-served basis. Tee times for Saturday can be made starting Tuesday and tee times for Sunday can be made starting Wednesday.
DRESS CODE: Nonmetal spikes are required.
COURSE DESCRIPTION: This course is mostly flat and narrow, with out-of-bounds on every hole. The greens are quite small.
NOTES: The course record is 61, set by Arlie Morris.
LOCATION: From Highway 99 or Highway 65, take Exit 190 east to Plano Road in Porterville. Turn left onto Plano and then right on Date Street. Drive to Leggett Road and turn left. Continue to Isham Avenue and the course.
. . . ● **TOURNAMENTS:** No shotgun starts are allowed.

8. PORTERVILLE GOLF COURSE

9 RIVER ISLAND COUNTRY CLUB
ARCHITECT: ROBERT DEAN PUTMAN, 1964

31989 River Island Drive
Porterville, CA 93257

PRO SHOP: 559-784-9425

Terry Treece, PGA Professional
Bill Trask, Superintendent

Driving Range ●
Practice Greens ●
Clubhouse ●
Food / Beverage ●
Accommodations ●
Pull Carts
Power Carts ●
Club Rental
$pecial Offers

	1	2	3	4	5	6	7	8	9	OUT
BACK	415	418	490	409	410	540	205	447	168	3502
REGULAR	395	375	466	385	398	525	162	352	138	3196
par	4	4	5	4	4	5	3	4	3	36
handicap	5	7	11	1	3	9	15	13	17	-
FORWARD	297	354	454	325	377	515	132	343	126	2923
par	4	4	5	4	4	5	3	4	3	36
handicap	13	7	5	9	1	3	15	11	17	-

	10	11	12	13	14	15	16	17	18	IN
BACK	443	165	547	380	625	385	185	392	401	3523
REGULAR	421	155	502	361	564	345	151	380	358	3237
par	4	3	5	4	5	4	3	4	4	36
handicap	4	16	8	14	2	12	18	6	10	-
FORWARD	363	147	413	348	507	295	134	346	325	2878
par	4	3	5	4	5	4	3	4	4	36
handicap	12	16	14	10	2	8	18	4	6	-

BACK	
yardage	7025
par	72
rating	72.8
slope	127

REGULAR	
yardage	6433
par	72
rating	69.9
slope	119

FORWARD	
yardage	5801
par	72
rating	73.0
slope	128

10 DELANO PUBLIC GOLF COURSE
ARCHITECT: BERT STAMPS, 1962

P.O. Box 927/Memorial   104 South Lexington
Delano, CA 93216

PRO SHOP: 661-725-7527

Thom Casey, Professional/Manager
Ramon Terrazas, Superintendent

Driving Range ●
Practice Greens ●
Clubhouse ●
Food / Beverage ●
Accommodations
Pull Carts ●
Power Carts ●
Club Rental ●
$pecial Offers

	1	2	3	4	5	6	7	8	9	OUT
BACK	-	-	-	-	-	-	-	-	-	-
REGULAR	148	279	209	485	277	163	163	276	177	2177
par	3	4	3	5	4	3	3	4	3	32
handicap	14	12	2	6	16	4	8	18	10	-
FORWARD	138	262	200	468	266	144	112	264	139	1993
par	3	4	3	5	4	3	4	3	3	32
handicap	18	8	2	4	16	6	10	12	14	-

	10	11	12	13	14	15	16	17	18	IN
BACK	-	-	-	-	-	-	-	-	-	-
REGULAR	158	295	219	501	319	187	175	265	182	2301
par	3	4	3	5	4	3	3	4	3	32
handicap	13	11	1	5	15	3	7	17	9	-
FORWARD	148	279	209	485	277	163	163	276	145	2145
par	3	4	3	5	4	3	4	3	3	32
handicap	17	7	1	3	15	5	9	11	13	-

BACK	
yardage	-
par	-
rating	-
slope	-

REGULAR	
yardage	4478
par	64
rating	60.8
slope	94

FORWARD	
yardage	4138
par	64
rating	63.1
slope	108

PLAY POLICY & FEES: Outside play is welcome after 10 a.m. every day except Monday. The course is closed on Monday. Reciprocal play is accepted with members of other private clubs. Guest fees are $30. Carts are $11. Green fees for public play are $45 including cart.

TEE TIMES: Reservations can be booked seven days in advance.

DRESS CODE: Collared shirts and nonmetal spikes are required. Shorts must be to mid-thigh, and no blue jeans are allowed on the course.

COURSE DESCRIPTION: This long, sprawling course wanders through old oak trees and offers a variety of holes. The Tule River flows through the terrain. You cross the river 11 times, and it comes into play on nine holes. The course is walkable, but there is a lot of distance between holes.

NOTES: Terry Harrelson holds the course record with a 64.

LOCATION: Take Highway 190 and drive past Porterville for 10 miles. The entrance to this private country club resort course is on the right.

. . . ● **TOURNAMENTS:** This course is available for outside tournaments.

9. RIVER ISLAND COUNTRY CLUB

PLAY POLICY & FEES: Green fees are $5 for nine holes and $8 for 18 holes weekdays, and $7 for nine holes and $10 for 18 holes weekends and holidays Senior , junior, and twilight rates are available.

TEE TIMES: Reservations can be booked seven days in advance.

DRESS CODE: Nonmetal spikes are mandatory.

COURSE DESCRIPTION: This level course offers undulating fairways. Ponds come into play on the first, eighth, and ninth holes. The third hole is a 209-yard par 3 with trees on the left and right, making for tight play. The fourth is a par-5, 485-yard challenge. This traditional course boasts eucalyptus trees along the fairways.

LOCATION: Take Highway 99 north to the Woollomes Avenue exit. Head east to Lexington and take a left. The course is on the right.

. . . ● **TOURNAMENTS:** This course is available for outside tournaments. A minimum of 20 players is needed to book a tournament. Tournaments may be booked 12 months in advance. ● **TRAVEL:** Aldo's is recommended for dining after your round. The Comfort Inn (800-228-5150) and the Shilo Inn are (800-222-2244) recommended.

10. DELANO PUBLIC GOLF COURSE

WASCO VALLEY ROSE GOLF COURSE
ARCHITECT: ROBERT DEAN PUTMAN, 1991

301 North Leonard Avenue
Wasco, CA 93280

PRO SHOP: 661-758-8301

Joe Haggerty, PGA Professional

Driving Range ●
Practice Greens ●
Clubhouse ●
Food / Beverage ●
Accommodations
Pull Carts ●
Power Carts ●
Club Rental ●
$pecial Offers

	1	2	3	4	5	6	7	8	9	OUT
BACK	436	188	361	522	155	416	413	403	551	3445
REGULAR	380	163	325	468	118	392	381	375	484	3086
par	4	3	4	5	3	4	4	4	5	36
handicap	3	1	13	11	17	9	5	7	15	-
FORWARD	352	96	285	422	102	334	305	341	432	2669
par	4	3	4	5	3	4	4	4	5	36
handicap	4	2	6	16	18	14	12	10	8	-

	10	11	12	13	14	15	16	17	18	IN
BACK	401	363	500	160	437	410	162	414	570	3417
REGULAR	370	332	482	135	403	378	137	387	520	3144
par	4	4	5	3	4	4	3	4	5	36
handicap	4	18	10	16	6	2	12	14	8	-
FORWARD	325	293	423	84	355	325	108	325	449	2687
par	4	4	5	3	4	4	3	4	5	36
handicap	3	15	7	17	5	1	11	13	9	-

BACK	
yardage	6862
par	72
rating	74.1
slope	126

REGULAR	
yardage	6230
par	72
rating	70.8
slope	122

FORWARD	
yardage	5356
par	72
rating	70.5
slope	119

NORTH KERN GOLF COURSE
ARCHITECT: KERMIT STYBER, 1953

17412 Quality Road
Bakersfield, CA 93308

PRO SHOP: 661-399-0347

Tony Emma, PGA Professional
Richard Koop, Superintendent

Driving Range ●
Practice Greens ●
Clubhouse ●
Food / Beverage ●
Accommodations
Pull Carts ●
Power Carts ●
Club Rental ●
$pecial Offers

	1	2	3	4	5	6	7	8	9	OUT
BACK	500	355	345	545	213	442	178	429	390	3397
REGULAR	480	333	336	525	198	428	156	408	373	3237
par	5	4	4	5	3	4	3	4	4	36
handicap	17	13	9	15	5	1	11	3	7	-
FORWARD	451	326	318	508	184	422	134	385	365	3093
par	5	4	4	5	3	5	3	5	4	38
handicap	3	13	9	1	15	5	17	7	11	-

	10	11	12	13	14	15	16	17	18	IN
BACK	375	193	390	435	395	490	454	165	475	3372
REGULAR	356	181	374	411	384	469	440	151	458	3224
par	4	3	4	4	4	5	4	3	5	36
handicap	6	12	8	4	10	16	2	14	18	-
FORWARD	344	168	362	400	374	459	437	139	406	3089
par	4	3	4	5	4	5	5	3	5	38
handicap	14	16	10	8	12	4	6	18	2	-

BACK	
yardage	6769
par	72
rating	71.4
slope	115

REGULAR	
yardage	6461
par	72
rating	69.9
slope	109

FORWARD	
yardage	6182
par	76
rating	72.7
slope	116

PLAY POLICY & FEES: Green fees are $12 weekdays and $14 weekends. Twilight rates are available. Carts are $18.

TEE TIMES: Reservations can be booked seven days in advance.

DRESS CODE: Nonmetal spikes are required.

COURSE DESCRIPTION: Six lakes come into play on this course. There are several undulating fairways, elevated tees, and spectacular greens. The ninth provides an exciting finish to the front nine, particularly if you survive the sloping fairway, a large lake, and bunker, all of which come into play off the tee.

NOTES: The men's course record is 65.

LOCATION: From Highway 99 take the Highway 46 exit west. Drive two miles west of Wasco and take the Leonard Avenue exit to the course. The course is about 20 miles northwest of Bakersfield.

. . . ● **TOURNAMENTS:** A 30-player minimum is needed to book an event and 144-player field for a shotgun start. ● **TRAVEL:** The Ramada Inn in Bakersfield is located 35 minutes from the golf course. For reservations call 661-327-0681.

11. WASCO VALLEY ROSE GOLF COURSE

PLAY POLICY & FEES: Green fees are $11 50 weekdays and $14.75 weekends. Call for special rates. Carts are $18.

TEE TIMES: Reservations can be booked seven days in advance.

DRESS CODE: Shirts and nonmetal spikes are required.

COURSE DESCRIPTION: This course is packed with trees and bunkers. Nevertheless, the fairways are wide and level, leading to small greens. The sixth hole is a devil. It's a 442-yard par 4 that plays uphill and into the wind. The green is heavily bunkered in front, leaving only a narrow opening. Pin placement can add more yardage to an already long hole.

NOTES: The Kern County Amateur Championships are held here each October, and the Kern County Two-Man Tournament is held each April. The course record is 63, set in 1985 by former head pro Bill McKinley.

LOCATION: From Bakersfield travel north on Highway 99 for 12 miles to the Shafter exit. Head east for 2.5 miles on Laredo Highway to Quality Road. Turn north on Quality Road and continue one-half mile to the course.

. . . ● **TOURNAMENTS:** This course is available for outside tournaments.

12. NORTH KERN GOLF COURSE

⑬ THE LINKS AT RIVERLAKES RANCH
ARCHITECT: RON FREAM-GOLF PLAN, 1999

5201 Riverlakes Drive
Bakersfield, CA 93312

PRO SHOP: 661-587-5465

Curtis Rowe, Director of Golf

Driving Range ●
Practice Greens ●
Clubhouse ●
Food / Beverage ●
Accommodations
Pull Carts
Power Carts ●
Club Rental ●
Special Offers

	1	2	3	4	5	6	7	8	9	OUT
BACK	350	365	180	570	155	435	345	390	510	3300
REGULAR										
par	4	4	3	5	3	4	4	4	5	36
handicap										-
FORWARD										
par										
handicap										-

	10	11	12	13	14	15	16	17	18	IN
BACK	585	460	425	210	375	165	335	440	530	3525
REGULAR										
par	5	4	4	3	4	3	4	4	5	36
handicap										-
FORWARD										
par										
handicap										-

BACK	
yardage	6825
par	72
rating	
slope	

REGULAR	
yardage	
par	72
rating	
slope	

FORWARD	
yardage	
par	
rating	
slope	

⑭ KERN RIVER GOLF COURSE
ARCHITECT: WILLIAM P. BELL, 1953

P.O. Box 6339
Bakersfield, CA 93306

PRO SHOP: 661-872-5128

Alan Sorensen, Head Professional, PGA
Jim Foss, Director of Golf
Chris Hansen, Superintendent

Driving Range ●
Practice Greens ●
Clubhouse ●
Food / Beverage ●
Accommodations
Pull Carts ●
Power Carts ●
Club Rental ●
Special Offers ●

	1	2	3	4	5	6	7	8	9	OUT
BACK	529	138	465	453	293	163	395	543	200	3179
REGULAR	516	129	454	436	282	152	388	534	180	3071
par	5	3	4	4	4	3	4	5	3	35
handicap	9	17	1	3	15	13	5	7	11	-
FORWARD	492	118	435	400	267	135	376	519	165	2907
par	5	3	5	4	4	3	4	5	3	36
handicap	7	17	11	5	13	15	3	1	9	-

	10	11	12	13	14	15	16	17	18	IN
BACK	381	235	365	339	459	366	382	222	530	3279
REGULAR	376	225	358	332	436	359	373	218	510	3187
par	4	3	4	4	4	4	4	3	5	35
handicap	10	4	8	18	2	12	14	6	16	-
FORWARD	361	211	344	320	424	346	357	205	496	3064
par	4	3	4	4	5	4	4	4	5	37
handicap	10	6	14	12	16	8	4	18	2	-

BACK	
yardage	6458
par	70
rating	70.7
slope	120

REGULAR	
yardage	6258
par	70
rating	69.6
slope	118

FORWARD	
yardage	5971
par	73
rating	72.3
slope	123

PLAY POLICY & FEES: This course is projected to be open in the fall of 1999. Green fees are expected to be $29 weekdays and $44 weekends and holidays. Cart fees are $11 per rider.

DRESS CODE: This will be a nonmetal spike facility.

COURSE DESCRIPTION: The course plays over 200 acres featuring existing almond orchards, redwoods, Canary Island pines and 12 lakes. Bunker placement and green design will make this course challenging for players of all skill levels.

LOCATION: In Bakersfield from Highway 99 take the Oliver Street exit and head west to Riverlakes Drive. Go left on Riverlakes Drive. The course will be on the right.

. . . ● **TOURNAMENTS:** A 20-player minimum will be required to book an event.
● **TRAVEL:** The Courtyard Marriot and the DoubleTree Hotel are both recommended. For reservations at the Courtyard call 661-324-6660. For reservations at the DoubleTree call 661-323-7111.

13. THE LINKS AT RIVERLAKES RANCH

PLAY POLICY & FEES: Green fees are $11.50 weekdays and $14.75 weekends Carts are $9 per person. Kern River offers special rates for seniors and juniors.

TEE TIMES: Reservations can be booked seven days in advance.

COURSE DESCRIPTION: This public facility will test your golf skill. It is one of two courses in the area that are rated over par. It was originally designed in the 1920s as a nine-hole course. Nine more holes were added in the 1950s. The course features rolling terrain and an abundance of mature trees. One word of caution: There are two long par-3 holes on the back nine that can ruin your day. A hole to remember is the 11th, which is 235 yards from the back tees. If you miss the green to the right, you're stymied behind trees. The green is sharply sloped downhill and difficult to putt. Don't leave the ball above the hole.

NOTES: The course record is 62 for men, held by Ron Baker, and 71 for women, held by Jacque Servadio.

LOCATION: From Highway 99 in Bakersfield, take Highway 178 east to Alfred Herrall Highway. Follow the signs to Lake Ming.

. . . ● **TOURNAMENTS:** Shotgun tournaments are available weekdays only. A 20-player minimum is needed to book a tournament. Tournaments can be booked after December 1 for the following year. ● **TRAVEL:** The Rio Bravo Resort is located one-quarter mile from the golf course. For reservations call 805-872-5000. ● **$PECIAL OFFERS:** Golf packages are available with the Rio Bravo Resort. Call the resort for more information.

14. KERN RIVER GOLF COURSE

Visalia/North Bakersfield Area (map page 510)   **525**

P.O. Box 6007
Bakersfield, CA 93306

4200 Country Club Drive
Bakersfield, CA 93306

PRO SHOP: 661-871-4121
CLUBHOUSE: 661-871-4000

Richard Moore, Director of Golf, PGA
Steve Scarbrough, Superintendent
John Hahn, Tournament Director

Driving Range ●
Practice Greens ●
Clubhouse ●
Food / Beverage ●
Accommodations
Pull Carts
Power Carts ●
Club Rental ●
$pecial Offers

	1	2	3	4	5	6	7	8	9	OUT
BACK	375	529	177	454	455	597	342	184	348	3461
REGULAR	361	493	164	448	415	548	314	162	325	3230
par	4	5	3	4	4	5	4	3	4	36
handicap	5	9	13	1	3	7	15	11	17	-
FORWARD	352	485	156	443	400	473	306	132	302	3049
par	4	5	3	5	4	5	4	3	4	37
handicap	5	3	15	11	1	7	9	17	13	-

	10	11	12	13	14	15	16	17	18	IN
BACK	394	516	350	220	443	528	297	190	420	3358
REGULAR	381	502	334	201	432	515	294	168	401	3228
par	4	5	4	3	4	5	4	3	4	36
handicap	8	16	12	6	2	10	18	14	4	-
FORWARD	371	496	328	198	429	511	294	154	326	3107
par	4	5	4	6	5	5	4	3	4	40
handicap	6	4	12	8	14	2	16	18	10	-

BACK	
yardage	6819
par	72
rating	72.6
slope	127

REGULAR	
yardage	6458
par	72
rating	70.8
slope	123

FORWARD	
yardage	6156
par	77
rating	75.8
slope	129

15200 Casa Club Drive
Bakersfield, CA 93306

PRO SHOP: 661-871-4653
CLUBHOUSE: 661-871-4900

Leisa Kiger, Operations Manager
Jim Kiger, Director of Golf, PGA
Trini Hernandez, Superintendent

Driving Range ●
Practice Greens ●
Clubhouse ●
Food / Beverage ●
Accommodations ●
Pull Carts
Power Carts ●
Club Rental ●
$pecial Offers ●

	1	2	3	4	5	6	7	8	9	OUT
BACK	406	387	568	426	223	552	410	192	372	3536
REGULAR	373	370	548	406	191	529	388	162	354	3321
par	4	4	5	4	3	5	4	3	4	36
handicap	8	10	14	2	16	6	4	18	12	-
FORWARD	322	319	498	352	160	473	345	137	303	2909
par	4	4	5	4	3	5	4	3	4	36
handicap	14	12	4	8	16	2	6	18	10	-

	10	11	12	13	14	15	16	17	18	IN
BACK	405	616	392	244	446	345	155	358	521	3482
REGULAR	365	596	336	219	419	326	144	331	498	3234
par	4	5	4	3	4	4	3	4	5	36
handicap	17	1	11	5	3	13	15	7	9	-
FORWARD	313	526	302	157	370	278	109	289	451	2795
par	4	5	4	3	4	4	3	4	5	36
handicap	15	1	11	13	5	9	17	7	3	-

BACK	
yardage	7018
par	72
rating	74.4
slope	138

REGULAR	
yardage	6555
par	72
rating	70.9
slope	122

FORWARD	
yardage	5704
par	72
rating	72.5
slope	123

18 HOLES

PLAY POLICY & FEES: Reciprocal play is accepted with members of other private clubs; otherwise, members and guests only. Green fees for guests and reciprocators are $100. Carts are $20. Reservations are required. The course is closed on Monday.

DRESS CODE: Appropriate golf attire and nonmetal spikes are required.

COURSE DESCRIPTION: This well-maintained, mature course is situated on a hill. The layout requires good shot-making ability. Every club in the bag comes into play. Several long par 4s highlight the course.

NOTES: The course record is 63.

LOCATION: From Highway 99 at Bakersfield, go east on Highway 178 about six miles. Take the Oswell Street exit and turn right to Country Club Drive to the club.

. . . ● **TOURNAMENTS:** Shotgun tournaments are available weekdays only. Carts are required. An 80-player minimum is required to book a tournament. Tournaments should be booked six months in advance. The banquet facility can hold 250 people. ● **TRAVEL:** The DoubleTree Hotel Bakersfield is 15 minutes from the course. For reservations call 805-323-7111.

15. BAKERSFIELD COUNTRY CLUB

---

18 HOLES

PLAY POLICY & FEES: Reciprocal play is accepted with members of other private clubs; otherwise, members and guests only. Guest fees are $30 weekdays and $35 weekends when accompanied by a member and $50 when unaccompanied. Fees are $50 for reciprocators, including carts. Carts are $22. The course is closed on Monday and Christmas.

TEE TIMES: Reservations can be booked seven days in advance.

DRESS CODE: T-shirts, denim, and metal spikes are not allowed.

COURSE DESCRIPTION: This is a beautiful championship layout set in the foothills of the Tehachapi Mountains. It plays long and has excellent greens. The hole to watch for is the 11th, affectionately known as "Big Bertha." It's par 5 and 616 yards uphill to a difficult green. There is no flat lie on this hole. The green, the most difficult on the course, is severely sloped left to right and tough to read.

NOTES: Rio Bravo has been the site of the PGA Tour Qualifying School, U.S. Open qualifying and the Southern California Open. The course record is 63, held by Mike Sugar.

LOCATION: From Highway 99 in Bakersfield, take Highway 178 east and drive about 15 miles to the Rio Bravo Resort Country Club. Continue past the airport and turn right on Mira Monte to the course.

. . . ● **TOURNAMENTS:** A 75-player minimum is needed to book an event. A 100-player minimum is needed to book a tournament on a Monday. The banquet facility can accommodate up to 300 people. ● **TRAVEL:** For reservations at the Rio Bravo Resort call 805-872-5000. ● **$PECIAL OFFERS:** Golf packages for the public are available for guests staying at the Rio Bravo Resort.

16. RIO BRAVO COUNTRY CLUB

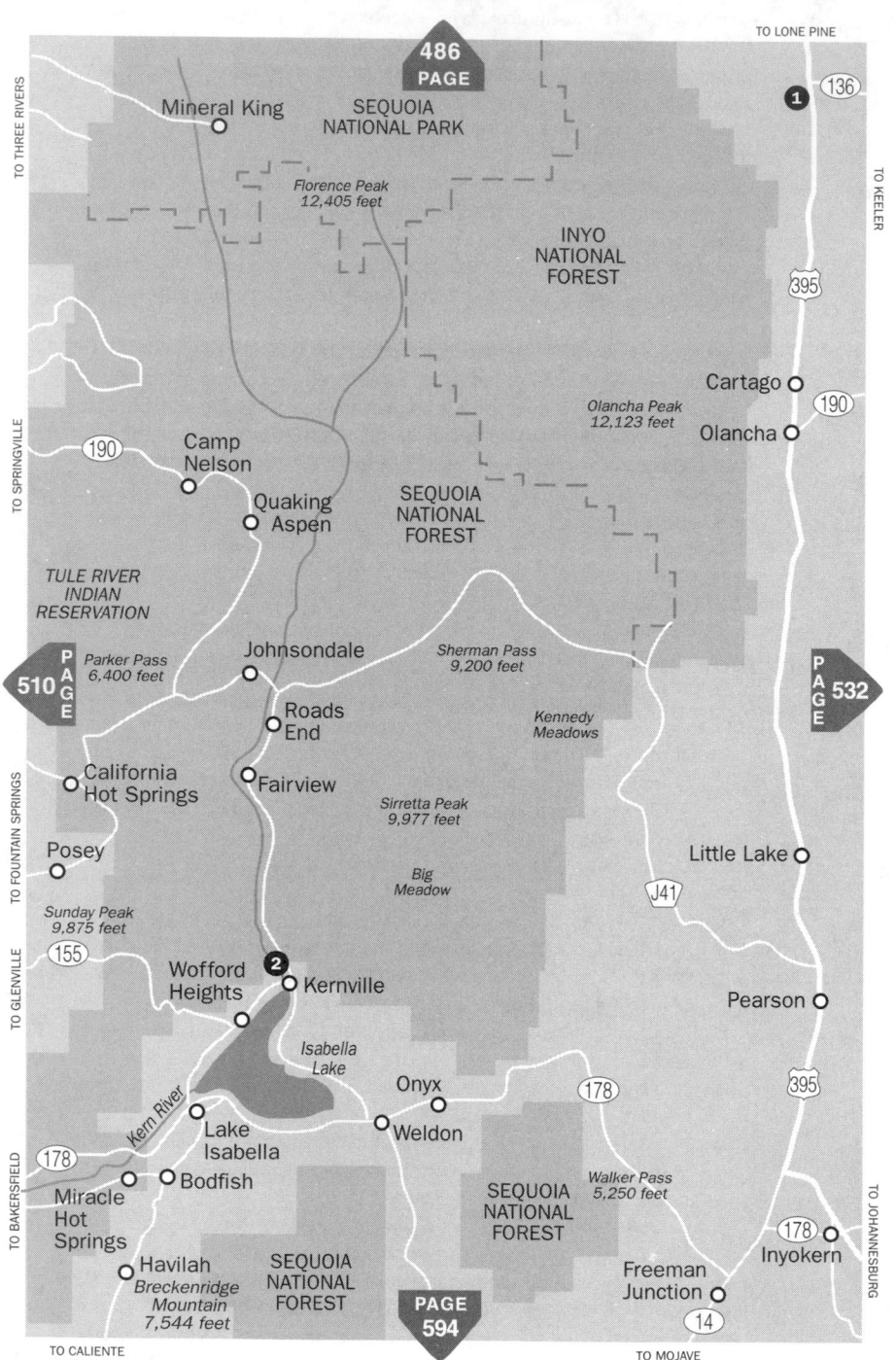

TO LONE PINE

TO THREE RIVERS

TO KEELER

TO SPRINGVILLE

TO FOUNTAIN SPRINGS

TO GLENVILLE

TO BAKERSFIELD

TO JOHANNESBURG

TO CALIENTE

TO MOJAVE

PAGE 486

Mineral King

SEQUOIA
NATIONAL PARK

Florence Peak
12,405 feet

INYO
NATIONAL
FOREST

1 · 136

Cartago

190

Olancha

Olancha Peak
12,123 feet

Camp
Nelson

190

Quaking
Aspen

SEQUOIA
NATIONAL
FOREST

395

TULE RIVER
INDIAN
RESERVATION

Johnsondale

Sherman Pass
9,200 feet

Kennedy
Meadows

PAGE 510

Parker Pass
6,400 feet

PAGE 532

Roads
End

California
Hot Springs

Fairview

Sirretta Peak
9,977 feet

Little Lake

Posey

Big
Meadow

J41

Sunday Peak
9,875 feet

155

Wofford
Heights

2 Kernville

Pearson

395

Isabella
Lake

Onyx

178

Kern River

Lake
Isabella

Weldon

Miracle
Hot
Springs

178

Bodfish

Walker Pass
5,250 feet

SEQUOIA
NATIONAL
FOREST

178

Inyokern

Havilah

Breckenridge
Mountain
7,544 feet

SEQUOIA
NATIONAL
FOREST

PAGE 594

Freeman
Junction

14

528

Kernville Area

❶ MOUNT WHITNEY GOLF COURSE
ARCHITECT: BOB BALDOCK, 1958

P.O. Box O
Lone Pine, CA 93545

1225 South Pine Road
Lone Pine, CA 93545

PRO SHOP: 760-876-5795

Brad Taylor, Head Professional
Brad Taylor, Superintendent

Driving Range ●
Practice Greens ●
Clubhouse ●
Food / Beverage ●
Accommodations
Pull Carts ●
Power Carts ●
Club Rental ●
$pecial Offers

	1	2	3	4	5	6	7	8	9	OUT
BACK										
REGULAR										
par										
handicap										
FORWARD										
par										
handicap										

	10	11	12	13	14	15	16	17	18	IN
BACK										
REGULAR										
par										
handicap										
FORWARD										
par										
handicap										

BACK	
yardage	6624
par	72
rating	70.1
slope	116

REGULAR	
yardage	6376
par	72
rating	69.3
slope	114

FORWARD	
yardage	5692
par	72
rating	71.0
slope	112

❷ KERN VALLEY COUNTRY CLUB
ARCHITECT: JACK E WING, 1957

P.O. Box 888
Kernville, CA 93238

9472 Burlando Road
Kernville, CA 93238

PRO SHOP: 760-376-2828

Mike Blanco, PGA Professional
Don Brown, Superintendent

Driving Range ●
Practice Greens ●
Clubhouse ●
Food / Beverage ●
Accommodations
Pull Carts ●
Power Carts ●
Club Rental ●
$pecial Offers

	1	2	3	4	5	6	7	8	9	OUT
BACK	-	-	-	-	-	-	-	-	-	-
REGULAR	379	295	200	494	362	325	163	423	543	3184
par	4	4	3	5	4	4	3	4	5	36
handicap	5	17	3	11	9	15	13	1	7	-
FORWARD	351	266	196	441	351	288	145	414	475	2927
par	4	4	3	5	4	4	3	5	5	37
handicap	2	15	9	5	7	11	17	13	3	-

	10	11	12	13	14	15	16	17	18	IN
BACK	-	-	-	-	-	-	-	-	-	-
REGULAR	397	259	194	485	356	315	144	411	510	3071
par	4	4	3	5	4	4	3	4	5	36
handicap	2	18	6	12	10	16	14	4	8	-
FORWARD	359	258	190	435	325	276	138	405	469	2855
par	4	4	3	5	4	4	3	5	5	37
handicap	1	16	10	6	8	12	18	14	4	-

BACK	
yardage	-
par	-
rating	-
slope	-

REGULAR	
yardage	6255
par	72
rating	68.0
slope	106

FORWARD	
yardage	5782
par	74
rating	
slope	116

PLAY POLICY & FEES: Green fees are $13 for nine holes and $17 for 18 holes weekdays, and $15 for nine holes and $21 for 18 holes weekends and holidays. Carts are $12 for nine holes and $18 for 18 holes. The course is closed Thanksgiving and Christmas.

TEE TIMES: Reservations can be booked seven days in advance.

COURSE DESCRIPTION: This scenic course is situated in the foothills of Mount Whitney. It's flat, with some water, bunkers, trees, and narrow fairways. Accurate iron play is essential.

NOTES: The course record is 64, held by Mike Sullivan.

LOCATION: Drive north on U.S. 395 to Lone Pine. The course is located on the left.

. . . ● **TOURNAMENTS:** This course is available for outside tournaments.

1. MOUNT WHITNEY GOLF COURSE

PLAY POLICY & FEES: Green fees are $10 for nine holes and $16 for 18 holes weekdays, and $14 for nine holes and $23 for 18 holes weekends. Call for special rates. Carts are $12 for nine holes and $20 for 18 holes.

TEE TIMES: Reservations can be booked three days in advance.

DRESS CODE: Proper golf attire is encouraged, and nonmetal spikes are required.

COURSE DESCRIPTION: Kern Valley is a well-maintained, fairly flat, short course. Many trees line the narrow fairways, demanding accuracy off the tees and a good short game.

NOTES: The course record is 64, held by Bob Salyer.

LOCATION: From Bakersfield travel northeast on Highway 178 for 50 miles. The course is located one-half mile south of Kernville on Highway 155.

. . . ● **TOURNAMENTS:** A 24-player minimum is required to book a tournament. The banquet facility can accommodate 100 people. ● **TRAVEL:** The Whispering Pines Bed and Breakfast is located five minutes from the course. For reservations call 760-376-3733.

2. KERN VALLEY COUNTRY CLUB

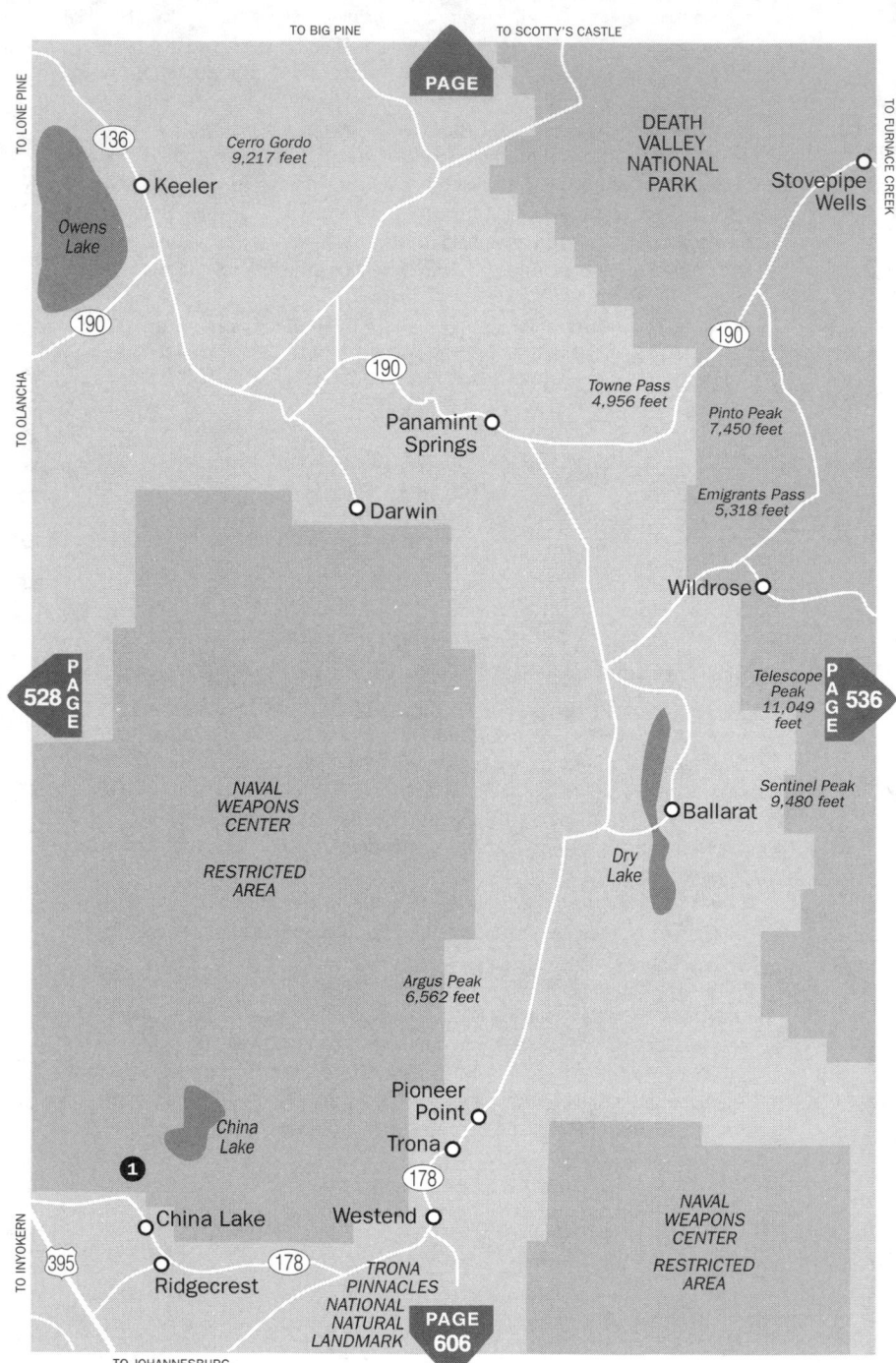

TO BIG PINE   TO SCOTTY'S CASTLE

PAGE

TO LONE PINE

(136)

Cerro Gordo
9,217 feet

O Keeler

DEATH
VALLEY
NATIONAL
PARK

Stovepipe
Wells

TO FURNACE CREEK

Owens
Lake

(190)

TO OLANCHA

(190)

(190)

Panamint
Springs

Towne Pass
4,956 feet

Pinto Peak
7,450 feet

O Darwin

Emigrants Pass
5,318 feet

Wildrose O

528 PAGE

PAGE 536

Telescope
Peak
11,049
feet

NAVAL
WEAPONS
CENTER

RESTRICTED
AREA

Sentinel Peak
9,480 feet

O Ballarat

Dry
Lake

Argus Peak
6,562 feet

China
Lake

Pioneer
Point O

Trona O

(178)

1

China Lake O

Westend O

NAVAL
WEAPONS
CENTER

RESTRICTED
AREA

TO INYOKERN

(395)

(178)

Ridgecrest O

TRONA
PINNACLES
NATIONAL
NATURAL
LANDMARK

PAGE 606

TO JOHANNESBURG

China Lake Area

CHINA LAKE GOLF COURSE
ARCHITECT: GEORGE BELL, 1957

P.O. Box 507
Ridgecrest, CA 93555

411 Midway Drive
Ridgecrest, CA 93555

PRO SHOP: 760-939-2990

Robert Booker, PGA Professional

Driving Range ●
Practice Greens ●
Clubhouse ●
Food / Beverage ●
Accommodations
Pull Carts ●
Power Carts ●
Club Rental ●
$pecial Offers

	1	2	3	4	5	6	7	8	9	OUT
BACK	489	365	404	335	444	191	537	182	420	3367
REGULAR	461	347	388	322	434	168	518	151	411	3200
par	5	4	4	4	4	3	5	3	4	36
handicap	17	7	5	15	1	11	9	13	3	-
FORWARD	420	308	323	283	324	112	446	140	351	2707
par	5	4	4	4	4	3	5	3	4	36
handicap	8	10	12	14	6	18	2	16	4	-

	10	11	12	13	14	15	16	17	18	IN
BACK	548	235	398	412	431	347	398	175	539	3483
REGULAR	523	216	381	408	413	340	380	164	516	3341
par	5	3	4	4	4	4	4	3	5	36
handicap	8	6	12	4	2	16	10	14	18	-
FORWARD	462	153	313	285	342	330	319	161	434	2799
par	5	3	4	4	4	4	4	3	5	36
handicap	1	17	5	15	3	7	11	13	9	-

BACK	
yardage	6850
par	72
rating	72.5
slope	119

REGULAR	
yardage	6541
par	72
rating	70.7
slope	114

FORWARD	
yardage	5506
par	72
rating	71.2
slope	120

PLAY POLICY & FEES: Outside play is accepted. Green fees are $16 weekdays and $18 weekends for civilian guests. Other fees vary according to military status. Twilight rates are available. Carts are $16.

TEE TIMES: Reservations can be made on weekends and every other Friday. Military personnel can make tee times on Wednesday before the weekend. Civilians can make tee times starting on Thursday. All other days are on a first-come, first-served basis.

DRESS CODE: No tank tops are allowed on the course.

COURSE DESCRIPTION: This is a flat, desert course with lots of bunkers and trees. There are no water hazards. Beware of the 10th hole, a 548-yard par 5. It is an uphill, dogleg right with two fairway traps. The two-tiered green has made more than one military commander wave the white flag and surrender. China Lake hosts a men's and women's club championship each year.

NOTES: Drew Martin and John Hemond share the men's course record of 65, and Jane Nechero holds the women's record of 76.

LOCATION: From the town of Mojave travel north on Highway 14 for approximately 40 miles to Highway 178. Turn right and drive east for about 13 miles to the entrance of China Lake Naval Weapons Station. Obtain a pass at the gate and continue to the course on Midway Drive.

. . . ● **TOURNAMENTS:** This course is available for outside tournaments.

1. CHINA LAKE GOLF COURSE

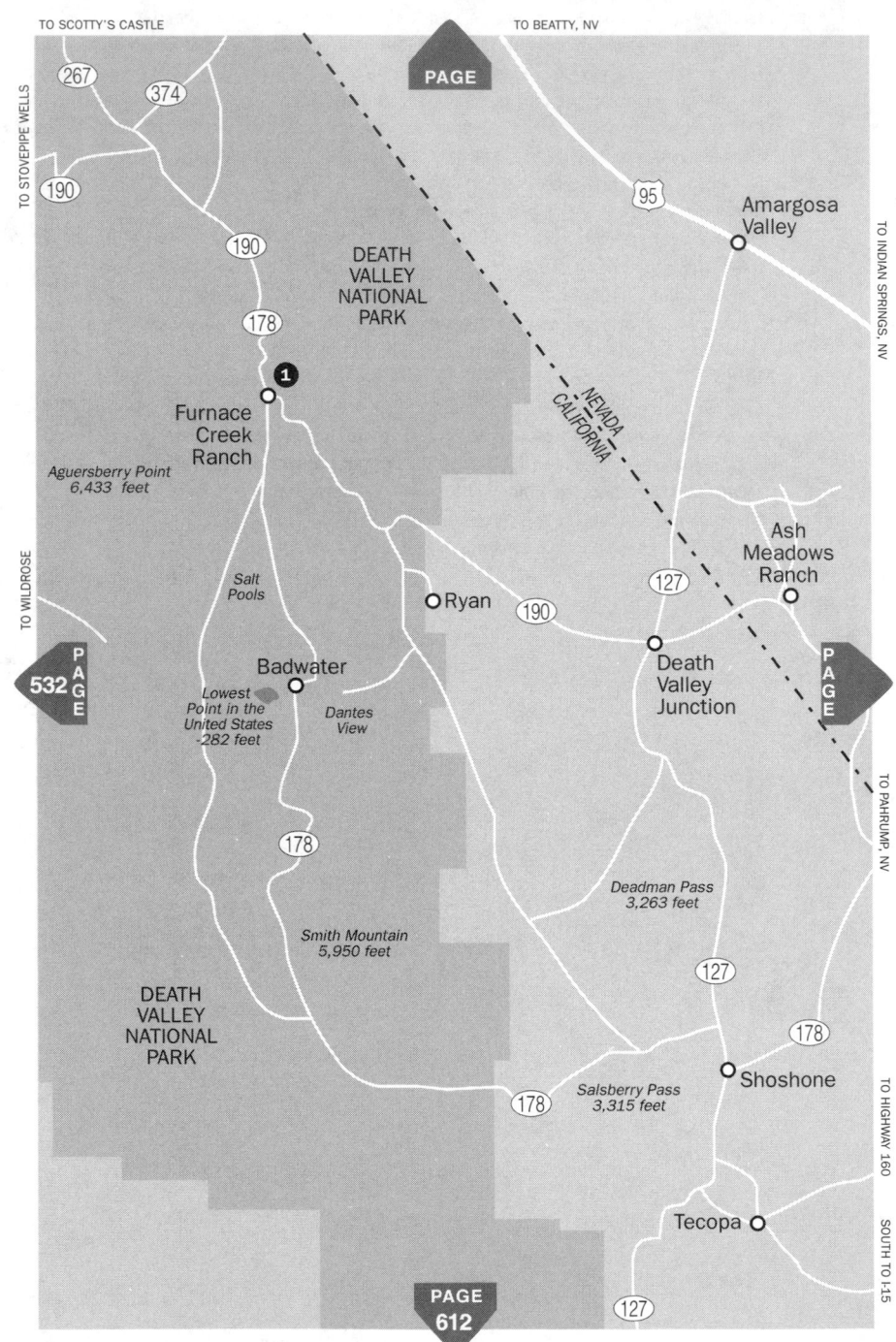

TO SCOTTY'S CASTLE

TO BEATTY, NV

PAGE

267

374

TO STOVEPIPE WELLS

190

190

178

DEATH
VALLEY
NATIONAL
PARK

95

Amargosa
Valley

TO INDIAN SPRINGS, NV

NEVADA
CALIFORNIA

1

Furnace
Creek
Ranch

Aguersberry Point
6,433 feet

TO WILDROSE

Salt
Pools

Ryan

190

127

Ash
Meadows
Ranch

Death
Valley
Junction

TO PAHRUMP, NV

Badwater

Lowest
Point in the
United States
-282 feet

Dantes
View

532 PAGE

PAGE

178

Smith Mountain
5,950 feet

DEATH
VALLEY
NATIONAL
PARK

Deadman Pass
3,263 feet

127

178

Shoshone

TO HIGHWAY 160

178

Salsberry Pass
3,315 feet

Tecopa

SOUTH TO I-15

PAGE
612

127

Death Valley Area

FURNACE CREEK GOLF COURSE

ARCHITECTS: WILLIAM P. BELL, 1939; WILLIAM F. BELL, 1969; PERRY DYE, 1997

GOLF 50

P.O. Box 187
Death Valley, CA 92328

Highway 190
Death Valley, CA 92328

PRO SHOP: 760-786-2301
OFFICE: 760-786-2345

Rick Heitzig, Director of Golf, PGA
Dave Parkinson, Superintendent

Driving Range ●
Practice Greens ●
Clubhouse ●
Food / Beverage ●
Accommodations ●
Pull Carts ●
Power Carts ●
Club Rental ●
$pecial Offers ●

	1	2	3	4	5	6	7	8	9	OUT
BACK	394	178	413	147	573	440	351	153	310	2959
REGULAR	388	144	404	137	542	421	307	145	302	2790
par	4	3	4	3	5	4	4	3	4	34
handicap	7	11	5	17	3	1	9	15	13	-
FORWARD	339	102	309	116	445	350	230	99	241	2231
par	4	3	4	3	5	4	4	3	4	34
handicap	7	11	5	17	3	1	9	15	13	-

	10	11	12	13	14	15	16	17	18	IN
BACK	571	435	329	334	226	304	333	310	414	3256
REGULAR	512	424	324	313	188	297	299	301	408	3066
par	5	4	4	4	3	4	4	4	4	36
handicap	4	2	16	18	8	10	12	14	6	-
FORWARD	476	322	302	236	118	239	228	247	325	2493
par	5	4	4	4	3	4	4	4	4	36
handicap	4	2	16	18	8	10	12	14	6	-

BACK	
yardage	6215
par	70
rating	69.6
slope	114

REGULAR	
yardage	5856
par	70
rating	67.8
slope	111

FORWARD	
yardage	4724
par	70
rating	66.0
slope	109

PLAY POLICY & FEES: Outside play is accepted. Green fees are $25 for nine holes and $45 for 18 holes. Carts are $10 for nine holes and $20 for 18 holes. Reduced rates are available in the summer. The course is now open year-round.

TEE TIMES: Tee times can be booked six months in advance.

DRESS CODE: No sleeveless shirts or cut-off shorts are allowed on the course.

COURSE DESCRIPTION: Perry Dye recently completed a redesign of the course. Wildlife, ranging from coyotes to Canadian geese, abounds on this desert course. From the 12th hole there is a spectacular view of the towering Panamint Mountains. The hardest hole at Furnace Creek is the sixth, a 440-yard par 4 that requires you carry over water off the tee to reach the fairway.

NOTES: At 214 feet below sea level, this is the world's lowest golf course.

LOCATION: This course is located in Death Valley National Park on California State Highway 190.

. . . ● **TOURNAMENTS:** A 20-player minimum is needed to book an event. Tournaments should be scheduled three months in advance. The banquet facility can accommodate up to 100 people. ● **TRAVEL:** For reservations at the Furnace Creek Inn and Ranch Resort call 760-786-2345. ● **$PECIAL OFFERS:** Stay-and-play packages are available. Prices vary depending on whether you stay at the Ranch or the Inn.

1. FURNACE CREEK GOLF COURSE

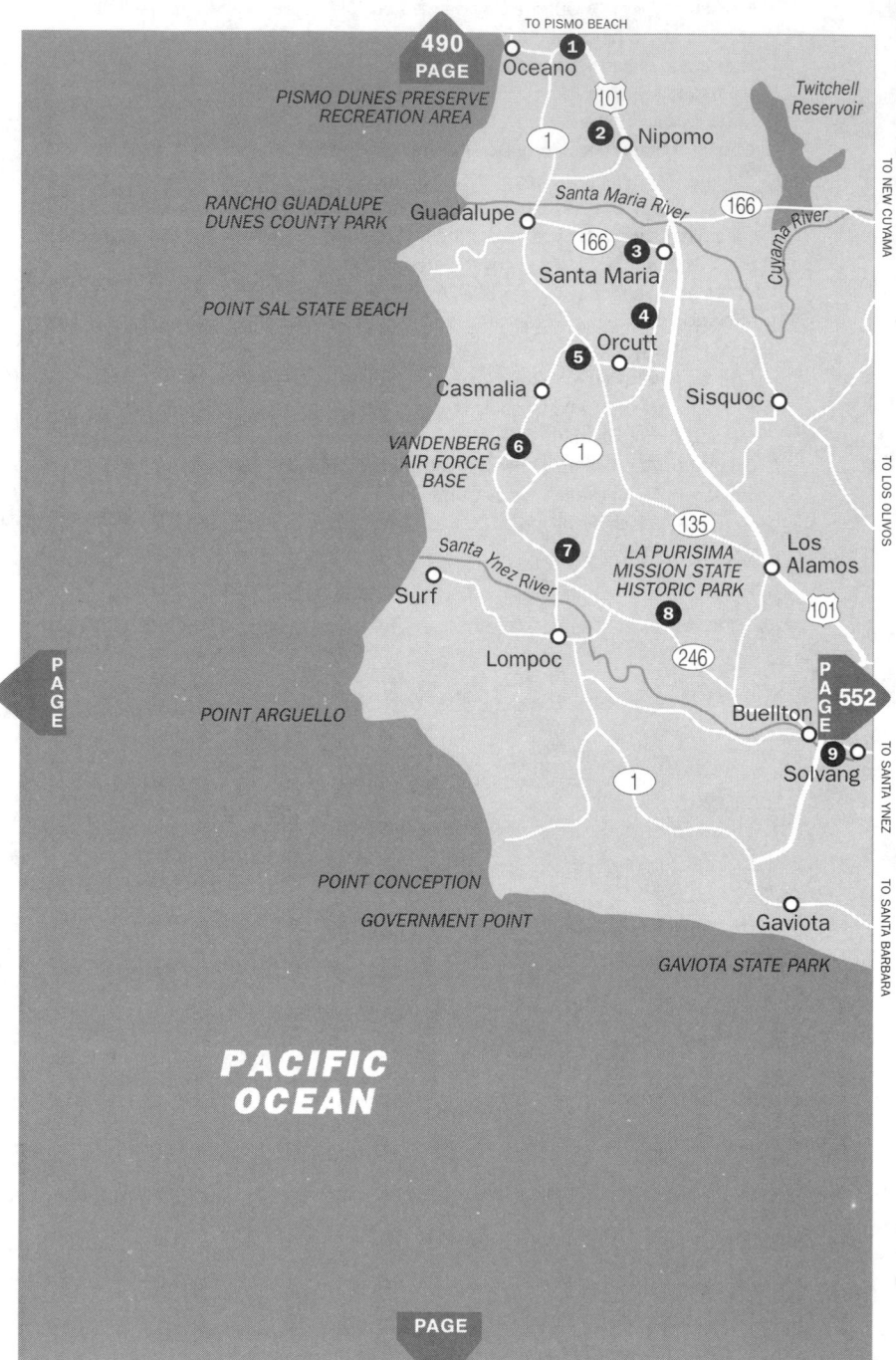

TO PISMO BEACH

490 PAGE

Oceano **1**

PISMO DUNES PRESERVE RECREATION AREA

Twitchell Reservoir

101

2 Nipomo

1

Santa Maria River

RANCHO GUADALUPE DUNES COUNTY PARK

Guadalupe

166

166 **3**

TO NEW CUYAMA

Cuyama River

Santa Maria

POINT SAL STATE BEACH

4

Orcutt

5

Casmalia

Sisquoc

VANDENBERG AIR FORCE BASE

6

1

135

7

Santa Ynez River

LA PURISIMA MISSION STATE HISTORIC PARK

Los Alamos

TO LOS OLIVOS

8

Surf

101

Lompoc

246

PAGE

PAGE 552

Buellton

POINT ARGUELLO

9

Solvang

TO SANTA YNEZ

1

POINT CONCEPTION

GOVERNMENT POINT

Gaviota

TO SANTA BARBARA

GAVIOTA STATE PARK

PACIFIC OCEAN

PAGE

Santa Maria/Solvang Area

CYPRESS RIDGE

ARCHITECTS: PETER JACOBSEN, 1999; JACOBSON/HARDY DESIGN

P.O. Box 179
Arroyo Grande, CA 93421

780 Cypress Ridge Parkway
Arryo Grande, CA 93420

PRO SHOP: 805-474-7979

Bonnie Lauer, General Manager, LPGA
Rick Ventura, Head Professional, PGA

Driving Range ●
Practice Greens ●
Clubhouse ●
Food / Beverage ●
Accommodations
Pull Carts
Power Carts ●
Club Rental
$pecial Offers

	1	2	3	4	5	6	7	8	9	OUT
BACK	430	216	534	154	330	436	300	432	524	3356
REGULAR	415	194	516	129	300	419	288	412	502	3175
par	4	3	5	3	4	4	4	4	5	36
handicap	3	9	5	17	15	7	13	1	11	-
FORWARD	323	139	422	88	244	324	233	336	411	2520
par	4	3	5	3	4	4	4	4	5	36
handicap	7	15	1	17	13	9	11	3	5	-

	10	11	12	13	14	15	16	17	18	IN
BACK	407	194	424	551	389	365	418	201	498	3447
REGULAR	384	171	411	531	368	344	400	184	475	3268
par	4	3	4	5	4	4	4	3	5	36
handicap	8	12	4	10	6	14	2	18	16	-
FORWARD	313	94	315	460	279	235	329	151	391	2567
par	4	3	4	5	4	4	4	3	5	36
handicap	10	16	8	2	12	14	4	18	6	-

BACK	
yardage	6803
par	72
rating	73.0
slope	133

REGULAR	
yardage	6443
par	72
rating	71.3
slope	129

FORWARD	
yardage	5087
par	72
rating	70.3
slope	120

BLACKLAKE GOLF RESORT

ARCHITECTS: TED ROBINSON, 1965; GARRET AND GILL, 1996

1490 Golf Course Lane
Nipomo, CA 93444

PRO SHOP: 805-343-1214
OFFICE: 805-481-4204

Norwood Eben, Manager
Tom Elliot, Superintendent
Barbara Oliver, Tournament Director

Driving Range ●
Practice Greens ●
Clubhouse ●
Food / Beverage ●
Accommodations
Pull Carts ●
Power Carts ●
Club Rental ●
$pecial Offers ●

	1	2	3	4	5	6	7	8	9	OUT
BACK	143	397	343	396	404	528	328	164	573	3276
REGULAR	125	358	323	378	396	518	314	136	527	3075
par	3	4	4	4	4	5	4	3	5	36
handicap	17	11	9	3	5	7	15	13	1	-
FORWARD	102	343	307	359	382	500	295	111	472	2871
par	3	4	4	4	4	5	4	3	5	36
handicap	17	11	9	7	5	3	13	15	1	-

	10	11	12	13	14	15	16	17	18	IN
BACK	380	505	367	442	173	407	335	158	358	3125
REGULAR	365	491	350	435	148	393	315	144	340	2981
par	4	5	4	5	3	4	4	3	4	36
handicap	6	4	10	12	14	2	16	18	8	-
FORWARD	346	445	332	420	122	374	302	121	295	2757
par	4	5	4	5	3	4	4	3	4	36
handicap	8	2	10	6	18	4	14	16	12	-

BACK	
yardage	6401
par	72
rating	70.9
slope	123

REGULAR	
yardage	6056
par	72
rating	69.2
slope	118

FORWARD	
yardage	5628
par	72
rating	72.9
slope	126

PLAY POLICY & FEES: Green fees are $45 Monday through Thursday, and $55 Friday through Sunday and holidays. Twilight green fees are $30 Monday through Thursday, and $40 Friday through Sunday. Carts are $12 per person.

TEE TIMES: Reservations can be made 10 days in advance.

DRESS CODE: Appropriate golf attire and nonmetal spikes are mandatory.

COURSE DESCRIPTION: Cypress Ridge is a links-style course with excellent ocean views. The course runs winds through 100-year-old cypress trees, giving you the feeling the course has been around for decades. Off-the-tee landing areas are ample, although fairly deep fairway bunkers come into play. If you miss the fairway, you will be playing out of thick native grass or possibly out of bounds. The greens are smallish with subtle slopes. All but two holes have bunkers, but players still have the opportunity to use a variety of shots around the green, including putting.

NOTES: Cypress Ridge has the distinction of being the 14th Audubon International Signature Sanctuary in the world.

LOCATION: Going south on U.S. 101 in San Luis Obispo, take El Campo exit. Stay on El Campo until you cross Los Berros Road. The next intersection will be Halcyon. Turn left; the course will be 400 yards on the right.

. . . ● **TOURNAMENTS:** A 24-player minimum is needed to book an event.

1. CYPRESS RIDGE

PLAY POLICY & FEES: Green fees are $30 Monday through Friday. Carts are $12. Green fees are $62 on weekends, cart included. Local resident, twilight, supertwilight and nine-hole rates are available. Call for special rates.

TEE TIMES: Reservations can be booked seven days in advance.

DRESS CODE: Appropriate golf attire is required.

COURSE DESCRIPTION: These well-designed courses offer tree-lined fairways, several lakes, and a rolling terrain. Among the holes to watch for is the par-5 second hole (Canyon Course), 506 yards with a narrow fairway, left lateral water hazard, and bunkered right side.

NOTES: The three nines are named the Lakes, Canyon, and Oaks Courses. The Oaks Course is 2,909 yards from the championship tees. See scorecard for information on the Lakes/Canyon Course.

LOCATION: Travel north on U.S. 101 from Los Angeles past Santa Maria to the Tefft Street exit in Nipomo. Turn left over the highway to Pomeroy. Turn left to Willow and right to the golf course.

. . . ● **TOURNAMENTS:** A 20-player minimum is needed to book a tournament. Events can be scheduled up to 12 months in advance. The banquet facility can accommodate up to 300 people. ● **TRAVEL:** The Santa Maria Hilton is located 15 minutes from the golf course. For reservations call 805-928-8000. ● **$PECIAL OFFERS:** Play-and-stay packages are available with the Santa Maria Hilton and several other hotels in the area. Call the pro shop for more information.

2. BLACKLAKE GOLF RESORT

❸ SUNSET RIDGE GOLF COURSE
ARCHITECT: LARRY POPOFF, 1994

1424 Fairway Drive
Santa Maria, CA 93455

PRO SHOP: 805-347-1070

Brad Fleisch, PGA Professional

Driving Range •
Practice Greens •
Clubhouse •
Food / Beverage •
Accommodations
Pull Carts •
Power Carts •
Club Rental •
$pecial Offers

	1	2	3	4	5	6	7	8	9	OUT
BACK	-	-	-	-	-	-	-	-	-	-
REGULAR	143	166	130	313	88	188	170	162	166	1526
par	3	3	3	4	3	3	3	3	3	28
handicap	13	11	15	1	17	3	9	7	5	-
FORWARD	-	-	-	-	-	-	-	-	-	
par	-	-	-	-	-	-	-	-	-	
handicap	-	-	-	-	-	-	-	-	-	-

BACK	
yardage	-
par	-
rating	-
slope	-

	10	11	12	13	14	15	16	17	18	IN
BACK	-	-	-	-	-	-	-	-	-	-
REGULAR	143	166	130	313	88	188	170	162	166	1526
par	3	3	4	3	3	3	3	3	3	28
handicap	14	12	16	2	18	4	10	8	6	-
FORWARD	-	-	-	-	-	-	-	-	-	
par	-	-	-	-	-	-	-	-	-	
handicap	-	-	-	-	-	-	-	-	-	-

REGULAR	
yardage	3052
par	56
rating	56.1
slope	84

FORWARD	
yardage	
par	
rating	-
slope	-

❹ SANTA MARIA COUNTRY CLUB

505 West Waller Lane
Santa Maria, CA 93455

PRO SHOP: 805-937-7872
CLUBHOUSE: 805-937-2025

Ken White, Head Professional

Driving Range •
Practice Greens •
Clubhouse •
Food / Beverage •
Accommodations
Pull Carts •
Power Carts •
Club Rental
$pecial Offers

	1	2	3	4	5	6	7	8	9	OUT
BACK	492	349	184	378	426	363	216	535	474	3417
REGULAR	483	335	180	367	406	330	194	526	471	3292
par	5	4	3	4	4	4	3	5	5	37
handicap	17	11	9	5	1	3	13	7	15	-
FORWARD	468	314	176	351	345	276	172	458	463	3023
par	5	4	3	4	4	4	3	5	5	37
handicap	1	11	15	9	5	13	17	7	3	-

BACK	
yardage	6495
par	72
rating	71.8
slope	129

	10	11	12	13	14	15	16	17	18	IN
BACK	423	509	337	115	380	372	185	353	404	3078
REGULAR	416	490	331	111	359	361	182	340	388	2978
par	4	5	4	3	4	4	3	4	4	35
handicap	4	2	14	18	10	8	12	16	6	-
FORWARD	406	473	326	105	335	350	179	333	377	2884
par	4	5	4	3	4	4	3	4	4	35
handicap	2	4	12	18	10	8	16	14	6	-

REGULAR	
yardage	6270
par	72
rating	70.0
slope	122

FORWARD	
yardage	5907
par	72
rating	74.3
slope	127

9
HOLES

PLAY POLICY & FEES: Green fees are $7 for nine holes and $10 for 18 holes on weekdays. Green fees on weekends and holidays are $8 for nine holes and $12 for 18 holes. Senior and junior rates are $5 for nine holes and $8 for 18 holes on weekdays and $7 for nine holes and $10 for 18 holes on weekends. A twilight rate of $5 begins at 5 p.m. Carts are $7 for nine holes.

TEE TIMES: Reservations can be made the day of play.

COURSE DESCRIPTION: This is a par-3 executive course with one par 4. Five of the par 3s are over 160 yards.

LOCATION: From U.S.101 in Santa Maria take the Betteravia exit and head west to Skyway Drive. Turn left on Skyway Drive. Take Skyway Drive to Fairway Drive, turn right, and go to the end of the street. Sunset Ridge is on the left.

. . . ● **TOURNAMENTS:** This course is available for outside tournaments. A 12-player minimum is needed to book an event. Tournaments should be booked 12 months in advance. The banquet facility can accommodate 50 people.

3. SUNSET RIDGE GOLF COURSE

18
HOLES

PLAY POLICY & FEES: Reciprocal play is accepted with members of other private clubs. Otherwise, members and guests only. Reciprocal green fees are $75. Guest fees are $35 weekdays and $50 weekends. Carts are $12 per rider. The course is closed on Monday.

DRESS CODE: Collared shirts and nonmetal spikes are required.

COURSE DESCRIPTION: This is a fairly level course, but don't let that fool you. It is heavily wooded, and more than one golfer has claimed to have lost a ball to a hungry chipmunk. The original nine holes were built in the 1920s, and the second nine holes were added in the 1950s.

LOCATION: Travel south of Santa Maria on U.S. 101 to the Betteravia exit. Turn west and drive to Broadway, then south to Waller Lane. From there go right to the club.

. . . ● **TOURNAMENTS:** Outside events are available on Monday only and must be board approved.

4. SANTA MARIA COUNTRY CLUB

5 RANCHO MARIA GOLF COURSE
ARCHITECT: BOB BALDOCK, 1965

1950 Casmalia Road
Santa Maria, CA 93455

PRO SHOP: 805-937-2019

Jack O'Keefe, PGA Professional
Dennis Brown, Superintendent

Driving Range ●
Practice Greens ●
Clubhouse ●
Food / Beverage ●
Accommodations
Pull Carts ●
Power Carts ●
Club Rental ●
$pecial Offers

	1	2	3	4	5	6	7	8	9	OUT
BACK	341	533	164	374	347	205	513	307	176	2960
REGULAR	329	498	155	363	338	197	499	297	158	2834
par	4	5	3	4	4	3	5	4	3	35
handicap	13	7	15	1	9	5	3	17	11	-
FORWARD	301	461	138	247	320	181	476	276	130	2530
par	4	5	3	4	4	3	5	4	3	35
handicap	11	3	15	13	5	9	1	7	17	-

	10	11	12	13	14	15	16	17	18	IN
BACK	348	358	191	438	488	163	424	498	522	3430
REGULAR	338	347	181	432	471	151	408	473	513	3314
par	4	4	3	4	5	3	4	5	5	37
handicap	10	14	6	2	16	18	4	12	8	-
FORWARD	237	326	166	415	418	132	378	411	488	2971
par	4	4	3	5	5	3	4	5	5	38
handicap	16	8	14	12	10	18	2	6	4	-

BACK	
yardage	6390
par	72
rating	70.0
slope	119

REGULAR	
yardage	6148
par	72
rating	68.9
slope	114

FORWARD	
yardage	5501
par	73
rating	70.3
slope	123

6 MARSHALLA RANCH GOLF COURSE
ARCHITECT: ROBERT DEAN PUTMAN, 1965

P.O. Box 5938
Vandenberg AFB, CA
93437
PRO SHOP: 805-734-1333
STARTER: 805-734-1333

Rick Vigil, Director of Golf
Rick Young, Superintendent

Driving Range ●
Practice Greens ●
Clubhouse ●
Food / Beverage ●
Accommodations ●
Pull Carts ●
Power Carts ●
Club Rental ●
$pecial Offers

	1	2	3	4	5	6	7	8	9	OUT
BACK	406	387	160	569	386	375	194	367	434	3278
REGULAR	385	366	140	526	351	361	174	332	403	3038
par	4	4	3	5	4	4	3	4	4	35
handicap	1	9	17	13	11	5	15	7	3	-
FORWARD	308	360	130	436	343	251	169	302	317	2616
par	4	4	3	5	4	4	3	4	4	35
handicap	9	3	17	5	1	15	13	11	7	-

	10	11	12	13	14	15	16	17	18	IN
BACK	366	359	489	217	436	586	416	206	492	3567
REGULAR	348	346	447	181	415	571	402	190	450	3350
par	4	4	5	3	4	5	4	3	5	37
handicap	10	8	18	12	4	6	2	14	16	-
FORWARD	245	304	345	171	315	465	379	181	383	2788
par	4	4	4	3	4	5	5	3	5	37
handicap	12	10	4	6	18	2	8	14	16	-

BACK	
yardage	6845
par	72
rating	74.1
slope	130

REGULAR	
yardage	6388
par	72
rating	71.1
slope	122

FORWARD	
yardage	5404
par	72
rating	72.5
slope	124

5. RANCHO MARIA GOLF COURSE

PLAY POLICY & FEES: Green fees are $22 weekdays and $28 weekends. Senior and twilight fees are available. Carts are $18.

TEE TIMES: Reservations can be booked seven days in advance.

COURSE DESCRIPTION: This course is located in the foothills southwest of Santa Maria. There are no parallel fairways, and the rolling greens can be very fast. Watch for the 13th hole in the afternoon. This par-4, 438-yard hole is dangerous in a confronting wind. The green, which slopes to the right, is also well bunkered on that side.

NOTES: The course record is 60, held by John McComish.

LOCATION: Take the Orcutt/Clark Avenue exit off U.S.101 in Santa Maria and drive west on Clark Avenue for 2.5 miles to Highway 1. Turn right and drive two miles to the course.

. . . ● **TOURNAMENTS:** A 24-player minimum is required to book a tournament.Tournaments should be booked six to twelve months in advance.

● **TRAVEL:** Holiday Inn (805-928-6000) and the Airport Hilton (805-928-8000) are recommended for lodging.

6. MARSHALLA RANCH GOLF COURSE

PLAY POLICY & FEES: Public play is allowed on a limited basis. Members' green fees range from $10 to $30, depending on military personnel status. Civilian green fees are $45 every day. Twilight rates for civilians are $23 every day. Carts are $16 for 18 holes. The course is closed on Monday.

TEE TIMES: Civilian play is on a space-available basis. No reservations are accepted.

DRESS CODE: No tank tops or short shorts are allowed.

COURSE DESCRIPTION: Set three miles from the ocean, this tight and heavily wooded course becomes increasingly difficult as the prevailing winds pick up. Each hole is separated by dense stands of trees. The course is fairly flat and walkable. The 9th and 16th holes are rated among the best in Santa Barbara County. The ninth is a par 4 through a chute to a narrow landing area and onto a green guarded by two large bunkers and surrounded by ice plant. The 16th is a par 4 straight uphill and into the wind. For most golfers it's unreachable in two. Morning and evening fog can cut short a day's play.

NOTES: The course record is 67, set by Rex Coldwell.

LOCATION: Follow U.S. 101 north to Highway 1 and take the Lompoc-Vandenberg exit (just beyond Gaviota coming from the south) north to Vandenberg AFB. Drive past the main gate about four miles to the exit for Marshalla Ranch. Go left to the course.

. . . ● **TOURNAMENTS:** This course is available for outside tournaments.

7 VILLAGE COUNTRY CLUB
ARCHITECT: TED ROBINSON, 1964

4300 Clubhouse Road
Lompoc, CA 93436

PRO SHOP: 805-733-3537
CLUBHOUSE: 805-733-3535

Dan Unrue, Head Professional, PGA
Bob Taeger, Superintendent
Tony Sable, Assistant Professional

Driving Range ●
Practice Greens ●
Clubhouse ●
Food / Beverage ●
Accommodations
Pull Carts ●
Power Carts ●
Club Rental ●
$pecial Offers

	1	2	3	4	5	6	7	8	9	OUT
BACK	343	171	504	417	520	368	204	411	371	3309
REGULAR	332	154	481	391	484	356	197	406	361	3162
par	4	3	5	4	5	4	3	4	4	36
handicap	11	17	7	1	13	15	9	3	5	-
FORWARD	310	134	371	323	437	351	120	312	288	2646
par	4	3	5	4	5	4	3	4	4	36
handicap	9	15	1	13	5	11	17	3	7	-

	10	11	12	13	14	15	16	17	18	IN
BACK	352	364	384	165	513	370	538	188	381	3255
REGULAR	343	358	371	155	493	355	517	141	374	3107
par	4	4	4	3	5	4	5	3	4	36
handicap	10	4	2	18	14	8	12	16	6	-
FORWARD	305	280	297	139	434	286	379	128	297	2545
par	4	4	4	3	5	4	5	3	4	36
handicap	8	4	2	18	10	12	6	16	14	-

BACK	
yardage	6564
par	72
rating	71.5
slope	126

REGULAR	
yardage	6269
par	72
rating	69.6
slope	118

FORWARD	
yardage	5191
par	72
rating	64.0
slope	104

8 LA PURISIMA GOLF COURSE
ARCHITECT: ROBERT MUIR GRAVES, 1986

GOLF 50

3455 State Highway 246
Lompoc, CA 93436

PRO SHOP: 805-735-8395

Michael McGinnis, Director of Golf, PGA
Paul Casas, Superintendent

Driving Range ●
Practice Greens ●
Clubhouse ●
Food / Beverage ●
Accommodations
Pull Carts ●
Power Carts ●
Club Rental ●
$pecial Offers

	1	2	3	4	5	6	7	8	9	OUT
BACK	542	432	158	340	433	566	427	437	227	3562
REGULAR	529	403	130	321	400	527	400	405	201	3316
par	5	4	3	4	4	5	4	4	3	36
handicap	9	3	17	13	1	7	5	11	15	-
FORWARD	447	337	98	274	344	457	353	353	165	2828
par	5	4	3	4	4	5	4	4	3	36
handicap	5	7	17	11	9	1	3	13	15	-

	10	11	12	13	14	15	16	17	18	IN
BACK	465	389	609	169	366	532	436	167	410	3543
REGULAR	438	371	587	149	366	503	395	145	387	3341
par	4	4	5	3	4	5	4	3	4	36
handicap	4	16	2	18	10	6	8	14	12	-
FORWARD	365	329	558	123	304	458	340	118	340	2935
par	4	4	5	3	4	5	4	3	4	36
handicap	10	16	4	18	12	6	8	14	2	-

BACK	
yardage	7105
par	72
rating	75.4
slope	142

REGULAR	
yardage	6657
par	72
rating	72.8
slope	132

FORWARD	
yardage	5763
par	72
rating	74.3
slope	131

PLAY POLICY & FEES: Reciprocal play is accepted with members of other private clubs. The fees for reciprocators are $35 weekdays and $60 weekends. Carts are $22.

DRESS CODE: Appropriate golf attire is required.

COURSE DESCRIPTION: Gently rolling terrain and fairways lined with mature pine and oak trees mark this interesting course. Driving accuracy is rewarded. The par-4 and par-5 holes are doglegs. The greens are mostly contoured and can be challenging. The par-4 15th is a tough water-hazard hole. Water is on the left within the landing zone. If you stray too far to the right, you're in the creek. Your second shot should be 130 to 140 yards uphill to a two-tiered green. Pin placement makes all the difference here. The green is fast and will hold if you find the top tier. If you find the lower tier, your ball will roll back.

LOCATION: Travel north from Lompoc on Harris Grade Road to Burton Mesa Boulevard and turn left. At Clubhouse Road, turn right and drive three-quarters of a mile to the club.

. . . ● **TOURNAMENTS:** Shotgun starts must have permission of the Golf Committee. An 18-player minimum is needed to book a tournament.

7. VILLAGE COUNTRY CLUB

PLAY POLICY & FEES: Green fees are $50 from Monday through Thursday and $60 from Friday through Sunday. Twilight fees after 2 p.m. are $30 weekdays and $40 weekends. Carts are $24 before 2 p.m. and $15 after 2 p.m.

TEE TIMES: Reservations can be booked seven days in advance.

DRESS CODE: Collared shirts are required.

COURSE DESCRIPTION: This is a highly rated public course. Overlooking Lompoc Valley, this scenic course meanders among the oak groves over rolling terrain. Three lakes come into play here, not to mention the wind, which can pick up in the afternoon.

NOTES: John McComish holds the course record with a 65. La Purisima hosted the 1996 PGA Tour final qualifying tournament and the 1998 and 1999 U.S. Open qualifier.

LOCATION: The course is 12 miles west of Buellton and four miles east of Lompoc on Highway 246.

. . . ● **TOURNAMENTS:** A 16-player minimum is required to book a tournament. Events can be scheduled two to 24 months in advance. The banquet facility can accommodate 100 people. ● **TRAVEL:** Anderson's Pea Soup, (805-688-3216), the Rancho Santa Barbara Marriott (805-688-1000) and the Royal Scandanavian (805-688-8000) are all recommended for lodging.

8. LA PURISIMA GOLF COURSE

⑨ ZACA CREEK GOLF COURSE

561 Amber Way
Solvang, CA 93427

223 Shadow Mountain
Buellton, CA 93463

PRO SHOP: 805-688-2575

Dennis Kleen, Professional/Manager

Driving Range ●
Practice Greens ●
Clubhouse
Food / Beverage ●
Accommodations
Pull Carts ●
Power Carts ●
Club Rental ●
$pecial Offers

	1	2	3	4	5	6	7	8	9	OUT
BACK	-	-	-	-	-	-	-	-	-	-
REGULAR	170	107	169	217	192	285	86	150	184	1560
par	3	3	3	4	3	4	3	3	3	29
handicap	5	15	7	17	1	9	13	11	3	-
FORWARD	170	107	169	217	192	269	86	150	184	1544
par	3	3	3	4	4	4	3	3	3	31
handicap	1	17	3	7	15	5	9	13	11	-

BACK	
yardage	-
par	-
rating	
slope	

REGULAR	
yardage	3090
par	58
rating	54.1
slope	

	10	11	12	13	14	15	16	17	18	IN
BACK	-	-	-	-	-	-	-	-	-	-
REGULAR	152	107	169	217	192	285	74	150	184	1530
par	3	3	3	4	3	4	3	3	3	29
handicap	6	16	8	18	2	10	14	12	4	-
FORWARD	152	90	169	217	164	207	74	108	184	1365
par	3	3	3	4	3	4	3	3	4	30
handicap	6	18	4	8	2	14	10	16	12	-

FORWARD	
yardage	2909
par	61
rating	56.5
slope	

PLAY POLICY & FEES: Green fees are $10 in the morning and $8.50 in the afternoon, weekdays. Fees are $11.50 mornings and $10 afternoons on weekends. Pull carts are $2.

TEE TIMES: Reservations are recommended.

COURSE DESCRIPTION: Nestled in the Santa Ynez Valley, this flat course offers seven par 3s and two par 4s that will test every club in your bag. The holes range from 90 to 285 yards. The men's record is 54.

LOCATION: Travel 37 miles northwest of Santa Barbara on U.S. 101 to the Highway 246 exit and turn west. Drive to the Avenue of Flags and go left. Continue to Shadow Mountain Drive and turn right.

. . . ● **TOURNAMENTS:** This course is available for outside tournaments.

9. ZACA CREEK GOLF COURSE

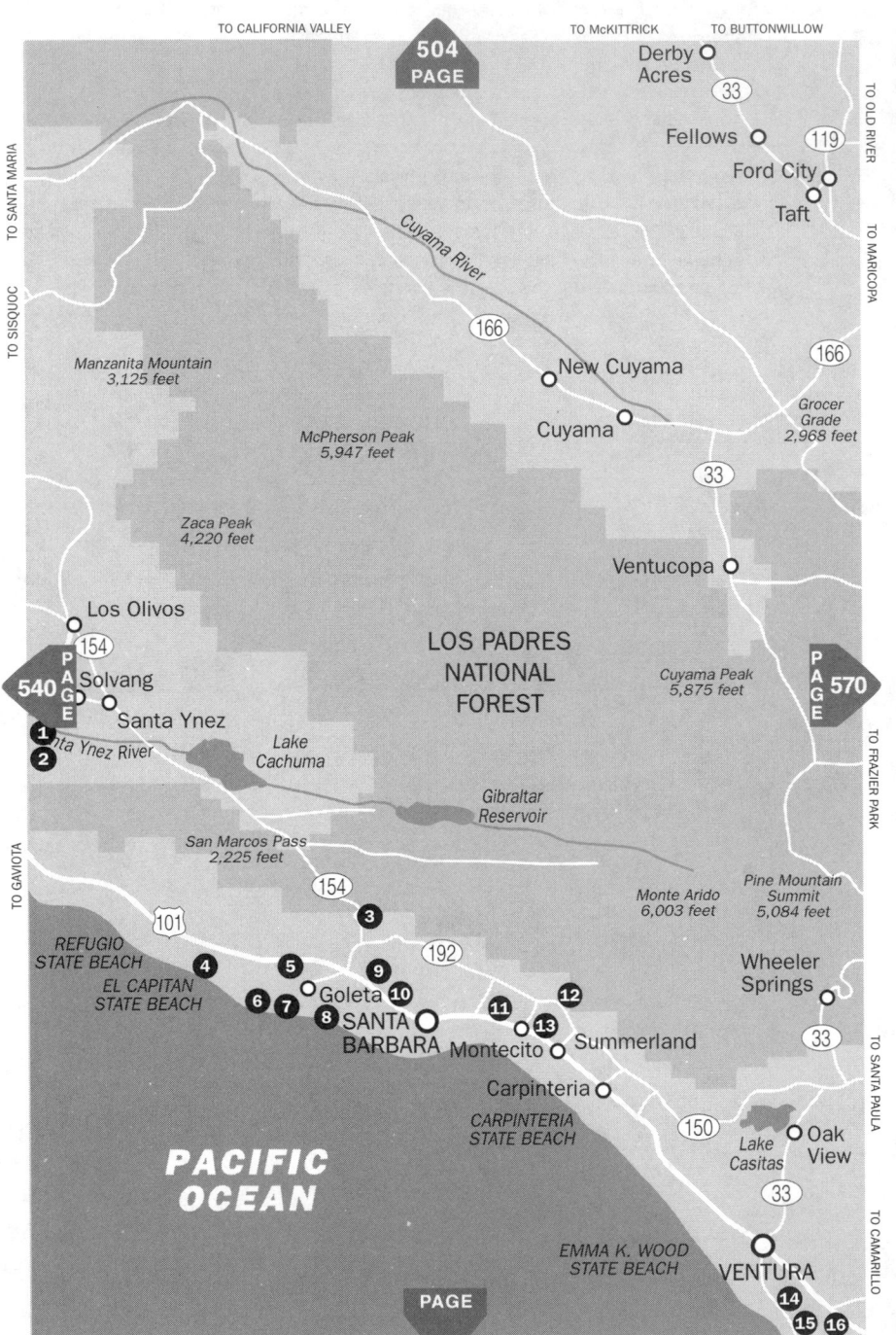

TO CALIFORNIA VALLEY   TO McKITTRICK   TO BUTTONWILLOW

Derby Acres

504 PAGE

33

Fellows

119

Ford City

Taft

TO OLD RIVER

TO MARICOPA

TO SANTA MARIA

TO SISQUOC

Cuyama River

166

Manzanita Mountain
3,125 feet

New Cuyama

Cuyama

166

Grocer Grade
2,968 feet

McPherson Peak
5,947 feet

33

Zaca Peak
4,220 feet

Ventucopa

Los Olivos

154

540 PAGE

Solvang

Santa Ynez

Santa Ynez River

Lake Cachuma

LOS PADRES NATIONAL FOREST

Cuyama Peak
5,875 feet

PAGE 570

TO FRAZIER PARK

Gibraltar Reservoir

San Marcos Pass
2,225 feet

154

192

Monte Arido
6,003 feet

Pine Mountain Summit
5,084 feet

Wheeler Springs

101

REFUGIO STATE BEACH

EL CAPITAN STATE BEACH

3

4

5

6 7

9

Goleta

10

8

SANTA BARBARA

11

13

12

Montecito

Summerland

33

TO SANTA PAULA

TO GAVIOTA

1

2

Carpinteria

CARPINTERIA STATE BEACH

150

Lake Casitas

Oak View

33

PACIFIC OCEAN

EMMA K. WOOD STATE BEACH

VENTURA

14

15 16

TO CAMARILLO

PAGE

Santa Barbara Area

❶ RIVER COURSE AT THE ALISAL
ARCHITECT: HALSEY/DAREY DESIGN GROUP, 1992

P.O. Box 1589
Solvang, CA 93464

150 Alisal Road
Solvang, CA 93463

PRO SHOP: 805-688-6042

Pamela Moore, Head Professional, LPGA
Dave Hartley, Assistant Professional

Driving Range ●
Practice Greens ●
Clubhouse ●
Food / Beverage ●
Accommodations
Pull Carts ●
Power Carts ●
Club Rental ●
$pecial Offers ●

	1	2	3	4	5	6	7	8	9	OUT
BACK	570	386	420	226	583	395	438	358	172	3548
REGULAR	563	368	400	206	563	376	407	331	150	3364
par	5	4	4	3	5	4	4	4	3	36
handicap	7	13	9	3	5	11	1	15	17	-
FORWARD	465	340	369	136	519	339	381	302	126	2977
par	5	4	4	3	5	4	4	4	3	36
handicap	7	13	9	3	5	11	1	15	17	-

	10	11	12	13	14	15	16	17	18	IN
BACK	430	539	147	391	523	356	399	123	374	3282
REGULAR	411	521	134	356	498	337	370	106	354	3087
par	4	5	3	4	5	4	4	3	4	36
handicap	2	8	18	10	4	12	6	16	14	-
FORWARD	384	450	111	325	476	250	346	82	309	2733
par	4	5	3	4	5	4	4	3	4	36
handicap	2	8	18	10	4	12	6	16	14	-

BACK	
yardage	6830
par	72
rating	73.1
slope	126

REGULAR	
yardage	6451
par	72
rating	70.6
slope	120

FORWARD	
yardage	5710
par	72
rating	73.1
slope	122

❷ ALISAL GUEST RANCH & GOLF COURSE
ARCHITECTS: WILLIAM F. BELL, 1955; STEVE HALSEY, 1995

P.O. Box 26
Solvang, CA 93463

1054 Alisal Road
Solvang, CA 93463

PRO SHOP: 805-688-4215
CLUBHOUSE: 805-688-6411

John Hardy, PGA Master Professional
David Lautensack, General Manager
David Rosenstraugh, Superintendent

Driving Range ●
Practice Greens ●
Clubhouse ●
Food / Beverage ●
Accommodations ●
Pull Carts ●
Power Carts ●
Club Rental ●
$pecial Offers ●

	1	2	3	4	5	6	7	8	9	OUT
BACK	528	165	386	496	161	482	339	416	208	3181
REGULAR	495	151	373	491	131	448	305	405	145	2944
par	5	3	4	5	3	5	4	4	3	36
handicap	5	11	3	13	15	9	17	1	7	-
FORWARD	418	140	359	458	126	407	305	384	133	2730
par	5	3	4	5	3	5	4	4	3	36
handicap	9	13	5	3	15	7	11	1	17	-

	10	11	12	13	14	15	16	17	18	IN
BACK	493	445	393	541	173	327	377	420	201	3370
REGULAR	474	430	353	494	156	311	367	405	188	3178
par	5	4	4	5	3	4	4	4	3	36
handicap	18	2	8	10	6	14	16	4	12	-
FORWARD	457	411	344	480	136	297	357	379	161	3022
par	5	5	4	5	3	4	4	4	3	37
handicap	10	18	6	2	16	12	8	4	14	-

BACK	
yardage	6551
par	72
rating	72.0
slope	133

REGULAR	
yardage	6122
par	72
rating	70.1
slope	127

FORWARD	
yardage	5752
par	73
rating	74.5
slope	133

PLAY POLICY & FEES: Green fees are $45 weekdays and $55 weekends and holidays. Thursday is senior day. All seniors 55 and over can play for $34 including cart. Junior rates are available. Children under seven are not permitted on the course. Carts are $24 for 18 holes.

TEE TIMES: Reservations can be booked seven days in advance.

DRESS CODE: Proper golf attire and nonmetal spikes are mandatory. Shorts must be Bermuda length.

COURSE DESCRIPTION: This course runs along a riverbed with views of nearby mountains and hillsides. The signature hole is the seventh, a 397-yard par 4 with a lake on the left and out-of-bounds on the right.

NOTES: The course record is 66, held by John Pate, brother of touring pro Steve Pate.

LOCATION: From U.S. 101 drive three miles east on Highway 246 into Solvang. Turn right on Alisal Road and drive one-quarter mile to the course on the left.

. . . ● **TOURNAMENTS:** A 20-player minimum is needed to book a tournament. Events can be scheduled up to 12 months in advance. The banquet facility can hold 150 people. ● **TRAVEL:** The Solvang Royal Scandinavian Inn is less than two blocks from the golf course. For reservations call 800-624-5572. The Alisal Guest Ranch (805-688-8000) is also recommended. ● **$PECIAL OFFERS:** Play-and-stay packages at the Royal Scandinavian include room, breakfast, green fees, and cart.

1. RIVER COURSE AT THE ALISAL

PLAY POLICY & FEES: Reciprocal play is accepted with members of private clubs. Otherwise, members and guests only. Alisal Guest Ranch guests are welcome. The fee for reciprocators is $90. Cars are $13 per rider.

TEE TIMES: Call seven days prior for reservations on weekdays or the prior Thursday after 12 p.m. for weekends.

DRESS CODE: Collared shirts are required for men, and short shorts are not allowed for women. Nonmetal spikes are required.

COURSE DESCRIPTION: Located on the 10,000-acre Alisal Guest Ranch, a working cattle ranch, this scenic course is set in a valley. When you're not watching for native birds and deer, keep an eye out for the fifth, a par-3, 160-yard hole that provides a view of Solvang and the Santa Ynez Valley from its elevated tee. Players hit across Alisal Creek to a green heavily bunkered on the front left. The tight fairways are lined with mature oaks and sycamores. The course is well maintained and usually uncrowded. An early morning round offers the chance to see numerous birds and other wildlife on this pleasant and walkable course.

LOCATION: From U.S. 101 in Solvang, take Mission Drive (in downtown Solvang). Turn south on Alisal Road and drive 1.75 miles to the course.

. . . ● **TOURNAMENTS:** Outside tournaments are limited to guests of the ranch. ● **TRAVEL:** For reservations at the ranch call 800-425-4725. ● **$PECIAL OFFERS:** Play-and-stay packages are available at the guest ranch.

2. ALISAL GUEST RANCH & GOLF COURSE

---

3 RANCHO SAN MARCOS GOLF COURSE
ARCHITECT: ROBERT TRENT JONES, JR., 1998

4600 Hwy. 154
Santa Barbara, CA 93105

PRO SHOP: 805-683-6334

Casey Paulson, Director of Golf
Douglas Crane, PGA Professional
Scott Nair, Superintendent

Driving Range ●
Practice Greens ●
Clubhouse ●
Food / Beverage ●
Accommodations
Pull Carts
Power Carts ●
Club Rental ●
$pecial Offers

	1	2	3	4	5	6	7	8	9	OUT
BACK	531	202	432	410	170	629	179	434	404	3391
REGULAR	491	172	417	379	166	585	165	388	387	3150
par	5	3	4	4	3	5	3	4	4	35
handicap	9	15	3	11	13	1	17	7	5	-
FORWARD	412	113	292	299	120	468	106	323	328	2461
par	5	3	4	4	3	5	3	4	4	35
handicap	5	15	3	11	13	1	17	7	5	-

	10	11	12	13	14	15	16	17	18	IN
BACK	491	447	528	145	175	410	223	450	542	3411
REGULAR	473	408	503	118	149	390	199	382	518	3140
par	5	4	5	3	3	4	3	4	5	36
handicap	10	12	6	18	16	2	14	8	4	-
FORWARD	394	309	460	88	78	292	145	359	432	2557
par	5	4	5	3	3	4	3	4	5	36
handicap	10	12	6	18	16	2	14	8	4	-

BACK	
yardage	6802
par	71
rating	73.1
slope	135

REGULAR	
yardage	6290
par	71
rating	70.2
slope	127

FORWARD	
yardage	5018
par	71
rating	69.2
slope	117

4 Sandpiper Golf Course
ARCHITECT: WILLIAM F. BELL, 1971

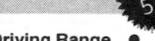

7925 Hollister Avenue
Goleta, CA 93117

PRO SHOP: 805-968-1541

Charlie Ortega, General Manager, PGA
Goyo Santa Maria, Superintendent

Driving Range ●
Practice Greens ●
Clubhouse ●
Food / Beverage ●
Accommodations
Pull Carts ●
Power Carts ●
Club Rental ●
$pecial Offers

	1	2	3	4	5	6	7	8	9	OUT
BACK	524	471	424	232	509	195	391	396	418	3560
REGULAR	505	429	395	205	491	171	364	366	398	3324
par	5	4	4	3	5	3	4	4	4	36
handicap	9	1	3	5	13	17	15	11	7	-
FORWARD	454	376	353	171	430	132	336	359	372	2983
par	5	4	4	3	5	3	4	4	4	36
handicap	5	1	13	15	7	17	9	11	3	-

	10	11	12	13	14	15	16	17	18	IN
BACK	381	224	341	532	444	599	392	421	174	3508
REGULAR	354	174	314	516	425	580	373	367	170	3273
par	4	3	4	5	4	5	4	4	3	36
handicap	4	14	18	6	2	8	10	16	12	-
FORWARD	315	148	252	399	413	471	341	304	99	2742
par	4	3	4	5	5	5	4	4	3	37
handicap	8	16	14	2	10	4	6	12	18	-

BACK	
yardage	7068
par	72
rating	74.5
slope	134

REGULAR	
yardage	6597
par	72
rating	71.7
slope	123

FORWARD	
yardage	5725
par	73
rating	73.3
slope	125

PUBLIC: $49-$100

18 HOLES

FAX: 805-692-8805   www.rsm1804.com

PLAY POLICY & FEES: Green fees Monday through Thursday for nonresidents are $85, and $100 Friday through Sunday. Resident green fees are $49 Monday through Thursday, $80 Friday through Sunday. Carts are $17 per player; $10 for nine holes. Call for special rates.

TEE TIMES: Reservations can be made 30 days in advance.

DRESS CODE: Collared shirts and nonmetal spikes are required.

COURSE DESCRIPTION: This course located in the Los Padres National Forest and offers centuries-old oak trees and views of the Santa Ynez River and Lake Cachuma. The front nine is fairly flat and easy to walk, but the back nine has some severe elevation changes. Pull out a driver with caution. A premium is placed on accuracy off the tee. With plenty of mounding, chances are you will not have a level lie.

NOTES: Rancho San Marcos has previosuly been nominated as "Top 10" in "Golf Digest" and "Golf Magazine." This course also has a 15-acre practice facility with all grass tees.

LOCATION: Take U.S. 101 to Santa Barbara and the State Street-San Marcos Pass exit. Cross State Street and turn toward the mountains on San Marcos Pass, Highway 154. The golf course entrance is 12.5 miles on the right.

. . . ● **TOURNAMENTS:** An 12-player minimum is required to book an event. Tournaments should be scheduled 12 months in advance.

3. RANCHO SAN MARCOS GOLF COURSE

PUBLIC: $40-$108

18 HOLES

FAX: 805-685-0044

PLAY POLICY & FEES: Green fees are $68 Monday through Thursday and $108 Friday through Sunday. Twilight green fees are $40 weekdays and $55 weekends. Carts are $24.

TEE TIMES: Reservations can be booked eight to 60 days in advance for a nonrefundable $10 per player fee; otherwise, reservations can be made seven days in advance.

DRESS CODE: Collared shirts and nonmetal spikes are required. Bermuda shorts are permitted.

COURSE DESCRIPTION: Championship golf takes you to the edge of the Pacific Ocean at this beautiful, challenging, and inspiring course. Sandpiper features beautiful, rolling fairways and challenging greens in a seaside links-style layout with breathtaking ocean and mountain views from every hole. Step off the green of the beautiful par-3 11th hole and onto the sand of the scenic Santa Barbara coastline.

NOTES: Sandpiper has been rated among the top 25 public golf courses in the nation and has hosted the final stage of the 1997 PGA Tour Qualifying.

LOCATION: Travel 12 miles north of Santa Barbara on U.S. 101 and exit at the Winchester Canyon Road/Hollister Avenue exit. Turn left at the stop sign and drive one-quarter mile on Hollister Avenue to the course on the right.

. . . ● **TOURNAMENTS:** A 16-player minimum is required to book a tournament. Tournaments can be booked 24 months in advance. ● **TRAVEL:** Pacifica Suites (805-683-6722), Santa Barbara Inn (805-866-2285) and Fess Parker Doubletree Inn (805-524-4333) are recommended for lodging.

4. SANDPIPER GOLF COURSE

Santa Barbara Area (map page 552)   **557**

GLEN ANNIE GOLF CLUB

ARCHITECTS: ROBERT MUIR GRAVES, 1997; DAMIEN PAZCUZZO, 1997

405 Glen Annie Road
Goleta, CA 93117

PRO SHOP: 805-968-6400

Ted Roderick, General Manager
Bill Krueger, Head Professional, PGA
Steve Montanez, Superintendent

Driving Range ●
Practice Greens ●
Clubhouse ●
Food / Beverage ●
Accommodations
Pull Carts
Power Carts ●
Club Rental ●
$pecial Offers

	1	2	3	4	5	6	7	8	9	OUT
BACK	447	143	340	347	568	149	533	439	207	3173
REGULAR	416	121	305	325	534	125	504	412	189	2931
par	4	3	4	4	5	3	5	4	3	35
handicap	1	13	15	11	9	17	5	7	3	-
FORWARD	337	86	267	283	454	95	449	326	124	2421
par	4	3	4	4	5	3	5	4	3	35
handicap	1	13	15	11	9	17	5	7	3	-

	10	11	12	13	14	15	16	17	18	IN
BACK	577	183	286	322	526	397	391	212	353	3247
REGULAR	554	152	266	304	497	352	374	180	330	3009
par	5	3	4	4	5	4	4	3	4	36
handicap	2	16	18	14	6	5	12	4	10	-
FORWARD	448	121	244	268	454	311	330	149	290	2615
par	5	3	4	4	5	4	4	3	4	36
handicap	2	16	18	14	6	8	12	4	10	-

BACK	
yardage	6420
par	71
rating	71.1
slope	122

REGULAR	
yardage	5940
par	71
rating	68.8
slope	117

FORWARD	
yardage	5036
par	71
rating	69.5
slope	118

 OCEAN MEADOWS GOLF COURSE

ARCHITECT: HARRY RAINVILLE, DAVID RAINVILLE, 1964

6925 Whittier Drive
Goleta, CA 93117

PRO SHOP: 805-968-6814

Mark Green, General Manager
Dave Grutzius, Head Professional, PGA
Simon Herrera, Superintendent

Driving Range ●
Practice Greens ●
Clubhouse ●
Food / Beverage ●
Accommodations
Pull Carts ●
Power Carts ●
Club Rental ●
$pecial Offers

	1	2	3	4	5	6	7	8	9	OUT
BACK	328	196	394	489	359	199	345	377	509	3196
REGULAR	320	163	372	474	339	170	329	354	480	3001
par	4	3	4	5	4	3	4	4	5	36
handicap	7	17	5	3	11	15	13	9	1	-
FORWARD	311	112	319	437	299	125	295	308	451	2657
par	4	3	4	5	4	3	4	4	5	36
handicap	5	17	7	3	11	15	13	9	1	-

	10	11	12	13	14	15	16	17	18	IN
BACK	328	196	394	489	359	199	345	377	509	3196
REGULAR	320	163	372	474	339	170	329	354	480	3001
par	4	3	4	5	4	3	4	4	5	36
handicap	10	14	6	4	12	16	18	8	2	-
FORWARD	311	112	319	437	299	125	295	308	451	2657
par	4	3	4	5	4	3	4	4	5	36
handicap	10	18	6	4	14	16	12	8	2	-

BACK	
yardage	6392
par	72
rating	70.0
slope	115

REGULAR	
yardage	6002
par	72
rating	68.2
slope	108

FORWARD	
yardage	5314
par	72
rating	65.1
slope	102

PLAY POLICY & FEES: Green fees are $60 Monday through Thursday, and $75 Friday, Saturday, Sunday, and holidays. Twilight and resident rates are available.

TEE TIMES: Tee times can be made seven days in advance.

DRESS CODE: Guests are asked to wear collared shirts, and no denim is allowed on the course. This is a nonmetal spike facility.

COURSE DESCRIPTION: Glen Annie offers excellent views of the Pacific Ocean and the Channel Islands, especially on the back nine, which takes the player up into the hills. This is a challenging course where fescue grass penalizes players who miss the fairways and greens. Because of the proximity to the ocean, wind can be a factor. The greens roll true with subtle undulations that make them tricky to read. The course is surrounded by environmentally sensitive areas (ESA). Players are not allowed to play out of an ESA and must take a drop. Don't let the sweeping views off the first hole distract you; this is a tough, long , uphill par 4 that demands two well-hit shots to reach the green.

LOCATION: From Santa Barbara take U.S. 101 north to the Glen Annie off-ramp north. Continue for one-half mile to the entry gate on the left.

. . . ● **TOURNAMENTS:** Shotgun tournaments are available. A 32-player minimum is needed to book a tournament. ● **TRAVEL:** The Doubletree Resort is one of many excellent hotels in the area; reservations can be made by calling 805-564-4333. Pacifica Suites is ten minutes from the course. Call 805-683-6722.

5. GLEN ANNIE GOLF CLUB

PLAY POLICY & FEES: Green fees are $15 for nine holes and $25 for 18 holes weekdays, and $17 for nine holes and $29 for 18 holes weekends and holidays. Call for special rates. Carts are $14 for nine holes and $20 for 18 holes.

TEE TIMES: Reservations can be booked seven days in advance.

COURSE DESCRIPTION: This relatively flat course has tree-lined fairways and mountain views. It is built within the boundaries of an ecologically rich ocean slough and consequently has numerous lateral water hazards.

NOTES: Bird watchers (not to be confused with birdie watchers) might want to bring binoculars to view the beautiful and abundant wildlife in the area, which includes blue herons and snowy egrets. It'll take more than binoculars to see an eagle. Mike McGinnis and Don Parsons share the course record of 64.

LOCATION: Go north of Santa Barbara on U.S. 101 to the Storke-Glen Annie exit. Drive south one mile to Whittier Drive.

. . . ● **TOURNAMENTS:** A 16-player minimum is required to book a tournament.

6. OCEAN MEADOWS GOLF COURSE

6034 Hollister Avenue
Goleta, CA 93117

PRO SHOP: 805-964-1414

James Ley, Golf Professional
Don Parson, Director of Instruction
Luciano Nungaray, Superintendent

Driving Range ●
Practice Greens ●
Clubhouse
Food / Beverage
Accommodations
Pull Carts ●
Power Carts
Club Rental ●
$pecial Offers

	1	2	3	4	5	6	7	8	9	OUT
BACK	-	-	-	-	-	-	-	-	-	-
REGULAR	95	134	94	335	126	109	360	89	132	1474
par	3	3	3	4	3	3	4	3	3	29
handicap	9	3	7	2	5	6	1	8	4	-
FORWARD	75	121	76	285	109	92	335	79	120	1292
par	3	3	3	4	3	3	4	3	3	29
handicap	9	3	7	2	5	6	1	8	4	-

	10	11	12	13	14	15	16	17	18	IN
BACK	-	-	-	-	-	-	-	-	-	-
REGULAR	95	134	94	335	126	109	360	89	132	1474
par	3	3	3	4	3	3	4	3	3	29
handicap	9	3	7	2	5	6	1	8	4	-
FORWARD	75	121	76	285	109	92	335	79	120	1292
par	3	3	3	4	3	3	4	3	3	29
handicap	9	3	7	2	5	6	1	8	4	-

BACK	
yardage	-
par	-
rating	-
slope	-

REGULAR	
yardage	2948
par	58
rating	53.6
slope	73

FORWARD	
yardage	2584
par	58
rating	53.6
slope	73

4760-G Calle Camarade
Santa Barbara, CA 93110

PRO SHOP: 805-967-3493

Cliff Carter, Director of Golf
Robin McMann, Professional
Ignacio Perez, Superintendent

Driving Range
Practice Greens ● ●
Clubhouse
Food / Beverage
Accommodations
Pull Carts ●
Power Carts
Club Rental ●
$pecial Offers

	1	2	3	4	5	6	7	8	9	OUT
BACK	-	-	-	-	-	-	-	-	-	-
REGULAR	85	112	115	139	156	122	80	136	173	1118
par	3	3	3	3	3	3	3	3	3	27
handicap	9	6	7	3	2	5	8	4	1	-
FORWARD	70	100	74	110	90	100	80	110	120	854
par	3	3	3	3	3	3	3	3	3	27
handicap	9	6	7	3	2	5	8	4	1	-

	10	11	12	13	14	15	16	17	18	IN
BACK	-	-	-	-	-	-	-	-	-	-
REGULAR	85	112	115	139	156	122	80	136	173	1118
par	3	3	3	3	3	3	3	3	3	27
handicap	9	6	7	3	2	5	8	4	1	-
FORWARD	70	100	74	110	90	100	80	110	120	854
par	3	3	3	3	3	3	3	3	3	27
handicap	9	6	7	3	2	5	8	4	1	-

BACK	
yardage	-
par	-
rating	-
slope	-

REGULAR	
yardage	2236
par	54
rating	-
slope	-

FORWARD	
yardage	1708
par	54
rating	-
slope	-

PLAY POLICY & FEES: Green fees are $9 weekdays and $10 weekends. Replays are $5. Ask for senior and junior discounts. Pull carts are $1.50.

TEE TIMES: Reservations can be booked seven days in advance.

DRESS CODE: Shirts and shoes are necessary.

COURSE DESCRIPTION: This is a par-29 course that has seven par 3s and two par 4s. This course has two lakes and a creek that come into play on four holes. The course is tight and will test all iron play.

NOTES: The course record is 23.

LOCATION: Take the Fairview exit off U.S. 101 north of Santa Barbara and drive west to the course.

. . . ● **TOURNAMENTS:** This course is available for outside tournaments.

7. TWIN LAKES GOLF COURSE

PLAY POLICY & FEES: Green fees are $8.50 weekdays and $9.50 weekends and holidays for nine holes. For 18 holes, fees are $15 weekdays and $17 weekends.

TEE TIMES: Reservations are limited to large groups; otherwise, play is on a first-come, first-served basis.

DRESS CODE: Shirts must be worn.

COURSE DESCRIPTION: This short course is all par 3s. There are bent greens and lush, narrow fairways. A well on the course provides year-round water, and in the drought years the course was the only green spot in the Santa Barbara area. The longest hole is the ninth at 173 yards. The sixth hole is tricky, shooting down 122 yards from an elevated tee to the green.

LOCATION: Off U.S. 101 heading south to Santa Barbara, take the Turnpike exit and turn left on Hollister. Turn right on Puente and follow it to Calle Camarade. Take a right turn to the course.

. . . ● **TOURNAMENTS:** A 36-player minimum is required to book a tournament. Events should be scheduled two months in advance.

8. HIDDEN OAKS GOLF COURSE

LA CUMBRE COUNTRY CLUB
ARCHITECT: WILLIAM P. BELL, 1957

4015 Via Laguna
Santa Barbara, CA 93110

PRO SHOP: 805-682-3131
CLUBHOUSE: 805-687-2421

Bryan Bahman, General Manager
Evan Colavincenzo, PGA Professional
Doug Weddle, Superintendent

Driving Range ●
Practice Greens ●
Clubhouse ●
Food / Beverage ●
Accommodations
Pull Carts ●
Power Carts ●
Club Rental ●
Special Offers

	1	2	3	4	5	6	7	8	9	OUT
BACK	415	358	393	364	154	522	156	402	472	3236
REGULAR	391	350	373	339	146	513	148	394	464	3118
par	4	4	4	4	3	5	3	4	5	36
handicap	5	3	9	13	17	7	15	1	11	-
FORWARD	389	316	363	321	138	503	126	324	443	2923
par	4	4	4	4	3	5	3	4	5	36
handicap	7	11	5	9	15	1	17	13	3	-

	10	11	12	13	14	15	16	17	18	IN
BACK	495	168	529	215	413	378	411	156	405	3170
REGULAR	483	148	479	190	381	363	401	144	385	2974
par	5	3	5	3	4	4	4	3	4	35
handicap	14	16	8	10	2	12	4	18	6	-
FORWARD	453	137	452	134	356	336	406	132	372	2778
par	5	3	5	3	4	4	5	3	4	36
handicap	6	16	2	14	8	10	12	18	4	-

BACK	
yardage	6406
par	71
rating	70.8
slope	128

REGULAR	
yardage	6092
par	71
rating	69.1
slope	120

FORWARD	
yardage	5701
par	72
rating	73.0
slope	128

 # SANTA BARBARA GOLF CLUB
ARCHITECT: LAWRENCE HUGHES, 1958

3500 McCaw Avenue
Santa Barbara, CA 93105

PRO SHOP: 805-687-7087

Richard Chavez, Director of Golf, PGA
Rich Barker, Head Professional, PGA
Bill Parker, Superintendent

Driving Range ●
Practice Greens ●
Clubhouse ●
Food / Beverage ●
Accommodations
Pull Carts ●
Power Carts ●
Club Rental ●
Special Offers

	1	2	3	4	5	6	7	8	9	OUT
BACK	346	290	112	362	368	481	435	193	511	3098
REGULAR	334	277	100	351	355	473	425	165	495	2975
par	4	4	3	4	4	5	4	3	5	36
handicap	9	15	17	3	7	11	1	13	5	-
FORWARD	318	260	86	341	349	466	416	143	479	2858
par	4	4	3	4	4	5	5	3	5	37
handicap	9	15	17	5	3	7	11	13	1	-

	10	11	12	13	14	15	16	17	18	IN
BACK	143	387	455	96	398	381	176	398	482	2916
REGULAR	133	370	440	86	386	373	167	385	467	2807
par	3	4	4	3	4	4	3	4	5	34
handicap	16	8	2	18	6	14	12	4	10	-
FORWARD	126	360	427	80	377	366	158	374	415	2683
par	3	4	5	3	4	4	3	4	5	35
handicap	14	10	16	18	4	12	8	2	6	-

BACK	
yardage	6014
par	70
rating	67.6
slope	113

REGULAR	
yardage	5782
par	70
rating	66.3
slope	109

FORWARD	
yardage	5541
par	72
rating	64.9
slope	105

9. LA CUMBRE COUNTRY CLUB

PLAY POLICY & FEES: Reciprocal play is accepted with members of other private clubs; otherwise, members and guests only. Green fees for reciprocators are $135. Carts are $17.50 per rider.

DRESS CODE: Appropriate golf attire and nonmetal spikes are required.

COURSE DESCRIPTION: This is a well-maintained course with a 30-acre lake coming into play on the back nine. Five holes border the lake. The course predates the surrounding homes of the Hope Ranch residential development.

NOTES: Al Geiberger holds the course record with a 61.

LOCATION: Heading into Santa Barbara on U.S. 101, take the Hope Avenue/La Cumbre Road exit. Turn left on Frontage Road and then left on La Cumbre Road and continue one-quarter mile past the arched entrance to Hope Ranch Park and Via Laguna. The club is on the left.

. . . ● **TOURNAMENTS:** This course is not available for outside events.

10. SANTA BARBARA GOLF CLUB

PLAY POLICY & FEES: Resident green fees are $18 weekdays and $22 on weekends. Nonresident fees are $25 weekdays and $35 weekends. Twilight, senior, junior, and nine-hole rates are available. Carts are $22. Pull carts are $2.50.

TEE TIMES: Reservations can be booked seven days in advance.

COURSE DESCRIPTION: This course is set in the foothills above Santa Barbara and offers a nice view of the Channel Islands. Trees border the holes, and the fairways are made up of Kikuyu grass, which limits roll. The course plays long.

NOTES: The Santa Barbara City Championship, the Santa Barbara Classic, the Santa Barbara Women's Open, and the Santa Barbara City Seniors Tournaments are held here. Jeff Hewes holds the men's course record of 59, and Peggy Hogan's 65 is the women's record.

LOCATION: Exit U.S. 101 at Las Positas Road in Santa Barbara and drive east for three-quarters of a mile to McCaw Avenue. Turn left and continue one-quarter mile to the course.

. . . ● **TOURNAMENTS:** Shotgun tournaments are available weekdays only. A 24-player minimum is required to book a tournament. Events can be scheduled up to 12 months in advance. The banquet facility can accommodate 100 people.

● **TRAVEL:** Best Western Pepper Tree Inn is located five minutes from the golf course. For reservations call 800-338-0030.

⑪ MONTECITO COUNTRY CLUB
ARCHITECT: MAX BEHR, 1922

P.O. Box 1170
Santa Barbara, CA 93102

920 Summit Road
Santa Barbara, CA 93108

PRO SHOP: 805-969-0800
CLUBHOUSE: 805-969-3216

Larry Talkington, PGA Professional
Vincente Ramirez, Superintendent

Driving Range
Practice Greens •
Clubhouse •
Food / Beverage •
Accommodations
Pull Carts
Power Carts •
Club Rental •
$pecial Offers

	1	2	3	4	5	6	7	8	9	OUT
BACK										
REGULAR										
par										
handicap										
FORWARD										
par										
handicap										

	10	11	12	13	14	15	16	17	18	IN
BACK										
REGULAR										
par										
handicap										
FORWARD										
par										
handicap										

BACK	
yardage	
par	
rating	
slope	

REGULAR	
yardage	6164
par	71
rating	69.9
slope	122

FORWARD	
yardage	5597
par	71
rating	74.3
slope	126

⑫ BIRNAM WOOD GOLF CLUB
ARCHITECT: ROBERT TRENT JONES SR., 1967

2031 Packing House Road
Santa Barbara, CA 93108

PRO SHOP: 805-969-0919
CLUBHOUSE: 805-969-2223

Paul Cronin, General Manager
John S. Diaz, Head Professional, PGA
Martin Moore, Superintendent

Driving Range •
Practice Greens •
Clubhouse •
Food / Beverage •
Accommodations •
Pull Carts •
Power Carts •
Club Rental •
$pecial Offers

	1	2	3	4	5	6	7	8	9	OUT
BACK	-	-	-	-	-	-	-	-	-	-
REGULAR	405	155	382	334	149	369	335	345	450	2924
par	4	3	4	4	3	4	4	4	5	35
handicap	1	11	3	7	17	5	13	9	15	-
FORWARD	409	121	354	302	127	312	310	288	434	2657
par	5	3	4	4	3	4	4	4	5	36
handicap	3	17	1	5	15	13	11	9	7	-

	10	11	12	13	14	15	16	17	18	IN
BACK	-	-	-	-	-	-	-	-	-	-
REGULAR	374	400	135	350	470	179	405	165	488	2966
par	4	4	3	4	5	3	4	3	5	35
handicap	6	2	18	8	12	14	4	10	16	-
FORWARD	342	376	111	322	434	163	373	128	458	2707
par	4	4	3	4	5	3	4	3	5	35
handicap	10	4	18	12	2	16	6	14	8	-

BACK	
yardage	-
par	-
rating	-
slope	-

REGULAR	
yardage	5890
par	70
rating	68.7
slope	121

FORWARD	
yardage	5364
par	71
rating	72.1
slope	127

PLAY POLICY & FEES: Reciprocal play is accepted with members of other private clubs. The reciprocator fee is $60. Guest fees are $30 walking and $40 with cart every day. Carts are $14 per person.

TEE TIMES: Guests should have their club professional make reservations with the Montecito pro shop. Tee times can be made three days in advance.

DRESS CODE: Appropriate golf attire is required.

COURSE DESCRIPTION: This is a challenging course that emphasizes shot making. Ocean and mountain views are abundant from the rolling, tree-lined fairways and well-kept undulating greens. The course plays much longer than yardage indicates. Accuracy and the ability to recover from troublesome lies are needed to score well here. Memorable holes include the par-4 third hole and the 18th, which is a top-notch finishing par 5.

LOCATION: From U.S. 101 take the Cabrillo Boulevard exit north and drive through the underpass, bearing right to Hot Springs Road (the first street). Turn left and drive one-half mile to Summit Road. Turn left and drive to the club.

. . . ● **TOURNAMENTS:** Shotgun tournaments are available weekdays only.

11. MONTECITO COUNTRY CLUB

PLAY POLICY & FEES: Members and guests only. Green fees are $40 when accompanied by a member or $95 when unaccompanied. Carts are $22 with a member and $28 without a member.

TEE TIMES: No reservations are taken.

DRESS CODE: Appropriate golf attire and nonmetal spikes are required.

COURSE DESCRIPTION: This is a short course that rewards accuracy. There are numerous out-of-bounds markers to the left and right. Barrancas are found in front of the greens, making it impossible to roll the ball on. Sharpen up your iron play before tackling this well-maintained, Robert Trent Jones Sr. beauty.

NOTES: Diane Wootton holds the women's record of 68, and Jim Cole holds the men's record of 60.

LOCATION: Take the Sheffield Drive exit off U.S. 101 in Santa Barbara and drive to the end. Turn left on East Valley Road and drive up the hill to the club entrance.

. . . ● **TOURNAMENTS:** All outside events must have a member sponsor.

12. BIRNAM WOOD GOLF CLUB

THE VALLEY CLUB OF MONTECITO
ARCHITECT: ALLISTER MACKENZIE, 1929

P.O. Box 5640
Santa Barbara, CA 93150

1901 East Valley Road
Santa Barbara, CA 93108

PRO SHOP: 805-969-4681

Scott Puailoa, PGA Professional
Sean McCormick, Superintendent

Driving Range ●
Practice Greens ●
Clubhouse ●
Food / Beverage ●
Accommodations ●
Pull Carts ●
Power Carts ●
Club Rental ●
$pecial Offers

	1	2	3	4	5	6	7	8	9	OUT
BACK	460	491	450	146	418	300	431	154	425	3275
REGULAR	451	473	436	133	404	285	409	135	405	3131
par	5	5	4	3	4	4	4	3	4	36
handicap	15	9	1	13	3	17	7	11	5	-
FORWARD	447	466	419	125	396	277	365	124	397	3016
par	5	5	5	3	4	4	4	3	4	37
handicap	9	5	11	17	1	13	7	15	3	-

	10	11	12	13	14	15	16	17	18	IN
BACK	476	176	360	386	177	506	455	373	419	3328
REGULAR	452	170	338	378	166	470	452	368	408	3202
par	5	3	4	4	3	5	4	4	4	36
handicap	16	18	8	6	14	10	2	12	4	-
FORWARD	405	130	329	330	160	412	371	366	294	2797
par	5	3	4	4	3	5	4	4	4	36
handicap	12	18	8	6	16	10	2	4	14	-

BACK	
yardage	6603
par	72
rating	72.1
slope	133

REGULAR	
yardage	6333
par	72
rating	70.0
slope	122

FORWARD	
yardage	5813
par	73
rating	74.3
slope	134

 OLIVAS PARK GOLF COURSE
ARCHITECT: WILLIAM F. BELL, 1969

3750 Olivas Park Drive
Ventura, CA 93003

PRO SHOP: 805-642-4303

Russ Clark, PGA Professional
Rueben Del Rio, Superintendent

Driving Range ●
Practice Greens ●
Clubhouse ●
Food / Beverage ●
Accommodations
Pull Carts ●
Power Carts ●
Club Rental ●
$pecial Offers

	1	2	3	4	5	6	7	8	9	OUT
BACK	535	359	142	531	194	397	372	389	405	3324
REGULAR	516	334	133	499	183	361	359	377	390	3152
par	5	4	3	5	3	4	4	4	4	36
handicap	11	15	17	9	7	5	13	3	1	-
FORWARD	435	330	112	449	153	303	349	302	330	2763
par	5	4	3	5	3	4	4	4	4	36
handicap	5	9	15	1	17	13	7	11	3	-

	10	11	12	13	14	15	16	17	18	IN
BACK	535	357	458	191	429	341	396	183	544	3434
REGULAR	506	328	425	174	404	313	384	162	505	3201
par	5	4	4	3	4	4	4	3	5	36
handicap	16	10	4	14	2	18	6	12	8	-
FORWARD	476	242	359	136	376	254	337	151	407	2738
par	5	4	4	3	4	4	4	3	5	36
handicap	10	12	8	18	4	16	2	14	6	-

BACK	
yardage	6758
par	72
rating	72.6
slope	124

REGULAR	
yardage	6353
par	72
rating	70.7
slope	119

FORWARD	
yardage	5501
par	72
rating	72.4
slope	119

PLAY POLICY & FEES: Members and guests only. Green fees are $150 for guests unaccompanied by a member. Fees are $35 with a member. Carts are $20. The course is closed on Monday.

DRESS CODE: Appropriate golf attire and nonmetal spikes are required.

COURSE DESCRIPTION: The course features small greens and a natural setting. A creek runs through about half the holes, and the narrow fairways are bordered by large cypress and pine trees. The ocean is visible from many holes.

NOTES: The course is very exclusive. Fewer than 100 members use it regularly. It is rated among the top 20 courses in the state. There have been no modifications to the course since it opened in 1929. The course record of 61 is held by John Pate.

LOCATION: Take the San Ysidro Road exit off U.S. 101 and travel north to East Valley Road. Turn right and drive one mile to Valley Club Road; then turn right to the club.

. . . ● **TOURNAMENTS:** This course is not available for outside events.

13. THE VALLEY CLUB OF MONTECITO

PLAY POLICY & FEES: Green fees are $18 weekdays and $23 weekends. Carts are $22. Resident rates are available. All rates are subject to change.

TEE TIMES: Reservations can be made seven days in advance.

DRESS CODE: Nonmetal spikes are encouraged.

COURSE DESCRIPTION: This beautiful and flat course is less than one-half mile from Ventura Harbor. Cool ocean breezes can play havoc with shots.

NOTES: Matt Eilson holds the course record of 62.

LOCATION: From Santa Barbara, drive about 26 miles south on U.S.101 to the Seaward exit in Ventura. Turn left onto Harbor Road and drive five miles to Olivas Park Drive. Turn left and drive 100 yards to the course.

. . . ● **TOURNAMENTS:** A 16-player minimum is needed to book a tournament. Tournaments should be booked 12 months in advance. A small additional charge is placed on shotgun starts.

14. OLIVAS PARK GOLF COURSE

BUENAVENTURA GOLF COURSE
ARCHITECT: WILLIAM F. BELL, 1932

5882 Olivas Park Drive
Ventura, CA 93003

PRO SHOP: 805-642-2231

Greg Gilmer, Manager
Lee Harlow, PGA Professional
Mark Cartrell, Superintendent

Driving Range
Practice Greens ●
Clubhouse ●
Food / Beverage ●
Accommodations
Pull Carts ●
Power Carts ●
Club Rental ●
$pecial Offers

	1	2	3	4	5	6	7	8	9	OUT
BACK	393	207	306	318	378	548	535	162	349	3196
REGULAR	383	191	294	309	367	537	527	149	330	3087
par	4	3	4	4	4	5	5	3	4	36
handicap	1	9	13	15	5	7	3	17	11	-
FORWARD	366	128	240	294	320	479	450	128	297	2702
par	4	3	4	4	4	5	5	3	4	36
handicap	5	17	13	11	7	3	1	15	9	-

	10	11	12	13	14	15	16	17	18	IN
BACK	397	225	341	378	144	293	529	483	426	3216
REGULAR	387	212	324	333	130	281	512	464	416	3059
par	4	3	4	4	3	4	5	5	4	36
handicap	8	4	14	12	16	18	6	10	2	-
FORWARD	359	171	309	314	89	262	417	439	381	2741
par	4	3	4	4	3	4	5	5	5	37
handicap	8	16	10	12	18	14	2	4	6	-

BACK	
yardage	6412
par	72
rating	70.7
slope	126

REGULAR	
yardage	6146
par	72
rating	69.1
slope	124

FORWARD	
yardage	5443
par	73
rating	71.8
slope	123

 RIVER RIDGE GOLF CLUB
ARCHITECT: WILLIAM F. BELL, 1986

2401 West Vineyard
Oxnard, CA 93030

PRO SHOP: 805-983-4653

Otto Kanny, General Manager
Marc A. Sipes, PGA Professional
Chris Harvey, Tournament Director

Driving Range ●
Practice Greens ●
Clubhouse ●
Food / Beverage ●
Accommodations ●
Pull Carts ●
Power Carts ●
Club Rental ●
$pecial Offers

	1	2	3	4	5	6	7	8	9	OUT
BACK	553	402	165	454	187	465	501	182	523	3432
REGULAR	534	326	148	377	172	401	460	140	497	3055
par	5	4	3	4	3	4	5	3	5	36
handicap	3	9	17	1	11	7	13	15	5	-
FORWARD	409	287	127	425	150	338	308	112	407	2563
par	5	4	3	5	3	4	4	3	5	36
handicap	13	7	15	9	5	3	11	17	1	-

	10	11	12	13	14	15	16	17	18	IN
BACK	445	506	383	386	191	388	351	139	497	3286
REGULAR	413	467	353	361	158	368	323	133	473	3049
par	4	5	4	4	3	4	4	3	5	36
handicap	2	14	8	12	6	4	10	18	16	-
FORWARD	382	420	324	346	122	328	296	119	451	2788
par	4	5	4	4	3	4	4	3	5	36
handicap	4	2	12	6	16	10	14	18	8	-

BACK	
yardage	6718
par	72
rating	72.3
slope	121

REGULAR	
yardage	6104
par	72
rating	69.3
slope	114

FORWARD	
yardage	5351
par	72
rating	71.3
slope	124

PLAY POLICY & FEES: Green fees are $16 weekdays and $20 weekends and holidays. Carts are $22 and optional.

TEE TIMES: Reservations can be made seven days in advance.

DRESS CODE: Collared shirts are required.

COURSE DESCRIPTION: Eight lakes come into play on nine holes. Large cypress, pine, and eucalyptus trees line the narrow fairways. Many bunkers guard the small, smooth, quick, and undulating greens. Eight of the greens have two tiers. The signature hole on the course is the notorious 14th, a short but dangerous 130-yard par 3. This hole has ruined many a good round.

NOTES: Buenaventura and its sister course down the road, Olivas Park, hosted the 1984 and 1985 California State Open, won by touring professionals Greg Twiggs (1984) and Brad Greer (1985). The course record of 62 is held by former touring professional Brad Sherfy.

LOCATION: From U.S. 101 (Ventura Freeway) in Ventura, take the Victoria Avenue exit south for one mile to Olivas Park Drive. Turn left and go one-quarter mile to the course on the right.

. . . ● **TOURNAMENTS:** Shotgun tournaments are available. A 16-player minimum is required to book an event. Events should be booked 12 months in advance. The banquet facility can hold 280 people. ● **TRAVEL:** La Quinta Hotel (805-658-6200), the Double Tree Hotel (805-643-6000) and Holiday Inn (805-648-7731) are recommended for lodging.

15. BUENAVENTURA GOLF COURSE

PLAY POLICY & FEES: Green fees are $22 weekdays and $27 weekends and holidays. Carts are $24.

TEE TIMES: Reservations can be booked seven days in advance.

DRESS CODE: Nonmetal spikes are required.

COURSE DESCRIPTION: This is a rolling, links-style course with nearly eight acres of water. The 191-yard, par-3 14th features an island green. You'll need every club in the bag because of the wind and hills.

NOTES: The Oxnard City Championships are played here each July, and the Strawberry Classic is played here in April.

LOCATION: Take the Vineyard exit off U.S. 101 in Oxnard and drive west for three miles to the course.

. . . ● **TOURNAMENTS:** Shotgun tournaments are available weekdays only. A 28-player minimum is required to book a tournament. Events should be booked 12 months in advance. ● **TRAVEL:** The Marriott Residential Inn (805-278-2200) is recommended for lodging.

16. RIVER RIDGE GOLF CLUB

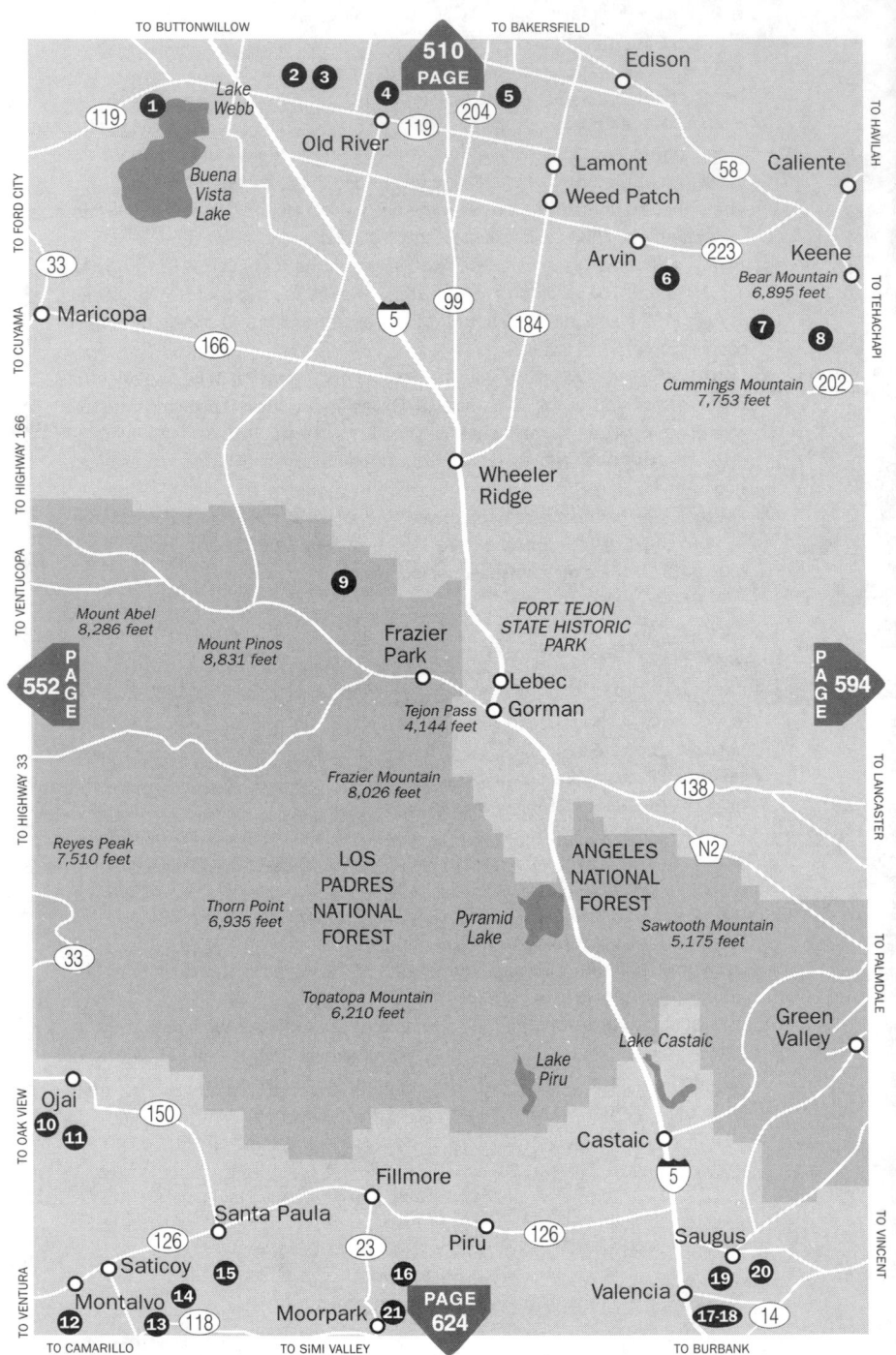

TO BUTTONWILLOW

TO BAKERSFIELD

510 PAGE

Edison

TO FORD CITY

119

① Lake Webb

② ③

④

⑤ 204

119

Old River

Buena Vista Lake

Lamont

TO HAVILAH

58 Caliente

Weed Patch

TO CUYAMA

33

Maricopa

166

5

99

184

Arvin

⑥

223 Keene

Bear Mountain 6,895 feet

⑦

⑧

TO TEHACHAPI

Cummings Mountain 7,753 feet

202

TO HIGHWAY 166

Wheeler Ridge

TO VENTUCOPA

⑨

FORT TEJON STATE HISTORIC PARK

Mount Abel 8,286 feet

Mount Pinos 8,831 feet

Frazier Park

Lebec

PAGE 552

Tejon Pass 4,144 feet

Gorman

PAGE 594

TO LANCASTER

TO HIGHWAY 33

Frazier Mountain 8,026 feet

138

N2

Reyes Peak 7,510 feet

LOS PADRES NATIONAL FOREST

ANGELES NATIONAL FOREST

Thorn Point 6,935 feet

Pyramid Lake

Sawtooth Mountain 5,175 feet

TO PALMDALE

33

Topatopa Mountain 6,210 feet

Lake Piru

Lake Castaic

Green Valley

TO OAK VIEW

Ojai

⑩ ⑪

150

Castaic

5

Fillmore

TO VENTURA

Santa Paula

126

23

Piru

126

Saugus

⑲ ⑳

Saticoy

⑮

⑯

Valencia

⑫

Montalvo

⑭

PAGE 624

⑰-⑱ 14

TO VINCENT

⑬

118

Moorpark

㉑

TO CAMARILLO

TO SIMI VALLEY

TO BURBANK

570

South Bakersfield/ Los Padres Area

BUENA VISTA GOLF COURSE
ARCHITECT: GEORGE MIFFLIN, 1953

10256 Golf Course Road
Taft, CA 93268

PRO SHOP: 661-398-9720

Dave James, Director of Golf
Ray George, Head Professional, PGA

Driving Range ●
Practice Greens ●
Clubhouse ●
Food / Beverage ●
Accommodations
Pull Carts ●
Power Carts ●
Club Rental ●
$pecial Offers

	1	2	3	4	5	6	7	8	9	OUT
BACK	363	216	409	513	525	120	440	420	423	3429
REGULAR	355	185	391	500	470	116	420	405	409	3251
par	4	3	4	5	5	3	4	4	4	36
handicap	15	9	3	11	13	17	5	1	7	-
FORWARD	328	161	324	467	425	99	358	345	388	2895
par	4	3	4	5	5	3	4	4	4	36
handicap	5	15	11	1	7	17	9	13	3	-

	10	11	12	13	14	15	16	17	18	IN
BACK	410	518	340	167	400	560	320	151	373	3239
REGULAR	363	488	330	151	387	536	307	143	362	3067
par	4	5	4	3	4	5	4	3	4	36
handicap	12	6	10	16	4	2	14	18	8	-
FORWARD	330	408	323	125	328	433	281	120	338	2686
par	4	5	4	3	4	5	4	3	4	36
handicap	12	6	14	16	2	4	10	18	8	-

BACK	
yardage	6668
par	72
rating	71
slope	118

REGULAR	
yardage	6318
par	72
rating	69.8
slope	113

FORWARD	
yardage	5581
par	72
rating	71.8
slope	117

STOCKDALE COUNTRY CLUB
ARCHITECT: LLOYD TEVIS, 1925

P.O. Box 9457
Bakersfield, CA 93309

7001 Stockdale Highway
Bakersfield, CA 93309

PRO SHOP: 661-832-0587
CLUBHOUSE: 661-832-0310

Rolly Allen, PGA Professional
Jodie Hale, Superintendent

Driving Range ●
Practice Greens ●
Clubhouse ●
Food / Beverage ●
Accommodations
Pull Carts ●
Power Carts ●
Club Rental
$pecial Offers

	1	2	3	4	5	6	7	8	9	OUT
BACK	341	400	365	341	414	407	168	506	337	3279
REGULAR	328	392	349	347	406	398	153	500	340	3213
par	4	4	4	4	4	4	3	5	4	36
handicap	11	1	7	13	3	5	9	17	15	-
FORWARD	291	344	335	329	382	382	138	484	323	3008
par	4	4	4	4	4	4	3	5	4	36
handicap	13	5	7	15	1	3	17	9	11	-

	10	11	12	13	14	15	16	17	18	IN
BACK	119	391	496	297	450	169	533	372	221	3048
REGULAR	124	378	476	295	429	141	526	380	210	2959
par	3	4	5	4	4	3	5	4	3	35
handicap	18	4	14	16	2	12	10	8	6	-
FORWARD	108	361	465	273	386	122	483	363	195	2756
par	3	4	5	4	4	3	5	4	3	35
handicap	18	4	10	12	2	16	6	8	14	-

BACK	
yardage	6327
par	71
rating	70.4
slope	120

REGULAR	
yardage	6172
par	71
rating	69.2
slope	116

FORWARD	
yardage	5764
par	71
rating	74.0
slope	124

PLAY POLICY & FEES: Green fees are $11.50 weekdays and $14.75 weekends. Carts are $18. The course is closed Christmas Day.

TEE TIMES: Reservations can be booked seven days in advance.

DRESS CODE: Nonmetal spikes are required.

COURSE DESCRIPTION: Originally a nine-hole layout, this course is the only green spot in the whole desert, thanks to irrigation from an on-site well. The course begins with a 355-yard par 4. This is not a mirage. The green sits on top of a hill 50 yards up, the highest point on the golf course. Hit your tee shot to the flat area of the fairway in order to avoid an uphill lie, and then go for the large, flat green at the top. Overall, the course offers a rolling layout dotted with many palm trees.

NOTES: Chris Zumbro holds the course record of 63.

LOCATION: Take Interstate 5 to Highway 119. Drive west on Highway 119 for about five miles and turn left onto Golf Course Road (just past the California Aqueduct).

. . . ● **TOURNAMENTS:** A 24-player minimum is required to book an outside event.

1. BUENA VISTA GOLF COURSE

PLAY POLICY & FEES: Reciprocal play is accepted with members of other private clubs. Have your club pro call for arrangements. The fee is $60 for reciprocators. Guest fees are $30 with a member and $60 without. Carts are $20.

TEE TIMES: Reservations can be booked three days in advance for reciprocal play.

DRESS CODE: Appropriate golf attire and nonmetal spikes are required.

COURSE DESCRIPTION: This course has numerous trees and a few water hazards on a traditional layout.

LOCATION: From the north, take the Stockdale exit off Highway 99 in Bakersfield. Travel west to the Stockdale Highway. Turn right and drive one-half mile to the club entrance.

. . . ● **TOURNAMENTS:** This course is not available for outside events.

2. STOCKDALE COUNTRY CLUB

③ SUNDALE COUNTRY CLUB
ARCHITECT: DEL WEBB, 1962

6218 Sundale Avenue
Bakersfield, CA 93309

PRO SHOP: 661-831-5224
CLUBHOUSE: 661-831-4200

Irene Ohr, Manager
Dave Bolar, PGA Professional

Driving Range ●
Practice Greens ●
Clubhouse ●
Food / Beverage ●
Accommodations
Pull Carts ●
Power Carts ●
Club Rental ●
$pecial Offers

	1	2	3	4	5	6	7	8	9	OUT
BACK	395	509	398	364	546	227	420	198	388	3445
REGULAR	382	496	384	355	534	211	392	185	378	3317
par	4	5	4	4	5	3	4	3	4	36
handicap	5	17	3	15	13	7	1	9	11	-
FORWARD	363	441	332	338	438	163	366	136	330	2907
par	4	5	4	4	5	3	4	3	4	36
handicap	5	9	7	13	3	15	1	17	11	-

	10	11	12	13	14	15	16	17	18	IN
BACK	471	198	388	379	521	366	386	162	485	3356
REGULAR	463	191	378	372	508	352	379	155	474	3272
par	4	3	4	4	5	4	4	3	5	36
handicap	2	6	8	10	16	12	4	18	14	-
FORWARD	449	158	339	319	444	286	336	102	403	2836
par	5	3	4	4	5	4	4	3	5	37
handicap	12	16	6	8	10	14	2	18	4	-

BACK	
yardage	6801
par	72
rating	71.8
slope	120

REGULAR	
yardage	6589
par	72
rating	70.7
slope	115

FORWARD	
yardage	5743
par	73
rating	72.7
slope	122

④ SEVEN OAKS COUNTRY CLUB
ARCHITECT: ROBERT MUIR GRAVES, 1992

2000 Grand Lakes Avenue
Bakersfield, CA 93311

PRO SHOP: 661-664-6474
CLUBHOUSE: 661-644-6404

Tony Murphy, Director of Golf, PGA
Bruce Burroughs, Head Professional, PGA
Gordon Carter, General Manager

Driving Range ●
Practice Greens ●
Clubhouse ●
Food / Beverage ●
Accommodations
Pull Carts
Power Carts ●
Club Rental ●
$pecial Offers

	1	2	3	4	5	6	7	8	9	OUT
BACK	414	376	385	175	540	456	384	219	620	3569
REGULAR	385	348	351	155	498	430	349	195	581	3292
par	4	4	4	3	5	4	4	3	5	36
handicap	9	11	15	17	7	3	13	5	1	-
FORWARD	319	287	293	113	425	370	286	141	507	2741
par	4	4	4	3	5	4	4	3	5	36
handicap	7	11	9	17	5	3	15	13	1	-

	10	11	12	13	14	15	16	17	18	IN
BACK	384	425	155	518	416	228	476	567	381	3550
REGULAR	359	397	132	490	391	200	429	537	351	3286
par	4	4	3	5	4	3	4	5	4	36
handicap	14	6	18	16	10	4	2	8	12	-
FORWARD	295	333	95	415	324	151	363	464	282	2722
par	4	4	3	5	4	3	4	5	4	36
handicap	14	6	18	16	8	12	2	4	10	-

BACK	
yardage	7119
par	72
rating	73.7
slope	128

REGULAR	
yardage	6578
par	72
rating	71.0
slope	119

FORWARD	
yardage	5463
par	72
rating	71.6
slope	125

PLAY POLICY & FEES: Outside play is accepted after 10:30 Monday through Thursday and after 11 a.m. Friday through Sunday. Green fees are the same as reciprocal play. Reciprocal play is accepted with members of other private clubs. Otherwise, members and guests only. Green fees are $25 with a member. Reciprocal play is $30 weekdays and $35 weekends. Carts are $10 per person. The course is closed on Monday.

DRESS CODE: Shorts must come to mid-thigh. Collared shirts and nonmetal spikes are required. No T-shirts are allowed.

COURSE DESCRIPTION: Formerly a public course known as Kern City, this layout is mostly flat with water and mature trees. The front nine has no parallel holes. Water can be found on six holes, and there is one long par 3. The course is deceptively difficult because the par-4 holes are long and the par-3 holes are tough.

NOTES: James Kiger holds the men's course record of 64. Val Skinner fired a 68 for the women's course record during a mini-tour event. The Bakersfield City Championship has been held at Sundale since 1980.

LOCATION: Take the Ming Avenue exit off Highway 99 in Bakersfield and travel west to New Stine Road. Turn right. Drive one-quarter mile to Sundale Avenue. Turn left and drive one-half mile to the club.

. . . ● **TOURNAMENTS:** This course is available for outside tournaments.

3. SUNDALE COUNTRY CLUB

PLAY POLICY & FEES: Limited reciprocal play is accepted by prior arrangement only. Guest fees for those accompanied by a member are $35, otherwise, guest fees are $60. Carts are $10 per player.

TEE TIMES: Reservations can be booked five days in advance.

DRESS CODE: Appropriate golf attire and nonmetal spikes are required.

COURSE DESCRIPTION: This mostly flat, traditional course played host to a Nike Tour event in 1993. Water comes into play on seven holes, notably in the par-5 ninth. Two lakes guard the green on this 620-yard tester, the signature hole of the course.

LOCATION: From Highway 99 in Bakersfield, take the Ming Avenue exit west. Continue about five miles to the intersection with Grand Lakes Avenue. The course is on the left.

. . . ● **TOURNAMENTS:** Outside events are limited to charity events on Monday. Carts are mandatory. An 80-player minimum is required. The banquet facility can accommodate 325 people. ● **TRAVEL:** The Sheraton Four Points Hotel in Bakersfield is located seven minutes from the course. For reservations call 805-325-9700.

4. SEVEN OAKS COUNTRY CLUB

⑤ VALLE GRANDE GOLF COURSE
ARCHITECTS: WILLIAM P. BELL, 1952; WILLIAM F. BELL

1119 Watts Drive
Bakersfield, CA 93307

PRO SHOP: 661-832-2259

Leon Mata, General Manager
Roland Reese, PGA Professional
Isaac Camarillo, Tournament Director

Driving Range ●
Practice Greens ●
Clubhouse ●
Food / Beverage ●
Accommodations
Pull Carts ●
Power Carts ●
Club Rental
$pecial Offers

	1	2	3	4	5	6	7	8	9	OUT
BACK	324	402	175	479	222	574	419	337	150	3082
REGULAR	310	396	164	449	211	555	395	330	130	2940
par	4	4	3	5	3	5	4	4	3	35
handicap	15	3	11	7	5	1	9	13	17	-
FORWARD	286	325	155	413	132	467	370	287	93	2528
par	4	4	3	4	3	5	4	4	3	34
handicap	11	7	13	3	15	1	5	9	17	-

	10	11	12	13	14	15	16	17	18	IN
BACK	519	184	371	359	487	320	109	472	428	3249
REGULAR	509	171	355	354	454	304	102	463	418	3130
par	5	3	4	4	5	4	3	5	4	37
handicap	4	8	10	14	6	16	18	12	2	-
FORWARD	496	119	328	325	385	246	94	423	374	2790
par	5	3	4	4	5	4	3	5	4	37
handicap	2	16	10	12	4	14	18	8	6	-

BACK	
yardage	6331
par	72
rating	116
slope	

REGULAR	
yardage	6070
par	72
rating	68.4
slope	112

FORWARD	
yardage	5318
par	72
rating	68.9
slope	115

⑥ SYCAMORE CANYON GOLF CLUB
ARCHITECT: ROBERT DEAN PUTMAN, 1989

500 Kenmar Lane
Arvin, CA 93203

PRO SHOP: 661-854-3163

Curtis Rowe, Professional/Manager
Steve Smith, Superintendent

Driving Range ●
Practice Greens ●
Clubhouse ●
Food / Beverage ●
Accommodations
Pull Carts ●
Power Carts ●
Club Rental ●
$pecial Offers

	1	2	3	4	5	6	7	8	9	OUT
BACK	382	388	198	505	330	425	417	181	602	3428
REGULAR	342	361	146	457	309	373	398	167	527	3080
par	4	4	3	5	4	4	4	3	5	36
handicap	13	9	11	7	17	1	5	15	3	-
FORWARD	324	330	127	398	291	336	359	107	480	2752
par	4	4	3	5	4	4	4	3	5	36
handicap	7	11	15	3	13	9	5	17	1	-

	10	11	12	13	14	15	16	17	18	IN
BACK	460	457	536	440	226	518	400	206	429	3672
REGULAR	417	412	516	379	192	500	385	136	411	3348
par	4	4	5	4	3	5	4	3	4	36
handicap	6	8	2	10	16	4	14	18	12	-
FORWARD	384	403	473	358	145	417	331	108	373	2992
par	4	5	5	4	3	5	4	3	4	37
handicap	6	8	2	10	16	4	14	18	12	-

BACK	
yardage	7100
par	72
rating	74.2
slope	123

REGULAR	
yardage	6428
par	72
rating	69.9
slope	117

FORWARD	
yardage	5744
par	73
rating	71.6
slope	120

PLAY POLICY & FEES: Green fees are $12 on weekdays and $15 on weekends. Call for special rates. Carts are $18.

TEE TIMES: Reservations can be booked 14 days in advance.

DRESS CODE: Collared shirts and nonmetal spikes are required.

COURSE DESCRIPTION: This course is level and appears simple to play, but don't be fooled. Out-of-bounds and an abundance of trees make accuracy a must. There are also two water channels running through the fairways, which add to the course's charm and difficulty.

LOCATION: Travel east on Highway 58 from Bakersfield, turn right on Cottonwood Road, and drive 1.25 miles. Turn left on Watts Drive to the club.

. . . ● **TOURNAMENTS:** A 44-player minimum is required to book a tournament. Carts are required. Events should be scheduled two months in advance.

5. VALLE GRANDE GOLF COURSE

PLAY POLICY & FEES: Green fees are $12 weekdays and $20 weekends. Twilight and senior rates are available. Carts are $20 and $25 on weekends. Call for special rates which include a cart.

TEE TIMES: Reservations can be booked seven days in advance.

DRESS CODE: No tank tops or sweats are allowed. Nonmetal spikes are required.

COURSE DESCRIPTION: Twenty acres of water come into play on 14 holes. Beware of the 548-yard ninth hole. It doglegs around a lake that runs 300 yards parallel to the hole. This par 5 is the number-one handicap hole on this course. This demanding course is made up of long par-4 and par-3 holes, and every green has at least two bunkers.

LOCATION: Take Highway 99 south of Bakersfield to the Bear Mountain/Arvin exit. Go 10 miles east to South Derby Street, then south 3.5 miles to Kenmar Lane. Turn left and drive to the course.

. . . ● **TOURNAMENTS:** A full field of 144 players is needed to book a weekend shotgun tournament.

6. SYCAMORE CANYON GOLF CLUB

HORSE THIEF GOLF & COUNTRY CLUB
ARCHITECT: BOB BALDOCK, 1974

P.O. Box 1487
Tehachapi, CA 93561

18100 Lucaya Way
Tehachapi, CA 93561

PRO SHOP: 800-244-0864

Alex Christ, General Manager
Leon Fourne, PGA Professional
Tim Kelley, Superintendent

Driving Range ●
Practice Greens ●
Clubhouse ●
Food / Beverage ●
Accommodations ●
Pull Carts ●
Power Carts ●
Club Rental ●
$pecial Offers ●

	1	2	3	4	5	6	7	8	9	OUT
BACK	378	405	562	416	194	563	145	365	385	3413
REGULAR	353	370	540	406	185	541	131	351	329	3206
par	4	4	5	4	3	5	3	4	4	36
handicap	13	9	1	5	11	3	17	7	15	-
FORWARD	311	326	492	365	147	481	96	340	265	2823
par	4	4	5	4	3	5	3	4	4	36
handicap	11	9	1	5	15	3	17	7	13	-

	10	11	12	13	14	15	16	17	18	IN
BACK	380	134	511	398	167	401	422	380	472	3265
REGULAR	370	127	493	383	155	385	402	369	458	3142
par	4	3	5	4	3	4	4	4	5	36
handicap	14	18	4	2	16	10	6	12	8	-
FORWARD	342	119	460	344	132	357	362	300	438	2854
par	4	3	5	4	3	4	4	4	5	36
handicap	10	18	4	6	16	12	8	14	2	-

BACK	
yardage	6678
par	72
rating	72.1
slope	124

REGULAR	
yardage	6348
par	72
rating	69.9
slope	117

FORWARD	
yardage	5677
par	72
rating	72.1
slope	124

 OAK TREE COUNTRY CLUB
ARCHITECT: TED ROBINSON, 1972

29541 Rolling Oak Drive
Tehachapi, CA 93561

PRO SHOP: 661-821-5144

Duane Gore, PGA Professional
Tom Bowers, General Manager
Micheal Greer, Superintendent

Driving Range ●
Practice Greens ●
Clubhouse ●
Food / Beverage ●
Accommodations
Pull Carts ●
Power Carts ●
Club Rental ●
$pecial Offers

	1	2	3	4	5	6	7	8	9	OUT
BACK	-	-	-	-	-	-	-	-	-	-
REGULAR	373	159	370	210	483	362	287	494	338	3076
par	4	3	4	3	5	4	4	5	4	36
handicap	5	11	1	3	17	13	15	9	7	-
FORWARD	348	118	351	193	403	329	260	414	331	2747
par	4	3	4	3	5	4	4	5	4	36
handicap	4	18	2	6	16	14	10	8	12	-

	10	11	12	13	14	15	16	17	18	IN
BACK	-	-	-	-	-	-	-	-	-	-
REGULAR	452	170	378	225	490	366	292	506	343	3222
par	4	3	4	3	5	4	4	5	4	36
handicap	2	16	4	6	18	12	14	10	8	-
FORWARD	434	134	362	193	456	300	277	479	293	2928
par	5	3	4	3	5	4	4	5	4	37
handicap	9	15	5	7	3	17	11	1	13	-

BACK	
yardage	-
par	-
rating	-
slope	-

REGULAR	
yardage	6298
par	72
rating	69.3
slope	113

FORWARD	
yardage	5675
par	73
rating	72.8
slope	125

PLAY POLICY & FEES: This course is affiliated with the Resort at Stallion Springs. Outside play is also accepted. Green fees are $20 weekdays and $30 weekends. Call for special rates. Carts are $20.

TEE TIMES: Reservations can be booked 10 days in advance.

DRESS CODE: Collared shirts are required. No short shorts are allowed.

COURSE DESCRIPTION: Horse Thief is a mountain course, elevation 4,000 feet. Although this course is not particularly long, it requires accuracy. The most prominent features are the oak trees and rocks that come into play. Water is also a factor on four holes.

LOCATION: From Bakersfield travel east on Highway 58 for 38 miles to Tehachapi and take the Highway 202 exit. Follow the signs for 16 miles to the Stallion Springs Resort.

. . . ● **TOURNAMENTS:** A 20-player minimum is required to book a tournament. The banquet facility can accommodate 40 people. ● **TRAVEL:** The Resort at Stallion Springs is located minutes away from the golf course. ● **$PECIAL OFFERS:** Golf packages are available with the Resort at Stallion Springs. Packages include lodging, breakfast, green fees, and cart.

7. HORSE THIEF GOLF & COUNTRY CLUB

PLAY POLICY & FEES: Reciprocal play is accepted with members of other private clubs. Green fees are $10 for nine holes and $15 for 18 on weekdays. Weekend green fees are $15 for nine holes and $20 for 18 holes. Carts are $10 for nine holes and $16 for 18 holes.

TEE TIMES: Reservations can be booked seven days in advance.

DRESS CODE: Collared shirts are required for men. Ladies must have either a collared shirt or sleeves. Shorts must be at least to mid-thigh. Nonmetal spikes are required.

COURSE DESCRIPTION: The course, set at 4,000 feet, is rimmed by mountains. It's a level layout set around a small lake. Trees dot the fairways, and jutting rocks add to the mountainous look of the course, but they rarely come into play.

LOCATION: From Bakersfield travel east on Highway 58 for 38 miles to the town of Tehachapi and take the Highway 202 exit. Follow the signs for about 14 miles to Bear Valley Springs.

. . . ● **TOURNAMENTS:** Outside events are held on a limited basis.

8. OAK TREE COUNTRY CLUB

P.O. Box P
Pine Mountain, CA 93222

2524 Beechwood Way
Pine Mountain, CA 93222

PRO SHOP: 661-242-3734
CLUBHOUSE: 661-242-3788

Bob Peterson, Manager
Chad Sorensen, PGA Professional
Jim Gordon, Superintendent

Driving Range ●
Practice Greens ●
Clubhouse ●
Food / Beverage ●
Accommodations
Pull Carts ●
Power Carts ●
Club Rental ●
$pecial Offers

	1	2	3	4	5	6	7	8	9	OUT
BACK	-	-	-	-	-	-	-	-	-	-
REGULAR	175	256	130	122	157	285	162	219	285	1791
par	3	4	3	3	3	4	3	3	4	30
handicap	11	13	17	15	7	9	5	3	1	-
FORWARD	157	176	111	79	141	211	152	219	325	1571
par	3	3	3	3	3	4	3	4	4	30
handicap	5	3	13	15	11	9	7	17	1	-

	10	11	12	13	14	15	16	17	18	IN
BACK	-	-	-	-	-	-	-	-	-	-
REGULAR	207	271	144	132	134	285	152	209	285	1819
par	3	4	3	3	3	4	3	3	4	30
handicap	4	12	18	14	16	10	8	6	2	-
FORWARD	167	128	125	72	134	285	134	215	325	1585
par	3	3	3	3	3	4	3	4	4	30
handicap	4	12	14	16	10	6	8	18	2	-

BACK	
yardage	-
par	-
rating	-
slope	-

REGULAR	
yardage	3610
par	60
rating	58.8
slope	100

FORWARD	
yardage	3156
par	60
rating	57.2
slope	95

GOLF 50

905 Country Club Drive
Ojai, CA 93023

PRO SHOP: 805-646-2420

Mark Wipf, Head Professional, PGA
Mark Greenslit, Director of Golf, PGA
Sam Williamson, Superintendent

Driving Range ●
Practice Greens ●
Clubhouse ●
Food / Beverage ●
Accommodations ●
Pull Carts
Power Carts ●
Club Rental ●
$pecial Offers ●

	1	2	3	4	5	6	7	8	9	OUT
BACK	405	203	563	442	177	359	402	227	487	3265
REGULAR	399	186	546	397	167	327	387	181	458	3048
par	4	3	5	4	3	4	4	3	5	35
handicap	7	13	9	1	17	3	5	15	11	-
FORWARD	364	152	471	359	145	300	350	133	435	2709
par	4	3	5	4	3	4	4	3	5	35
handicap	7	13	1	5	15	11	9	17	3	-

	10	11	12	13	14	15	16	17	18	IN
BACK	412	358	115	297	440	312	392	128	517	2971
REGULAR	406	330	105	274	433	299	379	119	499	2844
par	4	4	3	4	4	4	4	3	5	35
handicap	6	10	18	14	4	12	2	16	8	-
FORWARD	404	297	98	128	416	283	352	103	435	2516
par	5	4	3	3	5	4	4	3	5	36
handicap	8	6	16	14	10	12	2	18	4	-

BACK	
yardage	6236
par	70
rating	70.2
slope	122

REGULAR	
yardage	5892
par	70
rating	68.5
slope	117

FORWARD	
yardage	5225
par	71
rating	71.0
slope	129

PLAY POLICY & FEES: Guests must be accompanied by a member. Guest fees are $8 for nine holes and $13 for 18 holes weekdays, and $10 for nine holes and $15 for 18 holes weekends and holidays. Carts are $11 for nine holes and $17 for 18 holes.

DRESS CODE: No tank tops or halter tops allowed. Spikeless shoes are required.

COURSE DESCRIPTION: This is an interesting course set at 5,500 feet and nestled among the beautiful pine trees. (You may want to pack mountaineering boots.) The fifth hole is known as "Cardiac Hill," obviously because of its steepness. This hole is one of the reasons that the club now has power carts.

NOTES: Chad Sorensen holds the course record of 54.

LOCATION: Travel 40 miles south of Bakersfield on Interstate 5 and take the Frazier Park exit to Frazier Mountain Road. Drive west five miles and continue west on Cuddly Valley Road for another six miles to the top of the mountain. Turn right on Mill Potrero Road and drive five miles to the course.

. . . ● **TOURNAMENTS:** This course is not available for outside events. ● **TRAVEL:** The Pine Mountain Inn (661-242-2500) is recommended for lodging.

9. PINE MOUNTAIN CLUB

PLAY POLICY & FEES: Outside play is accepted; green fees are $130. For resort guests, green fees are $110, including cart, range balls, and club storage.

TEE TIMES: Reservations for hotel guests can be booked 90 days in advance; otherwise, 7 days in advance.

DRESS CODE: Nonmetal spikes are required.

COURSE DESCRIPTION: This beautiful, mountainside course was built in the 1920s by George C. Thomas and was improved by Jay Morrish in 1988. Among the holes to watch for is the par-4 fourth. The drive from the back tee must carry a barranca. Part of the hole is hidden by the barranca and large oak trees. If you're not in the fairway, you're cooked. The 11th par 4 crosses a barranca not once, but twice. The tee shot from the back tee must carry 200 yards to a safe landing area. Everything kicks toward the barranca, so you have to play down the left side.

NOTES: This course has been home to seven Senior PGA Tour events. It is the home of the EMC Squared Skills Challenge. The course record of 61 was set by Buddy Allin in the 1996 FHP Health Care Classic.

LOCATION: From Ventura travel north 13 miles on Highway 33 to Ojai. Turn right on Country Club Road.

. . . ● **TOURNAMENTS:** A 16-player minimum is needed to book a tournament. Events should be scheduled 12 months in advance. The banquet facility can accommodate 300 people. ● **TRAVEL:** The resort's world-class spa has recently opened. For reservations at the Ojai Valley Inn & Spa call 805-646-5511. ● **$PECIAL OFFERS:** Take advantage of "The Best of Ojai" play-and-stay package.

10. OJAI VALLEY INN & SPA

SOULE PARK GOLF COURSE
ARCHITECT: WILLIAM P. BELL, 1962

P.O. Box 758
Ojai, CA 93023

1033 East Ojai Avenue
Ojai, CA 93023

PRO SHOP: 805-646-5633
CLUBHOUSE: 805-646-5685

Dane Sonerson, PGA Professional
Don Miller, General Manager
Roger Specter, Superintendent

Driving Range ●
Practice Greens ●
Clubhouse ●
Food / Beverage ●
Accommodations
Pull Carts ●
Power Carts ●
Club Rental ●
$pecial Offers

	1	2	3	4	5	6	7	8	9	OUT
BACK	-	-	-	-	-	-	-	-	-	-
REGULAR	341	373	135	517	409	211	568	293	309	3156
par	4	4	3	5	4	3	5	4	4	36
handicap	9	7	17	5	3	13	1	15	11	-
FORWARD	332	322	114	493	333	190	538	286	302	2910
par	4	4	3	5	4	3	5	4	4	36
handicap	9	5	17	3	7	15	1	13	11	-

	10	11	12	13	14	15	16	17	18	IN
BACK	-	-	-	-	-	-	-	-	-	-
REGULAR	146	526	395	347	383	396	167	505	377	3242
par	3	5	4	4	4	4	3	5	4	36
handicap	18	10	6	16	4	2	14	8	12	-
FORWARD	132	461	374	277	374	377	154	496	339	2984
par	3	5	4	4	4	4	3	5	4	36
handicap	16	4	10	14	8	6	18	2	12	-

BACK	
yardage	-
par	-
rating	-
slope	-

REGULAR	
yardage	6398
par	72
rating	70.1
slope	120

FORWARD	
yardage	5894
par	72
rating	73.2
slope	124

SATICOY REGIONAL GOLF COURSE
ARCHITECTS: GEORGE C. THOMAS, 1921; WILLIAM F. BELL

1025 South Wells Road
Ventura, CA 93004

PRO SHOP: 805-647-6678

Kelly Sorenson, Manager
Matt Mulvany, Superintendent

Driving Range ●
Practice Greens ●
Clubhouse
Food / Beverage ●
Accommodations
Pull Carts ●
Power Carts ●
Club Rental ●
$pecial Offers

	1	2	3	4	5	6	7	8	9	OUT
BACK	-	-	-	-	-	-	-	-	-	-
REGULAR	310	322	461	428	168	112	425	169	328	2723
par	4	4	5	4	3	3	4	3	4	34
handicap	11	9	7	3	13	17	1	15	5	-
FORWARD	310	333	466	395	148	92	417	158	323	2642
par	4	4	5	4	3	3	4	3	4	35
handicap	7	9	11	1	15	13	5	17	3	-

	10	11	12	13	14	15	16	17	18	IN
BACK	-	-	-	-	-	-	-	-	-	-
REGULAR	342	308	461	394	142	112	413	156	342	2670
par	4	4	4	4	3	3	4	3	4	33
handicap	6	12	8	4	16	18	2	14	10	-
FORWARD	344	300	400	425	132	92	401	151	312	2557
par	4	4	4	5	3	3	5	3	4	35
handicap	8	10	2	14	16	6	12	18	4	-

BACK	
yardage	-
par	-
rating	-
slope	-

REGULAR	
yardage	5393
par	67
rating	65.4
slope	109

FORWARD	
yardage	5199
par	70
rating	67.9
slope	112

PLAY POLICY & FEES: Green fees are $22 weekdays and $28 weekends. Senior and twilight rates are available. Carts are $24. The course is closed Christmas Day.

TEE TIMES: Reservations can be booked seven days in advance starting at 7 a.m.

COURSE DESCRIPTION: This course is set at the base of the mountains in the Ojai Valley and traverses a rolling terrain. A creek runs through the course, and mature trees line the fairways. A hole that will stagger many a golfer is the 568-yard, par-5 seventh. This is a three-shot hole with a creek running in front of the green, requiring a 120-yard carry. The green is guarded by a huge oak tree. It is definitely a position hole.

NOTES: Soule Park's record is 62, held by Jim Hopper.

LOCATION: From Ventura travel north 16 miles on Highway 33 to the town of Ojai. Turn right on East Ojai Avenue and drive two miles to the course.

. . . ● **TOURNAMENTS:** A 20-player minimum is required to book a tournament. The banquet facility holds 150 people.

11. SOULE PARK GOLF COURSE

PLAY POLICY & FEES: Green fees are $10 for nine holes and $15 for 18 holes weekdays, and $12 for nine holes and $18 for 18 holes weekends. Carts are $6 for nine holes and $9 for 18 holes. Seniors (over 60) pay $8 for nine holes and $11 for 18 holes.

TEE TIMES: Reservations for 18-hole rounds must be booked seven days in advance.

DRESS CODE: Appropriate golf attire is required.

COURSE DESCRIPTION: This course was built in 1921 as the Saticoy Golf and Country Club. It has narrow fairways, gradual slopes, and quick, traditional greens. Water, bunkers, and trees make this a shot-maker's course from start to finish.

LOCATION: Take the Central Avenue exit off U.S. 101 south of Ventura and continue for five miles until it dead-ends at Vineyard. Make a right turn and drive until Vineyard dead-ends at Highway 118. Turn left on Highway 118 and drive one mile to the course on the left.

. . . ● **TOURNAMENTS:** A 20-player minimum is needed to book an event. Tournaments should be scheduled at least three months in advance. ● **TRAVEL:** Andria's restaurant is recommended for seafood. La Quinta Inn in Ventura is 15 minutes from the course.

12. SATICOY REGIONAL GOLF COURSE

⑬ SATICOY COUNTRY CLUB
ARCHITECT: WILLIAM F. BELL, 1964

4450 Clubhouse Drive
Camarillo, CA 93010

PRO SHOP: 805-485-5216

Jim Swagerty, PGA Professional
Rich Wagner, Superintendent

Driving Range ●
Practice Greens ●
Clubhouse ●
Food / Beverage ●
Accommodations
Pull Carts
Power Carts ●
Club Rental
$pecial Offers

	1	2	3	4	5	6	7	8	9	OUT
BACK	407	354	425	205	405	511	387	563	189	3446
REGULAR	376	325	401	172	376	480	375	528	162	3195
par	4	4	4	3	4	5	4	5	3	36
handicap	7	9	1	13	5	15	3	11	17	-
FORWARD	347	272	394	122	340	468	335	473	137	2888
par	4	4	4	3	4	5	4	5	3	36
handicap	7	13	1	17	5	3	9	11	15	-

	10	11	12	13	14	15	16	17	18	IN
BACK	178	404	359	207	536	410	341	474	569	3478
REGULAR	164	365	330	190	502	378	323	439	521	3212
par	3	4	4	3	5	4	4	4	5	36
handicap	18	4	16	12	6	8	14	2	10	-
FORWARD	137	355	289	186	464	345	309	434	440	2959
par	3	4	4	3	5	4	4	5	5	37
handicap	18	4	16	12	2	10	6	14	8	-

BACK	
yardage	6924
par	72
rating	74.5
slope	138

REGULAR	
yardage	6407
par	72
rating	71.0
slope	124

FORWARD	
yardage	5847
par	73
rating	74.3
slope	128

⑭ LAS POSAS COUNTRY CLUB
ARCHITECT: LAWRENCE HUGHES, 1958

955 Fairway Drive
Camarillo, CA 93010

PRO SHOP: 805-482-4518
CLUBHOUSE: 805-388-2901

Jon Fiedler, PGA Professional

Driving Range ●
Practice Greens ●
Clubhouse ●
Food / Beverage ●
Accommodations
Pull Carts ●
Power Carts ●
Club Rental ●
$pecial Offers ●

	1	2	3	4	5	6	7	8	9	OUT
BACK	-	-	-	-	-	-	-	-	-	-
REGULAR	382	126	367	498	376	210	483	363	205	3010
par	4	3	4	5	4	3	5	4	3	35
handicap	7	17	3	13	1	5	15	9	11	-
FORWARD	356	103	349	485	337	152	434	342	171	2729
par	4	3	4	5	4	3	5	4	3	35
handicap	11	117	5	1	3	15	7	9	13	-

	10	11	12	13	14	15	16	17	18	IN
BACK	-	-	-	-	-	-	-	-	-	-
REGULAR	485	135	536	164	333	390	387	396	375	3201
par	5	3	5	3	4	4	4	4	4	36
handicap	8	18	4	12	14	2	6	10	16	-
FORWARD	464	114	503	139	303	378	375	359	278	2913
par	5	3	5	3	4	4	4	4	4	36
handicap	4	18	6	16	12	2	8	10	14	-

BACK	
yardage	-
par	-
rating	-
slope	-

REGULAR	
yardage	6211
par	71
rating	70.1
slope	124

FORWARD	
yardage	5642
par	71
rating	73.1
slope	126

PRIVATE: $50-$100

18 HOLES

PLAY POLICY & FEES: Reciprocal play is accepted with members of other private clubs. Green fees are $50 with a member and $100 without a member. Carts are $12. The course is closed on Monday.

DRESS CODE: Collared shirts and nonmetal spikes are required. No denim is allowed on the course.

COURSE DESCRIPTION: Make sure your tee shots are accurate or you will be in for a long day. The fairways are tight and demanding. Greens are large and undulating. Many of the greens are elevated. The par-3 10th is 178 yards from the back tees, dropping about 100 feet over water to the green. Situated on the side of a mountain, this is the course to play in Ventura County if you're looking for golf and not scenery.

LOCATION: Take the Central Avenue exit off U.S. 101 just south of Ventura and drive north for two miles to Santa Clara Avenue. Turn right and travel 1.25 miles to Los Angeles Avenue and turn left. Drive one-half mile to the club.

. . . ● **TOURNAMENTS:** This course is available for outside events on a very limited basis. Call the general manager for details.

13. SATICOY COUNTRY CLUB

PRIVATE: $70-$

FAX: 805-388-1378

18 HOLES

PLAY POLICY & FEES: Reciprocal play is accepted with members of other private clubs; otherwise, members and quests only. Green fees are $70 for reciprocators. Carts are $10 per person.

DRESS CODE: Appropriate golf attire is required. No metal spikes are allowed.

COURSE DESCRIPTION: The front nine is hilly with narrow fairways. The back nine is flatter but well bunkered. The greens are soft, quick, and true.

NOTES: This is the home course of Corey Pavin.

LOCATION: Take the Las Posas Road exit off U.S.101 in Camarillo and drive north for one-half mile to Crestview Avenue. Turn right and drive one-quarter mile to Valley Vista Drive and turn right. Continue one mile to Fairway Drive and turn left to the club.

. . . ● **TOURNAMENTS:** This course is available for outside tournaments on Monday only. A 72-player minimum is needed to book an event. Tournaments should be scheduled six months in advance. A banquet facility is available that can accommodate 300 people.

14. LAS POSAS COUNTRY CLUB

15 MOUNTAIN VIEW GOLF CLUB
ARCHITECT: TONY PAWLAK, PAUL MCGRATH, 1969

16799 South Mountain
Santa Paula, CA 93060

PRO SHOP: 805-525-1571

Andrea Smith, Director of Golf
Ralph Corona, Pro/Superintendent

Driving Range
Practice Greens ●
Clubhouse ●
Food / Beverage ●
Accommodations
Pull Carts ●
Power Carts ●
Club Rental ●
$pecial Offers

	1	2	3	4	5	6	7	8	9	OUT
BACK	-	-	-	-	-	-	-	-	-	-
REGULAR	373	494	182	298	261	168	386	331	377	2870
par	4	5	3	4	4	3	4	4	4	35
handicap	5	9	13	11	17	15	1	7	3	-
FORWARD	340	449	154	211	216	143	373	289	344	2519
par	4	5	3	4	4	3	4	4	4	35
handicap	9	1	15	5	17	11	3	7	13	-

	10	11	12	13	14	15	16	17	18	IN
BACK	-	-	-	-	-	-	-	-	-	-
REGULAR	294	218	292	262	283	472	163	392	121	2497
par	4	3	4	4	4	5	3	4	3	34
handicap	8	4	10	14	18	6	12	2	16	-
FORWARD	268	170	260	232	236	417	147	371	90	2191
par	4	3	4	4	4	5	3	4	3	34
handicap	8	12	6	14	16	2	10	4	18	-

BACK	
yardage	-
par	-
rating	-
slope	-

REGULAR	
yardage	5367
par	69
rating	65.0
slope	112

FORWARD	
yardage	4710
par	69
rating	66.9
slope	112

16 ELKINS RANCH GOLF COURSE
ARCHITECT: WILLIAM TUCKER JR., 1962

P.O. Box 695   1386 Chambersburg Road
Fillmore, CA 93016-0695   Fillmore, CA 93015

PRO SHOP: 805-524-1440
STARTER: 805-524-1121

Dan Hodapp, Head Professional, PGA
Jay Jamison, Superintendent

Driving Range ●
Practice Greens ●
Clubhouse
Food / Beverage ●
Accommodations
Pull Carts ●
Power Carts ●
Club Rental ●
$pecial Offers

	1	2	3	4	5	6	7	8	9	OUT
BACK	329	416	199	521	403	464	169	355	416	3272
REGULAR	318	388	187	507	392	447	158	345	395	3137
par	4	4	3	5	4	5	3	4	4	36
handicap	17	1	7	11	5	15	13	9	3	-
FORWARD	309	383	162	483	365	432	145	311	385	2975
par	4	5	3	5	4	5	3	4	5	38
handicap	11	13	17	3	1	5	15	7	9	-

	10	11	12	13	14	15	16	17	18	IN
BACK	363	190	394	381	298	374	127	430	473	3030
REGULAR	355	166	371	355	280	361	116	423	447	2874
par	4	3	4	4	4	4	3	4	5	35
handicap	10	12	2	4	16	8	18	6	14	-
FORWARD	344	153	360	336	268	291	96	384	438	2670
par	4	3	4	4	4	4	3	4	5	35
handicap	6	16	2	8	12	14	18	4	10	-

BACK	
yardage	6302
par	71
rating	69.9
slope	117

REGULAR	
yardage	6011
par	71
rating	68.3
slope	112

FORWARD	
yardage	5645
par	73
rating	66.5
slope	107

PLAY POLICY & FEES: Green fees are $18 weekdays and $25 weekends. Twilight, senior, and junior rates are available. Carts are $18 weekdays and $20 weekends.

TEE TIMES: Reservations can be booked seven days in advance.

DRESS CODE: Shirts and shoes are necessary.

COURSE DESCRIPTION: This is a short course set in a narrow valley at the base of South Mountain. Mature trees border the fairways of this wandering course. The course may seem short, but it's difficult. Accuracy is essential to scoring well.

NOTES: Senior cards are $20 per year. They entitle anyone over 60 years of age to $8 green fees Monday through Friday. Carts are not included.

LOCATION: Take the Highway 126 exit off U.S. 101 just south of Ventura and drive east to the 10th Street exit. Turn left under the freeway, drive to Harvard Boulevard, and turn right. At 12th Street, turn right and drive one-half mile to South Mountain Road. Turn right to the course.

. . . ● **TOURNAMENTS:** Shotgun tournaments are available weekdays only.

15. MOUNTAIN VIEW GOLF CLUB

PLAY POLICY & FEES: Green fees are $23 weekdays and $29 weekends. Call for special rates. Carts are $22.

TEE TIMES: Reservations are recommended and should be made 10 days in advance.

DRESS CODE: Golfers must wear collared shirts. Bermuda shorts are allowed, but no cutoffs.

COURSE DESCRIPTION: This course is set in a canyon in the country. There are lots of water holes and few parallel fairways. It's a very challenging course with five lakes, elevated tees, and demanding greens. Fun for all levels of play, it's quiet and scenic. It's a great getaway course that sees 60,000 rounds a year.

NOTES: Chad Sorenson of Pine Mountain Golf Course holds the course record of 64.

LOCATION: Take Interstate 5 north to Highway 126 and turn west. Drive 19 miles to Fillmore. At Highway 23, the third stoplight, turn left. The course is 1.5 miles on the left.

. . . ● **TOURNAMENTS:** Shotgun tournaments are available weekdays only. Carts are required. A 28-player minimum is required to book a regular tournament. The outside banquet facility can accommodate 200 people. Events should be booked 12 months in advance.

16. ELKINS RANCH GOLF COURSE

THE GREENS AT VALENCIA
ARCHITECT: TED ROBINSON, 1999

26501 McBean Parkway
Valencia, CA 91355

PRO SHOP: 661-222-2900

John Perkins, Head Professional, PGA

Driving Range
Practice Greens
Clubhouse   x
Food / Beverage   x
Accommodations
Pull Carts
Power Carts
Club Rental
$pecial Offers

	1	2	3	4	5	6	7	8	9	OUT
BACK										
REGULAR										
par										
handicap										
FORWARD										
par										
handicap										

	10	11	12	13	14	15	16	17	18	IN
BACK										
REGULAR										
par										
handicap										
FORWARD										
par										
handicap										

BACK	
yardage	
par	
rating	
slope	

REGULAR	
yardage	
par	
rating	
slope	

FORWARD	
yardage	
par	
rating	
slope	

 VALENCIA COUNTRY CLUB
ARCHITECT: ROBERT TRENT JONES SR., 1965

27330 North Tourney Road
Valencia, CA 91355

PRO SHOP: 661-287-1880

Ken Kikuchi, General Manager
Rick Smith, Director of Golf, PGA
Wayne Mills, Superintendent

Driving Range   ●
Practice Greens   ●
Clubhouse   ●
Food / Beverage   ●
Accommodations
Pull Carts
Power Carts   ●
Club Rental   ●
$pecial Offers

	1	2	3	4	5	6	7	8	9	OUT
BACK	540	400	237	422	367	427	185	369	512	3459
REGULAR	511	390	180	386	356	414	172	354	500	3263
par	5	4	3	4	4	4	3	4	5	36
handicap	5	3	7	11	15	1	13	9	17	-
FORWARD	479	346	97	336	257	371	132	308	415	2741
par	5	4	3	4	4	4	3	4	5	36
handicap	5	3	17	11	13	1	15	7	9	-

	10	11	12	13	14	15	16	17	18	IN
BACK	470	400	387	386	211	529	202	466	566	3617
REGULAR	458	356	366	381	204	515	185	449	546	3460
par	4	4	4	4	3	5	3	4	5	36
handicap	2	16	18	14	12	6	10	4	8	-
FORWARD	400	305	327	325	158	452	114	398	482	2961
par	5	4	4	4	3	5	3	5	5	38
handicap	10	12	6	8	16	4	18	14	2	-

BACK	
yardage	7076
par	72
rating	74.7
slope	138

REGULAR	
yardage	6723
par	72
rating	72.8
slope	123

FORWARD	
yardage	5702
par	74
rating	74.4
slope	133

PLAY POLICY & FEES: Green fees are $10 Monday through Thursday, and $13 Friday through Sunday. Discount memberships are available.

TEE TIMES: Reservations can be made but are not necessary.

COURSE DESCRIPTION: This is a 27-hole putting course designed by Ted Robinson. Only 18 holes are used at one time. The course features lots of water and sand. The signature hole features a waterfall and an island green.

NOTES: The course is open until 9 p.m. Sunday through Thursday, and 11 p.m. Friday and Saturday.

LOCATION: Rrom Los Angeles take the Interstate 405 north to Interstate 5 north. Exit at Valencia Boulevard and turn right (east). Make a left on McBean Parkway. The course is right across from the Valencia Town Center.

. . . ● **TOURNAMENTS:** Call the pro shop for more information. A banquet facility is available that can accommodate up to 350 people.

17. THE GREENS AT VALENCIA

PLAY POLICY & FEES: Members and guests only. Guests must be accompanied by a member while playing. Green fees are $72 weekdays and $102 weekends, carts included.

DRESS CODE: Appropriate golf attire and nonmetal spikes are required.

COURSE DESCRIPTION: This Robert Trent Jones Sr. design offers a scenic, natural layout with lots of trees. Water comes into play on eight holes. It's always a love-hate relationship with Jones, so take your pick on the third. There is no bailout on this 180-yard par 3 from the back tees. Watch out for water and bunkers on the right and trees on the left. It's considered one of the toughest par-3 holes in Southern California.

NOTES: From the championship tees, the course record is 63, held by Bob Burns. From the tournament tees, the course record is 67, held by Jeff Flesher.

LOCATION: From San Fernando travel north on Interstate 5 for 12 miles to Magic Mountain Parkway and turn east on Tourney Road to the club.

. . . ● **TOURNAMENTS:** Outside events are scheduled for Monday only. Carts are required. A 72-player minimum is needed to book a shotgun tournament.

18. VALENCIA COUNTRY CLUB

24700 West Trevino Drive
Valencia, CA 91355

PRO SHOP: 661-253-1870
CLUBHOUSE: 661-253-0781

Warren Leary, General Manager
Les Johnson, Head Professional
Rojelio Alba, Superintendent

Driving Range ●
Practice Greens ●
Clubhouse ●
Food / Beverage ●
Accommodations
Pull Carts
Power Carts ●
Club Rental ●
$pecial Offers

	1	2	3	4	5	6	7	8	9	OUT
BACK	373	222	196	374	104	167	320	145	423	2324
REGULAR	350	200	184	368	86	144	303	126	397	2158
par	4	3	3	4	3	3	4	3	4	31
handicap	9	5	7	3	15	17	11	13	1	-
FORWARD	335	181	174	359	69	120	290	111	373	2012
par	4	4	3	4	3	3	4	3	5	33
handicap	5	17	3	1	15	11	7	9	13	-

	10	11	12	13	14	15	16	17	18	IN
BACK	452	194	92	81	144	344	396	158	181	2042
REGULAR	427	163	88	75	130	316	388	147	172	1906
par	4	3	3	3	3	4	4	3	3	30
handicap	2	8	18	16	14	6	4	12	10	-
FORWARD	400	142	76	67	114	290	376	118	163	1746
par	5	3	3	3	3	4	4	3	3	31
handicap	10	4	18	16	14	12	2	8	6	-

BACK	
yardage	4366
par	61
rating	61.4
slope	104

REGULAR	
yardage	4064
par	61
rating	60.5
slope	102

FORWARD	
yardage	3758
par	64
rating	61.1
slope	96

19345 Avenue of the Oaks
Newhall, CA 91321

PRO SHOP: 661-252-9859

Dean Dotson, Manager

Driving Range
Practice Greens ●
Clubhouse ●
Food / Beverage
Accommodations
Pull Carts ●
Power Carts
Club Rental ●
$pecial Offers

	1	2	3	4	5	6	7	8	9	OUT
BACK	-	-	-	-	-	-	-	-	-	-
REGULAR	132	187	153	140	273	103	152	175	110	1425
par	3	3	3	3	4	3	3	3	3	28
handicap	7	2	6	4	5	9	3	1	8	-
FORWARD	87	157	123	124	246	78	142	164	91	1212
par	3	3	3	3	4	3	3	3	3	28
handicap	7	2	6	4	5	9	3	1	8	-

	10	11	12	13	14	15	16	17	18	IN
BACK	-	-	-	-	-	-	-	-	-	-
REGULAR	132	187	153	140	273	103	152	175	110	1425
par	3	3	3	3	4	3	3	3	3	28
handicap	7	2	6	4	5	9	3	1	8	-
FORWARD	87	157	123	124	246	78	142	164	91	1212
par	3	3	3	3	4	3	3	3	3	28
handicap	7	2	6	4	5	9	3	1	8	-

BACK	
yardage	-
par	-
rating	-
slope	-

REGULAR	
yardage	2850
par	56
rating	-
slope	-

FORWARD	
yardage	2424
par	56
rating	-
slope	-

PLAY POLICY & FEES: Green fees are $21 Monday through Thursday, $23 Friday, and $28 weekends. Carts are $11 per rider. Discount memberships are available.

TEE TIMES: Reservations can be booked seven days in advance.

DRESS CODE: Shirts must be worn; no tank tops are allowed.

COURSE DESCRIPTION: This is a short course that requires good iron play. Five lakes, 88 bunkers, and one island green are found on the layout. The course is always in good condition.

NOTES: Paved cart paths have recently been added. The course record is 52, held by Donny Hinson.

LOCATION: In Valencia traveling north on Interstate 5, exit at Lyons Avenue. Drive east for one-half mile to Wiley Canyon Road. Turn left and then left again at Tournament Road. Drive one-half mile to Trevino Road and turn left again; then drive one-half mile to the club.

. . . ● **TOURNAMENTS:** A 12-player minimum is needed to book a tournament. Carts are required.

19. VISTA VALENCIA GOLF CLUB

PLAY POLICY & FEES: Members and guests only. This is a private retirement village.

DRESS CODE: Appropriate golf attire is required.

COURSE DESCRIPTION: This is a good opportunity for members to practice up on their short game. It features eight par 3s and is walkable.

NOTES: Friendly Valley also has a pitch-and-putt course.

LOCATION: Take Highway 126 off Interstate 5 and follow it to San Fernando Road. From there travel 1.5 miles to Avenue of the Oaks. Turn left and look for the course.

. . . ● **TOURNAMENTS:** This course is not available for outside events.

20. FRIENDLY VALLEY GOLF COURSE

21 TIERRA REJADA GOLF CLUB
ARCHITECT: BOB CUPP, 1999

15187 Tierra Rejada Golf
MoorPark, CA 93021

PRO SHOP: 805-531-9300

Driving Range
Practice Greens
Clubhouse
Food / Beverage
Accommodations
Pull Carts
Power Carts
Club Rental
$pecial Offers

	1	2	3	4	5	6	7	8	9	OUT
BACK										
REGULAR										
par										
handicap										
FORWARD										
par										
handicap										

	10	11	12	13	14	15	16	17	18	IN
BACK										
REGULAR										
par										
handicap										
FORWARD										
par										
handicap										

BACK	
yardage	
par	
rating	
slope	

REGULAR	
yardage	
par	
rating	
slope	

FORWARD	
yardage	
par	
rating	
slope	

PLAY POLICY & FEES: This course is due to open in the fall of 1999. No information on the course was available at time of press.

COURSE DESCRIPTION:

LOCATION:

21. TIERRA REJADA GOLF CLUB

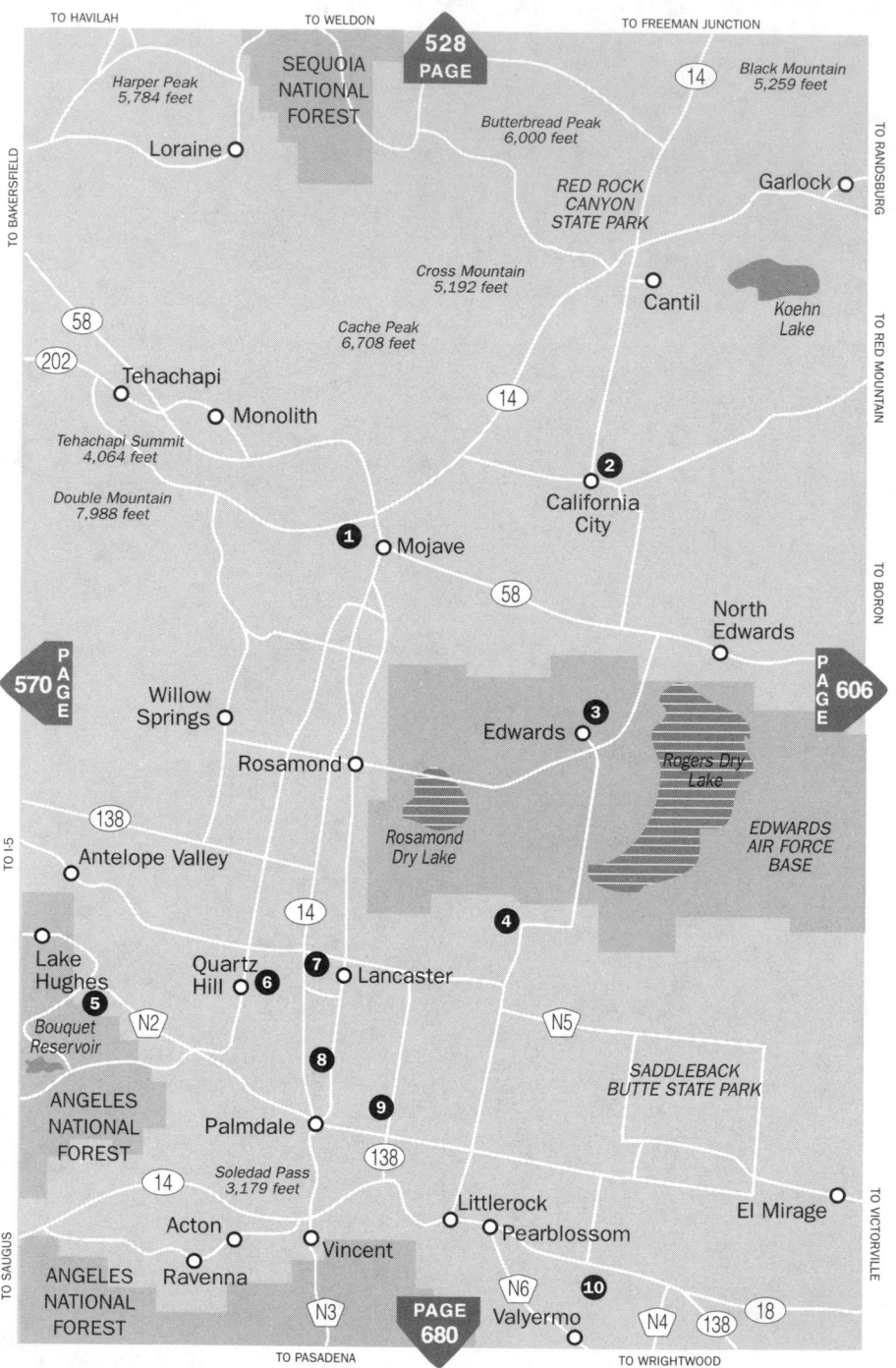

TO HAVILAH

TO WELDON

528 PAGE

TO FREEMAN JUNCTION

14 Black Mountain
5,259 feet

Harper Peak
5,784 feet

SEQUOIA
NATIONAL
FOREST

Butterbread Peak
6,000 feet

Loraine ○

RED ROCK
CANYON
STATE PARK

Garlock ○

TO RANDSBURG

TO BAKERSFIELD

Cross Mountain
5,192 feet

Cantil ○

Koehn
Lake

58

Cache Peak
6,708 feet

14

TO RED MOUNTAIN

202

Tehachapi ○

Monolith ○

Tehachapi Summit
4,064 feet

14

2

California
City

Double Mountain
7,988 feet

1 ○ Mojave

58

TO BORON

North
Edwards ○

PAGE 570

Willow
Springs ○

Rosamond ○

3

Edwards ○

Rogers Dry
Lake

PAGE 606

TO I-5

138

Antelope Valley ○

Rosamond
Dry Lake

EDWARDS
AIR FORCE
BASE

14

Lake
Hughes ○

5

Quartz
Hill ○ 6

7
○ Lancaster

4

N5

Bouquet
Reservoir

N2

8

SADDLEBACK
BUTTE STATE PARK

ANGELES
NATIONAL
FOREST

Palmdale ○

9

14

Soledad Pass
3,179 feet

138

Littlerock ○

El Mirage ○

TO VICTORVILLE

TO SAUGUS

Acton ○

Vincent ○

Pearblossom

ANGELES
NATIONAL
FOREST

Ravenna ○

N3

N6

10

N4

138

18

PAGE 680

Valyermo ○

TO PASADENA

TO WRIGHTWOOD

Lower Central Valley Area

① CAMELOT GOLF COURSE

3430 Camelot Boulevard
Mojave, CA 93501

PRO SHOP: 661-824-4107

Kathy Moulton, Manager
Jim Grier, Professional

Driving Range ●
Practice Greens ●
Clubhouse ●
Food / Beverage ●
Accommodations
Pull Carts ●
Power Carts ●
Club Rental ●
$pecial Offers

	1	2	3	4	5	6	7	8	9	OUT
BACK	-	-	-	-	-	-	-	-	-	-
REGULAR	375	500	454	392	169	249	128	369	448	3084
par	4	5	4	4	3	4	3	4	5	36
handicap	4	14	2	8	6	16	18	10	12	-
FORWARD	273	415	415	370	147	231	79	363	370	2663
par	4	5	5	4	3	4	3	4	4	36
handicap	3	9	15	1	7	17	11	5	13	-

	10	11	12	13	14	15	16	17	18	IN
BACK	-	-	-	-	-	-	-	-	-	-
REGULAR	386	517	462	400	194	256	167	378	487	3247
par	4	5	4	4	3	4	3	4	5	36
handicap	3	15	1	9	5	17	7	11	13	-
FORWARD	361	417	400	389	170	248	100	265	381	2731
par	4	5	5	4	3	4	3	4	4	36
handicap	4	10	12	2	8	16	18	6	14	-

BACK	
yardage	-
par	-
rating	-
slope	-

REGULAR	
yardage	6331
par	72
rating	70.4
slope	124

FORWARD	
yardage	5394
par	72
rating	72.5
slope	111

② TIERRA DEL SOL
ARCHITECT: BRUCE DEVLIN, ROBERT VON HAGGE, 1977

10300 North Loop Drive
California City, CA 93505

PRO SHOP: 760-373-2384

Bob Dacey, PGA Professional

Driving Range ●
Practice Greens ●
Clubhouse ●
Food / Beverage ●
Accommodations
Pull Carts ●
Power Carts ●
Club Rental ●
$pecial Offers

	1	2	3	4	5	6	7	8	9	OUT
BACK										
REGULAR										
par										
handicap										
FORWARD										
par										
handicap										

	10	11	12	13	14	15	16	17	18	IN
BACK										
REGULAR										
par										
handicap										
FORWARD										
par										
handicap										

BACK	
yardage	6908
par	72
rating	74.1
slope	130

REGULAR	
yardage	6300
par	72
rating	70.6
slope	121

FORWARD	
yardage	5227
par	72
rating	68.4
slope	122

PLAY POLICY & FEES: Green fees are $8 for nine holes and $12 for 18 holes weekdays, and $10 for nine holes and $15 for 18 holes weekends. Call for special rates. Carts are $15. Pull carts are $2 for nine holes and $3 for 18 holes.

TEE TIMES: Reservations can be booked up to seven days in advance.

DRESS CODE: Nonmetal spikes are required, and golf attire is encouraged.

COURSE DESCRIPTION: This course features tree-lined, narrow fairways. The greens, which are in excellent shape, are extremely difficult to read and putt. The par-3 fifth hole offers a tough and humbling green.

NOTES: Located on the course is the world's largest Joshua tree.

LOCATION: Drive one mile south of the town of Mojave on Highway 14. Turn west on Camelot Boulevard and drive two miles to the course.

. . . ● **TOURNAMENTS:** Saturday shotgun tournaments must start after noon. A 40-player minimum is needed to book an event. Tournaments should be scheduled two months in advance.

1. CAMELOT GOLF COURSE

PLAY POLICY & FEES: Green fees are $14 weekdays and $18 weekends. Carts are $20. Twilight rates are $15 on weekdays after 1 p.m. and $17 on weekends after 2 p.m. Twilight rates include cart. Resident, nonresident, military, junior, senior, and corporate memberships are available.

TEE TIMES: Reservations can be booked 14 days in advance.

DRESS CODE: Appropriate golf attire is required.

COURSE DESCRIPTION: This links-style course is level, long, and open. There is water on 12 holes, there are 146 bunkers, and most of the greens are elevated.

NOTES: All the bunkers have recently been renovated with a new drainage system and sand.

LOCATION: Drive north on Highway 14 from Lancaster to Mojave. Continue on Highway 14 five more miles to California City Boulevard and turn right. Drive 8.5 miles to North Loop, turn left, and continue two miles to the clubhouse.

. . . ● **TOURNAMENTS:** This course is available for outside events. Carts are mandatory. ● **TRAVEL:** If calling from outside the area, you can reach the pro shop by calling 800-465-3837.

2. TIERRA DEL SOL

P.O. Box 207/Edwards AFB
Edwards, CA 93523

PRO SHOP: 805-277-3469
CLUBHOUSE: 805-277-3467

Larry Cruise, PGA Professional
Sean Moore, Superintendent

Driving Range •
Practice Greens •
Clubhouse •
Food / Beverage •
Accommodations
Pull Carts •
Power Carts •
Club Rental •
$pecial Offers

	1	2	3	4	5	6	7	8	9	OUT
BACK	326	407	530	456	376	231	557	216	404	3503
REGULAR	316	396	508	444	359	202	493	157	394	3269
par	4	4	5	4	4	3	5	3	4	36
handicap	13	3	11	1	9	7	15	17	5	-
FORWARD	311	325	386	438	345	231	409	153	301	2899
par	4	4	4	5	4	4	5	3	4	37
handicap	9	11	1	7	3	17	5	15	13	-

	10	11	12	13	14	15	16	17	18	I N
BACK	571	374	222	435	347	498	437	199	368	3451
REGULAR	539	365	180	425	338	478	427	158	361	3271
par	5	4	3	4	4	5	4	3	4	36
handicap	8	6	10	4	14	18	2	16	12	-
FORWARD	454	360	174	358	333	422	342	97	324	2864
par	5	4	3	4	4	5	4	3	4	36
handicap	16	4	6	8	2	10	12	18	14	-

BACK	
yardage	6954
par	72
rating	
slope	

REGULAR	
yardage	6540
par	72
rating	
slope	

FORWARD	
yardage	5763
par	73
rating	
slope	

47205 60th Street East
Lancaster, CA 93535

PRO SHOP: 661-946-1080

Daniel Johnston, General Manager
Mark Karge, PGA Professional

Driving Range •
Practice Greens •
Clubhouse •
Food / Beverage •
Accommodations
Pull Carts •
Power Carts •
Club Rental •
$pecial Offers

	1	2	3	4	5	6	7	8	9	OUT
BACK	-	-	-	-	-	-	-	-	-	-
REGULAR	304	462	290	107	293	158	313	353	320	2600
par	4	5	4	3	4	3	4	4	4	35
handicap	11	1	13	17	15	7	9	3	5	-
FORWARD	304	462	290	107	293	158	313	353	320	2600
par	4	5	4	3	4	3	4	4	4	35
handicap	11	1	13	17	15	7	9	3	5	-

	10	11	12	13	14	15	16	17	18	I N
BACK	-	-	-	-	-	-	-	-	-	-
REGULAR	304	462	290	107	293	158	313	353	320	2600
par	4	5	4	3	4	3	4	4	4	35
handicap	12	2	14	18	16	8	10	4	6	-
FORWARD	304	462	290	107	293	158	313	353	320	2600
par	4	5	4	3	4	3	4	4	4	35
handicap	12	2	14	18	16	8	10	4	6	-

BACK	
yardage	-
par	-
rating	
slope	

REGULAR	
yardage	5200
par	70
rating	63.4
slope	100

FORWARD	
yardage	5200
par	70
rating	70.7
slope	115

PLAY POLICY & FEES: Military personnel and guests only. Reciprocal play is accepted with members of other Air Force bases. Green fees vary from $8 to $16 depending on mlitary status. Call for special rates. Carts are $14 for a single rider.

DRESS CODE: Collared shirts are required.

COURSE DESCRIPTION: This is the greenest place in this part of the Mojave Desert, and it's not because of all the military uniforms. The course is well maintained and features a small lake and numerous mature trees that line the fairways. Tall trees, which offer a welcome relief from the afternoon sun, are spaced every 20 yards on both sides of the fairways. If you hit through the trees, you're at the mercy of the desert.

LOCATION: Between the towns of Lancaster and Mojave, on Highway 14, take the Rosamond exit and travel northeast for 15 miles to Lancaster Boulevard. Turn left and drive to Fitzgerald Boulevard. Turn left again and drive to Yucca Street and follow the signs.

. . . ● **TOURNAMENTS:** Outside events must be sponsored by someone affiliated with the base.

3. MUROC LAKE

PLAY POLICY & FEES: Green fees are $11.50 tor nine holes and $17.50 for 18 holes weekdays, and $15 for nine holes and $21.50 for 18 holes weekends. Power carts are $12 weekdays, $15 weekends. Pull carts are $2.50.

TEE TIMES: Reservations can be booked seven days in advance.

COURSE DESCRIPTION: This is a flat, interesting course with narrow fairways. It features four lakes, and water comes into play on all but three holes. Mature trees line the fairways, and the bunkers are all grass.

LOCATION: Take the Avenue G exit off Highway 14 in the town of Lancaster, and travel east for about nine miles to 60th Street. Turn left and drive one-quarter mile to the course.

. . . ● **TOURNAMENTS:** A 12-player minimum is needed to book a tournament.

4. RANCHO SIERRA GOLF CLUB

5 LAKE ELIZABETH GOLF & RANCH CLUB

42505 Ranch Club Road
Lake Elizabeth, CA 93532

PRO SHOP: 661-724-1221
OFFICE: 661-724-1251

Mitchell Simon, General Manager
George Pallas, PGA Professional
Tom Zurcher, Superintendent

Driving Range ●
Practice Greens ●
Clubhouse ●
Food / Beverage ●
Accommodations
Pull Carts
Power Carts ●
Club Rental
$pecial Offers

	1	2	3	4	5	6	7	8	9	OUT
BACK	364	235	326	199	434	224	503	391	509	3185
REGULAR	353	175	317	192	342	212	490	366	493	2940
par	4	3	4	3	4	3	5	4	5	35
handicap	13	11	17	3	15	1	5	7	9	-
FORWARD	318	163	286	158	300	170	474	296	477	2642
par	4	3	4	3	4	3	5	4	5	35
handicap	1	17	11	6	15	13	9	5	7	-

	10	11	12	13	14	15	16	17	18	IN
BACK	175	405	481	166	474	135	366	171	479	2852
REGULAR	139	393	474	149	463	122	351	164	463	2718
par	3	4	5	3	5	3	4	3	5	35
handicap	14	8	2	16	4	18	6	12	10	-
FORWARD	117	376	423	131	455	113	263	147	407	2432
par	3	4	5	3	5	3	4	3	5	35
handicap	14	2	8	16	6	18	10	12	4	-

BACK	
yardage	6037
par	70
rating	68.8
slope	118

REGULAR	
yardage	5658
par	70
rating	67.1
slope	114

FORWARD	
yardage	5074
par	70
rating	72.9
slope	115

6 MEADOWLARK GOLF & RECREATION

43625 60th Street W
Quartz Hill, CA 93536

PRO SHOP: 661-943-2022

Jeanene Roelen, Manager

Driving Range ●
Practice Greens
Clubhouse ●
Food / Beverage ●
Accommodations
Pull Carts ●
Power Carts
Club Rental ●
$pecial Offers

	1	2	3	4	5	6	7	8	9	OUT
BACK										
REGULAR										
par										
handicap										
FORWARD										
par										
handicap										

	10	11	12	13	14	15	16	17	18	IN
BACK										
REGULAR										
par										
handicap										
FORWARD										
par										
handicap										

BACK	
yardage	
par	
rating	
slope	

REGULAR	
yardage	2024
par	27
rating	
slope	

FORWARD	
yardage	1858
par	27
rating	
slope	

PLAY POLICY & FEES: Standard green fees are $25 weekdays and $35 weekends, including carts. Call for special rates. The course is closed Thanksgiving, Christmas, and Easter.

TEE TIMES: Reservations can be made seven days in advance by phone and one year in advance by event contract.

DRESS CODE: No cutoffs or short shorts are allowed. Nonmetal spikes are preferred.

COURSE DESCRIPTION: This medium-length course is very challenging and fairly hilly with small greens. Seven lakes come into play. The par-4 fifth hole is 434 yards from the championship tees, which doesn't seem significant except for the fact that there is a 200-foot drop from tee to fairway. Many golfers have been fooled into thinking their tee shot traveled farther.

LOCATION: From Interstate 5 north of Los Angeles take the Valencia Boulevard exit. Go east on Valencia Boulevard one mile to McBean Parkway. Turn left on McBean and drive four miles to San Francisquito. Turn left onto San Francisquito, go 19 miles to Elizabeth Lake Road, and drive one mile to Ranch Club Road. Turn left on Ranch Club Road and proceed one mile to the clubhouse. . . . ● **TOURNAMENTS:** This course is available for outside tournaments that include exclusive use of the facilities. Carts are required. A 24-player minimum is needed to book an event. The banquet facility can hold 200 people. Tournaments should be scheduled at least two months in advance. ● **TRAVEL:** The Hyatt at Valencia and the Hilton at Valencia are recommended for lodging.

5. LAKE ELIZABETH GOLF & RANCH CLUB

PLAY POLICY & FEES: Green fees are $6 for nine holes and $2 for a replay on weekdays. Weekend green fees are $7 with a $3 replay fee. Senior, junior, and twilight rates are offered.

TEE TIMES: Reservations are made on a first-come, first-served basis.

COURSE DESCRIPTION: This par-3 course has small, angled greens, lots of trees, one sand trap, and one grass bunker. Water comes into play on three holes, and wind is a factor. This is a popular course with seniors, juniors, and those who wish to improve their short game.

LOCATION: From Los Angeles take Interstate 5 north to Highway 14 north. Exit at Avenue K, turn west on Avenue K, and proceed to 60th Avenue. Turn right on 60th Avenue. The course is on the left. . . . ● **TOURNAMENTS:** A 36-player minimum is needed for a shotgun tournament.

6. MEADOWLARK GOLF & RECREATION

7 LANCASTER GOLF CENTER

431 East Ave K-4
Lancaster, CA 93535

PRO SHOP: 661-726-3131

Andy Ash, Manager
Doug Martin, Head Professional, PGA

Driving Range •
Practice Greens
Clubhouse •
Food / Beverage •
Accommodations
Pull Carts •
Power Carts
Club Rental •
$pecial Offers

	1	2	3	4	5	6	7	8	9	OUT
BACK	-	-	-	-	-	-	-	-	-	-
REGULAR	87	82	66	110	97	93	81	65	112	793
par	3	3	3	3	3	3	3	3	3	27
handicap	5	6	8	1	3	4	7	9	2	-
FORWARD	-	-	-	-	-	-	-	-	-	
par	-	-	-	-	-	-	-	-	-	
handicap	-	-	-	-	-	-	-	-	-	-

	10	11	12	13	14	15	16	17	18	IN
BACK	-	-	-	-	-	-	-	-	-	-
REGULAR	-	-	-	-	-	-	-	-	-	
par	-	-	-	-	-	-	-	-	-	
handicap	-	-	-	-	-	-	-	-	-	-
FORWARD	-	-	-	-	-	-	-	-	-	
par	-	-	-	-	-	-	-	-	-	
handicap	-	-	-	-	-	-	-	-	-	-

BACK	
yardage	-
par	-
rating	
slope	

REGULAR	
yardage	793
par	27
rating	-
slope	-

FORWARD	
yardage	
par	
rating	-
slope	-

8 ANTELOPE VALLEY COUNTRY CLUB
ARCHITECT: WILLIAM F. BELL, 1957

39800 Country Club Drive
Palmdale, CA 93551

PRO SHOP: 661-947-3400

Steven Applegate, Head Professional, PGA
Larry Jost, Assistant Professional
Buzz Barker, Superintendent

Driving Range •
Practice Greens •
Clubhouse •
Food / Beverage •
Accommodations
Pull Carts •
Power Carts •
Club Rental
$pecial Offers

	1	2	3	4	5	6	7	8	9	OUT
BACK	400	177	348	561	161	432	383	344	509	3315
REGULAR	382	167	332	539	149	400	366	321	487	3143
par	4	3	4	5	3	4	4	4	5	36
handicap	5	9	11	7	17	1	3	15	13	-
FORWARD	366	164	322	525	119	390	356	309	477	3028
par	4	3	4	5	3	4	4	4	5	36
handicap	9	15	11	1	17	3	7	13	5	-

	10	11	12	13	14	15	16	17	18	IN
BACK	467	183	393	353	502	414	434	179	500	3425
REGULAR	443	171	378	325	478	394	425	167	484	3265
par	4	3	4	4	5	4	4	3	5	36
handicap	2	12	6	10	18	8	4	14	16	-
FORWARD	454	120	367	314	460	377	418	155	477	3142
par	5	3	4	4	5	4	5	3	5	38
handicap	10	18	2	12	8	4	14	16	6	-

BACK	
yardage	6740
par	72
rating	72.8
slope	129

REGULAR	
yardage	6408
par	72
rating	70.6
slope	122

FORWARD	
yardage	6170
par	74
rating	75.0
slope	125

PLAY POLICY & FEES: Green fees are $6 for nine holes and $10 for 18 holes on weekdays and $8 for nine holes and $14 for 18 holes on weekends. Junior green fees are $4 for nine holes and $8 for 18 holes on weekdays and $6 for nine holes and $10 for 18 holes on weekends. Seniors can play at junior rates with the purchase of a $10 senior card.

TEE TIMES: Reservations are not taken.

DRESS CODE: No steel spikes are permitted.

COURSE DESCRIPTION: This pitch-and-putt golf course is good for juniors, seniors, and those who want to sharpen their short game. The longest hole is 112 yards, and players have the option of teeing off either mats or grass. Because the course is young, wear a hat; you won't find much shade.

NOTES: Lancaster features a night-lit covered driving range.

LOCATION: From Los Angeles drive north on Interstate 5 and take Highway 14 north to Lancaster. Take the K Avenue exit. Take a right on K and then another right on Fifth, heading east to the course.

7. LANCASTER GOLF CENTER

PLAY POLICY & FEES: Reciprocal play is accepted with members of other private clubs; otherwise, members and guests only. Guest fees are $35 on weekdays, $45 weekends and holidays. Reciprocators are $45 weekdays, $55 weekends and holidays. Carts are $10 for one rider and $20 for two.

DRESS CODE: Shorts must be midthigh in length, and shirts must be collared. Nonmetal spikes are required.

COURSE DESCRIPTION: Don't forget to bring a sand wedge to this course. It is well bunkered but level, with many trees lining the fairways. Water can be found on several holes of this challenging course. The lake has been enlarged on the par-3, 183-yard 11th. You must hit over the water to the large green. Wind makes every hole on this course play differently each day.

NOTES: The men's course record is 64, and the women's is 66.

LOCATION: Take Avenue P east off Highway 14 in Palmdale and drive east for one block to Country Club Drive. Turn left and drive one-fourth mile to the club.

. . . ● **TOURNAMENTS:** All outside events must be approved by the head professional and the board.

8. ANTELOPE VALLEY COUNTRY CLUB

DESERT AIRE GOLF COURSE
ARCHITECT: TED ROBINSON, 1960

3620 East Avenue P
Palmdale, CA 93550

PRO SHOP: 661-538-0370
CLUBHOUSE: 661-266-9814

Christina McEnaney, Head Professional, LPGA
Mike Evinger, PGA Professional

Driving Range •
Practice Greens •
Clubhouse •
Food / Beverage •
Accommodations
Pull Carts •
Power Carts •
Club Rental •
$pecial Offers

	1	2	3	4	5	6	7	8	9	OUT
BACK	-	-	-	-	-	-	-	-	-	-
REGULAR	494	388	363	155	370	152	392	401	463	3178
par	5	4	4	3	4	3	4	4	5	36
handicap	10	4	16	18	6	12	8	2	14	-
FORWARD	430	352	345	132	336	126	326	343	385	2775
par	5	4	4	3	4	3	4	4	5	35
handicap	12	4	8	18	2	16	10	6	14	-

	10	11	12	13	14	15	16	17	18	IN
BACK	-	-	-	-	-	-	-	-	-	-
REGULAR	479	366	353	142	350	138	372	384	447	3031
par	5	4	4	3	4	3	4	4	5	36
handicap	9	3	15	17	5	11	7	1	13	-
FORWARD	479	366	353	142	350	138	372	384	447	3031
par	5	4	4	3	4	3	4	4	5	36
handicap	11	3	7	17	1	15	9	5	13	-

BACK	
yardage	-
par	-
rating	-
slope	-

REGULAR	
yardage	6209
par	72
rating	68.1
slope	102

FORWARD	
yardage	5806
par	71
rating	69.8
slope	116

 CRYSTALAIRE COUNTRY CLUB
ARCHITECT: WILLIAM F. BELL, 1956

15701 Boca Raton Avenue
Llano, CA 93544

PRO SHOP: 661-944-2111
OFFICE: 661-944-3091

Michael Hegarty, General Manager
Alan Arvesen, PGA Professional
Manuel Delgado, Superintendent

Driving Range •
Practice Greens •
Clubhouse •
Food / Beverage •
Accommodations
Pull Carts •
Power Carts •
Club Rental
$pecial Offers

	1	2	3	4	5	6	7	8	9	OUT
BACK	526	425	428	353	579	174	447	166	379	3477
REGULAR	505	415	411	339	561	150	437	152	366	3336
par	5	4	4	4	5	3	4	3	4	36
handicap	9	7	5	17	1	13	3	15	11	-
FORWARD	364	337	374	257	431	106	404	106	298	2677
par	4	4	4	4	5	3	5	3	4	36
handicap	3	11	9	15	1	13	7	17	5	-

	10	11	12	13	14	15	16	17	18	IN
BACK	416	173	571	374	440	222	421	355	513	3485
REGULAR	396	131	535	356	428	204	406	333	504	3293
par	4	3	5	4	4	3	4	4	5	36
handicap	10	18	6	12	2	8	4	16	14	-
FORWARD	339	95	418	286	329	124	314	283	412	2600
par	4	3	5	4	4	3	4	4	5	36
handicap	10	18	4	14	6	16	8	12	2	-

BACK	
yardage	6962
par	72
rating	73.1
slope	131

REGULAR	
yardage	6629
par	72
rating	71.4
slope	122

FORWARD	
yardage	5277
par	72
rating	71.5
slope	123

PLAY POLICY & FEES: Green fees are $9.50 weekdays and $12.50 weekends. Special rates are available. Call for more information. Carts are $9 for nine holes and $17 for 18 holes.

TEE TIMES: Reservations are not accepted. All play is on a first-come, first-served basis.

DRESS CODE: No tank tops are allowed on the course.

COURSE DESCRIPTION: This level desert course is well bunkered and has one lake. Mature trees line the fairways and offer welcome shade in the afternoon. The toughest hole is the 401-yard, par-4 eighth. It's straight and narrow, with out-of-bounds to the right. Accuracy on a windy day is a must on this hole.

LOCATION: Take Avenue P east off Highway 14 in Palmdale and drive four miles to the course.

. . . ● **TOURNAMENTS:** A 144-player minimum is needed for a shotgun tournament.

9. DESERT AIRE GOLF COURSE

PLAY POLICY & FEES: Reciprocal play is accepted with members of other private clubs. Reciprocal fees are $30 weekdays and $40 weekends. Carts are $16 on weekdays, $20 weekends.

DRESS CODE: Appropriate golf attire and nonmetal spikes are required.

COURSE DESCRIPTION: This scenic country course is set in the high desert, surrounded by mountains. The terrain is rolling to hilly, with lots of mature trees and three lakes. Watch for the par-3, 150-yard sixth. Players must carry the lake to reach the hole. This hole has been the downfall of many, but it has also recorded more holes in one than any other hole on the course. The course is situated at a 3,500-foot elevation and is usually open in the winter.

NOTES: The course record is 64.

LOCATION: Heading south of Lancaster, take the Pearblossom exit off Highway 14 and travel about 16 miles east to the town of Llano. Turn south on 165th Street and drive one mile to Crystalaire Drive. Take Crystalaire to Boca Raton Avenue and turn right to the course.

. . . ● **TOURNAMENTS:** This course is available for outside tournaments Monday and Tuesday. Carts are required. A 24-player minimum is needed to book an event. Tournaments should be scheduled six months in advance. A banquet facility is available that can accommodate 120 players.

10. CRYSTALAIRE COUNTRY CLUB

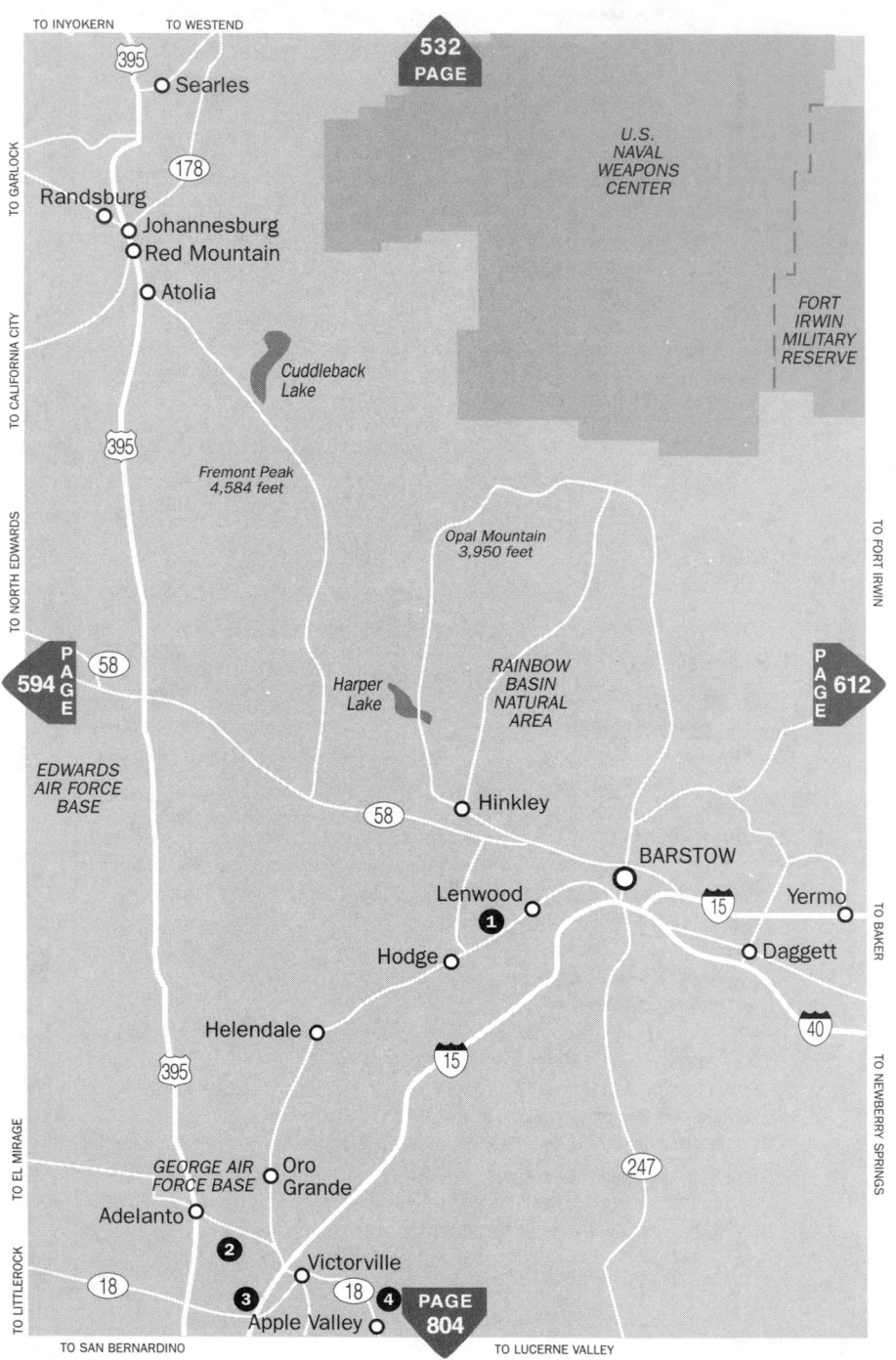

TO INYOKERN   TO WESTEND

395

○ Searles

178

Randsburg ○
○ Johannesburg
○ Red Mountain
○ Atolia

532 PAGE

U.S.
NAVAL
WEAPONS
CENTER

FORT
IRWIN
MILITARY
RESERVE

TO GARLOCK

TO CALIFORNIA CITY

TO NORTH EDWARDS

Cuddleback
Lake

395

Fremont Peak
4,584 feet

Opal Mountain
3,950 feet

TO FORT IRWIN

P A G E 594

58

Harper
Lake

RAINBOW
BASIN
NATURAL
AREA

P A G E 612

EDWARDS
AIR FORCE
BASE

58 ○ Hinkley

Lenwood ○
❶

BARSTOW ◎

15 Yermo ○

TO BAKER

Hodge ○

○ Daggett

Helendale ○

15

40

TO NEWBERRY SPRINGS

395

GEORGE AIR
FORCE BASE

Oro
Grande ○

247

TO EL MIRAGE

Adelanto ○

❷

TO LITTLEROCK

18

❸

Victorville ○
18 ❹ **PAGE 804**

Apple Valley ○

TO SAN BERNARDINO   TO LUCERNE VALLEY

Barstow/Victorville Area

SUN & SKY COUNTRY CLUB
ARCHITECT: TED ROBINSON, 1959

2781 Country Club Drive
Barstow, CA 92311

PRO SHOP: 760-253-5201

Ken Krol, Manager
Craig Radcliffe, Superintendent

Driving Range ●
Practice Greens ●
Clubhouse ●
Food / Beverage ●
Accommodations
Pull Carts ●
Power Carts ●
Club Rental ●
Special Offers

	1	2	3	4	5	6	7	8	9	OUT
BACK										
REGULAR										
par										
handicap										
FORWARD										
par										
handicap										

	10	11	12	13	14	15	16	17	18	IN
BACK										
REGULAR										
par										
handicap										
FORWARD										
par										
handicap										

BACK	
yardage	
par	
rating	-
slope	-

REGULAR	
yardage	3190
par	36
rating	69.0
slope	114

FORWARD	
yardage	3014
par	36
rating	71.9
slope	112

SILVER LAKES COUNTRY CLUB
ARCHITECT: TED ROBINSON, 1974

P.O. Box 2130
Helendale, CA 92342

14814 Clubhouse Drive
Helendale, CA 92342

PRO SHOP: 760-245-7435

Dave Ferrell, PGA Professional
Brad Rook, Superintendent

Driving Range ●
Practice Greens ●
Clubhouse ●
Food / Beverage ●
Accommodations ●
Pull Carts
Power Carts ●
Club Rental ●
Special Offers

	1	2	3	4	5	6	7	8	9	OUT
BACK	416	483	364	345	171	417	578	216	400	3390
REGULAR	395	465	342	336	154	396	541	201	374	3204
par	4	5	4	4	3	4	5	3	4	36
handicap	1	13	9	11	17	3	15	7	5	-
FORWARD	305	406	280	311	136	345	424	179	312	2698
par	4	5	4	4	3	4	5	3	4	36
handicap	11	5	13	3	17	1	15	9	7	-

	10	11	12	13	14	15	16	17	18	IN
BACK	401	207	380	530	197	382	409	545	410	3461
REGULAR	379	178	354	510	173	369	389	524	382	3258
par	4	3	4	5	3	4	4	5	4	36
handicap	3	17	11	13	5	15	7	9	1	-
FORWARD	340	151	318	456	146	337	324	442	352	2866
par	4	3	4	5	3	4	4	5	4	36
handicap	5	17	7	3	15	11	13	9	1	-

BACK	
yardage	6851
par	72
rating	73.0
slope	125

REGULAR	
yardage	6462
par	72
rating	70.5
slope	120

FORWARD	
yardage	5564
par	72
rating	70.9
slope	118

9
HOLES

PLAY POLICY & FEES: Green fees are $7 for nine holes and $10 for 18 holes weekdays, and $9 for nine holes and $12 for 18 holes weekends. Carts are $9 for nine holes and $15 for 18 holes.

TEE TIMES: Play is on a first-come, first-served basis during the week. Reservations are needed weekends and holidays.

DRESS CODE: Tank tops are allowed on the course.

COURSE DESCRIPTION: This is a straight, flat, tree-lined course that's perfect for beginners. The greens are small.

NOTES: The course record is 61, held by Mark Johnson.

LOCATION: From Interstate 15 traveling north at Barstow, take the Lenwood Road exit west. Turn left on Main Street. Drive on Main Street to Country Club Drive and the course.

. . . ● **TOURNAMENTS:** A 50-player minimum is needed to book a shotgun tournament. Events should be scheduled two months in advance.

1. SUN & SKY COUNTRY CLUB

27
HOLES

PLAY POLICY & FEES: Reciprocal play is accepted with members of private clubs. Guests at the Inn at Silver Lakes are welcome. Green fees are $25 weekdays and $35 weekends. Carts are $20.

TEE TIMES: Have your pro call ahead to make reservations up to five days in advance.

DRESS CODE: Appropriate golf attire and nonmetal spikes are required.

COURSE DESCRIPTION: All combinations are very distinctive. The South Course has lots of water. The East Course has one hole with water, and the North Course has two holes with water. All three courses have a good mix of long, tight, and challenging holes.

NOTES: This private facility has 27 holes and par is 72 for each of the 18-hole combinations. The North/South Course: See scorecard for yardage and rating information. The East/South Course is 6,395 yards and rated 69.9 from the regular tees with a slope 118. The forward tees are 5,635 yards and rated 71.1. The slope rating is 116. The East/North Course is 6,341 yards and rated 69.5 from the regular tees with a slope 116. The forward tees are 5,467 yards and rated 70.4. The slope rating is 114.

LOCATION: Take Interstate 15 north from San Bernardino to the D Street/Apple Valley exit in Victorville. Turn left on Apple Valley/Highway 66 and continue for 14 miles to Vista Road. Turn left to the club.

. . . ● **TOURNAMENTS:** This course is available for outside tournaments with board approval.

2. SILVER LAKES COUNTRY CLUB

GREENTREE GOLF COURSE
ARCHITECT: WILLIAM P. BELL, 1962

14144 Greentree
Victorville, CA 92392

PRO SHOP: 760-245-4860

Ray Echols Jr., Head Professional, PGA
Ray Salberg, Manager/Superintendent

Driving Range
Practice Greens •
Clubhouse •
Food / Beverage •
Accommodations
Pull Carts •
Power Carts •
Club Rental •
$pecial Offers

	1	2	3	4	5	6	7	8	9	OUT
BACK	393	398	573	376	175	399	425	202	491	3432
REGULAR	376	362	535	356	154	386	418	172	477	3236
par	4	4	5	4	3	4	4	3	5	36
handicap	9	5	3	13	17	11	1	7	15	-
FORWARD	365	330	470	345	133	374	410	153	467	3047
par	4	4	5	4	3	4	5	3	5	37
handicap	7	13	3	11	17	9	5	15	1	-

	10	11	12	13	14	15	16	17	18	IN
BACK	333	372	561	376	155	530	172	402	310	3211
REGULAR	333	351	549	367	146	517	160	382	291	3096
par	4	4	5	4	3	5	3	4	4	36
handicap	12	8	2	10	16	4	14	6	18	-
FORWARD	313	339	482	317	137	460	147	360	276	2831
par	4	4	5	4	3	5	3	4	4	36
handicap	14	6	2	10	18	4	16	8	12	-

BACK	
yardage	6643
par	72
rating	71.2
slope	121

REGULAR	
yardage	6332
par	72
rating	69.3
slope	117

FORWARD	
yardage	5878
par	73
rating	72.7
slope	118

 APPLE VALLEY COUNTRY CLUB
ARCHITECT: WILLIAM P. BELL, 1949

15200 Rancherias Road
Apple Valley, CA 92507

PRO SHOP: 760-242-3125
CLUBHOUSE: 760-242-3653

Larry Delmont, Head Professional, PGA
Jerry Moore, Superintendent

Driving Range •
Practice Greens •
Clubhouse •
Food / Beverage •
Accommodations
Pull Carts •
Power Carts •
Club Rental •
$pecial Offers

	1	2	3	4	5	6	7	8	9	OUT
BACK	403	155	429	398	492	205	461	385	395	3323
REGULAR	385	141	397	358	486	171	426	381	379	3124
par	4	3	4	4	5	3	4	4	4	35
handicap	5	17	3	13	7	15	1	9	11	-
FORWARD	365	113	267	321	475	146	420	372	327	2806
par	4	3	4	4	5	3	5	4	4	36
handicap	5	15	3	13	1	17	7	9	11	-

	10	11	12	13	14	15	16	17	18	IN
BACK	222	432	440	332	514	376	460	176	528	3480
REGULAR	206	423	426	315	507	367	446	169	494	3353
par	3	4	4	4	5	4	4	3	5	36
handicap	12	6	2	16	10	8	4	14	18	-
FORWARD	187	359	415	307	474	326	365	125	465	3023
par	3	4	5	4	5	4	4	3	5	37
handicap	16	8	4	14	2	12	10	18	6	-

BACK	
yardage	6803
par	71
rating	73.2
slope	129

REGULAR	
yardage	6477
par	71
rating	70.9
slope	123

FORWARD	
yardage	5829
par	73
rating	75.0
slope	128

PLAY POLICY & FEES: Green fees are $12 for nine holes and $19 for 18 holes weekdays, and $15 for nine holes and $23 for 18 holes weekends. Carts are $11 to $22, depending on the number of people and day of the week. Twilight green fees are $9 for nine holes and $12 for 18 holes on weekdays, and $11 for nine holes and $17 for 18 holes on weekends.

TEE TIMES: Reservations can be booked 14 days in advance.

DRESS CODE: No cutoffs, short shorts, or tank tops are allowed.

COURSE DESCRIPTION: This is a mostly flat, traditional course lined by trees and out-of-bounds on both sides. It is also a user-friendly course noted for its well-maintained greens.

NOTES: The course record for men is 64 and for women is 66.

LOCATION: From San Bernardino, drive north on Interstate 15 to Victorville. Exit at Palmdale Road and turn left to Greentree Boulevard; turn right. The course is 100 yards down the road.

. . . ● **TOURNAMENTS:** Carts are required for tournament play on certain days. Call the pro shop for more details.

3. GREENTREE GOLF COURSE

PLAY POLICY & FEES: Reciprocal play is accepted with members of other private clubs; otherwise, members and guests only. Green fees are $30 weekdays and $30 weekends. Carts are $9 weekdays and $11 weekends.

TEE TIMES: Reciprocal players can make reservations seven days in advance.

DRESS CODE: Appropriate golf attire is enforced. No cutoffs, short shorts, or blue jeans are allowed on the course. Collared shirts and nonmetal spikes are required.

COURSE DESCRIPTION: This is a fairly level course with wide fairways, mature trees, and some water. The greens can be hard and fast. The course plays much more difficult than it looks, especially when the wind is blowing.

NOTES: The men's course record is 64.

LOCATION: From San Bernardino drive north on Interstate 15 to the Apple Valley exit. Head east on Highway 18 to Rancherias Road and turn right. The course is on the right.

. . . ● **TOURNAMENTS:** A 72-player maximum is allowed for tournament play. Events should be scheduled 12 months in advance. The banquet facility can accommodate 180 people.

4. APPLE VALLEY COUNTRY CLUB

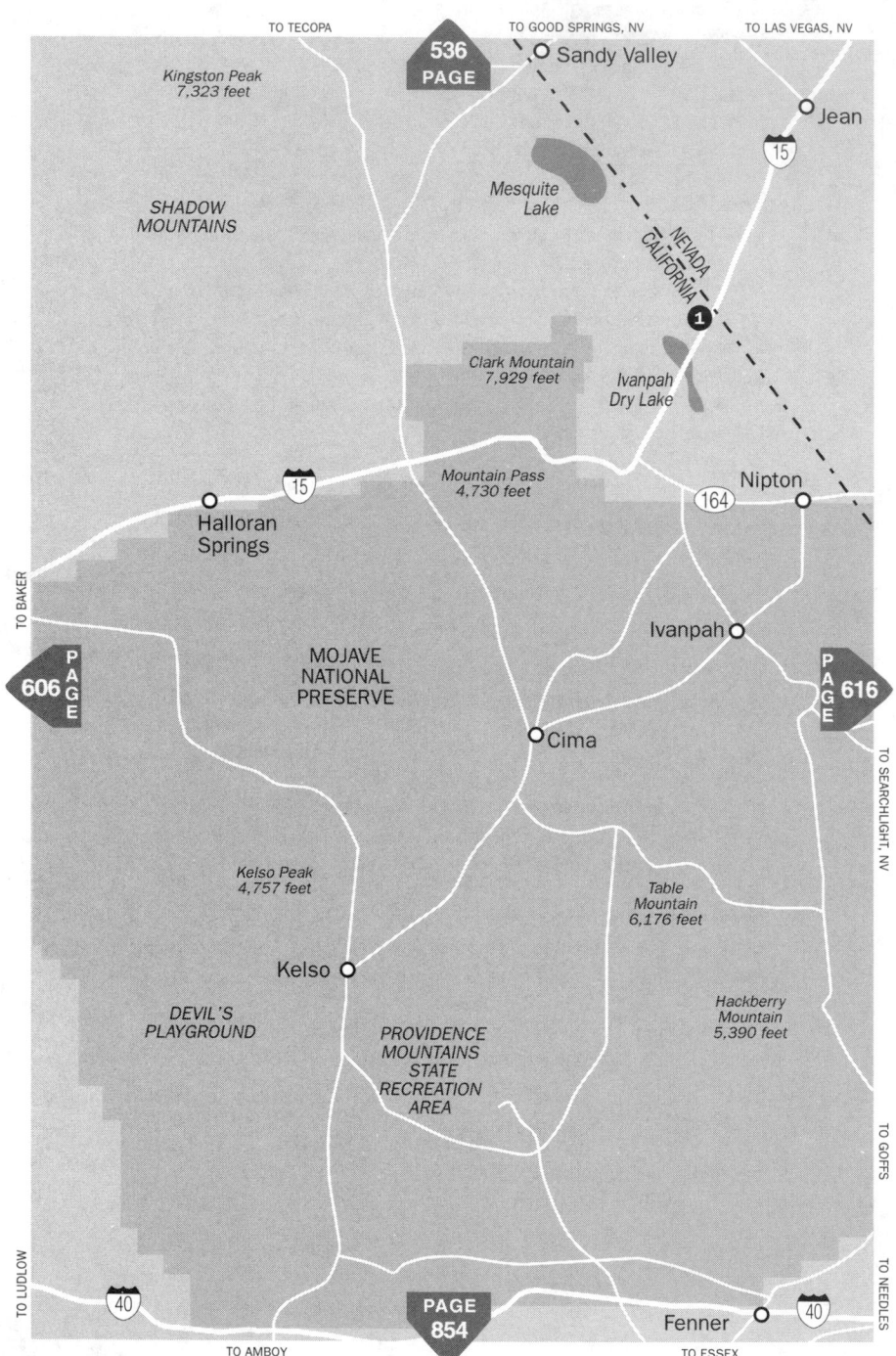

TO TECOPA

TO GOOD SPRINGS, NV

TO LAS VEGAS, NV

536 PAGE

Sandy Valley

Jean

15

Kingston Peak
7,323 feet

SHADOW
MOUNTAINS

Mesquite
Lake

NEVADA
CALIFORNIA

Clark Mountain
7,929 feet

Ivanpah
Dry Lake

1

Mountain Pass
4,730 feet

Nipton

15

164

Halloran
Springs

TO BAKER

606 PAGE

MOJAVE
NATIONAL
PRESERVE

Ivanpah

PAGE 616

TO SEARCHLIGHT, NV

Cima

Kelso Peak
4,757 feet

Table
Mountain
6,176 feet

Kelso

DEVIL'S
PLAYGROUND

Hackberry
Mountain
5,390 feet

TO GOFFS

PROVIDENCE
MOUNTAINS
STATE
RECREATION
AREA

TO LUDLOW

40

PAGE 854

Fenner

40

TO NEEDLES

TO AMBOY

TO ESSEX

Primm Valley Area

PRIMM VALLEY GOLF CLUB
ARCHITECT: TOM FAZIO, 1997

GOLF 50

P.O. Box 19129
Primm Valley , CA 89019

1 Yeates Well Road
Primm Valley , CA 19129

PRO SHOP: 702-679-5510

Mark Yelenich, Director of Golf, PGA
Jay Irvine, Superintendent

Driving Range ●
Practice Greens ●
Clubhouse ●
Food / Beverage ●
Accommodations ●
Pull Carts
Power Carts ●
Club Rental ●
$pecial Offers ●

	1	2	3	4	5	6	7	8	9	OUT
BACK	433	435	352	188	372	389	530	565	222	3486
REGULAR	407	414	324	160	345	336	506	545	181	3218
par	4	4	4	3	4	4	5	5	3	36
handicap	11	1	15	17	13	5	7	3	9	-
FORWARD	340	321	272	129	306	294	409	422	127	2620
par	4	4	4	3	4	4	5	5	3	36
handicap	11	1	15	17	13	5	7	3	9	-

	10	11	12	13	14	15	16	17	18	IN
BACK	473	216	455	575	397	196	431	385	517	3645
REGULAR	432	185	409	520	368	170	406	340	492	3322
par	4	3	4	5	4	3	4	4	5	36
handicap	2	16	6	4	14	8	10	18	12	-
FORWARD	363	143	353	463	291	128	336	284	416	2777
par	4	3	4	5	4	3	4	4	5	36
handicap	2	16	6	4	14	8	10	18	12	-

BACK	
yardage	7131
par	72
rating	74.6
slope	138

REGULAR	
yardage	6540
par	72
rating	71.7
slope	126

FORWARD	
yardage	5397
par	72
rating	
slope	

PLAY POLICY & FEES: Green fees for hotel guests range from $55 to $115. Green fees for nonguests range from $75 to $150. There are special rates for Las Vegas residents. Special seasonal golf packages are available.

TEE TIMES: Reservations can be made 60 days in advance for hotel guests and golf packages. Nonguest reservations can be made 21 days in advance.

DRESS CODE: Collared shirts and nonmetal spikes are required. No jeans are allowed on the course, and shorts must be appropiate length.

COURSE DESCRIPTION: The Lakes Course and the Desert Course contrast in both design and playability. The Lakes Course is a traditional design, showcased by rolling fairways, waterfalls, streams, lakes, and a forest of trees. The Desert Course is landscaped to blend with the surrounding cacti, desert plants, and grasses, and it features plenty of sand, desert waste areas, and well-placed lakes. Although the Desert Course has a higher slope rating, the low handicapper may find the Lakes Course more difficult. The Lakes Course is far more demanding on and around the greens, while the biggest challenge on the Desert Course is getting to the green.

NOTES: The Lakes Course is 6,945 yards from the back tees, with a rating of 74.0 and slope of 134. For more information on the Desert Course: see the scorecard.

LOCATION: From Los Angeles heading toward Las Vegas on Interstate 15, exit left on Yeates Well Road. Follow Yeates Well Road until it ends. Take a right to the golf course and another right to the front gate.

. . . ● **TOURNAMENTS:** A 12-player minimum is needed to book an event. Tournaments with 12 to 48 players can be booked up to nine months in advance. Tournaments with 48 or more players can be booked up to one year in advance. Tournament packages can include scoring, box lunches, tee prizes, special events, and banquets. ● **TRAVEL:** For reservations at Primadonna Resorts call 800-386-7867. ● **$PECIAL OFFERS:** Golf packages are available; call the resort for more information.

1. PRIMM VALLEY GOLF CLUB

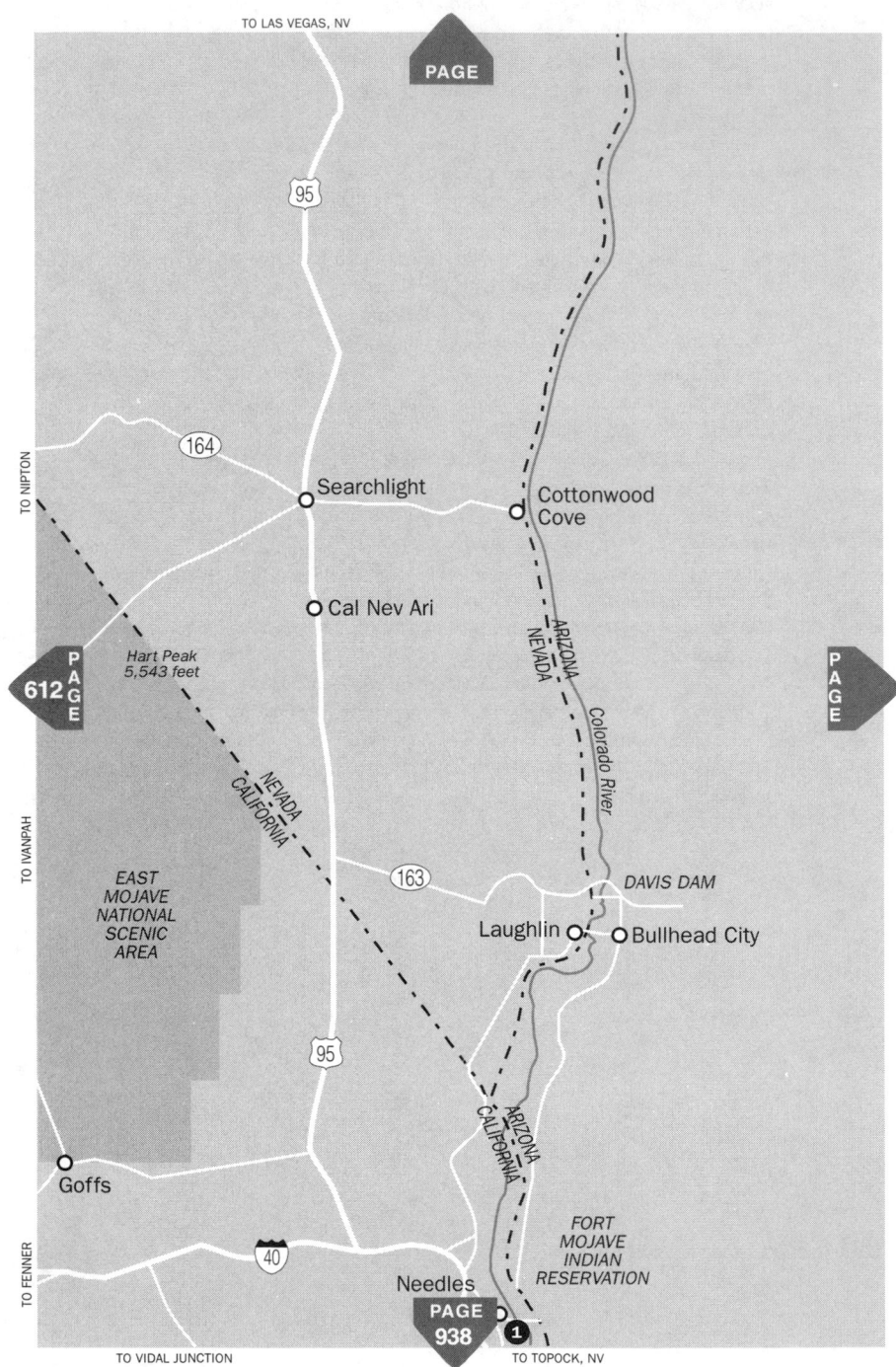

TO LAS VEGAS, NV

PAGE

95

TO NIPTON

164

Searchlight

Cottonwood Cove

PAGE 612

Hart Peak 5,543 feet

Cal Nev Ari

ARIZONA NEVADA

Colorado River

PAGE

TO IVANPAH

NEVADA CALIFORNIA

DAVIS DAM

EAST MOJAVE NATIONAL SCENIC AREA

163

Laughlin

Bullhead City

95

ARIZONA CALIFORNIA

Goffs

TO FENNER

FORT MOJAVE INDIAN RESERVATION

40

Needles

PAGE 938

1

TO VIDAL JUNCTION

TO TOPOCK, NV

Mojave Area

NEEDLES MUNICIPAL GOLF COURSE
ARCHITECT: HARRY RAINVILLE, DAVID RAINVILLE, 1964

144 Marina Drive
Needles, CA 92363

PRO SHOP: 760-326-3931

J.C. Bacon, PGA Professional

Driving Range ●
Practice Greens ●
Clubhouse ●
Food / Beverage ●
Accommodations
Pull Carts ●
Power Carts ●
Club Rental ●
$pecial Offers

	1	2	3	4	5	6	7	8	9	OUT
BACK	507	405	420	390	161	382	396	395	211	3267
REGULAR	500	386	410	377	145	374	384	382	191	3149
par	5	4	4	4	3	4	4	4	3	35
handicap	13	7	1	5	17	11	9	3	15	-
FORWARD	455	337	357	333	135	349	368	336	146	2816
par	5	4	4	4	3	4	4	4	3	35
handicap	3	9	5	11	17	7	1	13	15	-

BACK	
yardage	6515
par	70
rating	71.4
slope	117

	10	11	12	13	14	15	16	17	18	IN
BACK	193	547	152	382	404	409	401	563	197	3248
REGULAR	187	531	144	373	386	397	382	490	183	3073
par	3	5	3	4	4	4	4	5	3	35
handicap	16	6	18	8	10	2	4	12	14	-
FORWARD	155	485	133	332	363	364	376	425	154	2787
par	3	5	3	4	4	4	4	5	3	35
handicap	16	2	18	12	8	6	10	4	14	-

REGULAR	
yardage	6222
par	70
rating	70.1
slope	112

FORWARD	
yardage	5603
par	70
rating	71.1
slope	114

PLAY POLICY & FEES: Green fees are $25. Carts are $10 per person. The senior rate is $20. Reservations are recommended November through April. Reduced fees are offered during summer months. Fees are subject to change. Call in advance.

TEE TIMES: Reservations can be made seven days in advance.

DRESS CODE: Shirts must be worn.

COURSE DESCRIPTION: This well-maintained course has generous, fairly level fairways with mature trees. Lateral hazards are in play on five holes. The greens are overseeded with rye in the winter months and Bermuda in the summer months. This course is walkable and is a fair test for the average golfer.

LOCATION: From Interstate 40 in Needles, take the West Broadway exit and drive one mile east on Needles Highway. Cross K Street and proceed to the course entrance on the left.

. . . ● **TOURNAMENTS:** This course is available for outside tournaments. Tournaments should be booked six months in advance. ● **TRAVEL:** The Riverside Casino (702-298-2535) and the Avi Casino (800-AVI2WIN) are recommended.

1. NEEDLES MUNICIPAL GOLF COURSE

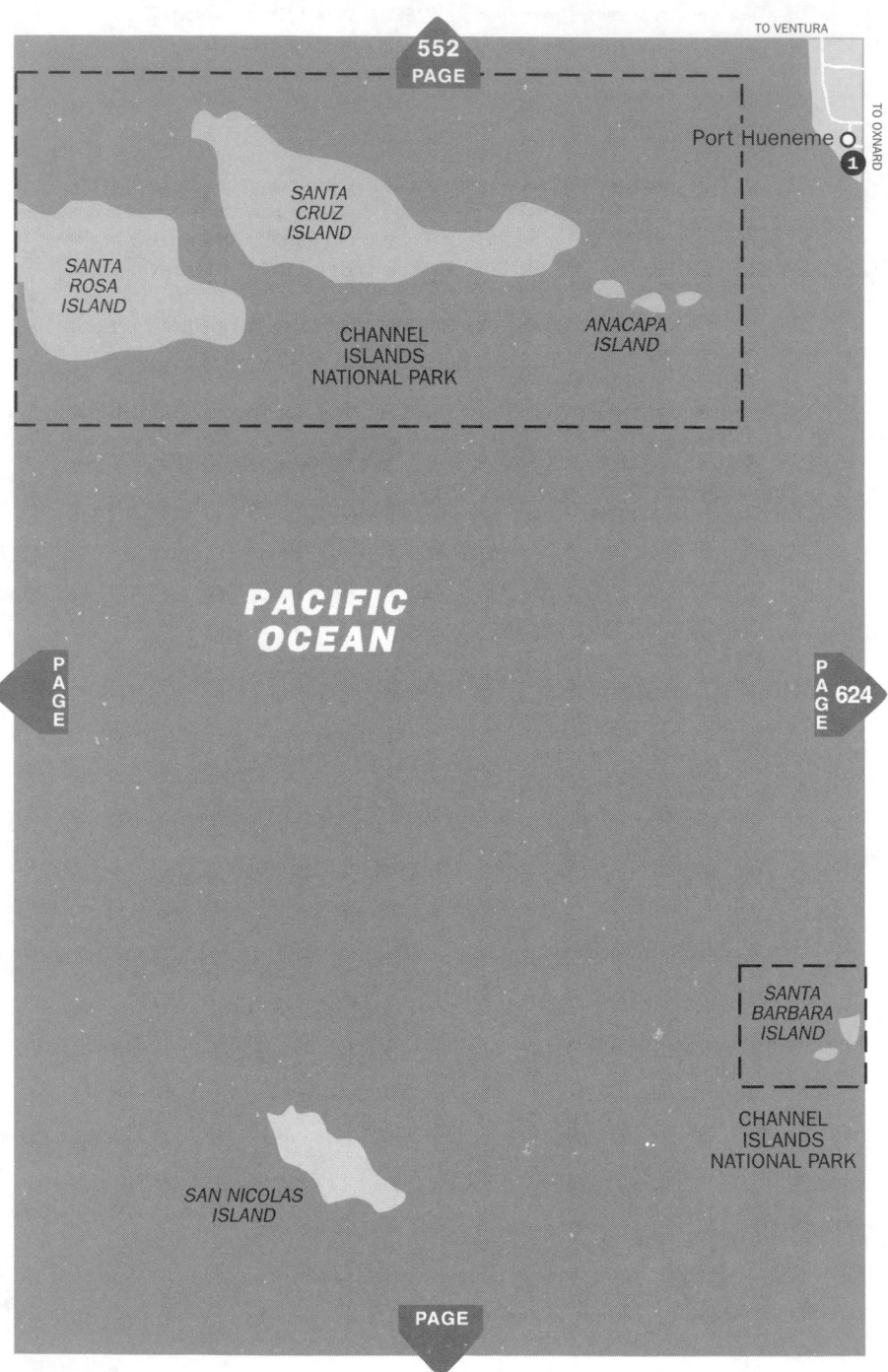

552
PAGE

TO VENTURA

Port Hueneme

TO OXNARD

1

SANTA
CRUZ
ISLAND

SANTA
ROSA
ISLAND

CHANNEL
ISLANDS
NATIONAL PARK

ANACAPA
ISLAND

PAGE

PAGE 624

PACIFIC
OCEAN

SANTA
BARBARA
ISLAND

CHANNEL
ISLANDS
NATIONAL PARK

SAN NICOLAS
ISLAND

PAGE

Port Hueneme Area

CBC PORT HUENEME GOLF CLUB

ARCHITECT: JACK DARAY, 1957

1000 23rd Avenue
Port Hueneme, CA
93043-4300
PRO SHOP: 805-982-2620

Manuel Quezada, Professional/Manager
George Garcia, Superintendent

Driving Range ●
Practice Greens ●
Clubhouse ●
Food / Beverage ●
Accommodations
Pull Carts ●
Power Carts ●
Club Rental ●
$pecial Offers

	1	2	3	4	5	6	7	8	9	OUT
BACK	365	222	326	423	360	180	356	505	300	3037
REGULAR	342	205	314	412	351	139	339	481	292	2875
par	4	3	4	4	4	3	4	5	4	35
handicap	11	13	15	3	5	7	9	1	17	-
FORWARD	317	150	303	402	339	110	321	388	284	2614
par	4	3	4	5	4	3	4	5	4	36
handicap	11	13	9	3	5	17	7	1	15	-

	10	11	12	13	14	15	16	17	18	IN
BACK	367	341	574	179	352	350	387	180	509	3239
REGULAR	359	331	516	168	344	342	357	153	500	3070
par	4	4	5	3	4	4	4	3	5	36
handicap	8	10	2	6	14	12	16	18	4	-
FORWARD	352	321	508	158	336	334	301	123	406	2839
par	4	4	5	3	4	4	4	3	5	36
handicap	6	10	2	8	14	12	16	18	4	-

BACK	
yardage	6276
par	71
rating	69.1
slope	112

REGULAR	
yardage	5945
par	71
rating	67.4
slope	107

FORWARD	
yardage	5453
par	72
rating	70.5
slope	119

1. CBC PORT HUENEME GOLF CLUB

PLAY POLICY & FEES: This was formerly a military course. Green fees for the public are $16 weekdays and $22 on weekends. Green fees vary according to military status. Carts are $20. Closed Christmas.

TEE TIMES: Reservations can be booked seven days in advance for civilians and retired military. Active military can make reservations eight days in advance.

DRESS CODE: No tank tops are allowed. Nonmetal spikes are preferred.

COURSE DESCRIPTION: This is a deceptive course. Although flat, it plays tough because of green and bunker placement. The prevailing west wind off the ocean and numerous trees add to the challenge. Jack Daray built the original nine holes here in 1957. In mid-1990 it was expanded to 18 holes. Give careful study to the 13th. It's a par 3, 179 yards from the championship tees. The large green appears to be surrounded by water, and it's tough getting there. The green is not only guarded by water, but there are also front bunkers, left and right, and out-of-bounds left and behind the green.

LOCATION: Take Ventura Road off U.S. 101 in Oxnard and drive south on Ventura Road to the Sunkist gate. Turn right and proceed to Pacific Street. Turn right on Pacific Street and drive to Port Hueneme Naval Base and the course.

. . . ● **TOURNAMENTS:** This course is available for outside tournaments.

Ventura/San Fernando/ West Los Angeles Area

STERLING HILLS GOLF CLUB
ARCHITECT: GRAVES & PASCUZZO, 1999

901 Sterling Hills Drive
Camarillo, CA 93010

PRO SHOP: 805-987-3446

TBD, Director of Golf, PGA

Driving Range ●
Practice Greens ●
Clubhouse ●
Food / Beverage ●
Accommodations
Pull Carts
Power Carts ●
Club Rental ●
$pecial Offers

	1	2	3	4	5	6	7	8	9	OUT
BACK	433	417	223	523	444	378	348	183	386	3335
REGULAR	416	400	202	490	424	355	332	167	368	3154
par	4	4	3	5	4	4	4	3	4	35
handicap										-
FORWARD	336	347	162	439	363	303	289	135	329	2703
par	4	4	3	5	4	4	4	3	4	35
handicap										-

	10	11	12	13	14	15	16	17	18	IN
BACK	382	163	407	407	448	181	495	457	522	3462
REGULAR	355	144	375	392	420	168	464	429	494	3241
par	4	3	4	4	4	3	5	4	5	36
handicap										-
FORWARD	301	105	315	349	340	123	407	370	432	2742
par	4	3	4	4	4	3	5	4	5	36
handicap										-

BACK	
yardage	6797
par	71
rating	
slope	

REGULAR	
yardage	6395
par	71
rating	
slope	

FORWARD	
yardage	5445
par	71
rating	
slope	

SPANISH HILLS GOLF & COUNTRY CLUB
ARCHITECT: ROBERT CUPP, 1993

999 Crestview Avenue
Camarillo, CA 93010

PRO SHOP: 805-388-5000

Mike Putnam, Director of Golf, PGA
Bruce Hamilton, PGA Teaching Professional
Scott Jorgensen, Superintendent

Driving Range ●
Practice Greens ●
Clubhouse ●
Food / Beverage ●
Accommodations
Pull Carts
Power Carts ●
Club Rental ●
$pecial Offers

	1	2	3	4	5	6	7	8	9	OUT
BACK	382	511	369	183	406	254	375	419	362	3261
REGULAR	332	469	332	125	370	179	324	372	327	2830
par	4	5	4	3	4	3	4	4	4	35
handicap	15	7	3	17	9	11	13	1	5	-
FORWARD	332	413	274	95	329	158	275	312	217	2405
par	4	5	4	3	4	3	4	4	4	35
handicap	13	7	3	17	9	15	11	1	5	-

	10	11	12	13	14	15	16	17	18	IN
BACK	425	194	392	146	512	643	431	388	357	3488
REGULAR	372	161	359	120	476	547	393	337	300	3065
par	4	3	4	3	5	5	4	4	4	36
handicap	8	16	10	18	14	2	4	12	6	-
FORWARD	336	139	298	105	417	476	358	297	191	2617
par	4	3	4	3	5	5	4	4	4	36
handicap	6	16	8	18	12	2	4	10	14	-

BACK	
yardage	6749
par	71
rating	72.9
slope	132

REGULAR	
yardage	5895
par	71
rating	68.7
slope	121

FORWARD	
yardage	5022
par	71
rating	69.9
slope	122

PLAY POLICY & FEES: Green fees have not yet been determined.

DRESS CODE: This will be a nonmetal-spike facility.

COURSE DESCRIPTION: The course is due open in late fall of 1999.

LOCATION: From Los Angeles take U.S.101 north to Camarillo and the Central Avenue exit. Turn right on Central Avenue and drive until you get to Beardsley Road. Take a right on Beardsley and another right on Sterling Hills Drive to the golf course.

. . . ● **TOURNAMENTS:** The course will feature a 2,900-square-foot banquet facility seating 180 people comfortably.

1. STERLING HILLS GOLF CLUB

PLAY POLICY & FEES: Guests must be accompanied by a member.

DRESS CODE: No denim is allowed. Women must wear either a collared or sleeved shirt. Men's shorts must be Bermuda length. Nonmetal spikes are required.

COURSE DESCRIPTION: This is a challenging but fair course with beautiful vistas and numerous changes in elevation. Architect Robert Cupp has made artistic use of water and bunkers. The talk of the course is the uphill, par-4 finishing hole, which features a green surrounded by water and flanked by a spectacular clubhouse.

LOCATION: This course is located 45 miles north of Los Angeles. Heading north on U.S. 101, exit on Las Posas Road. Turn right on Las Posas. Turn left on Ponderosa. Turn left on Crestview Avenue and continue to the course.

. . . ● **TOURNAMENTS:** Outside events are limited to Monday. A 100-player minimum is needed to book a tournament. Carts are a must. Events must be scheduled six months in advance. A banquet facility is available that can accommodate 240 people.

2. SPANISH HILLS GOLF & COUNTRY CLUB

3 CAMARILLO SPRINGS GOLF COURSE
ARCHITECT: TED ROBINSON, 1972

791 Camarillo Springs
Camarillo, CA 93012

PRO SHOP: 805-484-1075

Vernice Vasquez, Manager
Brian Reed, PGA Professional
Carl Waite, Superintendent

Driving Range •
Practice Greens •
Clubhouse •
Food / Beverage •
Accommodations
Pull Carts •
Power Carts •
Club Rental •
$pecial Offers

	1	2	3	4	5	6	7	8	9	OUT
BACK	372	382	382	379	193	512	377	195	535	3327
REGULAR	345	357	358	352	169	464	331	161	518	3055
par	4	4	4	4	3	5	4	3	5	36
handicap	11	9	1	5	3	13	7	17	-	
FORWARD	322	319	305	330	141	406	286	108	467	2684
par	4	4	4	4	3	5	4	3	5	36
handicap	9	5	11	7	13	1	15	17	3	-

	10	11	12	13	14	15	16	17	18	IN
BACK	155	342	509	194	169	345	525	334	475	3048
REGULAR	145	335	502	168	154	308	496	318	450	2876
par	3	4	5	3	3	4	5	4	5	36
handicap	18	16	4	6	14	10	2	12	8	-
FORWARD	135	329	484	147	115	264	410	299	430	2613
par	3	4	5	3	3	4	5	4	5	36
handicap	16	8	4	14	18	12	6	10	2	-

BACK	
yardage	6375
par	72
rating	70.2
slope	115

REGULAR	
yardage	5931
par	72
rating	67.9
slope	108

FORWARD	
yardage	5297
par	72
rating	70.2
slope	116

4 SUNSET HILLS COUNTRY CLUB
ARCHITECT: TED ROBINSON, 1974

4155 Erbes Road North
Thousand Oaks, CA 91360

PRO SHOP: 805-495-5407
OFFICE: 805-523-7450

Chris Kaczke, PGA Professional
Steve Holley, Superintendent
Steve Boveri, Tournament Director

Driving Range
Practice Greens •
Clubhouse •
Food / Beverage •
Accommodations
Pull Carts
Power Carts •
Club Rental •
$pecial Offers

	1	2	3	4	5	6	7	8	9	OUT
BACK	363	410	544	350	155	391	368	292	162	3035
REGULAR	357	393	534	342	145	358	322	288	143	2882
par	4	4	5	4	3	4	4	4	3	35
handicap	9	1	3	13	15	5	7	17	11	-
FORWARD	347	335	523	332	145	348	314	287	134	2765
par	4	4	5	4	3	4	4	4	3	35
handicap	7	3	1	11	17	5	9	13	15	-

	10	11	12	13	14	15	16	17	18	IN
BACK	333	457	138	326	374	489	347	210	357	3031
REGULAR	313	448	136	317	366	480	321	202	339	2922
par	4	5	3	4	4	5	4	3	4	36
handicap	14	18	16	8	2	4	6	10	12	-
FORWARD	308	448	128	223	365	471	321	192	322	2778
par	4	5	3	4	4	5	4	3	4	36
handicap	16	8	18	12	2	4	6	14	10	-

BACK	
yardage	6066
par	71
rating	69.3
slope	121

REGULAR	
yardage	5804
par	71
rating	68.0
slope	118

FORWARD	
yardage	5543
par	71
rating	72.2
slope	124

PLAY POLICY & FEES: Green fees are $36 weekdays and $45 weekends, including cart. Walking is allowed weekdays only for $24. Twilight and nine-hole rates are available.

TEE TIMES: Reservations can be booked seven days in advance.

DRESS CODE: Collared shirts are required.

COURSE DESCRIPTION: This is a well-maintained, easily walkable course with lots of trees. Water comes into play on 14 holes. The sixth is a knockout. This par 5 is 512 yards from the championship tees and aims toward a beautiful mountain range. There are two lakes on the left; one is not visible. Out-of-bounds is on the right and so are two fairway bunkers.

LOCATION: In Camarillo take the Camarillo Springs Road exit off U.S. 101 and drive south to the course.

. . . ● **TOURNAMENTS:** A 16-player minimum is need to book a tournament. A 100-player minimum is needed for a shotgun tournament. Carts are mandatory, and events should be scheduled 12 months in advance. The banquet facility can accommodate 120 people.

3. CAMARILLO SPRINGS GOLF COURSE

PLAY POLICY & FEES: Reciprocal play is accepted with members of other private clubs. Green fees are $50 weekdays and $65 weekends. Carts are $22.

DRESS CODE: Golfers must wear collared shirts. No jeans are allowed. Shorts must have a six-inch inseam. Nonmetal spikes are encouraged.

COURSE DESCRIPTION: This well-maintained course offers narrow fairways, fast greens, and blind tee shots. All the holes are fun but challenging.

NOTES: Tennis is also available.

LOCATION: From U.S. 101 (Ventura Freeway), take the Fillmore exit (Highway 23) and drive north for 4.5 miles to Olsen Road. Turn left and drive one-half mile to Erbes Road. Turn left to the club.

. . . ● **TOURNAMENTS:** This course is available for outside tournaments on Monday only. The banquet facility can accommodate 250 people.

4. SUNSET HILLS COUNTRY CLUB

SINALOA GOLF COURSE
ARCHITECT: GEOFF SHACKELFORD, 1994

980 Madera Road
Simi, CA 93065

PRO SHOP: 805-581-2662

Lynn Shackelford, Director of Golf

Driving Range ●
Practice Greens ●
Clubhouse ●
Food / Beverage ●
Accommodations
Pull Carts ●
Power Carts
Club Rental ●
$pecial Offers

	1	2	3	4	5	6	7	8	9	OUT
BACK	-	-	-	-	-	-	-	-	-	-
REGULAR	100	85	134	131	120	87	107	110	135	1009
par	3	3	3	3	3	3	3	3	3	27
handicap	7	6	2	3	1	4	8	9	5	-
FORWARD	100	85	134	131	120	87	107	110	135	1009
par	3	3	3	3	3	3	3	3	3	27
handicap	7	6	2	3	1	4	8	9	5	-

	10	11	12	13	14	15	16	17	18	IN
BACK	-	-	-	-	-	-	-	-	-	-
REGULAR	100	85	134	131	120	87	107	110	135	1009
par	3	3	3	3	3	3	3	3	3	27
handicap	7	6	2	3	1	4	8	9	5	-
FORWARD	100	85	134	131	120	87	107	110	135	1009
par	3	3	3	3	3	3	3	3	3	27
handicap	7	6	2	3	1	4	8	9	5	-

BACK	
yardage	-
par	-
rating	-
slope	-

REGULAR	
yardage	2018
par	54
rating	-
slope	-

FORWARD	
yardage	2018
par	54
rating	-
slope	-

 WOOD RANCH GOLF CLUB
ARCHITECT: TED ROBINSON, 1985

P.O. Box 1749
Simi Valley, CA 93065

301 Wood Ranch Parkway
Simi Valley, CA 93065

PRO SHOP: 805-522-7262

David Foster, General Manager, PGA
Don Fiala, PGA Professional
Ed Kutt, Superintendent

Driving Range ●
Practice Greens ●
Clubhouse ●
Food / Beverage ●
Accommodations
Pull Carts
Power Carts ●
Club Rental ●
$pecial Offers

	1	2	3	4	5	6	7	8	9	OUT
BACK	437	526	179	366	431	540	170	342	434	3425
REGULAR	402	459	152	344	380	461	150	310	358	3016
par	4	5	3	4	4	5	3	4	4	36
handicap	3	13	15	5	1	11	17	9	7	-
FORWARD	354	397	132	312	339	404	122	298	299	2657
par	4	5	3	4	4	5	3	4	4	36
handicap	3	9	17	7	1	15	13	5	11	-

	10	11	12	13	14	15	16	17	18	IN
BACK	418	428	415	196	365	537	460	207	521	3547
REGULAR	366	374	371	155	343	494	363	159	485	3110
par	4	4	4	3	4	5	4	3	5	36
handicap	2	6	4	8	14	16	10	18	12	-
FORWARD	341	347	338	115	300	436	291	115	452	2735
par	4	4	4	3	4	5	4	3	5	36
handicap	2	14	4	12	10	8	16	18	6	-

BACK	
yardage	6972
par	72
rating	74.4
slope	137

REGULAR	
yardage	6126
par	72
rating	69.7
slope	126

FORWARD	
yardage	5392
par	72
rating	72.4
slope	131

PLAY POLICY & FEES: Green fees are $7 for nine holes and $10 for 18 holes weekdays, and $9 for nine holes and $14 for 18 holes weekends. Call for special rates.

TEE TIMES: Reservations can be booked seven days in advance.

COURSE DESCRIPTION: In the morning the area teaching pros come to sharpen their short games. The fifth hole is patterned after the 12th hole at Augusta National. The eighth hole is patterned after the 10th hole at Winged Foot West.

LOCATION: From Simi Valley drive west on Highway 118 to the Madera Road exit. Go south and follow the road for about two miles to the course.

. . . ● **TOURNAMENTS:** Shotgun tournaments are available weekdays only. A 12-player minimum is needed to book an event.

5. SINALOA GOLF COURSE

PLAY POLICY & FEES: Reciprocal play is accepted with members of other private clubs. Guests must be accompanied by a member. Guest fees are $65 weekdays and $90 weekends. Carts are $12. Reservations are recommended.

TEE TIMES: Have your professional call in advance for tee times.

DRESS CODE: Appropriate golf attire is required.

COURSE DESCRIPTION: This course is considered one of the toughest in the Los Angeles area. This is an excellent target golf course with water hazards on 11 holes, lots of deep pot bunkers, few trees, and deep rough. It's long and demanding with a links-style flavor. The pride of this course is the 410-yard, par-4 16th hole. It drops 120 feet from the tee and requires a testy second shot to a severe, two-tiered green.

NOTES: Designed by Ted Robinson in 1985, the course is often rated among the top 20 in the state. The course record from the gold tees of 65 is held by Rob Sullivan. Wood Ranch was the site of the 1987 and 1988 GTE Senior Classic and the 1986 Pac-10 Championship.

LOCATION: From Los Angeles travel north on U.S. 101 to Highway 23. Head north to the Olsen Road exit and turn right. At Wood Ranch Parkway, turn right and drive to the club.

. . . ● **TOURNAMENTS:** This course is available for outside tournaments on Monday only.

6. WOOD RANCH GOLF CLUB

⑦ NORTH RANCH COUNTRY CLUB
ARCHITECT: TED ROBINSON, 1975

4761 Valley Spring Drive
Westlake Village, CA
91362
PRO SHOP: 818-889-9421
CLUBHOUSE: 818-889-3531

John Mook, General Manager
Scott Mendenhall, Superintendent

Driving Range ●
Practice Greens ●
Clubhouse ●
Food / Beverage ●
Accommodations
Pull Carts
Power Carts ●
Club Rental ●
Special Offers

	1	2	3	4	5	6	7	8	9	OUT
BACK										
REGULAR										
par										
handicap										
FORWARD										
par										
handicap										

	10	11	12	13	14	15	16	17	18	IN
BACK										
REGULAR										
par										
handicap										
FORWARD										
par										
handicap										

BACK	
yardage	6886
par	72
rating	72.8
slope	130

REGULAR	
yardage	6363
par	72
rating	70.4
slope	117

FORWARD	
yardage	5379
par	72
rating	73.5
slope	125

⑧ SIMI HILLS GOLF COURSE
ARCHITECT: TED ROBINSON, 1981

5031 Alamo Street
Simi Valley, CA 93063

PRO SHOP: 805-522-0803

Kelly Sorensen, Director of Golf, PGA
Brian Mahoney, Head Professional
Kim Lamoree, Tournament Director

Driving Range ●
Practice Greens ●
Clubhouse ●
Food / Beverage ●
Accommodations
Pull Carts ●
Power Carts ●
Club Rental ●
Special Offers ●

	1	2	3	4	5	6	7	8	9	OUT
BACK	515	391	396	366	362	193	407	180	544	3354
REGULAR	499	367	365	350	340	163	389	158	515	3146
par	4	5	4	3	4	4	4	3	4	35
handicap	17	3	15	9	5	13	7	11	1	-
FORWARD	462	327	333	313	297	137	349	140	464	2822
par	5	4	4	4	4	3	4	3	5	36
handicap	13	5	11	9	7	15	1	17	3	-

	10	11	12	13	14	15	16	17	18	IN
BACK	390	541	353	155	308	417	422	182	387	3155
REGULAR	363	512	343	146	290	415	398	159	361	2987
par	5	4	4	4	4	3	4	3	5	36
handicap	6	12	8	14	16	2	4	18	10	-
FORWARD	336	467	295	138	260	357	353	137	340	2683
par	4	5	4	3	4	4	4	3	4	35
handicap	10	2	14	18	16	6	4	12	8	-

BACK	
yardage	6509
par	71
rating	70.6
slope	125

REGULAR	
yardage	6133
par	71
rating	69.1
slope	121

FORWARD	
yardage	5505
par	71
rating	71.1
slope	120

PLAY POLICY & FEES: Members and guests only. Green fees are $55 weekdays and $75 weekends. Carts are $22. The course is closed on Monday.

DRESS CODE: Appropriate golf attire and nonmetal spikes are required.

COURSE DESCRIPTION: This course is known for its smooth, fast greens and tight fairways. Players who miss the fairway can find themselves in big trouble.

NOTES: The 1988 Men's NCAA Championship was held here. The Southwest Intercollegiate Championships are held here each spring. This private club has 27 holes, which break into three nines. Par is 72 on each of the 18-hole combinations. The Valley/Oak Course is 6,678 yards and rated 72.6 from the championship tees, and 6,238 yards and rated 70.7 from the regular tees. The slope ratings are 131 championship and 125 regular. Forward tees are 5,447 yards and unrated. The Valley/Lake Course is 6,879 yards and rated 73.1 from the championship tees, and 6,352 yards and rated 70.4 from the regular tees. The slope ratings are 130 championship and 124 regular. Forward tees are 5,328 yards and rated 73.4. The slope rating is 129. The Lake/Oak Course: See scorecard for more information.

LOCATION: From Westlake travel north on U.S. 101 to the Westlake Boulevard exit and drive north for two miles to Valley Spring Drive. Turn right and drive one mile to the club.

. . . ● **TOURNAMENTS:** This course is available for outside tournaments on Monday only.

7. NORTH RANCH COUNTRY CLUB

PLAY POLICY & FEES: Green fees are $22 weekdays and $32 weekends. Carts are $12 per person.

TEE TIMES: Reservations can be booked seven days in advance on weekdays and five days in advance on weekends. Residents can call at 7 a.m., nonresidents at 9 a.m.

DRESS CODE: Collared shirts must be worn on the course.

COURSE DESCRIPTION: The course makes use of the natural terrain and is set on what was once a Chumash Indian reservation. Many of the ancient trees were kept in place to enhance the beauty and increase the difficulty of the course, which winds its way through the hills and valleys.

NOTES: Several golf videos have been made at this course, including Tom Sharp's "I Hate Golf." This course was voted the number-one course in Ventura County for 1998. It has been the site of a number of commercials.

LOCATION: From Interstate 5 north of Los Angeles, travel west on Highway 118 for about 15 miles to the Stearns Street exit and turn right. Drive to Alamo Street and turn left to the course.

. . . ● **TOURNAMENTS:** Shotgun tournaments are available weekdays only. Carts are required. A 16-player minimum is required to book a regular tournament. Tournaments can be booked 11 months in advance. ● **TRAVEL:** The Simi Valley Radisson Hotel is seven minutes from the golf course. Call 805-583-2000 for reservations. ● **$PECIAL OFFERS:** Golf packages are available with the Radisson.

8. SIMI HILLS GOLF COURSE

9 PORTER VALLEY COUNTRY CLUB
ARCHITECT: TED ROBINSON, 1968

19216 Singing Hills Drive
Northridge, CA 91326

PRO SHOP: 818-368-2919
CLUBHOUSE: 818-360-1071

Jim Sweiter, Manager
Rick Booth, PGA Professional
Julie Morin, Banquet Manager

Driving Range •
Practice Greens •
Clubhouse •
Food / Beverage •
Accommodations •
Pull Carts
Power Carts •
Club Rental •
$pecial Offers

	1	2	3	4	5	6	7	8	9	OUT
BACK	337	412	139	352	366	391	570	193	395	3155
REGULAR	316	395	135	337	353	381	537	173	377	3004
par	4	4	3	4	4	4	5	3	4	35
handicap	9	3	17	7	13	11	1	15	5	-
FORWARD	275	380	113	323	335	377	486	169	367	2825
par	4	4	3	4	4	4	5	3	4	35
handicap	14	6	18	12	10	8	2	16	4	-

	10	11	12	13	14	15	16	17	18	IN
BACK	504	277	200	455	217	377	176	328	401	2935
REGULAR	488	260	176	433	200	341	160	321	386	2765
par	5	4	3	5	3	4	3	4	4	35
handicap	2	18	14	10	4	8	16	12	6	-
FORWARD	476	253	160	411	186	333	145	313	374	2651
par	5	4	3	5	3	4	3	4	4	35
handicap	1	13	15	3	11	9	17	5	7	-

BACK	
yardage	6090
par	70
rating	69.3
slope	116

REGULAR	
yardage	5769
par	70
rating	67.5
slope	113

FORWARD	
yardage	5476
par	70
rating	69.1
slope	115

10 MISSION HILLS LITTLE LEAGUE GOLF COURSE

P.O. Box 2642
Mission Hills, CA 91343

PRO SHOP: 818-892-3019

Jim Bracken, Manager

Driving Range
Practice Greens •
Clubhouse
Food / Beverage •
Accommodations
Pull Carts •
Power Carts
Club Rental •
$pecial Offers

	1	2	3	4	5	6	7	8	9	OUT
BACK										
REGULAR										
par										
handicap										
FORWARD										
par										
handicap										

	10	11	12	13	14	15	16	17	18	IN
BACK										
REGULAR										
par										
handicap										
FORWARD										
par										
handicap										

BACK	
yardage	
par	
rating	
slope	

REGULAR	
yardage	3300
par	54
rating	
slope	

FORWARD	
yardage	
par	
rating	
slope	

PLAY POLICY & FEES: Members and guests only. Guest fees are $50 Monday through Thursday and $70 Friday through Sunday and holidays. Carts are $22. The course is closed on Monday.

TEE TIMES: Reservations can be booked seven days in advance for members and guests.

DRESS CODE: No denim is allowed, and shirts must have collars. Nonmetal spikes are required.

COURSE DESCRIPTION: This is a short course offering tight fairways and well-bunkered greens. There are a few water hazards. The course sits up in the hills, offering golfers a beautiful view of the entire San Fernando Valley. But the course itself is especially hilly. It is a fun little course that can be more difficult than it looks.

NOTES: The course record is 62.

LOCATION: Take Interstate 5 or Interstate 405 to Highway 118 west to Northridge. Exit at Tampa Road and drive north to the first light. Make a right turn on Rinaldi Drive, and take a left onto Porter Valley Drive to the club.

. . . ● **TOURNAMENTS:** Outside events can be held on Monday only. Carts required. A 60-player minimum is required to book an event. Tournaments should be scheduled 12 months in advance. A banquet facility is available that can accommodate up to 300 people.

9. PORTER VALLEY COUNTRY CLUB

PLAY POLICY & FEES: Green fees are $5 weekdays and $6 weekends. Senior green fees are $4.50 Monday through Friday. Green fees for juniors under 18 are $3.50. Replays are $2.50 Monday through Friday.

TEE TIMES: Reservations are not accepted. All play is on a first-come, first-served basis.

COURSE DESCRIPTION: This short, flat course is good for beginners. A few trees dot the course, but there are no traps. All nine holes are par 3s.

LOCATION: Off Interstate 405 take the Nordoff exit west. Turn right on Woodley and you'll see the course near the Veterans Administration Hospital.

. . . ● **TOURNAMENTS:** This course is available for outside tournaments.

10. MISSION HILLS LITTLE LEAGUE GOLF

⑪ KNOLLWOOD COUNTRY CLUB

ARCHITECT: WILLIAM F. BELL, 1956

12040 Balboa Boulevard
Granada Hills, CA 91344

PRO SHOP: 818-363-8161

Kevin McGraw, General Manager
Garry Finneran, PGA Professional
Annie Barker, Tournament Director

Driving Range ●
Practice Greens ●
Clubhouse ●
Food / Beverage ●
Accommodations
Pull Carts ●
Power Carts ●
Club Rental ●
Special Offers

	1	2	3	4	5	6	7	8	9	OUT
BACK	438	493	340	562	383	162	386	154	376	3294
REGULAR	413	483	316	542	355	150	360	144	341	3104
par	4	5	4	5	4	3	4	3	4	36
handicap	1	5	13	3	11	15	9	17	7	-
FORWARD	405	460	289	495	346	135	345	135	325	2935
par	5	5	4	5	4	3	4	3	4	37
handicap	9	1	13	3	11	17	5	15	7	-

	10	11	12	13	14	15	16	17	18	IN
BACK	361	476	353	155	307	407	517	137	369	3082
REGULAR	352	461	313	147	304	391	499	134	349	2950
par	4	5	4	3	4	4	5	3	4	36
handicap	4	6	8	16	14	2	12	18	10	-
FORWARD	334	452	296	140	293	382	463	87	332	2779
par	4	5	4	3	4	4	5	3	4	36
handicap	6	2	12	16	14	4	8	18	10	-

BACK	
yardage	6376
par	72
rating	70.5
slope	125

REGULAR	
yardage	6054
par	72
rating	68.9
slope	120

FORWARD	
yardage	5714
par	73
rating	72.6
slope	118

⑫ CASCADE GOLF CLUB

ARCHITECTS: STEVE TIMM, 1999; BOB CUPP

16325 Silver Oak Drive
Sylmar, CA 91342

PRO SHOP: 818-833-8900

Driving Range ●
Practice Greens ●
Clubhouse
Food / Beverage ●
Accommodations
Pull Carts
Power Carts ●
Club Rental ●
Special Offers

	1	2	3	4	5	6	7	8	9	OUT
BACK										
REGULAR										
par										
handicap										
FORWARD										
par										
handicap										

	10	11	12	13	14	15	16	17	18	IN
BACK										
REGULAR										
par										
handicap										
FORWARD										
par										
handicap										

BACK	
yardage	6750
par	71
rating	
slope	

REGULAR	
yardage	
par	
rating	
slope	

FORWARD	
yardage	
par	
rating	
slope	

PLAY POLICY & FEES: Green fees are $20 weekdays and $25 weekends for 18 holes. Carts are $22.

TEE TIMES: Reservations can be booked seven days in advance.

DRESS CODE: No tank tops are allowed.

COURSE DESCRIPTION: No holes on this course overlap. Instead they run single file through a string of homes. Many approach shots are uphill, making it tough to judge distance.

NOTES: This course was originally built and owned by Bob Hope and Dean Martin. Dave Berganio holds the men's course record of 64. Donna Caponi holds the women's record of 70.

LOCATION: From Los Angeles take Interstate 5 north to Highway 118. Go west and exit at Balboa Boulevard and go north three-quarters of a mile to the course.

. . . ● **TOURNAMENTS:** Shotgun tournaments are available weekdays only. Carts are required. A 24-player minimum is required to book a tournament. Events should be scheduled 12 months in advance. The banquet facility can accommodate up to 500 people.

11. KNOLLWOOD COUNTRY CLUB

PLAY POLICY & FEES: This will be a public course with green fees expected to be $80 on weekdays and $90 on weekends. The course is expected to open in fall of 1999.

TEE TIMES: Reservations policy was not available at time of press.

COURSE DESCRIPTION: Cascade will be a traditional layout with lots of elevation changes. The bent-grass greens will be ample size and allow players with a good touch to make putts. However, for golfers who choose not to use the fairways, getting to the putting surface and scoring well will be a challenge.

LOCATION: From West Los Angeles take Interstate 405 north until it turns into Interstate 5. Take Interstate 5 to Highway 210. Take Highway 210 east and get off at the Yarnell exit. Go right on Foothill for one mile and take another right on Balboa. Follow Balboa to Silver Oaks Drive. Turn right to the course.

. . . ● **TOURNAMENTS:** A 12-player minimum is required to book an event.

12. CASCADE GOLF CLUB

EL CARISO GOLF COURSE
ARCHITECT: ROBERT MUIR GRAVES, 1977

13100 Eldridge Avenue
Sylmar, CA 91342

PRO SHOP: 818-367-6157
CLUBHOUSE: 818-367-2140

Michael O'Keefe, Head Professional, PGA
Joe Cuevas, Superintendent

Driving Range ●
Practice Greens ●
Clubhouse ●
Food / Beverage ●
Accommodations
Pull Carts ●
Power Carts ●
Club Rental ●
$pecial Offers

	1	2	3	4	5	6	7	8	9	OUT
BACK	353	347	161	196	389	127	345	139	233	2290
REGULAR	336	329	128	161	338	115	321	107	213	2048
par	4	4	3	3	4	3	4	3	3	31
handicap	7	3	13	11	1	15	5	17	9	-
FORWARD	295	265	118	147	287	101	282	100	178	1773
par	4	4	3	3	4	3	4	3	3	31
handicap	7	3	13	11	1	15	5	17	9	-

	10	11	12	13	14	15	16	17	18	IN
BACK	359	152	290	196	177	316	176	140	397	2203
REGULAR	347	134	270	172	163	293	160	122	376	2037
par	4	3	4	3	3	4	3	3	4	31
handicap	4	16	6	10	14	8	12	18	2	-
FORWARD	311	97	234	156	133	257	135	112	332	1767
par	4	3	4	3	3	4	3	3	4	31
handicap	4	16	6	10	14	8	12	18	2	-

BACK	
yardage	4493
par	62
rating	61.1
slope	97

REGULAR	
yardage	4085
par	62
rating	59.7
slope	92

FORWARD	
yardage	3540
par	62
rating	58.9
slope	87

HANSEN DAM GOLF COURSE

10400 Glenoaks Boulevard
Pacoima, CA 91331

PRO SHOP: 818-896-0050
STARTER: 818-899-2200

Phil Riggs, Manager
Jim Anderson, PGA Professional
Rod Binkier, Superintendent

Driving Range ●
Practice Greens ●
Clubhouse ●
Food / Beverage ●
Accommodations
Pull Carts ●
Power Carts ●
Club Rental ●
$pecial Offers

	1	2	3	4	5	6	7	8	9	OUT
BACK										
REGULAR										
par										
handicap										
FORWARD										
par										
handicap										

	10	11	12	13	14	15	16	17	18	IN
BACK										
REGULAR										
par										
handicap										
FORWARD										
par										
handicap										

BACK	
yardage	6662
par	72
rating	70.8
slope	115

REGULAR	
yardage	6345
par	72
rating	67.9
slope	112

FORWARD	
yardage	6084
par	72
rating	73.8
slope	123

PLAY POLICY & FEES: Green fees are $16.50 weekdays and $21.50 weekends. Call ahead for special twilight and senior rates. Carts are $19 for 18 holes.

TEE TIMES: Reservations can be booked seven days in advance.

DRESS CODE: Shirts and shoes are required.

COURSE DESCRIPTION: A well-placed tee shot is important on this course. Five lakes come into play, and each green is well bunkered. The fifth is a tough 389-yard par 4 that doglegs left and has water to the right. El Cariso is usually very well maintained. It is one of the tougher executive courses around.

NOTES: The course record is 54 held by PGA Tour player David Berganio, who grew up playing at El Cariso.

LOCATION: Take Interstate 210 to Hubbard and exit right. Go east for one mile. At Eldridge Avenue turn right and go one block to the course. The course is on the left.

. . . ● **TOURNAMENTS:** A 24-player minimum is required to book a tournament. Events should be booked nine months in advance. The banquet facility can hold up to 153 people.

13. EL CARISO GOLF COURSE

PLAY POLICY & FEES: Green fees are $18 weekdays and $23 weekends. The nine-hole rates are $11 weekdays and $14 weekends. Twilight rates are available. Carts are $21.

TEE TIMES: Reservations can be booked seven days in advance with a Los Angeles reservation card.

DRESS CODE: Shirts must be worn. Nonmetal spikes are preferred.

COURSE DESCRIPTION: This course plays longer than it looks. Big hitters must be careful about staying on the fairways. The greens tend to be small, so chipping skills are important. The ninth hole is the number-one handicap hole on this course. It's a par-4, 450-yarder from the championship tees that requires the second shot to carry a swale onto an elevated green.

LOCATION: From Interstate 5 take Osborne and go east 1.5 miles to Glenoaks Boulevard and turn right. Turn left to Montague and turn left to the course.

. . . ● **TOURNAMENTS:** No shotgun tournaments are allowed. A 24-player minimum is needed to book an event.

14. HANSEN DAM GOLF COURSE

15 POINT MUGU GOLF CLUB
ARCHITECT: MARLIN COX, 1963

NAWS, Building 153
Point Mugu, CA 93042

PRO SHOP: 805-989-7109

Gerry A. Garcia, Head Professional

Driving Range ●
Practice Greens ●
Clubhouse
Food / Beverage ●
Accommodations
Pull Carts ●
Power Carts ●
Club Rental ●
$pecial Offers

	1	2	3	4	5	6	7	8	9	OUT
BACK	-	-	-	-	-	-	-	-	-	-
REGULAR	323	158	365	420	513	150	381	337	320	2967
par	4	3	4	4	5	3	4	4	4	35
handicap	11	13	5	3	7	15	1	17	9	-
FORWARD	318	140	360	325	490	150	375	325	300	2783
par	4	3	4	4	5	3	5	4	4	36
handicap	15	9	1	13	3	7	5	11	17	-

	10	11	12	13	14	15	16	17	18	IN
BACK	-	-	-	-	-	-	-	-	-	-
REGULAR	318	143	364	332	511	183	425	337	278	2891
par	4	3	4	4	5	3	4	4	4	35
handicap	14	10	4	12	8	6	2	18	16	-
FORWARD	315	150	360	325	490	150	375	325	265	2755
par	4	3	4	4	5	3	5	4	4	36
handicap	16	10	2	14	4	8	6	12	18	-

BACK	
yardage	-
par	-
rating	-
slope	-

REGULAR	
yardage	5858
par	70
rating	67.7
slope	112

FORWARD	
yardage	5538
par	72
rating	-
slope	-

16 LOS ROBLES GOLF COURSE
ARCHITECT: BOB BALDOCK, 1964

299 South Moorpark Road
Thousand Oaks, CA 91361

PRO SHOP: 805-495-6421

Steve Butler, Director of Golf, PGA
Jose Ortiz, Superintendent

Driving Range ●
Practice Greens ●
Clubhouse ●
Food / Beverage ●
Accommodations
Pull Carts ●
Power Carts ●
Club Rental ●
$pecial Offers

	1	2	3	4	5	6	7	8	9	OUT
BACK	412	191	471	352	621	403	188	462	212	3312
REGULAR	379	174	453	336	573	371	168	411	183	3048
par	4	3	5	4	5	4	3	4	3	35
handicap	7	15	9	13	5	3	17	1	11	-
FORWARD	356	161	375	301	529	347	115	379	156	2719
par	4	3	4	4	5	4	3	4	3	34
handicap	11	15	1	9	7	3	17	5	13	-

	10	11	12	13	14	15	16	17	18	IN
BACK	480	163	395	340	353	193	446	159	293	2822
REGULAR	470	152	381	319	341	166	435	148	266	2678
par	5	3	4	4	4	3	4	3	4	34
handicap	14	18	4	6	8	10	2	16	12	-
FORWARD	420	133	360	294	327	131	419	132	249	2465
par	5	3	4	4	4	3	5	3	4	35
handicap	8	14	2	4	10	18	6	16	12	-

BACK	
yardage	6134
par	69
rating	68.7
slope	116

REGULAR	
yardage	5726
par	69
rating	66.5
slope	108

FORWARD	
yardage	5184
par	69
rating	69.0
slope	115

PLAY POLICY & FEES: Public play is accepted. Green fees for military vary according to military status. Green fees for public play are $10 for nine holes, and $12 for 18 holes on weekdays. On weekends green fees are $12 for nine holes, and $15 for 18 holes. Twilight green fees are $9 weekdays and $11 weekends.

TEE TIMES: Reservations can be booked seven days in advance.

DRESS CODE: Collared shirts and nonmetal spikes are encouraged.

COURSE DESCRIPTION: This short course is wide open and flat. The course has nine greens but 15 different tee boxes. Four water hazards line the course, but the biggest obstacle is the sound of low-flying aircraft going to and from the nearby airstrip. Bring ear plugs.

LOCATION: Take the Wood Road-USN Point Mugu exit off Highway 1 north of Camarillo Beach. Obtain a guest pass from the Visitor Information Center and enter the base at Mugu Road. Turn right at Third Street and drive to the course.

. . . ● **TOURNAMENTS:** This course is available for outside tournaments. A 48-player minimum is needed to book a tournament. Tournaments should be booked two months in advance.

15. POINT MUGU GOLF CLUB

PLAY POLICY & FEES: Green fees are $16 weekdays and $20 weekends for Thousand Oaks residents, and $22 weekdays and $27 weekends for nonresidents. Call for special rates. Carts are $22.

TEE TIMES: Reservations can be booked seven days in advance.

COURSE DESCRIPTION: This is a moderately hilly course with three lakes and fairways flanked by trees. There are six par 3s. The course features a variety of holes, requiring players to both fade and draw the ball. It is a scenic course with many old oak trees.

NOTES: The course is in excellent condition, considering 90,000 rounds are played here annually. The Thousand Oaks City Championships are played here each October.

LOCATION: Travel north on U.S. 101 (Ventura Freeway) to the Moorpark Road exit and turn left under the freeway. Drive one block and turn right to the club.

. . . ● **TOURNAMENTS:** A 24-player minimum is required to book a tournament. Carts required. Tournaments should be booked 12 months in advance. The banquet facility holds 250 people.

16. LOS ROBLES GOLF COURSE

17 SHERWOOD COUNTRY CLUB
ARCHITECT: JACK NICKLAUS, 1989

320 West Stafford Road
Thousand Oaks, CA
91361
PRO SHOP: 805-496-3036

John Phillips, Director of Golf, PGA
Bob Marshall, Superintendent

Driving Range •
Practice Greens •
Clubhouse •
Food / Beverage •
Accommodations
Pull Carts
Power Carts •
Club Rental •
$pecial Offers

	1	2	3	4	5	6	7	8	9	OUT
BACK	316	512	186	435	499	384	422	211	405	3370
REGULAR	298	491	146	407	457	359	383	162	355	3058
par	4	5	3	4	5	4	4	3	4	36
handicap	15	9	17	1	13	5	7	11	3	-
FORWARD	268	440	116	364	414	345	342	132	276	2697
par	4	5	3	4	5	4	4	3	4	36
handicap	13	7	17	5	11	3	1	15	9	-

	10	11	12	13	14	15	16	17	18	IN
BACK	362	496	159	524	428	170	513	145	427	3224
REGULAR	327	429	120	497	392	151	490	127	412	2945
par	4	5	3	5	4	3	5	3	4	36
handicap	12	14	18	6	2	10	8	16	4	-
FORWARD	294	408	93	388	358	130	453	121	336	2581
par	4	5	3	5	4	3	5	3	4	36
handicap	10	12	18	8	6	14	2	16	4	-

BACK	
yardage	6594
par	72
rating	72.9
slope	136

REGULAR	
yardage	6003
par	72
rating	69.5
slope	127

FORWARD	
yardage	5278
par	72
rating	70.9
slope	127

18 MALIBU COUNTRY CLUB
ARCHITECT: WILLIAM F. BELL, 1977

901 Encinal Canyon Road
Malibu, CA 90265

PRO SHOP: 818-889-6680

Nori Koda, Director of Golf
Efrain Barragan, Superintendent
Dan Meherin, Tournament Director

Driving Range
Practice Greens •
Clubhouse •
Food / Beverage •
Accommodations •
Pull Carts •
Power Carts •
Club Rental •
$pecial Offers

	1	2	3	4	5	6	7	8	9	OUT
BACK	398	357	413	488	236	476	194	349	378	3289
REGULAR	364	338	377	472	204	435	172	326	343	3031
par	4	4	4	5	3	5	3	4	4	36
handicap	3	15	5	11	1	17	7	13	9	-
FORWARD	346	296	344	415	136	391	153	262	313	2656
par	4	4	4	5	3	5	3	4	4	36
handicap	7	15	5	11	13	1	9	17	3	-

	10	11	12	13	14	15	16	17	18	IN
BACK	412	369	193	504	444	158	366	463	433	3342
REGULAR	391	337	162	487	419	135	346	448	400	3125
par	4	4	3	5	4	3	4	5	4	36
handicap	6	18	8	16	2	14	12	10	4	-
FORWARD	370	322	145	467	386	118	273	417	369	2867
par	4	4	3	5	4	3	4	5	4	36
handicap	4	12	14	6	2	16	18	8	10	-

BACK	
yardage	6631
par	72
rating	72.3
slope	130

REGULAR	
yardage	6156
par	72
rating	69.3
slope	121

FORWARD	
yardage	5523
par	72
rating	71.4
slope	120

PLAY POLICY & FEES: Members and guests only. Guests must be accompanied by a member. Reciprocal play is not accepted. Guest fees are $70 any day. Caddies are required. The course is closed on Monday.

DRESS CODE: Appropriate golf attire and nonmetal spikes are required.

COURSE DESCRIPTION: Sherwood was built on the site used for the original movie "Robin Hood," a spectacular setting with huge oak trees that have been there for more than 100 years. Jack Nicklaus designed the course so that it appears to have been there that long as well, though it only opened in 1989. It is a typical Nicklaus layout, featuring flawless bent-grass greens and fairways, several holes that favor the left-to-right player (of which Nicklaus is one), and tiered greens surrounded by severe slopes and mounds certain to penalize those who miss them with approach shots. The course's signature hole is the 170-yard, par-3 15th. From an elevated tee, the drive must carry a series of seven ponds, pools, and waterfalls and hold a wide but shallow green.

NOTES: This course is the site of the annual Franklin Funds Shark Shootout hosted by Greg Norman, held in November.

LOCATION: Take U.S.101 to Westlake Boulevard. Drive south two miles to Potrero Road. Turn right and drive three miles to Stafford Road and left to the club.

. . . ● **TOURNAMENTS:** This course is available on Monday for charity events.

17. SHERWOOD COUNTRY CLUB

PLAY POLICY & FEES: Green fees are $52 Monday through Thursday and $77 Friday through Sunday. Carts are included and mandatory. Players should check in 20 minutes prior to teeing off.

TEE TIMES: Reservations can be booked 10 days in advance.

DRESS CODE: Men must wear collared shirts. No jeans, sweat suits, or cutoffs are allowed. Shorts must be Bermuda length.

COURSE DESCRIPTION: Nestled in the Santa Monica Mountains, this scenic, hilly course features two natural lakes and interesting sloping topography. The weather stays fair and warm at this course because the hills block the ocean breezes.

LOCATION: Off U.S. 101 in Malibu, exit on Kanan Road and drive six miles toward the beach. After the second tunnel, turn right on Mulholland Highway. When the road forks, stay left. The course is two miles on the right, on Encinal Canyon Road.

. . . ● **TOURNAMENTS:** A 12-player minimum is needed to book an event. Shotgun tournaments are available weekdays only with a minimum of 72 players. The staff can help arrange catering.

18. MALIBU COUNTRY CLUB

WESTLAKE VILLAGE GOLF COURSE
ARCHITECT: TED ROBINSON, 1967

4812 Lakeview Canyon
Westlake Village, CA
91361
PRO SHOP: 818-889-0770

Chris Vatcher, Manager
Clint Airey, PGA Professional
Rudy Ruiz, Superintendent

Driving Range •
Practice Greens •
Clubhouse •
Food / Beverage •
Accommodations
Pull Carts •
Power Carts •
Club Rental •
$pecial Offers

	1	2	3	4	5	6	7	8	9	OUT
BACK	293	171	410	304	271	552	159	319	125	2604
REGULAR	282	153	374	282	240	506	139	290	105	2371
par	4	3	4	4	4	5	3	4	3	34
handicap	13	15	3	11	17	1	7	5	9	-
FORWARD	282	153	374	282	240	506	139	290	105	2371
par	4	3	4	4	4	5	3	4	3	34
handicap	9	15	3	11	13	1	7	5	17	-

	10	11	12	13	14	15	16	17	18	IN
BACK	320	406	313	174	155	450	164	282	185	2449
REGULAR	305	369	286	157	150	429	148	264	162	2270
par	4	4	4	3	3	5	3	4	3	33
handicap	10	2	8	4	16	14	12	18	6	-
FORWARD	305	369	286	157	150	429	148	264	162	2270
par	4	4	4	3	3	5	3	4	3	33
handicap	8	2	6	18	16	4	10	12	14	-

BACK	
yardage	5053
par	67
rating	63.4
slope	99

REGULAR	
yardage	4641
par	67
rating	61.2
slope	95

FORWARD	
yardage	4641
par	67
rating	66.0
slope	111

LAKE LINDERO COUNTRY CLUB
ARCHITECT: TED ROBINSON, 1976

5719 Lake Lindero Drive
Agoura Hills, CA 91301

PRO SHOP: 818-889-1158

Kristy Park, Director of Golf, PGA
Gregory Feet, Manager
Arnold Quintanilla, Superintendent

Driving Range •
Practice Greens •
Clubhouse •
Food / Beverage •
Accommodations
Pull Carts •
Power Carts
Club Rental •
$pecial Offers

	1	2	3	4	5	6	7	8	9	OUT
BACK	129	123	170	152	336	164	282	144	167	1667
REGULAR	117	113	161	141	328	146	271	135	145	1557
par	3	3	3	3	4	3	4	3	3	29
handicap	15	17	1	9	3	7	13	11	5	-
FORWARD	106	103	153	135	323	136	262	110	125	1453
par	3	3	3	3	4	3	4	3	3	29
handicap	13	15	1	9	3	7	5	17	11	-

	10	11	12	13	14	15	16	17	18	IN
BACK	129	123	170	152	336	164	282	144	167	1667
REGULAR	117	113	161	141	328	146	271	135	145	1557
par	3	3	3	3	4	3	4	3	3	29
handicap	16	18	2	10	4	8	14	12	6	-
FORWARD	106	103	153	135	323	136	262	110	125	1453
par	3	3	3	3	4	3	4	3	3	29
handicap	14	16	2	10	4	8	6	18	12	-

BACK	
yardage	3334
par	58
rating	54.8
slope	83

REGULAR	
yardage	3114
par	58
rating	54.8
slope	83

FORWARD	
yardage	2906
par	58
rating	55.0
slope	87

PLAY POLICY & FEES: Green fees are $20 weekdays and $30 weekends. Call for special rates. Carts are $21.

TEE TIMES: Reservations can be booked seven days in advance.

DRESS CODE: Appropriate golf attire is required.

COURSE DESCRIPTION: This course offers well-kept greens, three lakes, and scenic, tree-lined fairways. The trees make this course competitive and tough. Slice or hook and you'll be forced to execute a recovery shot. There are seven par 3s, nine par 4s, and two par 5s. The par 5s, thank goodness, are straight.

LOCATION: Travel north on U.S. 101 (Ventura Freeway) and take the Lindero Canyon Road exit. Drive south to Agoura Road and turn right. Continue three-quarters of a mile to Lakeview Canyon Road and turn right to the course.

. . . ● **TOURNAMENTS:** A 16-player minimum is needed to book a tournament. Carts are required. Events can be booked up to 12 months in advance. The banquet facility can accommodate 100 people. ● **TRAVEL:** The Hyatt Westlake is located five minutes from the golf course. For reservations call 805-497-9991. The Westlake Village Inn (818-889-0230) is also recommended.

19. WESTLAKE VILLAGE GOLF COURSE

PLAY POLICY & FEES: Outside play is accepted. Green fees for 18 holes are $12 weekdays and $16 weekends. Call for special rates.

TEE TIMES: Reservations can be booked six days in advance.

DRESS CODE: Golf attire is encouraged, and collared shirts and nonmetal spikes are required.

COURSE DESCRIPTION: This is a tight but rolling course with lots of trees and relatively small greens. Don't expect to tear it up. Accuracy is important. The toughest hole is the par-3 third. You hit from a slightly elevated tee to a small green guarded on the right by a huge oak and bunker. To the left is a creek that flows through the course. If your tee shot strays on this course, you're in trouble.

NOTES: The driving range is covered and lighted.

LOCATION: Travel north on U.S. 101 (Ventura Freeway) to the Reyes Adobe exit. Turn right and drive to Thousand Oaks Boulevard. Turn left and continue to Lake Lindero Drive. The course will be on your right.

. . . ● **TOURNAMENTS:** This course is available for tournaments.

20. LAKE LINDERO COUNTRY CLUB

CALABASAS GOLF & COUNTRY CLUB
ARCHITECT: ROBERT TRENT JONES SR. & JR., 1968

4515 Park Entrada
Calabasas Park, CA 91302

PRO SHOP: 818-222-3222
CLUBHOUSE: 818-222-3200

Yoshi Machida, Manager
David Bartholomew, PGA Professional
Ron Parker, Superintendent

Driving Range •
Practice Greens •
Clubhouse •
Food / Beverage •
Accommodations
Pull Carts •
Power Carts •
Club Rental •
$pecial Offers

	1	2	3	4	5	6	7	8	9	OUT
BACK	384	387	183	513	307	501	162	359	438	3234
REGULAR	361	377	165	507	296	486	151	352	431	3126
par	4	4	3	5	4	5	3	4	4	36
handicap	5	1	13	17	15	9	11	7	3	-
FORWARD	322	336	133	267	162	460	342	309	412	2743
par	4	4	3	4	3	5	4	4	5	36
handicap	7	5	17	9	13	1	15	11	3	-

	10	11	12	13	14	15	16	17	18	IN
BACK	357	371	150	302	206	490	394	384	435	3089
REGULAR	347	359	150	292	186	478	380	345	419	2956
par	4	4	3	4	3	5	4	4	5	36
handicap	12	10	16	18	4	8	2	6	14	-
FORWARD	322	336	133	267	162	460	342	309	412	2743
par	4	4	3	4	3	5	4	4	5	36
handicap	8	12	18	16	10	2	4	14	6	-

BACK	
yardage	6323
par	72
rating	70.8
slope	127

REGULAR	
yardage	6082
par	72
rating	69.6
slope	123

FORWARD	
yardage	5486
par	72
rating	72.8
slope	128

 WOODLAND HILLS COUNTRY CLUB
ARCHITECT: WILLIAM P. BELL, 1924

21150 Dumetz Road
Woodland Hills, CA 91364

PRO SHOP: 818-347-1476

Kerry Hopps, PGA Professional
Steve Sinclair, Superintendent

Driving Range •
Practice Greens •
Clubhouse •
Food / Beverage •
Accommodations
Pull Carts
Power Carts •
Club Rental
$pecial Offers

	1	2	3	4	5	6	7	8	9	OUT
BACK	381	159	473	483	306	196	177	375	355	2905
REGULAR	368	138	470	461	300	193	160	358	331	2779
par	4	3	5	5	4	3	3	4	4	35
handicap	10	18	4	2	16	8	14	12	6	-
FORWARD	314	126	464	401	296	183	132	313	265	2494
par	4	3	5	5	4	3	3	4	4	35
handicap	10	16	2	4	12	14	18	6	8	-

	10	11	12	13	14	15	16	17	18	IN
BACK	400	356	179	411	404	148	469	398	533	3298
REGULAR	389	332	165	400	394	137	450	388	513	3168
par	4	4	3	4	4	3	4	4	5	35
handicap	9	7	15	13	1	17	3	5	11	-
FORWARD	375	317	133	339	360	75	414	264	451	2728
par	4	4	3	4	5	3	5	4	5	37
handicap	1	11	15	5	9	17	13	3	7	-

BACK	
yardage	6203
par	70
rating	70.5
slope	126

REGULAR	
yardage	5947
par	70
rating	69.3
slope	124

FORWARD	
yardage	5222
par	72
rating	71.5
slope	129

18
HOLES

PLAY POLICY & FEES: Reciprocal play is accepted with members of other private clubs; otherwise, members and guests only. Prior arrangements are required for reciprocal play. Green fees are $55 weekdays and $85 weekends, cart included. The course is closed on Monday.

TEE TIMES: Reservations can be booked seven days in advance for reciprocal play.

DRESS CODE: Collared shirts and nonmetal spikes are required. Shorts must be Bermuda length, and no jeans or tank tops are allowed on the course.

COURSE DESCRIPTION: This challenging layout is located in a rapidly developing residential area. It is well maintained with many trees, lakes and rolling terrain. Although it isn't especially long, it can be difficult.

LOCATION: Travel north on U.S. 101 (Ventura Freeway) from Los Angeles to Parkway Calabasas, turn at the first right, and drive to the club.

. . . ● **TOURNAMENTS:** This course is available for outside tournaments on Monday.

21. CALABASAS GOLF & COUNTRY CLUB

18
HOLES

PLAY POLICY & FEES: Members and guests only. Green fees are $35 weekdays and $50 weekends. Carts are $20. The course is closed on Monday.

DRESS CODE: Appropriate golf attire is strictly enforced. Nonmetal spikes are required.

COURSE DESCRIPTION: Located in a parklike setting, this course features rolling hills and oak trees. The greens are among the most severe in Southern California. It is advisable to leave the ball below the hole or you probably will pay a penalty of three putts.

LOCATION: Travel north on U.S. 101 (Ventura Freeway) in Woodland Hills to the DeSoto Avenue exit. Drive south past Ventura Boulevard three-fourths of a mile and turn right on Dumetz Road. Drive one-quarter mile to the club.

. . . ● **TOURNAMENTS:** Shotgun tournaments are available on Monday. Carts are required. A 72-player minimum is needed to book a tournament. Tournaments should be booked 12 months in advance.

22. WOODLAND HILLS COUNTRY CLUB

BRAEMAR COUNTRY CLUB
ARCHITECT: TED ROBINSON, 1963

P.O. Box 570217
Tarzana, CA 91357

4001 Reseda Boulevard
Tarzan, CA 91357

PRO SHOP: 818-345-6520

Mark Murphy, Manager
Tom Swedzinski, PGA Professional

Driving Range ●
Practice Greens ●
Clubhouse ●
Food / Beverage ●
Accommodations
Pull Carts
Power Carts ●
Club Rental
$pecial Offers

	1	2	3	4	5	6	7	8	9	OUT
BACK	306	375	448	355	447	314	112	360	462	3179
REGULAR	296	352	436	339	422	304	112	348	437	3046
par	4	4	5	4	4	4	3	4	5	37
handicap	15	1	7	5	3	11	17	13	9	-
FORWARD	282	341	412	320	412	295	101	325	428	2916
par	4	4	5	4	4	4	3	4	5	37
handicap	9	3	5	17	1	7	15	11	13	-

	10	11	12	13	14	15	16	17	18	IN
BACK	323	211	433	398	330	163	295	366	151	2670
REGULAR	314	198	406	392	324	135	286	357	135	2547
par	4	3	5	4	4	3	4	4	3	34
handicap	10	6	12	2	8	14	16	4	18	-
FORWARD	305	185	390	353	320	111	258	349	119	2390
par	4	3	5	4	4	3	4	4	3	34
handicap	10	2	8	6	12	18	14	4	16	-

BACK	
yardage	5849
par	71
rating	68.7
slope	126

REGULAR	
yardage	5593
par	71
rating	67.3
slope	118

FORWARD	
yardage	5306
par	71
rating	70.6
slope	121

 VAN NUYS GOLF COURSE

6550 Odessa Avenue
Van Nuys, CA 91406

PRO SHOP: 818-785-3685
STARTER: 818-785-8871

Paul Tanner, General Manager
Wayne Tyni, Professional

Driving Range ●
Practice Greens ●
Clubhouse ●
Food / Beverage ●
Accommodations
Pull Carts ●
Power Carts
Club Rental ●
$pecial Offers

	1	2	3	4	5	6	7	8	9	OUT
BACK	-	-	-	-	-	-	-	-	-	-
REGULAR	-	-	-	-	-	-	-	-	-	
par	-	-	-	-	-	-	-	-	-	
handicap	-	-	-	-	-	-	-	-	-	-
FORWARD	-	-	-	-	-	-	-	-	-	
par	-	-	-	-	-	-	-	-	-	
handicap	-	-	-	-	-	-	-	-	-	-

	10	11	12	13	14	15	16	17	18	IN
BACK	-	-	-	-	-	-	-	-	-	-
REGULAR	-	-	-	-	-	-	-	-	-	
par	-	-	-	-	-	-	-	-	-	
handicap	-	-	-	-	-	-	-	-	-	-
FORWARD	-	-	-	-	-	-	-	-	-	
par	-	-	-	-	-	-	-	-	-	
handicap	-	-	-	-	-	-	-	-	-	-

BACK	
yardage	-
par	-
rating	-
slope	-

REGULAR	
yardage	2181
par	30
rating	-
slope	-

FORWARD	
yardage	1691
par	30
rating	-
slope	-

PLAY POLICY & FEES: Members and guests only. Green fees are $40 weekdays and $60 weekends. Carts are $22.

DRESS CODE: No jeans or short shorts are allowed on the course. Men must wear collared shirts.

COURSE DESCRIPTION: Both courses are short, tight, and hilly. There are mature trees and a few parallel fairways. There is virtually no room for error because of a plethora of out-of-bounds, water hazards, and other assorted obstacles.

NOTES: The East Course is 6,109 yards and rated 70.5 from the championship tees, and 5,808 yards and rated 68.8 from the regular tees. The slope ratings are 134 championship and 130 regular. Par is 70. The forward tees are 5,403 yards and rated 71.7. The slope rating is 127. The West Course: See scorecard for yardage and rating information.

LOCATION: Travel north on U.S. 101 (Ventura Freeway) and take the Reseda Boulevard exit. Drive south for 2.5 miles to the club entrance on the right.

. . . ● **TOURNAMENTS:** This course is available for outside tournaments on Monday.

23. BRAEMAR COUNTRY CLUB

PLAY POLICY & FEES: Green fees for the 18-hole course are $6 weekdays for nine holes and $10 for 18 holes. Weekend green fees for 18 holes are $12. After 6 p.m. on weekdays and weekends, green fees are $7 for nine holes and $11 for 18 holes. Green fees for the executive course are $7 weekdays and $9 weekends. The executive course rates are for nine holes only. Senior rates are $6 on the executive course Monday, Wednesday, and Friday. On the 18-hole course senior rates are $5 on weekdays and $8 weekends for nine holes. Pull carts are $1.50.

TEE TIMES: Reservations can be booked seven days in advance for the executive course.

COURSE DESCRIPTION: The executive course is one of the prominent par-3 courses in the area. The longest hole on this pitch-and-putt is 142 yards. The average playing time is under two hours. The 18-hole course is lined with trees and is relatively flat, with lakes and ducks. The course is good for beginners.

LOCATION: From Interstate 405 in Van Nuys take the Victory exit west. Drive about one mile to Odessa Avenue. Turn right onto Odessa and drive to the course.

. . . ● **TOURNAMENTS:** A 12- to 16-player minimum is needed to book an event. No shotgun tournaments are allowed.

24. VAN NUYS GOLF COURSE

WOODLEY LAKES GOLF COURSE
ARCHITECT: RAY GOATES

6331 Woodley Avenue
Van Nuys, CA 91406

PRO SHOP: 818-787-8163
STARTER: 818-780-6886

Brad Booth, PGA Professional
John Marquez, Superintendent

Driving Range ●
Practice Greens ●
Clubhouse ●
Food / Beverage ●
Accommodations
Pull Carts ●
Power Carts ●
Club Rental ●
$pecial Offers

	1	2	3	4	5	6	7	8	9	OUT
BACK										
REGULAR										
par										
handicap										
FORWARD										
par										
handicap										

	10	11	12	13	14	15	16	17	18	IN
BACK										
REGULAR										
par										
handicap										
FORWARD										
par										
handicap										

BACK	
yardage	6803
par	72
rating	70.4
slope	109

REGULAR	
yardage	6523
par	72
rating	69.0
slope	106

FORWARD	
yardage	6242
par	72
rating	74.3
slope	112

 SEPULVEDA GOLF COURSE
ARCHITECT: WILLIAM P. BELL, 1953

16821 Burbank Boulevard
Encino, CA 91436

PRO SHOP: 818-986-4560
STARTER: 818-995-1170

Troy Rodvold, PGA Professional
Jim Dodds, Manager
Mark Thorton, Superintendent

Driving Range ●
Practice Greens ●
Clubhouse ●
Food / Beverage ●
Accommodations
Pull Carts ●
Power Carts ●
Club Rental ●
$pecial Offers

	1	2	3	4	5	6	7	8	9	OUT
BACK	391	335	327	200	503	431	390	409	378	3364
REGULAR	375	324	319	193	489	429	372	396	369	3266
par	4	4	4	3	5	4	4	4	4	36
handicap	5	15	17	7	13	1	9	3	11	-
FORWARD	369	313	309	172	478	413	362	390	357	3163
par	4	4	4	3	5	5	4	4	4	37
handicap	7	13	15	17	1	11	9	3	5	-

	10	11	12	13	14	15	16	17	18	IN
BACK	370	330	443	149	389	336	368	220	359	2964
REGULAR	362	297	426	135	374	327	355	207	348	2831
par	4	4	4	3	4	4	4	3	4	34
handicap	8	16	2	18	10	14	6	4	12	-
FORWARD	353	275	405	127	359	314	345	200	339	2717
par	4	4	5	3	4	4	4	3	4	35
handicap	4	16	8	18	2	12	6	14	10	-

BACK	
yardage	6328
par	70
rating	68.8
slope	107

REGULAR	
yardage	6097
par	70
rating	67.7
slope	105

FORWARD	
yardage	5880
par	72
rating	70.9
slope	115

PLAY POLICY & FEES: Green fees are $18 weekdays and $23 weekends. Carts are $22.

TEE TIMES: Reservations can be made up to seven days in advance with a Los Angeles Recreation and Parks reservation card.

DRESS CODE: Nonmetal spikes are encouraged.

COURSE DESCRIPTION: This is a relatively long and flat course with large greens. Many of the greens are elevated. The course is not too demanding unless you hit into one or more of its six lakes.

NOTES: The course record, 62, was set by former UCLA golfer Duffy Waldorf.

LOCATION: From Interstate 405 in Van Nuys exit at Victory Boulevard and drive one-half mile to Woodley Avenue. Turn left to the course. The course is located about two miles from Van Nuys Airport.

. . . ● **TOURNAMENTS:** A 24-player minimum is needed to book a tournament.

25. WOODLEY LAKES GOLF COURSE

PLAY POLICY & FEES: Green fees are $18 weekdays and $23 weekends. Carts are $21. Twilight green fees are $11 weekdays and $13 weekends.

TEE TIMES: Reservations are recommended one week in advance, but can only be made by holders of a Los Angeles Recreation and Park reservation card.

COURSE DESCRIPTION: The Balboa Course is the shorter of the two, with small greens and tight fairways. Shot placement is crucial. The greens are well bunkered, and there are overhanging trees. The Encino Course, although longer, is much easier. It's wide open.

NOTES: The Balboa Course: See scorecard for yardage and rating information. At par 72, the Encino Course is 6,863 yards from the championship tees and rated 70.8, and 6,508 yards from the regular tees and rated 69.3. The slope ratings are 112 championship and 109 regular. The forward tees are 6,185 yards and rated 74.6. The slope rating is 120.

LOCATION: Take Highway 134 to the Burbank Boulevard exit in Encino and turn right. Go about one-half mile to course.

. . . ● **TOURNAMENTS:** All events must be booked through the Los Angeles reservations office; call 213-485-5515.

26. SEPULVEDA GOLF COURSE

EL CABALLERO COUNTRY CLUB
ARCHITECT: WILLIAM H. JOHNSON, 1957

18300 Tarzana Drive
Tarzana, CA 91356

PRO SHOP: 818-345-2770

Mark Taylor, Head Professional, PGA
Doug Meadows, Superintendent

Driving Range ●
Practice Greens ●
Clubhouse ●
Food / Beverage ●
Accommodations ●
Pull Carts
Power Carts ●
Club Rental ●
$Special Offers

	1	2	3	4	5	6	7	8	9	OUT
BACK	510	434	383	407	361	216	514	212	456	3493
REGULAR	498	412	374	377	341	175	502	181	425	3285
par	5	4	4	4	4	3	5	3	4	36
handicap	11/5	1/1	7/9	5/7	15/1	9/17	17/1	13/1	3/3	-
FORWARD	473	393	357	346	285	133	495	137	390	3009
par	5	4	4	4	4	3	5	3	4	36
handicap	5	1	11	9	13	15	3	17	7	-

	10	11	12	13	14	15	16	17	18	IN
BACK	167	402	528	381	386	419	173	458	423	3337
REGULAR	143	383	503	364	363	397	151	425	404	3133
par	3	4	5	4	4	4	3	4	4	35
handicap	14/1	4/8	12/6	16/1	10/1	6/4	18/1	2/2	8/10	-
FORWARD	121	337	468	333	348	369	124	415	379	2894
par	3	4	5	4	4	4	3	5	4	36
handicap	16	12	2	14	4	8	18	10	6	-

BACK	
yardage	6830
par	71
rating	73.2
slope	132

REGULAR	
yardage	6418
par	71
rating	70.9
slope	125

FORWARD	
yardage	5903
par	72
rating	74.9
slope	137

 MOUNTAINGATE COUNTRY CLUB
ARCHITECT: TED ROBINSON, 1974

12445 Mountaingate Drive
Los Angeles, CA 90049

PRO SHOP: 310-476-2800

Marianne Huning, Director of Golf, PGA
Doug Hoffort, Professional
Scott Randal, Tournament Director

Driving Range ●
Practice Greens ●
Clubhouse ●
Food / Beverage ●
Accommodations
Pull Carts
Power Carts ●
Club Rental ●
$Special Offers

	1	2	3	4	5	6	7	8	9	OUT
BACK	539	422	165	358	527	171	469	219	414	3284
REGULAR	512	384	150	321	510	138	453	193	378	3039
par	5	4	3	4	5	3	5	3	4	36
handicap	4	3	9	8	1	7	5	6	2	-
FORWARD	485	363	121	303	456	113	408	175	333	2757
par	5	4	3	4	5	3	5	3	4	36
handicap	3	6	9	5	1	8	4	7	2	-

	10	11	12	13	14	15	16	17	18	IN
BACK	343	190	363	300	518	390	173	420	478	3175
REGULAR	322	169	348	289	504	374	154	408	460	3028
par	4	3	4	4	5	4	3	4	5	36
handicap	9	4	3	8	5	1	6	3	7	-
FORWARD	294	154	294	266	465	369	130	401	404	2777
par	4	3	4	4	5	4	3	5	5	37
handicap	9	5	3	7	2	1	6	8	4	-

BACK	
yardage	6459
par	72
rating	70.4
slope	118

REGULAR	
yardage	6067
par	72
rating	68.5
slope	110

FORWARD	
yardage	5534
par	73
rating	72.2
slope	125

PLAY POLICY & FEES: Members and guests only. Guests must be accompanied by a member. Green fees are $50 weekdays and $85 weekends. Carts are $11 per person. The course is closed on Monday.

DRESS CODE: Collared shirts and nonmetal spikes are required. No short shorts are allowed.

COURSE DESCRIPTION: This rolling course is challenging with large greens. It is one of the highest-slope rated courses in Southern California and is also among the most demanding. Long and flanked by trees, this course was remodeled by Robert Trent Jones Sr. in 1964.

LOCATION: Traveling north on U.S. 101 (Ventura Freeway) in Tarzana, exit on Reseda Boulevard south (it becomes Mecca Avenue). At Tarzana Drive, turn left to the club.

. . . ● **TOURNAMENTS:** This course is available for charity tournaments only. Carts are required.

27. EL CABALLERO COUNTRY CLUB

PLAY POLICY & FEES: Reciprocal play is accepted with members of other private clubs; otherwise, members and guests only. Green fees for reciprocators are $125 Monday through Thursday, $175 Friday, and $225 weekends. Carts are $12. Guest fees are $80 Monday through Thursday, $95 Friday, $105 Saturday, and $125 on Sunday. Reservations are mandatory.

TEE TIMES: You can have your club pro call up to three months in advance.

DRESS CODE: Appropriate golf attire and nonmetal spikes are preferred.

COURSE DESCRIPTION: This course is characterized by rolling fairways and difficult, undulating greens. Overall, the South is the most difficult of the courses. There are elevated greens and rolling hills. Wherever you hit, don't expect to get a flat lie.

NOTES: This private course has 27 holes, and par is 72 for each 18-hole combination. The three courses are the North, South, and Lake. The Senior PGA Tour has held tournaments here in the past, including the Johnny Mathis Classic and the GTE Senior Classic.

LOCATION: Travel north on Interstate 405 to the Getty Center exit. Follow the exit to Sepulveda Boulevard and turn left, driving 1.5 miles to Mountaingate Drive. From there, turn left to the club.

. . . ● **TOURNAMENTS:** This course is available for outside tournaments on Monday only. A 100-player minimum is needed to book a tournament. Tournaments should be booked 12 to 18 months in advance. The banquet facility can hold 200 people.

28. MOUNTAINGATE COUNTRY CLUB

4141 Whitsett Avenue
Studio City, CA 91604

PRO SHOP: 818-761-3250

George McAllister, Manager

Driving Range ●
Practice Greens ●
Clubhouse ●
Food / Beverage ●
Accommodations
Pull Carts ●
Power Carts
Club Rental ●
$pecial Offers

	1	2	3	4	5	6	7	8	9	OUT
BACK	-	-	-	-	-	-	-	-	-	-
REGULAR	105	130	75	105	115	105	115	135	90	975
par	3	3	3	3	3	3	3	3	3	27
handicap	6	1	9	2	5	7	4	3	8	-
FORWARD	105	130	75	105	115	105	115	135	90	975
par	3	3	3	3	3	3	3	3	3	27
handicap	6	1	9	2	5	7	4	3	8	-

	10	11	12	13	14	15	16	17	18	IN
BACK	-	-	-	-	-	-	-	-	-	-
REGULAR	105	130	75	105	115	105	115	135	90	975
par	3	3	3	3	3	3	3	3	3	27
handicap	6	1	9	2	5	7	4	3	8	-
FORWARD	105	130	75	105	115	105	115	135	90	975
par	3	3	3	3	3	3	3	3	3	27
handicap	6	1	9	2	5	7	4	3	8	-

BACK	
yardage	-
par	-
rating	-
slope	-

REGULAR	
yardage	1950
par	54
rating	-
slope	-

FORWARD	
yardage	1950
par	54
rating	-
slope	-

30 LAKESIDE GOLF CLUB
ARCHITECT: MAX BEHR, 1926

P.O. Box 2386/Toluca Lake   4500 Lakeside Drive
Toluca Lake, CA 91610   Burbank, CA 91602

PRO SHOP: 818-985-3335

David Allaire, PGA Professional
Brent Weston, Superintendent

Driving Range ●
Practice Greens ●
Clubhouse ●
Food / Beverage ●
Accommodations
Pull Carts
Power Carts ●
Club Rental ●
$pecial Offers

	1	2	3	4	5	6	7	8	9	OUT
BACK										
REGULAR										
par										
handicap										
FORWARD										
par										
handicap										

	10	11	12	13	14	15	16	17	18	IN
BACK										
REGULAR										
par										
handicap										
FORWARD										
par										
handicap										

BACK	
yardage	6534
par	70
rating	71.9
slope	129

REGULAR	
yardage	6272
par	70
rating	70.1
slope	121

FORWARD	
yardage	5949
par	70
rating	74.3
slope	123

PLAY POLICY & FEES: Green fees are $7 weekdays and $8 weekends and holidays. The senior rate is $6 weekdays.

TEE TIMES: Reservations are not accepted. All play is on a first-come, first-served basis.

COURSE DESCRIPTION: This is a nine-hole, par-3 course with no hole longer than 135 yards.

NOTES: The adjoining driving range is open until 11 p.m. For those interested in a quick set of tennis, a tennis club is affiliated with the golf course.

LOCATION: Take U.S. 101 west to Coldwater Canyon. Turn right and drive to the first light (Moorpark Road). Turn left and drive to Whitsett Avenue. Turn right onto Whitsett and drive two blocks to the course.

. . . ● **TOURNAMENTS:** This course is not available for outside events. ●

TRAVEL: The Sportsman Lodge and the Universal Hilton are recommended for lodging.

29. STUDIO CITY GOLF COURSE

PLAY POLICY & FEES: Members and guests only. Guests must be accompanied by a member. Guest fees are $55 Monday and Tuesday, and $65 Wednesday through Sunday. Carts are $22.

DRESS CODE: Appropriate golf attire and nonmetal spikes are required.

COURSE DESCRIPTION: Built in 1926, this traditional rolling course has small undulating greens. Although short in yardage, it plays longer and demands accuracy.

NOTES: These fairways were once a haven for Hollywood's heroes and rogues: Bing Crosby, Dean Martin, Bob Hope—just about anybody who ever had a golf tournament named for him.

LOCATION: Travel north on U.S. 101 (Hollywood Freeway) to the Barham Boulevard exit and drive north to Lakeside Drive. Turn left and drive to the club. Or take Ventura Boulevard (Highway 134) to Pass Avenue south, crossing Riverside to Lakeside Drive. Turn right to the club.

. . . ● **TOURNAMENTS:** This course is available for outside tournaments on Monday. Carts are required.

30. LAKESIDE GOLF CLUB

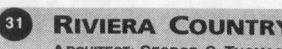

RIVIERA COUNTRY CLUB
ARCHITECT: GEORGE C. THOMAS, 1926

1250 Capri Drive
Pacific Palisades, CA
90272
PRO SHOP: 310-459-5395
CLUBHOUSE: 310-454-6591

Todd Yoshitake, Director of Golf, PGA
Paul Ramira, Superintendent
Gordon Krah, Tournament Director

Driving Range ●
Practice Greens ●
Clubhouse ●
Food / Beverage ●
Accommodations ●
Pull Carts
Power Carts ●
Club Rental ●
$pecial Offers

	1	2	3	4	5	6	7	8	9	OUT
BACK	503	463	434	236	419	175	408	370	420	3428
REGULAR	497	445	405	230	408	144	370	346	406	3251
par	5	4	4	3	4	3	4	4	4	35
handicap	17	1	5	7	9	15	11	13	3	-
FORWARD	451	396	378	187	385	130	318	286	385	2916
par	5	5	4	3	4	3	4	4	5	37
handicap	5	15	1	7	3	17	9	13	11	-

	10	11	12	13	14	15	16	17	18	IN
BACK	315	564	410	421	176	443	166	576	451	3522
REGULAR	301	513	367	402	159	430	148	512	422	3254
par	4	5	4	4	3	4	3	5	4	36
handicap	16	8	10	4	18	2	14	12	6	-
FORWARD	281	486	316	358	143	413	122	499	331	2949
par	4	5	4	4	3	5	3	5	4	37
handicap	12	4	6	2	18	4	16	8	10	-

BACK	
yardage	6950
par	71
rating	74.3
slope	139

REGULAR	
yardage	6505
par	71
rating	71.9
slope	130

FORWARD	
yardage	5865
par	74
rating	73.9
slope	129

PLAY POLICY & FEES: Very limited reciprocal play is accepted with members of other private clubs. Please call in advance. Fees for accompanied guests are $85 weekdays and $110 weekends.

DRESS CODE: Appropriate golf attire and nonmetal spikes are required.

COURSE DESCRIPTION: This well-maintained course is nearly 70 years old and has been played by scores of Hollywood's rich and famous. George C. Thomas designed the long and tough layout in 1926. The fairways and rough are planted with Kikuyu grass so there's not much roll. The 165-yard, par-3 sixth hole features a bunker in the middle of the green. If that doesn't frighten you, maybe the par-4 18th will. It is considered one of the toughest holes in golf.

NOTES: The 1948 U.S. Open was played here and won by the great Ben Hogan. After Hogan won the Los Angeles Open here in 1947 and 1948, the course became known as Hogan's Alley. The Los Angeles Open is played here annually. The course record of 61 is held by Ted Tryba. Riviera was also the site of the 1995 PGA Championship and the 1998 USGA Senior Open. Riviera has been rated the 24th best course in the country by "Golf Digest."

LOCATION: Take the Sunset Boulevard exit off Interstate 405 and travel west for three miles to Capri Drive; then turn left to the club.

. . . ● **TOURNAMENTS:** This course is available for outside tournaments on Monday only. A 100-player minimum is needed to book an event. Events should be scheduled 18 to 24 months in advance. A banquet facility is available that can accommodate 125 people. ● **TRAVEL:** El Moro is recommended for dining. Riviera Country Club has hotel rooms available for guests and reciprocal members. The Holiday Inn in Brentwood is five minutes from the course. For reservations call 310-476-6411.

31. RIVIERA COUNTRY CLUB

32

BRENTWOOD COUNTRY CLUB

590 South Burlingame
Los Angeles, CA 90049

PRO SHOP: 310-451-8011
STARTER: 310-393-6614

Richard Ameny, Manager
Bob Harrison, PGA Professional
Bob O'Connell, Superintendent

Driving Range ●
Practice Greens ●
Clubhouse ●
Food / Beverage ●
Accommodations
Pull Carts
Power Carts ●
Club Rental ●
Special Offers ●

	1	2	3	4	5	6	7	8	9	OUT
BACK	369	190	351	461	529	401	148	471	352	3272
REGULAR	356	170	342	456	508	369	145	464	345	3155
par	4	3	4	4	5	4	3	5	4	36
handicap	5	13	7	1	9	3	17	15	11	-
FORWARD	347	115	322	440	440	304	134	456	322	2880
par	4	3	4	4	5	4	3	5	4	36
handicap	5	13	7	1	9	3	17	15	11	-

	10	11	12	13	14	15	16	17	18	IN
BACK	407	435	509	379	576	219	406	167	385	3483
REGULAR	391	410	492	369	570	201	385	145	382	3345
par	4	4	5	4	5	3	4	3	4	36
handicap	6	2	14	12	10	16	4	18	8	-
FORWARD	388	372	361	366	473	182	402	118	370	3032
par	4	4	5	4	5	3	4	3	4	36
handicap	6	2	14	12	10	16	4	18	8	-

BACK	
yardage	6755
par	72
rating	71.9
slope	124

REGULAR	
yardage	6500
par	72
rating	70.5
slope	120

FORWARD	
yardage	5912
par	72
rating	68.0
slope	112

PENMAR GOLF COURSE

1233 Rose Avenue
Venice, CA 90291

PRO SHOP: 310-396-6228

Jim Hookstratten, Manager

Driving Range
Practice Greens ●
Clubhouse ●
Food / Beverage ●
Accommodations
Pull Carts ●
Power Carts
Club Rental ●
Special Offers ●

	1	2	3	4	5	6	7	8	9	OUT
BACK	-	-	-	-	-	-	-	-	-	-
REGULAR	271	338	140	288	177	423	368	141	350	2496
par	4	4	3	4	3	4	4	3	4	33
handicap	6	3	8	9	2	1	4	7	5	-
FORWARD	257	317	121	270	149	398	336	126	337	2311
par	4	4	3	4	3	5	4	3	4	34
handicap	6	3	8	9	2	1	4	7	5	-

	10	11	12	13	14	15	16	17	18	IN
BACK	-	-	-	-	-	-	-	-	-	-
REGULAR	271	338	140	288	177	423	368	141	350	2496
par	4	4	3	4	3	4	4	3	4	33
handicap	6	2	7	5	8	1	3	9	4	-
FORWARD	257	317	121	270	149	398	336	126	337	2311
par	4	4	3	4	3	5	4	3	4	34
handicap	5	2	7	6	8	1	3	9	4	-

BACK	
yardage	-
par	-
rating	-
slope	-

REGULAR	
yardage	4992
par	66
rating	63.4
slope	99

FORWARD	
yardage	4622
par	68
rating	61.9
slope	94

PLAY POLICY & FEES: Members and guests only. Guest fees are $40 Monday through Thursday and $60 Friday through Sunday. Carts are $10 per person.

DRESS CODE: Appropriate golf attire and nonmetal spikes are required.

COURSE DESCRIPTION: Accurate tee shots are important here. The course is fairly tight with lots of trees. The back nine is especially narrow and long. A small lake borders nine holes. The course also gets hilly in spots. What makes this a particularly good course are the greens: they are fast and true.

LOCATION: Take the Sunset Boulevard exit off Interstate 405 north of L.A. and travel west for 1.5 miles to Burlingame Avenue. Turn left and travel one-half mile to the club.

. . . ● **TOURNAMENTS:** This course is not available for outside events.

32. BRENTWOOD COUNTRY CLUB

PLAY POLICY & FEES: Green fees are $9 for nine holes weekdays and $12 weekends. Call for special rates.

TEE TIMES: Reservations can be booked seven days in advance with a City of Los Angeles Recreation and Parks membership card.

DRESS CODE: Nonmetal spikes are encouraged.

COURSE DESCRIPTION: This nine-hole course offers an interesting and challenging layout in the heart of wild and wacky Venice.

LOCATION: In Venice drive north on Lincoln Boulevard (Highway 1) to Rose Avenue, turn right, and go two blocks to the course.

. . . ● **TOURNAMENTS:** This course is available for outside tournaments, but shotgun starts are not allowed. A 24-player minimum is needed to book an event. Tournaments should be scheduled 12 months in advance.

33. PENMAR GOLF COURSE

ARCHITECT: GEORGE C. THOMAS, 1926

10768 Bellagio Road
Los Angeles, CA 90077

PRO SHOP: 310-440-2423
CLUBHOUSE: 310-476-9563

Charles Bernold, Manager
Ed Merrins, Head Professional, PGA
Brian Sullivan, Superintendent

Driving Range
Practice Greens •
Clubhouse •
Food / Beverage •
Accommodations
Pull Carts
Power Carts •
Club Rental •
$pecial Offers

	1	2	3	4	5	6	7	8	9	OUT
BACK	482	393	170	434	165	371	391	477	338	3221
REGULAR	453	382	156	424	154	353	373	465	326	3086
par	5	4	3	4	3	4	4	5	4	36
handicap	17	3	11	1	13	5	7	15	9	-
FORWARD	434	370	128	417	141	311	327	453	315	2896
par	5	4	3	5	3	4	4	5	4	37
handicap	6	2	18	8	16	12	14	4	10	-

	10	11	12	13	14	15	16	17	18	IN
BACK	200	392	375	213	577	448	195	468	393	3261
REGULAR	195	384	347	193	562	436	174	449	384	3124
par	3	4	4	3	5	4	3	4	4	34
handicap	8	12	16	14	6	2	18	4	10	-
FORWARD	94	366	323	171	530	424	152	422	392	2874
par	3	4	4	3	5	5	3	5	5	37
handicap	17	3	5	13	1	7	15	11	9	-

BACK	
yardage	6482
par	70
rating	72.0
slope	133

REGULAR	
yardage	6210
par	70
rating	70.5
slope	127

FORWARD	
yardage	5770
par	74
rating	73.6
slope	128

ARCHITECT: GEORGE C. THOMAS, 1921

10101 Wilshire Boulevard
Los Angeles, CA 90024

PRO SHOP: 310-276-6104

James Brewer, Manager
Jim Schaeffer, PGA Professional
Bruce Williams, Superintendent

Driving Range •
Practice Greens •
Clubhouse •
Food / Beverage •
Accommodations •
Pull Carts
Power Carts •
Club Rental •
$pecial Offers

	1	2	3	4	5	6	7	8	9	OUT
BACK										
REGULAR										
par										
handicap										
FORWARD										
par										
handicap										

	10	11	12	13	14	15	16	17	18	IN
BACK										
REGULAR										
par										
handicap										
FORWARD										
par										
handicap										

BACK	
yardage	6913
par	71
rating	75.1
slope	143

REGULAR	
yardage	6610
par	71
rating	72.9
slope	136

FORWARD	
yardage	6224
par	71
rating	76.5
slope	143

PLAY POLICY & FEES: Reciprocal play is accepted on a limited basis and must be approved by the professional or manager; otherwise, members and guests only.
DRESS CODE: Appropriate golf attire and nonmetal spikes are required.
COURSE DESCRIPTION: This austere, hilly course has narrow fairways and lots of trees. It's well bunkered with small greens and places a premium on accuracy. Designed by George C. Thomas in 1926, it rates among the top 20 courses in the state. One of the landmark holes is the 10th, a par-3, 200-yard nerve wracker, known as the "Swinging Bridge." You park your cart on one side of a canyon, walk back to the tee, and hope your drive clears the canyon. The tee is next to the club grill, where there is always a critical gallery.
NOTES: Bel-Air was the site of the 1976 U.S. Amateur Championship and is the home course of the UCLA Bruins golf team.
LOCATION: Take the Sunset Boulevard exit off Interstate 405 north of L.A. and travel east for three-quarters of a mile to Bellagio Road. Turn left and bear right. You'll shortly find the club entrance on the right.
... ● **TOURNAMENTS:** This course is not available for outside events.

34. BEL-AIR COUNTRY CLUB

PLAY POLICY & FEES: Members and guests only. Guest fees are $45 Monday through Friday, and $60 on weekends. Carts are $25.
DRESS CODE: No shorts are allowed on the golf course. Women must wear skirts. Nonmetal spikes are required.
COURSE DESCRIPTION: These are beautiful courses designed in 1921 by George C. Thomas. The North Course is often ranked the number-one course in Southern California and has been the home of five Los Angeles Open championships. It is regarded as among the best courses in the country. The USGA has repeatedly expressed an interest in playing the U.S. Open here. The North Course is the more difficult of the two. It features long, tight fairways and small greens with hilly terrain and lots of trees. The South Course is flatter and more open.
NOTES: The North Course records are 64 for men and 68 for women. This private club has two 18-hole courses. Par is 71 on the North Course and 70 on the South Course. The North Course: See scorecard. The South Course is 5,940 yards and rated 68.8 from the championship tees with a slope of 120 championship and 112 regular. Forward tees are 5,638 yards and rated 71.6. The slope rating is 112.
LOCATION: Take the Wilshire Boulevard exit off Interstate 405 and drive east to the club.
... ● **TOURNAMENTS:** This course is not available for outside events.

35. THE LOS ANGELES COUNTRY CLUB

HILLCREST COUNTRY CLUB
ARCHITECT: WILLIE WATSON, 1920

10000 West Pico
Los Angeles, CA 90064

PRO SHOP: 310-553-8911 EXT. 246

Leonard Fisher, Manager
Paul Wise, PGA Professional

Driving Range •
Practice Greens •
Clubhouse •
Food / Beverage •
Accommodations •
Pull Carts
Power Carts •
Club Rental
$pecial Offers

	1	2	3	4	5	6	7	8	9	OUT
BACK	384	169	338	548	431	174	317	490	377	3228
REGULAR	376	152	316	536	411	142	307	469	365	3074
par	4	3	4	5	4	3	4	5	4	36
handicap	9	15	13	1	5	17	7	11	3	-
FORWARD	373	145	305	470	371	126	270	459	360	2879
par	4	3	4	5	4	3	4	5	4	36
handicap	9	17	13	1	5	15	11	7	3	-

	10	11	12	13	14	15	16	17	18	IN
BACK	298	441	189	422	534	384	150	311	416	3145
REGULAR	288	436	172	406	509	367	129	299	389	2995
par	4	4	3	4	5	4	3	4	4	35
handicap	12	2	16	4	10	8	18	14	6	-
FORWARD	279	431	169	396	490	365	120	294	420	2964
par	4	5	3	4	5	4	3	4	5	37
handicap	12	6	16	4	2	8	18	14	10	-

BACK	
yardage	6373
par	71
rating	70.5
slope	122

REGULAR	
yardage	6069
par	71
rating	68.7
slope	115

FORWARD	
yardage	5843
par	73
rating	73.0
slope	122

 THE WILSHIRE COUNTRY CLUB
ARCHITECT: NORMAN MACBETH, 1919

301 North Rossmore
Los Angeles, CA 90004

PRO SHOP: 323-934-1121

Matthew Allmatt, General Manager
Patrick J. Rielly Jr., PGA Professional
Alex Galaviz Jr., Superintendent

Driving Range •
Practice Greens •
Clubhouse •
Food / Beverage •
Accommodations
Pull Carts •
Power Carts •
Club Rental •
$pecial Offers

	1	2	3	4	5	6	7	8	9	OUT
BACK	390	530	345	193	379	436	142	383	426	3224
REGULAR	378	520	325	185	366	426	135	366	419	3120
par	4	5	4	3	4	4	3	4	4	35
handicap	5	9	13	15	7	1	17	11	3	-
FORWARD	366	510	310	165	346	420	128	349	409	3003
par	4	5	4	3	4	5	3	4	5	37
handicap	7	1	13	15	3	5	17	9	11	-

	10	11	12	13	14	15	16	17	18	IN
BACK	155	362	405	188	509	329	555	365	439	3307
REGULAR	139	355	393	152	502	316	541	359	418	3175
par	3	4	4	3	5	4	5	4	4	36
handicap	18	8	2	16	12	14	6	10	4	-
FORWARD	115	317	377	129	492	304	519	348	404	3005
par	3	4	4	3	5	4	5	4	5	37
handicap	16	8	6	18	2	14	4	10	12	-

BACK	
yardage	6531
par	71
rating	71.5
slope	126

REGULAR	
yardage	6295
par	71
rating	70.0
slope	120

FORWARD	
yardage	6008
par	74
rating	75.6
slope	140

PLAY POLICY & FEES: Members and guests only. Guest fees are $45 Monday through Thursday and $65 Friday through Sunday. Carts are $10 for nine holes and $20 for 18 holes.

DRESS CODE: Appropriate golf attire and nonmetal spikes are required.

COURSE DESCRIPTION: This is a relatively short and tree-lined course, and it can be testy. The fairways are lush and well maintained. There is also a pitch-and-putt, six-hole, par-3 course.

NOTES: The 18-hole course record is 63 and is held by Eric Monty and Greg Starkman. The Los Angeles Open qualifier was formerly held here.

LOCATION: Take the Pico Boulevard exit off Interstate 405 southbound and travel east to the club. From northbound on Interstate 405, take the Venice Boulevard exit to Motor Street, which turns into Pico Boulevard, and drive to the club.

. . . ● **TOURNAMENTS:** A 140-player minimum is needed to book a tournament. Carts are required.

36. HILLCREST COUNTRY CLUB

PLAY POLICY & FEES: Members and guests only. Fees are $45 weekdays and $60 on weekends for guests of members. Carts are $10 per person.

DRESS CODE: Appropriate golf attire and nonmetal spikes are required.

COURSE DESCRIPTION: Built in 1919, this course was used for the Los Angeles Open in 1926. The mostly level fairways are lined with mature trees, and the greens are well maintained. A barranca runs through 14 of the 18 fairways.

LOCATION: Take the Santa Monica Boulevard exit off U.S. 101 (Hollywood Freeway) and travel west for one mile to Vine Street. Turn left and drive one mile (Vine becomes Rossmore Avenue) to the club on the right.

. . . ● **TOURNAMENTS:** All outside events must be approved by the general manager.

37. THE WILSHIRE COUNTRY CLUB

RANCHO PARK GOLF COURSE
ARCHITECTS: WILLIAM P. BELL , 1947; WILLIAM H. JOHNSON

10460 West Pico
Los Angeles, CA 90064

PRO SHOP: 310-839-4374

Mary Keener, Manager
Ron Weiner, PGA Professional
Steve Ball, Superintendent

Driving Range ●
Practice Greens ●
Clubhouse ●
Food / Beverage ●
Accommodations
Pull Carts ●
Power Carts ●
Club Rental ●
$pecial Offers

	1	2	3	4	5	6	7	8	9	OUT
BACK	380	440	192	520	395	372	357	213	389	3258
REGULAR	366	408	170	497	371	352	341	191	374	3070
par	4	4	3	5	4	4	4	3	4	35
handicap	7	1	15	17	3	13	11	9	5	-
FORWARD	346	403	141	450	359	351	340	153	361	2904
par	4	5	3	5	4	4	4	3	4	36
handicap	9	11	17	1	5	7	13	15	3	-

	10	11	12	13	14	15	16	17	18	IN
BACK	383	451	211	376	355	433	176	513	479	3377
REGULAR	363	435	300	360	344	419	165	488	414	3288
par	4	4	3	4	4	4	3	5	5	36
handicap	6	2	8	12	10	4	18	14	16	-
FORWARD	351	426	173	354	339	376	158	465	455	3097
par	4	5	3	4	4	5	3	5	5	38
handicap	9	11	17	1	5	7	13	15	3	-

BACK	
yardage	6585
par	71
rating	71.2
slope	124

REGULAR	
yardage	6312
par	71
rating	69.9
slope	117

FORWARD	
yardage	6003
par	71
rating	74.4
slope	124

 MANHATTAN BEACH MARRIOT GOLF COURSE

1400 Parkview Avenue
Manhattan Beach, CA
90267
PRO SHOP: 310-546-4551

Calvin Thepyasuwan, Head Professional, PGA

Driving Range
Practice Greens ●
Clubhouse
Food / Beverage ●
Accommodations
Pull Carts
Power Carts
Club Rental ●
$pecial Offers

	1	2	3	4	5	6	7	8	9	OUT
BACK	-	-	-	-	-	-	-	-	-	-
REGULAR	139	98	138	131	133	158	150	177	96	1220
par	3	3	3	3	3	3	3	3	3	27
handicap	2	9	4	6	8	1	5	3	7	-
FORWARD	-	-	-	-	-	-	-	-	-	-
par	-	-	-	-	-	-	-	-	-	-
handicap	-	-	-	-	-	-	-	-	-	-

	10	11	12	13	14	15	16	17	18	IN
BACK	-	-	-	-	-	-	-	-	-	-
REGULAR	-	-	-	-	-	-	-	-	-	-
par	-	-	-	-	-	-	-	-	-	-
handicap	-	-	-	-	-	-	-	-	-	-
FORWARD	-	-	-	-	-	-	-	-	-	-
par	-	-	-	-	-	-	-	-	-	-
handicap	-	-	-	-	-	-	-	-	-	-

BACK	
yardage	-
par	-
rating	-
slope	-

REGULAR	
yardage	1220
par	27
rating	-
slope	-

FORWARD	
yardage	
par	
rating	-
slope	-

PLAY POLICY & FEES: Green fees are $18 weekdays and $23 weekends for 18 holes. Twilight rates are offered. Call for temporarily lowered fees due to temporary greens. Pull carts are $3, electric $20, and personal remote control $6.

TEE TIMES: Reservations can be made one week in advance, but only by holders of a Los Angeles Recreation and Parks reservation card. Standbys are welcome for non-card holders.

COURSE DESCRIPTION: This course is one of the most heavily played courses in the country, so expect slow play. The course features many trees and rolling terrain.

NOTES: The course is currently rebiulding all greens, so expect temporaries. The completion of this greens project is expected by the end of 2000. This facility also offers a nine-hole, par-3 course. Par is 27. Rancho Park is the site of the Ralphs Senior Classic, an October stop on the Senior PGA Tour. Arnold Palmer once made a 12 on the par-5 18th hole (ninth hole during professional events) here during the Los Angeles Open. Asked how he made 12, he replied, "I missed a three-footer for 11." A plaque is near the tee at the 18th to commemorate the event. Because of the heavy play, each hole on the championship course has an alternate green.

LOCATION: Take the Santa Monica Freeway to the Overland exit. Travel north on Overland approximately 1.5 miles to Pico Boulevard. Turn right and drive one-half mile to the course.

. . . ● **TOURNAMENTS:** All reservations must be made through the Los Angeles Recreation and Parks Department. Call 213-485-5566.

38. RANCHO PARK GOLF COURSE

PLAY POLICY & FEES: Green fees are $7 weekdays and $9 weekends and holidays. Carts are not available. Pull carts are $2.

TEE TIMES: Reservations can be booked 14 days in advance.

DRESS CODE: Proper golf attire is required.

COURSE DESCRIPTION: This short par-3 course is hilly but walkable. There are few flat lies. Lake Kathleen comes into play on the first and eighth holes. The latter measures 177 yards and is the longest hole on the course.

LOCATION: From Los Angeles International Airport take Interstate 405 south. Exit at Rosecrans Avenue. Drive west approximately five minutes to the course. The course is directly behind the Radisson Hotel.

. . . ● **TOURNAMENTS:** This course is available for outside tournaments.

39. MANHATTAN BEACH MARRIOT GOLF

40 WESTCHESTER GOLF COURSE

6900 West Manchester
Los Angeles, CA 90045

PRO SHOP: 310-649-9168

Bruce Dunham, General Manager
Lynn Ralston, Head Professional, LPGA
Jesse Martinez, Superintendent

Driving Range ●
Practice Greens ●
Clubhouse ●
Food / Beverage ●
Accommodations
Pull Carts ●
Power Carts ●
Club Rental ●
$pecial Offers

	1	2	3	4	5	6	7	8	9	OUT
BACK										
REGULAR										
par										
handicap										
FORWARD										
par										
handicap										

	10	11	12	13	14	15	16	17	18	IN
BACK										
REGULAR										
par										
handicap										
FORWARD										
par										
handicap										

BACK	
yardage	
par	
rating	
slope	

REGULAR	
yardage	3470
par	53
rating	
slope	

FORWARD	
yardage	3470
par	53
rating	
slope	

41 THE LAKES AT EL SEGUNDO

400 South Sepulveda
El Segundo, CA 90245

PRO SHOP: 310-322-0202

Larry Greibenow, General Manager
Jennefer Jones, Head Professional, LPGA

Driving Range ●
Practice Greens ●
Clubhouse ●
Food / Beverage ●
Accommodations
Pull Carts ●
Power Carts
Club Rental ●
$pecial Offers

	1	2	3	4	5	6	7	8	9	OUT
BACK	-	-	-	-	-	-	-	-	-	-
REGULAR	128	112	178	269	96	78	103	115	261	1340
par	3	3	3	4	3	3	3	4	29	
handicap	5	7	4	2	8	9	3	6	1	-
FORWARD	128	112	178	233	96	78	103	115	225	1268
par	3	3	3	4	3	3	3	3	4	29
handicap	5	7	4	2	8	9	3	6	1	-

	10	11	12	13	14	15	16	17	18	IN
BACK	-	-	-	-	-	-	-	-	-	-
REGULAR	-	-	-	-	-	-	-	-	-	-
par	-	-	-	-	-	-	-	-	-	-
handicap	-	-	-	-	-	-	-	-	-	-
FORWARD	-	-	-	-	-	-	-	-	-	-
par	-	-	-	-	-	-	-	-	-	-
handicap	-	-	-	-	-	-	-	-	-	-

BACK	
yardage	-
par	-
rating	
slope	

REGULAR	
yardage	1340
par	29
rating	-
slope	-

FORWARD	
yardage	1268
par	29
rating	-
slope	-

PLAY POLICY & FEES: Green fees are $12 from Monday through Thursday, $13 Friday, and $17 weekends. Twilight and nine-hole rates are available. Carts are $15. Pull carts are $3.

TEE TIMES: Reservations can be booked seven days in advance.

COURSE DESCRIPTION: This very popular 15-hole, executive-length, night-lit course is located adjacent to the Los Angeles International Airport. Winchester lost three holes to the airport in 1990. The course has one lake, nice greens, and is open until 10 p.m.

NOTES: Westchester features a large driving range and practice facility from which six teaching professionals operate. A club repair shop is also on site.

LOCATION: From Interstate 405 in Westchester (near Inglewood), exit on Manchester Boulevard heading west and drive to the course on the left. From Interstate 105 west take the Sepulveda Boulevard exit heading north, under the airport runway. Turn left (west) on Manchcester Boulevard, and the course is on the left.

. . . ● **TOURNAMENTS:** A 12-player minimum is needed to book an event.

40. WESTCHESTER GOLF COURSE

PLAY POLICY & FEES: Green fees are $9 weekdays and $11 weekends. Senior and junior rates are $7 from Monday through Thursday. Pull carts are $2 with a $1 deposit.

TEE TIMES: Reservations can be booked seven days in advance.

DRESS CODE: No tank tops are allowed on the golf course.

COURSE DESCRIPTION: This executive course has two par 4s, the longest of which is the 269-yard fourth hole. Three lakes and many sand bunkers make this course a challenge. Greens are big and mostly forgiving.

NOTES: The course features a superb, two-tiered, lighted driving range and practice facility that is open until 11 p.m.

LOCATION: From Los Angeles International Airport take Sepulveda Boulevard south. Follow Sepulveda Boulevard one-half mile past El Segundo Boulevard to the course. The course is on Sepulveda Boulevard between El Segundo Boulevard and Rosecrans Avenue.

. . . ● **TOURNAMENTS:** This course is available for outside tournaments.

41. THE LAKES AT EL SEGUNDO

⁴² CHESTER WASHINGTON GOLF COURSE

1930 West 120th Street
Los Angeles, CA 90047

PRO SHOP: 323-756-6975
CLUBHOUSE: 213-756-2516

Danny Harris, General Manager
William Ensly, Tournament Director

Driving Range ●
Practice Greens ●
Clubhouse ●
Food / Beverage ●
Accommodations
Pull Carts ●
Power Carts ●
Club Rental ●
$pecial Offers

	1	2	3	4	5	6	7	8	9	OUT
BACK	342	181	339	195	337	363	422	353	445	2977
REGULAR	333	169	319	135	330	356	415	351	439	2847
par	4	3	4	3	4	4	4	4	4	34
handicap	9	15	11	17	13	5	3	7	1	-
FORWARD	311	156	305	115	321	328	387	333	420	2676
par	4	3	4	3	4	4	5	4	5	36
handicap	13	15	11	17	7	5	3	9	1	-

	10	11	12	13	14	15	16	17	18	IN
BACK	144	394	494	194	360	417	409	444	488	3344
REGULAR	139	385	482	185	315	408	376	429	447	3166
par	3	4	5	3	4	4	4	4	5	36
handicap	16	12	14	18	8	4	10	2	6	-
FORWARD	138	371	459	148	306	383	352	405	435	2997
par	3	4	5	3	4	4	4	5	5	37
handicap	18	10	4	16	14	8	12	6	2	-

BACK	
yardage	6321
par	70
rating	69.8
slope	119

REGULAR	
yardage	6013
par	70
rating	68.3
slope	115

FORWARD	
yardage	5673
par	73
rating	72.2
slope	120

⁴³ ALONDRA PARK GOLF COURSE
ARCHITECTS: WILLIAM P. BELL , 1947; WILLIAM H. JOHNSON

16400 South Prairie
Lawndale, CA 90260

PRO SHOP: 310-217-9915

Jim Dennerline, Head Professional, PGA
Salvador Flores, Superintendent

Driving Range ●
Practice Greens ●
Clubhouse ●
Food / Beverage ●
Accommodations
Pull Carts ●
Power Carts ●
Club Rental ●
$pecial Offers

	1	2	3	4	5	6	7	8	9	OUT
BACK	381	525	188	372	389	387	331	179	495	3247
REGULAR	372	517	183	365	381	376	323	175	482	3174
par	4	5	3	4	4	4	4	3	5	36
handicap	5	9	11	7	3	1	17	13	15	-
FORWARD	361	511	179	360	372	362	305	169	465	3084
par	4	5	3	4	4	4	4	3	5	36
handicap	9	1	15	11	5	3	13	17	7	-

	10	11	12	13	14	15	16	17	18	IN
BACK	406	295	142	371	395	363	426	350	502	3250
REGULAR	393	285	137	356	391	353	417	335	482	3149
par	4	4	3	4	4	4	4	4	5	36
handicap	4	12	16	10	8	6	2	18	14	-
FORWARD	346	297	132	347	386	343	398	324	472	3045
par	4	4	3	4	4	4	5	4	5	37
handicap	8	16	18	10	2	6	12	14	4	-

BACK	
yardage	6497
par	72
rating	68.1
slope	106

REGULAR	
yardage	6323
par	72
rating	67.4
slope	104

FORWARD	
yardage	6129
par	73
rating	73.0
slope	109

PLAY POLICY & FEES: Green fees are $20 weekdays and $25 weekends. Junior, senior, twilight, and supertwilight rates are available. Carts are $23.

TEE TIMES: Reservations can be booked seven days in advance.

DRESS CODE: Collared shirts are required.

COURSE DESCRIPTION: This is a wide-open course for free swingers and a confidence booster for everyone. There are few hazards to worry about.

LOCATION: From Interstate 405 driving south (near Inglewood and Hawthorne), take the Imperial Highway exit and drive west. Turn right on Western Avenue to the course.

. . . ● **TOURNAMENTS:** A 12-player minimum is needed to book an event. Tournaments should be booked 12 months in advance. The banquet facility can hold 250 people seated and 300 people for cocktails.

42. CHESTER WASHINGTON GOLF COURSE

PLAY POLICY & FEES: The green fees are $20 weekdays and $25 weekends and holidays for the main course, and $11 weekdays and $14 weekends for the executive course. Carts are $22.

TEE TIMES: Reservations can be booked seven days in advance starting at 6 a.m. on weekdays and 5 a.m. on weekends.

DRESS CODE: Appropriate golf attire is required.

COURSE DESCRIPTION: The main course is level and open with ocean breezes from two miles away. It is not a difficult course, and there are very few places where golfers can get into trouble. The executive course is also flat and offers a good practice round. It is a good course for beginners and seniors.

NOTES: Architect Cecil B. Hollingsworth built the executive course in 1950.

LOCATION: Off Interstate 405 in Redondo Beach take the Redondo Beach Boulevard exit and drive northeast. The course is located on the corner of Prairie and Redondo Beach Boulevard.

. . . ● **TOURNAMENTS:** A 24-player minimum is needed to book an event. Shotgun tournaments are not allowed.

43. ALONDRA PARK GOLF COURSE

44 SEA AIRE PARK GOLF COURSE

22730 Lupine Drive
Torrance, CA 90505

PRO SHOP: 310-316-9779

Larry Johnson, Manager

Driving Range
Practice Greens ●
Clubhouse
Food / Beverage
Accommodations
Pull Carts
Power Carts
Club Rental ●
$pecial Offers

	1	2	3	4	5	6	7	8	9	OUT
BACK										
REGULAR										
par										
handicap										
FORWARD										
par										
handicap										

	10	11	12	13	14	15	16	17	18	IN
BACK										
REGULAR										
par										
handicap										
FORWARD										
par										
handicap										

BACK	
yardage	
par	
rating	
slope	

REGULAR	
yardage	628
par	27
rating	
slope	

FORWARD	
yardage	
par	
rating	
slope	

45 PALOS VERDES GOLF CLUB
ARCHITECTS: WILLIAM P. BELL, 1924; GEORGE THOMAS, 1924

3301 Via Campesina
Palos Verdes Estates, CA
90274
PRO SHOP: 310-375-2759
CLUBHOUSE: 310-375-2533

Ross Kroeker, Head Professional, PGA
Michelle Nichol, Banquet Manager

Driving Range ●
Practice Greens ●
Clubhouse ●
Food / Beverage ●
Accommodations
Pull Carts
Power Carts ●
Club Rental ●
$pecial Offers

	1	2	3	4	5	6	7	8	9	OUT
BACK	381	200	388	210	484	325	510	146	364	3008
REGULAR	342	169	356	190	455	312	443	130	339	2736
par	4	3	4	3	5	4	5	3	4	35
handicap	5	15	7	13	1	9	11	17	3	-
FORWARD	337	157	301	164	455	278	441	110	255	2498
par	4	3	4	3	5	4	5	3	4	35
handicap	5	15	7	13	1	9	11	17	3	-

	10	11	12	13	14	15	16	17	18	IN
BACK	354	360	247	407	401	169	450	325	390	3103
REGULAR	333	347	130	386	332	132	435	314	361	2770
par	4	4	4	4	4	3	5	4	4	36
handicap	10	12	16	2	14	18	8	6	-	
FORWARD	319	289	96	336	263	96	383	241	343	2366
par	4	4	3	4	4	3	5	4	4	35
handicap	10	12	16	2	14	18	6	4	8	-

BACK	
yardage	6111
par	71
rating	70.1
slope	128

REGULAR	
yardage	5506
par	71
rating	67.3
slope	121

FORWARD	
yardage	4864
par	70
rating	70.8
slope	126

PLAY POLICY & FEES: Green fees are $3.50 for Torrance residents and $4 for nonresidents. Senior and junior rates are available.

TEE TIMES: Reservations are not accepted. All play is on a first-come, first-served basis.

COURSE DESCRIPTION: This is a very short, par-3 course. So short in fact, they used to have a rule that you could only bring three clubs. The longest hole is 85 yards. It is a good practice course for your short iron game. The course caters to beginners, and the price is right.

LOCATION: In Torrance drive west on Sepulveda. Cross Anza and turn left on Reynolds, then left on Lupine Drive to the course.

. . . ● **TOURNAMENTS:** This course is available for outside tournaments.

44. SEA AIRE PARK GOLF COURSE

PLAY POLICY & FEES: Outside play is accepted but limited to after 10 a.m. on Monday and after 2 p.m. Tuesday through Friday. Green fees are $135, carts included.

TEE TIMES: Reservations can be booked three days in advance.

DRESS CODE: Appropriate golf attire and nonmetal spikes are required.

COURSE DESCRIPTION: This course offers spectacular views, tree-lined fairways, small, fast greens and plenty of sand. Do not let the yardage fool you—Palos Verdes is a challenge! Most fairways have generous landing areas, but to score well, hitting it down the middle is not enough. You must know what side of the fairway to play to save strokes. Water comes into play on only one hole. A steady ocean breeze can be expected throughout your round.

NOTES: Average and low handicappers will enjoy this course, but beginners may struggle no matter which tees are chosen. An excellent driving range is offered with many targets and both grass and mats, depending on conditions. Want to be a member? Patience—the wait is two years and you must be a resident of the community.

LOCATION: From Interstate 405 south of the Los Angeles International Airport, take the Hawthorne Boulevard (Highway 107) exit. Go south six miles and take a right on Palos Verdes Drive. Stay on Palos Verdes Drive and take a left onto Via Campesina. The course is on the left.

. . . ● **TOURNAMENTS:** Shotgun tournaments are available Monday only on a limited basis, and carts are required. A 128-player minimum is required to book a shotgun tournament. Events should be scheduled 12 months in advance. The banquet facility can accommodate 250 people. ● **TRAVEL:** The Torrance Marriott is located 15 minutes from the golf course. For reservations call 310-316-3636.

45. PALOS VERDES GOLF CLUB

Los Verdes Golf & Country Club
ARCHITECT: WILLIAM F. BELL, 1964

7000 West Los Verdes
Rancho Palos Verdes, CA
90275
PRO SHOP: 310-377-7888
STARTER: 310-377-7370

Matt Stevens, General Manager
Mike Buroza, Head Professional, PGA
Christine Johnson, LPGA Professional

Driving Range ●
Practice Greens ●
Clubhouse ●
Food / Beverage ●
Accommodations
Pull Carts ●
Power Carts ●
Club Rental ●
$Special Offers

	1	2	3	4	5	6	7	8	9	OUT
BACK	491	365	183	444	189	559	381	355	411	3378
REGULAR	469	355	169	432	152	520	368	342	400	3207
par	5	4	3	4	3	5	4	4	4	36
handicap	11/7	9/15	15/1	1	13/17	7/11	3	17/9	5	-
FORWARD	455	326	111	318	138	426	360	333	391	2858
par	5	4	3	4	3	5	4	4	4	36
handicap	5	11	17	13	15	7	1	9	3	-

	10	11	12	13	14	15	16	17	18	IN
BACK	378	308	155	431	420	437	474	225	420	3248
REGULAR	370	293	139	378	385	425	433	206	412	3041
par	4	4	3	4	4	4	5	3	4	35
handicap	14/1	18	16	2/8	6/4	4/2	12	10/1	8/6	-
FORWARD	334	287	121	367	368	417	422	192	372	2880
par	4	4	3	4	4	5	5	3	4	36
handicap	10	16	16/1	2	4	14	6	12	8	-

BACK	
yardage	6626
par	71
rating	72.4
slope	122

REGULAR	
yardage	6248
par	71
rating	69.5
slope	119

FORWARD	
yardage	5738
par	72
rating	71.8
slope	118

 ## Victoria Park Golf Course
ARCHITECT: EDWIN H. RIPPERDAN, 1966

340 East 192nd Street
Carson, CA 90746

PRO SHOP: 310-323-6981

Anna McGrath, Head Professional, LPGA
Tom Levin, Superintendent

Driving Range ●
Practice Greens ●
Clubhouse ●
Food / Beverage ●
Accommodations
Pull Carts ●
Power Carts ●
Club Rental ●
$Special Offers

	1	2	3	4	5	6	7	8	9	OUT
BACK	515	406	368	381	156	547	448	199	392	3412
REGULAR	500	394	358	368	144	536	433	184	378	3295
par	5	4	4	4	3	5	4	3	4	36
handicap	15	7	13	3	17	11	1	9	5	-
FORWARD	482	362	334	355	125	468	417	169	365	3077
par	5	4	4	4	3	5	5	3	4	37
handicap	1	7	11	5	17	3	13	15	9	-

	10	11	12	13	14	15	16	17	18	IN
BACK	512	353	391	421	174	486	226	375	437	3375
REGULAR	499	334	376	409	157	473	216	359	413	3236
par	5	4	4	4	3	5	3	4	4	36
handicap	16	18	8	2	12	14	6	10	4	-
FORWARD	482	313	358	392	125	456	180	345	326	2977
par	5	4	4	4	3	5	3	4	4	36
handicap	2	10	6	12	18	4	16	8	14	-

BACK	
yardage	6787
par	72
rating	70.7
slope	111

REGULAR	
yardage	6531
par	72
rating	69.5
slope	109

FORWARD	
yardage	6054
par	73
rating	73.0
slope	115

PLAY POLICY & FEES: Green fees are $20 weekdays and $25 weekends. Twilight, senior, and junior rates are available. Carts are $22.

TEE TIMES: Reservations can be booked seven days in advance.

DRESS CODE: No tank tops are allowed.

COURSE DESCRIPTION: This course offers one of the best golf values in the state. It has views of the Pacific Ocean which are matched only by Pebble Beach. The course is well maintained with excellent putting surfaces. The 13th, 14th, and 15th present a tough three-hole sequence in addition to offering spectacular views of Catalina Island on clear days.

NOTES: The course record for men is 63. The course record for women is 71.

LOCATION: Travel on Interstate 405 to Rancho Palos Verdes. Exit on Hawthorne Boulevard, turn south and drive 11 miles to Los Verdes Drive. Turn right and follow it to the club. Or take Interstate 110 (Harbor Freeway) south to Pacific Coast Highway (Highway 1), then west to Hawthorne Boulevard. Turn south and drive 5.5 miles to Los Verdes Drive. Turn right and follow Los Verdes Drive around to the course.

. . . ● **TOURNAMENTS:** Shotgun tournaments are available weekdays only. A 24-player minimum is required for tournament play.

46. LOS VERDES GOLF & COUNTRY CLUB

PLAY POLICY & FEES: The course was recently purchased by Arnold Palmer Golf Management. The course will close in the fall of 1999 for a complete reconstruction. Look for the course to reopen in 2001. Green fees for nine holes are $13 weekdays and $16 weekends. Green fees for 18 holes are $20 for weekdays and $25 for weekends. The twilight rate is $14 weekdays and $17 weekends. Seniors and juniors with a resident card receive discounted green fees on weekdays. Carts are $22.

TEE TIMES: Reservations can be made at any time.

COURSE DESCRIPTION: Most greens are protected by sand at this course. There are no water holes. The 515-yard first hole may put you in a sour mood right off the bat if you're not aware of the fairway bunkers. It is an easy course to walk. The course features large greens and wide fairways. The wind usually comes up in the afternoon.

NOTES: The course record is 64.

LOCATION: Take Interstate 405 sout of L.A. International Airport to the Avalon exit. Go north on Avalon to 192nd Street. Turn left on 192nd Street to the course.

. . . ● **TOURNAMENTS:** This course is available for outside tournaments.

47. VICTORIA PARK GOLF COURSE

48 NEW HORIZONS GOLF COURSE

22727 Maple Avenue
Torrance, CA 90505

PRO SHOP: 310-325-3080

Driving Range
Practice Greens
Clubhouse
Food / Beverage
Accommodations
Pull Carts
Power Carts
Club Rental
$pecial Offers

	1	2	3	4	5	6	7	8	9	OUT
BACK	-	-	-	-	-	-	-	-	-	-
REGULAR	56	53	54	63	66	71	83	60	46	552
par	3	3	3	3	3	3	3	3	3	27
handicap	13	9	11	15	3	5	1	7	17	-
FORWARD	56	53	54	63	66	71	83	60	46	552
par	3	3	3	3	3	3	3	3	3	27
handicap	9	13	15	11	3	5	1	7	17	-

	10	11	12	13	14	15	16	17	18	IN
BACK	-	-	-	-	-	-	-	-	-	-
REGULAR	56	53	54	63	66	71	83	60	46	552
par	3	3	3	3	3	3	3	3	3	27
handicap	14	10	12	16	4	6	2	8	18	-
FORWARD	56	53	54	63	66	71	83	60	46	552
par	3	3	3	3	3	3	3	3	3	27
handicap	10	14	16	12	4	6	2	8	18	-

BACK	
yardage	-
par	-
rating	-
slope	-

REGULAR	
yardage	1104
par	54
rating	-
slope	-

FORWARD	
yardage	1104
par	54
rating	-
slope	-

49 DOMINGUEZ GOLF COURSE

19800 South Main Street
Carson, CA 90745

PRO SHOP: 310-719-1942

Mark Siebert, Head Professional, PGA
Eric Manley, Professional

Driving Range ●
Practice Greens ●
Clubhouse ●
Food / Beverage ●
Accommodations
Pull Carts ●
Power Carts
Club Rental ●
$pecial Offers

	1	2	3	4	5	6	7	8	9	OUT
BACK	-	-	-	-	-	-	-	-	-	-
REGULAR	126	119	118	118	97	107	119	121	97	1022
par	3	3	3	3	3	3	3	3	3	27
handicap	1	9	5	11	17	13	7	3	15	-
FORWARD	-	-	-	-	-	-	-	-	-	-
par	-	-	-	-	-	-	-	-	-	-
handicap	-	-	-	-	-	-	-	-	-	-

	10	11	12	13	14	15	16	17	18	IN
BACK	-	-	-	-	-	-	-	-	-	-
REGULAR	89	111	71	103	116	135	112	108	124	969
par	3	3	3	3	3	3	3	3	3	27
handicap	10	18	16	4	8	2	12	14	6	-
FORWARD	-	-	-	-	-	-	-	-	-	-
par	-	-	-	-	-	-	-	-	-	-
handicap	-	-	-	-	-	-	-	-	-	-

BACK	
yardage	-
par	-
rating	
slope	

REGULAR	
yardage	1991
par	54
rating	51.6
slope	

FORWARD	
yardage	
par	
rating	
slope	

PLAY POLICY & FEES: This is a private course for residents of the surrounding development only.

COURSE DESCRIPTION: The course has narrow fairways and undulating greens, making it a difficult layout for anyone with shoddy iron play or an unsteady putting stroke.

LOCATION: Take Interstate 110 north to Torrance Boulevard. Follow Torrance Boulevard about one mile to Maple Avenue. Turn right and go about three-fourths of a mile to the club.

. . . ● **TOURNAMENTS:** This course is not available for outside events.

48. NEW HORIZONS GOLF COURSE

PLAY POLICY & FEES: Green fees are $8 for nine holes and $10 for 18 holes weekdays. On weekends and holidays green fees are $12 for 18 holes. Twilight, senior, and junior rates are available.

TEE TIMES: Reservations can be booked seven days in advance.

COURSE DESCRIPTION: This tight course has a lot of gullies with some bunkers. It's a tough par-3 course with undulating greens. It was built on landfill, which may have had some effect on the settling of the greens.

NOTES: The course has lights and is open from 6 a.m. to 10 p.m.

LOCATION: From Interstate 405 north exit on Main Street in Carson. The course is south of the freeway on the left.

. . . ● **TOURNAMENTS:** This course is available for outside tournaments.

49. DOMINGUEZ GOLF COURSE

HARBOR PARK GOLF COURSE
ARCHITECT: WILLIAM H. TOOMEY, 1957

1235 North Figueroa Place
Wilmington, CA 90744

PRO SHOP: 310-549-9163
STARTER: 310-549-4953

George Smith, Professional
Ed Mallera, Superintendent
Bev Cox, Director of Golf

Driving Range •
Practice Greens •
Clubhouse •
Food / Beverage •
Accommodations
Pull Carts •
Power Carts •
Club Rental •
$pecial Offers

	1	2	3	4	5	6	7	8	9	OUT
BACK	-	-	-	-	-	-	-	-	-	-
REGULAR	316	444	488	314	507	189	364	155	384	3161
par	4	4	5	4	5	3	4	3	4	36
handicap	8	1	4	6	3	2	7	9	5	-
FORWARD	305	426	461	304	497	161	347	145	364	3010
par	4	5	5	4	5	3	4	3	4	37
handicap	8	3	1	5	4	2	7	9	6	-

	10	11	12	13	14	15	16	17	18	IN
BACK	-	-	-	-	-	-	-	-	-	-
REGULAR	-	-	-	-	-	-	-	-	-	-
par	-	-	-	-	-	-	-	-	-	-
handicap	-	-	-	-	-	-	-	-	-	-
FORWARD	-	-	-	-	-	-	-	-	-	-
par	-	-	-	-	-	-	-	-	-	-
handicap	-	-	-	-	-	-	-	-	-	-

BACK	
yardage	-
par	-
rating	-
slope	-

REGULAR	
yardage	3161
par	36
rating	69.6
slope	115

FORWARD	
yardage	3010
par	37
rating	74.4
slope	121

 ## ROLLING HILLS COUNTRY CLUB
ARCHITECT: TED ROBINSON, 1969

27000 Palos Verdes Drive
Rolling Hills Estates, CA
90274
PRO SHOP: 310-326-7731
CLUBHOUSE: 310-326-4343

Pat Chartrand, Director of Golf, PGA
Jack Hollis, PGA Professional
Jim Neal, Superintendent

Driving Range •
Practice Greens •
Clubhouse •
Food / Beverage •
Accommodations
Pull Carts •
Power Carts •
Club Rental •
$pecial Offers

	1	2	3	4	5	6	7	8	9	OUT
BACK	363	337	355	183	487	211	370	414	350	3070
REGULAR	337	332	344	164	459	190	354	397	341	2918
par	4	4	4	3	5	3	4	4	4	35
handicap	15	9	13	5	17	7	3	1	11	-
FORWARD	320	317	330	146	410	170	340	378	326	2737
par	4	4	4	3	5	3	4	4	4	35
handicap	11	5	9	17	13	15	3	1	7	-

	10	11	12	13	14	15	16	17	18	IN
BACK	325	181	426	172	515	193	505	324	370	3011
REGULAR	311	154	416	157	487	172	499	306	356	2858
par	4	3	4	3	5	3	5	4	4	35
handicap	16	8	2	18	4	12	10	14	6	-
FORWARD	282	140	367	144	469	153	494	280	343	2672
par	4	3	4	3	5	3	5	4	4	35
handicap	12	14	2	18	8	16	4	10	6	-

BACK	
yardage	6081
par	70
rating	69.8
slope	122

REGULAR	
yardage	5776
par	70
rating	68.2
slope	119

FORWARD	
yardage	5409
par	70
rating	71.7
slope	126

PLAY POLICY & FEES: Green fees are $10 weekdays and $13 weekends. Carts are $10.

TEE TIMES: Reservations can be made one week in advance with a reservation card from the Los Angeles City Recreation and Parks Department.

DRESS CODE: Nonmetal spikes are recommended.

COURSE DESCRIPTION: This is a long nine-hole course. Those who find the fairway can tame it, but the greens can be difficult, especially in summer when they tend to dry out.

NOTES: Harbor Park is located on a National Bird Migration flight path; over 263 different species of birds can be seen.

LOCATION: Take the Anaheim Street exit from Highway 110 south of Los Angeles. Turn right. Drive two blocks north. The course is on the left.

. . . ● **TOURNAMENTS:** This course is available for outside tournaments. Call the Los Angeles City Recreation and Parks Department at 213-473-7055 for more information.

50. HARBOR PARK GOLF COURSE

PLAY POLICY & FEES: Members and guests only. Guest fees are $40 weekdays and $60 weekends. Carts are $12.

DRESS CODE: No jeans, halter tops, or short shorts are allowed on the course. Walking shorts are acceptable (17 inches minimum length). Men must wear collared shirts. Nonmetal spikes are required.

COURSE DESCRIPTION: This is a well-manicured course that appears short, but it's tricky because of narrow, tree-lined fairways. Watch out for the 181-yard 11th hole. The green is surrounded by a pond that's filled with errant golf balls. Many holes feature large double greens and rolling fairways.

NOTES: The men's course record is 63, held by PGA Tour regular John Cook, and the women's record is 67, held by Mary Enright.

LOCATION: South of Carson on Interstate 110, turn onto the Pacific Coast Highway west (Highway 1) and drive for 2.25 miles to Narbonne. Turn left and drive one mile to the club.

. . . ● **TOURNAMENTS:** This course is available for outside tournaments when sponsored by a member. A 100-player minimum is needed to book an event. Tournaments should be scheduled 15 months in advance. A banquet facility is available that can accommodate 250 people.

51. ROLLING HILLS COUNTRY CLUB

52 OCEAN TRAILS GOLF CLUB AT PALOS VERDES
ARCHITECT: PETE DYE, 1999

One Ocean Trails Drive
Palos Verde, CA 90275

PRO SHOP: 877-799-GOLF

Robert Heath, Director of Golf, PGA
Ken Joersz, Head Professional, PGA

Driving Range ●
Practice Greens ●
Clubhouse ●
Food / Beverage ●
Accommodations
Pull Carts
Power Carts ●
Club Rental ●
$pecial Offers

	1	2	3	4	5	6	7	8	9	OUT
BACK										
REGULAR										
par										
handicap										
FORWARD										
par										
handicap										

	10	11	12	13	14	15	16	17	18	IN
BACK										
REGULAR										
par										
handicap										
FORWARD										
par										
handicap										

BACK	
yardage	6800
par	72
rating	
slope	

REGULAR	
yardage	
par	
rating	
slope	

FORWARD	
yardage	
par	
rating	
slope	

53 CATALINA ISLAND GOLF COURSE
ARCHITECT: JOHN DUNCAN DUNN, 1925

P.O. Box 2019
Avalon, CA 90704

One Country Club Road
Avalon, CA 90704

PRO SHOP: 310-510-0530
OFFICE: 310-510-7421

Brian Delamarter, Director of Golf
Jose Morones, Superintendent
Mike Melinger, Superintendent

Driving Range
Practice Greens ●
Clubhouse
Food / Beverage ●
Accommodations
Pull Carts ●
Power Carts ●
Club Rental ●
$pecial Offers

	1	2	3	4	5	6	7	8	9	OUT
BACK	-	-	-	-	-	-	-	-	-	-
REGULAR	322	114	305	312	276	124	203	270	159	2085
par	4	3	4	4	4	3	3	4	3	32
handicap	3	15	5	1	9	17	11	7	13	-
FORWARD	322	114	305	312	276	124	203	270	159	2085
par	4	3	4	4	4	3	3	4	3	32
handicap	3	15	5	1	9	17	11	7	13	-

	10	11	12	13	14	15	16	17	18	IN
BACK	-	-	-	-	-	-	-	-	-	-
REGULAR	334	122	314	323	287	137	157	278	166	2118
par	4	3	4	4	4	3	3	4	3	32
handicap	4	18	6	2	10	16	12	8	14	-
FORWARD	334	122	314	323	287	137	157	278	166	2118
par	4	3	4	4	4	3	3	4	3	32
handicap	4	18	6	2	10	16	12	8	14	-

BACK	
yardage	-
par	-
rating	-
slope	-

REGULAR	
yardage	4203
par	64
rating	60.0
slope	98

FORWARD	
yardage	4203
par	64
rating	60.0
slope	98

52. OCEAN TRAILS GOLF CLUB AT PALOS

PLAY POLICY & FEES: Green fees Monday through Thursday are $150, and $200 Friday through Sunday and holidays. Twilight green fees are $90 Monday through Thursday, and $110 Friday through Sunday and holidays. Starting times vary through the year. Carts are included.

TEE TIMES: Reservations can be made seven days in advance. For premuim tee times, 8 to 60 days, there is a $20 charge.

DRESS CODE: Appropriate golf attire is required.

COURSE DESCRIPTION: This course is set to be one of the best new courses in the state, but due to a landslide that took away the 18th hole, the course has not yet opened. Call the golf course for more information, or better yet, check their website at www.oceantrails.com. The website is updated weekly.

NOTES: Ocean Trails will play host to the Michael Douglas and Friends Celebrity Golf Event.

LOCATION: From Los Angeles take Interstate 405 south to Interstate 110. Head west on Interstate 110 to Gaffey Street. Follow Gaffey Street west to 25th Street. Take a right on 25th Street, which turns into Palos Verdes Drive south. The course is on the ocean side.

. . . ● **TOURNAMENTS:** Groups of 36 players or more may book tee times up to one year in advance.

RESORT: $25-$45

FAX: 310-510-0530

9

HOLES

53. CATALINA ISLAND GOLF COURSE

PLAY POLICY & FEES: Outside play is accepted. Green fees are $25 for nine holes and $45 for 18 holes. Carts are $14 for nine holes and $28 for 18 holes.

TEE TIMES: Reservations can be booked seven days in advance.

DRESS CODE: Appropriate golf attire and nonmetal spikes are required.

COURSE DESCRIPTION: This scenic canyon course is short but demanding. Greens are small and surrounded by traps, offering a challenge to any adventurous golfer.

NOTES: Celebrities have long been attracted to this course. William Wrigley of chewing-gum fame sponsored tournaments here in the 1920s. The Catalina Island Junior Championship is held here during Easter week and the Catalina Island Invitational is held here each October.

LOCATION: Take the boat from San Pedro Bay or Long Beach (Catalina Express or Catalina Cruises) to Catalina Island, 26 miles off the mainland. In the summer, boats leave from Redondo and Newport Beaches. Helicopters are available from Long Beach and San Pedro.

. . . ● **TOURNAMENTS:** This course is available for outside tournaments. Events should be booked three months in advance.

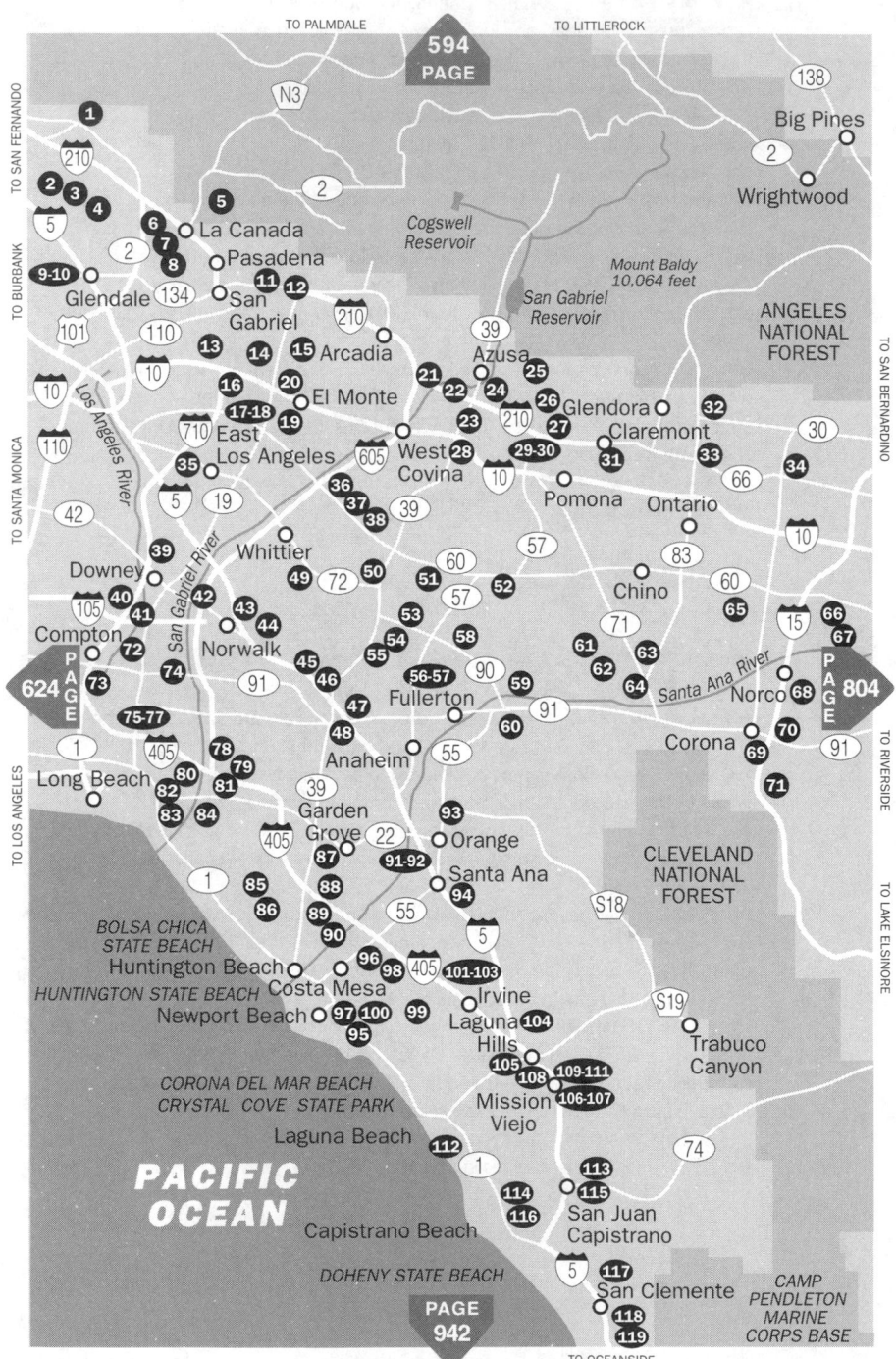

Pasadena/Los Angeles/ Orange County Area

681

1 VERDUGO HILLS GOLF COURSE

6433 La Tuna Canyon Road
Tujunga, CA 91042

PRO SHOP: 818-352-3282
STARTER: 818-352-3161

Richard Saatzer, Manager
Richard Contreras, Professional

Driving Range ●
Practice Greens ●
Clubhouse ●
Food / Beverage ●
Accommodations
Pull Carts
Power Carts
Club Rental ●
$pecial Offers

	1	2	3	4	5	6	7	8	9	OUT
BACK	-	-	-	-	-	-	-	-	-	-
REGULAR	140	120	105	100	100	95	85	115	85	945
par	3	3	3	3	3	3	3	3	3	27
handicap	1	7	3	9	11	13	15	5	17	-
FORWARD	140	120	105	100	100	95	85	115	85	945
par	3	3	3	3	3	3	3	3	3	27
handicap	1	7	3	9	11	13	15	5	17	-

	10	11	12	13	14	15	16	17	18	IN
BACK	-	-	-	-	-	-	-	-	-	-
REGULAR	70	110	95	75	100	115	75	110	110	860
par	3	3	3	3	3	3	3	3	3	27
handicap	16	4	8	14	6	2	18	10	12	-
FORWARD	70	110	95	75	100	115	75	110	110	860
par	3	3	3	3	3	3	3	3	3	27
handicap	16	4	8	14	6	2	18	10	12	-

BACK	
yardage	-
par	-
rating	-
slope	-

REGULAR	
yardage	1805
par	54
rating	-
slope	-

FORWARD	
yardage	1805
par	54
rating	-
slope	-

2 DE BELL GOLF COURSE
ARCHITECT: WILLIAM F. BELL, 1958

1500 Walnut Avenue
Burbank, CA 91504

PRO SHOP: 818-845-5052

Phil Scozzola, PGA Professional
Ray Lucero, Banquet Manager

Driving Range ●
Practice Greens ●
Clubhouse ●
Food / Beverage ●
Accommodations
Pull Carts ●
Power Carts ●
Club Rental ●
$pecial Offers

	1	2	3	4	5	6	7	8	9	OUT
BACK	-	-	-	-	-	-	-	-	-	-
REGULAR	389	445	164	441	135	337	278	213	384	2786
par	4	5	3	4	3	4	4	3	4	34
handicap	1	3	13	9	15	11	17	7	5	-
FORWARD	387	433	157	430	124	320	271	204	378	2704
par	5	5	3	5	3	4	4	3	4	36
handicap	5	1	15	9	13	7	17	11	3	-

	10	11	12	13	14	15	16	17	18	IN
BACK	-	-	-	-	-	-	-	-	-	-
REGULAR	462	310	277	313	239	132	232	506	261	2732
par	5	4	4	4	4	3	4	5	4	37
handicap	8	12	10	6	16	18	4	2	14	-
FORWARD	459	280	264	304	226	110	225	503	249	2620
par	5	4	4	4	4	3	4	5	4	37
handicap	6	10	8	4	14	18	16	2	12	-

BACK	
yardage	-
par	-
rating	-
slope	-

REGULAR	
yardage	5518
par	71
rating	67.4
slope	108

FORWARD	
yardage	5324
par	73
rating	70.8
slope	118

PLAY POLICY & FEES: Green fees are $6 for nine holes and $8 for 18 holes on weekdays. Green fees for weekends are $8 for nine holes and $10 for 18 holes. Senior and junior green fees are $4 for nine holes and $6 for 18 holes before 6 p.m.

TEE TIMES: Reservations can be booked 30 days in advance.

COURSE DESCRIPTION: This hilly, well-kept course has lots of trees and small greens. There are no bunkers or water hazards to slow you down. It's walkable. The longest hole is 140 yards. This course is considered to be one of the best-conditioned par-3 courses in Southern California.

NOTES: The course and range are lighted in the evening, and both are open until 9:30 p.m. in the fall and winter and 10:30 p.m. in the spring and summer.

LOCATION: From Interstate 210 in Tujunga, take the Lowell Avenue exit. Drive one block and turn left on La Tuna Canyon Road. Veer left to the course, which is located at the junction of La Tuna Canyon Road and Tujunga Canyon Road.

. . . ● **TOURNAMENTS:** This course is available for outside tournaments.

1. VERDUGO HILLS GOLF COURSE

PLAY POLICY & FEES: Green fees for Burbank residents are $15 weekdays and $20 weekends. Nonresident green fees are $20 weekdays and $23 weekends. Carts are $20.

TEE TIMES: Reservations can be booked five days in advance.

DRESS CODE: Nonmetal spikes are recommended.

COURSE DESCRIPTION: This is a fairly straight course with a minimum of sand traps and no water hazards. Although it is a short course, it is demanding, and course management is important. It has been called a thinking person's course.

LOCATION: From Interstate 5 take the Olive Avenue exit east about 2.5 miles to Walnut Avenue. Turn right on Walnut and follow it to the course.

. . . ● **TOURNAMENTS:** A 24-player minimum is needed to book an event. Tournaments can be scheduled up to 10 months in advance. The banquet facility can accommodate up to 150 people. ● **TRAVEL:** The Holiday Inn in Burbank is located seven minutes from the golf course. For reservations call 818-841-4770.

2. DE BELL GOLF COURSE

③ OAKMONT COUNTRY CLUB
ARCHITECT: MAX BEHR, 1924

3100 Country Club Drive
Glendale, CA 91208

PRO SHOP: 818-542-4292

Greg Frederick, PGA Professional
Dave Flaxbeard, Superintendent

Driving Range ●
Practice Greens ●
Clubhouse ●
Food / Beverage ●
Accommodations
Pull Carts
Power Carts ●
Club Rental
$pecial Offers

	1	2	3	4	5	6	7	8	9	OUT
BACK										
REGULAR										
par										
handicap										
FORWARD										
par										
handicap										

	10	11	12	13	14	15	16	17	18	IN
BACK										
REGULAR										
par										
handicap										
FORWARD										
par										
handicap										

BACK	
yardage	6758
par	72
rating	73.2
slope	130

REGULAR	
yardage	6480
par	72
rating	71.3
slope	124

FORWARD	
yardage	6033
par	72
rating	75.5
slope	136

④ SCHOLL CANYON GOLF & TENNIS CLUB
ARCHITECT: GEORGE WILLIAMS, 1994

1300 East Glenoaks
Glendale, CA 91206

PRO SHOP: 818-243-4100

Mike Konjoyan, Manager
Ted Eleftheriou, Professional

Driving Range ●
Practice Greens ●
Clubhouse ●
Food / Beverage ●
Accommodations
Pull Carts ●
Power Carts ●
Club Rental ●
$pecial Offers

	1	2	3	4	5	6	7	8	9	OUT
BACK	-	-	-	-	-	-	-	-	-	-
REGULAR	259	103	324	122	167	127	83	140	262	1587
par	4	3	4	3	3	3	3	3	4	30
handicap	7	15	1	11	3	13	17	9	5	-
FORWARD	233	83	294	84	126	101	61	107	228	1317
par	4	3	4	3	3	3	3	3	4	30
handicap	7	15	1	11	3	13	17	9	5	-

	10	11	12	13	14	15	16	17	18	IN
BACK	-	-	-	-	-	-	-	-	-	-
REGULAR	253	89	145	289	108	252	87	125	104	1452
par	4	3	3	4	3	4	3	3	3	30
handicap	8	18	10	2	4	6	16	12	14	-
FORWARD	231	64	78	218	64	206	49	81	92	1083
par	4	3	3	4	3	4	3	3	3	30
handicap	8	18	10	2	4	6	16	12	14	-

BACK	
yardage	-
par	-
rating	
slope	

REGULAR	
yardage	3039
par	60
rating	56.6
slope	81

FORWARD	
yardage	2400
par	60
rating	-
slope	-

PLAY POLICY & FEES: Members and guests only. Guest fees are $50 weekdays and $60 Friday and weekends. Carts are $10 per person.

DRESS CODE: Appropriate golf attire and nonmetal spikes are required.

COURSE DESCRIPTION: This mature course has tight fairways and well-maintained, tricky greens. Good ball placement is a must because of an abundance of trees.

NOTES: The LPGA Tour and Senior PGA Tour have held tournaments here in the past.

LOCATION: From the Ventura Freeway take the Glendale Avenue exit and drive north on Verdugo/Cañada Road for 3.5 miles to Country Club Drive. Turn left and drive one-half mile to the club.

. . . ● **TOURNAMENTS:** Outside tournaments are limited to charity events.

3. OAKMONT COUNTRY CLUB

PLAY POLICY & FEES: Green fees are $13 weekdays and $18 weekends. Twilight green fees are $10 weekdays and $13 weekends. Supertwilight rates are $7 weekdays and $9 weekends. Carts are $18.

TEE TIMES: Reservations can be booked seven days in advance.

DRESS CODE: Shirts must be worn.

COURSE DESCRIPTION: This course has exceptional character, bent-grass greens, and tremendous views. On the back nine you are hitting from elevated boxes over canyons. This course was built on a landfill. There are six par 4s and 12 par 3s.

NOTES: The course record is 51.

LOCATION: From Highway 134 in Glendale, take the Harvey Drive exit and head north to Glenoaks. Turn right onto Glenoaks Boulevard. Drive three miles to the club.

. . . ● **TOURNAMENTS:** A 16-player minimum is required to book a tournament.

4. SCHOLL CANYON GOLF & TENNIS CLUB

LA CAÑADA–FLINTRIDGE COUNTRY CLUB
ARCHITECT: LAWRENCE HUGHES, 1962

5500 Godbey Drive
La Cañada, CA 91011

PRO SHOP: 818-790-0155

Peter Fuller, Manager
Mark Saatzer, PGA Professional
Salvador Macias, Superintendent

Driving Range
Practice Greens •
Clubhouse •
Food / Beverage •
Accommodations
Pull Carts
Power Carts •
Club Rental •
$Special Offers

	1	2	3	4	5	6	7	8	9	OUT
BACK	171	418	333	285	368	546	191	347	121	2780
REGULAR	158	406	329	276	362	535	171	335	114	2686
par	3	4	4	4	4	5	3	4	3	34
handicap	11	1	15	13	5	3	7	9	17	-
FORWARD	158	354	333	283	368	546	140	347	121	2650
par	3	4	4	4	4	5	3	4	3	34
handicap	11	3	9	13	5	1	15	7	17	-

	10	11	12	13	14	15	16	17	18	IN
BACK	455	147	462	401	328	280	145	430	345	2993
REGULAR	445	135	437	392	316	274	140	409	332	2880
par	4	3	5	4	4	4	3	5	4	36
handicap	2	14	10	4	8	12	18	16	6	-
FORWARD	445	147	332	392	202	280	145	404	233	2580
par	5	3	4	4	4	4	3	5	4	36
handicap	12	14	4	2	16	6	18	8	10	-

BACK	
yardage	5773
par	70
rating	69.6
slope	134

REGULAR	
yardage	5566
par	70
rating	68.2
slope	128

FORWARD	
yardage	5230
par	70
rating	72.4
slope	132

 ## CHEVY CHASE COUNTRY CLUB
ARCHITECTS: WILLIAM F. BELL , 1927; WILLIAM P. BELL

3067 East Chevy Chase
Glendale, CA 91206

PRO SHOP: 818-244-8461
CLUBHOUSE: 818-246-5566

Mark Campbell, Manager
Dustin Schilling, Head Professional, PGA

Driving Range
Practice Greens •
Clubhouse •
Food / Beverage •
Accommodations
Pull Carts
Power Carts •
Club Rental
$Special Offers

	1	2	3	4	5	6	7	8	9	OUT
BACK	-	-	-	-	-	-	-	-	-	-
REGULAR	422	406	159	348	205	135	346	187	313	2521
par	5	4	3	4	3	3	4	3	4	33
handicap	9	1	15	5	7	17	3	11	13	-
FORWARD	422	406	159	348	205	135	346	187	313	2521
par	5	5	3	4	3	3	4	3	4	34
handicap	3	9	13	5	7	17	1	11	15	-

	10	11	12	13	14	15	16	17	18	IN
BACK	-	-	-	-	-	-	-	-	-	-
REGULAR	412	395	146	333	187	104	338	180	303	2398
par	5	4	3	4	3	3	4	3	4	33
handicap	10	2	16	6	8	18	4	12	14	-
FORWARD	412	395	146	333	187	104	338	180	303	2398
par	5	5	3	4	3	3	4	3	4	34
handicap	4	10	14	6	8	18	2	12	16	-

BACK	
yardage	-
par	-
rating	-
slope	-

REGULAR	
yardage	4919
par	66
rating	64.2
slope	116

FORWARD	
yardage	4919
par	68
rating	68.9
slope	114

PLAY POLICY & FEES: Reciprocal play is accepted with members of other private clubs; otherwise, members and guests only. Green fees are $36 weekdays and $55 weekends including carts. Carts are $10 per person on weekdays. Reservations are required.

DRESS CODE: Appropriate golf attire is mandatory.

COURSE DESCRIPTION: This short and narrow course makes up for lack of length with hills and tight fairways. Cart use is mandatory. On the back nine, watch for the par-5 12th. You tee off from an elevated tee to a narrow landing area, but first you must clear at least 160 yards of brush. The hole then opens up and is reachable in two shots for longer hitters.

LOCATION: From Pasadena drive west on Interstate 210 (Foothill Freeway) and take the Angeles Crest Highway exit. Drive north for 1.5 miles to Starlight Crest Drive. Turn right and drive one-fourth mile to Godbey Drive. Turn right to the club.

. . . ● **TOURNAMENTS:** A 72-player minimum is needed to book a tournament. All shotgun starts are on Monday only. Carts are required.

5. LA CAÑADA–FLINTRIDGE COUNTRY CLUB

PLAY POLICY & FEES: Members and guests only. Guests must be accompanied by a member. Green fees are $20 weekdays and $25 weekends for guests accompanied by a member. Carts are $16. The course is closed on Monday.

DRESS CODE: Appropriate golf attire and nonmetal spikes are required.

COURSE DESCRIPTION: This course was built in 1927 and has a variety of holes that traverse the rolling terrain of this area. The course is short and extremely tight, with out-of-bounds on virtually every hole.

LOCATION: From Highway 134 in Glendale take the Harvey exit and travel north for three blocks to Chevy Chase Drive. Turn right and drive two miles to the club.

. . . ● **TOURNAMENTS:** Outside events are held on Monday only. A 40-player minimum is needed to book a tournament. Tournaments should be booked six months in advance.

6. CHEVY CHASE COUNTRY CLUB

BROOKSIDE GOLF COURSE
ARCHITECT: WILLIAM P. BELL, 1928

1133 Rosemont Avenue
Pasadena, CA 91103

PRO SHOP: 626-796-8151
STARTER: 626-796-0177

Don Brown, Manager
Tim Terwilliger, PGA Professional
Gary Otto, Superintendent

Driving Range ●
Practice Greens ●
Clubhouse ●
Food / Beverage ●
Accommodations
Pull Carts
Power Carts ●
Club Rental ●
$pecial Offers

	1	2	3	4	5	6	7	8	9	OUT
BACK	314	423	461	423	361	509	425	199	344	3459
REGULAR	301	398	447	406	305	492	410	191	341	3291
par	4	4	4	4	4	5	4	3	4	36
handicap	15	11	1	5	17	9	3	7	13	-
FORWARD	282	375	438	377	285	462	365	118	331	3033
par	4	4	5	4	4	5	4	3	4	37
handicap	15	7	5	1	13	9	11	17	3	-

	10	11	12	13	14	15	16	17	18	IN
BACK	421	525	480	205	372	522	409	178	466	3578
REGULAR	403	515	466	186	358	510	393	169	441	3441
par	4	5	4	3	4	5	4	3	4	36
handicap	6	14	2	8	16	12	10	18	4	-
FORWARD	413	441	442	142	316	467	358	149	353	3081
par	5	5	5	3	4	5	4	3	4	38
handicap	6	4	10	16	14	2	8	18	12	-

BACK	
yardage	7037
par	72
rating	73.6
slope	128

REGULAR	
yardage	6732
par	72
rating	72.0
slope	123

FORWARD	
yardage	6114
par	75
rating	74.7
slope	128

ANNANDALE GOLF COURSE

1 N. San Rafael Avenue
Pasadena, CA 91105

PRO SHOP: 626-795-8253
CLUBHOUSE: 626-796-6125

Gino Zenobi, Manager
Patrick Rielly, PGA Professional
Scott Williams, Superintendent

Driving Range ●
Practice Greens ●
Clubhouse ●
Food / Beverage ●
Accommodations
Pull Carts
Power Carts ●
Club Rental
$pecial Offers

	1	2	3	4	5	6	7	8	9	OUT
BACK	338	412	408	404	171	458	460	334	165	3150
REGULAR	328	384	392	393	160	450	450	312	144	3013
par	4	4	4	4	3	5	4	4	3	35
handicap	11	5	3	7	15	13	1	9	17	-
FORWARD	320	371	392	380	151	434	447	298	137	2930
par	4	4	4	4	3	5	5	4	3	36
handicap	11	5	3	7	15	1	13	9	17	-

	10	11	12	13	14	15	16	17	18	IN
BACK	358	425	219	490	431	139	427	241	538	3268
REGULAR	342	417	191	481	416	132	392	201	3089	5661
par	4	4	3	5	4	3	4	3	5	35
handicap	16	6	10	14	4	18	2	8	12	-
FORWARD	315	409	184	464	397	125	367	176	503	2940
par	4	5	3	5	5	3	4	3	5	37
handicap	8	10	14	2	12	18	6	16	4	-

BACK	
yardage	6418
par	70
rating	71.9
slope	139

REGULAR	
yardage	8674
par	70
rating	70.1
slope	129

FORWARD	
yardage	5870
par	73
rating	74.0
slope	126

PLAY POLICY & FEES: Green fees for residents are $20 weekdays and $25 weekends. Green fees for nonresidents are $30 weekdays and $40 weekends. Twilight and senior rates are available. Cart fees are $24.

TEE TIMES: Reservations can be booked seven days in advance on weekdays. A special reservation system is set up for weekends. Reservations: 800-468-7952 or 818-585-3595.

DRESS CODE: Bermuda-type shorts are allowed, but no tank tops.

COURSE DESCRIPTION: The first hole is long and wide open, with mature trees lining the fairways. A lake comes into play. Well-placed bunkers guard both courses.

NOTES: The Los Angeles Open was held here in 1968. Par is 72 for the Number One Course and 70 for the Number Two Course. The Number One Course: See scorecard for yardage and rating information. The Number Two Course is 5,735 yards and rated 66.7 from the regular tees. The slope rating is 107. Women's tees are 5,377 yards and rated 70.5. The slope rating is 117.

LOCATION: From Interstate 210 in Pasadena, take the Seco/Mountain exit. Travel south on Seco to Rosemont; the course is adjacent to the Rose Bowl.

. . . ● **TOURNAMENTS:** A 16-player minimum is needed to book a tournament on weekdays, and 24 players on weekends. Shotgun tournaments on the weekend are booked on a very limited basis.

7. BROOKSIDE GOLF COURSE

PLAY POLICY & FEES: Members and guests only. Guests must be accompanied by members at time of play. Green fees are $50. Carts are $22. Reservations are required.

DRESS CODE: Appropriate golf attire is required. Nonmetal spikes are encouraged.

COURSE DESCRIPTION: This classic, hilly, and narrow course is known for its fast, sloping greens. The memorable 14th and 16th holes are set in a canyon with a lake in front of the 16th green.

NOTES: Arnold Palmer plays here annually in a charity event. Head pro Patrick Rielly is a former president of the PGA of America. Seven architects have remodeled this course, including Willie Watson, William Park Bell, and Robert Trent Jones Jr.

LOCATION: Take the San Rafael exit off Highway 134 in Pasadena. Turn left to the entrance gate.

. . . ● **TOURNAMENTS:** This course is not available for outside events.

8. ANNANDALE GOLF COURSE

9 GRIFFITH PARK GOLF COURSE
ARCHITECT: W. JOHNSON, G. THOMAS, 1941

4730 Crystal Springs Drive
Los Angeles, CA 90027

PRO SHOP: 323-664-2255
STARTER: 323-663-2555

Tom Barber, PGA Professional
Roger Barber, Professional

Driving Range ●
Practice Greens ●
Clubhouse ●
Food / Beverage ●
Accommodations
Pull Carts ●
Power Carts ●
Club Rental ●
$pecial Offers

	1	2	3	4	5	6	7	8	9	OUT
BACK										
REGULAR										
par										
handicap										
FORWARD										
par										
handicap										

	10	11	12	13	14	15	16	17	18	IN
BACK										
REGULAR										
par										
handicap										
FORWARD										
par										
handicap										

BACK	
yardage	6942
par	72
rating	72.7
slope	115

REGULAR	
yardage	6682
par	72
rating	70.9
slope	109

FORWARD	
yardage	6483
par	72
rating	76.0
slope	119

10 FRANKLIN D. ROOSEVELT MUNICIPAL

2650 N. Vermont Avenue
Los Angeles, CA 92007

PRO SHOP: 323-665-2011

Driving Range
Practice Greens ●
Clubhouse
Food / Beverage ●
Accommodations
Pull Carts ●
Power Carts
Club Rental ●
$pecial Offers

	1	2	3	4	5	6	7	8	9	OUT
BACK	-	-	-	-	-	-	-	-	-	-
REGULAR	275	392	156	340	339	310	158	346	162	2478
par	4	4	3	4	4	4	3	4	3	33
handicap	6	2	9	3	4	5	7	1	8	-
FORWARD	275	392	156	340	339	310	158	346	162	2478
par	4	4	3	4	4	4	3	4	3	33
handicap	6	2	9	3	4	5	7	1	8	-

	10	11	12	13	14	15	16	17	18	IN
BACK	-	-	-	-	-	-	-	-	-	-
REGULAR	275	392	156	340	339	310	158	346	162	2478
par	4	4	3	4	4	4	3	4	3	33
handicap	6	2	9	3	4	5	7	1	8	-
FORWARD	375	392	156	340	339	310	158	346	162	2578
par	4	4	3	4	4	4	3	4	3	33
handicap	6	2	9	3	4	5	7	1	8	-

BACK	
yardage	-
par	-
rating	-
slope	-

REGULAR	
yardage	4956
par	66
rating	62.6
slope	-

FORWARD	
yardage	5056
par	66
rating	66.8
slope	-

PLAY POLICY & FEES: Green fees are $18 weekdays and $23 weekends for 18 holes. Fees for the executive course are $10 weekdays and $13 weekends. The par-3 course is $4 weekdays and $5 weekends. Twilight rates are also available. Reservations are recommended.

TEE TIMES: A Los Angeles Recreation and Parks reservation card is required.

COURSE DESCRIPTION: Both championship courses are fairly open, with lots of trees lining the fairways. Water comes into play on both. The Wilson Course is the more difficult of the two championship courses. They both receive substantially heavy play. The 18th at Harding parallels the Griffith Park Zoo, so expect animal noises.

NOTES: This public facility has two 18-hole courses (Harding and Wilson) and par is 72 on both. There is also a nine-hole course (Los Felix), par 27, and an executive course (Roosevelt), par 33. The Harding Course is 6,536 yards and rated 70.4 with a slope of 112. The Wilson Course: See scorecard for more information. These courses are used for the annual Los Angeles City Amateur Championship.

LOCATION: Take Interstate 5 north and exit at Griffith Park. Turn right and drive two blocks and turn left. Follow the road for 1.5 miles to the parking lot.

. . . ● **TOURNAMENTS:** All tournaments are weekdays only. A 24-player minimum is needed to book an event.

9. GRIFFITH PARK GOLF COURSE

PLAY POLICY & FEES: Green fees are $10 weekdays and $13 weekends and holidays. Senior, junior, and twilight rates are available. Call the pro shop for information.

TEE TIMES: Reservations can be booked seven days in advance with a City of Los Angeles reservation card.

DRESS CODE: A neat appearance is appropriate.

COURSE DESCRIPTION: This nine-hole executive course is tree lined and surrounded by hillside terrain. The longest hole is number two, a 392-yard par 4.

LOCATION: From Interstate 5 take the Los Feliz Boulevard exit. Go west on Los Feliz and turn right onto Vermont Avenue, and drive to Griffith Park. The golf course is located in the park, on the right, soon after entering the park.

. . . ● **TOURNAMENTS:** Shotgun tournaments (62-player minimum) are available weekdays only. A 24-player minimum is needed to book a regular tournament. All tournaments must be booked through the Los Angeles City Reservation Office at 213-473-7055.

10. FRANKLIN D. ROOSEVELT MUNICIPAL

11 ALTADENA GOLF COURSE
ARCHITECT: WILLIAM P. BELL, 1939

1456 East Mendocino Drive
Altadena, CA 91001

PRO SHOP: 626-797-3821

Dave Brown, General Manager, PGA
Sam Morgan, Superintendent

Driving Range ●
Practice Greens ●
Clubhouse
Food / Beverage ●
Accommodations
Pull Carts ●
Power Carts ●
Club Rental ●
$pecial Offers

	1	2	3	4	5	6	7	8	9	OUT
BACK	448	164	301	175	447	301	370	298	491	2995
REGULAR	440	145	281	166	433	288	334	275	478	2840
par	4	3	4	3	5	4	4	4	5	36
handicap	3	11	9	7	13	17	1	15	5	-
FORWARD	434	129	267	159	418	277	317	275	433	2709
par	5	3	4	3	5	4	4	4	5	37
handicap	7	17	9	13	3	15	5	11	1	-

	10	11	12	13	14	15	16	17	18	IN
BACK	448	164	301	175	447	301	370	298	491	2995
REGULAR	440	145	281	166	433	288	334	275	478	2840
par	4	3	4	3	5	4	4	4	5	36
handicap	4	12	10	8	14	18	2	16	6	-
FORWARD	434	129	267	159	418	277	317	275	433	2709
par	5	3	4	3	5	4	4	4	5	37
handicap	8	18	10	14	4	16	6	12	2	-

BACK	
yardage	5990
par	72
rating	66.6
slope	111

REGULAR	
yardage	5680
par	72
rating	65.2
slope	108

FORWARD	
yardage	5418
par	74
rating	68.0
slope	-

12 EATON CANYON GOLF COURSE
ARCHITECT: WILLIAM F. BELL, 1959

1150 North Sierra Madre
Pasadena, CA 91107

PRO SHOP: 626-794-6773

Larry Salmi, PGA Professional
Sam Morgan, Superintendent

Driving Range ●
Practice Greens ●
Clubhouse ●
Food / Beverage ●
Accommodations
Pull Carts ●
Power Carts ●
Club Rental ●
$pecial Offers

	1	2	3	4	5	6	7	8	9	OUT
BACK	404	317	164	370	175	449	330	170	483	2862
REGULAR	379	250	150	355	158	425	319	152	472	2660
par	4	4	3	4	3	5	4	3	5	35
handicap	1	13	11	15	9	7	5	17	3	-
FORWARD	374	278	143	337	156	431	305	148	475	2647
par	4	4	3	4	3	5	4	3	5	35
handicap	3	15	11	9	13	7	5	17	1	-

	10	11	12	13	14	15	16	17	18	IN
BACK	404	317	164	370	175	449	330	170	483	2862
REGULAR	379	250	150	355	158	425	319	152	472	2660
par	4	4	3	4	3	5	4	3	5	35
handicap	2	14	12	16	10	8	6	18	4	-
FORWARD	357	239	113	322	139	412	298	125	448	2453
par	4	4	3	4	3	5	4	3	5	35
handicap	4	16	12	10	14	8	6	18	2	-

BACK	
yardage	5724
par	70
rating	67.0
slope	112

REGULAR	
yardage	5320
par	70
rating	65.4
slope	108

FORWARD	
yardage	5100
par	70
rating	67.4
slope	114

PLAY POLICY & FEES: Green fees are $12.50 weekdays and $14.50 weekends for nine holes. Replay fees are $6.50 weekdays and $8.50 weekends. Carts are $12 for nine holes and $10 for replays for two riders. Single rider carts are available weekdays for $8.

TEE TIMES: Reservations can be booked seven days in advance.

DRESS CODE: Shirts and shoes are necessary. Nonmetal spikes are encouraged.

COURSE DESCRIPTION: This is a flat, wide-open golf course with tree-lined fairways and very challenging greens. The San Gabriel Mountains provide a pleasant backdrop with Mount Wilson as the focal point.

LOCATION: Travel on Interstate 210 to the Lake Avenue exit in Pasadena. Drive 2.5 miles to Mendocino. Turn right, and the course is 1.5 miles on the right.

. . . ● **TOURNAMENTS:** A 20-player minimum is required to book a tournament.

11. ALTADENA GOLF COURSE

PLAY POLICY & FEES: Green fees are $12.50 for nine holes weekdays and $14.50 for nine holes weekends. Replay fees are $6.50 weekdays and $8.50 weekends.Twilight, senior, and junior rates are available. Single carts (weekdays only) are $7 with a replay fee of $6.

TEE TIMES: Reservations can be booked seven days in advance.

COURSE DESCRIPTION: The first four holes are flat and the last five are hilly on this tight course. There are lots of trees. The longest hole measures 483 yards.

LOCATION: Heading east of Pasadena on Interstate 210, take the Madre exit and turn left (north) on Madre Avenue. Then turn right onto North Sierra Madre Villa Avenue.

. . . ● **TOURNAMENTS:** A 20-player minimum is needed to book an event. Carts are mandatory for shotgun tournaments.

12. EATON CANYON GOLF COURSE

ARROYO SECO GOLF COURSE
ARCHITECT: WILLIAM B. JOHNSON, 1955

1055 Lohman Lane
South Pasadena, CA
91030
PRO SHOP: 323-257-0475

Gary Bailes, Manager
John De La Torre, Superintendent

Driving Range ●
Practice Greens ●
Clubhouse ●
Food / Beverage ●
Accommodations
Pull Carts ●
Power Carts
Club Rental ●
$Special Offers

	1	2	3	4	5	6	7	8	9	OUT
BACK	-	-	-	-	-	-	-	-	-	-
REGULAR	92	94	102	121	117	106	114	117	128	991
par	3	3	3	3	3	3	3	3	3	27
handicap	17	15	13	1	7	11	3	9	5	-
FORWARD	92	94	102	121	117	106	114	117	128	991
par	3	3	3	3	3	3	3	3	3	27
handicap	17	15	13	1	7	11	3	9	5	-

	10	11	12	13	14	15	16	17	18	IN
BACK	-	-	-	-	-	-	-	-	-	-
REGULAR	98	98	106	116	91	143	122	127	117	1018
par	3	3	3	3	3	3	3	3	3	27
handicap	14	18	12	2	16	8	6	4	10	-
FORWARD	98	98	106	116	91	143	122	127	117	1018
par	3	3	3	3	3	3	3	3	3	27
handicap	14	18	12	2	16	8	6	4	10	-

BACK	
yardage	-
par	-
rating	-
slope	-

REGULAR	
yardage	2009
par	54
rating	-
slope	-

FORWARD	
yardage	2009
par	54
rating	-
slope	-

SAN GABRIEL COUNTRY CLUB
ARCHITECT: NORMAN MACBETH, 1919

411 East Las Tunas Drive
San Gabriel, CA 91776

PRO SHOP: 626-287-6052
CLUBHOUSE: 626-287-9671

Alistair Philip, Head Professional, PGA
Robin Henry, Superintendent

Driving Range ●
Practice Greens ●
Clubhouse ●
Food / Beverage ●
Accommodations ●
Pull Carts
Power Carts ●
Club Rental ●
$Special Offers

	1	2	3	4	5	6	7	8	9	OUT
BACK	280	507	371	504	177	340	437	385	165	3166
REGULAR	272	486	363	484	163	323	422	365	157	3035
par	4	5	4	5	3	4	4	4	3	36
handicap	17	7	9	3	11	13	1	5	15	-
FORWARD	272	486	363	484	163	323	422	365	157	3035
par	4	5	4	5	3	4	5	4	3	37
handicap	11	1	7	3	15	9	13	5	17	-

	10	11	12	13	14	15	16	17	18	IN
BACK	420	144	345	457	182	314	415	441	375	3093
REGULAR	404	125	340	437	157	305	410	422	365	2965
par	4	3	4	5	3	4	4	4	4	35
handicap	2	18	10	12	14	16	6	4	8	-
FORWARD	404	125	340	437	157	305	410	422	365	2965
par	5	3	4	5	3	4	5	5	4	38
handicap	10	18	12	2	16	14	8	4	6	-

BACK	
yardage	6259
par	71
rating	70.6
slope	125

REGULAR	
yardage	6000
par	71
rating	68.9
slope	118

FORWARD	
yardage	6000
par	75
rating	75.0
slope	129

PLAY POLICY & FEES: Green fees are $8 for nine holes and $10 for 18 holes weekdays and $9.50 for nine holes and $12 for 18 holes weekends. Twilight and senior rates are available.

TEE TIMES: Reservations can be booked seven days in advance. Reservations can be made by calling 213-255-1506.

DRESS CODE: Nonmetal spikes are required.

COURSE DESCRIPTION: This flat course has a small creek near the 15th hole. The holes range in distance from 91 yards (14th) to 143 yards (15th).

LOCATION: On Highway 110 (Pasadena Freeway) in South Pasadena, take the Orange Grove Boulevard exit south. Turn right on Mission Street. On Mission Street stay in the right lane. Go down the hill and around to the right. Turn left at the tennis courts.

. . . ● **TOURNAMENTS:** This course is available for outside tournaments. Events should be scheduled two to three months in advance.

13. ARROYO SECO GOLF COURSE

PLAY POLICY & FEES: Members and guests only. Guests must be accompanied by members during play. Green fees are $45 weekdays and $60 weekends and holidays. Carts are $24.

DRESS CODE: Golfers must wear collared shirts, and nonmetal spikes are required. No jeans are allowed. Bermuda shorts to the knee are acceptable.

COURSE DESCRIPTION: This historic course was built in 1919 and renovated in 1972 by Robert Trent Jones Jr. It plays longer than it looks because of the bunkers. Lots of mature trees line the fairways, and the greens are well maintained. Fairways have been seeded with Kikuyu grass. Among the holes to watch for is the 437-yard seventh that features a dogleg right. Both sides of the fairway are out-of-bounds. The 420-yard 10th hole, which features an uphill second shot to a heavily bunkered green, will test the skills of any player.

NOTES: The course record of 59 is held by Bruce McCormick. The prestigious Cravens Invitational is held here each May, and the Mission Bell Tournament is played in October.

LOCATION: Travel on Interstate 10 to San Gabriel and take the San Gabriel Boulevard exit. Drive north to Las Tunas Drive, and turn left to the club.

. . . ● **TOURNAMENTS:** This course is not available for outside events.

14. SAN GABRIEL COUNTRY CLUB

405 South Santa Anita
Arcadia, CA 91006

PRO SHOP: 626-447-7156
STARTER: 626-447-2331

Scott Henderson, Managing General Partner
Terry Moeller, Head Professional, PGA
Judy Walters, Tournament Director

Driving Range ●
Practice Greens ●
Clubhouse ●
Food / Beverage ●
Accommodations
Pull Carts ●
Power Carts ●
Club Rental ●
$pecial Offers

	1	2	3	4	5	6	7	8	9	OUT
BACK	-	-	-	-	-	-	-	-	-	-
REGULAR	368	365	547	129	370	408	370	193	474	3224
par	4	4	5	3	4	4	4	3	5	36
handicap	9	11	3	17	5	1	13	7	15	-
FORWARD	308	351	533	111	290	390	350	177	427	2937
par	4	4	5	3	4	5	4	3	5	37
handicap	11	3	1	17	13	9	5	15	7	-

	10	11	12	13	14	15	16	17	18	IN
BACK	-	-	-	-	-	-	-	-	-	-
REGULAR	354	408	204	510	323	185	439	291	434	3148
par	4	4	3	5	4	3	4	4	4	35
handicap	12	6	10	8	16	14	2	18	4	-
FORWARD	322	392	184	478	308	170	426	274	417	2971
par	4	4	3	5	4	3	5	4	5	37
handicap	12	4	8	2	14	16	6	18	10	-

BACK	
yardage	-
par	-
rating	-
slope	-

REGULAR	
yardage	6372
par	71
rating	70.4
slope	122

FORWARD	
yardage	5908
par	74
rating	73.1
slope	121

630 South Almansor Street
Alhambra, CA 91801

PRO SHOP: 626-570-5059

Jerry Wisz, Director of Golf, PGA

Driving Range ●
Practice Greens ●
Clubhouse ●
Food / Beverage ●
Accommodations
Pull Carts ●
Power Carts ●
Club Rental ●
$pecial Offers

	1	2	3	4	5	6	7	8	9	OUT
BACK	283	467	254	256	296	485	128	150	336	2655
REGULAR	270	445	230	242	277	470	119	134	317	2504
par	4	5	4	4	4	5	3	3	4	36
handicap	7	3	11	13	9	1	17	15	5	-
FORWARD	253	427	212	230	261	455	111	121	302	2372
par	4	5	4	4	4	5	3	3	4	36
handicap	7	3	11	13	9	1	17	15	5	-

	10	11	12	13	14	15	16	17	18	IN
BACK	285	171	337	182	296	133	478	284	393	2559
REGULAR	270	152	304	151	266	118	452	268	371	2352
par	4	3	4	3	4	3	5	4	4	34
handicap	14	16	6	8	12	18	2	10	4	-
FORWARD	258	127	286	124	252	100	376	241	365	2129
par	4	3	4	3	4	3	5	4	5	35
handicap	14	16	6	8	10	18	2	12	4	-

BACK	
yardage	5214
par	70
rating	64.5
slope	107

REGULAR	
yardage	4856
par	70
rating	62.8
slope	103

FORWARD	
yardage	4501
par	71
rating	64.7
slope	105

PLAY POLICY & FEES: Green fees are $20 weekdays and $25 weekends. Twilight, senior, junior, and nine-hole rates are available. Carts are $22.

TEE TIMES: Reservations can be booked seven days in advance.

DRESS CODE: No tank tops are allowed.

COURSE DESCRIPTION: This is a well-maintained course with tight fairways, undulating and smallish greens, and several well-placed bunkers. It is long and challenging. It has rolling terrain and is more of a links-style course without the ocean. The Santa Anita Racetrack is next door, and the San Gabriel Mountains provide a pleasant backdrop.

NOTES: The course record is 62 set by Elsworth Vines.

LOCATION: Take Santa Anita Avenue off Interstate 210 and drive south to the course.

. . . ● **TOURNAMENTS:** No shotgun tournaments are allowed. A 24-player minimum is required to book a tournament.

15. SANTA ANITA GOLF COURSE

PLAY POLICY & FEES: Green fees are $19.50 weekdays and $24 weekends. Carts are $8 per person for nine holes and $11 per person for 18 holes; Alhambra residents get a discount. Twilight and supertwilight afternoon rates are available.

TEE TIMES: Reservations can be booked seven days in advance.

DRESS CODE: No tank tops, gym shorts, or metal spikes are allowed.

COURSE DESCRIPTION: This short regulation course features three par 5s and five par 3s. There are three lakes and 33 bunkers. The front nine is flat and easy to walk, with large groves of eucalyptus and black acacias. The back nine is composed of rolling hills with more sand and water. The two nines are distinctly different, although both have well-maintained greens. The greens are small and quick, requiring a soft touch.

NOTES: One unique feature of this course is the three-tiered, night-lighted driving range, believed to be America's first. This is a shot-maker's layout. The course also has a strong junior program.

LOCATION: From downtown Los Angeles take Interstate 10 east to the Garfield Avenue exit to Alhambra. Turn right on Valley Boulevard and go one-half mile to Almansor Street. Turn left on Almansor and go three-quarters of a mile.

. . . ● **TOURNAMENTS:** A 16-player minimum is required to book a regular tournament. Shotgun tournaments are available. Carts are required. Events can be booked 12 months in advance. The banquet facility can accommodate up to 1500 people. ● **TRAVEL:** The Ritz Carlton Huntington Hotel (626-568-3900) and the Alhambra Quality Inn (626-300-0003) are recommended for lodging.

16. ALHAMBRA GOLF COURSE

17 MONTEREY PARK GOLF COURSE

3600 Ramona Boulevard
Monterey Park, CA 91754

PRO SHOP: 323-266-2241
STARTER: 323-266-4632

Val Kim, Director of Golf
Ken Im, Professional

Driving Range ●
Practice Greens ●
Clubhouse
Food / Beverage ●
Accommodations
Pull Carts
Power Carts
Club Rental
$pecial Offers

	1	2	3	4	5	6	7	8	9	OUT
BACK	-	-	-	-	-	-	-	-	-	-
REGULAR	295	150	115	130	110	105	130	110	255	1400
par	4	3	3	3	3	3	3	3	4	29
handicap	2	1	6	4	8	9	5	7	3	-
FORWARD	295	150	115	130	110	105	130	110	255	1400
par	4	3	3	3	3	3	3	3	4	29
handicap	2	1	6	4	8	9	5	7	3	-

	10	11	12	13	14	15	16	17	18	IN
BACK	-	-	-	-	-	-	-	-	-	-
REGULAR	295	150	115	130	110	105	130	110	255	1400
par	4	3	3	3	3	3	3	3	4	29
handicap	2	1	6	4	8	9	5	7	3	-
FORWARD	295	150	115	130	110	105	130	110	255	1400
par	4	3	3	3	3	3	3	3	4	29
handicap	2	1	6	4	8	9	5	7	3	-

BACK	
yardage	-
par	-
rating	-
slope	-

REGULAR	
yardage	2800
par	58
rating	-
slope	-

FORWARD	
yardage	2800
par	58
rating	-
slope	-

18 WHITTIER NARROWS GOLF COURSE
ARCHITECT: WILLIAM F. BELL, 1960

8640 East Rush Street
Rosemead, CA 91770

PRO SHOP: 626-288-1044

Margaret Ryan, Manager
Todd Yoshitaki, Professional
Bill Houlihan, Superintendent

Driving Range ●
Practice Greens ●
Clubhouse ●
Food / Beverage ●
Accommodations
Pull Carts ●
Power Carts ●
Club Rental ●
$pecial Offers

	1	2	3	4	5	6	7	8	9	OUT
BACK										
REGULAR										
par										
handicap										
FORWARD										
par										
handicap										

	10	11	12	13	14	15	16	17	18	IN
BACK										
REGULAR										
par										
handicap										
FORWARD										
par										
handicap										

BACK	
yardage	6328
par	71
rating	68.8
slope	114

REGULAR	
yardage	6083
par	71
rating	67.9
slope	112

FORWARD	
yardage	5487
par	71
rating	73.6
slope	117

PLAY POLICY & FEES: Green fees are $7 weekdays and $8 weekends. Call for special rates.

TEE TIMES: Reservations can be booked seven days in advance.

DRESS CODE: Nonmetal spikes or spikeless shoes are required on the practice green.

COURSE DESCRIPTION: This is an executive course consisting of seven par 3s and two par 4s. The course and adjoining driving range are lighted for night play.

LOCATION: From Interstate 710 (Long Beach Freeway) in Monterey Park, take the Ramona Boulevard exit. The course is directly off the freeway on Ramona Boulevard.

. . . ● **TOURNAMENTS:** Shotgun tournaments are not available. A 16-player minimum is needed to book an event.

17. MONTEREY PARK GOLF COURSE

PLAY POLICY & FEES: Green fees are $11 weekdays and $16 weekends and holidays for nine holes. For 18 holes, fees are $20 to walk and $31 to ride weekdays and $25 to walk and $36 to ride weekends. Senior and twilight rates are available.

TEE TIMES: Reservations can be booked seven days in advance.

COURSE DESCRIPTION: These courses are flat and narrow with lots of trees and elevated greens. They are not especially difficult.

NOTES: Par is 72 on the River/Pine Course and 71 on the Pine/Mountain Course. The River/Pine Course is 6,864 yards and rated 72.3 from the blue tees, and 6,670 yards and rated 71.4 from the white tees. The slope ratings are 121 blue and 119 white. The Pine/Mountain Course: See scorecard for more information.

LOCATION: Off Highway 60 in Rosemead take the San Gabriel Boulevard exit and drive north to Walnut Grove Street. Drive to Rush Street and turn right to the course.

. . . ● **TOURNAMENTS:** Shotgun tournaments are available weekdays only. A 24-player minimum is needed to book a tournament.

18. WHITTIER NARROWS GOLF COURSE

⑲ RIVER RIDGE GOLF COURSE

3260 Fairway Drive
Pico Rivera, CA 90660

PRO SHOP: 562-692-9933
STARTER: 562-695-3206

Larry Conkings, General Manager
Brian Sanchez, Operations Manager

Driving Range ●
Practice Greens ●
Clubhouse ●
Food / Beverage ●
Accommodations
Pull Carts ●
Power Carts
Club Rental ●
$pecial Offers

	1	2	3	4	5	6	7	8	9	OUT
BACK	-	-	-	-	-	-	-	-	-	-
REGULAR	103	148	118	135	270	162	129	264	101	1430
par	3	3	3	3	4	3	3	4	3	29
handicap	5	2	4	3	7	1	9	8	6	-
FORWARD	88	148	118	135	270	101	103	248	83	1294
par	3	3	3	3	4	3	3	4	3	29
handicap	6	2	5	3	4	1	9	7	8	-

	10	11	12	13	14	15	16	17	18	IN
BACK	-	-	-	-	-	-	-	-	-	-
REGULAR	-	-	-	-	-	-	-	-	-	-
par	-	-	-	-	-	-	-	-	-	-
handicap	-	-	-	-	-	-	-	-	-	-
FORWARD	-	-	-	-	-	-	-	-	-	-
par	-	-	-	-	-	-	-	-	-	-
handicap	-	-	-	-	-	-	-	-	-	-

BACK	
yardage	-
par	-
rating	-
slope	-

REGULAR	
yardage	1430
par	29
rating	-
slope	-

FORWARD	
yardage	1294
par	29
rating	-
slope	-

⑳ ARCADIA PAR-3

620 East Live Oak
Arcadia, CA 91006

PRO SHOP: 626-443-9367

Chad Hackman, Manager
Dan Martin, Director of Instruction
Anly Hernandez, Superintendent

Driving Range ●
Practice Greens ●
Clubhouse
Food / Beverage ●
Accommodations
Pull Carts ●
Power Carts
Club Rental ●
$pecial Offers

	1	2	3	4	5	6	7	8	9	OUT
BACK	-	-	-	-	-	-	-	-	-	-
REGULAR	93	101	153	102	95	82	97	111	93	927
par	3	3	3	3	3	3	3	3	3	27
handicap	5	11	1	7	15	17	13	3	9	-
FORWARD	93	101	125	102	95	82	97	111	93	899
par	3	3	3	3	3	3	3	3	3	27
handicap										-

	10	11	12	13	14	15	16	17	18	IN
BACK	-	-	-	-	-	-	-	-	-	-
REGULAR	126	100	123	100	105	106	119	108	112	999
par	3	3	3	3	3	3	3	3	3	27
handicap	6	12	4	16	10	18	2	14	8	-
FORWARD	126	100	123	100	105	106	119	98	112	989
par	3	3	3	3	3	3	3	3	3	27
handicap	6	12	4	16	10	18	2	14	8	-

BACK	
yardage	-
par	-
rating	-
slope	-

REGULAR	
yardage	1926
par	54
rating	-
slope	-

FORWARD	
yardage	1888
par	54
rating	-
slope	-

PLAY POLICY & FEES: Green fees are $7 weekdays and $8 weekends and holidays. Senior, junior, and twilight rates are offered.

TEE TIMES: Reservations can be made seven days in advance. Walk-on play is okay.

DRESS CODE: No tank tops or boots are allowed on the course.

COURSE DESCRIPTION: All the greens are elevated on this short little course. The longest hole is 270 yards, which is the fifth. Finishing holes eight and nine are surrounded by lakes.

NOTES: The course is lighted for night play.

LOCATION: From Interstate 605, take the Beverly Boulevard exit onto San Gabriel River Parkway to Fairway Drive. The course is off Fairway Drive.

. . . ● **TOURNAMENTS:** This course is available for outside tournaments. A 16-player minimum is required to book an event. A banquet facility is available that can accommodate up to 130 people.

19. RIVER RIDGE GOLF COURSE

PLAY POLICY & FEES: Green fees are $9 weekdays and $12 weekends. Senior and junior rates are $7.50.

TEE TIMES: Reservations can be booked 21 days in advance.

DRESS CODE: Collared shirts are required. No short shorts are allowed on the course.

COURSE DESCRIPTION: This flat course has no bunkers or water. You tee off from mats. It's good practice for irons.

NOTES: The course is lighted for night play and is open until 10 P.M. The last tee time is 8 P.M.

LOCATION: Off Interstate 10 in Arcadia exit on Santa Anita Avenue and drive south for two miles until you reach Live Oak. Follow Live Oak east 1.5 miles to the course on the right.

. . . ● **TOURNAMENTS:** This course is available for outside tournaments.

20. ARCADIA PAR-3

21 RANCHO DUARTE GOLF CLUB
ARCHITECT: WILLIAM F. BELL, 1982

1000 Las Lomas
Duarte, CA 91010

PRO SHOP: 626-357-9981

Doug Ruff, Owner
Alex Quintina, Superintendent

Driving Range •
Practice Greens •
Clubhouse •
Food / Beverage •
Accommodations
Pull Carts •
Power Carts
Club Rental •
$pecial Offers

	1	2	3	4	5	6	7	8	9	OUT
BACK	68	112	329	143	222	126	109	282	244	1635
REGULAR	62	102	315	130	210	116	92	261	230	1518
par	3	3	4	3	4	3	3	4	4	31
handicap	9	8	2	4	5	6	7	1	3	-
FORWARD	56	92	301	99	198	85	75	240	195	1341
par	3	3	4	3	4	3	3	4	4	31
handicap	9	8	2	4	5	6	7	1	3	-

	10	11	12	13	14	15	16	17	18	IN
BACK	68	112	329	143	222	126	109	282	244	1635
REGULAR	62	102	315	130	210	116	92	261	230	1518
par	3	3	4	3	4	3	3	4	4	31
handicap	9	8	2	4	5	6	7	1	3	-
FORWARD	56	92	301	99	198	85	75	240	195	1341
par	3	3	4	3	4	3	3	4	4	31
handicap	9	8	2	4	5	6	7	1	3	-

BACK	
yardage	3270
par	62
rating	53.8
slope	76

REGULAR	
yardage	3036
par	62
rating	53.8
slope	76

FORWARD	
yardage	2682
par	62
rating	53.8
slope	76

22 AZUSA GREENS COUNTRY CLUB
ARCHITECT: BOB BALDOCK, 1965

919 West Sierra Madre
Azusa, CA 91702

PRO SHOP: 626-969-1727

Jerry Herrera, Head Professional, PGA
Bob Maycock, Tournament Director

Driving Range •
Practice Greens •
Clubhouse •
Food / Beverage •
Accommodations
Pull Carts
Power Carts •
Club Rental •
$pecial Offers •

	1	2	3	4	5	6	7	8	9	OUT
BACK	414	370	210	296	472	208	448	406	166	2990
REGULAR	382	355	199	276	463	193	435	388	149	2840
par	4	4	3	4	5	3	4	4	3	34
handicap	7	13	5	15	9	11	1	3	17	-
FORWARD	375	340	160	224	424	176	424	373	121	2617
par	4	4	3	4	5	3	5	4	3	35
handicap	9	11	13	5	1	15	3	7	17	-

	10	11	12	13	14	15	16	17	18	IN
BACK	280	501	277	124	385	380	435	396	365	3143
REGULAR	274	477	269	118	369	356	426	390	346	3025
par	4	5	4	3	4	4	4	4	4	36
handicap	14	6	16	18	10	8	2	4	12	-
FORWARD	260	459	263	110	349	336	421	340	327	2865
par	4	5	4	3	4	4	5	4	4	37
handicap	14	2	16	18	8	12	6	4	10	-

BACK	
yardage	6133
par	70
rating	69.0
slope	109

REGULAR	
yardage	5865
par	70
rating	67.4
slope	105

FORWARD	
yardage	5482
par	72
rating	69.0
slope	109

PLAY POLICY & FEES: Green fees are $9 weekdays and $12 weekends. Seniors are $6 weekdays.

TEE TIMES: Reservations can be made seven days in advance.

DRESS CODE: Shirts and shoes are necessary.

COURSE DESCRIPTION: This well-bunkered course offers undulating fairways and greens. There are five par 3s and four par 4s. The longest hole is 329 yards.

LOCATION: Driving on Interstate 210 in Duarte, take Mount Olive Drive and go right on Huntington. At the first stoplight, turn left on Las Lomas and drive a half block to the course on the right.

. . . ● **TOURNAMENTS:** A 72-player minimum is needed to book a shotgun tournament. Carts are required.

21. RANCHO DUARTE GOLF CLUB

PLAY POLICY & FEES: Green fees are $23 weekdays and $33 weekends, carts included. Senior rates are $19.50 weekdays. Call for excellent twilight and nine-hole rates starting at $14.

TEE TIMES: Reservations can be booked seven days in advance.

DRESS CODE: Collared shirts are required. No cutoffs are allowed on the course.

COURSE DESCRIPTION: Set at the base of the San Gabriel Valley foothills, this course is fairly level with straight, tree-lined fairways. Bunkers come into play on every hole, and the undulating greens will test players of all abilities.

NOTES: The course record is 63.

LOCATION: From Pasadena travel east on Interstate 210 to the Azusa Avenue exit. Drive north three miles to Sierra Madre Avenue and turn left. Drive four blocks to the clubhouse on the right.

. . . ● **TOURNAMENTS:** A 16-player minimum is required to book an event. Tournaments can be scheduled 12 months in advance. The banquet facility can accommodate up to 250 people. ● **$PECIAL OFFERS:** Call Charlotte Apo at the golf course for more information on golf packages and accommodations.

22. AZUSA GREENS COUNTRY CLUB

㉓ GLENOAKS GOLF COURSE

200 West Dawson
Glendora, CA 91740

PRO SHOP: 626-335-7565

Howard J. Perrin, Manager
Bruce Perrin, Professional

Driving Range	●
Practice Greens	●
Clubhouse	
Food / Beverage	●
Accommodations	
Pull Carts	●
Power Carts	
Club Rental	●
$pecial Offers	

	1	2	3	4	5	6	7	8	9	OUT
BACK	-	-	-	-	-	-	-	-	-	-
REGULAR	88	125	188	155	156	110	116	87	95	1120
par	3	3	3	3	3	3	3	3	3	27
handicap	9	5	1	3	2	6	4	8	7	-
FORWARD	88	125	188	155	156	110	116	87	95	1120
par	3	3	3	3	3	3	3	3	3	27
handicap	9	5	1	3	2	6	4	8	7	-

	10	11	12	13	14	15	16	17	18	IN
BACK	-	-	-	-	-	-	-	-	-	-
REGULAR	88	125	188	155	156	110	116	87	95	1120
par	3	3	3	3	3	3	3	3	3	27
handicap	9	5	1	3	2	6	4	8	7	-
FORWARD	88	125	188	155	156	110	116	87	95	1120
par	3	3	3	3	3	3	3	3	3	27
handicap	9	5	1	3	2	6	4	8	7	-

BACK	
yardage	-
par	-
rating	-
slope	-

REGULAR	
yardage	2240
par	54
rating	-
slope	-

FORWARD	
yardage	2240
par	54
rating	-
slope	-

㉔ SIERRA LA VERNE COUNTRY CLUB
ARCHITECT: DAN MURRAY, 1976

6300 Country Club Drive
La Verne, CA 91750

PRO SHOP: 909-596-2100

Dennis Troy, Director of Golf, PGA
Kenneth Conant, PGA Professional
Don Johnson, Superintendent

Driving Range	●
Practice Greens	●
Clubhouse	●
Food / Beverage	●
Accommodations	
Pull Carts	
Power Carts	●
Club Rental	●
$pecial Offers	

	1	2	3	4	5	6	7	8	9	OUT
BACK	508	391	139	362	163	340	426	493	333	3155
REGULAR	483	354	132	338	152	332	417	484	324	3016
par	5	4	3	4	3	4	4	5	4	36
handicap	7	3	17	5	15	11	1	9	13	-
FORWARD	450	347	124	314	148	314	412	472	289	2870
par	5	4	3	4	3	4	5	5	4	37
handicap	3	5	17	7	13	9	15	1	11	-

	10	11	12	13	14	15	16	17	18	IN
BACK	202	371	209	495	327	195	408	545	430	3182
REGULAR	178	338	169	478	310	179	386	530	412	2980
par	3	4	3	5	4	3	4	5	4	35
handicap	12	14	8	16	18	4	10	2	6	-
FORWARD	158	315	149	469	285	118	370	486	380	2730
par	3	4	3	5	4	3	4	5	4	35
handicap	18	10	16	2	12	14	6	8	4	-

BACK	
yardage	6337
par	71
rating	70.3
slope	124

REGULAR	
yardage	5996
par	71
rating	68.5
slope	119

FORWARD	
yardage	5600
par	72
rating	73.1
slope	127

PLAY POLICY & FEES: Green fees are $4 weekdays and $6 weekends. Senior and junior rates are available.

TEE TIMES: Reservations are not accepted. All play is on a first-come, first-served basis.

DRESS CODE: No tank tops or cutoffs are allowed.

COURSE DESCRIPTION: This is a well-maintained, par-3 course. The longest hole here is 188 yards, so leave your woods at home.

NOTES: Tennis and racquetball courts are nearby.

LOCATION: From Highway 210 exit at Grand Avenue. Go one block to Glendora Avenue, turn right and go to Dawson Avenue. Turn right and you're at the course.

. . . ● **TOURNAMENTS:** This course is available for outside tournaments. A 36-player minimum is needed. Tournaments can be booked two months in advance.

23. GLENOAKS GOLF COURSE

PLAY POLICY & FEES: Members and guests only. Guests must be accompanied by a member. Green fees are $30 Monday through Thursday and $50 Friday, Saturday, Sunday and holidays. Carts are $22.

DRESS CODE: Appropriate golf attire and nonmetal spikes are required.

COURSE DESCRIPTION: Set in the foothills of La Verne, this course is both picturesque and challenging. The front nine is more open and not as difficult as the back nine, which requires accuracy with irons and good putting on the well-manicured greens. The greens are severe, however, and it is difficult to read the break and speed.

LOCATION: From Pasadena travel east on Interstate 210. Exit at Foothill Boulevard heading east and drive to Wheeler Road north. Take Wheeler Road to Birdie and follow Birdie to Country Club Drive. Turn left on Country Club Drive and proceed to the clubhouse.

. . . ● **TOURNAMENTS:** This course is available for outside tournaments on Monday and Thursday. A 72-player minimum is needed to book an event, and carts are mandatory. Tournaments should be scheduled six months to a year in advance. A banquet facility is available that can accommodate 200 people.

24. SIERRA LA VERNE COUNTRY CLUB

SAN DIMAS CANYON GOLF COURSE
ARCHITECT: JEFF BRAUER, 1991

2100 Terrebonne Avenue
San Dimas, CA 91773

PRO SHOP: 909-599-2313

Mike Orloff, Director of Golf, PGA
Trip Stevens, Tournament Director
Dave Nobbs, Superintendent

Driving Range
Practice Greens ●
Clubhouse ●
Food / Beverage ●
Accommodations
Pull Carts ●
Power Carts ●
Club Rental ●
$pecial Offers

	1	2	3	4	5	6	7	8	9	OUT
BACK	341	141	552	382	203	447	211	351	442	3070
REGULAR	312	129	523	357	185	434	183	334	430	2887
par	4	3	5	4	3	5	3	4	5	36
handicap	10	16	2	4	8	18	6	12	14	-
FORWARD	300	125	483	340	168	406	124	301	402	2649
par	4	3	5	4	3	5	3	4	5	36
handicap	9	15	1	3	13	11	17	7	5	-

	10	11	12	13	14	15	16	17	18	IN
BACK	195	379	459	402	416	380	161	463	384	3239
REGULAR	172	357	441	384	377	362	134	443	372	3042
par	3	4	5	4	4	4	3	5	4	36
handicap	11	7	13	5	1	9	15	17	3	-
FORWARD	147	341	431	334	383	351	97	438	368	2890
par	3	4	5	4	5	4	3	5	5	38
handicap	16	4	12	10	2	8	18	14	6	-

BACK	
yardage	6309
par	72
rating	70.3
slope	118

REGULAR	
yardage	5929
par	72
rating	68.3
slope	103

FORWARD	
yardage	5539
par	74
rating	72.9
slope	123

 GLENDORA COUNTRY CLUB
ARCHITECTS: E. WARREN BEACH, 1955; ROBERT TRENT JONES JR., 1970

310 South Amelia Avenue
Glendora, CA 91740

PRO SHOP: 626-335-3713
CLUBHOUSE: 626-335-4051

Dave Enderby, Manager
Dave Carollo, PGA Professional
Condie Lopez, Superintendent

Driving Range ●
Practice Greens ●
Clubhouse ●
Food / Beverage ●
Accommodations
Pull Carts ●
Power Carts ●
Club Rental ●
$pecial Offers

	1	2	3	4	5	6	7	8	9	OUT
BACK	565	151	324	439	481	472	165	322	404	3323
REGULAR	544	142	311	424	475	441	144	304	397	3182
par	5	3	4	4	5	4	3	4	4	36
handicap	5	15	9	3	11	1	17	13	7	-
FORWARD	497	115	290	378	463	424	118	274	388	2947
par	5	3	4	4	5	5	3	4	4	37
handicap	7	17	9	1	5	11	15	13	3	-

	10	11	12	13	14	15	16	17	18	IN
BACK	458	327	520	219	420	172	317	303	538	3274
REGULAR	449	312	511	210	412	163	309	299	530	3195
par	4	4	5	3	4	3	4	4	5	36
handicap	2	14	8	10	4	16	12	18	6	-
FORWARD	428	299	495	180	386	151	305	278	523	3045
par	5	4	3	4	3	4	4	4	5	36
handicap	12	10	2	14	6	16	8	18	4	-

BACK	
yardage	6597
par	72
rating	72.2
slope	128

REGULAR	
yardage	6377
par	72
rating	71.1
slope	125

FORWARD	
yardage	5992
par	73
rating	75.5
slope	135

PLAY POLICY & FEES: Green fees are $22 weekdays and $30 weekends. Carts are $12 per person.

TEE TIMES: Reservations can be booked seven days in advance.

DRESS CODE: No tank tops or cut-off jeans are allowed.

COURSE DESCRIPTION: This course offers a distinctive, interesting layout over a relatively level front nine and a hilly back nine. Four water hazards come into play. The 165-yard 16th hole is a real challenge. From an elevated tee, you hit over a lake to a green faced by a rock retaining wall and surrounded by mounds and pot bunkers.

NOTES: The course record is 66 for men and 70 for women.

LOCATION: Travel east on Interstate 210 (Foothill Freeway) and Highway 30 to the San Dimas Avenue exit. Travel north to Foothill Boulevard, turn right. Drive three-quarters of a mile to San Dimas Canyon Road. Go left and continue one mile to the Terrebonne Avenue entrance to Gray Oaks; then turn left to the club.

. . . ● **TOURNAMENTS:** Shotgun tournaments are available on weekdays. Carts are required. A 16-player minimum is needed to book an event. Tournaments should be scheduled three to 12 months in advance. A banquet facility is available that can accommodate 300 people.

25. SAN DIMAS CANYON GOLF COURSE

PLAY POLICY & FEES: Members and guests only. Guest fees are $50. Carts are $20 for two people.

DRESS CODE: Collared shirts and nonmetal spikes are required. No jeans or short shorts are allowed on the course.

COURSE DESCRIPTION: This picturesque course is set at the foot of the San Gabriel Mountains. The narrow, tree-lined fairways are fairly level and easy to walk. It is a traditional east-coast type of course, with gently rolling fairways and small greens.

LOCATION: Travel east on Interstate 210. (Stay in the middle lane.) At the "End of Freeway/Foothill Boulevard" sign, take the Lone Hill exit and drive north for one-half mile to Alosta Avenue. Turn right and drive one-half mile to Amelia Avenue and turn left to the club.

. . . ● **TOURNAMENTS:** This course is available for outside tournaments on Monday. A 120-player minimum is needed to book an event. Tournaments should be scheduled 12 months in advance. The banquet facility can accommodate 350 people. ● **TRAVEL:** The Golden Spur is recommended for dining.

26. GLENDORA COUNTRY CLUB

㉗ MARSHALL CANYON GOLF CLUB

6100 Stephens Ranch Road
La Verne, CA 91750

PRO SHOP: 909-593-6914
CLUBHOUSE: 909-593-8211

Jamie Deffin, Manager
Daniel Larsen, PGA Professional
Jerry Wolfenden, Superintendent

Driving Range ●
Practice Greens ●
Clubhouse ●
Food / Beverage ●
Accommodations
Pull Carts ●
Power Carts ●
Club Rental ●
$pecial Offers

	1	2	3	4	5	6	7	8	9	OUT
BACK	471	163	356	368	414	313	207	303	352	2947
REGULAR	462	154	340	356	404	304	195	290	342	2847
par	5	3	4	4	4	4	3	4	4	35
handicap	11	17	3	5	1	13	9	15	7	-
FORWARD	450	145	314	351	401	304	185	287	323	2760
par	5	3	4	4	5	4	3	4	4	36
handicap	3	17	7	1	11	13	5	15	9	-

	10	11	12	13	14	15	16	17	18	IN
BACK	485	177	318	424	352	376	175	460	404	3171
REGULAR	469	161	297	417	342	351	161	405	393	2996
par	5	3	4	4	4	4	3	5	4	36
handicap	6	18	14	2	10	8	16	12	4	-
FORWARD	461	138	296	402	329	340	117	402	319	2804
par	5	3	4	5	4	4	3	5	4	37
handicap	2	16	12	4	8	10	18	6	14	-

BACK	
yardage	6118
par	71
rating	68.5
slope	111

REGULAR	
yardage	5843
par	71
rating	67.2
slope	107

FORWARD	
yardage	5564
par	73
rating	72.3
slope	117

㉘ SOUTH HILLS COUNTRY CLUB
ARCHITECT: WILLIAM P. BELL, 1954

2655 South Citrus Avenue
West Covina, CA 91791

PRO SHOP: 626-332-3222
CLUBHOUSE: 626-339-1231

Campbell Wright, General Manager, PGA
Todd Turner, PGA Professional
Dan Dau Jr., Superintendent

Driving Range ●
Practice Greens ●
Clubhouse ●
Food / Beverage ●
Accommodations
Pull Carts
Power Carts ●
Club Rental
$pecial Offers

	1	2	3	4	5	6	7	8	9	OUT
BACK	-	-	-	-	-	-	-	-	-	-
REGULAR	316	334	152	523	200	514	313	487	387	3226
par	4	4	3	4	3	5	4	5	4	36
handicap	9	5	17	1	13	11	15	7	3	-
FORWARD	286	312	122	454	170	476	300	429	356	2905
par	4	4	3	5	3	5	4	5	4	37
handicap	11	7	17	5	15	1	13	9	3	-

	10	11	12	13	14	15	16	17	18	IN
BACK	-	-	-	-	-	-	-	-	-	-
REGULAR	150	328	446	313	521	205	400	151	561	3075
par	3	4	4	4	5	3	4	3	5	35
handicap	18	10	2	14	4	8	6	16	12	-
FORWARD	122	286	407	301	449	137	371	131	494	2698
par	3	4	4	4	5	3	4	3	5	35
handicap	16	12	2	10	4	18	6	14	8	-

BACK	
yardage	-
par	-
rating	-
slope	-

REGULAR	
yardage	6301
par	71
rating	69.7
slope	120

FORWARD	
yardage	5603
par	72
rating	73.4
slope	133

PLAY POLICY & FEES: Green fees are $20 weekdays and $25 weekends. Twilight and senior rates are available. Carts are $18 weekdays and $20 weekends.

TEE TIMES: Reservations can be booked seven days in advance.

DRESS CODE: Appropriate golf attire is required.

COURSE DESCRIPTION: This course is located in a canyon at the base of the San Gabriel Mountains, which offer a spectacular backdrop. The greens have a great deal of contour and are extremely tricky because of the mountains, which cause optical illusions. The par-3, 177-yard 11th hole plays over part of the canyon and is particularly scenic.

NOTES: Marshall Canyon has a remodeled grass driving range.

LOCATION: Take Interstate 210 east to Wheeler; then go north to Golden Hills. Go east on Golden Hills to Stephens Ranch Road and north to the course.

. . . ● **TOURNAMENTS:** A 16-player minimum is needed to book a tournament.

27. MARSHALL CANYON GOLF CLUB

PLAY POLICY & FEES: Members and guests only. Guests must be accompanied by a member at time of play. Guest fees are $50. Carts are $20. The course is closed on Monday.

DRESS CODE: Men must wear collared shirts. Jeans are not allowed. Women's skirts must be no shorter than four inches above the knee. No halter or tank tops are allowed. Nonmetal spikes are mandatory.

COURSE DESCRIPTION: This is a course for shot-makers. It requires precision iron play and a great imagination on and around the greens. The fairways are medium width over rolling terrain. A fair number of bunkers surround the well-groomed, fast greens. It is a right-to-left course favoring players who hook the ball.

NOTES: The course hosts the Hustlers Invitational Tournament in April, the Mr. and Mrs. Invitational in August, and the Tres Dias in September.

LOCATION: From Los Angeles travel on Interstate 10 (San Bernardino Freeway) to the Citrus Avenue exit and drive south for one mile to the club at the Lark Hill Drive intersection.

. . . ● **TOURNAMENTS:** A 100-player minimum is required to book a tournament. Carts are required. Tournament fees are $140 per person. Tournaments should be booked four months in advance.

28. SOUTH HILLS COUNTRY CLUB

ARCHITECT: LAWRENCE HUGHES, 1968

1400 Avenida Entrada
San Dimas, CA 91773

PRO SHOP: 909-599-8486

Tim R. Haas, Director of Golf, PGA
Rafael Martinez, Superintendent

Driving Range ●
Practice Greens ●
Clubhouse ●
Food / Beverage ●
Accommodations
Pull Carts ●
Power Carts
Club Rental ●
$pecial Offers

	1	2	3	4	5	6	7	8	9	OUT
BACK	355	517	197	412	368	551	359	379	170	3308
REGULAR	345	500	166	400	356	540	351	370	162	3190
par	4	5	3	4	4	5	4	4	3	36
handicap	15	13	11	1	7	3	5	9	17	-
FORWARD	330	476	155	349	345	468	326	361	150	2960
par	4	5	3	4	4	5	4	4	3	36
handicap	13	3	17	1	9	7	5	11	15	-

	10	11	12	13	14	15	16	17	18	IN
BACK	495	173	321	187	354	349	374	376	496	3125
REGULAR	482	161	318	169	346	337	366	362	484	3025
par	5	3	4	3	4	4	4	4	5	36
handicap	10	14	16	18	6	2	12	4	8	-
FORWARD	439	156	316	163	328	280	360	309	391	2742
par	5	3	4	3	4	4	4	4	5	36
handicap	6	16	12	18	4	14	2	8	10	-

BACK	
yardage	6433
par	72
rating	70.9
slope	124

REGULAR	
yardage	6215
par	72
rating	69.3
slope	120

FORWARD	
yardage	5702
par	72
rating	73.7
slope	126

ARCHITECT: TED ROBINSON, 1975

1875 Fairplex Drive
Pomona, CA 91768

PRO SHOP: 909-623-3704
STARTER: 909-629-1166

Brian Bode, Director of Golf, PGA
Joe Lerma, Superintendent
John Van Blitter, Tournament Director

Driving Range ●
Practice Greens ●
Clubhouse ●
Food / Beverage ●
Accommodations
Pull Carts ●
Power Carts ●
Club Rental ●
$pecial Offers

	1	2	3	4	5	6	7	8	9	OUT
BACK	523	353	344	384	438	179	365	514	162	3262
REGULAR	509	346	331	362	424	157	355	493	145	3122
par	5	4	4	4	4	3	4	5	3	36
handicap	7	5	11	3	1	13	9	17	15	-
FORWARD	461	313	319	342	355	136	333	469	128	2856
par	5	4	4	4	4	3	4	5	3	36
handicap	5	3	13	7	11	15	9	1	17	-

	10	11	12	13	14	15	16	17	18	IN
BACK	372	476	370	213	356	490	365	159	377	3178
REGULAR	342	460	343	200	335	464	344	145	358	2991
par	4	5	4	3	4	5	4	3	4	36
handicap	14	10	2	4	8	18	12	16	6	-
FORWARD	319	422	242	150	302	441	321	128	338	2663
par	4	5	4	3	4	5	4	3	4	36
handicap	12	2	4	16	8	6	10	18	14	-

BACK	
yardage	6440
par	72
rating	70.4
slope	120

REGULAR	
yardage	6113
par	72
rating	68.7
slope	113

FORWARD	
yardage	5519
par	72
rating	71.4
slope	122

PLAY POLICY & FEES: Reciprocal play is accepted, otherwise members and guests only. Reciprocal and guest fees are $30 weekdays and $50 weekends. Carts are $10 per person.

DRESS CODE: Appropriate golf attire is required.

COURSE DESCRIPTION: This course, set on a hill, is well bunkered with narrow fairways and rolling terrain. It is set within a residential community. The greens are extremely fast and usually in excellent condition. Water comes into play on two holes. It is primarily a target golf course; accuracy is imperative.

NOTES: Via Verde features a brand-new clubhouse and banquet facility that can seat 400 people.

LOCATION: From San Bernardino drive west on Interstate 10 (San Bernardino Freeway) to the Via Verde exit. Drive north one mile to Avenida Entrada and turn left. Drive three-fourths of a mile to the end and turn left to the club.

. . . ● **TOURNAMENTS:** This course is available for outside tournaments on Monday. A 72-player minimum is needed to book an event. The banquet facility can accommodate 400 people. Carts are required. ● **TRAVEL:** The Sheraton Suites at Fairplex is located 15 minutes from the golf course. For reservations call 909-622-2220.

29. VIA VERDE COUNTRY CLUB

PLAY POLICY & FEES: Green fees are $20 weekdays and $25 weekends. Carts are $22.

TEE TIMES: Reservations can be booked seven days in advance.

DRESS CODE: No tank tops or short shorts are allowed.

COURSE DESCRIPTION: This is a hilly course with numerous trees flanking the fairways. For scenery and difficulty, watch out for the 13th. It's a 213-yard par 3 over a canyon, overlooking part of the San Gabriel Valley.

NOTES: This course was awarded the Los Angeles County Course of the Year three out of the last six years.

LOCATION: Travel on Interstate 10 (San Bernardino Freeway) to the Fairplex Drive exit. Go north on Fairplex for about one mile to the club.

. . . ● **TOURNAMENTS:** Shotgun tournaments are available. A 24-player minimum is needed to book a regular tournament. Events should be booked 12 months in advance. The banquet facility holds 300 people. ● **TRAVEL:** The Sheraton Fairplex is recommended for lodging.

30. MOUNTAIN MEADOWS GOLF COURSE

31 CLAREMONT GOLF COURSE

1550 N. Indian Hill Blvd.
Claremont, CA 91711

PRO SHOP: 909-624-2748

Dennis E. Bishop, President
Bruce Thompson, Golf Instructor

Driving Range ●
Practice Greens ●
Clubhouse
Food / Beverage ●
Accommodations
Pull Carts ●
Power Carts ●
Club Rental ●
$pecial Offers

	1	2	3	4	5	6	7	8	9	OUT
BACK	-	-	-	-	-	-	-	-	-	-
REGULAR	102	146	123	273	223	389	239	108	82	1685
par	3	3	3	4	3	4	3	3	3	29
handicap	7	5	6	4	3	1	2	8	9	-
FORWARD	102	146	123	273	223	389	239	108	82	1685
par	3	3	3	4	4	4	4	3	3	31
handicap	7	5	6	2	4	1	3	8	9	-

	10	11	12	13	14	15	16	17	18	IN
BACK	-	-	-	-	-	-	-	-	-	-
REGULAR	117	165	149	298	263	426	274	124	99	1915
par	3	3	3	4	4	4	4	3	3	31
handicap	7	5	6	2	4	1	3	8	9	-
FORWARD	117	165	149	298	263	426	274	124	99	1915
par	3	3	3	4	4	5	4	3	3	32
handicap	7	5	6	2	4	1	3	8	9	-

BACK	
yardage	-
par	-
rating	-
slope	-

REGULAR	
yardage	3600
par	60
rating	-
slope	-

FORWARD	
yardage	3600
par	63
rating	-
slope	-

32 UPLAND HILLS COUNTRY CLUB
ARCHITECT: DAVID RAINVILLE, 1983

1231 East 16th Street
Upland, CA 91786

PRO SHOP: 909-946-4711
CLUBHOUSE: 909-946-3057

Brian Bode, Head Professional
Carol Gundlach, Superintendent

Driving Range ●
Practice Greens ●
Clubhouse ●
Food / Beverage ●
Accommodations
Pull Carts ●
Power Carts ●
Club Rental ●
$pecial Offers

	1	2	3	4	5	6	7	8	9	OUT
BACK	-	-	-	-	-	-	-	-	-	-
REGULAR	373	379	320	477	343	186	404	138	328	2948
par	4	4	4	5	4	3	4	3	4	35
handicap	5	3	15	11	7	13	1	17	9	-
FORWARD	317	308	257	425	287	145	359	106	259	2463
par	4	4	4	5	4	3	4	3	4	35
handicap	5	7	13	3	11	15	1	17	9	-

	10	11	12	13	14	15	16	17	18	IN
BACK	-	-	-	-	-	-	-	-	-	-
REGULAR	359	166	336	422	352	545	158	379	339	3056
par	4	3	4	4	4	5	3	4	4	35
handicap	10	18	14	2	12	6	16	4	8	-
FORWARD	307	137	279	340	287	475	123	320	279	2547
par	4	3	4	4	4	5	3	4	4	35
handicap	8	18	14	2	12	4	16	6	10	-

BACK	
yardage	-
par	-
rating	-
slope	-

REGULAR	
yardage	6004
par	70
rating	67.1
slope	111

FORWARD	
yardage	5010
par	70
rating	66.5
slope	106

PLAY POLICY & FEES: Green fees are $9 for nine holes and $14 for 18 holes on weekdays. Weekend green fees are $10 for nine holes and $17 for 18 holes on weekends. Senior and junior rates are available all week, and ladies' rates are available on Wednesday.

TEE TIMES: Reservations can be made seven days in advance.

DRESS CODE: Casual attire is OK, but no tank tops or short shorts are allowed on the course.

COURSE DESCRIPTION: This challenging nine-hole course has two sets of tee boxes so that the course can be played as 18 holes. The hardest hole on the course is the sixth hole from the blue tees, a 426-yard par-4 dogleg left.

LOCATION: The course is located 40 miles east of Los Angeles. From Los Angeles take Interstate 10 east to Indian Hill Boulevard exit. Drive north on Indian Hill Boulevard for three miles to the course.

. . . ● **TOURNAMENTS:** Claremont is available for outside events. Tournaments should be scheduled at least one month in advance. ● **TRAVEL:** The Claremont Inn is located just two blocks from the course. For reservations call 909-626-2411.

31. CLAREMONT GOLF COURSE

PLAY POLICY & FEES: Outside play is accepted. Monday through Thursday green fees are $23 walking, and $34 with a cart. Friday green fees are $25 walking and $36 with a cart. Green fees are $45 weekends and holidays including a cart. Twilight rates are available

TEE TIMES: Reservations can be booked nine days in advance.

DRESS CODE: No jeans or cutoffs are allowed on the course; collared shirts are mandatory.

COURSE DESCRIPTION: Located in the foothills, this relatively young course is fairly flat and easy to walk. Six lakes and fast greens make it a challenge. It is short and tight, causing lots of trouble, but it's always in good condition. Out-of-bounds line both sides of the fairways on 15 holes.

NOTES: The course record is 59.

LOCATION: Travel east on Interstate 10 (San Bernardino Freeway) to Euclid Avenue in Upland. Turn north to 16th Street; then head east for one mile to the club.

. . . ● **TOURNAMENTS:** A 16-player minimum is required to book a tournament.

32. UPLAND HILLS COUNTRY CLUB

33 RED HILL COUNTRY CLUB
ARCHITECT: GEORGE C. THOMAS, 1921

8358 Red Hill Country Club
Rancho Cucamonga, CA
91730
PRO SHOP: 909-982-1358

James Porter, PGA Professional
Ernie Pacheco, Superintendent

Driving Range ●
Practice Greens ●
Clubhouse ●
Food / Beverage ●
Accommodations
Pull Carts ●
Power Carts ●
Club Rental
$pecial Offers

	1	2	3	4	5	6	7	8	9	OUT
BACK										
REGULAR										
par										
handicap										
FORWARD										
par										
handicap										

	10	11	12	13	14	15	16	17	18	IN
BACK										
REGULAR										
par										
handicap										
FORWARD										
par										
handicap										

BACK	
yardage	6613
par	72
rating	72.1
slope	125

REGULAR	
yardage	6391
par	72
rating	70.4
slope	119

FORWARD	
yardage	6020
par	72
rating	75.0
slope	130

34 EMPIRE LAKES GOLF COURSE
ARCHITECT: ARNOLD PALMER, 1996

11015 6th Street
Rancho Cucamonga, CA
91730
PRO SHOP: 909-481-6663

Michael Lautenbach, Director of Golf
Pat Truchan, Superintendent

Driving Range ●
Practice Greens ●
Clubhouse ●
Food / Beverage ●
Accommodations
Pull Carts
Power Carts ●
Club Rental ●
$pecial Offers ●

	1	2	3	4	5	6	7	8	9	OUT
BACK	403	159	334	364	533	388	206	530	432	3349
REGULAR	381	153	320	356	524	362	194	521	407	3218
par	4	3	4	4	5	4	3	5	4	36
handicap	5	15	9	11	7	13	3	17	1	-
FORWARD	324	112	244	275	405	294	150	414	317	2535
par	4	3	4	4	5	4	3	5	4	36
handicap	5	15	9	11	7	13	3	17	1	-

	10	11	12	13	14	15	16	17	18	IN
BACK	404	601	460	397	169	420	381	225	517	3574
REGULAR	382	576	449	367	164	411	357	214	490	3410
par	4	5	4	4	3	4	4	3	5	36
handicap	12	2	6	14	18	10	16	4	8	-
FORWARD	300	453	342	281	137	337	256	158	401	2665
par	4	5	4	4	3	4	4	3	5	36
handicap	12	2	6	14	18	10	16	4	8	-

BACK	
yardage	6923
par	72
rating	73.4
slope	133

REGULAR	
yardage	6628
par	72
rating	68.8
slope	124

FORWARD	
yardage	5200
par	72
rating	70.5
slope	125

PLAY POLICY & FEES: Members and guests only. Guests must be accompanied by a member at time of play. Guest fees are $50. Carts are $20.

DRESS CODE: Appropriate golf attire and nonmetal spikes are required.

COURSE DESCRIPTION: This deceptive course offers a challenging test. It's a traditional layout, void of railroad ties or other gimmicks. There are lots of trees and undulating greens. Watch out for the two ponds that have been incorporated into the seventh and eighth holes.

LOCATION: Take Interstate 10 (San Bernardino Freeway) to the Euclid Avenue exit (west of San Bernardino) and drive north to Foothill Boulevard. Turn right and drive 1.5 miles to Red Hill Country Club Drive and turn left to the club.

. . . ● TOURNAMENTS: This course authorizes 20 outside events a year. A 100-player minimum is needed to book an event.

33. RED HILL COUNTRY CLUB

PLAY POLICY & FEES: Green fees are $55 Monday through Thursday and $80 Friday through Sunday. Twilight rates are available. Carts are included in all green fees.

TEE TIMES: Reservations can be booked seven days in advance.

DRESS CODE: Collared shirts and nonmetal spikes are required. No blue jeans are allowed on the course.

COURSE DESCRIPTION: This course has undulations in the fairways and greens with finger-shaped bunkers throughout. If you're hitting your driver remotely straight, bring it on because the fairways are wide open. For those with a driver that refuses to do anything but hook or slice, keep it in the bag, or you'll find yourself trying to hack back into the fairway.

LOCATION: From Interstate 10 in Ontario take the Haven exit. Follow Haven north one mile to Sixth Street. Take a right on Sixth; the course is on the right.

. . . ● TOURNAMENTS: A 13-player minimum is needed to book a tournament. The banquet facility can accommodate up to 200 people. ● TRAVEL: The Ontario Hiltion is located five minutes from the golf course. For reservations call 909-980-0400. ● $PECIAL OFFERS: Play-and-stay packages with the Ontario Hiltion include: accommodations, green fees, golf towel, a sleeve of golf balls, range balls, and transportation. Other play-and-stay packages with nearby hotels are available. Call the pro shop for more information.

34. EMPIRE LAKES GOLF COURSE

MONTEBELLO GOLF COURSE
ARCHITECT: MAX BEHR, 1928

901 Via San Clemente
Montebello, CA 90640

PRO SHOP: 323-887-4565

Thomas Camacho, Professional/Manager
Ted Spaceff, Superintendent

Driving Range ●
Practice Greens ●
Clubhouse ●
Food / Beverage ●
Accommodations
Pull Carts ●
Power Carts ●
Club Rental
$pecial Offers

	1	2	3	4	5	6	7	8	9	OUT
BACK	437	421	531	461	447	157	380	404	105	3343
REGULAR	406	388	501	400	408	140	341	369	96	3049
par	4	4	5	4	4	3	4	4	3	35
handicap	11	7	15	1	3	9	13	5	17	-
FORWARD	376	374	467	380	385	126	319	336	89	2852
par	4	4	5	4	4	3	4	4	3	35
handicap	9	7	5	3	1	15	11	13	17	-

	10	11	12	13	14	15	16	17	18	IN
BACK	371	478	351	366	216	382	155	496	458	3273
REGULAR	353	445	320	339	178	347	137	460	402	2981
par	4	5	4	4	3	4	3	5	4	36
handicap	8	16	10	14	16	18	8	6	4	-
FORWARD	326	422	294	314	156	324	125	434	377	2772
par	4	5	4	4	3	4	3	5	4	36
handicap	12	2	10	14	16	18	8	6	4	-

BACK	
yardage	6616
par	71
rating	71.6
slope	124

REGULAR	
yardage	6030
par	71
rating	68.9
slope	119

FORWARD	
yardage	5624
par	71
rating	71.8
slope	121

CALIFORNIA COUNTRY CLUB
ARCHITECT: WILLIAM P. BELL, 1956

P.O. Box 31
Whittier, CA 90680

1509 S. Workman Mill
Whittier, CA 90601

PRO SHOP: 626-968-4222

Donald Brubaker, PGA Professional
Bob Johnson, Superintendent

Driving Range ●
Practice Greens ●
Clubhouse ●
Food / Beverage ●
Accommodations
Pull Carts
Power Carts ●
Club Rental ●
$pecial Offers

	1	2	3	4	5	6	7	8	9	OUT
BACK	506	151	356	461	176	387	359	381	501	3278
REGULAR	503	141	344	448	138	375	353	356	487	3145
par	5	3	4	4	3	4	4	4	5	36
handicap	9	11	15	1	17	13	5	3	7	-
FORWARD	501	129	323	438	127	323	342	338	478	2999
par	5	3	4	5	3	4	4	4	5	37
handicap	1	15	11	5	17	13	7	9	3	-

	10	11	12	13	14	15	16	17	18	IN
BACK	167	567	417	454	427	337	480	214	463	3526
REGULAR	152	555	401	444	411	317	468	186	452	3386
par	3	5	4	4	4	4	5	3	4	36
handicap	18	10	8	6	2	14	16	12	4	-
FORWARD	129	545	351	438	372	297	409	170	387	3098
par	3	5	4	5	4	4	5	3	4	37
handicap	18	2	8	12	6	16	10	14	4	-

BACK	
yardage	6804
par	72
rating	72.7
slope	128

REGULAR	
yardage	6531
par	72
rating	70.9
slope	121

FORWARD	
yardage	6097
par	74
rating	75.2
slope	129

PLAY POLICY & FEES: Green fees are $28 weekdays and $38 weekends. Carts are $12.

TEE TIMES: Reservations can be booked seven days in advance on weekdays and on Monday morning for that weekend.

DRESS CODE: Collared shirts and nonmetal spikes are required.

COURSE DESCRIPTION: Built in 1928, this flat course is one of the better-maintained courses in the area. It is fairly long for a public course. Trees line many of the fairways, placing a premium on accuracy off the tee.

NOTES: The course underwent major renovations in 1999. Three new lakes were added as well as many new bunkers, and the course has all new greens.

LOCATION: In Montebello, traveling on Highway 60 (Pomona Freeway), exit at Garfield Avenue and drive south for one block. Turn right on Via San Clemente at the club sign.

. . . ● **TOURNAMENTS:** A 24-player minimum is needed for a tournament and events should be booked four to six months in advance. The banquet facilities can accommodate up to 1200 people.

35. MONTEBELLO GOLF COURSE

PLAY POLICY & FEES: Reciprocal play is allowed on a limited basis, otherwise, Members and guests only. Green fees are $43 weekdays and $70 weekends. Carts are $20.

DRESS CODE: Appropriate golf attire is required, and nonmetal spikes are encouraged.

COURSE DESCRIPTION: This is a mostly flat course except for a few elevated tees. Water hazards are minimal. Built in the old traditional style, it plays extremely long, although it is fairly wide open.

LOCATION: From Los Angeles travel on Highway 60 (Pomona Freeway) east to the Crossroads Parkway exit; head left over freeway. Turn left at the stoplight onto Workman Mill Road. Turn right and go to Coleford Avenue, then left to the club.

. . . ● **TOURNAMENTS:** This course is available for outside tournaments on Monday, Thursday, and Friday. A 24-player minimum is needed to book an event. Carts are required.

36. CALIFORNIA COUNTRY CLUB

901 South 6th Avenue
Hacienda Heights, CA
91745
PRO S HOP: 626-968-2338

Judy and Harold Hink, Managers

Driving Range
Practice Greens ●
Clubhouse ●
Food / Beverage
Accommodations
Pull Carts
Power Carts
Club Rental
$pecial Offers

	1	2	3	4	5	6	7	8	9	OUT
BACK	-	-	-	-	-	-	-	-	-	-
REGULAR	63	128	123	116	143	175	133	193	116	1190
par	3	3	3	3	3	3	3	3	3	27
handicap	17	5	11	15	9	1	7	3	13	-
FORWARD	63	128	123	116	143	175	133	137	116	1134
par	3	3	3	3	3	3	3	3	3	27
handicap	17	7	11	15	9	1	3	5	13	-

	10	11	12	13	14	15	16	17	18	IN
BACK	-	-	-	-	-	-	-	-	-	-
REGULAR	63	128	123	116	143	175	133	193	116	1190
par	3	3	3	3	3	3	3	3	3	27
handicap	18	6	12	16	10	2	8	4	14	-
FORWARD	63	128	123	116	143	175	133	193	116	1190
par	3	3	3	3	3	3	3	3	3	27
handicap	18	8	12	16	10	2	4	6	14	-

BACK	
yardage	-
par	-
rating	-
slope	-

REGULAR	
yardage	2380
par	54
rating	-
slope	-

FORWARD	
yardage	2324
par	54
rating	-
slope	-

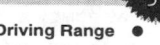

1 Industry Hills Parkway
City of Industry, CA 91744

PRO S HOP: 626-810-4653

David Youpa, Director of Golf, PGA
Detlef Reck, General Manager

Driving Range ●
Practice Greens ●
Clubhouse ●
Food / Beverage ●
Accommodations ●
Pull Carts
Power Carts ●
Club Rental ●
$pecial Offers

	1	2	3	4	5	6	7	8	9	OUT
BACK	504	345	342	446	206	460	437	490	130	3360
REGULAR	487	335	314	418	136	413	415	472	126	3116
par	5	4	4	4	3	4	4	5	3	36
handicap	11	9	7	3	15	1	5	13	17	-
FORWARD	460	266	295	383	115	351	371	397	94	2732
par	5	4	4	4	3	4	4	5	3	36
handicap	7	3	13	11	17	1	5	9	15	-

	10	11	12	13	14	15	16	17	18	IN
BACK	529	330	462	194	360	154	403	325	618	3375
REGULAR	489	318	450	167	325	138	393	297	569	3146
par	5	4	4	3	4	3	4	4	5	36
handicap	8	12	2	14	10	18	4	16	6	-
FORWARD	458	265	430	141	311	115	356	275	505	2856
par	5	4	5	3	4	3	4	4	5	37
handicap	4	14	2	16	10	18	8	12	6	-

BACK	
yardage	6735
par	72
rating	73.5
slope	138

REGULAR	
yardage	6262
par	72
rating	70.9
slope	130

FORWARD	
yardage	5588
par	73
rating	73.0
slope	126

PLAY POLICY & FEES: Members and guests only. This is a resident course. Memberships are available at $56 per year. There are no daily fees.

COURSE DESCRIPTION: This mostly flat course can be intimidating because it is so narrow. There's a fence on one side and mobile homes on the other. Only two holes measure more than 150 yards, so it's a good chance to fine-tune your irons.

LOCATION: This course is located off Highway 60 (Pomona Freeway) in Hacienda Heights. Take the Seventh Avenue exit north. At the first light, turn left on Clark Street, which runs into the course.

. . . ● **TOURNAMENTS:** This course is not available for outside events.

37. WILDWOOD MOBILE COUNTRY CLUB

PLAY POLICY & FEES: Green fees are $50 Monday through Thursday and $65 Friday, Saturday, Sunday, and holidays. Fees include carts. Reservations are recommended.

TEE TIMES: Reservations can be booked three days in advance.

DRESS CODE: Appropriate golf attire and nonmetal spikes are required.

COURSE DESCRIPTION: The Eisenhower Course has been rated one of the top 25 public courses in the United States by "Golf Digest." It's long and extremely demanding. The greens are huge, but they're often tiered and undulating. The Zaharias Course is tighter and trickier. A shot-maker will excel here. Both courses cover rolling and hilly terrain and make use of a funicular, imported from Switzerland, to transport players.

NOTES: This public club has two 18-hole courses. Par is 72 on the Eisenhower Course and 71 on the Zaharias Course. The Eisenhower Course: See scorecard for yardage and rating information. The Zaharias Course is 6,600 yards and rated 72.9 from the championship tees with a slope of 137. The U.S. Open qualifying is frequently held here.

LOCATION: Travel on Highway 60 (Pomona Freeway) to the Azusa Avenue exit north. Drive 1.5 miles and turn left on Industry Hills Parkway and continue to the club. From Interstate 10 (San Bernardino Freeway), take the Azusa Avenue exit; drive south on Azusa for three miles and turn right on Industry Hills Parkway to the club.

. . . ● **TOURNAMENTS:** This course is available for outside tournaments.

38. INDUSTRY HILLS GOLF CLUB

39 FORD PARK GOLF COURSE

8000 Park Lane
Bell Gardens, CA 90202

PRO SHOP: 562-927-8811

Rick Romas, Manager

Driving Range
Practice Greens ●
Clubhouse
Food / Beverage ●
Accommodations
Pull Carts ●
Power Carts
Club Rental
$pecial Offers

	1	2	3	4	5	6	7	8	9	OUT
BACK										
REGULAR										
par										
handicap										
FORWARD										
par										
handicap										

BACK	
yardage	
par	
rating	
slope	

	10	11	12	13	14	15	16	17	18	IN
BACK										
REGULAR										
par										
handicap										
FORWARD										
par										
handicap										

REGULAR	
yardage	1017
par	27
rating	
slope	

FORWARD	
yardage	
par	
rating	
slope	

40 SOUTH GATE MUNICIPAL GOLF COURSE
ARCHITECT: WILLIAM H. JOHNSON, 1948

9615 Pinehurst Avenue
South Gate, CA 90280

PRO SHOP: 323-357-9613

Art Pedrosa, Golf Instructor
Ruth McAllister, Senior Starter
Cindy Tally, Superintendent

Driving Range
Practice Greens ●
Clubhouse
Food / Beverage ●
Accommodations
Pull Carts ●
Power Carts
Club Rental ●
$pecial Offers

	1	2	3	4	5	6	7	8	9	OUT
BACK	-	-	-	-	-	-	-	-	-	-
REGULAR	82	99	105	102	100	120	136	156	110	1010
par	3	3	3	3	3	3	3	3	3	27
handicap	17	15	9	11	13	5	3	1	7	-
FORWARD	82	99	105	102	100	120	136	156	110	1010
par	3	3	3	3	3	3	3	3	3	27
handicap	17	15	9	11	13	5	3	1	7	-

BACK	
yardage	-
par	-
rating	-
slope	-

	10	11	12	13	14	15	16	17	18	IN
BACK	-	-	-	-	-	-	-	-	-	-
REGULAR	82	99	105	102	100	120	136	156	110	1010
par	3	3	3	3	3	3	3	3	3	27
handicap	18	16	10	12	14	6	4	2	8	-
FORWARD	82	99	105	102	100	120	136	156	110	1010
par	3	3	3	3	3	3	3	3	3	27
handicap	18	16	10	12	14	6	4	2	8	-

REGULAR	
yardage	2020
par	54
rating	-
slope	-

FORWARD	
yardage	2020
par	54
rating	-
slope	-

PLAY POLICY & FEES: Green fees are $3.75 weekdays and $4 weekends. Juniors and seniors are $2 weekdays.

TEE TIMES: Reservations are not accepted. All play is on a first-come, first-served basis.

COURSE DESCRIPTION: This is a short, par-3 course, excellent for working on your short game. Leave your woods and long irons at home.

LOCATION: In Bell Gardens take the Garfield Avenue exit off Interstate 5 and travel west about three miles to Park Lane. From there, take a right and you'll see the course.

. . . ● **TOURNAMENTS:** This course is available for outside tournaments.

39. FORD PARK GOLF COURSE

PLAY POLICY & FEES: Green fees are $4 weekdays and $5 weekends for nine holes. Senior bargain rates are available. Call for information.

TEE TIMES: Reservations are not accepted. All play is on a first-come, first-served basis.

COURSE DESCRIPTION: This short par-3 course is excellent for sharpening your short game. The longest hole, the eighth, measures 156 yards. Several large trees come into play.

LOCATION: From Highway 710 in South Gate take the Imperial Highway off-ramp to Wright Road. The road merges into Atlantic Avenue. Turn left on Tweedy Boulevard, then right onto Pinehurst Avenue. The course is on the left.

. . . ● **TOURNAMENTS:** A 36-player minimum is needed to book a tournament.

40. SOUTH GATE MUNICIPAL GOLF COURSE

41 RIO HONDO GOLF CLUB

ARCHITECTS: JOHN DUNCAN DUNN, 1923; GERRY PERKL, 1994

10629 Old River School
Downey, CA 90241

PRO SHOP: 562-927-2329
STARTER: 562-927-2420

Bruce MacDonald, Head Professional, PGA
Scott Wally, Tournament Director
John Rodriquez, Superintendent

Driving Range •
Practice Greens •
Clubhouse •
Food / Beverage •
Accommodations
Pull Carts •
Power Carts •
Club Rental •
$pecial Offers

	1	2	3	4	5	6	7	8	9	OUT
BACK	418	403	492	535	403	342	165	232	416	3406
REGULAR	401	390	471	495	393	326	146	218	393	3233
par	4	4	5	5	4	4	3	3	4	36
handicap	9	11	5	1	7	13	17	15	3	-
FORWARD	340	336	409	418	339	277	118	191	344	2772
par	4	4	5	5	4	4	3	3	4	36
handicap	7	9	3	1	11	13	17	15	5	-

	10	11	12	13	14	15	16	17	18	IN
BACK	194	490	310	368	204	489	321	138	424	2938
REGULAR	174	478	296	354	165	477	310	117	406	2777
par	3	5	4	4	3	5	4	3	4	35
handicap	14	2	16	8	10	6	12	18	4	-
FORWARD	131	413	275	285	124	412	243	79	346	2308
par	3	5	4	4	3	5	4	3	4	35
handicap	16	4	10	12	18	2	8	14	6	-

BACK	
yardage	6344
par	71
rating	70.2
slope	119

REGULAR	
yardage	6010
par	71
rating	68.5
slope	115

FORWARD	
yardage	5080
par	71
rating	69.4
slope	117

42 LOS AMIGOS COUNTRY CLUB

ARCHITECT: RON RIEGE, 1965

7295 Quill Drive
Downey, CA 90242

PRO SHOP: 562-862-1717
STARTER: 562-869-0302

Don Duffin, Manager
Frank Gomez, Head Professional, PGA
LaVern Hockett, Tournament Director

Driving Range •
Practice Greens •
Clubhouse •
Food / Beverage •
Accommodations
Pull Carts •
Power Carts •
Club Rental •
$pecial Offers

	1	2	3	4	5	6	7	8	9	OUT
BACK	512	402	160	364	377	376	151	493	240	3075
REGULAR	486	383	144	354	368	350	137	477	227	2926
par	5	4	3	4	4	4	3	5	3	35
handicap	5	1	15	3	7	11	17	13	9	-
FORWARD	499	370	145	346	362	350	132	486	225	2915
par	5	4	3	4	4	4	3	5	4	36
handicap	1	5	15	9	7	11	17	3	13	-

	10	11	12	13	14	15	16	17	18	IN
BACK	333	314	119	398	335	495	370	187	380	2931
REGULAR	318	304	109	358	324	466	359	171	359	2768
par	4	4	3	4	4	5	4	3	4	35
handicap	16	14	18	2	4	10	6	12	8	-
FORWARD	315	303	115	366	319	473	351	149	340	2731
par	4	4	3	4	4	5	4	3	4	35
handicap	12	14	18	6	10	2	4	16	8	-

BACK	
yardage	6006
par	70
rating	67.5
slope	110

REGULAR	
yardage	5694
par	70
rating	66.4
slope	108

FORWARD	
yardage	5646
par	71
rating	71.5
slope	112

PLAY POLICY & FEES: Green fees are $30 weekdays and $40 weekends. Carts are $22.

TEE TIMES: Reservations can be booked seven days in advance.

DRESS CODE: Collared shirts and nonmetal spikes are required.

COURSE DESCRIPTION: This is a level course with narrow, tree-lined fairways. Architect Gerry Perkl directed an extensive remodeling program that included the addition of four lakes and a new irrigation system. The course has been lengthened by 400 yards. It reopened in 1994 with new bentgrass greens.

LOCATION: Take Interstate 710 (Long Beach Freeway) in Downey to the Firestone Boulevard exit. Drive east for one mile to Old River School Road. Turn left and continue a half mile to the club.

. . . ● **TOURNAMENTS:** Shotgun tournaments are available weekdays only. Carts are required. A 24-player minimum is required to book a regular tournament. Events should be scheduled 12 months in advance. The banquet facility can accommodate 400 people. ● **TRAVEL:** The Embassy Suites is located five minutes from the course. For reservations call 562-861-1900.

41. RIO HONDO GOLF CLUB

PLAY POLICY & FEES: Green fees are $19 weekdays and $23 weekends. Senior rates are available. Carts are $22.

TEE TIMES: Reservations can be booked seven days in advance.

DRESS CODE: No tank tops are allowed.

COURSE DESCRIPTION: This is a well-maintained public golf facility with large greens. It plays long, requiring significant approach shots to reach the greens in regulation. The greens can be quick when baked under the hot summer sun. Water comes into play frequently.

NOTES: This is one of the busier courses in Southern California with about 135,000 rounds played annually.

LOCATION: From the Long Beach Freeway (Interstate 710) take the Imperial Highway east to Old River School Road. Turn left to the course on Quill Drive.

. . . ● **TOURNAMENTS:** Shotgun tournaments are available weekdays only. A 24-player minimum is required to book a tournament.

42. LOS AMIGOS COUNTRY CLUB

ARCHITECT: H. RAINVILLE, D. RAINVILLE, 1952

14000 E. Telegraph Road
Whittier, CA 90604

PRO SHOP: 562-941-5310
CLUBHOUSE: 562-941-1228

Rudy Sangston, General Manager
Mark Blakely, PGA Professional
Mike Caranci, Superintendent

Driving Range ●
Practice Greens ●
Clubhouse ●
Food / Beverage ●
Accommodations
Pull Carts
Power Carts ●
Club Rental ●
$pecial Offers

	1	2	3	4	5	6	7	8	9	OUT
BACK	382	379	181	348	388	371	555	170	328	3102
REGULAR	374	355	150	327	377	371	545	140	304	2943
par	4	4	3	4	4	4	5	3	4	35
handicap	7	5	13	11	3	9	1	17	15	-
FORWARD	367	342	118	320	361	365	536	124	303	2836
par	4	4	3	4	4	4	5	3	4	35
handicap	7	11	17	9	3	5	1	15	13	-

	10	11	12	13	14	15	16	17	18	IN
BACK	145	557	391	206	377	421	379	328	283	3087
REGULAR	135	529	381	189	364	401	369	328	273	2969
par	3	5	4	3	4	4	4	4	4	35
handicap	18	2	6	14	8	4	10	12	16	-
FORWARD	130	522	378	185	355	363	363	319	269	2884
par	3	5	4	3	4	4	4	4	4	35
handicap	16	2	4	14	8	6	10	12	18	-

BACK	
yardage	6189
par	70
rating	69.3
slope	120

REGULAR	
yardage	5912
par	70
rating	68.1
slope	117

FORWARD	
yardage	5720
par	70
rating	74.0
slope	128

13717 Shoemaker Avenue
Norwalk, CA 90650

PRO SHOP: 562-921-6500

Ken McCreary, Manager
Tom Whieldon, Professional
Mike Webb, Superintendent

Driving Range ●
Practice Greens ●
Clubhouse
Food / Beverage ●
Accommodations
Pull Carts ●
Power Carts
Club Rental ●
$pecial Offers

	1	2	3	4	5	6	7	8	9	OUT
BACK										
REGULAR										
par										
handicap										
FORWARD										
par										
handicap										

	10	11	12	13	14	15	16	17	18	IN
BACK										
REGULAR										
par										
handicap										
FORWARD										
par										
handicap										

BACK	
yardage	
par	
rating	
slope	

REGULAR	
yardage	1990
par	27
rating	51.0
slope	-

FORWARD	
yardage	
par	
rating	
slope	

PLAY POLICY & FEES: Reciprocal play is accepted with members of other private clubs (have your pro call to make arrangements); otherwise, members and guests only. Green fees are $45 Monday through Thursday and $55 Friday through Sunday and holidays. Carts are $10.

DRESS CODE: Appropriate golf attire and nonmetal spikes are required.

COURSE DESCRIPTION: Lots of mature trees line the narrow fairways, and a canal runs through the back nine. This course is not especially long, but it can be difficult in spots. Beware of the seventh hole, a par-5, 545-yarder, a double dogleg with water in front of the green. The most difficult shot on this hole is the approach, which most likely will require a short iron over water to the sizable green. But you're hitting downhill with out-of-bounds to the right and left—so beware.

NOTES: Candlewood was the first course to host an LPGA event in 1958. The winner was Patty Berg. The course record is 60.

LOCATION: Travel on Interstate 605 to the Telegraph Road exit east and drive about 3.5 miles to the club.

. . . ● TOURNAMENTS: This course is available for outside events on Monday. A 72-player minimum is needed to book a tournament. Carts are required. Events should be scheduled 12 months in advance. A banquet facility is available that can accommodate 300 people.

43. CANDLEWOOD COUNTRY CLUB

PLAY POLICY & FEES: Green fees are $4.50 weekdays and $5.50 weekends. Juniors and senior rates are offered.

TEE TIMES: Reservations are not accepted. All play is on a first-come, first-served basis.

DRESS CODE: The dress can be casual but should always be appropiate.

COURSE DESCRIPTION: This pitch-and-putt course is excellent for beginners, seniors, and those wishing to practice their short games. The longest hole is 130 yards.

NOTES: This course is lighted for night play.

LOCATION: Off Interstate 5 in Norwalk, exit on Rosecrans Avenue. Go east on Rosecrans to Shoemaker Avenue and left to the course.

. . . ● TOURNAMENTS: A 36-player minimum is needed to book an event.

44. NORWALK GOLF CENTER

45 LA MIRADA GOLF COURSE
ARCHITECT: WILLIAM F. BELL, 1961

15501 East Alicante Road
La Mirada, CA 90638

PRO SHOP: 562-943-7123
CLUBHOUSE: 562-943-3731

Mario Marquez, General Manager
John Mahoney, PGA Professional
Virginia Brunt, Tournament Director

Driving Range ●
Practice Greens ●
Clubhouse ●
Food / Beverage ●
Accommodations
Pull Carts ●
Power Carts ●
Club Rental ●
$pecial Offers

	1	2	3	4	5	6	7	8	9	OUT
BACK	387	384	188	495	158	412	515	426	165	3130
REGULAR	370	368	174	488	150	400	495	421	151	3017
par	4	4	3	5	3	4	5	4	3	35
handicap	9	3	5	13	17	7	11	1	15	-
FORWARD	369	359	163	475	138	384	484	418	143	2933
par	4	4	3	5	3	4	5	4	3	35
handicap	3	9	15	5	13	11	1	7	17	-

	10	11	12	13	14	15	16	17	18	IN
BACK	359	186	550	168	343	326	475	136	371	2914
REGULAR	345	155	532	152	334	306	450	122	357	2753
par	4	3	5	3	4	4	5	3	4	35
handicap	8	4	2	10	16	14	12	18	6	-
FORWARD	339	138	525	148	326	316	431	128	356	2707
par	4	3	5	3	4	4	5	3	4	35
handicap	8	14	2	18	6	10	4	16	12	-

BACK	
yardage	6044
par	70
rating	68.6
slope	114

REGULAR	
yardage	5770
par	70
rating	67.4
slope	111

FORWARD	
yardage	5640
par	70
rating	71.6
slope	117

46 BUENA PARK GOLF CENTER

5151 Beach Boulevard
Buena Park, CA 90621

PRO SHOP: 714-562-0840

John MacMillan, General Manager
Kim Lasken, Tournament Director

Driving Range ●
Practice Greens ●
Clubhouse
Food / Beverage ●
Accommodations
Pull Carts ●
Power Carts ●
Club Rental ●
$pecial Offers

	1	2	3	4	5	6	7	8	9	OUT
BACK	-	-	-	-	-	-	-	-	-	-
REGULAR	96	113	140	115	145	114	131	150	94	1098
par	3	3	3	3	3	3	3	3	3	27
handicap	15	11	1	7	5	13	3	9	17	-
FORWARD	96	113	140	115	145	114	131	150	94	1098
par	3	3	3	3	3	3	3	3	3	27
handicap	15	11	1	7	5	13	3	9	17	-

	10	11	12	13	14	15	16	17	18	IN
BACK	-	-	-	-	-	-	-	-	-	-
REGULAR	96	113	140	115	145	114	131	150	94	1098
par	3	3	3	3	3	3	3	3	3	27
handicap	16	12	2	8	6	14	4	10	18	-
FORWARD	96	113	140	115	145	114	131	150	94	1098
par	3	3	3	3	3	3	3	3	3	27
handicap	16	12	2	8	6	14	4	10	18	-

BACK	
yardage	-
par	-
rating	-
slope	-

REGULAR	
yardage	2196
par	54
rating	-
slope	-

FORWARD	
yardage	2196
par	54
rating	-
slope	-

18
HOLES

PLAY POLICY & FEES: Green fees are $20 weekdays and $25 weekends. Seniors are $10 Monday through Friday. Twilight and junior rates are available. Carts are $22.

TEE TIMES: Reservations can be booked seven days in advance.

DRESS CODE: No tank tops are allowed.

COURSE DESCRIPTION: This is a well-maintained course with some trees. The greens are bunkered on most holes. Water comes into play on one hole, No. 10. The par 5s generally are reachable in two shots for longer hitters. This course permits fivesomes—play can be slow, even during the week, taking up to five hours.

NOTES: The course record of 61 is held by Blaine McAllister. The tournament record of 63 belongs to Tiger Woods.

LOCATION: From Interstate 5 take Highway 39 east to Norwalk Boulevard. Go left on Norwalk for about one mile to La Mirada and follow it to the course.

. . . ● **TOURNAMENTS:** Shotgun tournaments are available weekdays only. A 24-player minimum is required to book a tournament.

45. LA MIRADA GOLF COURSE

9
HOLES

PLAY POLICY & FEES: Green fees are $6.50 on weekdays before 5 p.m. and $7 on weekdays after 5 p.m. Green fees are $7 on weekends for nine holes.

TEE TIMES: Reservations are not accepted. All play is on a first-come, first-served basis.

COURSE DESCRIPTION: This is a beginner course. The eighth hole is the longest at 150 yards. The course is flat and has many trees, as well as lights for night play until 10:30 p.m.

NOTES: The driving range is lighted and covered. For information about lessons, call the Teaching Center at 714-670-1052.

LOCATION: On Highway 91 or Interstate 5 heading east in Buena Park, take the Beach Boulevard exit north and drive four miles to La Mirada Boulevard. The course is located on the corner of La Mirada and Beach Boulevard.

. . . ● **TOURNAMENTS:** This course is available for outside events.

46. BUENA PARK GOLF CENTER

LOS COYOTES COUNTRY CLUB
ARCHITECT: WILLIAM F. BELL, 1958

8888 Los Coyotes Drive
Buena Park, CA 90621

PRO SHOP: 714-523-7780

Chuck Conway, Manager
Bradley Shupe, PGA Professional
Bill Gallegos, Superintendent

Driving Range ●
Practice Greens ●
Clubhouse ●
Food / Beverage ●
Accommodations
Pull Carts
Power Carts ●
Club Rental ●
$pecial Offers

	1	2	3	4	5	6	7	8	9	OUT
BACK	523	176	574	382	182	431	442	426	425	3561
REGULAR	504	158	545	363	170	409	427	404	408	3388
par	5	3	5	4	3	4	4	4	4	36
handicap	11	17	3	13	15	5	1	7	9	-
FORWARD	465	126	449	312	161	382	355	374	368	2992
par	5	3	5	4	3	4	4	4	4	36
handicap	3	17	7	13	15	5	11	1	9	-

	10	11	12	13	14	15	16	17	18	IN
BACK	417	369	193	531	408	401	171	414	504	3408
REGULAR	400	360	185	501	393	392	153	400	478	3262
par	4	4	3	5	4	4	3	4	4	35
handicap	8	16	10	12	4	2	18	6	14	-
FORWARD	388	341	153	481	387	379	137	389	448	3103
par	4	4	3	5	4	4	3	4	5	36
handicap	10	16	14	2	12	4	18	6	8	-

BACK	
yardage	6969
par	71
rating	73.7
slope	129

REGULAR	
yardage	6650
par	71
rating	71.5
slope	119

FORWARD	
yardage	6095
par	72
rating	75.5
slope	130

 ANAHEIM "DAD" MILLER GOLF COURSE
ARCHITECT: DICK MILLER, 1961

430 North Gilbert Street
Anaheim, CA 92801

PRO SHOP: 714-765-3481

Bob Johns, Director of Golf, PGA
Gary Wimberly, Superintendent

Driving Range ●
Practice Greens ●
Clubhouse ●
Food / Beverage ●
Accommodations
Pull Carts ●
Power Carts ●
Club Rental ●
$pecial Offers

	1	2	3	4	5	6	7	8	9	OUT
BACK	326	372	385	259	300	429	227	455	172	2925
REGULAR	305	357	372	251	293	411	205	440	150	2784
par	4	4	4	4	4	4	3	5	3	35
handicap	9	7	3	17	15	1	5	13	11	-
FORWARD	284	328	359	244	277	368	162	426	125	2573
par	4	4	4	4	4	4	3	5	3	35
handicap	9	7	1	15	11	3	13	5	17	-

	10	11	12	13	14	15	16	17	18	IN
BACK	468	107	359	131	348	369	193	614	507	3096
REGULAR	457	100	341	119	337	348	168	607	495	2972
par	5	3	4	3	4	4	3	5	5	36
handicap	14	18	4	16	12	8	10	2	6	-
FORWARD	440	92	322	100	289	329	147	600	470	2789
par	5	3	4	3	4	4	3	6	5	37
handicap	2	16	8	18	12	10	14	4	6	-

BACK	
yardage	6021
par	71
rating	68.0
slope	108

REGULAR	
yardage	5756
par	71
rating	66.4
slope	105

FORWARD	
yardage	5362
par	72
rating	70.0
slope	107

PLAY POLICY & FEES: Reciprocal play is accepted with members of other private clubs (weekdays only); otherwise, members and guests only. Fees for reciprocators are $60 weekdays. Guests on weekends are $90. Carts are $10 per rider.

DRESS CODE: Appropriate golf attire and nonmetal spikes are required.

COURSE DESCRIPTION: These courses are set around the top of a small hill. The rolling fairways are seeded with Kikuyu grass, and the rough is tough. All three layouts are well bunkered and interesting. They play long from any set of tees.

NOTES: Par is 72 on the Valley/Vista Course and 67 on the Vista/Lake and Lake/Valley Courses. The Valley/Vista Course: See scorecard for yardage and rating information. The Vista/Lake Course is 5,272 yards and rated 64.6 from the regular tees with a slope of 100. The Lake/Valley Course is 5,423 yards and rated 65.3 from the regular tees with a slope rating of 101. The Valley/Vista Course was the site of the annual Los Coyotes LPGA Classic from 1989 to 1992, won twice by Nancy Lopez and once by Pat Bradley.

LOCATION: Take Highway 91 or Interstate 5 to the Beach Boulevard exit. Drive north for three miles from Highway 91 or two miles from Interstate 5 to Los Coyotes Drive and turn right, and continue one mile to the club.

. . . ● **TOURNAMENTS:** This course is available for outside tournaments on Monday.

47. LOS COYOTES COUNTRY CLUB

PLAY POLICY & FEES: Green fees are $20 weekdays and $26 weekends. Twilight fees are available. Call for special senior rates. Carts are $24.

TEE TIMES: Reservations can be booked seven days in advance through the computer reservations system. For tee times call 714-748-8900.

DRESS CODE: Casual attire is OK, but nonmetal spikes are required.

COURSE DESCRIPTION: This course is not long, except for the 614-yard, par-5 17th hole, but it is challenging for the average golfer. The tree-lined fairways are level and well kept for a public course. It's flat and easy to walk.

NOTES: This course is located close to Disneyland and Knotts Berry Farm.

LOCATION: Travel on Interstate 5 (Santa Ana Freeway) to the Brookhurst Street exit. Drive south one-half mile to Crescent Avenue and turn right. Continue one-half mile to Gilbert Street and turn left to the course.

. . . ● **TOURNAMENTS:** Shotgun tournaments are available weekdays only. A 12-player minimum is required to book a tournament. Tournaments should be booked 12 months in advance. The banquet facility holds 100 people.

48. ANAHEIM "DAD" MILLER GOLF COURSE

49 WESTRIDGE GOLF CLUB
ARCHITECT: GRAVES & PASCUZZO, 1999

1400 S. La Habra Hills
La Habra, CA 90631

PROSHOP: 562-690-4200

Tom Arnold, Head Professional, PGA

Driving Range
Practice Greens
Clubhouse
Food / Beverage
Accommodations
Pull Carts
Power Carts
Club Rental
$pecial Offers

	1	2	3	4	5	6	7	8	9	OUT
BACK	347	553	127	447	500	296	175	450	353	3248
REGULAR	320	523	107	410	463	263	158	420	337	3001
par	4	5	3	4	5	4	3	4	4	36
handicap										-
FORWARD	290	460	83	373	406	230	110	367	290	2609
par	4	5	3	4	5	4	3	4	4	36
handicap										-

	10	11	12	13	14	15	16	17	18	IN
BACK	367	120	357	340	537	120	337	430	510	3118
REGULAR	347	100	323	320	500	110	313	400	477	2890
par	4	3	4	4	5	3	4	4	5	36
handicap										-
FORWARD	297	80	293	283	447	80	273	350	447	2550
par	4	3	4	4	5	3	4	4	5	36
handicap										-

BACK	
yardage	6366
par	72
rating	
slope	

REGULAR	
yardage	5891
par	72
rating	
slope	

FORWARD	
yardage	5159
par	72
rating	
slope	

50 FRIENDLY HILLS COUNTRY CLUB
ARCHITECT: JIMMY HINES

8500 Villaverde Drive
Whittier, CA 90605

PROSHOP: 562-693-3623

Luis Izurieta, General Manager
Jay Prestella, PGA Professional
Vince Santo Pietro, Tournament Director, PGA

Driving Range ●
Practice Greens ●
Clubhouse ●
Food / Beverage ●
Accommodations
Pull Carts
Power Carts ●
Club Rental
$pecial Offers

	1	2	3	4	5	6	7	8	9	OUT
BACK	567	191	360	462	317	438	381	173	373	3262
REGULAR	544	183	350	450	301	415	369	146	363	3121
par	5	3	4	4	4	4	4	3	4	35
handicap	3	11	9	1	15	7	5	17	13	-
FORWARD	396	162	339	430	285	389	353	125	351	2830
par	5	3	4	5	4	4	4	3	4	36
handicap	9	11	3	15	13	7	1	17	5	-

	10	11	12	13	14	15	16	17	18	IN
BACK	342	390	353	195	394	486	221	380	389	3150
REGULAR	336	368	335	179	377	473	309	364	374	3115
par	4	4	4	3	4	5	3	4	4	35
handicap	16	2	10	14	4	6	12	18	8	-
FORWARD	330	339	322	170	359	454	156	349	350	2829
par	4	4	4	3	4	5	3	4	4	35
handicap	8	6	14	16	2	4	18	10	12	-

BACK	
yardage	6412
par	70
rating	71.3
slope	132

REGULAR	
yardage	6236
par	70
rating	69.7
slope	128

FORWARD	
yardage	5659
par	71
rating	74.4
slope	131

PLAY POLICY & FEES: The course is scheduled to open in the late fall of 1999. Green fees have not been established at time of press.

COURSE DESCRIPTION: The course will play around large hills and valleys with three lakes placed along fairways and greens. The location and layout will take full advantage of surrounding views.

LOCATION: From Los Angeles head south on Interstate 5. Take the Beach Boulevard exit and head north to the Imperial Highway. Make a right on the Imperial Highway and another right on La Habra Drive, and follow it to the course.

. . . ● **TOURNAMENTS:** A 20-player minimum will be required to book an event. The banquet room will hold 160 golfers, plus another 150 on the terrace.

49. WESTRIDGE GOLF CLUB

PLAY POLICY & FEES: Members and guests only. Green fees are $50 weekdays and $60 weekends. Guests must be accompanied by a member. The course is closed on Monday.

DRESS CODE: Appropriate golf attire and nonmetal spikes are required.

COURSE DESCRIPTION: This club features rolling terrain, undulating greens, and narrow fairways. The course gets off to a fast start at the first hole, a par-5, 558-yard heavyweight. The hole is straight uphill to a green heavily bunkered on both sides, with a creek on the left. The greens are treacherous. The course, in the hills above Whittier, is usually in immaculate condition.

LOCATION: From the Pomona Freeway (Highway 60) in Whittier, take the Hacienda Boulevard South exit and go south for three miles to Colima Road. Turn right and drive 2.25 miles to Mar Vista. Go left to Villaverde Drive and the club.

. . . ● **TOURNAMENTS:** This course is available for outside tournaments on Monday only.

50. FRIENDLY HILLS COUNTRY CLUB

51 LOS ANGELES ROYAL VISTA GOLF COURSE
ARCHITECT: WILLIAM F. BELL, 1965

20055 East Colima Road
Walnut, CA 91789

PRO SHOP: 909-595-7441

Don Crooker, Director of Golf, PGA
Fred Kim, PGA Professional
Jose Santana, Superintendent

Driving Range ●
Practice Greens ●
Clubhouse ●
Food / Beverage ●
Accommodations
Pull Carts ●
Power Carts ●
Club Rental ●
$Special Offers

	1	2	3	4	5	6	7	8	9	OUT
BACK	498	423	193	352	402	168	521	387	360	3304
REGULAR	471	395	173	340	370	136	496	350	345	3076
par	5	4	3	4	4	3	5	4	4	36
handicap	7	1	9	13	3	11	17	5	15	-
FORWARD	453	382	152	327	348	118	473	329	330	2912
par	5	4	3	4	4	3	5	4	4	36
handicap	1	3	13	11	5	15	7	9	17	-

	10	11	12	13	14	15	16	17	18	IN
BACK	418	210	375	490	205	585	360	420	170	3233
REGULAR	375	160	335	448	165	544	326	385	150	2888
par	4	3	4	5	3	5	4	4	3	35
handicap	2	14	8	12	4	6	16	10	18	-
FORWARD	285	128	320	432	140	510	315	364	139	2633
par	4	3	4	5	3	5	4	4	3	35
handicap	4	18	8	6	14	2	12	10	16	-

BACK	
yardage	6537
par	71
rating	70.6
slope	121

REGULAR	
yardage	5964
par	71
rating	68
slope	114

FORWARD	
yardage	5545
par	71
rating	71.3
slope	118

52 DIAMOND BAR GOLF COURSE
ARCHITECT: WILLIAM F. BELL, 1962

22801 East Golden Springs
Diamond Bar, CA 91765

PRO SHOP: 909-861-8282
CLUBHOUSE: 909-861-5757

Scott Kliesen, Director of Golf, PGA

Driving Range ●
Practice Greens ●
Clubhouse ●
Food / Beverage ●
Accommodations
Pull Carts ●
Power Carts ●
Club Rental ●
$Special Offers

	1	2	3	4	5	6	7	8	9	OUT
BACK	476	387	191	559	378	480	391	420	188	3470
REGULAR	449	372	180	552	365	416	374	399	161	3268
par	5	4	3	5	4	4	4	4	3	36
handicap	9	5	11	7	17	3	13	1	15	-
FORWARD	365	324	119	538	354	412	346	368	142	2968
par	4	4	3	5	4	5	4	4	3	36
handicap	5	15	17	1	11	7	9	3	13	-

	10	11	12	13	14	15	16	17	18	IN
BACK	345	424	530	197	354	486	414	150	440	3340
REGULAR	334	410	518	181	343	476	401	140	404	3207
par	4	4	5	3	4	5	4	3	4	36
handicap	16	6	8	10	14	12	4	18	2	-
FORWARD	320	350	487	163	332	463	397	123	406	3041
par	4	4	5	3	4	5	4	3	5	37
handicap	16	4	2	14	10	6	12	18	8	-

BACK	
yardage	6810
par	72
rating	72.8
slope	125

REGULAR	
yardage	6475
par	72
rating	70.4
slope	119

FORWARD	
yardage	6009
par	73
rating	73.9
slope	122

PLAY POLICY & FEES: Outside play is accepted. Green fees are $22 weekdays and $33 weekends. Carts are $12 per person.

TEE TIMES: Reservations can be booked seven days in advance. You can make reservations by calling 800-334-6533.

DRESS CODE: No tank tops are allowed on the course.

COURSE DESCRIPTION: All of the courses are moderately hilly with mature trees and some water. The shorter South Course is the narrowest, and the East Course plays the longest. On the South Course, watch out for the second hole. It's a par-3, 199-yarder that requires a delicate tee shot over a lake to a green tucked between two hills. The first hole on the East Course is a difficult starting hole. There is water on the left, a major dogleg left after the tee shot, and a straight, uphill approach to a shallow, extremely elevated green.

NOTES: Los Angeles Royal Vista used to be a private facility. The facility offers showers, banquets, and a sports bar. Par is 71 on the East/North Course and on the North/South course. Par is 72 on the South/East Course.

LOCATION: From Los Angeles travel on Highway 60 (Pomona Freeway) east to the Fairway Drive exit and turn right on the Brea Canyon cutoff. At Colima Road, turn left to the club.

. . . ● **TOURNAMENTS:** Shotgun tournaments are available weekdays only. Carts are required before 11 a.m. on weekends. A 12-player minimum is required to book a tournament. The banquet facility can accommodate 500 people.

51. LOS ANGELES ROYAL VISTA GOLF

PLAY POLICY & FEES: Green fees are $20 weekdays and $25 weekends. Los Angeles County senior citizens play for $9 for nine holes and $10 for 18 holes. Carts are $16 for nine holes and $22 for 18 holes.

TEE TIMES: Reservations can be booked seven days in advance.

DRESS CODE: Collared shirts and nonmetal spikes are preferred.

COURSE DESCRIPTION: This is a tree-lined course with water hazards on four holes and doglegs on several others. The course is very open, so errant tee shots are salvageable.

NOTES: New forward tees that play at 4,700 yards have been added to accommodate golfers of every level.

LOCATION: From downtown Los Angeles take Highway 60 (Pomona Freeway) east 24 miles to Grand Avenue. Turn right, go to the next light, and turn left to the course.

. . . ● **TOURNAMENTS:** Shotgun tournaments are available weekdays only. A 24-player minimum is required to book a tournament. Events can be scheduled 12 months in advance. The banquet facility can accommodate up to 250 people.

● **TRAVEL:** The Country Suites by Ayer in Diamond Bar is located one-quarter mile from the golf course. For reservations call 909-860-6290.

52. DIAMOND BAR GOLF COURSE

53 HACIENDA GOLF CLUB
ARCHITECT: MAX BEHR, 1920

718 East Road
La Habra Heights, CA
90631
PRO SHOP: 562-697-3610
CLUBHOUSE: 562-694-1081

Malcolm Smith, Manager
Andrew Thuney, PGA Professional
Rafael Barajas, Superintendent

Driving Range ●
Practice Greens ●
Clubhouse ●
Food / Beverage ●
Accommodations
Pull Carts
Power Carts ●
Club Rental ●
$pecial Offers

	1	2	3	4	5	6	7	8	9	OUT
BACK	410	433	325	187	460	202	516	448	392	3373
REGULAR	390	418	308	174	435	190	511	432	383	3241
par	4	4	4	3	4	3	5	4	4	35
handicap	9	5	15	11	1	17	13	3	7	-
FORWARD	369	339	286	128	362	175	494	427	373	2953
par	4	4	4	3	4	3	5	5	4	36
handicap	9	13	7	17	5	11	1	15	3	-

	10	11	12	13	14	15	16	17	18	IN
BACK	520	321	148	419	426	379	194	470	410	3287
REGULAR	503	305	133	394	411	367	170	457	398	3138
par	5	4	3	4	4	4	3	5	4	36
handicap	10	14	18	2	4	6	12	16	8	-
FORWARD	470	259	122	370	401	330	161	440	357	2910
par	5	4	3	4	4	4	3	5	4	36
handicap	6	14	18	4	2	10	16	8	12	-

BACK	
yardage	6660
par	71
rating	73.2
slope	132

REGULAR	
yardage	6379
par	71
rating	71.1
slope	127

FORWARD	
yardage	5863
par	72
rating	74.2
slope	129

54 BREA GOLF COURSE
ARCHITECT: WILLIAM THOMPSON, 1955

501 West Fir Street
Brea, CA 92621

PRO SHOP: 714-529-3003

Tony Lopez, Professional

Driving Range ●
Practice Greens ●
Clubhouse ●
Food / Beverage ●
Accommodations
Pull Carts ●
Power Carts ●
Club Rental ●
$pecial Offers

	1	2	3	4	5	6	7	8	9	OUT
BACK	-	-	-	-	-	-	-	-	-	-
REGULAR	132	167	310	132	385	183	139	114	121	1683
par	3	3	4	3	4	3	3	3	3	29
handicap	17	5	9	11	1	3	7	13	15	-
FORWARD	122	120	290	125	319	131	128	86	110	1431
par	3	3	4	3	4	3	3	3	3	29
handicap	18	6	10	12	2	4	8	14	16	-

	10	11	12	13	14	15	16	17	18	IN
BACK	-	-	-	-	-	-	-	-	-	-
REGULAR	132	167	310	132	385	183	139	114	121	1683
par	3	3	4	3	4	3	3	3	3	29
handicap	17	5	9	11	1	3	7	13	15	-
FORWARD	122	120	290	125	319	131	128	86	110	1431
par	3	3	4	3	4	3	3	3	3	29
handicap	18	6	10	12	2	4	8	14	16	-

BACK	
yardage	-
par	-
rating	-
slope	-

REGULAR	
yardage	3366
par	58
rating	-
slope	-

FORWARD	
yardage	2862
par	58
rating	-
slope	-

PLAY POLICY & FEES: Members and guests only. Guest fees are $50 weekdays and $60 weekends. Carts are $20.

DRESS CODE: Proper attire for golfers is collared shirts and slacks. Bermuda shorts are acceptable. Nonmetal spikes are mandatory.

COURSE DESCRIPTION: This course was built in 1920, during the golden age of golf. It is a classic old-style layout, with narrow, tree-lined fairways that traverse a rolling terrain. The 16th hole is a gem. It's 194 yards over a lake to a two-tiered green.

NOTES: The USGA Women's Amateur Championship was held here in 1966. The McGregor Men's Tournament is held each June, and the Jewel of the Canyon Invitational is played each August. The course record is 62 for men and 70 for women.

LOCATION: Travel on Highway 60 (Pomona Freeway) to La Habra Heights and exit on Hacienda Boulevard south. Drive four miles to East Road and turn left. Continue three-fourths of a mile to the club.

. . . ● **TOURNAMENTS:** This course is available for outside tournaments on Monday. A 100-player minimum is needed to book a tournament. Events should be booked 12 months in advance. The banquet facility can accommodate up to 280 people.

53. HACIENDA GOLF CLUB

PLAY POLICY & FEES: Green fees are $9 weekdays and $10 weekends. Seniors, junior, and twilight rates are available. Carts are $6 weekdays and $7 weekends.

TEE TIMES: Reservations can be booked seven days in advance.

COURSE DESCRIPTION: This mostly flat course has a storm channel running through its center. There are few trees. The course consists of two par 4s and seven par 3s.

LOCATION: From Highway 57 heading south toward Brea, take the Imperial Highway exit west to Brea Boulevard and turn left. At the second signal, turn right on West Fir, which will dead end at the course.

. . . ● **TOURNAMENTS:** This course is available for outside events.

54. BREA GOLF COURSE

FULLERTON GOLF CLUB
ARCHITECT: WILLIAM F. BELL, 1963

2700 N. Harbor Boulevard
Fullerton, CA 92635

PROSHOP: 714-871-7411

Randy Richardson, Manager
Henry Woodrome, Head Professional, PGA
Art Fuertes, Superintendent

Driving Range ●
Practice Greens ●
Clubhouse ●
Food / Beverage ●
Accommodations
Pull Carts ●
Power Carts ●
Club Rental ●
Special Offers

	1	2	3	4	5	6	7	8	9	OUT
BACK	-	-	-	-	-	-	-	-	-	-
REGULAR	369	501	373	284	195	166	137	174	352	2551
par	4	5	4	4	3	3	3	3	4	33
handicap	9	7	1	15	5	13	17	11	3	-
FORWARD	365	500	352	276	176	154	130	165	346	2464
par	4	5	4	4	3	3	3	3	4	33
handicap	7	3	1	9	11	15	17	13	5	-

	10	11	12	13	14	15	16	17	18	IN
BACK	-	-	-	-	-	-	-	-	-	-
REGULAR	348	139	533	336	391	152	356	294	142	2691
par	4	3	5	4	4	3	4	4	3	34
handicap	8	18	4	12	2	10	6	16	14	-
FORWARD	321	131	497	326	382	146	342	285	138	2568
par	4	3	5	4	4	3	4	4	3	34
handicap	8	18	6	10	4	16	2	12	14	-

BACK	
yardage	-
par	-
rating	-
slope	-

REGULAR	
yardage	5242
par	67
rating	65.1
slope	105

FORWARD	
yardage	5032
par	67
rating	70.1
slope	112

 COYOTE HILLS GOLF COURSE
ARCHITECT: CAL OLSON, PAYNE STEWART, 1996

1440 Bastanchury
Fullerton, CA 92835

PROSHOP: 714-672-6800

Trevor Baker, Director of Golf
Jamie Mulligan, PGA Professional
Scott Bourgeois, Superintendent

Driving Range ●
Practice Greens ●
Clubhouse ●
Food / Beverage ●
Accommodations
Pull Carts
Power Carts ●
Club Rental ●
Special Offers

	1	2	3	4	5	6	7	8	9	OUT
BACK	415	381	150	396	386	366	403	205	414	3116
REGULAR	351	314	120	333	337	327	361	178	349	2670
par	4	4	3	4	4	4	4	3	4	34
handicap	9	5	17	15	1	11	13	7	3	-
FORWARD	298	289	83	293	275	257	302	86	294	2177
par	4	4	3	4	4	4	4	3	4	34
handicap	9	5	17	15	1	11	13	7	3	-

	10	11	12	13	14	15	16	17	18	IN
BACK	395	506	420	392	215	526	360	161	419	3394
REGULAR	334	426	377	359	161	478	323	121	369	2948
par	4	5	4	4	3	5	4	3	4	36
handicap	8	10	2	16	12	6	14	18	4	-
FORWARD	249	368	260	298	108	388	259	85	245	2260
par	4	5	4	4	3	5	4	3	4	36
handicap	8	10	2	16	12	6	14	18	4	-

BACK	
yardage	6510
par	70
rating	77.1
slope	128

REGULAR	
yardage	5618
par	70
rating	66.5
slope	113

FORWARD	
yardage	4437
par	70
rating	-
slope	-

PLAY POLICY & FEES: Green fees are $18 Monday through Thursday, $19 Friday, and $26 weekends. Senior rates are $11 Monday through Thursday and before 9 a.m. on Friday. Twilight rates are $12 from Monday through Thursday, $13 Friday, and $15 weekends. Carts are $22. Reservations are recommended.

TEE TIMES: Reservations can be booked seven days in advance.

DRESS CODE: Golf attire is encouraged.

COURSE DESCRIPTION: This is a tight, narrow course with a creek coming into play on 14 holes. The course is generally in good condition.

NOTES: The Fullerton City Championship is played here. This course also features one of the best junior golf programs in Southern California.

LOCATION: From Highway 91 in Fullerton, take the Harbor Boulevard exit. Go north for three miles to the course, just past the Greenview Terrace condo development.

. . . ● **TOURNAMENTS:** Shotgun tournaments are available weekdays only. A 120-player minimum is needed for a shotgun start. For a regular tournament a 16-player minimum is needed.

55. FULLERTON GOLF CLUB

PLAY POLICY & FEES: Green fees are $80 weekdays and $95 weekends and holidays. Price includes cart and driving range. Twilight rates are $60 weekdays and $65 weekends. Junior rates and nine-hole rates are available.

TEE TIMES: Reservations can be booked 45 days in advance.

DRESS CODE: Collared shirts and nonmetal spikes are a must. No denim is allowed on the course, and shorts must be country club length.

COURSE DESCRIPTION: Coyote Hills is located in a wildlife preserve that features cascading streams and spectacular views. Imagine standing on an elevated tee box at the ninth hole, looking down at a wildlife preserve. Now picture yourself hitting the ball down the middle of the fairway. If you don't, trouble awaits. The wildlife preserve along the left side turns into water with sand guarding the front of the green. If you hit the ball too far right, you'll get to tee it up again, plus a two-shot penalty.

NOTES: This course has been recognized by "Golf For Women" as one of its "100 Women-Friendly Golf Courses."

LOCATION: This course is located five miles north of Disneyland. From Highway 57 take the Yorba Linda exit. Take a right on State College Boulevard and a left on Bastanchury. The course will be on the left.

. . . ● **TOURNAMENTS:** A 16-player minimum is needed for a tournament. Carts are mandatory. Events should be booked 16 months in advance. The banquet facility can accommodate 250 people. ● **TRAVEL:** The Anaheim Marriott is about 20 minutes from the golf course. For reservations call 714-750-8000. The Embassay Suites (714-990-6000) and the Disneyland Hotel (714-956-6000) are also recommended.

56. COYOTE HILLS GOLF COURSE

ALTA VISTA COUNTRY CLUB
ARCHITECT: HARRY RAINVILLE, 1961

777 East Alta Vista Street
Placentia, CA 92670

PRO SHOP: 714-528-1103

Ted Debus, PGA Professional
Paul Mandry, PGA Professional

Driving Range ●
Practice Greens ●
Clubhouse ●
Food / Beverage ●
Accommodations
Pull Carts
Power Carts ●
Club Rental ●
$pecial Offers

	1	2	3	4	5	6	7	8	9	OUT
BACK	540	201	414	195	314	392	480	375	548	3459
REGULAR	501	180	388	165	305	365	460	360	516	3240
par	5	3	4	3	4	4	5	4	5	37
handicap	7	9	3	13	17	1	15	11	5	-
FORWARD	483	171	371	155	294	355	451	352	481	3113
par	5	3	4	3	4	4	5	4	5	37
handicap	3	15	9	17	13	7	1	11	5	-

	10	11	12	13	14	15	16	17	18	IN
BACK	371	487	141	349	167	440	538	185	402	3080
REGULAR	335	471	127	318	147	394	495	148	359	2794
par	4	5	3	4	3	4	5	3	4	35
handicap	8	12	18	10	14	2	4	16	6	-
FORWARD	347	420	107	306	127	344	424	143	322	2540
par	4	5	3	4	3	4	5	3	4	35
handicap	10	4	18	2	14	12	6	16	8	-

BACK	
yardage	6539
par	72
rating	71.1
slope	124

REGULAR	
yardage	6034
par	72
rating	68.8
slope	116

FORWARD	
yardage	5653
par	72
rating	73.0
slope	128

 # BIRCH HILLS GOLF COURSE
ARCHITECT: HARRY RAINVILLE, 1975

2250 East Birch Street
Brea, CA 92621

PRO SHOP: 714-990-0201

Bill Marsh, General Manager
Steve LaBarge, Director of Golf, PGA
Lisa Campbell, Tournament Director

Driving Range ●
Practice Greens ●
Clubhouse ○
Food / Beverage ●
Accommodations
Pull Carts ●
Power Carts ●
Club Rental ●
$pecial Offers

	1	2	3	4	5	6	7	8	9	OUT
BACK	132	128	152	369	337	98	139	127	143	1625
REGULAR	127	119	147	361	317	92	135	119	140	1557
par	3	3	3	4	4	3	3	3	3	29
handicap	9	17	5	1	3	15	11	13	7	-
FORWARD	116	102	132	313	276	86	123	109	129	1386
par	3	3	3	4	4	3	3	3	3	29
handicap	9	17	7	1	3	13	11	15	5	-

	10	11	12	13	14	15	16	17	18	IN
BACK	178	341	191	137	333	161	187	258	149	1935
REGULAR	172	327	177	128	326	150	180	251	142	1853
par	3	4	3	3	4	3	3	4	3	30
handicap	12	2	6	18	4	14	10	8	16	-
FORWARD	163	288	138	94	295	126	149	230	134	1617
par	3	4	3	3	4	3	3	4	3	30
handicap	10	2	8	18	4	14	12	6	16	-

BACK	
yardage	3560
par	59
rating	57.1
slope	89

REGULAR	
yardage	3410
par	59
rating	55.0
slope	89

FORWARD	
yardage	3003
par	59
rating	57.6
slope	-

18
HOLES

PLAY POLICY & FEES: Reciprocal play is accepted with members of other private clubs after 12:30 p.m. weekdays and 1 p.m. weekends; otherwise, members and guests only. Reciprocator fees are $50 weekdays and $60 weekends. Carts are $22.

TEE TIMES: Reservations for reciprocal play can be booked four days in advance.

DRESS CODE: All shirts must have a collar. No blue jeans are allowed.

COURSE DESCRIPTION: This is a rolling course with mature trees, lots of out-of-bounds, and some lakes. Homes line the perimeter. The back nine was redesigned in 1992 to create a more challenging home stretch.

LOCATION: Travel on Highway 91 to Placentia and take the Kraemar Boulevard exit. Drive north two miles to Alta Vista Street and turn right. Turn left on Sue Drive and continue one-half block to the club.

. . . ● **TOURNAMENTS:** This course is available for outside tournaments on Monday. Carts are required. A 48-player minimum is needed to book a tournament. Events should be booked 12 months in advance.

57. ALTA VISTA COUNTRY CLUB

18
HOLES

PLAY POLICY & FEES: Green fees are $17 weekdays and $24 weekends for 18 holes. Senior and twilight rates are available. Carts are $15 weekdays and $18 weekends.

TEE TIMES: Reservations can be booked seven days in advance.

DRESS CODE: Shirts must be worn.

COURSE DESCRIPTION: This short executive course is hilly and has good greens that can be tricky to putt. The course has five par 4s, and golfers can use their drivers—fairways are fairly wide. Some water comes into play on the front nine. The course is right across the street from Imperial Golf Course. It is an excellent course for seniors and is walkable.

NOTES: Birch Hills offers an excellent practice facility.

LOCATION: Driving south on Highway 57 from Brea, exit at Imperial Highway east. Turn left on Associated Road and right on Birch Street to the course.

. . . ● **TOURNAMENTS:** A 16-player minimum is required to book a tournament.

58. BIRCH HILLS GOLF COURSE

YORBA LINDA COUNTRY CLUB
ARCHITECT: HARRY RAINVILLE, DAVID RAINVILLE, 1957

19400 Mountain View
Yorba Linda, CA 92886

PRO SHOP: 714-779-2467
CLUBHOUSE: 714-779-2461

Tim Hughes, Manager
William Hulbert, PGA Professional
Tim Wren, Superintendent

Driving Range ●
Practice Greens ●
Clubhouse ●
Food / Beverage ●
Accommodations
Pull Carts
Power Carts ●
Club Rental ●
$pecial Offers

	1	2	3	4	5	6	7	8	9	OUT
BACK	436	405	380	426	217	377	198	387	542	3368
REGULAR	421	399	366	400	191	356	175	376	521	3205
par	4	4	4	4	3	4	3	4	5	35
handicap	1	5	7	3	11	13	15	9	17	-
FORWARD	402	382	300	321	155	343	122	361	480	2866
par	5	4	4	4	3	4	3	4	5	36
handicap	13	1	11	9	15	7	17	5	3	-

	10	11	12	13	14	15	16	17	18	IN
BACK	469	377	458	158	526	397	422	129	530	3466
REGULAR	451	356	436	153	508	385	397	122	514	3322
par	4	4	4	3	5	4	4	3	5	36
handicap	2	10	4	14	12	6	8	18	16	-
FORWARD	416	319	382	133	419	320	382	114	479	2964
par	5	4	4	3	5	4	4	3	5	37
handicap	14	8	2	16	10	12	6	18	4	-

BACK	
yardage	6834
par	71
rating	72.8
slope	125

REGULAR	
yardage	6527
par	71
rating	70.5
slope	119

FORWARD	
yardage	5830
par	73
rating	74.0
slope	126

ANAHEIM HILLS GOLF COURSE
ARCHITECT: RICHARD BIGLER, 1972

6501 Nohl Ranch Road
Anaheim, CA 92807

PRO SHOP: 714-998-3041

Bob Johns, Director of Golf, PGA
Scott Stubbs, Head Professional, PGA
Tom Mathiew, Superintendent

Driving Range ●
Practice Greens ●
Clubhouse ●
Food / Beverage ●
Accommodations
Pull Carts
Power Carts ●
Club Rental ●
$pecial Offers

	1	2	3	4	5	6	7	8	9	OUT
BACK	484	383	428	296	254	347	142	295	424	3053
REGULAR	467	373	410	287	245	340	134	288	419	2963
par	5	4	4	4	3	4	3	4	4	35
handicap	15	7	1	13	5	11	17	9	3	-
FORWARD	441	283	327	264	183	331	117	274	415	2635
par	5	4	4	4	3	4	3	4	5	36
handicap	5	7	1	3	15	9	17	13	11	-

	10	11	12	13	14	15	16	17	18	IN
BACK	359	398	501	207	375	366	350	164	472	3192
REGULAR	339	349	490	200	362	360	338	139	465	3042
par	4	4	5	3	4	4	4	3	5	36
handicap	12	16	2	8	4	14	6	18	10	-
FORWARD	330	325	441	134	320	329	324	122	401	2726
par	4	4	5	3	4	4	4	3	5	36
handicap	10	12	2	14	4	16	8	18	6	-

BACK	
yardage	6245
par	71
rating	69.6
slope	117

REGULAR	
yardage	6005
par	71
rating	68.4
slope	114

FORWARD	
yardage	5361
par	72
rating	70.0
slope	115

PLAY POLICY & FEES: Members and guests only. Green fees are $65 weekdays and $75 weekends. Carts are $10 per person.

DRESS CODE: Appropriate golf attire is required. No denim is allowed on the course. Nonmetal spikes are required.

COURSE DESCRIPTION: This old-style course is nestled among numerous homes. There are tree-lined fairways, hills, bunkers, and a little water. It's walkable.

NOTES: For information on memberships, contact Membership Director Carol Bond.

LOCATION: Take the Riverside Freeway (Highway 91) to Imperial Highway (Highway 90). Drive north to Kellogg and turn right to Mountain View and the club.

. . . ● **TOURNAMENTS:** This course is available for outside tournaments on Monday only, and carts are required. A 100-player minimum is needed. Tournaments should be scheduled 12 months in advance. The banquet facility can accommodate 200 people.

59. YORBA LINDA COUNTRY CLUB

PLAY POLICY & FEES: Green fees are $34 Monday through Thursday and $40 Friday through Sunday; carts are included and mandatory. The course has added a GPS system for $2.50 per player. It is mandatory, but refundable.

TEE TIMES: Reservations can be made seven days in advance either through the pro shop or the computer reservations system. For the computer reservations system, call 714-748-8900

DRESS CODE: No tank tops, short shorts, or cutoffs are allowed. Nonmetal spikes are required.

COURSE DESCRIPTION: Most of the fairways are separated on this hilly course (only four are parallel). The greens are undulating and can be fast in the summer. The first hole is a short par 5, but because the tee is elevated, errant tee shots can easily wind up lost or out-of-bounds. Local knowledge is imperative.

NOTES: The course offers great views and lots of wildlife.

LOCATION: Take the Riverside Freeway (Highway 91) to the Imperial Highway exit south. Drive one-half mile to Nohl Ranch Road, and turn left and travel one-half mile to the club.

. . . ● **TOURNAMENTS:** Shotgun tournaments are available weekdays only. Events should be booked 12 months in advance. Carts are required. The banquet facility holds 150 people.

60. ANAHEIM HILLS GOLF COURSE

WESTERN HILLS GOLF & COUNTRY CLUB
ARCHITECT: H. RAINVILLE, D. RAINVILLE, 1963

1800 Carbon Canyon Road
Chino, CA 91709

PRO SHOP: 714-528-6400

Michael Donovan, Manager
Scott Stevenson, PGA Professional
Vincent Vazquez, Superintendent

Driving Range •
Practice Greens •
Clubhouse •
Food / Beverage •
Accommodations
Pull Carts
Power Carts •
Club Rental •
$pecial Offers

	1	2	3	4	5	6	7	8	9	OUT
BACK	399	355	382	403	363	165	510	159	374	3110
REGULAR	380	350	378	382	351	145	497	124	366	2973
par	4	4	4	4	4	3	5	3	4	35
handicap	3	13	11	1	5	15	7	17	9	-
FORWARD	359	343	371	324	301	131	463	119	331	2742
par	4	4	4	4	4	3	5	3	4	35
handicap	3	5	11	13	9	15	1	17	7	-

	10	11	12	13	14	15	16	17	18	IN
BACK	365	403	409	400	155	503	400	524	400	3559
REGULAR	356	376	380	388	148	490	380	512	385	3415
par	4	4	4	4	3	5	4	5	4	37
handicap	10	8	2	12	18	16	4	14	6	-
FORWARD	349	362	360	343	143	469	315	494	294	3129
par	4	4	4	4	3	5	4	5	4	37
handicap	10	6	2	14	16	8	12	4	18	-

BACK	
yardage	6669
par	72
rating	72.3
slope	128

REGULAR	
yardage	6388
par	72
rating	70.6
slope	122

FORWARD	
yardage	5871
par	72
rating	73.9
slope	126

 LOS SERRANOS LAKES GOLF & COUNTRY CLUB
ARCHITECT: JOHN DUNN, W. EATON (S), 1925 (N)

GOLF 50

15656 Yorba Avenue
Chino, CA 91709

PRO SHOP: 909-597-1711
CLUBHOUSE: 909-597-1769

David Kramer, Manager
John Powell, PGA Professional
Steven Hall, Superintnedent

Driving Range •
Practice Greens •
Clubhouse •
Food / Beverage •
Accommodations
Pull Carts •
Power Carts •
Club Rental •
$pecial Offers

	1	2	3	4	5	6	7	8	9	OUT
BACK	526	469	393	405	457	174	368	573	207	3572
REGULAR	499	457	315	362	431	168	356	573	166	3327
par	5	5	4	4	4	3	4	5	3	37
handicap	9	17	11	3	1	13	15	7	5	-
FORWARD	428	417	271	353	296	159	353	431	144	2852
par	5	5	4	4	4	3	4	5	3	37
handicap	5	3	13	1	9	15	11	7	17	-

	10	11	12	13	14	15	16	17	18	IN
BACK	347	402	183	475	402	380	505	179	591	3464
REGULAR	339	376	163	460	388	360	473	149	534	3242
par	4	4	3	5	4	4	5	3	5	37
handicap	8	2	10	18	12	6	14	16	4	-
FORWARD	330	356	155	448	382	335	445	130	524	3105
par	4	4	3	5	4	4	5	3	5	37
handicap	10	14	16	2	12	4	8	18	6	-

BACK	
yardage	7036
par	74
rating	73.7
slope	134

REGULAR	
yardage	6569
par	74
rating	71.3
slope	131

FORWARD	
yardage	5957
par	74
rating	73.9
slope	128

PLAY POLICY & FEES: Reciprocal play is accepted with members of other private clubs Monday through Friday; otherwise, members and guests only. Green fees are $35 weekdays and $60 weekends. Carts are $11 per person.

DRESS CODE: Collared shirts and nonmetal spikes are required. No jeans are allowed on the course.

COURSE DESCRIPTION: This rolling course has mature trees and is well bunkered. There is a double green that serves two holes, the 12th and 14th. Water comes into play on only one hole.

NOTES: The U.S. Amateur qualifier has been held here in the past.

LOCATION: From Highway 71 take Chino Hills Parkway west to Carbon Canyon Road. Turn left and drive two miles to the club. From Highway 57, take Lambert Road east 11 miles to the club.

. . . ● **TOURNAMENTS:** The course is available for outside tournaments on Monday.

61. WESTERN HILLS GOLF & COUNTRY CLUB

PLAY POLICY & FEES: Green fees for the North Course are $22 Monday through Thursday, and $26 Friday. Fees for the South Course are $26 Monday through Thursday, and $29 Friday. Both courses are $50 including carts on weekends. Carts are mandatory on weekend play. Carts are $26 for two riders during the week.

TEE TIMES: Reservations are accepted seven days in advance.

DRESS CODE: No tank tops or cut-off shorts are allowed.

COURSE DESCRIPTION: The South Course is long and hilly and gets breezy in the afternoons. The North Course was built in 1925 and is scenic and rolling. The South Course has six par 5s, including the first two holes, each of them reachable in two for the longer hitter.

NOTES: This public club has two 18-hole courses. Par is 74 on the South Course and 72 on the North Course. The North Course is 6,440 yards and rated 71.2 with a slope of 129 from the championship tees. The South Course: See scorecard for yardage and rating information. Jack Kramer of tennis fame owns these courses.

LOCATION: From Highway 60 (Pomona Freeway), take the Pomona/Corona Highway 71 exit and travel south on Highway 71 for five miles to the Soquel Canyon Parkway exit. Take a right on Soquel Canyon Parkway to Los Serranos Road. Turn right to the club.

. . . ● **TOURNAMENTS:** Shotgun tournaments are available Monday and Tuesday only. A 20-player minimum is needed to book an event.

62. LOS SERRANOS LAKES GOLF & COUNTRY

EL PRADO GOLF COURSE
ARCHITECT: HARRY RAINVILLE, 1976

6555 Pine Avenue
Chino, CA 91710

PRO SHOP: 909-597-1753

Bruce Janke, Manager, PGA
Rich Tharp, PGA Professional
Dennis Jobert, Superintendent

Driving Range ●
Practice Greens ●
Clubhouse ●
Food / Beverage ●
Accommodations
Pull Carts ●
Power Carts ●
Club Rental ●
$pecial Offers

	1	2	3	4	5	6	7	8	9	OUT
BACK	374	377	399	178	527	371	149	429	514	3318
REGULAR	364	339	389	144	517	358	142	399	504	3156
par	4	4	4	3	5	4	3	4	5	36
handicap	7	11	3	17	5	15	9	1	13	-
FORWARD	306	306	341	118	470	313	118	335	460	2767
par	4	4	4	3	5	4	3	4	5	36
handicap	7	5	11	17	3	15	13	9	1	-

	10	11	12	13	14	15	16	17	18	IN
BACK	385	370	401	520	164	413	148	512	440	3353
REGULAR	368	350	384	506	150	406	141	442	393	3140
par	4	4	4	5	3	4	3	5	4	36
handicap	4	8	12	14	16	2	18	10	6	-
FORWARD	321	310	333	458	124	360	121	409	393	2829
par	4	4	5	5	3	4	3	5	5	37
handicap	4	12	10	8	18	2	16	6	14	-

BACK	
yardage	6671
par	72
rating	71.5
slope	119

REGULAR	
yardage	6296
par	72
rating	69.3
slope	114

FORWARD	
yardage	5596
par	73
rating	70.8
slope	115

 GREEN RIVER GOLF CLUB
ARCHITECT: HENRY BICKLER, 1958

5215 Green River Road
Corona, CA 91720

PRO SHOP: 714-970-8411
CLUBHOUSE: 714-737-5000

Howard Smith, Director of Golf, PGA
George Apodaca, Tournament Director
Greg Arrowsmith, Superintendent

Driving Range ●
Practice Greens ●
Clubhouse ●
Food / Beverage ●
Accommodations
Pull Carts ●
Power Carts ●
Club Rental ●
$pecial Offers

	1	2	3	4	5	6	7	8	9	OUT
BACK	506	391	161	521	214	350	498	413	168	3222
REGULAR	497	382	151	507	198	342	488	394	157	3116
par	5	4	3	5	3	4	5	4	3	36
handicap	11	3	13	7	5	15	17	1	9	-
FORWARD	488	373	134	486	137	334	429	356	104	2841
par	5	4	3	5	3	4	5	4	3	36
handicap	3	5	17	1	13	11	9	7	15	-

	10	11	12	13	14	15	16	17	18	IN
BACK	371	357	198	499	170	561	437	500	155	3248
REGULAR	361	348	170	488	160	547	427	490	149	3140
par	4	4	3	5	3	5	4	4	3	35
handicap	10	18	4	16	12	6	2	8	14	-
FORWARD	358	322	148	475	150	457	372	475	127	2884
par	4	4	3	5	3	5	5	4	3	36
handicap	10	12	16	4	18	2	6	8	14	-

BACK	
yardage	6470
par	71
rating	70.4
slope	119

REGULAR	
yardage	6256
par	71
rating	69.0
slope	114

FORWARD	
yardage	5725
par	72
rating	72.8
slope	125

PLAY POLICY & FEES: Green fees are $13 weekdays and $17 weekends for nine holes, and $22 weekdays and $28 weekends for 18 holes. Carts are $23.

TEE TIMES: Reservations can be booked seven days in advance. On weekends, reservations can be made on the Monday prior starting at 8 a.m.

DRESS CODE: Nonmetal spikes are required.

COURSE DESCRIPTION: The Chino Creek Course is longer and a bit more challenging than the Butterfield Stage Course, with water hazards and several out-of-bounds. There are rolling hills, but the course is very walkable. The Butterfield Stage Course is slightly shorter (6,508 yards), flatter, and more forgiving, making it receptive to beginning golfers. It, too, has water. Greens are usually well maintained. See the scorecard for yardage and rating information on the Chino Creek Course.

NOTES: On weekdays the courses play very fast.

LOCATION: From Los Angeles travel east on Highway 60 (Pomona Freeway) to the Corona Freeway/Highway 71 exit. Turn right and drive six miles to Euclid Avenue. Turn left on Euclid Avenue to Pine Street. Turn left to the course.

. . . ● **TOURNAMENTS:** Shotgun tournaments are available weekdays only. A 24-player minimum is needed to book a tournament. Events should be scheduled 12 months in advance. The banquet facility can accommodate 600 people. ● **TRAVEL:** The Ontario Hilton is about 15 minutes from the golf course. For reservations call 909-980-0400.

63. EL PRADO GOLF COURSE

PLAY POLICY & FEES: Green fees are $24 Monday through Thursday and $32 Friday through Sunday and holidays. Carts are $22.

TEE TIMES: Reservations can be booked seven days in advance for weekdays and five days in advance for weekends.

DRESS CODE: Appropriate golf attire and nonmetal spikes are required.

COURSE DESCRIPTION: These two courses feature gently rolling slopes with many trees and lakes. An errant tee shot means trouble. The Santa Ana River runs through both courses. The first hole on the Orange Course features trees down the right side and the river down the left side. These courses are in a narrow valley with hills on each side and therefore can get quite windy.

NOTES: The Orange Course: See scorecard for yardage and rating information. The Riverside Course is 6,275 yards and rated 69.2 from the championship tees.

LOCATION: From the Riverside Freeway (Highway 91), take the Green River Drive exit north and travel one mile to the entrance.

. . . ● **TOURNAMENTS:** Shotgun tournaments are available weekdays only. A 20-player minimum is needed to book an event. Carts are required. The banquet facility can accommodate up to 450 people. Events should be scheduled 12 months in advance. ● **TRAVEL:** The Dynasty Suites is located 10 minutes from the golf course. For reservations call 909-371-7185.

64. GREEN RIVER GOLF CLUB

WHISPERING LAKES GOLF COURSE

ARCHITECT: WILLIAM TUCKER, JR., 1959

2525 Riverside Drive
Ontario, CA 91761

PRO SHOP: 909-923-3673
CLUBHOUSE: 909-923-3675

Tim McBride, General Manager
Tim Walsh, Head Professional, PGA
Mark Fowler, PGA Professional

Driving Range •
Practice Greens •
Clubhouse •
Food / Beverage •
Accommodations
Pull Carts •
Power Carts •
Club Rental •
Special Offers

	1	2	3	4	5	6	7	8	9	OUT
BACK	384	407	380	183	389	385	186	497	410	3221
REGULAR	373	385	365	170	339	350	167	456	398	3003
par	4	4	4	3	4	4	3	5	4	35
handicap	13	1	7	5	15	9	11	17	3	-
FORWARD	358	375	350	150	310	339	160	455	394	2891
par	4	4	4	3	4	4	3	5	4	35
handicap	11	1	5	3	15	13	17	9	7	-

	10	11	12	13	14	15	16	17	18	IN
BACK	424	395	223	338	435	476	172	475	567	3505
REGULAR	417	364	212	325	426	460	165	460	478	3307
par	4	4	3	4	4	5	3	5	5	37
handicap	4	12	2	18	6	16	14	10	8	-
FORWARD	380	360	163	311	419	432	165	430	455	3115
par	4	4	3	4	4	5	3	5	5	37
handicap	2	12	14	18	10	8	16	6	4	-

BACK	
yardage	6726
par	72
rating	71.4
slope	122

REGULAR	
yardage	6310
par	72
rating	68.8
slope	114

FORWARD	
yardage	6006
par	72
rating	72.8
slope	117

 THE COUNTRY VILLAGE GOLF COURSE

10301 Country Club Drive
Mira Loma, CA 91752

PRO SHOP: 909-685-7466

Janice Koontz, Assistant Manager

Driving Range
Practice Greens •
Clubhouse •
Food / Beverage
Accommodations
Pull Carts •
Power Carts
Club Rental
Special Offers

	1	2	3	4	5	6	7	8	9	OUT
BACK	-	-	-	-	-	-	-	-	-	-
REGULAR	48	149	146	78	146	85	148	130	143	1073
par	3	3	3	3	3	3	3	3	3	27
handicap	9	4	5	7	2	8	1	6	3	-
FORWARD	48	132	112	76	123	71	99	87	130	878
par	3	3	3	3	3	3	3	3	3	27
handicap	9	6	5	7	2	8	1	4	3	-

	10	11	12	13	14	15	16	17	18	IN
BACK	-	-	-	-	-	-	-	-	-	-
REGULAR	-	-	-	-	-	-	-	-	-	-
par	-	-	-	-	-	-	-	-	-	-
handicap	-	-	-	-	-	-	-	-	-	-
FORWARD	-	--	-	-	-	-	-	-	-	-
par	-	-	-	-	-	-	-	-	-	-
handicap	-	-	-	-	-	-	-	-	-	-

BACK	
yardage	-
par	-
rating	-
slope	-

REGULAR	
yardage	1073
par	27
rating	-
slope	-

FORWARD	
yardage	878
par	27
rating	-
slope	-

PLAY POLICY & FEES: Green fees are $16 weekdays and $19 weekends for residents, and $19 weekdays and $23 weekends for nonresidents. Senior, student and twilight rates are available. Carts are $22.

TEE TIMES: Reservations can be booked seven days in advance for weekdays.

DRESS CODE: No tank tops are allowed on the course. Nonmetal spikes are required.

COURSE DESCRIPTION: This course has level terrain, mature trees, and wide-open fairways. It plays long because the ball gets little roll. The driving range has lights.

LOCATION: Travel east of Los Angeles on Highway 60 (Pomona Freeway) to the Vineyard exit near Ontario. Turn left on Riverside Drive, travel two blocks, and turn left to the club.

. . . ● **TOURNAMENTS:** A 20-player minimum is needed to book an event.

65. WHISPERING LAKES GOLF COURSE

PLAY POLICY & FEES: This course is part of a private senior residential community; residents and guests only. Guest fees are $5 every day.

COURSE DESCRIPTION: This short par-3 course has plenty of trees, sand traps, but no water as it winds through a senior apartment complex.

LOCATION: From Los Angeles take Highway 60 east for 50 miles, and take the Country Village exit. Turn left; the apartment complex is on the left.

. . . ● **TOURNAMENTS:** This course is available for outside events. The banquet facility can accommodate 300 people.

66. THE COUNTRY VILLAGE GOLF COURSE

GOOSE CREEK GOLF CLUB
ARCHITECT: BRIAN CURLEY, 1999

11418 68th Street
Mira Loma, CA 91752

PRO SHOP: 909-735-3982

Ross Fisher, Director of Golf, PGA
Chad Center, Tournament Director

Driving Range ●
Practice Greens ●
Clubhouse
Food / Beverage ●
Accommodations
Pull Carts ●
Power Carts ●
Club Rental
Special Offers

	1	2	3	4	5	6	7	8	9	OUT
BACK	381	185	389	533	179	361	532	357	188	3105
REGULAR	370	165	363	520	148	340	518	345	169	2938
par	4	3	4	5	3	4	5	4	3	35
handicap	8	18	6	2	16	12	4	14	10	-
FORWARD	268	95	305	449	87	265	396	255	88	2208
par	4	3	4	5	3	4	5	4	3	35
handicap	8	18	6	2	14	10	4	12	16	-

	10	11	12	13	14	15	16	17	18	IN
BACK	352	184	479	425	326	422	220	541	466	3415
REGULAR	340	155	440	405	310	398	200	505	430	3183
par	4	3	4	4	4	4	3	5	4	35
handicap	13	17	7	11	15	5	9	1	3	-
FORWARD	288	93	305	310	185	316	94	461	285	2337
par	4	3	4	5	3	4	5	4	3	35
handicap	11	13	7	9	17	5	15	1	3	-

BACK	
yardage	6520
par	70
rating	
slope	

REGULAR	
yardage	6121
par	70
rating	
slope	

FORWARD	
yardage	4545
par	70
rating	
slope	

HIDDEN VALLEY GOLF CLUB
ARCHITECT: CASEY O'CALLAGHAN, 1997

10 Clubhouse Drive
Norco, CA 91760

PRO SHOP: 909-737-1010

Mark Hoesing, General Manager
Harold Vaubel, Superintendent
Charlie Gallagher, Tournament Director

Driving Range ●
Practice Greens ●
Clubhouse ●
Food / Beverage ●
Accommodations
Pull Carts
Power Carts ●
Club Rental ●
Special Offers

	1	2	3	4	5	6	7	8	9	OUT
BACK	495	437	377	387	217	492	314	177	462	3358
REGULAR	495	388	352	387	196	455	314	166	401	3154
par	5	4	4	4	3	5	4	3	4	36
handicap	11/9	3/5	15/13	9/11	5/1	7	17	13/15	1/3	-
FORWARD	331	232	234	267	104	409	213	114	343	2247
par	4	4	4	4	3	5	4	3	4	35
handicap	5	3	13	11	9	7	17	15	1	-

	10	11	12	13	14	15	16	17	18	IN
BACK	376	556	362	172	312	574	188	384	439	3363
REGULAR	376	505	321	148	312	574	179	322	439	3176
par	4	5	4	3	4	5	3	4	4	36
handicap	6	14/10	12/8	16	18	8/4	10/12	4/14	2	-
FORWARD	248	421	258	87	232	476	152	254	282	2410
par	4	5	4	3	4	5	3	4	4	36
handicap	12	2	14	18	10	4	16	6	8	-

BACK	
yardage	6721
par	72
rating	-
slope	-

REGULAR	
yardage	6330
par	72
rating	-
slope	-

FORWARD	
yardage	4657
par	71
rating	-
slope	-

PLAY POLICY & FEES: Green fees are $40 Monday through through Thursday, $50 Friday, and $60 weekends and holidays. Senior green fees are $27 Monday through Thursday and $30 Friday. Junior rates are $22 weekdays and $25 weekends. Twilight green fees are $27 Monday through Thursday, $32 Friday, and $35 weekends and holidays. Carts are included

TEE TIMES: Reservations can be made seven days in advance.

DRESS CODE: Casual dress is OK, but shirts and shoes are required.

COURSE DESCRIPTION: Goose Creek is a privately owned public course that has a links feel, giving players plenty of options for reaching the green. The front nine is shorter than the back, with a marsh coming into play on several holes. For the most part the course is open off the tee, and although the bunkers are imposing, they are playable. Trouble awaits the golfer who misses the greens off the wrong side. Getting back to the green can be an experience involving many clubs and plenty of strokes.

NOTES: Goose Creek will offer one of the largest practice facilities in Southern California.

LOCATION: From Anaheim take Highway 91 east to Interstate 15. Take interstate 15 north for five miles and exit at Limonite. Follow Limonite to Wineville and take a right. Wineville turns into 68th Street. The course will be on the right-hand side.

. . . ● **TOURNAMENTS:** Events can be booked one year in advance. A 20-player minimum is required to book an event. The banquet facility can accommodate up to 150 people.

67. GOOSE CREEK GOLF CLUB

PLAY POLICY & FEES: Green fees are $70 Monday through Thursday, and $90 Friday through Sunday. Twilight rates are available. All fees include cart with computer yardage system.

TEE TIMES: Reservations can be made 14 days in advance.

DRESS CODE: Collared shirts and nonmetal spikes are mandatory. Shorts should be knee length.

COURSE DESCRIPTION: This target golf course, cut out of the hills, features constant elevation changes, rock outcroppings, and fair but challenging greens. Water comes into play on two holes. The signature hole is the 15th, a severe down-hill, dog-leg right that drops in elevation 220 feet from tee to green. Five sets of tees meet the needs of all golfers.

NOTES: In the 1998 March issue of "Golf Magazine," Hidden Valley was selected as a must-play course in Southern California. "Golf Digest" gave this course three-and-half-stars out of five in its "Places to Play" guide.

LOCATION: From Los Angeles take Highway 91 east for 35 miles. Take the McKinley exit and head north through five stoplights. Turn right on Parkview Avenue to the course.

. . . ● **TOURNAMENTS:** A 16-player minimum is required to book an event, and 144 players are required for shotgun tournaments. Events should be booked 12 months in advance. The banquet facility can accommodate 150 people. ●

TRAVEL: The Countryside Inn is located two miles from the course. For reservations call 909-734-2140. The Mission Inn (909-784-0300) is also recommended.

68. HIDDEN VALLEY GOLF CLUB

MOUNTAIN VIEW COUNTRY CLUB
ARCHITECT: WILLIAM F. BELL, 1955

2121 Mountain View Drive
Corona, CA 91720

PRO SHOP: 909-737-9798

Emil Scodeller, Professional
Carlos Briseno, Superintendent

Driving Range •
Practice Greens •
Clubhouse •
Food / Beverage •
Accommodations
Pull Carts •
Power Carts •
Club Rental •
$pecial Offers

	1	2	3	4	5	6	7	8	9	OUT
BACK	419	337	116	554	481	329	162	308	498	3204
REGULAR	409	329	108	543	466	321	155	300	482	3113
par	4	4	3	5	5	4	3	4	5	37
handicap	3	13	11	5	15	17	9	7	1	-
FORWARD	405	320	100	440	387	311	140	245	469	2817
par	5	4	3	5	5	4	3	4	5	38
handicap	3	7	17	5	11	15	13	9	1	-

	10	11	12	13	14	15	16	17	18	IN
BACK	203	466	133	375	327	371	586	220	548	3229
REGULAR	191	401	107	363	319	362	573	198	540	3054
par	3	4	3	4	4	4	5	3	5	35
handicap	6	2	18	4	16	8	14	10	12	-
FORWARD	127	394	100	284	300	302	553	187	310	2557
par	3	5	3	4	4	4	5	3	4	35
handicap	16	14	18	6	12	4	2	10	8	-

BACK	
yardage	6433
par	72
rating	70.8
slope	124

REGULAR	
yardage	6167
par	72
rating	69.4
slope	119

FORWARD	
yardage	5374
par	73
rating	71.7
slope	120

 CRESTA VERDE GOLF CLUB
ARCHITECT: RANDOLPH SCOTT, 1927

1295 Cresta Road
Corona, CA 91719

PRO SHOP: 909-737-2255

Michael McKinlay, PGA Professional
Carlos Moreno, Superintendent

Driving Range •
Practice Greens •
Clubhouse •
Food / Beverage •
Accommodations
Pull Carts •
Power Carts •
Club Rental •
$pecial Offers

	1	2	3	4	5	6	7	8	9	OUT
BACK	503	342	144	199	469	119	363	404	486	3029
REGULAR	486	332	118	183	457	101	348	343	431	2799
par	5	4	3	3	5	3	4	4	5	36
handicap	5	7	13	1	11	15	9	3	17	-
FORWARD	481	285	107	176	381	85	317	333	418	2583
par	5	4	3	3	5	3	4	4	5	36
handicap	1	13	15	7	9	17	11	3	5	-

	10	11	12	13	14	15	16	17	18	IN
BACK	321	312	335	283	124	429	341	184	438	2767
REGULAR	314	292	329	278	119	423	302	179	419	2655
par	4	4	4	4	3	4	4	3	5	35
handicap	14	10	8	16	12	2	6	4	18	-
FORWARD	308	217	241	274	114	404	291	166	405	2420
par	4	4	4	4	3	5	4	3	5	36
handicap	6	16	14	12	18	8	4	10	2	-

BACK	
yardage	5796
par	71
rating	67.3
slope	111

REGULAR	
yardage	5454
par	71
rating	65.3
slope	102

FORWARD	
yardage	5003
par	72
rating	69.1
slope	109

PLAY POLICY & FEES: Green fees are $19 walking and $29 with a cart on weekdays and $39 with a cart on weekends. Carts are mandatory on weekends. Senior and twilight rates are available.

TEE TIMES: Reservations can be booked seven days in advance.

DRESS CODE: Collared shirts and golf shoes are required.

COURSE DESCRIPTION: This course has tight fairways, tiny greens, and lots of trees. The front nine winds through homes, while the back nine is hilly. It is a traditional course that offers a challenge to players of any skill level.

NOTES: This course annually hosts six Southern California PubLinks team events. The course record is 61, shot before changes were made to the layout in the late '70s.

LOCATION: From the Riverside Freeway (Highway 91) east of Orange County, go south on Serfas Club Drive exit and travel east 400 yards to Pinecrest. Turn left and drive to the club entrance at the end of the street.

. . . ● **TOURNAMENTS:** A 144-player minimum is needed to book a shotgun tournament.

69. MOUNTAIN VIEW COUNTRY CLUB

PLAY POLICY & FEES: Green fees are $27 weekdays and $37 weekends including cart. Senior rates are $25 on weekdays including cart. Twilight green fees are $15 weekdays, and $25 weekends.

TEE TIMES: Reservations can be booked seven days in advance.

DRESS CODE: No tank tops are allowed on the course.

COURSE DESCRIPTION: The course offers a rolling terrain with some steep slopes, many mature trees, and winding fairways. It is not for the casual walker. The 17th hole has a 400-foot elevated tee.

NOTES: Here's a course with Hollywood history. Henry Fonda and Randolph Scott started this course back in 1927. In fact, Scott, who was a star attraction at the early Bing Crosby National Pro-Am at Pebble Beach, is credited with being the architect. The men's record stands at 61 and the women's at 72.

LOCATION: From the Riverside Freeway (Highway 91) take the Main Street North/Norco exit and travel north for one mile to Parkridge Avenue. Turn right and drive 1.25 miles to Cresta Road. Turn left and drive to the club entrance.

. . . ● **TOURNAMENTS:** This course is available for outside tournaments.

70. CRESTA VERDE GOLF CLUB

71 EAGLE GLEN GOLF CLUB
ARCHITECT: GARY ROGER BAIRD, 1999

1800 Eagle Glen Parkway
Corona, CA 91719

PRO SHOP: 909-272-4653

Archie Cart, Facility Manager, PGA
T.J. Baggett, Head Professional, PGA
Kelly McCaffrey, Superintendent

Driving Range ●
Practice Greens ●
Clubhouse ●
Food / Beverage ●
Accommodations
Pull Carts
Power Carts ●
Club Rental ●
$pecial Offers

	1	2	3	4	5	6	7	8	9	OUT
BACK	416	325	549	203	554	363	371	167	395	3343
REGULAR	389	298	520	187	523	335	354	151	363	3120
par	4	4	5	3	5	4	4	3	4	36
handicap	8	16	2	10	6	12	14	18	4	-
FORWARD	326	242	445	113	425	275	286	72	293	2477
par	4	4	5	3	5	4	4	3	4	36
handicap	8	16	2	10	6	12	14	16	4	-

	10	11	12	13	14	15	16	17	18	IN
BACK	203	399	650	343	441	477	365	166	543	3587
REGULAR	157	343	584	314	403	393	357	152	467	3170
par	3	4	5	4	4	4	4	3	5	36
handicap	15	11	3	13	1	5	9	17	7	-
FORWARD	106	286	460	262	320	326	240	108	413	2521
par	3	4	5	4	4	4	4	3	5	36
handicap	15	11	3	13	1	5	9	17	7	-

BACK	
yardage	6930
par	72
rating	
slope	

REGULAR	
yardage	6290
par	72
rating	
slope	

FORWARD	
yardage	4998
par	72
rating	
slope	

72 COMPTON GOLF COURSE
ARCHITECT: JOHN HILBUR, 1958

6400 E Compton Blvd.
Compton, CA 90221

PRO SHOP: 562-633-6721

Willy Forge, Professional

Driving Range
Practice Greens ●
Clubhouse
Food / Beverage ●
Accommodations
Pull Carts ●
Power Carts
Club Rental ●
$pecial Offers

	1	2	3	4	5	6	7	8	9	OUT
BACK										
REGULAR										
par										
handicap										
FORWARD										
par										
handicap										

	10	11	12	13	14	15	16	17	18	IN
BACK										
REGULAR										
par										
handicap										
FORWARD										
par										
handicap										

BACK	
yardage	
par	
rating	-
slope	-

REGULAR	
yardage	1500
par	27
rating	
slope	

FORWARD	
yardage	
par	
rating	-
slope	-

PLAY POLICY & FEES: Green fees are $75 Monday through Thursday and $90 Friday through Sunday. Rates include cart, range balls, divot repair tool, bag tag, tees, ball markers, and yardage book. Reduced rates are available in the afternoon.

TEE TIMES: Standard tee times can be booked seven days in advance. Preferred tee times may be reserved 8 to 60 days in advance. A $15 premium is required but includes a sleeve to Titleist golf balls.

DRESS CODE: Proper golf attire is required.

COURSE DESCRIPTION: Part of the continuing trend of upscale courses with wide fairways, minimal rough, and multi-level, undulating greens, Eagle Glen lies partially next to a new housing development and partially at the base of the Cleveland National Forest, with homes near the 1st, 5th, 6th, and 10th tees. The course has a number of memorable holes: the 9th, which feels like you are on top of the world; the 14th, a long par 4 into a prevailing wind; and a reachable par-5 finishing hole that requires a carry over water on both shots. Walking is virtually impossible due to a 400-foot elevation gain on the front side. If you insist on walking and it's a hot smoggy day, make sure you pre-register at Corona Regional Medical Center.

LOCATION: Take Highway 91 to Corona, turn south on Interstate 15 to the Cajalco Road exit, and then head west. Follow Eagle Glen Parkway to the clubhouse.

71. EAGLE GLEN GOLF CLUB

PLAY POLICY & FEES: Green fees are $3.50 for nine holes and $6.50 for 18 holes on weekdays. Weekend green fees are $4 for nine holes and $7.50 for 18 holes.

TEE TIMES: Reservations are on a first-come, first-served basis.

DRESS CODE: Nonmetal spikes are preferred.

COURSE DESCRIPTION: Although all the holes are par 3s, this is not a pitch and putt. The holes average 170 yards in length.

NOTES: Every Saturday Compton Golf Course offers a junior program for children 7 to 14 years of age. Children are given a golf lesson, and from 9 a.m. to 10 a.m., a teacher volunteers time in assisting students with classwork.

LOCATION: From Los Angeles take Interstate 405 south to the Alondra exit in Compton. Go west on Alondra Boulevard until you reach Atlantic Avenue. Go north on Atlantic Avenue until you reach Compton Boulevard. Take Compton Boulevard back over the freeway to the course.

72. COMPTON GOLF COURSE

73 VIRGINIA COUNTRY CLUB
ARCHITECTS: WILLIAM P. BELL, 1923; A.W. TILLINGHAST

4602 Virginia Road
Long Beach, CA 90807

PRO SHOP: 562-424-5211
CLUBHOUSE: 562-427-0924

H. Jeff Schlicht, General Manager
Michael Bacica, PGA Professional
Stephen McVey, Superintendent

Driving Range ●
Practice Greens ●
Clubhouse ●
Food / Beverage ●
Accommodations
Pull Carts
Power Carts ●
Club Rental ●
$pecial Offers

	1	2	3	4	5	6	7	8	9	OUT
BACK	387	393	206	362	526	433	196	374	367	3244
REGULAR	378	373	192	347	511	412	160	368	354	3095
par	4	4	3	4	5	4	3	4	4	35
handicap	3	5	13	15	9	1	17	7	11	-
FORWARD	358	262	186	333	415	402	125	352	334	2767
par	4	4	3	4	5	5	3	4	4	36
handicap	3	17	11	13	7	5	15	1	9	-

	10	11	12	13	14	15	16	17	18	IN
BACK	171	375	502	400	308	140	398	390	540	3224
REGULAR	167	366	496	374	306	124	383	369	524	3109
par	3	4	5	4	4	3	4	4	5	36
handicap	16	4	12	2	10	18	6	8	14	-
FORWARD	159	351	495	349	304	107	367	353	489	2974
par	3	4	5	4	4	3	4	4	5	36
handicap	16	4	2	14	12	18	8	6	10	-

BACK	
yardage	6468
par	71
rating	71.1
slope	124

REGULAR	
yardage	6204
par	71
rating	69.6
slope	120

FORWARD	
yardage	5741
par	72
rating	73.4
slope	129

74 BELLFLOWER MUNICIPAL GOLF

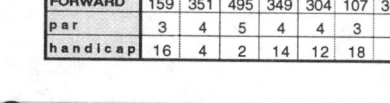

9030 East Compton
Bellflower, CA 90706

PRO SHOP: 562-920-8882

Tong Oh, Professional

Driving Range ●
Practice Greens ●
Clubhouse ●
Food / Beverage ●
Accommodations
Pull Carts ●
Power Carts
Club Rental ●
$pecial Offers

	1	2	3	4	5	6	7	8	9	OUT
BACK	134	115	167	155	120	111	167	154	192	1315
REGULAR	114	102	137	132	109	107	138	140	177	1156
par	3	3	3	3	3	3	3	3	3	27
handicap	13	7	5	9	15	17	1	11	3	-
FORWARD	114	102	137	132	109	107	138	140	177	1156
par	3	3	3	3	3	3	3	3	3	27
handicap	13	7	5	9	15	17	1	11	3	-

	10	11	12	13	14	15	16	17	18	IN
BACK	134	115	167	155	120	111	167	154	192	1315
REGULAR	114	102	137	132	109	107	138	140	177	1156
par	3	3	3	3	3	3	3	3	3	27
handicap	14	8	6	10	16	18	2	12	4	-
FORWARD	114	102	137	132	109	107	138	140	177	1156
par	3	3	3	3	3	3	3	3	3	27
handicap	14	8	6	10	16	18	2	12	4	-

BACK	
yardage	2630
par	54
rating	-
slope	-

REGULAR	
yardage	2312
par	54
rating	-
slope	-

FORWARD	
yardage	2312
par	54
rating	-
slope	-

PRIVATE: $45-$60

18
HOLES

PLAY POLICY & FEES: Members and guests only. Guest fees are $45 weekdays and $60 weekends. Carts are $9.

DRESS CODE: Appropriate golf attire and nonmetal spikes are required. Footjoy's Turf-Mate Plus soft spikes are preferred.

COURSE DESCRIPTION: This is a medium-length, testy course designed in the old, traditional style.

NOTES: The property is the site of Lynx's testing facility.

LOCATION: Travel on Interstate 405 to Long Beach Boulevard north. Turn left on San Antonio Road and right on Virginia Road to the course.

. . . ● **TOURNAMENTS:** All outside events must be member sponsored.

73. VIRGINIA COUNTRY CLUB

PUBLIC: $3-$5

9
HOLES

PLAY POLICY & FEES: Green fees are $4.50 weekdays and $5.50 weekends. Those with a Bellflower senior's card pay $3.50. After 3 p.m. green fees are $3.

TEE TIMES: Reservations can be made at any time.

DRESS CODE: Nonmetal spikes are required.

COURSE DESCRIPTION: This flat course is all par 3s, although it is not necessarily easy. Golfers can use virtually all their irons. The longest hole from the regular tees is 177 yards.

LOCATION: Take Highway 91 to Lakewood Boulevard. Drive north to Compton Boulevard, turn right and go about a half mile to the course on the right.

. . . ● **TOURNAMENTS:** Shotgun tournaments are available weekdays only. A 20-player minimum is needed to book a regular tournament. A banquet facility can hold 40 people. Events should be booked at least one month in advance.

74. BELLFLOWER MUNICIPAL GOLF

LAKEWOOD COUNTY GOLF COURSE
ARCHITECT: WILLIAM P. BELL, 1933

3101 Carson Street
Lakewood, CA 90712

PRO SHOP: 562-429-9711

Len Kennet, Director of Golf, PGA
Jorge Badel, PGA Professional
Craig McDonald, General Manager

Driving Range ●
Practice Greens ●
Clubhouse ●
Food / Beverage ●
Accommodations
Pull Carts ●
Power Carts ●
Club Rental ●
$pecial Offers

	1	2	3	4	5	6	7	8	9	OUT
BACK	415	415	162	349	225	443	506	364	497	3376
REGULAR	407	398	140	339	217	434	489	346	486	3256
par	4	4	3	4	3	4	5	4	5	36
handicap	7	3	15	17	5	1	11	9	13	-
FORWARD	365	374	116	316	189	418	464	313	436	2991
par	4	4	3	4	3	5	5	4	5	37
handicap	5	3	17	13	15	9	1	11	7	-

	10	11	12	13	14	15	16	17	18	IN
BACK	408	376	216	421	487	343	373	197	542	3363
REGULAR	389	363	200	402	473	324	352	178	508	3189
par	4	4	3	4	5	4	4	3	5	36
handicap	8	10	4	2	16	18	14	12	6	-
FORWARD	362	343	155	374	453	308	339	148	447	2929
par	4	4	3	4	5	4	4	3	5	36
handicap	6	10	16	2	14	12	8	18	4	-

BACK	
yardage	6739
par	72
rating	71.5
slope	110

REGULAR	
yardage	6445
par	72
rating	70.2
slope	108

FORWARD	
yardage	5920
par	73
rating	74.1
slope	121

SKYLINKS GOLF COURSE
ARCHITECT: WILLIAM F. BELL, 1959

4800 Wardlow Road
Long Beach, CA 90808

PRO SHOP: 562-429-0030

Andrew Valainis, Manager, PGA
Bob Chaffee, PGA Professional
Jorge Morales, Superintendent

Driving Range ●
Practice Greens ●
Clubhouse ●
Food / Beverage ●
Accommodations
Pull Carts ●
Power Carts ●
Club Rental ●
$pecial Offers

	1	2	3	4	5	6	7	8	9	OUT
BACK	322	507	342	417	159	490	383	372	180	3172
REGULAR	314	497	324	405	150	477	368	358	170	3063
par	4	5	4	4	3	5	4	4	3	36
handicap	13	3	15	1	17	11	9	7	5	-
FORWARD	307	473	301	408	127	472	364	349	160	2961
par	4	5	4	5	3	5	4	4	3	37
handicap	13	5	11	7	17	1	9	3	15	-

	10	11	12	13	14	15	16	17	18	IN
BACK	350	516	368	165	314	176	468	397	428	3182
REGULAR	340	495	348	148	304	164	458	384	421	3062
par	4	5	4	3	4	3	5	4	4	36
handicap	10	2	8	16	18	14	12	4	6	-
FORWARD	327	496	343	138	291	148	449	364	401	2957
par	4	5	4	3	4	3	5	4	4	37
handicap	12	4	8	18	14	16	2	6	10	-

BACK	
yardage	6354
par	72
rating	69.3
slope	111

REGULAR	
yardage	6125
par	72
rating	68.2
slope	109

FORWARD	
yardage	5918
par	74
rating	73.5
slope	119

PLAY POLICY & FEES: Greens fees are $20 weekdays and $25 weekends. Twilight rates are $14 weekdays, and $17 weekends. Senior rates are $10, and junior rates are $5 weekdays only. Carts are $22.

TEE TIMES: Reservations can be made seven days in advance. Be persistent and call early.

DRESS CODE: No tank tops are allowed on the course.

COURSE DESCRIPTION: This is a fairly flat course built alongside an 11-acre lake that brings water into play on the second, third, sixth, ninth, 10th, 11th, and 12th holes.

NOTES: This course can be noisy because it is located near Long Beach Airport. It is the site of the annual Queen Mary Open.

LOCATION: Take the Lakewood Boulevard (Highway 19) exit off Interstate 405 near the Long Beach Airport and head north. At Carson Street turn left and drive about two miles to the club.

. . . ● **TOURNAMENTS:** Shotgun tournaments are available weekdays only. A 24-player minimum is required to book a tournament.

75. LAKEWOOD COUNTY GOLF COURSE

PLAY POLICY & FEES: Green fees are $14.50 weekdays and $18.50 weekends for Long Beach residents, and $19 weekdays and $23 weekends for nonresidents. Carts are $21. Pull carts are $2.

TEE TIMES: Tee times can be booked six days in advance with a reservation card through the reservation office. Otherwise tee times can be booked three days in advance at the course.

DRESS CODE: Tank tops and short shorts are not allowed.

COURSE DESCRIPTION: This is a fairly flat course with tree-lined fairways and water on three holes. Severe doglegs spice up this layout. It can be noisy because it is located near Long Beach Airport.

NOTES: Four greens have recently been rebuilt on holes 2, 5, 8 and 9.

LOCATION: Take Interstate 405 south to Long Beach. Exit on Lakewood Boulevard north. The course is located three blocks down on the right, across from the Long Beach Airport.

. . . ● **TOURNAMENTS:** This course is available for tournaments. Tournaments can be booked one month in advance. ● **TRAVEL:** The Mission Inn, Days Inn, and Best Western are convenient lodging facilities.

76. SKYLINKS GOLF COURSE

77 HEARTWELL GOLF PARK
ARCHITECT: WILLIAM F. BELL, 1962

6700 East Carson Street
Long Beach, CA 90808

PRO SHOP: 562-421-8855

Craig Hatfield, Head Professional, PGA
Shanna Robb, General Manager

Driving Range ●
Practice Greens ●
Clubhouse ●
Food / Beverage ●
Accommodations
Pull Carts ●
Power Carts ●
Club Rental ●
$pecial Offers

	1	2	3	4	5	6	7	8	9	OUT
BACK	-	-	-	-	-	-	-	-	-	
REGULAR	128	135	91	126	125	121	121	140	150	1137
par	3	3	3	3	3	3	3	3	3	27
handicap	5	3	17	7	13	15	11	9	1	
FORWARD	128	135	91	126	125	121	121	140	150	1137
par	3	3	3	3	3	3	3	3	3	27
handicap	5	3	17	7	13	15	11	9	1	

	10	11	12	13	14	15	16	17	18	IN
BACK	-	-	-	-	-	-	-	-	-	
REGULAR	119	103	85	130	85	118	119	136	121	1016
par	3	3	3	3	3	3	3	3	3	27
handicap	10	18	14	2	16	12	6	4	8	
FORWARD	119	103	85	130	85	118	119	136	121	1016
par	3	3	3	3	3	3	3	3	3	27
handicap	10	18	14	2	16	12	6	4	8	

BACK	
yardage	-
par	-
rating	-
slope	-

REGULAR	
yardage	2153
par	54
rating	50.1
slope	-

FORWARD	
yardage	2153
par	54
rating	50.1
slope	-

78 CYPRESS GOLF CLUB
ARCHITECT: PETER DYE, 1992

4921 Katella Avenue
Los Alamitos, CA 90720

PRO SHOP: 714-527-1800

Steve Shimand, Manager
Keith McDuff, PGA Professional

Driving Range ●
Practice Greens ●
Clubhouse ●
Food / Beverage ●
Accommodations
Pull Carts
Power Carts ●
Club Rental ●
$pecial Offers

	1	2	3	4	5	6	7	8	9	OUT
BACK	348	407	182	502	116	416	268	325	372	2936
REGULAR	316	399	167	485	105	378	260	306	337	2753
par	4	4	3	5	3	4	4	4	4	35
handicap	11	3	5	9	15	1	17	13	7	-
FORWARD	264	303	116	405	82	298	220	249	270	2207
par	4	4	3	5	3	4	4	4	4	35
handicap	11	1	9	5	17	3	15	13	7	-

	10	11	12	13	14	15	16	17	18	IN
BACK	493	196	283	345	360	554	302	140	430	3103
REGULAR	479	179	275	322	344	545	271	122	403	2940
par	5	3	4	4	4	5	4	3	4	36
handicap	10	6	18	12	8	4	14	16	2	-
FORWARD	406	121	228	255	275	427	207	93	350	2362
par	5	3	4	4	4	5	4	3	4	36
handicap	8	10	16	12	6	4	14	18	2	-

BACK	
yardage	6039
par	71
rating	69.0
slope	122

REGULAR	
yardage	5693
par	71
rating	67.2
slope	118

FORWARD	
yardage	4569
par	71
rating	68.2
slope	115

PLAY POLICY & FEES: Green fees are $7.50 weekdays and $8.50 weekends for 18 holes for Long Beach residents, and $9.50 weekdays and $10.50 weekends for 18 holes for nonresidents. Carts are $7.50 for nine holes and $10.50 for 18 holes.

TEE TIMES: Reservations can be booked seven days in advance.

DRESS CODE: Golf attire is encouraged.

COURSE DESCRIPTION: This well-conditioned course has elevated greens. The longest holes are the eighth and ninth at 140 yards. The course and driving range are lighted for night play.

NOTES: This is a course Tiger Woods began playing virtually from infancy.

LOCATION: Off Interstate 405 in Long Beach, take the Lakewood Boulevard exit north. Follow Lakewood two miles to Carson Street and turn right. The course is 1.5 miles on the right.

. . . ● **TOURNAMENTS:** All shotgun tournaments must have approval of the golf commission. A 16-player minimum is needed to book a tournament.

77. HEARTWELL GOLF PARK

PLAY POLICY & FEES: Green fees are $55 weekdays and $80 weekends. Twilight tees are $45 weekdays and $65 weekends. Cypress offers an early-bird special of $45 Monday through Friday if you tee off before 7:30 A.M. All green fees include carts.

TEE TIMES: Reservations can be booked 14 days in advance.

DRESS CODE: Appropriate golf attire and nonmetal spikes are required. No denim is allowed.

COURSE DESCRIPTION: Cypress is a spectacular and challenging championship 18-hole golf course. A combination of water hazards, bunkers, and mounds have been used to create scenic and demanding holes. The greens are large with subtle breaks sure to challenge every golfer.

NOTES: The course record of 63 was set by Tiger Woods.

LOCATION: From Interstate 605 near Interstate 405, take the Katella Avenue exit to the racetrack and turn left.

. . . ● **TOURNAMENTS:** A 13-player minimum is needed to book a tournament. A banquet facility is available that can accomodate 200 people.

78. CYPRESS GOLF CLUB

NAVY GOLF COURSES: LONG BEACH
ARCHITECT: JOESPH B. WILLIAMS, 1966

5660 Orangewood Avenue
Cypress, CA 90630

PRO SHOP: 714-527-4401

Paul Moreno, Manager
Don Rasmussen, Professional
Gilbert Quintero, Superintendent

Driving Range ●
Practice Greens ●
Clubhouse ●
Food / Beverage ●
Accommodations
Pull Carts ●
Power Carts ●
Club Rental ●
$pecial Offers

	1	2	3	4	5	6	7	8	9	OUT
BACK	398	342	532	383	366	570	412	391	186	3580
REGULAR	388	298	506	367	359	550	393	380	157	3398
par	4	4	5	4	4	5	4	4	3	37
handicap	3	15	7	13	11	1	5	9	17	-
FORWARD	379	293	457	352	351	497	341	357	125	3152
par	4	4	5	4	4	5	4	4	3	37
handicap	11	15	3	13	9	1	5	7	17	-

BACK									
yardage	6830
par	72
rating	73.5
slope	131

	10	11	12	13	14	15	16	17	18	IN
BACK	371	179	373	516	422	162	444	218	565	3250
REGULAR	355	163	352	493	410	157	435	203	549	3117
par	4	3	4	5	4	3	4	3	5	35
handicap	6	18	12	10	8	16	2	14	4	-
FORWARD	346	134	285	448	395	107	377	192	478	2762
par	4	3	4	5	4	3	4	3	5	35
handicap	6	16	12	2	8	18	10	14	4	-

REGULAR	
yardage	6515
par	72
rating	71.2
slope	124

FORWARD	
yardage	5914
par	72
rating	73.6
slope	126

 EL DORADO GOLF COURSE

2400 Studebaker Road
Long Beach, CA 90815

PRO SHOP: 562-430-5411

Spencer McDaniel, PGA Professional

Driving Range ●
Practice Greens ●
Clubhouse ●
Food / Beverage ●
Accommodations
Pull Carts ●
Power Carts ●
Club Rental ●
$pecial Offers

	1	2	3	4	5	6	7	8	9	OUT
BACK	366	352	156	512	365	371	496	440	190	3248
REGULAR	348	338	148	496	355	356	485	425	181	3132
par	4	4	3	5	4	4	5	4	3	36
handicap	5	11	15	13	9	3	17	1	7	-
FORWARD	340	330	139	485	347	349	422	459	171	3042
par	4	4	3	5	4	4	5	5	3	37
handicap	11	13	17	3	7	5	9	1	15	-

BACK	
yardage	6474
par	72
rating	71.0
slope	121

	10	11	12	13	14	15	16	17	18	IN
BACK	544	381	197	395	373	377	325	151	483	3226
REGULAR	531	370	183	382	367	366	317	142	477	3135
par	5	4	3	4	4	4	4	3	5	36
handicap	4	8	12	2	16	6	18	14	10	-
FORWARD	505	280	169	373	352	360	394	130	402	2965
par	5	4	3	4	4	4	4	3	5	36
handicap	2	12	16	4	10	8	14	18	6	-

REGULAR	
yardage	6267
par	72
rating	69.8
slope	118

FORWARD	
yardage	6007
par	73
rating	74.3
slope	126

27

HOLES

PLAY POLICY & FEES: Military personnel and guests only. Green fees are $6 to $14 for military personnel and $26 to $29 for guests. Carts are $17.

DRESS CODE: Appropriate golf attire is required.

COURSE DESCRIPTION: Tree-lined fairways, numerous water hazards, and offshore breezes add to the character and challenge of the Destroyer Course. Beware of the par-3, 186-yard ninth hole. Tee shots must carry over water to a bunker-lined green.

NOTES: There is also a par-32, nine-hole executive course. The Destroyer Course: See scorecard for yardage and rating information. The Cruiser Course is 4,031 yards and rated 55.8 from the regular tees. The slope rating is 85. Tiger Woods often played here; his father, Earl, was a career Army officer. This is a busy course, with over 90,000 rounds played each year.

LOCATION: Heading south on Interstate 405 (San Diego Freeway), bear right at the intersection with the Garden Grove Freeway to the Cypress–Valley View exit. Drive north 1.5 miles to Orangewood Avenue, then left to the course.

. . . ● **TOURNAMENTS:** This course is available for charity events. Reservations must be made one year in advance. No weekend shotguns are allowed.

79. NAVY GOLF COURSES: LONG BEACH

18

HOLES

PLAY POLICY & FEES: Green fees are $18.50 weekdays and $22.50 weekends for nonresidents and $14.50 weekdays and $18 weekends for residents. Weekday twilight rates are $10 for residents and $12 for nonresidents after 4 p.m. Weekend twilight rates are $12.50 for residents and $14.50 for nonresidents after 4 p.m. To obtain resident rates, players must present a discount card from Long Beach's Recreation and Parks Department. The discount card fee is $10. Carts are $21.

TEE TIMES: Reservations can be booked six days in advance with a reservation card and three days without.

DRESS CODE: Appropriate golf attire is required.

COURSE DESCRIPTION: This course is mostly level with lots of doglegs and trees at least 50 years old lining the fairways. Water comes into play on five holes.

NOTES: The Long Beach Open is played here annually.

LOCATION: From Los Angeles travel south on Interstate 405 (San Diego Freeway) to the Studebaker Road exit. Turn north and drive three-fourths of a mile to the club.

. . . ● **TOURNAMENTS:** A 64-player minimum is needed to book a tournament. A few shotgun tournaments are allowed each year.

80. EL DORADO GOLF COURSE

OLD RANCH COUNTRY CLUB
ARCHITECT: TED ROBINSON, 1965

3901 Lampson Avenue
Seal Beach, CA 90740

PRO SHOP: 562-596-4611
CLUBHOUSE: 562-596-4425

Bill Elvins, Manager
Robert Silver, Director of Golf, PGA
Don Parsons, Superintendent

Driving Range ●
Practice Greens ●
Clubhouse ●
Food / Beverage ●
Accommodations ●
Pull Carts
Power Carts ●
Club Rental
$pecial Offers

	1	2	3	4	5	6	7	8	9	OUT
BACK	337	371	168	545	316	383	211	537	402	3270
REGULAR	330	359	150	512	299	362	184	521	380	3097
par	4	4	3	5	4	4	3	5	4	36
handicap	15	1	17	9	13	3	11	5	7	-
FORWARD	319	346	142	500	291	354	140	503	367	2962
par	4	4	3	5	4	4	3	5	4	36
handicap	13	1	11	7	17	5	15	3	9	-

	10	11	12	13	14	15	16	17	18	IN
BACK	375	135	383	380	530	205	400	413	524	3345
REGULAR	347	126	364	353	503	160	362	380	504	3099
par	4	3	4	4	5	3	4	4	5	36
handicap	12	18	8	16	2	14	4	10	6	-
FORWARD	326	116	357	319	487	142	346	351	471	2915
par	4	3	4	4	5	3	4	4	5	36
handicap	14	18	2	16	6	12	4	10	8	-

BACK	
yardage	6615
par	72
rating	71.8
slope	126

REGULAR	
yardage	6196
par	72
rating	69.4
slope	118

FORWARD	
yardage	5877
par	72
rating	74.5
slope	133

 RECREATION PARK GOLF COURSE
ARCHITECT: WILLIAM F. BELL, 1969

5001 Deukmejian Drive
Long Beach, CA 90804

PRO SHOP: 562-494-5000

David McGrady, General Manager
Bruce McDaniel, PGA Professional
Sam Zeller, Tournament Director

Driving Range ●
Practice Greens ●
Clubhouse ●
Food / Beverage ●
Accommodations
Pull Carts ●
Power Carts ●
Club Rental ●
$pecial Offers

	1	2	3	4	5	6	7	8	9	OUT
BACK	289	304	408	355	131	456	427	412	477	3259
REGULAR	282	295	392	342	127	444	416	399	443	3140
par	4	4	4	4	3	4	4	4	5	36
handicap	15	13	5	9	17	1	3	7	11	-
FORWARD	267	272	377	317	124	414	416	381	425	2993
par	4	4	4	4	3	5	5	4	5	38
handicap	15	13	3	7	17	9	5	1	11	-

	10	11	12	13	14	15	16	17	18	IN
BACK	421	359	130	300	510	324	147	480	387	3058
REGULAR	407	338	124	286	498	319	139	449	375	2935
par	4	4	3	4	5	4	3	5	4	36
handicap	2	10	16	14	4	12	18	6	8	-
FORWARD	389	306	124	271	494	310	119	426	361	2800
par	4	4	3	4	5	4	3	5	4	36
handicap	6	10	16	14	2	12	18	8	4	-

BACK	
yardage	6317
par	72
rating	69.9
slope	111

REGULAR	
yardage	6075
par	72
rating	68.8
slope	108

FORWARD	
yardage	5793
par	74
rating	72.4
slope	119

PLAY POLICY & FEES: Members and guests only. Guest fees are $70 weekdays and $80 Friday, weekends, and holidays. Carts are $20 for two riders. Call ahead. The course is being remodeled and may be closed.

DRESS CODE: Appropriate golf attire and nonmetal spikes are required.

COURSE DESCRIPTION: This course is level, but don't let that fool you. Because of its proximity to the ocean, winds can greatly affect playing conditions. The holes are tight, and the well-maintained greens are protected by water. The best holes on the course are the four finishing holes.

NOTES: The course is under construction as it is being completely redesigned by Ted Robinson. The layout will be completely different. The course will remain private, but will have a double-ended driving range with one end open to the public. The scheduled completion date is June 2000.

LOCATION: Near Long Beach take the Seal Beach exit off Interstate 405 (San Diego Freeway) and turn right. Drive a half mile to Lampson Avenue. Turn right again and drive a half mile to the club.

. . . ● **TOURNAMENTS:** This course is not available for outside events. ●
TRAVEL: The Fish Market restaurant is recommended in Los Alamitos.

81. OLD RANCH COUNTRY CLUB

PLAY POLICY & FEES: Green fees for 18 holes are $18.50 weekdays and $22.50 weekends. Resident rates are available.

TEE TIMES: Reservations can be booked six days in advance with a reservation card and three days in advance without.

DRESS CODE: Spikeless shoes are preferred.

COURSE DESCRIPTION: This course features rolling terrain and undulating greens. The course is fairly wide open and features many trees. It is usually well maintained.

LOCATION: Follow the Pacific Coast Highway (Highway 1) north from Seal Beach and exit at Seventh Street. Drive one-half mile on Seventh to the course entrance. From the Interstate 405 take the highway 22 exit west. Highway 22 becomes Seventh Street. Follow signs to the course.

. . . ● **TOURNAMENTS:** This course is available for outside tournaments and offers a full banquet facility that can accommodate 200 people. A 64-player minimum is needed to book a tournament. Events should be booked 12 months in advance.

82. RECREATION PARK GOLF COURSE

BIXBY VILLAGE GOLF COURSE

ARCHITECTS: RON FREAM, 1979; PETER THOMPSON, 1979; MICHAEL WOLVERIDGE, 1979

6180 Bixby Village Drive
Long Beach, CA 90803

PRO SHOP: 562-498-7003

Robert Jones, Professional

Driving Range
Practice Greens •
Clubhouse •
Food / Beverage •
Accommodations
Pull Carts •
Power Carts
Club Rental •
$pecial Offers

	1	2	3	4	5	6	7	8	9	OUT
BACK	-	-	-	-	-	-	-	-	-	-
REGULAR	146	121	158	284	148	99	184	322	105	1567
par	3	3	3	4	3	3	3	4	3	29
handicap	7	3	6	2	5	9	1	4	8	-
FORWARD	136	101	148	259	130	89	169	290	95	1417
par	3	3	3	4	3	3	3	4	3	29
handicap	7	4	6	2	5	9	3	1	8	-

	10	11	12	13	14	15	16	17	18	IN
BACK	-	-	-	-	-	-	-	-	-	-
REGULAR	146	121	158	284	148	99	184	322	105	1567
par	3	3	3	4	3	3	3	4	3	29
handicap	7	3	6	2	5	9	1	4	8	-
FORWARD	136	101	148	259	130	89	169	290	95	1417
par	3	3	3	4	3	3	3	4	3	29
handicap	7	4	6	2	5	9	3	1	8	-

BACK	
yardage	-
par	-
rating	
slope	

REGULAR	
yardage	3134
par	58
rating	57.5
slope	86

FORWARD	
yardage	2834
par	58
rating	55.1
slope	82

 LEISURE WORLD GOLF COURSE

13580 St. Andrews Drive
Seal Beach, CA 90740

PRO SHOP: 562-431-6586

Fred Cooper, Director of Golf

Driving Range
Practice Greens •
Clubhouse
Food / Beverage
Accommodations
Pull Carts
Power Carts
Club Rental
$pecial Offers

	1	2	3	4	5	6	7	8	9	OUT
BACK	-	-	-	-	-	-	-	-	-	-
REGULAR	105	54	95	115	104	83	79	76	118	829
par	3	3	3	3	3	3	3	3	3	27
handicap	3	17	11	1	7	15	9	13	5	-
FORWARD	105	54	95	115	104	83	79	76	118	829
par	3	3	3	3	3	3	3	3	3	27
handicap	3	17	11	1	7	15	9	13	5	-

	10	11	12	13	14	15	16	17	18	IN
BACK	-	-	-	-	-	-	-	-	-	-
REGULAR	105	54	95	115	104	83	79	76	118	829
par	3	3	3	3	3	3	3	3	3	27
handicap	6	14	10	4	12	18	8	16	2	-
FORWARD	105	54	95	115	104	83	79	76	118	829
par	3	3	3	3	3	3	3	3	3	27
handicap	6	14	10	4	12	18	8	16	2	-

BACK	
yardage	-
par	-
rating	-
slope	-

REGULAR	
yardage	1658
par	54
rating	-
slope	-

FORWARD	
yardage	1658
par	54
rating	-
slope	-

PLAY POLICY & FEES: Green fees are $6.50 weekdays and $9.75 weekends. Replay rate is $5.50 weekdays and $6.50 weekends. Seniors pay $5.75 weekdays.

TEE TIMES: Reservations can be booked seven days in advance.

DRESS CODE: Shirts and shoes are necessary. Nonmetal spikes are encouraged.

COURSE DESCRIPTION: This hilly course has undulating greens and two lakes. The longest hole is the par-4 eighth at 322 yards.

LOCATION: On Interstate 405 south in Long Beach, exit on Bellflower Boulevard and drive south. Veer left on the Pacific Coast Highway (Highway 1). Turn left on Loynes Drive and drive one-quarter mile to Bixby Village Drive. Turn left on Bixby Village Drive to the course.

. . . ● TOURNAMENTS: A 16-player minimum is required to book an event. Tournaments should be booked three months in advance. ● TRAVEL: Best Western Golden Sails is located across the street from the golf course. For reservations call 562-596-1631.

83. BIXBY VILLAGE GOLF COURSE

PLAY POLICY & FEES: Members only. This is a resident course. No reciprocal play is allowed.

COURSE DESCRIPTION: This residential course is flat. A pond offers some excitement on four or five holes.

LOCATION: On Interstate 405 heading south to Seal Beach, exit on Seal Beach Boulevard east. Turn left (south) and drive two blocks to the course on the right.

. . . ● TOURNAMENTS: This course is not available for outside events.

84. LEISURE WORLD GOLF COURSE

MEADOWLARK GOLF COURSE
ARCHITECT: WILLIAM P. BELL, 1922

16782 Graham Street
Huntington Beach, CA
92649
PRO SHOP: 714-846-1364
CLUBHOUSE: 714-846-4450

Mez White, General Manager
Dan Yenny, PGA Professional
Sarah Nordachi, Tournament Director

Driving Range ●
Practice Greens ●
Clubhouse ●
Food / Beverage ●
Accommodations
Pull Carts ●
Power Carts ●
Club Rental ●
$pecial Offers

	1	2	3	4	5	6	7	8	9	OUT
BACK	-	-	-	-	-	-	-	-	-	-
REGULAR	450	176	246	484	350	255	222	262	395	2840
par	4	3	4	5	4	4	3	4	4	35
handicap	1	7	17	11	9	15	5	13	3	-
FORWARD	438	144	238	480	341	239	222	242	384	2728
par	5	3	4	5	4	4	3	4	4	36
handicap	3	17	9	1	13	7	15	11	5	-

	10	11	12	13	14	15	16	17	18	IN
BACK	-	-	-	-	-	-	-	-	-	-
REGULAR	357	294	378	174	400	315	155	361	476	2910
par	4	4	4	3	4	4	3	4	5	35
handicap	12	18	8	4	2	14	10	16	6	-
FORWARD	354	287	364	166	392	302	146	352	440	2803
par	4	4	4	3	4	4	3	4	5	35
handicap	10	14	6	16	4	8	18	12	2	-

BACK	
yardage	-
par	-
rating	-
slope	-

REGULAR	
yardage	5750
par	70
rating	66.2
slope	104

FORWARD	
yardage	5531
par	71
rating	71.2
slope	116

 SEACLIFF COUNTRY CLUB
ARCHITECT: PRESS MAXWELL, 1965

6501 Palm Avenue
Huntington Beach, CA
92648
PRO SHOP: 714-536-7575
CLUBHOUSE: 714-536-8866

Kevitt Sale, General Manager
Travis Brasher, Professional
Kevin Neal, Superintendent

Driving Range ●
Practice Greens ●
Clubhouse ●
Food / Beverage ●
Accommodations
Pull Carts
Power Carts ●
Club Rental ●
$pecial Offers

	1	2	3	4	5	6	7	8	9	OUT
BACK	514	359	167	542	392	375	355	410	139	3253
REGULAR	458	343	145	502	346	359	340	378	120	2991
par	5	4	3	5	4	4	4	4	3	36
handicap	7	15	9	5	3	13	11	1	17	-
FORWARD	439	331	108	464	330	340	323	351	92	2778
par	5	4	3	5	4	4	4	4	3	36
handicap	3	11	15	1	13	9	7	5	17	-

	10	11	12	13	14	15	16	17	18	IN
BACK	385	373	502	178	373	375	409	189	481	3265
REGULAR	355	350	478	165	352	343	383	168	461	3055
par	4	4	5	3	4	4	4	3	5	36
handicap	6	10	14	16	4	12	2	18	8	-
FORWARD	330	333	416	151	309	319	360	138	438	2794
par	4	4	5	3	4	4	4	3	5	36
handicap	8	10	12	16	2	14	6	18	4	-

BACK	
yardage	6518
par	72
rating	73.5
slope	126

REGULAR	
yardage	6046
par	72
rating	68.7
slope	114

FORWARD	
yardage	5572
par	72
rating	72.3
slope	123

18
HOLES

PLAY POLICY & FEES: Green fees are $24 Monday through Thursday, $25 Friday, and $33 weekends and holidays. Twilight, senior, and junior rates are available. Carts are $12 per person.

TEE TIMES: Reservations are available 21 days in advance beginning at 6 a.m.

DRESS CODE: No tank tops are allowed.

COURSE DESCRIPTION: Established in the early 1920s, this is a rolling course with narrow, tree-lined fairways. The greens are small, so shot placement is essential. There are several water hazards. The course is located close to the ocean in Huntington Beach, so it is subject to ocean breezes. The upside is that the air is usually clean and clear.

NOTES: This is a busy course, with 125,000 rounds played here per year.

LOCATION: From south Orange County, drive north on Interstate 405 to the Warner Avenue exit and go west four miles to Graham Street. Turn right to the club.

. . . ● **TOURNAMENTS:** This course is available for outside tournaments.

85. MEADOWLARK GOLF COURSE

18
HOLES

PLAY POLICY & FEES: Reciprocal play is accepted with members of other private clubs; otherwise, members and guests only. Reciprocators' green fees are $70 every day. Guest fees are $50 weekdays and $70 weekends and holidays. Carts are $12.

DRESS CODE: Appropriate golf attire is required. Nonmetal spikes are encouraged.

COURSE DESCRIPTION: This course was formerly a public layout under the Huntington Seacliff name but has been private for over a decade. It was remodeled in 1985 by Ron Fream and is long with undulating greens. It is well maintained.

LOCATION: In Huntington Beach travel south on Interstate 405 (San Diego Freeway) to the Golden West exit. Turn right and drive seven miles to Palm Avenue. Turn right and drive to the club.

. . . ● **TOURNAMENTS:** This course is available for outside tournaments on Monday. A 100-player minimum is needed to book a tournament.

86. SEACLIFF COUNTRY CLUB

MILE SQUARE GOLF COURSE

ARCHITECT: H. RAINVILLE, D. RAINVILLE, 1969

10401 Warner Avenue
Fountain Valley, CA 92708

PRO SHOP: 714-968-4556
CLUBHOUSE: 714-575-7106

Scott Chaffin, Director of Golf, PGA

Driving Range •
Practice Greens •
Clubhouse •
Food / Beverage •
Accommodations
Pull Carts •
Power Carts •
Club Rental •
Special Offers

	1	2	3	4	5	6	7	8	9	OUT
BACK	380	423	383	508	180	394	366	176	527	3337
REGULAR	369	410	365	495	171	383	358	165	514	3230
par	4	4	4	5	3	4	4	3	5	36
handicap	5	3	11	15	17	1	9	7	13	-
FORWARD	313	340	321	450	136	329	313	132	456	2790
par	5	4	4	3	5	3	4	5	3	36
handicap	6	8	4	14	2	16	10	12	18	-

	10	11	12	13	14	15	16	17	18	IN
BACK	545	379	391	153	524	190	407	504	199	3292
REGULAR	531	369	380	144	511	175	396	494	180	3180
par	5	4	4	3	5	3	4	5	3	36
handicap	8	4	6	16	14	12	2	18	10	-
FORWARD	449	315	339	121	487	142	334	436	132	2755
par	4	4	4	5	3	4	4	3	5	36
handicap	9	7	11	3	17	1	13	15	5	-

BACK	
yardage	6629
par	72
rating	71.0
slope	119

REGULAR	
yardage	6410
par	72
rating	69.6
slope	117

FORWARD	
yardage	5545
par	72
rating	70.5
slope	109

 DAVID L. BAKER MEMORIAL GOLF COURSE

ARCHITECTS: GARRET GILL, 1989; GEORGE B. WILLIAMS

10410 Edinger Avenue
Fountain Valley, CA 92708

PRO SHOP: 714-418-2152

Michael Shank, General Manager
Larry Brown , Head Professional, PGA

Driving Range •
Practice Greens •
Clubhouse •
Food / Beverage •
Accommodations
Pull Carts •
Power Carts •
Club Rental •
Special Offers

	1	2	3	4	5	6	7	8	9	OUT
BACK	-	-	-	-	-	-	-	-	-	-
REGULAR	138	297	118	279	191	281	147	145	316	1912
par	3	4	3	4	3	4	3	3	4	31
handicap	15	3	17	7	5	9	11	13	1	-
FORWARD	138	297	118	279	191	281	147	145	316	1912
par	3	4	3	4	3	4	3	3	4	31
handicap	15	3	17	7	5	9	11	13	1	-

	10	11	12	13	14	15	16	17	18	IN
BACK	-	-	-	-	-	-	-	-	-	-
REGULAR	133	315	137	313	209	147	260	281	187	1982
par	3	4	3	4	3	3	4	4	3	31
handicap	18	2	16	4	6	14	12	10	8	-
FORWARD	133	315	137	313	209	147	260	281	187	1982
par	3	4	3	4	3	3	4	4	3	31
handicap	18	2	16	4	6	14	12	10	8	-

BACK	
yardage	-
par	-
rating	-
slope	-

REGULAR	
yardage	3894
par	62
rating	57.7
slope	91

FORWARD	
yardage	3894
par	62
rating	54.6
slope	91

PLAY POLICY & FEES: Green fees are $24 Monday through Thursday and $30 Friday through Sunday and holidays. Carts are $22.

TEE TIMES: Weekday reservations can be booked seven days in advance, Monday for Saturday, and Tuesday for Sunday.

DRESS CODE: Shirts must be worn.

COURSE DESCRIPTION: This is a fairly open and level course. There are numerous mature trees, a small creek, and three lakes that add to the course's challenge and scenery. You can find water off the 4th, 15th, and 17th tees if you're not careful. The course is usually in good condition. Afternoon breezes usually make the back nine difficult. Many fairways parallel one another, so errant tee shots can still be played.

NOTES: Red foxes inhabit the course. They are quite tame and have been known to steal golf balls and resell them in the pro shop.

LOCATION: In Fountain Valley take the Brookhurst Street/Fountain Valley exit off Interstate 405 (San Diego Freeway) and follow the Brookhurst Street north off-ramp. Continue north one mile to Warner Avenue and turn right. Drive a half mile to Ward Street and turn left to the course.

. . . ● **TOURNAMENTS:** This course does not allow shotgun starts. A 24-player minimum is needed to book a tournament.

87. MILE SQUARE GOLF COURSE

PLAY POLICY & FEES: Green fees are $16 from Monday through Thursday, $17 Friday, and $22 on weekends and holidays. Senior, junior, twilight, and supertwilight rates are available. Power carts are $20 and pull carts are $3. The course is lighted for night play.

TEE TIMES: Reservations can be booked seven days in advance.

COURSE DESCRIPTION: This course has five lakes which come into play on nine holes and has many well-placed bunkers. There are no par 5s.

NOTES: David L. Baker Memorial Golf Course has a banquet facility that holds 250 people.

LOCATION: Off Interstate 405 near Fountain Valley, take the Brookhurst exit north for two miles and turn right on Edinger Avenue.

. . . ● **TOURNAMENTS:** Shotgun tournaments are available weekdays only. A 12-player minimum is required to book a tournament.

88. DAVID L. BAKER MEMORIAL GOLF

COSTA MESA GOLF & COUNTRY CLUB
ARCHITECT: WILLIAM F. BELL, 1967

1701 Golf Course Drive
Costa Mesa, CA 92626

PRO SHOP: 714-540-7500
STARTER: 714-754-5267

Scott Henderson, Managing General Partner
Brad Booth, PGA Professional
Jim Fetlerly, Superintendent

Driving Range ●
Practice Greens ●
Clubhouse ●
Food / Beverage ●
Accommodations
Pull Carts ●
Power Carts ●
Club Rental ●
$pecial Offers

	1	2	3	4	5	6	7	8	9	OUT
BACK	528	531	412	178	359	545	209	304	344	3410
REGULAR	509	509	390	161	343	510	195	290	331	3238
par	5	5	4	3	4	5	3	4	4	37
handicap	11	5	1	9	13	7	3	17	15	-
FORWARD	496	489	362	149	309	490	172	279	317	3063
par	5	5	4	3	4	5	3	4	4	37
handicap	5	1	7	17	9	3	15	13	11	-

	10	11	12	13	14	15	16	17	18	IN
BACK	371	164	357	373	560	193	414	183	522	3137
REGULAR	357	150	337	355	542	189	404	168	502	3004
par	4	3	4	4	5	3	4	3	5	35
handicap	14	12	16	6	4	8	2	10	18	-
FORWARD	345	142	310	342	526	155	391	152	489	2852
par	4	3	4	4	5	3	4	3	5	35
handicap			8	18	12	6	2	14	4	-

BACK	
yardage	6547
par	72
rating	70.5
slope	117

REGULAR	
yardage	6242
par	72
rating	68.9
slope	111

FORWARD	
yardage	5915
par	72
rating	73.3
slope	118

 MESA VERDE COUNTRY CLUB
ARCHITECT: WILLIAM F. BELL, 1958

3000 Club House Road
Costa Mesa, CA 92626

PRO SHOP: 714-549-0522
CLUBHOUSE: 714-549-0377

Kim Porter, Manager, PGA
Tom Sargent, PGA Professional
Eric Lover, Superintendent

Driving Range ●
Practice Greens ●
Clubhouse ●
Food / Beverage ●
Accommodations
Pull Carts ●
Power Carts ●
Club Rental
$pecial Offers

	1	2	3	4	5	6	7	8	9	OUT
BACK	465	360	169	574	453	383	222	402	390	3418
REGULAR	451	343	155	505	408	365	201	384	357	3169
par	5	4	3	5	4	4	3	4	4	36
handicap	17	7	15	9	1	11	13	5	3	-
FORWARD	434	321	148	461	321	302	154	322	314	2777
par	5	4	3	5	4	4	3	4	4	36
handicap	11	3	15	5	9	13	17	7	1	-

	10	11	12	13	14	15	16	17	18	IN
BACK	446	585	134	576	419	367	176	405	200	3308
REGULAR	424	552	123	550	373	344	165	391	175	3097
par	4	5	3	5	4	4	3	4	3	35
handicap	2	6	18	4	12	14	16	10	8	-
FORWARD	376	460	116	456	330	316	149	345	134	2682
par	4	5	3	5	4	4	3	4	3	35
handicap	2	4	16	6	10	12	18	8	14	-

BACK	
yardage	6726
par	71
rating	72.4
slope	130

REGULAR	
yardage	6266
par	71
rating	69.9
slope	124

FORWARD	
yardage	5459
par	71
rating	72.0
slope	135

36
HOLES

PLAY POLICY & FEES: Los Lagos green fees are $24 Monday through Thursday, $26 Friday, and $33 weekends. Mesa Linda green fees are $18 Monday through Thursday, $21 Friday, and $25 on weekends. Resident, twilight, and senior rates are available. Carts are $22.

TEE TIMES: Reservations can be booked seven days in advance.

DRESS CODE: Nonmetal spikes are preferred.

COURSE DESCRIPTION: Los Lagos is the older of the two courses and it features many trees, three lakes, and a rolling layout. When the wind comes up, as it often does, this course can be extremely difficult. It is a short, flat course that is excellent for seniors.

NOTES: The Los Lagos Course: See scorecard for yardage and rating information. The par-70 Mesa Linda Course is 5,529 yards and rated 66.1 from the championship tees with a slope of 107. Costa Mesa is the site of the annual Costa Mesa City Championship. The driving range is lighted for night practice.

LOCATION: Traveling south on Interstate 405 (near Huntington Beach and Costa Mesa), exit on Harbor Boulevard. Continue south one mile to Adams Avenue and turn right. Drive one-quarter of a mile to Mesa Verde Drive; turn left and then right on Golf Course Drive.

. . . ● **TOURNAMENTS:** Shotgun tournaments are available weekdays only. A 24-player minimum is needed to book a tournament.

89. COSTA MESA GOLF & COUNTRY CLUB

18
HOLES

PLAY POLICY & FEES: Members and guests only. Green fees are $70 weekdays and $90 weekends. Carts are included.

DRESS CODE: Appropriate golf attire and nonmetal spikes are required.

COURSE DESCRIPTION: This mature course offers a variety of holes and hazards and is easy walking. The 18th is a par-3, 200-yarder fronted by water with out-of-bounds left. It usually plays into the wind to a sizable green that slopes toward the water. Overall, the course can be very difficult.

NOTES: The LPGA has played several tournaments here, including the Women's Kemper Open. It was the site of the 1993 USGA Junior Girls Championship.

LOCATION: Travel south on Interstate 405 (San Diego Freeway) to Costa Mesa and take the Harbor Boulevard exit. Drive south and turn right on Adams Street. Continue three-quarters of a mile to Mesa Verde West and turn right on Club House Road.

. . . ● **TOURNAMENTS:** This course is available for outside tournaments on Monday only. Carts are required. A 100-player minimum is needed to book a tournament. Tournaments should be booked at least one year in advance. The banquet facility can accommodate 250 people.

90. MESA VERDE COUNTRY CLUB

91 RIVER VIEW GOLF

1800 West Santa Clara
Santa Ana, CA 92706

Pro Shop: 714-543-1115

Lou Cooper, Professional
Steve Hart, Superintendent

Driving Range ●
Practice Greens ●
Clubhouse ●
Food / Beverage ●
Accommodations
Pull Carts ●
Power Carts ●
Club Rental ●
$pecial Offers

	1	2	3	4	5	6	7	8	9	OUT
BACK	325	178	199	392	545	195	375	525	110	2844
REGULAR	305	164	185	363	528	181	355	477	96	2654
par	4	3	3	4	5	3	4	5	3	34
handicap	7	11	9	15	5	1	3	13	17	-
FORWARD	289	157	165	350	457	156	317	464	91	2446
par	4	3	3	4	5	3	4	5	3	34
handicap	7	11	9	15	5	1	3	13	17	-

	10	11	12	13	14	15	16	17	18	IN
BACK	198	340	470	548	172	480	418	538	194	3358
REGULAR	184	328	447	486	162	461	374	513	181	3136
par	3	4	4	5	3	4	4	5	3	36
handicap	4	10	18	12	6	16	2	8	14	-
FORWARD	172	313	436	454	150	434	357	429	169	2914
par	3	4	4	5	3	5	4	5	3	36
handicap	4	10	18	12	6	16	2	8	14	-

BACK	
yardage	6202
par	70
rating	69.0
slope	109

REGULAR	
yardage	5790
par	70
rating	67.2
slope	106

FORWARD	
yardage	5360
par	70
rating	-
slope	-

92 WILLOWICK GOLF COURSE
Architect: William P. Bell, 1924

3017 West Fifth Street
Santa Ana, CA 92703

Pro Shop: 714-554-0672

Chris Donovan, Manager
Ken Kobayashi, PGA Professional
Roy Haines, Superintendent

Driving Range ●
Practice Greens ●
Clubhouse ●
Food / Beverage ●
Accommodations
Pull Carts ●
Power Carts ●
Club Rental
$pecial Offers

	1	2	3	4	5	6	7	8	9	OUT
BACK	-	-	-	-	-	-	-	-	-	-
REGULAR	327	195	502	155	387	463	183	281	375	2868
par	4	3	5	3	4	5	3	4	4	35
handicap	11	9	3	17	1	7	15	13	5	-
FORWARD	320	190	481	144	349	444	149	267	367	2711
par	4	3	5	3	4	5	3	4	4	35
handicap	13	11	1	17	3	7	15	9	5	-

	10	11	12	13	14	15	16	17	18	IN
BACK	-	-	-	-	-	-	-	-	-	-
REGULAR	520	541	154	388	330	397	286	178	399	3193
par	5	5	3	4	4	4	4	3	4	36
handicap	10	4	18	6	16	2	14	12	18	-
FORWARD	510	532	147	381	323	382	270	157	329	3031
par	5	5	3	4	4	4	4	3	4	36
handicap	4	2	18	8	14	6	16	10	12	-

BACK	
yardage	-
par	-
rating	-
slope	-

REGULAR	
yardage	6061
par	71
rating	67.4
slope	102

FORWARD	
yardage	5742
par	71
rating	71.5
slope	116

18

HOLES

PLAY POLICY & FEES: Green fees are $17 walking and $27 riding on weekdays. Weekend green fees are $34 including carts. Carts are mandatory before noon. After noon green fees are $24 to walk.

TEE TIMES: Reservations can be booked 10 days in advance.

DRESS CODE: No tank tops are allowed on the course.

COURSE DESCRIPTION: This challenging short course crisscrosses the bed of the Santa Ana River. The front nine requires good ball placement, and the back nine is wide open. Because of its proximity to the Santa Ana River, the course is sometimes subject to closing several holes during heavy rains.

LOCATION: Travel south from L.A. on Interstate 5 (Santa Ana Freeway) to the Bristol exit. Head south to Santa Clara Street, then west to the club.

. . . ● **TOURNAMENTS:** This course is available for outside tournaments. Carts are required on weekends.

91. RIVER VIEW GOLF

18

HOLES

PLAY POLICY & FEES: Green fees are $18 weekdays and $28 weekends for 18 holes, and $13 weekdays and $19 weekends for nine holes. Twilight rates are available. Carts are $22.

TEE TIMES: Reservations can be booked seven days in advance.

COURSE DESCRIPTION: This course is wide open and level, with many trees and bunkers. It is an established course that has been a favorite of Southern Californians since the 1920s. It is short and walkable, good for exercising the legs.

NOTES: The course record is 60.

LOCATION: In Santa Ana take the Harbor exit off Highway 22 (Garden Grove Freeway) and travel one mile south to Fifth Street. Turn left on Fifth Street and drive a half mile to the course on the left.

. . . ● **TOURNAMENTS:** A 24-player minimum is needed to book a tournament.

92. WILLOWICK GOLF COURSE

1051 N. Meads
Orange, CA 92869

PRO SHOP: 714-538-5030

John McClendon, Manager
Lynn Stone, Director of Golf, PGA
Tomas Garcia, Superintendent

Driving Range ●
Practice Greens ●
Clubhouse ●
Food / Beverage ●
Accommodations
Pull Carts ●
Power Carts ●
Club Rental ●
$pecial Offers

	1	2	3	4	5	6	7	8	9	OUT
BACK	-	-	-	-	-	-	-	-	-	-
REGULAR	125	143	320	113	235	395	90	305	105	1831
par	3	3	4	3	4	4	3	4	3	31
handicap	7	5	4	6	3	2	9	1	8	-
FORWARD	125	135	320	113	170	395	90	305	105	1758
par	3	3	4	3	4	5	3	4	3	32
handicap	6	5	4	7	3	2	9	1	8	-

	10	11	12	13	14	15	16	17	18	IN
BACK	-	-	-	-	-	-	-	-	-	-
REGULAR	-	-	-	-	-	-	-	-	-	-
par	--	-	-	-	-	-	-	-	-	-
handicap	-	-	-	-	-	-	-	-	-	-
FORWARD	-	-	-	-	-	-	-	-	-	-
par	-	-	-	-	-	-	-	-	-	-
handicap	-	-	-	-	-	-	-	-	-	-

BACK	
yardage	-
par	-
rating	-
slope	-

REGULAR	
yardage	1831
par	31
rating	-
slope	-

FORWARD	
yardage	1758
par	32
rating	-
slope	-

12442 Tustin Ranch Road
Tustin, CA 92782

PRO SHOP: 714-730-1611
CLUBHOUSE: 714-730-4725

Randy Chang, Director of Golf, PGA
Steve Puck, Head Professional, PGA
Skip Anderson, Tournament Director

Driving Range ●
Practice Greens ●
Clubhouse ●
Food / Beverage ●
Accommodations
Pull Carts
Power Carts ●
Club Rental ●
$pecial Offers

	1	2	3	4	5	6	7	8	9	OUT
BACK	409	510	191	401	332	206	394	451	537	3431
REGULAR	372	468	163	353	306	177	348	377	489	3053
par	4	5	3	4	4	3	4	4	5	36
handicap	3	11	15	9	17	7	13	1	5	-
FORWARD	314	430	144	299	280	144	274	322	446	2653
par	4	5	3	4	4	3	4	4	5	36
handicap	5	3	15	11	17	7	9	13	1	-

	10	11	12	13	14	15	16	17	18	IN
BACK	509	170	442	332	392	556	376	198	397	3372
REGULAR	480	136	383	301	343	521	348	151	348	3011
par	5	3	4	4	4	5	4	3	4	36
handicap	16	6	2	18	12	8	14	10	4	-
FORWARD	434	111	309	280	302	449	307	119	299	2610
par	5	3	4	4	4	5	4	3	4	36
handicap	4	10	2	16	12	8	14	18	6	-

BACK	
yardage	6803
par	72
rating	72.4
slope	129

REGULAR	
yardage	6064
par	72
rating	68.7
slope	119

FORWARD	
yardage	5263
par	72
rating	65
slope	110

PLAY POLICY & FEES: Green fees on weekdays are $12 for nine holes and $18 for 18 holes. Green fees on weekends are $18 for nine holes and $26 for 18 holes.
TEE TIMES: Tee times can be made one week in advance.
DRESS CODE: Shirts and shoes are required.
COURSE DESCRIPTION: This slightly hilly executive course is popular among seniors, juniors, and families. Although not long in yardage, Ridgeline is a challenge and requires an accurate short game. This course also offers young players a chance to learn how to hit from uphill, downhill, and side hill lies.
LOCATION: From Highway 55 in Newport Beach, exit at Katella Ave. Head east 3.5 miles and turn right on Meads Avenue. The course is three blocks on the left.
. . . ● **TOURNAMENTS:** This course is available for outside events. Events should be booked one month in advance. The banquet facility can accommodate 200 people.

93. RIDGELINE COUNTRY CLUB

PLAY POLICY & FEES: Green fees are $85 Monday through Wednesday, $95 Thursday and Friday, and $125 weekends and holidays, including carts. Caddies are available and can be reserved 48 hours in advance.
TEE TIMES: Reservations can be made seven days in advance. For reservations over seven days, a $20 fee per player is required.
DRESS CODE: Golf attire is encouraged, but absolutely no T-shirts are allowed. Nonmetal spikes are required.
COURSE DESCRIPTION: Architect Ted Robinson took a flat parcel of land and sculpted an excellent public course from it. Carts are not permitted on fairways, so the course is maintained in country-club-quality condition. The signature hole is the par-3 11th, which requires tee shots to carry a pond that includes waterscapes to an undulating green.
LOCATION: Take Interstate 5 to the Tustin Ranch Road exit. Go left 1.6 miles to Township Drive on the right. From Highway 55 near Tustin, take the 4th Street/Irvine Boulevard exit and go east. Drive three miles and turn left on Tustin Ranch Road. Turn right on Township Drive.
. . . ● **TOURNAMENTS:** A 13-player minimum is required to book a tournament.
● **TRAVEL:** Sutton Place Hotel (949-476-2001), Doubletree Hotel (714-438-4910) and the Hyatt Newporter (949-729-1234) are all recommended for lodging.

94. TUSTIN RANCH GOLF CLUB

PELICAN HILL GOLF CLUB
ARCHITECT: TOM FAZIO, 1991

GOLF 50

22651 Pelican Hill Road
Newport Coast, CA 92657

PRO SHOP: 949-760-0707

Robert Ford, Director of Golf, PGA
Gary Newman, Tournament Director
Joe Hough, Head Professional

Driving Range •
Practice Greens •
Clubhouse •
Food / Beverage •
Accommodations
Pull Carts
Power Carts •
Club Rental •
$pecial Offers •

	1	2	3	4	5	6	7	8	9	OUT
BACK	428	342	332	143	335	396	178	550	434	3138
REGULAR	409	306	310	135	304	374	165	511	422	2936
par	4	4	4	3	4	4	3	5	4	35
handicap	7	13	15	17	9	3	11	5	1	-
FORWARD	395	306	310	122	295	337	153	426	397	2741
par	4	4	4	3	4	4	3	5	4	35
handicap	3	11	13	17	9	7	15	5	1	-

BACK		
yardage	6305
par	70
rating	70.3
slope	125

	10	11	12	13	14	15	16	17	18	IN
BACK	440	348	193	112	516	385	208	547	418	3167
REGULAR	421	329	174	101	471	357	166	533	395	2947
par	4	4	3	3	5	4	3	5	4	35
handicap	2	16	14	18	12	8	10	6	4	-
FORWARD	386	303	155	93	413	311	147	465	395	2668
par	4	4	3	3	5	4	3	5	4	35
handicap	2	12	14	18	6	10	16	4	8	-

REGULAR		
yardage	5883
par	70
rating	72.5
slope	124

FORWARD		
yardage	5409
par	70
rating	68.7
slope	116

PLAY POLICY & FEES: Green fees are $155 Monday through Thursday and $225 Friday through Sunday and holidays, including cart. Twilight rates are available.

TEE TIMES: Reservations can be made seven days in advance without a charge. Tee times can be made up to 60 days in advance with a $20 fee per player. For reservations call 949-760-0707.

DRESS CODE: Appropriate golf attire and nonmetal spikes are required. No denim is allowed.

COURSE DESCRIPTION: The Ocean South Course offers spectacular ocean views from every hole. Designed by Tom Fazio, the course is a good test of golf and can be difficult when the ocean breezes are stiff. More often it is user-friendly. The Ocean North Course is longer, tighter, flatter, and offers spectacular ocean views on every hole. A lighted driving range is available.

NOTES: Par is 70 on the Ocean North Course and 71 on the Ocean South Course. The Ocean North Course is 6,856 yards and rated 73.3 from the gold tees with a slope of 133. The women's tees are 5,800 yards and rated 73.0 with a slope of 125. The Ocean South Course is 6,634 yards and rated 72.1 with a slope of 130 from the gold tees. See scorecard for additional yardage and rating information.

LOCATION: Take Interstate 405 or Highway 55 to Highway 73 (a toll road). Exit at Newport Coast Road. Turn right on Pelican Hill Road South.

. . . ● **TOURNAMENTS:** A 36-player minimum is needed to book a tournament. Tournaments can be booked 12 months in advance. The banquet facility can accommodate 300 people. ● **TRAVEL:** The Hyatt Regency Newport Beach is located 10 minutes from the golf course. Call 714-729-1234 for reservations. The Four Seasons (949-975-1234) is also recommended. ● **$PECIAL OFFERS:** Play-and-stay packages with the Hyatt Regency are available.

95. PELICAN HILL GOLF CLUB

20382 Newport Boulevard
Santa Ana, CA 92707

PRO SHOP: 714-545-7260
CLUBHOUSE: 714-556-3000

Jack Downing, Manager
Mike Reehl, PGA Professional
Dave Zahrte, Superintendent

Driving Range •
Practice Greens •
Clubhouse •
Food / Beverage •
Accommodations
Pull Carts •
Power Carts •
Club Rental •
$Special Offers

	1	2	3	4	5	6	7	8	9	OUT
BACK	536	163	372	423	417	188	390	368	503	3360
REGULAR	518	142	351	402	382	177	377	350	477	3176
par	5	3	4	4	4	3	4	4	5	36
handicap	5	13	17	1	3	15	9	7	11	-
FORWARD	497	124	321	377	361	159	364	334	455	2992
par	5	3	4	4	4	3	4	4	5	36
handicap	1	17	11	3	7	15	9	13	5	-

	10	11	12	13	14	15	16	17	18	IN
BACK	508	150	337	368	208	522	418	192	473	3176
REGULAR	488	134	329	348	187	486	398	181	438	2989
par	5	3	4	4	3	5	4	3	5	36
handicap	8	18	12	4	10	14	2	16	6	-
FORWARD	473	120	314	330	150	463	377	170	420	2817
par	5	3	4	4	3	5	4	3	5	36
handicap	2	18	10	12	16	4	8	14	6	-

BACK	
yardage	6536
par	72
rating	71.7
slope	128

REGULAR	
yardage	6165
par	72
rating	69.9
slope	123

FORWARD	
yardage	5809
par	72
rating	75.2
slope	136

1600 Pacific Coast
Newport Beach, CA 92660

PRO SHOP: 949-644-9680
CLUBHOUSE: 949-644-9550

Jerry Anderson, Director of Golf, PGA
Paul Hahn, Head Professional, PGA
Ron Benedict, Superintendent

Driving Range •
Practice Greens •
Clubhouse •
Food / Beverage •
Accommodations
Pull Carts
Power Carts •
Club Rental •
$Special Offers

	1	2	3	4	5	6	7	8	9	OUT
BACK	339	390	549	143	455	418	360	202	407	3263
REGULAR	332	381	522	134	421	398	335	178	386	3087
par	4	4	5	3	4	4	4	3	4	35
handicap	13	9	7	17	1	3	11	15	5	-
FORWARD	318	339	507	103	452	355	287	139	367	2867
par	4	4	5	3	5	4	4	3	4	36
handicap	11	7	1	17	3	9	13	15	5	-

	10	11	12	13	14	15	16	17	18	IN
BACK	429	344	370	170	397	492	437	185	515	3339
REGULAR	393	326	355	152	377	473	415	158	496	3145
par	4	4	4	3	4	5	4	3	5	36
handicap	4	16	8	18	6	10	2	12	14	-
FORWARD	383	309	337	131	344	431	375	140	479	2929
par	4	4	4	3	4	5	4	3	5	36
handicap	2	16	10	18	12	8	6	14	4	-

BACK	
yardage	6602
par	71
rating	71.5
slope	126

REGULAR	
yardage	6232
par	71
rating	69.5
slope	119

FORWARD	
yardage	5796
par	72
rating	73.7
slope	126

18
HOLES

PLAY POLICY & FEES: Members and guests only. Green fees for guests accompanied by a member are $55 weekdays and $80 weekends. Carts are $20.

DRESS CODE: Nonmetal spikes are mandatory.

COURSE DESCRIPTION: This course has many old trees and five lakes. Water comes into play on several holes. The course is relatively flat, exquisitely maintained, and sometimes noisy; John Wayne Airport is nearby.

NOTES: When PGA Tour star Fred Couples lived in Newport Beach, he played and practiced here frequently.

LOCATION: Travel south from L.A. on Interstate 405 to the Newport Freeway (Highway 55). Exit at Mesa Drive, turn left, and drive 100 yards to Newport Boulevard. Turn left and drive 100 yards to the club.

. . . ● **TOURNAMENTS:** This course is not available for outside events.

96. SANTA ANA COUNTRY CLUB

18
HOLES

PLAY POLICY & FEES: Reciprocal play is accepted with members of other private clubs. Guest fees with a member are $75 weekdays and $85 weekends and holidays. The reciprocal fee is $125. Reservations are required.

TEE TIMES: Reservations are accepted on weekdays with a call from the guest's PGA professional.

DRESS CODE: Nonmetal spikes are mandatory.

COURSE DESCRIPTION: This is an older, traditional course, with trees lining both sides of most fairways and water coming into play on a few par 3s. It is located about a mile from the Pacific Ocean and therefore is subject to ocean breezes, especially in the afternoon.

NOTES: This is the home of the Toshiba Senior Classic, a PGA Senior Tour event.

LOCATION: Travel north from Laguna Beach on Highway 1, one-half mile past MacArthur Boulevard. The course is located between Jamboree Road and MacArthur Boulevard on Pacific Coast Highway next to Fashion Island Shopping Center.

. . . ● **TOURNAMENTS:** This course is available for outside tournaments on Monday only. Carts are required. A 100-player minimum is needed to book a tournament.

97. THE NEWPORT BEACH COUNTRY CLUB

98 NEWPORT BEACH GOLF COURSE

3100 Irvine Avenue
Newport Beach, CA 92660

PRO SHOP: 949-852-8689
STARTER: 949-852-8681

Steve Lane, Manager
John Leonard, PGA Professional
Manuel Mendoza, Superintendent

Driving Range ●
Practice Greens ●
Clubhouse ●
Food / Beverage ●
Accommodations
Pull Carts ●
Power Carts
Club Rental ●
$pecial Offers

	1	2	3	4	5	6	7	8	9	OUT
BACK	-	-	-	-	-	-	-	-	-	-
REGULAR	146	110	89	291	112	114	276	130	152	1420
par	3	3	3	4	3	3	4	3	3	29
handicap	3	11	17	1	15	13	5	9	7	-
FORWARD	146	110	89	291	112	114	276	130	152	1420
par	3	3	3	4	3	3	4	3	3	29
handicap	3	11	17	1	15	13	5	9	7	-

	10	11	12	13	14	15	16	17	18	IN
BACK	-	-	-	-	-	-	-	-	-	-
REGULAR	207	129	92	182	147	316	271	235	217	1796
par	3	3	3	3	3	4	4	4	3	30
handicap	4	16	18	12	14	6	8	10	2	-
FORWARD	207	129	92	182	147	316	271	235	217	1796
par	3	3	3	3	3	4	4	4	3	30
handicap	4	16	18	12	14	6	8	10	2	-

BACK	
yardage	-
par	-
rating	
slope	

REGULAR	
yardage	3216
par	59
rating	54.7
slope	-

FORWARD	
yardage	3216
par	59
rating	57.2
slope	-

99 RANCHO SAN JOAQUIN GOLF COURSE
ARCHITECT: WILLIAM F. BELL, 1969

One Sandburg Way
Irvine, CA 92715

PRO SHOP: 949-786-5522
CLUBHOUSE: 949-786-1224

Scot Woodward, Manager
Joe Cannon, PGA Professional
Frank Page, Superintendent

Driving Range ●
Practice Greens ●
Clubhouse ●
Food / Beverage ●
Accommodations
Pull Carts ●
Power Carts ●
Club Rental ●
$pecial Offers

	1	2	3	4	5	6	7	8	9	OUT
BACK	515	140	328	338	502	384	353	168	421	3149
REGULAR	498	123	313	315	421	362	328	155	365	2880
par	5	3	4	4	5	4	4	3	4	36
handicap	5	17	15	11	1	3	9	13	7	-
FORWARD	498	123	313	315	421	362	328	155	365	2880
par	5	3	4	4	5	4	4	3	4	36
handicap	3	17	9	13	7	1	11	15	5	-

	10	11	12	13	14	15	16	17	18	IN
BACK	355	385	525	160	348	158	404	289	456	3080
REGULAR	348	334	518	121	330	146	388	284	445	2914
par	4	4	5	3	4	3	4	4	5	36
handicap	10	6	2	14	8	12	4	18	16	-
FORWARD	348	334	518	121	330	146	388	284	445	2914
par	4	4	5	3	4	3	4	4	5	36
handicap	12	8	2	18	10	14	4	16	6	-

BACK	
yardage	6229
par	72
rating	68.9
slope	112

REGULAR	
yardage	5794
par	72
rating	66.7
slope	109

FORWARD	
yardage	5794
par	72
rating	73.1
slope	121

PLAY POLICY & FEES: Green fees are $14 weekdays and $18 weekends. Pull carts are $2.

TEE TIMES: Reservations can be booked seven days in advance.

DRESS CODE: Nonmetal spikes are required.

COURSE DESCRIPTION: This executive course offers well-maintained and well-contoured holes, with bunkers and water often coming into play. The course is lighted for night play, and players can start until 8 p.m. The course features five par 4s. The 18th hole is among the most difficult—225 yards, downhill. There are no grass tees here; golfers tee off from mats.

LOCATION: In Newport Beach from the Newport Freeway (Highway 55), exit at Highway 73/South Corona Del Mar and drive south to Irvine Avenue. Turn right and drive one-half mile to the club.

. . . ● **TOURNAMENTS:** Shotgun tournaments are available weekdays only.

98. NEWPORT BEACH GOLF COURSE

PLAY POLICY & FEES: Walking green fees are $33 Monday though Thursday and $42 Friday. Riding green fees are $44 Monday through Thursday and $53 Friday. On weekends green fees are $60, including cart. Twilight rates are $20 to walk, $28 to ride Monday through Thursday, and $28 to walk, $36 to ride Friday through Sunday.

TEE TIMES: Reservations can be booked seven days in advance with no charge and 14 days in advance with a $5 per player fee.

DRESS CODE: No tank tops are allowed on the course.

COURSE DESCRIPTION: This is an interesting and challenging course. It features large, undulating greens, hilly terrain, and some water hazards. The par-5 fifth hole is among the best holes in Orange County. It requires a layup second shot with water on each side of the fairway.

LOCATION: Travel south on Interstate 405 from Santa Ana to the Culver Drive exit west. Turn right and drive to the second traffic light on Sandburg Way. Turn right again and drive to the course.

. . . ● **TOURNAMENTS:** This course is available for outside events.

99. RANCHO SAN JOAQUIN GOLF COURSE

BIG CANYON COUNTRY CLUB
ARCHITECT: ROBERT MUIR GRAVES, 1971

1 Big Canyon Drive
Newport Beach, CA 92660

PRO SHOP: 949-720-1003
CLUBHOUSE: 949-644-5404

Bob Lovejoy, Director of Golf
Kelly Manos, Head Professional, PGA
Jeff Beardsley, Superintendent

Driving Range ●
Practice Greens ●
Clubhouse ●
Food / Beverage ●
Accommodations
Pull Carts
Power Carts ●
Club Rental ●
$pecial Offers

	1	2	3	4	5	6	7	8	9	OUT
BACK										
REGULAR										
par										
handicap										
FORWARD										
par										
handicap										

	10	11	12	13	14	15	16	17	18	IN
BACK										
REGULAR										
par										
handicap										
FORWARD										
par										
handicap										

BACK	
yardage	7018
par	72
rating	75.4
slope	139

REGULAR	
yardage	6748
par	72
rating	73.4
slope	123

FORWARD	
yardage	6382
par	72
rating	70.9
slope	129

STRAWBERRY FARMS GOLF CLUB
ARCHITECT: JIM LIPE, 1997

11 Strawberry Farms Road
Irvine, CA 92612

PRO SHOP: 949-551-1811
CLUBHOUSE: 949-551-2560

Rick Howard, Director of Golf
Jim Wood, PGA Professional
Charlotte McCauliff, Tournament Director

Driving Range ●
Practice Greens ●
Clubhouse ●
Food / Beverage ●
Accommodations
Pull Carts
Power Carts ●
Club Rental ●
$pecial Offers

	1	2	3	4	5	6	7	8	9	OUT
BACK	418	410	215	424	445	527	170	312	545	3466
REGULAR	403	372	200	414	431	501	153	385	515	3374
par	4	4	3	4	4	5	3	4	5	36
handicap	13	5	9	1	3	11	17	15	7	-
FORWARD	337	273	112	354	323	417	92	209	432	2549
par	4	4	3	4	4	5	3	4	5	36
handicap	9	13	15	1	5	7	17	11	3	-

	10	11	12	13	14	15	16	17	18	IN
BACK	410	182	631	433	360	160	481	185	404	3246
REGULAR	353	162	592	412	340	146	443	177	388	3013
par	4	3	5	4	4	3	5	3	4	35
handicap	12	14	2	6	8	18	10	16	4	-
FORWARD	286	122	543	302	290	97	414	110	317	2481
par	4	3	6	4	4	3	5	3	4	36
handicap	12	14	6	8	10	18	2	16	4	-

BACK	
yardage	6712
par	71
rating	-
slope	-

REGULAR	
yardage	6387
par	71
rating	-
slope	-

FORWARD	
yardage	5030
par	72
rating	-
slope	-

PLAY POLICY & FEES: Reciprocal play is accepted on a very limited basis, otherwise members and guests only. The green fee for reciprocators and guests accompanied by a member is $75, cart included. Unaccompanied guests pay $150 every day, and caddies are mandatory.

DRESS CODE: Appropriate golf attire and nonmetal spikes are required.

COURSE DESCRIPTION: This course was built in 1971. It's a traditional layout with many trees and bunkers. There are several water hazards as well. It has rolling fairways and many blind shots to the greens. It is among the more exclusive country clubs in the state.

LOCATION: From Interstate 405 at Newport Beach take the MacArthur Boulevard exit south and drive five miles to San Joaquin Hills Road. Turn right and drive to Big Canyon Drive and the course.

. . . ● **TOURNAMENTS:** This course is not available for outside events.

100. BIG CANYON COUNTRY CLUB

PLAY POLICY & FEES: Weekday green fees are $85 Monday through Thursday and $125 Friday through Sunday and holidays. Twilight rates are $65 weekdays and $85 weekends. Nine-hole rates are available. All green fees include carts. Carts are equipped with Pro-Shot computerized yardage system.

TEE TIMES: Reservations can be made 30 days in advance for Sunday through Thursday and seven days in advance for Friday and Saturday.

DRESS CODE: Collared shirts and nonmetal spikes are required.

COURSE DESCRIPTION: Situated around Sand Canyon Reservoir, this course is surrounded by lakes, wildlife, natural waterfalls, and vegetation. Accuracy is a must to score well, and wind can be a factor, especially in the afternoon.

NOTES: This public course was conceived by Doug DeCinces, former California Angels' third baseman. Strawberry Farms offers diverse golf instruction for both adults and juniors. In the summer months, free junior clinics are available. Call the pro shop for more information.

LOCATION: From Interstate 405 in Irvine take the University/Jeffrey exit and head west. The course will be on the left.

. . . ● **TOURNAMENTS:** A 20-player minimum is required to book an event. Tournaments should be scheduled three months in advance. The banquet facility can accommodate 150 people.

101. STRAWBERRY FARMS GOLF CLUB

THE GREENS AT PARK PLACE
ARCHITECT: TED ROBINSON, 1995

3301 Michelson Drive
Irvine, CA 92715

PRO SHOP: 949-250-PUTT

David Hunter, Professional

Driving Range
Practice Greens
Clubhouse x
Food / Beverage x
Accommodations
Pull Carts
Power Carts
Club Rental
$pecial Offers

	1	2	3	4	5	6	7	8	9	OUT
BACK	94	85	109	89	57	123	120	89	119	885
REGULAR										
par	3	3	3	3	2	4	3	3	4	28
handicap	10	16	18	2	12	4	6	8	14	-
FORWARD										
par										
handicap										-

BACK	
yardage	1678
par	56
rating	
slope	

REGULAR	
yardage	
par	56
rating	
slope	

	10	11	12	13	14	15	16	17	18	IN
BACK	97	89	97	127	71	83	82	53	94	793
REGULAR										
par	3	3	3	4	3	3	3	3	3	28
handicap	15	1	9	7	13	11	5	3	17	-
FORWARD										
par										
handicap										-

FORWARD	
yardage	
par	
rating	
slope	

 OAK CREEK GOLF CLUB
ARCHITECT: TOM FAZIO, 1996

1 Golf Club Drive
Irvine , CA 92620

PRO SHOP: 949-653-7300

Perry Hallmeyer, Head Professional, PGA
Kent Coffman, Superintendent

Driving Range ●
Practice Greens ●
Clubhouse ●
Food / Beverage ●
Accommodations
Pull Carts
Power Carts ●
Club Rental ●
$pecial Offers ●

	1	2	3	4	5	6	7	8	9	OUT
BACK	525	209	430	384	344	434	370	228	500	3424
REGULAR	513	189	400	368	316	415	360	211	489	3261
par	5	3	4	4	4	4	4	3	5	36
handicap	11	5	3	15	17	1	13	7	9	-
FORWARD	468	170	347	335	284	373	311	139	439	2866
par	5	3	4	4	4	4	4	3	5	36
handicap	11	5	3	15	17	1	13	7	9	-

BACK	
yardage	6834
par	71
rating	71.9
slope	127

REGULAR	
yardage	6515
par	71
rating	70.3
slope	123

	10	11	12	13	14	15	16	17	18	IN
BACK	384	387	173	429	434	558	222	367	456	3410
REGULAR	360	371	163	415	419	541	199	355	431	3254
par	4	4	3	4	4	5	3	4	4	35
handicap	12	16	14	10	2	4	8	18	6	-
FORWARD	291	327	122	358	355	447	157	305	377	2739
par	4	4	3	4	4	5	3	4	4	35
handicap	12	16	14	10	2	4	8	18	6	-

FORWARD	
yardage	5605
par	71
rating	71.2
slope	121

PLAY POLICY & FEES: Green fees are $10 Monday through Thursday and $12 Friday through Sunday and holidays. Memberships are available that entitle players to discount green fees

TEE TIMES: Reservations are for members only. The public is served on a first-come, first-served basis.

DRESS CODE: No spikes of any kind are allowed; only tennis shoes are permitted.

COURSE DESCRIPTION: Do you want to play 18 holes in less than two hours and putt on some of the best greens anywhere? The Greens at Park Place is an 18-hole putting course built to USGA standards and designed by renowned architect Ted Robinson. The course comes complete with bunkers, water hazards, and, of course, undulating greens.

NOTES: The course is lit for night play and open until 11 p.m. on weekends. The Greens offers a lunch and play special, call for details.

LOCATION: From the John Wayne Airport go south on Interstate 405. Take the Jamboree exit and turn right on Jamboree, then left on Michelson. Take Michelson to Carlson and make a left.

. . . ● **TOURNAMENTS:** The banquet facility can accommodate up to 90 people, and shotgun tournaments are available.

102. THE GREENS AT PARK PLACE

PLAY POLICY & FEES: Green fees are $90 Monday through Thursday and $125 Friday through Sunday. Twilight green fees are $65 Monday through Thursday, and $80 Friday through Sunday. Senior, junior, and nine-hole rates are available.

TEE TIMES: Reservations can be made seven days in advance. Premium tee times can be made with a credit card 8 to 60 days in advance for a $15 nonrefundable fee.

DRESS CODE: No denim is allowed on the course. Collared shirts and nonmetal spikes are required.

COURSE DESCRIPTION: Oak Creek is a picturesque course where good shots are rewarded and bad shots are penalized. Tee shots are generally wide open and driver friendly. If you miss fairways, bring plenty of golf balls, because the holes are surrounded by fescue and tall native grass. To score well, you must stay out of the well-placed bunkers and survive the par threes. Researcher Brad Sevier also gives this piece of advice: "Stay out of the right fairway bunker on the long par-4 sixth."

NOTES: Oak Creek features a large practice facility.

LOCATION: From Highway 405 in Newport Beach, head south and take the Sand Canyon Avenue exit. Head east on Sand Canyon Avenue to Irvine Center Drive. Take a left on Irvine Center Drive. The golf course will be on the right.

. . . ● **TOURNAMENTS:** A 36-player minimum is required to book a tournament. The banquet facility can accommodate 60 people. Events can be scheduled up to one year in advance. ● **TRAVEL:** The Hyatt Regency Irvine is located five minutes from the golf course. Call 714-975-1234 for reservations. ● **$PECIAL OFFERS:** The Hyatt Regency Irvine offers play-and-stay golf packages.

103. OAK CREEK GOLF CLUB

EL TORO GOLF COURSE
ARCHITECT: WILLIAM P. BELL, 1949

El Toro Marine Memorial
Santa Ana, CA 92709

PRO SHOP: 949-726-2577

Wally Bradley, PGA Professional
Wally Bradley, Superintendent
Jaime Hernandez, Maintenance Leader

Driving Range ●
Practice Greens ●
Clubhouse ●
Food / Beverage ●
Accommodations
Pull Carts ●
Power Carts ●
Club Rental ●
$pecial Offers

	1	2	3	4	5	6	7	8	9	OUT
BACK	397	512	417	384	433	331	228	497	195	3394
REGULAR	383	500	402	371	411	320	195	485	184	3251
par	4	5	4	4	4	4	3	5	3	36
handicap	5	11	3	7	1	15	13	9	17	-
FORWARD	368	452	358	340	344	283	155	445	155	2900
par	4	5	4	4	4	4	3	5	3	36
handicap	3	5	1	11	7	13	17	9	15	-

	10	11	12	13	14	15	16	17	18	IN
BACK	377	332	533	143	421	185	516	407	442	3356
REGULAR	343	315	520	127	397	176	506	400	433	3217
par	4	4	5	3	4	3	5	4	4	36
handicap	12	14	8	18	2	16	10	6	4	-
FORWARD	324	274	443	120	419	166	318	365	328	2757
par	4	4	5	3	5	3	4	4	4	36
handicap	12	14	8	18	6	16	10	2	4	-

BACK	
yardage	6750
par	72
rating	71.5
slope	114

REGULAR	
yardage	6468
par	72
rating	69.7
slope	111

FORWARD	
yardage	5657
par	72
rating	71.8
slope	117

 # LAGUNA WOODS GOLF CLUB
ARCHITECT: HARRY & DAVID RAINVILLE, 1974

P.O. Box 2307   24112 Moulton Parkway
Laguna Hills, CA 92653   Laguna Hills, CA 92653

PRO SHOP: 949-597-4336

Bob Vogel, Operations Manager, PGA
Kurt Rahn, Superintendent

Driving Range ●
Practice Greens ●
Clubhouse ●
Food / Beverage ●
Accommodations
Pull Carts ●
Power Carts ●
Club Rental ●
$pecial Offers

	1	2	3	4	5	6	7	8	9	OUT
BACK	392	176	369	487	180	478	380	174	471	3107
REGULAR	392	161	369	480	169	478	380	168	471	3068
par	4	3	4	5	3	5	4	3	5	36
handicap	2	9	6	3	5	8	1	7	4	-
FORWARD	338	136	355	452	142	457	340	137	442	2799
par	4	3	4	5	3	45	4	3	5	76
handicap	5	8	6	1	7	3	2	9	4	-

	10	11	12	13	14	15	16	17	18	IN
BACK	412	199	353	485	373	153	485	140	363	2963
REGULAR	406	180	353	485	373	149	485	140	363	2934
par	4	3	4	5	4	3	5	3	4	35
handicap	1	4	7	6	2	8	3	9	5	-
FORWARD	388	151	325	459	342	131	472	123	344	2735
par	4	3	4	5	4	3	5	3	4	35
handicap	4	7	6	3	2	8	1	9	5	-

BACK	
yardage	6070
par	71
rating	-
slope	-

REGULAR	
yardage	6002
par	71
rating	67.7
slope	107

FORWARD	
yardage	5534
par	111
rating	71.0
slope	113

PLAY POLICY & FEES: Military personnel and guests only. Green fees vary according to military status. Carts are $16.

DRESS CODE: There is a strict dress code: no tank tops, cutoffs, or clothing with obscene or anti-American sentiments. Nonmetal spikes are mandatory.

COURSE DESCRIPTION: This relatively flat course has mature trees and a few doglegs. The course plays host to 75,000 rounds a year.

LOCATION: Take the Santa Ana Freeway (Interstate 5) south from Santa Ana to the Sand Canyon exit east. At Trabuco Road, turn south to the main gate and take the perimeter road south for 2.5 miles to the course.

. . . ● **TOURNAMENTS:** Shotgun tournaments are available weekdays only.

104. EL TORO GOLF COURSE

PLAY POLICY & FEES: Members and guests only. Green fees are $25 for guests. Carts are $20 for guests.

DRESS CODE: Appropriate golf attire is required, and nonmetal spikes are recommended.

COURSE DESCRIPTION: Located in a retirement community, Leisure World, this rolling course is slightly hilly with mature trees. All three nines have different pars—36 for the first, 35 for the second, and 34 for the third. The course is closed Christmas.

NOTES: This private facility has 27 holes, and par is 71, 69, and 70 for each of the 18-hole combinations. The One and Two Combination: See scorecard for yardage and rating information. The Three and One Combination is 5,559 yards and rated 65.2 from the regular tees with a slope of 96. Women's tees are 5,369 yards and rated 65.2 with a slope of 109. The Two and Three Combination is 5,454 yards and rated 64.7 from the regular tees with a slope of 96. Women's tees are 5,331 yards and rated 64.7 with a slope of 109.

LOCATION: Take the El Toro Road exit off Interstate 5 at Laguna Hills and travel west to Moulton Parkway. Turn right one-quarter mile to the club.

. . . ● **TOURNAMENTS:** This course is not available for outside events.

105. LAGUNA WOODS GOLF CLUB

CASTA DEL SOL GOLF COURSE
ARCHITECT: TED ROBINSON, 1963

27601 Casta Del Sol Rd.
Mission Viejo, CA 92692

PROSHOP: 949-470-4996
STARTER: 949-470-4996

Mario Marquez, General Manager
Jose Cañedo, Superintendent
Judy Gavel, Tournament Director

Driving Range
Practice Greens ●
Clubhouse ●
Food / Beverage ●
Accommodations
Pull Carts ●
Power Carts ●
Club Rental ●
$pecial Offers

	1	2	3	4	5	6	7	8	9	OUT
BACK	-	-	-	-	-	-	-	-	-	-
REGULAR	288	177	151	282	170	289	148	179	321	2005
par	4	3	3	4	3	4	3	3	4	31
handicap	11	9	15	13	1	7	17	3	5	-
FORWARD	271	157	135	259	163	283	138	160	299	1865
par	4	3	3	4	3	4	3	3	4	31
handicap	3	11	15	13	5	7	17	9	1	-

	10	11	12	13	14	15	16	17	18	IN
BACK	-	-	-	-	-	-	-	-	-	-
REGULAR	243	176	125	290	163	162	131	195	225	1710
par	4	3	3	4	3	3	3	3	3	29
handicap	16	6	18	8	10	12	14	4	2	-
FORWARD	225	158	117	271	142	126	115	175	203	1532
par	4	3	3	4	3	3	3	3	4	30
handicap	12	8	18	2	4	16	10	6	14	-

BACK	
yardage	-
par	-
rating	-
slope	-

REGULAR	
yardage	3715
par	60
rating	57.8
slope	90

FORWARD	
yardage	3397
par	61
rating	58.7
slope	91

 COTO DE CAZA GOLF CLUB
ARCHITECT: ROBERT TRENT JONES, JR. 1987 (NC), 1995 (SC)

25291 Vista del Verde
Coto de Caza, CA 92679

PROSHOP: 949-858-2770
CLUBHOUSE: 949-858-4100

Mike Mitzel, General Manager
Bill Hancock, Head Professional, PGA

Driving Range ●
Practice Greens ●
Clubhouse ●
Food / Beverage ●
Accommodations
Pull Carts
Power Carts ●
Club Rental ●
$pecial Offers

	1	2	3	4	5	6	7	8	9	OUT
BACK	560	323	385	175	522	170	370	377	281	3163
REGULAR	539	308	358	160	457	165	352	364	275	2978
par	5	4	4	3	5	3	4	4	4	36
handicap	1	11	3	9	13	15	7	5	17	-
FORWARD	429	288	308	135	426	143	291	336	239	2595
par	5	4	4	3	5	3	4	4	4	36
handicap	1	9	7	5	13	17	11	3	15	-

	10	11	12	13	14	15	16	17	18	IN
BACK	503	162	537	418	424	139	369	388	379	3319
REGULAR	482	153	492	399	395	132	350	368	361	3132
par	5	3	5	4	4	3	4	4	4	36
handicap	14	16	10	6	4	18	8	2	12	-
FORWARD	440	115	455	361	370	87	296	333	317	2774
par	5	3	5	4	4	3	4	4	4	36
handicap	14	16	4	10	8	18	6	2	12	-

BACK	
yardage	6482
par	72
rating	71.9
slope	133

REGULAR	
yardage	6110
par	72
rating	69.5
slope	124

FORWARD	
yardage	5369
par	72
rating	71.2
slope	126

PLAY POLICY & FEES: Green fees are $17 Monday through Thursday, $18 Friday, and $29 weekends and holidays. Senior, junior, and twilight rates are available. Carts are $22.

TEE TIMES: Reservations can be made seven days in advance without a reservation fee. Reservations made more than seven days in advance are charged a $2 non-refundable fee per player.

DRESS CODE: Shirts and shoes are required.

COURSE DESCRIPTION: This rolling course has several streams and lakes. It's a testy, short course and extremely busy, with more than 100,000 rounds played here a year.

NOTES: This rolling course has several streams and lakes. It's a testy, short course but extremely busy, with more than 100,000 rounds played here a year.

LOCATION: Take the La Paz Road exit off Interstate 5 and travel east for one mile to Marguerite Parkway. Turn left and drive 1.5 miles to Casta del Sol Road. Turn right and drive to the course.

. . . ● **TOURNAMENTS:** A 16-player minimum is needed to book a tournament. Events should be booked three months in advance. A banquet facility is available that can accommodate 80 people.

106. CASTA DEL SOL GOLF COURSE

PLAY POLICY & FEES: Limited reciprocal play is accepted with members of other private clubs; otherwise, members and guests only. The green fee for reciprocal play is $110. Guest fees are $75 Monday through Thursday and $100 Friday through Sunday and holidays. Guests must be accompanied by a member. Carts are included.

TEE TIMES: Have your pro call for arrangements.

DRESS CODE: Appropriate golf attire and nonmetal spikes are required.

COURSE DESCRIPTION: Designed by Robert Trent Jones Jr. with Johnny Miller as a consultant, Coto is set in canyons in south Orange County and features native California oak trees. The North Course's par-5 first hole requires a tee shot through a chute and over one of the canyons, with trees and more canyon guarding the left side. The wonderful new South Course complements the North Course. Most consider it several shots easier. Small, traditional greens have subtle mounding and offer makable putts.

NOTES: The par-72 South Course is 6,317 yards and rated 70.3 from the blue tees with a slope of 123. The North Course: See scorecard for yardage and rating information.

LOCATION: From Mission Viejo take Interstate 5 south to the Oso Parkway exit. Drive east for six miles until Oso Parkway ends. Turn left on Coto de Caza Drive. Turn right into the club.

. . . ● **TOURNAMENTS:** This course is available for outside tournaments on Monday.

107. COTO DE CAZA GOLF CLUB

ALISO VIEJO GOLF CLUB
ARCHITECT: NICKLAUS DESIGN, 1999

25002 Golf Course Drive
Aliso Viejo, CA CA

PRO SHOP: 949-598-9200

Jeff Whitt, Head Professional, PGA
Bob Blalock, Superintendent
Kendra Goss, Tournament Director

Driving Range ●
Practice Greens ●
Clubhouse ●
Food / Beverage ●
Accommodations
Pull Carts
Power Carts ●
Club Rental ●
$pecial Offers ●

	1	2	3	4	5	6	7	8	9	OUT
BACK	344	297	359	188	434	391	537	141	522	3213
REGULAR	334	286	354	178	424	365	527	130	517	3115
par	4	4	4	3	4	4	5	3	5	36
handicap	8	6	6	7	1	3	4	5	2	-
FORWARD	251	235	255	130	285	338	448	97	402	2441
par	4	4	4	3	4	4	5	3	5	36
handicap	8	9	6	7	1	3	4	5	2	-

	10	11	12	13	14	15	16	17	18	IN
BACK	409	186	461	370	309	158	414	409	506	3222
REGULAR	404	181	439	354	301	143	409	404	501	3136
par	4	3	4	4	4	3	4	4	5	35
handicap	4	5	1	6	9	8	2	3	7	-
FORWARD	314	117	329	246	255	122	314	319	421	2437
par	4	3	4	4	4	3	4	4	5	35
handicap	4	5	1	6	9	8	2	3	7	-

BACK	
yardage	6435
par	71
rating	
slope	

REGULAR	
yardage	6251
par	71
rating	
slope	

FORWARD	
yardage	4878
par	71
rating	
slope	

PLAY POLICY & FEES: Green fees are $50 Monday through Thursday for nine holes, and $85 for 18 holes. Friday through Sunday green fees are $65 for nine holes and $125 for 18 holes. Twilight and resident rates are also available. All green fees include a cart.

TEE TIMES: Reservations can be made for free up to six days in advance. A $15 fee is charged for tee times made seven to 14 days in advance, and a $20 fee is charged for tee times 15 to 30 days in advance.

DRESS CODE: No jeans are allowed on the course, and collared shirts are required. Dress shorts are OK.

COURSE DESCRIPTION: Aliso Viejo is 27 holes of thoughtfully and at times inspired design, not overly long (no nine measures over 3,300 yards), with wide fairways and large contoured greens that guarantee a lot of three putts if your approach is not accurate. Bunkers are well placed and somewhat deep, though you can always see whatever trouble lies ahead. Lots of holes you'll remember after the round.

NOTES: The three nines are named the Valley, Creek, and Ridge. The Ridge nine is 3,055 yard from the back tees. A 408-room hotel is due to open sometime in 2001.

LOCATION: From San Clemente head north on Interstate 5 to the El Toro Road exit. Turn left on El Torro to the Moulton Parkway. Turn left on the Moulton Parkway to Glenwood Drive. Turn right on Glenwood to the golf course.

. . . ● **TOURNAMENTS:** A minimum of 13 players is required to book an event. Tournament rates are $110 weekdays and $150 on weekends. All tournaments include personal tournament coordinator, scoring, and unlimited advanced booking. The banquet facility can accommodate up to 320 people. ● **$PECIAL OFFERS:** Play-and-stay packages are available with local hotels. Call the pro shop for details.

108. ALISO VIEJO GOLF CLUB

TIJERAS CREEK GOLF CLUB
ARCHITECT: TED ROBINSON, 1990

29082 Tijeras Creek Road
Rancho Santa Margarita,
CA 92688
PRO SHOP: 949-589-9321

Jennifer Alderson, General Manager
Marty LaRoche, Head Professional, PGA
Justin Alderson, Tournament Director

Driving Range ●
Practice Greens ●
Clubhouse ●
Food / Beverage ●
Accommodations
Pull Carts
Power Carts ●
Club Rental ●
$pecial Offers

	1	2	3	4	5	6	7	8	9	OUT
BACK	507	346	442	402	162	393	200	550	414	3416
REGULAR	491	326	410	369	151	366	174	524	388	3199
par	5	4	4	4	3	4	3	5	4	36
handicap	15	17	1	9	11	13	5	7	3	-
FORWARD	414	280	336	308	110	312	118	442	330	2650
par	5	4	4	4	3	4	3	5	4	36
handicap	15	17	1	9	11	13	5	7	3	-

	10	11	12	13	14	15	16	17	18	IN
BACK	342	516	342	519	165	343	172	399	399	3197
REGULAR	327	493	328	505	142	321	149	376	380	3021
par	4	5	4	5	3	4	3	4	4	36
handicap	10	8	4	16	14	18	6	2	12	-
FORWARD	275	399	281	426	111	275	119	311	283	2480
par	4	5	4	5	3	4	3	4	4	36
handicap	10	8	4	16	14	18	6	2	12	-

BACK	
yardage	6613
par	72
rating	71.7
slope	126

REGULAR	
yardage	6220
par	72
rating	69.5
slope	120

FORWARD	
yardage	5130
par	72
rating	69.8
slope	120

 DOVE CANYON COUNTRY CLUB
ARCHITECT: JACK NICKLAUS, 1990

22682 Golf Club Drive
Dove Canyon, CA 92679

PRO SHOP: 949-858-2888
CLUBHOUSE: 949-858-2800

Mike Carey, Manager
Ken Ferrell, PGA Professional
Eric Lover, Superintendent

Driving Range ●
Practice Greens ●
Clubhouse ●
Food / Beverage ●
Accommodations
Pull Carts
Power Carts ●
Club Rental ●
$pecial Offers

	1	2	3	4	5	6	7	8	9	OUT
BACK	497	431	464	184	437	355	207	406	556	3537
REGULAR	485	411	443	170	416	328	182	396	525	3356
par	5	4	4	3	4	4	3	4	5	36
handicap	11	7	3	15	1	13	17	9	5	-
FORWARD	424	346	355	146	271	269	133	300	446	2690
par	5	4	5	3	4	4	3	4	5	37
handicap	5	1	7	15	9	11	17	13	3	-

	10	11	12	13	14	15	16	17	18	IN
BACK	212	574	428	146	545	394	429	208	429	3365
REGULAR	202	554	401	138	512	363	420	167	385	3142
par	3	5	4	3	5	4	4	3	4	35
handicap	14	4	12	16	2	6	10	18	8	-
FORWARD	100	459	315	102	457	320	366	122	334	2575
par	3	5	4	3	5	4	4	3	4	35
handicap	18	6	12	14	2	4	10	16	8	-

BACK	
yardage	6902
par	71
rating	74.0
slope	137

REGULAR	
yardage	6498
par	71
rating	71.2
slope	130

FORWARD	
yardage	5265
par	72
rating	71.9
slope	129

PLAY POLICY & FEES: Green fees are $75 Monday through Thursday and $110 Friday through Sunday and holidays, cart included.

TEE TIMES: Reservations can be booked one year in advance.

DRESS CODE: Collared shirts and nonmetal spikes are required. No denim is allowed on the course.

COURSE DESCRIPTION: The course has distinctly different nines. The front nine winds through a housing development, while the back nine is surrounded by natural terrain that will not be developed. Deer are frequently spotted on the back nine. Tijeras Creek is regarded as one of the best public courses in Orange County.

LOCATION: From Interstate 5 take the Oso Parkway exit east. Drive three miles to Antonio. Turn left on Antonio and drive two miles to Tijeras Creek Road. Turn left and follow the road to the golf club.

. . . ● **TOURNAMENTS:** Tournament packages are available. Carts are required.

109. TIJERAS CREEK GOLF CLUB

PLAY POLICY & FEES: Reciprocal play is accepted on a very limited basis, otherwise members and guests only. Guest fees are $70 weekdays and $110 weekends and holidays, including cart and range balls. The course is closed on Monday.

DRESS CODE: Appropriate golf attire and nonmetal spikes are required, and the dress code is strictly enforced.

COURSE DESCRIPTION: This course backs up to Cleveland National Forest, so count on plenty of wildlife. There are both barrancas and bunnies. The course is rolling, with some water and beautiful old oaks. A lake and a waterfall flank the finishing hole. It is among Nicklaus' more user-friendly courses, although from the championship tees, combined with tough pin placements, the course can play extremely difficult.

NOTES: Several members of the California Angels and other baseball teams are members here. This is a nonsmoking course.

LOCATION: From Interstate 5 south take the Alicia Road exit east. Drive to Santa Margarita Parkway. Turn south on Santa Margarita to Plano Trabuco and turn right. Take Plano Trabuco to Dove Canyon Drive and turn left. Follow Dove Canyon to the guard gate and the course.

. . . ● **TOURNAMENTS:** This course is available for outside tournaments. A 40-player minimum is needed to book an event. Tournaments should be scheduled at least two months in advance. The banquet facility can accommodate approximately 150 people.

110. DOVE CANYON COUNTRY CLUB

111 MISSION VIEJO COUNTRY CLUB
ARCHITECT: ROBERT TRENT JONES SR., 1967

26200 Country Club Drive
Mission Viejo, CA 92691

PRO SHOP: 949-582-1020
CLUBHOUSE: 949-582-1550

Rick Sussman, Manager
Rob Heslar, PGA Professional
Bruce Douglas, Tournament Director

Driving Range ●
Practice Greens ●
Clubhouse ●
Food / Beverage ●
Accommodations
Pull Carts
Power Carts ●
Club Rental ●
$Special Offers

	1	2	3	4	5	6	7	8	9	OUT
BACK	509	378	195	469	330	196	408	545	391	3421
REGULAR	489	366	177	430	320	177	376	525	376	3236
par	5	4	3	4	4	3	4	5	4	36
handicap	13	11	7	1	15	17	3	9	5	-
FORWARD	453	326	128	385	291	152	307	451	326	2819
par	5	4	3	4	4	3	4	5	4	36
handicap	4	14	16	2	10	18	8	6	12	-

	10	11	12	13	14	15	16	17	18	IN
BACK	398	394	417	194	519	371	196	488	416	3393
REGULAR	378	368	402	179	497	361	170	472	393	3220
par	4	4	4	3	5	4	3	5	4	36
handicap	2	12	4	16	6	10	18	14	8	-
FORWARD	311	349	344	132	430	332	120	453	368	2839
par	4	4	4	3	5	4	3	5	4	36
handicap	7	9	13	15	1	11	17	5	3	-

BACK	
yardage	6814
par	72
rating	73.5
slope	132

REGULAR	
yardage	6456
par	72
rating	71.1
slope	124

FORWARD	
yardage	5658
par	72
rating	75.7
slope	141

112 ALISO CREEK GOLF COURSE

31106 Pacific Coast
South Laguna Beach, CA
92677
PRO SHOP: 949-499-1919
OFFICE: 949-499-2271

Mark Slymen, General Manager

Driving Range ●
Practice Greens ●
Clubhouse ●
Food / Beverage ●
Accommodations
Pull Carts ●
Power Carts ●
Club Rental ●
$Special Offers

	1	2	3	4	5	6	7	8	9	OUT
BACK	-	-	-	-	-	-	-	-	-	-
REGULAR	301	208	310	197	313	118	310	207	259	2223
par	4	3	4	3	4	3	4	3	4	32
handicap	9	1	13	5	7	15	11	3	17	-
FORWARD	301	208	310	197	313	118	310	207	259	2223
par	4	3	4	3	4	3	4	3	4	32
handicap	9	1	13	5	7	15	11	3	17	-

	10	11	12	13	14	15	16	17	18	IN
BACK	-	-	-	-	-	-	-	-	-	-
REGULAR	286	177	269	184	259	105	207	191	249	1927
par	4	3	4	3	4	3	4	3	4	32
handicap	10	2	14	6	8	16	12	4	18	-
FORWARD	286	177	269	184	259	105	207	191	249	1927
par	4	3	4	3	4	3	4	3	4	32
handicap	10	2	14	6	8	16	12	4	18	-

BACK	
yardage	-
par	-
rating	-
slope	-

REGULAR	
yardage	4150
par	64
rating	59.7
slope	104

FORWARD	
yardage	4150
par	64
rating	59.7
slope	104

PLAY POLICY & FEES: Members and guests only. Green fees are $75 Tuesday through Thursday and $85 Friday through Sunday and holidays. Carts are $12 per person.

DRESS CODE: All shirts must have collars. No jeans are allowed on the course, and shorts must have a 17-inch inseam. Metal spikes are prohibited.

COURSE DESCRIPTION: This is a long and demanding course. The fairways are hilly and parallel. The greens are well maintained, very fast, and usually elevated. It was once dubbed "Mission Impossible" by Johnny Miller.

NOTES: This course responds to the nickname "Mission Impossible." Mission Viejo has been host to the local U.S. Open qualifying for the past two years and will also host the U.S. Open women's qualifying.

LOCATION: Take the Oso Parkway exit off Interstate 5 near Mission Viejo, and travel east one-half mile to Country Club Drive and turn right to the club.

. . . ● **TOURNAMENTS:** This course is available for outside tournaments, requiring a 100-player minimum. Tournaments should be scheduled at least eight months in advance. A banquet facility can accommodate 200 people.

111. MISSION VIEJO COUNTRY CLUB

PLAY POLICY & FEES: Green fees are $17 for nine holes Monday through Thursday, $20 Friday, and $25 weekends.

TEE TIMES: Reservations can be booked seven days in advance.

DRESS CODE: Collared shirts and nonmetal spikes are required.

COURSE DESCRIPTION: This traditional course is set in a heavily foliaged canyon with a meandering creek. There are 19 bunkers and lots of trees. With the ocean just 400 yards away, a sea breeze adds to the quiet atmosphere.

LOCATION: Take Interstate 5 or Interstate 405 southbound in Orange County to Highway 133 (Laguna Freeway). Take Highway 133 west to Highway 1 (Pacific Coast Highway). Drive south on Highway 1 almost three miles to the green overpass. Take an immediate left turn at Ben Brown's sign. From northbound Interstate 5, take the Beach Cities exit. Drive north on Highway 1 about six miles. Turn right at the sign across from the Aliso State Beach Pier.

. . . ● **TOURNAMENTS:** Shotgun tournaments are not allowed.

112. ALISO CREEK GOLF COURSE

MARBELLA GOLF & COUNTRY CLUB

ARCHITECT: TOM WEISKOPF, JAY MORRISH, 1989

30800 Golf Club Drive
San Juan Capistrano, CA
92675
PRO SHOP: 949-248-3700

John Sullivan, General Manager
Chris Herald, PGA Professional
Jeff Stroup, Superintendent

Driving Range ●
Practice Greens ●
Clubhouse ●
Food / Beverage ●
Accommodations
Pull Carts
Power Carts ●
Club Rental ●
$pecial Offers

	1	2	3	4	5	6	7	8	9	OUT
BACK	366	404	302	186	475	360	143	430	415	3081
REGULAR	352	389	292	165	460	332	132	392	393	2907
par	4	4	4	3	5	4	3	4	4	35
handicap	5	1	13	15	9	11	17	3	7	-
FORWARD	307	338	271	142	449	305	122	345	360	2639
par	4	4	4	3	5	4	3	4	4	35
handicap	9	5	13	15	1	11	17	7	3	-

	10	11	12	13	14	15	16	17	18	IN
BACK	434	150	286	392	521	426	199	396	428	3232
REGULAR	418	127	271	380	506	408	180	380	414	3084
par	4	3	4	4	5	4	3	4	4	35
handicap	4	18	16	10	2	8	14	6	12	-
FORWARD	354	99	251	321	423	365	143	315	375	2646
par	4	3	4	4	5	4	3	4	4	35
handicap	4	18	16	12	2	6	14	8	10	-

BACK	
yardage	6313
par	70
rating	69.4
slope	121

REGULAR	
yardage	5991
par	70
rating	67.1
slope	

FORWARD	
yardage	5285
par	70
rating	-
slope	-

 EL NIGUEL COUNTRY CLUB

ARCHITECT: DAVID KENT, 1963

23700 Clubhouse Drive
Laguna Niguel, CA 92677

PRO SHOP: 949-496-5767

John Shuki, PGA Professional
Brian Archibald, Superintendent

Driving Range ●
Practice Greens ●
Clubhouse ●
Food / Beverage ●
Accommodations
Pull Carts
Power Carts ●
Club Rental ●
$pecial Offers

	1	2	3	4	5	6	7	8	9	OUT
BACK	393	520	380	426	183	505	404	183	452	3446
REGULAR	374	490	373	404	168	483	380	165	421	3258
par	4	5	4	4	3	5	4	3	4	36
handicap	9	11	5	1	15	13	7	17	3	-
FORWARD	289	428	345	376	154	402	327	134	368	2823
par	4	5	4	4	3	5	4	3	4	36
handicap	13	1	11	5	15	3	9	17	7	-

	10	11	12	13	14	15	16	17	18	IN
BACK	431	389	562	416	158	459	518	214	417	3564
REGULAR	412	380	524	388	151	430	500	193	393	3371
par	4	4	5	4	3	4	5	3	4	36
handicap	2	10	12	8	18	4	16	14	6	-
FORWARD	366	359	457	348	112	366	437	145	318	2908
par	4	4	5	4	3	4	5	3	4	36
handicap	6	10	2	12	18	8	4	16	14	-

BACK	
yardage	7010
par	72
rating	73.8
slope	134

REGULAR	
yardage	6629
par	72
rating	72.1
slope	128

FORWARD	
yardage	5731
par	72
rating	74.2
slope	134

PLAY POLICY & FEES: Reciprocal play is accepted on a very limited basis with local clubs; otherwise, members and guests only. Guests must be accompanied by a member. Guest fees are $60 weekdays and $90 weekends. Carts are $11 per person for 18 holes.

DRESS CODE: Appropriate golf attire and nonmetal spikes are required.

COURSE DESCRIPTION: This long, hilly course features undulating fairways and large bent-grass greens. The front nine is mostly flat while the back nine is hillier. The pride of the course is the 428-yard, par-4 18th hole. This downhill hole is guarded by water and is a test for any player.

NOTES: Masters and British Open Champion Mark O'Meara holds the course record with a 62.

LOCATION: From Interstate 5 in Los Angeles drive south to the Ortega Highway/Highway 74 exit. Drive east to Rancho Viejo Road. Turn left on Rancho Viejo Road. Drive one mile to the club, which is on the right.

. . . ● **TOURNAMENTS:** This course is available for outside tournaments on Monday.

113. MARBELLA GOLF & COUNTRY CLUB

PLAY POLICY & FEES: Members and guests only. Guest fees are $50 weekdays and $70 weekends. Carts are $20.

DRESS CODE: Appropriate golf attire and nonmetal spikes are required.

COURSE DESCRIPTION: This is a challenging course that is well bunkered with level fairways and lots of trees. The greens are some of the toughest west of the Rockies. You'll need a fortune teller to help you read them. The par-3 holes are exceptionally good. Fairways and roughs are Kikuyu grass, which makes them unwieldy. The course is beautifully maintained, and at one time was considered the finest course in Orange County.

LOCATION: Take the Crown Valley Parkway exit off Interstate 5 in Laguna Niguel and drive west for 4.5 miles to Clubhouse Drive. Turn left to the club.

. . . ● **TOURNAMENTS:** This course is available for outside tournaments with board approval. Submit a request in writing to the general manager. A 100-player minimum is needed.

114. EL NIGUEL COUNTRY CLUB

SAN JUAN HILLS COUNTRY CLUB
ARCHITECT: H. RAINVILLE, D. RAINVILLE, 1966

32120 San Juan Creek
San Juan Capistrano, CA
92675
PRO SHOP: 949-493-1167

Buzz Grifith, Director of Golf, PGA
Bill Gruenert, PGA Professional
Gary Bugg, Superintendent

Driving Range •
Practice Greens •
Clubhouse •
Food / Beverage •
Accommodations
Pull Carts •
Power Carts •
Club Rental •
$pecial Offers

	1	2	3	4	5	6	7	8	9	OUT
BACK	342	360	367	342	344	563	175	513	193	3199
REGULAR	316	351	357	328	327	546	164	479	177	3045
par	4	4	4	4	4	5	3	5	3	36
handicap	11	3	5	9	7	1	15	17	13	-
FORWARD	299	312	316	268	312	485	150	464	159	2765
par	4	4	4	4	4	5	3	5	3	36
handicap	7	5	13	11	3	1	17	9	15	-

	10	11	12	13	14	15	16	17	18	IN
BACK	369	419	483	355	142	436	170	517	205	3096
REGULAR	352	399	474	338	117	413	144	497	181	2915
par	4	4	5	4	3	4	3	5	3	35
handicap	10	4	14	8	18	2	12	6	16	-
FORWARD	331	369	466	273	72	387	128	462	149	2637
par	4	4	5	4	3	4	3	5	3	35
handicap	8	10	6	12	18	2	14	4	16	-

BACK	
yardage	6295
par	71
rating	69.5
slope	116

REGULAR	
yardage	5960
par	71
rating	67.7
slope	111

FORWARD	
yardage	5402
par	71
rating	71.4
slope	122

 MONARCH BEACH GOLF LINKS
ARCHITECT: ROBERT TRENT JONES JR., 1983

33033 Niguel Rd.
Monarch Beach, CA 92677

PRO SHOP: 949-240-8247

Greg Winter, Head Professional, PGA
Craig Luckey, Tournament Director
Tom Sadey, Superintendent

Driving Range •
Practice Greens •
Clubhouse •
Food / Beverage •
Accommodations
Pull Carts
Power Carts •
Club Rental •
$pecial Offers

	1	2	3	4	5	6	7	8	9	OUT
BACK	376	446	315	183	217	392	602	417	499	3447
REGULAR	354	401	293	162	193	366	537	357	472	3135
par	4	4	4	3	3	4	5	4	5	36
handicap	15	7	17	13	11	9	1	3	5	-
FORWARD	319	346	258	132	164	340	499	296	436	2790
par	4	4	4	3	3	4	5	4	5	36
handicap	7	3	15	17	9	13	1	11	5	-

	10	11	12	13	14	15	16	17	18	IN
BACK	373	405	526	146	381	185	366	157	358	2897
REGULAR	346	342	496	127	354	137	305	133	330	2570
par	4	4	4	3	4	3	4	4	5	36
handicap	14	6	18	16	12	10	2	8	4	-
FORWARD	306	303	456	90	323	105	268	117	288	2256
par	4	4	4	3	3	4	5	4	5	36
handicap	8	4	2	16	6	14	12	18	10	-

BACK	
yardage	6344
par	72
rating	69.2
slope	128

REGULAR	
yardage	5705
par	72
rating	66.9
slope	121

FORWARD	
yardage	5046
par	72
rating	70.3
slope	119

PLAY POLICY & FEES: Monday through Wednesday green fees are $22 walking, $32 riding. Green fees on Thursday are $32, Friday $36, and $45 on weekends and holidays. Twilight and senior rates are available. Carts are mandatory Thursday through Sunday.

TEE TIMES: Reservations can be booked 10 days in advance.

DRESS CODE: Collared shirts are required.

COURSE DESCRIPTION: The front and back nines are as different as night and day. The front nine is flat, with trees lining the fairway. The back nine is hilly, with an abundance of trees to get in your way. This course is fairly close to the ocean, so the air is clean, but afternoon winds can make the course difficult.

NOTES: The course record of 63 from the blue tees belongs to Rick Parillo. From the white tees the course record is 63 by Ray Ricardo, and from the red tees the course record is 69 by Linda Healios.

LOCATION: From Interstate 5 near Juan Capistrano take the exit for San Juan Creek Road. Go to the light and turn right. Take the next right and go a quarter of a mile to the course.

. . . ● **TOURNAMENTS:** Shotgun tournaments are not allowed. A 24-player minimum is needed to book a tournament. Tournaments can be booked one month in advance. The banquet facility can accommodate 70 people.

115. SAN JUAN HILLS COUNTRY CLUB

PLAY POLICY & FEES: Outside play is accepted. Green fees are $115 Monday through Thursday, and $145 Friday through Sunday. Carts are included.

TEE TIMES: Reservations can be booked seven days in advance without a prebooking fee. For reservations up to 30 days, there is a $15 prebooking fee.

DRESS CODE: Appropriate golf attire is required.

COURSE DESCRIPTION: Most of the course offers a nice view of the ocean, and one hole runs alongside it. The course was built to conform nicely to the terrain. Watch out for the seventh hole. It's a par-5, 537-yard twister with a creek intersecting the fairway. To reach the green in regulation, it is necessary to clear the creek twice. Long hitters might reach the green in two, but if they miss, they will be appropriately penalized.

NOTES: The course is located on both sides of scenic Pacific Coast Highway.

LOCATION: Take the Crown Valley Parkway exit off Interstate 5. Drive 3.5 miles to Niguel Road. Turn left and travel another three miles. Turn right into the entryway across from the tennis club.

. . . ● **TOURNAMENTS:** Shotgun tournaments are available. A 36-player minimum is needed to book a tournament. Carts are recommended. A banquet facility is available that can accommodate up to 200 people. ● **TRAVEL:** The course is located next to the Ritz-Carlton Hotel.

116. MONARCH BEACH GOLF LINKS

SAN CLEMENTE GOLF COURSE
ARCHITECT: WILLIAM P. BELL, 1928

150 East Magdalena
San Clemente, CA 92672

PRO SHOP: 949-361-8380
STARTER: 949-361-8384

Gus Nelson, Golf Course Manager
Dave Cook, PGA Professional
Peggy O'Neill, Tournament Director

Driving Range ●
Practice Greens ●
Clubhouse ●
Food / Beverage ●
Accommodations
Pull Carts ●
Power Carts ●
Club Rental ●
$pecial Offers

	1	2	3	4	5	6	7	8	9	OUT
BACK	343	145	337	384	535	378	492	418	173	3205
REGULAR	336	126	311	366	520	356	474	410	159	3058
par	4	3	4	4	5	4	5	4	3	36
handicap	11	17	13	7	1	5	9	3	15	-
FORWARD	328	101	278	304	499	335	453	402	147	2847
par	4	3	4	4	5	4	5	5	3	37
handicap	7	17	13	11	3	5	9	1	15	-

	10	11	12	13	14	15	16	17	18	IN
BACK	385	488	483	205	304	196	405	358	418	3242
REGULAR	378	477	473	180	294	172	346	343	393	3056
par	4	5	5	3	4	3	4	4	4	36
handicap	12	4	8	14	18	16	2	10	6	-
FORWARD	366	465	461	138	268	156	323	330	368	2875
par	4	5	5	3	4	3	4	4	4	36
handicap	8	2	4	18	14	16	12	10	6	-

BACK	
yardage	6447
par	72
rating	70.6
slope	121

REGULAR	
yardage	6114
par	72
rating	68.9
slope	117

FORWARD	
yardage	5722
par	73
rating	73.0
slope	120

PACIFIC GOLF & COUNTRY CLUB
ARCHITECTS: GARY PLAYER, 1988; CARL LITTON

200 Avenida La Pata
San Clemente, CA 92673

PRO SHOP: 949-498-3771
CLUBHOUSE: 949-498-6604

Frank Adlesh, Manager
Scott Hoiseth, Head Professional, PGA
Rameka Fornaro, Tournament Director

Driving Range ●
Practice Greens ●
Clubhouse ●
Food / Beverage ●
Accommodations
Pull Carts
Power Carts ●
Club Rental ●
$pecial Offers

	1	2	3	4	5	6	7	8	9	OUT
BACK	329	567	305	142	349	411	443	139	439	3124
REGULAR	273	536	241	131	239	341	403	132	407	2703
par	4	5	4	3	4	4	5	3	4	36
handicap	1	3	7	9	2	4	5	6	8	-
FORWARD	273	536	202	131	316	341	403	98	407	2707
par	4	5	4	3	4	4	5	3	4	36
handicap	4	1	9	7	5	3	2	8	6	-

	10	11	12	13	14	15	16	17	18	IN
BACK	540	348	150	385	370	397	148	308	535	3181
REGULAR	502	308	130	301	340	359	112	250	499	2801
par	5	4	3	4	4	4	3	4	5	36
handicap	2	4	7	6	5	1	9	8	3	-
FORWARD	502	308	97	301	261	278	112	250	499	2608
par	5	4	3	4	4	4	3	4	5	36
handicap	1	3	8	4	6	7	9	5	2	-

BACK	
yardage	6305
par	72
rating	71.0
slope	132

REGULAR	
yardage	5504
par	72
rating	67.2
slope	120

FORWARD	
yardage	5315
par	72
rating	70.9
slope	124

PLAY POLICY & FEES: Green fees are $25 weekdays and $30 weekends. Twilight rates and resident discounts are available. Carts are $20.

TEE TIMES: Reservations can be booked seven days in advance.

DRESS CODE: Nonmetal spikes are required.

COURSE DESCRIPTION: This is a scenic course offering delightful ocean views. The par-3, 196-yard 15th hole has an elevated tee with a spectacular view of the Pacific Ocean. The back nine is more enjoyable and challenging than the front nine. It is a heavily played course; reservations are often difficult to secure. However, three tee times an hour are left open for walk-on traffic only.

NOTES: The men's course record is 63, set in 1996 by Kirk Rose. The women's record is 69, set in 1989 by Jayne Thobois. The San Clemente City Championship is held here in October.

LOCATION: From San Diego travel north on Interstate 5 and take the Avenida Magdalena exit. Turn right on El Camino Real and go one block. Turn left on Magdalena to the course. Coming from Los Angeles on Interstate 5, exit at Avenida Calfia and turn right. Take another right over the freeway, a right on El Camino Real for one block to Avenida Magdalena, and a left to the course.

. . . ● **TOURNAMENTS:** Five shotgun tournaments are allowed per year. A 24-player minimum is required to book a tournament. Events should be booked 12 months in advance. The banquet facility can accommodate 25 to 175 people.

● **TRAVEL:** Quality Suites is located right behind the course. For reservations call 714-366-1000.

117. SAN CLEMENTE GOLF COURSE

PLAY POLICY & FEES: Reciprocal play with other private clubs is accepted; otherwise, members and guests only. Reciprocal green fees are $100. Guest fees are $45 Monday through Thursday and $65 Friday through Sunday.

TEE TIMES: Have your golf pro call Monday through Thursday to arrange starting times.

DRESS CODE: Appropriate golf attire is required.

COURSE DESCRIPTION: This 27-hole course offers a traditional links layout that rolls through meadows. The first hole at Carnoustie/Muirfield gives some golfers a scare. It's an uphill par 4 to an undulating, sloping green. To make par, your second shot had better be a good one. All three nines are distinctly different. Wind can be a factor here.

NOTES: The course record is 66, set by Gary Player on opening day. Par is 72 for each of the 18-hole combinations. The Muirfield/Royal Course is 5,499 yards and rated 67.4 from the regular tees with a slope of 125. The Royal/Carnoustie Course is 5,467 yards and rated 67.3 from the regular tees with a slope of 124. The Carnoustie/Muirfield Course: See scorecard for yardage and rating information.

LOCATION: Take the Pico exit off Interstate 5 in San Clemente and travel two miles east to Avenida La Pata. Turn right and drive one mile to the club.

. . . ● **TOURNAMENTS:** A 12-player minimum is needed to book a tournament. Carts are required. No shotgun starts are allowed on weekends.

118. PACIFIC GOLF & COUNTRY CLUB

501 Avenida Vaquero
San Clemente, CA 92672

PRO SHOP: 949-492-1177
CLUBHOUSE: 949-492-5216

Fon Leong, Owner
Phil Vigil, PGA Professional
Fred Pinon, Superintendent

Driving Range ●
Practice Greens ●
Clubhouse ●
Food / Beverage ●
Accommodations
Pull Carts ●
Power Carts ●
Club Rental ●
$Special Offers

	1	2	3	4	5	6	7	8	9	OUT
BACK	545	361	332	199	315	307	169	386	426	3040
REGULAR	528	322	299	186	261	280	151	370	415	2812
par	5	4	4	3	4	4	3	4	4	35
handicap	3	13	15	7	11	9	17	5	1	-
FORWARD	487	310	288	173	252	251	138	286	404	2589
par	5	4	4	3	4	4	3	4	5	36
handicap	1	7	9	15	11	13	17	5	3	-

	10	11	12	13	14	15	16	17	18	IN
BACK	357	504	380	179	304	182	465	376	353	3100
REGULAR	343	494	273	148	294	175	450	360	341	2878
par	4	5	4	3	4	3	5	4	4	36
handicap	14	2	4	6	18	10	8	12	16	-
FORWARD	329	429	273	141	284	135	417	299	295	2602
par	4	5	4	3	4	3	5	4	4	36
handicap	6	4	12	16	10	18	2	14	8	-

BACK	
yardage	6140
par	71
rating	70.4
slope	130

REGULAR	
yardage	5690
par	71
rating	67.8
slope	122

FORWARD	
yardage	5191
par	72
rating	70.6
slope	120

PLAY POLICY & FEES: This is one of the few courses that offer you a discount for having a friend. Green fees are $35 for a single player and $60 for two players weekdays. On weekends green fees are $60 for a single player and $110 for two players. On weekdays seniors play for $30. Carts are included and mandatory.

TEE TIMES: Reservations can be booked seven days in advance.

DRESS CODE: Appropriate golf attire is required.

COURSE DESCRIPTION: This is a course that demands accuracy. It is short and tight and meanders in and out of canyons. Hook a tee shot and you might find yourself in a canyon with the coyotes. There are lots of out-of-bounds and several water hazards. The yardage of this course makes it look easier than it plays.

NOTES: This was one of President Nixon's favorite courses.

LOCATION: Take the Camino de Estrella exit off Interstate 5 and drive east to Avenida Vaquero. Turn right to the course.

. . . ● **TOURNAMENTS:** This course is available for outside tournaments.

119. SHORECLIFFS GOLF COURSE

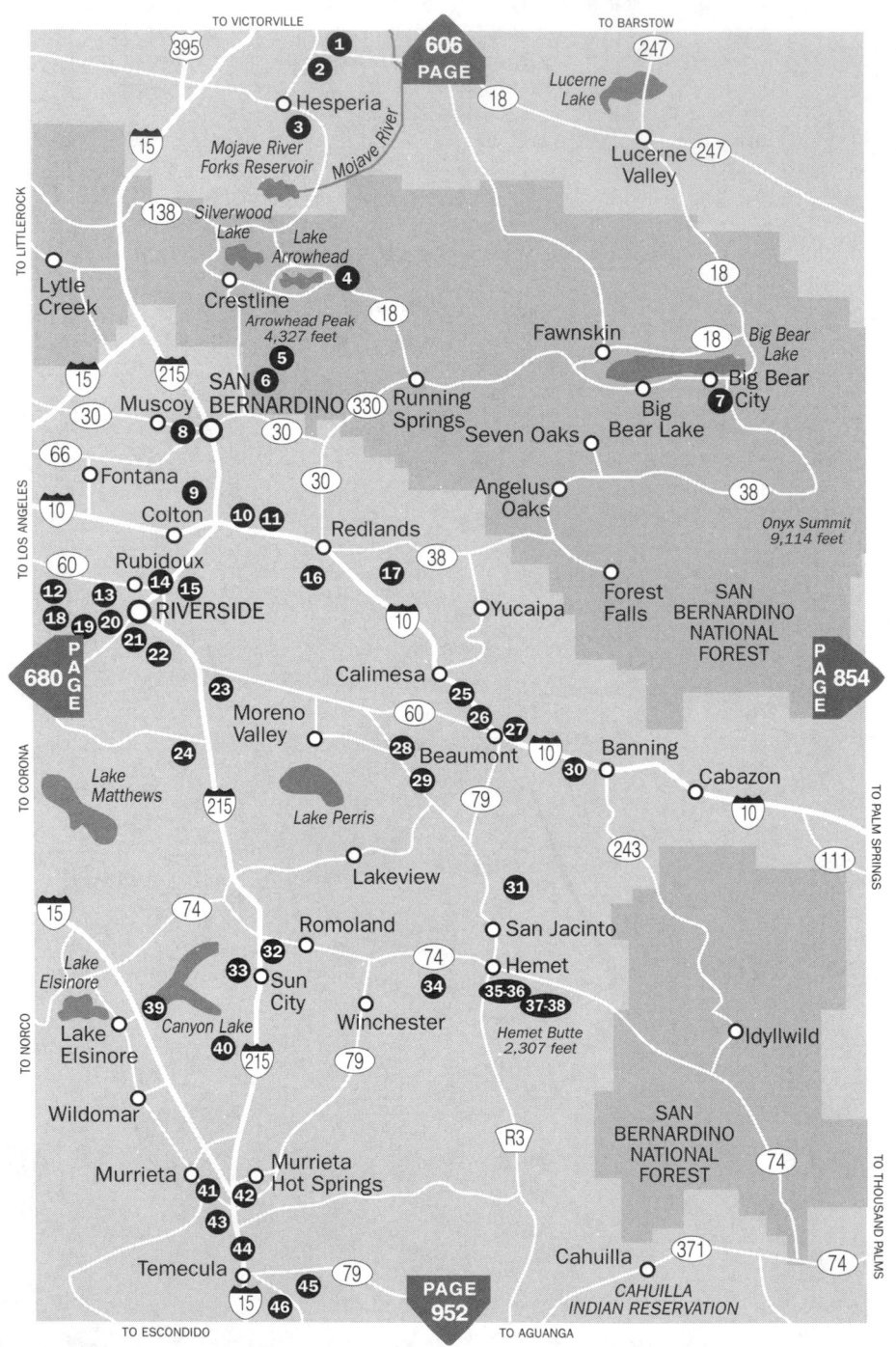

TO VICTORVILLE

TO BARSTOW

395

1
2

606
PAGE

247

Lucerne
Lake

18

Hesperia

3

247

Mojave River
Forks Reservoir

Mojave River

Lucerne
Valley

15

Silverwood
Lake

138

18

Lake
Arrowhead

Lytle
Creek

Crestline

4

Fawnskin

18

Big Bear
Lake

Arrowhead Peak
4,327 feet

18

15

5

Big Bear
City

215

SAN
BERNARDINO

6

330

Running
Springs

Big
Bear Lake

7

30

Muscoy

8

30

Seven Oaks

66

30

Angelus
Oaks

38

Fontana

9

30

Onyx Summit
9,114 feet

10

Colton

10 **11**

Redlands

TO LITTLEROCK

TO LOS ANGELES

60

Rubidoux

14 **15**

16

38

Forest
Falls

SAN
BERNARDINO
NATIONAL
FOREST

12 **13**

17

18
19 **20**

RIVERSIDE

10

Yucaipa

21

10

22

680
PAGE

854
PAGE

23

Calimesa

TO CORONA

24

Moreno
Valley

60

25

26 **27**

Banning

Cabazon

Lake
Matthews

28

Beaumont

10

30

215

29

10

Lake Perris

79

243

TO PALM SPRINGS

15

74

Lakeview

31

111

TO NORCO

Lake
Elsinore

Romoland

San Jacinto

32

74

Hemet

33

Sun
City

34

35-36

39

Canyon Lake

Winchester

37-38

Idyllwild

Lake
Elsinore

40

215

79

Hemet Butte
2,307 feet

Wildomar

SAN
BERNARDINO
NATIONAL
FOREST

Murrieta

Murrieta
Hot Springs

R3

74

41
42

43

TO THOUSAND PALMS

44

Cahuilla

371

74

Temecula

45

79

PAGE
952

15

46

CAHUILLA
INDIAN RESERVATION

TO ESCONDIDO

TO AGUANGA

San Bernardino/Riverside/ Temecula Area

❶ JESS RANCH GOLF CLUB
ARCHITECT: DAVID RAINVILLE, 1993

10885 Apple Valley Road
Apple Valley, CA 92308

PRO SHOP: 760-240-1800

Tim Brito, Manager

Driving Range ●
Practice Greens ●
Clubhouse ●
Food / Beverage ●
Accommodations
Pull Carts ●
Power Carts ●
Club Rental ●
$Special Offers

	1	2	3	4	5	6	7	8	9	OUT
BACK	386	292	195	386	140	205	349	434	155	2542
REGULAR	358	267	168	356	118	178	309	389	121	2264
par	4	4	3	4	3	3	4	4	3	32
handicap	1	13	3	9	15	5	11	7	17	-
FORWARD	289	214	141	279	94	155	274	343	95	1884
par	4	4	3	4	3	3	4	4	3	32
handicap	3	9	13	5	17	11	7	1	15	-

	10	11	12	13	14	15	16	17	18	IN
BACK	363	361	198	318	134	360	297	155	280	2466
REGULAR	328	325	160	291	111	326	255	131	255	2182
par	4	4	3	4	3	4	4	3	4	33
handicap	4	10	12	8	16	2	14	6	18	-
FORWARD	277	254	130	226	105	261	220	113	229	1815
par	4	4	3	4	3	4	4	3	4	33
handicap	2	4	14	8	18	6	10	16	12	-

BACK	
yardage	5008
par	65
rating	63.3
slope	101

REGULAR	
yardage	4446
par	65
rating	61.0
slope	98

FORWARD	
yardage	3699
par	65
rating	63.7
slope	105

❷ SPRING VALLEY LAKE COUNTRY CLUB
ARCHITECT: ROBERT TRENT JONES JR., 1970

13229 Spring Valley
Victorville, CA 92392

PRO SHOP: 760-245-7921
CLUBHOUSE: 760-245-5356

Joe Hough, Manager
Greg Combs, PGA Professional
Greg Day, Superintendent

Driving Range ●
Practice Greens ●
Clubhouse ●
Food / Beverage ●
Accommodations
Pull Carts ●
Power Carts ●
Club Rental ●
$Special Offers

	1	2	3	4	5	6	7	8	9	OUT
BACK	396	348	178	505	404	199	522	419	391	3362
REGULAR	346	339	167	498	388	167	495	395	374	3169
par	4	4	3	5	4	3	5	4	4	36
handicap	5	17	13	15	1	11	7	3	9	-
FORWARD	321	333	109	474	354	153	450	357	359	2910
par	4	4	3	5	4	3	5	4	4	36
handicap	5	13	17	9	3	15	1	7	11	-

	10	11	12	13	14	15	16	17	18	IN
BACK	478	337	188	521	413	399	318	329	190	3173
REGULAR	468	327	174	504	388	365	306	316	162	3010
par	5	4	3	5	4	4	4	4	3	36
handicap	10	12	14	6	2	4	18	16	8	-
FORWARD	394	313	134	486	371	351	298	305	134	2786
par	5	4	3	5	4	4	4	4	3	36
handicap	10	8	18	2	4	6	12	14	16	-

BACK	
yardage	6535
par	72
rating	71.2
slope	123

REGULAR	
yardage	6179
par	72
rating	69.3
slope	115

FORWARD	
yardage	5696
par	72
rating	72.7
slope	122

PLAY POLICY & FEES: Green fees are $9 for nine holes and $15 for 18 holes on weekdays. On weekends green fees are $11 for nine holes and $20 for 18 holes. Senior rates are $9 for nine and $10 for 18 holes. Junior rates are $6 for nine or 18 holes. Twilight rates are available; call for more information. Carts are $6 per player for nine holes and $10 per player for 18 holes.

TEE TIMES: Reservations can be booked seven days in advance.

DRESS CODE: Collared shirts are required. No cutoffs or tank tops are allowed on the course.

COURSE DESCRIPTION: This is a links-style course with bent-grass greens. Water comes into play on seven holes. There are no par 5s but several long par 4s. The first hole is the number-one handicap hole measuring 386 yards.

NOTES: The course record is 58 and is held by Rick Lawubenstien.

LOCATION: Exit off Interstate 15 on Bear Valley Road. Take Bear Valley Road east eight miles to Apple Valley Road and make a right turn. Take Apple Valley Road until it ends. The course entrance will be at the end of the road.

. . . ● **TOURNAMENTS:** A 16-player minimum is needed to book an event.

1. JESS RANCH GOLF CLUB

PLAY POLICY & FEES: Reciprocal play is accepted with members of other private clubs; otherwise, members and guests only. Green fees are $50. Carts are included.

DRESS CODE: Shorts must be Bermuda length, and no denim is allowed on the course.

COURSE DESCRIPTION: Traditionally in excellent condition, this course has plenty of water on the front nine and is relatively hilly on the back. It all toughens up when the winds blow, as they often will. Greens are medium sized, fast, and true.

LOCATION: From Victorville take Interstate 10 to Interstate 15. Drive north on Interstate 15 to the Lucerne Valley exit. Turn right and travel east for five miles on Bear Valley Road to Spring Valley Parkway. Turn left through the big archway to Spring Valley Lake and turn left on Country Club Drive.

. . . ● **TOURNAMENTS:** On Monday a minimum of 50 players is needed to book a tournament. During the rest of the week, a tournament will consist of no more than 50 players. Events are allowed only in the afternoons.

2. SPRING VALLEY LAKE COUNTRY CLUB

HESPERIA GOLF & COUNTRY CLUB
ARCHITECT: WILLIAM F. BELL, 1955

17970 Bangor Avenue
Hesperia, CA 92345

PRO SHOP: 760-244-9301

Alexander Rickards Sr., General Manager
Alexander Rickards Jr., Superintendent

Driving Range ●
Practice Greens ●
Clubhouse ●
Food / Beverage ●
Accommodations
Pull Carts ●
Power Carts ●
Club Rental ●
$pecial Offers

	1	2	3	4	5	6	7	8	9	OUT
BACK	409	421	519	387	159	525	173	377	429	3399
REGULAR	390	410	501	366	150	494	159	362	416	3248
par	4	4	5	4	3	5	3	4	4	36
handicap	5	1	7	13	17	9	15	11	3	-
FORWARD	373	399	462	346	139	468	137	321	399	3044
par	4	4	5	4	3	5	3	4	4	36
handicap	5	1	7	11	17	9	15	13	3	-

	10	11	12	13	14	15	16	17	18	IN
BACK	399	461	211	575	188	438	369	512	444	3597
REGULAR	384	444	196	558	170	424	355	500	416	3447
par	4	4	3	5	3	4	4	5	4	36
handicap	14	4	10	8	18	6	16	12	2	-
FORWARD	372	389	135	499	151	394	341	455	356	3092
par	4	4	3	5	3	4	4	5	4	36
handicap	12	10	16	6	18	2	14	8	4	-

BACK	
yardage	6996
par	72
rating	73.5
slope	131

REGULAR	
yardage	6695
par	72
rating	71.9
slope	128

FORWARD	
yardage	6136
par	72
rating	74.5
slope	128

PLAY POLICY & FEES: Reciprocal play is accepted with members of other private clubs. Outside play is also accepted. Green fees are $17 weekdays, $22 on weekends and holidays. Junior, senior, and nine-hole rates are available.

TEE TIMES: Reservations can be booked 14 days in advance.

DRESS CODE: Golf attire and nonmetal spikes are encouraged. No tank tops are allowed on the course.

COURSE DESCRIPTION: This former PGA Tour stop offers a championship layout. It was designed and built in 1957 and is still a tough test. The fairways are separated by mature trees. The course is well bunkered and features three lakes and rolling terrain. The toughest hole is the 18th. Trees guard each side of the fairway. Rumor has it that pro Doug Sanders once took a 12 on this hole.

NOTES: In the mid-1950s and early 1960s legends like Arnold Palmer, Gary Player, Billy Casper, Gene Littler, Sam Snead, and Julius Boros played in the Hesperia Open Invitational. "Golf Digest" gave Hesperia three and a half stars for 1996–1997 and 1998-1999. In the 1998-1999 issue, CALIFORNIA GOLF recognized this course as one of the "California 50."

LOCATION: From Los Angeles take Interstate 10 to Interstate 15 and travel 33 miles north on Interstate 15 to the first Hesperia exit. Turn right on Main Street and go 5.5 miles to I Avenue and turn right. Go 1.5 miles to Bangor Avenue and turn left.

. . . ● **TOURNAMENTS:** This course is available for outside tournaments. A 12-player minimum is needed. Events should be scheduled 12 months in advance. The banquet facility can hold 145 people. ● **TRAVEL:** For lodging, Days Inn (760-956-8645) and Red Roof Inn (760-241-1577) are recommended.

3. HESPERIA GOLF & COUNTRY CLUB

4 LAKE ARROWHEAD COUNTRY CLUB
ARCHITECT: WILLIAM F. BELL, 1963

P.O. Box 670
Lake Arrowhead, CA
92352
PRO SHOP: 909-337-3515

250 Golf Course Road
Lake Arrowhead, CA
92352

Kelly B. Jensen, PGA Professional
Hank Ott Devries, General Manager
Emilio Castorena, Superintendent

Driving Range •
Practice Greens •
Clubhouse •
Food / Beverage •
Accommodations
Pull Carts
Power Carts •
Club Rental
$pecial Offers

	1	2	3	4	5	6	7	8	9	OUT
BACK	433	178	478	437	379	185	359	463	289	3201
REGULAR	430	168	466	421	374	182	355	461	285	3142
par	4	3	5	4	4	3	4	4	4	35
handicap	5	11	13	3	7	9	15	1	17	-
FORWARD	420	117	437	388	312	147	323	459	284	2887
par	5	3	5	4	4	3	4	5	4	37
handicap	7	15	5	1	13	11	9	3	17	-

	10	11	12	13	14	15	16	17	18	IN
BACK	309	363	476	284	143	489	373	436	168	3041
REGULAR	309	348	472	282	134	455	340	405	155	2900
par	4	4	5	4	3	5	4	4	3	36
handicap	16	6	10	12	18	2	8	4	14	-
FORWARD	308	314	456	269	121	426	314	336	111	2655
par	4	4	5	4	3	5	4	4	3	36
handicap	14	8	4	12	16	2	6	10	18	-

BACK	
yardage	6242
par	71
rating	70.5
slope	128

REGULAR	
yardage	6042
par	71
rating	69.2
slope	124

FORWARD	
yardage	5542
par	73
rating	70.2
slope	131

5 ARROWHEAD COUNTRY CLUB

3433 Parkside Drive
San Bernardino, CA 92404

PRO SHOP: 909-882-1638
CLUBHOUSE: 909-882-1735

Brian Miskell, Head Professional, PGA
Dan Vasquez, Superintendent

Driving Range •
Practice Greens •
Clubhouse •
Food / Beverage •
Accommodations
Pull Carts •
Power Carts •
Club Rental •
$pecial Offers

	1	2	3	4	5	6	7	8	9	OUT
BACK	390	404	485	196	351	560	513	202	403	3504
REGULAR	373	372	465	165	344	551	494	202	387	3353
par	4	4	5	3	4	5	5	3	4	37
handicap	5	1	15	11	17	9	13	7	3	-
FORWARD	364	345	450	140	331	472	437	194	372	3105
par	4	4	5	3	4	5	5	3	4	37
handicap	3	5	9	17	13	7	11	15	1	-

	10	11	12	13	14	15	16	17	18	IN
BACK	194	499	212	487	338	174	420	363	382	3069
REGULAR	176	479	195	470	325	140	401	347	361	2894
par	3	5	3	5	4	3	4	4	4	35
handicap	8	18	4	16	6	14	2	10	12	-
FORWARD	162	457	170	424	290	116	376	321	338	2654
par	3	5	3	5	4	3	4	4	4	35
handicap	18	4	8	10	6	16	2	14	12	-

BACK	
yardage	6573
par	72
rating	71.5
slope	124

REGULAR	
yardage	6247
par	72
rating	69.6
slope	117

FORWARD	
yardage	5759
par	72
rating	72.8
slope	125

PLAY POLICY & FEES: Members and guests only. Green fees are $75. Carts are $14. The course is open from April to November.

DRESS CODE: Nonmetal spikes are mandatory.

COURSE DESCRIPTION: Originally a 1930s nine-hole course, it became 18 holes in 1963. The front nine is level and open while the back nine is hilly. There is a small lake on the course that comes into play. All the holes are dotted with bunkers.

LOCATION: Drive northeast of San Bernardino on Interstate 215 to the Mountain Resorts exit. Continue to Highway 18 (Waterman Avenue) and turn left, following it to the Blue Jay exit. Bear left to the stop signal, turn left, and drive one-half mile to Grass Valley Road. Bear right and continue 1.5 miles to Golf Course Road. Turn left and drive 100 yards to the club.

. . . ● **TOURNAMENTS:** This course is not available for outside events.

4. LAKE ARROWHEAD COUNTRY CLUB

PLAY POLICY & FEES: Reciprocal play is accepted with members of other private clubs; otherwise, members and guests only. Guest and reciprocal fees are $50. Carts are $10.

DRESS CODE: Collared shirts and nonmetal spikes are required. No blue jeans or short shorts are allowed on the course.

COURSE DESCRIPTION: This course in one form or another has been around since the 1920s. It first opened for memberships in 1944. It has level terrain, mature trees, and water hazards. It is set at the foot of the mountains in a desert area, so the heat can become unbearable.

NOTES: In the winter, several ski areas are open 30 minutes away in the San Bernardino Mountains.

LOCATION: From San Bernardino travel east on Highway 30 to Waterman Avenue north. Drive one-half mile and turn right on 34th Street. Continue to Parkside Drive and the entrance to the club.

. . . ● **TOURNAMENTS:** This course is not available for outside events.

5. ARROWHEAD COUNTRY CLUB

6 SHANDIN HILLS GOLF CLUB
ARCHITECT: HENRY BICKLER, 1982

3380 Little Mountain Drive
San Bernardino, CA 92407

PRO SHOP: 909-886-0669
CLUBHOUSE: 909-886-2322

Joe Baumbach, Manager
Rick Clawson, Superintendent
Thomas Mainez, Director of Golf

Driving Range •
Practice Greens •
Clubhouse •
Food / Beverage •
Accommodations
Pull Carts •
Power Carts •
Club Rental •
$pecial Offers

	1	2	3	4	5	6	7	8	9	OUT
BACK	490	385	147	363	385	350	178	556	380	3234
REGULAR	467	370	135	345	376	341	166	530	360	3090
par	5	4	3	4	4	4	3	5	4	36
handicap	17	3	11	9	1	5	15	7	13	-
FORWARD	420	336	126	325	353	320	105	501	296	2782
par	5	4	3	4	4	4	3	5	4	36
handicap	11	7	13	9	1	3	17	5	15	-

	10	11	12	13	14	15	16	17	18	IN
BACK	425	190	373	338	514	165	408	530	340	3283
REGULAR	400	171	360	320	490	145	396	500	320	3102
par	4	3	4	4	5	3	4	5	4	36
handicap	4	10	18	16	12	8	2	6	14	-
FORWARD	380	123	350	306	433	115	375	480	248	2810
par	4	3	4	4	5	3	4	5	4	36
handicap	6	18	8	10	12	16	4	2	14	-

BACK	
yardage	6517
par	72
rating	70.3
slope	120

REGULAR	
yardage	6192
par	72
rating	68.7
slope	114

FORWARD	
yardage	5592
par	72
rating	71.6
slope	122

7 BEAR MOUNTAIN GOLF COURSE

43100 Goldmine Drive
Big Bear Lake, CA 92315

PRO SHOP: 909-585-8002

Brent Tregaskis, Manager
Tekla Dilday, Director of Golf
Jack Culler, Superintendent

Driving Range •
Practice Greens •
Clubhouse
Food / Beverage •
Accommodations
Pull Carts •
Power Carts •
Club Rental •
$pecial Offers

	1	2	3	4	5	6	7	8	9	OUT
BACK	379	527	315	457	138	382	143	137	252	2730
REGULAR	368	484	309	448	128	361	138	117	248	2601
par	4	5	4	5	3	4	3	3	4	35
handicap	13	1	5	7	17	3	9	11	15	-
FORWARD	242	455	279	412	123	329	94	53	221	2208
par	4	5	4	5	3	4	3	3	4	35
handicap	13	1	5	7	17	3	9	11	15	-

	10	11	12	13	14	15	16	17	18	IN
BACK	379	527	315	457	138	382	143	137	252	2730
REGULAR	368	484	309	448	128	361	138	117	248	2601
par	4	5	4	5	3	4	3	3	4	35
handicap	14	2	6	8	18	4	10	12	16	-
FORWARD	242	455	279	412	123	329	94	53	221	2208
par	4	5	4	5	3	4	3	3	4	35
handicap	14	2	6	8	18	4	10	12	16	-

BACK	
yardage	5460
par	70
rating	65.4
slope	108

REGULAR	
yardage	5202
par	70
rating	64.2
slope	105

FORWARD	
yardage	4416
par	70
rating	-
slope	-

PLAY POLICY & FEES: Green fees are $24 walking and $33 riding Monday through Thursday. Friday green fees are $26 walking and $34 riding. Saturday and Sunday and holiday green fees are $43 riding.

TEE TIMES: Reservations can be booked seven days in advance.

DRESS CODE: Collared shirts are required, and nonmetal spikes are preferred.

COURSE DESCRIPTION: This is a challenging course with 79 bunkers. The rough is well developed, so accuracy is essential. Narrow tree-lined fairways lead from elevated tees to elevated greens. Interstate 215 bisects the two nines, but scenic views of the San Bernardino Mountains abound.

NOTES: PGA Tour pro Kirk Triplett set the course record of 61 while playing a Golden State Mini-Tour event in 1987.

LOCATION: From Los Angeles travel east on Interstate 10 to Interstate 215. In San Bernardino take the Mount Vernon/27th Street off-ramp and turn right on 27th Street, then immediately left on Little Mountain. Travel one mile to the club.

. . . ● **TOURNAMENTS:** This course is available for outside tournaments. A 12-player minimum is needed to book a tournament. Tournaments can be booked up to 12 months in advance. The banquet facility holds up to 250 people.

● **TRAVEL:** The San Bernadino Hilton and the San Bernadino Radisson are recommended for lodging.

6. SHANDIN HILLS GOLF CLUB

PLAY POLICY & FEES: Green fees are $20 for nine holes weekdays and $22 for nine holes weekends. The 18-hole rates are $30 weekdays and $32 weekends. Carts are $14 for nine holes and $20 for 18 holes. Pull carts are $3 for nine holes and $5 for 18 holes. The course is closed from November to March depending on the weather.

TEE TIMES: Reservations are encouraged and can be made up to one month in advance.

DRESS CODE: No tank tops or sandals are allowed on the golf course. T-shirts are OK, but golf attire and golf shoes are encouraged.

COURSE DESCRIPTION: The elevation here is 7,200 feet, and the course closes when it snows. It offers long par 3s and gently rolling hills. This course was formerly known as Goldmine Golf Course.

LOCATION: In San Bernardino take Highway 330 to Highway 18 and head east to Moonridge Road. Drive 1.25 miles to Club View Drive. Turn left on Goldmine Drive and left into the parking lot. It is about 40 miles from San Bernardino.

. . . ● **TOURNAMENTS:** Weekend shotgun tournaments are not allowed during the peak season, July through September.

7. BEAR MOUNTAIN GOLF COURSE

355 E. Country Club Drive
Rialto, CA 92377

PRO SHOP: 909-875-5346
CLUBHOUSE: 909-875-7111

David Sarricks, Manager, PGA
Ben Carson, Professional
Julio Silva, Superintendent

Driving Range ●
Practice Greens ●
Clubhouse ●
Food / Beverage ●
Accommodations
Pull Carts
Power Carts ●
Club Rental ●
$pecial Offers

	1	2	3	4	5	6	7	8	9	OUT
BACK	381	455	516	195	393	438	498	389	167	3432
REGULAR	370	446	505	161	385	429	491	376	156	3319
par	4	4	5	3	4	4	5	4	3	36
handicap	17	1	13	7	9	5	15	3	11	-
FORWARD	311	386	457	124	279	369	457	336	143	2862
par	4	4	5	3	4	4	5	4	3	36
handicap	9	3	1	15	13	7	5	11	17	-

	10	11	12	13	14	15	16	17	18	IN
BACK	378	368	226	415	512	168	389	430	526	3412
REGULAR	367	353	209	406	503	149	377	420	512	3296
par	4	4	3	4	5	3	4	4	5	36
handicap	10	8	2	6	18	12	16	4	14	-
FORWARD	267	306	177	355	380	114	310	357	461	2727
par	4	4	3	4	4	3	4	4	5	35
handicap	16	14	4	10	2	18	12	6	8	-

BACK	
yardage	6844
par	72
rating	72.9
slope	124

REGULAR	
yardage	6615
par	72
rating	71.6
slope	122

FORWARD	
yardage	5589
par	71
rating	71.9
slope	124

1901 Valley Boulevard
Colton, CA 92324

PRO SHOP: 909-877-1712

Bob Mastalski, General Manager
Tad Juday, Superintendent

Driving Range ●
Practice Greens ●
Clubhouse ●
Food / Beverage ●
Accommodations
Pull Carts ●
Power Carts ●
Club Rental ●
$pecial Offers

	1	2	3	4	5	6	7	8	9	OUT
BACK	-	-	-	-	-	-	-	-	-	-
REGULAR	180	305	141	163	146	179	139	245	142	1640
par	3	4	3	3	3	3	3	4	3	29
handicap	2	16	12	6	8	4	10	18	14	-
FORWARD	162	285	99	117	123	143	120	219	117	1385
par	3	4	3	3	3	3	3	4	3	29
handicap	2	16	12	6	8	4	10	18	14	-

	10	11	12	13	14	15	16	17	18	IN
BACK	-	-	-	-	-	-	-	-	-	-
REGULAR	124	143	197	146	107	269	126	154	202	1468
par	3	3	3	3	3	4	3	3	3	28
handicap	9	5	1	15	13	17	11	7	3	-
FORWARD	101	117	180	112	83	240	106	120	182	1241
par	3	3	3	3	3	4	3	3	3	28
handicap	9	5	1	15	13	17	11	7	3	-

BACK	
yardage	-
par	-
rating	-
slope	-

REGULAR	
yardage	3108
par	57
rating	54.8
slope	82

FORWARD	
yardage	2626
par	57
rating	54.8
slope	82

PLAY POLICY & FEES: Green fees are $17 weekdays and $30 weekends. Green fees including a cart are $25 weekdays and $40 weekends. Fees are subject to change.

TEE TIMES: Reservations can be booked seven days in advance.

DRESS CODE: No tank tops are allowed. Nonmetal spikes are preferred.

COURSE DESCRIPTION: This course offers gentle, rolling hills with many pine and eucalyptus trees on the front nine and orange groves on the back nine. It boasts tough par 3s and a view of the San Bernardino Mountains. The 12th, for instance, is set 226 yards uphill, with an orange grove to the left and out-of-bounds to the right.

NOTES: The facility includes a lighted driving range open to 10 p.m.

LOCATION: From Los Angeles drive east on Interstate 10 (San Bernardino Freeway) to Riverside Avenue in the town of Rialto. Turn left and drive six miles to Country Club Drive.

. . . ● **TOURNAMENTS:** This course is available for outside tournaments. A 24-player minimum is required to book a tournament. Events should be scheduled 12 months in advance. The banquet facility can accommodate 300 people.

8. EL RANCHO VERDE ROYAL VISTA GOLF

PLAY POLICY & FEES: Green fees are $14 weekdays and $17 weekends. Carts are $14 weekdays and $17 weekends. Senior, nine-hole, and other special rates are available. Call for more information.

TEE TIMES: Reservations can be booked seven days in advance.

DRESS CODE: Shirts must be worn.

COURSE DESCRIPTION: This is an executive course designed for those who want to test almost every club in the bag. This Robert Trent Jones Sr. layout offers all his usual challenges in short form, including sculpted, well-protected greens. It's short, but still a championship course.

NOTES: Colton Golf Club was once owned by Sam Snead. The course record is 50.

LOCATION: Take Interstate 10 to Colton and exit at Riverside Avenue. Follow Riverside to Valley Boulevard, turn right, and go about one mile to the course. Alternatively, take the Pepper exit off Interstate 10 and proceed to Valley Boulevard.

. . . ● **TOURNAMENTS:** Shotgun tournaments are available weekdays only. A 20-player minimum is required to book a tournament. ● **TRAVEL:** The Best Western Empire Inn is a couple blocks away from the golf course. For reservations call 909-877-0690.

9. COLTON GOLF CLUB

10 SAN BERNARDINO GOLF COURSE
ARCHITECT: DAN BROWN, 1968

1494 South Waterman
San Bernardino, CA 92408

PRO SHOP: 909-885-2414

Tomas Self, Manager
Cheryl Thomas, Professional
Frank Hillpot, Tournament Director

Driving Range ●
Practice Greens ●
Clubhouse ●
Food / Beverage ●
Accommodations
Pull Carts ●
Power Carts ●
Club Rental ●
$pecial Offers

	1	2	3	4	5	6	7	8	9	OUT
BACK	422	455	323	191	429	329	162	329	328	2968
REGULAR	415	445	317	176	419	320	152	319	318	2881
par	4	5	4	3	4	4	3	4	4	35
handicap	3	11	13	7	1	15	17	9	5	-
FORWARD	404	404	308	154	409	304	137	304	308	2732
par	5	5	4	3	5	4	3	4	4	37
handicap	5	1	11	13	3	15	17	9	7	-

	10	11	12	13	14	15	16	17	18	IN
BACK	334	298	266	412	125	376	191	358	450	2810
REGULAR	324	273	255	404	112	365	170	350	424	2677
par	4	4	4	4	3	4	3	4	5	35
handicap	18	10	8	2	16	4	12	6	14	-
FORWARD	308	244	248	384	104	294	148	334	426	2490
par	4	4	4	4	3	4	3	4	5	35
handicap	8	16	10	2	18	6	14	12	4	-

BACK	
yardage	5778
par	70
rating	67.4
slope	112

REGULAR	
yardage	5558
par	70
rating	66.4
slope	109

FORWARD	
yardage	5222
par	72
rating	68.7
slope	109

11 PALM MEADOWS GOLF CLUB
ARCHITECT: WILLIAM F. BELL, 1958

1964 East Palm Meadows
San Bernardino, CA 92408

PRO SHOP: 909-382-2002

Troy Burton, G.M./Head Professional, PGA
Bev Carlson, Banquet Manager
Bruce Atkin, Superintendent

Driving Range ●
Practice Greens ●
Clubhouse ●
Food / Beverage ●
Accommodations
Pull Carts ●
Power Carts ●
Club Rental ●
$pecial Offers

	1	2	3	4	5	6	7	8	9	OUT
BACK	381	400	430	570	175	522	432	347	195	3452
REGULAR	370	396	411	557	146	511	369	337	180	3277
par	4	4	4	5	3	5	4	4	3	36
handicap	7	1	3	11	17	13	5	9	15	-
FORWARD	337	387	407	460	122	448	362	330	159	3012
par	4	4	5	5	3	5	4	4	3	37
handicap	7	1	11	5	17	9	3	13	15	-

	10	11	12	13	14	15	16	17	18	IN
BACK	557	361	295	370	377	190	478	189	405	3222
REGULAR	552	347	295	350	369	180	471	183	392	3139
par	5	4	4	4	4	3	5	3	4	36
handicap	4	6	18	10	8	14	16	12	2	-
FORWARD	425	281	290	314	361	172	460	152	384	2839
par	5	4	4	4	4	3	5	3	4	36
handicap	4	6	12	16	14	10	8	18	2	-

BACK	
yardage	6674
par	72
rating	71.5
slope	124

REGULAR	
yardage	6416
par	72
rating	70.4
slope	120

FORWARD	
yardage	5851
par	73
rating	73.0
slope	124

PLAY POLICY & FEES: On weekdays, green fees are $17 walking and $26 riding. On weekends and holidays, green fees are $26 walking and $35 riding. Green fees are more expensive in the morning. Senior, student, afternoon, and twilight rates are available. Reservations are recommended.

TEE TIMES: Reservations can be booked seven days in advance.

DRESS CODE: No tank tops, half shirts, altered T-shirts, halter tops, or bathing suits are allowed. Nonmetal spikes are preferred.

COURSE DESCRIPTION: This course has only four bunkers but five holes with water. Don't be fooled by the apparent short length. Typically, scores here are higher on average than on neighboring courses. Stay in the fairways or you're in tall rough.

NOTES: The men's course record of 60 is held by Walt "Sonny" Hammond, set in 1985. The women's course record of 64 is held by Kathy Dougherty. The San Bernardino County Men's Amateur Championships are held here the last weekend in August.

LOCATION: In San Bernardino take Interstate 10 (San Bernardino Freeway) to the Waterman Avenue exit north and travel three-quarters of a mile to the course.

. . . ● **TOURNAMENTS:** A 144-player minimum is needed to book a shotgun tournament. Carts are required.

10. SAN BERNARDINO GOLF COURSE

PLAY POLICY & FEES: Green fees are $17 walking and $27 riding. Weekend fees are $25 walking and $35 riding. Military personnel discounts are offered. Senior, afternoon, and twilight rates are also available. Carts are $16 for two riders. Reservations are recommended.

TEE TIMES: Reservations can be booked seven days in advance.

DRESS CODE: Collared shirts are required. No cutoffs are allowed.

COURSE DESCRIPTION: This well-manicured course is set on the old Norton Air Force Base. It has gentle rolling fairways surrounded by a unique combination of eucalyptus and palm trees. Palm Meadow is an ideal course for golfers of all skill levels.

NOTES: The clubhouse has recently been remodeled.

LOCATION: Drive southeast of San Bernardino on Interstate 10 to the Tippecanoe exit. Turn North and proceed 1.5 miles. Turn right on Palm Meadows Drive.

. . . ● **TOURNAMENTS:** This course is available for outside tournaments. A 24-player minimum is required to book a tournament. Events can be scheduled three to 24 months in advance. A banquet facility is available that can accommodate up to 180 people. ● **TRAVEL:** The Black Angus is recommended for dinner. The San Bernardino Hilton is 10 minutes from the course. Call 909-889-0133.

11. PALM MEADOWS GOLF CLUB

12 INDIAN HILLS GOLF CLUB
ARCHITECT: WILLIAM P. BELL, 1964

5700 Clubhouse Drive
Riverside, CA 92509

PRO SHOP: 909-360-2090

Paul Dietsche, Head Professional, PGA
Erik Wolf, Tournament Director
Scott Vlahos, Superintendent

Driving Range
Practice Greens •
Clubhouse •
Food / Beverage •
Accommodations
Pull Carts
Power Carts •
Club Rental •
$pecial Offers

	1	2	3	4	5	6	7	8	9	OUT
BACK	402	285	199	390	217	401	297	505	451	3147
REGULAR	400	278	176	379	162	386	292	495	437	3005
par	4	4	3	4	3	4	4	5	4	35
handicap	5	15	7	3	11	9	17	13	1	-
FORWARD	387	274	165	368	158	397	287	488	423	2947
par	4	4	3	4	3	5	4	5	5	37
handicap	5	9	11	7	15	17	13	3	1	-

	10	11	12	13	14	15	16	17	18	IN
BACK	320	156	286	406	314	164	408	418	515	2987
REGULAR	311	147	260	390	302	148	398	408	497	2861
par	4	3	4	4	4	3	4	4	5	35
handicap	8	16	18	12	6	14	4	2	10	-
FORWARD	307	137	240	376	291	133	383	330	418	2615
par	4	3	4	4	4	3	4	4	5	35
handicap	5	9	11	7	15	17	13	3	1	-

BACK	
yardage	6134
par	70
rating	70.0
slope	123

REGULAR	
yardage	5866
par	70
rating	68.1
slope	117

FORWARD	
yardage	5562
par	72
rating	70.7
slope	118

13 FAIRMOUNT PARK GOLF CLUB

2681 Dexter Drive
Riverside, CA 92501

PRO SHOP: 909-682-2202

Bill Shoemaker, Manager
John Welter, Superintendent

Driving Range •
Practice Greens •
Clubhouse •
Food / Beverage •
Accommodations
Pull Carts •
Power Carts •
Club Rental •
$pecial Offers

	1	2	3	4	5	6	7	8	9	OUT
BACK	371	183	355	527	176	342	304	493	467	3218
REGULAR	351	110	340	489	139	329	280	487	448	2973
par	4	3	4	5	3	4	4	5	4	36
handicap	5	7	11	13	3	9	15	17	1	-
FORWARD	320	91	309	432	107	309	204	458	380	2610
par	4	3	4	5	3	4	4	5	4	36
handicap	9	17	3	5	7	11	15	3	1	-

	10	11	12	13	14	15	16	17	18	IN
BACK	371	183	355	527	176	342	304	493	467	3218
REGULAR	351	110	340	489	139	329	280	487	448	2973
par	4	3	4	5	3	4	4	5	4	36
handicap	4	16	10	18	8	6	14	12	2	-
FORWARD	320	91	309	432	107	309	204	458	380	2610
par	4	3	4	5	3	4	4	5	4	36
handicap	10	18	14	6	8	12	16	2	4	-

BACK	
yardage	6436
par	72
rating	-
slope	-

REGULAR	
yardage	5946
par	72
rating	68.6
slope	103

FORWARD	
yardage	5220
par	72
rating	-
slope	-

PLAY POLICY & FEES: Green fees are $27 weekdays and $43 weekends. Twilight rates are $20 weekdays and $27 weekends after 1 p.m. The senior rate is $24 weekdays. All fees include cart.

TEE TIMES: Reservations can be booked seven days in advance by calling 909-360-2089.

DRESS CODE: Collared shirts are required.

COURSE DESCRIPTION: This is a rolling course with numerous mature trees and no parallel fairways. The two nines loop out and back from the clubhouse. The greens are undulating and can be tough. Walking on this hilly course is for the adventurous.

NOTES: The course record is 64.

LOCATION: From Los Angeles take Highway 60 (Pomona Freeway) east to the Van Buren/Etiwanda Avenue exit in Riverside. Travel south on Van Buren Boulevard for 4.5 miles to Limonite Avenue and turn left. Drive to Clay Street and turn left, then right on Lakeside Drive. Follow the signs to the club on top of the hill.

. . . ● **TOURNAMENTS:** Shotgun tournaments are available. Carts are required. A 20-player minimum is needed to book a regular tournament. Tournaments can be booked 12 months in advance. ● **TRAVEL:** The Mission Inn in Riverside is recommended for lodging.

12. INDIAN HILLS GOLF CLUB

PLAY POLICY & FEES: Green fees are $6 for nine holes and $8 for 18 holes weekdays, and $8 for nine holes and $10 for 18 holes weekends. Carts are $8 for nine holes and $14 for 18 holes weekdays, and $11 for nine holes and $18 for 18 holes on weekends.

TEE TIMES: Reservations can be booked seven days in advance.

DRESS CODE: Casual dress is accepted, but shirts must worn at all times.

COURSE DESCRIPTION: This is an older course, but it has character. Numerous mature palm and cypress trees line the level fairways. It's a left-to-right course with mean doglegs and more trees. The first hole can be a tester thanks to a large tree in the middle of the fairway.

NOTES: The course includes a 60-stall, night-lighted driving range.

LOCATION: From Los Angeles travel east on Highway 60 (Pomona Freeway) to Riverside. Take the Market Street exit to the course.

. . . ● **TOURNAMENTS:** Shotgun tournaments are available weekdays only. A 72-player minimum is needed to book a shotgun tournament. A $2 surcharge is added for all events.

13. FAIRMOUNT PARK GOLF CLUB

⑭ EL RIVINO COUNTRY CLUB
ARCHITECT: JOSEPH CALWELL, 1956

P.O. Box 3369
Riverside, CA 92519

5530 El Rivino Road
Riverside, CA 92519

PRO SHOP: 909-684-8905

David Williams, Professional
William Anderson, Superintendent

Driving Range
Practice Greens ●
Clubhouse ●
Food / Beverage ●
Accommodations
Pull Carts
Power Carts ●
Club Rental
$pecial Offers

	1	2	3	4	5	6	7	8	9	OUT
BACK	626	374	162	420	304	347	281	493	153	3160
REGULAR	595	367	125	408	290	339	266	484	142	3016
par	6	4	3	4	4	4	4	5	3	37
handicap	5	3	17	1	11	13	9	7	15	-
FORWARD	580	360	119	400	281	285	254	479	128	2886
par	6	4	3	4	4	4	4	5	3	37
handicap	5	3	17	1	11	13	9	7	15	-

	10	11	12	13	14	15	16	17	18	IN
BACK	243	347	425	374	339	514	477	186	372	3277
REGULAR	218	327	408	362	332	501	447	176	355	3126
par	3	4	4	4	4	5	5	3	4	36
handicap	4	14	2	16	12	8	10	18	6	-
FORWARD	206	313	392	311	325	488	434	168	340	2977
par	3	4	4	4	4	5	5	3	4	36
handicap	10	14	2	16	12	6	4	18	8	-

BACK	
yardage	6437
par	73
rating	70.8
slope	111

REGULAR	
yardage	6142
par	73
rating	69.4
slope	108

FORWARD	
yardage	5863
par	73
rating	71.8
slope	116

⑮ RIVERSIDE GOLF CLUB
ARCHITECT: CHARLES MAUD, 1948

P.O. Box 391
Riverside, CA 92501

PRO SHOP: 909-682-3748

Deborah Eschrich, General Manager
Dennis Kahn, PGA Professional
Greg Aerosmith, Superintendent

Driving Range ●
Practice Greens ●
Clubhouse ●
Food / Beverage ●
Accommodations
Pull Carts ●
Power Carts ●
Club Rental ●
$pecial Offers

	1	2	3	4	5	6	7	8	9	OUT
BACK	366	166	500	406	389	405	407	433	349	3421
REGULAR	350	149	492	396	374	398	395	423	346	3323
par	4	3	5	4	4	4	4	4	4	36
handicap	9	13	15	3	11	5	7	1	17	-
FORWARD	332	140	474	385	356	391	382	415	342	3217
par	4	3	5	4	4	4	4	5	4	37
handicap	13	15	1	5	11	3	7	17	9	-

	10	11	12	13	14	15	16	17	18	IN
BACK	393	369	423	146	394	377	537	204	496	3339
REGULAR	382	320	410	143	382	367	492	202	473	3171
par	4	4	4	3	4	4	5	3	5	36
handicap	6	12	2	18	4	14	16	10	8	-
FORWARD	372	288	400	139	369	347	475	182	413	2985
par	4	4	4	3	4	4	5	3	5	36
handicap	10	16	4	18	6	14	2	12	8	-

BACK	
yardage	6760
par	72
rating	71.9
slope	122

REGULAR	
yardage	6494
par	72
rating	70.2
slope	117

FORWARD	
yardage	6202
par	73
rating	74.8
slope	120

PLAY POLICY & FEES: Green fees are $20 weekdays and $33 weekends. Carts are $24. Reservations are recommended.

TEE TIMES: Reservations can be booked 14 days in advance on weekdays and seven days in advance on weekends.

DRESS CODE: Golfers must wear sleeved shirts. Short shorts are not allowed. Nonmetal spikes are required.

COURSE DESCRIPTION: Built in 1956, this wide-open course has five lakes, level terrain, and mature trees. The first hole is a long, 626-yard par 6 designed to scare off the fainthearted. If the first hole doesn't send you packing, wait until the fourth. The green is surrounded on three sides by water.

LOCATION: From Los Angeles travel east on Interstate 10 (San Bernardino Freeway) to the Cedar Avenue exit in Bloomington. Head south on Cedar Avenue for three miles to El Rivino Road and then turn east on El Rivino Road to the club.

. . . ● **TOURNAMENTS:** No shotgun tournaments are allowed. Tournaments should be booked at least four months in advance.

14. EL RIVINO COUNTRY CLUB

PLAY POLICY & FEES: Green fees are $17 weekdays and $22 weekends. Twilight green fees are $12 weekdays and $16 weekends. Call for special senior rates. Carts are $20. Reservations are recommended.

TEE TIMES: Reservations can be booked seven days in advance.

DRESS CODE: Collard shirts must be worn. Nonmetal spikes are required.

COURSE DESCRIPTION: This course is long but fairly level. It is lined with pine and mulberry trees. It is wide open, as are its mostly level greens.

NOTES: A new clubhouse with complete banquet facilities just opened.

LOCATION: Driving toward Riverside, take the Columbia Avenue exit off the Riverside Freeway (Highway 91) and travel north on Orange Street to the club.

. . . ● **TOURNAMENTS:** A 24-player minimum is needed to book a tournament. Shotgun tournaments are available. Tournaments should be booked six to 12 months in advance. ● **TRAVEL:** The Mission Inn (909-784-8300) and the Holiday Inn Select (909-784-8000) are recommended.

15. RIVERSIDE GOLF CLUB

16 REDLANDS COUNTRY CLUB
ARCHITECT: A.E. STERLING, J.H. FISHER, 1896

1749 Garden Street
Redlands, CA 92373

PRO SHOP: 909-793-1295
CLUBHOUSE: 909-793-2661

Dan Monday, Head Professional, PGA
Richard Ray, Superintendent

Driving Range ●
Practice Greens ●
Clubhouse ●
Food / Beverage ●
Accommodations
Pull Carts ●
Power Carts ●
Club Rental
$pecial Offers

	1	2	3	4	5	6	7	8	9	OUT
BACK										
REGULAR										
par										
handicap										
FORWARD										
par										
handicap										

	10	11	12	13	14	15	16	17	18	IN
BACK										
REGULAR										
par										
handicap										
FORWARD										
par										
handicap										

BACK	
yardage	6276
par	70
rating	70.0
slope	122

REGULAR	
yardage	6061
par	70
rating	68.9
slope	118

FORWARD	
yardage	5730
par	70
rating	73.0
slope	121

17 YUCAIPA GOLF CLUB
ARCHITECT: RAINVILLE-BYE, 1999

Yucaipa, CA

PRO SHOP: 877-790-6522

Driving Range ●
Practice Greens ●
Clubhouse
Food / Beverage ●
Accommodations
Pull Carts
Power Carts ●
Club Rental
$pecial Offers

	1	2	3	4	5	6	7	8	9	OUT
BACK										
REGULAR										
par										
handicap										
FORWARD										
par										
handicap										

	10	11	12	13	14	15	16	17	18	IN
BACK										
REGULAR										
par										
handicap										
FORWARD										
par										
handicap										

BACK	
yardage	6910
par	72
rating	
slope	

REGULAR	
yardage	
par	
rating	
slope	

FORWARD	
yardage	
par	
rating	
slope	

PLAY POLICY & FEES: Limited reciprocal play is accepted; otherwise, members and guests only. Guests must be accompanied by a member. Green fees are $50 weekdays and $60 weekends, carts included.

DRESS CODE: Collared shirts and nonmetal spikes are required. Shorts can be no more than four inches above the knee. No denim is allowed on the course.

COURSE DESCRIPTION: This course was originally built as a nine-hole layout by old money just before the turn of the century. In 1927 it was expanded to an 18-hole course under the direction of club member Raven Hornby with the consultation of Alister Mackenzie, according to club records. It has similar characteristics to the Lake Course at the Olympic Club and Cherry Hills Country Club near Denver, Colorado. There are lots of oaks and many tall cypress and pine trees.

LOCATION: Take the Ford exit off Interstate 10 east of San Bernardino and travel south for 1.5 miles. Bear right at the fork on Garden Hill and turn left on Garden Street to the club.

. . . ● **TOURNAMENTS:** This course is not available for outside events.

16. REDLANDS COUNTRY CLUB

PLAY POLICY & FEES: Green fees were not available at time of press. The course is expected to open in late 1999.

COURSE DESCRIPTION: A course description was not available at time of press.

LOCATION: Directions were not available at time of press.

. . . ● **TOURNAMENTS:** Yucaipa Valley will be available for tournament play.

17. YUCAIPA GOLF CLUB

18 JURUPA HILLS COUNTRY CLUB
ARCHITECT: WILLIAM F. BELL, 1960

6161 Moraga Avenue
Riverside, CA 92509-6263

PRO SHOP: 909-685-7214
OFFICE: 909-685-7214

Ron Robinson, Director of Golf, PGA
Jason Taylor, Head Professional, PGA
Jim Fareio, Superintendent

Driving Range ●
Practice Greens ●
Clubhouse ●
Food / Beverage ●
Accommodations
Pull Carts ●
Power Carts ●
Club Rental ●
$pecial Offers

	1	2	3	4	5	6	7	8	9	OUT
BACK	-	-	-	-	-	-	-	-	-	-
REGULAR	376	355	159	347	372	377	499	161	341	2987
par	4	4	3	4	4	4	5	3	4	35
handicap	2	4	16	14	12	10	8	18	6	-
FORWARD	366	345	139	323	356	364	483	148	329	2853
par	4	4	3	4	4	4	5	3	4	35
handicap	3	1	17	13	7	5	9	15	11	-

	10	11	12	13	14	15	16	17	18	IN
BACK	-	-	-	-	-	-	-	-	-	-
REGULAR	363	441	336	378	134	512	362	368	141	3035
par	4	4	4	4	3	5	4	4	3	35
handicap	3	1	11	5	15	3	7	9	17	-
FORWARD	350	429	327	358	121	507	350	354	124	2920
par	4	5	4	4	3	5	4	4	3	36
handicap	2	14	12	8	16	10	4	6	18	-

BACK	
yardage	-
par	-
rating	-
slope	-

REGULAR	
yardage	6022
par	70
rating	69.5
slope	122

FORWARD	
yardage	5773
par	71
rating	73.4
slope	123

19 PARADISE KNOLLS GOLF COURSE

9330 Limonite Avenue
Riverside, CA 92509

PRO SHOP: 909-685-7034

Joe Carricoza, General Manager
Ryan Wendel, Superintendent

Driving Range
Practice Greens
Clubhouse ●
Food / Beverage ●
Accommodations
Pull Carts ●
Power Carts ●
Club Rental ●
$pecial Offers

	1	2	3	4	5	6	7	8	9	OUT
BACK	-	-	-	-	-	-	-	-	-	-
REGULAR	343	490	301	336	305	389	183	349	364	3060
par	4	5	4	4	4	4	3	4	4	36
handicap	5	17	13	7	11	1	3	15	9	-
FORWARD	323	472	283	306	291	379	167	330	351	2902
par	4	5	4	4	4	4	3	4	4	36
handicap	7	3	17	13	11	1	15	9	5	-

	10	11	12	13	14	15	16	17	18	IN
BACK	-	-	-	-	-	-	-	-	-	-
REGULAR	299	157	213	394	506	385	363	470	344	3131
par	4	3	3	4	5	4	4	5	4	36
handicap	18	10	2	4	8	12	6	16	14	-
FORWARD	290	136	205	369	486	362	342	448	325	2963
par	4	3	4	4	5	4	4	5	4	37
handicap	14	18	16	4	2	12	8	10	6	-

BACK	
yardage	-
par	-
rating	-
slope	-

REGULAR	
yardage	6191
par	72
rating	68.3
slope	104

FORWARD	
yardage	5865
par	73
rating	73.9
slope	126

PUBLIC: $24-$41
FAX: 909-685-4752

18
HOLES

PLAY POLICY & FEES: Green fees are $26 weekdays and $41 weekends including cart. Senior rates are $24 weekdays including cart.

TEE TIMES: Reservations can be booked seven days in advance.

DRESS CODE: Golf attire is encouraged.

COURSE DESCRIPTION: Trees of all sizes outline this mostly level course. Locally the course is known for its well-kept, fast greens. It's a favorite spot for local tournaments.

NOTES: The SCPGA Senior's Championship is held here. Olin Dutra, the club's first pro, was a former U.S. Open champ. Dutra, Gary McCord, and Bill Lytle share the course record of 62.

LOCATION: From Ontario take Highway 60 (Pomona Freeway) east to the Van Buren/Etiwanda Avenue exit in Riverside. Travel east on Van Buren Boulevard for 4.5 miles and turn left on Limonite Avenue. Drive 1.5 miles to Camino Real. Turn right and drive to Linares. Turn left to the club.

. . . ● **TOURNAMENTS:** This course is available for outside tournaments. Tournaments can be booked two years in advance, and should be booked at least six months in advance. Carts are required on weekend tournaments. The Banquet facility can accommodate 160 people. ● **TRAVEL:** The Riverside Marriot Courtyard Inn is located 20 minutes from the golf course. For reservations call 909-276-1200. The Riverside Holiday Inn (909-784-8000) is also recommended.

18. JURUPA HILLS COUNTRY CLUB

PUBLIC: $25-$39
FAX: 909-685-0504

18
HOLES

PLAY POLICY & FEES: Green fees are $25 walking and $32 riding on weekdays and $30 walking and $39 riding on weekends. Twilight and senior rates are available.

TEE TIMES: Reservations can be booked seven days in advance.

COURSE DESCRIPTION: This is a pretty course with an interesting mix of mature eucalyptus, palm, and pepper trees that act as natural dividers between the fairways. The course is fairly level with parallel fairways and small greens.

NOTES: Paradise Knolls recently spent over $500,000 in renovations of the course and facility.

LOCATION: From Riverside travel east on Highway 60 (Pomona Freeway) to Interstate 15 south. Take the Limonite exit and turn left. Drive about three miles to the course.

. . . ● **TOURNAMENTS:** A 16-player minimum is needed to book a tournament.

19. PARADISE KNOLLS GOLF COURSE

6720 Van Buren Blvd.
Riverside, CA 92503

PRO SHOP: 909-688-2563

Mike Yaklin, General Manager
Mike Hancock, Professional
Scott Vlahos, Superintendent

Driving Range ●
Practice Greens ●
Clubhouse ●
Food / Beverage ●
Accommodations
Pull Carts ●
Power Carts ●
Club Rental ●
$pecial Offers

	1	2	3	4	5	6	7	8	9	OUT
BACK	92	83	115	50	107	163	234	141	131	1116
REGULAR	84	72	103	45	99	123	200	135	112	973
par	3	3	3	3	3	3	4	3	3	28
handicap	11	17	9	15	13	1	3	5	7	-
FORWARD	72	61	94	45	89	97	183	119	98	858
par	3	3	3	3	3	3	4	3	3	28
handicap	11	17	9	15	13	1	3	5	7	-

	10	11	12	13	14	15	16	17	18	IN
BACK	304	140	122	78	132	145	316	108	127	1472
REGULAR	297	132	110	70	126	137	304	95	118	1389
par	4	3	3	3	3	4	3	3	3	29
handicap	4	8	10	16	12	6	2	18	14	-
FORWARD	272	111	100	64	98	105	286	85	84	1205
par	4	3	3	3	3	3	4	3	3	29
handicap	4	8	10	16	12	6	2	18	14	-

BACK	
yardage	2588
par	57
rating	-
slope	-

REGULAR	
yardage	2362
par	57
rating	-
slope	-

FORWARD	
yardage	2063
par	57
rating	-
slope	-

2521 Arroyo Drive
Riverside, CA 92506

PRO SHOP: 909-684-5035
CLUBHOUSE: 909-683-5323

Jeff Cross, PGA Professional
Mark Livingston, Superintendent

Driving Range ●
Practice Greens ●
Clubhouse ●
Food / Beverage ●
Accommodations
Pull Carts ●
Power Carts ●
Club Rental
$pecial Offers

	1	2	3	4	5	6	7	8	9	OUT
BACK	361	300	363	542	140	448	370	200	382	3106
REGULAR	340	300	340	530	118	440	355	180	382	2985
par	4	4	4	5	3	4	4	3	4	35
handicap	4	18	2	12	8	10	14	16	6	-
FORWARD	328	293	333	520	109	437	341	147	378	2886
par	11	9	5	1	17	13	7	15	3	81
handicap	328	293	333	520	109	437	341	147	378	-

	10	11	12	13	14	15	16	17	18	IN
BACK	415	165	400	190	482	498	192	494	544	3380
REGULAR	400	145	390	174	476	480	187	484	530	3266
par	4	3	4	3	5	5	3	5	5	37
handicap	4	18	2	12	8	10	14	16	6	-
FORWARD	396	136	385	120	390	459	156	459	428	2929
par	4	3	4	3	5	5	3	5	5	37
handicap	6	16	4	18	12	2	14	8	10	-

BACK	
yardage	6486
par	72
rating	71.3
slope	125

REGULAR	
yardage	6251
par	72
rating	69.8
slope	121

FORWARD	
yardage	5815
par	118
rating	73.4
slope	127

PLAY POLICY & FEES: Weekday morning green fees are $14, and afternoon fees are $12. On weekends, morning green fees are $17, and afternoon fees are $14. Seniors play for $10 on weekdays, and juniors play for $7. Night play is $11 weekdays and $12 weekends.

TEE TIMES: Reservations can be made 14 days in advance.

DRESS CODE: Collared shirts are required.

COURSE DESCRIPTION: This straight-forward executive course has 15 par 3s and three par 4s. Water comes into play on two holes.

NOTES: The course is 11 holes long for night play.

LOCATION: From Los Angeles take Highway 60 east and get off at VanBuren Boulevard. Turn right on VanBuren and drive 6.5 miles. The course is on the right, just past Central Avenue.

. . . ● **TOURNAMENTS:** A 16-player minimum is required to book an event. The banquet facility can accommodate 50 people.

20. SKYLINKS EXECUTIVE GOLF COURSE

PLAY POLICY & FEES: Reciprocal play is accepted with members of other private clubs on Tuesday and Thursday; otherwise, members and guests only. Reciprocal fees are $65. Guest fees are $45 with a member weekdays and $65 on weekends. Guest fees without a member are $100. Carts are $20. Reservations are required.

DRESS CODE: Collared shirts and nonmetal spikes are required. Bermuda shorts must be 18 inches in length.

COURSE DESCRIPTION: This course has that old-style look to it. There are many interesting holes. There is a lake on the first hole, and a large creekbed meanders through the course. Accurate placement is crucial because of flanking trees.

LOCATION: In Riverside take the Central Avenue exit off Highway 91 (Riverside Freeway), travel east for one mile to the first traffic light (Victoria), and turn left. From there go one-half mile to Arroyo Drive and turn right to the club entrance.

. . . ● **TOURNAMENTS:** Outside events are limited to Monday.

21. VICTORIA GOLF CLUB

22 CANYON CREST COUNTRY CLUB
ARCHITECT: OLIN DUTRA, 1964

975 Country Club Drive
Riverside, CA 92506

PRO SHOP: 909-274-7906
CLUBHOUSE: 909-274-7900

Dick Watson, Manager
John Renslow, PGA Professional
Bob MacBeth, Superintendent

Driving Range ●
Practice Greens ●
Clubhouse ●
Food / Beverage ●
Accommodations
Pull Carts ●
Power Carts ●
Club Rental ●
$pecial Offers

	1	2	3	4	5	6	7	8	9	OUT
BACK	391	490	365	185	389	391	198	495	365	3269
REGULAR	373	465	355	148	356	384	172	485	345	3083
par	4	5	4	3	4	4	3	5	4	36
handicap	1	7	15	11	9	13	17	5	3	-
FORWARD	366	443	347	136	323	378	162	362	382	2899
par	4	5	4	3	4	4	3	4	5	36
handicap	5	1	13	15	9	7	17	11	3	-

	10	11	12	13	14	15	16	17	18	IN
BACK	414	204	448	471	371	337	194	367	495	3301
REGULAR	400	191	435	456	362	331	168	362	479	3184
par	4	3	4	5	4	4	3	4	5	36
handicap	6	18	2	4	8	12	14	16	10	-
FORWARD	392	120	390	412	355	327	158	336	466	2956
par	4	3	4	5	4	4	3	4	5	36
handicap	10	18	2	8	12	4	16	14	6	-

BACK	
yardage	6570
par	72
rating	71.4
slope	124

REGULAR	
yardage	6267
par	72
rating	70.2
slope	122

FORWARD	
yardage	5855
par	72
rating	76.1
slope	136

23 MORENO VALLEY RANCH GOLF CLUB
ARCHITECT: PETE DYE, 1988

GOLF 50

28095 John F. Kennedy
Moreno Valley, CA 92555

PRO SHOP: 909-924-4444

Hank Schiller, Director of Golf, PGA
Mark Williams, Tournament Director
Joe Wagner, Superintendent

Driving Range ●
Practice Greens ●
Clubhouse ●
Food / Beverage ●
Accommodations
Pull Carts ●
Power Carts ●
Club Rental ●
$pecial Offers

	1	2	3	4	5	6	7	8	9	OUT
BACK	427	143	499	333	434	425	509	125	320	3215
REGULAR	349	140	475	318	401	364	475	123	310	2955
par	4	3	5	4	4	4	5	3	4	36
handicap	1	4	5	7	3	2	6	9	8	-
FORWARD	329	117	454	279	332	314	437	105	300	2667
par	4	3	5	4	4	4	5	3	4	36
handicap	1	4	5	7	3	2	6	9	8	-

	10	11	12	13	14	15	16	17	18	IN
BACK	333	374	150	359	404	489	165	515	334	3123
REGULAR	279	334	144	343	380	472	115	498	313	2878
par	4	4	3	4	4	5	3	5	4	36
handicap	8	2	7	4	1	3	6	5	9	-
FORWARD	264	315	114	278	322	420	91	439	286	2529
par	4	4	3	4	4	5	3	5	4	36
handicap	8	2	7	4	1	3	6	5	9	-

BACK	
yardage	6338
par	72
rating	71.5
slope	129

REGULAR	
yardage	5833
par	72
rating	68.6
slope	123

FORWARD	
yardage	5196
par	72
rating	70.1
slope	122

PLAY POLICY & FEES: Members and guests only. Reciprocal play with other private clubs is accepted. Green fees are $45 weekdays and $55 weekends. Carts are $24. The course is closed on Monday.

DRESS CODE: Appropriate golf attire and nonmetal spikes are required.

COURSE DESCRIPTION: This course is very hilly, with lots of mature trees and numerous bunkers. Accurate shot placement is critical or your round could become a nightmare. A brush-filled dry creek bed runs through the course, lining six holes. Homes line the perimeter, which means out-of-bounds on nearly every hole. Carts are advisable because the hills make for strenuous walking.

LOCATION: In Riverside take the Martin Luther King Drive exit off Highway 60 (Pomona Freeway). Go west for about one-quarter mile to Canyon Crest Drive and turn left. Drive about 1.5 miles and turn right on Country Club Drive.

. . . ● TOURNAMENTS: Outside events are on Monday only. A 72-player minimum is needed to book a tournament.

22. CANYON CREST COUNTRY CLUB

PLAY POLICY & FEES: Green fees are $42 Monday through Thursday, $45 Friday and $65 weekends and holidays. Junior, senior, and twilight rates are offered.

TEE TIMES: Reservations can be booked seven days in advance.

DRESS CODE: Collared shirts are required.

COURSE DESCRIPTION: This is a well-maintained course with fast, sloping greens. The fairways are tight in some places, demanding accurate tee shots. The Valley and Lake Courses are rolling, with elevated tees and greens. The Mountain Course is tight with many elevation changes.

NOTES: This course was the host site for the Nike Inland Empire Open 1994 through 1997, a PGA-sponsored event. Par is 36 on each nine. The Lake/Valley Course is 5,907 yards and rated 68.6 from the regular tees with a slope of 123. Women's tees are 5,246 yards and rated 70.1. The slope rating is 122. The Mountain/Lake Course is 5,830 yards and rated 68.5 from the regular tees with a slope of 123. Women's tees are 5,108 yards and rated 69.6. The slope rating is 121. See scorecard for rating and yardage information for the Valley/Mountian Course.

LOCATION: From Riverside take Highway 60 (Pomona Freeway) east. Exit south on Moreno Beach Drive. Go two miles to John F. Kennedy Avenue and turn left to the course.

. . . ● TOURNAMENTS: Shotgun tournaments are available weekdays only, requiring a 72-player minimum.

23. MORENO VALLEY RANCH GOLF CLUB

6104 Village West Drive
Riverside, CA 92518

PROSHOP: 909-697-6690

Sue Cloonan, General Manager
Kiki Garcia, Professional

Driving Range ●
Practice Greens ●
Clubhouse ●
Food / Beverage ●
Accommodations
Pull Carts ●
Power Carts ●
Club Rental ●
$pecial Offers

	1	2	3	4	5	6	7	8	9	OUT
BACK	434	196	395	541	357	376	158	382	538	3377
REGULAR	424	187	386	522	336	367	149	366	457	3194
par	4	3	4	5	4	4	3	4	5	36
handicap	2	16	4	8	14	10	18	12/6	6/12	-
FORWARD	410	178	370	507	317	345	131	348	429	3035
par	4	3	4	5	4	4	3	4	5	36
handicap	12	16	2	8	10	6	18	4	14	-

	10	11	12	13	14	15	16	17	18	IN
BACK	504	197	387	439	546	388	335	181	399	3376
REGULAR	489	190	380	429	535	382	322	171	390	3288
par	5	3	4	4	5	4	4	3	4	36
handicap	13	9	11	1	7	5	17	15	3	-
FORWARD	425	167	331	379	489	340	281	130	346	2888
par	5	3	4	4	5	4	4	3	4	36
handicap	13	11	9	1	5	7	15	17	3	-

BACK	
yardage	6753
par	72
rating	71.9
slope	118

REGULAR	
yardage	6482
par	72
rating	70.5
slope	115

FORWARD	
yardage	5923
par	72
rating	73.1
slope	120

1300 South Third Street
Calimesa, CA 92320

PROSHOP: 909-795-2488

Bill Bracy, General Manager
Bryan Williams, Professional
David Cruz, Superintendent

Driving Range ●
Practice Greens ●
Clubhouse ●
Food / Beverage ●
Accommodations
Pull Carts ●
Power Carts ●
Club Rental
$pecial Offers

	1	2	3	4	5	6	7	8	9	OUT
BACK	534	181	336	420	358	201	290	414	125	2859
REGULAR	519	139	321	410	333	163	280	402	115	2682
par	5	3	4	4	4	3	4	4	3	34
handicap	5	15	9	3	7	13	11	1	17	-
FORWARD	486	125	313	418	328	156	257	379	93	2555
par	5	3	4	5	4	3	4	4	3	35
handicap	1	17	9	5	7	13	11	3	15	-

	10	11	12	13	14	15	16	17	18	IN
BACK	198	305	418	371	282	383	314	305	535	3111
REGULAR	185	288	410	337	273	361	278	295	499	2926
par	3	4	4	4	4	4	4	4	5	36
handicap	8	12	2	6	14	4	16	18	10	-
FORWARD	134	268	404	314	258	354	265	178	484	2659
par	3	4	5	4	4	5	4	3	5	37
handicap	8	12	16	2	10	6	14	18	4	-

BACK	
yardage	5970
par	70
rating	67.3
slope	114

REGULAR	
yardage	5608
par	70
rating	65.6
slope	110

FORWARD	
yardage	5214
par	72
rating	69.2
slope	112

PLAY POLICY & FEES: This former military course in now open to public play. Public play green fees are $18 walking and $29 riding on weekdays. On weekends public play is $27 walking and $38 riding. Military, senior, and twilight rates are available.

TEE TIMES: Reservations can be booked seven days in advance.

COURSE DESCRIPTION: There are numerous doglegs and bunkers at this championship layout. There are seven holes that must be reached over or around water. The front nine is relatively flat, and the back nine is up and down.

LOCATION: From Riverside drive southeast on Interstate 215 four miles to Van Buren Boulevard, the first exit past the main gate to March AFB. Turn right and drive one mile to Village West Drive and turn left to the golf course.

. . . ● **TOURNAMENTS:** A 24-player minimum is needed to book a tournament. Shotgun tournaments are not available. Tournaments can be booked 12 months in advance.

24. GENERAL OLD GOLF COURSE

PLAY POLICY & FEES: Green fees are $16 weekdays and $23 weekends. Twilight rates are available. Carts are $10 per person.

TEE TIMES: Reservations can be booked seven days in advance.

DRESS CODE: Collared shirts are required.

COURSE DESCRIPTION: This scenic little course is set in a canyon. It shows lots of character with its up-and-down layout and mature trees. You can have fun on this course.

LOCATION: Travel eight miles east of Redlands on Interstate 10 to Calimesa. Turn east on County Line Road to Third Street and travel south to the club.

. . . ● **TOURNAMENTS:** This course is available for outside tournaments.

25. CALIMESA GOLF & COUNTRY CLUB

10370 1/2 Chisholm Trail
Cherry Valley, CA 92223

PRO SHOP: 909-845-8044

Burdette Bushman, Manager

Driving Range
Practice Greens ●
Clubhouse ●
Food / Beverage ●
Accommodations
Pull Carts
Power Carts
Club Rental
$pecial Offers

	1	2	3	4	5	6	7	8	9	OUT
BACK	-	-	-	-	-	-	-	-	-	-
REGULAR	188	255	190	163	128	176	213	160	181	1654
par	3	4	3	3	3	3	3	3	3	28
handicap	5	17	7	13	15	9	3	11	1	-
FORWARD	188	255	190	163	128	176	213	160	181	1654
par	3	4	3	3	3	3	4	3	3	29
handicap	7	5	9	15	17	3	11	13	1	-

	10	11	12	13	14	15	16	17	18	IN
BACK	-	-	-	-	-	-	-	-	-	-
REGULAR	179	250	178	155	120	161	206	150	135	1534
par	3	4	3	3	3	3	3	3	3	28
handicap	4	18	6	12	14	8	2	10	16	-
FORWARD	179	250	178	155	120	161	206	150	135	1534
par	3	4	3	3	3	3	4	3	3	29
handicap	4	2	8	12	18	6	10	14	16	-

BACK	
yardage	-
par	-
rating	-
slope	-

REGULAR	
yardage	3188
par	56
rating	56.1
slope	94

FORWARD	
yardage	3188
par	58
rating	56.1
slope	94

27 OAK VALLEY GOLF CLUB
ARCHITECT: LANDMARK, 1988

1888 Golf Club Dr.
Beaumont, CA 92223

PRO SHOP: 909-769-7200

Tim Helwig, Director of Golf, PGA
Scott Arnold, PGA Professional
John Harkness, Superintendent

Driving Range ●
Practice Greens ●
Clubhouse ●
Food / Beverage ●
Accommodations
Pull Carts
Power Carts ●
Club Rental ●
$pecial Offers

	1	2	3	4	5	6	7	8	9	OUT
BACK	369	360	185	374	581	170	474	442	557	3512
REGULAR	346	340	139	346	539	148	392	400	524	3174
par	4	4	3	4	5	3	4	4	5	36
handicap	13	11	17	7	5	15	1	3	9	-
FORWARD	311	274	71	258	456	122	353	366	439	2650
par	4	4	3	4	5	3	4	4	5	36
handicap	13	11	17	7	5	15	1	3	9	-

	10	11	12	13	14	15	16	17	18	IN
BACK	349	199	416	557	210	411	523	355	471	3491
REGULAR	319	159	386	530	180	384	493	329	418	3198
par	4	3	4	5	3	4	5	4	4	36
handicap	18	14	4	6	16	8	10	12	2	-
FORWARD	294	101	313	475	103	340	424	256	393	2699
par	4	3	4	5	3	4	5	4	4	36
handicap	18	14	4	6	16	8	10	12	2	-

BACK	
yardage	7003
par	72
rating	74.0
slope	138

REGULAR	
yardage	6372
par	72
rating	71.0
slope	131

FORWARD	
yardage	5349
par	72
rating	71.1
slope	122

PLAY POLICY & FEES: Members and guests only. Guests must be accompanied by a member. Guest fees are $4 for nine holes and $8 for 18 holes. The course is closed on Monday.

DRESS CODE: Golfers must wear collared shirts. No tank tops or short shorts are allowed. Nonmetal spikes are preferred.

COURSE DESCRIPTION: This short executive course wanders through olive trees, and two lakes keep things interesting. There are eight par 3s and one par 4 from the back tees, and seven par 3s and two par 4s from the forward tees. The course is tight and mostly flat except for the first and ninth holes.

LOCATION: From Beaumont take Highland Springs Boulevard three miles north to the course. The course is located in Highland Springs Village.

. . . ● **TOURNAMENTS:** This course is not available for outside events.

26. HIGHLAND SPRINGS VILLAGE GOLF

PLAY POLICY & FEES: Green fees are $55 Monday through Thursday, $75 Friday, amd $85 Saturday, Sunday and holidays. Range use and carts are included. Twilight rates are available. Starting times vary throughout the year.

TEE TIMES: Reservations can be booked seven days in advance.

DRESS CODE: Collared shirts and nonmetal spikes are required.

COURSE DESCRIPTION: This is a links-style course with rolling terrain. The signature hole is the seventh, a 474-yard par 4. From the tee, you are hitting downhill. The next shot is uphill to a shelved green with traps guarding the left side and brush hovering off the right side.

NOTES: Oak Valley features a brand new 11,000 square foot clubhouse, locker room, and restaurant. Oak Valley received a four-star rating from "Golf Digest."

LOCATION: From Interstate 10, take the San Timoteo exit north one-third of a mile to the course.

. . . ● **TOURNAMENTS:** This course is available for outside tournaments. A 16-player minimum is needed. Large tournaments are limited to 144 players. Events should be booked four to 12 months in advance. A banquet facility is available that can accommodate 144 people. ● **TRAVEL:** The Best Western is located five minutes from the golf course. For reservations call 909-845-2176.

27. OAK VALLEY GOLF CLUB

QUAIL RANCH COUNTRY CLUB
ARCHITECT: DESMOND MUIRHEAD, 1969

15960 Gilman Springs
Moreno Valley, CA 92355

PRO SHOP: 909-654-2727

Frank Bruno, G.M./Head Professional, PGA
Steve Domenigoni, Superintendent

Driving Range •
Practice Greens •
Clubhouse •
Food / Beverage •
Accommodations
Pull Carts
Power Carts •
Club Rental •
$pecial Offers

	1	2	3	4	5	6	7	8	9	OUT
BACK	536	387	175	372	481	143	387	337	398	3216
REGULAR	534	348	139	350	474	131	362	298	368	3004
par	5	4	3	4	5	3	4	4	4	36
handicap	11	1	13	3	9	15	7	17	5	-
FORWARD	452	315	108	332	375	97	311	251	322	2563
par	5	4	3	4	4	3	4	4	4	35
handicap	9	5	13	7	1	17	3	15	11	-

	10	11	12	13	14	15	16	17	18	IN
BACK	423	190	359	385	344	184	471	435	513	3304
REGULAR	404	170	341	376	327	154	458	427	492	3149
par	4	3	4	4	4	3	5	4	5	36
handicap	4	16	18	10	6	14	8	2	12	-
FORWARD	386	113	294	285	296	150	412	356	436	2728
par	4	3	4	4	4	3	5	4	5	36
handicap	2	16	10	14	12	18	4	6	8	-

BACK	
yardage	6520
par	72
rating	72.2
slope	133

REGULAR	
yardage	6153
par	72
rating	70.4
slope	128

FORWARD	
yardage	5291
par	71
rating	70.0
slope	117

 GOLDEN ERA GOLF COURSE
ARCHITECT: STEVE HALSEY, 1991

19871 Highway 79
Gilman Hot Springs, CA
92583
PRO SHOP: 909-654-0130

Bruce Martin, PGA Professional
Jaime Danien, Superintendent

Driving Range
Practice Greens •
Clubhouse •
Food / Beverage •
Accommodations
Pull Carts •
Power Carts •
Club Rental •
$pecial Offers

	1	2	3	4	5	6	7	8	9	OUT
BACK	507	296	199	350	348	353	188	525	312	3078
REGULAR	496	258	188	342	338	331	161	514	302	2930
par	5	4	3	4	4	4	3	5	4	36
handicap	3	13	17	9	7	5	15	1	11	-
FORWARD	486	252	177	333	328	322	138	503	293	2832
par	5	4	3	4	4	4	3	5	4	36
handicap	3	13	15	5	7	9	17	1	11	-

	10	11	12	13	14	15	16	17	18	IN
BACK	507	296	199	350	348	353	188	525	312	3078
REGULAR	496	258	188	342	338	331	161	514	302	2930
par	5	4	3	4	4	4	3	5	4	36
handicap	4	14	16	10	8	6	18	2	12	-
FORWARD	486	252	177	333	328	322	138	503	293	2832
par	5	4	3	4	4	4	3	5	4	36
handicap	4	14	16	6	8	10	18	2	12	-

BACK	
yardage	6156
par	72
rating	-
slope	-

REGULAR	
yardage	5860
par	72
rating	68.8
slope	116

FORWARD	
yardage	5664
par	72
rating	72.7
slope	128

PLAY POLICY & FEES: Green fees are $29 weekdays and $45 weekends and holidays. Twilight rates are offered. Carts are included.

TEE TIMES: Reservations can be booked seven days in advance.

DRESS CODE: Appropriate golf attire and nonmetal spikes are required.

COURSE DESCRIPTION: This course was originally known as Quail Ranch Resort and Country Club, but changed its name to Palm Crest when the course was renovated in mid-1991 and 1,000 full-grown palm trees were planted in clusters around the greens and along the fairways. In 1993, new owners changed the name back to the original one. It's a Scottish links-style course with rolling terrain and undulating greens.

NOTES: The Southern California Golf Association rated this course as one of its top 10 public golf facilities in 1988. The PGA Tour School qualifier and the U.S. Open qualifier have been held here. Craig Stadler impressed the locals once when he finished a round in the dark and asked the pro staff if they would park their cars around the 18th green with their headlights on so he could finish his round. CBS golf analyst Gary McCord holds the course record of 64.

LOCATION: From Moreno Valley take Highway 91 to Highway 60 (Pomona Freeway). Take Highway 60 east about 14 miles to the Gilman Springs exit. Drive four miles south to the club.

. . . ● **TOURNAMENTS:** This course is available for outside tournaments.

28. QUAIL RANCH COUNTRY CLUB

PLAY POLICY & FEES: Green fees for nine holes are $11.50 walking and $19 with a cart weekdays and $13.50 walking and $21 with a cart weekends. Green fees for 18 holes are $17.50 walking and $28 with a cart weekdays and $21.50 walking and $25 with a cart weekends. Twilight, senior and junior rates are available. Call for special off-season rates.

TEE TIMES: Reservations can be booked seven days in advance.

DRESS CODE: Casual attire is accepted. Nonmetal spikes are mandatory.

COURSE DESCRIPTION: This challenging, well-conditioned course has three lakes and an abundance of cottonwood trees to keep golfers honest. The undulating greens are quick, so stay below the hole. The pride of the course is the 353-yard, par-4 sixth hole, a dogleg left around water. Beware of the oak tree guarding the left side of the green.

LOCATION: From Highway 60 (Pomona Freeway) in Los Angeles drive east to the Gilman Springs Road exit. Follow Gilman Springs Road east for 12 miles. The course is on the right.

. . . ● **TOURNAMENTS:** This course is available for outside tournaments.

29. GOLDEN ERA GOLF COURSE

SUN LAKES COUNTRY CLUB
ARCHITECT: DAVID RAINVILLE, 1987

850 South Country Club
Banning, CA 92220

PRO SHOP: 909-845-2135

Roger Work, Manager
Tommy Jackson, PGA Professional
Mike Snyder, Superintendent

Driving Range ●
Practice Greens ●
Clubhouse ●
Food / Beverage ●
Accommodations
Pull Carts
Power Carts ●
Club Rental
$pecial Offers

	1	2	3	4	5	6	7	8	9	OUT
BACK	373	586	442	408	166	560	440	174	396	3545
REGULAR	338	533	385	328	124	481	381	125	340	3035
par	4	5	4	4	3	5	4	3	4	36
handicap	13	3	5	11	17	1	7	15	9	-
FORWARD	294	496	364	306	107	457	356	104	313	2797
par	4	5	4	4	3	5	4	3	4	36
handicap	13	3	5	7	15	1	11	17	9	-

	10	11	12	13	14	15	16	17	18	IN
BACK	382	385	436	193	415	555	388	174	533	3461
REGULAR	323	349	385	136	328	510	334	135	506	3006
par	4	4	4	3	4	5	4	3	5	36
handicap	16	6	2	18	8	10	12	14	4	-
FORWARD	298	325	362	110	308	495	297	108	450	2753
par	4	4	4	3	4	5	4	3	5	36
handicap	14	6	12	18	10	2	8	16	4	-

BACK	
yardage	7006
par	72
rating	73.6
slope	129

REGULAR	
yardage	6041
par	72
rating	68.4
slope	115

FORWARD	
yardage	5550
par	72
rating	71.9
slope	120

SOBOBA SPRINGS ROYAL VISTA
ARCHITECT: DESMOND MUIRHEAD, 1967

1020 Soboba Road
San Jacinto, CA 92583

PRO SHOP: 909-654-9354
CLUBHOUSE: 909-654-7111

Dan Hornig, General Manager, PGA
Sherman Sabie, Professional
Jesse Trejo, Superintendent

Driving Range ●
Practice Greens ●
Clubhouse ●
Food / Beverage ●
Accommodations
Pull Carts
Power Carts ●
Club Rental ●
$pecial Offers ●

	1	2	3	4	5	6	7	8	9	OUT
BACK	366	395	410	199	410	206	502	382	515	3385
REGULAR	351	370	394	140	331	190	489	338	487	3090
par	4	4	4	3	4	3	5	4	5	36
handicap	13/1	5/1	9/3	7/17	3/13	1/5	11/7	15	17/9	-
FORWARD	344	331	388	116	306	158	424	325	404	2796
par	4	4	4	3	4	3	5	4	5	36
handicap	9	3	1	17	15	11	7	13	5	-

	10	11	12	13	14	15	16	17	18	IN
BACK	392	421	448	140	538	445	514	175	430	3503
REGULAR	378	361	417	128	518	361	455	136	388	3142
par	4	4	4	3	5	4	5	3	4	36
handicap	12/1	2/14	4/2	18	14/4	6/8	8/12	16	10/6	-
FORWARD	367	301	413	118	429	341	445	117	346	2877
par	4	4	5	3	5	4	5	3	4	37
handicap	6	14	8	18	12	2	10	16	4	-

BACK	
yardage	6888
par	72
rating	72.8
slope	133

REGULAR	
yardage	6232
par	72
rating	70.2
slope	126

FORWARD	
yardage	5673
par	73
rating	72.7
slope	130

PLAY POLICY & FEES: Outside play is accepted. All guest fees are $50 and include a cart.

TEE TIMES: Reservations can be booked four days in advance for public play.

DRESS CODE: Appropriate golf attire is required. Nonmetal spikes are encouraged.

COURSE DESCRIPTION: This is a long traditional layout. Bring sand-moving equipment—there are 104 bunkers. There are also seven lakes and smallish greens to make this challenging course even more difficult. The winds make this an interesting test, especially in winter, but the rough areas have been trimmed in recent years, making this a playable layout.

LOCATION: Take the Highlands Springs Avenue exit off Interstate 10 in Banning (east of San Bernardino) and travel south to Sun Lakes Boulevard. Head east and turn on Country Club Drive south to the club.

. . . ● **TOURNAMENTS:** Outside events are limited to 25 players. Carts are required. Tournaments must start after 12 p.m.

30. SUN LAKES COUNTRY CLUB

PLAY POLICY & FEES: Reciprocal play is accepted with members of other private clubs. Outside play is accepted. Green fees are $35 weekdays, $50 weekends. Carts are included. Reduced rates after 1 p.m. and special twilight rates after 3 p.m. are available. Seasonal rates and one-month memberships are also available.

TEE TIMES: Reservations can be booked seven days in advance.

DRESS CODE: No T-shirts or tank tops are allowed, and nonmetal spikes are mandatory.

COURSE DESCRIPTION: The course lies at the base of the San Jacinto Mountains. It has a traditional layout with beautiful mature trees and 22 acres of lakes that come into play on nine of the 18 holes. This is a good test of golf for all skill levels.

NOTES: The course record is 61 set by Joe Walsh in 1996.

LOCATION: Travel east of San Bernardino on Interstate 10 to the town of Beaumont. Drive south on Highway 79 and turn left on Romona Expressway. Drive to Lake Park, turn left, and turn left again on Soboba Road. Follow it to the course.

. . . ● **TOURNAMENTS:** A 16-player minimum is needed to book a tournament. Carts are mandatory and included in price. ● **TRAVEL:** For lodging the Hemet Super 8 (800-769-6346), the Ramada Inn (800-858-8574) and the Hemet Inn (800-909-6366) are recommended. ● **$PECIAL OFFERS:** Play-and-stay packages are available. Call the pro shop for information.

31. SOBOBA SPRINGS ROYAL VISTA

32 CHERRY HILLS GOLF CLUB
ARCHITECT: DEL WEBB, 1962

26583 Cherry Hills
Sun City, CA 92586

PRO SHOP: 909-679-1182
OFFICE: 909-672-1265

Penny Lee, Manager
Dave Smith, Superintendent

Driving Range ●
Practice Greens ●
Clubhouse ●
Food / Beverage ●
Accommodations
Pull Carts
Power Carts ●
Club Rental
$pecial Offers

	1	2	3	4	5	6	7	8	9	OUT
BACK	378	572	465	165	397	404	216	542	381	3520
REGULAR	362	517	445	144	395	381	185	508	366	3303
par	4	5	4	3	4	4	3	5	4	36
handicap	9	15	1	11	5	3	17	13	7	-
FORWARD	319	409	335	124	336	308	127	445	316	2719
par	4	5	4	3	4	4	3	5	4	36
handicap	11	3	5	15	13	7	17	1	9	-

	10	11	12	13	14	15	16	17	18	IN
BACK	395	546	221	426	393	328	404	147	528	3388
REGULAR	381	500	213	404	360	319	384	115	504	3180
par	4	5	3	4	4	4	4	3	5	36
handicap	6	12	8	2	10	16	4	18	14	-
FORWARD	327	403	135	329	290	275	332	93	405	2589
par	4	5	3	4	4	4	4	3	5	36
handicap	12	4	16	14	8	10	6	18	2	-

BACK	
yardage	6908
par	72
rating	72.6
slope	122

REGULAR	
yardage	6483
par	72
rating	69.8
slope	114

FORWARD	
yardage	5308
par	72
rating	69.4
slope	106

33 NORTH GOLF COURSE
ARCHITECT: DEL WEBB, 1975

26660 McCall Boulevard
Sun City, CA 92586

PRO SHOP: 909-679-5111
OFFICE: 909-679-9668

Rod Stark, Business Manager
Roger Miller, Superintendent

Driving Range
Practice Greens ●
Clubhouse
Food / Beverage
Accommodations
Pull Carts ●
Power Carts
Club Rental
$pecial Offers

	1	2	3	4	5	6	7	8	9	OUT
BACK	-	-	-	-	-	-	-	-	-	-
REGULAR	395	131	370	95	336	134	165	119	371	2116
par	4	3	4	3	4	3	3	3	4	31
handicap	1	13	3	17	7	11	9	15	5	-
FORWARD	302	117	324	73	287	98	140	109	313	1763
par	4	3	4	3	4	3	3	3	4	31
handicap	5	13	1	17	7	15	9	11	3	-

	10	11	12	13	14	15	16	17	18	IN
BACK	-	-	-	-	-	-	-	-	-	-
REGULAR	177	380	188	121	171	291	189	266	111	1894
par	3	4	3	3	3	4	3	4	3	30
handicap	8	2	4	12	6	14	10	16	18	-
FORWARD	160	350	174	101	140	271	173	241	94	1704
par	3	4	3	3	3	4	3	4	3	30
handicap	8	2	10	16	14	6	4	12	18	-

BACK	
yardage	-
par	-
rating	-
slope	-

REGULAR	
yardage	4010
par	61
rating	58.2
slope	90

FORWARD	
yardage	3467
par	61
rating	59.0
slope	89

PLAY POLICY & FEES: Outside play is accepted. Green fees are $30 weekdays and $35 weekends and holidays. Carts are included. Call for special rates after 10 a.m. and after 1 p.m.

TEE TIMES: Reservations can be booked seven days in advance.

DRESS CODE: Collared shirts and nonmetal spikes are required.

COURSE DESCRIPTION: The course is now contour-mowed. That new look, numerous bunkers, and a daily southern breeze in the afternoons increase the difficulty of this course.

LOCATION: In Sun City take the McCall Boulevard/Sun City exit off Interstate 215 and travel west on McCall for one-quarter mile to Sun City Boulevard. Turn left and drive one-quarter mile to Cherry Hills Boulevard. Turn right and go one block to the club.

. . . ● **TOURNAMENTS:** Shotgun tournaments are available on a very limited basis. Carts are required. A 24-player minimum is needed to book a regular tournament. Tournaments can be booked one month in advance.

32. CHERRY HILLS GOLF CLUB

PLAY POLICY & FEES: Outside play is accepted. Green fees are $17 weekdays and $20 weekends and holidays. Senior, junior, and nine-hole rates are available. No carts; walking is mandatory. Closed Wednesday and Thursday until noon.

TEE TIMES: Reservations can be booked three days in advance.

DRESS CODE: No halter tops, tank tops, short shorts, or metal spikes are allowed on the golf course.

COURSE DESCRIPTION: This level, executive course features small, well-maintained greens. There are seven par 4s and 11 par 3s. This course is challenging for players of all skill levels.

LOCATION: From Riverside, take Interstate 215 south to Sun City. Exit at McCall Boulevard, take a right, and drive three blocks to the golf course. From San Diego, take Interstate 15 to Interstate 215 north to Sun City and exit McCall Boulevard. Turn left and go three blocks to the golf course.

. . . ● **TOURNAMENTS:** A 12-player minimum is needed to book a tournament. Shotgun tournaments are not allowed. Events should be booked 12 months in advance. The banquet facility can accommodate 125 people.

33. NORTH GOLF COURSE

34 COLONIAL COUNTRY CLUB

25115 Kirby Street
Hemet, CA 92545

PRO SHOP: 909-925-2664

Jim Folenius, Manager

Driving Range
Practice Greens
Clubhouse
Food / Beverage
Accommodations
Pull Carts
Power Carts
Club Rental
$pecial Offers

	1	2	3	4	5	6	7	8	9	OUT
BACK	-	-	-	-	-	-	-	-	-	-
REGULAR	55	65	80	78	255	85	260	79	66	1023
par	3	3	3	3	4	3	4	3	3	29
handicap	9	8	4	6	2	3	1	5	7	-
FORWARD	55	65	80	78	255	85	260	79	66	1023
par	3	3	3	3	4	3	4	3	3	29
handicap	9	8	4	6	2	3	1	5	7	-

	10	11	12	13	14	15	16	17	18	IN
BACK	-	-	-	-	-	-	-	-	-	-
REGULAR	240	100	92	120	120	124	110	79	245	1230
par	3	3	3	3	3	3	4	3	3	28
handicap	8	12	9	6	18	10	4	14	13	-
FORWARD	240	100	92	120	120	124	110	79	245	1230
par	3	3	3	3	3	3	4	3	3	28
handicap	8	12	9	6	18	10	4	14	13	-

BACK	
yardage	-
par	-
rating	-
slope	-

REGULAR	
yardage	2253
par	57
rating	-
slope	-

FORWARD	
yardage	2253
par	57
rating	-
slope	-

35 ECHO HILLS GOLF CLUB
ARCHITECT: ED DOVER, 1958

545 East Thornton Avenue
Hemet, CA 92543

PRO SHOP: 909-652-2203

Chris Bennington, Manager

Driving Range
Practice Greens ●
Clubhouse ●
Food / Beverage ●
Accommodations
Pull Carts ●
Power Carts ●
Club Rental ●
$pecial Offers

	1	2	3	4	5	6	7	8	9	OUT
BACK	-	-	-	-	-	-	-	-	-	-
REGULAR	323	135	231	252	270	237	263	263	255	2229
par	4	3	4	4	4	4	4	4	4	35
handicap	2	5	7	8	3	9	6	4	1	-
FORWARD	251	133	219	240	272	235	252	253	253	2108
par	4	3	4	4	4	4	4	4	4	35
handicap	3	5	7	6	8	9	2	4		-

	10	11	12	13	14	15	16	17	18	IN
BACK	-	-	-	-	-	-	-	-	-	-
REGULAR	323	135	231	252	270	237	263	263	255	2229
par	4	3	4	4	4	4	4	4	4	35
handicap	2	5	7	8	3	9	6	4	1	-
FORWARD	251	133	219	240	272	235	252	253	253	2108
par	4	3	4	4	4	4	4	4	4	35
handicap	3	5	7	6	8	9	2	4	1	-

BACK	
yardage	-
par	-
rating	
slope	

REGULAR	
yardage	4458
par	70
rating	58.4
slope	92

FORWARD	
yardage	4216
par	70
rating	58.4
slope	92

PLAY POLICY & FEES: Members and guests only. Green fees are $7 for nine holes and $14 for 18 holes.
DRESS CODE: Appropriate golf attire is required.
COURSE DESCRIPTION: These are short, executive courses. One features a pair of par 4s. Both courses are reserved for residents and guests of the adjoining mobile home park.
LOCATION: In Hemet, take Florida Avenue (Highway 74) to Warren Avenue. Turn left and continue three-fourths mile to Kirby Street and turn right. Follow Kirby to the course.
. . . ● **TOURNAMENTS:** This course is not available for outside events.

34. COLONIAL COUNTRY CLUB

PLAY POLICY & FEES: Green fees are $6.50 for nine holes and $10 for 18 holes. Carts are $8 for nine holes and $12 for 18 holes.
TEE TIMES: Reservations can be booked seven days in advance.
DRESS CODE: Shirts and shoes are necessary.
COURSE DESCRIPTION: This course is short enough to walk, but long enough to provide a challenge. The course has narrow fairways and many mature trees. It is a good nine-hole track for beginners and serious golfers.
LOCATION: From Interstate 215 take the Highway 74 exit to the town of Hemet and drive through town. Turn right on Buena Vista Street and drive 1.5 miles to Thornton Avenue; then go left to the club.
. . . ● **TOURNAMENTS:** Shotgun tournaments are available weekdays only. A 36-player minimum is needed for a regular tournament. Events must be booked two months in advance.

35. ECHO HILLS GOLF CLUB

36 DIAMOND VALLEY GOLF CLUB
ARCHITECTS: ART MAGNUSON, 1998; BILL MARTIN

31220 Sage Road
Hemet, CA 92543

PRO SHOP: 909-767-0828

Mike Gallivan, Head Professional
Collette Muscara, Tournament Director

Driving Range ●
Practice Greens ●
Clubhouse ●
Food / Beverage ●
Accommodations
Pull Carts
Power Carts ●
Club Rental
$pecial Offers

	1	2	3	4	5	6	7	8	9	OUT
BACK	595	335	296	189	459	159	342	430	559	3364
REGULAR	565	320	290	178	429	149	338	422	526	3217
par	5	4	4	3	4	3	4	4	5	36
handicap	5	13	15	9	1	17	11	3	7	-
FORWARD	503	266	222	135	370	102	310	296	467	2671
par	5	4	4	3	4	3	4	4	5	36
handicap	5	13	15	9	1	17	11	3	7	-

	10	11	12	13	14	15	16	17	18	IN
BACK	377	446	611	128	307	408	430	144	505	3356
REGULAR	366	421	589-	121	307	392	421	128	490	3235
par	4	4	5	3	4	4	4	3	5	36
handicap	14	4	6	18	12	8	2	16	10	-
FORWARD	296	339	512	94	215	337	351	93	405	2642
par	4	4	5	3	4	4	4	3	5	36
handicap	14	4	6	18	12	8	2	16	10	-

BACK	
yardage	6720
par	72
rating	73.0
slope	135

REGULAR	
yardage	6452
par	72
rating	71.8
slope	131

FORWARD	
yardage	5313
par	72
rating	70.5
slope	124

37 SEVEN HILLS GOLF CLUB
ARCHITECT: HARRY RAINVILLE, 1970

1537 South Lyon Avenue
Hemet, CA 92545

PRO SHOP: 909-925-4815
CLUBHOUSE: 909-925-5469

Jeff Kasper, Tournament Director
Mike Jauregui, Superintendent

Driving Range ●
Practice Greens ●
Clubhouse ●
Food / Beverage ●
Accommodations
Pull Carts ●
Power Carts ●
Club Rental ●
$pecial Offers ●

	1	2	3	4	5	6	7	8	9	OUT
BACK	382	162	370	508	152	378	350	381	499	3182
REGULAR	366	155	360	502	141	367	341	369	495	3096
par	4	3	4	5	3	4	4	4	5	36
handicap	5	15	3	9	17	7	13	1	11	-
FORWARD	350	138	352	435	135	361	328	324	438	2861
par	4	3	4	5	3	4	4	4	5	36
handicap	5	15	1	7	17	3	9	13	11	-

	10	11	12	13	14	15	16	17	18	IN
BACK	374	511	192	382	432	390	164	384	546	3375
REGULAR	366	504	162	374	401	363	155	376	515	3216
par	4	5	4	4	4	3	4	4	5	36
handicap	6	12	16	4	2	10	18	8	14	-
FORWARD	348	449	148	359	318	348	124	364	452	2910
par	4	3	4	5	3	4	4	4	5	36
handicap	4	16	2	6	18	8	12	14	10	-

BACK	
yardage	6557
par	72
rating	70.2
slope	116

REGULAR	
yardage	6312
par	72
rating	69.0
slope	113

FORWARD	
yardage	5771
par	72
rating	72.0
slope	113

PLAY POLICY & FEES: Green fees are $30 weekdays and $40 weekends and holidays. Twilight green fees are $25 weekdays and $30 weekends. Supertwilight green fees are $18 on weekdays only. Carts are $11 per player. Senior green fees are $35 Monday through Thursday and include a cart. Nine-hole and replay rates are also available.

TEE TIMES: Reservations can be made seven days in advance.

DRESS CODE: No jeans are allowed on the course. Collared shirts and nonmetal spikes are required.

COURSE DESCRIPTION: Diamond Valley Golf Club is a links-style public course with a country club feel. At 6,720 yards from the back tees, it isn't long by new course standards, instead chooses to challenge players in a traditional manner by making them think. The key to scoring well here is keeping the ball in the fairway, even if you have to leave your $400 driver in the bag.

LOCATION: From Los Angeles take Interstate10 east to Highway 79 south. Follow Highway 79 to the end. Take a left on Domenigoni Parkway. Take a right on State Street. State Street turns into Sage Road. The course will be on your left.

. . . ● **TOURNAMENTS:** A 24-player minimum is required to book an event. Tournaments should be booked at least 12 months in advance. ● **TRAVEL:** The Hemet Inn is located is 15 minutes from the golf course. For reservations call 800-909-6366.

36. DIAMOND VALLEY GOLF CLUB

PLAY POLICY & FEES: Green fees are $14 for nine holes and $20 for 18 holes weekdays, and $16 for nine holes and $25 for 18 holes weekends. Twilight, senior, and junior rates are available. Carts are $6 for nine holes and $10 for 18 holes per player.

TEE TIMES: Reservations can be booked seven days in advance.

DRESS CODE: Collared shirts are preferred, and nonmetal spikes are required.

COURSE DESCRIPTION: This is a flat course that is easy to walk. It is medium short with trees and water—four water hazards—and a few bunkers. The greens are small, which can make approach shots demanding.

LOCATION: Take the Highway 79 exit off Interstate 10 east of San Bernardino and travel south to Highway 74 in Hemet. Turn left and drive to Lyon Avenue, then right to the club.

. . . ● **TOURNAMENTS:** This course is available for outside tournaments. A 24-player minimum is needed to book a tournament. Tournaments should be booked 12 months in advance. The banquet facility can accommodate up to 110 people.

37. SEVEN HILLS GOLF CLUB

42751 East Florida
Hemet, CA 92544

CLUBHOUSE: 909-927-1610

Al Martin, Manager

Driving Range
Practice Greens •
Clubhouse
Food / Beverage
Accommodations
Pull Carts
Power Carts
Club Rental
$pecial Offers

	1	2	3	4	5	6	7	8	9	OUT
BACK	-	-	-	-	-	-	-	-	-	-
REGULAR	90	122	105	170	95	112	110	80	145	1029
par	3	3	3	3	3	3	3	3	3	27
handicap	-	-	-	-	-	-	-	-	-	-
FORWARD	90	122	105	127	95	112	60	105	108	924
par	3	3	3	3	3	3	3	3	3	27
handicap	-	-	-	-	-	-	-	-	-	-

	10	11	12	13	14	15	16	17	18	IN
BACK	-	-	-	-	-	-	-	-	-	-
REGULAR	90	122	105	170	95	112	110	80	145	1029
par	3	3	3	3	3	3	3	3	3	27
handicap	-	-	-	-	-	-	-	-	-	-
FORWARD	90	122	105	127	95	112	60	105	108	924
par	3	3	3	3	3	3	3	3	3	27
handicap	-	-	-	-	-	-	-	-	-	-

BACK	
yardage	-
par	-
rating	
slope	

REGULAR	
yardage	2058
par	54
rating	
slope	-

FORWARD	
yardage	1848
par	54
rating	-
slope	-

39 CANYON LAKE COUNTRY CLUB
ARCHITECT: TED ROBINSON, 1968

32001 Railroad Canyon
Canyon Lake, CA 92587

PRO SHOP: 909-246-1782
CLUBHOUSE: 909-244-6841

David Lindeman, PGA Professional
Troy Mullare, Superintendent

Driving Range •
Practice Greens •
Clubhouse •
Food / Beverage •
Accommodations
Pull Carts
Power Carts •
Club Rental •
$pecial Offers

	1	2	3	4	5	6	7	8	9	OUT
BACK	235	300	170	342	407	392	285	463	480	3074
REGULAR	163	241	170	270	386	370	265	404	480	2749
par	3	4	3	4	4	4	4	4	5	35
handicap	6	14	12	16	8	2	18	4	10	-
FORWARD	122	241	107	240	344	336	258	285	409	2342
par	3	4	3	4	4	4	4	4	5	35
handicap										-

	10	11	12	13	14	15	16	17	18	IN
BACK	235	300	170	342	407	392	285	463	480	3074
REGULAR	203	250	155	240	353	382	258	340	480	2661
par	3	4	3	4	4	4	4	4	5	35
handicap	7	13	15	11	5	1	17	3	9	-
FORWARD	163	221	155	191	294	344	222	219	409	2218
par	3	4	3	3	4	4	4	4	5	34
handicap	9	11	13	1	5	3	15	17	7	-

BACK	
yardage	6148
par	70
rating	-
slope	-

REGULAR	
yardage	5410
par	70
rating	-
slope	-

FORWARD	
yardage	4560
par	69
rating	-
slope	-

PLAY POLICY & FEES: Members and guests only. Green fees are $2 for nine holes and $3 for 18 holes.

COURSE DESCRIPTION: This is a pitch-and-putt layout reserved for residents and their guests staying at the adjoining mobile home park. It is well maintained with lots of trees and bunkers.

LOCATION: In Hemet follow Florida Avenue (Highway 74) east to the course.

. . . ● **TOURNAMENTS:** This course is not available for outside events.

38. ARROYO FAIRWAYS MOBILE HOME CLUB

PLAY POLICY & FEES: Reciprocal play is accepted; otherwise members and guests of residents only. Green fees are $20 for members and $35 for guests. Carts are $20 for members and $25 for guests. Reservations are recommended.

DRESS CODE: Golfers must wear collared shirts.

COURSE DESCRIPTION: This hilly course is short and tight with many hidden greens. Watch for the 15th. It is a par-3, 185-yard hole with a drop of 200 feet. The green is surrounded by trees and bunkers.

LOCATION: From Riverside travel south on Interstate 215 to Newport Road. Turn right, head west to the last stop, and turn left. The club entrance is 300 yards past the traffic light.

. . . ● **TOURNAMENTS:** This course is not available for outside tournaments.

39. CANYON LAKE COUNTRY CLUB

MENIFEE LAKES COUNTRY CLUB
ARCHITECT: TED ROBINSON, 1989

29875 Menifee Lakes Drive
Menifee, CA 92584

PRO SHOP: 909-672-3090
CLUBHOUSE: 909-672-4824

Stan Gonzales, PGA Professional
John Welter, Superintendent

Driving Range ●
Practice Greens ●
Clubhouse ●
Food / Beverage ●
Accommodations
Pull Carts
Power Carts ●
Club Rental ●
$pecial Offers

	1	2	3	4	5	6	7	8	9	OUT
BACK	401	385	150	302	393	502	414	149	466	3162
REGULAR	370	359	133	287	367	487	391	130	444	2968
par	4	4	3	4	4	5	4	3	5	36
handicap	7/8	5/6	17/1	9/10	1/2		3/4	13/1	15/1	-
FORWARD	347	326	114	267	316	449	366	102	399	2686
par	4	4	3	4	4	5	4	3	5	36
handicap	5/6	7/8	17/1	11/1	9/10	3/4	1/2	15/1	13/1	-

	10	11	12	13	14	15	16	17	18	IN
BACK	377	361	380	147	522	369	181	368	525	3230
REGULAR	350	344	360	134	498	350	153	348	496	3033
par	4	4	4	3	5	4	3	4	5	36
handicap	5/6	7/8	1/2	17/1	9/10	3/4	15/1	13/1	11/1	-
FORWARD	324	316	330	103	438	305	115	311	440	2682
par	4	4	4	3	5	4	3	4	5	36
handicap	9/10	5/6	1/2	15/1		7/8	17/1	13/1	3/4	-

BACK	
yardage	6392
par	72
rating	70.5
slope	120

REGULAR	
yardage	6001
par	72
rating	68.0
slope	115

FORWARD	
yardage	5368
par	72
rating	71.5
slope	120

 TEMEKU HILLS GOLF COURSE
ARCHITECT: TED ROBINSON, 1989

41687 Temeku Drive
Temecula, CA 92591

PRO SHOP: 909-693-1440
CLUBHOUSE: 909-694-9998

Betty Lou Iverson, General Manager
Mark Johnson, PGA Professional

Driving Range ●
Practice Greens ●
Clubhouse ●
Food / Beverage ●
Accommodations
Pull Carts
Power Carts ●
Club Rental ●
$pecial Offers

	1	2	3	4	5	6	7	8	9	OUT
BACK	365	194	380	572	358	199	374	341	516	3299
REGULAR	345	176	359	545	341	185	357	328	498	3134
par	4	3	4	5	4	3	4	4	5	36
handicap	6	10	2	4	12	14	16	18	8	-
FORWARD	308	142	298	458	264	144	308	283	397	2602
par	4	3	4	5	4	3	4	4	5	36
handicap	6	16	4	8	10	18	14	12	2	-

	10	11	12	13	14	15	16	17	18	IN
BACK	345	414	202	478	544	182	381	318	359	3223
REGULAR	327	400	181	462	528	167	375	301	341	3082
par	4	4	3	5	5	3	4	4	4	36
handicap	9	1	7	13	5	11	3	17	15	-
FORWARD	243	320	126	401	490	121	312	253	271	2537
par	4	4	3	5	5	3	4	4	4	36
handicap	9	3	15	7	1	17	5	11	13	-

BACK	
yardage	6522
par	72
rating	70.3
slope	118

REGULAR	
yardage	6216
par	72
rating	68.7
slope	115

FORWARD	
yardage	5139
par	72
rating	68.8
slope	109

PLAY POLICY & FEES: Green fees are $35 weekdays and $56 weekends. Twilight green fees are $24 weekdays and $34 weekends. Carts are included.

TEE TIMES: Reservations can be booked six days in advance.

DRESS CODE: Collared shirts are required. No denim is allowed on the course.

COURSE DESCRIPTION: This Ted Robinson–designed course features tight fairways and plenty of signature water and sand.

NOTES: Par is 72 on each of the 18-hole combinations. The Lakes/Palms Course: See scorecard for yardage and rating information. The Palms/Falls Course is 6,503 yards and rated 71.1 from the championship tees, with a slope of 122. The Falls/Lakes Course is 6,435 yards and rated 70.7 from the championship tees with a slope of 121. There are two practice holes reserved for club members in need of preround tune-ups, and a marvelous driving range.

LOCATION: From Perris take the Newport Road exit off Interstate 215 south; follow it about one-half mile to Menifee Lakes Drive. Turn left and follow the road to the course.

. . . ● **TOURNAMENTS:** This course is available for outside tournaments.

40. MENIFEE LAKES COUNTRY CLUB

PLAY POLICY & FEES: Green fees are $40 weekdays, $50 Friday, and $65 weekends, including cart.

TEE TIMES: Reservations can be booked seven days in advance.

DRESS CODE: Collared shirts and nonmetal spikes are required. No blue jeans or tank tops are allowed. Bermuda shorts are permitted.

COURSE DESCRIPTION: Carts are mandatory on this hilly course, which features multi-tiered greens and five lakes. As always, architect Ted Robinson has incorporated waterfalls (four), which are visually pleasing but also dangerous for those easily distracted. The pride of the course is the downhill 345-yard, par-4 10th hole, a dogleg right with water in front and behind the green.

NOTES: The nines were switched in 1999.

LOCATION: From San Diego take Interstate 15 north. Exit at Rancho California Road. Drive east three miles to the course.

. . . ● **TOURNAMENTS:** A 16-player minimum is required to book a tournament. Events can be scheduled 12 months in advance. The banquet facility can accommodate 450 people. ● **TRAVEL:** Embassy Suites in Temecula is located 10 minutes from the golf course. For reservations call 909-676-5656.

41. TEMEKU HILLS GOLF COURSE

42 SCGA Members' Club at Rancho California

ARCHITECT: ROBERT TRENT JONES SR., 1972

38275 Murrieta Hot Springs
Murrieta, CA 92563

PRO SHOP: 909-677-7446

Clint Whitehill, Head Professional, PGA
Scott Mallory, PGA Professional
John Martinez, Superintendent

Driving Range ●
Practice Greens ●
Clubhouse ●
Food / Beverage ●
Accommodations
Pull Carts
Power Carts ●
Club Rental ●
$pecial Offers

	1	2	3	4	5	6	7	8	9	OUT
BACK	546	174	387	539	420	160	324	420	356	3326
REGULAR	514	146	372	527	392	144	309	350	317	3071
par	5	3	4	5	4	3	4	4	4	36
handicap	9	13	3	7	5	17	15	1	11	-
FORWARD	473	113	213	426	351	110	280	303	294	2563
par	5	3	4	5	4	3	4	4	4	36
handicap	1	17	11	9	3	13	7	5	15	-

	10	11	12	13	14	15	16	17	18	IN
BACK	191	380	411	565	408	343	189	499	411	3397
REGULAR	135	369	377	542	398	319	164	459	401	3164
par	3	4	4	5	4	4	3	5	4	36
handicap	12	10	2	8	6	18	14	16	4	-
FORWARD	102	348	367	489	318	277	155	429	307	2792
par	3	4	4	5	4	4	3	5	4	36
handicap	18	4	6	2	8	16	14	12	10	-

BACK	
yardage	6723
par	72
rating	72.0
slope	126

REGULAR	
yardage	6235
par	72
rating	69.4
slope	117

FORWARD	
yardage	5355
par	72
rating	70.5
slope	116

43 Bear Creek Golf Club

ARCHITECT: JACK NICKLAUS, 1983

22640 North Bear Creek
Murrieta, CA 92562

PRO SHOP: 909-677-8631
CLUBHOUSE: 909-677-8621

Roy Shoemaker, Manager
Scott Mallory, Head Professional, PGA
Mike Beauchman, Tournament Director

Driving Range ●
Practice Greens ●
Clubhouse ●
Food / Beverage ●
Accommodations
Pull Carts ●
Power Carts ●
Club Rental ●
$pecial Offers

	1	2	3	4	5	6	7	8	9	OUT
BACK	412	424	499	414	434	132	433	172	547	3467
REGULAR	383	398	473	391	390	112	371	153	510	3181
par	4	4	5	4	4	3	4	3	5	36
handicap	5	7	13	1	3	17	9	15	11	-
FORWARD	339	306	465	307	312	68	357	124	443	2721
par	4	4	5	4	4	3	4	3	5	36
handicap	9	7	1	3	5	17	13	15	11	-

	10	11	12	13	14	15	16	17	18	IN
BACK	414	531	210	351	542	424	210	425	428	3535
REGULAR	398	483	174	330	496	396	164	392	408	3241
par	4	5	3	4	5	4	3	4	4	36
handicap	4	6	16	14	8	2	18	12	10	-
FORWARD	309	431	128	317	429	316	123	327	325	2705
par	4	5	3	4	5	4	3	4	4	36
handicap	2	4	16	8	6	14	18	12	10	-

BACK	
yardage	7002
par	72
rating	75.3
slope	145

REGULAR	
yardage	6422
par	72
rating	71.6
slope	136

FORWARD	
yardage	5426
par	72
rating	73.3
slope	137

42. SCGA MEMBERS' CLUB AT RANCHO

PUBLIC: $21-$70

18 HOLES

PLAY POLICY & FEES: Green fees for SCGA members are $40 weekdays and $55 weekends. Fees for nonmembers are $55 weekdays and $70 weekends. Fees include carts. Twilight rates are available. All green fees are subject to change.

TEE TIMES: Reservations can be booked seven days in advance for nonmembers and 10 days in advance for SCGA members.

DRESS CODE: Collared shirts and slacks are required. Bermuda shorts are OK. Nonmetal spikes will be required January 1, 2000.

COURSE DESCRIPTION: Acquired by the Southern California Golf Association in February 1994, this classic Robert Trent Jones, Sr. course is long, open, and traverses rolling terrain. New back tees have been added, stretching the layout to 7,059 yards. The pride of the course is the par-4 third hole, which features an elevation drop of about 150 feet from tee to fairway. This hole also provides great views of the valley.

NOTES: The course has hosted numerous qualifiers for the U.S. PubLinks, SCGA, and U.S. Amateur.

LOCATION: The course is located in Murrieta, off Interstate 15 and Highway 215. Take the Murrieta Hot Springs Road exit east for 1.5 miles to Via Princessa and the course.

. . . ● **TOURNAMENTS:** A 16-player minimum is needed to book a tournament. Carts are required.

43. BEAR CREEK GOLF CLUB

PRIVATE: $55-$112

18 HOLES

privategolfcourses.com/bearcreekcc

PLAY POLICY & FEES: Limited reciprocal play is accepted with members of other private clubs; otherwise, members and guests only. Green fees are $55 when accompanied by a member and $112 unaccompanied, including carts.

DRESS CODE: Proper dress code is strictly enforced. Nonmetal spikes are required.

COURSE DESCRIPTION: This championship course is aptly named because it's a bear to play. It was designed by Jack Nicklaus in 1983 and features a natural rolling terrain with pot bunkers, mounds, and creeks. Water guards half the course, and the greens are large and tricky. Nicklaus's favorite hole is the 391-yard, par-4 fourth hole. It has a split-level fairway divided by grass bunkers. Bear Creek rates among the top 20 courses in the state, although the wind picks up considerably in the afternoons, often making this an angry bear. Immaculately conditioned, it hosts only about 35,000 rounds per year.

NOTES: The course was the site of the 1985 Skins Game and is used regularly for PGA Tour qualifying.

LOCATION: From Temecula take Interstate 15 to the Clinton Keith exit in Murrieta; then travel west to Bear Creek Drive and turn north to the club.

. . . ● **TOURNAMENTS:** Shotgun tournaments are available Monday only. Carts are required. A 100-player minimum is required to book a tournament. Events should be scheduled 12 months in advance. A banquet facility is available that can accommodate up to 220 people.

ARCHITECT: DAVID RAINVILLE, 1989

40603 Colony Drive
Murrieta, CA 92562

PRO SHOP: 909-677-2221

Tom Williams, Professional/Manager
Jim Blacketer, Superintendent

Driving Range
Practice Greens ●
Clubhouse ●
Food / Beverage ●
Accommodations
Pull Carts ●
Power Carts ●
Club Rental ●
$pecial Offers

	1	2	3	4	5	6	7	8	9	OUT
BACK	361	165	299	356	120	163	384	333	175	2356
REGULAR	339	144	284	333	108	147	354	317	164	2190
par	4	3	4	4	3	3	4	4	3	32
handicap	7	5	17	3	13	15	1	9	11	-
FORWARD	296	126	258	285	95	127	314	290	149	1940
par	4	3	4	4	3	3	4	4	3	32
handicap	3	7	9	5	13	17	1	11	15	-

	10	11	12	13	14	15	16	17	18	IN
BACK	189	301	317	278	317	95	286	332	210	2325
REGULAR	173	301	305	260	296	86	265	314	155	2155
par	3	4	4	4	4	3	4	4	3	33
handicap	8	4	2	14	12	18	10	6	16	-
FORWARD	147	283	293	226	244	77	219	280	134	1903
par	3	4	4	4	4	3	4	4	3	33
handicap	6	4	2	14	12	18	10	6	16	-

BACK	
yardage	4681
par	65
rating	62.3
slope	108

REGULAR	
yardage	4345
par	65
rating	60.4
slope	103

FORWARD	
yardage	3843
par	65
rating	62.0
slope	100

ARCHITECT: RON FREAM, 1991

GOLF 50

45100 Redhawk Parkway
Temecula, CA 92592

PRO SHOP: 909-302-3850

J.B. Sneve, Manager

Driving Range ●
Practice Greens ●
Clubhouse
Food / Beverage ●
Accommodations
Pull Carts
Power Carts ●
Club Rental ●
$pecial Offers ●

	1	2	3	4	5	6	7	8	9	OUT
BACK	505	375	350	130	450	390	565	150	445	3360
REGULAR	465	350	320	110	415	365	550	140	425	3140
par	5	4	4	3	4	4	5	3	4	36
handicap	15	5	13	17	1	9	7	11	3	-
FORWARD	430	315	300	100	375	300	450	100	350	2720
par	5	4	4	3	4	4	5	3	4	36
handicap	1	11	13	17	9	15	3	7	5	-

	10	11	12	13	14	15	16	17	18	IN
BACK	425	535	145	445	340	355	420	195	535	3395
REGULAR	410	500	145	410	320	325	375	180	505	3170
par	4	5	3	4	4	4	4	3	5	36
handicap	8	6	18	2	16	14	4	12	10	-
FORWARD	360	460	120	340	275	305	335	135	465	2795
par	4	5	3	4	4	4	4	3	5	36
handicap	10	2	12	4	14	18	6	16	8	-

BACK	
yardage	6755
par	72
rating	72.7
slope	137

REGULAR	
yardage	6310
par	72
rating	69.5
slope	125

FORWARD	
yardage	5515
par	72
rating	72.0
slope	124

PLAY POLICY & FEES: Outside play is accepted. Green fees are $15 walking and $23 riding everyday. Senior, junior, and twilight rates are offered.

TEE TIMES: Reservations can be booked five days in advance.

DRESS CODE: Collared shirts and nonmetal spikes are required.

COURSE DESCRIPTION: Five lakes and a channel keep golfers honest on this executive course. Although mostly flat, trees and bunkers can be a problem for errant shots. The toughest hole is the par-4 seventh, which is bordered by trees on both sides of the fairway, and a large eucalyptus tree looms off the tee.

LOCATION: From Temecula, take Interstate 15 five miles north to California Oaks Road. The course is one block east of the freeway.

. . . ● **TOURNAMENTS:** A 20-player minimum is needed to book a tournament.

44. THE COLONY COUNTRY CLUB

PLAY POLICY & FEES: Green fees are $50 Monday through Thursday, $60 Friday, and $80 weekends and holidays. Twilight rates are $30 Monday through Thursday, $35 Friday, and $45 weekends. Carts are included. Reservations are required.

TEE TIMES: Reservations can be booked seven days in advance by calling the phone number listed above the scorecard or by calling 800-451-HAWK.

DRESS CODE: Collared shirts and nonmetal spikes are required. No blue jeans are allowed on the course.

COURSE DESCRIPTION: Its rolling terrain features several elevated tees and greens. There are generous landing areas, but tiered and sloping greens present a real challenge.

NOTES: Redhawk has the largest putting green in California. This course has been rated as high as seventh among public courses in the state.

LOCATION: From Highway 15 in Temecula, take the Highway 79 south exit. Travel east on Highway 79 for 2.5 miles, and turn right on Redhawk Parkway and drive straight to the course.

. . . ● **TOURNAMENTS:** A 16-player minimum is needed to book a tournament. Carts are required. Events can be booked two weeks in advance. ● **TRAVEL:** The Embassy Suites in Temecula is located 10 minutes from the golf course. For reservations call 909-676-5656. ● **$PECIAL OFFERS:** Play-and-stay packages are available.

45. REDHAWK GOLF CLUB

TEMECULA CREEK INN GOLF COURSE
ARCHITECTS: DICK ROSSEN, 1970; TED ROBINSON, 1989

44501 Rainbow Canyon
Temecula, CA 92592

PRO SHOP: 909-676-2405
OFFICE: 800-962-7335

Bill Sloan, Head Professional, PGA
Phil Fitzgerald, Superintendent
Chris Clark, Tournament Director

Driving Range ●
Practice Greens ●
Clubhouse ●
Food / Beverage ●
Accommodations ●
Pull Carts
Power Carts ●
Club Rental ●
$pecial Offers ●

	1	2	3	4	5	6	7	8	9	OUT
BACK	372	498	171	404	443	212	520	411	405	3436
REGULAR	357	482	153	378	387	174	507	368	386	3192
par	4	5	3	4	4	3	5	4	4	36
handicap	9/10	15/1	17/1	1/2	3/4	13/1	11/1	5/6	7/8	-
FORWARD	343	465	109	348	323	148	445	340	346	2867
par	4	5	3	4	4	3	5	4	4	36
handicap	5/6	11/1	17/1	1/2	9/10	15/1	13/1	7/8	3/4	-

	10	11	12	13	14	15	16	17	18	IN
BACK	505	352	402	331	180	416	351	165	555	3257
REGULAR	488	333	380	315	165	396	333	153	540	3103
par	5	4	4	4	3	4	4	3	5	36
handicap	11/1	9/10	3/4	13/1	15/1	1/2	7/8	17/1	5/6	-
FORWARD	455	313	330	280	147	330	305	136	520	2816
par	5	4	4	4	3	4	4	3	5	36
handicap	7/8	9/10	3/4	17/1	11/1	5/6	13/1	15/1	1/2	-

BACK	
yardage	6693
par	72
rating	72.6
slope	130

REGULAR	
yardage	6295
par	72
rating	70.1
slope	116

FORWARD	
yardage	5683
par	72
rating	72.4
slope	125

PLAY POLICY & FEES: Outside play is accepted. Green fees are $50 from Monday through Thursday, $60 Friday, and $80 weekends and holidays. Carts are included.

TEE TIMES: Reservations can be booked seven days in advance.

DRESS CODE: Collared shirts are required. No cutoffs or blue jeans are allowed on the course, and nonmetal spikes are recommended.

COURSE DESCRIPTION: Each of the nines is distinctly different. They range in character from flat and rolling to hilly with lots of trees to more hills and more trees.

LOCATION: From the junction of Interstate 15 and Highway 79 south, travel east one mile to Pala Road and turn right. Take Pala Road to Rainbow Canyon Road. Take a right and follow to the golf course.

. . . ● **TOURNAMENTS:** A 16-player minimum is required to book a tournament. Carts are required. Events should be booked 12 months in advance. The banquet facility can accommodate up to 200 people. ● **TRAVEL:** The Temecula Inn has 80 rooms and 10 junior suites. For more information or reservations call 800-698-9295. ● **$PECIAL OFFERS:** The Temecula Inn has play-and-stay golf packages that include lodging, green fees, dinner, and breakfast. For more information call 800-698- 9295.

46. TEMECULA CREEK INN GOLF COURSE

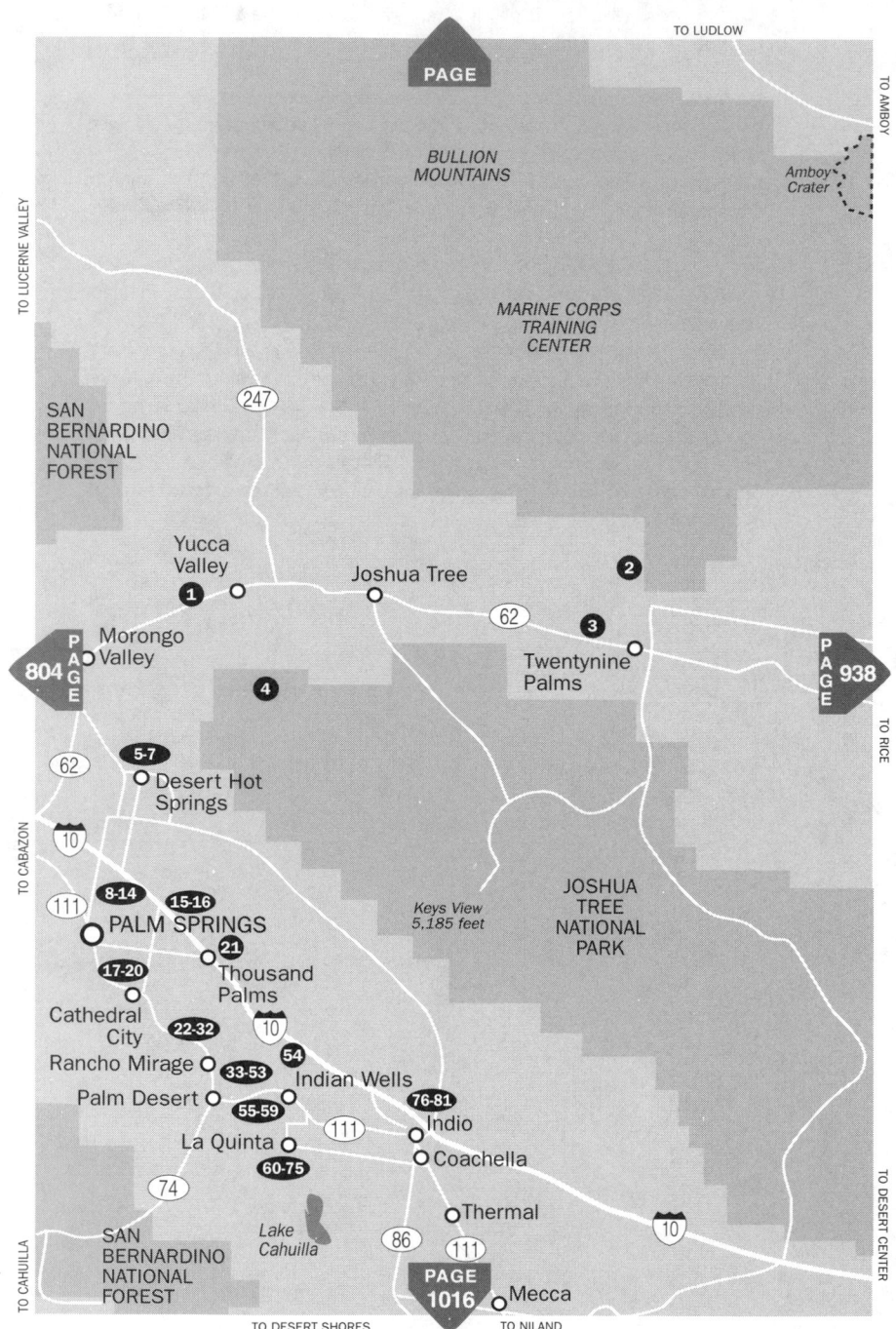

TO LUDLOW

PAGE

TO AMBOY

BULLION
MOUNTAINS

Amboy
Crater

TO LUCERNE VALLEY

MARINE CORPS
TRAINING
CENTER

247

SAN
BERNARDINO
NATIONAL
FOREST

Yucca
Valley
1

Joshua Tree

2

62

3

P
A
G
E
804

Morongo
Valley

4

Twentynine
Palms

P
A
G
E
938

TO RICE

62

5-7
Desert Hot
Springs

TO CABAZON

10

111

8-14

15-16

PALM SPRINGS

21

17-20

Thousand
Palms

Keys View
5,185 feet

JOSHUA
TREE
NATIONAL
PARK

Cathedral
City

22-32

10

Rancho Mirage

33-53

54

Palm Desert

Indian Wells

55-59

76-81

La Quinta

Indio

60-75

111

Coachella

74

Thermal

10

TO DESERT CENTER

SAN
BERNARDINO
NATIONAL
FOREST

Lake
Cahuilla

86

111

PAGE
1016

Mecca

TO CAHUILLA

TO DESERT SHORES

TO NILAND

Palm Springs Area

BLUE SKIES COUNTRY CLUB
ARCHITECT: ROSCOE SMITH, 1958

55100 Martinez Trail
Yucca Valley, CA 92284

PRO SHOP: 760-365-0111

Mark Elliott, Head Professional, PGA
Bob Robbins, Superintendent

Driving Range ●
Practice Greens ●
Clubhouse ●
Food / Beverage ●
Accommodations
Pull Carts ●
Power Carts ●
Club Rental ●
$pecial Offers

	1	2	3	4	5	6	7	8	9	OUT
BACK	324	421	368	312	221	427	417	166	459	3115
REGULAR	307	412	358	300	209	418	400	155	451	3010
par	4	4	4	4	3	4	4	3	5	35
handicap	18	4	12	14	2	6	16	10	12	-
FORWARD	286	403	348	274	151	401	390	134	444	2831
par	4	5	4	4	3	5	4	3	5	37
handicap	12	8	10	14	18	2	4	16	6	-

	10	11	12	13	14	15	16	17	18	IN
BACK	401	325	192	546	354	320	414	344	389	3285
REGULAR	388	315	153	515	339	306	397	330	362	3105
par	4	4	3	5	4	4	4	4	4	36
handicap	1	5	7	9	13	17	3	15	11	-
FORWARD	361	302	102	493	323	296	390	316	343	2926
par	4	4	3	5	4	4	4	4	4	36
handicap	5	15	17	1	9	13	3	11	7	-

BACK	
yardage	6400
par	71
rating	69.8
slope	115

REGULAR	
yardage	6115
par	71
rating	68.7
slope	108

FORWARD	
yardage	5757
par	73
rating	71.6
slope	119

 ROADRUNNER DUNES GOLF CLUB
ARCHITECT: LAWRENCE HUGHES, 1964

4733 Desert Knoll Road
Twentynine Palms, CA
92277
PRO SHOP: 760-367-5770

Rich Mellott, Assitant Manager

Driving Range ●
Practice Greens ●
Clubhouse ●
Food / Beverage ●
Accommodations
Pull Carts ●
Power Carts ●
Club Rental ●
$pecial Offers

	1	2	3	4	5	6	7	8	9	OUT
BACK	-	-	-	-	-	-	-	-	-	-
REGULAR	303	182	380	398	481	364	361	492	143	3104
par	4	3	4	4	5	4	4	5	3	36
handicap	18	14	6	2	12	10	4	8	16	-
FORWARD	266	160	350	352	410	203	340	434	121	2636
par	4	3	4	4	5	4	4	5	3	36
handicap	12	18	10	4	6	16	8	2	14	-

	10	11	12	13	14	15	16	17	18	IN
BACK	-	-	-	-	-	-	-	-	-	-
REGULAR	313	170	393	391	491	354	371	490	153	3126
par	4	3	4	4	5	4	4	5	3	36
handicap	17	13	1	3	11	9	5	7	15	-
FORWARD	297	120	368	345	470	198	345	429	126	2698
par	4	3	4	4	5	4	4	5	3	36
handicap	13	11	7	1	5	17	9	3	15	-

BACK	
yardage	-
par	-
rating	-
slope	-

REGULAR	
yardage	6230
par	72
rating	70.1
slope	115

FORWARD	
yardage	5334
par	72
rating	70.2
slope	117

PLAY POLICY & FEES: Reciprocal play is accepted with members of other private clubs. Outside play is accepted. Green fees for nine holes are $8 weekdays and $15 weekends and holidays. Green fees for 18 holes are $15 weekdays and $20 weekends and holidays. Senior rates are $11 for 18 holes on weekdays and $13 on weekends. Carts are $12 per person.

TEE TIMES: Reservations can be booked seven days in advance. Reservations can be made by calling 800-877-1412.

DRESS CODE: Shirts with sleeves are required.

COURSE DESCRIPTION: This upgraded course has tree-lined fairways and two lakes. The fairways are fairly open. The third is a scenic lake hole. It is par 3 and 164 yards from an elevated tee over a lake. The green is bunkered in the front, and the tee is situated in a chute of trees. And what trees—towering cottonwoods and Chinese elms line every fairway.

LOCATION: Take the Twenty-Nine Palms/Yucca Valley exit off Interstate 10 and drive about 18 miles north on Highway 62. Turn left at the Yucca Inn sign and continue to the club.

. . . ● **TOURNAMENTS:** This course is available for outside tournaments.

1. BLUE SKIES COUNTRY CLUB

PLAY POLICY & FEES: Green fees are $10 for nine holes and $14 for 18 holes. Call for special rates.

TEE TIMES: This course is located in a motor home park, so reservations are a must in the winter months and can be made seven days in advance.

DRESS CODE: Nonmetal spikes are required.

COURSE DESCRIPTION: This challenging, short course offers large greens with water coming into play on two holes.

LOCATION: Take the Twentynine Palms/Yucca Valley exit off Interstate 10 and drive about 40 miles to the town of Twentynine Palms. Turn left on Adobe Road and drive two miles. Turn right on Amboy and then left on Desert Knoll Avenue.

. . . ● **TOURNAMENTS:** A 16-player minimum is required to book an event. The banquet facility can accommodate 130 people.

2. ROADRUNNER DUNES GOLF CLUB

③ DESERT WINDS GOLF COURSE

MCAGCC Golf Course,
Twentynine Palms, CA
92278
PRO SHOP: 760-830-6132
CLUBHOUSE: 760-830-7353

Stony Hoffman, Manager/Superintendent
Joe Vincent, Professional

Driving Range ●
Practice Greens ●
Clubhouse ●
Food / Beverage ●
Accommodations
Pull Carts ●
Power Carts ●
Club Rental ●
$pecial Offers

	1	2	3	4	5	6	7	8	9	OUT
BACK	341	396	173	563	414	151	445	370	542	3395
REGULAR	328	375	167	540	396	142	422	342	526	3238
par	4	4	3	5	4	3	4	4	5	36
handicap	10	4	16	8	6	18	2	12	14	-
FORWARD	315	355	159	516	376	132	398	317	508	3076
par	4	4	3	5	4	3	4	4	5	36
handicap	16	8	14	6	4	18	2	12	10	-

	10	11	12	13	14	15	16	17	18	IN
BACK	484	389	213	569	405	180	401	397	475	3513
REGULAR	434	330	200	495	382	173	345	338	435	3132
par	4	4	3	5	4	3	4	4	5	36
handicap	15	7	5	11	3	17	13	9	1	-
FORWARD	384	325	170	479	371	161	331	326	375	2922
par	4	4	3	5	4	3	4	4	5	36
handicap	1	5	9	7	3	17	11	13	15	-

BACK	
yardage	6908
par	72
rating	72.7
slope	121

REGULAR	
yardage	6370
par	72
rating	70.2
slope	116

FORWARD	
yardage	5998
par	72
rating	-
slope	113

④ DESERT DUNES GOLF CLUB
ARCHITECT: ROBERT T. JONES JR., 1989

19300 Palm Drive
Desert Hot Springs, CA
92240
PRO SHOP: 760-251-5368

Kerry Walker, PGA Professional
Olen Bartley, General Manager
Bill Kostes, Superintendent

Driving Range ●
Practice Greens ●
Clubhouse ●
Food / Beverage ●
Accommodations
Pull Carts ●
Power Carts ●
Club Rental ●
$pecial Offers

	1	2	3	4	5	6	7	8	9	OUT
BACK	517	386	328	394	167	349	390	171	536	3238
REGULAR	503	366	305	367	141	338	363	162	518	3063
par	5	4	4	4	3	4	4	3	5	36
handicap	8	2	14	10	18	12	4	16	6	-
FORWARD	459	287	254	322	119	315	308	104	466	2634
par	5	4	4	4	3	4	4	3	5	36
handicap	4	10	14	8	18	12	6	16	2	-

	10	11	12	13	14	15	16	17	18	IN
BACK	376	346	365	576	184	411	517	187	414	3376
REGULAR	349	321	333	530	164	397	484	166	398	3142
par	4	4	4	5	3	4	5	3	4	36
handicap	7	13	11	5	17	3	9	15	1	-
FORWARD	297	279	296	492	126	318	443	131	343	2725
par	4	4	4	5	3	4	5	3	4	36
handicap	9	13	11	3	17	5	7	15	1	-

BACK	
yardage	6614
par	72
rating	72.7
slope	134

REGULAR	
yardage	6205
par	72
rating	70.2
slope	124

FORWARD	
yardage	5359
par	72
rating	70.7
slope	116

PLAY POLICY & FEES: Military personnel and guests only. Civilian guests pay $8.50 for nine holes and $11 for 18 holes weekdays, $9.50 for nine holes and $12 for 18 holes weekends. Military personnel fees are based on rank. Juniors pay $5 for nine holes and $7.50 for 18 holes. Carts are $13.

TEE TIMES: Reservations are required up to a week in advance for weekends and holidays.

DRESS CODE: No tank tops or cutoffs are allowed on the course. Nonmetal spikes are required.

COURSE DESCRIPTION: If you like toying with the elements, this course is for you. Built on the side of a hill in the middle of the desert, it is wide open but challenging, with out-of-bounds, desert-style rough, and seasonal winds. Five ponds come into play, but during the summer the water is a welcome sight.

NOTES: Approximately 20,000 rounds are played per year at Desert Winds.

LOCATION: Take the Twentynine Palms/Yucca Valley exit off Interstate 10 and drive about 40 miles to the town of Twentynine Palms. Turn left at Adobe Road and drive five miles to the main gate at the Marine Combat Center. Continue through the main gate for three miles to the flashing light. Turn left and drive one-half mile to the first paved road, then right to the course.

. . . ● **TOURNAMENTS:** All outside events must have a military sponsor.

3. DESERT WINDS GOLF COURSE

PLAY POLICY & FEES: Green fees are $100 Monday through Thursday and $115 Friday through Sunday, and holidays during peak season. Call for special seasonal rates. Reservations are recommended.

TEE TIMES: Reservations can be booked seven days in advance.

DRESS CODE: Collared shirts and nonmetal spikes are required. No blue jeans are allowed.

COURSE DESCRIPTION: This course has a unique Scottish-links flavor. Natural sand dunes and mesquite brush line the fairways. There is an abundance of wildlife including jackrabbits, roadrunners, and coyotes in the surrounding desert. The par-3 fifth hole requires a long tee shot over a desert setting to a severely undulating green with a mesquite backdrop. It's a terrific layout.

NOTES: In 1996 Desert Dunes hosted the second stage of PGA Tour Qualifying School, and in 1994 it hosted the first stage of U.S. Open qualifying.

LOCATION: From Interstate 10 in Palm Springs, take Gene Autry Trail and cross over the freeway. When you cross the freeway, the name changes to Palm Drive. Continue on Palm Drive two miles to the course.

. . . ● **TOURNAMENTS:** A 16-player minimum is needed to book a tournament. Carts are required.

4. DESERT DUNES GOLF CLUB

MISSION LAKES COUNTRY CLUB
ARCHITECT: TED ROBINSON, 1971

8484 Clubhouse Drive
Desert Hot Springs, CA
92240
PRO SHOP: 760-329-8061
CLUBHOUSE: 760-329-6481

Jack Elser, Manager
Robert Duncan, PGA Professional
Ray Cymbalisty, Superintendent

Driving Range ●
Practice Greens ●
Clubhouse ●
Food / Beverage ●
Accommodations ●
Pull Carts
Power Carts ●
Club Rental ●
$pecial Offers

	1	2	3	4	5	6	7	8	9	OUT
BACK	540	202	402	146	380	363	389	219	506	3147
REGULAR	520	180	384	135	368	343	353	204	483	2970
par	5	3	4	3	4	4	4	3	5	35
handicap	9	3	1	17	5	11	13	7	15	-
FORWARD	503	121	347	122	354	313	336	179	448	2723
par	5	3	4	3	4	4	4	3	5	35
handicap	1	17	7	15	9	11	5	13	3	-

	10	11	12	13	14	15	16	17	18	IN
BACK	503	427	200	411	515	249	628	226	431	3590
REGULAR	483	404	180	384	506	234	608	209	418	3426
par	5	4	3	4	5	3	5	3	4	36
handicap	14	2	16	8	18	10	4	12	6	-
FORWARD	454	360	150	353	377	133	439	133	268	2667
par	5	5	3	4	5	3	5	3	4	37
handicap	2	8	16	4	12	18	6	14	10	-

BACK	
yardage	6737
par	71
rating	72.8
slope	131

REGULAR	
yardage	6396
par	71
rating	70.6
slope	124

FORWARD	
yardage	5390
par	72
rating	71.2
slope	122

SANDS RV
ARCHITECT: RON GARL, 1983

16400 Bubbling Wells Road
Desert Hot Springs, CA
92240
PRO SHOP: 760-251-1173

Larry Violette, Manager

Driving Range ●
Practice Greens ●
Clubhouse
Food / Beverage
Accommodations
Pull Carts ●
Power Carts
Club Rental ●
$pecial Offers

	1	2	3	4	5	6	7	8	9	OUT
BACK	-	-	-	-	-	-	-	-	-	-
REGULAR	280	310	363	120	141	321	168	141	283	2127
par	4	4	4	3	3	4	3	3	4	32
handicap	5	6	1	9	8	2	4	7	3	-
FORWARD	261	287	320	96	112	273	110	124	249	1832
par	4	4	4	3	3	4	3	3	4	32
handicap	5	6	2	9	8	1	4	7	3	-

	10	11	12	13	14	15	16	17	18	IN
BACK	-	-	-	-	-	-	-	-	-	-
REGULAR	-	-	-	-	-	-	-	-	-	-
par	-	-	-	-	-	-	-	-	-	-
handicap	-	-	-	-	-	-	-	-	-	-
FORWARD	-	-	-	-	-	--	-	-	-	-
par	-	-	-	-	-	-	-	-	-	-
handicap	-	-	-	-	-	-	-	-	-	-

BACK	
yardage	-
par	-
rating	
slope	

REGULAR	
yardage	2127
par	32
rating	57.7
slope	-

FORWARD	
yardage	1832
par	32
rating	-
slope	-

PLAY POLICY & FEES: Outside play is accepted. Green fees are $20 every day from June to September. Winter rates were not yet decided by time of press.
DRESS CODE: Appropriate golf attire and nonmetal spikes are required.
COURSE DESCRIPTION: This is a high-desert course, which means you can expect searing sun and wicked wind. Three holes climb into the mountains. Long par 3s also make this a demanding course; five measure 200 yards or longer.
LOCATION: Take the Indian Avenue exit off Interstate 10 at Palm Springs. Drive north to Mission Lakes Avenue east and turn north on Clubhouse Drive.
. . . ● **TOURNAMENTS:** This course is available for outside events. Restrictions apply for weekend shotgun tournaments.

5. MISSION LAKES COUNTRY CLUB

PLAY POLICY & FEES: Green fees are $12 for nonresidents.
TEE TIMES: Reservations can be booked 24 hours in advance.
COURSE DESCRIPTION: This is an executive course adjoining an RV park. It is short and wide open, with a few trees and no bunkers. It's a beginner's paradise. A lake on the seventh offers some suspense.
LOCATION: Take the Palm Drive exit north off Interstate 10. Turn right on Dillon Road and drive three-fourths mile to Bubbling Wells Road. The entrance to the RV park and the course is on the corner.
. . . ● **TOURNAMENTS:** This course is not available for outside events.

6. SANDS RV RESORT

7 DESERT CREST COUNTRY CLUB

69400 S. Country Club
Desert Hot Springs, CA
92241

CLUBHOUSE: 760-329-8711

Penny Moore, Manager

Driving Range
Practice Greens
Clubhouse
Food / Beverage ●
Accommodations
Pull Carts
Power Carts
Club Rental
$pecial Offers

	1	2	3	4	5	6	7	8	9	OUT
BACK	-	-	-	-	-	-	-	-	-	-
REGULAR	101	80	120	123	110	102	131	122	110	999
par	3	3	3	3	3	3	3	3	3	27
handicap	11	17	13	1	9	15	7	3	5	-
FORWARD	101	80	120	123	110	102	131	122	110	999
par	3	3	3	3	3	3	3	3	3	27
handicap	11	17	13	1	9	15	7	3	5	-

	10	11	12	13	14	15	16	17	18	IN
BACK	-	-	-	-	-	-	-	-	-	-
REGULAR	-	-	-	-	-	-	-	-	-	-
par	-	-	-	-	-	-	-	-	-	-
handicap	-	-	-	-	-	-	-	-	-	-
FORWARD	-	-	-	-	-	-	-	-	-	-
par	-	-	-	-	-	-	-	-	-	-
handicap	-	-	-	-	-	-	-	-	-	-

BACK	
yardage	-
par	-
rating	
slope	

REGULAR	
yardage	999
par	27
rating	48.8
slope	--

FORWARD	
yardage	999
par	27
rating	51.2-
slope	-

8 O'DONNELL GOLF CLUB
ARCHITECTS: J. DAWSON, 1934; T. O'DONNELL

301 North Belardo Road
Palm Springs, CA 92262

PRO SHOP: 760-325-2259

Sally Mahoney, PGA Professional
Remedios Munez, Superintendent

Driving Range
Practice Greens ●
Clubhouse ●
Food / Beverage ●
Accommodations
Pull Carts
Power Carts ●
Club Rental ●
$pecial Offers

	1	2	3	4	5	6	7	8	9	OUT
BACK	-	-	-	-	-	-	-	-	-	-
REGULAR	312	357	130	207	125	468	197	504	301	2601
par	4	4	3	4	3	5	3	5	4	35
handicap	7	1	15	13	17	5	11	3	9	-
FORWARD	312	357	130	207	125	468	197	504	301	2601
par	4	4	3	4	3	5	3	5	4	35
handicap	7	1	15	13	17	5	11	3	9	-

	10	11	12	13	14	15	16	17	18	IN
BACK	-	-	-	-	-	-	-	-	-	-
REGULAR	320	367	150	250	130	472	207	508	305	2709
par	4	4	3	4	3	5	3	5	4	35
handicap	8	2	16	14	18	6	12	4	10	-
FORWARD	320	367	150	250	130	472	207	508	305	2709
par	4	4	3	4	3	5	3	5	4	35
handicap	8	2	16	14	18	6	12	4	10	-

BACK	
yardage	-
par	-
rating	-
slope	-

REGULAR	
yardage	5310
par	70
rating	65.3
slope	98

FORWARD	
yardage	5310
par	70
rating	69.6
slope	110

PLAY POLICY & FEES: The course is open to members only Tuesday, Wednesday, and Friday from 7 a.m. to noon; otherwise, the public is welcome. Green fees are $8 for nine holes and $11 for 18 holes. Children under 15 are not allowed.

TEE TIMES: Reservations are not accepted.

DRESS CODE: Appropriate golf attire is required.

COURSE DESCRIPTION: This level course has four lakes, lots of trees, and is well maintained. Desert Crest is part of a mobile home community and very popular among seniors.

LOCATION: From Los Angeles on Interstate 10, take the Palm Drive exit and head north. Follow Palm Drive until you reach Dillon Road. Take a right on Dillon Road and head east three miles. Stay on Dillon one mile past Mt. View. The course is on the left.

. . . ● **TOURNAMENTS:** Events should be scheduled at least eight months in advance. The banquet facility can accommodate up to 190 people.

7. DESERT CREST COUNTRY CLUB

PLAY POLICY & FEES: Members and guests only. Guest fees are $43, cart included.

DRESS CODE: Nonmetal spikes are required.

COURSE DESCRIPTION: This is a tranquil course in downtown Palm Springs, set against the base of the mountains. It is a peaceful spot for some mellow golfing. This was the first course in the Springs and a mecca for the Hollywood set 60 years ago. Today, it's a sporty course with two par 5s and a 207-yard par 3.

LOCATION: From Interstate 10, take Highway 111 east on Palm Canyon Drive into the town of Palm Springs. Turn west on Amado Road and drive one block to the club.

. . . ● **TOURNAMENTS:** This course is not available for outside events.

8. O'DONNELL GOLF CLUB

PALM SPRINGS COUNTRY CLUB
ARCHITECT: ROBERT BELL, 1957

2500 Whitewater Club
Palm Springs, CA 92262

PRO SHOP: 760-323-2626

Jeff Thush, Operations Manager

Driving Range ●
Practice Greens ●
Clubhouse ●
Food / Beverage ●
Accommodations
Pull Carts
Power Carts ●
Club Rental ●
$pecial Offers

	1	2	3	4	5	6	7	8	9	OUT
BACK	531	381	146	440	391	192	533	379	519	3512
REGULAR	499	359	129	398	371	174	514	356	481	3281
par	5	4	3	4	4	3	5	4	5	37
handicap	5	11	17	1	3	15	13	9	7	-
FORWARD	410	320	96	352	314	142	474	246	435	2789
par	5	4	3	4	4	3	5	4	5	37
handicap	5	11	17	1	3	15	13	9	7	-

	10	11	12	13	14	15	16	17	18	IN
BACK	370	155	480	185	291	517	195	334	337	2864
REGULAR	355	159	389	155	261	484	167	322	312	2604
par	4	3	5	3	4	5	3	4	4	35
handicap	2	14	12	16	18	4	10	8	6	-
FORWARD	345	115	401	116	244	459	134	318	307	2439
par	4	3	5	3	4	5	3	4	4	35
handicap	2	16	8	12	18	6	14	4	10	-

BACK	
yardage	6376
par	72
rating	68.9
slope	115

REGULAR	
yardage	5885
par	72
rating	66.6
slope	110

FORWARD	
yardage	5228
par	72
rating	67.0
slope	109

 CANYON COUNTRY CLUB
ARCHITECT: WILLIAM F. BELL, 1962

1100 Murray Canyon Drive
Palm Springs, CA 92264

PRO SHOP: 760-327-5831
CLUBHOUSE: 760-327-1321

Vicki Woodcock, Head Professional, LPGA
David Reardon, Director of Golf, PGA
Som Bali, Superintendent

Driving Range ●
Practice Greens ●
Clubhouse ●
Food / Beverage ●
Accommodations
Pull Carts
Power Carts ●
Club Rental
$pecial Offers

	1	2	3	4	5	6	7	8	9	OUT
BACK	379	396	440	190	447	552	164	395	397	3360
REGULAR	357	376	416	171	427	527	153	379	375	3181
par	4	4	4	3	4	5	3	4	4	35
handicap	13	5	3	15	1	9	17	11	7	-
FORWARD	332	332	388	125	393	470	100	345	336	2821
par	4	4	4	3	4	5	3	4	4	35
handicap	7	9	3	15	1	11	17	13		-

	10	11	12	13	14	15	16	17	18	IN
BACK	500	423	433	560	204	341	189	377	482	3509
REGULAR	478	394	411	539	176	332	151	357	469	3307
par	5	4	4	5	3	4	3	4	5	37
handicap	12	4	2	8	16	18	14	6	10	-
FORWARD	463	359	384	488	148	304	113	323	459	3041
par	5	4	4	5	3	4	3	4	5	37
handicap	12	4	2	10	16	14	18	8	6	-

BACK	
yardage	6869
par	72
rating	73.5
slope	129

REGULAR	
yardage	6488
par	72
rating	71.1
slope	122

FORWARD	
yardage	5862
par	72
rating	74.0
slope	125

PLAY POLICY & FEES: Green fees range from $10 to $50, depending on the time of year. Carts are included. Reservations are recommended.

TEE TIMES: Reservations can be booked seven days in advance.

DRESS CODE: Collared shirts are required, and nonmetal spikes recommended.

COURSE DESCRIPTION: This is a mature desert course with tree-lined fairways. The well-conditioned greens are also well protected.

NOTES: This was the second course built in this desert.

LOCATION: Take the Palm Drive exit off Interstate 10 and go south a half mile to Vista Chino. Turn right and drive one-quarter mile to Whitewater Club Drive. Turn right and continue to the club.

. . . ● **TOURNAMENTS:** A 40-player minimum is required to book a tournament. Carts are required.

9. PALM SPRINGS COUNTRY CLUB

PLAY POLICY & FEES: Members and guests only. Guest fees are $65. Carts are $15.

DRESS CODE: Appropriate golf attire and nonmetal spikes are required.

COURSE DESCRIPTION: This mature course is beautifully maintained. It's set among million-dollar homes, with out-of-bounds on all but one hole.

LOCATION: Take the Indian Avenue exit off Interstate 10 near Palm Springs and drive south to Murray Canyon. Turn left and drive six blocks to the club.

. . . ● **TOURNAMENTS:** This course is not available for outside events.

10. CANYON COUNTRY CLUB

CANYON SOUTH GOLF COURSE
ARCHITECT: WILLIAM P. BELL, 1962

1097 Murray Canyon Drive
Palm Springs, CA 92264

PRO SHOP: 760-327-2019

Mary Ann Quijada, Professional, LPGA
Bob Burgess, Superintendent
Jeff Thush, Operations Manager

Driving Range ●
Practice Greens ●
Clubhouse
Food / Beverage ●
Accommodations
Pull Carts
Power Carts ●
Club Rental ●
$pecial Offers

	1	2	3	4	5	6	7	8	9	OUT
BACK	515	435	375	195	412	407	303	147	557	3346
REGULAR	495	415	355	170	382	386	290	140	537	3170
par	5	4	4	3	4	4	4	3	5	36
handicap	9	3	11	15	1	5	13	17	7	-
FORWARD	480	375	340	150	360	355	280	130	520	2990
par	5	4	4	3	4	4	4	3	5	36
handicap	9	3	11	15	1	5	13	17	7	-

	10	11	12	13	14	15	16	17	18	IN
BACK	471	366	216	389	360	345	204	452	387	3190
REGULAR	451	351	201	378	335	330	190	432	367	3035
par	5	4	3	4	4	4	3	4	4	35
handicap	18	14	6	4	10	16	12	2	8	-
FORWARD	440	300	180	325	325	260	175	350	340	2695
par	5	4	3	4	4	4	3	4	4	35
handicap	18	14	6	4	10	16	12	2	8	-

BACK	
yardage	6536
par	71
rating	70.8
slope	119

REGULAR	
yardage	6205
par	71
rating	68.6
slope	109

FORWARD	
yardage	5685
par	71
rating	72.0
slope	116

 ## MESQUITE GOLF & COUNTRY CLUB
ARCHITECT: BERT STAMPS, 1984

2700 East Mesquite
Palm Springs, CA 92264

PRO SHOP: 760-323-9377

Todd Connelly, Head Professional, PGA

Driving Range ●
Practice Greens ●
Clubhouse ●
Food / Beverage ●
Accommodations
Pull Carts
Power Carts ●
Club Rental ●
$pecial Offers

	1	2	3	4	5	6	7	8	9	OUT
BACK	516	220	526	187	370	334	487	170	374	3184
REGULAR	497	169	481	172	357	322	476	155	354	2983
par	5	3	5	3	4	4	5	3	4	36
handicap	5	3	1	13	11	15	17	9	7	-
FORWARD	480	140	346	141	344	295	458	141	327	2672
par	5	3	4	3	4	4	5	3	4	35
handicap	1	17	5	13	7	15	3	11	9	-

	10	11	12	13	14	15	16	17	18	IN
BACK	512	203	284	375	168	485	200	485	432	3144
REGULAR	470	189	278	360	150	467	174	454	419	2961
par	5	3	4	4	3	5	3	5	4	36
handicap	8	6	18	14	16	12	4	10	2	-
FORWARD	370	164	260	342	109	442	169	346	407	2609
par	4	3	4	4	3	5	3	4	5	35
handicap	2	14	16	12	18	8	6	10	4	-

BACK	
yardage	6328
par	72
rating	69.5
slope	122

REGULAR	
yardage	5944
par	72
rating	68.0
slope	118

FORWARD	
yardage	5281
par	70
rating	70.8
slope	120

11. CANYON SOUTH GOLF COURSE

PLAY POLICY & FEES: Green fees are $50 to $65 during peak season (January to April). Off-season rates (June through September) are $25 all day every day.

TEE TIMES: Reservations can be booked seven days in advance.

DRESS CODE: Collared shirts are required.

COURSE DESCRIPTION: Set in at the base of Indian Canyons, this is one of the most scenic and least windy courses in the area. It's a good test of golf with some tough par 3s.

NOTES: This facility now has a fully stocked pro shop.

LOCATION: Take the Highway 111 exit off Interstate 10 near Palm Springs and drive south on Palm Canyon Drive to Murray Canyon. Turn left and drive three blocks to the club.

. . . ● **TOURNAMENTS:** This course is available for outside tournaments. ●

TRAVEL: The Spa Hotel and Casino is recommended. Call 800-854-1279.

---

12. MESQUITE GOLF & COUNTRY CLUB

PLAY POLICY & FEES: From June 17 to October green fees are $45 every day, with twilight green fees of $25 starting after 4 p.m. In October green fees are $30 for nine holes and $40 for 18 holes. Only nine holes are open in October. From November through Christmas green fees are $65 Monday through Thursday and $75 Friday through Sunday. Twilight green fees are $40 Monday through Thursday, and $45 Friday through Sunday starting at 12:30 p.m.. From April until June green fees are $60 Monday through Thursday and $70 Friday through Sunday. Twilight green fees are $45.

TEE TIMES: Reservations can be booked seven days in advance. For tee times call 760-325-GOLF.

DRESS CODE: No cutoffs or tank tops are allowed on the course. Golfers must wear collared shirts. Nonmetal spikes are preferred.

COURSE DESCRIPTION: This is a flat course with beautiful mountain scenery. It is well bunkered, with eight small lakes and many palm trees. The course plays over and along a stream bed, so it's considerably tougher when the water flows.

NOTES: Mac O'Grady and Wayne Byrd share the course record of 62.

LOCATION: Take the Palm Drive exit off Interstate 10 and drive south to Ramon Road and turn west. At Farrell, turn south and drive to the course at Mesquite Avenue.

. . . ● **TOURNAMENTS:** A 16-player minimum is needed to book an event.

1001 South El Cielo Road
Palm Springs, CA 92264

PRO SHOP: 760-322-6062

Tommy Jacobs, Director of Golf, PGA
John Hulbert, Head Professional, PGA

Driving Range ●
Practice Greens ●
Clubhouse ●
Food / Beverage ●
Accommodations
Pull Carts ●
Power Carts
Club Rental ●
$pecial Offers

	1	2	3	4	5	6	7	8	9	OUT
BACK	262	103	145	125	182	185	176	288	302	1768
REGULAR	247	102	126	120	160	158	150	232	275	1570
par	4	3	3	3	4	4	3	4	4	32
handicap	3	7	6	5	8	9	2	4	1	-
FORWARD	207	83	116	104	147	128	145	212	255	1397
par	4	3	3	3	4	4	3	4	4	32
handicap	3	7	6	5	8	9	2	4	1	-

	10	11	12	13	14	15	16	17	18	IN
BACK	262	103	145	125	182	185	176	288	302	1768
REGULAR	247	102	126	120	160	158	150	232	275	1570
par	4	3	3	3	4	4	3	4	4	32
handicap	3	7	6	5	8	9	2	4	1	-
FORWARD	207	83	116	104	147	128	145	212	255	1397
par	4	3	3	3	4	4	3	4	4	32
handicap	3	7	6	5	8	9	2	4	1	-

BACK	
yardage	3536
par	64
rating	-
slope	-

REGULAR	
yardage	3140
par	64
rating	57.0
slope	92

FORWARD	
yardage	2794
par	64
rating	55.0
slope	88

⑭ TAHQUITZ CREEK GOLF RESORT
ARCHITECTS: WILLIAM F. BELL, 1959; TED ROBINSON, 1995

1885 Golf Club Drive
Palm Springs, CA 92264

PRO SHOP: 760-328-1005

Mike Reeder, Manager
Neil Finch, PGA Professional
Gerry Tarsitano, Superintendent

Driving Range ●
Practice Greens ●
Clubhouse ●
Food / Beverage ●
Accommodations ●
Pull Carts
Power Carts ●
Club Rental ●
$pecial Offers

	1	2	3	4	5	6	7	8	9	OUT
BACK	349	371	175	551	390	531	384	196	416	3363
REGULAR	330	356	152	519	367	503	361	167	392	3147
par	4	4	3	5	4	5	4	3	4	36
handicap	17	13	15	9	3	11	1	5	7	-
FORWARD	291	316	111	428	311	431	307	123	301	2619
par	4	4	3	5	4	5	4	3	4	36
handicap	15	7	17	11	3	13	1	5	9	-

	10	11	12	13	14	15	16	17	18	IN
BACK	404	362	317	179	562	400	411	130	577	3342
REGULAR	378	336	288	158	537	375	391	110	536	3109
par	4	4	4	3	5	4	4	3	5	36
handicap	2	12	18	16	6	8	4	14	10	-
FORWARD	312	278	236	109	474	311	331	81	455	2587
par	4	4	4	3	5	4	4	3	5	36
handicap	2	14	16	18	8	6	4	12	10	-

BACK	
yardage	6705
par	72
rating	71.4
slope	120

REGULAR	
yardage	6256
par	72
rating	69.2
slope	116

FORWARD	
yardage	5206
par	72
rating	70.0
slope	119

PLAY POLICY & FEES: Green fees are $9 any day from the end of May until October. From October through December green fees are $16 for nine holes and $26 for 18 holes. January through April 19 green fees are $19 for nine holes and $31 for 18 holes. From April 20 through May green fees are $16 for nine holes and $26 for 18 holes. Pull carts are $3.50.

TEE TIMES: Reservations can be booked 14 days in advance.

DRESS CODE: Shirts and shoes are necessary.

COURSE DESCRIPTION: This is a well-maintained nine-hole course with small, quick greens and narrow fairways. It is one of the most scenic courses in the desert with mature trees and a lot of water.

NOTES: This is truly a course for all ages. An 18-hole miniature golf course is part of the complex.

LOCATION: In Palm Springs, take Highway 111 (East Palm Canyon Drive) to Escoba Drive. Follow Escoba one-third mile to El Cielo and turn left. Go one-half mile to the course. The course is located one-half mile south of the Palm Springs Airport.

. . . ● **TOURNAMENTS:** Shotgun tournaments are available weekdays only.

13. TOMMY JACOBS' BEL AIR GREENS

PLAY POLICY & FEES: Green fees range from $25 to $90. Call for seasonal rates.

TEE TIMES: Reservations can be booked 30 days in advance.

DRESS CODE: Collared shirts and golf shoes are required.

COURSE DESCRIPTION: The Legend Course is a well-maintained, tree-lined course, providing some much-needed shade in the summer. Water comes into play on seven holes on the Resort Course. The seventh hole features an island fairway. If you miss the fairway right, left, short, or long, you will find yourself reaching in your bag for another ball.

NOTES: This public resort has 36 holes. Par is 72 on each 18-hole course. The Resort Course: See scorecard for yardage and rating information. The Legend Course is 6,660 yards and rated 71.0, with a slope of 117 from the back tees. It plays 6,422 yards from the regular tees, with a rating of 69.7 and a slope of 114. The forward tees play 6,077 and have a rating of 74.0 and a slope of 120.

LOCATION: From Interstate 10 near Palm Springs take the Date Palm Drive exit and drive south 4.5 miles to Ramon Road and turn left. Drive one-half mile to Crossley Road, turn right, and drive one mile to the club.

. . . ● **TOURNAMENTS:** A 16-player minimum is required to book a tournament. A banquet facility can accommodate up to 100 people.

14. TAHQUITZ CREEK GOLF RESORT

SUN CITY PALM DESERT
ARCHITECTS: BILLY CASPER, 1992; G. NASH

38180 Del Webb Boulevard
Bermuda Dunes, CA 92203

PRO SHOP: 760-772-2200

Robbie Powell, Director of Golf
Nancy Dickens, Superintendent

Driving Range •
Practice Greens •
Clubhouse •
Food / Beverage •
Accommodations
Pull Carts
Power Carts •
Club Rental •
$pecial Offers

	1	2	3	4	5	6	7	8	9	OUT
BACK	375	562	142	368	387	322	299	214	563	3232
REGULAR	352	516	132	336	353	274	263	193	518	2937
par	4	5	3	4	4	4	4	3	5	36
handicap	5	13	17	11	1	7	9	3	15	-
FORWARD	316	458	89	297	311	242	228	133	457	2531
par	4	5	3	4	4	4	4	3	5	36
handicap	7	3	17	9	5	13	11	15	1	-

	10	11	12	13	14	15	16	17	18	IN
BACK	427	378	173	526	448	366	203	516	451	3488
REGULAR	399	356	131	489	406	338	187	490	427	3225
par	4	4	3	5	4	4	3	5	4	36
handicap	4	6	10	12	8	16	14	18	2	-
FORWARD	340	309	97	439	369	304	105	448	363	2774
par	4	4	3	5	4	4	3	5	4	36
handicap	12	6	16	4	10	14	18	2	8	-

BACK	
yardage	6720
par	72
rating	73.0
slope	131

REGULAR	
yardage	6162
par	72
rating	70.0
slope	123

FORWARD	
yardage	5305
par	72
rating	70.3
slope	118

 ## BERMUDA DUNES COUNTRY CLUB
ARCHITECT: WILLIAM F. BELL, 1957

42-360 Adams Street
Bermuda Dunes, CA 92201

PRO SHOP: 760-345-2771

Greg VanNatta, Head Professional, PGA
Robert Durkee, Superintendent

Driving Range •
Practice Greens •
Clubhouse •
Food / Beverage •
Accommodations
Pull Carts
Power Carts •
Club Rental
$pecial Offers

	1	2	3	4	5	6	7	8	9	OUT
BACK	538	418	377	209	432	368	176	540	389	3447
REGULAR	507	399	354	192	401	353	164	520	344	3234
par	5	4	4	3	4	4	3	5	4	36
handicap	15	3	13	7	1	5	17	11	9	-
FORWARD	473	357	332	161	364	337	138	477	322	2961
par	5	4	4	3	4	4	3	5	4	36
handicap	7	11	13	15	5	3	17	1	9	-

	10	11	12	13	14	15	16	17	18	IN
BACK	414	382	160	564	385	399	451	212	513	3480
REGULAR	409	368	143	549	361	379	421	178	500	3308
par	4	4	3	5	4	4	4	5	4	37
handicap	4	12	18	8	10	6	2	16	14	-
FORWARD	398	354	129	461	345	366	416	169	482	3120
par	4	4	3	5	4	4	5	3	5	37
handicap	2	8	18	6	12	10	14	16	4	-

BACK	
yardage	6927
par	73
rating	73.5
slope	126

REGULAR	
yardage	6542
par	73
rating	70.8
slope	118

FORWARD	
yardage	6081
par	73
rating	75.0
slope	126

PLAY POLICY & FEES: Outside play is accepted. Green fees are $60 November and December, $90 January through March, $60 in April, and $30 May through September. The 18-hole course is closed in October. Players can play the new nine-hole course.

TEE TIMES: Call two days in advance Monday through Thursday for reservations and seven days in advance Friday through Sunday.

DRESS CODE: No denim is allowed on the course, and collared shirts are required.

COURSE DESCRIPTION: This spacious, mostly flat course features large greens and few elevation changes. Most holes are bordered by houses. Water comes into play on 11 holes, notably the 451-yard, par-4 18th, which usually plays into the wind.

NOTES: A new nine-hole course is due to open in the fall.

LOCATION: Take Interstate 10 southeast of Palm Springs to the Washington Street exit. Drive one-half mile to the course.

. . . ● **TOURNAMENTS:** A 16-player minimum is needed for tournament play.

15. SUN CITY PALM DESERT

PLAY POLICY & FEES: Members and guests only. Guest fees are $65 during the summer season and $80 during the winter. Carts are $24. The course is closed in October.

DRESS CODE: Appropriate golf attire and nonmetal spikes are required.

COURSE DESCRIPTION: This is not a typical desert course. It offers rolling hills with an assortment of trees guarding the fairways. There is some water. You can expect a lot of variation from hole to hole.

NOTES: Bermuda Dunes is one of the courses used in the Bob Hope Classic rotation. Par is 72 for each 18-hole combination. The One and Two Course: See scorecard for yardage and rating information. The One and Three Course is 6,716 yards and rated 72.2 from the championship tees, and 6,360 yards and rated 69.8 from the regular tees. The slope ratings are 123 championship and 115 regular. Forward tees are 5,857 yards and rated 74.0. The slope rating is 126. The Two and Three Course is 6,749 yards and rated 72.4 from the championship tees, and 6,434 yards and rated 70.1 from the regular tees. The slope ratings are 124 championship and 116 regular. Forward tees are 6,016 yards and rated 74.8. The slope rating is 127.

LOCATION: Southeast of Palm Springs take the Washington Street exit off Interstate 10 and drive south to Avenue 42. Turn left and drive one mile to the club.

. . . ● **TOURNAMENTS:** This course is not available for outside events.

16. BERMUDA DUNES COUNTRY CLUB

Palm Springs Area (map page 854)

CATHEDRAL CANYON COUNTRY CLUB
ARCHITECT: DAVID RAINVILLE, 1975

68311 Paseo Real
Cathedral City, CA 92234

PRO SHOP: 760-328-6571

Ray Miller, Manager
Terry Ferraro, PGA Professional
Tom Shephard, Superintendent

Driving Range ●
Practice Greens ●
Clubhouse ●
Food / Beverage ●
Accommodations
Pull Carts
Power Carts ●
Club Rental ●
$Special Offers

	1	2	3	4	5	6	7	8	9	OUT
BACK	552	366	374	156	508	385	328	349	179	3197
REGULAR	537	334	364	143	496	368	313	339	169	3063
par	5	4	4	3	5	4	4	4	3	36
handicap	2	7	1	9	3	4	8	5	6	-
FORWARD	493	290	314	114	461	331	286	298	125	2712
par	5	4	4	3	5	4	4	4	3	36
handicap	1	5	2	9	3	4	8	7	6	-

	10	11	12	13	14	15	16	17	18	IN
BACK	553	371	163	176	555	358	423	205	504	3308
REGULAR	526	362	150	157	523	340	393	170	488	3109
par	5	4	4	3	5	4	4	4	3	36
handicap	2	6	8	9	5	44	1	3	7	-
FORWARD	472	319	138	132	469	296	325	112	448	2711
par	5	4	3	3	5	4	4	3	5	36
handicap	3	6	8	9	2	4	1	7	5	-

BACK	
yardage	6505
par	72
rating	71.6
slope	128

REGULAR	
yardage	6172
par	72
rating	69.5
slope	117

FORWARD	
yardage	5423
par	72
rating	71.6
slope	127

 OUTDOOR RESORT & COUNTRY CLUB
ARCHITECT: KELLY JOHNSON, 1986

69-411 Ramon Road
Cathedral City, CA 92234

PRO SHOP: 760-324-4005
OFFICE: 760-328-3834

Ed Brock, General Manager

Driving Range
Practice Greens ●
Clubhouse ●
Food / Beverage ●
Accommodations
Pull Carts ●
Power Carts
Club Rental ●
$Special Offers

	1	2	3	4	5	6	7	8	9	OUT
BACK	-	-	-	-	-	-	-	-	-	-
REGULAR	94	145	100	140	116	127	74	76	60	932
par	3	3	3	3	3	3	3	3	3	27
handicap	9	3	11	1	7	5	15	13	17	-
FORWARD	92	146	96	95	115	130	79	86	60	899
par	3	3	3	3	3	3	3	3	3	27
handicap	7	3	11	1	9	5	15	13	17	-

	10	11	12	13	14	15	16	17	18	IN
BACK	-	-	-	-	-	-	-	-	-	-
REGULAR	60	70	97	100	139	121	102	74	106	869
par	3	3	3	3	3	3	3	3	3	27
handicap	12	16	8	10	2	4	14	18	6	-
FORWARD	82	75	93	100	105	125	107	75	110	872
par	3	3	3	3	3	3	3	3	3	27
handicap	12	16	8	10	2	4	14	18	6	-

BACK	
yardage	-
par	-
rating	-
slope	-

REGULAR	
yardage	1801
par	54
rating	-
slope	-

FORWARD	
yardage	1771
par	54
rating	-
slope	-

PLAY POLICY & FEES: Outside play is accepted. Green fees are $25 during the summer and $70 during peak season. Call for seasonal rates. Carts are included.
TEE TIMES: Reservations can be booked seven days in advance. call 760-328-6571.
DRESS CODE: Appropriate golf attire is required.
COURSE DESCRIPTION: These scenic, tree-lined courses are fairly tight and require a variety of shot-making skills. Refreshingl water comes into play on almost every hole.
NOTES: This facility has hosted several major California state tournaments. Par is 72 for each of the three 18-hole combinations. The Lake/Mountain Course: See scorecard for yardage and rating information. The Mountain/Arroyo Course is 6,477 yards and rated 70.9 from the championship tee with a slope of 119. Forward tees are 5,182 yards and rated 70.8. The slope rating is 124. The Lake/Arroyo Course is 6,021 yards and rated 68.5 from the regular tees with a slope of 110. Forward tees are 5,183 and rated 70.1. The slope rating is 124.
LOCATION: Take the Date Palm exit off Interstate 10 near Palm Springs. Drive south to Dinah Shore Drive and turn right. Drive one mile to Cathedral Canyon Drive and turn left. Continue one mile to the club.
. . . ● **TOURNAMENTS:** A 16-player minimum is required to book a regular tournament. Sixty players are required to book a shotgun tournament. Carts are required.

17. CATHEDRAL CANYON COUNTRY CLUB

PLAY POLICY & FEES: Members and guests only. The guest fee is $9 for nine holes and $18 for 18 holes.
DRESS CODE: Collared shirts are required.
COURSE DESCRIPTION: The par-3 course is very short with no hole over 145 yards. The greens are small and well protected.
NOTES: A skins game was held here with local pros, including Mac O'Grady and Mark Pfeil. The nine-hole course is par 27 and 561 yards. The course is unrated.
LOCATION: Take Interstate 10 to Date Palm Drive and go south to Ramon Road. Turn left and drive one-half mile to the resort.
. . . ● **TOURNAMENTS:** This course is not available for outside events.

18. OUTDOOR RESORT & COUNTRY CLUB

19 DATE PALM COUNTRY CLUB
ARCHITECT: TED ROBINSON, 1970

36-200 Date Palm Drive
Cathedral City, CA 92234

PRO SHOP: 760-328-1315

Jim Wheeler, Manager
Bobby Reyes, Superintendent
Vic Falo, Head Starter

Driving Range
Practice Greens ●
Clubhouse ●
Food / Beverage ●
Accommodations
Pull Carts ●
Power Carts ●
Club Rental ●
$pecial Offers

	1	2	3	4	5	6	7	8	9	OUT
BACK										
REGULAR										
par										
handicap										
FORWARD										
par										
handicap										

	10	11	12	13	14	15	16	17	18	IN
BACK										
REGULAR										
par										
handicap										
FORWARD										
par										
handicap										

BACK	
yardage	
par	
rating	
slope	

REGULAR	
yardage	3083
par	58
rating	54.9
slope	90

FORWARD	
yardage	2517
par	58
rating	57.2
slope	93

20 DESERT PRINCESS COUNTRY CLUB
ARCHITECT: DAVID RAINVILLE, 1985

28-555 Landau Boulevard
Cathedral City, CA 92234

PRO SHOP: 760-322-2280
CLUBHOUSE: 760-322-1655

Bob Breidenbach, Head Professional, PGA
Craig Hanson, Superintendent

Driving Range ●
Practice Greens ●
Clubhouse ●
Food / Beverage ●
Accommodations ●
Pull Carts
Power Carts ●
Club Rental ●
$pecial Offers ●

	1	2	3	4	5	6	7	8	9	OUT
BACK	567	386	155	370	418	359	161	517	409	3342
REGULAR	490	399	142	340	87	343	505	325	396	3027
par	5	4	3	4	3	4	5	4	4	36
handicap	3	1	7	2	9	6	4	8	5	-
FORWARD	465	373	130	289	74	297	453	280	363	2724
par	5	4	3	4	3	4	5	4	4	36
handicap	1	3	8	5	9	6	2	7	4	-

	10	11	12	13	14	15	16	17	18	IN
BACK	543	454	177	397	143	375	550	367	433	3439
REGULAR	510	345	120	321	377	297	116	452	347	2885
par	5	4	3	4	4	4	3	5	4	36
handicap	2	3	7	8	4	6	9	1	5	-
FORWARD	464	290	105	284	361	281	109	431	324	2649
par	5	4	3	4	4	4	3	5	4	36
handicap	1	3	8	7	4	6	9	2	5	-

BACK	
yardage	6781
par	72
rating	72.5
slope	126

REGULAR	
yardage	5912
par	72
rating	67.6
slope	114

FORWARD	
yardage	5373
par	72
rating	71.0
slope	119

PLAY POLICY & FEES: Reciprocal play is accepted with members of other private clubs. Outside play is also accepted. Green fees are seasonal and range from $20 to $40.

DRESS CODE: No tank tops are allowed on the course.

COURSE DESCRIPTION: This course is set in a retirement area, so it is quiet, private, and walkable. Seven lakes dot the course, and many trees line the fairways, including eucalyptus, olive, and pine trees—some are 300 years old. The 175-yard eighth hole is a standout. It takes an accurate tee shot over a beautiful lake. The green is guarded by trees on two sides. The course is closed for three weeks in late October.

LOCATION: Take the Date Palm Drive exit off Interstate 10 in Cathedral City and drive south for four miles to the club entrance on the left.

. . . ● **TOURNAMENTS:** This course is available for outside events.

19. DATE PALM COUNTRY CLUB

PLAY POLICY & FEES: Green fees are seasonal and range from $45 to $115. Call for current rates.

TEE TIMES: Reservations can be booked two days in advance.

DRESS CODE: Appropriate golf attire and nonmetal spikes are required.

COURSE DESCRIPTION: These courses are well maintained and mostly flat. Water comes into play on 17 holes. The Cielo Course is located in a wash and features six holes with a Scottish-links flair. The well-bunkered greens and bent grass make the course a challenge.

NOTES: Par is 72 for each 18-hole combination. The Vista/Cielo Course: See scorecard. The Cielo/Lagos Course is 6,587 yards from the back tees with a slope of 121. The Vista/Lagos Course has a slope of 123 and is 6,684 yards long from the back tees.

LOCATION: Take the Date Palm exit off Interstate 10 southeast of Palm Springs. Turn right and drive to Vista Chino. Turn right and drive to Landau Boulevard. Go left to the club.

. . . ● **TOURNAMENTS:** A 72-player minimum is needed to book a tournament. Events should be scheduled 12 months in advance. The banquet facility can accommodate 200 people. ● **$PECIAL OFFERS:** Play-and-stay packages are available with the Doral Hotel. For reservations call 800-637-0577.

20. DESERT PRINCESS COUNTRY CLUB

21 IVEY RANCH COUNTRY CLUB
ARCHITECT: WILLIAM F. BELL, 1985

74-580 Varner Road
Thousand Palms, CA
92276
PRO SHOP: 760-343-2013

Dennis Foster, Head Professional, PGA

Driving Range ●
Practice Greens ●
Clubhouse ●
Food / Beverage ●
Accommodations
Pull Carts
Power Carts ●
Club Rental ●
$pecial Offers

	1	2	3	4	5	6	7	8	9	OUT
BACK	-	-	-	-	-	-	-	-	-	-
REGULAR	327	149	211	246	338	132	502	346	440	2691
par	4	3	3	4	4	3	5	4	5	35
handicap	11	13	3	15	5	17	1	7	9	-
FORWARD	266	120	193	220	313	111	472	303	400	2398
par	4	3	3	4	4	3	5	4	5	35
handicap	11	13	3	15	5	17	1	7	9	-

	10	11	12	13	14	15	16	17	18	IN
BACK	-	-	-	-	-	-	-	-	-	-
REGULAR	327	149	211	246	338	132	502	346	440	2691
par	4	3	3	4	4	3	5	4	5	35
handicap	12	14	4	16	6	18	2	8	10	-
FORWARD	266	120	193	220	313	111	472	303	400	2398
par	4	3	3	4	4	3	5	4	5	35
handicap	12	14	4	16	6	18	2	8	10	-

BACK	
yardage	-
par	-
rating	-
slope	-

REGULAR	
yardage	5382
par	70
rating	68.0
slope	100

FORWARD	
yardage	4796
par	70
rating	64.0
slope	114

22 WESTIN MISSION HILLS: PETE DYE COURSE
ARCHITECT: PETE DYE, 1986

71-501 Dinah Shore Drive
Rancho Mirage, CA 92270

PRO SHOP: 760-328-3198

Alan Deck, Director of Golf, PGA
Randy Duncan, PGA Professional
Scott Tuggle, Superintendent

Driving Range ●
Practice Greens ●
Clubhouse ●
Food / Beverage ●
Accommodations ●
Pull Carts ●
Power Carts ●
Club Rental ●
$pecial Offers ●

	1	2	3	4	5	6	7	8	9	OUT
BACK										
REGULAR										
par										
handicap										
FORWARD										
par										
handicap										

	10	11	12	13	14	15	16	17	18	IN
BACK										
REGULAR										
par										
handicap										
FORWARD										
par										
handicap										

BACK	
yardage	6706
par	70
rating	73.5
slope	137

REGULAR	
yardage	6158
par	70
rating	70.3
slope	126

FORWARD	
yardage	4841
par	70
rating	67.4
slope	107

PLAY POLICY & FEES: Outside play is accepted. Green fees range from $15 to $35 depending on the season. Discounts are available. Call for rates.

TEE TIMES: Reservations can be booked seven days in advance.

DRESS CODE: Appropriate golf attire is required.

COURSE DESCRIPTION: This well-maintained course has bent-grass greens, strategically placed trees, and fairly narrow fairways. It's a regulation nine-hole course, with doglegs and out-of-bounds on several holes.

LOCATION: Take the Monterey Avenue exit off Interstate 10 near Thousand Palms and drive east to Varner Road. Turn north and take the frontage road 1.5 miles to the club.

. . . ● **TOURNAMENTS:** This course is available for outside tournaments. A 15-player minimum is needed. Tournaments can be booked one month in advance. The banquet facility can accommodate 150 people.

21. IVEY RANCH COUNTRY CLUB

PLAY POLICY & FEES: Guests of the Westin Mission Hills Resort have priority on tee times. Public play is welcome at the course. Green fees are seasonal and range from $35 to $175. Call for current rates.

TEE TIMES: Hotel guests can book times 90 days in advance; otherwise 30 days in advance.

DRESS CODE: Appropriate golf attire is required. Nonmetal spikes are recommended.

COURSE DESCRIPTION: This course is a links-style layout with rolling fairways and large, undulating greens. There are also numerous pot bunkers and railroad ties.

NOTES: The Pete Dye Course has recently replaced 18 greens with Tiff Dwarf Bermuda grass. It is the first course in the desert to use this new type of grass. This grass is heat resistant, less disease prone, faster, and better able to hold shots.

LOCATION: Take the Bob Hope Drive/Ramon Road exit off Interstate 10 southeast of Palm Springs and drive south on Bob Hope Drive to Dinah Shore Drive. Then turn right and drive one-half mile to the resort entrance.

. . . ● **TOURNAMENTS:** A 12-player minimum is required to book an event. An advance deposit is required. The banquet facility can accommodate 1000 people. ● **TRAVEL:** The Westin Mission Hills has 512 rooms. For reservations call 760-328-5955. ● **$PECIAL OFFERS:** Golf packages are available. The Westin is also home to a five-star tennis school.   ·

22. WESTIN MISSION HILLS: PETE DYE

WESTIN MISSION HILLS: GARY PLAYER COURSE
ARCHITECT: GARY PLAYER, 1991

70-705 Dinah Shore Drive
Rancho Mirage, CA 92270

PRO SHOP: 760-770-9496

Alan Deck, Director of Golf, PGA
Craig Freeman, PGA Professional
Scott Tuggle, Superintendent

Driving Range •
Practice Greens •
Clubhouse •
Food / Beverage •
Accommodations •
Pull Carts
Power Carts •
Club Rental •
$pecial Offers •

	1	2	3	4	5	6	7	8	9	OUT
BACK	423	403	513	428	160	371	510	156	429	3393
REGULAR	386	380	482	385	126	345	487	127	398	3116
par	4	4	5	4	3	4	5	3	4	36
handicap	3	11	7	5	17	15	9	13	1	-
FORWARD	281	306	372	290	101	278	428	80	351	2487
par	4	4	5	4	3	4	5	3	4	36
handicap	3	11	7	5	17	15	9	13	1	-

	10	11	12	13	14	15	16	17	18	IN
BACK	337	548	130	341	382	145	419	566	382	3250
REGULAR	292	471	111	298	357	130	384	539	346	2928
par	4	5	3	4	4	3	4	5	4	36
handicap	16	4	14	12	10	18	2	8	6	-
FORWARD	254	428	74	238	280	86	327	477	256	2420
par	4	5	3	4	4	3	4	5	4	36
handicap	16	4	14	12	10	18	2	8	6	-

BACK	
yardage	6643
par	72
rating	71.3
slope	124

REGULAR	
yardage	6044
par	72
rating	68.0
slope	114

FORWARD	
yardage	4907
par	72
rating	68.0
slope	118

 ## MISSION HILLS COUNTRY CLUB
ARCHITECT: DESMOND MUIRHEAD, 1970 (DS)

34-600 Mission Hills Drive
Rancho Mirage, CA 92270

PRO SHOP: 760-324-7336

Chipper Cecil, Director of Golf, PGA
Jeff Harrison, PGA Professional
Steve Jacobson, Tournament Director

Driving Range •
Practice Greens •
Clubhouse •
Food / Beverage •
Accommodations
Pull Carts
Power Carts •
Club Rental •
$pecial Offers

	1	2	3	4	5	6	7	8	9	OUT
BACK	406	418	512	166	413	517	174	372	434	3412
REGULAR	385	382	480	147	384	492	141	341	402	3154
par	4	4	5	3	4	5	3	4	4	36
handicap	9	7	13	17	3	11	15	5	1	-
FORWARD	306	337	423	123	367	436	119	298	376	2785
par	4	4	5	3	4	5	3	4	4	36
handicap	11	7	13	17	1	5	15	9	3	-

	10	11	12	13	14	15	16	17	18	IN
BACK	370	175	379	389	384	494	387	208	545	3331
REGULAR	354	152	346	367	369	481	324	167	457	3017
par	4	3	4	4	4	5	4	3	5	36
handicap	12	18	4	6	8	14	2	10	16	-
FORWARD	339	121	312	291	350	433	306	136	409	2697
par	4	3	4	4	4	5	4	3	5	36
handicap	14	18	4	10	8	6	2	16	12	-

BACK	
yardage	6743
par	72
rating	72.4
slope	126

REGULAR	
yardage	6171
par	72
rating	69.5
slope	119

FORWARD	
yardage	5482
par	72
rating	71.7
slope	123

PLAY POLICY & FEES: Guests of the Westin Mission Hills Resort have priority on tee times. Public play is welcome at the course. Green fees are seasonal and range from $35 to $175. Call for current rates.

TEE TIMES: Hotel guests can book times 90 days in advance; otherwise 30 days in advance.

DRESS CODE: Appropriate golf attire is required. Nonmetal spikes are recommended.

COURSE DESCRIPTION: This course features nine lakes and four waterfalls. It is as challenging as the Westin Mission Hills Pete Dye Course, but more forgiving on the greens.

LOCATION: Take the Bob Hope Drive/Ramon Road exit off Interstate 10 southeast of Palm Springs and drive west on Ramon Road for one mile to the club.

. . . ● **TOURNAMENTS:** Outside tournaments are available, requiring a 12-player minimum. An advance deposit is required. The banquet facility can accommodate 1000 people. ● **TRAVEL:** The Westin Mission Hills has 512 rooms. For reservations call 760-328-3198. ● **$PECIAL OFFERS:** Golf packages are available. The Westin is also home to a five-star tennis school.

23. WESTIN MISSION HILLS: GARY PLAYER

PLAY POLICY & FEES: Reciprocal play is accepted. Guest fees are seasonal and range from $35 to $115. Reciprocators' fees range from $70 to $215. Carts are included.

DRESS CODE: Appropriate golf attire and nonmetal spikes are required.

COURSE DESCRIPTION: The Arnold Palmer Course was designed by Arnie along with Ed Seay and opened in 1978. It's a links-style layout. It is a relatively flat course, heavily bunkered, and features Tiff Dwarf greens. It's immaculate. The Pete Dye Challenge Course, designed by Pete Dye, opened in 1988. It's a stadium-type course with big rolling hills and deep bunkers. The Tiff Eagle greens on this course are small but undulating. The rough and surrounding area are natural desert. The Dinah Shore Tournament Course has rolling terrain, mature trees, and undulating Bermuda greens.

NOTES: Mission Hills is the home of the LPGA Nabisco Dinah Shore Tournament and LPGA qualifying. Par is 72 on all three courses. The Arnold Palmer Course: See scorecard for yardage and rating Information. The Pete Dye Challenge Course is 6,065 yards from the regular tees. Forward tees are 5,079 yards. The Dinah Shore Tournament Course is 6,286 yards from the regular tees.

LOCATION: Take the Date Palm Drive/Cathedral City exit south off Interstate 10 and drive three miles to Dinah Shore Drive. Turn left and drive 1.5 miles to the club.

. . . ● **TOURNAMENTS:** This course is available for outside tournaments. Carts are required.

24. MISSION HILLS COUNTRY CLUB

25 RANCHO MIRAGE COUNTRY CLUB
ARCHITECT: HAROLD HEERS JR., 1984

38-500 Bob Hope Drive
Rancho Mirage, CA 92270

PRO SHOP: 760-324-4711
CLUBHOUSE: 760-328-1444

Bill Olds, General Manager
Eric Charos, PGA Professional
Pete Izadora, Superintendent

Driving Range ●
Practice Greens ●
Clubhouse ●
Food / Beverage ●
Accommodations
Pull Carts
Power Carts ●
Club Rental ●
$pecial Offers

	1	2	3	4	5	6	7	8	9	OUT
BACK	315	101	360	471	447	142	469	416	313	3034
REGULAR	300	91	346	471	412	133	451	388	306	2898
par	4	3	4	5	4	3	4	4	4	35
handicap	11	17	9	7	3	15	1	5	13	-
FORWARD	292	77	338	403	383	125	391	306	280	2595
par	4	3	4	5	4	3	4	4	4	35
handicap	13	17	9	7	3	15	1	5	11	-

	10	11	12	13	14	15	16	17	18	IN
BACK	385	401	418	176	336	123	364	485	389	3077
REGULAR	367	381	406	164	310	100	345	478	374	2925
par	4	4	4	3	4	3	4	5	4	35
handicap	10	6	2	14	12	18	16	8	4	-
FORWARD	355	356	389	145	299	79	324	432	335	2714
par	4	4	4	3	4	3	4	5	4	35
handicap	10	4	2	16	12	18	14	8	6	-

BACK	
yardage	6111
par	70
rating	69.5
slope	119

REGULAR	
yardage	5823
par	70
rating	67.7
slope	111

FORWARD	
yardage	5309
par	70
rating	70.6
slope	119

26 TAMARISK COUNTRY CLUB
ARCHITECT: WILLIAM P. BELL, 1952

70-240 Frank Sinatra Drive
Rancho Mirage, CA 92270

PRO SHOP: 760-328-2141

F. Cameron Janati, Manager
John Shelden, PGA Professional
Rick Sall, Superintendent

Driving Range ●
Practice Greens ●
Clubhouse ●
Food / Beverage ●
Accommodations
Pull Carts
Power Carts ◉
Club Rental
$pecial Offers

	1	2	3	4	5	6	7	8	9	OUT
BACK										
REGULAR										
par										
handicap										
FORWARD										
par										
handicap										

	10	11	12	13	14	15	16	17	18	IN
BACK										
REGULAR										
par										
handicap										
FORWARD										
par										
handicap										

BACK	
yardage	6881
par	72
rating	72.6
slope	123

REGULAR	
yardage	6555
par	72
rating	70.9
slope	119

FORWARD	
yardage	5940
par	72
rating	74.0
slope	125

PLAY POLICY & FEES: Public play is welcome. Reciprocal play is accepted with members of other private clubs. Green fees for guests range from $25 to $95. Carts are included. The course is closed during October.

TEE TIMES: Reservations for the public can be made three days in advance. Members can make tee times 14 days in advance.

DRESS CODE: Appropriate golf attire is required.

COURSE DESCRIPTION: This gently rolling course has narrow fairways and small greens. Water comes into play on nine holes. Centrally located in the valley, the course offers views of the Santa Rosa and San Jacinto Mountains. It's a good test for both the advanced and beginning golfer.

LOCATION: Take the Bob Hope Drive/Ramon Road exit off Interstate 10 southeast of Palm Springs. Head south on Bob Hope Drive and drive four miles to the club entrance on the left.

. . . ● **TOURNAMENTS:** This course is available for outside tournaments.

25. RANCHO MIRAGE COUNTRY CLUB

PLAY POLICY & FEES: Members and guests only. Green fees are $75 with a member and $100 if sponsored. Carts are $20. This course closes for part of the summer. Call ahead.

DRESS CODE: Appropriate golf attire is required.

COURSE DESCRIPTION: This is one of the Bob Hope Classic tournament courses and one of the oldest in the desert. It's a very challenging, mature course with lots of trees.

NOTES: The club's first golf pro was Ben Hogan.

LOCATION: Take the Bob Hope Drive/Ramon Road exit off Interstate 10 southeast of Palm Springs and drive south on Bob Hope Drive. Turn right on Frank Sinatra Drive and drive one mile to the club on the right.

. . . ● **TOURNAMENTS:** This course is not available for outside events.

26. TAMARISK COUNTRY CLUB

One Duke Drive
Rancho Mirage, CA 92270

PRO SHOP: 760-328-0590
CLUBHOUSE: 760-324-8292

Doug Hart, Professional
Mike Kocour, Superintendent

Driving Range ●
Practice Greens ●
Clubhouse ●
Food / Beverage ●
Accommodations
Pull Carts
Power Carts ●
Club Rental ●
$pecial Offers

	1	2	3	4	5	6	7	8	9	OUT
BACK	477	432	385	399	191	400	352	172	510	3318
REGULAR	474	409	378	380	174	372	335	133	479	3134
par	5	4	4	4	3	4	4	3	5	36
handicap	17	1	5	7	9	3	13	15	11	-
FORWARD	442	356	314	339	140	342	310	98	439	2780
par	5	4	4	4	3	4	4	3	5	36
handicap	5	1	11	3	17	9	13	15	7	-

	10	11	12	13	14	15	16	17	18	IN
BACK	420	484	170	384	359	218	354	375	555	3319
REGULAR	392	466	158	360	348	189	345	356	531	3145
par	4	5	3	4	4	3	4	4	5	36
handicap	2	18	16	4	14	12	8	6	10	-
FORWARD	371	414	102	329	304	175	313	334	485	2827
par	4	5	3	4	4	3	4	4	5	36
handicap	2	16	18	8	12	14	10	6	4	-

BACK	
yardage	6637
par	72
rating	72.3
slope	128

REGULAR	
yardage	6279
par	72
rating	70.1
slope	122

FORWARD	
yardage	5607
par	72
rating	72.5
slope	126

28 THE CLUB AT MORNINGSIDE
ARCHITECT: JACK NICKLAUS, 1982

Morningside Drive
Rancho Mirage, CA 92270

PRO SHOP: 760-321-1555
STARTER: 760-321-1556

Sterling Jarden, Manager
Vern Fraser, PGA Professional

Driving Range ●
Practice Greens ●
Clubhouse ●
Food / Beverage ●
Accommodations
Pull Carts
Power Carts ●
Club Rental ●
$pecial Offers

	1	2	3	4	5	6	7	8	9	OUT
BACK	363	492	158	354	382	406	180	486	362	3183
REGULAR	342	480	142	344	376	396	162	486	355	3083
par	4	5	3	4	4	4	3	5	4	36
handicap	13	5	17	7	1	3	15	9	11	-
FORWARD	327	421	129	291	327	356	138	419	343	2751
par	4	5	3	4	4	4	3	5	4	36
handicap	13	3	17	9	7	5	15	1	11	-

	10	11	12	13	14	15	16	17	18	IN
BACK	487	372	162	377	389	362	178	399	533	3259
REGULAR	475	346	156	369	379	350	166	393	523	3157
par	5	4	3	4	4	4	3	5	4	36
handicap	6	14	18	12	2	10	16	4	8	-
FORWARD	422	332	142	320	322	291	136	325	451	2741
par	5	4	3	4	4	4	3	5	4	36
handicap	2	10	18	8	6	14	16	12	4	-

BACK	
yardage	6442
par	72
rating	70.8
slope	122

REGULAR	
yardage	6240
par	72
rating	69.9
slope	120

FORWARD	
yardage	5492
par	72
rating	71.8
slope	124

18
HOLES

PLAY POLICY & FEES: Members and guests only. The guest fees are $25 June through October and $50 the rest of the year. Carts are $25.

DRESS CODE: Appropriate golf attire and nonmetal spikes are required.

COURSE DESCRIPTION: Water comes into play on 11 holes. The greens are well bunkered and undulating. The tree-lined fairways are well maintained.

LOCATION: Take the Bob Hope Drive/Ramon Road exit off Interstate 10 southeast of Palm Springs and drive south on Bob Hope Drive four miles to the club entrance on the right.

. . . ● **TOURNAMENTS:** This course is not available for outside events.

27. THE SPRINGS CLUB

18
HOLES

PLAY POLICY & FEES: Members and guests only. Green fees for guests are $75. Carts are $15 per person. The pro shop closes at 12:30 p.m. during summer season. The course is closed Monday and Tuesday from July through October.

TEE TIMES: Reservations can be booked seven days in advance.

DRESS CODE: Appropriate golf attire and nonmetal spikes are required.

COURSE DESCRIPTION: Jack Nicklaus designed this links-style course. It's immaculate and scenic. Almost every hole provides an option to gamble or play it safe. Contoured fairways, deep bunkers, and water make this a challenge from start to finish.

NOTES: A nine-hole practice course is scheduled to be finished at press time.

LOCATION: Take the Bob Hope Drive/Ramon Road exit off Interstate 10 southeast of Palm Springs and drive south on Bob Hope Drive. Turn right on Frank Sinatra Drive and travel one-half mile to Morningside Drive. Turn left and travel one-quarter mile to the club entrance on the right.

. . . ● **TOURNAMENTS:** This course is not available for outside events.

28. THE CLUB AT MORNINGSIDE

RANCHO LAS PALMAS COUNTRY CLUB
ARCHITECT: TED ROBINSON, 1976

42000 Bob Hope Drive
Rancho Mirage, CA 92270

PRO SHOP: 760-862-4551
CLUBHOUSE: 760-568-2727

John Faulk, Director of Golf
Mark Ophoven, Professional

Driving Range ●
Practice Greens ●
Clubhouse ●
Food / Beverage ●
Accommodations ●
Pull Carts
Power Carts ●
Club Rental ●
$pecial Offers

	1	2	3	4	5	6	7	8	9	OUT
BACK	510	350	330	143	502	327	332	120	390	3004
REGULAR	495	336	320	135	490	315	320	110	375	2896
par	5	4	4	3	5	4	4	3	4	36
handicap	1	5	7	8	2	6	4	9	3	-
FORWARD	444	322	291	124	453	275	284	96	371	2660
par	5	4	4	3	5	4	4	3	4	36
handicap	2	3	5	8	4	6	7	9	1	-

	10	11	12	13	14	15	16	17	18	IN
BACK	376	360	390	187	338	537	355	133	339	3015
REGULAR	349	342	360	154	321	517	334	124	319	2820
par	4	4	4	3	4	5	4	3	4	35
handicap	3	7	2	5	8	1	6	9	4	-
FORWARD	300	306	341	140	299	494	325	106	293	2604
par	4	4	4	3	4	5	4	3	4	35
handicap	3	7	6	8	4	2	5	9	1	-

BACK	
yardage	6019
par	71
rating	67.2
slope	115

REGULAR	
yardage	5716
par	71
rating	65.7
slope	103

FORWARD	
yardage	5264
par	71
rating	70.8
slope	118

 DESERT ISLAND GOLF & COUNTRY CLUB
ARCHITECT: DESMOND MUIRHEAD, 1972

71-777 Frank Sinatra Drive
Rancho Mirage, CA 92270

PRO SHOP: 760-328-0841
CLUBHOUSE: 760-328-2111

Carol Hogan, Head Professional
Dennis Callahan, General Manager, PGA
Jim Lindblad, Superintendent

Driving Range ●
Practice Greens ●
Clubhouse ●
Food / Beverage ●
Accommodations
Pull Carts
Power Carts ●
Club Rental ●
$pecial Offers

	1	2	3	4	5	6	7	8	9	OUT
BACK	342	388	371	368	197	559	494	166	400	3285
REGULAR	339	373	365	362	190	544	474	156	381	3184
par	4	4	4	4	3	5	5	3	4	36
handicap	15	5	11	7	9	1	13	17	3	-
FORWARD	313	335	306	316	142	498	399	114	337	2760
par	4	4	4	4	3	5	5	3	4	36
handicap	15	5	9	7	13	1	11	17	3	-

	10	11	12	13	14	15	16	17	18	IN
BACK	345	524	197	352	434	186	557	402	404	3401
REGULAR	335	502	184	339	372	164	525	342	363	3126
par	4	5	3	4	4	3	5	4	4	36
handicap	16	6	10	12	2	18	4	8/14	14/8	-
FORWARD	311	442	144	314	325	137	496	330	345	2844
par	4	5	3	4	4	3	5	4	4	36
handicap	12	4	16	10	8	18	2	14	6	-

BACK	
yardage	6686
par	72
rating	71.7
slope	123

REGULAR	
yardage	6310
par	72
rating	69.8
slope	118

FORWARD	
yardage	5604
par	72
rating	72.2
slope	120

PLAY POLICY & FEES: Reciprocal play is accepted with members of other private clubs. A Marriott hotel is affiliated with this course, and hotel guests are welcome. Guest fees range from $69 to $129, including carts.

TEE TIMES: Reservations are recommended seven days in advance, one day in advance for reciprocators.

DRESS CODE: Appropriate golf attire is required.

COURSE DESCRIPTION: The North nine is the longest and has the most hills. The South nine is the narrowest and threads through condominiums. The West nine is the shortest and most scenic. It also has the most water. Numerous palm trees are spread throughout this well-maintained course.

NOTES: This facility has 27 holes and par is 71, 69, or 70, depending on the 18-hole combination played. The North/South Course: See scorecard for yardage and rating information. The South/West Course is 5,569 yards and rated 65.6 from the championship tees with a slope of 106. Forward tees are 4,772 yards and rated 66.7 with a slope rating of 112. The West/North Course is 5,558 yards and rated 65.3 from the championship tees with a slope rating of 105. Forward tees are 4,828 yards and rated 67.0. The slope rating is 112.

LOCATION: Take the Bob Hope/Ramon Road exit off Interstate 10 southeast of Palm Springs and drive five miles south to the resort entrance on the left.

. . . ● **TOURNAMENTS:** This course is available for outside tournaments. ●
TRAVEL: Rancho Las Palmas is affiliated with a local Marriot hotel. Call the pro shop for more information.

29. RANCHO LAS PALMAS COUNTRY CLUB

PLAY POLICY & FEES: Members and guests only. Guest fees in season are $75 with a member and $125 without a member. Guest fees out of season (June to October) are $65 with a member and $80 without a member. Carts are included. The course is closed in October. Reservations are recommended.

DRESS CODE: A dress code is strictly enforced. Nonmetal spikes are required.

COURSE DESCRIPTION: This well-maintained course is set around an enormous lake with an island in the middle; condominiums are on the island. It is challenging, with narrow fairways and numerous bunkers surrounding the greens. This course also offers panoramic views of the mountains.

LOCATION: Take the Bob Hope Drive/Ramon Road exit off Interstate 10 southeast of Palm Springs and drive south on Bob Hope Drive to Frank Sinatra Drive. Turn right and drive one block to the entrance on the left.

. . . ● **TOURNAMENTS:** This course is not available for outside events.

30. DESERT ISLAND GOLF & COUNTRY CLUB

THUNDERBIRD COUNTRY CLUB

ARCHITECTS: JOHNNY DAWSON, 1952; TED ROBINSON, 1982

70-612 Highway 111
Rancho Mirage, CA 92270

PRO SHOP: 760-328-2161

Don Callahan, PGA Professional

Driving Range ●
Practice Greens ●
Clubhouse ●
Food / Beverage ●
Accommodations ●
Pull Carts
Power Carts ●
Club Rental
$pecial Offers

	1	2	3	4	5	6	7	8	9	OUT
BACK										
REGULAR										
par										
handicap										
FORWARD										
par										
handicap										

BACK	
yardage	6460
par	71
rating	71.5
slope	126

REGULAR	
yardage	6185
par	71
rating	69.6
slope	119

	10	11	12	13	14	15	16	17	18	IN
BACK										
REGULAR										
par										
handicap										
FORWARD										
par										
handicap										

FORWARD	
yardage	5854
par	71
rating	73.9
slope	124

 SUNRISE COUNTRY CLUB

ARCHITECT: TED ROBINSON, 1971

71-601 Country Club Drive
Rancho Mirage, CA 92270

PRO SHOP: 760-328-1139
CLUBHOUSE: 760-328-6549

Chris Hudson, PGA Professional
John Hernandez, Superintendent

Driving Range ●
Practice Greens ●
Clubhouse ●
Food / Beverage ●
Accommodations
Pull Carts
Power Carts ●
Club Rental ●
$pecial Offers

	1	2	3	4	5	6	7	8	9	OUT
BACK	-	-	-	-	-	-	-	-	-	-
REGULAR	252	116	253	299	235	147	295	123	291	2011
par	4	3	4	4	4	3	4	3	4	33
handicap	9	17	7	1	13	11	3	15	5	-
FORWARD	252	116	253	299	235	147	295	123	291	2011
par	4	3	4	4	4	3	4	3	4	33
handicap	9	17	7	1	13	11	3	15	5	-

BACK	
yardage	-
par	-
rating	
slope	

REGULAR	
yardage	3837
par	64
rating	57.3
slope	95

	10	11	12	13	14	15	16	17	18	IN
BACK	-	-	-	-	-	-	-	-	-	-
REGULAR	204	135	139	263	260	120	295	140	270	1826
par	3	3	3	4	4	3	4	3	4	31
handicap	4	14	16	10	2	18	6	12	8	-
FORWARD	204	135	139	263	260	120	295	140	270	1826
par	3	3	3	4	4	3	4	3	4	31
handicap	4	14	16	10	2	18	6	12	8	-

FORWARD	
yardage	3837
par	64
rating	61.3
slope	101

PLAY POLICY & FEES: Members and guests only. Guests must be accompanied by a member at time of play. Green fees for guests are $45 from June to October and $90 the rest of the year. Carts are $30.

DRESS CODE: Appropriate golf attire and nonmetal spikes are required.

COURSE DESCRIPTION: This is one of the very first and most exclusive courses in the area. It is the home course of former President Gerald Ford. Water, bunkers, and palm trees make this mostly flat, narrow course an interesting challenge.

LOCATION: Take the Bob Hope Drive/Ramon exit off Interstate 10 southeast of Palm Springs and drive south on Bob Hope Drive. Turn right on Country Club Drive and travel 1.5 miles to the club entrance on the left.

. . . ● **TOURNAMENTS:** This course is not available for outside events.

31. THUNDERBIRD COUNTRY CLUB

PLAY POLICY & FEES: Reciprocal play is accepted with members of other private clubs; otherwise, members and guests only. Green fees are $40 for guests and $50 for reciprocators. Carts are $10 per player any time. Reservations are recommended. Summer hours are June 1 through October 1, 6 a.m. to 1 p.m.

DRESS CODE: Appropriate golf attire and nonmetal spikes are required.

COURSE DESCRIPTION: This is a mature, 18-hole executive course with water and lots of sand. It boasts 10 par 4s and eight par 3s. If you drive the ball 180 to 190 yards and want to use every club in your bag, this is the course for you.

LOCATION: Take the Bob Hope Drive/Ramon Road exit off Interstate 10 southeast of Palm Springs and drive about six miles south on Bob Hope Drive. Turn right on Country Club Drive and travel several yards to the entrance on the left.

. . . ● **TOURNAMENTS:** This course is not available for outside events.

32. SUNRISE COUNTRY CLUB

PALM DESERT GREENS COUNTRY CLUB

ARCHITECT: TED ROBINSON, 1971

73-750 Country Club Drive
Palm Desert, CA 92260

PRO SHOP: 760-346-2941

Joseph Casey, PGA Professional

Driving Range
Practice Greens •
Clubhouse •
Food / Beverage •
Accommodations
Pull Carts •
Power Carts •
Club Rental •
$pecial Offers

	1	2	3	4	5	6	7	8	9	OUT
BACK										
REGULAR	287	323	216	158	208	188	122	270	254	2026
par	4	4	3	3	3	3	3	4	4	31
handicap	13	5	1	9	3	7	17	15	11	
FORWARD	267	295	176	130	184	124	115	244	231	1766
par	4	4	3	3	3	3	3	4	4	31
handicap	4	2	12	14	10	16	18	8	6	

	10	11	12	13	14	15	16	17	18	IN
BACK										
REGULAR	282	158	190	262	155	347	254	154	251	2053
par	4	3	3	4	3	4	4	3	4	32
handicap	12	6	4	16	8	2	14	10	18	
FORWARD	250	150	176	249	140	327	238	144	241	1915
par	4	3	3	4	3	4	4	3	4	32
handicap	3	15	11	7	13	1	9	17	5	

BACK	
yardage	
par	63
rating	
slope	

REGULAR	
yardage	4079
par	63
rating	58.5
slope	90

FORWARD	
yardage	3681
par	63
rating	59.6
slope	95

 DESERT FALLS COUNTRY CLUB

ARCHITECT: RON FREAM, 1984

1111 Desert Falls Parkway
Palm Desert, CA 92211

PRO SHOP: 760-340-4653
CLUBHOUSE: 760-340-5646

Jack Deal, Manager
Trent Traylor, PGA Professional
Mike Ritchie, Tournament Director

Driving Range •
Practice Greens •
Clubhouse •
Food / Beverage •
Accommodations
Pull Carts
Power Carts •
Club Rental •
$pecial Offers

	1	2	3	4	5	6	7	8	9	OUT
BACK	349	393	163	458	361	197	304	417	521	3163
REGULAR	328	382	154	430	336	185	290	401	497	3003
par	4	4	3	5	4	3	4	4	5	36
handicap	6	8	16	14	2	12	18	4	10	-
FORWARD	302	318	101	415	290	164	235	348	445	2618
par	4	4	3	5	4	3	4	4	5	36
handicap	6	8	16	14	2	12	18	4	10	-

	10	11	12	13	14	15	16	17	18	IN
BACK	387	494	130	397	204	523	382	437	438	3392
REGULAR	375	464	110	382	170	501	357	405	407	3171
par	4	5	3	4	3	5	4	4	4	36
handicap	9	15	17	11	13	3	5	7	1	-
FORWARD	334	416	72	346	132	420	286	356	333	2695
par	4	5	3	4	3	5	4	4	4	36
handicap	9	15	17	11	13	3	5	7	1	-

BACK	
yardage	6555
par	72
rating	71.3
slope	128

REGULAR	
yardage	6174
par	72
rating	69.3
slope	121

FORWARD	
yardage	5313
par	72
rating	71.7
slope	124

PLAY POLICY & FEES: Members and guests only. Guests must be accompanied by members at time of play. Guest fees are seasonal and range from $15 to $30. The course is closed in October. Carts are $16.

DRESS CODE: Golf attire and nonmetal spikes are mandatory.

COURSE DESCRIPTION: This 18-hole executive course is flat with several lakes and mature trees. It's a fun layout and usually in great shape.

LOCATION: Take the Monterey Avenue exit off Interstate 10 southeast of Palm Springs and drive south to Country Club Drive. Turn left to the club entrance.

. . . ● **TOURNAMENTS:** This course is not available for outside events.

33. PALM DESERT GREENS COUNTRY CLUB

PLAY POLICY & FEES: Outside play is accepted. Green fees are seasonal, ranging from $30 during the off-season (summer) to $180 during the high season (winter). Call for rates. Carts are included. Reservations are recommended. This course is closed in October.

TEE TIMES: Reservations can be booked three days in advance.

DRESS CODE: Collared shirts are required. No jeans are allowed on the course.

COURSE DESCRIPTION: This course will truly test your golf skills. It is long and one of the few desert courses with a Scottish-style layout. The greens sport Tiff Dwarf Bermuda grass and are big enough to play football on. The 14th green is 18,000 square feet. It is one of the best tracks in the Coachella Valley.

NOTES: This course has served as a Stage I PGA Tour qualifying site.

LOCATION: Take the Cook Street exit off Interstate 10 southeast of Palm Springs and drive south to Country Club Drive. Turn left and travel one-half mile to the club.

. . . ● **TOURNAMENTS:** Carts are required. A 24-player minimum is required to book a tournament.

34. DESERT FALLS COUNTRY CLUB

SANTA ROSA COUNTRY CLUB
ARCHITECT: LEONARD GERKIN, 1978

38-105 Portola Avenue
Palm Desert, CA 92260

PRO SHOP: 760-568-5717
OFFICE: 760-568-5707

Rick Downes, PGA Professional
Kimberly Sandmann, General Manager
Lupe Franco, Superintendent

Driving Range ●
Practice Greens ●
Clubhouse ●
Food / Beverage ●
Accommodations
Pull Carts
Power Carts ●
Club Rental ●
$pecial Offers

	1	2	3	4	5	6	7	8	9	OUT
BACK	-	-	-	-	-	-	-	-	-	-
REGULAR	403	310	160	367	179	512	287	181	371	2770
par	4	4	3	4	3	5	4	3	4	34
handicap	3	5	13	9	17	1	15	11	7	-
FORWARD	403	299	148	345	155	493	272	169	349	2633
par	5	4	3	4	3	5	4	3	4	35
handicap	9	5	15	7	17	1	11	13	3	-

	10	11	12	13	14	15	16	17	18	IN
BACK	-	-	-	-	-	-	-	-	-	-
REGULAR	358	200	390	159	177	491	371	161	366	2673
par	4	3	4	3	3	5	4	3	4	33
handicap	6	8	2	16	14	12	10	18	4	-
FORWARD	341	174	369	152	168	470	357	143	354	2528
par	4	3	4	3	3	5	4	3	4	33
handicap	8	12	2	16	14	6	10	18	4	-

BACK	
yardage	-
par	-
rating	-
slope	-

REGULAR	
yardage	5443
par	67
rating	65.6
slope	103

FORWARD	
yardage	5161
par	68
rating	70.2
slope	119

 AVONDALE GOLF CLUB
ARCHITECT: JIMMY HINES, 1969

75-800 Avondale Drive
Palm Desert, CA 92260

PRO SHOP: 760-345-3712
CLUBHOUSE: 760-345-2727

Fred Scherzer, PGA Professional
Mike Tellier, Superintendent

Driving Range ●
Practice Greens ●
Clubhouse ●
Food / Beverage ●
Accommodations
Pull Carts
Power Carts ●
Club Rental ●
$pecial Offers

	1	2	3	4	5	6	7	8	9	OUT
BACK	545	370	225	350	370	406	381	201	542	3390
REGULAR	529	349	206	330	356	389	363	158	516	3196
par	5	4	3	4	4	4	4	3	5	36
handicap	7	11	9	17	5	1	13	15	3	-
FORWARD	493	330	188	314	342	311	319	144	447	2888
par	5	4	3	4	4	4	4	3	5	36
handicap	4	10	16	8	6	12	14	18	2	-

	10	11	12	13	14	15	16	17	18	IN
BACK	391	407	341	217	483	174	415	415	549	3392
REGULAR	343	396	329	199	466	156	399	384	532	3204
par	4	4	4	3	5	3	4	4	5	36
handicap	6	2	14	12	16	18	8	4	10	-
FORWARD	303	321	312	176	432	145	374	369	461	2893
par	4	4	4	3	5	3	4	4	5	36
handicap	1	11	13	15	9	17	7	5	3	-

BACK	
yardage	6782
par	72
rating	72.4
slope	127

REGULAR	
yardage	6400
par	72
rating	70.5
slope	122

FORWARD	
yardage	5781
par	72
rating	74.7
slope	125

18
HOLES

PLAY POLICY & FEES: Reciprocal play is accepted with members of other private clubs; otherwise, members and guests only. Guest fees are $15 in summer and $35 the rest of the year. Reciprocal fees are $60. Carts are $20 and mandatory for guests.

TEE TIMES: Guest reservations are recommended one day in advance.

DRESS CODE: Appropriate golf attire and nonmetal spikes are required.

COURSE DESCRIPTION: This desert course has tree-lined fairways and two large lakes. It's challenging and offers a view of the Santa Rosa Mountains. Adding new tees is the latest step in a program to upgrade the course. A rarity in the desert, this course consists of 80 acres of golf course and clubhouse—no homes are built on or around it.

LOCATION: Take the Monterey Avenue exit off Interstate 10 southeast of Palm Springs and drive south to Gerald Ford Drive. Turn left on Portola and right on Frank Sinatra Drive. The course is on the right.

. . . ● **TOURNAMENTS:** This course is available for outside events during the off season—May through September. A 12-player minimum is required. Tournaments can be booked three months in advance. The banquet facility can hold 100 people. ● **TRAVEL:** The Holiday Inn Express is recommended for lodging. Call 760-340-4303 for reservations.

35. SANTA ROSA COUNTRY CLUB

18
HOLES

PLAY POLICY & FEES: Members and guests only. Guest fees are $32 June 1 through mid-September, and $77 November 1 through May 31. Carts are included. The course is closed from mid-September to early November.

DRESS CODE: Collared shirts and nonmetal spikes are required.

COURSE DESCRIPTION: This is not a typical desert course. There are water hazards and lots of trees dispersed on rolling terrain.

LOCATION: Take the Washington Street exit off Interstate 10 southeast of Palm Springs and drive south. Turn right on Country Club Drive and travel 2.5 miles to El Dorado. Turn right to the course.

. . . ● **TOURNAMENTS:** Outside events must have board approval.

36. AVONDALE GOLF CLUB

SUNCREST COUNTRY CLUB
ARCHITECT: RICHARD WATSON, 1980

73-450 Country Club Drive
Palm Desert, CA 92260

PRO SHOP: 760-340-2467
STARTER: 760-340-2467

Peggy Mayo, LPGA Professional
Juan Martinez, Superintendent
Tina Wassenmiller, Banquet Manager

Driving Range ●
Practice Greens ●
Clubhouse ●
Food / Beverage ●
Accommodations
Pull Carts ●
Power Carts ●
Club Rental ●
$pecial Offers

	1	2	3	4	5	6	7	8	9	OUT
BACK	375	166	337	118	336	178	451	150	362	2473
REGULAR	350	144	303	101	311	141	436	122	342	2250
par	4	3	4	3	4	3	5	3	4	33
handicap	1	15	7	17	13	5	11	9	3	-
FORWARD	301	121	271	94	269	105	408	88	291	1948
par	4	3	4	3	4	3	5	3	4	33
handicap	1	15	7	17	13	5	11	9	3	-

	10	11	12	13	14	15	16	17	18	IN
BACK	375	166	337	118	336	178	451	150	362	2473
REGULAR	350	144	303	101	311	141	436	122	342	2250
par	4	3	4	3	4	3	5	3	4	33
handicap	2	16	8	18	14	6	12	10	4	-
FORWARD	301	121	271	94	269	105	408	88	291	1948
par	4	3	4	3	4	3	5	3	4	33
handicap	2	16	8	18	14	6	12	10	4	-

BACK	
yardage	4946
par	66
rating	62.3
slope	101

REGULAR	
yardage	4500
par	66
rating	60.6
slope	98

FORWARD	
yardage	3896
par	66
rating	-
slope	-

 PALM VALLEY COUNTRY CLUB
ARCHITECT: T. ROBINSON, 1984 (S), 1986 (N)

76-200 Country Club Drive
Palm Desert, CA 92260

PRO SHOP: 760-345-2742

Malia Folquet, PGA, LPGA Professional
Brian Riek, Superintendent

Driving Range ●
Practice Greens ●
Clubhouse ●
Food / Beverage ●
Accommodations
Pull Carts ●
Power Carts ●
Club Rental ●
$pecial Offers

	1	2	3	4	5	6	7	8	9	OUT
BACK	365	390	501	384	151	394	204	518	372	3279
REGULAR	344	363	480	364	129	368	176	501	357	3082
par	4	4	5	4	3	4	3	5	4	36
handicap	7	15	3	5	17	1	9	11	13	-
FORWARD	303	312	442	327	115	326	131	431	307	2694
par	4	4	5	4	3	4	3	5	4	36
handicap	7	15	1	9	17	3	13	5	11	-

	10	11	12	13	14	15	16	17	18	IN
BACK	402	356	149	390	538	504	358	147	422	3266
REGULAR	372	340	134	376	520	491	344	138	394	3109
par	4	4	3	4	5	5	4	3	4	36
handicap	2	8	16	6	12	14	10	18	4	-
FORWARD	304	277	119	301	456	440	319	107	306	2629
par	4	4	3	4	5	5	4	3	4	36
handicap	4	2	12	16	14	10	8	18	6	-

BACK	
yardage	6545
par	72
rating	70.9
slope	120

REGULAR	
yardage	6191
par	72
rating	68.9
slope	117

FORWARD	
yardage	5323
par	72
rating	71.8
slope	127

PLAY POLICY & FEES: Green fees are $20 for nine holes, $30 for 18 holes. Carts are $12 for nine holes and $20 for 18 holes. Reservations are recommended. The course is closed during September and October.

TEE TIMES: Reservations can be booked three days in advance.

DRESS CODE: No tank tops or short shorts are allowed on the course.

COURSE DESCRIPTION: Set in Suncrest Park, this nicely maintained course is flat, with trees and two lakes. The course is elevated and provides a nice view.

NOTES: The course record is 57.

LOCATION: Take the Monterey Avenue exit off Interstate 10 southeast of Palm Springs and drive south to Country Club Drive. Turn left and travel one-half mile to the club on the left.

. . . ● **TOURNAMENTS:** A 20-player minimum is required to book a tournament. Events should be scheduled one month in advance. The banquet facility can accommodate 140 people. ● **TRAVEL:** The Desert Springs Marriot is located one mile from the golf course. For reservations call 760-341-2211. Deep Canyon Inn (760-346-8061) and Rancho Las Palmas Marriott (760-568-2727) are also recommended.

37. SUNCREST COUNTRY CLUB

PLAY POLICY & FEES: Reciprocal play is accepted for the Challenge Course only. The Championship Course is for members and guest only. During the summer, guest fees are $55 for the Championship Course and $38 for the Challenge Course. During the peak winter season, fees are $110 for the Championship Course and $60 for the Challenge Course. Carts are included.

DRESS CODE: Appropriate golf attire and nonmetal spikes are required.

COURSE DESCRIPTION: The Championship Course has surprising undulation for a desert course and offers beautiful panoramic views of the area. The Challenge Course is a difficult short course with water hazards coming into play on 15 holes. It's a tough challenge for mid- to low-handicap players.

NOTES: The par-63 Challenge Course is 4,232 yards and rated 58.0 from the championship tees, and 3,909 yards and rated 56.2 from the regular tees. The slope ratings are 96 championship and 93 regular. Forward tees are 3,467 yards and rated 61.0. The slope rating is 99. The Championship Course: See Scorecard for more information.

LOCATION: Take the Washington Street exit off Interstate 10 southeast of Palm Springs and drive south to Country Club Drive. Turn right and travel one mile to the club on the right.

. . . ● **TOURNAMENTS:** This course is available for outside tournaments on Monday from November to May. Off-season outside tournaments can be booked Monday through Friday.

38. PALM VALLEY COUNTRY CLUB

DESERT WILLOW GOLF RESORT
ARCHITECTS: DR. MICHAEL HURDZAN ; DANA FRY; JOHN COOK, 1997

GOLF 50

P.O. Box 14062
Palm Desert, CA 92255

38-500 Portola Avenue
Palm Desert, CA 92260

PRO SHOP: 760-346-7060
OFFICE: 760-346-0015

Rodney Young, Head Professional, PGA

Driving Range ●
Practice Greens ●
Clubhouse ●
Food / Beverage ●
Accommodations
Pull Carts
Power Carts ●
Club Rental ●
$pecial Offers

	1	2	3	4	5	6	7	8	9	OUT
BACK	535	410	194	446	429	331	569	155	455	3524
REGULAR	489	364	139	387	380	279	520	119	408	3085
par	5	4	3	4	4	4	5	3	4	36
handicap	12	10	18	2	8	14	4	16	6	-
FORWARD	417	312	107	313	304	233	465	82	323	2556
par	5	4	3	4	4	4	5	3	4	36
handicap	14	12	16	4	8	10	2	18	6	-

	10	11	12	13	14	15	16	17	18	IN
BACK	435	452	427	550	176	332	420	204	536	3532
REGULAR	393	396	371	502	141	279	368	170	468	3088
par	4	4	4	5	3	4	4	3	5	36
handicap	5	1	9	13	15	17	3	7	11	-
FORWARD	323	329	311	425	97	227	297	129	385	2523
par	4	4	4	5	3	4	4	3	5	36
handicap	5	1	13	9	15	17	3	11	7	-

BACK	
yardage	7056
par	72
rating	73.9
slope	131

REGULAR	
yardage	6173
par	72
rating	69.5
slope	122

FORWARD	
yardage	5079
par	72
rating	69.0
slope	120

CHAPARRAL COUNTRY CLUB
ARCHITECT: TED ROBINSON, 1979

100 Chaparral Drive
Palm Desert, CA 92260

PRO SHOP: 760-340-1501
CLUBHOUSE: 760-340-1893

Mike O'Shea, Manager, PGA
David M. James, Director of Golf, PGA
Mike Jensen, Superintendent

Driving Range ●
Practice Greens ●
Clubhouse ●
Food / Beverage ●
Accommodations
Pull Carts
Power Carts ●
Club Rental ●
$pecial Offers

	1	2	3	4	5	6	7	8	9	OUT
BACK	309	152	188	195	320	215	315	149	201	2044
REGULAR	290	147	178	182	313	211	305	142	165	1933
par	4	3	3	3	4	3	4	3	3	30
handicap	15	13	11	9	1	3	7	17	5	-
FORWARD	274	139	159	159	313	215	229	85	104	1677
par	4	3	3	3	4	4	4	3	3	31
handicap	3	13	7	9	1	11	5	17	15	-

	10	11	12	13	14	15	16	17	18	IN
BACK	203	275	212	278	204	275	129	115	181	1872
REGULAR	198	248	183	272	197	260	111	100	162	1731
par	3	4	3	4	3	4	3	3	3	30
handicap	4	14	6	10	2	8	16	18	12	-
FORWARD	115	159	120	272	150	260	95	100	155	1426
par	3	3	3	4	3	4	3	3	3	29
handicap	14	6	12	4	8	2	16	18	10	-

BACK	
yardage	3916
par	60
rating	59.0
slope	94

REGULAR	
yardage	3664
par	60
rating	57.9
slope	90

FORWARD	
yardage	3103
par	60
rating	56.8
slope	90

PLAY POLICY & FEES: Off-season green fees are $50 weekdays and $60 weekends and holidays. In-season, October through December, green fees are $120 weekdays and $145 on weekends. From December through April green fees are $130 weekdays and $145 on weekends. Carts are included. Twilight and junior rates are available.

TEE TIMES: Reservations can be booked 14 days in advance.

DRESS CODE: Appropriate golf attire is required.

COURSE DESCRIPTION: Showcasing a painstaking commitment to the preservation of the native desert surroundings, this beautiful course rewards those who stay in the fairway. When you miss the fairway, you're liable to find yourself in the most common obstacle found in the desert, sand. With five sets of tees, there is plenty of room for golfers of all levels.

LOCATION: From Interstate 10 near Palm Desert take the Monterey exit. Take a right on Monterey and continue to Frank Sinatra Drive. Turn left on Frank Sinatra Drive and then right on Portola Drive. The course is a quarter of a mile on the left.

. . . ● **TOURNAMENTS:** A 12-player minimum is needed to book a tournament. Tournaments may be booked 12 months in advance. ● **TRAVEL:** The Marriot Desert Springs Resort is located across the street. For reservations call 760-341-2211.

39. DESERT WILLOW GOLF RESORT

PLAY POLICY & FEES: Reciprocal play is not accepted. Guest fees range from $35 to $65. The course is closed in October.

DRESS CODE: Appropriate golf attire is required.

COURSE DESCRIPTION: Known as the "Little Monster," this tough executive course is well bunkered with water on 13 holes. It's a shot-maker's course.

NOTES: The men's course record is 52, held by Jim Fairfield. The women's course record is 55, held by Shelly Rule.

LOCATION: Take the Monterey Drive exit off Interstate 10 near Palm Desert and drive south to Country Club Drive. Turn left and drive to Portola Road; then turn right and drive 1.5 miles to the club.

. . . ● **TOURNAMENTS:** This course is not available for outside events.

40. CHAPARRAL COUNTRY CLUB

THE LAKES COUNTRY CLUB
ARCHITECT: TED ROBINSON, 1982

161 Old Ranch Road
Palm Desert, CA 92211

PRO SHOP: 760-568-4321
CLUBHOUSE: 760-568-4321

Buzz Radoff, Manager
Mike Clifford, Director of Golf, PGA
Mike Donahue

Driving Range ●
Practice Greens ●
Clubhouse ●
Food / Beverage ●
Accommodations
Pull Carts
Power Carts ●
Club Rental ●
Special Offers

	1	2	3	4	5	6	7	8	9	OUT
BACK	522	376	365	172	348	365	504	438	155	3245
REGULAR	502	359	347	147	324	341	486	404	135	3045
par	5	4	4	3	4	4	5	4	3	36
handicap	13	3	5	11	17	7	9	1	15	-
FORWARD	444	324	300	125	286	319	458	332	115	2703
par	5	4	4	3	4	4	5	4	3	36
handicap	7	1	9	13	15	11	3	5	17	-

	10	11	12	13	14	15	16	17	18	IN
BACK	486	357	170	375	359	558	158	312	392	3167
REGULAR	462	342	150	356	321	537	140	297	373	2978
par	5	4	3	4	4	5	3	4	4	36
handicap	14	8	12	4	16	2	10	18	6	-
FORWARD	416	317	117	324	292	471	125	278	348	2688
par	5	4	3	4	4	5	3	4	4	36
handicap	14	4	18	10	2	6	8	16	12	-

BACK	
yardage	6412
par	72
rating	70.4
slope	117

REGULAR	
yardage	6023
par	72
rating	68.5
slope	113

FORWARD	
yardage	5391
par	72
rating	71.8
slope	128

 ## MONTEREY COUNTRY CLUB
ARCHITECT: TED ROBINSON, 1978

41500 Monterey Avenue
Palm Desert, CA 92260

PRO SHOP: 760-346-1115
CLUBHOUSE: 760-568-9311

Patrick Casey, PGA Professional
Graham Leibowitz, General Manager
Jess Troche, Superintendent

Driving Range ●
Practice Greens ●
Clubhouse ●
Food / Beverage ●
Accommodations ●
Pull Carts
Power Carts ●
Club Rental ●
Special Offers

	1	2	3	4	5	6	7	8	9	OUT
BACK	375	488	126	361	196	480	355	364	296	3041
REGULAR	354	477	121	348	155	470	331	348	288	2892
par	4	5	3	4	3	5	4	4	4	36
handicap	3	5	9	1	4	7	2	6	8	-
FORWARD	330	452	121	333	118	417	316	325	280	2692
par	4	5	3	4	3	5	4	4	4	36
handicap	4	1	9	5	8	2	6	7	3	-

	10	11	12	13	14	15	16	17	18	IN
BACK	342	519	342	152	475	372	378	390	174	3144
REGULAR	324	505	327	135	458	356	360	371	148	2984
par	4	5	4	3	5	4	4	4	3	36
handicap	7	6	8	9	4	1	3	2	5	-
FORWARD	303	490	309	118	414	308	338	336	109	2725
par	4	5	4	3	5	4	4	4	3	36
handicap	7	1	6	9	2	3	4	5	8	-

BACK	
yardage	6185
par	72
rating	69.4
slope	119

REGULAR	
yardage	5876
par	72
rating	67.9
slope	117

FORWARD	
yardage	5417
par	72
rating	71.8
slope	125

PLAY POLICY & FEES: Members and guests only.

DRESS CODE: Appropriate golf attire and nonmetal spikes are required. Men's and women's shorts must be no more than four inches above the knee.

COURSE DESCRIPTION: These well-bunkered courses have lots of water and spectacular views of the Santa Rosa Mountains. Two of the nines are set among the condos.

NOTES: Par is 72 for each of the 18-hole combinations. The North/East Course: See scorecard for yardage and rating information. The South/North Course is 6,679 yards and rated 71.8 from the championship tees, and 6,275 yards and rated 69.6 from the regular tees. The slope ratings are 121 championship and 116 regular. Women's tees are 5,703 yards and rated 73.1. The slope rating is 127. The East/South Course is 6,601 yards and rated 71.4 from the championship tees, and 6,208 yards and rated 69.4 from the regular tees. The slope ratings are 120 championship and 115 regular. Women's tees are 5,688 yards and rated 73.4. The slope rating is 126.

LOCATION: Take the Cook Street exit off Interstate 10 southeast of Palm Springs and drive south to Country Club Drive. Turn left and go one-half mile to the course.

. . . ● **TOURNAMENTS:** This course is not available for outside events.

41. THE LAKES COUNTRY CLUB

PLAY POLICY & FEES: Reciprocal play is accepted with members of other private clubs by the general manager or the head pro. Reciprocal fees are $110 per person. Green fees for guests are $80. Carts and range balls are included. Reservations are required.

DRESS CODE: Appropriate golf attire and nonmetal spikes are required.

COURSE DESCRIPTION: This tight, target course has strategically placed bunkers and water hazards. The narrow fairways are lined with condos on both sides.

NOTES: Par is 72 on the South/West Course and 71 on the other 18-hole combinations. The South/West Course: See scorecard for additional yardage and rating information. The East/West Course is 6,108 yards and rated 68.9 from the championship tees, and 5,790 yards and rated 67 from the regular tees. The slope ratings are 117 championship and 114 regular. Forward tees are 5,259 yards and rated 70.5. The slope rating is 120. The East/South Course is 6,005 yards and rated 68 from the championship tees, and 5,720 yards and rated 66.6 from the regular tees. The slope ratings are 116 championship and 111 regular. Forward tees are 5,226 yards and rated 70.4. The slope rating is 124.

LOCATION: Take the Monterey Avenue exit off Interstate 10 near Palm Desert and drive south four miles to the club.

. . . ● **TOURNAMENTS:** You must contact the pro for tournament reservations. Shotgun tournaments are available weekdays only. A 16-player minimum is needed for a regular tournament. Events can be booked one to 12 months in advance. The banquet facility can accommodate 220 people. ● **TRAVEL:** The Holiday Inn Express (760-340-4303) is recommended for lodging.

42. MONTEREY COUNTRY CLUB

43 PORTOLA COUNTRY CLUB

42-500 Portola Avenue
Palm Desert, CA 92260

PRO SHOP: 760-568-1592
OFFICE: 760-346-5481

Jim E. Manning, Manager
Gary Stevenson
Oscar T. Hernandez, Superintendent

Driving Range
Practice Greens ●
Clubhouse ●
Food / Beverage ●
Accommodations
Pull Carts ●
Power Carts ●
Club Rental
$pecial Offers

	1	2	3	4	5	6	7	8	9	OUT
BACK	-	-	-	-	-	-	-	-	-	-
REGULAR	89	82	149	150	121	107	180	121	141	1140
par	3	3	3	3	3	3	3	3	3	27
handicap	17	15	7	5	9	11	1	13	3	-
FORWARD	80	76	142	113	114	100	110	111	130	976
par	3	3	3	3	3	3	3	3	3	27
handicap	13	17	1	9	5	7	11	15	3	-

	10	11	12	13	14	15	16	17	18	IN
BACK	-	-	-	-	-	-	-	-	-	-
REGULAR	114	126	143	113	116	76	109	122	75	994
par	3	3	3	3	3	3	3	3	3	27
handicap	18	4	2	14	6	16	10	8	12	-
FORWARD	110	120	131	108	110	70	109	11	75	844
par	3	3	3	3	3	3	3	3	3	27
handicap	16	4	2	18	6	12	8	14	10	-

BACK	
yardage	-
par	-
rating	-
slope	-

REGULAR	
yardage	2134
par	54
rating	50.2
slope	

FORWARD	
yardage	1820
par	54
rating	50.7
slope	

44 INDIAN RIDGE COUNTRY CLUB
ARCHITECT: ARNOLD PALMER, 1992

76-375 Country Club Drive
Palm Desert, CA 92211

PRO SHOP: 760-772-7272

Dennis Alexander, General Manager
Martin Chuck, PGA Professional

Driving Range ●
Practice Greens ●
Clubhouse ●
Food / Beverage ●
Accommodations
Pull Carts
Power Carts ●
Club Rental ●
$pecial Offers

	1	2	3	4	5	6	7	8	9	OUT
BACK										
REGULAR										
par										
handicap										
FORWARD										
par										
handicap										

	10	11	12	13	14	15	16	17	18	IN
BACK										
REGULAR										
par										
handicap										
FORWARD										
par										
handicap										

BACK	
yardage	7010
par	72
rating	74.3
slope	137

REGULAR	
yardage	6739
par	72
rating	72.5
slope	132

FORWARD	
yardage	5506
par	72
rating	71.6
slope	124

PLAY POLICY & FEES: Members and guests only. Green fees are $10 weekdays and $15 weekends. Pull carts are $2.

TEE TIMES: Reservations are not accepted. All play is on a first-come, first-served basis.

DRESS CODE: Golf attire and nonmetal spikes are mandatory.

COURSE DESCRIPTION: Situated on 27 acres, this par-3 course is somewhat rolling, with many lakes and water hazards. It is set in a mobile home park.

LOCATION: From Interstate 10 southeast of Palm Springs, take the Cook exit and turn right on Country Club. Drive to Portola Avenue. Go left on Portola and follow it about one mile to the club.

. . . ● **TOURNAMENTS:** This course is not available for outside events.

43. PORTOLA COUNTRY CLUB

PLAY POLICY & FEES: Members and guests only.

DRESS CODE: Appropriate golf attire and nonmetal spikes are required.

COURSE DESCRIPTION: This is a typical Palmer design with lots of undulations and lots of water that seldom comes into play.

NOTES: Besides a beautiful golf course, Indian Ridge Country Club offers clay tennis courts and croquet.

LOCATION: From Interstate 10 southeast of Palm Springs and near Palm Desert, take the Washington Street exit. Take a right on Washington, then another right on Country Club. The entrance is on the left.

. . . ● **TOURNAMENTS:** This course is not available for outside events.

44. INDIAN RIDGE COUNTRY CLUB

SHADOW MOUNTAIN GOLF CLUB
ARCHITECT: GENE SARAZEN, 1959

73-800 Ironwood Street
Palm Desert, CA 92260

PRO SHOP: 760-346-8242
CLUBHOUSE: 760-346-0766

Tony Schieffer, PGA Professional/Manager
Gaylord Moller, Superintendent

Driving Range •
Practice Greens •
Clubhouse •
Food / Beverage •
Accommodations
Pull Carts •
Power Carts •
Club Rental •
$pecial Offers

	1	2	3	4	5	6	7	8	9	OUT
BACK	-	-	-	-	-	-	-	-	-	-
REGULAR	335	328	285	138	333	347	179	155	437	2537
par	4	4	4	3	4	4	3	3	5	34
handicap	6	12	14	18	2	4	10	16	8	-
FORWARD	324	302	275	131	328	341	175	150	425	2451
par	4	4	4	3	4	4	3	3	5	34
handicap	8	10	12	18	6	2	14	16	4	-

	10	11	12	13	14	15	16	17	18	IN
BACK	-	-	-	-	-	-	-	-	-	-
REGULAR	292	285	364	309	318	363	127	402	444	2904
par	4	4	4	4	4	4	3	4	5	36
handicap	15	9	3	11	7	5	17	1	13	-
FORWARD	283	282	356	304	312	348	120	402	436	2843
par	4	4	4	4	4	4	3	5	5	37
handicap	13	11	5	9	7	1	17	15	3	-

BACK	
yardage	-
par	-
rating	-
slope	-

REGULAR	
yardage	5441
par	70
rating	66.3
slope	114

FORWARD	
yardage	5294
par	71
rating	64.5
slope	106

 MARRAKESH COUNTRY CLUB
ARCHITECT: TED ROBINSON

47-000 Marrakesh Drive
Palm Desert, CA 92260

47001 Portola Avenue
Palm Desert, CA

PRO SHOP: 760-568-2660
OFFICE: 760-568-2688

Daniel J. Cooper, CCM, Exec. VP & GM
Willy Gatherum, PGA Professional
John Figgen, Superintendent

Driving Range •
Practice Greens •
Clubhouse •
Food / Beverage •
Accommodations
Pull Carts •
Power Carts •
Club Rental •
$pecial Offers

	1	2	3	4	5	6	7	8	9	OUT
BACK	-	-	-	-	-	-	-	-	-	-
REGULAR	304	157	170	162	190	145	194	269	155	1746
par	4	3	3	3	3	3	3	4	3	29
handicap	5	15	7	11	1	17	3	13	9	-
FORWARD	257	146	152	116	178	140	181	256	104	1530
par	4	3	3	3	3	3	3	4	3	29
handicap	3	11	7	17	1	13	5	9	15	-

	10	11	12	13	14	15	16	17	18	IN
BACK	-	-	-	-	-	-	-	-	-	-
REGULAR	158	260	165	276	198	229	126	171	285	1868
par	3	4	3	4	3	4	3	3	4	31
handicap	14	12	10	8	2	18	16	6	4	-
FORWARD	131	248	153	246	182	217	113	132	268	1690
par	3	4	3	4	3	4	3	3	4	31
handicap	14	8	12	10	2	18	16	6	4	-

BACK	
yardage	-
par	-
rating	-
slope	-

REGULAR	
yardage	3614
par	60
rating	56.8
slope	86

FORWARD	
yardage	3220
par	60
rating	57.9
slope	92

PLAY POLICY & FEES: Reciprocal play is accepted with members of other private clubs. Green fees are $55 during the winter season and $25 during the summer season. Carts are $10 per person. Reservations are mandatory. The course is closed during October.

TEE TIMES: Reservations can be booked two days in advance.

DRESS CODE: Appropriate golf attire and nonmetal spikes are required.

COURSE DESCRIPTION: This course is well bunkered, with some water and lots of palm trees. It's a challenging course for the average player. The 402-yard 17th hole, which winds slightly uphill through rock gardens, is the signature hole on this well-hidden gem. The course is lined with 700 50-foot palm trees, but is so protected that it's the last place the wind blows or the rain falls. The course is walkable.

NOTES: The men's course record of 55 is held by Fred Hawkins. Sherry Wilder holds the women's record of 65.

LOCATION: Take the Monterey Avenue exit off Interstate 10 southeast of Palm Springs, drive south to Highway 111 in Palm Desert, and turn left. At San Luis Rey Avenue, turn right and drive to the end of the road. Turn left into the club.

. . . ● **TOURNAMENTS:** This course is not available for outside events.

45. SHADOW MOUNTAIN GOLF CLUB

PLAY POLICY & FEES: Reciprocal play is accepted with members of other private clubs. The reciprocal fee is $90; a guest with a member is $40. An unaccompanied guest of a member is $55.

TEE TIMES: Call the pro shop for availability of tee times.

DRESS CODE: Collared shirts are required, and metal spikes are not allowed. Bermuda-length shorts are OK.

COURSE DESCRIPTION: This hilly course with excellent mountain views is located in a community of 364 homes. The longest of the six par 4s is 304 yards, and the par 3s range between 126 and 198 yards. The course is well bunkered, has four lakes and many trees, so it's a test. The course plays much tougher than it looks. You'll need every club in the bag on this fine 18-hole executive course.

NOTES: Non-resident membership applications are available. The clubhouse has been completely remodeled.

LOCATION: From Palm Desert, take Interstate 10 to the Monterey Avenue exit. Take Monterey Avenue south to Country Club Drive. Turn left on Country Club Drive and proceed to Portola Avenue. Turn right on Portola Avenue to the club.

. . . ● **TOURNAMENTS:** This course is not available for outside events.

46. MARRAKESH COUNTRY CLUB

47

IRONWOOD COUNTRY CLUB
ARCHITECT: DESMOND MUIRHEAD, TED ROBINSON , 1973 (S)

73-735 Irontree Drive
Palm Desert, CA 92260

PRO SHOP: 760-346-0551

Michael Oberlander, Director of Golf, PGA
Mark Cupit, Superintendent
Bob Malloch, Clubhouse Manager

Driving Range ●
Practice Greens ●
Clubhouse ●
Food / Beverage ●
Accommodations
Pull Carts
Power Carts ●
Club Rental ●
$Special Offers

	1	2	3	4	5	6	7	8	9	OUT
BACK	390	473	345	176	499	168	433	417	429	3330
REGULAR	370	455	334	159	487	156	416	404	405	3186
par	4	5	4	3	5	3	4	4	4	36
handicap	3	17	9	13	11	15	1	7	5	-
FORWARD	346	410	310	134	471	123	363	363	351	2871
par	4	5	4	3	5	3	4	4	4	36
handicap	9	11	13	15	1	17	3	7	5	-

	10	11	12	13	14	15	16	17	18	IN
BACK	510	390	393	382	174	549	415	214	453	3480
REGULAR	490	380	374	345	162	525	397	185	406	3264
par	5	4	4	4	3	5	4	3	4	36
handicap	16	6	12	10	18	8	2	14	4	-
FORWARD	470	353	362	329	109	490	373	168	366	3020
par	5	4	4	4	3	5	4	3	4	36
handicap	6	14	10	12	18	2	4	16	8	-

BACK	
yardage	6810
par	72
rating	72.6
slope	125

REGULAR	
yardage	6450
par	72
rating	70.7
slope	120

FORWARD	
yardage	5891
par	72
rating	74.6
slope	132

PALM DESERT RESORT COUNTRY CLUB
ARCHITECT: JOE MOLLENEAUX, 1980

77-333 Country Club Drive
Palm Desert, CA 92260

PRO SHOP: 760-345-2791
CLUBHOUSE: 760-345-2781

Brent Grindleland, General Manager, PGA
Robert Burke, PGA Professional
Sam Zigler, Superintendent

Driving Range ●
Practice Greens ●
Clubhouse ●
Food / Beverage ●
Accommodations ●
Pull Carts
Power Carts ●
Club Rental ●
$Special Offers

	1	2	3	4	5	6	7	8	9	OUT
BACK										
REGULAR										
par										
handicap										
FORWARD										
par										
handicap										

	10	11	12	13	14	15	16	17	18	IN
BACK										
REGULAR										
par										
handicap										
FORWARD										
par										
handicap										

BACK	
yardage	6585
par	72
rating	70.8
slope	117

REGULAR	
yardage	6291
par	72
rating	69.2
slope	112

FORWARD	
yardage	5670
par	72
rating	70.8
slope	123

PLAY POLICY & FEES: Members and guests only. Guest fees are $70 with a member and $150 without during the winter season, and $50 with a member and $60 without during the summer season. Carts are included. Reservations are required.

DRESS CODE: Appropriate golf attire and nonmetal spikes are required.

COURSE DESCRIPTION: Situated above the desert floor, the South Course is very scenic. It's long and winds through the desert. Arnold Palmer was the original designer of the course, but after the great flood of the early 1970s, it was reconstructed by Desmond Muirhead and Ted Robinson. There are several tough holes from the back tees. The North Course is also very scenic with mountain and desert valley views. There are some water hazards and the fairways are lined with condos and homes, but it isn't as tough as the South Course, which has been rated among the state's toughest.

NOTES: The clubhouse has been remodeled, and the fitness center and offices have been expanded. Par is 70 on the North Course. The North Course ranges from 5,342 from the women's tees to 5,770 yards from the regular tees. See scorecard for additional yardage and rating information on the South Course.

LOCATION: Take the Monterey Drive exit off Interstate 10 southeast of Palm Springs and drive south to Highway 111. Turn left and drive to Portola Avenue. Turn right and drive about two miles to the club.

... ● **TOURNAMENTS:** This course is not available for outside events.

47. IRONWOOD COUNTRY CLUB

PLAY POLICY & FEES: Outside play is accepted. November and December green fees are $50 Monday through Thursday and $60 Friday through Sunday. January through April green fees are $60 Monday through Thursday and $75 Friday through Sunday. In May green fees are $40 Monday through Thursday and $50 Friday through Sunday. June through September green fees are $30 Monday through Sunday and $40 Friday through Sunday. The course is closed in October. Carts are included.

TEE TIMES: Reservations can be booked five days in advance.

DRESS CODE: Golfers are not allowed to wear tank tops or cutoffs. Nonmetal spikes are recommended.

COURSE DESCRIPTION: This course has fairly wide fairways, bent-grass greens, and nine lakes that come into play. It's well bunkered and in excellent condition. It challenges good and average players alike.

LOCATION: Take the Washington Street exit off Interstate 10 and drive south to Country Club Drive. Turn right and travel three-quarters of a mile to the club on the left.

... ● **TOURNAMENTS:** A 40-player minimum is needed to book an event. Weekend shotgun tournaments must be approved by the homeowners' association.

48. PALM DESERT RESORT COUNTRY CLUB

WOODHAVEN COUNTRY CLUB
ARCHITECT: HAROLD HEERS JR., 1985

41-555 Woodhaven Drive
Palm Desert, CA 92211

PRO SHOP: 760-345-7513
CLUBHOUSE: 760-345-7636

J.B. Kemp, Head Professional, LPGA
Jim Holub, Superintendent

Driving Range •
Practice Greens •
Clubhouse •
Food / Beverage •
Accommodations
Pull Carts
Power Carts •
Club Rental •
$pecial Offers

	1	2	3	4	5	6	7	8	9	OUT
BACK	-	-	-	-	-	-	-	-	-	-
REGULAR	361	368	137	394	263	152	489	395	356	2915
par	4	4	3	4	4	3	5	4	4	35
handicap	7	5	17	1	15	9	13	3	11	-
FORWARD	341	357	114	362	244	115	440	360	336	2669
par	4	4	3	4	4	3	5	4	4	35
handicap	7	1	17	5	15	13	11	3	9	-

	10	11	12	13	14	15	16	17	18	IN
BACK	-	-	-	-	-	-	-	-	-	-
REGULAR	347	357	141	335	178	331	306	494	346	2835
par	4	4	3	4	3	4	4	5	4	35
handicap	6	2	18	8	14	16	12	4	10	-
FORWARD	303	331	128	288	163	316	279	460	317	2585
par	4	4	3	4	3	4	4	5	4	35
handicap	12	4	18	10	16	8	14	2	6	-

BACK	
yardage	-
par	-
rating	-
slope	-

REGULAR	
yardage	5750
par	70
rating	66.6
slope	111

FORWARD	
yardage	5254
par	70
rating	70.0
slope	117

 PALM DESERT COUNTRY CLUB
ARCHITECT: WILLIAM P. BELL, 1962

77-200 California Drive
Palm Desert, CA 92211

PRO SHOP: 760-345-2525

Monique Gibb, Manager
Susan Tevyan, Manager
Rusty Uhl, Professional

Driving Range •
Practice Greens •
Clubhouse •
Food / Beverage •
Accommodations
Pull Carts •
Power Carts •
Club Rental •
$pecial Offers

	1	2	3	4	5	6	7	8	9	OUT
BACK	503	392	357	180	470	425	188	405	405	3325
REGULAR	490	388	345	166	450	411	163	390	395	3198
par	5	4	4	3	5	4	3	4	4	36
handicap	9	5	11	15	13	1	17	7	3	-
FORWARD	420	354	329	147	433	399	137	373	348	2940
par	5	4	4	3	5	4	3	4	4	36
handicap	11	3	13	15	9	1	17	5	7	-

	10	11	12	13	14	15	16	17	18	IN
BACK	554	490	179	406	401	389	163	315	421	3318
REGULAR	524	476	167	394	379	3770	149	303	410	6572
par	5	5	3	4	4	4	3	4	4	36
handicap	10	18	12	2	4	8	14	16	6	-
FORWARD	461	426	150	385	370	343	131	292	345	2903
par	5	5	3	4	4	4	3	4	4	36
handicap	8	12	14	2	4	6	18	16	10	-

BACK	
yardage	6643
par	72
rating	70.9
slope	116

REGULAR	
yardage	6360
par	72
rating	69.3
slope	111

FORWARD	
yardage	5843
par	72
rating	72.5
slope	121

PLAY POLICY & FEES: Reciprocal play is accepted for members of other clubs. The fees for reciprocators and guests are seasonal and range from $35 to $70. Carts and range balls are included. The course is closed in October.

TEE TIMES: Reservations can be booked four days in advance.

DRESS CODE: Collared shirts are required. No denim shorts are allowed on course.

COURSE DESCRIPTION: This is a well-maintained, challenging course that offers narrow fairways, trees, bunkers, small greens, and some water. It's set among numerous condominiums.

LOCATION: Take the Washington Street exit off Interstate 10 near Palm Desert and drive south three-quarters of a mile to the club on the right.

. . . ● **TOURNAMENTS:** Carts are required. Afternoon shotgun tournaments only.

49. WOODHAVEN COUNTRY CLUB

PLAY POLICY & FEES: Outside play is accepted. Hotel guests are welcome. From November through April green fees are $55 weekdays and $65 weekends. During the summer green fees are $20. Carts are included in the green fees.

TEE TIMES: Reservations can be booked seven days in advance.

DRESS CODE: Collared shirts are required. No denim is allowed on the course.

COURSE DESCRIPTION: These are mature courses designed by William Park Bell. The wide, tree-lined fairways are well laid out and challenging. The executive nine, like the Championship Course, is bordered by homes. Recent bunker, tree, and flower bed additions have boosted the ratings.

NOTES: Par is 72 for each 18-hole combination. For information on the Championship Course (First/Second): see scorecard. The First/Third course is 5,435 yards and rated 65.1 from the championship tees, and 5,288 yards and rated 63.8 from the regular tees. The slope ratings are 100 championship and 94 regular. Forward tees are 4,987 yards and are unrated. The Second/Third Course is 5,719 yards and rated 65.0 from the championship tees, and 5,173 yards and rated 63.6 from the regular tees. The slope ratings are 101 championship and 99 regular. Forward tees are 4,914 yards and are unrated.

LOCATION: Take the Washington Street exit off Interstate 10, turn right, and drive 1.5 miles to Avenue of the States. Turn right and merge into California Drive and continue one mile to the club entrance.

. . . ● **TOURNAMENTS:** This course is available for outside tournaments.

50. PALM DESERT COUNTRY CLUB

51 THE OASIS COUNTRY CLUB
ARCHITECT: DAVID RAINVILLE, 1984

42-330 Casbah Way
Palm Desert, CA 92211

PRO SHOP: 760-345-2715
CLUBHOUSE: 760-345-5661

Judy Grum, Manager
Steve Toth, PGA Professional
Larry Ruiz, Superintendent

Driving Range ●
Practice Greens ●
Clubhouse ●
Food / Beverage ●
Accommodations
Pull Carts ●
Power Carts ●
Club Rental ●
$pecial Offers

	1	2	3	4	5	6	7	8	9	OUT
BACK	295	132	177	275	140	104	292	122	161	1698
REGULAR	278	110	159	255	125	90	269	99	141	1526
par	4	3	3	4	3	3	4	3	3	30
handicap	5	13	3	9	11	17	1	15	7	-
FORWARD	254	93	139	227	106	79	248	89	117	1352
par	4	3	3	4	3	3	4	3	3	30
handicap	3	13	5	9	11	17	1	15	7	-

	10	11	12	13	14	15	16	17	18	IN
BACK	127	116	309	168	136	113	326	156	340	1791
REGULAR	110	99	294	148	109	83	296	131	322	1592
par	3	3	4	3	3	3	4	3	4	30
handicap	14	16	4	6	12	18	8	10	2	-
FORWARD	90	83	262	122	92	69	256	110	292	1376
par	3	3	4	3	3	3	4	3	4	30
handicap	14	16	6	8	12	18	4	10	2	-

BACK	
yardage	3489
par	60
rating	57.3
slope	97

REGULAR	
yardage	3118
par	60
rating	55.0
slope	88

FORWARD	
yardage	2728
par	60
rating	-
slope	-

52 BIGHORN GOLF CLUB
ARCHITECTS: ARTHUR HILLS, 1991; TOM FAZIO, 1999

255 Palowet Drive
Palm Desert, CA 92260

PRO SHOP: 760-773-2468
CLUBHOUSE: 760-341-4653

Ray Pennington, PGA Professional
Dennis Osborne, Superintendent

Driving Range ●
Practice Greens ●
Clubhouse ●
Food / Beverage ●
Accommodations
Pull Carts
Power Carts ●
Club Rental ●
$pecial Offers

	1	2	3	4	5	6	7	8	9	OUT
BACK	421	197	551	391	425	505	436	166	426	3518
REGULAR	395	162	506	373	399	492	408	145	400	3280
par	4	3	5	4	4	5	4	3	4	36
handicap	5	15	13	11	7	17	3	9	1	-
FORWARD	305	96	405	325	312	433	306	101	321	2604
par	4	3	5	4	4	5	4	3	4	36
handicap	3	17	11	9	7	15	5	13	1	-

	10	11	12	13	14	15	16	17	18	IN
BACK	503	346	501	185	280	505	369	205	459	3353
REGULAR	490	325	494	173	270	480	364	189	452	3237
par	5	4	5	3	4	4	4	3	4	36
handicap	16	8	4	14	18	2	10	12	6	-
FORWARD	418	241	436	87	228	338	259	110	257	2374
par	5	4	5	3	4	4	4	3	4	36
handicap	10	8	4	16	18	2	6	12	14	-

BACK	
yardage	6871
par	72
rating	73.4
slope	140

REGULAR	
yardage	6517
par	72
rating	71.3
slope	134

FORWARD	
yardage	4978
par	72
rating	69.6
slope	125

PLAY POLICY & FEES: Outside play is accepted. In-season green fees run around $45. The course is closed in October. During the summer months green fees are $20, and the pro shop closes at 5 p.m. Carts are $10.

TEE TIMES: Reservations can be booked three days in advance.

DRESS CODE: Appropriate golf attire and nonmetal spikes are required.

COURSE DESCRIPTION: This is a fun and challenging executive course with some of the finest greens to be found in the desert. There are 22 lakes guarding six par 4s and 12 par 3s.

LOCATION: Take the Washington Street exit off Interstate 10 and drive south to Avenue 42. Turn right and drive one mile to Casbah Way. Turn left to the club.

. . . ● **TOURNAMENTS:** This course is available for outside tournaments.

51. THE OASIS COUNTRY CLUB

PLAY POLICY & FEES: Reciprocal play is not accepted. Members and guests only. The course is open Wednesday through Sunday, June 1 to September 30, and Monday through Sunday, November 1 to May 31.

DRESS CODE: Appropriate golf attire and nonmetal spikes are required.

COURSE DESCRIPTION: This dramatic desert course is part of a private residential community. Carved into the Santa Rosa Mountains (with elevation changes of up to 400 feet) the course provides spectacular views of the mountains and the Coachella Valley.

NOTES: Bighorn was the host of the PGA Skins Game from 1992 to 1995 and the Senior World Match Play Championship in 1998.

LOCATION: From Interstate 10 near Palm Desert, exit on Monterey Avenue. Drive south on Monterey Avenue/Highway 74. The club is 3.5 miles south on Highway 74.

. . . ● **TOURNAMENTS:** This course is not available for outside events. ●

TRAVEL: The Ritz-Carlton (619-321-8282) and the Hyatt Grand Champions (760-341-1000) are recommended.

52. BIGHORN GOLF CLUB

53 EMERALD DESERT COUNTRY CLUB
ARCHITECT: JAMES LAIER JR., 1990

76-000 Frank Sinatra Drive
Palm Desert, CA 92260

PRO SHOP: 760-345-4770

Don McCalla, Owner

Driving Range ●
Practice Greens ●
Clubhouse ●
Food / Beverage ●
Accommodations
Pull Carts ●
Power Carts ●
Club Rental ●
$pecial Offers

	1	2	3	4	5	6	7	8	9	OUT
BACK	153	187	272	135	268	263	161	257	127	1823
REGULAR	132	169	256	105	262	259	143	248	106	1680
par	3	3	4	3	4	4	3	4	3	31
handicap	13	7	5	15	3	1	11	9	17	-
FORWARD	95	165	171	100	253	254	141	243	97	1519
par	3	4	4	3	4	4	3	4	3	32
handicap	9	11	5	17	3	1	15	7	13	-

	10	11	12	13	14	15	16	17	18	IN
BACK	153	187	272	135	268	263	161	257	127	1823
REGULAR	132	169	256	105	262	259	143	248	106	1680
par	3	3	4	3	4	4	3	4	3	31
handicap	14	8	6	16	4	2	12	10	18	-
FORWARD	95	165	171	100	253	254	141	243	97	1519
par	3	4	4	3	4	4	3	4	3	32
handicap	10	12	6	18	4	2	16	8	14	-

BACK	
yardage	3646
par	62
rating	56.3
slope	92

REGULAR	
yardage	3360
par	62
rating	56.3
slope	92

FORWARD	
yardage	3038
par	64
rating	-
slope	-

54 MARRIOTT'S DESERT SPRINGS RESORT AND SPA
ARCHITECTS: TED ROBINSON (PALMS), 1987; TED ROBINSON (VALLEY), 1988

74-855 Country Club Drive
Palm Desert, CA 92260

PRO SHOP: 760-341-1756

Tim Skogen, Director of Golf, PGA
Drew Hudgens, Head Professional, PGA
Bob Tamblyn, Tournament coordinator

Driving Range ●
Practice Greens ●
Clubhouse ●
Food / Beverage ●
Accommodations ●
Pull Carts
Power Carts ●
Club Rental ●
$pecial Offers ●

	1	2	3	4	5	6	7	8	9	OUT
BACK										
REGULAR										
par										
handicap										
FORWARD										
par										
handicap										

	10	11	12	13	14	15	16	17	18	IN
BACK										
REGULAR										
par										
handicap										
FORWARD										
par										
handicap										

BACK	
yardage	
par	
rating	
slope	

REGULAR	
yardage	
par	
rating	
slope	

FORWARD	
yardage	
par	
rating	
slope	

PLAY POLICY & FEES: Green fees are $10 for nine holes and $15 for 18 holes weekdays, and $15 for nine holes and $20 for 18 holes weekends. Call for summer rates. Carts are $10 weekdays and $15 on weekends.

TEE TIMES: Reservations can be booked four days in advance.

DRESS CODE: Collared shirts and nonmetal spikes are required.

COURSE DESCRIPTION: This course features six lakes, bent-grass greens protected by numerous sand traps, and narrow fairways. The par-4, 263-yard sixth hole demands good shot placement. The steeply elevated green is protected front and left by water.

LOCATION: From Interstate 10 take the Monterey Avenue exit near Palm Desert to Frank Sinatra Drive. Go east approximately four miles to the course.

... ● **TOURNAMENTS:** This course is available for outside tournaments.

53. EMERALD DESERT COUNTRY CLUB

PLAY POLICY & FEES: Green fees for resort guests range from $32 in the summer to $155 in prime season. All green fees include range balls and a cart. Prime season rates are January 30 to April 2.

TEE TIMES: Reservations can be made up to 60 days in advance for hotel guests and three days in advance for nonguests.

COURSE DESCRIPTION: Both the Palms and Valley Courses are well maintained fairly level. Players have ample room for error off the tee, so swinging away with the driver is OK. For those who stray too far outside the generous fairways, you can find bunkers, lakes, and palm trees. These are fun courses that can give you a challenge but will not overwhelm the average golfer.

NOTES: Marriott Desert Springs also offers an 18-hole putting course.

LOCATION: Take Interstate 10 to Palm Desert. Exit at Cook Street . Go south on Cook Street to Country Club Drive. Turn right on Country Club Drive to the entrance.

● **TRAVEL:** For reservations at the resort call 760-341-2211. ● **$PECIAL OFFERS:** Play-and-stay packages are available through the resort.

54. MARRIOTT'S DESERT SPRINGS RESORT

THE GOLF RESORT AT INDIAN WELLS
ARCHITECT: TED ROBINSON, 1986

44-500 Indian Wells Lane
Indian Wells, CA 92210

PRO SHOP: 760-346-4653

Mike Pease, Manager
Jon Darrah, PGA Professional
Glenn Miller, Superintendent

Driving Range ●
Practice Greens ●
Clubhouse ●
Food / Beverage ●
Accommodations ●
Pull Carts
Power Carts ●
Club Rental ●
$pecial Offers ●

	1	2	3	4	5	6	7	8	9	OUT
BACK	375	410	391	171	388	496	196	536	423	3386
REGULAR	353	370	371	151	361	482	165	497	391	3141
par	4	4	4	3	4	5	3	5	4	36
handicap	15	5	7	17	13	11	9	3	1	-
FORWARD	319	330	334	135	321	430	139	437	342	2787
par	4	4	4	3	4	5	3	5	4	36
handicap	15	5	7	17	13	11	9	3	1	-

BACK		
yardage		6631
par		72
rating		71.7
slope		122

	10	11	12	13	14	15	16	17	18	IN
BACK	418	207	400	370	511	343	362	149	485	3245
REGULAR	404	182	378	352	494	325	347	141	468	3091
par	4	3	4	4	5	4	4	3	5	36
handicap	2	4	12	6	10	16	14	18	8	-
FORWARD	353	151	332	290	436	297	322	112	436	2729
par	4	3	4	4	5	4	4	3	5	36
handicap	2	4	12	6	10	16	14	18	8	-

REGULAR		
yardage		6232
par		72
rating		69.5
slope		117

FORWARD		
yardage		5516
par		72
rating		70.7
slope		113

 # DESERT HORIZONS COUNTRY CLUB
ARCHITECT: TED ROBINSON, 1979

44-900 Desert Horizons
Indian Wells, CA 92210

PRO SHOP: 760-340-4651

Rick Ruppert, Director of Golf, PGA
Wil Friedner, Superintendent

Driving Range ●
Practice Greens ●
Clubhouse ●
Food / Beverage ●
Accommodations
Pull Carts
Power Carts ●
Club Rental ●
$pecial Offers

	1	2	3	4	5	6	7	8	9	OUT
BACK	476	417	185	423	370	516	381	349	206	3323
REGULAR	463	377	158	391	347	496	361	316	157	3066
par	5	4	3	4	4	5	4	4	3	36
handicap	17	3	15	1	5	11	9	13	7	-
FORWARD	443	334	136	349	313	453	332	293	133	2786
par	75	4	3	4	4	5	4	4	3	106
handicap	7	5	17	3	11	1	13	15	9	-

BACK		
yardage		6613
par		72
rating		71.7
slope		125

	10	11	12	13	14	15	16	17	18	IN
BACK	335	418	192	339	540	516	215	344	391	3290
REGULAR	313	398	152	312	498	496	192	320	370	3051
par	4	4	3	4	5	5	3	4	4	36
handicap	18	2	16	14	4	12	10	8	6	-
FORWARD	294	337	133	295	440	439	164	298	312	2712
par	4	4	3	4	5	5	3	4	4	36
handicap	14	4	16	12	2	10	18	8	6	-

REGULAR		
yardage		6117
par		72
rating		68.9
slope		116

FORWARD		
yardage		5498
par		142
rating		71.6
slope		121

PLAY POLICY & FEES: Green fees are seasonal and range from $30 to $140. Call for current rates.

TEE TIMES: Reservations can be booked three days in advance.

DRESS CODE: T-shirts, denim, or swimwear are not allowed.

COURSE DESCRIPTION: Both courses were designed by Ted Robinson and feature beautiful greens, rolling fairways, and a natural desert setting. There are many parallel fairways but plenty of mounding to separate them.

NOTES: Adjacent to the Hyatt Grand Champions and Renaissance Hotels, the resort was awarded a silver medal listing of the nation's best resorts by "Golf Magazine" for 1996/97. This resort facility hosted the California State Open, from 1994 to 1998. The facility has two 18-hole courses with a par of 72 on both. See scorecard for yardage and rating information for the East Course. The West Course is 6,157 yards and rated 69.0 from the regular tees. The slope rating is 115. The course is 5,408 yards and rated 70.0 from the forward tees. The slope rating is 127.

LOCATION: From Interstate 10 near Palm Springs take the Cook Street exit three miles to Highway 111. Turn left on Highway 111 to Indian Wells Lane.

. . . ● **TOURNAMENTS:** This course is available for guests of the Indian Wells Hotel. ● **TRAVEL:** Hyatt Grand Champions Resort and the Renaissance Palm Springs are located on either side of the course. For reservations at the Hyatt call 760-341-1000. For reservations at the Renaissance call 760-773-4444. ● **SPECIAL OFFERS:** Both the Hyatt and the Renaissance have stay-and-play golf packages available.

55. THE GOLF RESORT AT INDIAN WELLS

PLAY POLICY & FEES: Members and guests only. Green fees are $65 for guests accompanied by a member and $125 for guests unaccompanied by a member. This course is closed in October.

DRESS CODE: Appropriate golf attire and nonmetal spikes are required.

COURSE DESCRIPTION: This championship course has more sand than Iwo Jima and lots of water. In other words, it is very challenging. Beware of the ninth hole. It's a par-3, 206-yard brute that demands a 180-yard carry over water to a three-tiered, hourglass green. The green is bunkered on the left, with water on the right.

NOTES: Course architect Ted Robinson lives in this development. The facility also features an 18-hole putting course complete with water and bunkers. Par is 44; the course record is 40.

LOCATION: Travel one mile west of Indian Wells on Highway 111. At Desert Horizons Drive, turn north and drive to the club.

. . . ● **TOURNAMENTS:** This course is not available for outside events.

56. DESERT HORIZONS COUNTRY CLUB

ELDORADO COUNTRY CLUB
ARCHITECT: LAWRENCE HUGHES, 1957

Fairway Drive
Indian Wells, CA 92210

PRO SHOP: 760-346-8081

Jack Peat, Jr., Owner
Terry Beardsley, PGA Professional

Driving Range ●
Practice Greens ●
Clubhouse ●
Food / Beverage ●
Accommodations ●
Pull Carts
Power Carts ●
Club Rental ●
$pecial Offers

	1	2	3	4	5	6	7	8	9	OUT
BACK	507	178	440	393	379	368	191	385	520	3361
REGULAR	486	163	406	365	362	353	167	367	457	3126
par	5	3	4	4	4	4	3	4	5	36
handicap	13	15	3	1	7	5	17	9	11	-
FORWARD	431	110	339	288	293	293	131	299	402	2586
par	5	3	4	4	4	4	3	4	5	36
handicap	3	15	5	1	11	7	17	9	13	-

	10	11	12	13	14	15	16	17	18	IN
BACK	377	438	200	510	407	391	186	430	508	3447
REGULAR	358	397	182	488	382	374	166	403	470	3220
par	4	4	3	5	4	4	3	4	5	36
handicap	10	4	16	14	6	8	18	2	12	-
FORWARD	298	350	147	432	327	324	119	277	420	2694
par	4	4	3	5	4	4	3	4	5	36
handicap	14	6	18	2	10	12	16	4	8	-

BACK	
yardage	6808
par	72
rating	73.0
slope	129

REGULAR	
yardage	6346
par	72
rating	70.0
slope	119

FORWARD	
yardage	5280
par	72
rating	70.0
slope	117

 # THE VINTAGE CLUB
ARCHITECT: TOM FAZIO, 1981 (M), 1984 (D)

75-001 Vintage Drive West
Indian Wells, CA 92210

PRO SHOP: 760-862-2076
CLUBHOUSE: 760-340-0500

Paul Lemcke, Director of Golf
Doug Anderson, Superintendent

Driving Range ●
Practice Greens ●
Clubhouse ●
Food / Beverage ●
Accommodations
Pull Carts
Power Carts ●
Club Rental ●
$pecial Offers

	1	2	3	4	5	6	7	8	9	OUT
BACK	369	396	424	375	190	539	136	344	524	3297
REGULAR	346	364	400	360	174	483	123	315	503	3068
par	4	4	4	4	3	5	3	4	5	36
handicap	9	3	1	7	13	5	17	15	11	-
FORWARD	291	273	365	274	144	422	102	265	373	2509
par	4	4	4	4	3	5	3	4	5	36
handicap	9	3	1	7	15	5	17	13	11	-

	10	11	12	13	14	15	16	17	18	IN
BACK	392	167	383	295	402	491	387	126	482	3125
REGULAR	384	163	353	281	389	473	370	109	455	2977
par	4	3	4	4	4	5	4	3	5	36
handicap	6	10	4	18	8	12	2	16	14	-
FORWARD	341	123	292	251	365	443	314	83	424	2636
par	4	3	4	4	4	5	4	3	5	36
handicap	6	16	8	14	4	10	2	18	12	-

BACK	
yardage	6422
par	72
rating	70.6
slope	122

REGULAR	
yardage	6045
par	72
rating	68.4
slope	112

FORWARD	
yardage	5145
par	72
rating	68.7
slope	117

PLAY POLICY & FEES: Members and guests only. The guest fees are $75 with a member and $150 without. Carts are $25. This course is open from November 1 to May 31.

DRESS CODE: Proper golf attire and nonmetal spikes are mandatory. No short shorts are allowed on the course.

COURSE DESCRIPTION: This is a mature course that is fairly level with out-of-bounds on every hole. A fairway returns to the clubhouse every four or five holes for those in need of refreshments. This is probably the oldest course in the Palm Springs area south of Tamarisk.

NOTES: This course was used in the Bob Hope Classic rotation for almost 30 years.

LOCATION: Take the Monterey Avenue exit off Interstate 10. Drive south to Highway 111 in Palm Desert and turn left. At Eldorado Drive, turn right and drive one-half mile to Fairway Drive. Turn right and drive one-half block to the club on the left.

. . . ● **TOURNAMENTS:** This course is not available for outside events.

57. ELDORADO COUNTRY CLUB

PLAY POLICY & FEES: Members and guests only. Guests must be accompanied by a member. Guest fees are $100. Carts are $15 per rider.

DRESS CODE: Appropriate golf attire and nonmetal spikes are required.

COURSE DESCRIPTION: The Desert Course is short but deceptive, requiring precise shot-making to the very small greens. It has Scottish flavor, with deep pot bunkers, sand, and shrubbery. The Mountain Course is a wide- open, easy-driving course with a British accent. It features deep pot bunkers, sprawling fairways, natural rock formations, citrus groves, indigenous shrubs, colorful flowers, and waterfalls. The 387-yard, par-4 16th hole is flanked by three lakes and two greenside waterfalls, while the scenic 126-yard, par-3 17th is fronted by a lake and affords a panoramic view.

NOTES: This club was used for the Senior PGA Tour's Vintage Invitational from 1981 to 1992. Par is 72 on both. The Desert Course is 6,301 yards and rated 70.2 from the regular tees with a slope of 129. Forward tees are 5,664 yards and rated 73.7 with a slope of 132. The Mountain Course: See scorecard for additional yardage and rating information.

LOCATION: Take the Monterey Avenue exit off Interstate 10. Drive south to Highway 111 in Palm Desert and turn left. At Cook Street, turn right and drive one-half mile to the club at the end of the road.

. . . ● **TOURNAMENTS:** This course is not available for outside events.

58. THE VINTAGE CLUB

INDIAN WELLS COUNTRY CLUB
ARCHITECT: HARRY RAINVILLE, 1955

46-000 Indian Wells Lane
Indian Wells, CA 92210

PRO SHOP: 760-360-0861
CLUBHOUSE: 760-345-2561

Mark Neneman, Manager
John Kyle, PGA Professional

Driving Range ●
Practice Greens ●
Clubhouse ●
Food / Beverage ●
Accommodations
Pull Carts
Power Carts ●
Club Rental ●
$pecial Offers

	1	2	3	4	5	6	7	8	9	OUT
BACK	388	355	382	162	517	167	548	391	405	3315
REGULAR	373	337	373	145	491	151	533	381	379	3163
par	4	4	4	3	5	3	5	4	4	36
handicap	3	13	1	15	11	17	7	5	9	-
FORWARD	360	319	356	117	464	138	505	344	356	2959
par	4	4	4	3	5	3	5	4	4	36
handicap	5	11	1	17	7	15	3	9	13	-

	10	11	12	13	14	15	16	17	18	IN
BACK	357	415	173	499	361	140	338	515	398	3196
REGULAR	350	405	151	472	340	128	326	498	379	3049
par	4	4	3	5	4	3	4	5	4	36
handicap	6	2	16	14	12	18	10	8	4	-
FORWARD	338	359	123	454	277	113	305	481	354	2804
par	4	4	3	5	4	3	4	5	4	36
handicap	10	6	18	2	14	16	12	8	4	-

BACK	
yardage	6511
par	72
rating	71.8
slope	127

REGULAR	
yardage	6212
par	72
rating	69.9
slope	118

FORWARD	
yardage	5763
par	72
rating	73.6
slope	127

 # INDIAN SPRINGS COUNTRY CLUB
ARCHITECT: JOHN GURLEY, HOAGY CARMICHAEL, 1960

46-080 Jefferson Street
La Quinta, CA 92253

PRO SHOP: 760-775-3360

Dennis Pogue, Director of Golf, PGA
Ron Stevenson, Superintendent

Driving Range ●
Practice Greens ●
Clubhouse ●
Food / Beverage ●
Accommodations
Pull Carts ●
Power Carts ●
Club Rental ●
$pecial Offers

	1	2	3	4	5	6	7	8	9	OUT
BACK	339	451	197	510	203	521	413	443	367	3444
REGULAR	329	445	179	486	194	511	364	433	349	3290
par	4	4	3	5	3	5	4	4	4	36
handicap	15	1	17	5	13	7	11	3	9	-
FORWARD	308	421	104	426	149	499	354	338	335	2934
par	4	5	3	5	3	5	4	4	4	37
handicap	13	3	17	9	15	1	5	7	11	-

	10	11	12	13	14	15	16	17	18	IN
BACK	173	372	211	182	501	465	299	386	376	2965
REGULAR	154	366	167	169	493	459	294	372	365	2839
par	3	4	3	3	5	5	4	4	4	35
handicap	18	10	12	16	4	6	14	2	8	-
FORWARD	143	361	143	134	435	451	285	366	357	2675
par	3	4	3	4	4	4	3	5	5	35
handicap	18	8	12	14	2	6	16	10	4	-

BACK	
yardage	6409
par	71
rating	69.8
slope	112

REGULAR	
yardage	6129
par	71
rating	68.6
slope	109

FORWARD	
yardage	5609
par	72
rating	72.4
slope	117

PLAY POLICY & FEES: Members and guests only. The green fee is $225 without a member and $80 with a member in season. Seasonal rates apply after April. Rates include cart and use of the range.

DRESS CODE: Country club attire is required; Bermuda shorts are permitted, and nonmetal spikes are preferred.

COURSE DESCRIPTION: The five layouts are distinctly different. The Classic 18 is the oldest and has tree-lined fairways. The Cove/West Course has a desert layout. The Cove nine is set at the base of the mountains. The Classic Course is configured from a selection of holes from all three nines. Choose your poison. The courses are not long, but they demand accuracy and a deft short game.

NOTES: The Bob Hope Classic Course is 6,095 yards and rated 69.4 from the regular tees with a slope of 117. The Cove/West Course: See scorecard for yardage and rating information. The North/Cove Course is 6,208 yards and rated 70.0 from the regular tees with a slope of 118. The West/North Course is 6,094 yards and rated 69.3 from the regular tees with a slope of 117. The late Bert Yancey set the course record of 61. The Bob Hope Classic is held here each year.

LOCATION: From Interstate 10, take the Washington Avenue exit. Go south to Highway 111, then west to Club Drive.

. . . ● **TOURNAMENTS:** Carts are required. Outside events are limited to summer months.

59. INDIAN WELLS COUNTRY CLUB

PLAY POLICY & FEES: Green fees are $20 June through September. From October through December green fees are $30 Monday through Friday and $40 Friday through Sunday. From January through mid-April green fees are $40 Monday through Thursday and $50 Friday through Sunday. From mid-April through May green fees are $40. Carts are included.

TEE TIMES: Reservations can be booked seven days in advance.

DRESS CODE: Collared shirts are required. No cutoffs are allowed on the course.

COURSE DESCRIPTION: This older course has some trees and a few bunkers. Sand guards many fairways. Small greens demand a creative short game. It's a sporty, casual place with active men's and women's clubs.

LOCATION: Take the Jefferson Street exit off Interstate 10 southeast of Palm Springs and drive south about 2.5 miles to the course.

. . . ● **TOURNAMENTS:** Shotgun tournaments are available weekdays only.

60. INDIAN SPRINGS COUNTRY CLUB

PALM ROYALE COUNTRY CLUB
ARCHITECT: TED ROBINSON, 1985

78-259 Indigo Drive
La Quinta , CA 92253

PRO SHOP: 760-345-9701

Dean Mayo, Director of Golf
Garrett Gross, Head Professional

Driving Range ●
Practice Greens ●
Clubhouse ●
Food / Beverage ●
Accommodations
Pull Carts ●
Power Carts
Club Rental ●
$pecial Offers

	1	2	3	4	5	6	7	8	9	OUT
BACK	-	-	-	-	-	-	-	-	-	-
REGULAR	82	106	96	86	120	107	150	95	81	923
par	3	3	3	3	3	3	3	3	3	27
handicap	11	5	9	13	3	7	1	15	17	-
FORWARD	71	92	80	71	81	90	130	82	72	769
par	3	3	3	3	3	3	3	3	3	27
handicap	11	5	9	13	3	7	1	15	17	-

	10	11	12	13	14	15	16	17	18	IN
BACK	-	-	-	-	-	-	-	-	-	-
REGULAR	101	98	150	102	120	117	130	126	125	1069
par	3	3	3	3	3	3	3	3	3	27
handicap	10	18	2	16	8	12	6	14	4	-
FORWARD	87	86	132	87	101	99	107	109	112	920
par	3	3	3	3	3	3	3	3	3	27
handicap	10	18	2	16	8	12	6	14	4	-

BACK	
yardage	-
par	-
rating	-
slope	-

REGULAR	
yardage	1992
par	54
rating	-
slope	-

FORWARD	
yardage	1689
par	54
rating	-
slope	-

 LA QUINTA COUNTRY CLUB
ARCHITECT: LAWRENCE HUGHES, 1959

P.O. Box 99
La Quinta, CA 92253

77-750 Avenue 50
La Quinta, CA 92253

PRO SHOP: 760-564-4151

Bob Moore, Manager
Jeff Jackson, PGA Professional
Ty Broadhead, Superintendent

Driving Range ●
Practice Greens ●
Clubhouse ●
Food / Beverage ●
Accommodations
Pull Carts
Power Carts ●
Club Rental ●
$pecial Offers

	1	2	3	4	5	6	7	8	9	OUT
BACK	382	433	186	397	498	521	174	391	391	3373
REGULAR	365	416	165	367	485	507	150	375	373	3203
par	4	4	3	4	5	5	3	4	4	36
handicap	7	1	11	3	17	15	13	5	9	-
FORWARD	348	404	120	325	479	504	123	351	357	3011
par	4	5	3	4	5	5	3	4	4	37
handicap	5	15	17	11	3	1	13	9	7	-

	10	11	12	13	14	15	16	17	18	IN
BACK	393	530	200	540	436	194	420	419	396	3528
REGULAR	382	492	191	490	422	177	389	406	380	3329
par	4	5	3	5	4	3	4	4	4	36
handicap	6	18	8	14	2	16	12	4	10	-
FORWARD	369	483	171	426	402	147	326	398	372	3094
par	4	5	3	5	5	3	4	4	4	37
handicap	4	6	10	12	18	16	14	2	8	-

BACK	
yardage	6901
par	72
rating	72.9
slope	128

REGULAR	
yardage	6532
par	72
rating	71.3
slope	123

FORWARD	
yardage	6105
par	74
rating	75.6
slope	133

PLAY POLICY & FEES: Green fees are $25 in season and $10 in June, July, August, and September. Green fees for juniors are $17.50 in season and $7.50 off-season. A twilight rate of $15 is in effect after 3 p.m. in season. This course is closed the first two weeks of October.

TEE TIMES: Reservations can be booked three days in advance in season and seven days in advance off-season.

DRESS CODE: No tank tops are allowed on the course.

COURSE DESCRIPTION: This is a short par-3 course with water on nine holes. It's a scaled-down version of the Marriott Desert Springs courses, with palms backing the greens, 26 bunkers, grass moguls, and water hazards.

LOCATION: Take Interstate 10 and exit at Washington Street near La Quinta. Follow Washington Street for about three-quarters of a mile to the club at the intersection of Washington and Fred Waring Road.

. . . ● **TOURNAMENTS:** This course is available for outside tournaments.

61. PALM ROYALE COUNTRY CLUB

PLAY POLICY & FEES: Members and guests only. Guests must be accompanied by a member at time of play. Guest fees are $75. Carts are $20. The course is closed in October.

DRESS CODE: Appropriate golf attire and nonmetal spikes are required.

COURSE DESCRIPTION: This mature, immaculately maintained course has tree-lined fairways, lakes, bunkers, and undulating greens. The emphasis is on driving accuracy.

NOTES: La Quinta has been used in the Bob Hope Classic and is one of the top courses in the desert.

LOCATION: Take the Washington Street exit off Interstate 10 near La Quinta. Drive south for six miles to Avenue 50 and turn right. Drive one mile to the club on the right.

. . . ● **TOURNAMENTS:** This course is not available for outside events.

62. LA QUINTA COUNTRY CLUB

RANCHO LA QUINTA GOLF COURSE
ARCHITECT: ROBERT TRENT JONES JR., 1993

79-325 Cascades Circle
La Quinta, CA 92253

PRO SHOP: 760-777-7799

Mike Hulme, Project Director
Fred Rodriguez, PGA Professional
John Cummings, General Manager

Driving Range ●
Practice Greens ●
Clubhouse ●
Food / Beverage ●
Accommodations
Pull Carts
Power Carts ●
Club Rental ●
$pecial Offers

	1	2	3	4	5	6	7	8	9	OUT
BACK	368	151	517	162	411	330	392	536	400	3267
REGULAR	352	125	498	145	395	312	363	507	355	3052
par	4	3	5	3	4	4	4	5	4	36
handicap	11	17	7	15	1	13	5	9	3	-
FORWARD	312	114	442	118	361	266	332	451	311	2707
par	4	3	5	3	4	4	4	5	4	36
handicap	11	17	7	15	1	13	5	9	3	-

	10	11	12	13	14	15	16	17	18	IN
BACK	510	419	141	340	525	185	381	158	523	3182
REGULAR	493	394	120	306	497	169	352	137	486	2954
par	5	4	3	4	5	3	4	3	5	36
handicap	10	2	18	16	6	12	4	14	8	-
FORWARD	428	364	94	258	443	130	268	124	440	2549
par	5	4	3	4	5	3	4	3	5	36
handicap	10	2	18	16	6	12	4	14	8	-

BACK	
yardage	6449
par	72
rating	71.0
slope	124

REGULAR	
yardage	6006
par	72
rating	68.5
slope	124

FORWARD	
yardage	5256
par	72
rating	68.5
slope	116

 LA QUINTA HOTEL GOLF CLUB: DUNES
ARCHITECT: PETE DYE, 1981

50-200 Vista Bonita
La Quinta, CA 92253

PRO SHOP: 760-564-7686
CLUBHOUSE: 760-564-7610

Tim Walton, General Manager, PGA

Driving Range ●
Practice Greens ●
Clubhouse ●
Food / Beverage ●
Accommodations ●
Pull Carts
Power Carts ●
Club Rental ●
$pecial Offers ●

	1	2	3	4	5	6	7	8	9	OUT
BACK	358	506	312	385	342	173	513	159	466	3214
REGULAR	343	504	290	319	292	148	466	124	431	2917
par	4	5	4	4	4	3	5	3	5	37
handicap	5	7	15	3	17	11	1	13	9	-
FORWARD	290	450	236	246	252	105	456	101	412	2548
par	4	5	4	4	4	3	5	3	5	37
handicap	5	7	11	3	15	17	1	13	9	-

	10	11	12	13	14	15	16	17	18	IN
BACK	327	404	345	122	354	520	187	414	363	3036
REGULAR	291	365	333	106	331	479	149	393	348	2795
par	4	4	4	3	4	5	3	4	4	35
handicap	10	4	16	18	12	6	14	2	8	-
FORWARD	295	289	312	88	296	423	121	360	273	2457
par	4	4	4	3	4	5	3	4	4	35
handicap	10	4	16	18	12	6	14	2	8	-

BACK	
yardage	6250
par	72
rating	70.1
slope	124

REGULAR	
yardage	5712
par	72
rating	67.1
slope	114

FORWARD	
yardage	5005
par	72
rating	68.0
slope	114

PLAY POLICY & FEES: Member guest fees are $75 weekdays and $95 weekends November through May . Fees are $30 June through September. Sponsored fees are $150. The golf course is closed in October.

DRESS CODE: Appropriate golf attire and nonmetal spikes are required.

COURSE DESCRIPTION: This course is located in a desert setting and features wide fairways, rolling hills, and great views of the Santa Rosa Mountains. The signature hole is the 16th, a long par 4 with a water hazard.

NOTES: The course record is 64, held by Jeff Hart.

LOCATION: From Highway 111 in La Quinta, drive one mile south on Washington Street to the course.

. . . ● **TOURNAMENTS:** This course is not available for outside events.

63. RANCHO LA QUINTA GOLF COURSE

PLAY POLICY & FEES: Outside play is accepted. Members have priority. There are reduced fees for hotel guests. Green fees range from $60 to $265, depending on time of year. Fees include cart and use of the driving range.

TEE TIMES: Members and hotel guests have first priority.

DRESS CODE: Appropriate golf attire and nonmetal spikes are required and strictly enforced.

COURSE DESCRIPTION: This course is well bunkered, with railroad ties and lots of water. The PGA of America rated the 414-yard, par-4 17th one of the country's toughest holes.

NOTES: The PGA Tour Qualifying School was held here in 1990. "Golf Magazine" rated La Quinta and its three courses a silver medalist for 1991–92.

LOCATION: Take the Washington Street exit off Interstate 10 near La Quinta. Drive south past Highway 111 to Avenue 50 and turn right. Continue past Eisenhower Drive to the gate and follow the road to the club.

. . . ● **TOURNAMENTS:** A 12-player minimum is needed to book an event. Carts are required. The tournament office can be reached at 760-564-7660. ●

TRAVEL: For reservations at the La Quinta Resort call 800-598-3828. ● **$PECIAL OFFERS:** Play-and-stay packages are available with the resort.

64. LA QUINTA HOTEL GOLF CLUB: DUNES

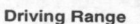 GOLF 50

50-200 Vista Bonita
La Quinta, CA 92253

PRO SHOP: 760-564-7686
CLUBHOUSE: 760-564-7610

Tim Walton, General Manager, PGA

Driving Range ●
Practice Greens ●
Clubhouse ●
Food / Beverage ●
Accommodations ●
Pull Carts
Power Carts ●
Club Rental ●
$pecial Offers ●

	1	2	3	4	5	6	7	8	9	OUT
BACK	335	190	336	494	151	352	471	367	403	3099
REGULAR	310	156	305	452	112	321	404	307	300	2667
par	4	3	4	5	3	4	5	4	4	36
handicap	11	13	15	7	17	1	9	5	3	-
FORWARD	293	132	265	402	104	272	404	282	300	2454
par	4	3	4	5	3	4	5	4	4	36
handicap	7	13	15	1	17	3	11	5	9	-

BACK	
yardage	6320
par	72
rating	71.5
slope	130

	10	11	12	13	14	15	16	17	18	IN
BACK	361	375	373	162	383	508	157	407	495	3221
REGULAR	304	344	311	140	313	465	91	326	444	2738
par	4	4	4	3	4	5	3	4	5	36
handicap	14	6	12	18	2	8	16	4	10	-
FORWARD	285	292	300	111	304	465	91	274	434	2556
par	4	4	4	3	4	5	3	4	5	36
handicap	12	6	14	16	4	2	18	10	8	-

REGULAR	
yardage	5405
par	72
rating	67.0
slope	113

FORWARD	
yardage	5010
par	72
rating	68.4
slope	120

50-503 Jefferson Street
La Quinta, CA 92253

PRO SHOP: 760-564-7620

Desi Howe, Head Professional, PGA

Driving Range ●
Practice Greens ●
Clubhouse ●
Food / Beverage ●
Accommodations ●
Pull Carts
Power Carts ●
Club Rental ●
$pecial Offers ●

	1	2	3	4	5	6	7	8	9	OUT
BACK	379	495	189	440	359	392	139	540	353	3286
REGULAR	340	456	135	355	351	319	105	517	340	2918
par	4	5	3	4	4	4	3	5	4	36
handicap	9	11	7	1	15	3	13	5	17	-
FORWARD	287	418	104	315	326	319	99	450	288	2606
par	4	5	3	4	4	4	3	5	4	36
handicap	11	3	15	9	7	5	17	1	13	-

BACK	
yardage	6479
par	72
rating	71.0
slope	123

	10	11	12	13	14	15	16	17	18	IN
BACK	372	379	351	145	517	358	136	513	422	3193
REGULAR	350	354	290	114	435	308	107	414	365	2737
par	4	4	4	3	5	4	3	5	4	36
handicap	16	4	14	12	10	8	18	6	2	-
FORWARD	314	280	290	94	435	277	74	414	322	2500
par	4	4	4	3	5	4	3	5	4	36
handicap	8	10	12	16	2	14	18	4	6	-

REGULAR	
yardage	5655
par	72
rating	67.9
slope	113

FORWARD	
yardage	5106
par	72
rating	69.0
slope	115

PLAY POLICY & FEES: Members only until 9:30 a.m. in season and 8 a.m. off-season. Members receive preference in tee times. Guests may play only after members' tee times. Guest fees vary from $60 to $265 according to time of year, but include cart and range fees. Reservations are recommended.

TEE TIMES: Reservations can be made up to one year in advance with a credit card.

DRESS CODE: Dress code is strictly enforced.

COURSE DESCRIPTION: This is a challenging desert course noted for pot bunkers, rock formations, sand, and water. The large, undulating greens are set naturally against the mountains. Accuracy is the key. Watch for the par-3 16th hole. The green is surrounded by mountain rocks.

NOTES: This has been the home of the World Cup, the PGA National Club Pro Championships, and the California State Open. Many golf pros and superintendents rate it the top course in the desert. The Seniors Skins Game was held here in 1989. Fred Couples holds the course record with a 63.

LOCATION: Take the Washington Street exit off Interstate 10 southeast of Palm Springs. Drive south past Highway 111 to Avenue 50 and turn right. Drive past Eisenhower Drive to the gate and follow the road to the club.

. . . ● **TOURNAMENTS:** This course is available for outside tournaments. ● **TRAVEL:** For reservations at the La Quinta Resort call 800-598-3828. ● **$PECIAL OFFERS:** Play-and-stay packages are available with the resort.

65. LA QUINTA HOTEL GOLF CLUB: MTN.

PLAY POLICY & FEES: Reciprocal play is accepted after 11 a.m. with members of other clubs. Reciprocal fees are $260. Guest fees, when playing with a member, are $50. All rates apply November through the end of April.

DRESS CODE: Appropriate golf attire and nonmetal spikes are required.

COURSE DESCRIPTION: This is a level course carved out of a citrus orchard, and it is anything but a lemon. In fact, this is one of the more scenic courses in the area. A typically challenging Pete Dye-design, the course features rolling contours, bent-grass greens, and scenic views of the Santa Rosa Mountains. This layout has plenty of character with a mix of sand and water, but it's more forgiving than the neighboring Mountain and Dunes Courses.

LOCATION: Take the Jefferson Street exit off Interstate 10 and drive south for three miles to the course.

. . . ● **TOURNAMENTS:** This course is not available for outside events. ● **TRAVEL:** For reservations at the La Quinta Resort call 800-598-3828.

66. LA QUINTA HOTEL GOLF CLUB: CITRUS

THE QUARRY AT LA QUINTA
ARCHITECT: TOM FAZIO, 1994

1 Quarry Lane
La Quinta, CA 92253

PRO SHOP: 760-777-1100

George Van Valkenburg Jr., Head Professional, PGA
Mark Smith, Superintendent

Driving Range ●
Practice Greens ●
Clubhouse ●
Food / Beverage ●
Accommodations ●
Pull Carts
Power Carts ●
Club Rental ●
$pecial Offers

	1	2	3	4	5	6	7	8	9	OUT
BACK	531	202	371	385	529	451	424	143	440	3476
REGULAR	488	163	327	356	483	392	368	129	386	3092
par	5	3	4	4	5	4	4	3	4	36
handicap	11	9	15	13	5	1	7	17	3	-
FORWARD	412	123	296	290	427	359	330	121	277	2635
par	5	3	4	4	5	4	4	3	4	36
handicap	11	15	13	7	1	9	5	17	3	-

	10	11	12	13	14	15	16	17	18	IN
BACK	521	400	401	352	173	614	454	223	469	3607
REGULAR	488	375	324	335	143	539	391	160	401	3156
par	5	4	4	4	3	5	4	3	4	36
handicap	14	10	12/8	16	18	2	6	8/12	4	-
FORWARD	386	281	245	235	114	491	346	140	353	2591
par	5	4	4	4	3	5	4	3	4	36
handicap	14	10	12/8	16	18	2	6	8/12	4	-

BACK	
yardage	7083
par	72
rating	73.7
slope	135

REGULAR	
yardage	6248
par	72
rating	69.3
slope	124

FORWARD	
yardage	5226
par	72
rating	70.3
slope	120

 ## PGA WEST: JACK NICKLAUS RESORT
ARCHITECT: JACK NICKLAUS, 1987

56-150 PGA Boulevard
La Quinta, CA 92253

PRO SHOP: 760-564-7170

Joey Garon, General Manager
Dave Doerr, Head Professional, PGA
Steve Auckland, Superintendent

Driving Range ●
Practice Greens ●
Clubhouse ●
Food / Beverage ●
Accommodations
Pull Carts
Power Carts ●
Club Rental ●
$pecial Offers

	1	2	3	4	5	6	7	8	9	OUT
BACK	381	397	167	506	324	412	473	146	438	3244
REGULAR	351	388	156	482	300	379	451	130	390	3027
par	4	4	3	5	4	4	5	3	4	36
handicap	13	5	11	7	15	3	9	17	1	-
FORWARD	274	321	120	415	226	342	392	96	343	2529
par	4	4	3	5	4	4	5	3	4	36
handicap	3	13	17	1	11	7	5	15	9	-

	10	11	12	13	14	15	16	17	18	IN
BACK	328	488	165	381	387	504	433	194	432	3312
REGULAR	321	482	151	330	346	455	366	159	400	3010
par	4	5	3	4	4	5	4	3	4	36
handicap	18	12	16	10	6	8	4	14	2	-
FORWARD	239	401	105	293	302	406	307	100	361	2514
par	4	5	3	4	4	5	4	3	4	36
handicap	14	6	16	10	12	2	4	18	8	-

BACK	
yardage	6556
par	72
rating	72.0
slope	129

REGULAR	
yardage	6037
par	72
rating	69.2
slope	122

FORWARD	
yardage	5043
par	72
rating	69.0
slope	116

PLAY POLICY & FEES: Members and guests only. Guests must be accompanied by a member. The green fee for guests is $100.

DRESS CODE: Appropriate golf attire and nonmetal spikes are required.

COURSE DESCRIPTION: Nestled in the foothills, this Tom Fazio design is routed through an abandoned rock quarry and covers 375 acres. The entire course was sodded. A 70-foot waterfall serves as a backdrop for the 10th and 17th holes. The par-5 10th hole is considered the signature hole. A river and stream run through the course, a typical Fazio creation with subtle mounding and small, traditional greens.

NOTES: "Golf Digest" has ranked the Quarry at La Quinta 73rd in the United States and eighth in California in its best–golf courses listings.

LOCATION: From La Quinta, take the Jefferson Street exit south to 54th Avenue. Turn left on 54th Avenue and follow it to Madison. Turn right on Madison and continue to 58th Avenue. Turn right on 58th Avenue and drive 1.5 miles to the course.

. . . ● **TOURNAMENTS:** This course is not available for outside events. ●

TRAVEL: The Quarry offers course-side cottages. Call the pro shop for information.

67. THE QUARRY AT LA QUINTA

PLAY POLICY & FEES: Outside play is accepted. Green fees are seasonal and range from $60 to $265. Carts are included.

TEE TIMES: Reservations can be booked three days in advance for outside play.

DRESS CODE: Appropriate golf attire and nonmetal spikes are required

COURSE DESCRIPTION: This course is a tamer version of the adjacent Stadium Course. There are Jack Nicklaus's trademark elevated tees and Pete Dye's trademark railroad ties, forced carries over water, and huge, multi-tiered greens. The course can be as difficult as you choose to make it, depending on what tees you use.

NOTES: The course has hosted the PGA Tour Qualifying School.

LOCATION: Take the Indio Boulevard/Jefferson Street exit off Interstate 10 and drive south to the end of Jefferson Street.

. . . ● **TOURNAMENTS:** A 12-player minimum is required to book an event. ●

TRAVEL: Places to stay in the area include the La Quinta Resort & Club, 760-564-4111, the Desert Springs Marriot Resort and Spa, 760-341-2211, and the Hyatt Grand Champions, 760-341-1000.

68. PGA WEST: JACK NICKLAUS RESORT

PGA WEST: JACK NICKLAUS PRIVATE
ARCHITECT: JACK NICKLAUS, 1987

55-955 PGA Boulevard
La Quinta, CA 92253

PRO SHOP: 760-564-7100
CLUBHOUSE: 760-564-7111

John Cochrane, Director of Golf, PGA
Lisa Taggert, Head Professional, PGA
Brian Distel, Superintendent

Driving Range ●
Practice Greens ●
Clubhouse ●
Food / Beverage ●
Accommodations
Pull Carts
Power Carts ●
Club Rental ●
$pecial Offers

	1	2	3	4	5	6	7	8	9	OUT
BACK	342	375	153	514	405	364	145	479	380	3157
REGULAR	294	345	126	460	329	343	142	442	337	2818
par	4	4	3	5	4	4	3	5	4	36
handicap	13	7	15	9	1	3	17	11	5	-
FORWARD	235	275	110	407	285	287	113	407	296	2415
par	4	4	3	5	4	4	3	5	4	36
handicap	9	5	17	1	13	7	15	3	11	-

	10	11	12	13	14	15	16	17	18	IN
BACK	385	175	375	472	344	390	492	183	395	3211
REGULAR	326	151	324	437	308	352	443	155	350	2846
par	4	3	4	5	4	4	5	3	4	36
handicap	8	18	6	16	14	12	2	10	4	-
FORWARD	272	102	263	402	265	313	403	122	302	2444
par	4	3	4	5	4	4	5	3	4	36
handicap	14	16	12	4	6	8	2	18	10	-

BACK	
yardage	6368
par	72
rating	71.5
slope	137

REGULAR	
yardage	5664
par	72
rating	67.3
slope	123

FORWARD	
yardage	4859
par	72
rating	68.4
slope	122

 PGA WEST: TPC STADIUM COURSE
ARCHITECT: PETE DYE, 1986

56-150 PGA Boulevard
La Quinta, CA 92253

PRO SHOP: 760-564-7170

Joey Garon, General Manager
Dave Doerr, Head Professional, PGA
Steve Auckland, Superintendent

Driving Range ●
Practice Greens ●
Clubhouse ●
Food / Beverage ●
Accommodations
Pull Carts
Power Carts ●
Club Rental ●
$pecial Offers

	1	2	3	4	5	6	7	8	9	OUT
BACK	377	349	446	171	512	223	319	526	430	3353
REGULAR	353	328	378	152	493	192	296	484	381	3057
par	4	4	4	3	5	3	4	5	4	36
handicap	11	15	3	17	1	7	13	9	5	-
FORWARD	296	288	322	112	434	133	242	427	315	2569
par	4	4	4	3	5	3	4	5	4	36
handicap	11	13	7	17	1	15	9	3	5	-

	10	11	12	13	14	15	16	17	18	IN
BACK	381	593	346	198	375	439	521	147	400	3400
REGULAR	351	530	309	171	349	407	479	128	383	3107
par	4	5	4	3	4	4	5	3	4	36
handicap	12	2	16	10	18	8	6	14	4	-
FORWARD	294	443	247	105	295	339	436	85	274	2518
par	4	5	4	3	4	4	5	3	4	36
handicap	6	2	14	18	10	12	4	16	8	-

BACK	
yardage	6753
par	72
rating	74.4
slope	139

REGULAR	
yardage	6164
par	72
rating	71.2
slope	130

FORWARD	
yardage	5087
par	72
rating	70.3
slope	124

69. PGA WEST: JACK NICKLAUS PRIVATE

PLAY POLICY & FEES: Members and guests only. Guests must be accompanied by members at time of play. The fees range from $105 to $250 depending on the season. Guest play is allowed after 11:00 am.

DRESS CODE: Appropriate golf attire and nonmetal spikes are required.

COURSE DESCRIPTION: This is a unique course with flowers, tall desert grasses, and water off the fairways. There are huge desert bunkers throughout the course. You may need a dune buggy to get in and out of these traps. Many fairways are defined by large mounds of grass.

LOCATION: Take the Indio Boulevard/Jefferson Street exit off Interstate 10 or Highway 111 and drive south to the end of Jefferson Street and PGA Boulevard.

. . . ● **TOURNAMENTS:** This course is not available for outside events. ●

TRAVEL: Places to stay in the area include the La Quinta Resort & Club, 760-564-4111, the Desert Springs Marriot Resort and Spa, 760-341-2211, and the Hyatt Grand Champions, 760-341-1000.

70. PGA WEST: TPC STADIUM COURSE

PLAY POLICY & FEES: Outside play is accepted. Green fees are seasonal and range from $60 to $235. Carts and range balls are included.

TEE TIMES: Reservations can be booked three days in advance by calling Tee Time Central at (800) PGA-WEST from October 31 to May 31.

DRESS CODE: Collared shirts and nonmetal spikes are required. No blue jeans are allowed.

COURSE DESCRIPTION: This course opened in 1986 and immediately secured a place in golf lore. It is packed with pot bunkers, sand, water, and sidehill lies. Large, undulating greens with several tiers make putting a chore. Among the course highlights is a 19-foot-deep, greenside bunker that flanks the par-5 16th hole. The course is expensive, difficult, and time-consuming in the busy season, deathly hot in off-season, and one of the top-10 must-play courses in the country.

NOTES: The Skins Game was played here from 1986 to 1991. The Bob Hope Classic was held here in 1987.

LOCATION: Take the Indio Boulevard/Jefferson Street exit off Interstate 10 or Highway 111 and drive south to the end of Jefferson Street to PGA Boulevard. Follow PGA Boulevard to the Resort Golf House.

. . . ● **TOURNAMENTS:** A 12-player minimum is needed to book a tournament. ● **TRAVEL:** Places to stay in the area include the La Quinta Resort & Club, 760-564-4111, the Desert Springs Marriot Resort and Spa, 760-341-2211, and the Hyatt Grand Champions, 760-341-1000.

71 PGA WEST: ARNOLD PALMER COURSE
ARCHITECT: ARNOLD PALMER, 1986

55-955 PGA Boulevard
La Quinta, CA 92253

PRO SHOP: 760-564-7100
CLUBHOUSE: 760-564-7111

John Cochrane, Director of Golf, PGA
Lisa Taggert, Head Professional, PGA
Dean Miller, Superintendent

Driving Range •
Practice Greens •
Clubhouse •
Food / Beverage •
Accommodations
Pull Carts
Power Carts •
Club Rental •
Special Offers

	1	2	3	4	5	6	7	8	9	OUT
BACK	405	490	156	373	207	531	390	317	421	3290
REGULAR	378	451	134	356	170	501	382	302	393	3067
par	4	5	3	4	3	5	4	4	4	36
handicap	11	9	15	13	7	5	1	17	3	-
FORWARD	343	432	122	292	119	432	312	287	331	2670
par	4	5	3	4	3	5	4	4	4	36
handicap	5	11	15	1	17	7	9	13	3	-

BACK		
yardage	6474	
par	72	
rating	71.4	
slope	129	

	10	11	12	13	14	15	16	17	18	IN
BACK	422	503	198	423	525	128	342	121	522	3184
REGULAR	409	485	168	401	478	122	318	102	466	2949
par	4	5	3	4	5	3	4	3	5	36
handicap	2	8	14	6	4	16	12	18	10	-
FORWARD	277	434	144	306	475	105	259	100	449	2549
par	4	5	3	4	5	3	4	3	5	36
handicap	12	8	14	6	2	16	10	18	4	-

REGULAR		
yardage	6016	
par	72	
rating	68.9	
slope	120	

FORWARD		
yardage	5219	
par	72	
rating	71.6	
slope	126	

72 PGA WEST: GREG NORMAN COURSE
ARCHITECT: GREG NORMAN, 1999

n/a
La Quinta, CA

PRO SHOP: N/A

Joey Garon, General Manager
Dave Doerr, Head Professional, PGA
Steve Aukland, Superintendent

Driving Range •
Practice Greens •
Clubhouse •
Food / Beverage •
Accommodations
Pull Carts
Power Carts •
Club Rental •
Special Offers

	1	2	3	4	5	6	7	8	9	OUT
BACK										
REGULAR										
par										
handicap										
FORWARD										
par										
handicap										

BACK		
yardage		
par		
rating		
slope		

	10	11	12	13	14	15	16	17	18	IN
BACK										
REGULAR										
par										
handicap										
FORWARD										
par										
handicap										

REGULAR		
yardage		
par		
rating		
slope		

FORWARD		
yardage		
par		
rating		
slope		

PLAY POLICY & FEES: Members and guests only. Guests must be accompanied by members. The guest fees range from $105 to $250. Guest play is allowed after 11:00 am.

DRESS CODE: Appropriate golf attire and nonmetal spikes are required.

COURSE DESCRIPTION: This demanding course plays as long as any of the courses in the area, except perhaps the Stadium Course. Bunkers distinguish the front nine, and hills the back nine. The last four holes are tight against the Santa Rosa Mountains. The tees are elevated above large greens, just the way Arnie likes them. Some greens are backed by massive boulders.

NOTES: This course will be one of the sites for the Bob Hope Chrysler Classic.

LOCATION: Take the Indio Boulevard/Jefferson Street exit off Interstate 10 or Highway 111 and drive south to the end of Jefferson Street to PGA Boulevard.

. . . ● **TOURNAMENTS:** This course is not available for outside events. ● **TRAVEL:** Places to stay in the area include the La Quinta Resort & Club, 760-564-4111, the Desert Springs Marriot Resort and Spa, 760-341-2211, and the Hyatt Grand Champions, 760-341-1000.

71. PGA WEST: ARNOLD PALMER COURSE

PLAY POLICY & FEES: The course is expected to be open late fall of 1999. Outside play is accepted. Green fees are seasonal and will range from $35 to $235. Carts will be included.

TEE TIMES: Reservations can be booked three days in advance for outside play.

DRESS CODE: Appropriate golf attire and nonmetal spikes will be required.

COURSE DESCRIPTION: The course was not available for play at time of press.

NOTES: Walking will be allowed on the course, but caddies will be required.

LOCATION: From Interstate 10 take the Indio Boulevard/Jefferson Street exit and drive south on Jefferson. Turn left on Avenue 54 and right on Madison Avenue to the course.

. . . ● **TOURNAMENTS:** A 12-player minimum will be required to book an event. Events should be booked three to six months in advance. ● **TRAVEL:** Places to stay in the area include La Quinta Resort & Club, 760-564-4111, Desert Springs Marriot Resort and Spa, 760-341-2211, and Hyatt Grand Champions, 760-341-1000.

72. PGA WEST: GREG NORMAN COURSE

⑦ PGA WEST: TOM WEISKOPF COURSE
ARCHITECT: TOM WEISKOPF, 1996

55-955 PGA Boulevard
La Quinta, CA 92253

John Cochrane, Director of Golf, PGA
Lisa Taggart, Head Professional, PGA
Brian Distel, Superintendent

Driving Range ●
Practice Greens ●
Clubhouse ●
Food / Beverage ●
Accommodations
Pull Carts
Power Carts ●
Club Rental ●
Special Offers

	1	2	3	4	5	6	7	8	9	OUT
BACK	404	438	169	520	358	438	180	463	534	3504
REGULAR	379	398	145	486	325	409	165	431	501	3239
par	4	4	3	5	4	4	3	4	5	36
handicap	1	3	11	15	13	7	9	5	17	-
FORWARD	354	372	135	451	295	378	149	394	468	2996
par	4	4	3	5	4	4	3	4	5	36
handicap	5	3	17	9	13	7	15	1	11	-

	10	11	12	13	14	15	16	17	18	IN
BACK	593	439	200	454	329	461	518	224	442	3660
REGULAR	571	402	185	418	294	428	485	204	408	3395
par	5	4	3	4	4	4	5	3	4	36
handicap	8	2	12	10	18	4	16	14	6	-
FORWARD	532	381	165	386	259	389	455	186	380	3133
par	5	4	3	4	4	4	5	3	4	36
handicap	2	4	14	12	18	8	6	16	10	-

BACK	
yardage	7164
par	72
rating	
slope	

REGULAR	
yardage	6634
par	72
rating	
slope	

FORWARD	
yardage	6129
par	72
rating	
slope	

⑦ THE PALMS GOLF CLUB
ARCHITECTS: BRIAN CURLEY, 1999; FRED COUPLES

P.O. Box 29
La Quinta, CA 92253

1 Palms Drive
La Quinta, CA 92253

PRO SHOP: 760-399-8090

Brian Calhoun, Head Professional, PGA

Driving Range ●
Practice Greens ●
Clubhouse ●
Food / Beverage ●
Accommodations
Pull Carts
Power Carts ●
Club Rental
Special Offers

	1	2	3	4	5	6	7	8	9	OUT
BACK										
REGULAR										
par										
handicap										
FORWARD										
par										
handicap										

	10	11	12	13	14	15	16	17	18	IN
BACK										
REGULAR										
par										
handicap										
FORWARD										
par										
handicap										

BACK	
yardage	7050
par	70
rating	
slope	

REGULAR	
yardage	
par	
rating	
slope	

FORWARD	
yardage	
par	
rating	
slope	

PLAY POLICY & FEES: Members and guests only. Guests must be accompanied by members at time of play. The fees range from $105 to $250 depending on the season. Guest play is allowed after 11 am.

DRESS CODE: Appropriate golf attire and nonmetal spikes are required.

COURSE DESCRIPTION: The Weiskopf Course is a well-maintained, long, and challenging golf course, with plenty of desert areas to keep you on your toes. Although much of the challenge comes in the length of the course, the fairways are fairly wide open giving players a chance to use their drivers. The greens are spacious, and the ball rolls true for those who have a deft touch.

LOCATION: Take the Indio Boulevard/Jefferson Street exit off Interstate 10 or Highway 111 and drive south to the end of Jefferson Street to PGA Boulevard.

. . . ● **TOURNAMENTS:** This course is not available for outside events. ●

TRAVEL: Places to stay in the area include La Quinta Resort & Club, 760-564-4111, Desert Springs Marriot Resort and Spa, 760-341-2211, and Hyatt Grand Champions, 760-341-1000.

73. PGA WEST: TOM WEISKOPF COURSE

PLAY POLICY & FEES: Members and guests only; reciprocal play is not allowed.

DRESS CODE: Appropriate golf attire and nonmetal spikes are required.

COURSE DESCRIPTION: The course was not open at time of press. The Palms Golf Club will be a traditional layout, with small greens and tree-lined fairways.

LOCATION: Streets to the course had not been developed at time of press. The course is directly across from the PGA West facility.

. . . ● **TOURNAMENTS:** Outside events will not be allowed.

74. THE PALMS GOLF CLUB

75 TRADITION GOLF CLUB
ARCHITECT: ARNOLD PALMER/ED SEAY, 1998

78505 Old Ave. 52
La Quinta, CA 92253

PRO SHOP: 760-564-1067

Doug Mauch, Head Professional, PGA
John Reynolds, General Manager
Lane Stave, Superintendent

Driving Range ●
Practice Greens ●
Clubhouse ●
Food / Beverage ●
Accommodations
Pull Carts
Power Carts ●
Club Rental ●
$pecial Offers

	1	2	3	4	5	6	7	8	9	OUT
BACK										
REGULAR										
par										
handicap										
FORWARD										
par										
handicap										

	10	11	12	13	14	15	16	17	18	IN
BACK										
REGULAR										
par										
handicap										
FORWARD										
par										
handicap										

BACK	
yardage	6925
par	72
rating	72.6
slope	134

REGULAR	
yardage	6530
par	72
rating	70.9
slope	129

FORWARD	
yardage	5545
par	72
rating	70.6
slope	130

76 INDIO GOLF CLUB
ARCHITECT: LAWRENCE HUGHES, 1964

P.O. Box X
Indio, CA 92202

83-040 Avenue 42
Indio, CA 92202

PRO SHOP: 760-347-9156

Mike Carroll, General Manager

Driving Range ●
Practice Greens ●
Clubhouse ●
Food / Beverage ●
Accommodations
Pull Carts ●
Power Carts ●
Club Rental ●
$pecial Offers

	1	2	3	4	5	6	7	8	9	OUT
BACK	-	-	-	-	-	-	-	-	-	-
REGULAR	148	137	201	241	155	181	192	158	169	1582
par	3	3	3	3	3	3	3	3	3	27
handicap	15	17	3	1	13	7	5	11	9	-
FORWARD	138	123	185	210	136	161	173	143	149	1418
par	3	3	3	3	3	3	3	3	3	27
handicap	15	17	3	1	13	7	5	11	9	-

	10	11	12	13	14	15	16	17	18	IN
BACK	-	-	-	-	-	-	-	-	-	-
REGULAR	120	145	179	210	159	148	161	184	116	1422
par	3	3	3	3	3	3	3	3	3	27
handicap	18	12	6	2	10	16	8	4	14	-
FORWARD	108	132	146	197	147	121	146	149	98	1244
par	3	3	3	3	3	3	3	3	3	27
handicap	18	12	6	2	10	16	8	4	14	-

BACK	
yardage	-
par	-
rating	-
slope	-

REGULAR	
yardage	3004
par	54
rating	53.2
slope	71

FORWARD	
yardage	2662
par	54
rating	-
slope	-

PLAY POLICY & FEES: Members and guests only. All guests must play with a member. Guest fees are $85.

DRESS CODE: Appropriate golf attire and nonmetal spikes are mandatory.

COURSE DESCRIPTION: Set in the Santa Rosa Mountains, this layout is traditional yet unusual in that is has five par 5s and five par 3s. The signature hole is the 17th, a short par-4 set 150 feet above the green. Looking down from the tee, players see a lake that guards the left side and the mountains that guard the right. An accurate drive is a must. In general, this course offers generous fairways but punishes those players who miss the greens.

LOCATION: Take Highway 10 to the Washington Street exit to La Quinta. Go south on Washington Street and follow it six miles to the course.

. . . ● **TOURNAMENTS:** Outside events are not allowed.

75. TRADITION GOLF CLUB

PLAY POLICY & FEES: Summer green fees are $8 for nine holes and $12 for 18 holes. Winter green fees are $10 for nine holes and $15 for 18 holes. Carts are $10 for 18 holes. The junior rate is $2 for nine holes. The course closes at 6 p.m. weekends.

TEE TIMES: Reservations can be booked three days in advance.

DRESS CODE: No tank tops are allowed on the course.

COURSE DESCRIPTION: This great little track is one of the longest par-3 courses in the country. The holes range from 120 to 240 yards, so bring all your irons. There is one lake that intersects three or four holes, depending on your shot.

NOTES: The course is night-lighted, and the last weekday tee time is 8 p.m.

LOCATION: Take the Jackson Street exit off Interstate 10 near Indio, drive north to Avenue 42, and turn right to the course.

. . . ● **TOURNAMENTS:** A 72-player minimum is needed to book a shotgun tournament.

76. INDIO GOLF CLUB

PRESIDENTS CLUB AT INDIAN PALMS
ARCHITECT: J. COCHRAN, H. DETWEILER, 1948

48-630 Monroe Street
Indio, CA 92201

PRO S HOP: 760-347-2326

David Pfotenhauer, General Manager

Driving Range ●
Practice Greens ●
Clubhouse ●
Food / Beverage ●
Accommodations ●
Pull Carts
Power Carts ●
Club Rental ●
$pecial Offers

	1	2	3	4	5	6	7	8	9	OUT
BACK	320	217	394	456	448	419	390	206	498	3348
REGULAR	309	180	386	452	401	410	372	188	480	3178
par	4	3	4	5	4	4	4	3	5	36
handicap	7	5	2	8	3	1	4	9	6	-
FORWARD	297	154	345	447	375	389	328	148	409	2892
par	4	3	4	5	4	4	4	3	5	36
handicap	7	9	5	2	4	3	6	8	1	-

	10	11	12	13	14	15	16	17	18	IN
BACK	507	225	358	394	405	379	477	184	432	3361
REGULAR	499	152	349	384	395	369	464	163	406	3181
par	5	3	4	4	4	4	5	3	4	36
handicap	2	9	8	5	3	7	6	4	1	-
FORWARD	482	143	341	330	382	359	404	120	406	2967
par	5	3	4	4	4	4	5	3	5	37
handicap	1	8	6	7	4	5	2	9	3	-

BACK	
yardage	6709
par	72
rating	72.7
slope	131

REGULAR	
yardage	6359
par	72
rating	70.5
slope	119

FORWARD	
yardage	5859
par	73
rating	74.1
slope	120

 HERITAGE PALMS GOLF CLUB
ARCHITECT: ARTHUR HILLS, 1996

44-291 Heritage Palms
South Indio, CA 92201

PRO S HOP: 760-772-7334

D.B. Temple, PGA Professional
Mike Eskuchen, Tournament Coordinator

Driving Range ●
Practice Greens ●
Clubhouse ●
Food / Beverage ●
Accommodations
Pull Carts ●
Power Carts ●
Club Rental ●
$pecial Offers

	1	2	3	4	5	6	7	8	9	OUT
BACK	351	531	181	417	395	411	510	164	428	3388
REGULAR	337	509	157	388	379	378	481	139	396	3164
par	4	5	3	4	4	4	5	3	4	36
handicap	17	9	15	1	5	7	11	13	3	-
FORWARD	266	418	95	304	284	296	404	95	305	2467
par	4	5	3	4	4	4	5	3	4	36
handicap	17	9	15	1	5	7	11	13	3	-

	10	11	12	13	14	15	16	17	18	IN
BACK	503	194	453	351	203	400	330	529	376	3339
REGULAR	486	169	434	331	165	380	308	506	350	3129
par	5	3	4	4	3	4	4	5	4	36
handicap	12	16	2	18	10	4	14	6	8	-
FORWARD	407	113	342	243	101	285	221	439	267	2418
par	5	3	4	4	3	4	4	5	4	36
handicap	12	16	2	18	10	4	14	6	8	-

BACK	
yardage	6727
par	72
rating	74.1
slope	119

REGULAR	
yardage	6293
par	72
rating	69.3
slope	114

FORWARD	
yardage	4885
par	72
rating	66.6
slope	107

PLAY POLICY & FEES: Outside play is accepted. Green fees are $70 during the winter season, $35 during the spring, and $25 during the summer. Call for twilight rates. Carts are included. Reservations are recommended.

TEE TIMES: Reservations can be booked three days in advance.

DRESS CODE: Collared shirts and nonmetal spikes are required. No cutoffs or denim are allowed.

COURSE DESCRIPTION: The original nine-hole course, called Indian Palms, was built in 1948 by world-famous aviatrix Jackie Cochran on her ranch that once served as a retreat for the rich and famous of the 1940s and '50s. The White and the Blue nines were built around 1980. The Blue has eight holes where water comes into play. All the courses have mature trees and natural growth along gently rolling terrain, leading to elevated greens.

NOTES: Dwight D. Eisenhower stayed at Indian Palms to write his memoirs. This course also has a small pitch-and-putt. The Red/White Course: see scorecard for yardage and rating information. The White/Blue Course is 6,184 yards and rated 69.5 from the regular tees with a slope of 118. Forward tees are 5,622 yards and rated 72.1 with a slope of 123. The Blue/Red Course is 6,181 yards and rated 69.4 from the regular tees with a slope of 118. Forward tees are 5,547 yards and rated 72.1 with a slope of 119.

LOCATION: Take the Monroe Street/Central Indio exit off Interstate 10 near Indio. Drive south on Monroe for 2.5 miles.

. . . ● **TOURNAMENTS:** This course is available for outside tournaments.

77. PRESIDENTS CLUB AT INDIAN PALMS

PLAY POLICY & FEES: Christmas to mid April green fees are $110. Mid April to the end of May green fees are $65. From June to the end of September, green fees are $40, and from October until Christmas, green fees are $85. Twilight and replay rates are available. Shared carts are included.

TEE TIMES: Reservations can be booked seven days in advance.

DRESS CODE: Collared shirts are a must. No denim is allowed on the course and shorts must be Bermuda length.

COURSE DESCRIPTION: Heritage Palms is a manicured golf course with spectacular mountain views. The hardest hole is the fourth, a par 4 with a lake running down the the left side. But don't miss right—the ball may find a trap, or worse yet, out-of-bounds.

LOCATION: From Highway 10, take the Jefferson Street exit and head south. Make a left on Fred Waring Drive; the course is on the right.

. . . ● **TOURNAMENTS:** A 16-player minimum is needed to book a tournament. Carts are required. The banquet facility can accommodate 500 people.

78. HERITAGE PALMS GOLF CLUB

THE PLANTATION GOLF
ARCHITECTS: BRIAN CURLEY, 1998; FRED COUPLES

50994 Monroe Street
Indio, CA 92201

PRO SHOP: 760-775-3688

Mike Kingsrud, Director of Golf, PGA

Driving Range ●
Practice Greens ●
Clubhouse ●
Food / Beverage ●
Accommodations
Pull Carts
Power Carts ●
Club Rental
$pecial Offers

	1	2	3	4	5	6	7	8	9	OUT
BACK										
REGULAR										
par										
handicap										
FORWARD										
par										
handicap										

	10	11	12	13	14	15	16	17	18	IN
BACK										
REGULAR										
par										
handicap										
FORWARD										
par										
handicap										

BACK	
yardage	7040
par	72
rating	73.9
slope	134

REGULAR	
yardage	6590
par	72
rating	71.7
slope	127

FORWARD	
yardage	6196
par	72
rating	69.9
slope	124

 ## THE RESERVE
ARCHITECTS: JAY MORRISH, 1998; TOM WEISKOPF

74001 Drive
Indio, CA 92210

PRO SHOP: 760-776-6605

Bill Feil, PGA Professional

Driving Range ●
Practice Greens ●
Clubhouse ●
Food / Beverage ●
Accommodations
Pull Carts
Power Carts ●
Club Rental
$pecial Offers

	1	2	3	4	5	6	7	8	9	OUT
BACK										
REGULAR										
par										
handicap										
FORWARD										
par										
handicap										

	10	11	12	13	14	15	16	17	18	IN
BACK										
REGULAR										
par										
handicap										
FORWARD										
par										
handicap										

BACK	
yardage	
par	
rating	
slope	

REGULAR	
yardage	
par	
rating	
slope	

FORWARD	
yardage	
par	
rating	
slope	

PLAY POLICY & FEES: Members and guests only; no reciprocal play is allowed.

DRESS CODE: Appropriate golf attire is required.

COURSE DESCRIPTION: This Brian Curley–Fred Couple design is situated upon the flat desert floor, but subtle creative mounding and bunkering make it a compelling test of golf, one of the very best in the area. Couples' influence upon the design is reflected in his affection for Augusta National and Riviera. Date palms and citrus trees line the fairways of this former nursery, making it appear that the course has been around beyond its years.

LOCATION: From Interstate 10 in Indio take the Monroe exit and turn right on Monroe. The course is on the left-hand side just past 50th Avenue.

. . . ● **TOURNAMENTS:** No outside events are allowed.

79. THE PLANTATION GOLF CLUB

PLAY POLICY & FEES: Members and guests only. No reciprocal play is allowed.

DRESS CODE: Appropriate golf attire and nonmetal spikes are required.

COURSE DESCRIPTION: This course was built on one of the last pristine sites in the desert. Built up against the mountains, the course features elevation changes subtle to the eye, but dramatic in the way you must play the course. The slight elevations to some of the greens will find newcomers underclubbing. The fairways, for the most part, allow you to take out the driver, but a few holes give you the chance to hone your nerves. Is the risk worth the reward?

NOTES: The Reserve has three practice holes.

LOCATION: From Highway 10 southeast of Palm Springs, take Highway 111 east to Portola Avenue. Take Portola south. The golf course entrance will be on your left..

. . . ● **TOURNAMENTS:** No outside events are allowed.

80. THE RESERVE

84-000 Landmark Parkway
Indio, CA 92203

PRO SHOP: 760-775-2000

Jeff Walser, Director of Golf, PGA
Willie Lopez, Superintendent

Driving Range ●
Practice Greens ●
Clubhouse ●
Food / Beverage ●
Accommodations
Pull Carts
Power Carts ●
Club Rental ●
$pecial Offers

	1	2	3	4	5	6	7	8	9	OUT
BACK	386	411	539	185	478	229	437	577	448	3690
REGULAR	338	348	479	119	390	167	361	523	387	3112
par	4	4	5	3	4	3	4	5	4	36
handicap										-
FORWARD	303	269	445	97	327	139	317	499	333	2729
par	4	4	5	3	4	3	4	5	4	36
handicap										-

	10	11	12	13	14	15	16	17	18	IN
BACK	363	478	188	540	233	578	360	139	513	3392
REGULAR	338	348	479	119	390	167	361	523	387	3112
par	4	4	3	5	3	5	4	3	5	36
handicap										-
FORWARD	263	376	120	432	163	444	269	77	392	2536
par	4	4	3	5	3	5	4	3	5	36
handicap										-

BACK	
yardage	7082
par	72
rating	
slope	

REGULAR	
yardage	6224
par	72
rating	
slope	

FORWARD	
yardage	5265
par	72
rating	
slope	

PLAY POLICY & FEES: Green fees are $135 October 29 through December 25. From December 26 through April, green fees are $160. All rates include range balls and golf cart.

TEE TIMES: Reservations booked14 days in advance must be secured with a credit card.

DRESS CODE: Appropriate golf attire and nonmetal spikes are required.

COURSE DESCRIPTION: Landmark Golf Club is a 36-hole course located in the foothills of the Indio Hills. The facility is due to open in the fall of 1999, and by all accounts will soon become a "don't miss" course for golfers in the desert. The course features constant elevations changes, undulating greens, and views ranging from San Gorgonio Mountain to the Chocolate Mountains.

NOTES: Landmark Golf Club will host the the Skins Game for the next five seasons. The 1998 champion was Mark O'Meara, who earned $430,000. The bridges at Landmark are crafted from vintage railroad cars. The South Course yardages are shown above; the North Course yardages range from 5,272 yards to 7,021 yards.

LOCATION: From Interstate 10 heading east to Indio, take the Golf Center Parkway exit and head north one mile. The course is on the right.

. . . ● **TOURNAMENTS:** An eight-player minimum is required to book an event. Tournaments should be booked eight months in advance. The banquet facility can accommodate up to 350 people.

81. LANDMARK GOLF CLUB

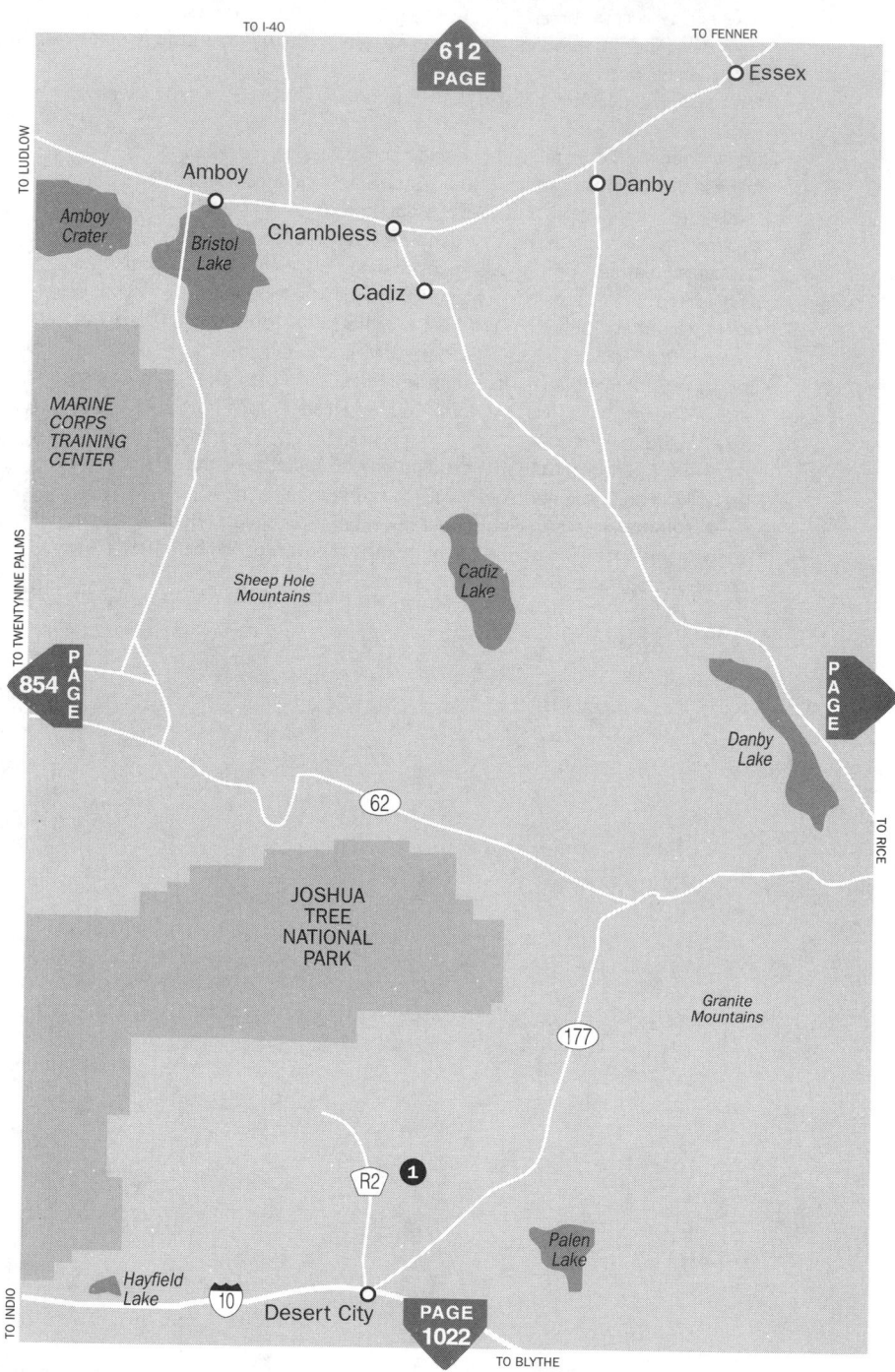

TO I-40

TO FENNER

**612
PAGE**

○ Essex

TO LUDLOW

Amboy
○

○ Danby

*Amboy
Crater*

Chambless ○

*Bristol
Lake*

Cadiz ○

MARINE
CORPS
TRAINING
CENTER

TO TWENTYNINE PALMS

*Sheep Hole
Mountains*

*Cadiz
Lake*

**P
854 A
G
E**

*Danby
Lake*

**P
A
G
E**

TO RICE

62

JOSHUA
TREE
NATIONAL
PARK

*Granite
Mountains*

177

R2 **1**

*Palen
Lake*

TO INDIO

*Hayfield
Lake*

10

Desert City

**PAGE
1022**

TO BLYTHE

Desert City Area

LAKE TAMARISK GOLF CLUB

ARCHITECT: ROBERT TRENT JONES SR., 1967

P.O. Box 316
Desert Center, CA 92239

26-251 Parkview Drive
Desert Center, CA 92239

PRO SHOP: 760-227-3203

Steve Jones, Manager

Driving Range
Practice Greens ●
Clubhouse ●
Food / Beverage
Accommodations
Pull Carts ●
Power Carts ●
Club Rental ●
$pecial Offers

	1	2	3	4	5	6	7	8	9	OUT
BACK	-	-	-	-	-	-	-	-	-	-
REGULAR	482	198	334	398	340	172	285	396	360	2965
par	5	3	4	4	4	3	4	4	4	35
handicap	5	7	13	3	15	8	17	1	9	-
FORWARD	455	135	313	395	324	153	285	396	330	2786
par	5	3	4	4	4	3	4	4	4	37
handicap	1	17	7	13	5	15	9	11	3	-

	10	11	12	13	14	15	16	17	18	IN
BACK	-	-	-	-	-	-	-	-	-	-
REGULAR	482	167	334	398	340	172	285	396	360	2934
par	5	3	4	4	4	3	4	4	4	35
handicap	6	12	14	4	16	11	18	2	10	-
FORWARD	455	135	313	395	324	153	285	396	330	2786
par	5	3	4	5	4	3	4	5	4	37
handicap	2	18	8	14	6	16	10	12	4	-

BACK	
yardage	-
par	-
rating	-
slope	-

REGULAR	
yardage	5899
par	70
rating	66.9
slope	100

FORWARD	
yardage	5572
par	74
rating	69.9
slope	104

PLAY POLICY & FEES: Green fees are $16 for 18 holes. Carts are $10 for nine holes and $12 for 18 holes. Reservations are recommended January through April.

TEE TIMES: Reservations can be booked 24 hours in advance.

DRESS CODE: Shirts must be worn.

COURSE DESCRIPTION: This is literally an oasis in the middle of the desert. Refreshing lakes line the course, and palm trees and oleanders flank the fairways. The course is fairly level, but the tees and greens are elevated.

NOTES: If "warm" weather doesn't bother you, head for Lake Tamarisk and play unlimited golf for $6 per day in June, July, and August.

LOCATION: Travel east from Indio on Interstate 10 for about 50 miles and take the Desert Center Road exit north. Bear left onto Kaiser Road and drive 1.5 miles to the entrance.

. . . ● **TOURNAMENTS:** Shotgun tournaments are available weekdays only.

1. LAKE TAMARISK GOLF CLUB

Desert City Area (map page 938)

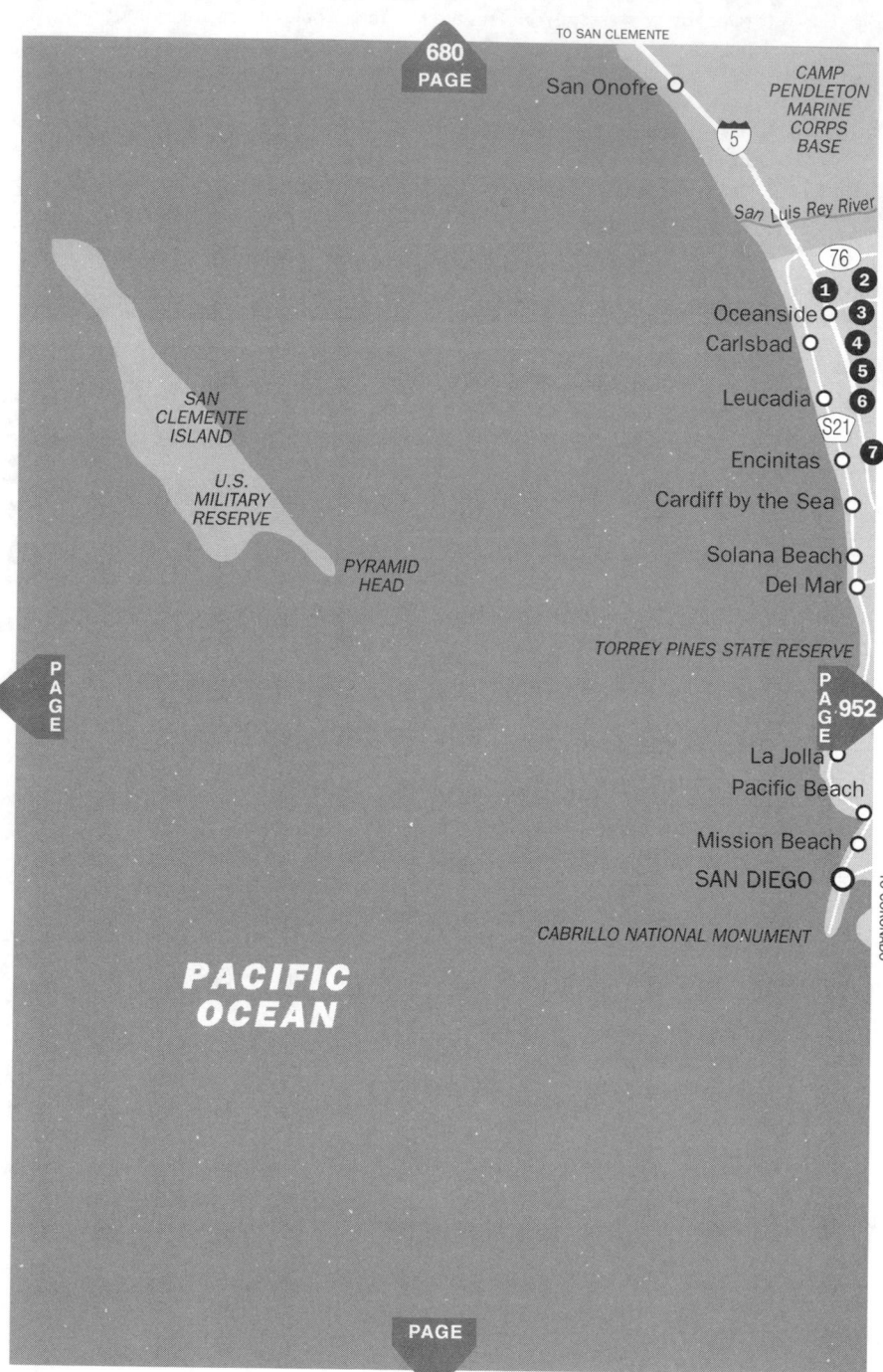

TO SAN CLEMENTE

680
PAGE

San Onofre ○

CAMP
PENDLETON
MARINE
CORPS
BASE

5

San Luis Rey River

TO BONSALL

76

1 2

Oceanside ○ 3

TO SAN MARCOS

Carlsbad ○ 4
5

Leucadia ○ 6

S21

Encinitas ○ 7

Cardiff by the Sea ○

Solana Beach ○

Del Mar ○

TORREY PINES STATE RESERVE

P
A
G
E

P
A
G
E **952**

La Jolla ○

Pacific Beach
○

Mission Beach ○

SAN DIEGO ○

TO CORONADO

CABRILLO NATIONAL MONUMENT

**PACIFIC
OCEAN**

*SAN
CLEMENTE
ISLAND*

*U.S.
MILITARY
RESERVE*

*PYRAMID
HEAD*

PAGE

Escondido/Oceanside/ Carlsbad Area

❶ CENTER CITY GOLF COURSE

P.O. Box 1088
Oceanside, CA 92054

Saratoga at Oceanside
Oceanside, CA 92054

PRO SHOP: 760-433-8590

Ludwig Keehn, Director of Golf, PGA
Debbie Herbert, Professional

Driving Range	●
Practice Greens	●
Clubhouse	●
Food / Beverage	●
Accommodations	
Pull Carts	●
Power Carts	●
Club Rental	●
$pecial Offers	

	1	2	3	4	5	6	7	8	9	OUT
BACK	332	165	325	327	146	185	158	335	138	2111
REGULAR	320	150	320	315	135	165	130	315	116	1966
par	4	3	4	4	3	3	3	4	3	31
handicap	17	1	13	7	11	3	9	5	15	-
FORWARD	305	145	320	305	125	180	101	305	103	1889
par	4	3	4	4	3	4	3	4	3	32
handicap	11	1	3	5	15	7	13	9	17	-

	10	11	12	13	14	15	16	17	18	IN
BACK	325	172	325	170	281	460	348	145	310	2536
REGULAR	310	156	315	155	253	430	325	135	300	2379
par	4	3	4	3	4	5	4	3	4	34
handicap	12	6	4	10	14	8	2	16	18	-
FORWARD	302	139	305	140	253	415	310	110	285	2259
par	4	3	4	3	4	5	4	3	4	34
handicap	10	12	4	14	8	2	6	16	18	-

BACK	
yardage	4647
par	65
rating	-
slope	-

REGULAR	
yardage	4345
par	65
rating	-
slope	-

FORWARD	
yardage	4148
par	66
rating	-
slope	-

❷ EL CAMINO COUNTRY CLUB
ARCHITECT: WILLIAM F. BELL, 1958

3202 Vista Way
Oceanside, CA 92056

PRO SHOP: 760-757-0321
CLUBHOUSE: 760-757-2100

Mike Carey, Manager
Cliff Myers, PGA Professional
Larry Jones, Superintendent

Driving Range	
Practice Greens	●
Clubhouse	●
Food / Beverage	●
Accommodations	
Pull Carts	●
Power Carts	●
Club Rental	●
$pecial Offers	

	1	2	3	4	5	6	7	8	9	OUT
BACK	503	375	418	375	423	164	533	392	435	3618
REGULAR	488	356	386	366	409	141	527	358	375	3406
par	5	4	4	4	4	3	5	4	4	37
handicap	5	15	7	13	1	17	3	11	9	-
FORWARD	430	343	343	354	361	136	471	337	366	3141
par	5	4	4	4	4	3	5	4	4	37
handicap	3	11	15	7	9	17	1	13	5	-

	10	11	12	13	14	15	16	17	18	IN
BACK	359	152	374	206	512	429	131	557	396	3116
REGULAR	351	134	362	199	478	412	126	540	354	2956
par	4	3	4	3	5	4	3	5	4	35
handicap	10	16	8	12	4	2	18	6	14	-
FORWARD	347	103	343	180	463	344	93	474	326	2673
par	4	3	4	3	5	4	3	5	4	35
handicap	12	18	6	14	4	2	16	8	10	-

BACK	
yardage	6734
par	72
rating	72.5
slope	130

REGULAR	
yardage	6362
par	72
rating	70.0
slope	119

FORWARD	
yardage	5814
par	72
rating	73.5
slope	130

PLAY POLICY & FEES: Green fees are $12 weekdays and $15 weekends for 18 holes.

TEE TIMES: Reservations are not accepted. All play is on a first-come, first-served basis.

DRESS CODE: No tank tops or short shorts are allowed.

COURSE DESCRIPTION: This 35-year-old course is executive length and includes nine par 4s and one par 5. The course is hilly, with greens on the large side—and there is only one bunker on the site.

LOCATION: Take linterstate 5 to the Oceanside Boulevard in Oceanside. Drive inland. Stay in the left lane and turn left on Saratoga. The course is two blocks from the freeway.

. . . ● **TOURNAMENTS:** This course is available for outside tournaments.

1. CENTER CITY GOLF COURSE

PLAY POLICY & FEES: Members, guests, and those sponsored by the professional only.

DRESS CODE: Nonmetal spikes are required.

COURSE DESCRIPTION: This course features a flat layout with plenty of trees and narrow fairways that offer little trouble. The course plays long, so be prepared. It's not laid out in a circle, but pretty close to it, so there are out-of-bounds areas to the left of every hole.

LOCATION: Take Interstate 5 to the Highway 78 exit in Oceanside. Drive to El Camino Real exit north and cross the overpass to Vista Way. Turn right and drive one-quarter mile to the club.

. . . ● **TOURNAMENTS:** This course is not available for outside events.

2. EL CAMINO COUNTRY CLUB

③ EMERALD ISLE GOLF
ARCHITECT: MIKE GANDY, 1986

660 South El Camino Real
Oceanside, CA 92054

PRO SHOP: 760-721-4700
OFFICE: 760-721-4774

Al Meddings, Manager
Jeff Sampson, PGA Professional
Raul Vargas, Superintendent

Driving Range ●
Practice Greens ●
Clubhouse ●
Food / Beverage ●
Accommodations
Pull Carts ●
Power Carts ●
Club Rental ●
$pecial Offers

	1	2	3	4	5	6	7	8	9	OUT
BACK	162	215	167	140	167	124	256	113	156	1500
REGULAR	147	205	145	125	140	115	245	108	135	1365
par	3	4	3	3	3	3	4	3	3	29
handicap	7	15	1	17	5	13	9	11	3	-
FORWARD	135	200	120	110	130	105	237	100	100	1237
par	3	4	3	3	3	3	4	3	3	29
handicap	9	7	1	15	11	13	3	17	5	-

	10	11	12	13	14	15	16	17	18	IN
BACK	160	105	137	128	145	185	136	90	117	1203
REGULAR	147	90	120	96	133	150	115	85	97	1033
par	3	3	3	3	3	3	3	3	3	27
handicap	4	10	8	12	6	2	14	16	18	-
FORWARD	135	85	115	85	115	110	90	85	80	900
par	3	3	3	3	3	3	3	3	3	27
handicap	4	12	8	10	6	2	16	14	18	-

BACK	
yardage	2703
par	56
rating	55.4
slope	-

REGULAR	
yardage	2398
par	56
rating	54.5
slope	-

FORWARD	
yardage	2137
par	56
rating	56.0
slope	-

④ LA COSTA RESORT & SPA
ARCHITECT: DICK WILSON, JOESPH LEE, 1964

GOLF 50

Costa del Mar Road
Carlsbad, CA 92009

PRO SHOP: 760-438-9111

Gary Glaser, Director of Golf, PGA
Scott Wilson, PGA Professional
Ernie Anaya, Superintendent

Driving Range ●
Practice Greens ●
Clubhouse ●
Food / Beverage ●
Accommodations ●
Pull Carts
Power Carts ●
Club Rental ●
$pecial Offers

	1	2	3	4	5	6	7	8	9	OUT
BACK	413	526	187	382	389	548	460	199	415	3519
REGULAR	396	506	161	373	376	527	446	169	392	3346
par	4	5	3	4	4	5	4	3	4	36
handicap	9	3	17	15	13	1	5	11	7	-
FORWARD	329	485	132	351	352	476	417	140	324	3006
par	4	5	3	4	4	5	5	3	4	37
handicap	11	3	17	7	9	1	13	15	5	-

	10	11	12	13	14	15	16	17	18	IN
BACK	539	384	221	387	447	363	189	398	540	3468
REGULAR	520	374	202	358	421	347	158	374	508	3262
par	5	4	3	4	4	4	3	4	5	36
handicap	6	8	14	10	2	12	18	16	4	-
FORWARD	498	326	158	322	332	323	133	354	487	2933
par	5	4	3	4	4	4	3	4	5	36
handicap	2	14	16	10	6	8	18	12	4	-

BACK	
yardage	6987
par	72
rating	74.8
slope	137

REGULAR	
yardage	6608
par	72
rating	72.1
slope	128

FORWARD	
yardage	5939
par	73
rating	74.0
slope	127

PLAY POLICY & FEES: Green fees are $16 weekdays and $21 weekends and holidays. The rate of $10 weekdays and $16 weekends and holidays is for senior members only. Carts are $18 weekdays and $20 weekends and holidays. Reservations are recommended.

TEE TIMES: Reservations are made the same day.

DRESS CODE: Shirts must be worn.

COURSE DESCRIPTION: This is a challenging course with two par 4s on the front nine, the longest measuring 245 yards. Water comes into play on seven holes, while trees, bunkers, and rolling terrain also keep golfers honest.

LOCATION: Take Interstate 5 south to Oceanside. Take the Highway 76 exit east and go two miles. Turn right on El Camino Real. Turn left at the first light, Vista Oceana, and drive one block to the course.

. . . ● **TOURNAMENTS:** Shotgun tournaments are available weekday mornings only. A 16-player minimum is needed to book a tournament. A 20 percent deposit is required for tournament play. ● **TRAVEL:** The Best Western Oceanside is seven minutes from the golf course. For reservations call 760-722-1821.

3. EMERALD ISLE GOLF

PLAY POLICY & FEES: Members and guests only. Hotel guests are welcome. Green fees are $140. Carts are $20.

TEE TIMES: If staying at the resort, golfers can make tee times when reservations are made.

DRESS CODE: No denim, short shorts, or T-shirts are allowed on the course.

COURSE DESCRIPTION: The North Course is wide open and rolling, while the South Course is tighter and more demanding. Water and tree-lined fairways make accuracy a must.

NOTES: This is the site of the PGA Tour's Anderson Consulting Match Play World Golf Championship. Nine holes of each course are used for the tournament. See scorecard for additional yardage and rating information on the North Course. The South Course is 6,894 yards and rated 74.4 from the tournament tees, 6,524 yards and rated 72.0 from the championship tees, and 6,198 yards and rated 69.8 from the regular tees. The slope ratings are 138 tournament, 129 championship, and 121 regular. Women's tees are 5,612 yards and rated 72.1. The slope rating is 123.

LOCATION: Drive 20 miles north of San Diego on Interstate 5 to the La Costa Avenue exit east. Go 1.5 miles to El Camino Real and turn left to the club.

. . . ● **TOURNAMENTS:** This course is not available for outside events. The banquet facility can accommodate up to 800 people.

4. LA COSTA RESORT & SPA

FOUR SEASONS RESORT AVIARA GOLF CLUB
ARCHITECT: ARNOLD P ALMER, ED S EAY, 1991

7447 Batiquitos Drive
Carlsbad, CA 92009

PRO S HOP: 760-603-6900
CLUBHOUSE: 760-603-6911

Jim Bellington, Director of Golf, PGA
Bill Crist, Head Professional, PGA
Dick Rudolph, Superintendent

Driving Range ●
Practice Greens ●
Clubhouse ●
Food / Beverage ●
Accommodations ●
Pull Carts
Power Carts ●
Club Rental ●
$pecial Offers ●

	1	2	3	4	5	6	7	8	9	OUT
BACK	389	420	149	393	543	195	404	536	375	3404
REGULAR	351	391	147	362	508	188	393	519	348	3207
par	4	4	3	4	5	3	4	5	4	36
handicap	9	3	17	7	1	11	13	5	15	-
FORWARD	260	310	107	294	430	133	291	417	284	2526
par	4	4	3	4	5	3	4	5	4	36
handicap	9	3	17	7	1	11	13	5	15	-

	10	11	12	13	14	15	16	17	18	IN
BACK	515	189	405	374	201	473	418	585	443	3603
REGULAR	489	178	368	346	190	445	387	568	413	3384
par	5	3	4	4	3	4	4	5	4	36
handicap	8	18	12	14	10	6	16	4	15	-
FORWARD	386	128	228	269	138	319	290	414	309	2481
par	5	3	4	4	3	4	4	5	4	36
handicap	8	18	12	14	10	6	16	4	2	-

BACK	
yardage	7007
par	72
rating	74.2
slope	137

REGULAR	
yardage	6591
par	72
rating	71.8
slope	130

FORWARD	
yardage	5007
par	72
rating	69.1
slope	119

RANCHO CARLSBAD GOLF COURSE

5200 El Camino Real
Carlsbad, CA 92008

PRO S HOP: 760-438-1772

Howard T. Fujimoto, Director of Golf, PGA
Rito Mendoza, Superintendent

Driving Range ●
Practice Greens ●
Clubhouse
Food / Beverage ●
Accommodations
Pull Carts ●
Power Carts
Club Rental ●
$pecial Offers

	1	2	3	4	5	6	7	8	9	OUT
BACK	232	74	68	155	137	74	166	67	307	1280
REGULAR	222	71	60	141	126	67	144	57	254	1142
par	4	3	3	3	3	3	3	3	4	29
handicap	7	17	15	3	9	13	1	11	5	-
FORWARD	211	63	49	127	114	59	133	49	236	1041
par	4	3	3	3	3	3	3	3	4	29
handicap	3	11	15	9	7	13	5	17	1	-

	10	11	12	13	14	15	16	17	18	IN
BACK	101	167	96	176	151	82	138	132	73	1116
REGULAR	89	152	90	164	142	75	131	108	65	1016
par	3	3	3	3	3	3	3	3	3	27
handicap	10	4	18	2	6	14	8	16	12	-
FORWARD	66	129	84	155	136	65	121	101	57	914
par	3	3	3	3	3	3	3	3	3	27
handicap	8	6	18	2	4	12	10	16	14	-

BACK	
yardage	2396
par	56
rating	-
slope	-

REGULAR	
yardage	2158
par	56
rating	-
slope	-

FORWARD	
yardage	1955
par	56
rating	-
slope	-

RESORT: $95-$175 **18**
HOLES

PLAY POLICY & FEES: Outside play is accepted. Green fees are $175 including cart. Twilight green fees are $95.

TEE TIMES: Reservations can be booked six days in advance.

DRESS CODE: Appropriate golf attire and nonmetal spikes are required.

COURSE DESCRIPTION: An Arnold Palmer design, both "Golf Magazine" and "Golf Digest" rated this one of the best new resort courses in 1991 and 1992, and with good reason. It follows the coastal topography and features wide fairways and enormous greens. The course is in top condition.

LOCATION: From Interstate 5 at Carlsbad, take the Poinsettia Lane exit east for one mile to Aviara Parkway. Turn right and drive one mile to Batiquitos Drive.

. . . ● **TOURNAMENTS:** Outside events are allowed for guests of the hotel. ●

TRAVEL: For reservations at this award-winning resort call 760-603-6800. ●

$PECIAL OFFERS: Besides traditional play-and-stay packages, the Four Seasons offers a golf and spa getaway.

5. FOUR SEASONS RESORT AVIARA GOLF

PUBLIC: $9.5-$14.5 **18**
FAX: 760-438-4750   **www.birdie.com/rancarl**   HOLES

PLAY POLICY & FEES: Green fees are $11.50 weekdays and $14.50 weekends. Twilight fees are $9.50 weekdays and $11.50 weekends. Junior and resident rates are also available.

TEE TIMES: Reservations can be booked seven days in advance.

DRESS CODE: No tank tops are allowed on the course.

COURSE DESCRIPTION: This is a well-maintained course with flat terrain. It's challenging for any caliber of golfer. It's a tight, tree-lined course, but a good shot is rewarded. The greens tend to be fast and tricky to putt. The two par 4s are 260 and 225 yards.

LOCATION: From Interstate 5 take Highway 78 east to El Camino Real (County Road S-11). Drive south to Rancho Carlsbad Drive and turn left to the course.

. . . ● **TOURNAMENTS:** A 72-player minimum is needed for a shotgun tournament. A 24-player minimum is needed for a regular tournament. Events should be booked three months in advance. ● **TRAVEL:** The Carlsbad Inn is seven miles from the golf course. For information or reservations call 760-434-7020.

6. RANCHO CARLSBAD GOLF COURSE

ENCINITAS RANCH GOLF COURSE

ARCHITECT: CARY BICKLER, 1998

1275 Quail Garden Drive
Encinitas, CA 92024

PRO SHOP: 760-944-1936
STARTER: 760-944-2964

Robert Powell, PGA Professional
Mark Warren, Superintendent
Scott Brand, Tournament Director

Driving Range ●
Practice Greens ●
Clubhouse
Food / Beverage ●
Accommodations
Pull Carts ●
Power Carts ●
Club Rental ●
$pecial Offers

	1	2	3	4	5	6	7	8	9	OUT
BACK	442	540	169	435	433	398	361	205	601	3584
REGULAR	434	532	159	398	420	373	353	185	495	3349
par	4	5	3	4	4	4	4	3	5	36
handicap	3	7	17	1	5	15	13	11	9	-
FORWARD	334	432	85	300	325	213	260	105	385	2439
par	4	5	3	4	4	4	4	3	5	36
handicap	9	7	17	3	5	13	11	15	1	-

	10	11	12	13	14	15	16	17	18	IN
BACK	391	168	527	342	380	160	365	407	497	3237
REGULAR	385	158	522	337	370	154	355	401	490	3172
par	4	3	5	4	4	3	4	4	5	36
handicap	12	16	6	14	8	18	4	2	10	-
FORWARD	271	106	415	224	258	109	252	206	393	2234
par	4	3	5	4	4	3	4	4	5	36
handicap	12	18	10	14	2	16	6	4	8	-

BACK	
yardage	6821
par	72
rating	72.2
slope	127

REGULAR	
yardage	6521
par	72
rating	71.0
slope	124

FORWARD	
yardage	4673
par	72
rating	68.5
slope	107

PLAY POLICY & FEES: Green fees for residents are $30 Monday through Thursday, $36 Friday, and $45 weekends. For nonresidents, green fees are $40 Monday through Thursday, $46 Friday, and $57 weekends and holidays. Twilight rates are available. Carts are $10 per rider.

TEE TIMES: Reservations can be made seven days in advance.

DRESS CODE: Shirts must have collars, and shorts must be Bermuda length. No jeans or metal spikes are allowed on the course.

COURSE DESCRIPTION: This course is one-half mile inland from the coast and offers excellent views of the ocean from 14 holes. At this time, Encinitas is extremely driver friendly due to the short, new trees lining the fairways. Take advantage while you can. The greens are firm, but roll true. The afternoon breeze can make this challenging course downright tough.

LOCATION: From Interstate 5 in Encinitas, take the Lacadia Drive exit. Head east one mile on Lacadia to Quail Gardens Drive.

. . . ● **TOURNAMENTS:** A 16-player minimum is required to book an event. The banquet facility can accommodate up to 200 people.

7. ENCINITAS RANCH GOLF COURSE

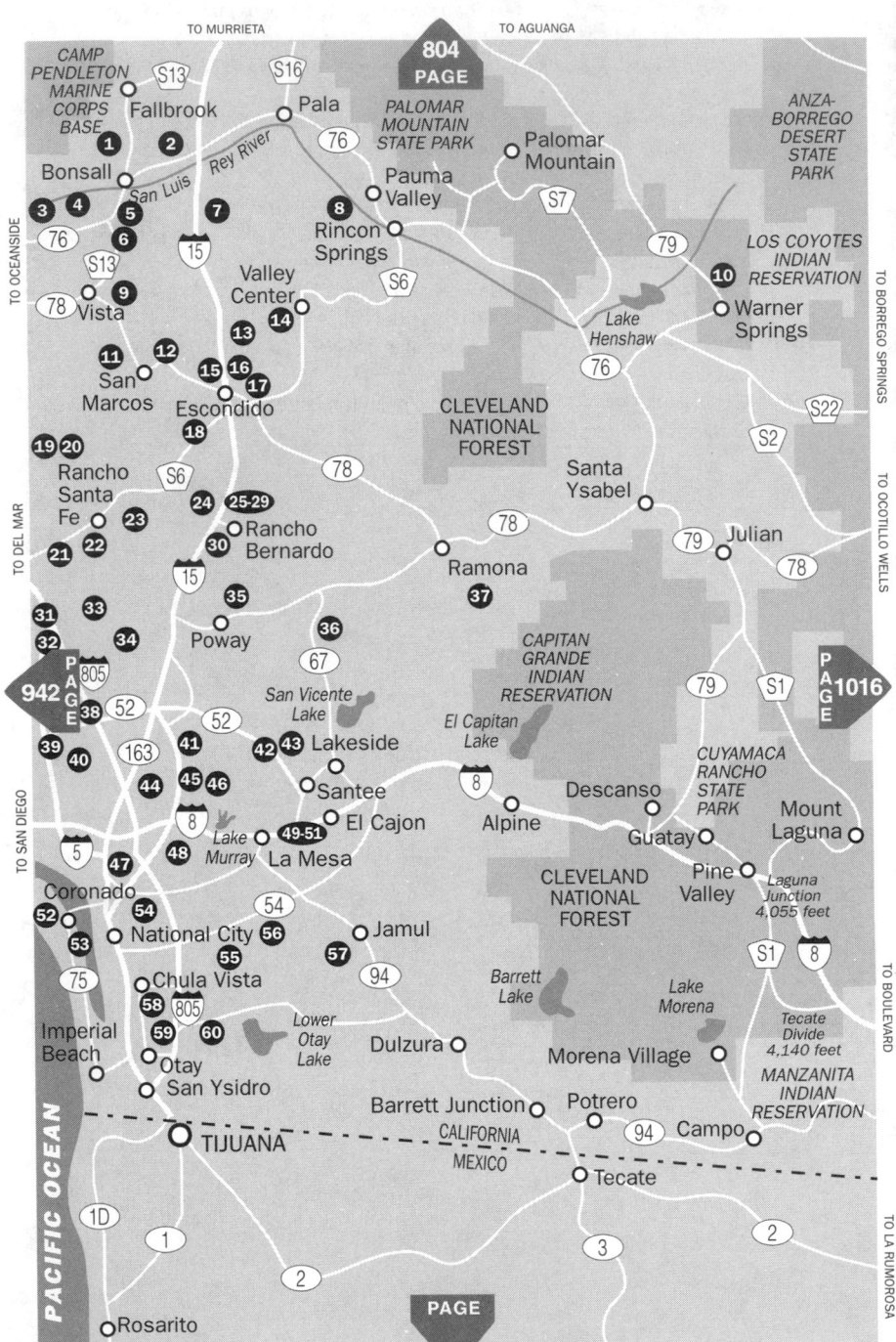

TO MURRIETA
TO AGUANGA

804 PAGE

CAMP PENDLETON MARINE CORPS BASE

S13
S16

Fallbrook
Pala

1
2

Bonsall
San Luis Rey River

3
4
5
6
7

76

S13

9

Vista

78

Valley Center

13
14

11
12

San Marcos

15
16
17

Escondido

18

19
20

Rancho Santa Fe

S6

23
24

22
21

25-29

Rancho Bernardo

30

15

35

Poway

31
33

32
34

805

942 PAGE

38

52

39
40

163

41

42
43
Lakeside

44
45
46

Santee

8

49-51
El Cajon
La Mesa

48

47

Lake Murray

Coronado

52
54
53

National City
56

75

55

Chula Vista

58
805

59
60

Imperial Beach

Otay
San Ysidro

TIJUANA

Rosarito

TO ENSENADA, MEXICO

PALOMAR MOUNTAIN STATE PARK

Palomar Mountain

Pauma Valley

8

Rincon Springs

76

S7

S6

ANZA-BORREGO DESERT STATE PARK

LOS COYOTES INDIAN RESERVATION

79

10

Warner Springs

76

S22

CLEVELAND NATIONAL FOREST

Santa Ysabel

78

78

Ramona

37

S2

79

Julian

78

CAPITAN GRANDE INDIAN RESERVATION

El Capitan Lake

San Vicente Lake

67

36

79

S1

P PAGE 1016

CUYAMACA RANCHO STATE PARK

8

Alpine

Descanso

Guatay

Mount Laguna

Pine Valley

Laguna Junction 4,055 feet

S1

8

54

Jamul

57

94

Barrett Lake

Lake Morena

Tecate Divide 4,140 feet

Dulzura

Morena Village

MANZANITA INDIAN RESERVATION

Lower Otay Lake

Barrett Junction

Potrero

94

Campo

CALIFORNIA
MEXICO

Tecate

1D

1

2

3

2

PAGE

952

TO ENSENADA, MEXICO

TO OCEANSIDE
TO DEL MAR
TO SAN DIEGO
PACIFIC OCEAN
TO BORREGO SPRINGS
TO OCOTILLO WELLS
TO BOULEVARD
TO LA RUMOROSA

San Diego Area

① PALA MESA RESORT
ARCHITECT: DICK ROSSEN, 1964

2001 Old Highway 395
Fallbrook, CA 92028

PRO SHOP: 800-722-4700

John Esgate, Manager
Dana Gunderson, Head Professional, PGA

Driving Range ●
Practice Greens ●
Clubhouse ●
Food / Beverage ●
Accommodations ●
Pull Carts
Power Carts ●
Club Rental ●
$pecial Offers ●

	1	2	3	4	5	6	7	8	9	OUT
BACK	407	540	390	189	326	392	173	525	414	3356
REGULAR	399	473	378	166	304	372	159	520	378	3149
par	4	5	4	3	4	4	3	5	4	36
handicap	3	13	1	15	9	7	17	11	5	-
FORWARD	391	451	357	128	285	342	145	489	365	2953
par	4	5	4	3	4	4	3	5	4	36
handicap	3	7	1	17	13	11	15	5	9	-

	10	11	12	13	14	15	16	17	18	IN
BACK	480	304	490	403	167	412	149	351	416	3172
REGULAR	464	298	468	386	151	396	137	334	411	3045
par	5	4	5	4	3	4	3	4	4	36
handicap	8	14	12	2	16	6	18	10	4	-
FORWARD	447	276	439	371	136	376	127	316	407	2895
par	5	4	5	4	3	4	3	4	5	37
handicap	4	14	8	6	16	2	18	10	12	-

BACK	
yardage	6528
par	72
rating	72.0
slope	131

REGULAR	
yardage	6194
par	72
rating	70.1
slope	125

FORWARD	
yardage	5848
par	73
rating	74.5
slope	134

② FALLBROOK GOLF CLUB
ARCHITECT: HARRY RAINVILLE, 1962

P.O. Box 2167
Fallbrook, CA 92088

2757 Gird Road
Fallbrook, CA 92028

PRO SHOP: 760-728-8334

Blair Cooke, Manager
Stacy O'Leary, Tournament Director
Ken Holloway, Superintendent

Driving Range ●
Practice Greens ●
Clubhouse ●
Food / Beverage ●
Accommodations
Pull Carts ●
Power Carts ●
Club Rental
$pecial Offers

	1	2	3	4	5	6	7	8	9	OUT
BACK	-	-	-	-	-	-	-	-	-	-
REGULAR	341	458	402	385	403	488	129	371	103	3080
par	4	5	4	4	4	5	3	4	3	36
handicap	9	13	7	3	1	11	15	5	17	-
FORWARD	268	454	354	324	378	470	125	334	84	2791
par	4	5	4	4	4	5	3	4	3	36
handicap	13	7	5	11	1	3	15	9	17	-

	10	11	12	13	14	15	16	17	18	IN
BACK	-	-	-	-	-	-	-	-	-	-
REGULAR	368	162	419	370	317	473	391	473	170	3143
par	4	3	4	4	4	5	4	5	3	36
handicap	6	16	4	8	10	14	2	12	18	-
FORWARD	339	151	380	325	274	434	355	403	145	2806
par	4	3	4	4	4	5	4	5	3	36
handicap	6	16	2	10	14	8	4	12	18	-

BACK	
yardage	-
par	-
rating	-
slope	-

REGULAR	
yardage	6223
par	72
rating	69.9
slope	119

FORWARD	
yardage	5597
par	72
rating	73.8
slope	130

RESORT: $20-$80
FAX: 760-723-8292

18

HOLES

PLAY POLICY & FEES: Outside play is accepted. Hotel guests are welcome. Green fees are $55 Monday through Thursday. Twilight is $35 after 2 p.m. On Friday green fees are $60; after 2 p.m. green fees are $40. Weekend and holiday rates are $80; after 2 p.m. green fees are $45. A supertwilight rate is $20 every day. Carts are included.

TEE TIMES: Reservations can be booked seven days in advance.

DRESS CODE: Collared shirts and nonmetal spikes are required. No denim, cutoffs, or halter tops are allowed on the course.

COURSE DESCRIPTION: This scenic, mature course rolls through oak woodlands with tight fairways and fast greens. It's a pretty course, a little more demanding than a garden-variety resort course.

NOTES: The course record is 62, set by Chris Starkjohann in 1988.

LOCATION: From San Diego drive north on Interstate 15 to Highway 76. Turn left to Old Highway 395. Turn right and drive two miles to the course.

. . . ● **TOURNAMENTS:** Carts are required. A 28-player minimum is required to book a tournament. ● **TRAVEL:** For reservations at the resort call 760-723-8292. ● **$PECIAL OFFERS:** Play-and-stay packages are available.

1. PALA MESA RESORT

PUBLIC: $25-$35
FAX: 760-728-2632   http://www.fallbrookgolf.com

18

HOLES

PLAY POLICY & FEES: Green fees are $25 weekdays and $35 weekends. Carts are $22.

TEE TIMES: Reservations can be booked 10 days in advance.

DRESS CODE: No tank tops, halter tops, metal spikes, or short shorts allowed on the course. Men must wear collared shirts. Coolers are not permitted.

COURSE DESCRIPTION: This course features greens tightly guarded by sand. Shot-makers will score well here, especially those with a good short game. It will offer a great challenge to all skill levels. Oak Creek runs through the layout. The creek and the hundreds of live oak trees add to the course's beauty and challenge.

NOTES: Clubhouse is to be remodeled by December 1999.

LOCATION: From Interstate 15 north of Escondido, take Highway 76 west for two miles to Gird Road; then drive north two miles to the course.

. . . ● **TOURNAMENTS:** No shotgun starts allowed. A 12-player minimum is needed to book a tournament. The banquet facility can accommodate up to 175 people. Events can be scheduled up to 24 months in advance.

2. FALLBROOK GOLF CLUB

③ MARINE MEMORIAL GOLF COURSE
ARCHITECT: WILLIAM P. BELL, 1949

Building 18415
Camp Pendleton, CA
92055
PRO SHOP: 760-725-4704
STARTER: 760-725-4756

Mike Bratschi, Director of Golf, PGA
Bob Hall, Superintendent

Driving Range ●
Practice Greens ●
Clubhouse ●
Food / Beverage ●
Accommodations
Pull Carts ●
Power Carts ●
Club Rental ●
$pecial Offers

	1	2	3	4	5	6	7	8	9	OUT
BACK	519	372	374	166	397	380	527	207	400	3342
REGULAR	508	359	335	148	380	374	508	195	388	3195
par	5	4	4	3	4	4	5	3	4	36
handicap	15	13	9	17	5	1	11	7	3	-
FORWARD	448	332	301	129	353	354	469	154	354	2894
par	5	4	4	3	4	4	5	3	4	36
handicap	11	9	13	17	3	7	5	15	1	-

	10	11	12	13	14	15	16	17	18	IN
BACK	525	353	416	390	183	529	395	161	417	3369
REGULAR	509	339	409	360	173	517	379	155	407	3248
par	5	4	4	4	3	5	4	3	4	36
handicap	10	16	2	8	14	12	6	18	4	-
FORWARD	451	331	333	315	143	459	308	137	345	2822
par	5	4	4	4	3	5	4	3	4	36
handicap	2	10	8	12	18	6	14	16	4	-

BACK	
yardage	6711
par	72
rating	72.3
slope	127

REGULAR	
yardage	6443
par	72
rating	70.1
slope	117

FORWARD	
yardage	5716
par	72
rating	73.1
slope	125

④ OCEANSIDE MUNICIPAL GOLF COURSE
ARCHITECT: RICHARD BIGLER, 1970

825 Douglas Drive
Oceanside, CA 92054

PRO SHOP: 760-433-1360

Rex Kinne, Manager
Fred Wood, PGA Professional
Jose Garcia, Superintendent

Driving Range ●
Practice Greens ●
Clubhouse ●
Food / Beverage ●
Accommodations
Pull Carts ●
Power Carts ●
Club Rental ●
$pecial Offers

	1	2	3	4	5	6	7	8	9	OUT
BACK	367	350	182	534	201	355	406	487	343	3225
REGULAR	349	334	168	521	191	340	396	444	331	3074
par	4	4	3	5	3	4	4	5	4	36
handicap	13	15	17	1	7	11	3	5	9	-
FORWARD	342	327	164	414	146	255	313	421	317	2699
par	4	4	3	5	3	4	4	5	4	36
handicap	7	9	13	5	15	17	3	1	11	-

	10	11	12	13	14	15	16	17	18	IN
BACK	370	153	303	135	497	459	429	501	378	3225
REGULAR	355	145	291	113	477	438	381	442	340	2982
par	4	3	4	3	5	4	4	5	4	36
handicap	10	16	12	18	8	4	2	6	14	-
FORWARD	344	125	216	90	472	382	342	424	304	2699
par	4	3	4	3	5	4	4	5	4	36
handicap	10	16	12	18	4	6	8	2	14	-

BACK	
yardage	6450
par	72
rating	70.8
slope	118

REGULAR	
yardage	6056
par	72
rating	68.7
slope	109

FORWARD	
yardage	5398
par	72
rating	71.6
slope	121

PLAY POLICY & FEES: Guests, with the exception of Department of Defense civilian employees, must be accompanied by military personnel. Military personnel are entitled to bring three guests. Fees vary according to military status.

DRESS CODE: No jeans are allowed on the course. Collared shirts and nonmetal spikes are required.

COURSE DESCRIPTION: This is a relatively level course set in a peaceful valley. Some holes are strategically placed along the hills and slopes of the fairway. The fairways are tight, and sand guards the greens.

LOCATION: From Highway 76 east of Oceanside, travel north on Douglas Drive for 1.25 miles. Turn right on North River Road and drive 3.5 miles to the San Luis Rey entrance. Drive one mile and turn left at the course sign.

. . . ● **TOURNAMENTS:** Outside events are limited to charity events. A 40-player minimum is required to book a tournament. Events should be scheduled six months in advance. The banquet facility can accommodate 300 people.

3. MARINE MEMORIAL GOLF COURSE

PLAY POLICY & FEES: Green fees are $18 weekdays and $24 weekends. Carts are $20.

TEE TIMES: Reservations by phone can be booked eight days in advance, starting at 6 p.m. Credit cards are required for reservations Friday through Sunday.

DRESS CODE: Collared shirts are required.

COURSE DESCRIPTION: This course has level terrain, but water comes into play on 13 holes. The greens are fairly large. Mature trees line the fairways. The booming in the background is probably the Marines practicing artillery fire at nearby Camp Pendleton.

NOTES: Oceanside allows fivesomes.

LOCATION: From Interstate 15 north of Escondido, travel west on Highway 76. Turn right onto Douglas Drive and go two miles to the course.

. . . ● **TOURNAMENTS:** A 16-player minimum is required to book a tournament. An outside banquet facility can accommodate up to 100 people. Events can be scheduled 12 months in advance. ● **TRAVEL:** Best Western Oceanside Inn is located about 15 minutes from the golf course. For reservations call 760-722-1821.

4. OCEANSIDE MUNICIPAL GOLF COURSE

SAN LUIS REY DOWNS GOLF & COUNTRY CLUB
ARCHITECT: WILLIAM F. BELL, 1965

31474 Golf Club Drive
Bonsall, CA 92003

PRO SHOP: 760-758-9699
CLUBHOUSE: 760-758-3762

Greg Milligan, General Manager
Mark Schaer, Superintendent
Anne Johnson, Tournament Director

Driving Range ●
Practice Greens ●
Clubhouse ●
Food / Beverage ●
Accommodations ●
Pull Carts ●
Power Carts ●
Club Rental ●
$Special Offers ●

	1	2	3	4	5	6	7	8	9	OUT
BACK	377	517	401	369	510	195	412	203	309	3293
REGULAR	369	496	386	352	498	185	377	187	299	3149
par	4	5	4	4	5	3	4	3	4	36
handicap	9	15	1	5	7	17	3	13	11	-
FORWARD	336	464	361	289	401	165	358	132	247	2753
par	4	5	4	4	5	3	4	3	4	36
handicap	13	1	7	11	3	15	5	17	9	-

	10	11	12	13	14	15	16	17	18	IN
BACK	377	176	522	187	576	447	230	427	515	3457
REGULAR	326	165	496	176	557	404	214	370	508	3216
par	4	3	5	3	5	4	3	4	5	36
handicap	10	16	6	18	8	2	12	4	14	-
FORWARD	264	123	468	135	485	320	162	297	486	2740
par	4	3	5	3	5	4	3	4	5	36
handicap	10	16	6	18	2	12	14	8	4	-

BACK	
yardage	6750
par	72
rating	72.6
slope	128

REGULAR	
yardage	6365
par	72
rating	70.5
slope	122

FORWARD	
yardage	5493
par	72
rating	72.1
slope	124

 ## VISTA VALLEY COUNTRY CLUB
ARCHITECT: TED ROBINSON, 1978

29354 Vista Valley Drive
Vista, CA 92084

PRO SHOP: 760-758-5275
CLUBHOUSE: 760-758-2800

Daton Dickey, Manager
Grant Garrison, PGA Professional
Ron Nolf, Superintendent

Driving Range ●
Practice Greens ●
Clubhouse ●
Food / Beverage ●
Accommodations
Pull Carts ●
Power Carts ●
Club Rental ●
$Special Offers

	1	2	3	4	5	6	7	8	9	OUT
BACK	528	360	173	433	352	369	338	156	532	3241
REGULAR	512	353	158	413	339	347	326	150	519	3117
par	5	4	3	4	4	4	4	3	5	36
handicap	13	9	15	1	3	5	11	17	7	-
FORWARD	477	327	118	384	310	316	305	123	416	2776
par	5	4	3	4	4	4	4	3	5	36
handicap	3	7	15	1	9	11	13	17	5	-

	10	11	12	13	14	15	16	17	18	IN
BACK	406	367	182	379	198	533	192	286	561	3104
REGULAR	384	332	169	362	179	511	167	269	545	2918
par	4	4	3	4	3	5	3	4	5	35
handicap	4	8	14	2	12	6	16	18	10	-
FORWARD	332	255	127	319	149	395	121	251	477	2426
par	4	4	3	4	3	5	3	4	5	35
handicap	4	16	18	8	14	2	12	10	6	-

BACK	
yardage	6345
par	71
rating	71.1
slope	130

REGULAR	
yardage	6035
par	71
rating	69.6
slope	125

FORWARD	
yardage	5202
par	71
rating	71.7
slope	130

PLAY POLICY & FEES: Outside play is accepted. Hotel guests are welcome. Green fees are $29 walking, $38 riding Monday through Thursday; $31 walking, $40 riding on Friday; and $55 weekends, which includes a mandatory cart.

TEE TIMES: Reservations can be booked seven days in advance.

DRESS CODE: Appropriate golf attire is required.

COURSE DESCRIPTION: The San Luis Rey River snakes through this level course, and water comes into play on nine holes. Five par 3s and five par 5s add a twist to this tree-lined layout.

NOTES: Adjacent to the course is the San Luis Rey Downs Training Center, where top-notch thoroughbred horses are trained.

LOCATION: From Interstate 15 north of Escondido, travel 4.5 miles west on Highway 76 to Camino Del Rey in the town of Bonsall. Turn left over the bridge and bear left at the sign for San Luis Rey Downs. Continue for three-fourths of a mile to the golf resort.

. . . ● **TOURNAMENTS:** Shotgun tournaments are available weekdays only. A 16-player minimum is required to book a tournament. The banquet facility can accommodate 150 people. ● **TRAVEL:** San Luis Rey Downs Resort also includes a golf school and complete tennis facility. For reservations call 800-78-DOWNS. ● **$PECIAL OFFERS:** Golf packages are available. Call the resort for more information.

5. SAN LUIS REY DOWNS GOLF & COUNTRY

PLAY POLICY & FEES: Reciprocal play is accepted with members of the other private clubs; otherwise, members and guests only. Guest fees are $50 when accompanied by a member and $70 unaccompanied. Carts and range balls are included.

TEE TIMES: Reservations can be booked seven days in advance.

DRESS CODE: Appropriate golf attire and nonmetal spikes are required.

COURSE DESCRIPTION: This course is nestled in a valley with a creek meandering through the hills. There are scenic mountain views. This is a good, challenging golf course for the low- and high-handicapper.

LOCATION: From Interstate 15 take the Gopher Canyon Road exit and travel west for 2.5 miles to Vista Valley Drive. Turn left and drive one-half mile to the club.

. . . ● **TOURNAMENTS:** This course is available for outside tournaments.

6. VISTA VALLEY COUNTRY CLUB

CASTLE CREEK COUNTRY CLUB
ARCHITECT: JACK DARAY, 1956

8797 Circle "R" Drive
Escondido, CA 92026

PRO SHOP: 760-749-2422
CLUBHOUSE: 760-749-2877

Makoto Kawasumi, Manager
Jesse L. Griffith, PGA Professional

Driving Range
Practice Greens ●
Clubhouse ●
Food / Beverage ●
Accommodations
Pull Carts ●
Power Carts ●
Club Rental ●
$pecial Offers

	1	2	3	4	5	6	7	8	9	OUT
BACK	394	526	282	404	158	596	382	151	377	3270
REGULAR	374	513	254	394	139	556	373	132	370	3105
par	4	5	4	4	3	5	4	3	4	36
handicap	7	9	13	3	15	1	11	17	5	-
FORWARD	360	507	224	348	124	485	291	115	352	2806
par	4	5	4	4	3	5	4	3	4	36
handicap	9	3	13	5	15	1	11	17	7	-

	10	11	12	13	14	15	16	17	18	IN
BACK	443	469	491	285	372	158	319	205	359	3101
REGULAR	418	453	476	264	277	147	276	177	345	2833
par	4	5	5	4	4	3	4	3	4	36
handicap	4	10	12	16	2	18	14	8	6	-
FORWARD	331	427	459	238	262	134	256	155	335	2597
par	4	5	5	4	4	3	4	3	4	36
handicap	8	4	2	12	10	18	14	16	6	-

BACK	
yardage	6371
par	72
rating	70.8
slope	124

REGULAR	
yardage	5938
par	72
rating	68.3
slope	116

FORWARD	
yardage	5403
par	72
rating	72.4
slope	124

 PAUMA VALLEY COUNTRY CLUB
ARCHITECT: ROBERT TRENT JONES SR., 1960

Pauma Valley Drive/P.O.
Pauma Valley, CA 92061

PRO SHOP: 760-742-1230

Mark Priester, Director of Golf, PGA
Don Berliner, General Manager
Doug Rudolph, Superintendent

Driving Range ●
Practice Greens ●
Clubhouse ●
Food / Beverage ●
Accommodations ●
Pull Carts
Power Carts ●
Club Rental
$pecial Offers

	1	2	3	4	5	6	7	8	9	OUT
BACK	532	392	187	449	452	425	187	443	411	3478
REGULAR	520	382	175	434	432	420	175	423	396	3357
par	5	4	3	4	4	5	3	4	4	36
handicap	9	13	15	5	7	1	17	3	11	-
FORWARD	462	345	114	398	371	402	129	355	342	2918
par	5	4	3	4	4	5	3	4	4	36
handicap	1	11	17	5	7	9	15	3	13	-

	10	11	12	13	14	15	16	17	18	IN
BACK	396	559	210	378	465	397	206	525	463	3599
REGULAR	380	549	190	358	450	377	190	513	447	3454
par	4	5	3	4	4	4	3	5	4	36
handicap	2	6	18	14	4	12	16	10	8	-
FORWARD	337	494	132	296	400	322	150	462	380	2973
par	4	5	3	4	4	4	3	5	4	36
handicap	2	4	18	14	8	12	16	6	10	-

BACK	
yardage	7077
par	72
rating	75.5
slope	137

REGULAR	
yardage	6811
par	72
rating	74.0
slope	135

FORWARD	
yardage	5891
par	72
rating	74.7
slope	130

PLAY POLICY & FEES: Green fees are $35 Monday through Thursday, and $40 Friday with a cart. Green fees are $40 weekends and holidays. Carts are $10 per rider.

TEE TIMES: Reservations can be booked nine days in advance.

DRESS CODE: Collared shirts and nonmetal spikes are mandatory.

COURSE DESCRIPTION: Castle Creek meanders through this well-maintained course. The front nine is flat, and the back nine is hilly. There are numerous trees (900) lining the fairways.

LOCATION: From Interstate 15 take the Old Castle Road/Gopher Canyon Road exit and travel east. Turn left and drive one-half mile to the club.

. . . ● **TOURNAMENTS:** Carts are required. A 20-player minimum is needed to book a tournament.

7. CASTLE CREEK COUNTRY CLUB

PLAY POLICY & FEES: Members and quests only. Green fees are $85. Carts are $20.

DRESS CODE: Standard country club attire is mandatory. Nonmetal spikes are required.

COURSE DESCRIPTION: Pick your trap; they are everywhere. With more than 120 bunkers, this difficult course is considered a ball-striker's course. It's an original Robert Trent Jones Sr. layout and plays very long. Very private, it's generally regarded as one of the premier courses in San Diego County.

LOCATION: From Interstate 15 travel east on Highway 76 for 14 miles to the town of Pauma Valley. Turn right on Pauma Valley Drive and continue three-fourths of a mile to the club.

. . . ● **TOURNAMENTS:** This course is not available for outside events.

8. PAUMA VALLEY COUNTRY CLUB

San Diego Area (map page 952)

SHADOWRIDGE COUNTRY CLUB
ARCHITECT: DAVID RAINVILLE, 1981

1980 Gateway Drive
Vista, CA 92083

PROSHOP: 760-727-7706
CLUBHOUSE: 760-727-7700

Perry Dickey, General Manager, PGA
Jim Letourneau, PGA Professional
Mike Rowher, Superintendent

Driving Range ●
Practice Greens ●
Clubhouse ●
Food / Beverage ●
Accommodations
Pull Carts
Power Carts ●
Club Rental ●
$pecial Offers

	1	2	3	4	5	6	7	8	9	OUT
BACK	507	376	407	174	364	419	540	199	396	3382
REGULAR	483	375	384	160	341	398	511	170	376	3198
par	5	4	4	3	4	4	5	3	4	36
handicap	9	11	1	17	13	3	7	15	5	-
FORWARD	457	353	329	136	314	326	481	121	299	2816
par	5	4	4	3	4	4	5	3	4	36
handicap	7	1	3	15	9	13	11	17	5	-

	10	11	12	13	14	15	16	17	18	IN
BACK	384	434	151	420	557	196	374	513	443	3472
REGULAR	359	381	133	384	521	160	355	489	394	3176
par	4	4	3	4	5	3	4	5	4	36
handicap	4	12	18	2	6	16	14	8	10	-
FORWARD	319	355	98	354	482	128	309	464	368	2877
par	4	4	3	4	5	3	4	5	4	36
handicap	10	12	18	2	6	16	14	4	8	-

BACK	
yardage	6854
par	72
rating	73.1
slope	124

REGULAR	
yardage	6374
par	72
rating	69.9
slope	114

FORWARD	
yardage	5693
par	72
rating	73.3
slope	127

 WARNER SPRINGS RANCH GOLF COURSE
ARCHITECT: DAVID RAINVILLE, 1965

P.O. Box 10
Warner Springs, CA 92086

31652 Highway 79
Warner Springs, CA

PROSHOP: 760-782-4270

Mike Mathison II, PGA Professional
Jay Navarro, Tournament Director
Randy Heasley, Superintendent

Driving Range ●
Practice Greens ●
Clubhouse ●
Food / Beverage ●
Accommodations
Pull Carts ●
Power Carts ●
Club Rental ●
$pecial Offers ●

	1	2	3	4	5	6	7	8	9	OUT
BACK	532	361	359	440	175	485	206	421	386	3365
REGULAR	511	334	350	375	143	477	180	388	372	3130
par	5	4	4	4	3	5	3	4	4	36
handicap	15	17	13	5	11	7	9	1	3	-
FORWARD	476	306	320	338	110	435	150	287	331	2753
par	5	4	4	4	3	5	3	4	4	36
handicap	3	13	9	7	17	1	15	11	5	-

	10	11	12	13	14	15	16	17	18	IN
BACK	386	496	184	319	391	230	404	418	508	3336
REGULAR	367	473	169	291	366	183	386	397	490	3122
par	4	5	3	4	4	3	4	4	5	36
handicap	14	12	18	8	10	16	4	6	2	-
FORWARD	312	433	152	258	322	160	325	323	432	2717
par	4	5	3	4	4	3	4	4	5	36
handicap	14	12	18	8	10	16	4	6	2	-

BACK	
yardage	6701
par	72
rating	71.1
slope	121

REGULAR	
yardage	6252
par	72
rating	69.1
slope	116

FORWARD	
yardage	5470
par	72
rating	70.9
slope	119

PLAY POLICY & FEES: Members and guests only. Green fees are $65. Carts are $11.

DRESS CODE: Collared shirts and nonmetal spikes are required. No jeans or short shorts allowed on the golf course.

COURSE DESCRIPTION: This is a rolling layout with eucalyptus-lined fairways and several picturesque lakes. The beautiful finishing hole features a stone-edged lake set in front of the green.

LOCATION: Travel north from San Diego on Interstate 5 or Interstate 15 to Highway 78 west. Take the Sycamore exit off Highway 78 and go south to Shadowridge Drive. Turn right and continue to Gateway Drive.

. . . ● **TOURNAMENTS:** Shotgun tournaments are available Monday only. Carts are required. A 72-player minimum is needed to book a tournament. Tournaments should be booked 12 months in advance. The banquet facility can hold 300 people.

9. SHADOWRIDGE COUNTRY CLUB

PLAY POLICY & FEES: Reciprocal play is accepted with members of other clubs. This course is open to outside play Monday through Thursday, excluding holidays, and green tees are $40. Twilight and senior rates are available. For guests with members, fees are $40 Friday, and $49 weekends and holidays. Carts are included.

TEE TIMES: Reservations can be booked seven days in advance.

DRESS CODE: Appropriate golf attire and nonmetal spikes are required and strictly enforced.

COURSE DESCRIPTION: Warner Springs has some of the best greens in Southern California. They tend to be fast. The signature hole, the par-3 fifth, can play anywhere from 110 to 190 yards. Do not get greedy on the 13th hole off the tee or you may lose a few balls.

NOTES: Warner Springs hosts the California State Amateur qualifying.

LOCATION: Take Interstate 15 north from San Diego. Turn right on Scripps Poway Parkway and left on Highway 67. Follow Highway 67 to Santa Ysabel, Highway 79, and turn left.

. . . ● **TOURNAMENTS:** Shotgun tournaments are available Monday through Thurday (excluding holidays), requiring an 60-player minimum. A 24-player minimum is needed for a regular tournament. Events can be scheduled six to 12 months in advance. ● **TRAVEL:** Warner Springs Ranch is located across the street from the golf course. For reservations call 760-782-4220. ● **$PECIAL OFFERS:** Warner Springs Ranch offers golf packages Sunday through Thursday.

10. WARNER SPRINGS RANCH GOLF COURSE

LAKE SAN MARCOS COUNTRY CLUB
ARCHITECT: H. RAINVILLE, D. RAINVILLE, 1963

1750 San Pablo Drive
Lake San Marcos, CA
92069
PRO SHOP: 760-744-1310
CLUBHOUSE: 760-744-9385

Ron Frazar, Manager
Marty McGee, Superintendent

Driving Range ●
Practice Greens ●
Clubhouse ●
Food / Beverage ●
Accommodations ●
Pull Carts ●
Power Carts ●
Club Rental ●
$pecial Offers ●

	1	2	3	4	5	6	7	8	9	OUT
BACK	460	174	606	167	369	466	412	210	480	3344
REGULAR	438	156	597	156	364	463	403	186	465	3228
par	4	3	5	3	4	5	4	3	5	36
handicap	3	17	1	15	11	13	5	7	9	-
FORWARD	425	144	502	131	359	455	387	160	454	3017
par	5	3	5	3	4	5	4	3	5	37
handicap	11	17	1	15	9	5	3	13	7	-

	10	11	12	13	14	15	16	17	18	IN
BACK	338	394	208	387	492	163	487	359	343	3171
REGULAR	321	375	195	379	477	148	478	340	331	3044
par	4	4	3	4	5	3	5	4	4	36
handicap	16	4	10	2	8	18	6	12	14	-
FORWARD	315	362	181	355	451	140	462	325	321	2912
par	4	4	3	4	5	3	5	4	4	36
handicap	16	4	10	2	8	18	6	12	14	-

BACK	
yardage	6515
par	72
rating	71.5
slope	124

REGULAR	
yardage	6272
par	72
rating	69.4
slope	116

FORWARD	
yardage	5929
par	73
rating	75.2
slope	131

 TWIN OAKS GOLF COURSE
ARCHITECT: TED ROBINSON, 1993

1425 N. Twin Oaks Valley
San Marcos, CA 92069

PRO SHOP: 800-662-6439

Scott Bentley, Director of Golf, PGA
Rick Danruther, Head Professional, PGA
Jim Nagle, Tournament Director

Driving Range ●
Practice Greens ●
Clubhouse ●
Food / Beverage ●
Accommodations
Pull Carts
Power Carts ●
Club Rental ●
$pecial Offers ●

	1	2	3	4	5	6	7	8	9	OUT
BACK	361	500	194	369	527	356	170	334	370	3181
REGULAR	344	475	173	352	501	333	142	319	353	2992
par	4	5	3	4	5	4	3	4	4	36
handicap	11	1	13	9	5	7	15	17	3	-
FORWARD	301	445	134	277	457	308	115	303	337	2677
par	4	5	3	4	5	4	3	4	4	36
handicap	7	3	15	11	1	9	13	17	5	-

	10	11	12	13	14	15	16	17	18	IN
BACK	207	374	352	373	388	350	555	194	561	3354
REGULAR	179	353	338	349	366	332	533	166	538	3154
par	3	4	4	4	4	4	5	3	5	36
handicap	8	10	18	12	6	14	2	16	4	-
FORWARD	155	319	317	304	327	310	459	125	430	2746
par	3	4	4	4	4	4	5	3	5	36
handicap	12	6	16	10	8	14	2	18	4	-

BACK	
yardage	6535
par	72
rating	71.2
slope	124

REGULAR	
yardage	6146
par	72
rating	68.8
slope	116

FORWARD	
yardage	5423
par	72
rating	71.6
slope	120

PLAY POLICY & FEES: Reciprocal play is accepted with members of other private clubs; otherwise, members and guests only. Hotel guests are welcome. Green fees are $50 weekdays and $60 weekends. Carts are included. Reservations are recommended.

TEE TIMES: Reservations can be booked three days in advance.

DRESS CODE: Appropriate golf attire is required.

COURSE DESCRIPTION: This gently rolling layout through a housing development is mature and well maintained. The 606-yard third hole is a double dogleg known as "the Monster." Greens tend to be elevated and contoured.

LOCATION: Take the Palomar Airport Road exit from Interstate 5 south of Oceanside. Travel seven miles east to Rancho Santa Fe Road and turn right. Continue to Lake San Marcos. To reach the executive course, continue to Camino del Arroyo. Turn left to the course.

. . . ● **TOURNAMENTS:** A 12-player minimum is required to book an event. Carts are required. Tournaments should be booked at least one month in advance. The banquet facility can accommodate up to 500 people. ● **TRAVEL:** The Quails Inn is part of the Lake San Marcos Country Club. For reservations call 760-744-0120. ● **$PECIAL OFFERS:** Play-and-stay golf packages are available at the Quails Inn.

11. LAKE SAN MARCOS COUNTRY CLUB

PLAY POLICY & FEES. Green fees are $44 Monday through Thursday, $49 Friday, and $67 weekends and holidays. Twilight green fees are $28 Monday through Thursday, and $38 Friday through Sunday and holidays. Green fees include mandatory golf cart.

TEE TIMES: Tee times can be made seven days in advance.

DRESS CODE: No jeans or running shorts are allowed. Shirts must have collars and sleeves. The course is a nonmetal spike facility.

COURSE DESCRIPTION: Located in a tranquil valley, Twin Oaks features elevation changes and undulating greens. Water comes into play on four holes. The seventh hole is a 170-yard par 3 from the back tees, over water, with a small but well-placed bunker guarding the left side of the green. If the pin is tucked left, the smart player will hit to the middle of the green to take par.

NOTES: Twin oaks is owned by JC Resorts, which owns and/or operates several other courses in the area including Temecula Creek, Rancho Bernardo Inn, and the new Encinitas Ranch Golf Course.

LOCATION: Take Interstate 5 south from L.A. to Highway 78 east. Take Highway 78 east for 11 miles and exit at Twin Oaks Valley Road. Turn north on Twin Oaks Valley Road for two miles. The course is on the right.

. . . ● **TOURNAMENTS:** A 16-player minimum is required to book an event. The banquet facility can accommodate up to 200 people. ● **TRAVEL:** For reservations at the Rancho Bernardo Inn call 800-542-6096. ● **$PECIAL OFFERS:** Play-and-stay packages are available with the Inn.

12. TWIN OAKS GOLF COURSE

MEADOW LAKE GOLF COURSE

ARCHITECT: TOM SANDERSON, 1965

10333 Meadow Glen Way
Escondido, CA 92026

PRO S HOP: 760-749-1620
CLUBHOUSE: 760-749-0983

Brad VanHorn, Head Professional, PGA
Gerald Ward, Superintendent
Scott Rethlake, General Manager

Driving Range ●
Practice Greens ●
Clubhouse ●
Food / Beverage ●
Accommodations ●
Pull Carts ●
Power Carts ●
Club Rental ●
$Special Offers

	1	2	3	4	5	6	7	8	9	OUT
BACK	545	159	508	314	448	546	142	377	366	3405
REGULAR	533	150	497	308	435	534	132	364	354	3307
par	5	3	5	4	4	5	3	4	4	37
handicap	1	17	9	13	3	5	15	7	11	-
FORWARD	409	139	483	290	422	463	125	345	298	2974
par	5	3	5	4	5	5	3	4	4	38
handicap	3	17	1	13	9	5	15	7	11	-

	10	11	12	13	14	15	16	17	18	IN
BACK	344	180	403	295	503	364	165	402	460	3116
REGULAR	331	166	394	283	485	346	159	393	448	3005
par	4	3	4	4	5	4	3	4	4	35
handicap	12	16	4	14	6	10	18	8	2	-
FORWARD	325	160	328	278	484	340	158	276	435	2784
par	4	3	4	4	5	4	3	4	5	36
handicap	10	18	4	12	2	8	16	14	6	-

BACK	
yardage	6521
par	72
rating	71.7
slope	130

REGULAR	
yardage	6312
par	72
rating	70.7
slope	127

FORWARD	
yardage	5758
par	74
rating	75.3
slope	135

 SKYLINE RANCH COUNTRY CLUB

18218 Paradise Mountain
Valley Center, CA 92082

PRO S HOP: 760-749-3233

Stan Johnson, Manager
Manuel Perez, Superintendent

Driving Range
Practice Greens ●
Clubhouse ●
Food / Beverage
Accommodations
Pull Carts
Power Carts ●
Club Rental
$Special Offers

	1	2	3	4	5	6	7	8	9	OUT
BACK	-	-	-	-	-	-	-	-	-	-
REGULAR	-	-	-	-	-	-	-	-	-	-
par	-	-	-	-	-	-	-	-	-	-
handicap	-	-	-	-	-	-	-	-	-	-
FORWARD	-	-	-	-	-	-	-	-	-	-
par	-	-	-	-	-	-	-	-	-	-
handicap	-	-	-	-	-	-	-	-	-	-

	10	11	12	13	14	15	16	17	18	IN
BACK	-	-	-	-	-	-	-	-	-	-
REGULAR	-	-	-	-	-	-	-	-	-	-
par	-	-	-	-	-	-	-	-	-	-
handicap	-	-	-	-	-	-	-	-	-	-
FORWARD	-	-	-	-	-	-	-	-	-	-
par	-	-	-	-	-	-	-	-	-	-
handicap	-	-	-	-	-	-	-	-	-	-

BACK	
yardage	-
par	-
rating	-
slope	-

REGULAR	
yardage	3032
par	29
rating	54.5
slope	85

FORWARD	
yardage	3032
par	30
rating	56.7
slope	87

PLAY POLICY & FEES: Outside play is accepted. Green fees are $38 weekdays and $50 weekends, including carts.

TEE TIMES: Reservations can be booked seven days in advance.

DRESS CODE: Collared shirts are required. No cutoffs are allowed on the course.

COURSE DESCRIPTION: This is a mountainous course with lots of doglegs. There are blind shots, but the variation between tight and open makes this a fair, sporting challenge. Don't be deceived by stated yardage—elevation changes call for every club in the bag.

LOCATION: Drive 33 miles north from San Diego on Interstate 15 and take the Mountain Meadows exit. Travel east 1.5 miles to the club, located on Meadow Glen Way.

. . . ● **TOURNAMENTS:** A 24-player minimum is needed to book a tournament. Carts are required. Events should be booked 12 months in advance. The banquet facility can hold 150 people.

13. MEADOW LAKE GOLF COURSE

PLAY POLICY & FEES: The course is restricted to members of the mobile home park and their guests. Guests must be accompanied by a member. Guest fees are $2 for nine holes.

DRESS CODE: Appropriate golf attire is required.

COURSE DESCRIPTION: This course is mostly level and walkable. Trees and water come into play on several holes, and there are two par 4s. There are front nine and back nine tees.

LOCATION: From Escondido take Valley Center Road north for 11 miles. Turn right on Lake Wolford Road. Turn right on Paradise Mountain Road to the club entrance.

. . . ● **TOURNAMENTS:** This course is not available for outside events.

14. SKYLINE RANCH COUNTRY CLUB

ESCONDIDO COUNTRY CLUB
ARCHITECT: HARRY RAINVILLE, 1962

1800 West Country Club
Escondido, CA 92026

PRO SHOP: 760-746-4212
CLUBHOUSE: 760-743-3301

Terry Clark, General Manager
David Cantrell, PGA Professional
Jose Canedo, Superintendent

Driving Range ●
Practice Greens ●
Clubhouse ●
Food / Beverage ●
Accommodations
Pull Carts
Power Carts ●
Club Rental
$pecial Offers

	1	2	3	4	5	6	7	8	9	OUT
BACK										
REGULAR										
par										
handicap										
FORWARD										
par										
handicap										

	10	11	12	13	14	15	16	17	18	IN
BACK										
REGULAR										
par										
handicap										
FORWARD										
par										
handicap										

BACK	
yardage	6140
par	70
rating	69.1
slope	111

REGULAR	
yardage	5884
par	70
rating	67.7
slope	107

FORWARD	
yardage	5536
par	70
rating	71.7
slope	124

 ## WELK RESORT CENTER
ARCHITECT: DAVID RAINVILLE, 1986

8860 Lawrence Welk Drive
Escondido, CA 92026

PRO SHOP: 760-749-3225

Ron Cropley, PGA Professional
Sergio Vasquez, Superintendent

Driving Range
Practice Greens ●
Clubhouse
Food / Beverage ●
Accommodations ●
Pull Carts ●
Power Carts ●
Club Rental ●
$pecial Offers ●

	1	2	3	4	5	6	7	8	9	OUT
BACK	144	268	122	165	352	169	313	152	326	2011
REGULAR	132	250	102	145	336	152	278	133	303	1831
par	3	4	3	3	4	3	4	3	4	31
handicap	9	7	17	11	3	13	5	15	1	-
FORWARD	100	216	92	114	300	124	258	115	268	1587
par	3	4	3	3	4	3	4	3	4	31
handicap	9	7	17	13	1	11	5	15	3	-

	10	11	12	13	14	15	16	17	18	IN
BACK	151	136	303	193	177	280	290	142	319	1991
REGULAR	138	119	282	169	137	253	270	114	268	1750
par	3	3	4	3	3	4	4	3	4	31
handicap	14	16	4	10	12	8	6	18	2	-
FORWARD	129	98	263	142	112	220	227	70	207	1468
par	3	3	4	3	3	4	4	3	4	31
handicap	12	16	2	10	14	6	4	18	8	-

BACK	
yardage	4002
par	62
rating	59.1
slope	99

REGULAR	
yardage	3581
par	62
rating	56.8
slope	93

FORWARD	
yardage	3055
par	62
rating	57.7
slope	90

PLAY POLICY & FEES: Members and guests only. Guest fees are $45 weekdays, $50 weekends. Carts are $24.

DRESS CODE: Appropriate golf attire and nonmetal spikes are required

COURSE DESCRIPTION: Escondido is sneaky and hard, with hills, wind, and subtle greens all in the mix—plus a stream that wanders through most of the course. Accuracy and patience pay off here. It doesn't look lethal, but it can be.

NOTES: The course record is 62.

LOCATION: Take the Centre City Parkway exit off Interstate 15 two miles north of Escondido. Turn left on Country Club Lane and drive one mile to the club.

. . . ● **TOURNAMENTS:** A 40-player minimum is needed to book a tournament. Shotgun tournaments are available weekdays only. Carts are required. Events should be booked three to four months in advance. The banquet facility holds 150 people.

15. ESCONDIDO COUNTRY CLUB

RESORT: $8-$40

36
HOLES

FAX: 760-749-4619

PLAY POLICY & FEES: Green fees for the Fountain Course are $35 weekdays and $40 weekends. The twilight rate is $12 walking and $23 with a cart after 2 p.m. Carts are $11 per person and mandatory until 2 p.m. The green fee for the Oaks Course is $14. The twilight rate is $8 walking. Carts are $8 per rider.

TEE TIMES: Reservations can be booked seven days in advance for local residents, 14 days in advance for time-share owners or guests, and 30 days or more with a hotel package.

DRESS CODE: Collared shirts and nonmetal spikes are required.

COURSE DESCRIPTION: The Fountain Executive Course has 10 par 3s and 8 par 4s. It is up and down and features lots of water, trees, and large rocks. The par-3 first hole is guarded by a lake which features a fountain shaped like a champagne glass. Cheers!

NOTES: The Oaks par-3 course is 1,837 yards from the back tees, and 1,652 yards from the forward tees.

LOCATION: on Interstate 15 from San Diego, drive 33 miles north and take the Mountain Meadow Road exit. Turn north on Champagne Boulevard.

. . . ● **TOURNAMENTS:** This course is available for outside tournaments. A 20-player minimum is needed to book an event. The banquet facility can accommodate up to 300 people. ● **TRAVEL:** For reservations at the hotel call 760-749-3000. ● **$PECIAL OFFERS:** The Welk Resort offers a unique play-and-stay package that includes tickets to productions at the Welk Resort Theatre.

16. WELK RESORT CENTER

THE VINEYARD AT ESCONDIDO
ARCHITECT: DAVID RAINVILLE, 1993

925 San Pasqual Road
Escondido, CA 92025

PRO SHOP: 760-735-9545

Ron Gorski, General Manager, PGA
Phillip White, PGA Professional
Rick Martinez, Tournament Director

Driving Range ●
Practice Greens ●
Clubhouse ●
Food / Beverage ●
Accommodations
Pull Carts
Power Carts ●
Club Rental ●
$pecial Offers ●

	1	2	3	4	5	6	7	8	9	OUT
BACK	420	351	125	404	401	152	295	419	503	3070
REGULAR	397	334	109	388	386	134	281	401	484	2914
par	4	4	3	4	4	3	4	4	5	35
handicap	7	11	13	9	5	15	17	3	1	-
FORWARD	336	263	79	332	304	110	245	326	420	2415
par	4	4	3	4	4	3	4	4	5	35
handicap	5	3	15	9	13	7	17	11	1	-

	10	11	12	13	14	15	16	17	18	IN
BACK	389	457	154	477	412	551	453	157	411	3461
REGULAR	374	436	124	455	381	523	425	136	392	3246
par	4	4	3	4	4	5	4	3	4	35
handicap	18	6	14	4	12	2	10	16	8	-
FORWARD	301	348	96	393	312	453	332	102	321	2658
par	4	4	3	4	4	5	4	3	4	35
handicap	18	6	14	4	12	2	10	16	8	-

BACK	
yardage	6531
par	70
rating	70.3
slope	125

REGULAR	
yardage	6160
par	70
rating	68.3
slope	119

FORWARD	
yardage	5073
par	70
rating	70.3
slope	117

 EAGLE CREST GOLF CLUB
ARCHITECT: DAVID RAINVILLE, 1993

1656 Cloverdale Road
Escondido, CA 92027

PRO SHOP: 760-737-9762

Jason Wood, General Manager, PGA
George Kenny, Superintendent

Driving Range ●
Practice Greens ●
Clubhouse ●
Food / Beverage ●
Accommodations
Pull Carts
Power Carts ●
Club Rental ●
$pecial Offers

	1	2	3	4	5	6	7	8	9	OUT
BACK										
REGULAR										
par										
handicap										
FORWARD										
par										
handicap										

	10	11	12	13	14	15	16	17	18	IN
BACK										
REGULAR										
par										
handicap										
FORWARD										
par										
handicap										

BACK	
yardage	6400
par	72
rating	71.6
slope	136

REGULAR	
yardage	6000
par	72
rating	69.3
slope	125

FORWARD	
yardage	4940
par	72
rating	69.9
slope	123

www.cobblestonegolf.com/vinyd-main.   HOLES

PLAY POLICY & FEES: Green fees are $37 walking on weekdays and $60 including carts on weekends. Twilight rates are $25 without a cart and $33 with a cart weekdays after 2:30 p.m. Weekend twilight rates are $29 walking and $37 with a cart. Carts are $12 per player. Twilight carts are $8.

TEE TIMES: Reservations can be booked seven days in advance.

DRESS CODE: Appropriate golf attire and nonmetal spikes are required.

COURSE DESCRIPTION: This scenic layout winds through acres of wetlands with stunning mountain back-drops. Five lakes, more than 70 bunkers, well-defined fairways, and perfect greens make this course a must on everyone's list.

NOTES: A lighted practice area features a driving range with target greens, as well as putting greens.

LOCATION: From Interstate 15 in Escondido take the Via Rancho Parkway east to San Pasqual Road. Turn right and proceed a quarter of a mile to the club entrance.

. . . ● **TOURNAMENTS:** A 16-player minimum is required to book a tournament. Carts are mandatory. Shotgun tournaments are available weekdays only. Events should be booked six months in advance. The banquet facility can accommodate 80 people. ● **$PECIAL OFFERS:** Tournament packages are available. Tournament activities can include driving range privileges, putting and closest-to-the-pin contests, and awards presentations. Call the pro shop for details.

17. THE VINEYARD AT ESCONDIDO

HOLES

PLAY POLICY & FEES: There are several different rates including, resident, nonresident, twilight, supertwilight, and early-bird rates. Call for current pricing. Carts are included and mandatory.

TEE TIMES: Reservations can be booked seven days in advance.

DRESS CODE: Appropriate golf attire and nonmetal spikes are required.

COURSE DESCRIPTION: Eight lakes and rolling terrain make this course a challenge for any player. No other hole is visible from the one you're playing, a rarity these days. The signature hole is the 518-yard, par-5 sixth, where a lake and waterfall guard the left side of the green.

LOCATION: From San Diego, take Highway 78 to Interstate 15 south. Exit at Via Rancho Parkway. Drive one mile east to San Pasqual Road. Turn right on San Pasqual Road and drive 5.5 miles to Rockwood. Drive one mile to the course.

. . . ● **TOURNAMENTS:** This course is available for outside tournaments.

18. EAGLE CREST GOLF CLUB

LOMAS SANTA FE COUNTRY CLUB
ARCHITECT: WILLIAM F. BELL, 1964

P.O. Box 1007
Solana Beach, CA 92075

PRO SHOP: 858-755-1547

Maria Harris, Manager
Ken Cherry, PGA Professional
Leslie Chocheles, Tournament Director

1505 Lomas Santa Fe
Solana Beach, CA 92075

Driving Range ●
Practice Greens ●
Clubhouse ●
Food / Beverage ●
Accommodations
Pull Carts
Power Carts ●
Club Rental
$pecial Offers

	1	2	3	4	5	6	7	8	9	OUT
BACK	499	341	355	386	203	411	333	160	478	3166
REGULAR	483	317	338	349	188	389	312	140	457	2973
par	5	4	4	4	3	4	4	3	5	36
handicap	9	15	7	1	11	3	13	17	5	-
FORWARD	463	310	325	325	176	383	297	109	443	2831
par	5	4	4	4	3	4	4	3	5	36
handicap	9	13	7	5	15	1	11	17	3	-

	10	11	12	13	14	15	16	17	18	IN
BACK	512	416	541	197	388	385	423	386	193	3441
REGULAR	497	401	512	160	356	363	400	370	176	3235
par	5	4	5	3	4	4	4	4	3	36
handicap	10	4	16	14	6	8	2	12	18	-
FORWARD	473	385	500	130	311	346	389	327	138	2999
par	5	4	5	3	4	4	4	4	3	36
handicap	10	2	4	18	14	8	6	12	16	-

BACK	
yardage	6607
par	72
rating	72.3
slope	128

REGULAR	
yardage	6208
par	72
rating	70.0
slope	122

FORWARD	
yardage	5830
par	72
rating	74.7
slope	129

 RANCHO SANTA FE GOLF CLUB
ARCHITECT: MAX BEHR, 1927

P.O. Box 598
Rancho Santa Fe, CA
92067
PRO SHOP: 858-756-3094

Chuck Courtney, PGA Professional
Tim Barrier, Superintendent

5827 Via de la Cumbre
Rancho Santa Fe, CA
92067

Driving Range ●
Practice Greens ●
Clubhouse ●
Food / Beverage ●
Accommodations ●
Pull Carts ●
Power Carts ●
Club Rental ●
$pecial Offers

	1	2	3	4	5	6	7	8	9	OUT
BACK										
REGULAR										
par										
handicap										
FORWARD										
par										
handicap										

	10	11	12	13	14	15	16	17	18	IN
BACK										
REGULAR										
par										
handicap										
FORWARD										
par										
handicap										

BACK	
yardage	6911
par	72
rating	74.3
slope	137

REGULAR	
yardage	6452
par	72
rating	71.3
slope	129

FORWARD	
yardage	5869
par	72
rating	74.8
slope	131

PLAY POLICY & FEES: Members and guests only. Green fees are $55 weekdays and $65 weekends. Carts are $11 per person. Executive green fees are $14 weekdays and $16 weekends for 18 holes. Carts are $15. Call for other special rates.

DRESS CODE: Appropriate golf attire and nonmetal spikes are required.

COURSE DESCRIPTION: This is a well-maintained course in a beautiful setting. The course offers rolling terrain with tight fairways.

LOCATION: Take the Lomas Santa Fe Drive exit off Interstate 5 and drive east one mile to the club.

. . . ● **TOURNAMENTS:** This course is available for outside events on Monday. Tournaments should be booked 12 months in advance. A banquet facility is available that can accommodate 400 people.

19. LOMAS SANTA FE COUNTRY CLUB

PLAY POLICY & FEES: Members and guests only. Guests at the Inn at Rancho Santa Fe are welcome to play in the afternoon at $125 weekdays and $135 on weekends, including cart.

TEE TIMES: Reservations can be booked seven days in advance for guests at the Inn.

DRESS CODE: Appropriate golf attire and nonmetal spikes are required.

COURSE DESCRIPTION: This course has a rolling layout among mature trees with very little water. Regarded locally as one of the top courses in the country—and certainly in Southern California—the design is a tribute to economy, demanding both strength and smarts. It is a true treasure.

NOTES: This course was the original site of the Bing Crosby National Pro-Am and the hangout of many Hollywood types during the 1940s and '50s.

LOCATION: Take Interstate 5 to Lomas Santa Fe Drive and travel east for four miles on Highway 8 to the Inn. Turn left on Avenida de Acacias and drive one-half mile to Via de la Cumbre. Go left one-fourth mile to the club. ●

. . . ● **TOURNAMENTS:** Outside play is limited to local charity events. ●

TRAVEL: The Inn at Rancho Santa Fe has 87 guest rooms. For reservations call 858-756-1131.

20. RANCHO SANTA FE GOLF CLUB

FAIRBANKS RANCH COUNTRY CLUB
ARCHITECT: TED ROBINSON, 1984

P.O. Box 8586
Rancho Santa Fe, CA
92067
PRO SHOP: 858-259-8819
CLUBHOUSE: 858-259-8811

15150 San Dieguito Road
Rancho Santa Fe, CA
92067

Driving Range ●
Practice Greens ●
Clubhouse ●
Food / Beverage ●
Accommodations
Pull Carts
Power Carts ●
Club Rental ●
$Special Offers

Tom Rutherford, Manager
Richard "Tag" Merritt, PGA Professional
Brian Darrock, Superintendent

	1	2	3	4	5	6	7	8	9	OUT
BACK	520	424	541	441	423	193	417	209	434	3602
REGULAR	497	356	514	400	397	171	366	161	359	3221
par	5	4	5	4	4	3	4	3	4	36
handicap	15	11	17	1	5	13	3	9	7	-
FORWARD	434	324	463	335	342	133	341	137	331	2840
par	5	4	5	4	4	3	4	3	4	36
handicap	13	11	3	9	7	17	1	15	5	-

	10	11	12	13	14	15	16	17	18	IN
BACK	391	433	210	545	380	225	560	457	422	3623
REGULAR	374	372	189	483	364	168	495	379	400	3224
par	4	4	3	5	4	3	5	4	4	36
handicap	4	10	18	14	6	16	2	12	8	-
FORWARD	334	343	140	454	324	142	460	343	344	2884
par	4	4	3	5	4	3	5	4	4	36
handicap	6	10	18	12	2	16	4	14	8	-

BACK	
yardage	7225
par	72
rating	75.0
slope	135

REGULAR	
yardage	6445
par	72
rating	70.1
slope	125

FORWARD	
yardage	5724
par	72
rating	74.4
slope	132

 DEL MAR COUNTRY CLUB
ARCHITECT: JOSEPH LEE, 1991

6001 Camino Sante Fe
Rancho Santa Fe, CA
92067
PRO SHOP: 858-759-2720

Driving Range ●
Practice Greens ●
Clubhouse ●
Food / Beverage ●
Accommodations
Pull Carts
Power Carts ●
Club Rental ●
$Special Offers

Jim Andrus, Club Manager
Tim Moher, Head Professional, PGA
David Major, superintendent

	1	2	3	4	5	6	7	8	9	OUT
BACK										
REGULAR										
par										
handicap										
FORWARD										
par										
handicap										

	10	11	12	13	14	15	16	17	18	IN
BACK										
REGULAR										
par										
handicap										
FORWARD										
par										
handicap										

BACK	
yardage	6508
par	72
rating	74.4
slope	133

REGULAR	
yardage	5972
par	72
rating	71.2
slope	123

FORWARD	
yardage	5381
par	72
rating	72.0
slope	123

PLAY POLICY & FEES: Members and guests only. Guest fees are $55 weekdays and $70 weekends. Carts are $21 for 18 holes.

DRESS CODE: Appropriate golf attire and nonmetal spikes are required.

COURSE DESCRIPTION: Ted Robinson designed this challenging course, which bears his trademarks; The greens are surrounded by mounds and palm trees, and there is quite a bit of water. The course can be about two shots tougher in the afternoon, but it's almost always in ideal condition.

NOTES: A new irrigation system has been installed, and new driving range has opened. This course was the site of the 1984 Olympic equestrian event.

LOCATION: Take the Via de la Valle exit off Interstate 5 and drive east to El Camino Real. Drive south to San Dieguito Road. Then drive east for one mile to the club.

. . . ● **TOURNAMENTS:** This course is available for outside charity events only. An 80-player minimum is needed to book an event. Tournaments should be scheduled 12 months in advance. A banquet facility is available that can accommodate 200 people.

21. FAIRBANKS RANCH COUNTRY CLUB

PLAY POLICY & FEES: Members and guests only. Reciprocal play is not accepted. Guest fees are $125, including cart.

DRESS CODE: Appropriate golf attire and nonmetal spikes are required.

COURSE DESCRIPTION: This course features bent grass from tee to green, and four lakes come into play on four holes. The course is situated in a natural valley. There are natural timbers and stands of old eucalyptus and new plantings. There are also 80 bunkers to contend with, so bring your sand wedge.

LOCATION: Take the Via de la Valle exit off Interstate 5 and drive east to El Camino Real south. At San Dieguito Road, travel one mile and turn east. The course is about 600 yards east of the entrance to the Fairbanks Country Club.

. . . ● **TOURNAMENTS:** This course is available for outside tournaments.

22. DEL MAR COUNTRY CLUB

MORGAN RUN RESORT & CLUB
ARCHITECTS: RAINVILLE , 1967 (E); L. JONES

5690 Cancha de Golf
Rancho Santa Fe, CA
92067
PRO SHOP: 858-756-3255

Gary Sowinski, PGA Professional
Dale Hahn, Superintendent

Driving Range ●
Practice Greens ●
Clubhouse ●
Food / Beverage ●
Accommodations ●
Pull Carts ●
Power Carts ●
Club Rental ●
$Special Offers

	1	2	3	4	5	6	7	8	9	OUT
BACK	186	350	191	472	377	381	478	124	560	3119
REGULAR	168	328	170	463	364	371	456	107	543	2970
par	3	4	3	5	4	4	5	3	5	36
handicap	8	6	4	7	5	3	2	9	1	-
FORWARD	154	320	119	413	324	333	443	94	510	2710
par	3	4	3	5	4	4	5	3	5	36
handicap	7	5	8	3	6	4	2	9	1	-

	10	11	12	13	14	15	16	17	18	IN
BACK	373	170	376	428	510	431	509	366	161	3324
REGULAR	345	162	362	406	496	413	490	353	134	3161
par	4	3	4	4	5	4	5	4	3	36
handicap	5	8	3	2	4	1	6	7	9	-
FORWARD	323	154	353	362	482	384	435	289	123	2905
par	4	3	4	4	5	4	5	4	3	36
handicap	5	9	2	3	4	1	6	7	8	-

BACK	
yardage	6443
par	72
rating	73.0
slope	132

REGULAR	
yardage	6131
par	72
rating	70.9
slope	124

FORWARD	
yardage	5615
par	72
rating	75.0
slope	132

DOUBLETREE CARMEL HIGHLAND RESORT
ARCHITECT: WILLIAM F. BELL, 1964

14455 Penasquitos Drive
San Diego, CA 92128

PRO SHOP: 858-672-2200

Michael Flanagan, PGA Professional
Mike Magnani, Superintendent

Driving Range
Practice Greens ●
Clubhouse ●
Food / Beverage ●
Accommodations ●
Pull Carts
Power Carts ●
Club Rental ●
$Special Offers ●

	1	2	3	4	5	6	7	8	9	OUT
BACK	340	442	316	217	502	522	438	420	162	3359
REGULAR	333	412	303	159	488	508	406	342	154	3105
par	4	4	4	3	5	5	4	4	3	36
handicap	13	1	17	15	5	7	3	9	11	-
FORWARD	325	396	286	137	437	441	314	321	107	2764
par	4	4	4	3	5	5	4	4	3	36
handicap	7	1	13	15	3	5	11	9	17	-

	10	11	12	13	14	15	16	17	18	IN
BACK	304	309	460	388	315	495	123	314	361	3069
REGULAR	293	289	445	367	295	470	115	307	332	2913
par	4	4	4	4	4	5	3	4	4	36
handicap	12	14	2	4	18	8	16	10	6	-
FORWARD	259	258	338	352	275	436	105	259	315	2597
par	4	4	4	4	4	5	3	4	4	36
handicap	12	16	2	6	14	4	18	10	8	-

BACK	
yardage	6428
par	72
rating	70.7
slope	123

REGULAR	
yardage	6018
par	72
rating	68.4
slope	116

FORWARD	
yardage	5361
par	72
rating	71.9
slope	125

PLAY POLICY & FEES: Outside play is accepted after 11 a.m. every day. The course is open to the public on Monday and after 2 p.m. on Saturday and Sunday. Hotel guests and guest of members can play before 11 a.m. every day. Green fees are $70 walking or riding Monday through Thursday, and $90 walking or riding Friday through Sunday and holidays.

TEE TIMES: Reservations can be booked seven days in advance.

DRESS CODE: Collared shirts are required, and no denim or metal spikes are allowed on the course.

COURSE DESCRIPTION: This flat course is easy to walk, but the narrow fairways and long rough make it challenging. A river snakes through two of the nines. Known locally for its slow greens, the internationally acclaimed San Diego Academy of Golf is based here.

NOTES: Par is 72 for the East/South and 71 for the South/North and North/East Courses. The East/South Course: See scorecard for yardage and rating information. Morgan Run has recently added a set of gold tee boxes.

LOCATION: From Interstate 5 in Del Mar, take the Via de la Valle exit. Drive east for three miles and turn right on Cancha de Golf.

. . . ● **TOURNAMENTS:** This course is available for outside tournaments. ●

TRAVEL: For reservations at the resort call 858-756-2471.

23. MORGAN RUN RESORT & CLUB

PLAY POLICY & FEES: Green fees are $50 weekdays and $65 weekends and holidays. Carts are included.

TEE TIMES: Reservations can be booked seven days in advance for public play and 30 days in advance for hotel guests.

DRESS CODE: Appropriate golf attire and nonmetal spikes are required.

COURSE DESCRIPTION: This rolling course is well groomed with exceptional greens. Water comes into play on four holes. The par-5 sixth hole has a lateral water hazard running alongside the fairway and a pond in front of the green. The eighth hole is a long par 4 up a hill to a sloped green.

LOCATION: Travel 23 miles north of San Diego on Interstate 15 to the Carmel Mountain Road exit. Drive west for a quarter mile to Penasquitos Drive and turn right to the club entrance.

. . . ● **TOURNAMENTS:** A 16-player minimum is needed to book a tournament. The banquet facility can accommodate up to 300 people. ● **TRAVEL:** For reservations at the resort call 858-672-9100. ● **$PECIAL OFFERS:** Golf packages are available.

24. DOUBLETREE CARMEL HIGHLAND RESORT

MIRAMAR MEMORIAL GOLF CLUB
ARCHITECT: JACK DARAY, 1963

MCAS Miramar P.O. Box
San Diego, CA 92145-2008

PRO SHOP: 858-577-4155

Robert Knight, PGA Professional
Steve Parker, Superintendent

Driving Range •
Practice Greens •
Clubhouse •
Food / Beverage •
Accommodations
Pull Carts •
Power Carts •
Club Rental •
$pecial Offers

	1	2	3	4	5	6	7	8	9	OUT
BACK	374	368	497	386	149	540	385	184	640	3523
REGULAR	355	356	478	378	111	510	354	169	553	3264
par	4	4	5	4	3	5	4	3	5	37
handicap	3	11	15	7	17	13	1	9	5	-
FORWARD	338	344	354	368	103	429	344	136	485	2901
par	4	4	4	4	3	5	4	3	5	36
handicap	9	11	13	7	15	3	5	17	1	-

	10	11	12	13	14	15	16	17	18	IN
BACK	416	366	417	340	202	520	150	443	441	3295
REGULAR	395	347	403	316	182	504	137	428	426	3138
par	4	4	4	4	3	5	3	4	4	35
handicap	4	12	8	14	16	2	18	10	6	-
FORWARD	377	329	396	300	150	490	126	418	411	2997
par	4	4	4	4	3	5	3	5	5	37
handicap	4	12	8	14	16	2	18	10	6	-

BACK	
yardage	6818
par	72
rating	72.2
slope	126

REGULAR	
yardage	6402
par	72
rating	70.0
slope	120

FORWARD	
yardage	5898
par	73
rating	73.9
slope	128

 STONERIDGE COUNTRY CLUB
ARCHITECT: TED ROBINSON, 1972

17166 Stoneridge Country
Poway, CA 92064

PRO SHOP: 858-487-2117
CLUBHOUSE: 858-487-2138

Eric Troll, Manager
Ben Stewart, Head Professional, PGA
Troy Mullane, Superintendent

Driving Range •
Practice Greens •
Clubhouse •
Food / Beverage •
Accommodations
Pull Carts
Power Carts •
Club Rental •
$pecial Offers

	1	2	3	4	5	6	7	8	9	OUT
BACK	502	415	165	386	540	422	175	443	279	3327
REGULAR	492	397	155	374	518	411	158	433	270	3208
par	5	4	3	4	5	4	3	4	4	36
handicap	9	7	15	13	3	5	11	1	17	-
FORWARD	473	366	148	347	471	380	145	411	255	2996
par	5	4	3	4	5	4	3	5	4	37
handicap	5	3	17	11	7	1	15	9	13	-

	10	11	12	13	14	15	16	17	18	IN
BACK	313	403	525	203	326	501	153	379	371	3174
REGULAR	306	388	508	186	321	492	148	361	356	3066
par	4	4	5	3	4	5	3	4	4	36
handicap	14	8	4	10	16	2	18	6	12	-
FORWARD	277	350	424	168	289	453	145	340	290	2736
par	4	4	5	3	4	5	3	4	4	36
handicap	10	8	6	14	16	2	18	4	12	-

BACK	
yardage	6501
par	72
rating	69.9
slope	118

REGULAR	
yardage	6274
par	72
rating	68.5
slope	111

FORWARD	
yardage	5732
par	73
rating	73.2
slope	128

25. MIRAMAR MEMORIAL GOLF CLUB

PLAY POLICY & FEES: Military personnel and guests only. Green fees are based on military status. Guest fees are $21 weekdays and $26 weekends.

DRESS CODE: Appropriate golf attire is required.

COURSE DESCRIPTION: The course was originally built as an emergency landing area. Today it's lined with trees. The course is flat, but wind and rough make it a firm test. The par-5 ninth hole was recently lengthened to 640 yards, making it the longest par 5 in Southern Califonia.

NOTES: The Marines recently took over the base from the Navy.

LOCATION: Take Interstate 15 or State Road 163 for 12 miles north of San Diego to Miramar Way. Exit and drive west to the main gate.

. . . ● **TOURNAMENTS:** This course is not available for outside events.

26. STONERIDGE COUNTRY CLUB

PLAY POLICY & FEES: Reciprocal play is accepted with members of other private clubs weekdays only with the approval of the head professional. Green fees are $70 for reciprocators, including cart. Green fees are $60 for guests with members, including cart. Reservations are recommended.

DRESS CODE: Appropriate golf attire and nonmetal spikes are required.

COURSE DESCRIPTION: The front nine is level and the back nine is hilly on this well-maintained course. Frequent afternoon winds can stiffen the challenge here.

NOTES: Stoneridge hosted the LPGA tour from 1988 to 1992.

LOCATION: From Interstate 15 south of Escondido, take the Rancho Bernardo Road exit and travel east for 2.5 miles to Stoneridge Country Club Lane.

. . . ● **TOURNAMENTS:** This course is available for outside tournaments on Monday.

RANCHO BERNARDO INN & COUNTRY CLUB

ARCHITECTS: WILLIAM F. BELL, 1962; SCHMIDT & CURLY, 1998

17550 Bernardo Oaks
San Diego, CA 92128

PRO SHOP: 858-675-8470
CLUBHOUSE: 800-662-6439

Scott Bentley, Director of Golf, PGA
Scott Murray, PGA Professional
Kent Graff, Superintendent

Driving Range ●
Practice Greens ●
Clubhouse ●
Food / Beverage ●
Accommodations ●
Pull Carts
Power Carts ●
Club Rental ●
$pecial Offers ●

	1	2	3	4	5	6	7	8	9	OUT
BACK	347	205	497	208	381	385	435	503	306	3267
REGULAR	312	136	471	144	356	323	370	471	271	2854
par	4	3	5	3	4	4	4	5	4	36
handicap	15	7	5	13	9	11	1	3	17	-
FORWARD	261	107	409	95	293	276	350	416	242	2449
par	4	3	4	3	4	4	5	5	4	36
handicap	15	7	5	3	9	11	1	3	17	-

	10	11	12	13	14	15	16	17	18	IN
BACK	409	178	505	141	438	377	395	361	544	3348
REGULAR	367	126	471	100	361	348	331	319	508	2931
par	4	3	5	3	4	4	4	4	5	36
handicap	6	16	4	18	2	8	14	12	10	-
FORWARD	302	80	422	84	314	301	275	284	434	2496
par	4	3	5	3	4	4	4	4	5	36
handicap	6	16	4	18	2	8	14	12	10	-

BACK	
yardage	6615
par	72
rating	72.1
slope	129

REGULAR	
yardage	5785
par	72
rating	69.2
slope	121

FORWARD	
yardage	4945
par	72
rating	70.6
slope	123

THE COUNTRY CLUB OF RANCHO BERNARDO

ARCHITECT: TED ROBINSON, 1967

12280 Green East Road
San Diego, CA 92128

PRO SHOP: 858-487-1212
CLUBHOUSE: 858-487-1134

Dan Sweetwood, Manager
Ron Cropley, PGA Professional
Sandy Clarke, Superintendent

Driving Range ●
Practice Greens ●
Clubhouse ●
Food / Beverage ●
Accommodations
Pull Carts ●
Power Carts ●
Club Rental ●
$pecial Offers

	1	2	3	4	5	6	7	8	9	OUT
BACK	-	-	-	-	-	-	-	-	-	-
REGULAR	-	-	-	-	-	-	-	-	-	-
par	-	-	-	-	-	-	-	-	-	-
handicap	-	-	-	-	-	-	-	-	-	-
FORWARD	-	-	-	-	-	-	-	-	-	-
par	-	-	-	-	-	-	-	-	-	-
handicap	-	-	-	-	-	-	-	-	-	-

	10	11	12	13	14	15	16	17	18	IN
BACK	-	-	-	-	-	-	-	-	-	-
REGULAR	-	-	-	-	-	-	-	-	-	-
par	-	-	-	-	-	-	-	-	-	-
handicap	-	-	-	-	-	-	-	-	-	-
FORWARD	-	-	-	-	-	-	-	-	-	-
par	-	-	-	-	-	-	-	-	-	-
handicap	-	-	-	-	-	-	-	-	-	-

BACK	
yardage	6428
par	72
rating	70.7
slope	124

REGULAR	
yardage	6163
par	72
rating	69.5
slope	121

FORWARD	
yardage	5663
par	72
rating	67.5
slope	115

PLAY POLICY & FEES: Outside play is accepted along with hotel guests and members. The green fees are $70 Monday through Thursday, $80 Friday, and $90 on weekends. Green fees include carts. Twilight rates are available.

TEE TIMES: Reservations can be booked seven days in advance.

DRESS CODE: No jeans or running shorts are allowed. Shirts must have collars and sleeves. This is a nonmetal spike facility.

COURSE DESCRIPTION: Set in a small, scenic valley and enclosed by homes, this course offers sloping fairways, a meandering creek, two lakes, natural vegetation areas and fast greens. It is well maintained and challenging, offering four sets of tees. The par-5 18th is a beautiful signature hole featuring a cascading waterfall.

NOTES: The Rancho Bernardo Inn is also a top-ranked tennis resort and spa, and has large, nicely appointed accommodations as well as some of the best food in San Diego. The Golf University Instructional Schools are also based here.

LOCATION: Travel eight miles south of the town of Escondido on Interstate 15 to Rancho Bernardo Road east. Drive one mile to Bernardo Oaks Drive and turn left to the Inn and golf course.

. . . ● **TOURNAMENTS:** This course is available for outside tournaments. A 16-player minimum is needed. Tournaments should be booked 12 months in advance. The banquet facility can accommodate 300 people. ● **TRAVEL:** For reservations at the resort call 858-675-8500. ● **$PECIAL OFFERS:** Play-and-stay packages that include golf, tennis, spa, and meals are available.

27. RANCHO BERNARDO INN & COUNTRY

PLAY POLICY & FEES: Members and guests only. Guests must be accompanied by a member. Green fees are $40 weekdays and $50 weekends. Carts are $20.

DRESS CODE: Appropriate golf attire and nonmetal spikes are required.

COURSE DESCRIPTION: This course is a fairly open layout where the short par 4s are uphill and the longer par 4s are downhill. It's known as hole-in-one paradise, although the par 3s range up to 190 yards.

NOTES: In 1999 a 20,000-square-foot clubhouse opened.

LOCATION: Travel eight miles south of the city of Escondido on Interstate 15 to Rancho Bernardo Road east. Drive one mile to Bernardo Oaks Drive and turn left to the club.

. . . ● **TOURNAMENTS:** This course is not available for outside events.

28. THE COUNTRY CLUB OF RANCHO

BERNARDO HEIGHTS COUNTRY CLUB
ARCHITECT: TED ROBINSON, 1983

16066 Bernardo Heights
San Diego, CA 92128

PRO SHOP: 858-487-3440

Russ Bloom, Head Professional, PGA
Robert Steele, Superintendent

Driving Range ●
Practice Greens ●
Clubhouse ●
Food / Beverage ●
Accommodations
Pull Carts
Power Carts ●
Club Rental ●
Special Offers

	1	2	3	4	5	6	7	8	9	OUT
BACK	434	439	165	551	386	350	383	376	184	3268
REGULAR	403	467	144	507	361	333	362	353	155	3085
par	4	4	3	5	4	4	4	4	3	35
handicap	3	1	13	15	11	17	5	9	7	-
FORWARD	340	414	124	465	337	300	324	315	130	2749
par	4	5	3	5	4	4	4	4	3	36
handicap	7	13	17	5	1	11	9	3	15	-

BACK	
yardage	6648
par	71
rating	71.9
slope	124

REGULAR	
yardage	6221
par	71
rating	69.7
slope	119

	10	11	12	13	14	15	16	17	18	IN
BACK	411	401	202	486	387	412	168	501	412	3380
REGULAR	389	361	166	459	365	392	146	487	371	3136
par	4	4	3	5	4	4	3	5	4	36
handicap	6	2	8	18	10	12	16	14	4	-
FORWARD	340	336	146	413	339	366	129	449	334	2852
par	4	4	3	5	4	4	3	5	4	36
handicap	14	12	16	4	10	8	18	2	6	-

FORWARD	
yardage	5601
par	72
rating	73.2
slope	127

 CARMEL MOUNTAIN RANCH COUNTRY CLUB
ARCHITECT: RON FREAM, 1986

14050 Carmel Ridge Road
San Diego, CA 92128

PRO SHOP: 858-487-9224
CLUBHOUSE: 858-451-8353

Jeff Perry, General Manager
Michael Winn, PGA Professional

19 mi
8.63 mi

Driving Range ●
Practice Greens ●
Clubhouse ●
Food / Beverage ●
Accommodations
Pull Carts
Power Carts ●
Club Rental ●
Special Offers

	1	2	3	4	5	6	7	8	9	OUT
BACK	384	460	391	175	488	221	310	469	395	3293
REGULAR	359	434	363	152	468	212	295	451	380	3114
par	4	4	4	3	5	3	4	5	4	36
handicap	12	2	10	8	4	6	18	16	14	-
FORWARD	337	398	329	91	324	166	255	411	351	2662
par	4	4	4	3	5	3	4	5	4	36
handicap	6	2	19	18	4	14	16	12	8	-

BACK	
yardage	6615
par	72
rating	72.9
slope	136

REGULAR	
yardage	6217
par	72
rating	70.5
slope	128

	10	11	12	13	14	15	16	17	18	IN
BACK	550	157	217	340	447	505	397	324	385	3322
REGULAR	521	134	198	310	419	479	362	300	380	3103
par	5	3	3	4	4	5	4	4	4	36
handicap	17	9	3	11	1	15	5	13	7	-
FORWARD	457	100	108	260	367	436	286	250	356	2620
par	5	3	3	4	4	5	4	4	4	36
handicap	9	15	17	13	5	1	11	7		-

FORWARD	
yardage	5282
par	72
rating	70.2
slope	121

PLAY POLICY & FEES: Reciprocal play is accepted with clubs that also have reciprocal play. The reciprocal fee is $75. Reciprocal play is only allowed weekdays. Green fees for guests are $40 weekdays and $55 weekends. Carts are $22. Reservations are required.

DRESS CODE: Appropriate golf attire and nonmetal spikes are required.

COURSE DESCRIPTION: This well-maintained course is hilly with a few trees, some water, and fast greens. Homes and condos line many fairways but are not intrusive. It's a big course, with large, sloping greens.

NOTES: Bernardo Heights hosted LPGA events in 1986 and 1987.

LOCATION: Take the Bernardo Center Drive exit off Interstate 15 and drive east to Bernardo Heights Parkway; then turn right to the club.

. . . ● **TOURNAMENTS:** This course is available for outside events on Monday. Carts are required.

29. BERNARDO HEIGHTS COUNTRY CLUB

PLAY POLICY & FEES: Outside play is accepted. Green fees are $40 Monday through Thursday, $50 Friday and Sunday, and $60 on Saturday and holidays for San Diego County residents. Nonresident rates are $65, $75 and $85, respectively. Carts are included. Twilight, senior, junior, and military rates are available.

TEE TIMES: Reservations can be booked 30 days in advance. An additional $5 per player reservation fee will apply to all reservations made prior to seven days in advance. All reservations must be guaranteed with a credit card.

DRESS CODE: Collared shirts are required. No jeans are allowed on the course. Nonmetal spikes are required.

COURSE DESCRIPTION: The holes on this rolling, narrow course follow the contours of the hills. There are no parallel fairways. The greens are well kept and fast. Homes line virtually every fairway, and there are some serious hills here, all of which demand accuracy and patience. The number five hole was rated the toughest par 4 in San Diego.

NOTES: Hole number eight now features two lakes and a waterfall. The course record is 64. Tour players Mark O'Meara and Bill Glasson have sharpened their games at this course.

LOCATION: Take Interstate 15 to the Carmel Mountain Road east. Drive past three stoplights and take a right on Highland Ranch Road. Drive past three more stoplights and take a right on Carmel Ridge Road. Drive to the top of the hill.

. . . ● **TOURNAMENTS:** This course is available for tournaments. Carts are required. `The banquet facility can accommodate 250 people.

30. CARMEL MOUNTAIN RANCH COUNTRY

TORREY PINES GOLF COURSE
ARCHITECT: WILLIAM F. BELL, 1957

GOLF 50

11480 North Torrey Pines
La Jolla, CA 92037

PRO SHOP: 800-985-4653
STARTER: 619-552-1784

Susan Casagranda, President
Joe DeBock, Director of Golf, PGA
Robert Bunn, Tournament Director

Driving Range ●
Practice Greens ●
Clubhouse ●
Food / Beverage ●
Accommodations ●
Pull Carts ●
Power Carts ●
Club Rental ●
Special Offers

	1	2	3	4	5	6	7	8	9	OUT
BACK	520	326	121	398	371	206	400	436	497	3275
REGULAR	511	313	112	384	355	150	354	418	480	3077
par	5	4	3	4	4	3	4	4	5	36
handicap	7	15	17	3	9	13	5	1	11	-
FORWARD	504	303	109	374	346	141	346	404	470	2997
par	5	4	3	4	4	3	4	4	5	36
handicap	3	13	17	7	11	15	5	1	9	-

	10	11	12	13	14	15	16	17	18	IN
BACK	416	437	190	430	507	397	338	172	485	3372
REGULAR	404	422	174	418	490	387	323	159	472	3249
par	4	4	3	4	5	4	4	3	5	36
handicap	6	2	10	4	14	8	18	12	11	-
FORWARD	391	410	159	407	478	377	314	125	460	3121
par	4	5	3	5	5	4	4	3	5	38
handicap	4	12	16	10	2	8	14	18	6	-

BACK	
yardage	6647
par	72
rating	72.1
slope	129

REGULAR	
yardage	6326
par	72
rating	70.0
slope	119

FORWARD	
yardage	6118
par	74
rating	75.4
slope	134

 LA JOLLA COUNTRY CLUB
ARCHITECT: WILLIAM P. BELL, 1927

P.O. Box 1760   7301 High Avenue
La Jolla, CA 92038   La Jolla, CA 92038

PRO SHOP: 858-454-2505

Pete Coe, Head Professional, PGA
Bruce Duenow, Superintendent

Driving Range ●
Practice Greens ●
Clubhouse ●
Food / Beverage ●
Accommodations
Pull Carts
Power Carts ●
Club Rental ●
Special Offers

	1	2	3	4	5	6	7	8	9	OUT
BACK	-	-	-	-	-	-	-	-	-	-
REGULAR	-	-	-	-	-	-	-	-	-	
par	-	-	-	-	-	-	-	-	-	
handicap	-	-	-	-	-	-	-	-	-	-
FORWARD	-	-	-	-	-	-	-	-	-	
par	-	-	-	-	-	-	-	-	-	
handicap	-	-	-	-	-	-	-	-	-	-

	10	11	12	13	14	15	16	17	18	IN
BACK	-	-	-	-	-	-	-	-	-	-
REGULAR	-	-	-	-	-	-	-	-	-	
par	-	-	-	-	-	-	-	-	-	
handicap	-	-	-	-	-	-	-	-	-	-
FORWARD	-	-	-	-	-	-	-	-	-	
par	-	-	-	-	-	-	-	-	-	
handicap	-	-	-	-	-	-	-	-	-	-

BACK	
yardage	6713
par	72
rating	72.9
slope	133

REGULAR	
yardage	6254
par	72
rating	70.2
slope	125

FORWARD	
yardage	5988
par	72
rating	75.8
slope	134

PLAY POLICY & FEES: Green fees are $95 Monday through Thursday and $110 Friday through Sunday.

TEE TIMES: Advance tee time package includes a guaranteed tee time, cart, green fees and a golf professional escort for three holes. Reservations can be made up to two months in advance.

DRESS CODE: Collared shirts are encouraged on the golf course.

COURSE DESCRIPTION: This is a top-notch public facility. The South Course is wide open but tough when the wind is blowing off the ocean. The North Course is shorter and more scenic. The 12th on the South Course at 486 yards into the wind has been rated one of the toughest holes in the country. The North Course is about two shots easier.

NOTES: Both courses are used for the PGA Tour's Buick Invitational of California in February. The South Course is 7,033 yards and rated 74.6 from the championship tees, and 6,705 yards and rated 72.6 from the regular tees. The slope ratings are 136 championship and 130 regular. The forward tees are 6,463 yards and rated 77.2. The slope rating is 128.

LOCATION: Drive north from San Diego on Interstate 5 to Genesse. Turn west to North Torrey Pines Road and turn north into the club.

. . . ● **TOURNAMENTS:** A 32-player minimum is needed to book a tournament, and carts are required. The Lodge at Torrey Pines and the Hilton La Jolla Torrey Pines Hotel are close and have banquet facilities. ● **TRAVEL:** For information on rooms call the Lodge at Torrey Pines at 619-453-4420 or the Grand Sheraton at 619-558-1500.

31. TORREY PINES GOLF COURSE

PLAY POLICY & FEES: Members and guests only. Green fees are $60 weekdays and $80 weekends. Carts are $18.

DRESS CODE: Appropriate golf attire and nonmetal spikes are required.

COURSE DESCRIPTION: This is an older traditional course perched on a bluff overlooking the Pacific. It is well maintained and relatively hilly with lots of trees and bunkers. When the wind picks up, it can be a tough course. The key here is accuracy and the ability to read the small, subtle, and quick greens.

LOCATION: Take the Ardath Road exit (it becomes Torrey Pines Road) off Interstate 5 north of San Diego and drive 3.25 miles. Turn left on Girard Street and then left on Pearl Street. Drive two blocks to High Avenue and turn right. Continue one block to the club.

. . . ● **TOURNAMENTS:** This course is not available for outside events.

32. LA JOLLA COUNTRY CLUB

San Diego Area (map page 952)   **985**

RANCHO SANTA FE FARMS GOLF CLUB
ARCHITECT: PETE DYE, 1988

P.O. Box 2769
Rancho Santa Fe, CA
92067
PRO SHOP: 858-756-5884

8500 Saint Andrews Road
Rancho Santa Fe, CA
92067

Glen Daugherty, PGA Professional
Dave Reidman, Superintendent

Driving Range ●
Practice Greens ●
Clubhouse ●
Food / Beverage ●
Accommodations
Pull Carts
Power Carts ●
Club Rental ●
$pecial Offers

	1	2	3	4	5	6	7	8	9	OUT
BACK	362	141	513	335	179	306	370	380	485	3071
REGULAR	323	129	482	309	166	289	330	351	430	2809
par	4	3	5	4	3	4	4	4	5	36
handicap	15	17	1	3	11	13	5	7	9	-
FORWARD	323	110	477	277	130	280	299	351	430	2677
par	4	3	5	4	3	44	4	4	5	76
handicap	13	17	1	9	11	15	3	5	7	-

	10	11	12	13	14	15	16	17	18	IN
BACK	411	367	524	381	163	364	171	430	508	3319
REGULAR	390	339	495	358	145	314	154	402	481	3078
par	4	4	5	4	3	4	3	4	5	36
handicap	8	18	4	10	16	6	14	2	12	-
FORWARD	353	301	455	333	117	314	139	365	457	2834
par	4	4	5	4	3	4	3	4	5	36
handicap	2	14	10	8	18	16	12	6	4	-

BACK	
yardage	6390
par	72
rating	71.1
slope	131

REGULAR	
yardage	5887
par	72
rating	68.6
slope	121

FORWARD	
yardage	5511
par	112
rating	71.6
slope	125

 ## NAVAL STATION SAN DIEGO GOLF COURSE

MWR Code 10, NSGC
San Diego, CA 92136

PRO SHOP: 858-556-7502

Mark Johnson, Director of Golf, PGA

Driving Range ●
Practice Greens ●
Clubhouse ●
Food / Beverage ●
Accommodations
Pull Carts ●
Power Carts
Club Rental ●
$pecial Offers

	1	2	3	4	5	6	7	8	9	OUT
BACK	506	334	387	407	366	556	199	405	207	3367
REGULAR	492	327	371	383	348	535	189	386	176	3207
par	5	4	4	4	4	5	3	4	3	36
handicap	17	13	11	3	9	5	7	1	15	-
FORWARD	444	276	356	372	330	480	127	355	167	2907
par	5	4	4	4	4	5	3	4	3	36
handicap	5	13	9	7	11	1	17	3	15	-

	10	11	12	13	14	15	16	17	18	IN
BACK	316	417	429	430	180	515	380	226	562	3455
REGULAR	284	400	404	409	168	493	365	212	544	3279
par	4	4	4	4	3	5	4	3	5	36
handicap	18	14	8	2	16	14	10	12	6	-
FORWARD	267	309	395	392	154	474	349	155	442	2937
par	4	4	5	4	3	5	4	3	5	37
handicap	14	12	10	6	16	2	8	18	4	-

BACK	
yardage	6822
par	72
rating	72.8
slope	126

REGULAR	
yardage	2500
par	27
rating	70.3
slope	-117

FORWARD	
yardage	5844
par	73
rating	67
slope	109

18
HOLES

PLAY POLICY & FEES: Members and guests only. The green fee for guests with members is $75. The fee for unaccompanied guests is $200. Carts are included.

DRESS CODE: Appropriate golf attire and nonmetal spikes are required.

COURSE DESCRIPTION: Members consider this maturing course a very private retreat. Michael Jordan and Janet Jackson are members. This very hilly course has three man-made lakes that come into play on five holes. This is one of the most scenic courses in the country. It demands accuracy to navigate rough-lined fairways and tiered greens, as well as some strength when the wind blows.

LOCATION: From Interstate 5, take the Carmel Valley Road exit and drive east four to five miles. Turn left on Rancho Santa Fe Road. At the dead end, turn right; the course is one-quarter mile farther.

. . . ● **TOURNAMENTS:** This course is not available for outside events.

33. RANCHO SANTA FE FARMS GOLF CLUB

9
HOLES

PLAY POLICY & FEES: Military personnel and guests only. Green fees vary according to military status.

DRESS CODE: No cutoffs are allowed on the course.

COURSE DESCRIPTION: This is a short course with open fairways and small greens. Holes vary between 110 and 175 yards. It's all tucked snugly into the 32nd Street Naval Station just south of downtown San Diego.

LOCATION: Going south from San Diego on Interstate 5, take the Main Street exit. Cross Main Street and drive directly to the gate.

. . . ● **TOURNAMENTS:** This course is not available for outside events.

34. NAVAL STATION SAN DIEGO GOLF

OAKS NORTH EXECUTIVE COURSE
ARCHITECT: TED ROBINSON, 1971

12602 Oaks North Drive
San Diego, CA 92128

PRO SHOP: 858-487-3021

Lloyd Porter, Professional/Manager
Glen Olson, Superintendent

Driving Range ●
Practice Greens ●
Clubhouse
Food / Beverage ●
Accommodations
Pull Carts ●
Power Carts ●
Club Rental ●
$pecial Offers

	1	2	3	4	5	6	7	8	9	OUT
BACK	-	-	-	-	-	-	-	-	-	-
REGULAR	163	254	306	125	147	143	140	185	286	1749
par	3	4	4	3	3	3	3	3	4	30
handicap	5	3	1	9	6	7	8	4	2	-
FORWARD	138	240	292	111	119	121	120	145	251	1537
par	3	4	4	3	3	3	3	3	4	30
handicap	5	3	1	9	6	7	8	4	2	-

	10	11	12	13	14	15	16	17	18	IN
BACK	-	-	-	-	-	-	-	-	-	-
REGULAR	252	119	156	179	279	251	126	171	132	1665
par	4	3	3	3	4	4	3	3	3	30
handicap	2	7	6	4	1	3	9	5	8	-
FORWARD	239	112	139	154	259	227	102	150	122	1504
par	4	3	3	3	4	4	3	3	3	30
handicap	2	7	6	4	1	3	9	5	8	-

BACK	
yardage	-
par	-
rating	-
slope	-

REGULAR	
yardage	3414
par	60
rating	55.8
slope	86

FORWARD	
yardage	3041
par	60
rating	57.6
slope	85

 # MOUNT WOODSON GOLF CLUB
ARCHITECT: L. SCHMIDT, B. CURLEY, 1991

16422 North Woodson
Ramona, CA 92065

PRO SHOP: 760-788-3555

David Johnson, PGA Professional
Vince Zelle Frow, Superintendent

Driving Range
Practice Greens ●
Clubhouse ●
Food / Beverage ●
Accommodations
Pull Carts
Power Carts ●
Club Rental ●
$pecial Offers ●

	1	2	3	4	5	6	7	8	9	OUT
BACK	301	308	186	501	398	164	311	293	181	2643
REGULAR	286	300	163	486	362	138	281	270	167	2453
par	4	4	3	5	4	3	4	4	3	34
handicap	18	8	6	4	2	16	14	12	10	-
FORWARD	278	241	91	430	316	102	247	235	101	2041
par	4	4	3	5	4	3	4	4	3	34
handicap	18	8	6	4	2	16	14	12	10	-

	10	11	12	13	14	15	16	17	18	IN
BACK	337	133	402	514	510	318	150	348	475	3187
REGULAR	314	117	267	500	486	286	132	325	404	2831
par	4	3	4	5	5	4	3	4	4	36
handicap	11	17	1	3	9	13	15	7	5	-
FORWARD	296	97	223	410	422	259	107	247	339	2400
par	4	3	4	5	5	4	3	4	4	36
handicap	11	17	1	3	9	13	15	7	5	-

BACK	
yardage	5830
par	70
rating	68.8
slope	130

REGULAR	
yardage	5284
par	70
rating	65.7
slope	121

FORWARD	
yardage	4441
par	70
rating	64.7
slope	108

PLAY POLICY & FEES: Green fees are $26 weekdays, $28 weekends. Junior green fees are $10 weekdays, $12 weekends. Twilight rate is $16 every day, and a supertwilight rate is $12 every day. Memberships are available. Member green fees are $16 weekdays, $18 weekends. Carts are $5 for nine holes, $8 for 18 holes.

TEE TIMES: Reservations can be booked seven days in advance.

DRESS CODE: Collared shirts and Bermuda-length shorts or slacks are required for men; no tank tops or short shorts for women are allowed. Nonmetal spikes are encouraged.

COURSE DESCRIPTION: These executive courses have tight fairways and undulating greens. The courses have regulation par 4s and par 3s, but no par 5s. Homes line some fairways. Greens are receptive—only two are tiered.

NOTES: There are three nines, and each 18-hole combination is par 60. The North/South Course is 3,608 yards and rated 56.8 from the regular tees. The slope rating is 88. The South/East Course is 3,524 yards and rated 56.5 from the regular tees. The slope rating is 87. The North/East Course: see scorecard for additional yardage and rating information.

LOCATION: From Interstate 15 in San Diego take Rancho Bernardo Road to Pomerado. Take a left on Pomerado to Oaks North Drive.

. . . ● **TOURNAMENTS:** A 72-player minimum is needed to book a tournament. Tournaments should be booked six months in advance. The banquet facility can hold 300 people.

35. OAKS NORTH EXECUTIVE COURSE

PLAY POLICY & FEES: Green fees are seasonal and range from $49 to $75. Twilight rates are available year-round.

TEE TIMES: Reservations can be booked seven days in advance.

DRESS CODE: Collared shirts and nonmetal spikes are required. Shorts must be Bermuda length. No denim is allowed.

COURSE DESCRIPTION: Tucked away in the mountains of Ramona at the base of Mount Woodson, this is a spectacular course in a natural setting. There are boulders, lakes, ancient oaks, and numerous elevation changes. The 150-yard bridge that links the second green to the third tee is a landmark. Holes 13, 15, and 17 offer superb views. Six lakes come into play. Both the fairways and the undulating greens are well bunkered. There are no parallel fairways.

LOCATION: From Interstate 15, take Scripps Poway Parkway east to Highway 67. Turn left on Highway 67 and drive for seven miles to Archie Moore Road. Turn left to the club entrance.

. . . ● **TOURNAMENTS:** A 16-player minimum is required to book a tournament. The banquet facility can accommodate 200 people. ● **TRAVEL:** The Rancho Bernardo Inn is located 20 minutes from the golf course. For reservations call 619-487-1611. ● **$PECIAL OFFERS:** The Rancho Bernardo Inn offers golf packages.

36. MOUNT WOODSON GOLF CLUB

37 SAN VICENTE INN & GOLF CLUB
ARCHITECT: TED ROBINSON, 1972

24157 San Vicente Road
Ramona, CA 92065

PRO SHOP: 760-789-3477

Al Powers, Manager
Bob Harchut, Head Professional, PGA
Pat Shannon, Superintendent

Driving Range ●
Practice Greens ●
Clubhouse ●
Food / Beverage ●
Accommodations ●
Pull Carts
Power Carts ●
Club Rental ●
$Special Offers ●

	1	2	3	4	5	6	7	8	9	OUT
BACK	540	168	342	506	397	346	391	207	387	3284
REGULAR	516	156	320	486	372	329	372	188	375	3114
par	5	3	4	5	4	4	4	3	4	36
handicap	7	13	17	1	11	5	9	15	3	-
FORWARD	434	137	305	447	313	293	341	141	325	2736
par	5	3	4	5	4	4	4	3	4	36
handicap	3	15	13	1	11	9	7	17	5	-

	10	11	12	13	14	15	16	17	18	IN
BACK	391	519	152	377	366	183	375	539	424	3326
REGULAR	351	496	130	358	345	166	341	521	388	3096
par	4	5	3	4	4	3	4	5	4	36
handicap	12	2	18	8	10	16	14	4	6	-
FORWARD	328	469	111	335	303	149	292	457	363	2807
par	4	5	3	4	4	3	4	5	4	36
handicap	10	2	18	8	12	16	14	4	6	-

BACK	
yardage	6610
par	72
rating	71.5
slope	123

REGULAR	
yardage	6210
par	72
rating	69.3
slope	116

FORWARD	
yardage	5543
par	72
rating	72.8
slope	128

38 LOMAS SANTA FE EXECUTIVE COURSE

1580 Sun Valley Road
Solana Beach, CA 92075

PRO SHOP: 858-755-0195

John O'Rourke, PGA Professional
Connie Hays, Tournament Director

Driving Range
Practice Greens ●
Clubhouse
Food / Beverage ●
Accommodations
Pull Carts ●
Power Carts ●
Club Rental
$Special Offers

	1	2	3	4	5	6	7	8	9	OUT
BACK										
REGULAR										
par										
handicap										
FORWARD										
par										
handicap										

	10	11	12	13	14	15	16	17	18	IN
BACK										
REGULAR										
par										
handicap										
FORWARD										
par										
handicap										

BACK	
yardage	
par	
rating	
slope	

REGULAR	
yardage	2295
par	56
rating	
slope	

FORWARD	
yardage	2097
par	56
rating	
slope	

PLAY POLICY & FEES: Outside play is accepted. Green fees are $47 Monday through Thursday and $57 Friday through Sunday, including cart. Twilight rates are available. Carts are $12 per person.

TEE TIMES: Reservations can be booked five days in advance.

DRESS CODE: Collared shirts and nonmetal spikes are preferred. No short shorts are allowed.

COURSE DESCRIPTION: This picturesque course is set in a valley and follows the topography of the land. Four lakes come into play on 14 of the holes, many of which are shaded by ancient live oaks. The sixth is a challenge: 329 yards uphill to the directional flag, then down to a bunkered green.

NOTES: A 26-room, on-site lodge is packed with winter guests from November through April.

LOCATION: From Main Street in downtown Ramona, drive south on 10th Street and continue six miles to the San Diego Country Estates.

. . . ● **TOURNAMENTS:** Carts are required. A 100-player minimum is needed to book a shotgun tournament. ● **TRAVEL:** For reservations at San Vicente Inn call 760-789-8290 or 800-776-1289. ● **$PECIAL OFFERS:** Play-and-stay golf packages are available.

37. SAN VICENTE INN & GOLF CLUB

PLAY POLICY & FEES: Weekday green fees are $19 until 3 p.m.. After 3 p.m. green fees are $15, and after 4 p.m. green fees are $10. On weekends green fees are $23 until 3 p.m., $17 after 3p.m., and $12 after 4 p.m. Carts are $20.

TEE TIMES: Reservations can be made at any time.

DRESS CODE: No tank tops are allowed on the course.

COURSE DESCRIPTION: This fairly level, but challenging executive course offers excellent greens and a chance to work on the short game.

LOCATION: From San Diego take Interstate 5 north to the Lomas Sante Fe Drive exit. Take Lomas Sante Fe Drive east one mile, turn left on Highland Drive and left on Sun Valley Road. The course will be on the left.

. . . ● **TOURNAMENTS:** Outside events and a banquet facility are available.

38. LOMAS SANTA FE EXECUTIVE COURSE

MISSION BAY GOLF COURSE
ARCHITECT: TED ROBINSON, 1964

2702 North Mission Bay
San Diego, CA 92109

PRO SHOP: 858-490-3370

Rick Irwin, Director of Golf, PGA
Rich Baxter, PGA Professional
Phil Ravenna, Superintendent

Driving Range •
Practice Greens •
Clubhouse •
Food / Beverage •
Accommodations
Pull Carts •
Power Carts •
Club Rental •
$pecial Offers

	1	2	3	4	5	6	7	8	9	OUT
BACK	-	-	-	-	-	-	-	-	-	-
REGULAR	262	90	134	95	121	75	265	135	124	1301
par	4	3	3	3	3	3	4	3	3	29
handicap	3	15	7	13	11	17	1	5	9	-
FORWARD	240	76	117	81	105	65	246	119	105	1154
par	4	3	3	3	3	3	4	3	3	29
handicap	3	15	7	13	9	17	1	5	11	-

BACK		
yardage	-
par	-
rating	-
slope	-

	10	11	12	13	14	15	16	17	18	IN
BACK	-	-	-	-	-	-	-	-	-	-
REGULAR	250	134	141	129	102	118	123	131	291	1419
par	4	3	3	3	3	3	3	3	4	29
handicap	4	12	6	8	18	16	14	10	2	-
FORWARD	234	115	121	105	91	102	109	113	283	1273
par	4	3	3	3	3	3	3	3	4	29
handicap	4	8	6	12	18	14	16	10	2	-

REGULAR		
yardage	2720
par	58
rating	-
slope	-

FORWARD		
yardage	2427
par	58
rating	-
slope	-

 TECOLOTE CANYON GOLF COURSE
ARCHITECT: ROBERT TRENT JONES SR., 1955

2755 Snead Avenue
San Diego, CA 92111

PRO SHOP: 858-279-1600

Don O'Rourke, PGA Professional
Tina Sanchez, Tournament Director

Driving Range •
Practice Greens •
Clubhouse •
Food / Beverage •
Accommodations
Pull Carts •
Power Carts •
Club Rental •
$pecial Offers

	1	2	3	4	5	6	7	8	9	OUT
BACK	-	-	-	-	-	-	-	-	-	-
REGULAR	105	114	152	158	305	137	129	339	142	1581
par	3	3	3	3	4	3	3	4	3	29
handicap	17	15	1	3	11	7	9	5	13	-
FORWARD	77	90	102	106	255	116	103	307	112	1268
par	3	3	3	3	4	3	3	4	3	29
handicap	17	15	9	11	5	7	1	3	13	-

BACK		
yardage	-
par	-
rating	-
slope	-

	10	11	12	13	14	15	16	17	18	IN
BACK	-	-	-	-	-	-	-	-	-	-
REGULAR	129	299	163	162	137	159	304	118	109	1580
par	3	4	3	3	3	3	4	3	3	29
handicap	14	6	4	8	12	10	2	16	18	-
FORWARD	95	269	143	139	106	136	287	91	91	1357
par	3	4	3	3	3	3	4	3	3	29
handicap	4	2	8	10	16	12	6	14	18	-

REGULAR		
yardage	3161
par	58
rating	-
slope	-

FORWARD		
yardage	2625
par	58
rating	-
slope	-

PLAY POLICY & FEES: Green fees are $10 for nine holes and $15 for 18 holes weekdays, $12 for nine holes and $17 for 18 holes weekends. Senior rates are $9 for nine holes and $13 for 18 holes weekdays. Juniors play for $8 for nine holes and $12 for 18 holes on weekdays. Carts are $9 for nine holes and $15 for 18 holes.

TEE TIMES: Reservations can be booked seven days in advance.

COURSE DESCRIPTION: Holes range between 75 and 291 yards, including four par 4s. Water and sand come into play often. The course, which is lighted for play until 10 p.m., is beautifully landscaped and located next to Mission Bay.

LOCATION: Take Interstate 5 from San Diego and go west on Clairmont Drive and north on Mission Bay Drive to the course.

. . . ● **TOURNAMENTS:** A 16-player minimum is required to book an event. Tournaments should be scheduled two to six months in advance. The banquet facility can accommodate up to 200 people. ● **TRAVEL:** The San Diego Hilton is located 10 minutes from the golf course. For reservations call 858-543-9000.

39. MISSION BAY GOLF COURSE

PLAY POLICY & FEES: Green fees are $15 weekdays and $21 weekends and holidays. Senior, junior, and twilight rates are offered. Carts are $18.

TEE TIMES: Reservations can be booked seven days in advance.

DRESS CODE: Nonmetal spikes are required.

COURSE DESCRIPTION: This well-maintained executive course is a great place for beginners and players of all skill levels. A 3.5-hour round is routine here during the week.

LOCATION: From downtown San Diego head north on Interstate 5 to the Clairmont Drive exit. Go east one-quarter mile to Bueguer Street; turn right. Take the first left on Field Street. Follow Field Street to the golf course.

. . . ● **TOURNAMENTS:** A 16-player minimum is needed to book a tournament.

40. TECOLOTE CANYON GOLF COURSE

NAVY GOLF COURSES: MISSION GORGE
ARCHITECT: JACK DARAY, 1957

Friars Road and Admiral
San Diego, CA 92021

PRO SHOP: 619-556-5520
STARTER: 619-556-5521

Mark Johnson, Director of Golf, PGA
Jim Higgins, Head Professional
Alan Andreason, Superintendent

Driving Range ●
Practice Greens ●
Clubhouse ●
Food / Beverage ●
Accommodations
Pull Carts ●
Power Carts ●
Club Rental ●
$pecial Offers

	1	2	3	4	5	6	7	8	9	OUT
BACK	506	334	387	407	366	556	199	405	207	3367
REGULAR	492	327	371	383	348	535	189	386	176	3207
par	5	4	4	4	4	5	3	4	3	36
handicap	17	13	11	3	9	5	7	1	15	-
FORWARD	444	276	356	372	330	480	127	355	167	2907
par	5	4	4	4	4	5	3	4	3	36
handicap	5	13	9	7	11	1	17	3	15	-

	10	11	12	13	14	15	16	17	18	IN
BACK	316	417	429	430	180	515	380	226	562	3455
REGULAR	284	400	404	409	168	493	365	212	544	3279
par	4	4	4	4	3	5	4	3	5	36
handicap	18	4	8	2	16	14	10	12	6	-
FORWARD	267	309	395	392	154	474	349	155	442	2937
par	4	4	5	4	3	5	4	3	5	37
handicap	14	12	10	6	16	2	8	18	4	-

BACK	
yardage	6822
par	72
rating	72.8
slope	126

REGULAR	
yardage	6486
par	72
rating	70.3
slope	117

FORWARD	
yardage	5844
par	73
rating	67.0
slope	109

CARLTON OAKS COUNTRY CLUB & LODGE
ARCHITECT: PETE DYE, 1989

9200 Inwood Drive
Santee, CA 92071

PRO SHOP: 619-448-8500
CLUBHOUSE: 619-448-4242

Susan Reid, General Manager
Rex Cole, PGA Professional
Jim Timke, Superintendent

Driving Range ●
Practice Greens ●
Clubhouse ●
Food / Beverage ●
Accommodations ●
Pull Carts
Power Carts ●
Club Rental ●
$pecial Offers ●

	1	2	3	4	5	6	7	8	9	OUT
BACK	392	164	510	419	294	364	182	366	527	3218
REGULAR	377	146	496	381	263	341	137	336	500	2977
par	4	3	5	4	4	4	3	4	5	36
handicap	3	17	5	1	13	7	15	11	9	-
FORWARD	289	103	356	275	173	232	78	225	425	2156
par	4	3	5	4	3	4	3	4	5	35
handicap	15	13	7	9	5	11	17	1	3	-

	10	11	12	13	14	15	16	17	18	IN
BACK	387	349	162	573	427	531	345	141	401	3316
REGULAR	372	322	129	528	380	491	335	128	363	3048
par	4	4	3	5	4	5	4	3	4	36
handicap	8	12	14	6	2	10	16	18	4	-
FORWARD	295	260	81	436	307	420	215	91	287	2392
par	4	4	3	5	4	5	4	3	4	36
handicap	14	6	12	10	4	8	18	16	2	-

BACK	
yardage	6534
par	72
rating	71.3
slope	127

REGULAR	
yardage	6025
par	72
rating	68.6
slope	118

FORWARD	
yardage	4548
par	71
rating	67.1
slope	114

PLAY POLICY & FEES: Military personnel and guests only. Green fees for military personnel vary depending on status. Green fees for retired military personnel are $12. Guests fees are $18 weekdays and $23 weekends. Carts are $16.

DRESS CODE: No tank tops or cutoffs are allowed. Nonmetal spikes are required.

COURSE DESCRIPTION: The North Course is the more interesting of the two and offers a variety of holes traversing rather hilly terrain. The South Course is shorter and more level.

NOTES: The South Course is 6,046 yards from the back tees with a 68.2 rating and 112 slope. The North Course: See scorecard for more information.

LOCATION: Take Interstate 5 from Interstate 8 and drive north for a quarter of a mile to the Friars Road East exit. Drive east to Admiral Baker Road and turn left past the security gate to the club.

. . . ● **TOURNAMENTS:** Outside events require a majority of military personnel.

41. NAVY GOLF COURSES: MISSION GORGE

PLAY POLICY & FEES: Outside play is accepted and hotel guests are welcome. Green fees are $55 Monday through Thursday, $65 Friday, and $75 Saturday, Sunday, and holidays. Twilight rates are offered. Carts are included.

TEE TIMES: Reservations can be booked seven days in advance.

DRESS CODE: Collared shirts and nonmetal spikes are required. Bermuda-length shorts are OK.

COURSE DESCRIPTION: This terrific layout has it all—water, wind, rough, and well-guarded greens. The 427-yard 14th hole is one of the hardest on the course. With a slight dogleg left to a narrow landing area, this hole demands accuracy off the tee. The second shot is a long iron to a green bunkered left and back. Oh, did I mention that the fairway is lined with trees? Good luck!

NOTES: Phil Mickelson rated the eighteenth hole as one of the best finishing holes in golf.

LOCATION: Take Highway 52 east to the Mast Boulevard exit. Drive one mile on Mast and turn right on Pebble Beach Drive. Turn right on Carlton Oaks Drive and drive to the course on the left.

. . . ● **TOURNAMENTS:** This course is available for outside tournaments. Carts are required for tournament play. ● **TRAVEL:** The phone number for the lodge is 619-448-4242. ● **$PECIAL OFFERS:** Packages are available that include lodging, meals, and green fees. Call the lodge for more information.

42. CARLTON OAKS COUNTRY CLUB &

WILLOWBROOK COUNTRY CLUB
ARCHITECTS: UNKNOWN, 1955; JACK DARAY JR., 1981

11905 Riverside Drive
Lakeside, CA 92040

PRO SHOP: 619-561-1061

Spero Tzathas, Manager
George Winters, Superintendent

Driving Range
Practice Greens ●
Clubhouse ●
Food / Beverage ●
Accommodations
Pull Carts ●
Power Carts ●
Club Rental ●
$pecial Offers

	1	2	3	4	5	6	7	8	9	OUT
BACK	-	-	-	-	-	-	-	-	-	-
REGULAR	306	362	116	292	500	379	172	381	447	2955
par	4	4	3	4	5	4	3	4	5	36
handicap	15	3	17	11	5	7	9	1	13	-
FORWARD	310	279	112	242	461	380	89	314	448	2635
par	4	4	3	4	5	4	3	4	5	36
handicap	9	11	15	13	3	1	17	7	5	-

	BACK	
yardage	-
par	-
rating	-
slope	-

	10	11	12	13	14	15	16	17	18	IN
BACK	-	-	-	-	-	-	-	-	-	-
REGULAR	308	345	129	272	509	373	181	368	451	2936
par	4	4	3	4	5	4	3	4	5	36
handicap	16	4	18	12	6	8	10	2	14	-
FORWARD	295	279	128	242	461	373	89	314	456	2637
par	4	4	3	4	5	4	3	4	5	36
handicap	10	12	16	14	4	2	18	8	6	-

	REGULAR	
yardage	5891
par	72
rating	67.3
slope	107

	FORWARD	
yardage	5272
par	72
rating	70.5
slope	116

FOUR POINTS SHERITAN HOTEL & GOLF COURSE

8110 Aero Drive
San Diego, CA 92123

PRO SHOP: 858-277-8888

Driving Range
Practice Greens ●
Clubhouse
Food / Beverage ●
Accommodations ●
Pull Carts
Power Carts
Club Rental ●
$pecial Offers

	1	2	3	4	5	6	7	8	9	OUT
BACK										
REGULAR										
par										
handicap										
FORWARD										
par										
handicap										

	BACK	
yardage	
par	
rating	
slope	

	10	11	12	13	14	15	16	17	18	IN
BACK										
REGULAR										
par										
handicap										
FORWARD										
par										
handicap										

	REGULAR	
yardage	775
par	27
rating	
slope	

	FORWARD	
yardage	
par	
rating	
slope	

PLAY POLICY & FEES: Green fees are $13 for nine holes and $17 for 18 holes weekdays, and $15 for nine holes and $22 for 18 holes weekends.

TEE TIMES: Reservations can be booked seven days in advance.

DRESS CODE: No tank tops for men are allowed on the course.

COURSE DESCRIPTION: This level course has water on four holes, five for the slightly errant. The 500-yard fifth can be a real monster if the afternoon winds pick up, as they often do. The 447-yard ninth features rough and water left off the tee and trees straight ahead. Better have your power fade working here.

LOCATION: Take Interstate 8 east from San Diego to the Highway 67 exit in El Cajon. Travel north to the Riverford Road exit (bear left). Make a left on Riverford Road and then turn right on Riverside Drive. The club is on the right side about one-half mile down.

. . . ● **TOURNAMENTS:** A 72-player minimum is needed to book a shotgun tournament. A 16-player minimum is needed for a regular tournament. Events should be scheduled two to three months in advance.

43. WILLOWBROOK COUNTRY CLUB

PLAY POLICY & FEES: Green fees for hotel guests are $5 weekdays and $6 weekends. For non-hotel guests, green fees are $7 weekdays and $8 weekends.

TEE TIMES: Reservations are made on a first-come, first-served basis.

COURSE DESCRIPTION: This is a short, par-3 course. The longest hole is 140 yards.

LOCATION: From the San Diego airport, take Interstate 805 north to Highway 163 north. Exit at Kearny Villa Road and take a right. Aero Drive will be on the right.

. . . ● **TOURNAMENTS:** Outside events are allowed.

44. FOUR POINTS SHERITAN HOTEL & GOLF

1150 Fashion Valley Road
San Diego, CA 92108

PRO SHOP: 619-296-4653

Jeff Perry, General Manager
Steve Marino, Head Professional, PGA
Monica Davis, Tournament Director

Driving Range ●
Practice Greens ●
Clubhouse ●
Food / Beverage ●
Accommodations
Pull Carts
Power Carts ●
Club Rental ●
$pecial Offers

	1	2	3	4	5	6	7	8	9	OUT
BACK	388	293	304	526	178	354	190	378	542	3153
REGULAR	376	274	285	510	143	329	161	357	521	2956
par	4	4	4	5	3	4	3	4	5	36
handicap	4	9	8	2	6	7	3	5	1	-
FORWARD	263	250	260	457	122	285	127	334	457	2555
par	4	4	4	5	3	4	3	4	5	36
handicap	4	9	8	2	6	7	3	5	1	-

	10	11	12	13	14	15	16	17	18	IN
BACK	398	178	511	440	393	538	374	148	417	3397
REGULAR	379	156	488	416	373	515	350	132	391	3200
par	4	3	5	4	4	5	4	3	4	36
handicap	7	4	3	1	6	5	8	9	2	-
FORWARD	353	125	416	378	313	502	297	111	377	2872
par	4	3	5	4	4	5	4	3	4	36
handicap	7	4	3	1	6	5	8	9	2	-

BACK	
yardage	6550
par	72
rating	71.5
slope	120

REGULAR	
yardage	6156
par	72
rating	69.7
slope	116

FORWARD	
yardage	5427
par	72
rating	71.3
slope	115

PLAY POLICY & FEES: Green fees are $75 Monday through Thursday, $85 Friday and Sunday, and $95 Saturday and holidays. Twilight, junior, early bird, and replay rates are also available.

TEE TIMES: Reservations can be made up to 30 days in advance. All reservations beyond seven days have an additional $5 reservation charge and must be guaranteed with a credit card.

DRESS CODE: Collared shirts and nonmetal spikes are required. No denim is allowed, and shorts must be Bermuda length.

COURSE DESCRIPTION: What was once a flat course now features undulating fairways, waterfalls, and well-protected, bent-grass greens. Water comes into play on 13 of the 27 holes. The San Diego River is a prominent feature running through the course. The hardest hole on the Mission Course is the 542-yard par 5 with the San Diego River running in front of the green, making it risky for even the longest hitter to reach it in two.

NOTES: This is a 27-hole facility. The Friars Course is 3,230 yards long from the back tees, 3,077 yards long from the middle tees, and 2,660 yards long from the forward tees. See the scorecard for information on the Mission Course and the Presidio Course. Formerly known as the Stardust Country Club, this course hosted the PGA Tour from 1955 until 1968.

LOCATION: Drive north on Interstate 5 from San Diego,. Take Interstate 8 east and exit at Hotel Circle North. Go north on Fashion Valley Road. The course is on the left.

. . . ● **TOURNAMENTS:** Riverwalk is available for outside events, and banquet facilities are available that can accommodate 250 people. A 24-player minimum is needed to book a tournament. ● **TRAVEL:** The course is located in Mission Valley's Hotel Circle and offers several play-and-stay packages with nearby hotels. Call the pro shop for more information.

45. RIVERWALK GOLF CLUB

MISSION TRAILS GOLF COURSE
ARCHITECT: WILLIAM P. BELL, 1966

7380 Golfcrest Place
San Diego, CA 92119

PRO SHOP: 619-460-5400

Rick Crochet, General Manager
Walt Willows, PGA Professional
Ed Kelly, Superintendent

Driving Range ●
Practice Greens ●
Clubhouse ●
Food / Beverage ●
Accommodations
Pull Carts ●
Power Carts ●
Club Rental ●
$Special Offers

	1	2	3	4	5	6	7	8	9	OUT
BACK	538	331	157	292	325	472	144	364	170	2793
REGULAR	528	315	146	252	293	456	129	333	158	2610
par	5	4	3	4	4	5	3	4	3	35
handicap	1	7	17	11	3	9	15	5	13	-
FORWARD	516	304	132	223	276	415	112	311	148	2437
par	5	4	3	4	4	5	3	4	3	35
handicap	1	7	17	13	5	3	15	11	9	-

BACK	
yardage	6004
par	71
rating	68.6
slope	114

	10	11	12	13	14	15	16	17	18	IN
BACK	197	353	467	370	574	347	391	237	275	3211
REGULAR	188	338	432	361	558	340	342	164	270	2993
par	3	4	5	4	5	4	4	3	4	36
handicap	14	2	10	4	6	8	12	18	16	-
FORWARD	182	324	411	351	457	325	319	132	237	2738
par	3	4	5	4	5	4	4	3	4	36
handicap	14	8	12	6	2	4	16	18	10	-

REGULAR	
yardage	5603
par	71
rating	66.4
slope	107

FORWARD	
yardage	5175
par	71
rating	71.1
slope	120

 PRESIDIO HILLS GOLF COURSE
ARCHITECT: GEORGE MARSTON, 1932

4136 Wallace Street
San Diego, CA 92210

PRO SHOP: 619-295-9476

Donna Abrego, Professional/Manager
Doug Broadley, Superintendent

Driving Range
Practice Greens ●
Clubhouse ●
Food / Beverage ●
Accommodations
Pull Carts
Power Carts
Club Rental ●
$Special Offers

	1	2	3	4	5	6	7	8	9	OUT
BACK	-	-	-	-	-	-	-	-	-	-
REGULAR	45	50	60	80	90	70	70	90	90	645
par	3	3	3	3	3	3	3	3	3	27
handicap	16	15	7	11	1	5	8	4	9	-
FORWARD	45	50	60	80	90	70	70	90	90	645
par	3	3	3	3	3	3	3	3	3	27
handicap	16	15	7	11	1	5	8	4	9	-

BACK	
yardage	-
par	-
rating	-
slope	-

	10	11	12	13	14	15	16	17	18	IN
BACK	-	-	-	-	-	-	-	-	-	-
REGULAR	60	90	80	100	70	65	70	90	55	680
par	3	3	3	3	3	3	3	3	3	27
handicap	18	3	10	6	12	13	14	2	17	-
FORWARD	60	90	80	100	70	65	70	90	55	680
par	3	3	3	3	3	3	3	3	3	27
handicap	18	3	10	6	12	13	14	2	17	-

REGULAR	
yardage	1325
par	54
rating	-
slope	-

FORWARD	
yardage	1325
par	54
rating	-
slope	-

PLAY POLICY & FEES: Green fees are $22 Monday through Thursday, $25 Friday, and $31 weekends and holidays. Senior rates are offered. Carts are $22. Reservations are recommended.

TEE TIMES: The general public may reserve tee times one week in advance, and AGPA (American Golf Players Association) members may reserve up to nine days in advance.

DRESS CODE: Collared shirts are preferred.

COURSE DESCRIPTION: Set in a valley, the layout of this scenic course follows the contours of the land, with two of the holes running alongside Lake Murray. Mature trees separate the fairways.

LOCATION: Drive on Interstate 8 inSan Diego to College Avenue. Turn north and drive one mile to Navajo Road. Turn right and drive two miles to Golfcrest Drive. Turn right again and continue one-quarter mile to Golfcrest Place. Turn left into the club.

. . . ● **TOURNAMENTS:** This course is available for outside tournaments. A banquet facility is available that can accommodate up to 200 people.

46. MISSION TRAILS GOLF COURSE

PLAY POLICY & FEES: Green fees are $7

TEE TIMES: Reservations are not accepted. All play is on a first-come, first-served basis.

DRESS CODE: Nonmetal spikes are required.

COURSE DESCRIPTION: This is the one of the oldest courses in the San Diego area. It's been a family operation for many years. Donna Abrego's grandfather was the first pro. This is a fun little pitch-and-putt course for tuning up the short game. Full-grown sycamore trees keep the course in welcome shade.

NOTES: The San Diego Junior Golf Association, one of the oldest and most successful in the nation, starts its youngsters here. Years after they made the PGA Tour, such players as Lon Hinkle and Morris Hatalsky returned here to polish their short games.

LOCATION: Take the Taylor Street exit off Interstate 8 in San Diego. Drive about one mile to Juan Street, turn left, and drive one block to the course. The course is on the left.

. . . ● **TOURNAMENTS:** This course is available for outside tournaments weekdays only.

47. PRESIDIO HILLS GOLF COURSE

COLINA PARK GOLF COURSE

4085 52nd Street
San Diego, CA 92105

PRO SHOP: 619-582-4704

Ann Bolzoni, Executive Director
Chip Boldin, PGA Professional
Chris Bailey, Superintendent

Driving Range
Practice Greens ●
Clubhouse ●
Food / Beverage ●
Accommodations
Pull Carts
Power Carts
Club Rental
$Special Offers

	1	2	3	4	5	6	7	8	9	OUT
BACK	76	74	122	132	92	67	85	85	75	808
REGULAR	76	74	77	112	71	67	85	85	75	722
par	3	3	3	3	3	3	3	3	3	27
handicap	3	13	9	1	5	17	7	15	11	-
FORWARD	76	74	77	100	64	67	85	85	75	703
par	3	3	3	3	3	3	3	3	3	27
handicap	3	13	9	1	5	17	7	15	11	-

BACK	
yardage	1546
par	54
rating	-
slope	-

	10	11	12	13	14	15	16	17	18	IN
BACK	61	73	100	80	124	78	80	69	73	738
REGULAR	61	73	100	80	69	78	80	69	73	683
par	3	3	3	3	3	3	3	3	3	27
handicap	18	14	2	4	8	10	6	12	16	-
FORWARD	61	73	100	80	69	78	80	69	73	683
par	3	3	3	3	3	3	3	3	3	27
handicap	18	14	2	4	8	10	6	12	16	-

REGULAR	
yardage	1405
par	54
rating	-
slope	-

FORWARD	
yardage	1386
par	54
rating	-
slope	-

SUN VALLEY GOLF COURSE

5080 Memorial Drive
La Mesa, CA 92041

PRO SHOP: 619-466-6102

Johnny Gonzales, Manager

Driving Range ●
Practice Greens ●
Clubhouse
Food / Beverage ●
Accommodations
Pull Carts
Power Carts
Club Rental ●
$Special Offers

	1	2	3	4	5	6	7	8	9	OUT
BACK	-	-	-	-	-	-	-	-	-	-
REGULAR	-	-	-	-	-	-	-	-	-	-
par	-	-	-	-	-	-	-	-	-	-
handicap	-	-	-	-	-	-	-	-	-	-
FORWARD	-	-	-	-	-	-	-	-	-	-
par	-	-	-	-	-	-	-	-	-	-
handicap	-	-	-	-	-	-	-	-	-	-

BACK	
yardage	-
par	-
rating	-
slope	-

	10	11	12	13	14	15	16	17	18	IN
BACK	-	-	-	-	-	-	-	-	-	-
REGULAR	-	-	-	-	-	-	-	-	-	-
par	-	-	-	-	-	-	-	-	-	-
handicap	-	-	-	-	-	-	-	-	-	-
FORWARD	-	-	-	-	-	-	-	-	-	-
par	-	-	-	-	-	-	-	-	-	-
handicap	-	-	-	-	-	-	-	-	-	-

REGULAR	
yardage	1085
par	27
rating	-
slope	-

FORWARD	
yardage	
par	
rating	-
slope	-

PLAY POLICY & FEES: The green fees are $5 any day. Junior fees are $2, and senior fees are $3 any day. Replays or second rounds are $2.50. Junior golfers certified through the Pro Kids Academy play free.

TEE TIMES: Reservations can be made at any time.

DRESS CODE: Shirts and shoes are necessary. Nonmetal spikes are required.

COURSE DESCRIPTION: This course is carved into a neighborhood in the middle of the city. It has rolling fairways, undulating greens, and trees—lots of trees. Bring your straight game. Colina Park is a delightful little track for seniors and juniors.

NOTES: Colina Park is the home of the Pro Kids Golf Academy and Learning Center. Colina Park is the site of the San Diego Chapter PGA "Clubs for Kids" program. Funded through foundations and corporations, a two-story clubhouse facility is underway that will include a community room, golf library, classrooms, computer learning center, patios, barbeque area, and a toddler golf area.

LOCATION: Take Interstate 805 to University Avenue and go east a few blocks. At 52nd Street, turn left to the course on the right.

48. COLINA PARK GOLF COURSE

PLAY POLICY & FEES: Green fees are $7 for nine holes and $11 for 18 holes Monday through Thursday. Friday through Sunday green fees are $8 for nine holes and $12 for 18 holes.

TEE TIMES: Reservations are accepted up to 30 days in advance.

DRESS CODE: Shirts are required at all times.

COURSE DESCRIPTION: This hilly course has nice, open fairways. It's part of a larger municipal park in a suburban San Diego neighborhood. The longest hole is 131 yards; the shortest, 96.

NOTES: Sun Valley just completed a major renovation that included a new driving range, new tee-box locations on several holes, new irrigation system, and remodeled pro-shop,

LOCATION: Take Interstate 8 east of San Diego to El Cajon Boulevard. Go left to La Mesa Boulevard and follow it to Memorial Drive and the course.

. . . ● **TOURNAMENTS:** This course is available for outside tournaments.

49. SUN VALLEY GOLF COURSE

3007 Dehesa Road
El Cajon, CA 92019

PRO SHOP: 619-442-3425

Mike Reinhardt, Head Professional, PGA
Holly Williams, Tournament Director

Driving Range ●
Practice Greens ●
Clubhouse ●
Food / Beverage ●
Accommodations ●
Pull Carts ●
Power Carts ●
Club Rental ●
$pecial Offers ●

	1	2	3	4	5	6	7	8	9	OUT
BACK	362	330	395	323	502	185	416	544	184	3241
REGULAR	341	311	374	308	481	167	387	518	159	3046
par	4	4	4	4	5	3	4	5	3	36
handicap	9	13	3	11	7	15	5	1	17	-
FORWARD	316	295	335	296	470	125	330	474	119	2760
par	4	4	4	4	5	3	4	5	3	36
handicap	7	13	9	3	5	15	11	1	17	-

	10	11	12	13	14	15	16	17	18	IN
BACK	506	403	169	395	358	406	413	547	167	3364
REGULAR	490	367	149	371	340	373	393	528	150	3161
par	5	4	3	4	4	4	4	5	3	36
handicap	16	8	14	12	10	2	6	4	18	-
FORWARD	435	334	134	341	307	337	337	464	136	2825
par	5	4	3	4	4	4	4	5	3	36
handicap	6	14	16	10	12	4	8	2	18	-

BACK	
yardage	6605
par	72
rating	72.0
slope	124

REGULAR	
yardage	6207
par	72
rating	69.5
slope	113

FORWARD	
yardage	5585
par	72
rating	72.8
slope	130

50. SINGING HILLS GOLF CLUB & RESORT

PLAY POLICY & FEES: Outside play is accepted. Hotel guests are welcome. Green fees are $35 Monday through Thursday, $37 Friday, and $42 Saturday, Sunday, and holidays. Carts are $20. Green fees for the Pine Glen course are $15. Senior and twilight rates are available. Senior rates are only available at the Pine Glen course.

TEE TIMES: Reservations can be booked seven days in advance Monday through Friday, and five days in advance on weekends.

DRESS CODE: No tank tops are allowed on the course. Shorts must be mid-thigh in length. Nonmetal spikes are preferred.

COURSE DESCRIPTION: Mature trees line the flat, straight fairways on the Oak Glen Course. The Willow Glen Course offers a rolling layout and is known for its elevated tee on the fourth hole and the par-3 12th with its tiered green beyond a lake ringed with flowers.

NOTES: This course is home to The School of Golf for Women and Seniors. "Golf For Women" put Singing Hills on its "Most Woman-Friendly" list for 1998. This semiprivate club has three 18-hole courses. Par is 72 on Oak Glen and Willow Glen, and 54 on Pine Glen. The Pine Glen Course is 3,000 yards. It is not rated. The Oak Glen Course is 5,749 yards and rated 66.9, with a slope rating of 107. Forward tees are 5,308 yards and rated 69.3. The slope rating is 112. The Willow Glen Course: See scorecard for yardage and rating information.

LOCATION: From Interstate 5 or Interstate 805, take Interstate 8 east to the El Cajon Boulevard exit. Drive to the second light and turn right on Washington Street. Washington Street turns into Dehesa Road.

. . . ● **TOURNAMENTS:** Shotgun tournaments are available weekdays only. A 72-player minimum is required for a shotgun tournament, and carts are required. The banquet facility can accommodate 300 people. ● **TRAVEL:** Singing Hills has 102 rooms and suites. Most rooms have golf course views. The resort also features a tennis facility. ● **$PECIAL OFFERS:** Several golf and tennis packages are available.

51

COTTONWOOD AT RANCHO SAN DIEGO GOLF

ARCHITECTS: O.W. MOORMAN , 1960; A.C. SEARS

3121 Willow Glen Drive
El Cajon, CA 92019

PRO SHOP: 619-442-9891

Chris Carlson, General Manager
Lori Coobeen, Tournament Director
Rick Sprouse, Director of Golf

Driving Range ●
Practice Greens ●
Clubhouse ●
Food / Beverage ●
Accommodations
Pull Carts ●
Power Carts ●
Club Rental ●
$pecial Offers

	1	2	3	4	5	6	7	8	9	OUT
BACK	388	537	427	219	367	410	389	566	262	3565
REGULAR	358	512	400	203	360	400	379	551	178	3341
par	4	5	4	3	4	4	4	5	3	36
handicap	11	9	1	5	13	7	15	3	17	-
FORWARD	292	450	364	178	330	355	363	453	137	2922
par	4	5	4	3	4	4	4	5	3	36
handicap	13	1	5	15	11	7	9	3	17	-

	10	11	12	13	14	15	16	17	18	IN
BACK	441	373	150	366	341	492	439	488	207	3297
REGULAR	432	364	136	353	330	474	425	457	197	3168
par	5	4	3	4	4	5	4	5	3	37
handicap	2	8	18	12	16	4	6	14	10	-
FORWARD	282	347	136	315	285	392	413	424	142	2736
par	4	4	3	4	4	5	5	5	3	37
handicap	14	6	18	10	12	4	8	2	16	-

BACK	
yardage	6862
par	73
rating	72.6
slope	126

REGULAR	
yardage	6509
par	73
rating	70.5
slope	116

FORWARD	
yardage	5658
par	73
rating	76.8
slope	128

52

CORONADO GOLF COURSE

ARCHITECTS: JACK DARAY, 1957; WILLIAM FRANCIS BELL, 1968

GOLF 50

P.O. Box 18190
Coronado, CA 92178

2000 Visalia Row
Coronado, CA 92118

PRO SHOP: 619-435-9485, EXT. 4

Dave Jones, Director of Golf
Ron Yarbrough, PGA Professional
Jim Robyn, Tournament Director, PGA

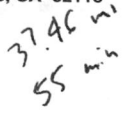
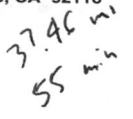

Driving Range ●
Practice Greens ●
Clubhouse ●
Food / Beverage ●
Accommodations
Pull Carts ●
Power Carts ●
Club Rental ●
$pecial Offers

	1	2	3	4	5	6	7	8	9	OUT
BACK	371	500	406	536	163	396	389	404	175	3340
REGULAR	361	485	389	516	136	380	375	383	153	3178
par	4	5	4	5	3	4	4	4	3	36
handicap	7	15	1	9	17	3	11	5	13	-
FORWARD	349	450	337	476	133	357	320	347	123	2892
par	4	5	4	5	3	4	4	4	3	36
handicap	7	3	9	1	17	5	13	11	15	-

	10	11	12	13	14	15	16	17	18	IN
BACK	409	142	300	543	391	175	370	427	493	3250
REGULAR	382	129	285	524	378	166	359	411	464	3098
par	4	3	4	5	4	3	4	4	5	36
handicap	8	18	16	6	4	12	10	2	14	-
FORWARD	356	117	269	488	355	145	322	363	435	2850
par	4	3	4	5	4	3	4	4	5	36
handicap	6	18	14	2	4	16	12	8	10	-

BACK	
yardage	6590
par	72
rating	71.5
slope	120

REGULAR	
yardage	6276
par	72
rating	70.0
slope	117

FORWARD	
yardage	5742
par	72
rating	67.4
slope	112

PLAY POLICY & FEES: Green fees for the Ivanhoe Course are $26 weekdays and $39 weekends. Green fees for the Monte Vista Course are $23 weekdays and $36 weekends. Twilight rates are available. Carts are $10 per person or $16 for a single rider.

TEE TIMES: Reservations are recommended two weeks in advance.

DRESS CODE: Collared shirts are required, and nonmetal spikes are encouraged.

COURSE DESCRIPTION: These courses have a lot of trees, ponds, and lakes, and a river runs through them in the winter. The Ivanhoe Course has numerous doglegs and is one of the best-maintained public courses in the area. The Monte Vista Course has tight fairways and is shorter.

NOTES: The range closes Mondays at 3 p.m. The par 71 Monte Vista Course is 6,248 yards and rated 71.3 from the back tees. The slope rating is 119. Forward tees are 5,503 yards and rated 72.0. The slope is 121. The Ivanhoe Course: See scorecard for yardage and rating information.

LOCATION: From Interstate 5 or Interstate 805 take Interstate 8 east to the Second Street exit in El Cajon. Drive south on Second Street for about four miles to Willow Glen Drive and turn left to the club.

. . . ● **TOURNAMENTS:** This course is available for outside tournaments. ● **TRAVEL:** Embassy Suites in La Jolla is located about 25 minutes from the course (during rush hour, travel time can be considerably longer). For reservations or more information call 619-453-0400.

51. COTTONWOOD AT RANCHO SAN DIEGO

PLAY POLICY & FEES: Green fees are $20. After 4 p.m. the green fees are $10. Carts are $24. Reservations are recommended. Closed on Independence Day.

TEE TIMES: Reservations can be made by calling 619-435-3121, ext. 3.

DRESS CODE: Nonmetal spikes are preferred.

COURSE DESCRIPTION: Open fairways and large greens typify this course. It hosts a whopping 110,000 rounds annually, but is in remarkably fine condition. Set beneath the Coronado Bay Bridge, it has some of the best views of San Diego and its harbor.

NOTES: President Clinton has been known to frequent this course. The course record is 62 by Jim Robyn. Douglas Clark's 64 is the tournament course record.

LOCATION: From Interstate 5 in SanDiego take the Coronado Bay Bridge west and turn left at the end of the bridge. Go left on Fifth Street to Glorietta Boulevard and turn right to the club.

. . . ● **TOURNAMENTS:** Carts are required. A 144-player minimum is needed to book a shotgun tournament, and a 16-player minimum is needed to book a regular tournament. Tournaments should be booked 12 to 48 months in advance. The banquet facility can accommodate 200 people. ● **TRAVEL:** Hotel Del Coronado (619-435-6611), Lowes (619-424-4000) and the Marriott (800-543-4300) are recommended for lodging.

52. CORONADO GOLF COURSE

Sea 'N Air

ARCHITECTS: JACK DARAY , 1981; STEPHEN HALSEY

P.O. Box 357081
Coronado, CA 92178

Building 800 NAS North
San Diego, CA 92135

PRO SHOP: 619-545-9659

Mark McCain, Superintendent

Driving Range ●
Practice Greens ●
Clubhouse ●
Food / Beverage ●
Accommodations
Pull Carts ●
Power Carts ●
Club Rental ●
$pecial Offers

	1	2	3	4	5	6	7	8	9	OUT
BACK	500	280	268	411	362	563	195	360	341	3280
REGULAR	486	265	261	393	347	546	188	352	329	3167
par	5	4	4	4	4	5	3	4	4	37
handicap	5	17	13	3	7	1	15	11	9	-
FORWARD	425	250	248	337	329	433	160	287	306	2775
par	5	4	4	4	4	5	3	4	4	37
handicap	5	15	11	3	7	1	13	17	9	-

	10	11	12	13	14	15	16	17	18	IN
BACK	393	163	544	173	393	487	356	191	349	3049
REGULAR	382	155	528	161	384	477	347	185	339	2958
par	4	3	5	3	4	5	4	3	4	35
handicap	4	18	2	14	6	10	8	16	12	-
FORWARD	369	106	451	150	374	467	330	183	334	2764
par	4	3	5	3	4	5	4	3	4	35
handicap	8	18	2	16	6	4	12	14	10	-

BACK	
yardage	6329
par	72
rating	70.3
slope	117

REGULAR	
yardage	6125
par	72
rating	69.2
slope	113

FORWARD	
yardage	5539
par	72
rating	72.2
slope	121

54 BALBOA PARK GOLF CLUB

2600 Golf Course Drive
San Diego, CA 92102

PRO SHOP: 619-239-1632

Michael Jory, PGA Professional
Nancy Marx, Tournament Director, PGA

Driving Range ●
Practice Greens ●
Clubhouse ●
Food / Beverage ●
Accommodations
Pull Carts ●
Power Carts ●
Club Rental ●
$pecial Offers

	1	2	3	4	5	6	7	8	9	OUT
BACK	344	502	379	354	296	207	470	323	177	3052
REGULAR	311	468	318	304	277	193	452	298	164	2785
par	4	5	4	4	4	3	5	4	3	36
handicap	14/1	6	12/8	8/12	18	2/4	4/2	10/1	16	-
FORWARD	301	434	293	261	253	179	398	281	158	2558
par	4	5	4	4	4	3	5	4	3	36
handicap	8	4	12	18	10	6	2	14	16	-

	10	11	12	13	14	15	16	17	18	IN
BACK	409	384	392	134	512	315	555	198	316	3215
REGULAR	379	356	379	105	494	299	534	167	303	3016
par	4	4	4	3	5	4	5	3	4	36
handicap	7	11	5/15	13/1	3	17/1	1	15/9	9/15	-
FORWARD	353	332	361	86	467	277	507	150	278	2811
par	4	4	4	3	5	4	5	3	4	36
handicap	5	11	7	17	3	15	1	13	9	-

BACK	
yardage	6267
par	72
rating	69.8
slope	119

REGULAR	
yardage	5801
par	72
rating	67.5
slope	114

FORWARD	
yardage	5369
par	72
rating	71.4
slope	119

PLAY POLICY & FEES: Military personnel and guests only. Rates vary according to military rank and status.

DRESS CODE: No tank tops or cutoffs are allowed.

COURSE DESCRIPTION: This flat course features a links-style feel, with three holes that run along the ocean. The course is directly below the North Island Naval Air Station's flight path.

LOCATION: Take the Coronado exit off Interstate 5 in San Diego and drive across the Coronado Bay Bridge through the toll gate. Continue on Third Avenue and turn left on Alameda Street. At Fourth Avenue, turn right through the main gate, drive one-quarter mile to Rogers Road, and turn left to the club.

. . . ● **TOURNAMENTS:** This course is available to outside events as long as at least 51 percent of the players in the tournament are military.

53. SEA 'N AIR

PLAY POLICY & FEES: Green fees are $30 weekdays and $35 weekends. Carts are $18 until 3 p.m. and $10 after 3 p.m. Resident and twilight rates are available.

TEE TIMES: Reservations can be booked seven days in advance. To make reservations, call 619-570-1234.

COURSE DESCRIPTION: Both courses are tight with small greens.

NOTES: Par is 32 on the nine-hole course.

LOCATION: Take the Pershing Drive exit off Interstate 5 and drive east to 26th Street. Turn right, drive to Golf Course Drive, and turn left. Continue to the club.

. . . ● **TOURNAMENTS:** A 16-player minimum is needed to book a tournament, and carts are required.

54. BALBOA PARK GOLF CLUB

CHULA VISTA GOLF COURSE
ARCHITECT: HARRY RAINVILLE, 1961

4475 Bonita Road
Bonita, CA 92002

PRO SHOP: 619-479-4141

Bob Jodice, Manager
Mark Aten, PGA Professional
Brad Holm, Superintendent

Driving Range •
Practice Greens •
Clubhouse •
Food / Beverage •
Accommodations
Pull Carts •
Power Carts •
Club Rental •
$pecial Offers

	1	2	3	4	5	6	7	8	9	OUT
BACK	339	491	347	141	505	421	522	408	172	3346
REGULAR	328	452	296	133	474	412	516	382	144	3137
par	4	5	4	3	5	4	5	4	3	37
handicap	7	5	11	17	13	1	9	3	15	-
FORWARD	323	435	278	90	412	407	509	375	138	2967
par	4	5	4	3	5	5	5	4	3	38
handicap	7	5	9	17	11	13	1	3	15	-

	10	11	12	13	14	15	16	17	18	IN
BACK	392	442	524	349	368	178	380	195	497	3325
REGULAR	367	411	513	324	357	157	368	187	490	3174
par	4	4	5	4	4	3	4	3	5	36
handicap	10	2	12	16	4	18	6	14	8	-
FORWARD	302	363	468	284	309	135	356	111	481	2809
par	4	4	5	4	4	3	4	3	5	36
handicap	12	2	6	16	8	14	10	18	4	-

BACK	
yardage	6671
par	73
rating	71.0
slope	123

REGULAR	
yardage	6311
par	73
rating	69.1
slope	116

FORWARD	
yardage	5776
par	74
rating	72.7
slope	124

BONITA GOLF CLUB
ARCHITECT: WILLIAM F. BELL, 1958

P.O. Box 455
Bonita, CA 91902

5540 Sweetwater Road
Bonita, CA 91902

PRO SHOP: 619-267-1103

Robert Scribner, Manager
Jim Crockett, Director of Golf, PGA
Bill Osgood, Head Professional, PGA

Driving Range •
Practice Greens •
Clubhouse •
Food / Beverage •
Accommodations
Pull Carts •
Power Carts •
Club Rental •
$pecial Offers

	1	2	3	4	5	6	7	8	9	OUT
BACK	346	195	418	502	304	434	522	286	177	3184
REGULAR	301	132	402	483	286	389	497	280	159	2929
par	4	3	4	5	4	4	5	4	3	36
handicap	3	9	1	7	15	5	11	17	13	-
FORWARD	287	115	387	470	271	343	471	270	145	2759
par	4	3	4	5	4	4	5	4	3	36
handicap	7	13	1	5	15	9	3	17	11	-

	10	11	12	13	14	15	16	17	18	IN
BACK	422	200	378	488	374	364	348	148	381	3103
REGULAR	396	175	364	464	326	355	310	114	348	2852
par	4	3	4	5	4	4	4	3	4	35
handicap	4	14	10	6	16	2	12	18	8	-
FORWARD	347	154	350	446	321	345	298	100	322	2683
par	4	3	4	5	4	4	4	3	4	35
handicap	4	16	8	2	10	6	14	18	12	-

BACK	
yardage	6287
par	71
rating	69.3
slope	110

REGULAR	
yardage	5781
par	71
rating	67.8
slope	104

FORWARD	
yardage	5442
par	71
rating	71.0
slope	119

PLAY POLICY & FEES: Green fees are $21 weekdays and $28 weekends. Carts are $8 per person for nine holes and $11 per person for 18 holes.

TEE TIMES: Reservations can be booked seven days in advance. For $1 per person, players can book tee times up to 30 days in advance on weekdays, and for $2 per person, players can book tee times 30 days in advance on weekends.

DRESS CODE: No tank tops are allowed on the golf course.

COURSE DESCRIPTION: This is a walkable, level course with five par 5s. It has large greens and wide-open, rolling terrain. A creek meanders through most of the course, which adds to the test already presented by the usual afternoon breeze.

NOTES: Fivesomes are allowed, but carts are mandatory.

LOCATION: From Interstate 805 in Chula Vista take the E Street and travel east two miles to the club.

. . . ● **TOURNAMENTS:** A 16-player minimum is needed to book a tournament. A banquet facility is available that can accommodate up to 350 people.

55. CHULA VISTA GOLF COURSE

PLAY POLICY & FEES: Outside play is accepted. Green fees are $20 weekdays and $28 weekends. Twilight and senior rates are offered. Carts are $20.

TEE TIMES: Reservations can be booked seven days in advance.

DRESS CODE: Collared shirts are required.

COURSE DESCRIPTION: This flat course is set in a river valley and has a few doglegs. The friendly greens do not have any bunkers set directly in front of them. There are two lakes on the course, and although the breeze tends to pick up, this is a user-friendly layout.

LOCATION: Drive on Interstate 805 south from San Diego to Highway 54. Drive east on Highway 54 to Sweetwater Road, turn right, and drive three-fourths of a mile to the course.

. . . ● **TOURNAMENTS:** Shotgun tournaments are available weekdays only and require a 120-player minimum.

56. BONITA GOLF CLUB

3199 Stonefield Drive
Jamul, CA 91935

PRO SHOP: 619-441-6900

Buzz Colton, General Manager
Sue Allen-Stultz, Head Professional, PGA
Amy Grigsby, Tournament Director

Driving Range ●
Practice Greens ●
Clubhouse ●
Food / Beverage ●
Accommodations ●
Pull Carts v
Power Carts ●
Club Rental ●
$pecial Offers ●

	1	2	3	4	5	6	7	8	9	OUT
BACK	409	552	182	524	214	360	171	390	404	3206
REGULAR	381	517	163	489	209	330	150	358	373	2970
par	4	5	3	5	3	4	3	4	4	35
handicap	6	1	5	2	9	8	4	3	7	-
FORWARD	304	422	121	380	116	297	60	271	250	2221
par	4	5	3	5	3	4	3	4	4	35
handicap	4	1	6	5	9	3	8	2	7	-

	10	11	12	13	14	15	16	17	18	IN
BACK	364	385	446	189	559	388	432	230	542	3535
REGULAR	329	323	401	174	533	371	414	204	509	3258
par	4	4	4	3	5	4	4	3	5	36
handicap	9	6	1	5	3	8	7	4	2	-
FORWARD	255	247	234	101	388	291	340	162	416	2434
par	4	4	4	3	5	4	4	3	5	36
handicap	9	3	8	7	4	6	2	5	1	-

BACK	
yardage	6741
par	71
rating	72.7
slope	135

REGULAR	
yardage	6228
par	71
rating	69.7
slope	122

FORWARD	
yardage	4655
par	71
rating	66.6
slope	112

58 **NATIONAL CITY GOLF COURSE**
ARCHITECTS: HARRY RAINVILLE, 1961; RICHARD BERMUDAS, 1985

1439 Sweetwater Road
National City, CA 91950

PRO SHOP: 619-474-1400

Rocco Tannone, Manager
Nonilon Taguiam, PGA Professional
Bobby Canedo, Superintendent

Driving Range ●
Practice Greens ●
Clubhouse
Food / Beverage ●
Accommodations
Pull Carts ●
Power Carts ●
Club Rental ●
$pecial Offers

	1	2	3	4	5	6	7	8	9	OUT
BACK	255	525	265	250	125	175	375	315	120	2405
REGULAR	235	505	245	230	105	155	350	295	100	2220
par	4	5	4	4	3	3	4	4	3	34
handicap	9	1	11	13	15	5	3	7	17	-
FORWARD	215	485	230	205	85	135	310	255	80	2000
par	4	5	4	4	3	3	4	4	3	34
handicap	9	1	11	13	15	5	3	7	17	-

	10	11	12	13	14	15	16	17	18	IN
BACK	255	525	265	250	125	175	375	315	120	2405
REGULAR	235	505	245	230	105	155	350	295	100	2220
par	4	5	4	4	3	3	4	4	3	34
handicap	10	2	12	14	16	6	4	8	18	-
FORWARD	215	485	230	205	85	135	310	255	80	2000
par	4	5	4	4	3	3	4	4	3	34
handicap	10	2	12	14	16	6	4	8	18	-

BACK	
yardage	4810
par	68
rating	60.5
slope	100

REGULAR	
yardage	4440
par	68
rating	59.9
slope	100

FORWARD	
yardage	4000
par	68
rating	60.5
slope	106

PLAY POLICY & FEES: Green fees are $65 Monday through Thursday, $75 Friday, and $85 weekends. Twilight rates are available.

TEE TIMES: Reservations can be booked seven days in advance.

DRESS CODE: Nonmetal spikes are mandatory.

COURSE DESCRIPTION: The Canyon Ranch nine features several significant elevation changes. The Meadow Ranch course is somewhat flatter, but has a couple of carries over gulches. The Canyon Meadow course places a premium on accuracy. The three combine for a top-flight layout. For information on the Canyon Ranch Course: See scorecard.

NOTES: The course received a four-star rating from "Golf Digest."

LOCATION: From Interstate 5 in San Diego, exit east onto Interstate 94 (which turns into Highway 54). Drive to Willow Glen Drive. Turn right and drive to Steele Canyon Drive. Turn right on Steele Canyon Drive to Jamul Drive (the first traffic light). Turn left and drive one mile to the club.

. . . ● **TOURNAMENTS:** A 20-player minimum is needed to book a tournament. Carts are required. Shotgun tournaments are available on weekdays only. Events should be booked nine months in advance. The banquet facility can accommodate up to 200 people. ● **TRAVEL:** The Mission Valley Marriott, the San Diego Marriott and the Sheraton Harbor Island Hotel are all recommended.

57. STEELE CANYON GOLF CLUB

PLAY POLICY & FEES. Green fees are $9 for nine holes weekdays and $12 weekends. The replay fee is $6 weekdays and $7 weekends. The senior rate is $7 weekdays and $9 after noon on weekends. Reservations are recommended.

TEE TIMES: Reservations can be booked seven days in advance.

DRESS CODE: Golf attire is encouraged.

COURSE DESCRIPTION: This course is extremely tight with out-of-bounds markers on almost every hole. The 525-yard second hole is very narrow and needs pinpoint placement for success.

LOCATION: Follow Interstate 805 south from San Diego to Sweetwater Road. Turn west and drive to the course.

. . . ● **TOURNAMENTS:** A 16-player minimum is needed to book a tournament. Events should be scheduled three months in advance.

58. NATIONAL CITY GOLF COURSE

SAN DIEGO COUNTRY CLUB
ARCHITECT: WILLIAM P. BELL, 1921

88 L Street
Chula Vista, CA 91911

PRO SHOP: 619-422-0108

Steve Nordstrom, Manager
Thomas Hust, PGA Professional
Gary Dalton, Superintendent

Driving Range ●
Practice Greens ●
Clubhouse ●
Food / Beverage ●
Accommodations
Pull Carts ●
Power Carts ●
Club Rental ●
$pecial Offers

	1	2	3	4	5	6	7	8	9	OUT
BACK	-	-	-	-	-	-	-	-	-	-
REGULAR	-	-	-	-	-	-	-	-	-	
par	-	-	-	-	-	-	-	-	-	
handicap	-	-	-	-	-	-	-	-	-	-
FORWARD	-	-	-	-	-	-	-	-	-	
par	-	-	-	-	-	-	-	-	-	
handicap	-	-	-	-	-	-	-	-	-	-

	10	11	12	13	14	15	16	17	18	IN
BACK	-	-	-	-	-	-	-	-	-	-
REGULAR	-	-	-	-	-	-	-	-	-	
par	-	-	-	-	-	-	-	-	-	
handicap	-	-	-	-	-	-	-	-	-	-
FORWARD	-	-	-	-	-	-	-	-	-	
par	-	-	-	-	-	-	-	-	-	
handicap	-	-	-	-	-	-	-	-	-	-

BACK	
yardage	6887
par	72
rating	74.2
slope	133

REGULAR	
yardage	6560
par	72
rating	71.9
slope	127

FORWARD	
yardage	4946
par	72
rating	68.9
slope	118

 EASTLAKE COUNTRY CLUB
ARCHITECT: TED ROBINSON, 1991

2375 Clubhouse Drive
Chula Vista, CA 91915

PRO SHOP: 619-482-5757

Craig Doyle, General Manager
John Rathbun, PGA Professional
Christina Jacobson, Tournament Director

Driving Range ●
Practice Greens ●
Clubhouse ●
Food / Beverage ●
Accommodations
Pull Carts ●
Power Carts ●
Club Rental ●
$pecial Offers

	1	2	3	4	5	6	7	8	9	OUT
BACK	302	363	310	154	530	415	160	365	513	3112
REGULAR	285	345	280	133	500	380	139	340	480	2882
par	4	4	4	3	5	4	3	4	5	36
handicap	15	5	17	7	3	1	13	11	9	-
FORWARD	255	295	270	111	440	340	122	310	425	2568
par	4	4	4	3	5	4	3	4	5	36
handicap	13	9	11	17	1	5	15	7	3	-

	10	11	12	13	14	15	16	17	18	IN
BACK	360	400	153	380	495	335	360	145	485	3113
REGULAR	340	390	134	355	470	325	340	128	470	2952
par	4	4	3	4	5	4	4	3	5	36
handicap	14	4	8	2	6	16	10	18	12	-
FORWARD	320	315	113	300	425	280	285	102	410	2550
par	4	4	3	4	5	4	4	3	5	36
handicap	8	10	14	6	2	12	16	18	4	-

BACK	
yardage	6225
par	72
rating	68.7
slope	109

REGULAR	
yardage	5834
par	72
rating	66.4
slope	105

FORWARD	
yardage	5118
par	72
rating	68.8
slope	114

PLAY POLICY & FEES: Members and guests only. Green fees for guests with members are $60, plus $10 per person for carts. The course is closed on Monday.

DRESS CODE: Call the pro shop if you have any questions about appropriate dress. Nonmetal spikes are mandatory.

COURSE DESCRIPTION: This course is the last golf stop before reaching the Mexican border. It was built in the 1920s, making it the oldest private course in San Diego County. Flat to gently rolling, it's a traditional layout with medium to large greens.

NOTES: This is the course on which the great PGA Tour player Billy Casper learned to play. It was the site of the 1993 U.S. Women's Amateur.

LOCATION: From Interstate 5 take the L Street exit and drive 1.5 miles east, or take the Telegraph Canyon/L Street exit off Interstate 805 and drive one mile west.

. . . ● **TOURNAMENTS:** This course is not available for outside events.

59. SAN DIEGO COUNTRY CLUB

PLAY POLICY & FEES: Green fees are $50 weekdays and $65 weekends, including cart. Twilight rates are available. Pull carts are allowed during twilight hours only. Monthly and annual memberships are available.

TEE TIMES: Reservations can be booked seven days in advance.

DRESS CODE: Collared shirts and nonmetal spikes are required.

COURSE DESCRIPTION: There are four sets of tees on this course. There are undulating fairways, bent-grass greens, and six lakes. Greens are huge, but not multitiered. The course is forgiving, although afternoon winds can be tough. It's a good test for players of all abilities.

LOCATION: Take Interstate 805 south to the Telegraph Canyon Road exit in Chula Vista. Drive east four miles to East Lake Greens Community/East Lake Parkway. Turn right and drive one-quarter mile to Clubhouse Drive. The course is on the left.

. . . ● **TOURNAMENTS:** This course is available for outside tournaments. Carts are required.

60. EASTLAKE COUNTRY CLUB

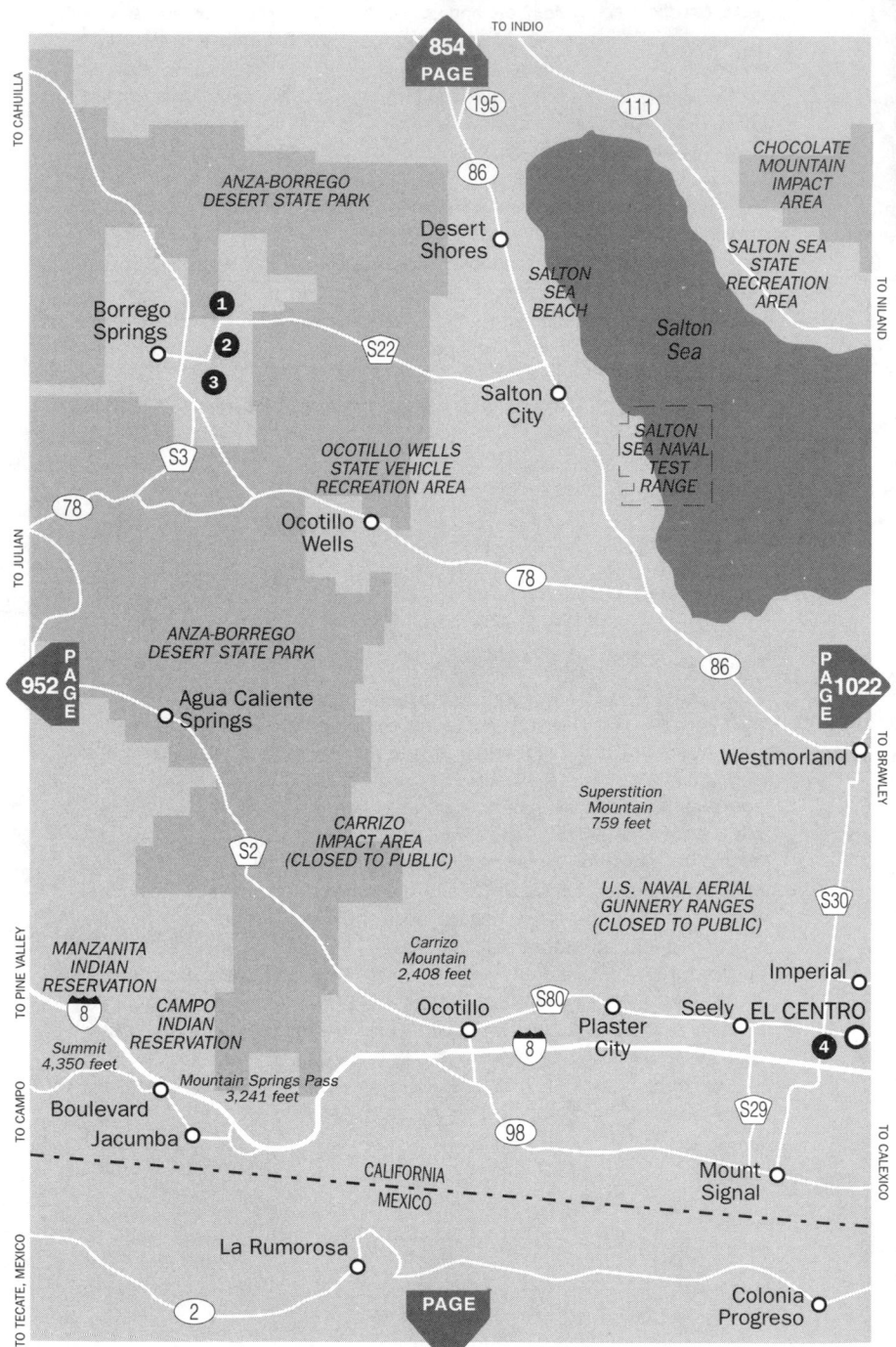

TO INDIO

854 PAGE

TO CAHUILLA

195

111

ANZA-BORREGO DESERT STATE PARK

86

CHOCOLATE MOUNTAIN IMPACT AREA

Desert Shores

SALTON SEA BEACH

SALTON SEA STATE RECREATION AREA

1 Borrego Springs

2

3

S22

Salton City

Salton Sea

SALTON SEA NAVAL TEST RANGE

S3

OCOTILLO WELLS STATE VEHICLE RECREATION AREA

TO NILAND

78

TO JULIAN

Ocotillo Wells

78

86

ANZA-BORREGO DESERT STATE PARK

952 PAGE

Agua Caliente Springs

1022 PAGE

Westmorland

TO BRAWLEY

CARRIZO IMPACT AREA (CLOSED TO PUBLIC)

S2

Superstition Mountain 759 feet

U.S. NAVAL AERIAL GUNNERY RANGES (CLOSED TO PUBLIC)

S30

TO PINE VALLEY

MANZANITA INDIAN RESERVATION

8

CAMPO INDIAN RESERVATION

Carrizo Mountain 2,408 feet

Imperial

Summit 4,350 feet

Ocotillo

S80

Seely

EL CENTRO

4

TO CAMPO

Mountain Springs Pass 3,241 feet

8

Plaster City

Boulevard

Jacumba

98

S29

CALIFORNIA

MEXICO

Mount Signal

TO CALEXICO

TO TECATE, MEXICO

La Rumorosa

PAGE

2

Colonia Progreso

Borrego Springs/ El Centro Area

1 DE ANZA COUNTRY CLUB
ARCHITECT: LAWRENCE HUGHES, 1959

P.O. Box 120
Borrego Spr., CA 92004

509 Catarina Drive
Borrego Spr., CA 92004

PRO SHOP: 760-767-5577

John Bitner, Manager
Denny Mays, PGA Professional
Lorne Olsen, Tournament Director

Driving Range ●
Practice Greens ●
Clubhouse ●
Food / Beverage ●
Accommodations
Pull Carts ●
Power Carts ●
Club Rental ●
$pecial Offers

	1	2	3	4	5	6	7	8	9	OUT
BACK	392	400	211	386	168	417	570	393	525	3462
REGULAR	376	382	173	366	160	392	537	371	495	3252
par	4	4	3	4	3	4	5	4	5	36
handicap	5	7	13	9	17	1	3	11	5	-
FORWARD	325	335	118	325	135	359	432	330	459	2818
par	4	4	3	4	3	4	5	4	5	36
handicap	5	11	17	13	15	1	9	7	3	-

BACK	
yardage	6778
par	72
rating	72.1
slope	123

	10	11	12	13	14	15	16	17	18	IN
BACK	373	386	190	544	380	393	167	501	382	3316
REGULAR	352	365	175	524	370	368	130	475	362	3121
par	4	4	3	5	4	4	3	5	4	36
handicap	12	4	16	8	6	2	18	14	10	-
FORWARD	311	330	155	460	313	318	111	416	325	2739
par	4	4	3	5	4	4	3	5	4	36
handicap	14	6	16	2	12	8	18	10	4	-

REGULAR	
yardage	6373
par	72
rating	69.8
slope	117

FORWARD	
yardage	5557
par	72
rating	71.4
slope	118

2 BORREGO SPRINGS RESORT & COUNTRY CLUB
ARCHITECT: CARY BICKLER, 1997

P.O. Box 981
Borrego Spr., CA 92004

1112 Tilting T Drive
Borrego Spr., CA 92004

PRO SHOP: 760-767-3330

Aaron Biggers, General Manager

Driving Range ●
Practice Greens ●
Clubhouse ●
Food / Beverage ●
Accommodations ●
Pull Carts
Power Carts ●
Club Rental ●
$pecial Offers ●

	1	2	3	4	5	6	7	8	9	OUT
BACK	329	518	255	507	367	142	425	459	330	3332
REGULAR	289	475	236	486	323	118	396	426	301	3050
par	4	5	3	5	4	3	4	4	4	36
handicap	15	7	5	9	11	17	3	1	13	-
FORWARD	218	401	149	408	283	88	236	366	249	2398
par	4	5	3	5	4	3	4	4	4	36
handicap	15	7	5	9	11	17	3	1	13	-

BACK	
yardage	6569
par	71
rating	70.4
slope	67.6

	10	11	12	13	14	15	16	17	18	IN
BACK	437	555	219	381	407	197	295	366	380	3237
REGULAR	412	515	192	338	362	182	287	348	366	3002
par	4	5	3	4	4	3	4	4	4	35
handicap	4	2	6	14	8	12	18	16	10	-
FORWARD	331	403	110	262	279	130	243	290	308	2356
par	4	5	3	4	4	3	4	4	4	35
handicap	4	2	16	14	12	18	8	10	6	-

REGULAR	
yardage	6052
par	71
rating	67.6
slope	112

FORWARD	
yardage	4754
par	71
rating	66.7
slope	104

PLAY POLICY & FEES: Members and guests only. Fees for sponsored guests are $60. Carts are $22. Reservations are required.

TEE TIMES: Guests can make tee times one day in advance. For reservations call 760-767-5105.

DRESS CODE: No blue jeans or short shorts are allowed. Nonmetal spikes are required.

COURSE DESCRIPTION: This flat course has plenty of mature trees and two lakes. It's surrounded by homes. One of the toughest challenges is the third hole, a 211-yard par 3. Players must hit over a lake and bunker to reach the green.

NOTES: The course is closed during the month of October.

LOCATION: From Palm Canyon Drive in Borrego Springs, turn north on Ocotillo Circle and drive one-half mile to Lazy S Drive. Turn right and travel 1.5 miles to Pointing Rock Drive and turn right.

. . . ● **TOURNAMENTS:** This course is not available for outside events.

1. DE ANZA COUNTRY CLUB

PLAY POLICY & FEES: Summer green fees are $30 Monday throughThursday and $40 Friday through Sunday. Winter rates are $54 Monday through Thursday and $64 Friday through Sunday. Green fees include cart. Call ahead. The course is closed mid-September to mid-October.

TEE TIMES: Reservations can be made 14 days in advance.

DRESS CODE: Collared shirts are required and nonmetal spikes are preferred.

COURSE DESCRIPTION: A desert course, Borrego Springs features 75 bunkers, and water comes into play on five holes. The hardest hole on the course is the 459-yard par-4 eighth hole. This slight dogleg right has a narrow landing area off the tee and four traps guarding a fairly large but undulating green.

NOTES: No matter what time of year, Borrego Springs rounds average less than four hours.

LOCATION: Take Highway 10 from Palm Springs south to Highway 86. Follow 86 south to County Road S-22 west. Take S-22 to Borrego Valley Road. Turn left; the course is one mile on the right.

. . . ● **TOURNAMENTS:** Outside events are welcome. A 16-player minimum is needed to book a tournament. Tournaments can be booked one month in advance. A banquet facility is available that can accommodate up to 300 people. ● **TRAVEL:** For reservations at the resort call 760-767-5700 ● **SPECIAL OFFERS:** Play-and-stay packages are available all year. Call the resort for more information.

2. BORREGO SPRINGS RESORT & COUNTRY

❸ RAMS HILL COUNTRY CLUB
ARCHITECT: TED ROBINSON, 1983

P.O. Box 2190
Borrego Spr., CA 92004

1881 Rams Hills Road
Borrego Spr., CA 92004

PRO SHOP: 760-767-5124

Tom Glaser, Manager
Ryan Wilson, Head Professional, PGA
Anthony Ashford, Superintendent

Driving Range ●
Practice Greens ●
Clubhouse ●
Food / Beverage ●
Accommodations ●
Pull Carts
Power Carts ●
Club Rental ●
$pecial Offers

	1	2	3	4	5	6	7	8	9	OUT
BACK	434	550	186	418	492	197	395	365	386	3423
REGULAR	398	518	164	385	468	168	371	349	357	3178
par	4	5	3	4	5	3	4	4	4	36
handicap	5	11	13	1	17	15	3	9	7	-
FORWARD	351	466	141	337	430	140	327	315	330	2837
par	4	5	3	4	5	3	4	4	4	36
handicap	7	1	17	3	5	15	13	9	11	-

	10	11	12	13	14	15	16	17	18	IN
BACK	377	419	517	170	384	424	220	527	405	3443
REGULAR	355	378	476	145	362	380	180	505	369	3150
par	4	4	5	3	4	4	3	5	4	36
handicap	6	4	18	12	14	2	10	16	8	-
FORWARD	331	343	436	133	323	332	156	460	343	2857
par	4	4	5	3	4	4	3	5	4	36
handicap	10	4	6	18	12	14	16	2	8	-

BACK	
yardage	6866
par	72
rating	74.0
slope	133

REGULAR	
yardage	6328
par	72
rating	70.7
slope	125

FORWARD	
yardage	5694
par	72
rating	72.9
slope	127

❹ LAKE VIEW GOLF COURSE

1589 Drew Road
El Centro, CA 92243

PRO SHOP: 760-352-6638

Keith Earle, Professional

Driving Range ●
Practice Greens ●
Clubhouse
Food / Beverage ●
Accommodations
Pull Carts ●
Power Carts ●
Club Rental ●
$pecial Offers

	1	2	3	4	5	6	7	8	9	OUT
BACK	-	-	-	-	-	-	-	-	-	-
REGULAR	-	-	-	-	-	-	-	-	-	-
par	-	-	-	-	-	-	-	-	-	-
handicap	-	-	-	-	-	-	-	-	-	-
FORWARD	-	-	-	-	-	-	-	-	-	-
par	-	-	-	-	-	-	-	-	-	-
handicap	-	-	-	-	-	-	-	-	-	-

	10	11	12	13	14	15	16	17	18	IN
BACK	-	-	-	-	-	-	-	-	-	-
REGULAR	-	-	-	-	-	-	-	-	-	-
par	-	-	-	-	-	-	-	-	-	-
handicap	-	-	-	-	-	-	-	-	-	-
FORWARD	-	-	-	-	-	-	-	-	-	-
par	-	-	-	-	-	-	-	-	-	-
handicap	-	-	-	-	-	-	-	-	-	-

BACK	
yardage	-
par	-
rating	-
slope	-

REGULAR	
yardage	2178
par	33
rating	60.6
slope	102

FORWARD	
yardage	2176
par	33
rating	60.6
slope	102

PLAY POLICY & FEES: Outside play is accepted. Green fees are seasonal and range from $40 to $105. The course is closed Monday and Tuesday, June through September, and it is closed for the month of October.

TEE TIMES: Reservations can be booked 14 days in advance.

DRESS CODE: Appropriate golf attire is required.

COURSE DESCRIPTION: This is a long, well-maintained course with sloping, palm-lined fairways and seven scenic water holes. The course closes in October for fairway reseeding.

NOTES: The course is managed by Troon Golf properties. Rams Hill hosted the first round of qualifying for the 1993, 1997, 1998, and 1999 U.S. Open.

LOCATION: Travel on Interstate 10 or Highway 111 to Indio. Turn on Highway 86 to Salton City. Turn right on County Road S-22 to Borrego Valley Road, turn left, and drive six miles to the club.

. . . ● **TOURNAMENTS:** A 12-player minimum is needed to book a tournament, and carts are required. Events should be scheduled six months in advance. ●

TRAVEL: La Casa Del Zorro is located two minutes from the golf course. For reservations call 760-767-5323. The Palm Canyon Resort (760-767-5341) and the Palms at Indian Head (760-767-7788) are also recommended.

3. RAMS HILL COUNTRY CLUB

PLAY POLICY & FEES: Summer rates begin on April 1. Green fees are $6 for nine holes and $10 for 18 holes. Carts are $6 for 9 holes and $9 for 18 holes. Please call for winter rates.

TEE TIMES: Reservations can be booked three to four days in advance.

DRESS CODE: Shirts and shoes are necessary.

COURSE DESCRIPTION: This unique executive course features lots of undulation and elevation changes. The pride of the course is the sixth hole, a 183-yard par 3 over water. Rabbits, skunks, and ground squirrels are regulars.

LOCATION: From El Centro, drive eight miles west to the Drew Road exit. Drive south on Drew Road for one mile to the course.

. . . ● **TOURNAMENTS:** This course is available for outside tournaments.

4. LAKE VIEW GOLF COURSE

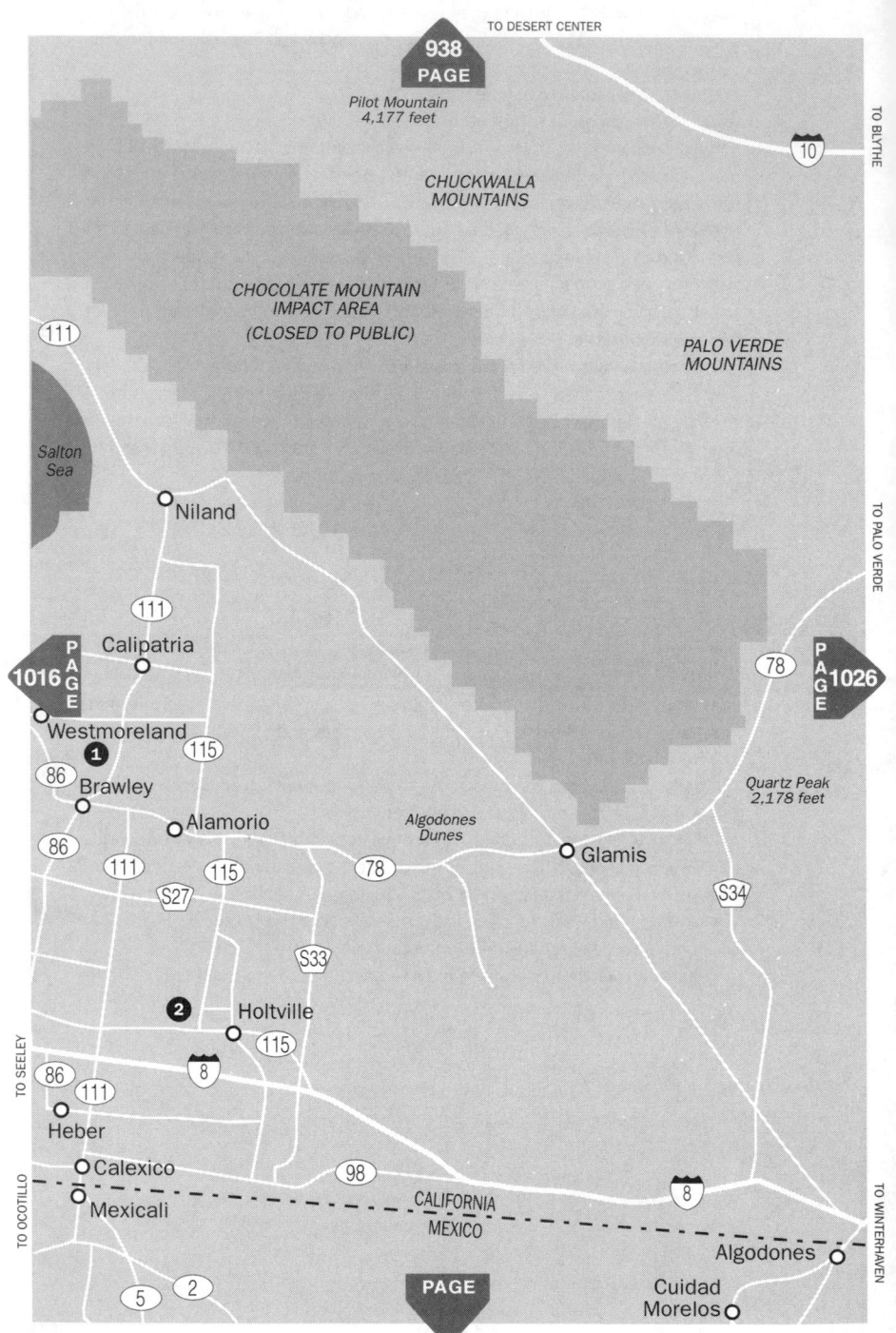

TO DESERT CENTER

938 PAGE

Pilot Mountain
4,177 feet

CHUCKWALLA
MOUNTAINS

CHOCOLATE MOUNTAIN
IMPACT AREA
(CLOSED TO PUBLIC)

PALO VERDE
MOUNTAINS

TO BLYTHE

(10)

(111)

Salton
Sea

Niland

(111)

Calipatria

TO PALO VERDE

PAGE 1016

PAGE 1026

(78)

Westmoreland

(115)

1

Quartz Peak
2,178 feet

(86)

Brawley

Alamorio

(86)

(111)

(115)

S27

Algodones
Dunes

(78)

Glamis

S34

S33

2

Holtville

(115)

(8)

(86)

(111)

Heber

Calexico

(98)

(8)

Mexicali

CALIFORNIA

MEXICO

PAGE

Algodones

(5)

(2)

Cuidad
Morelos

TO SEELEY

TO OCOTILLO

TO WINTERHAVEN

Brawley/Holtville Area

① DEL RIO COUNTRY CLUB
ARCHITECT: WILLIAM P. BELL, 1926

P.O. Box 38
Brawley, CA 92227

102 East Del Rio Road
Brawley, CA 92227

PRO SHOP: 760-344-0085

Bob Gelesko, PGA Professional
Tayno Aguilera, Superintendent

Driving Range ●
Practice Greens ●
Clubhouse ●
Food / Beverage ●
Accommodations
Pull Carts ●
Power Carts ●
Club Rental ●
Special Offers

	1	2	3	4	5	6	7	8	9	OUT
BACK	-	-	-	-	-	-	-	-	-	-
REGULAR	520	414	225	424	198	336	258	353	294	3022
par	5	4	3	4	3	4	4	4	4	35
handicap	9	3	11	1	16	7	17	5	15	-
FORWARD	511	406	217	414	189	323	244	344	287	2935
par	5	5	4	5	3	4	4	4	4	38
handicap	1	11	15	7	17	5	13	9	3	-

	10	11	12	13	14	15	16	17	18	IN
BACK	-	-	-	-	-	-	-	-	-	-
REGULAR	185	385	492	206	375	365	145	473	353	2979
par	3	4	5	3	4	4	3	5	4	35
handicap	10	2	8	16	6	4	18	12	14	-
FORWARD	138	376	480	196	351	345	128	456	333	2803
par	3	4	5	3	4	4	3	5	4	35
handicap	14	4	2	16	10	12	18	6	8	-

BACK	
yardage	-
par	-
rating	-
slope	-

REGULAR	
yardage	6001
par	70
rating	67.9
slope	105

FORWARD	
yardage	5738
par	73
rating	72.8
slope	118

② BARBARA WORTH GOLF RESORT
ARCHITECT: LAWRENCE HUGHES, 1928

2050 Country Club Drive
Holtville, CA 92250

PRO SHOP: 760-356-5842
CLUBHOUSE: 760-356-2806

Bill Adams, Manager
John Hildreth, Head Professional, PGA
Ignacio Martinez, Superintendent

Driving Range ●
Practice Greens ●
Clubhouse ●
Food / Beverage ●
Accommodations ●
Pull Carts ●
Power Carts ●
Club Rental ●
Special Offers

	1	2	3	4	5	6	7	8	9	OUT
BACK										
REGULAR										
par										
handicap										
FORWARD										
par										
handicap										

	10	11	12	13	14	15	16	17	18	IN
BACK										
REGULAR										
par										
handicap										
FORWARD										
par										
handicap										

BACK	
yardage	
par	
rating	
slope	

REGULAR	
yardage	6302
par	71
rating	70.0
slope	115

FORWARD	
yardage	5879
par	71
rating	72.6
slope	120

PLAY POLICY & FEES: Reciprocal play is accepted with members of other private clubs. Outside play is also accepted. Green fees during the summer are $21 every day. Twilight green fees are $16. During the winter season Green fees are $26 weekdays and $35 weekends, carts included.

TEE TIMES: Reservations can be booked seven days in advance.

DRESS CODE: No tank tops or short shorts are allowed.

COURSE DESCRIPTION: This course is short and tight, demanding strategic shot placement. It has fairly level terrain, tree-lined fairways, many doglegs, and small greens. Del Rio hosts approximately 25,000 rounds annually.

LOCATION: Travel east on Interstate 10 to the town of Indio and take Highway 86 south to Brawley. Take Highway 111 north and drive two miles to the course.

. . . ● **TOURNAMENTS:** A 50-player minimum is needed to book a tournament. Carts are mandatory. A banquet facility is available that can accommodate up to 330 people.

1. DEL RIO COUNTRY CLUB

PLAY POLICY & FEES: Outside play is accepted. Green fees are $19 weekdays and $24 weekends during the summer season (June through August), and $25 weekdays and $30 weekends during the winter season. Senior rates are available. Carts are $11 per rider.

TEE TIMES: Reservations can be booked seven days in advance.

DRESS CODE: Golf attire is encouraged, and nonmetal spikes are required.

COURSE DESCRIPTION: This older desert course has tree-lined fairways, good greens, and several ponds. It's nicely maintained. Have your bets won by the time you reach the par-3 17th. It's 150 yards over water. And the 18th hole covers 430 yards uphill to a small, well-bunkered green.

NOTES: Tony Lema is said to have won his first professional event here.

LOCATION: From Interstate 8 in San Diego, travel east about 125 miles to Bowker Road and turn left. At Interstate 80 turn right and drive to the club.

. . . ● **TOURNAMENTS:** This course is available for tournaments. Carts are required for weekend tournaments. Events should be booked six months in advance. The banquet facility can accommodate 800 people. ● **TRAVEL:** Barbara Worth has a motel with more than 104 rooms, three apartments, and four executive suites. For reservations call 760-356-2806.

2. BARBARA WORTH GOLF RESORT

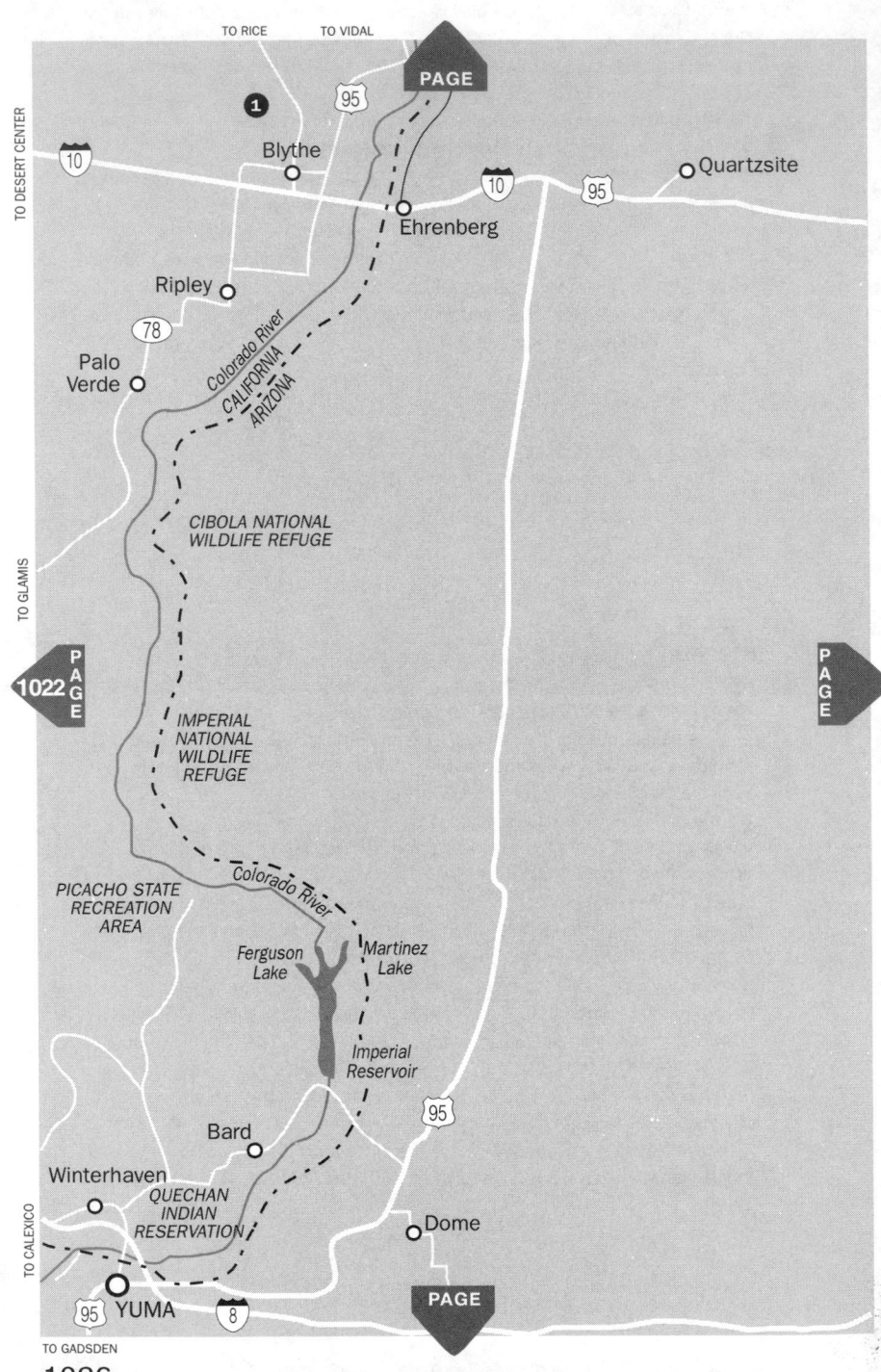

TO RICE   TO VIDAL

PAGE

95

1

TO DESERT CENTER

Blythe

10

Quartzsite

10   95

Ehrenberg

Ripley

78

Colorado River

Palo
Verde

CALIFORNIA
ARIZONA

TO GLAMIS

CIBOLA NATIONAL
WILDLIFE REFUGE

P
A
G
E

1022

P
A
G
E

IMPERIAL
NATIONAL
WILDLIFE
REFUGE

Colorado River

PICACHO STATE
RECREATION
AREA

Ferguson
Lake

Martinez
Lake

Imperial
Reservoir

Bard

95

Winterhaven

QUECHAN
INDIAN
RESERVATION

Dome

TO CALEXICO

PAGE

95   YUMA   8

TO GADSDEN

Blythe Area

BLYTHE MUNICIPAL GOLF COURSE
ARCHITECT: WILLIAM F. BELL, 1969

4708 Wells Road
Blythe, CA 92225

PRO SHOP: 760-922-7272

Anne Getchell, Manager
Willie Getchell, Head Professional, PGA
Vern Hansen, Superintendent

Driving Range ●
Practice Greens ●
Clubhouse ●
Food / Beverage ●
Accommodations ●
Pull Carts ●
Power Carts ●
Club Rental ●
Special Offers

	1	2	3	4	5	6	7	8	9	OUT
BACK	-	-	-	-	-	-	-	-	-	-
REGULAR	470	213	431	402	382	486	384	168	351	3287
par	5	3	4	4	4	5	4	3	4	36
handicap	17	9	1	3	7	11	5	13	15	-
FORWARD	411	148	401	371	332	409	300	125	332	2829
par	5	3	5	4	4	5	4	3	4	37
handicap	9	15	1	3	5	11	7	17	13	-

	10	11	12	13	14	15	16	17	18	IN
BACK	-	-	-	-	-	-	-	-	-	-
REGULAR	346	373	426	467	186	395	354	553	180	3280
par	4	4	4	5	3	4	4	5	3	36
handicap	16	8	2	18	14	6	4	10	12	-
FORWARD	336	361	387	462	127	380	164	418	220	2855
par	4	4	4	5	3	4	4	5	3	36
handicap	12	2	6	8	16	4	14	10	18	-

BACK	
yardage	-
par	-
rating	-
slope	-

REGULAR	
yardage	6567
par	72
rating	70.7
slope	109

FORWARD	
yardage	5684
par	73
rating	72.6
slope	117

PLAY POLICY & FEES: Green fees are $10 for nine holes and $20 for 18 holes.

TEE TIMES: Reservations can be booked one day in advance January through March.

COURSE DESCRIPTION: This nicely maintained course sits on top of a mesa overlooking the Palo Verde Valley. A moderate number of eucalyptus and pine trees line the fairways that go up and down the mesa. The 213-yard second hole drops 150 feet to a tiered green. The 384-yard seventh hole has a blind second shot, usually calling for two strong irons. There's lots of character here.

LOCATION: From Interstate 10 travel east of Palm Springs and take the Lovekin Boulevard exit north. Travel three miles to Sixth Avenue and turn left. At Wells Road turn right to the course.

. . . ● **TOURNAMENTS:** This course is available for outside tournaments. A 16-player minimum is needed to book a tournament. Tournaments can be booked one month in advance.

1. BLYTHE MUNICIPAL GOLF COURSE

Index

CLAREMONT GOLF COURSE, Claremont 712

Clark, Chris (Tournament Director) 852

Clark, Mike (Superintendent) 136

Clark, Roger (PGA Professional) 90

Clark, Russ (PGA Professional) 566

Clark, Terry (General Manager) 968

Clarke, Sandy (Superintendent) 980

Claus, George (General Manager) 270

Claveran, Derek (Professional/Manager) 394

Claveran, Felix (PGA Professional) 56

Clawson, Rick (Superintendent) 812

Clayton 280

CLEAR LAKE RIVIERA YACHT & GOLF CLUB, Kelseyville 122

Clifford, Ed (Architect) 100

Clifford, Mike (Director of Golf, PGA) 896

Clio 106

Cloonan, Sue (General Manager) 830

CLUB AT MORNINGSIDE, THE Rancho Mirage 882

Coalinga 508

Coarsegold 470

Cobb 124

Cobb, Rob (Superintendent) 388

Cochran, H. Detweiler, J. (Architect) 932

Cochrane, John (Director of Golf, PGA) 924, 926, 928

Coe, Pete (Head Professional, PGA) 984

Coffman, Kent (Superintendent) 784

Colavincenzo, Evan (PGA Professional) 562

COLD SPRINGS GOLF & COUNTRY CLUB, Placerville 226

Cole, Rex (PGA Professional) 994

Coles, Jim (Director of Instruction) 498

COLINA PARK GOLF COURSE, San Diego 1002

Collins, Dave (Director of Golf) 320

Collins, Jim (PGA Professional) 276

Collins, Kenny (PGA Professional) 478

Collins-Maurer, Linda (LPGA Professional) 380

Colma 286

COLONIAL COUNTRY CLUB, Hemet 840

COLONY COUNTRY CLUB, THE Murrieta 850

Colton 814

Colton, Buzz (General Manager) 1012

COLTON GOLF CLUB, Colton 814

Colusa 162

COLUSA COUNTRY CLUB, Colusa 162

Combs, Greg (PGA Professional) 806

Comerford, Pat (General Manager) 496, 498

Compton 752

COMPTON GOLF COURSE, Compton 752

Conant, Kenneth (PGA Professional) 704

Concord 262, 264

Condos, Mark (Superintendent) 368

Cone, Byron (Head Professional, PGA) 134

Conkings, Larry (General Manager) 700

Connelly, Todd (Head Professional, PGA) 866

Conrad, Bill (Superintendent) 328

CONTRA COSTA COUNTRY CLUB, Pleasant Hill 260

Contreras, Richard (Professional) 682

Conway, Chuck (Manager) 728

Coobeen, Lori (Tournament Director) 1006

Cook, Avery (Head Professional, PGA) 340

Cook, Dave (PGA Professional) 800

Cook, Mike (Director of Golf, PGA) 396

Cooke, Blair (Manager) 954

Cooke, Jim (PGA Professional) 478

Cool 222

Cooper, Daniel (CCM, Exec. VP & GM) 900

Cooper, Fred (Director of Golf) 764

Cooper, Lou (Professional) 772

COPPER RIVER COUNTRY CLUB, Fresno 474

Copperopolis 392

CORDEVALLE GOLF CLUB, San Jose 414

CORDOVA GOLF COURSE, Sacramento 204

Corona 744, 750, 752

Corona, Ralph (Pro/Superintendent) 586

Coronado 1006, 1008

CORONADO GOLF COURSE, Coronado 1006

CORRAL DE TIERRA COUNTRY CLUB, Salinas 442

Cosand, Rich (PGA Professional) 424

Costa, Eric (PGA Professional) 458

Costa, Jack (Banquet Manager) 478

Costa, Matt (Tournament Director) 90

Costa Mesa 770

COSTA MESA GOLF & COUNTRY CLUB, Costa Mesa 770

Coto de Caza 788

COTO DE CAZA GOLF CLUB, Coto de Caza 788

COTTONWOOD AT RANCHO SAN DIEGO GOLF

COUNTRY CLUB OF RANCHO BERNARDO, THE, San Diego 980

COUNTRY VILLAGE GOLF COURSE, THE, Mira Loma 746

COURSE, El Cajon 1006

COURSE AT WENTE VINEYARDS, THE, Livermore 370

Couples, Fred (Architect) 928, 934

Couples, Gene Bates, Fred (Architect) 448

COURSE AT RASPBERRY HILL, Auburn 220

Courtney, Chuck (PGA Professional) 972

Coward, Jim (Architect) 264

Cox, Bev (Director of Golf) 676

Cox, Bobby (Superintendent) 294

Cox, Marlin (Architect) 640

Coyote 342

COYOTE HILLS GOLF COURSE, Fullerton 736

Cozart, Gary (Superintendent) 154

Crane, Douglas (PGA Professional) 556

Crawford, Dan (Owner) 44

Crawford, Malcolm (Architect) 44

Crescent City 34

Cress, Mike (Manager) 90

CRESTA VERDE GOLF CLUB, Corona 750

Crist, Bill (Head Professional, PGA) 948

Crochet, Rick (General Manager) 1000

Crockett, Jim (Director of Golf, PGA) 1010

Cronin, Paul (General Manager) 564

Crooker, Don (Director of Golf, PGA) 732

Cropley, Ron (PGA Professional) 968, 980

Cross, Jeff (PGA Professional) 826

CROW CANYON COUNTRY CLUB, Danville 292

Cruise, Larry (PGA Professional) 598

Crump, Donald A. (Architect) 358

Cruz, David (Superintendent) 830

CRYSTAL SPRINGS GOLF COURSE, Burlingame 312

CRYSTALAIRE COUNTRY CLUB, Llano 604

Cuevas, Joe (Superintendent) 638

Cullen, Kevin (Director of Golf, PGA) 338

Culler, Jack (Superintendent) 812

Cummings, John (General Manager) 918

Cupertino 324

Cupit, Mark (Superintendent) 902

Cupp, Robert (Architect) 592, 626, 636

Curley, Brian (Architect) 748, 928, 934

& Curly, Schmidt (Architect) 980

Cursio, Gary (Director of Golf) 438

Curtola, Connie (Manager) 306

Curtola, Ron (Architect) 306

Cymbalisty, Ray (Superintendent) 860

Cypress 760

CYPRESS GOLF CLUB, Los Alamitos 758

CYPRESS GOLF COURSE, Colma 286

CYPRESS LAKES GOLF COURSE, Vacaville 158

CYPRESS POINT CLUB, Pebble Beach 430

CYPRESS RIDGE, Arroyo Grande 542

Dacey, Bob (PGA Professional) 596

Daily, Colleen (Tournament Director) 272

DAIRY CREEK GOLF COURSE, San Luis Obispo 498

Dalton, Bob (Superintendent) 514

Dalton, Gary (Superintendent) 1014

Daly City 284

Danien, Jaime (Superintendent) 834

Danruther, Rick (Head Professional, PGA) 964

Danville 282

Daray, Jack (Architect) 622, 960, 978, 994, 1006, 1008

Daray, Jack Jr. (Architect) 996

Darby, Mark (Head Professional, PGA) 438

DARKHORSE GOLF CLUB, Auburn 216

Darrah, Jon (PGA Professional) 910

Darrock, Brian (Superintendent) 974

DATE PALM COUNTRY CLUB, Cathedral City 874

Dau, Dan Jr. (Superintendent) 708

About the Author

Shaw Kobre—Author

Shaw Kobre is a freelance writer who lives in Santa Rosa, California, with his wife, Kim and their two sons, Alec and Rylan. Shaw has written the last three editions of CALIFORNIA GOLF and is currently helping produce HAWAII GOLF and the CALIFORNIA GOLF SERVICES GUIDE. Mr. Kobre spent five seasons, from 1991 to 1995, as coordinator and then director of the Sonoma County Open in Windsor, California. The Nike Sonoma County Open produced some of today's top PGA Touring professionals, including David Duval, Tom Lehman, and Ernie Els, to name a few.

Shannon Millhouse—Research Director

Shannon Phillips is an entrepreneur, freelance writer, director of research for CALIFORNIA GOLF, and grade-school teacher, who also finds time to golf. Shannon is a regular at the Windsor Golf Club where she has twice won the Women's Club Championship.

Bob Fagan—Article Submissions/Research

Bob was the Executive Director of the Northern California PGA from 1991-1998 and is now an executive with GolfPro International, Inc., the producer of the first robotic caddie. He resides in Pleasanton, California and has a daughter, Kelly, and a son, Matthew. A former golf professional, he has played golf for more than 35 years, with over 1,400 courses under his belt. A fine player, he owns more than 70 course records. Fagan is a member of the Golf Writers Association of America and the California Golf Writers Association.